AGENTS OF ATLAS

THE
COMPLETE COLLECTION
VOL. 1

AGENTS OF ATLAS

THE COMPLETE COLLECTION VOL. 1

Jeff Parker
WRITER

AGENTS OF ATLAS (2006) **#1-6, SPIDER-MAN FAMILY #4** & **SECRET INVASION: WHO DO YOU TRUST?**

Leonard Kirk
PENCILER

Kris Justice (#1-6, Spider-Man) with **Terry Pallot** (#6) & **Karl Kesel** (Secret Invasion)
INKERS

Tomm Coker (#1-6); **Leonard Kirk** & **Michelle Madsen** (Spider-Man); **Phil Jimenez, Andy Lanning** & **Christina Strain** (Secret Invasion)
COVER ART

Michelle Madsen
COLORIST

X-MEN: FIRST CLASS #8

Roger Cruz
ARTIST

Val Staples
COLORIST

Marko Djurdjević
COVER ART

WOLVERINE: AGENT OF ATLAS #1-3

Benton Jew
ARTIST

Elizabeth Dismang Breitweiser
COLORIST

DARK REIGN: NEW NATION & **AGENTS OF ATLAS** (2009) **#1-5**

Carlo Pagulayan (Dark Reign, #1-2, #5) & **Clayton Henry** (#3-4)
PENCILERS

Jason Paz (Dark Reign, #1-2, #5) & **Clayton Henry** (#3-4)
INKERS

Gabriel Hardman
ARTIST (1958 SCENES, #2-4)

Jana Schirmer
COLORIST

Elizabeth Dismang Breitweiser
COLORIST (1958 SCENES, #2-4)

Daniel Acuña (Dark Reign); **Arthur Adams** & **Guru-eFX** (#1); **Greg Land** & **Justin Ponsor** (#2); **Adi Granov** (#3); **Stuart Immonen** & **John Rauch** (#4); **Billy Tan** & **Frank D'Armata** (#5)
COVER ART

BONUS STORIES

Al Feldstein, Don Glut & co.
WRITERS

Ken Bald & **Syd Shores, George Klein** & **Lin Streeter, Russ Heath, Robert Q. Sale, John Romita Sr., Joe Maneely,** and **Alan Kupperberg** & **Bill Black**
ARTISTS

Carl Gafford & co.
COLORISTS

Tom Orzechowski & co.
LETTERERS

Bob Powell, George Klein, Russ Heath, Joe Maneely, and **Jack Kirby** & **Joe Sinnott**
COVER ART

Stan Lee & **Roy Thomas**
EDITORS

AGENTS OF ATLAS: THE MENACE FROM SPACE

Jeff Parker
WRITER

Artmonkeys' Dave Lanphear (Agents of Atlas 2006) & **Blambot's Nate Piekos** (X-Men, Spider-Man, Secret Invasion, Wolverine, Dark Reign, Agents of Atlas 2009)
LETTERERS

Nathan Cosby & **Lauren Sankovitch**
ASSISTANT EDITORS

Mark Paniccia & **Nathan Cosby**
EDITORS

John Cerilli
DIRECTOR OF DIGITAL CONTENT

Harry Go
DIGITAL COORDINATOR

Tim Smith 3
DIGITAL PRODUCTION MANAGER

COLLECTION EDITOR: **Mark D. Beazley**
ASSISTANT EDITOR: **Caitlin O'Connell**
ASSOCIATE MANAGING EDITOR: **Kateri Woody**
ASSOCIATE MANAGER, DIGITAL ASSETS: **Joe Hochstein**
MASTERWORKS EDITOR: **Cory Sedlmeier**

SENIOR EDITOR, SPECIAL PROJECTS: **Jennifer Grünwald**
VP PRODUCTION & SPECIAL PROJECTS: **Jeff Youngquist**
RESEARCH & LAYOUT: **Jeph York**
BOOK DESIGNER: **Adam Del Re**
SVP PRINT, SALES & MARKETING: **David Gabriel**

EDITOR IN CHIEF: **C.B. Cebulski**
CHIEF CREATIVE OFFICER: **Joe Quesada**
PRESIDENT: **Dan Buckley**
EXECUTIVE PRODUCER: **Alan Fine**

Special Thanks to **Gary Henderson, Crusher Hogan, Murray Ward** & **Dr. Michael J. Vassallo**

AGENTS OF ATLAS: THE COMPLETE COLLECTION VOL. 1. Contains material originally published in magazine form as AGENTS OF ATLAS (2006) #1-6, X-MEN: FIRST CLASS #8, WOLVERINE: AGENT OF ATLAS #1-3, AGENTS OF ATLAS (2009) #1-5, WHAT IF? #9, AGENTS OF ATLAS: MENACE FROM SPACE, SPIDER-MAN FAMILY #4, SECRET INVASION: WHO DO YOU TRUST?, DARK REIGN: NEW NATION, MARVEL MYSTERY COMICS #82, VENUS #1, MARVEL BOY #1, MEN'S ADVENTURES #26, MENACE #11 and YELLOW CLAW #1. First printing 2018. ISBN 978-1-302-91129-4. Published by MARVEL WORLDWIDE, INC., a subsidiary of MARVEL ENTERTAINMENT, LLC. OFFICE OF PUBLICATION: 135 West 50th Street, New York, NY 10020. Copyright © 2018 MARVEL No similarity between any of the names, characters, persons, and/or institutions in this magazine with those of any living or dead person or institution is intended, and any such similarity which may exist is purely coincidental. **Printed in the U.S.A.** DAN BUCKLEY, President, Marvel Entertainment; JOHN NEE, Publisher; JOE QUESADA, Chief Creative Officer; TOM BREVOORT, SVP of Publishing; DAVID BOGART, SVP of Business Affairs & Operations, Publishing & Partnership; DAVID GABRIEL, SVP of Sales & Marketing, Publishing; JEFF YOUNGQUIST, VP of Production & Special Projects; DAN CARR, Executive Director of Publishing Technology; ALEX MORALES, Director of Publishing Operations; SUSAN CRESPI, Production Manager; STAN LEE, Chairman Emeritus. For information regarding advertising in Marvel Comics or on Marvel.com, please contact Vit DeBellis, Custom Solutions & Integrated Advertising Manager, at vdebellis@marvel.com. For Marvel subscription inquiries, please call 888-511-5480. **Manufactured between 3/9/2018 and 4/10/2018 by LSC COMMUNICATIONS INC., KENDALLVILLE, IN, USA.**

10 9 8 7 6 5 4 3 2 1

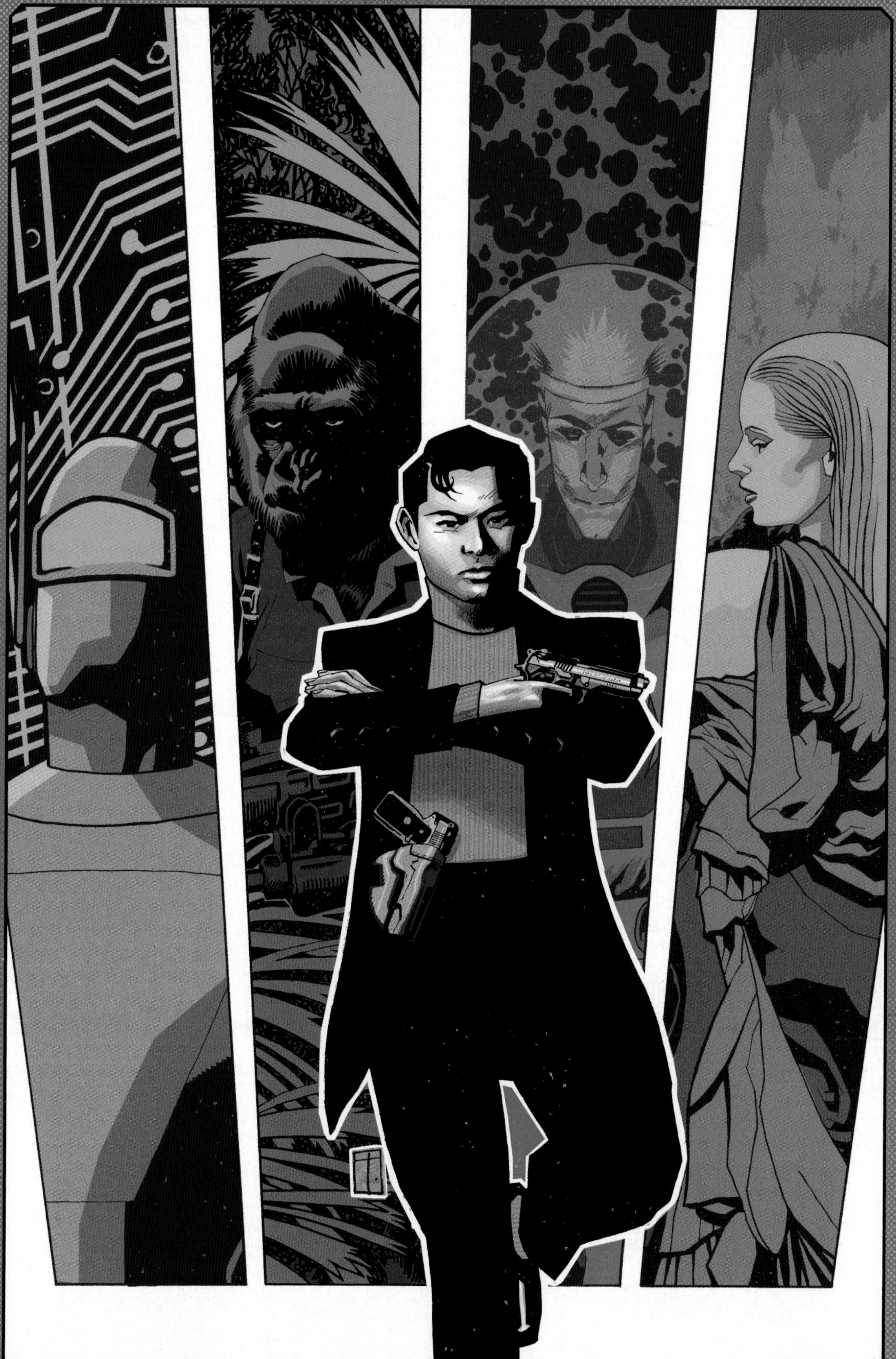

AGENTS OF ATLAS (2006) **1**

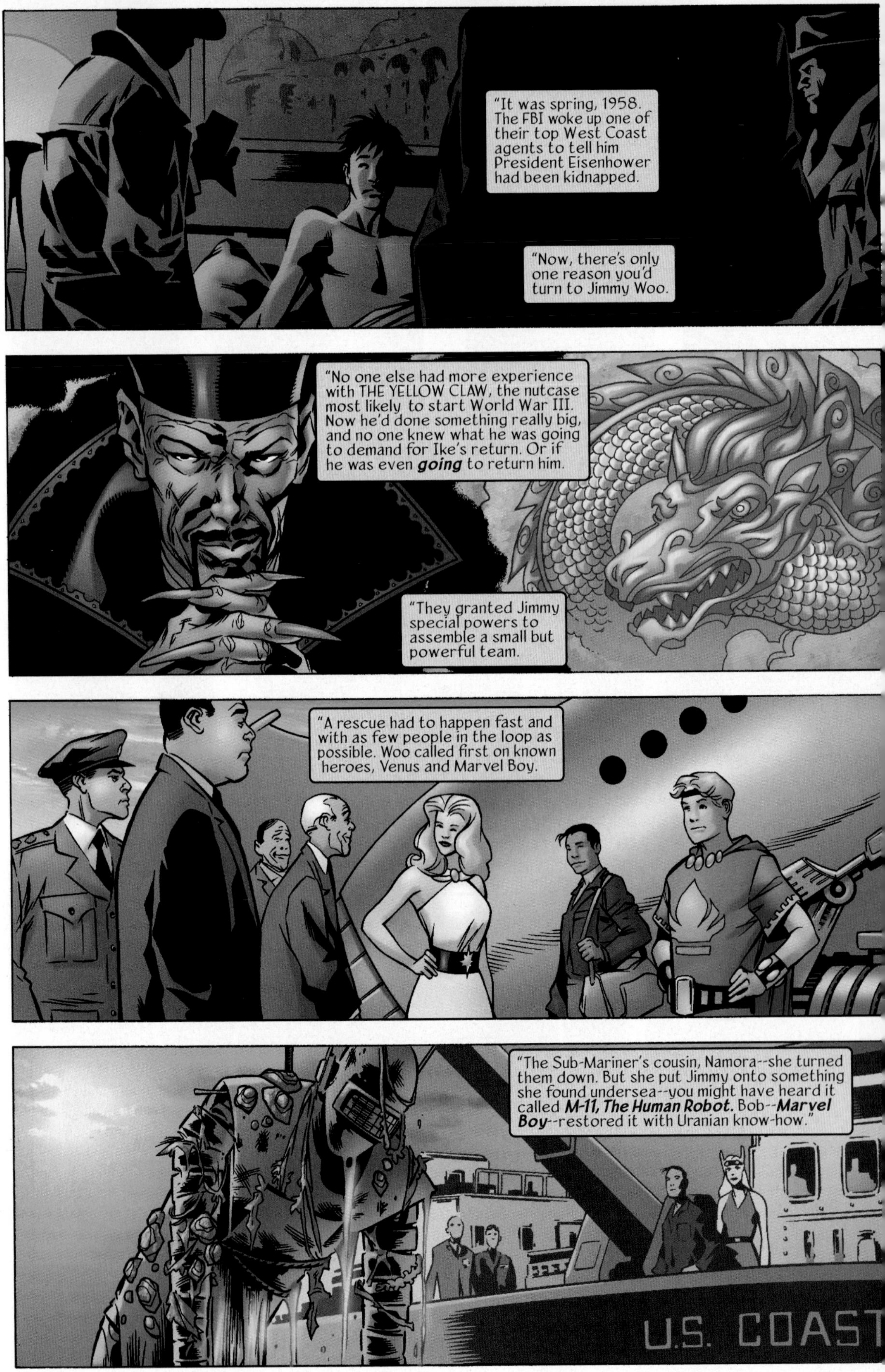
"It was spring, 1958. The FBI woke up one of their top West Coast agents to tell him President Eisenhower had been kidnapped.
"Now, there's only one reason you'd turn to Jimmy Woo.
"No one else had more experience with THE YELLOW CLAW, the nutcase most likely to start World War III. Now he'd done something really big, and no one knew what he was going to demand for Ike's return. Or if he was even ***going*** to return him.
"They granted Jimmy special powers to assemble a small but powerful team.
"A rescue had to happen fast and with as few people in the loop as possible. Woo called first on known heroes, Venus and Marvel Boy.
"The Sub-Mariner's cousin, Namora--she turned them down. But she put Jimmy onto something she found undersea--you might have heard it called ***M-11, The Human Robot.*** Bob--***Marvel Boy***--restored it with Uranian know-how."
U.S. COAST

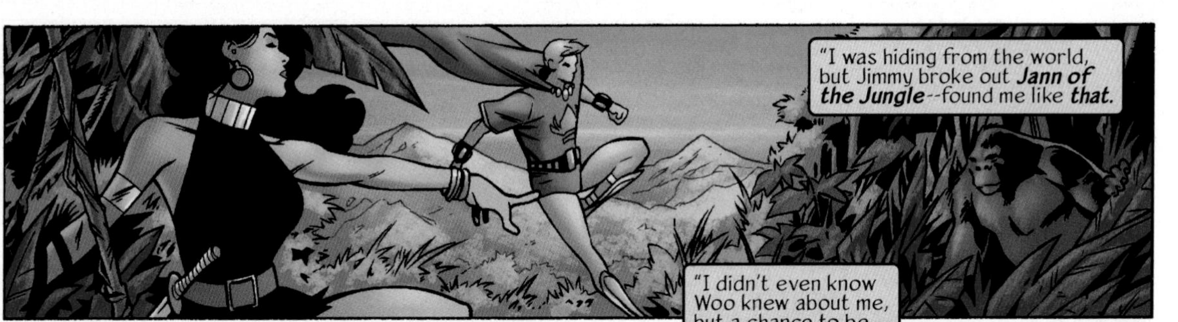
"I was hiding from the world, but Jimmy broke out **Jann of the Jungle**--found me like **that**.
"I didn't even know Woo knew about me, but a chance to be treated like a man?

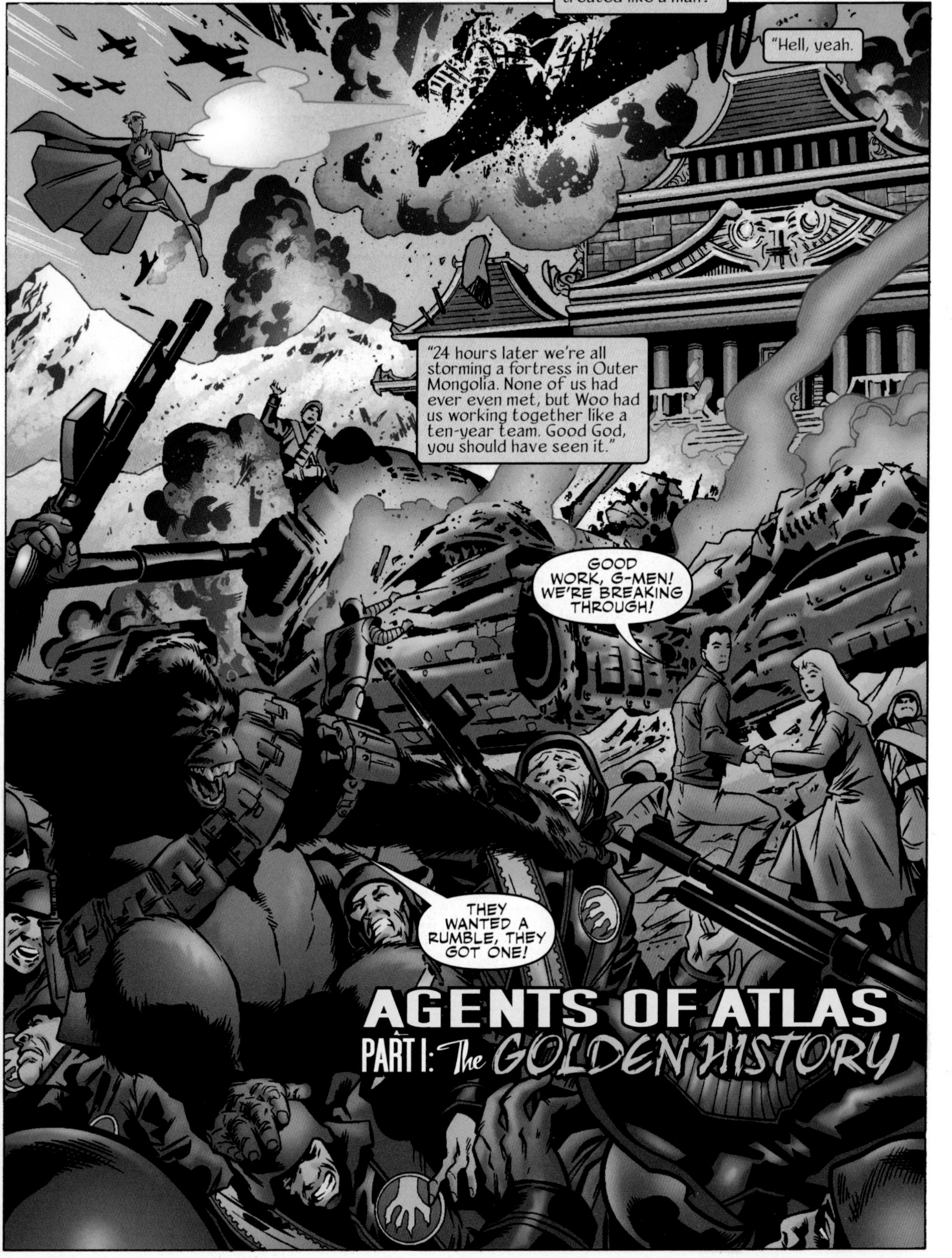
"Hell, yeah.
"24 hours later we're all storming a fortress in Outer Mongolia. None of us had ever even met, but Woo had us working together like a ten-year team. Good God, you should have seen it."
GOOD WORK, G-MEN! WE'RE BREAKING THROUGH!
THEY WANTED A RUMBLE, THEY GOT ONE!
AGENTS OF ATLAS
PART I: The GOLDEN HISTORY

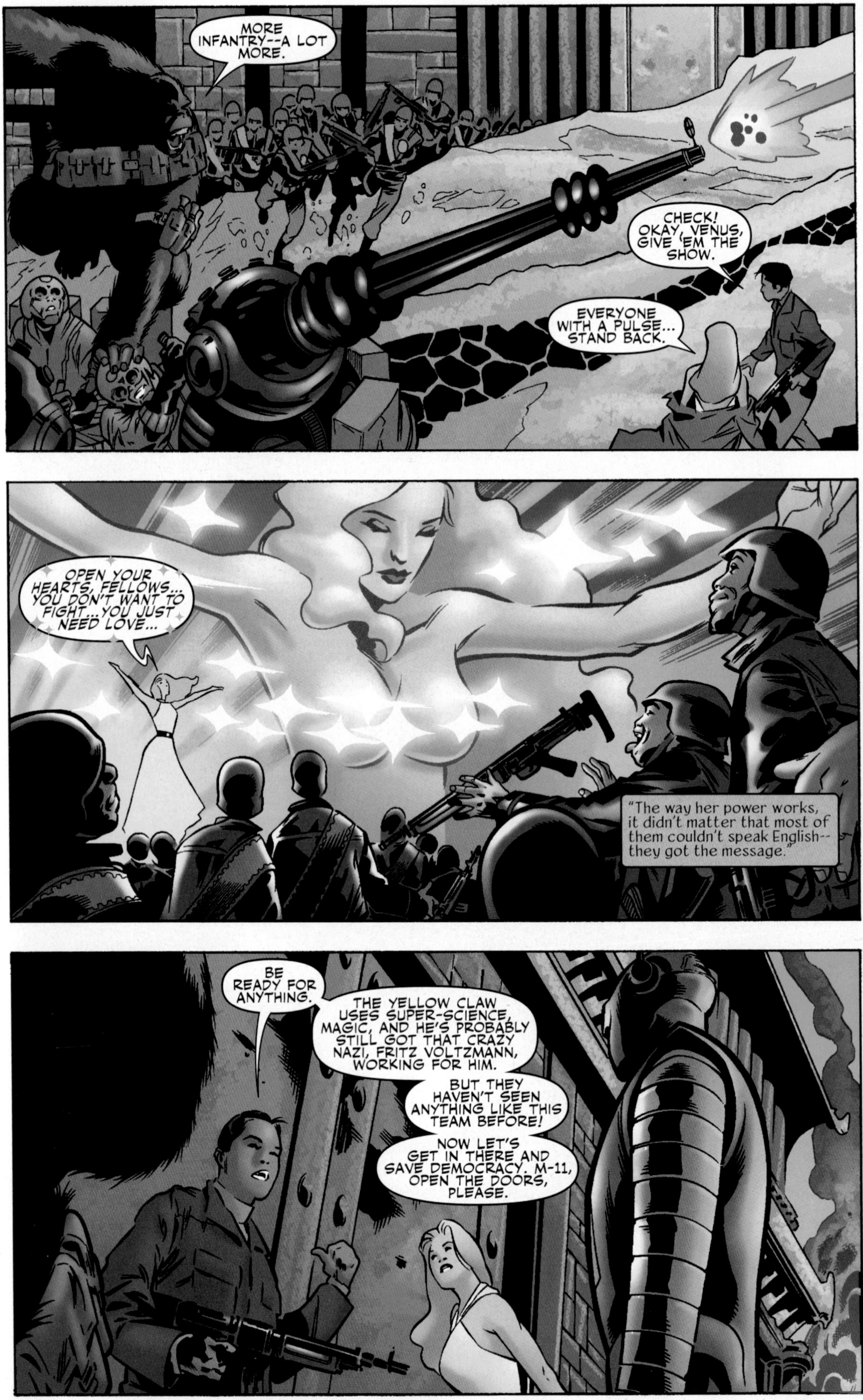

MORE INFANTRY--A LOT MORE.
CHECK! OKAY, VENUS, GIVE 'EM THE SHOW.
EVERYONE WITH A PULSE... STAND BACK.
OPEN YOUR HEARTS, FELLOWS... YOU DON'T WANT TO FIGHT... YOU JUST NEED LOVE...
"The way her power works, it didn't matter that most of them couldn't speak English-- they got the message."
BE READY FOR ANYTHING.
THE YELLOW CLAW USES SUPER-SCIENCE, MAGIC, AND HE'S PROBABLY STILL GOT THAT CRAZY NAZI, FRITZ VOLTZMANN, WORKING FOR HIM.
BUT THEY HAVEN'T SEEN ANYTHING LIKE THIS TEAM BEFORE!
NOW LET'S GET IN THERE AND SAVE DEMOCRACY. M-11, OPEN THE DOORS, PLEASE.

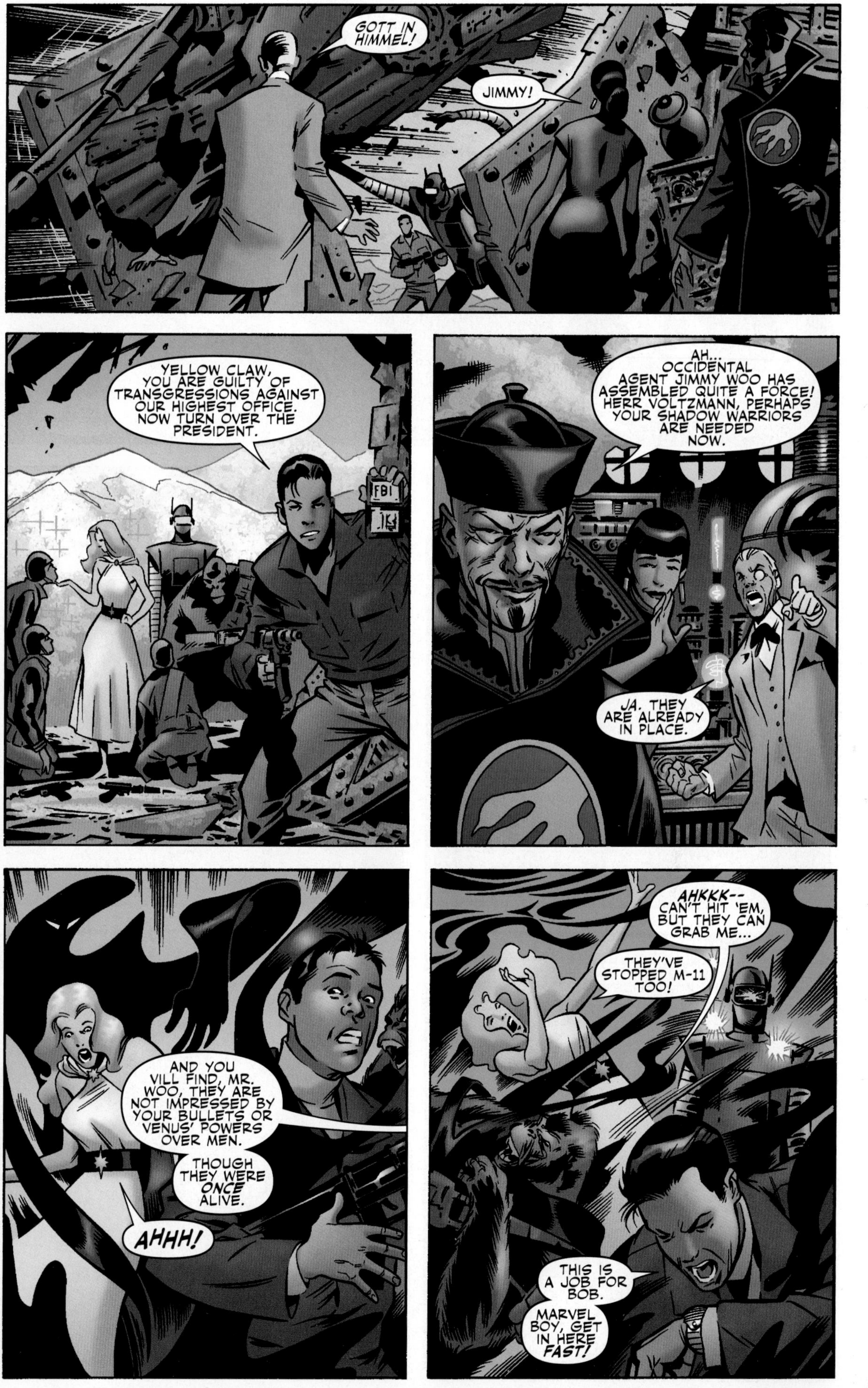
GOTT IN HIMMEL!
JIMMY!
YELLOW CLAW, YOU ARE GUILTY OF TRANSGRESSIONS AGAINST OUR HIGHEST OFFICE. NOW TURN OVER THE PRESIDENT.
FBI
AH... OCCIDENTAL AGENT JIMMY WOO HAS ASSEMBLED QUITE A FORCE! HERR VOLTZMANN, PERHAPS YOUR SHADOW WARRIORS ARE NEEDED NOW.
JA. THEY ARE ALREADY IN PLACE.
AND YOU VILL FIND, MR. WOO, THEY ARE NOT IMPRESSED BY YOUR BULLETS OR VENUS' POWERS OVER MEN.
THOUGH THEY WERE *ONCE* ALIVE.
AHHH!
AHKKK-- CAN'T HIT 'EM, BUT THEY CAN GRAB ME...
THEY'VE STOPPED M-11 TOO!
THIS IS A JOB FOR BOB.
MARVEL BOY, GET IN HERE *FAST!*

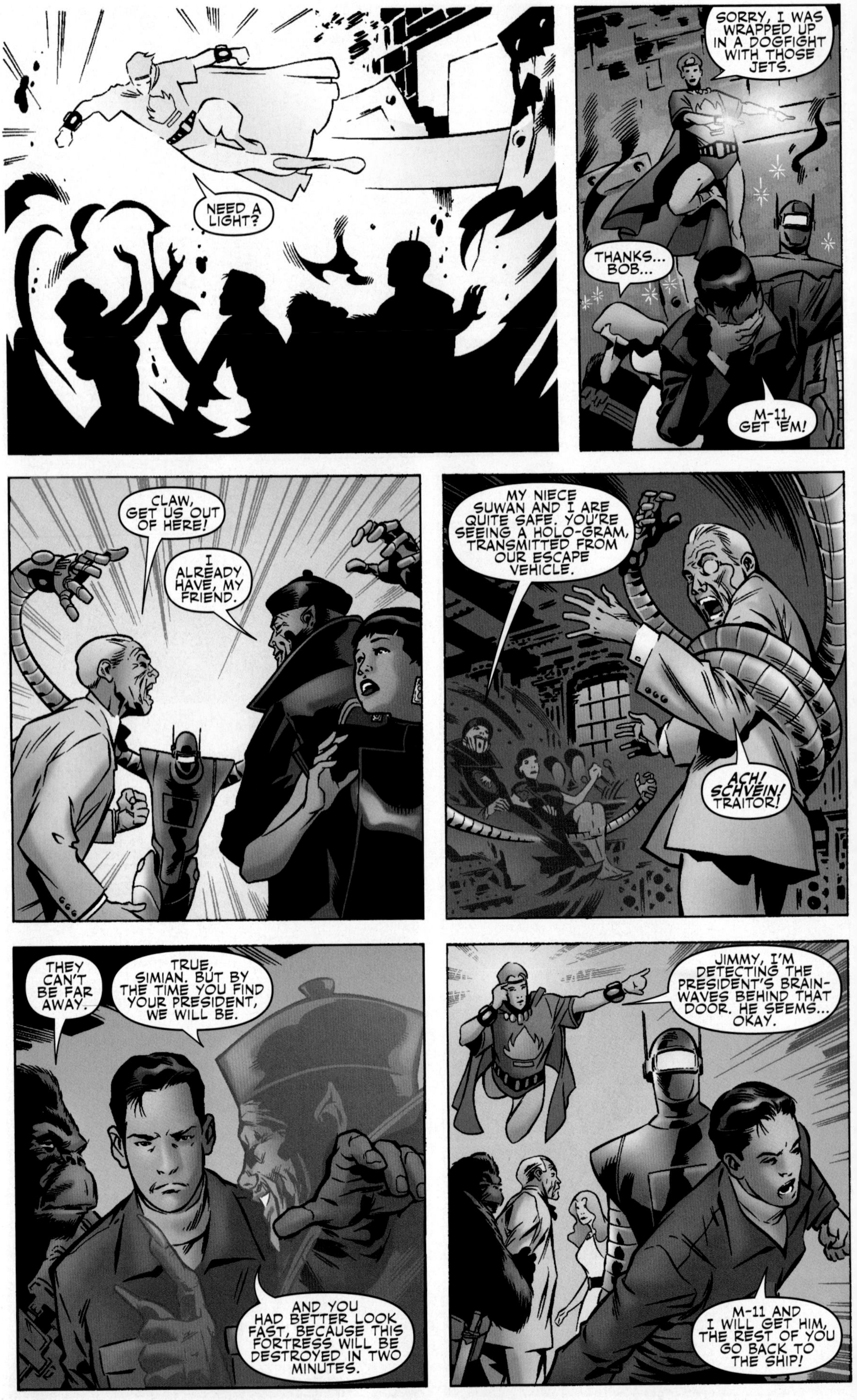
NEED A LIGHT?
SORRY, I WAS WRAPPED UP IN A DOGFIGHT WITH THOSE JETS.
THANKS... BOB...
M-11, GET 'EM!
CLAW, GET US OUT OF HERE!
I ALREADY HAVE, MY FRIEND.
MY NIECE SUWAN AND I ARE QUITE SAFE. YOU'RE SEEING A HOLO-GRAM, TRANSMITTED FROM OUR ESCAPE VEHICLE.
ACH! SCHVEIN! TRAITOR!
THEY CAN'T BE FAR AWAY.
TRUE, SIMIAN. BUT BY THE TIME YOU FIND YOUR PRESIDENT, WE WILL BE.
AND YOU HAD BETTER LOOK FAST, BECAUSE THIS FORTRESS WILL BE DESTROYED IN TWO MINUTES.
JIMMY, I'M DETECTING THE PRESIDENT'S BRAIN-WAVES BEHIND THAT DOOR. HE SEEMS... OKAY.
M-11 AND I WILL GET HIM, THE REST OF YOU GO BACK TO THE SHIP!

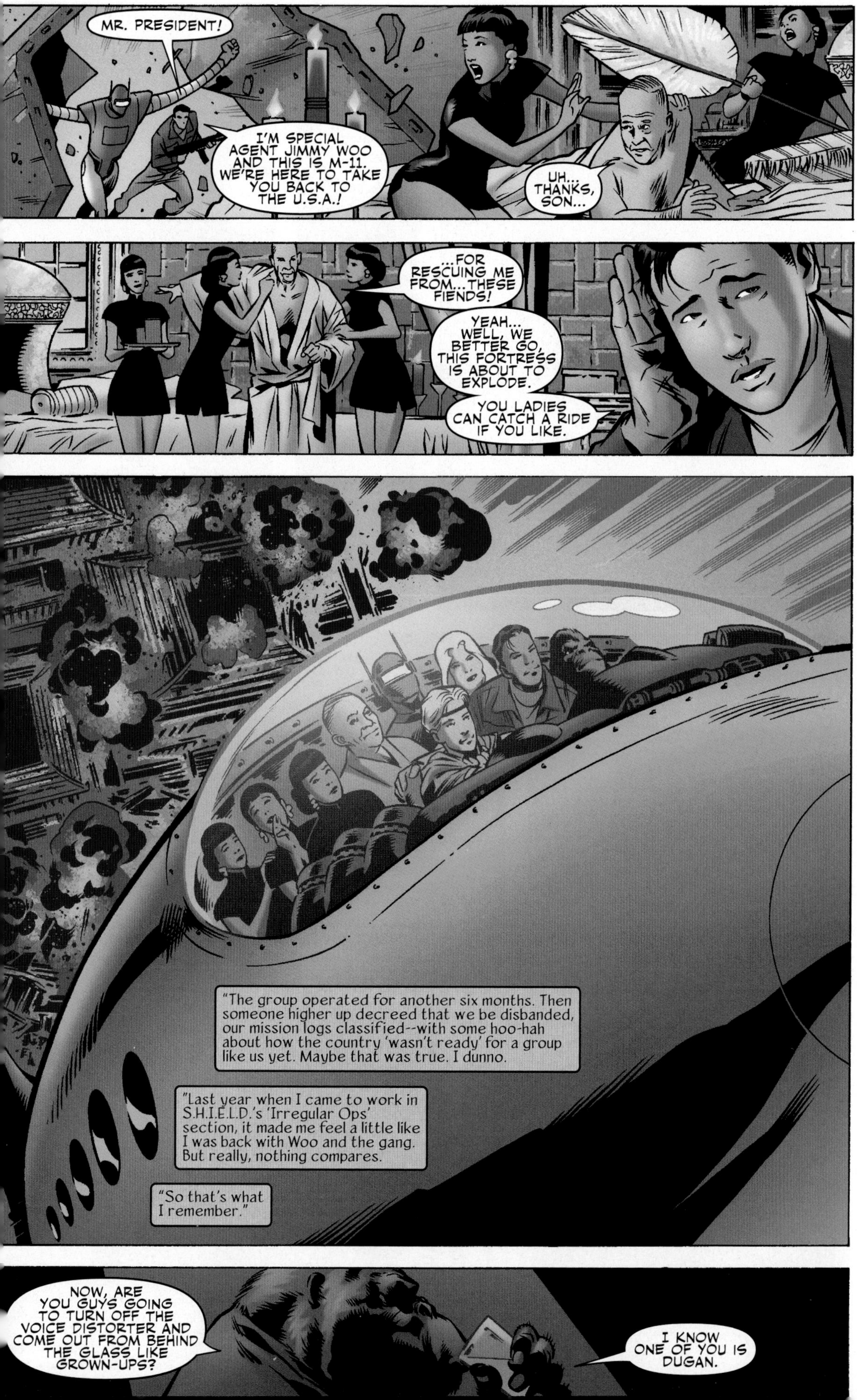
MR. PRESIDENT!
I'M SPECIAL AGENT JIMMY WOO AND THIS IS M-11. WE'RE HERE TO TAKE YOU BACK TO THE U.S.A.!
UH... THANKS, SON...
...FOR RESCUING ME FROM...THESE FIENDS!
YEAH... WELL, WE BETTER GO, THIS FORTRESS IS ABOUT TO EXPLODE.
YOU LADIES CAN CATCH A RIDE IF YOU LIKE.
"The group operated for another six months. Then someone higher up decreed that we be disbanded, our mission logs classified--with some hoo-hah about how the country 'wasn't ready' for a group like us yet. Maybe that was true. I dunno.
"Last year when I came to work in S.H.I.E.L.D.'s 'Irregular Ops' section, it made me feel a little like I was back with Woo and the gang. But really, nothing compares.
"So that's what I remember."
NOW, ARE YOU GUYS GOING TO TURN OFF THE VOICE DISTORTER AND COME OUT FROM BEHIND THE GLASS LIKE GROWN-UPS?
I KNOW ONE OF YOU IS DUGAN.

1600 HRS
STANDARD S.H.I.E.L.D. DEBRIEFING, HALE--YOU KNOW THAT. NOW, HOW'D YOU KNOW I WAS THERE?
SMELLED YA.
THIS IS AGENT DEREK KHANATA. HE'S HEADING THIS INVESTI-GATION.
MISTER HALE.
YOUR ACCOUNT LINES UP WITH WHAT WE LEARNED FROM THE FBI FILE, SEALED UNTIL YESTERDAY. TILL THEN, WE KNEW NOTHING ABOUT YOUR TEAM.
THEY MUST HAVE BEEN PRETTY PROUD OF US, HUH?
LOOK, IF S.H.I.E.L.D. IS MAD THAT I DIDN'T MENTION MY SERVICE RECORD--
NO, WE KNOW YOU WEREN'T ALLOWED TO TALK ABOUT IT. THIS AIN'T ABOUT YOU. IT'S ABOUT JIMMY WOO.
SUBDIRECTOR JAMES WOO
WOO'S BEEN WITH US SINCE THE '60'S. WORKED IN DIRECTORATE FOR THE LAST EIGHT YEARS.
EXTREMELY RELIABLE...UP UNTIL 48 HOURS AGO.
WOO HAD FORMED A SECRET STRIKE FORCE COMPRISED OF DISENFRANCHISED AND PROBLEM AGENTS WHO, AND I'M ASSUMING NOW, WOULD RISK GOING UNDERCOVER IN THEIR OWN AGENCY FOR THE PROMISE OF ACCEPTANCE--AND REAL ACTION.
HE ARRANGED FOR THE FIVE AGENTS TO MEET HIM IN SAN FRANCISCO TO RAID AN ORGANIZATION CALLED THE ATLAS FOUNDATION. BY THE TIME DIRECTORATE REALIZED SOMETHING WAS UP, WE RECEIVED A DISTRESS CALL. WHEN WE ARRIVED, WOO WAS THE ONLY ONE STILL ALIVE--BARELY.

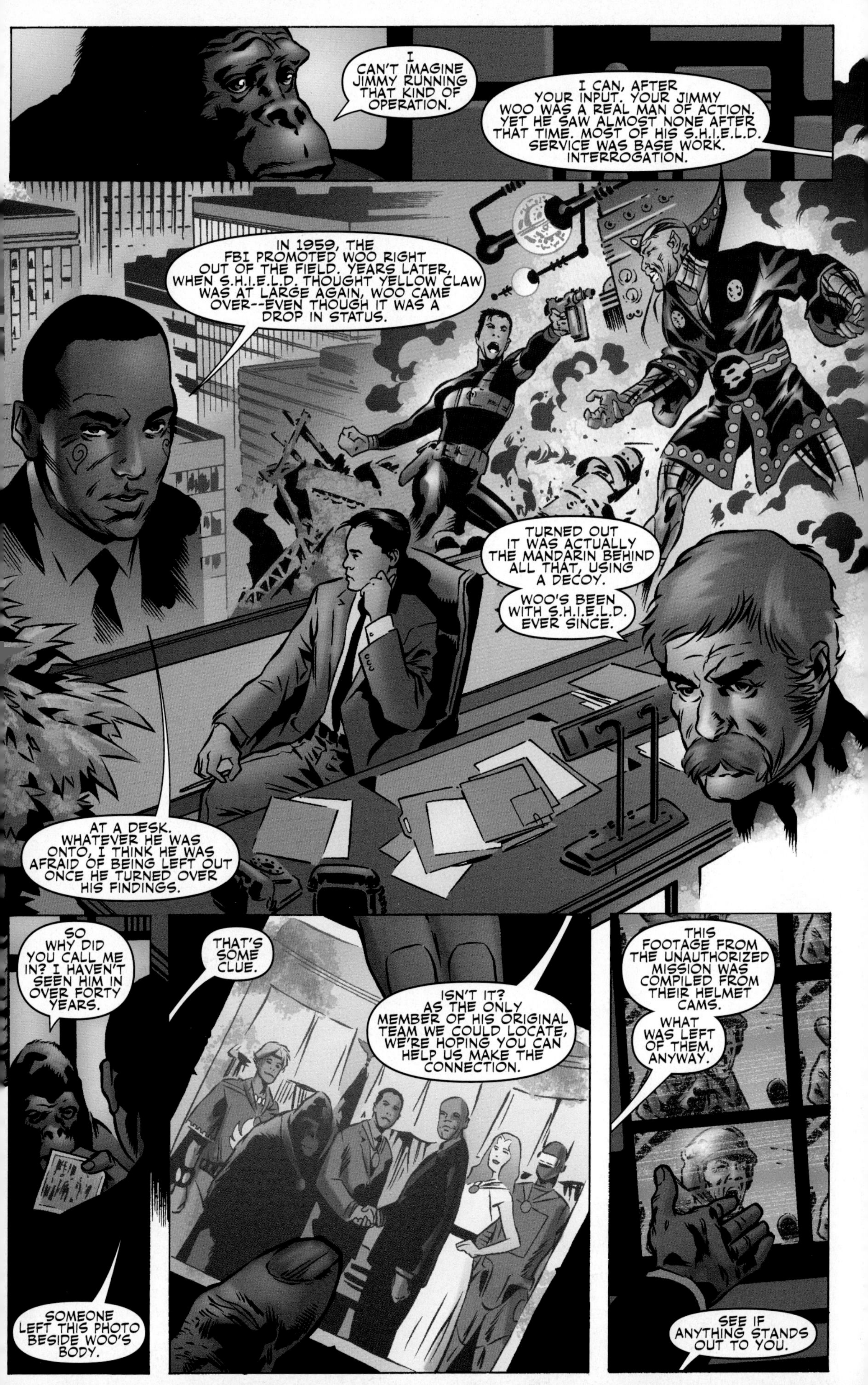
I CAN'T IMAGINE JIMMY RUNNING THAT KIND OF OPERATION.
I CAN, AFTER YOUR INPUT. YOUR JIMMY WOO WAS A REAL MAN OF ACTION. YET HE SAW ALMOST NONE AFTER THAT TIME. MOST OF HIS S.H.I.E.L.D. SERVICE WAS BASE WORK. INTERROGATION.
IN 1959, THE FBI PROMOTED WOO RIGHT OUT OF THE FIELD. YEARS LATER, WHEN S.H.I.E.L.D. THOUGHT YELLOW CLAW WAS AT LARGE AGAIN, WOO CAME OVER--EVEN THOUGH IT WAS A DROP IN STATUS.
TURNED OUT IT WAS ACTUALLY THE MANDARIN BEHIND ALL THAT, USING A DECOY.
WOO'S BEEN WITH S.H.I.E.L.D. EVER SINCE.
AT A DESK. WHATEVER HE WAS ONTO, I THINK HE WAS AFRAID OF BEING LEFT OUT ONCE HE TURNED OVER HIS FINDINGS.
SO WHY DID YOU CALL ME IN? I HAVEN'T SEEN HIM IN OVER FORTY YEARS.
SOMEONE LEFT THIS PHOTO BESIDE WOO'S BODY.
THAT'S SOME CLUE.
ISN'T IT? AS THE ONLY MEMBER OF HIS ORIGINAL TEAM WE COULD LOCATE, WE'RE HOPING YOU CAN HELP US MAKE THE CONNECTION.
THIS FOOTAGE FROM THE UNAUTHORIZED MISSION WAS COMPILED FROM THEIR HELMET CAMS.
WHAT WAS LEFT OF THEM, ANYWAY.
SEE IF ANYTHING STANDS OUT TO YOU.

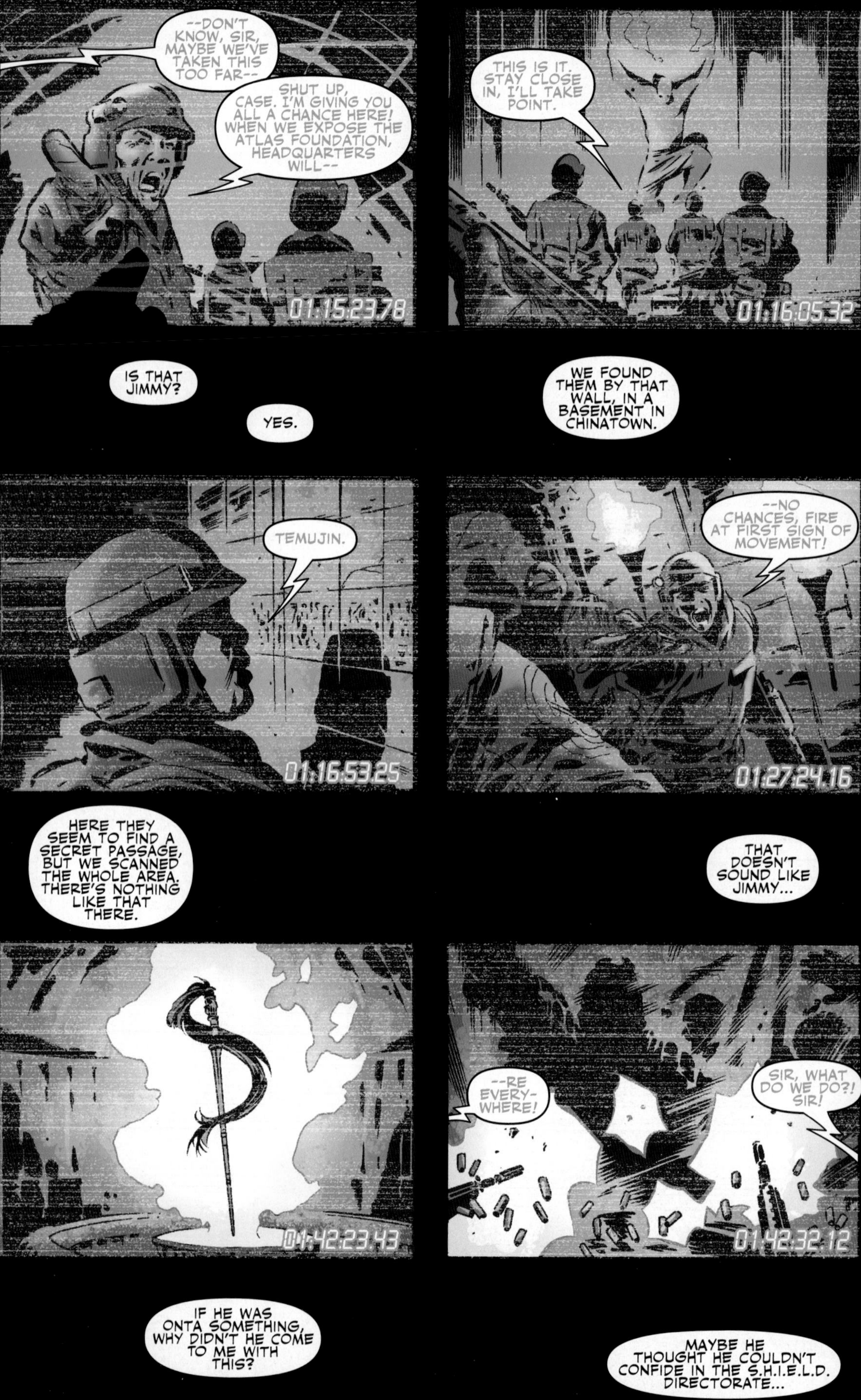
--DON'T KNOW, SIR, MAYBE WE'VE TAKEN THIS TOO FAR--
SHUT UP, CASE. I'M GIVING YOU ALL A CHANCE HERE! WHEN WE EXPOSE THE ATLAS FOUNDATION, HEADQUARTERS WILL--
01:15:23.78
THIS IS IT. STAY CLOSE IN, I'LL TAKE POINT.
01:16:05.32
IS THAT JIMMY?
YES.
WE FOUND THEM BY THAT WALL, IN A BASEMENT IN CHINATOWN.
TEMUJIN.
01:16:53.25
--NO CHANCES, FIRE AT FIRST SIGN OF MOVEMENT!
01:27:24.16
HERE THEY SEEM TO FIND A SECRET PASSAGE, BUT WE SCANNED THE WHOLE AREA. THERE'S NOTHING LIKE THAT THERE.
THAT DOESN'T SOUND LIKE JIMMY...
01:42:23.43
--RE EVERY-WHERE!
SIR, WHAT DO WE DO?! SIR!
01:42:32.12
IF HE WAS ONTA SOMETHING, WHY DIDN'T HE COME TO ME WITH THIS?
MAYBE HE THOUGHT HE COULDN'T CONFIDE IN THE S.H.I.E.L.D. DIRECTORATE...

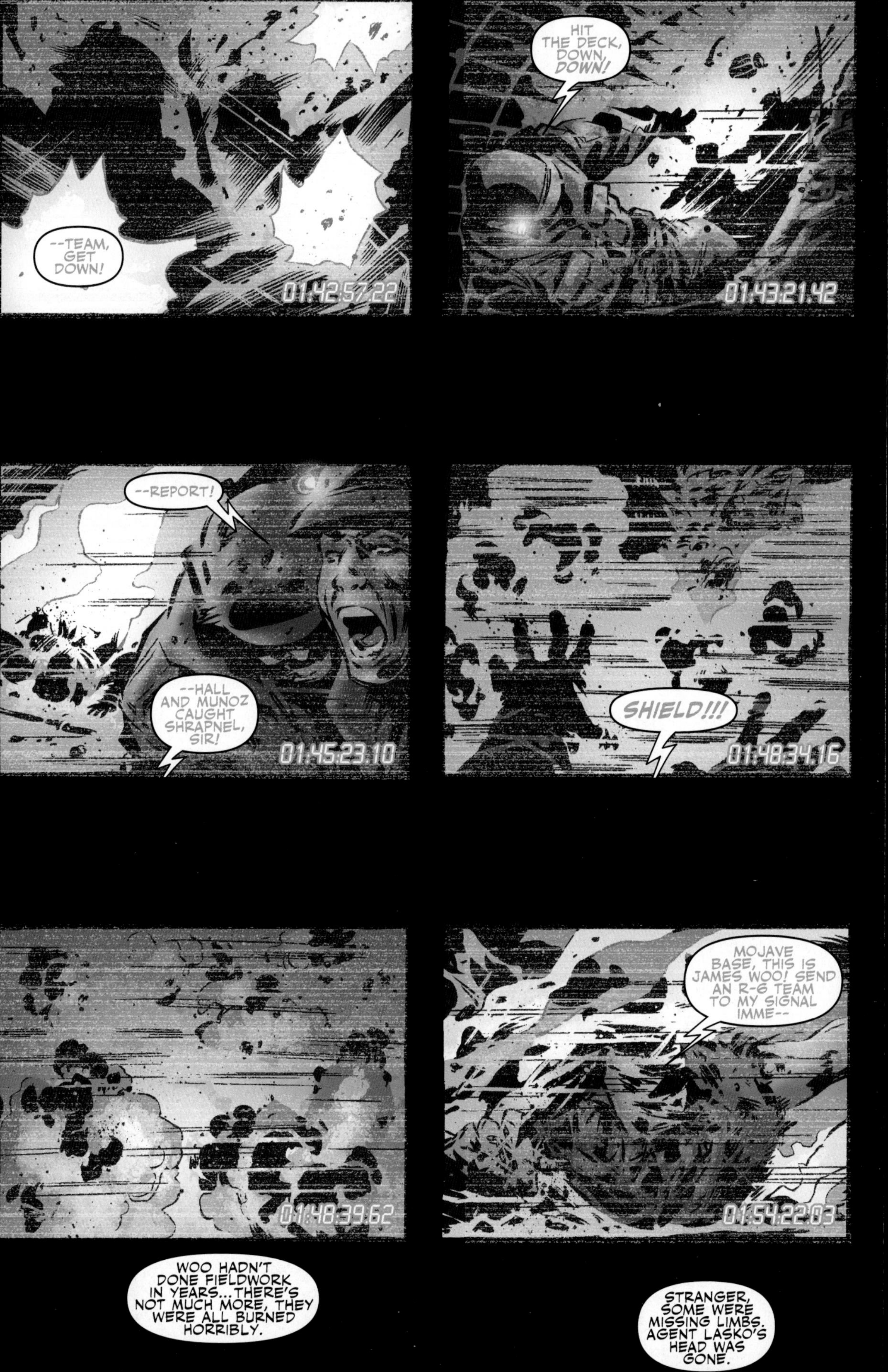
--TEAM, GET DOWN!
01:42:57.22
HIT THE DECK, DOWN, *DOWN!*
01:43:21.42
--REPORT!
--HALL AND MUNOZ CAUGHT SHRAPNEL, SIR!
01:45:23.10
SHIELD!!!
01:48:34.16
01:48:39.62
MOJAVE BASE, THIS IS JAMES WOO! SEND AN R-6 TEAM TO MY SIGNAL IMME--
01:54:22.03
WOO HADN'T DONE FIELDWORK IN YEARS... THERE'S NOT MUCH MORE, THEY WERE ALL BURNED HORRIBLY.
STRANGER, SOME WERE MISSING LIMBS. AGENT LASKO'S HEAD WAS GONE.

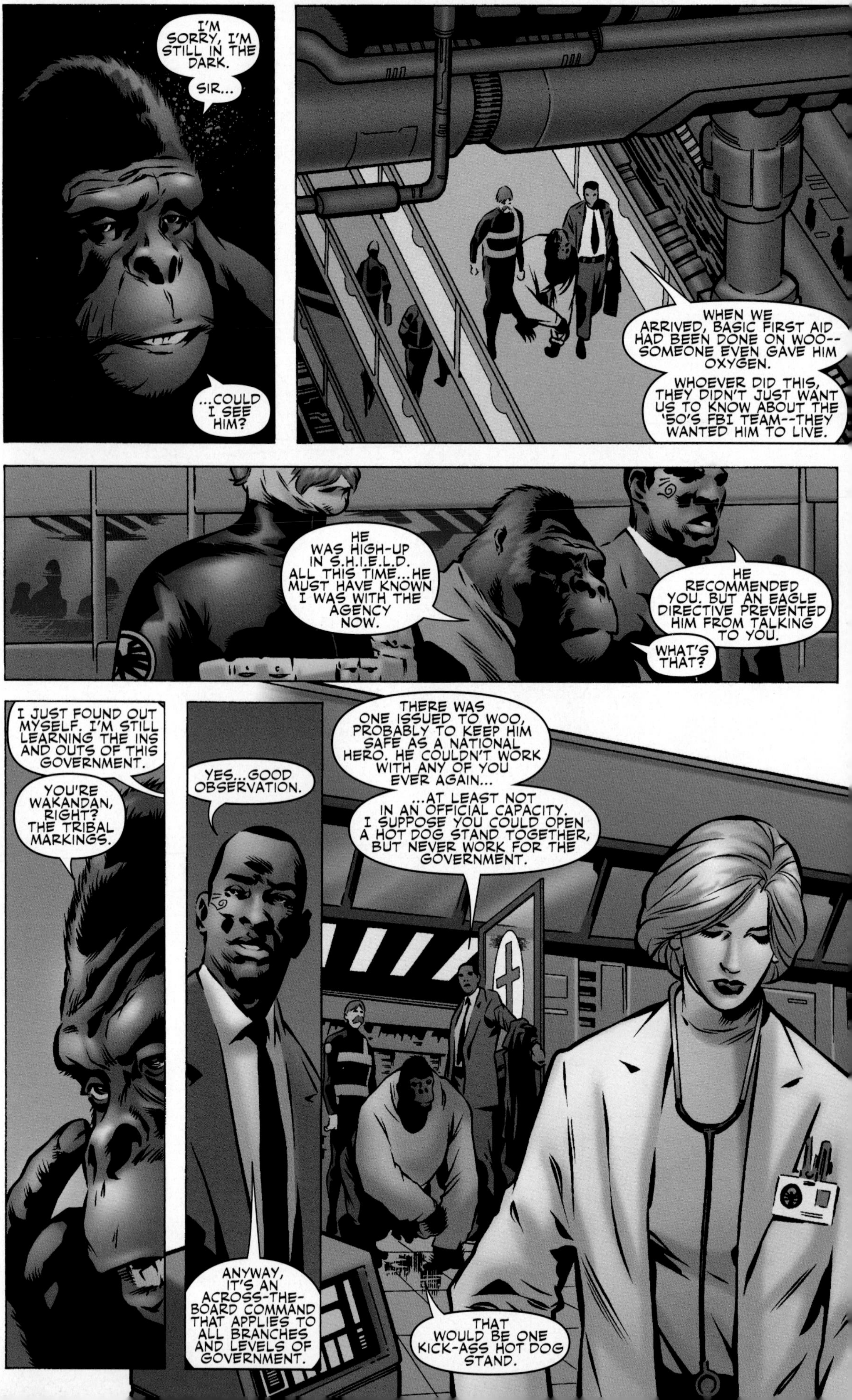
I'M SORRY, I'M STILL IN THE DARK.
SIR...
...COULD I SEE HIM?
WHEN WE ARRIVED, BASIC FIRST AID HAD BEEN DONE ON WOO--SOMEONE EVEN GAVE HIM OXYGEN.
WHOEVER DID THIS, THEY DIDN'T JUST WANT US TO KNOW ABOUT THE '50'S FBI TEAM--THEY WANTED HIM TO LIVE.
HE WAS HIGH-UP IN S.H.I.E.L.D. ALL THIS TIME...HE MUST HAVE KNOWN I WAS WITH THE AGENCY NOW.
HE RECOMMENDED YOU. BUT AN EAGLE DIRECTIVE PREVENTED HIM FROM TALKING TO YOU.
WHAT'S THAT?
I JUST FOUND OUT MYSELF. I'M STILL LEARNING THE INS AND OUTS OF THIS GOVERNMENT.
YOU'RE WAKANDAN, RIGHT? THE TRIBAL MARKINGS.
YES...GOOD OBSERVATION.
ANYWAY, IT'S AN ACROSS-THE-BOARD COMMAND THAT APPLIES TO ALL BRANCHES AND LEVELS OF GOVERNMENT.
THERE WAS ONE ISSUED TO WOO, PROBABLY TO KEEP HIM SAFE AS A NATIONAL HERO. HE COULDN'T WORK WITH ANY OF YOU EVER AGAIN...
...AT LEAST NOT IN AN OFFICIAL CAPACITY. I SUPPOSE YOU COULD OPEN A HOT DOG STAND TOGETHER, BUT NEVER WORK FOR THE GOVERNMENT.
THAT WOULD BE ONE KICK-ASS HOT DOG STAND.

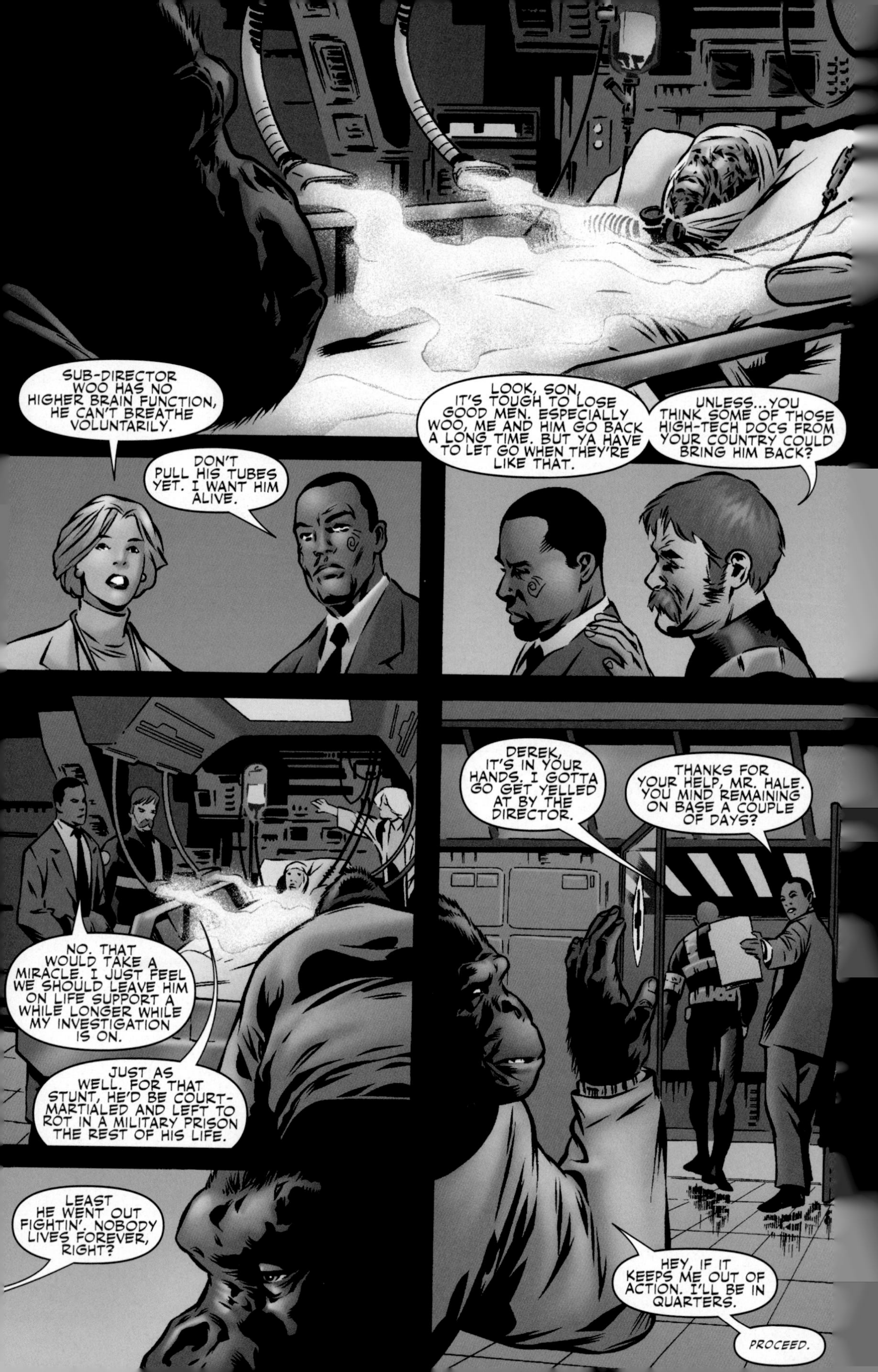
SUB-DIRECTOR WOO HAS NO HIGHER BRAIN FUNCTION, HE CAN'T BREATHE VOLUNTARILY.
DON'T PULL HIS TUBES YET. I WANT HIM ALIVE.
LOOK, SON, IT'S TOUGH TO LOSE GOOD MEN. ESPECIALLY WOO, ME AND HIM GO BACK A LONG TIME. BUT YA HAVE TO LET GO WHEN THEY'RE LIKE THAT.
UNLESS...YOU THINK SOME OF THOSE HIGH-TECH DOCS FROM YOUR COUNTRY COULD BRING HIM BACK?
NO. THAT WOULD TAKE A MIRACLE. I JUST FEEL WE SHOULD LEAVE HIM ON LIFE SUPPORT A WHILE LONGER WHILE MY INVESTIGATION IS ON.
JUST AS WELL. FOR THAT STUNT, HE'D BE COURT-MARTIALED AND LEFT TO ROT IN A MILITARY PRISON THE REST OF HIS LIFE.
LEAST HE WENT OUT FIGHTIN'. NOBODY LIVES FOREVER, RIGHT?
DEREK, IT'S IN YOUR HANDS. I GOTTA GO GET YELLED AT BY THE DIRECTOR.
THANKS FOR YOUR HELP, MR. HALE. YOU MIND REMAINING ON BASE A COUPLE OF DAYS?
HEY, IF IT KEEPS ME OUT OF ACTION. I'LL BE IN QUARTERS.
PROCEED.

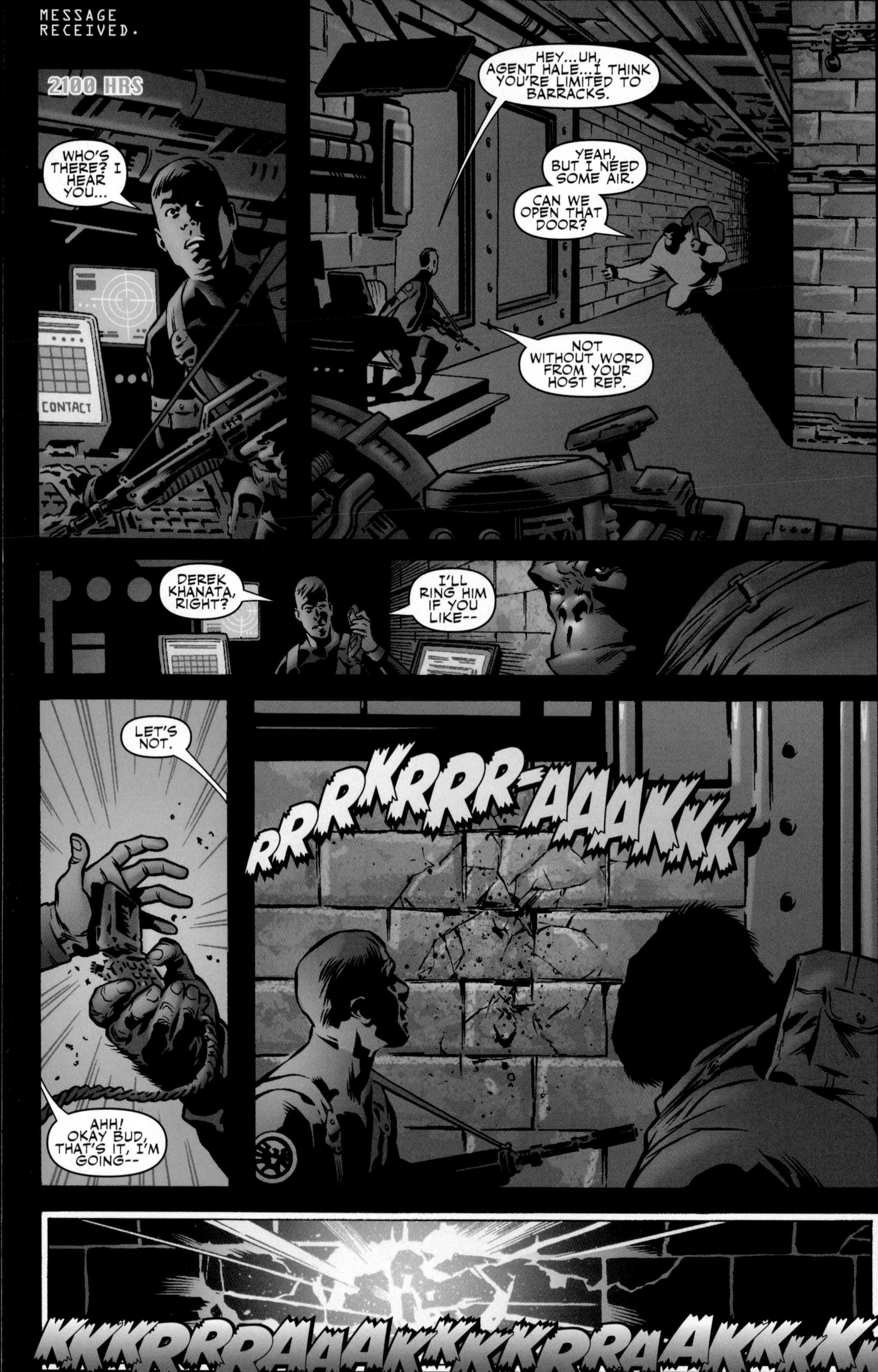
MESSAGE RECEIVED.
2100 HRS
WHO'S THERE? I HEAR YOU...
HEY...UH, AGENT HALE...I THINK YOU'RE LIMITED TO BARRACKS.
YEAH, BUT I NEED SOME AIR.
CAN WE OPEN THAT DOOR?
NOT WITHOUT WORD FROM YOUR HOST REP.
DEREK KHANATA, RIGHT?
I'LL RING HIM IF YOU LIKE--
LET'S NOT.
AHH! OKAY BUD, THAT'S IT, I'M GOING--
RRRKRRR-AAAKKK
KKKRRRAAAKKKKRRAAKKKK

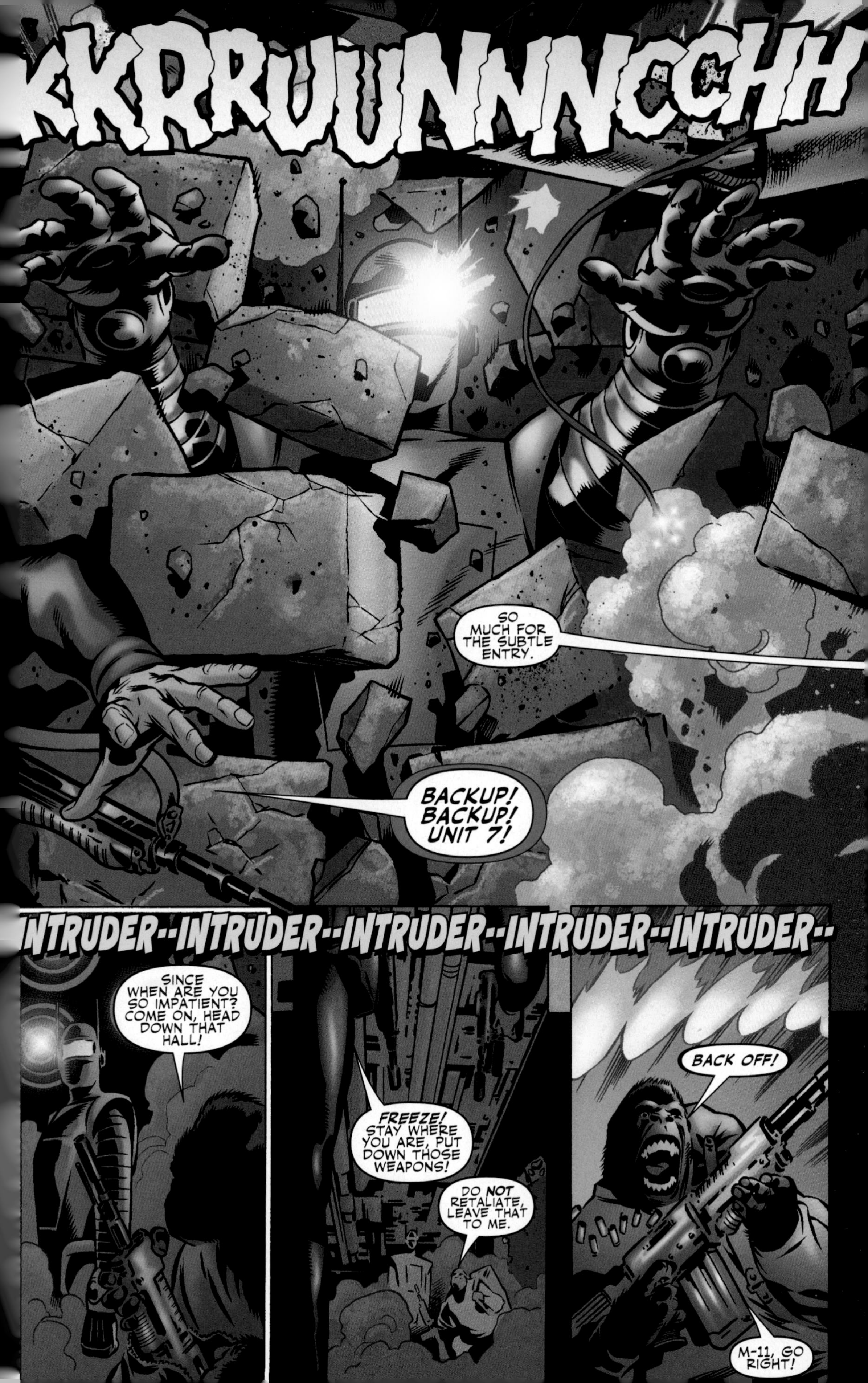
KKRRUUNNNCCHH
SO MUCH FOR THE SUBTLE ENTRY.
BACKUP! BACKUP! UNIT 7!
INTRUDER--INTRUDER--INTRUDER--INTRUDER--INTRUDER--
SINCE WHEN ARE YOU SO IMPATIENT? COME ON, HEAD DOWN THAT HALL!
FREEZE! STAY WHERE YOU ARE, PUT DOWN THOSE WEAPONS!
DO NOT RETALIATE, LEAVE THAT TO ME.
BACK OFF!
M-11, GO RIGHT!

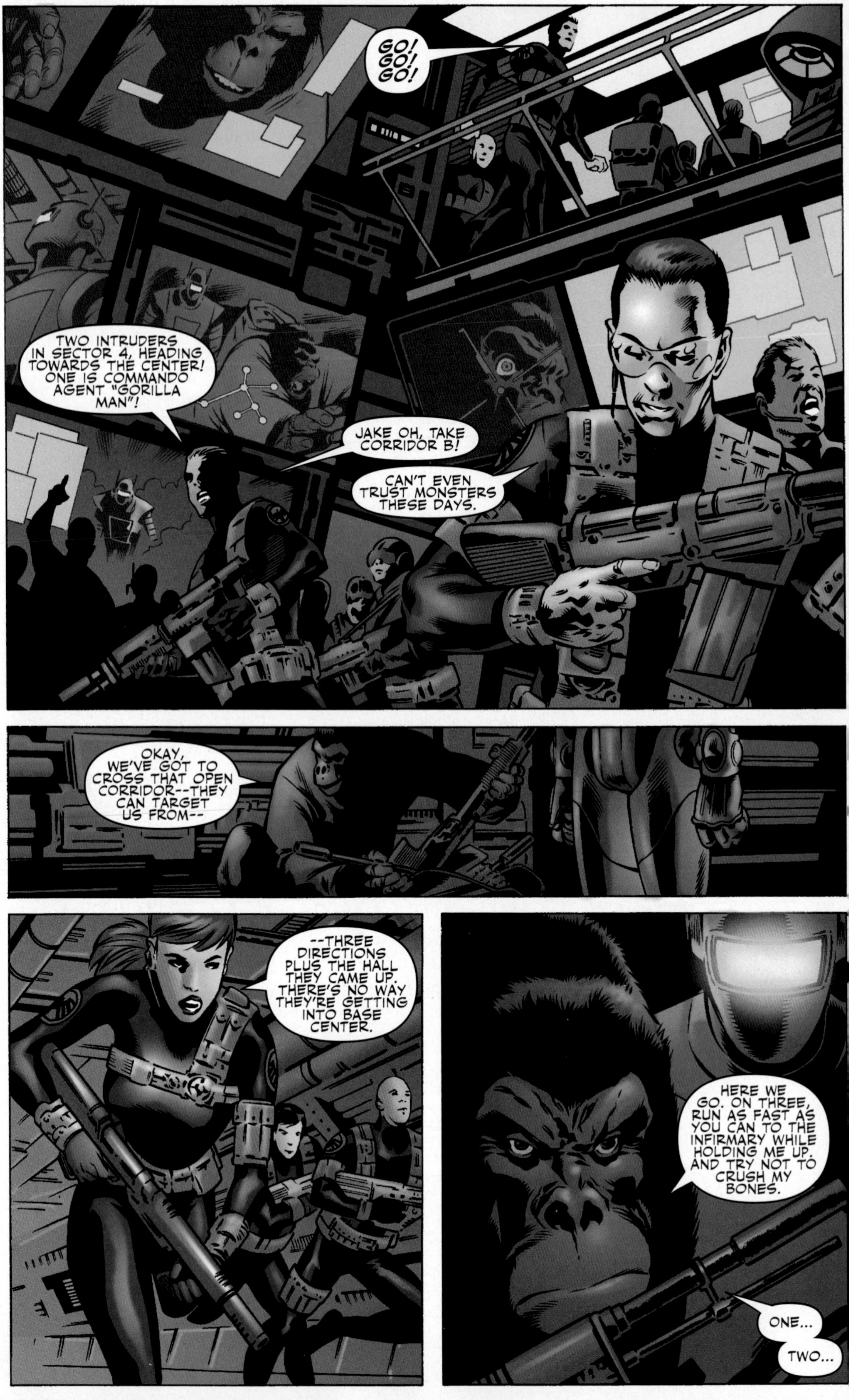
GO! GO! GO!
TWO INTRUDERS IN SECTOR 4, HEADING TOWARDS THE CENTER! ONE IS COMMANDO AGENT "GORILLA MAN"!
JAKE OH, TAKE CORRIDOR B!
CAN'T EVEN TRUST MONSTERS THESE DAYS.
OKAY, WE'VE GOT TO CROSS THAT OPEN CORRIDOR--THEY CAN TARGET US FROM--
--THREE DIRECTIONS PLUS THE HALL THEY CAME UP. THERE'S NO WAY THEY'RE GETTING INTO BASE CENTER.
HERE WE GO. ON THREE, RUN AS FAST AS YOU CAN TO THE INFIRMARY WHILE HOLDING ME UP. AND TRY NOT TO CRUSH MY BONES.
ONE...
TWO...

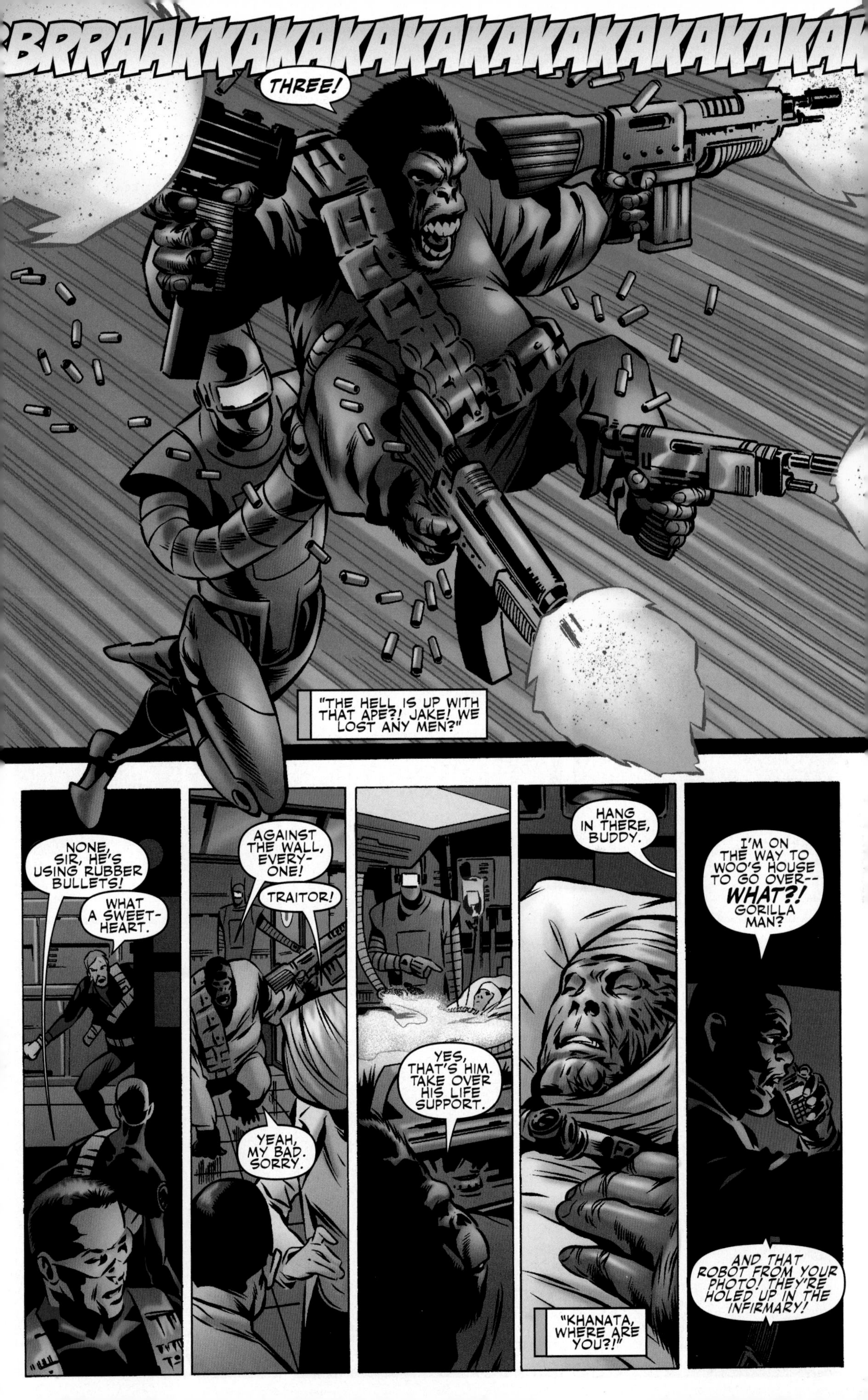
BRRAAKKAKAKAKAKAKAKAKAKAKAK
THREE!
"THE HELL IS UP WITH THAT APE?! JAKE! WE LOST ANY MEN?"
NONE, SIR, HE'S USING RUBBER BULLETS!
WHAT A SWEET-HEART.
AGAINST THE WALL, EVERY-ONE!
TRAITOR!
YEAH, MY BAD. SORRY.
YES, THAT'S HIM. TAKE OVER HIS LIFE SUPPORT.
HANG IN THERE, BUDDY.
"KHANATA, WHERE ARE YOU?!"
I'M ON THE WAY TO WOO'S HOUSE TO GO OVER-- WHAT?! GORILLA MAN?
AND THAT ROBOT FROM YOUR PHOTO! THEY'RE HOLED UP IN THE INFIRMARY!

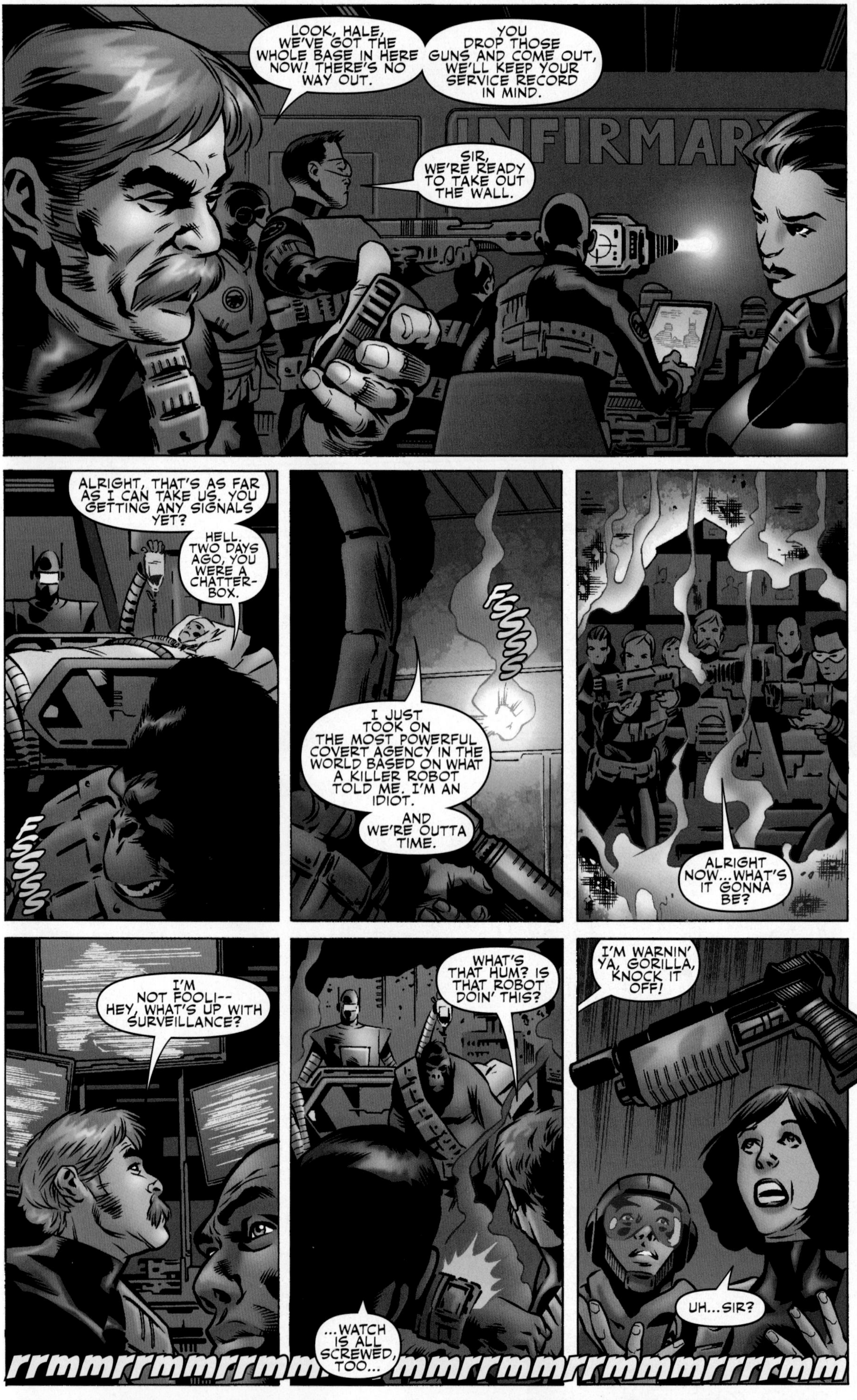
LOOK, HALE, WE'VE GOT THE WHOLE BASE IN HERE NOW! THERE'S NO WAY OUT.
YOU DROP THOSE GUNS AND COME OUT, WE'LL KEEP YOUR SERVICE RECORD IN MIND.
INFIRMARY
SIR, WE'RE READY TO TAKE OUT THE WALL.
ALRIGHT, THAT'S AS FAR AS I CAN TAKE US. YOU GETTING ANY SIGNALS YET?
HELL. TWO DAYS AGO, YOU WERE A CHATTER-BOX.
FSSSS
FSSSS
I JUST TOOK ON THE MOST POWERFUL COVERT AGENCY IN THE WORLD BASED ON WHAT A KILLER ROBOT TOLD ME. I'M AN IDIOT.
AND WE'RE OUTTA TIME.
ALRIGHT NOW...WHAT'S IT GONNA BE?
I'M NOT FOOLI-- HEY, WHAT'S UP WITH SURVEILLANCE?
WHAT'S THAT HUM? IS THAT ROBOT DOIN' THIS?
...WATCH IS ALL SCREWED, TOO...
I'M WARNIN' YA, GORILLA, KNOCK IT OFF!
UH...SIR?
rrmmrrmmrrmmmmrrmmrrmmmrrrrmm

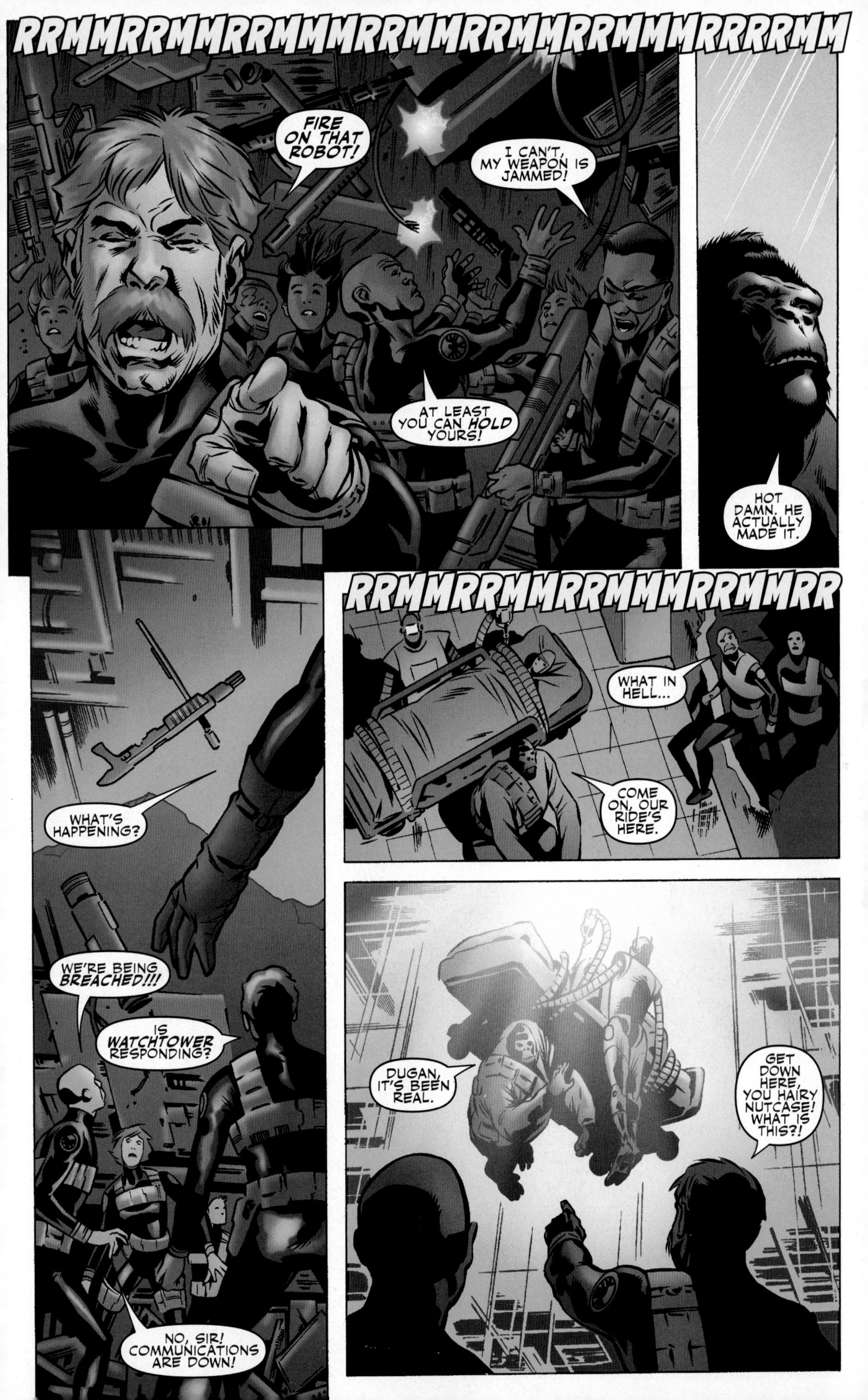
RRMMRRMMRRMMMRRMMRRMMRRMMMRRRRMM
FIRE ON THAT ROBOT!
I CAN'T, MY WEAPON IS JAMMED!
AT LEAST YOU CAN HOLD YOURS!
HOT DAMN. HE ACTUALLY MADE IT.
WHAT'S HAPPENING?
WE'RE BEING BREACHED!!!
IS WATCHTOWER RESPONDING?
NO, SIR! COMMUNICATIONS ARE DOWN!
RRMMRRMMRRMMMRRMMRR
WHAT IN HELL...
COME ON, OUR RIDE'S HERE.
DUGAN, IT'S BEEN REAL.
GET DOWN HERE, YOU HAIRY NUTCASE! WHAT IS THIS?!

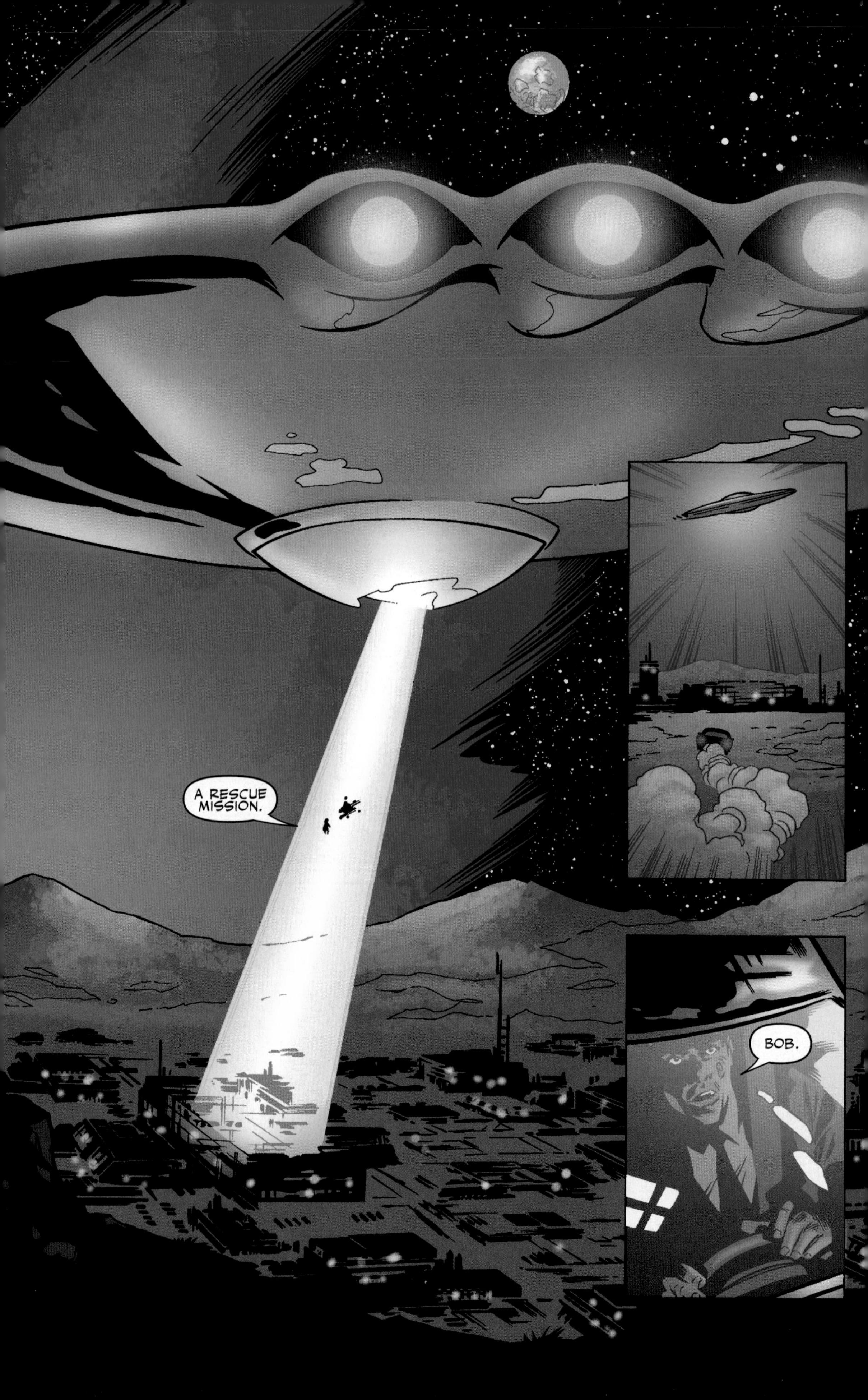
A RESCUE MISSION.
BOB.

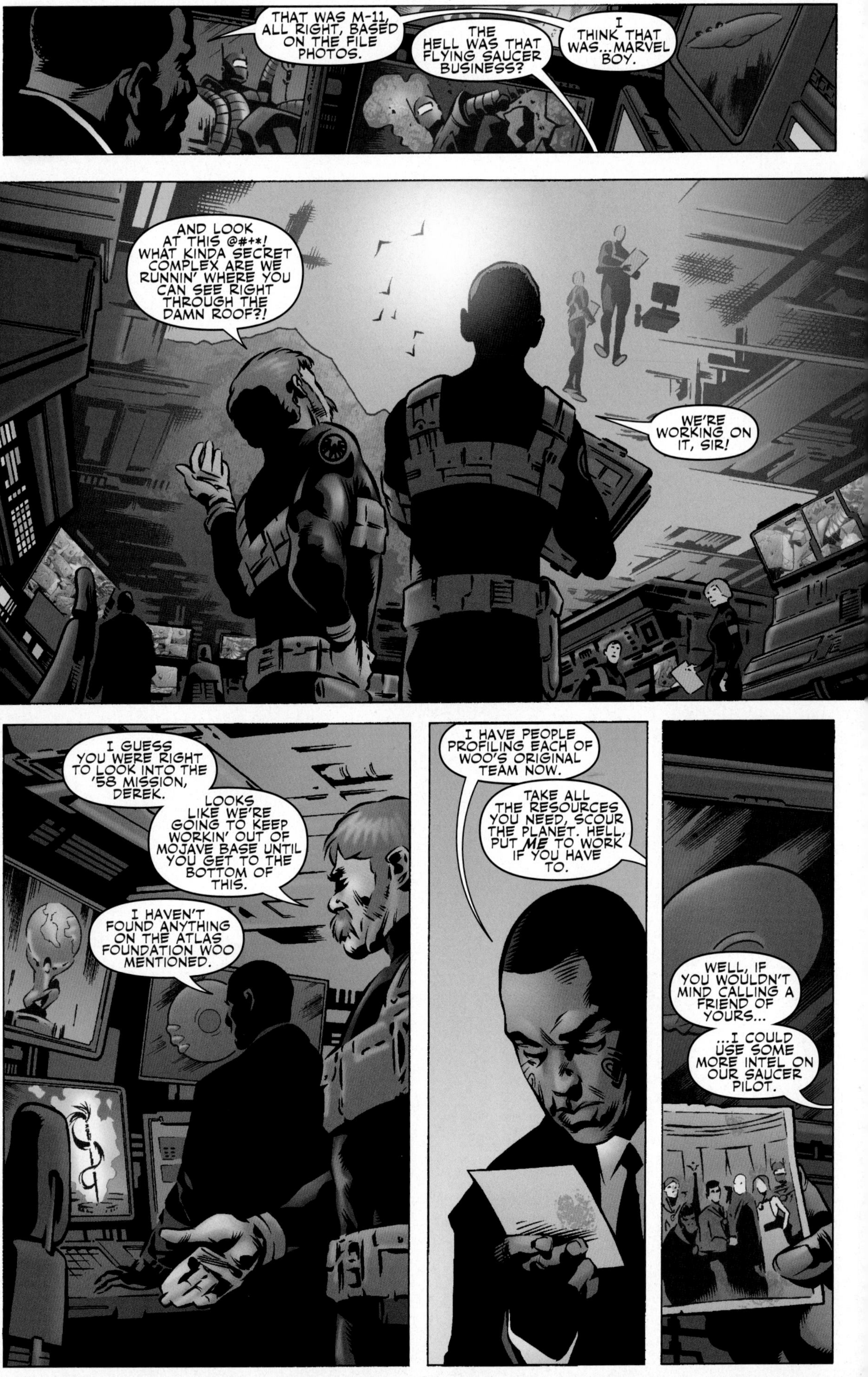
THAT WAS M-11, ALL RIGHT, BASED ON THE FILE PHOTOS.
THE HELL WAS THAT FLYING SAUCER BUSINESS?
I THINK THAT WAS...MARVEL BOY.
AND LOOK AT THIS @#+*! WHAT KINDA SECRET COMPLEX ARE WE RUNNIN' WHERE YOU CAN SEE RIGHT THROUGH THE DAMN ROOF?!
WE'RE WORKING ON IT, SIR!
I GUESS YOU WERE RIGHT TO LOOK INTO THE '58 MISSION, DEREK.
LOOKS LIKE WE'RE GOING TO KEEP WORKIN' OUT OF MOJAVE BASE UNTIL YOU GET TO THE BOTTOM OF THIS.
I HAVEN'T FOUND ANYTHING ON THE ATLAS FOUNDATION WOO MENTIONED.
I HAVE PEOPLE PROFILING EACH OF WOO'S ORIGINAL TEAM NOW.
TAKE ALL THE RESOURCES YOU NEED, SCOUR THE PLANET. HELL, PUT *ME* TO WORK IF YOU HAVE TO.
WELL, IF YOU WOULDN'T MIND CALLING A FRIEND OF YOURS...
...I COULD USE SOME MORE INTEL ON OUR SAUCER PILOT.

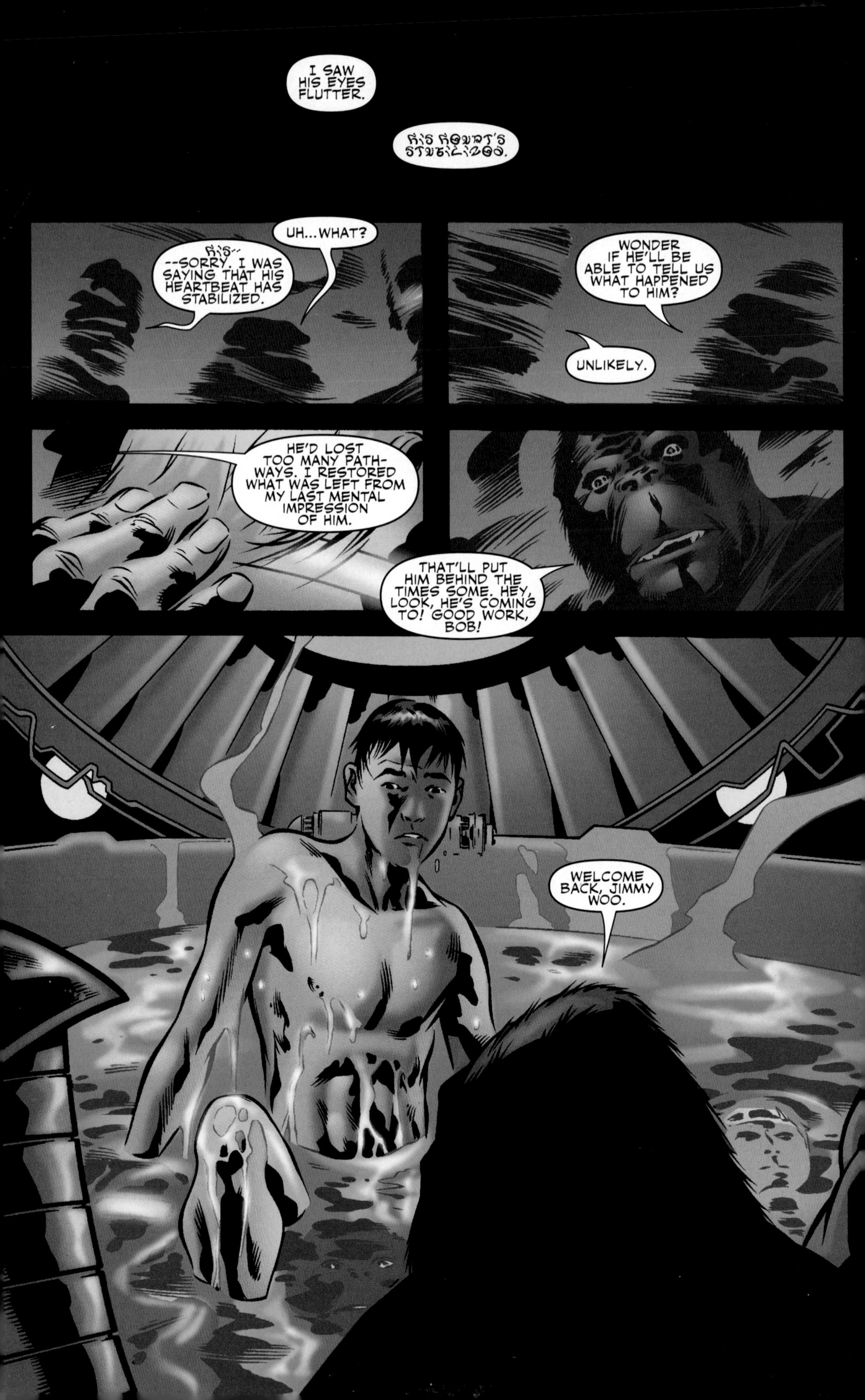
I SAW HIS EYES FLUTTER.
UH...WHAT?
--SORRY. I WAS SAYING THAT HIS HEARTBEAT HAS STABILIZED.
WONDER IF HE'LL BE ABLE TO TELL US WHAT HAPPENED TO HIM?
UNLIKELY.
HE'D LOST TOO MANY PATH-WAYS. I RESTORED WHAT WAS LEFT FROM MY LAST MENTAL IMPRESSION OF HIM.
THAT'LL PUT HIM BEHIND THE TIMES SOME. HEY, LOOK, HE'S COMING TO! GOOD WORK, BOB!
WELCOME BACK, JIMMY WOO.

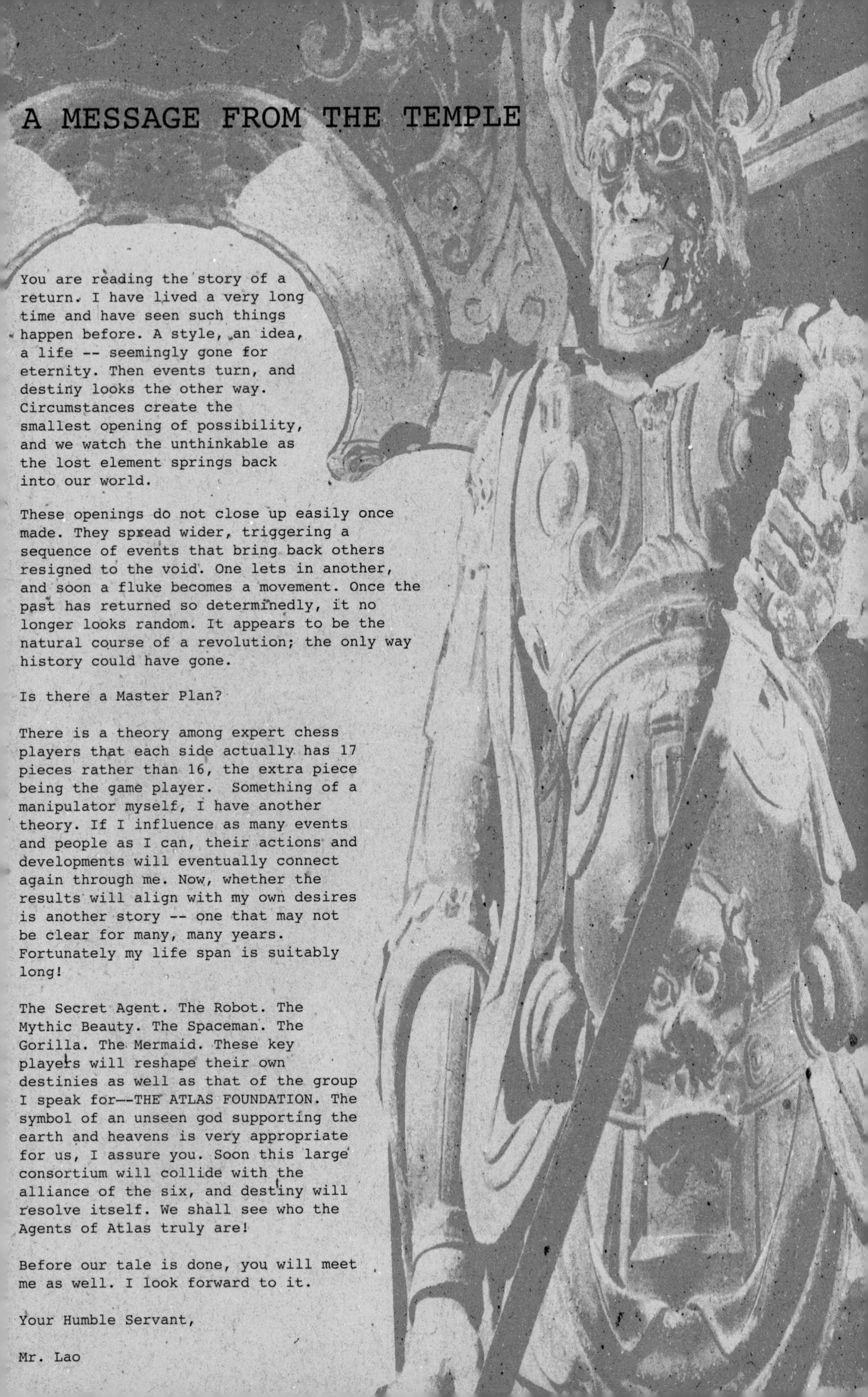

A MESSAGE FROM THE TEMPLE

You are reading the story of a return. I have lived a very long time and have seen such things happen before. A style, an idea, a life -- seemingly gone for eternity. Then events turn, and destiny looks the other way. Circumstances create the smallest opening of possibility, and we watch the unthinkable as the lost element springs back into our world.

These openings do not close up easily once made. They spread wider, triggering a sequence of events that bring back others resigned to the void. One lets in another, and soon a fluke becomes a movement. Once the past has returned so determinedly, it no longer looks random. It appears to be the natural course of a revolution; the only way history could have gone.

Is there a Master Plan?

There is a theory among expert chess players that each side actually has 17 pieces rather than 16, the extra piece being the game player. Something of a manipulator myself, I have another theory. If I influence as many events and people as I can, their actions and developments will eventually connect again through me. Now, whether the results will align with my own desires is another story -- one that may not be clear for many, many years. Fortunately my life span is suitably long!

The Secret Agent. The Robot. The Mythic Beauty. The Spaceman. The Gorilla. The Mermaid. These key players will reshape their own destinies as well as that of the group I speak for--THE ATLAS FOUNDATION. The symbol of an unseen god supporting the earth and heavens is very appropriate for us, I assure you. Soon this large consortium will collide with the alliance of the six, and destiny will resolve itself. We shall see who the Agents of Atlas truly are!

Before our tale is done, you will meet me as well. I look forward to it.

Your Humble Servant,

Mr. Lao

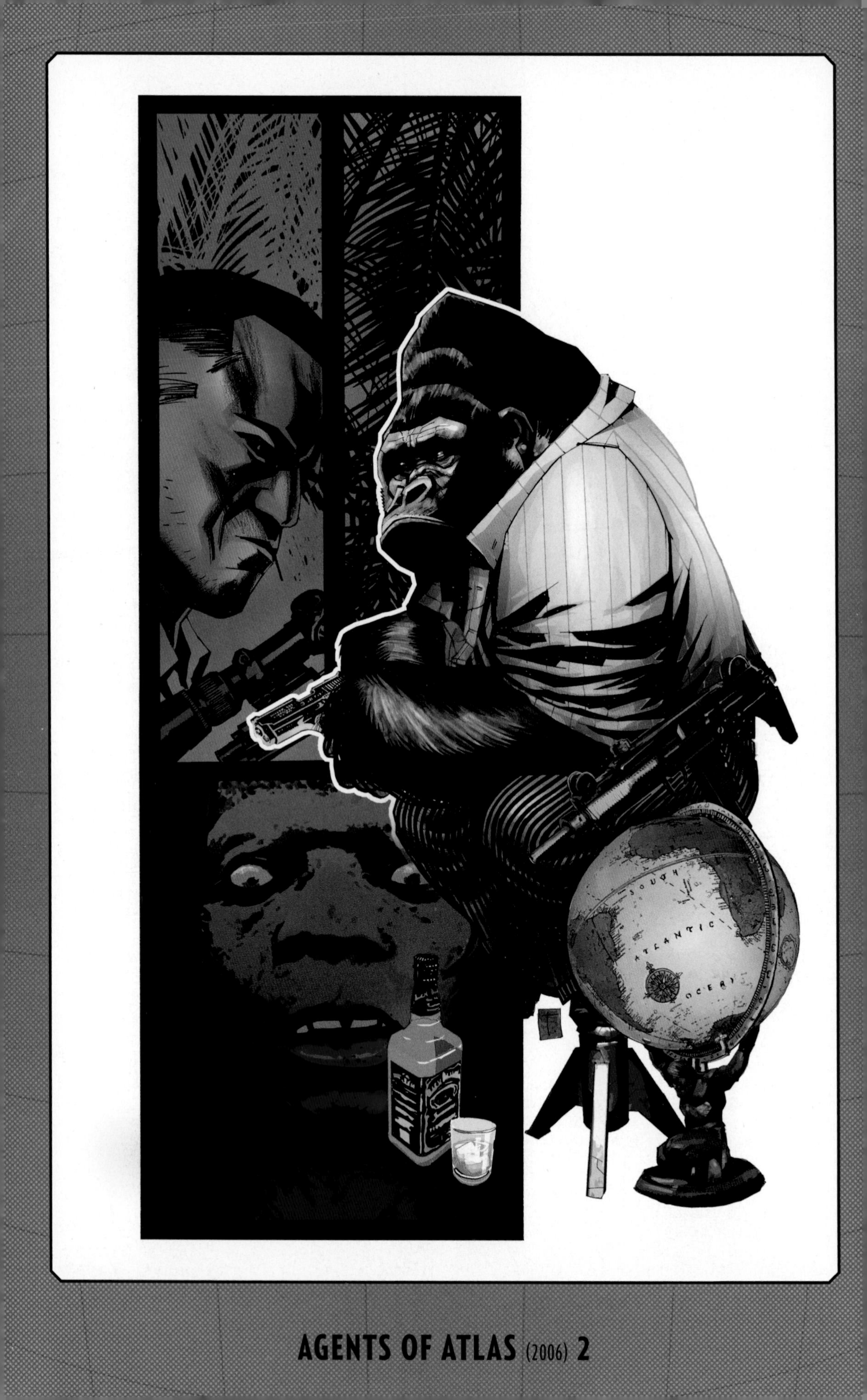
SOUTH
ATLANTIC

AGENTS OF ATLAS (2006) **2**

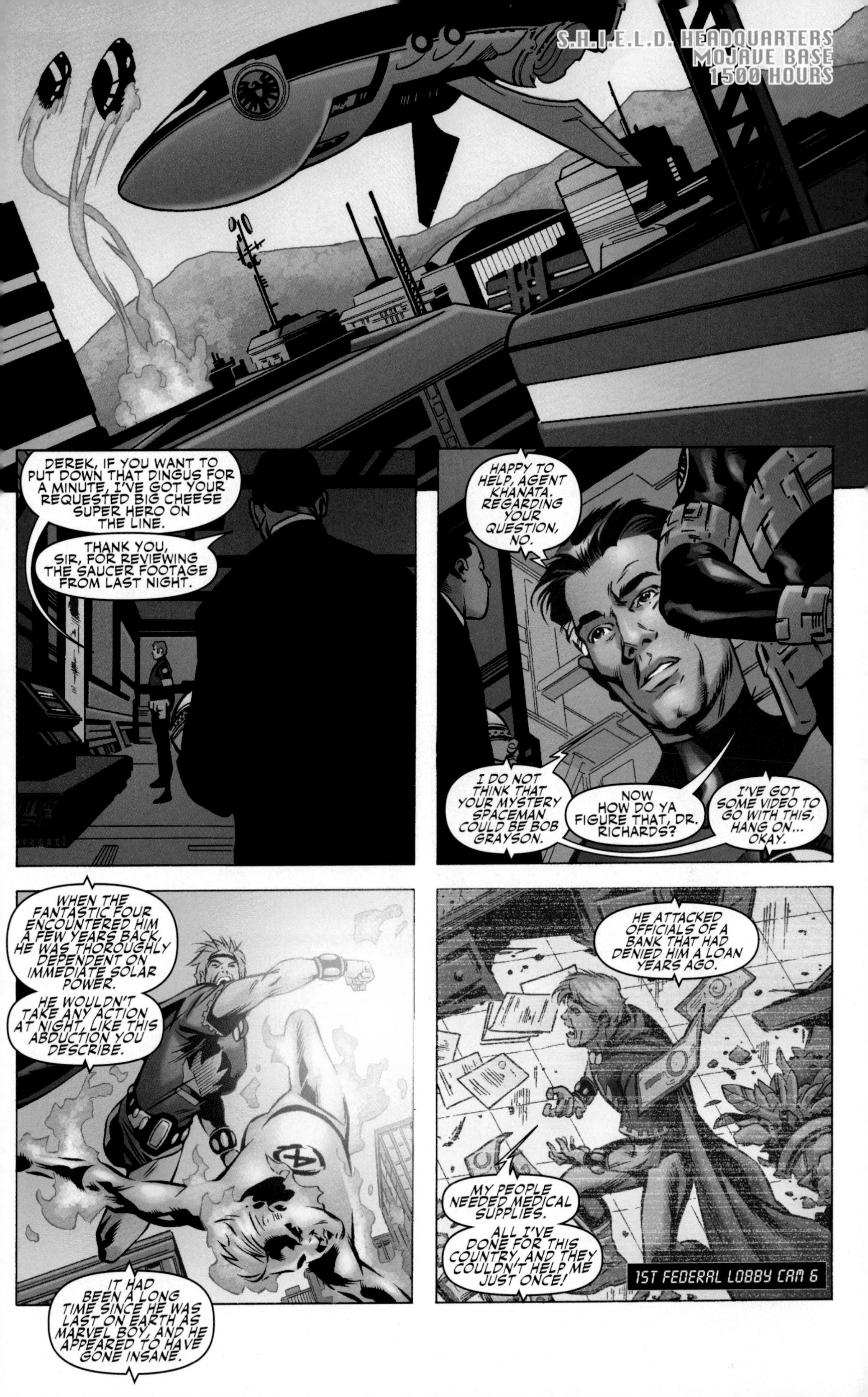
S.H.I.E.L.D. HEADQUARTERS
MOJAVE BASE
1500 HOURS
DEREK, IF YOU WANT TO PUT DOWN THAT DINGUS FOR A MINUTE, I'VE GOT YOUR REQUESTED BIG CHEESE SUPER HERO ON THE LINE.
THANK YOU, SIR, FOR REVIEWING THE SAUCER FOOTAGE FROM LAST NIGHT.
HAPPY TO HELP, AGENT KHANATA. REGARDING YOUR QUESTION, NO.
I DO NOT THINK THAT YOUR MYSTERY SPACEMAN COULD BE BOB GRAYSON.
NOW HOW DO YA FIGURE THAT, DR. RICHARDS?
I'VE GOT SOME VIDEO TO GO WITH THIS, HANG ON... OKAY.
WHEN THE FANTASTIC FOUR ENCOUNTERED HIM A FEW YEARS BACK, HE WAS THOROUGHLY DEPENDENT ON IMMEDIATE SOLAR POWER.
HE WOULDN'T TAKE ANY ACTION AT NIGHT, LIKE THIS ABDUCTION YOU DESCRIBE.
IT HAD BEEN A LONG TIME SINCE HE WAS LAST ON EARTH AS MARVEL BOY, AND HE APPEARED TO HAVE GONE INSANE.
HE ATTACKED OFFICIALS OF A BANK THAT HAD DENIED HIM A LOAN YEARS AGO.
MY PEOPLE NEEDED MEDICAL SUPPLIES.
ALL I'VE DONE FOR THIS COUNTRY, AND THEY COULDN'T HELP ME JUST ONCE!
1ST FEDERAL LOBBY CAM 6

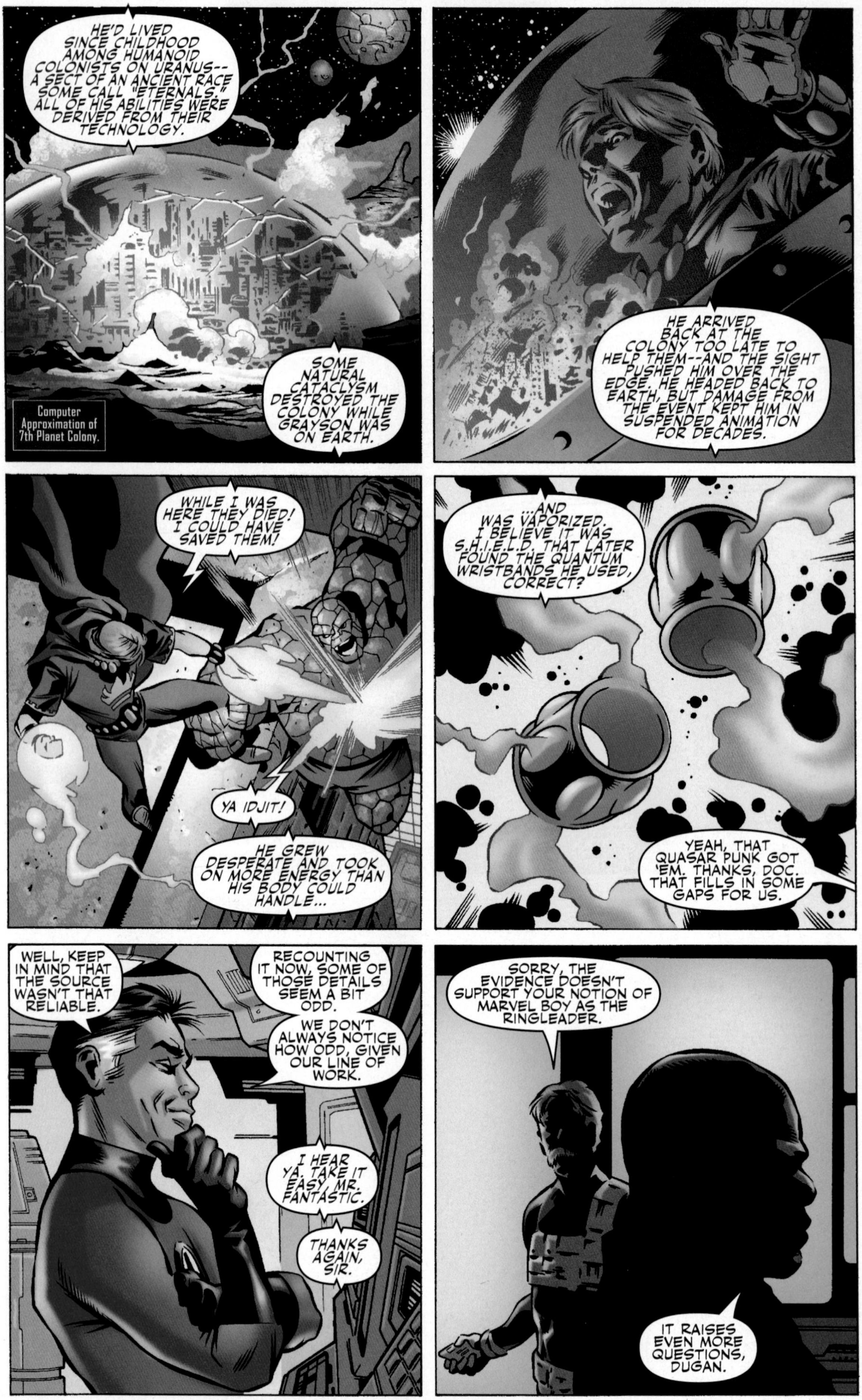
HE'D LIVED SINCE CHILDHOOD AMONG HUMANOID COLONISTS ON URANUS-- A SECT OF AN ANCIENT RACE SOME CALL "ETERNALS." ALL OF HIS ABILITIES WERE DERIVED FROM THEIR TECHNOLOGY.
Computer Approximation of 7th Planet Colony.
SOME NATURAL CATACLYSM DESTROYED THE COLONY WHILE GRAYSON WAS ON EARTH.
HE ARRIVED BACK AT THE COLONY TOO LATE TO HELP THEM--AND THE SIGHT PUSHED HIM OVER THE EDGE. HE HEADED BACK TO EARTH, BUT DAMAGE FROM THE EVENT KEPT HIM IN SUSPENDED ANIMATION FOR DECADES.
WHILE I WAS HERE THEY DIED! I COULD HAVE SAVED THEM!
YA IDJIT!
HE GREW DESPERATE AND TOOK ON MORE ENERGY THAN HIS BODY COULD HANDLE...
...AND WAS VAPORIZED. I BELIEVE IT WAS S.H.I.E.L.D. THAT LATER FOUND THE QUANTUM WRISTBANDS HE USED, CORRECT?
YEAH, THAT QUASAR PUNK GOT 'EM. THANKS, DOC. THAT FILLS IN SOME GAPS FOR US.
WELL, KEEP IN MIND THAT THE SOURCE WASN'T THAT RELIABLE.
RECOUNTING IT NOW, SOME OF THOSE DETAILS SEEM A BIT ODD.
WE DON'T ALWAYS NOTICE HOW ODD, GIVEN OUR LINE OF WORK.
I HEAR YA. TAKE IT EASY, MR. FANTASTIC.
THANKS AGAIN, SIR.
SORRY, THE EVIDENCE DOESN'T SUPPORT YOUR NOTION OF MARVEL BOY AS THE RINGLEADER.
IT RAISES EVEN MORE QUESTIONS, DUGAN.

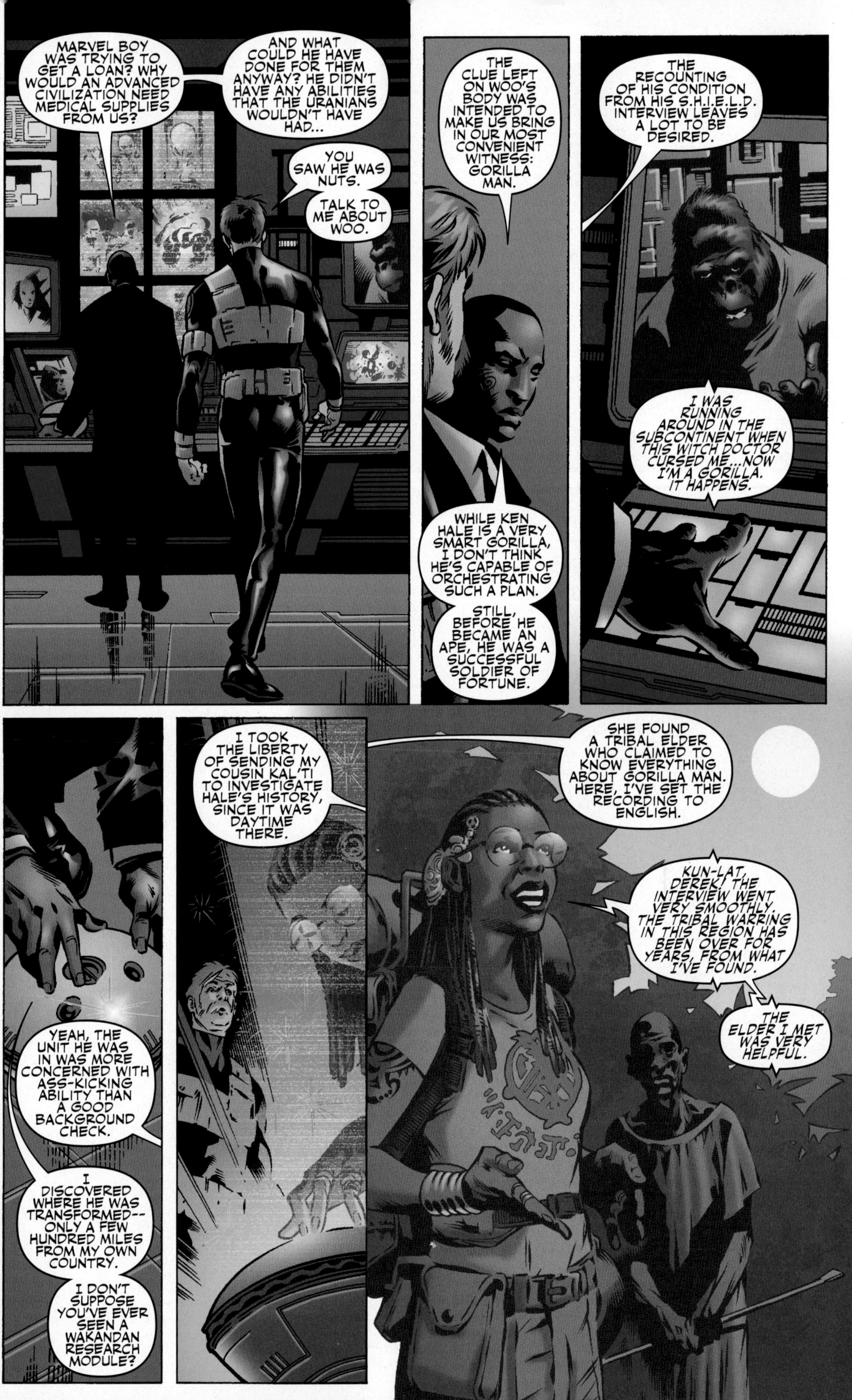
MARVEL BOY WAS TRYING TO GET A LOAN? WHY WOULD AN ADVANCED CIVILIZATION NEED MEDICAL SUPPLIES FROM US?
AND WHAT COULD HE HAVE DONE FOR THEM ANYWAY? HE DIDN'T HAVE ANY ABILITIES THAT THE URANIANS WOULDN'T HAVE HAD...
YOU SAW HE WAS NUTS.
TALK TO ME ABOUT WOO.
THE CLUE LEFT ON WOO'S BODY WAS INTENDED TO MAKE US BRING IN OUR MOST CONVENIENT WITNESS: GORILLA MAN.
WHILE KEN HALE IS A VERY SMART GORILLA, I DON'T THINK HE'S CAPABLE OF ORCHESTRATING SUCH A PLAN.
STILL, BEFORE HE BECAME AN APE, HE WAS A SUCCESSFUL SOLDIER OF FORTUNE.
THE RECOUNTING OF HIS CONDITION FROM HIS S.H.I.E.L.D. INTERVIEW LEAVES A LOT TO BE DESIRED.
I WAS RUNNING AROUND IN THE SUBCONTINENT WHEN THIS WITCH DOCTOR CURSED ME...NOW I'M A GORILLA. IT HAPPENS.
YEAH, THE UNIT HE WAS IN WAS MORE CONCERNED WITH ASS-KICKING ABILITY THAN A GOOD BACKGROUND CHECK.
I DISCOVERED WHERE HE WAS TRANSFORMED-- ONLY A FEW HUNDRED MILES FROM MY OWN COUNTRY.
I DON'T SUPPOSE YOU'VE EVER SEEN A WAKANDAN RESEARCH MODULE?
I TOOK THE LIBERTY OF SENDING MY COUSIN KAL'TI TO INVESTIGATE HALE'S HISTORY, SINCE IT WAS DAYTIME THERE.
SHE FOUND A TRIBAL ELDER WHO CLAIMED TO KNOW EVERYTHING ABOUT GORILLA MAN. HERE, I'VE SET THE RECORDING TO ENGLISH.
KUN-LAT, DEREK! THE INTERVIEW WENT VERY SMOOTHLY. THE TRIBAL WARRING IN THIS REGION HAS BEEN OVER FOR YEARS, FROM WHAT I'VE FOUND.
THE ELDER I MET WAS VERY HELPFUL.

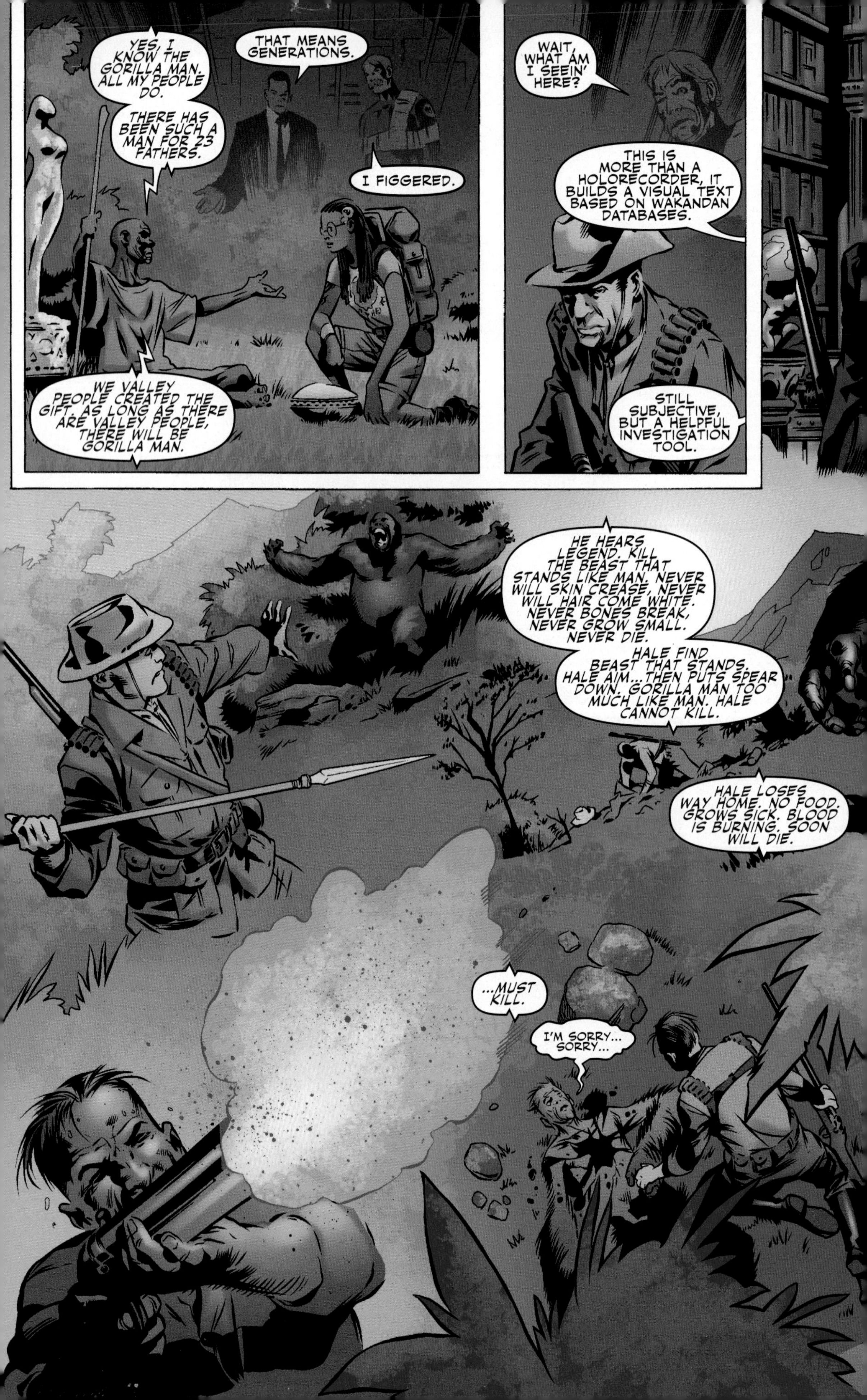

YES, I KNOW THE GORILLA MAN. ALL MY PEOPLE DO.
THERE HAS BEEN SUCH A MAN FOR 23 FATHERS.
THAT MEANS GENERATIONS.
I FIGGERED.
WE VALLEY PEOPLE CREATED THE GIFT. AS LONG AS THERE ARE VALLEY PEOPLE, THERE WILL BE GORILLA MAN.
WAIT, WHAT AM I SEEIN' HERE?
THIS IS MORE THAN A HOLORECORDER, IT BUILDS A VISUAL TEXT BASED ON WAKANDAN DATABASES.
STILL SUBJECTIVE, BUT A HELPFUL INVESTIGATION TOOL.
HE HEARS LEGEND. KILL THE BEAST THAT STANDS LIKE MAN. NEVER WILL SKIN CREASE, NEVER WILL HAIR COME WHITE. NEVER BONES BREAK, NEVER GROW SMALL. NEVER DIE.
HALE FIND BEAST THAT STANDS. HALE AIM...THEN PUTS SPEAR DOWN. GORILLA MAN TOO MUCH LIKE MAN. HALE CANNOT KILL.
HALE LOSES WAY HOME. NO FOOD. GROWS SICK. BLOOD IS BURNING. SOON WILL DIE.
...MUST KILL.
I'M SORRY... SORRY...

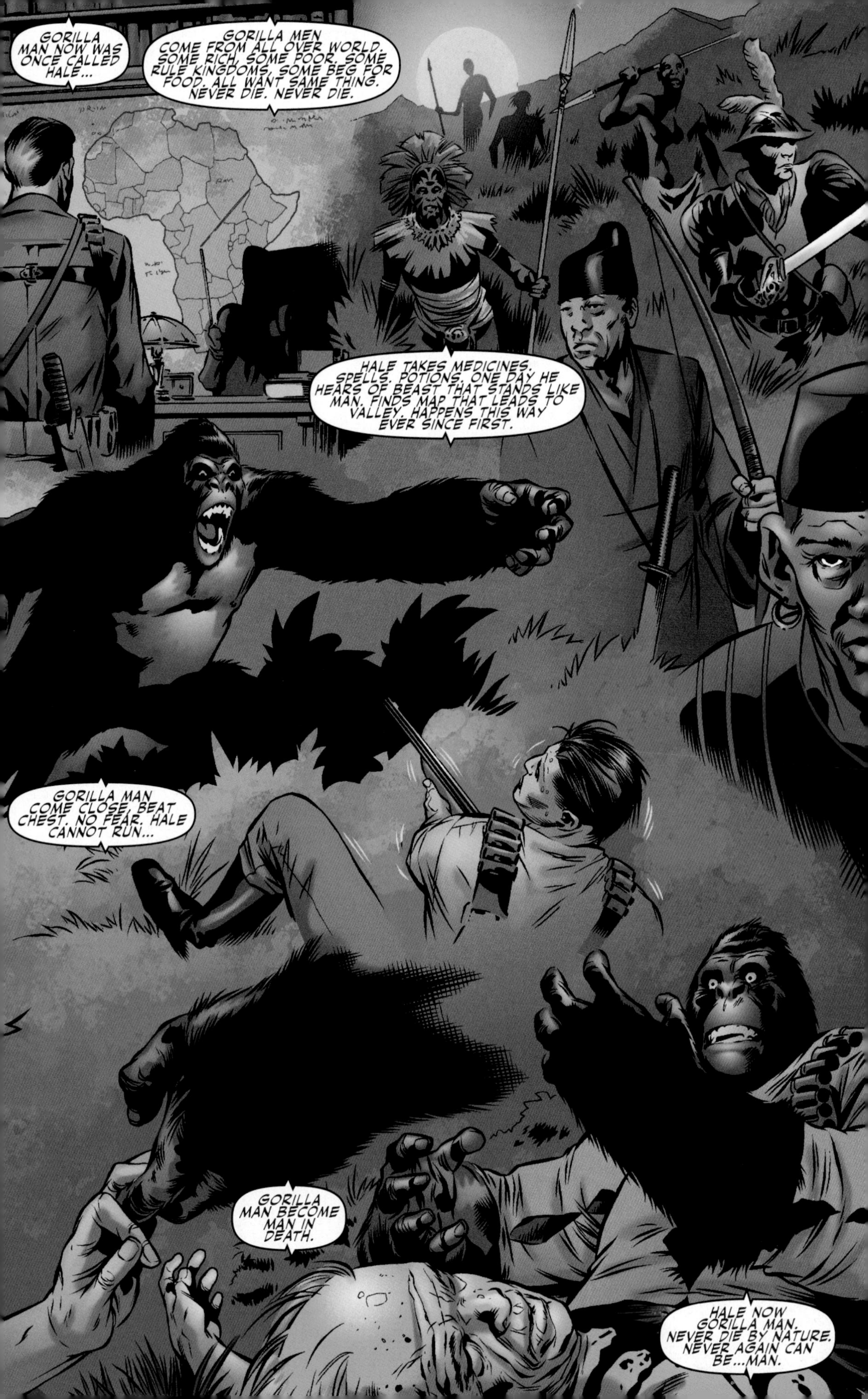
GORILLA MAN NOW WAS ONCE CALLED HALE...
GORILLA MEN COME FROM ALL OVER WORLD. SOME RICH, SOME POOR. SOME RULE KINGDOMS, SOME BEG FOR FOOD. ALL WANT SAME THING. NEVER DIE. NEVER DIE.
HALE TAKES MEDICINES. SPELLS. POTIONS. ONE DAY HE HEARS OF BEAST THAT STANDS LIKE MAN. FINDS MAP THAT LEADS TO VALLEY. HAPPENS THIS WAY EVER SINCE FIRST.
GORILLA MAN COME CLOSE, BEAT CHEST. NO FEAR. HALE CANNOT RUN...
GORILLA MAN BECOME MAN IN DEATH.
HALE NOW GORILLA MAN. NEVER DIE BY NATURE. NEVER AGAIN CAN BE...MAN.

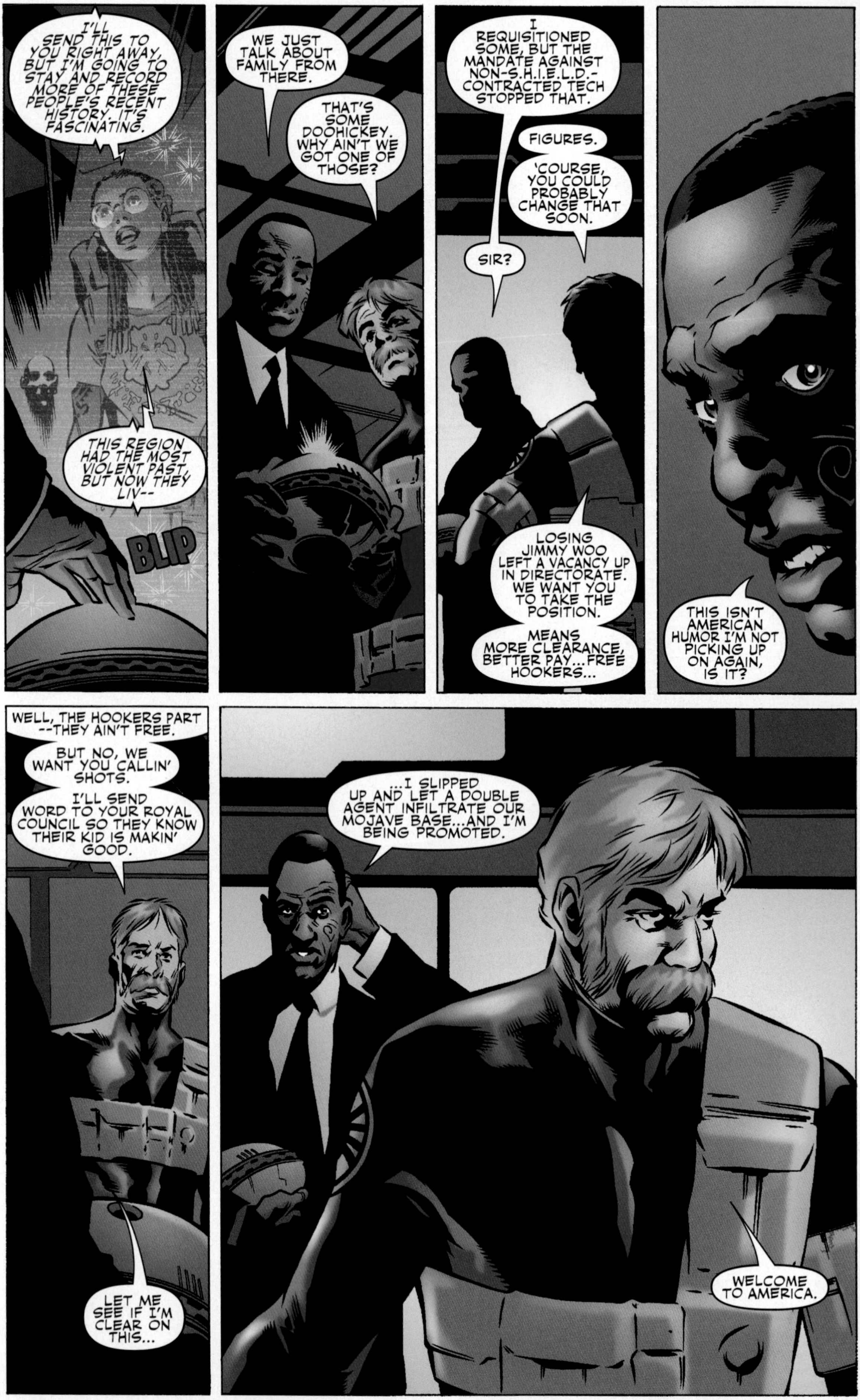
I'LL SEND THIS TO YOU RIGHT AWAY, BUT I'M GOING TO STAY AND RECORD MORE OF THESE PEOPLE'S RECENT HISTORY. IT'S FASCINATING.
THIS REGION HAD THE MOST VIOLENT PAST, BUT NOW THEY LIV--
BLIP
WE JUST TALK ABOUT FAMILY FROM THERE.
THAT'S SOME DOOHICKEY. WHY AIN'T WE GOT ONE OF THOSE?
I REQUISITIONED SOME, BUT THE MANDATE AGAINST NON-S.H.I.E.L.D.-CONTRACTED TECH STOPPED THAT.
FIGURES.
'COURSE, YOU COULD PROBABLY CHANGE THAT SOON.
SIR?
LOSING JIMMY WOO LEFT A VACANCY UP IN DIRECTORATE. WE WANT YOU TO TAKE THE POSITION.
MEANS MORE CLEARANCE, BETTER PAY...FREE HOOKERS...
THIS ISN'T AMERICAN HUMOR I'M NOT PICKING UP ON AGAIN, IS IT?
WELL, THE HOOKERS PART --THEY AIN'T FREE.
BUT NO, WE WANT YOU CALLIN' SHOTS.
I'LL SEND WORD TO YOUR ROYAL COUNCIL SO THEY KNOW THEIR KID IS MAKIN' GOOD.
LET ME SEE IF I'M CLEAR ON THIS...
...I SLIPPED UP AND LET A DOUBLE AGENT INFILTRATE OUR MOJAVE BASE...AND I'M BEING PROMOTED.
WELCOME TO AMERICA.

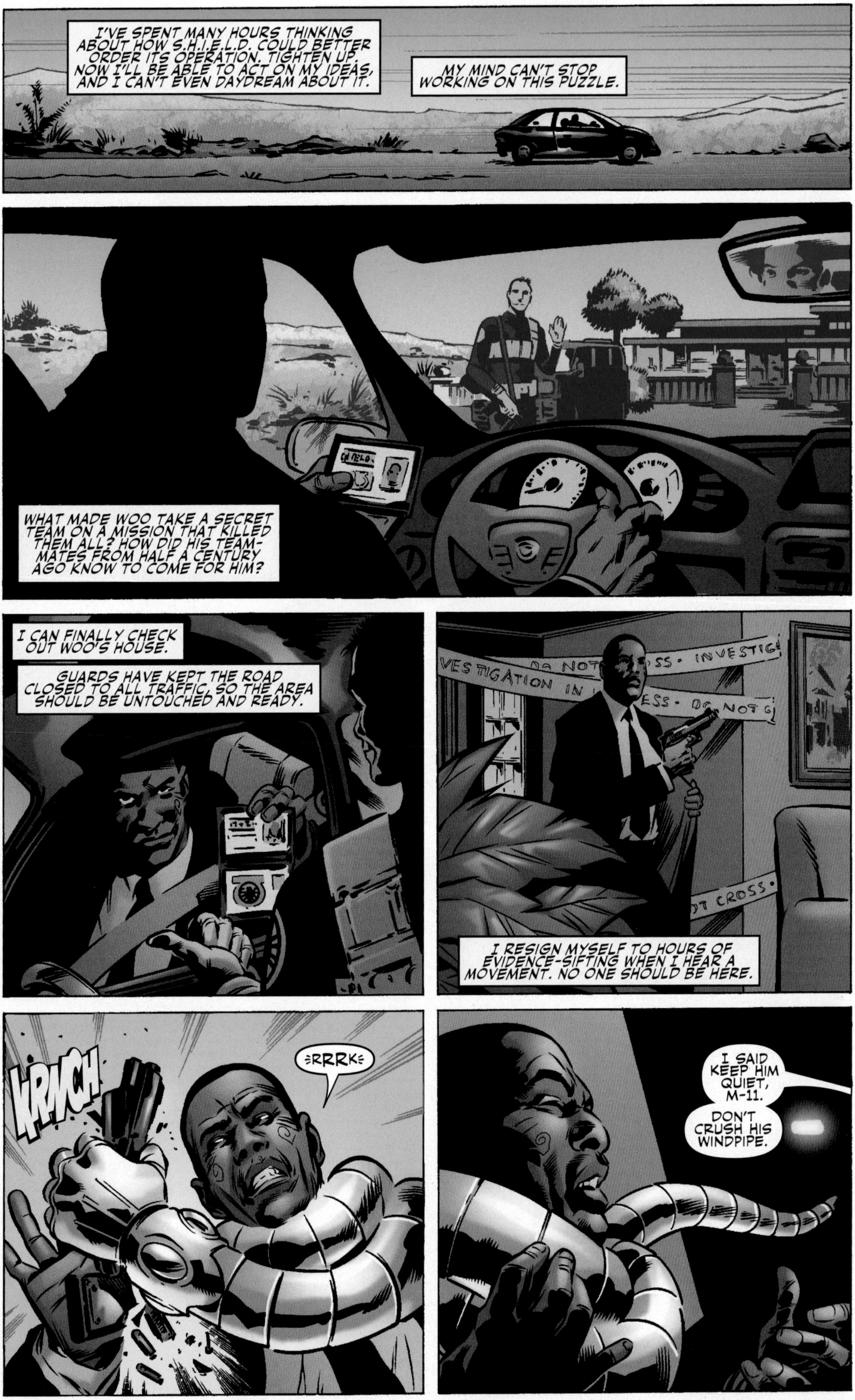
I'VE SPENT MANY HOURS THINKING ABOUT HOW S.H.I.E.L.D. COULD BETTER ORDER ITS OPERATION. TIGHTEN UP. NOW I'LL BE ABLE TO ACT ON MY IDEAS, AND I CAN'T EVEN DAYDREAM ABOUT IT.
MY MIND CAN'T STOP WORKING ON THIS PUZZLE.
WHAT MADE WOO TAKE A SECRET TEAM ON A MISSION THAT KILLED THEM ALL? HOW DID HIS TEAM-MATES FROM HALF A CENTURY AGO KNOW TO COME FOR HIM?
I CAN FINALLY CHECK OUT WOO'S HOUSE.
GUARDS HAVE KEPT THE ROAD CLOSED TO ALL TRAFFIC, SO THE AREA SHOULD BE UNTOUCHED AND READY.
I RESIGN MYSELF TO HOURS OF EVIDENCE-SIFTING WHEN I HEAR A MOVEMENT. NO ONE SHOULD BE HERE.
KRNCH
RRRK
I SAID KEEP HIM QUIET, M-11.
DON'T CRUSH HIS WINDPIPE.

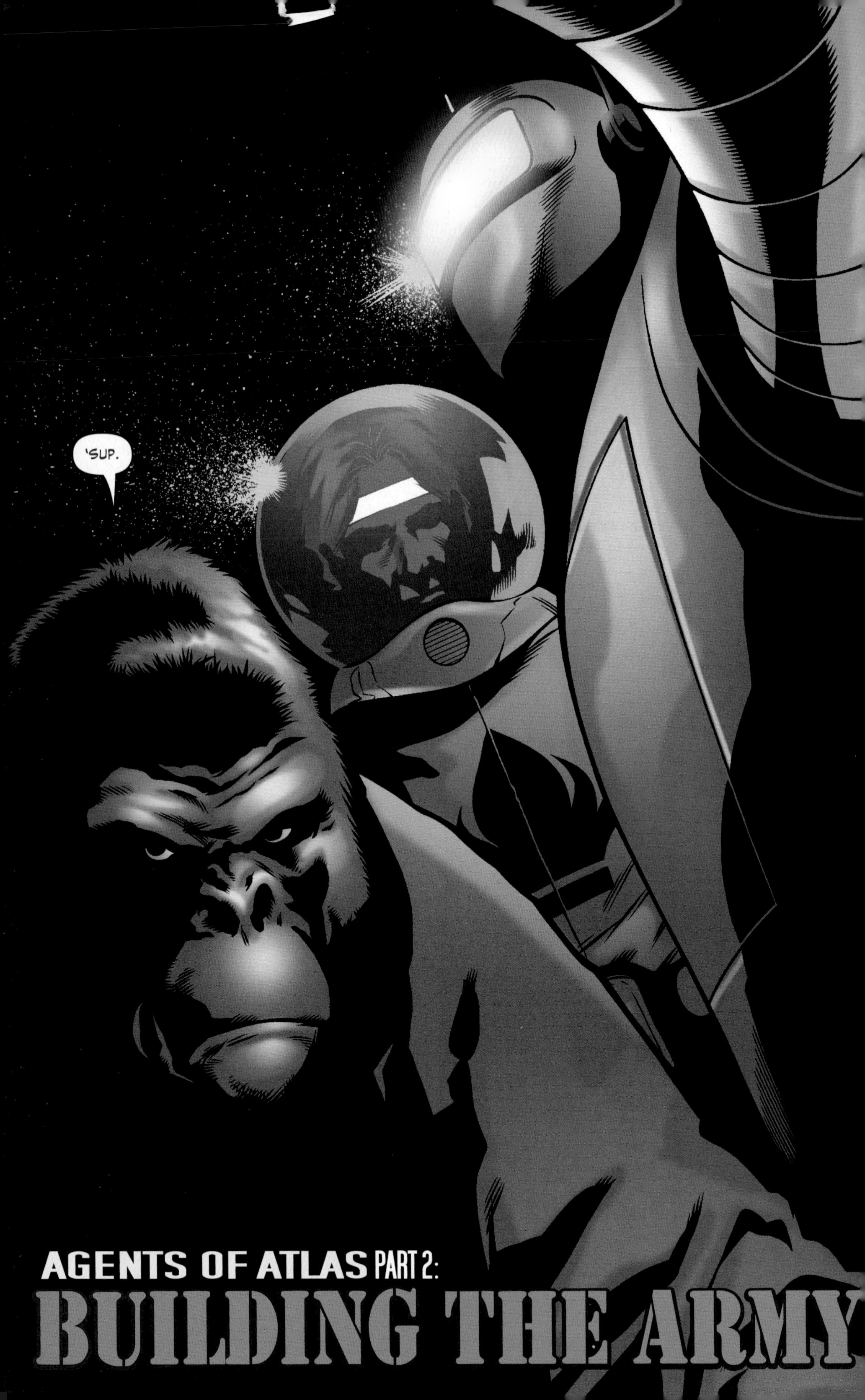
'SUP.
AGENTS OF ATLAS PART 2:
BUILDING THE ARMY

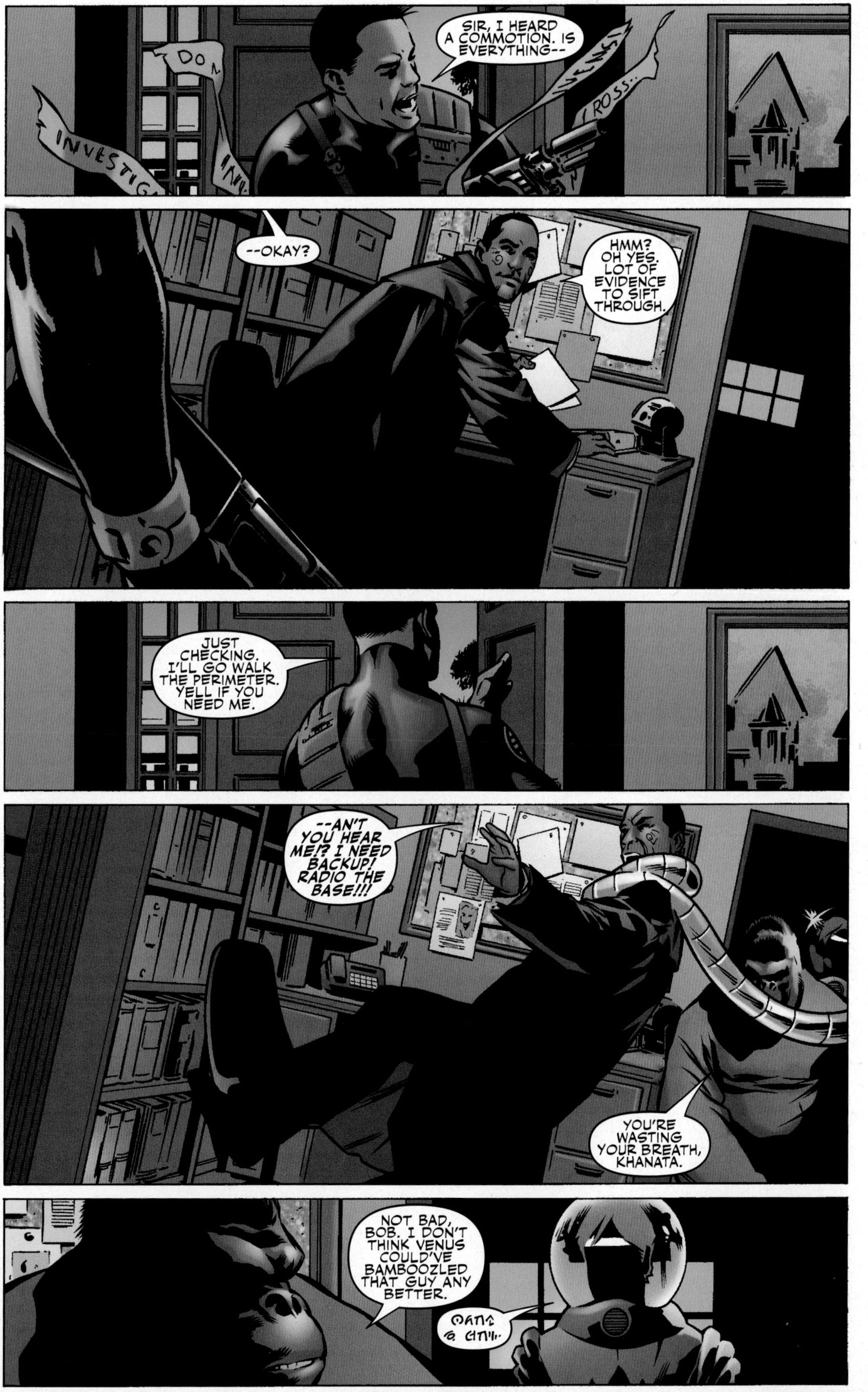
SIR, I HEARD A COMMOTION. IS EVERYTHING--
--OKAY?
HMM? OH YES. LOT OF EVIDENCE TO SIFT THROUGH.
JUST CHECKING. I'LL GO WALK THE PERIMETER. YELL IF YOU NEED ME.
--AN'T YOU HEAR ME!? I NEED BACKUP! RADIO THE BASE!!!
YOU'RE WASTING YOUR BREATH, KHANATA.
NOT BAD, BOB. I DON'T THINK VENUS COULD'VE BAMBOOZLED THAT GUY ANY BETTER.

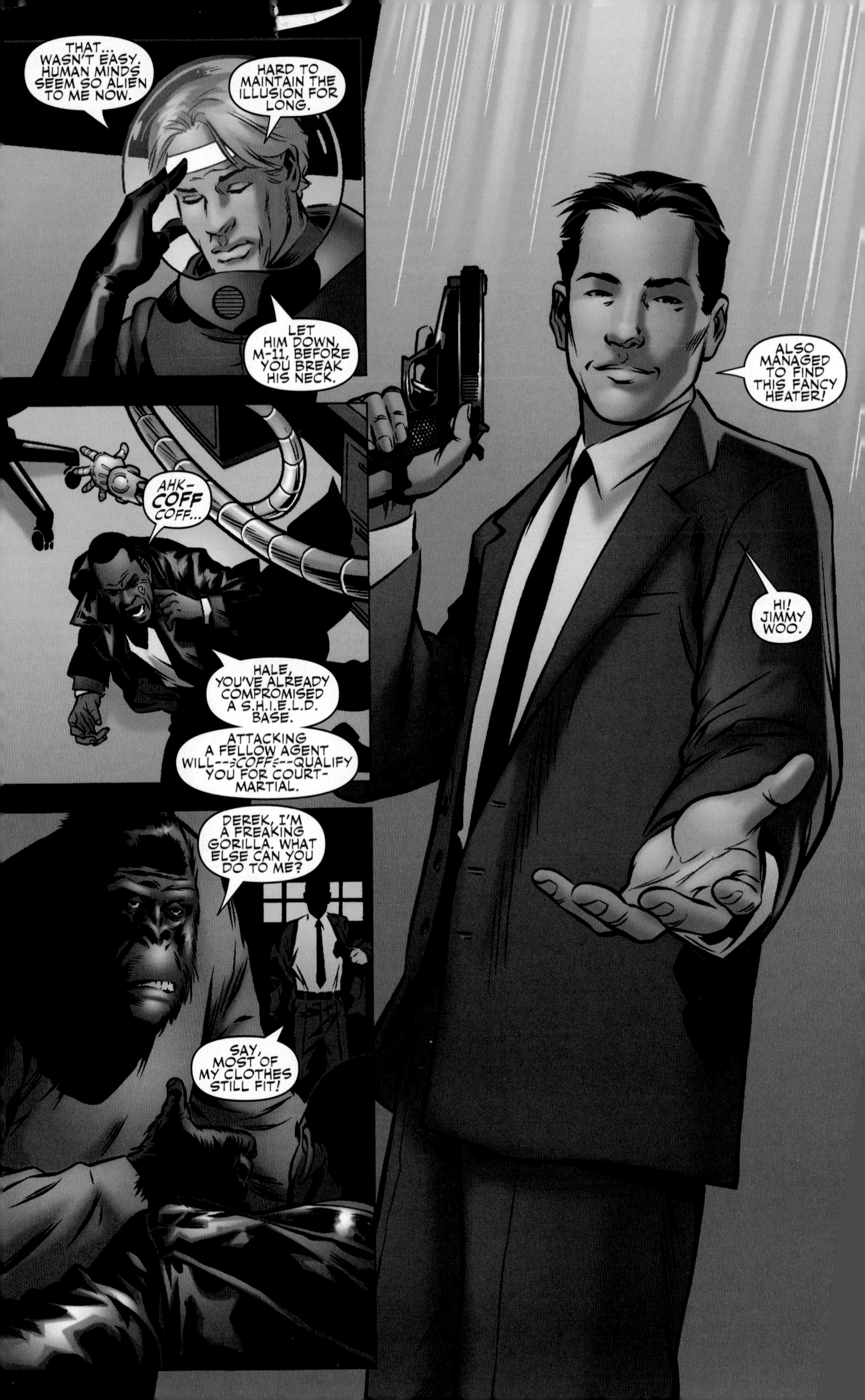
THAT... WASN'T EASY. HUMAN MINDS SEEM SO ALIEN TO ME NOW.
HARD TO MAINTAIN THE ILLUSION FOR LONG.
LET HIM DOWN, M-11, BEFORE YOU BREAK HIS NECK.
AHK-COFF COFF...
HALE, YOU'VE ALREADY COMPROMISED A S.H.I.E.L.D. BASE.
ATTACKING A FELLOW AGENT WILL--COFF--QUALIFY YOU FOR COURT-MARTIAL.
DEREK, I'M A FREAKING GORILLA. WHAT ELSE CAN YOU DO TO ME?
SAY, MOST OF MY CLOTHES STILL FIT!
ALSO MANAGED TO FIND THIS FANCY HEATER!
HI! JIMMY WOO.

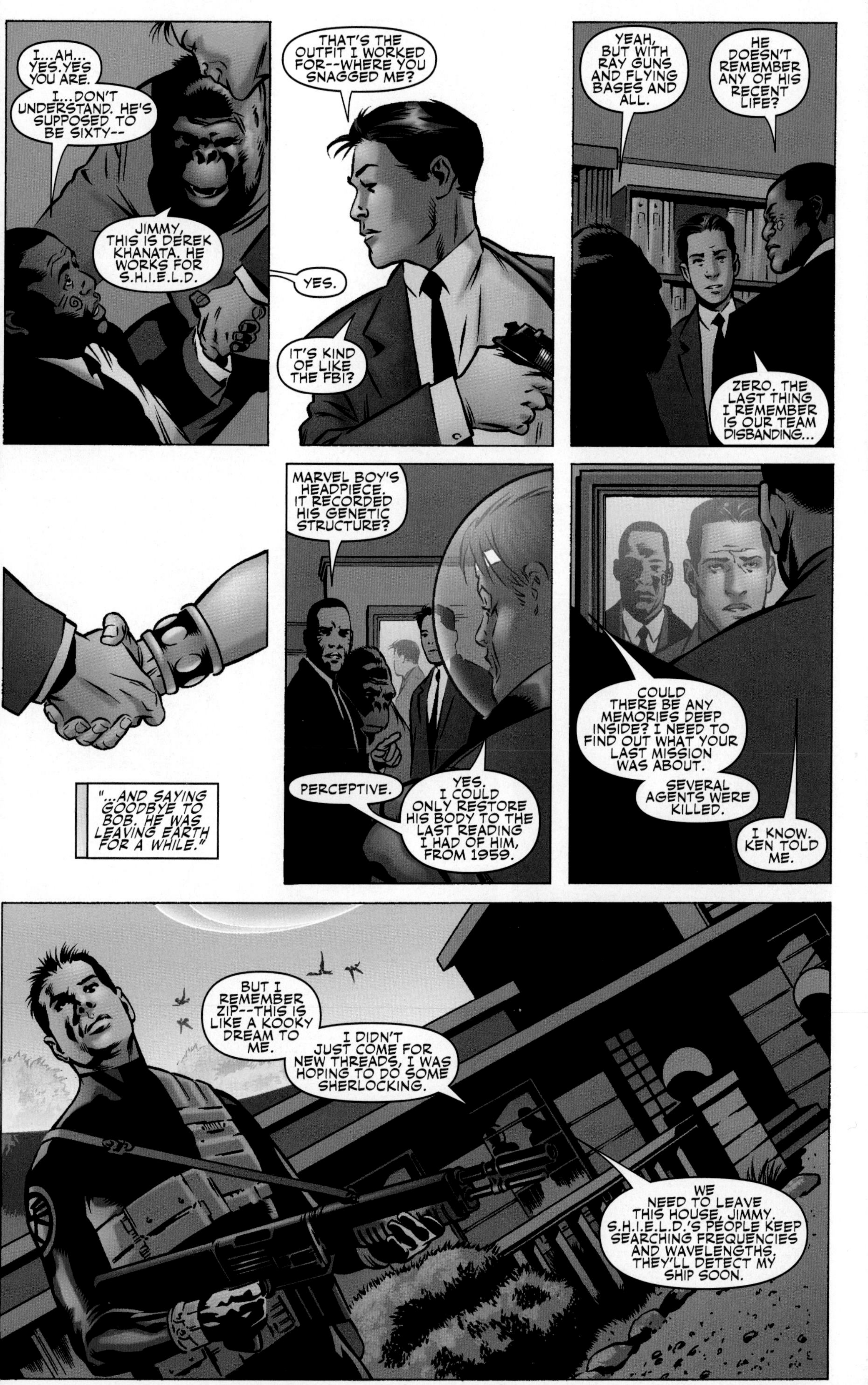

I...AH... YES. YES YOU ARE.
I...DON'T UNDERSTAND. HE'S SUPPOSED TO BE SIXTY--
JIMMY, THIS IS DEREK KHANATA. HE WORKS FOR S.H.I.E.L.D.
THAT'S THE OUTFIT I WORKED FOR--WHERE YOU SNAGGED ME?
YES.
IT'S KIND OF LIKE THE FBI?
YEAH, BUT WITH RAY GUNS AND FLYING BASES AND ALL.
HE DOESN'T REMEMBER ANY OF HIS RECENT LIFE?
ZERO. THE LAST THING I REMEMBER IS OUR TEAM DISBANDING...
"...AND SAYING GOODBYE TO BOB. HE WAS LEAVING EARTH FOR A WHILE."
MARVEL BOY'S HEADPIECE. IT RECORDED HIS GENETIC STRUCTURE?
PERCEPTIVE.
YES. I COULD ONLY RESTORE HIS BODY TO THE LAST READING I HAD OF HIM, FROM 1959.
COULD THERE BE ANY MEMORIES DEEP INSIDE? I NEED TO FIND OUT WHAT YOUR LAST MISSION WAS ABOUT.
SEVERAL AGENTS WERE KILLED.
I KNOW. KEN TOLD ME.
BUT I REMEMBER ZIP--THIS IS LIKE A KOOKY DREAM TO ME.
I DIDN'T JUST COME FOR NEW THREADS, I WAS HOPING TO DO SOME SHERLOCKING.
WE NEED TO LEAVE THIS HOUSE, JIMMY. S.H.I.E.L.D.'S PEOPLE KEEP SEARCHING FREQUENCIES AND WAVELENGTHS. THEY'LL DETECT MY SHIP SOON.

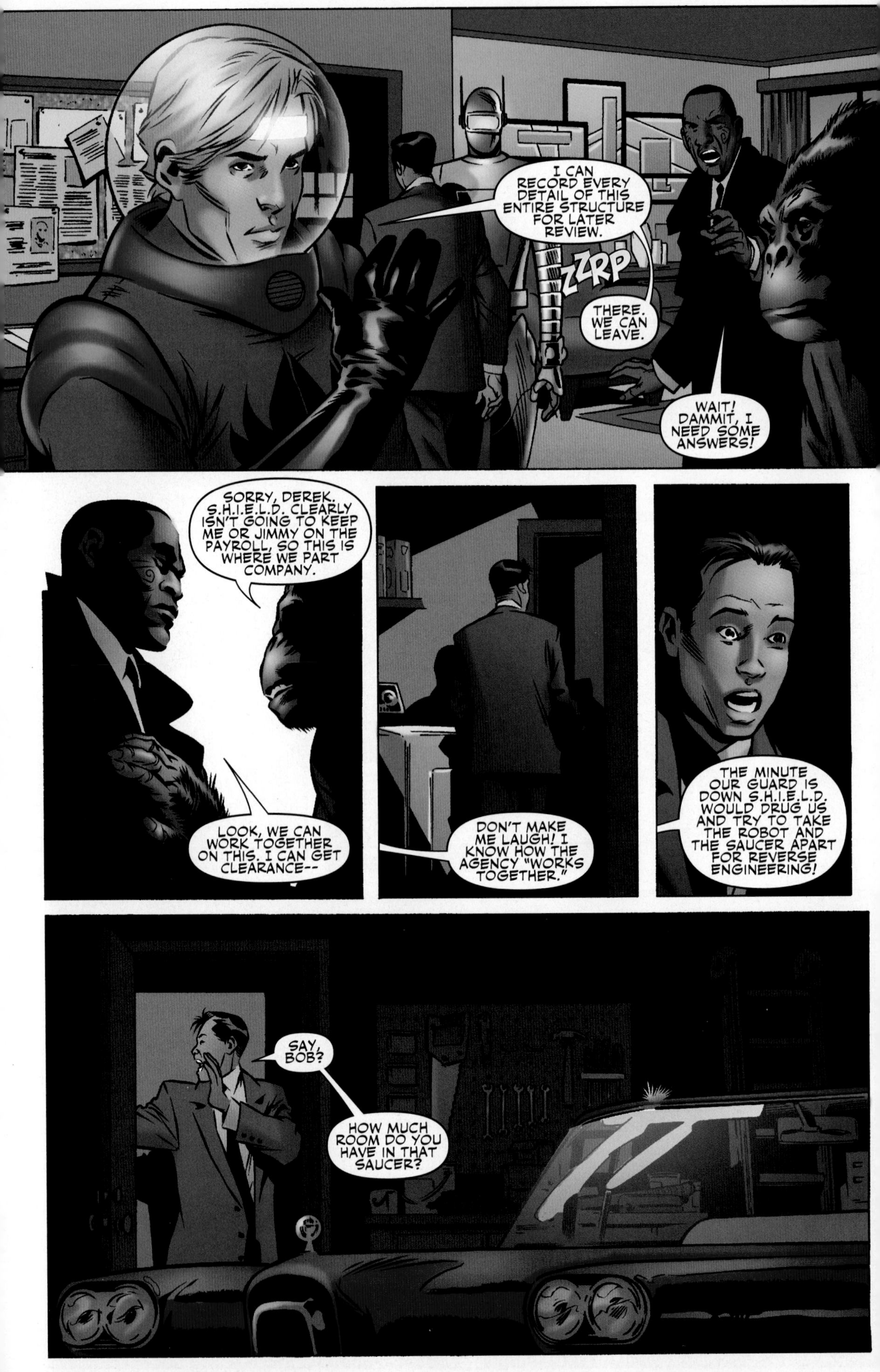

I CAN RECORD EVERY DETAIL OF THIS ENTIRE STRUCTURE FOR LATER REVIEW.
ZZRP
THERE. WE CAN LEAVE.
WAIT! DAMMIT, I NEED SOME ANSWERS!
SORRY, DEREK. S.H.I.E.L.D. CLEARLY ISN'T GOING TO KEEP ME OR JIMMY ON THE PAYROLL, SO THIS IS WHERE WE PART COMPANY.
LOOK, WE CAN WORK TOGETHER ON THIS. I CAN GET CLEARANCE--
DON'T MAKE ME LAUGH! I KNOW HOW THE AGENCY "WORKS TOGETHER."
THE MINUTE OUR GUARD IS DOWN S.H.I.E.L.D. WOULD DRUG US AND TRY TO TAKE THE ROBOT AND THE SAUCER APART FOR REVERSE ENGINEERING!
SAY, BOB?
HOW MUCH ROOM DO YOU HAVE IN THAT SAUCER?

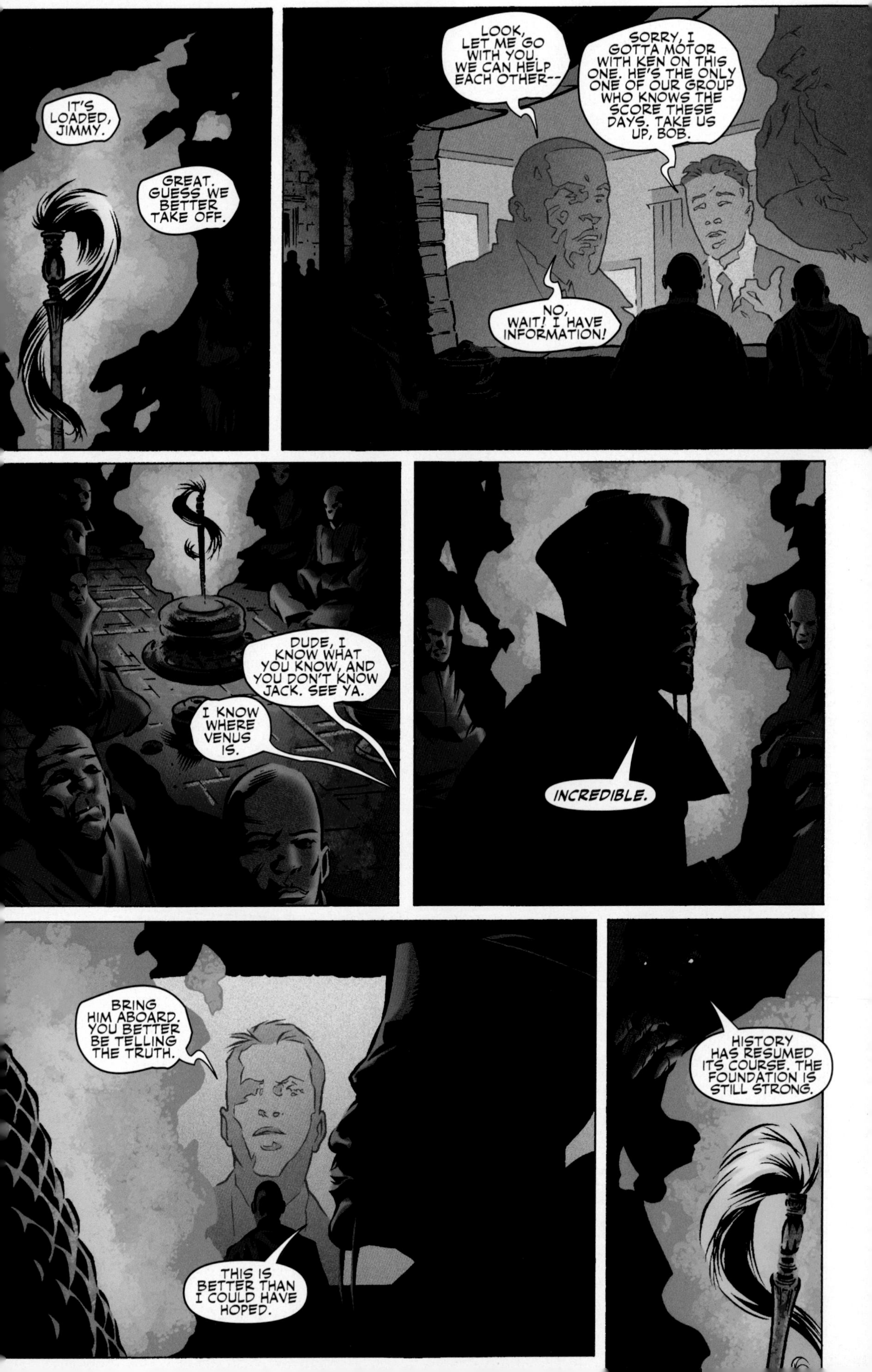
IT'S LOADED, JIMMY.
GREAT. GUESS WE BETTER TAKE OFF.
LOOK, LET ME GO WITH YOU. WE CAN HELP EACH OTHER--
SORRY, I GOTTA MOTOR WITH KEN ON THIS ONE. HE'S THE ONLY ONE OF OUR GROUP WHO KNOWS THE SCORE THESE DAYS. TAKE US UP, BOB.
NO, WAIT! I HAVE INFORMATION!
DUDE, I KNOW WHAT YOU KNOW, AND YOU DON'T KNOW JACK. SEE YA.
I KNOW WHERE VENUS IS.
INCREDIBLE.
BRING HIM ABOARD. YOU BETTER BE TELLING THE TRUTH.
THIS IS BETTER THAN I COULD HAVE HOPED.
HISTORY HAS RESUMED ITS COURSE. THE FOUNDATION IS STILL STRONG.

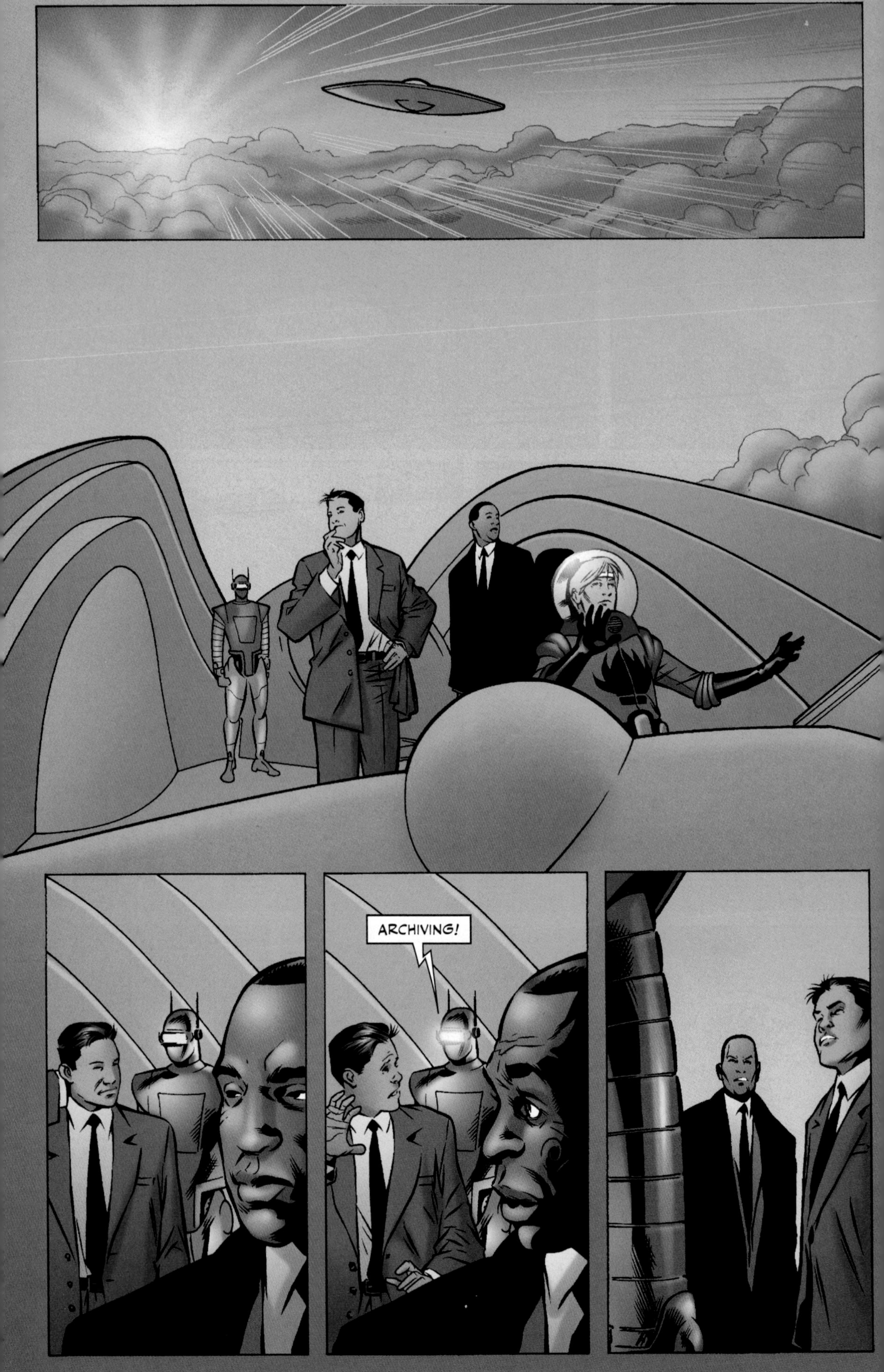
ARCHIVING!

IS HE DOING TAI CHI?

NO, THAT'S HOW BOB FLIES THE SAUCER. HE SAYS HIS HEADBAND MAKES CONTROLS ONLY HE CAN SEE OR TOUCH. CRAZY!

AH. A VIRTUAL REALITY INTERFACE.

YEAH, THAT'S WHAT HE CALLED IT! DO WE HAVE THAT ON EARTH NOW, TOO?

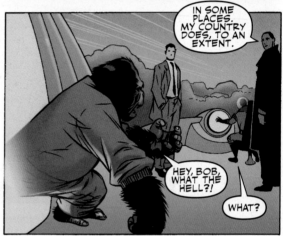

IN SOME PLACES. MY COUNTRY DOES, TO AN EXTENT.

HEY, BOB, WHAT THE HELL?!

WHAT?

YOU SAID I COULD GO TO THE JOHN IN THAT ROOM! THERE'S NO TOILET OR PAPER OR ANYTHING IN THERE!

YOU DON'T NEED ANYTHING, JUST GO BACK IN AND EXCRETE YOUR WASTE. THE SHIP WILL TAKE CARE OF IT.

I NEED WATER, SOMETHING TO CLEAN UP WITH!

NO YOU DON'T, TRUST ME.

BETTER DAMN NOT...

MEET US ON LEVEL 2 WHEN YOU'RE DONE.

JIMMY? PLEASE STEP ON THE CENTER DISK.

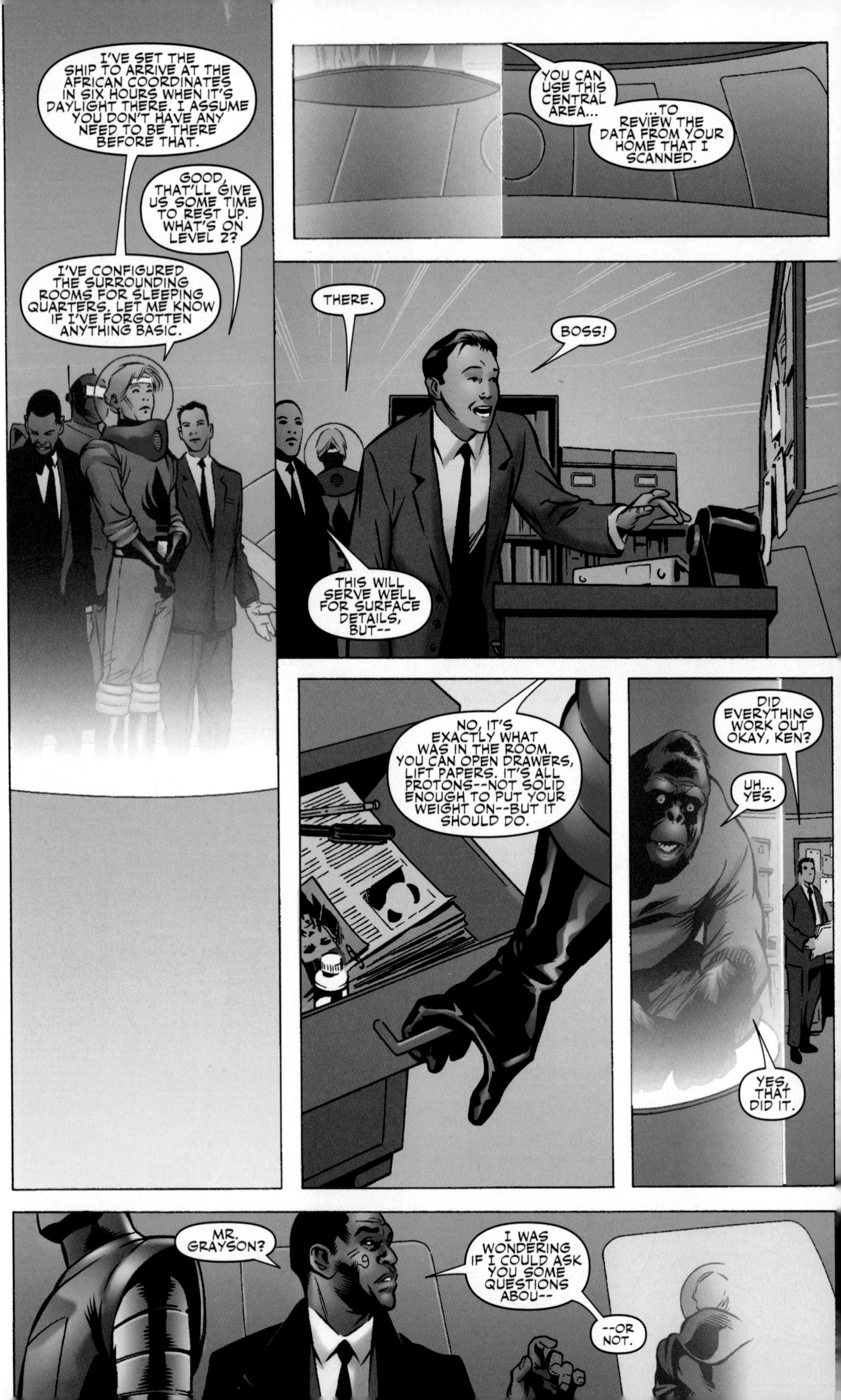
I'VE SET THE SHIP TO ARRIVE AT THE AFRICAN COORDINATES IN SIX HOURS WHEN IT'S DAYLIGHT THERE. I ASSUME YOU DON'T HAVE ANY NEED TO BE THERE BEFORE THAT.
GOOD, THAT'LL GIVE US SOME TIME TO REST UP. WHAT'S ON LEVEL 2?
I'VE CONFIGURED THE SURROUNDING ROOMS FOR SLEEPING QUARTERS. LET ME KNOW IF I'VE FORGOTTEN ANYTHING BASIC.
YOU CAN USE THIS CENTRAL AREA...
...TO REVIEW THE DATA FROM YOUR HOME THAT I SCANNED.
THERE.
BOSS!
THIS WILL SERVE WELL FOR SURFACE DETAILS, BUT--
NO, IT'S EXACTLY WHAT WAS IN THE ROOM. YOU CAN OPEN DRAWERS, LIFT PAPERS. IT'S ALL PROTONS--NOT SOLID ENOUGH TO PUT YOUR WEIGHT ON--BUT IT SHOULD DO.
DID EVERYTHING WORK OUT OKAY, KEN?
UH... YES.
YES, THAT DID IT.
MR. GRAYSON?
I WAS WONDERING IF I COULD ASK YOU SOME QUESTIONS ABOU--
--OR NOT.

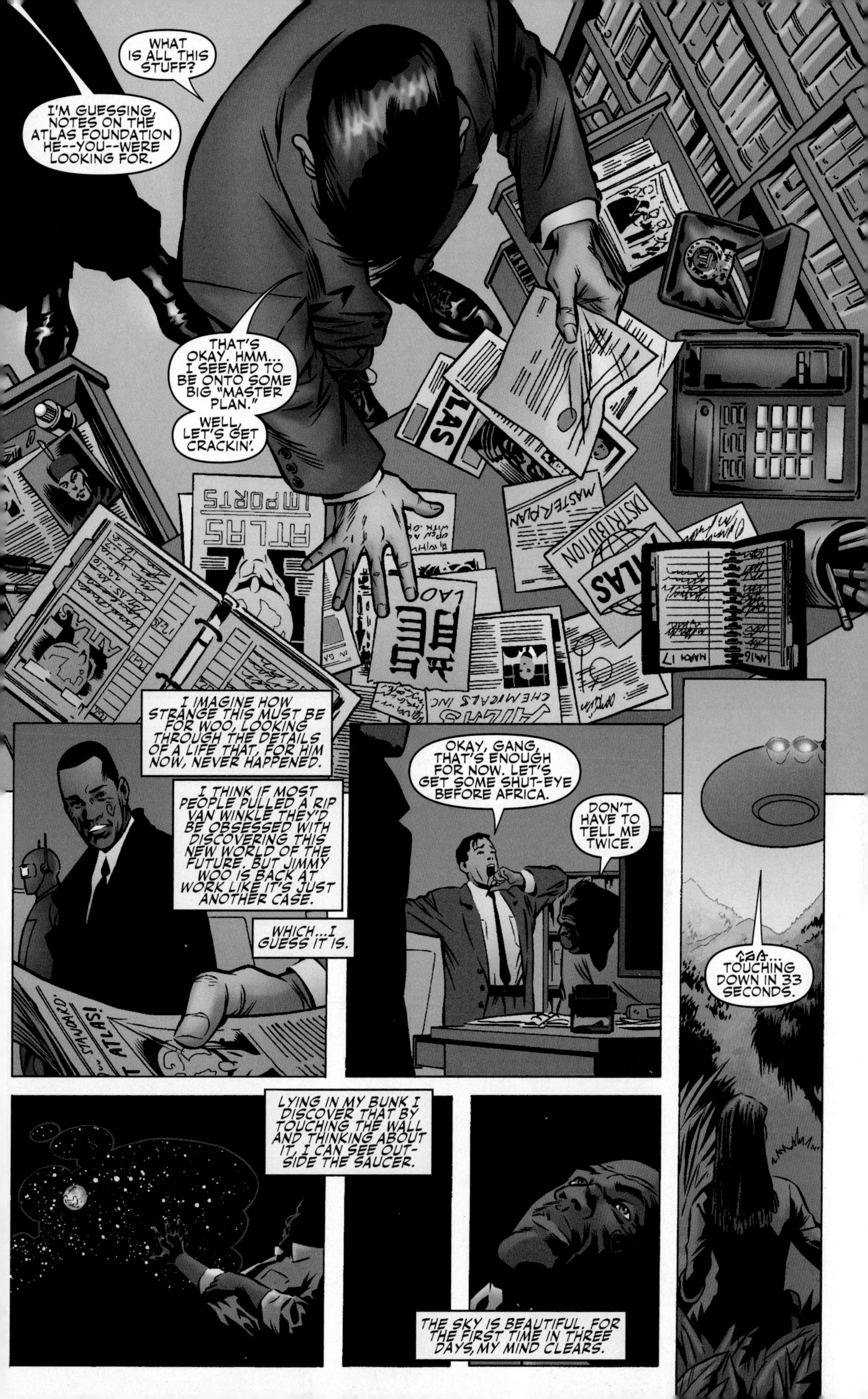

WHAT IS ALL THIS STUFF?
I'M GUESSING, NOTES ON THE ATLAS FOUNDATION HE--YOU--WERE LOOKING FOR.
THAT'S OKAY. HMM... I SEEMED TO BE ONTO SOME BIG "MASTER PLAN."
WELL, LET'S GET CRACKIN'.
I IMAGINE HOW STRANGE THIS MUST BE FOR WOO, LOOKING THROUGH THE DETAILS OF A LIFE THAT, FOR HIM NOW, NEVER HAPPENED.
I THINK IF MOST PEOPLE PULLED A RIP VAN WINKLE THEY'D BE OBSESSED WITH DISCOVERING THIS NEW WORLD OF THE FUTURE. BUT JIMMY WOO IS BACK AT WORK LIKE IT'S JUST ANOTHER CASE.
WHICH...I GUESS IT IS.
OKAY, GANG, THAT'S ENOUGH FOR NOW. LET'S GET SOME SHUT-EYE BEFORE AFRICA.
DON'T HAVE TO TELL ME TWICE.
LYING IN MY BUNK I DISCOVER THAT BY TOUCHING THE WALL AND THINKING ABOUT IT, I CAN SEE OUTSIDE THE SAUCER.
THE SKY IS BEAUTIFUL. FOR THE FIRST TIME IN THREE DAYS, MY MIND CLEARS.
TOUCHING DOWN IN 33 SECONDS.

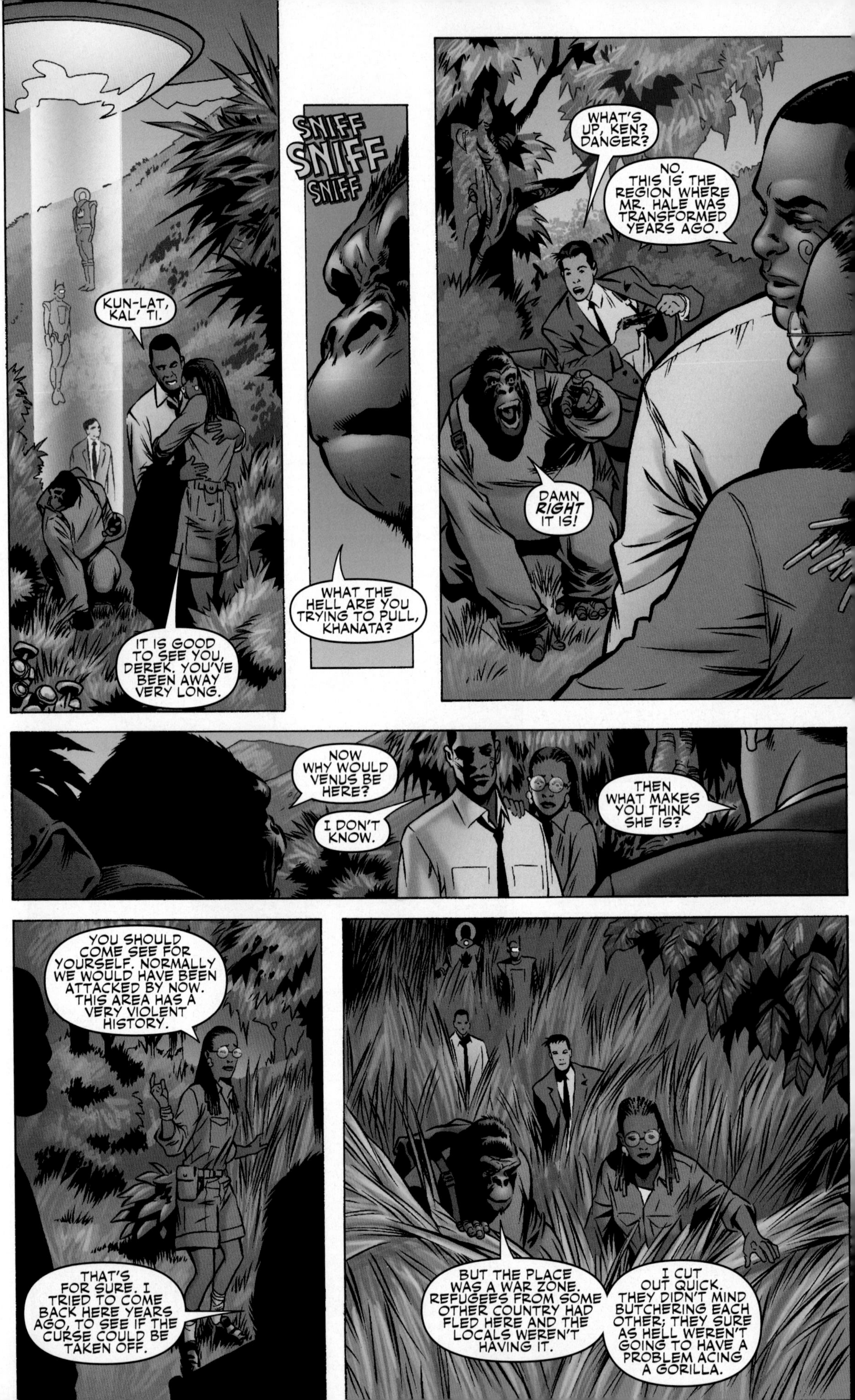
KUN-LAT, KAL' TI.
IT IS GOOD TO SEE YOU, DEREK. YOU'VE BEEN AWAY VERY LONG.
SNIFF SNIFF SNIFF
WHAT THE HELL ARE YOU TRYING TO PULL, KHANATA?
WHAT'S UP, KEN? DANGER?
NO. THIS IS THE REGION WHERE MR. HALE WAS TRANSFORMED YEARS AGO.
DAMN RIGHT IT IS!
NOW WHY WOULD VENUS BE HERE?
I DON'T KNOW.
THEN WHAT MAKES YOU THINK SHE IS?
YOU SHOULD COME SEE FOR YOURSELF. NORMALLY WE WOULD HAVE BEEN ATTACKED BY NOW. THIS AREA HAS A VERY VIOLENT HISTORY.
THAT'S FOR SURE. I TRIED TO COME BACK HERE YEARS AGO, TO SEE IF THE CURSE COULD BE TAKEN OFF.
BUT THE PLACE WAS A WAR ZONE. REFUGEES FROM SOME OTHER COUNTRY HAD FLED HERE AND THE LOCALS WEREN'T HAVING IT.
I CUT OUT QUICK. THEY DIDN'T MIND BUTCHERING EACH OTHER; THEY SURE AS HELL WEREN'T GOING TO HAVE A PROBLEM ACING A GORILLA.

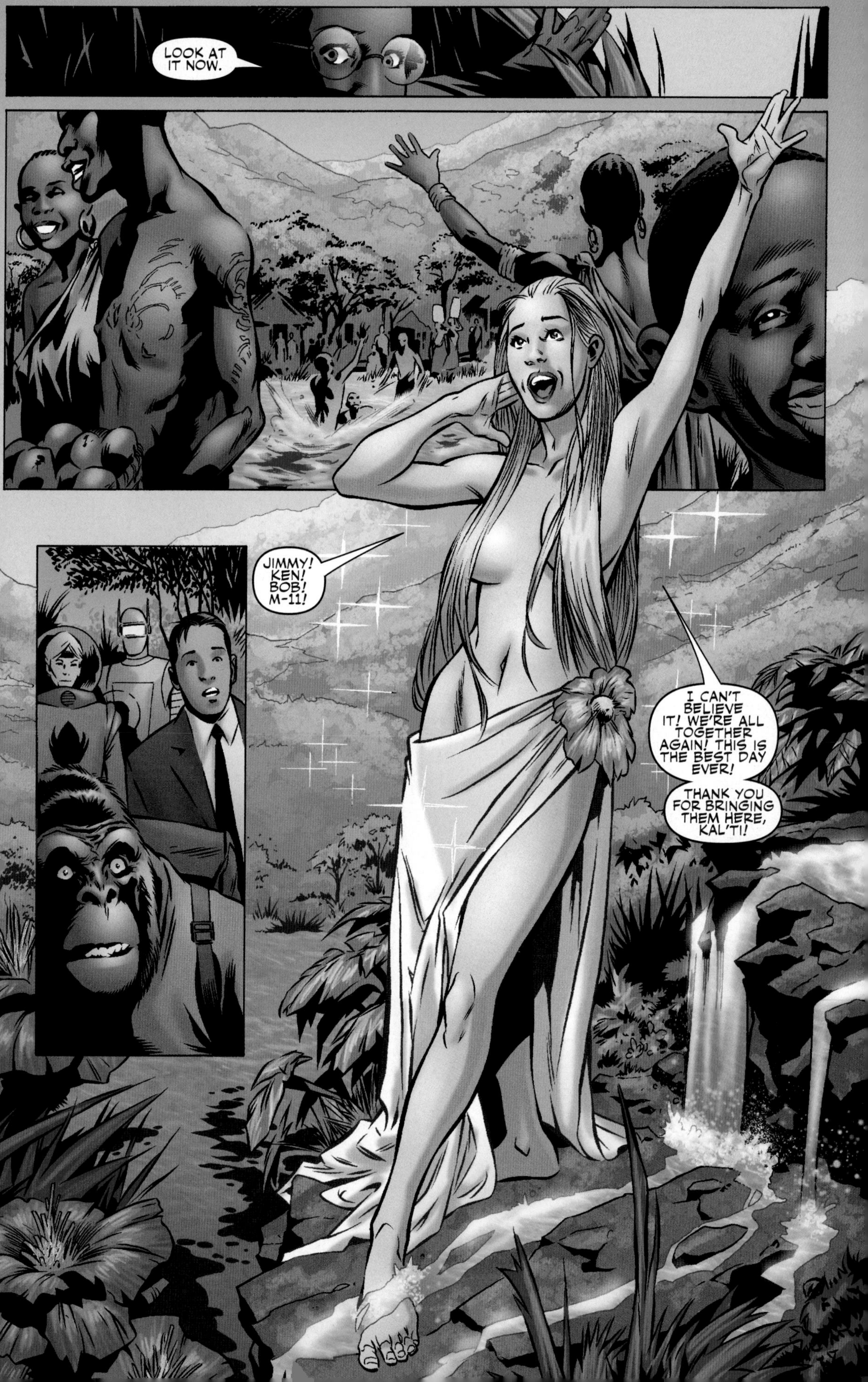
LOOK AT IT NOW.
JIMMY! KEN! BOB! M-11!
I CAN'T BELIEVE IT! WE'RE ALL TOGETHER AGAIN! THIS IS THE BEST DAY EVER!
THANK YOU FOR BRINGING THEM HERE, KAL'TI!

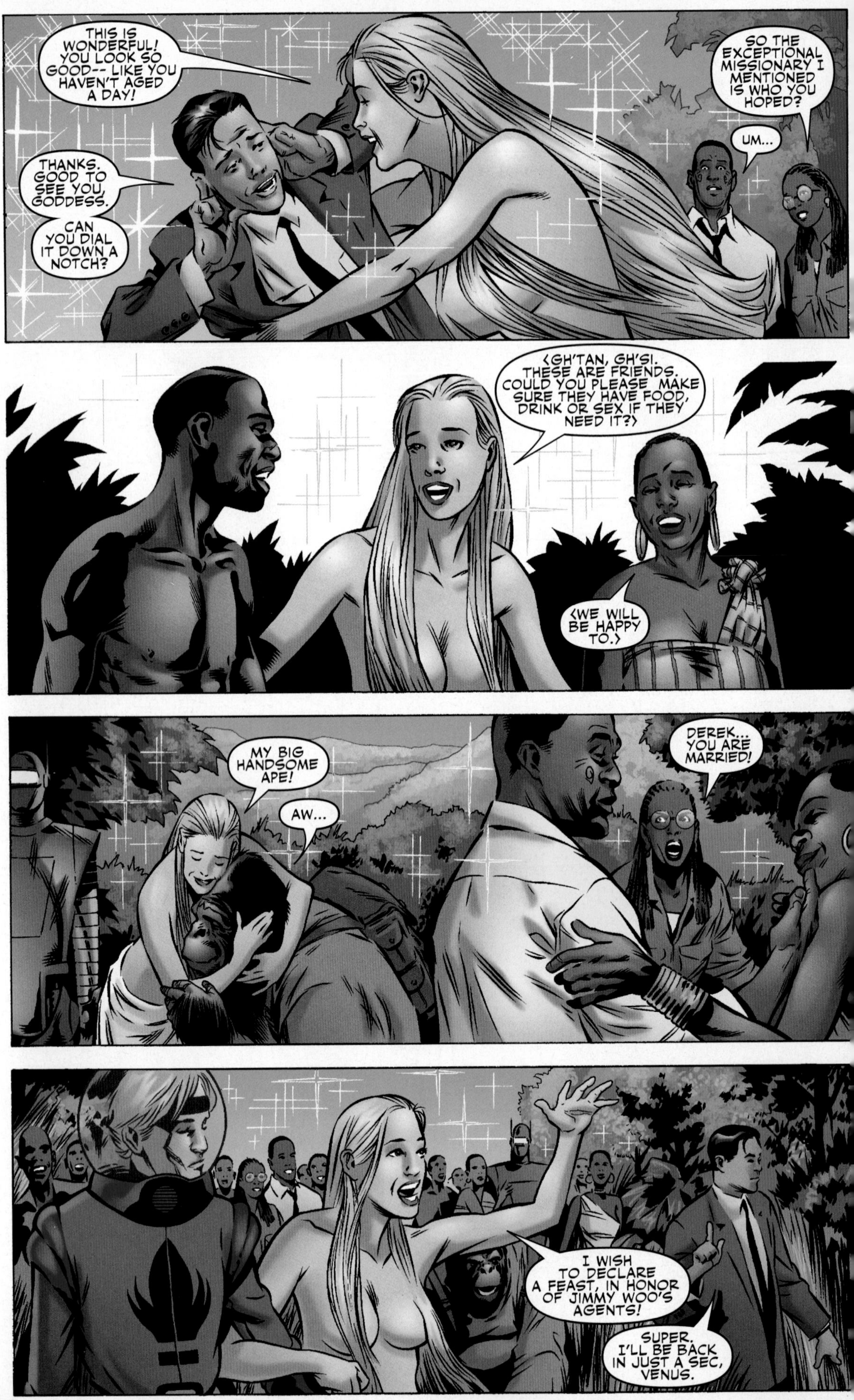

THIS IS WONDERFUL! YOU LOOK SO GOOD-- LIKE YOU HAVEN'T AGED A DAY!
THANKS. GOOD TO SEE YOU, GODDESS.
CAN YOU DIAL IT DOWN A NOTCH?
SO THE EXCEPTIONAL MISSIONARY I MENTIONED IS WHO YOU HOPED?
UM...
<GH'TAN, GH'SI. THESE ARE FRIENDS. COULD YOU PLEASE MAKE SURE THEY HAVE FOOD, DRINK OR SEX IF THEY NEED IT?>
<WE WILL BE HAPPY TO.>
MY BIG HANDSOME APE!
AW...
DEREK... YOU ARE MARRIED!
I WISH TO DECLARE A FEAST, IN HONOR OF JIMMY WOO'S AGENTS!
SUPER. I'LL BE BACK IN JUST A SEC, VENUS.

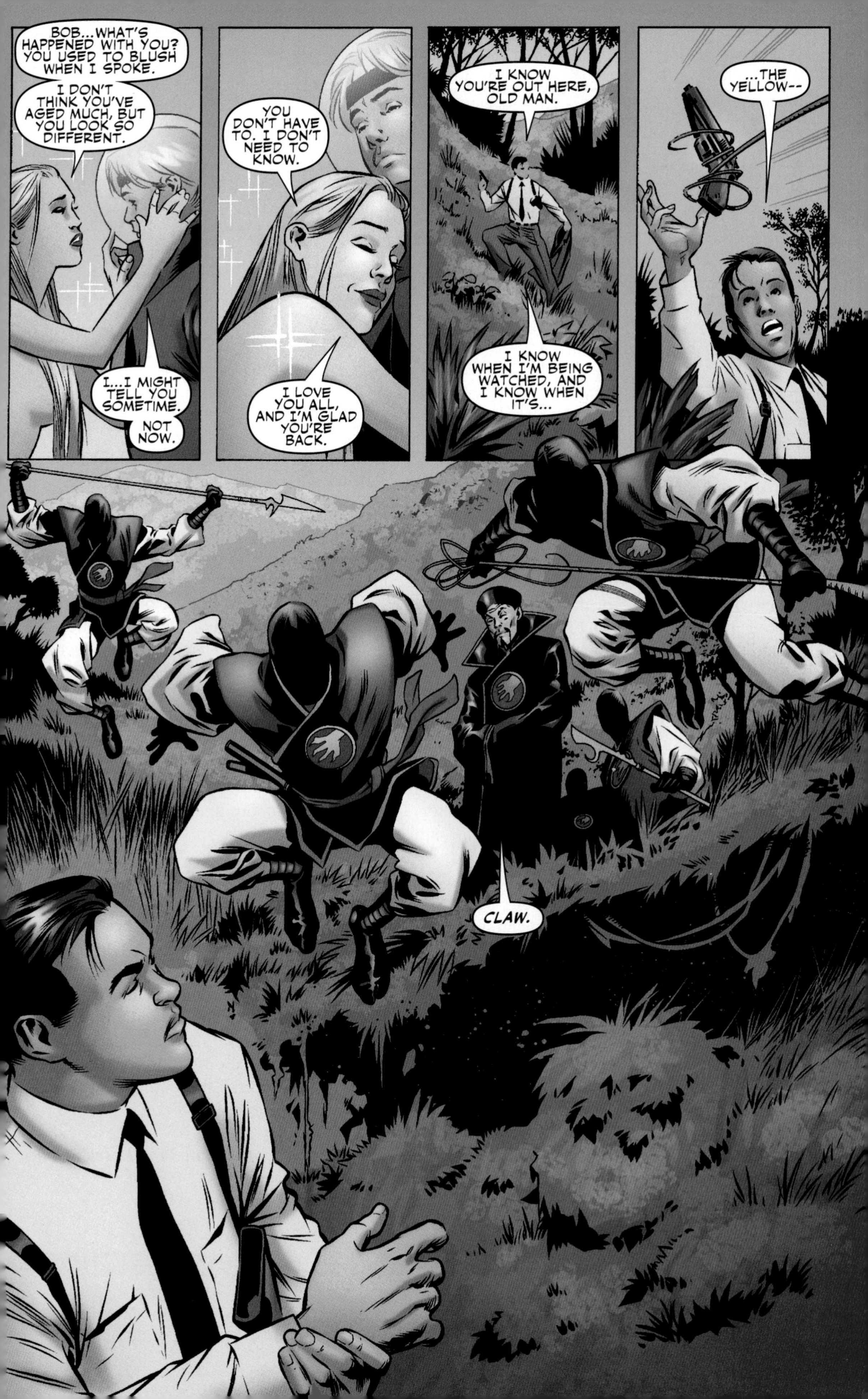
BOB...WHAT'S HAPPENED WITH YOU? YOU USED TO BLUSH WHEN I SPOKE.
I DON'T THINK YOU'VE AGED MUCH, BUT YOU LOOK SO DIFFERENT.
I...I MIGHT TELL YOU SOMETIME.
NOT NOW.
YOU DON'T HAVE TO. I DON'T NEED TO KNOW.
I LOVE YOU ALL, AND I'M GLAD YOU'RE BACK.
I KNOW YOU'RE OUT HERE, OLD MAN.
I KNOW WHEN I'M BEING WATCHED, AND I KNOW WHEN IT'S...
...THE YELLOW--
CLAW.

THE GODS WALK AMONG US

In 1958 at the Hunter's Point Naval Shipyard in San Francisco, I was a young officer susceptible to beautiful women. I had never been affected as profoundly, though, as when I saw a young lady riding in a convertible with a gorilla and a robot. I would later find this woman was an adventurer known as Venus, and many testify that she was in fact the actual deity who had given up many godly powers to walk among humans.

Some of her behavior was perplexing; primarily that Venus would show herself to ordinary humans at all. For the purpose of speculation, let's assume that the Greco-Roman gods were, in fact, real beings. By all accounts, they rarely interacted directly with mortals, preferring to use a go-between of some sort. At times the gods would speak to mortals through statues in their likeness, or through nature, such as animals with traits reflective of them.

Later I found some unreliable accounts of her living in Europe, but nothing concrete until 1948, when she came to New York City. She was in fact working as an editor for the popular magazine, *Beauty*, for publisher Whitney Hammond, under the name Victoria Starr. Searching a paper trail revealed the unfortunate middle name Nutley, which to me seemed an odd choice until one considers her frame of reference may be far different from that of

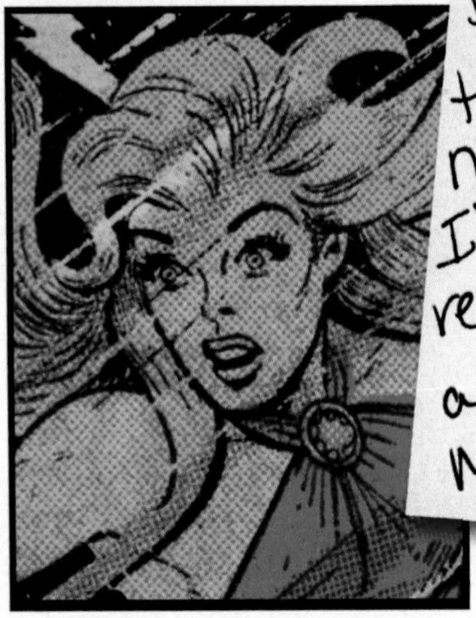

a modern woman. It is likely given her whimsical nature that the name is based on the initials, VNS, a winking sobriquet.

A trait that confuses the records is the changing of her hair color*, which apparently happens at regular intervals. I suspected at first this was due to subjective viewing, as many eyewitnesses could be rendered unreliable upon exposure to Venus. Photographs gathered support this, however.

An interview with the Dutch pop band, Shocking Blue, mentions that they based their 1969 chart-topping hit "Venus" (later covered by Bananarama) on a real woman traveling in their home city. I note this because Venus also seems to be an expert on world languages, soon mastering the local tongue wherever she goes.

Given my chosen life in academia, I was particularly surprised to run across a Vicki Starr in the early 1970's, a

Dugan—
this is the only
noteworthy writing
I've found on the woman
requested so far, from
a Literature Professor.
More coming, I hope.
—Coover

Professor of the Humanities at Pepperdine University**. By the time I made it to Southern California to follow this lead, the teacher in question had already moved on. I suspect this was the same Starr because campus interviews described the faculty member as more concerned with organizing peace rallies than in following a curriculum. The rallies were far more peaceful than other anti-war gatherings of the time, more akin to the "love-ins" of the day.

In my upcoming book I will provide documentation of all the possible appearances of Venus to the point I lost track of her in the late 20th-century. Many claim that this work is all in service of hopefully meeting the woman to experience her effect one last time, a final hurrah for an old man. I never said it wasn't.

–Associate Prof. Derek Schiller

*While it would be easy enough for Venus to dye her hair red, blonde, or brunette, one of the pictures- and many accounts- portray her with shimmering silver hair. I've not been made aware of any tonsorial tincture or pigment capable of creating this particular hue.

** An intriguing detail I found while going through her class roster (she only taught two semesters) was the presence of a student named Nita Prentiss. News from the recent catastrophe in Stamford, Connecticut reveal that name as being used by the young Atlantean heroine known as Namorita or Kymaera. The discrepancy in years would seem to refute this until one remembers that Merpeople age at a far slower rate than surface dwellers. That one heroine would have studied under another in a non-adventuring context is of interest, I think.

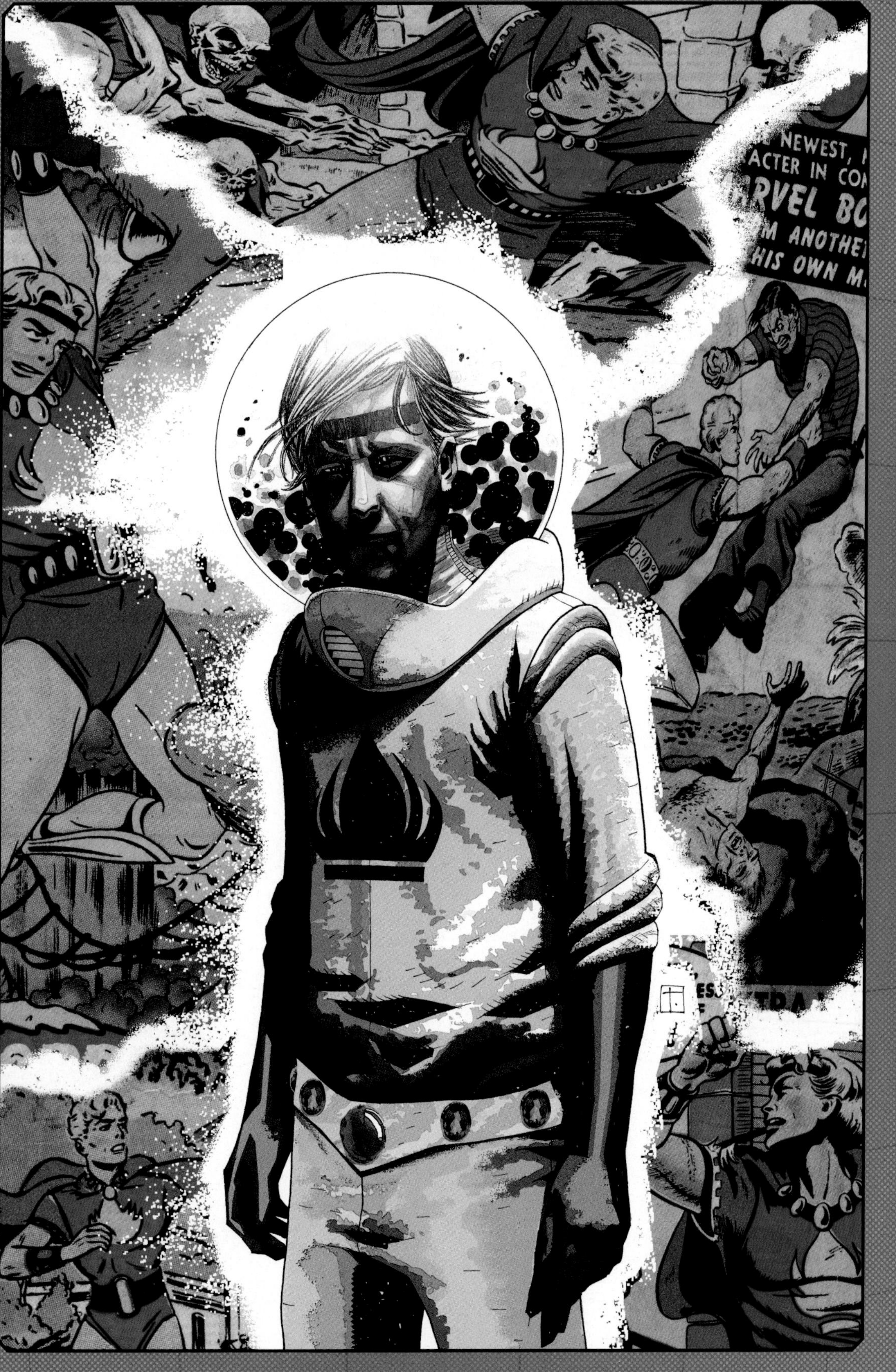

AGENTS OF ATLAS (2006) **3**

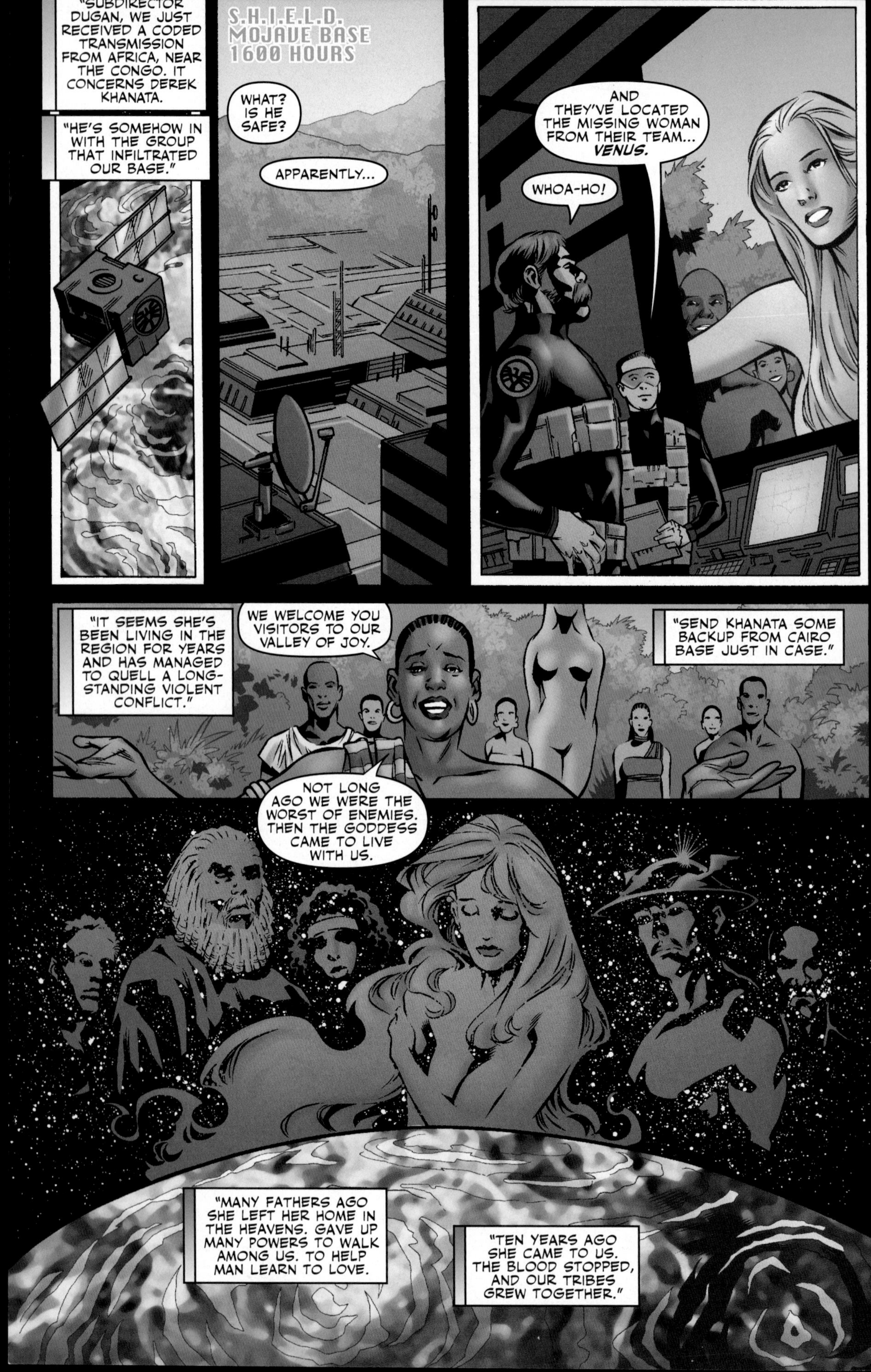
"SUBDIRECTOR DUGAN, WE JUST RECEIVED A CODED TRANSMISSION FROM AFRICA, NEAR THE CONGO. IT CONCERNS DEREK KHANATA.
"HE'S SOMEHOW IN WITH THE GROUP THAT INFILTRATED OUR BASE."
S.H.I.E.L.D. MOJAVE BASE 1600 HOURS
WHAT? IS HE SAFE?
APPARENTLY...
AND THEY'VE LOCATED THE MISSING WOMAN FROM THEIR TEAM... VENUS.
WHOA-HO!
"IT SEEMS SHE'S BEEN LIVING IN THE REGION FOR YEARS AND HAS MANAGED TO QUELL A LONG-STANDING VIOLENT CONFLICT."
WE WELCOME YOU VISITORS TO OUR VALLEY OF JOY.
"SEND KHANATA SOME BACKUP FROM CAIRO BASE JUST IN CASE."
NOT LONG AGO WE WERE THE WORST OF ENEMIES. THEN THE GODDESS CAME TO LIVE WITH US.
"MANY FATHERS AGO SHE LEFT HER HOME IN THE HEAVENS. GAVE UP MANY POWERS TO WALK AMONG US. TO HELP MAN LEARN TO LOVE.
"TEN YEARS AGO SHE CAME TO US. THE BLOOD STOPPED, AND OUR TRIBES GREW TOGETHER."

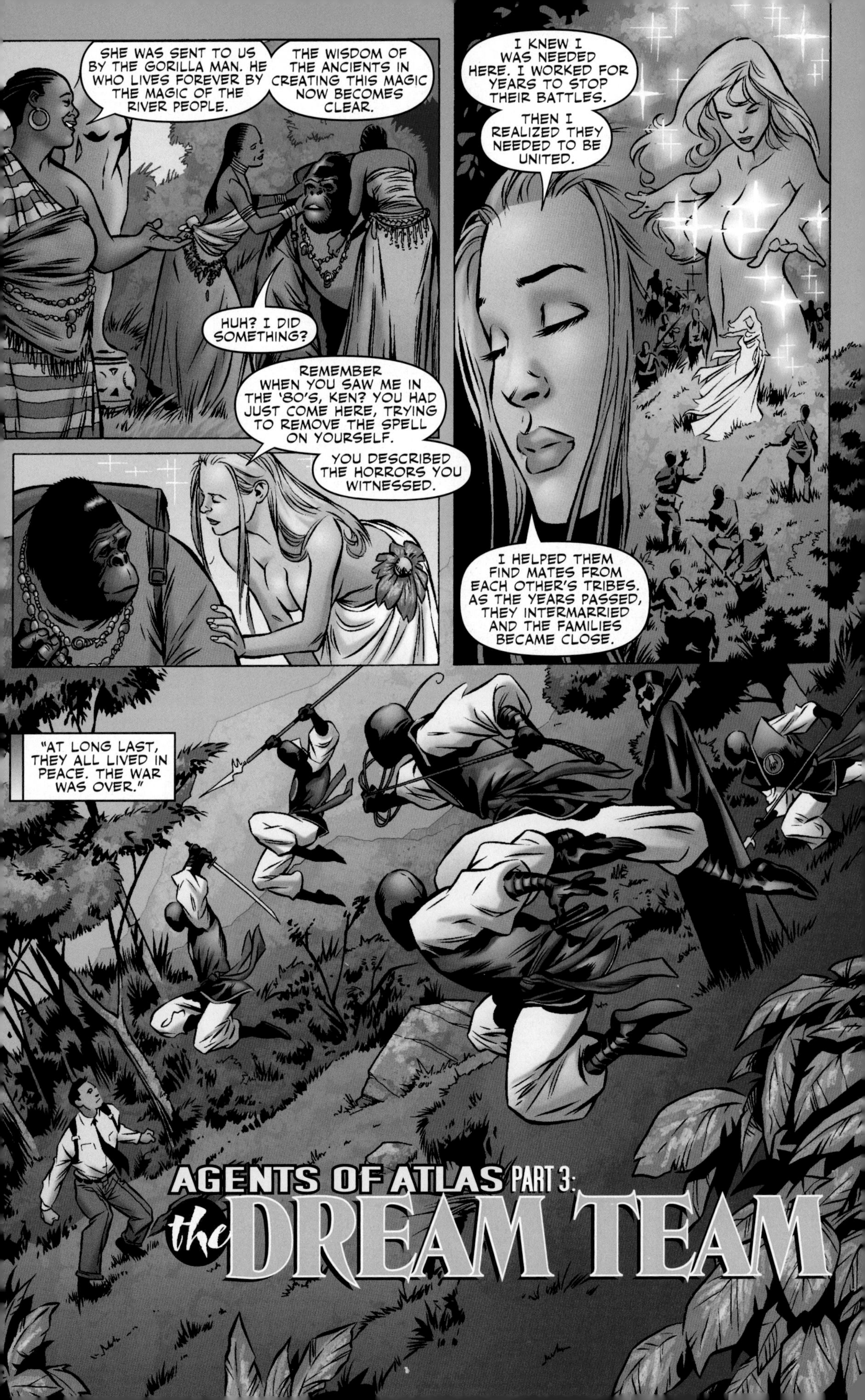
SHE WAS SENT TO US BY THE GORILLA MAN. HE WHO LIVES FOREVER BY THE MAGIC OF THE RIVER PEOPLE.
THE WISDOM OF THE ANCIENTS IN CREATING THIS MAGIC NOW BECOMES CLEAR.
HUH? I DID SOMETHING?
REMEMBER WHEN YOU SAW ME IN THE '80'S, KEN? YOU HAD JUST COME HERE, TRYING TO REMOVE THE SPELL ON YOURSELF.
YOU DESCRIBED THE HORRORS YOU WITNESSED.
I KNEW I WAS NEEDED HERE. I WORKED FOR YEARS TO STOP THEIR BATTLES.
THEN I REALIZED THEY NEEDED TO BE UNITED.
I HELPED THEM FIND MATES FROM EACH OTHER'S TRIBES. AS THE YEARS PASSED, THEY INTERMARRIED AND THE FAMILIES BECAME CLOSE.
"AT LONG LAST, THEY ALL LIVED IN PEACE. THE WAR WAS OVER."
AGENTS OF ATLAS PART 3:
the DREAM TEAM

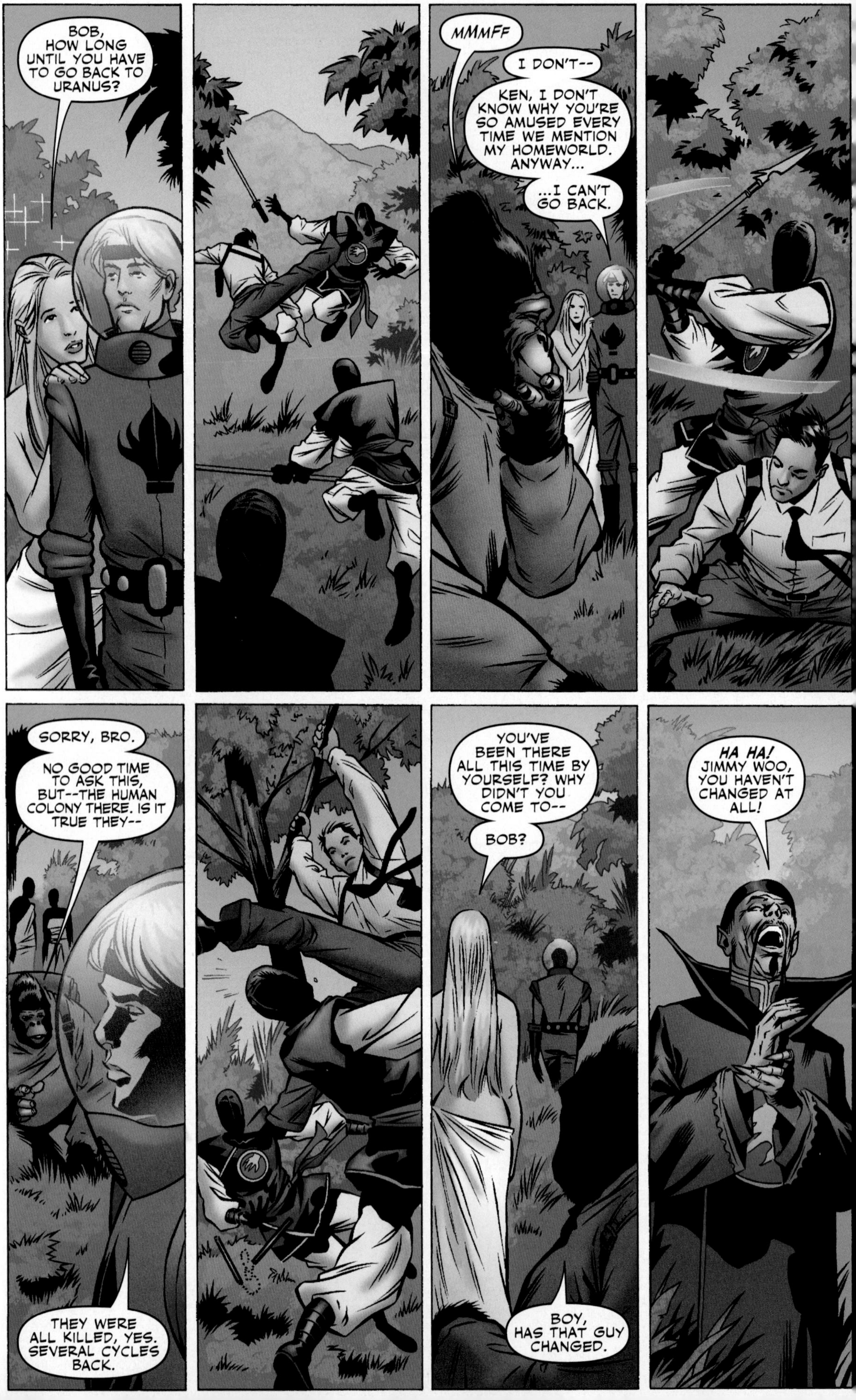
BOB, HOW LONG UNTIL YOU HAVE TO GO BACK TO URANUS?
MMMFF
I DON'T--
KEN, I DON'T KNOW WHY YOU'RE SO AMUSED EVERY TIME WE MENTION MY HOMEWORLD. ANYWAY...
...I CAN'T GO BACK.
SORRY, BRO.
NO GOOD TIME TO ASK THIS, BUT--THE HUMAN COLONY THERE. IS IT TRUE THEY--
THEY WERE ALL KILLED, YES. SEVERAL CYCLES BACK.
YOU'VE BEEN THERE ALL THIS TIME BY YOURSELF? WHY DIDN'T YOU COME TO--
BOB?
BOY, HAS THAT GUY CHANGED.
HA HA! JIMMY WOO, YOU HAVEN'T CHANGED AT ALL!

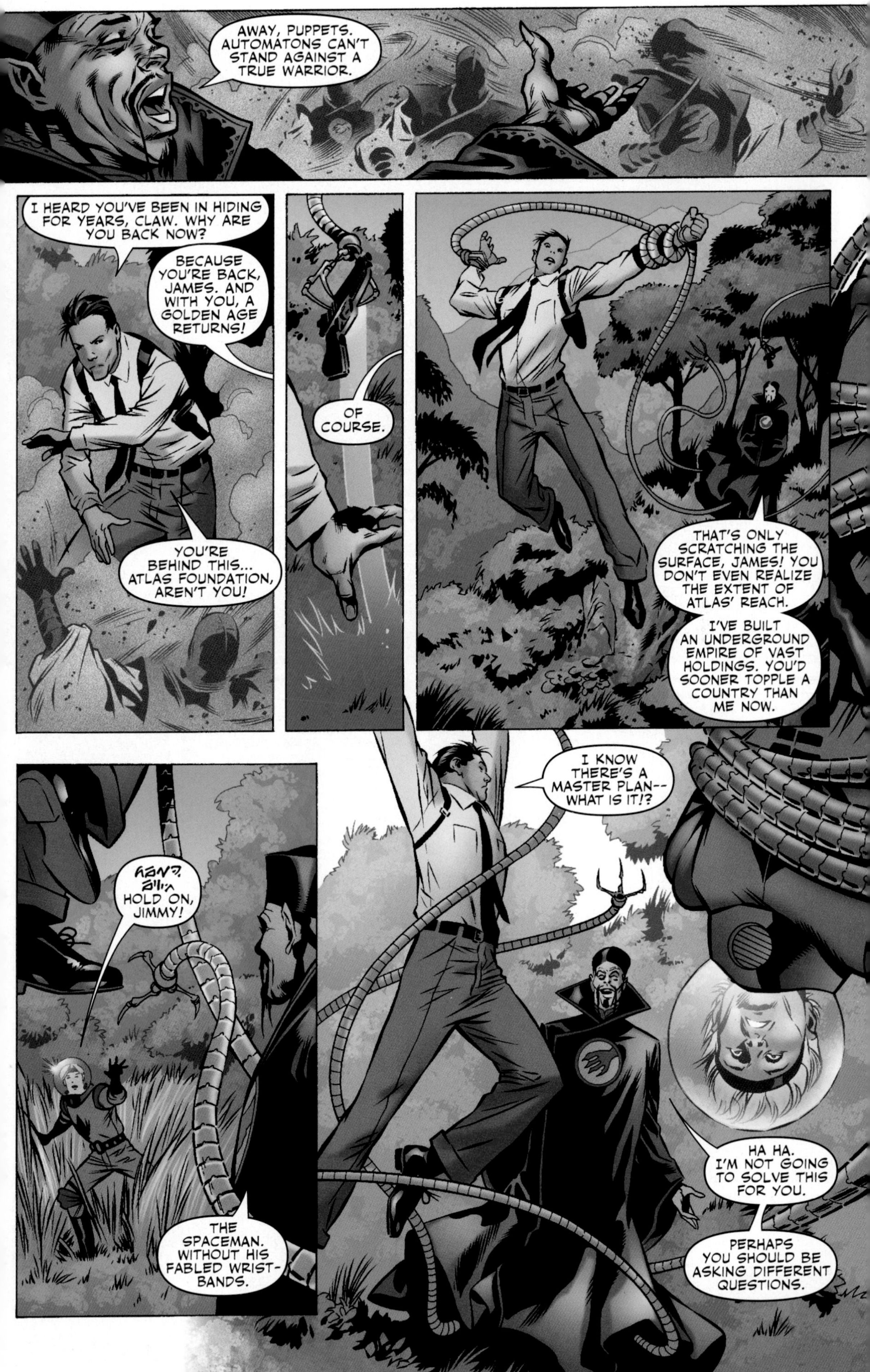
AWAY, PUPPETS. AUTOMATONS CAN'T STAND AGAINST A TRUE WARRIOR.
I HEARD YOU'VE BEEN IN HIDING FOR YEARS, CLAW. WHY ARE YOU BACK NOW?
BECAUSE YOU'RE BACK, JAMES. AND WITH YOU, A GOLDEN AGE RETURNS!
YOU'RE BEHIND THIS... ATLAS FOUNDATION, AREN'T YOU!
OF COURSE.
THAT'S ONLY SCRATCHING THE SURFACE, JAMES! YOU DON'T EVEN REALIZE THE EXTENT OF ATLAS' REACH.
I'VE BUILT AN UNDERGROUND EMPIRE OF VAST HOLDINGS. YOU'D SOONER TOPPLE A COUNTRY THAN ME NOW.
HOLD ON, JIMMY!
THE SPACEMAN. WITHOUT HIS FABLED WRIST-BANDS.
I KNOW THERE'S A MASTER PLAN-- WHAT IS IT!?
HA HA. I'M NOT GOING TO SOLVE THIS FOR YOU.
PERHAPS YOU SHOULD BE ASKING DIFFERENT QUESTIONS.

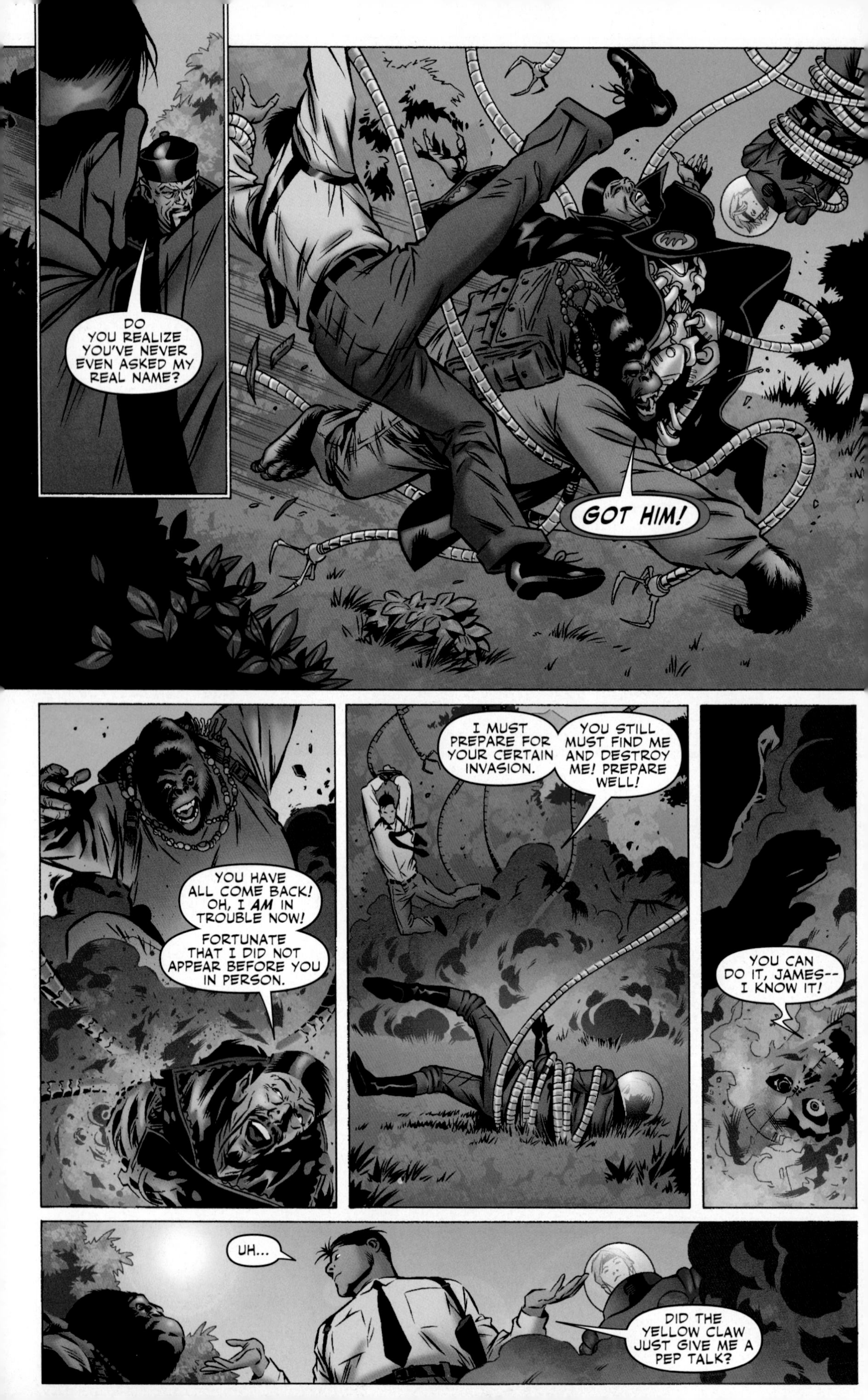
DO YOU REALIZE YOU'VE NEVER EVEN ASKED MY REAL NAME?
GOT HIM!
YOU HAVE ALL COME BACK! OH, I AM IN TROUBLE NOW!
FORTUNATE THAT I DID NOT APPEAR BEFORE YOU IN PERSON.
I MUST PREPARE FOR YOUR CERTAIN INVASION.
YOU STILL MUST FIND ME AND DESTROY ME! PREPARE WELL!
YOU CAN DO IT, JAMES-- I KNOW IT!
UH...
DID THE YELLOW CLAW JUST GIVE ME A PEP TALK?

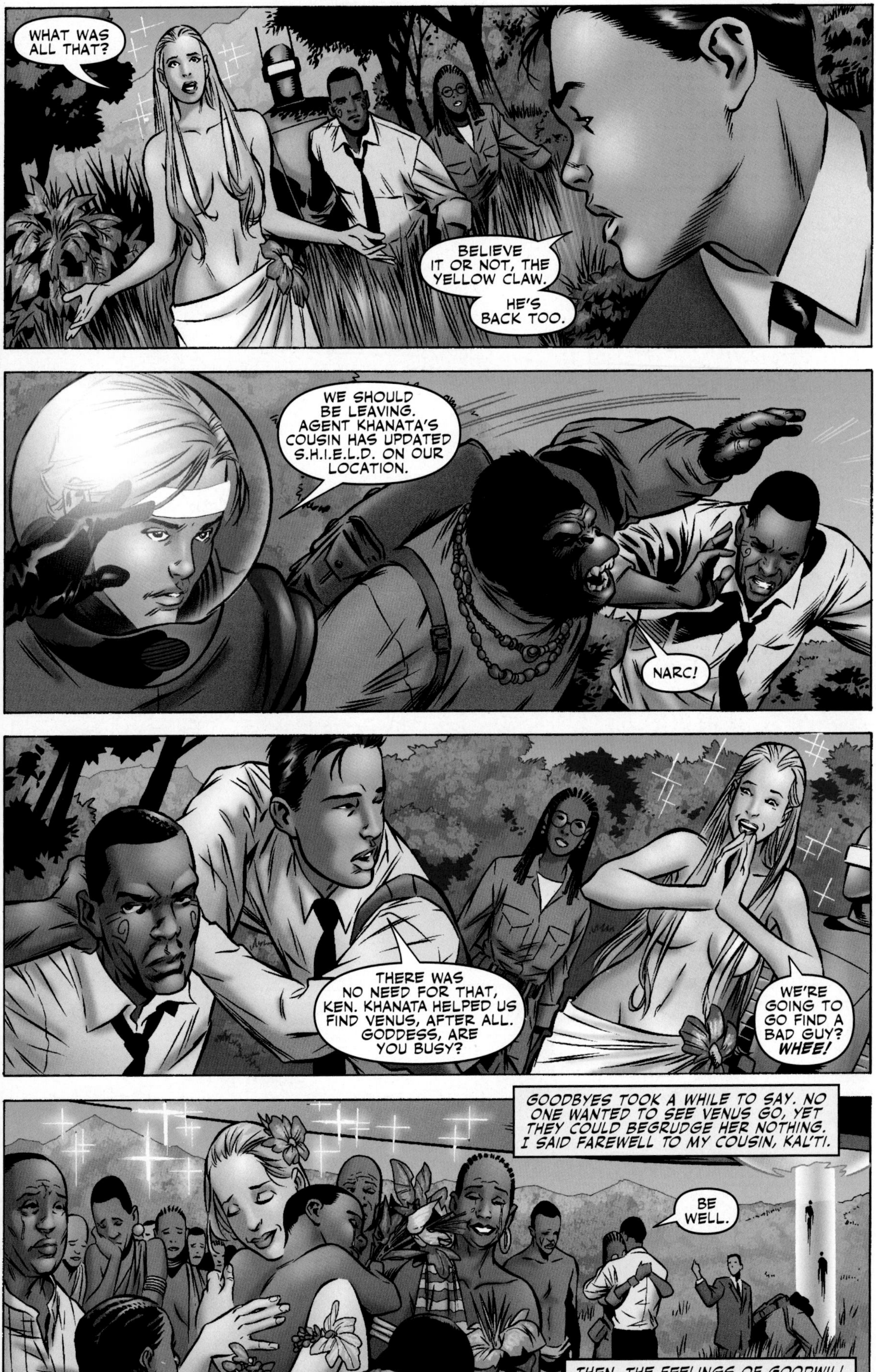
WHAT WAS ALL THAT?
BELIEVE IT OR NOT, THE YELLOW CLAW.
HE'S BACK TOO.
WE SHOULD BE LEAVING. AGENT KHANATA'S COUSIN HAS UPDATED S.H.I.E.L.D. ON OUR LOCATION.
NARC!
THERE WAS NO NEED FOR THAT, KEN. KHANATA HELPED US FIND VENUS, AFTER ALL. GODDESS, ARE YOU BUSY?
WE'RE GOING TO GO FIND A BAD GUY? *WHEE!*
GOODBYES TOOK A WHILE TO SAY. NO ONE WANTED TO SEE VENUS GO, YET THEY COULD BEGRUDGE HER NOTHING. I SAID FAREWELL TO MY COUSIN, KAL'TI.
BE WELL.
THEN, THE FEELINGS OF GOODWILL SEEMED TO PERMEATE JIMMY WOO, WHO INVITED ME TO CONTINUE ALONG WITH THE GROUP.

SAN FRANCISCO

MR. WOO, I HAVE A QUESTION.

FIRE AWAY, AGENT KHANATA.

HOW DID YOU PICK THIS SPECIFIC TEAM FOR THE RESCUE OF THE PRESIDENT BACK IN '59?

YEAH, ALWAYS WANTED TO KNOW THAT MYSELF.

YOU MAY THINK THIS IS WACKY, BUT...

...THE LINEUP CAME TO ME IN A DREAM.

REALLY?

SCOUT'S HONOR. I HAD TO PICK A KEY GROUP FOR THE MISSION--SMALL AND POWERFUL, SO THE MILITARY WOULDN'T HAVE TO BE CALLED IN.

"I WENT THROUGH ALL THE FILES OF PARANORMALS WHO MIGHT BE AVAILABLE TO HELP. THEN I LOCKED MY OFFICE DOOR FOR ABOUT AN HOUR, AND TOOK A NAP."

"THE PERFECT TEAM JUST... PRESENTED ITSELF TO ME. I KNOW IT SOUNDS KOOKY, BUT THAT'S THE WAY I'VE MADE A LOT OF MAJOR DECISIONS IN MY LIFE, AND IT ALWAYS WORKS."

BLAZING SKULL

PHANTOM

FURY

JACK FROST

MISS PATRIOT

FLEXO

THE SUBCONSCIOUS IS OFTEN MUCH BETTER AT SUCH SELECTIONS.

WE ARE ARRIVING AT THE BAY.

BUT M-11 HERE WAS ACTUALLY BROUGHT TO YOU BY THE ATLANTEAN, NAMORA, RIGHT?

THAT'S RIGHT, NAMORA WAS THE ONE I DREAMED OF, BUT SHE SAID SHE HAD NEGLECTED HER SEA PEOPLE TOO LONG.

SHE LED US TO M-11 AND BOB FIXED HIM UP.

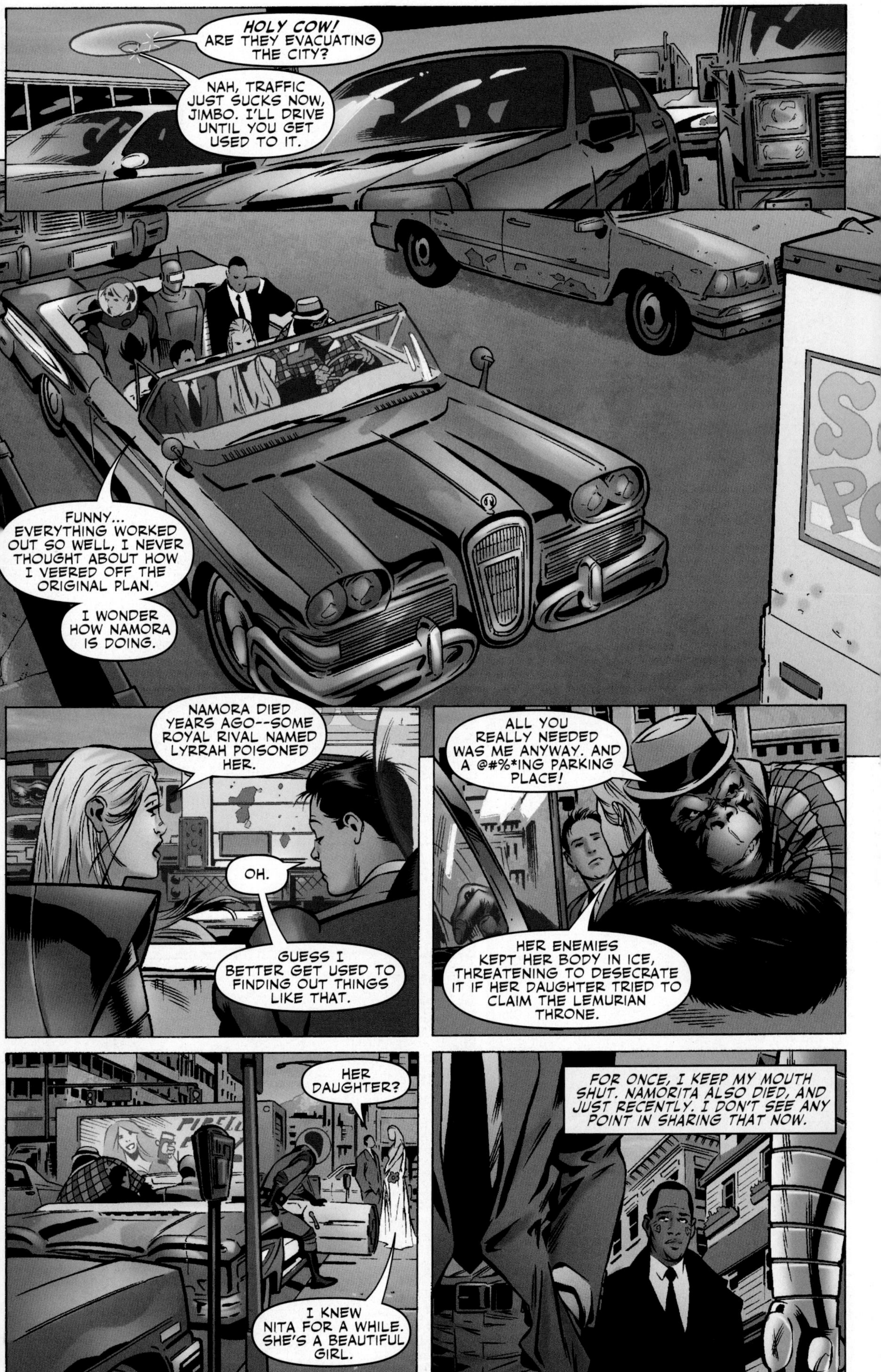
HOLY COW! ARE THEY EVACUATING THE CITY?
NAH, TRAFFIC JUST SUCKS NOW, JIMBO. I'LL DRIVE UNTIL YOU GET USED TO IT.
FUNNY... EVERYTHING WORKED OUT SO WELL, I NEVER THOUGHT ABOUT HOW I VEERED OFF THE ORIGINAL PLAN.
I WONDER HOW NAMORA IS DOING.
NAMORA DIED YEARS AGO--SOME ROYAL RIVAL NAMED LYRRAH POISONED HER.
OH.
GUESS I BETTER GET USED TO FINDING OUT THINGS LIKE THAT.
ALL YOU REALLY NEEDED WAS ME ANYWAY. AND A @#%*ING PARKING PLACE!
HER ENEMIES KEPT HER BODY IN ICE, THREATENING TO DESECRATE IT IF HER DAUGHTER TRIED TO CLAIM THE LEMURIAN THRONE.
HER DAUGHTER?
I KNEW NITA FOR A WHILE. SHE'S A BEAUTIFUL GIRL.
FOR ONCE, I KEEP MY MOUTH SHUT. NAMORITA ALSO DIED, AND JUST RECENTLY. I DON'T SEE ANY POINT IN SHARING THAT NOW.

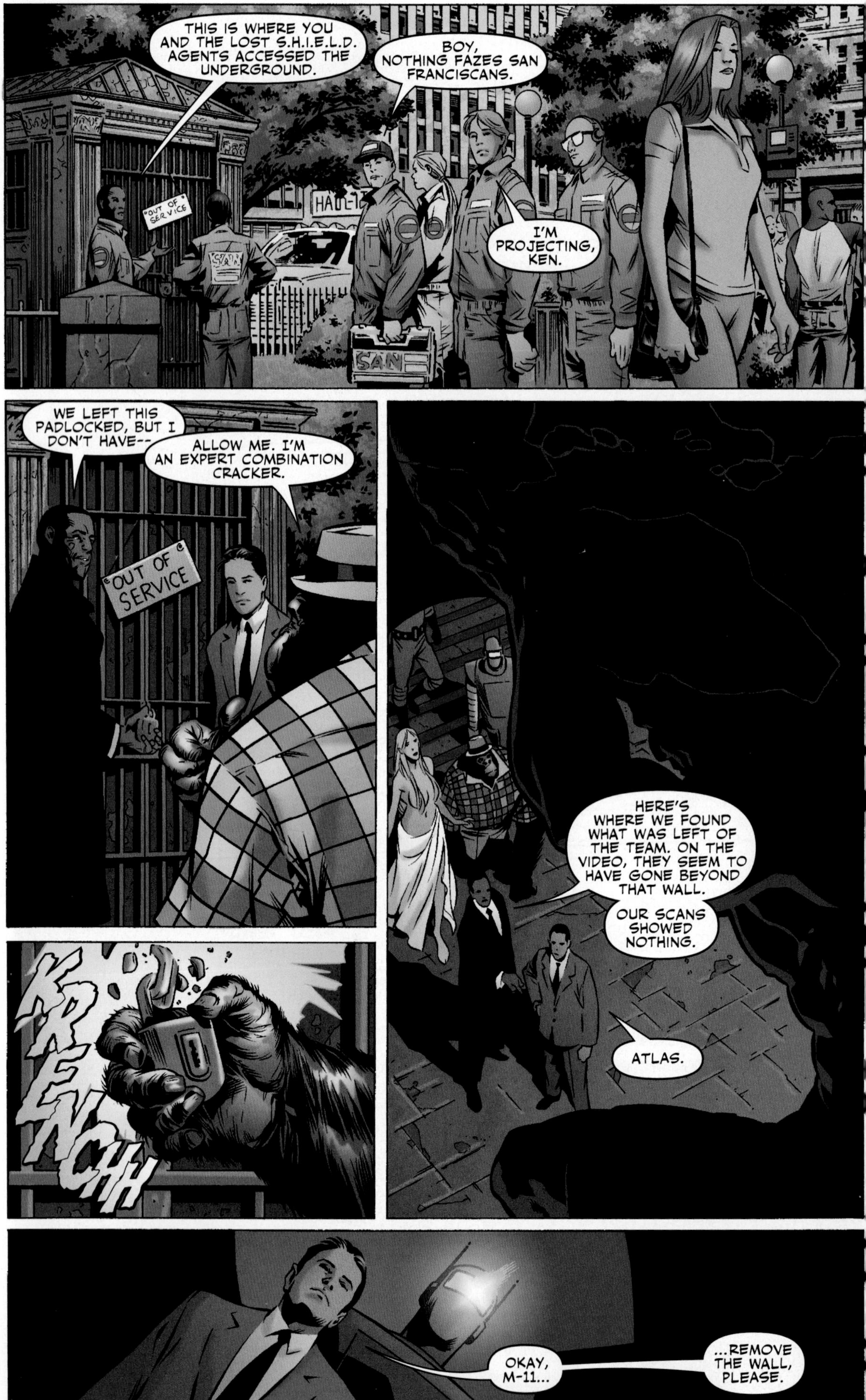
THIS IS WHERE YOU AND THE LOST S.H.I.E.L.D. AGENTS ACCESSED THE UNDERGROUND.
OUT OF SERVICE
BOY, NOTHING FAZES SAN FRANCISCANS.
I'M PROJECTING, KEN.
WE LEFT THIS PADLOCKED, BUT I DON'T HAVE--
ALLOW ME. I'M AN EXPERT COMBINATION CRACKER.
OUT OF SERVICE
KRENCHH
HERE'S WHERE WE FOUND WHAT WAS LEFT OF THE TEAM. ON THE VIDEO, THEY SEEM TO HAVE GONE BEYOND THAT WALL.
OUR SCANS SHOWED NOTHING.
ATLAS.
OKAY, M-11...
...REMOVE THE WALL, PLEASE.

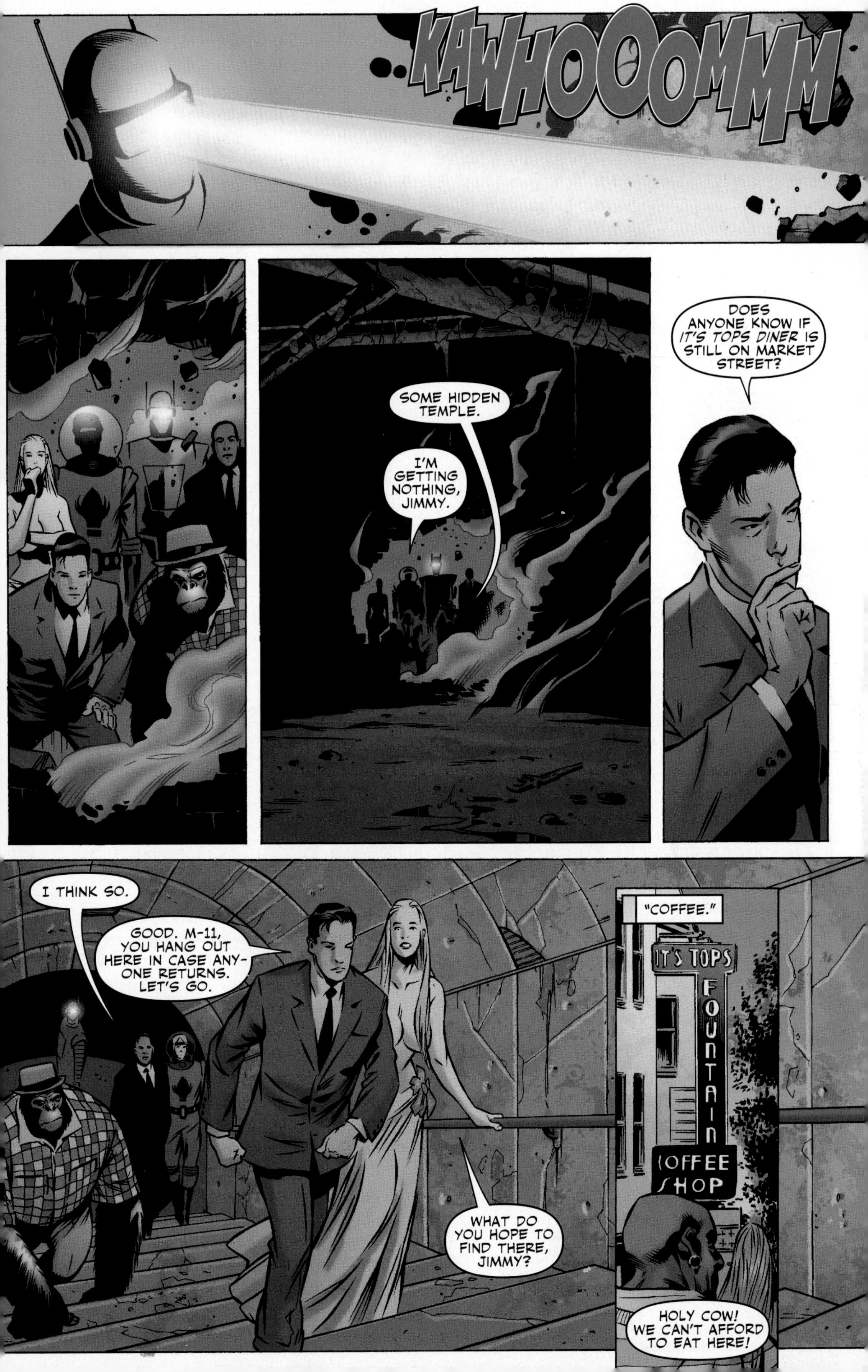
KAWHOOOOMMMM
SOME HIDDEN TEMPLE.
I'M GETTING NOTHING, JIMMY.
DOES ANYONE KNOW IF *IT'S TOPS DINER* IS STILL ON MARKET STREET?
I THINK SO.
GOOD. M-11, YOU HANG OUT HERE IN CASE ANYONE RETURNS. LET'S GO.
WHAT DO YOU HOPE TO FIND THERE, JIMMY?
"COFFEE."
IT'S TOPS
FOUNTAIN
COFFEE SHOP
HOLY COW! WE CAN'T AFFORD TO EAT HERE!

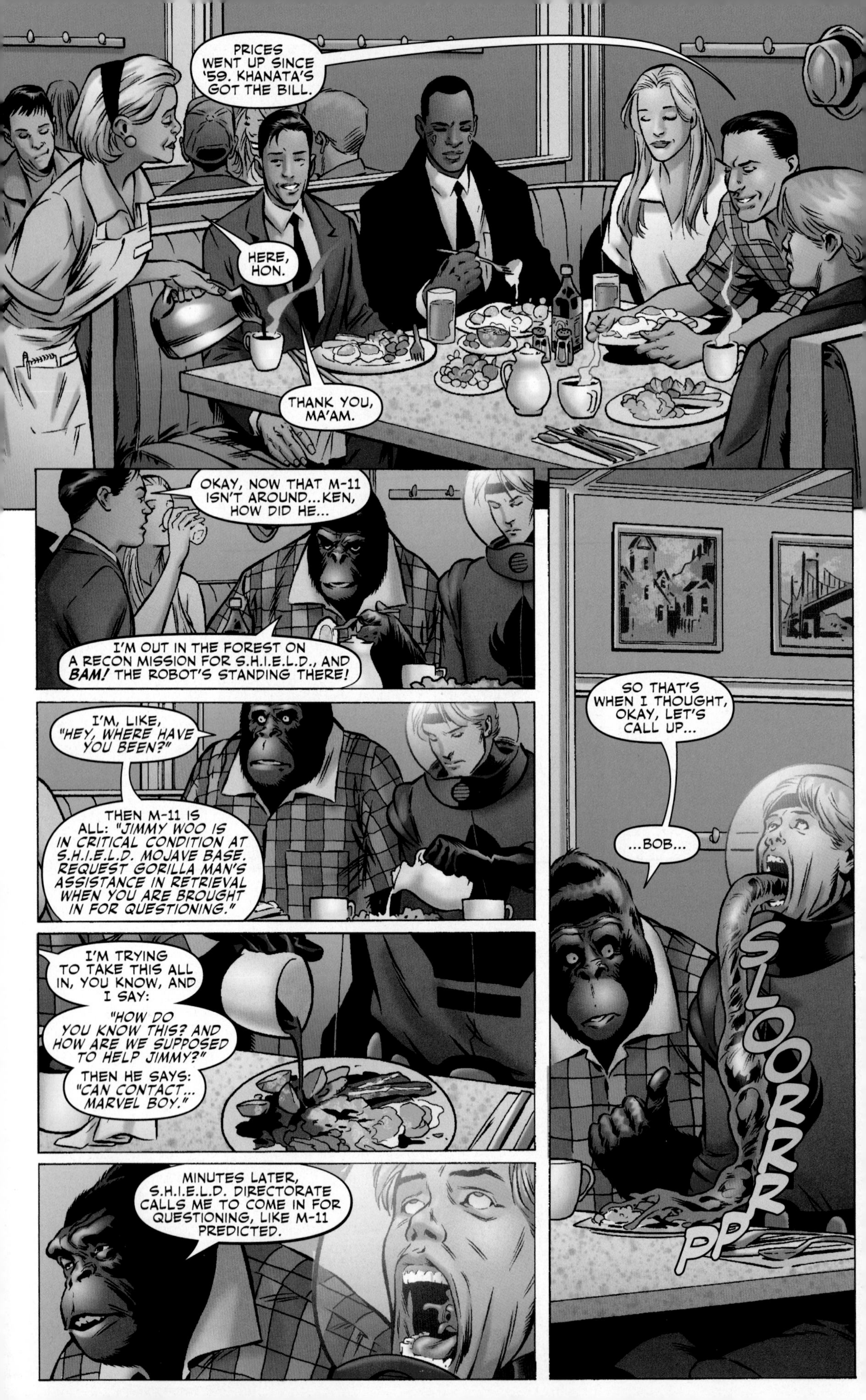

PRICES WENT UP SINCE '59. KHANATA'S GOT THE BILL.
HERE, HON.
THANK YOU, MA'AM.
OKAY, NOW THAT M-11 ISN'T AROUND...KEN, HOW DID HE...
I'M OUT IN THE FOREST ON A RECON MISSION FOR S.H.I.E.L.D., AND BAM! THE ROBOT'S STANDING THERE!
I'M, LIKE, "HEY, WHERE HAVE YOU BEEN?"
THEN M-11 IS ALL: "JIMMY WOO IS IN CRITICAL CONDITION AT S.H.I.E.L.D. MOJAVE BASE. REQUEST GORILLA MAN'S ASSISTANCE IN RETRIEVAL WHEN YOU ARE BROUGHT IN FOR QUESTIONING."
I'M TRYING TO TAKE THIS ALL IN, YOU KNOW, AND I SAY:
"HOW DO YOU KNOW THIS? AND HOW ARE WE SUPPOSED TO HELP JIMMY?"
THEN HE SAYS: "CAN CONTACT... MARVEL BOY."
MINUTES LATER, S.H.I.E.L.D. DIRECTORATE CALLS ME TO COME IN FOR QUESTIONING, LIKE M-11 PREDICTED.
SO THAT'S WHEN I THOUGHT, OKAY, LET'S CALL UP...
...BOB...
SLOORRRPP

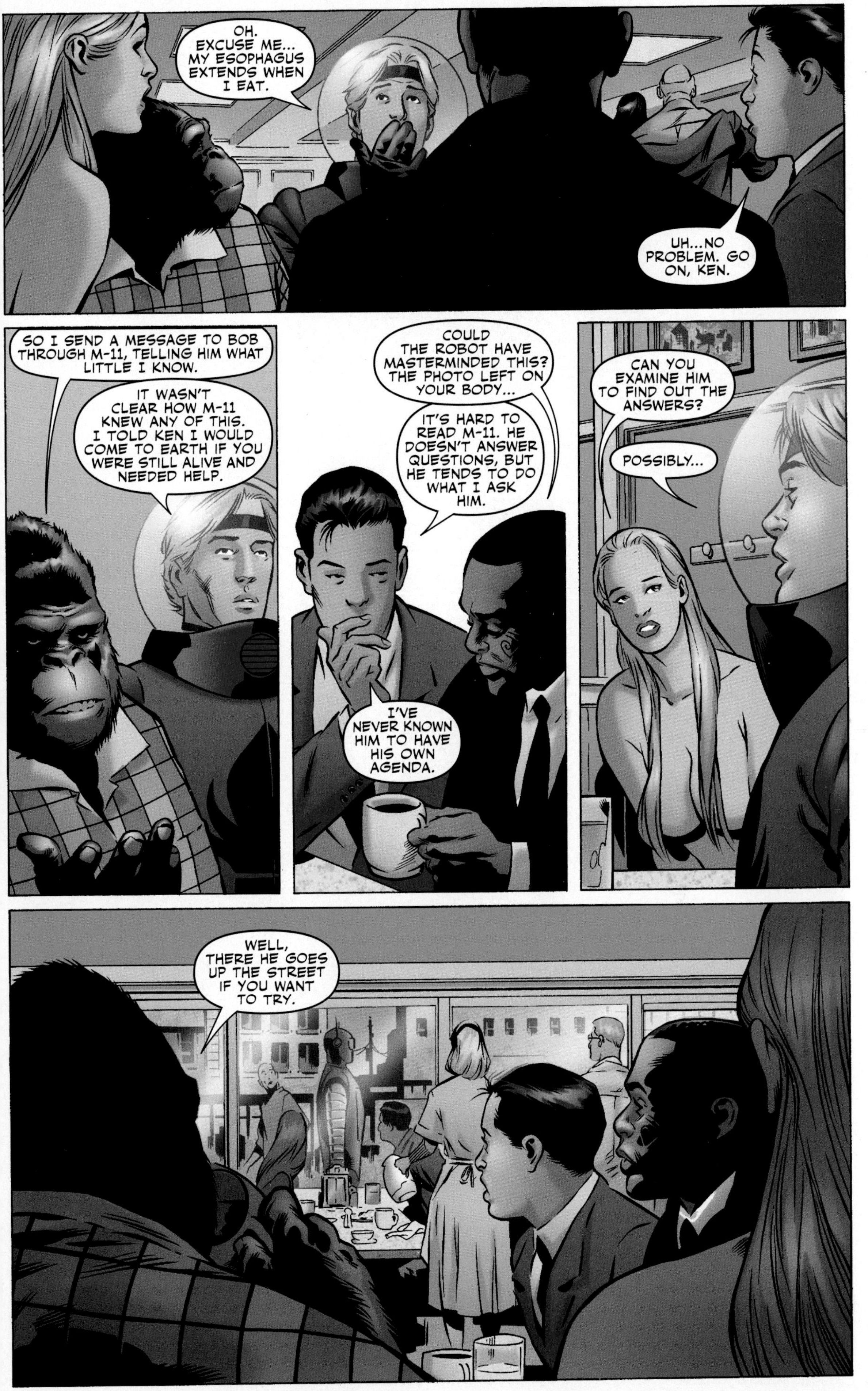
OH. EXCUSE ME... MY ESOPHAGUS EXTENDS WHEN I EAT.
UH...NO PROBLEM. GO ON, KEN.
SO I SEND A MESSAGE TO BOB THROUGH M-11, TELLING HIM WHAT LITTLE I KNOW.
IT WASN'T CLEAR HOW M-11 KNEW ANY OF THIS. I TOLD KEN I WOULD COME TO EARTH IF YOU WERE STILL ALIVE AND NEEDED HELP.
COULD THE ROBOT HAVE MASTERMINDED THIS? THE PHOTO LEFT ON YOUR BODY...
IT'S HARD TO READ M-11. HE DOESN'T ANSWER QUESTIONS, BUT HE TENDS TO DO WHAT I ASK HIM.
I'VE NEVER KNOWN HIM TO HAVE HIS OWN AGENDA.
CAN YOU EXAMINE HIM TO FIND OUT THE ANSWERS?
POSSIBLY...
WELL, THERE HE GOES UP THE STREET IF YOU WANT TO TRY.

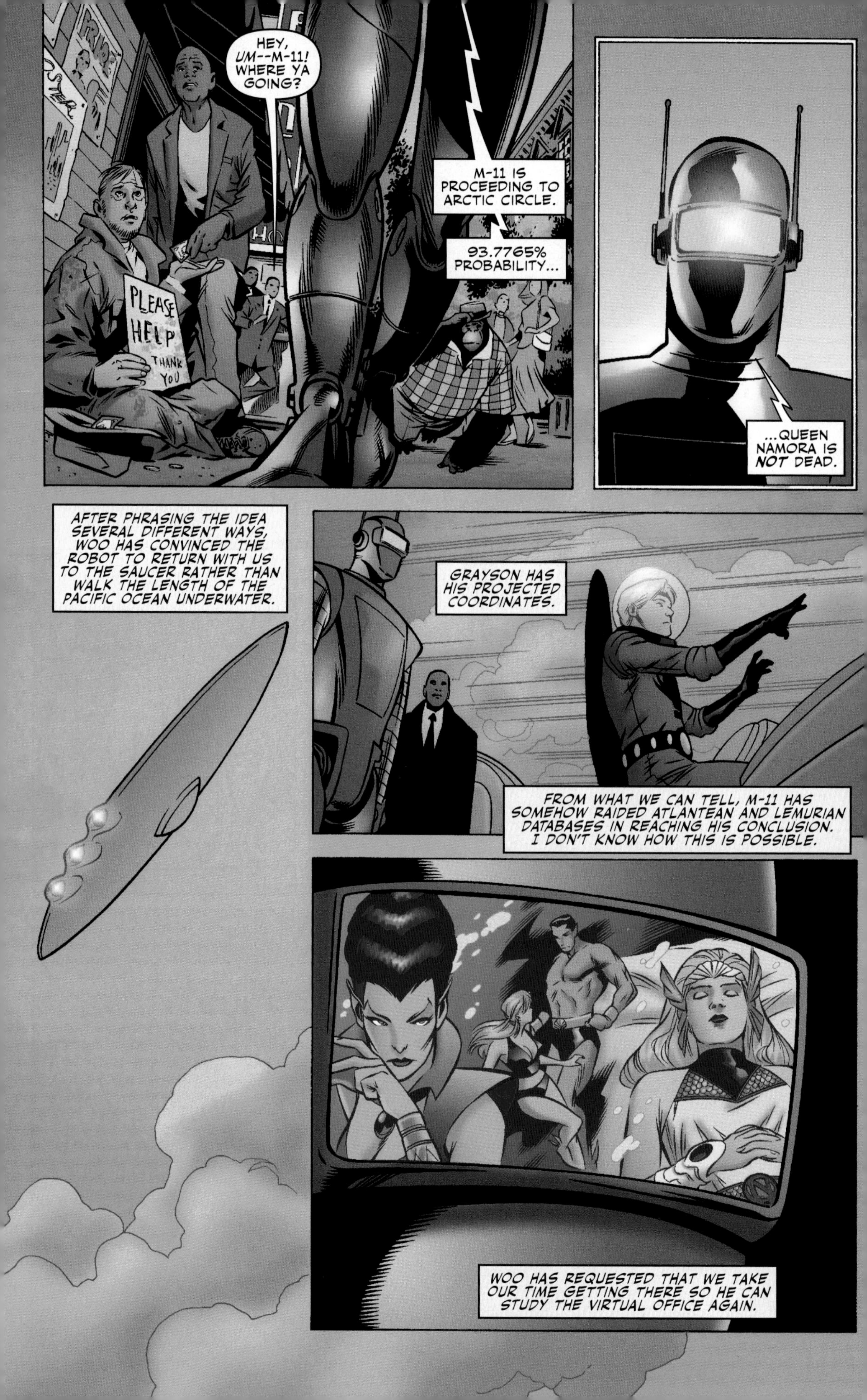

HEY, UM--M-11! WHERE YA GOING?
M-11 IS PROCEEDING TO ARCTIC CIRCLE.
93.7765% PROBABILITY...
PLEASE HELP THANK YOU
...QUEEN NAMORA IS NOT DEAD.
AFTER PHRASING THE IDEA SEVERAL DIFFERENT WAYS, WOO HAS CONVINCED THE ROBOT TO RETURN WITH US TO THE SAUCER RATHER THAN WALK THE LENGTH OF THE PACIFIC OCEAN UNDERWATER.
GRAYSON HAS HIS PROJECTED COORDINATES.
FROM WHAT WE CAN TELL, M-11 HAS SOMEHOW RAIDED ATLANTEAN AND LEMURIAN DATABASES IN REACHING HIS CONCLUSION. I DON'T KNOW HOW THIS IS POSSIBLE.
WOO HAS REQUESTED THAT WE TAKE OUR TIME GETTING THERE SO HE CAN STUDY THE VIRTUAL OFFICE AGAIN.

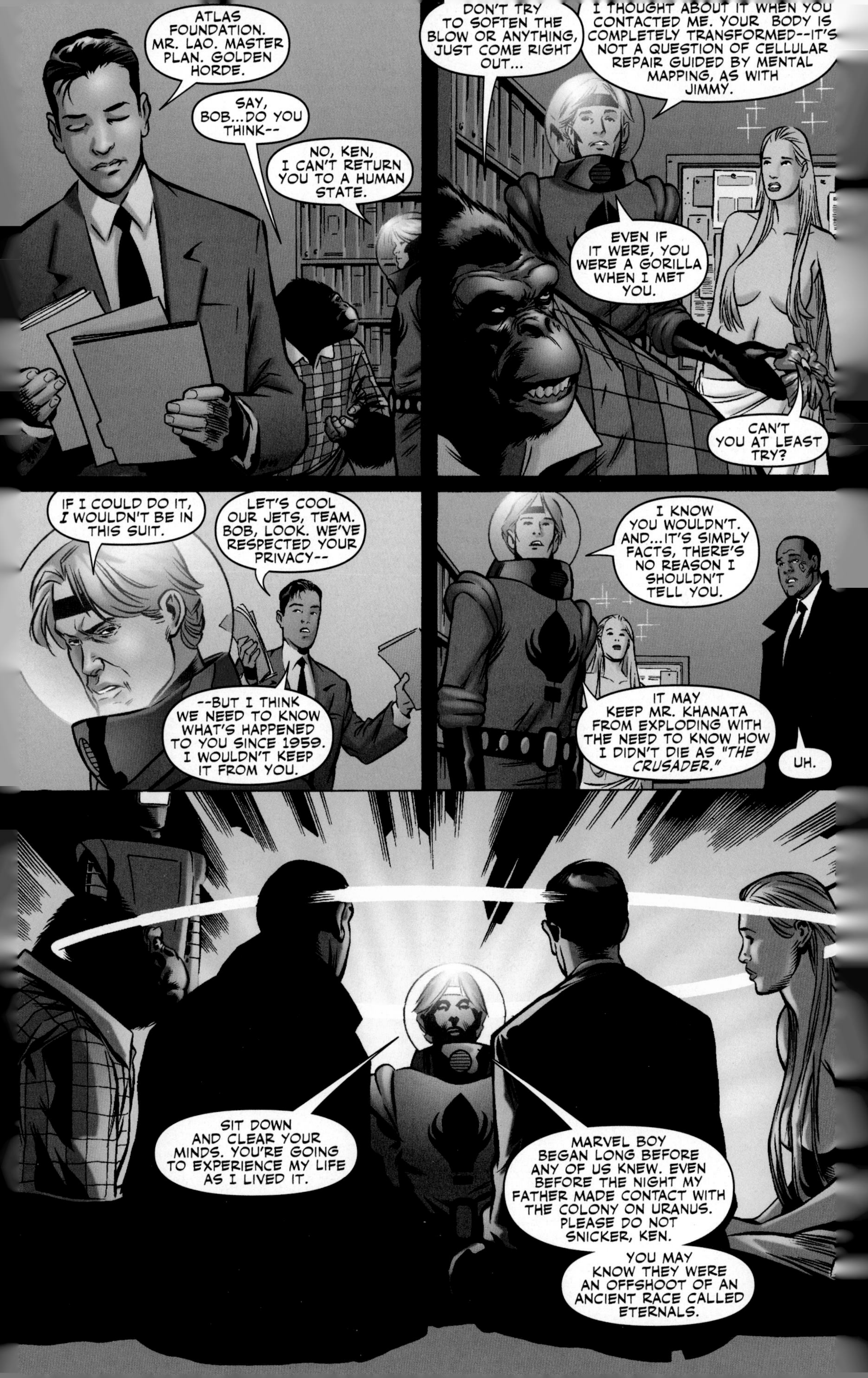
ATLAS FOUNDATION. MR. LAO. MASTER PLAN. GOLDEN HORDE.
SAY, BOB...DO YOU THINK--
NO, KEN, I CAN'T RETURN YOU TO A HUMAN STATE.
DON'T TRY TO SOFTEN THE BLOW OR ANYTHING, JUST COME RIGHT OUT...
I THOUGHT ABOUT IT WHEN YOU CONTACTED ME. YOUR BODY IS COMPLETELY TRANSFORMED--IT'S NOT A QUESTION OF CELLULAR REPAIR GUIDED BY MENTAL MAPPING, AS WITH JIMMY.
EVEN IF IT WERE, YOU WERE A GORILLA WHEN I MET YOU.
CAN'T YOU AT LEAST TRY?
IF I COULD DO IT, *I* WOULDN'T BE IN THIS SUIT.
LET'S COOL OUR JETS, TEAM. BOB, LOOK. WE'VE RESPECTED YOUR PRIVACY--
--BUT I THINK WE NEED TO KNOW WHAT'S HAPPENED TO YOU SINCE 1959. I WOULDN'T KEEP IT FROM YOU.
I KNOW YOU WOULDN'T. AND...IT'S SIMPLY FACTS, THERE'S NO REASON I SHOULDN'T TELL YOU.
IT MAY KEEP MR. KHANATA FROM EXPLODING WITH THE NEED TO KNOW HOW I DIDN'T DIE AS *"THE CRUSADER."*
UH.
SIT DOWN AND CLEAR YOUR MINDS. YOU'RE GOING TO EXPERIENCE MY LIFE AS I LIVED IT.
MARVEL BOY BEGAN LONG BEFORE ANY OF US KNEW. EVEN BEFORE THE NIGHT MY FATHER MADE CONTACT WITH THE COLONY ON URANUS. PLEASE DO NOT SNICKER, KEN.
YOU MAY KNOW THEY WERE AN OFFSHOOT OF AN ANCIENT RACE CALLED ETERNALS.

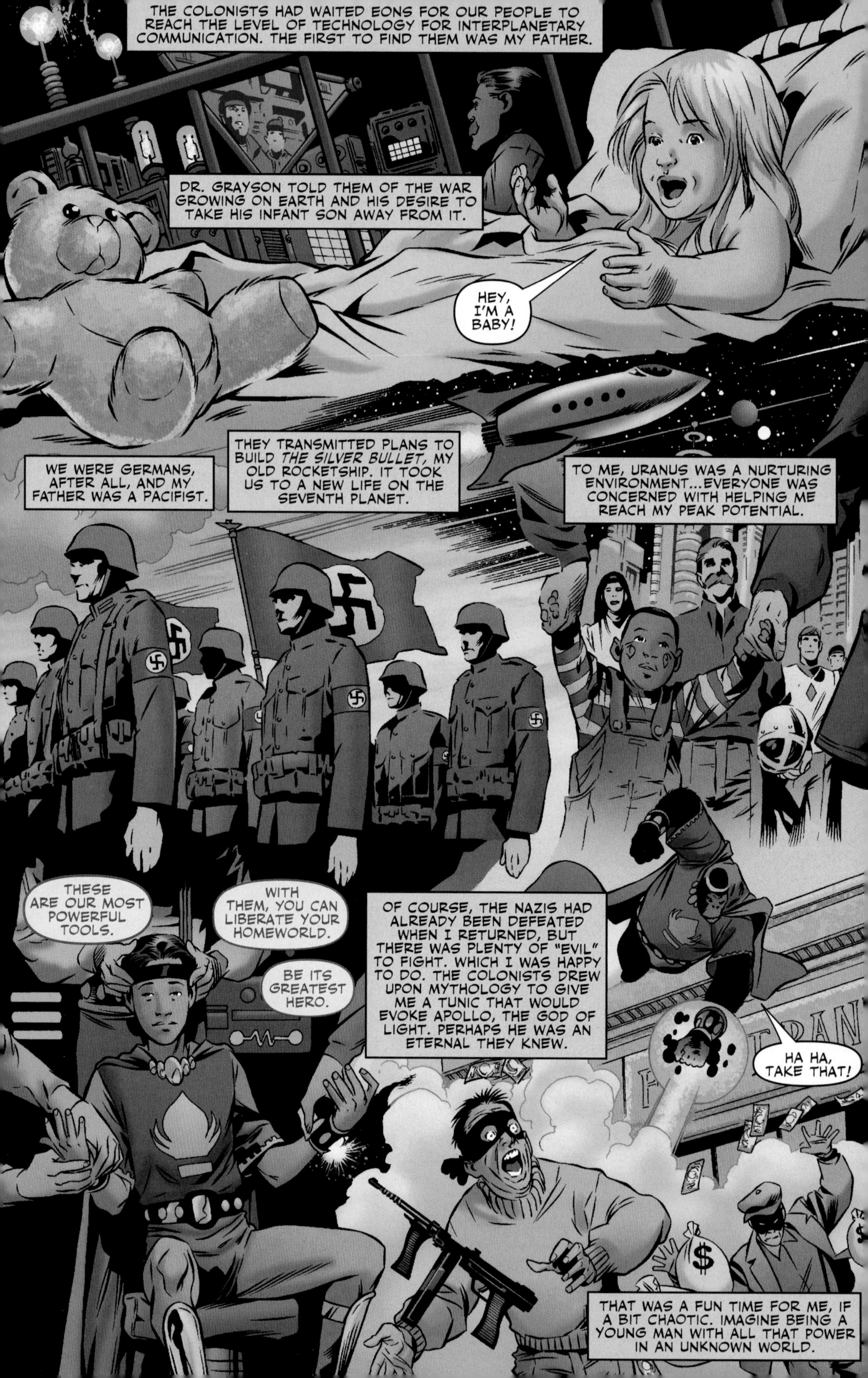
THE COLONISTS HAD WAITED EONS FOR OUR PEOPLE TO REACH THE LEVEL OF TECHNOLOGY FOR INTERPLANETARY COMMUNICATION. THE FIRST TO FIND THEM WAS MY FATHER.
DR. GRAYSON TOLD THEM OF THE WAR GROWING ON EARTH AND HIS DESIRE TO TAKE HIS INFANT SON AWAY FROM IT.
HEY, I'M A BABY!
WE WERE GERMANS, AFTER ALL, AND MY FATHER WAS A PACIFIST.
THEY TRANSMITTED PLANS TO BUILD *THE SILVER BULLET*, MY OLD ROCKETSHIP. IT TOOK US TO A NEW LIFE ON THE SEVENTH PLANET.
TO ME, URANUS WAS A NURTURING ENVIRONMENT...EVERYONE WAS CONCERNED WITH HELPING ME REACH MY PEAK POTENTIAL.
THESE ARE OUR MOST POWERFUL TOOLS.
WITH THEM, YOU CAN LIBERATE YOUR HOMEWORLD.
BE ITS GREATEST HERO.
OF COURSE, THE NAZIS HAD ALREADY BEEN DEFEATED WHEN I RETURNED, BUT THERE WAS PLENTY OF "EVIL" TO FIGHT. WHICH I WAS HAPPY TO DO. THE COLONISTS DREW UPON MYTHOLOGY TO GIVE ME A TUNIC THAT WOULD EVOKE APOLLO, THE GOD OF LIGHT. PERHAPS HE WAS AN ETERNAL THEY KNEW.
HA HA, TAKE THAT!
THAT WAS A FUN TIME FOR ME, IF A BIT CHAOTIC. IMAGINE BEING A YOUNG MAN WITH ALL THAT POWER IN AN UNKNOWN WORLD.

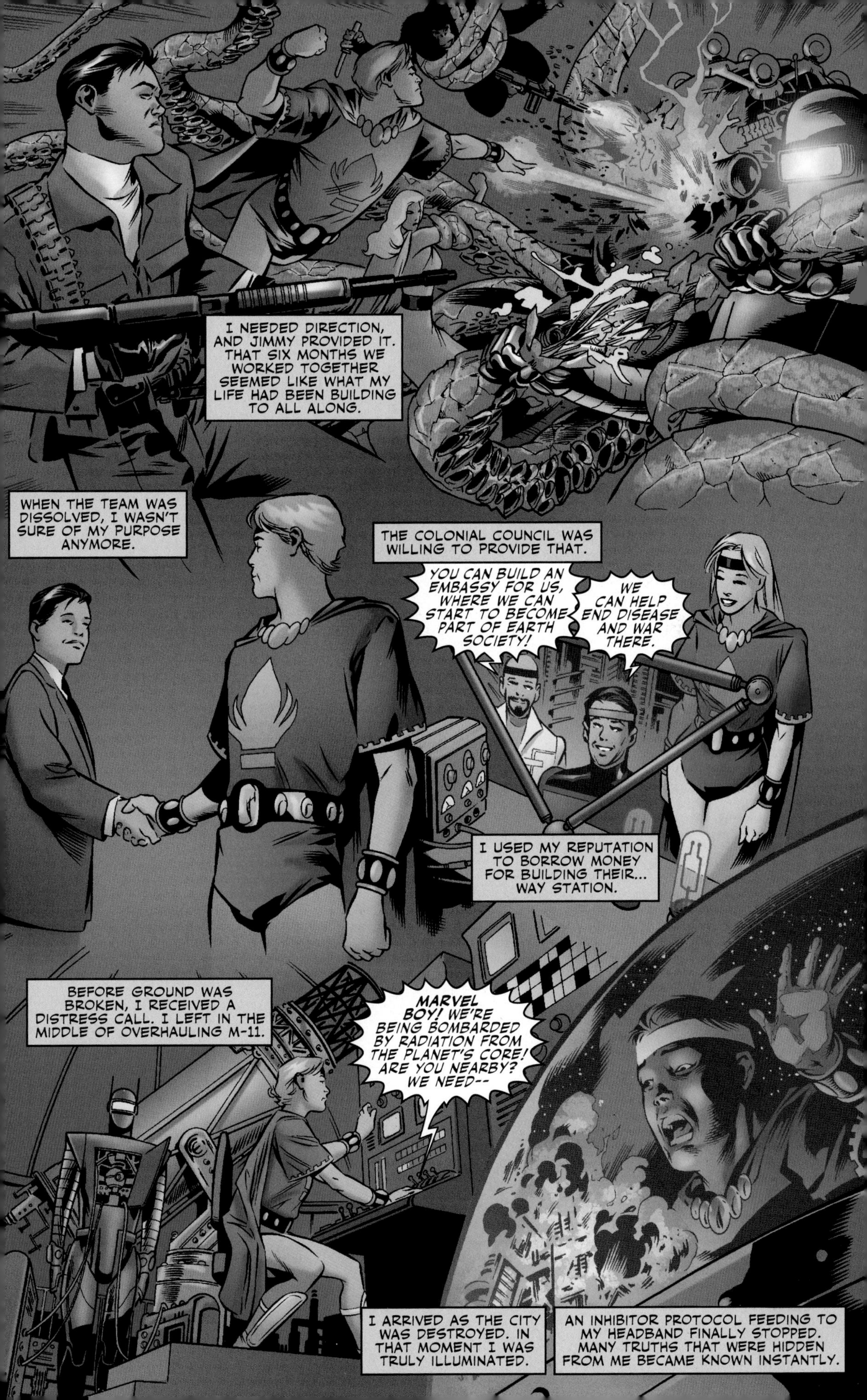
I NEEDED DIRECTION, AND JIMMY PROVIDED IT. THAT SIX MONTHS WE WORKED TOGETHER SEEMED LIKE WHAT MY LIFE HAD BEEN BUILDING TO ALL ALONG.
WHEN THE TEAM WAS DISSOLVED, I WASN'T SURE OF MY PURPOSE ANYMORE.
THE COLONIAL COUNCIL WAS WILLING TO PROVIDE THAT.
YOU CAN BUILD AN EMBASSY FOR US, WHERE WE CAN START TO BECOME PART OF EARTH SOCIETY!
WE CAN HELP END DISEASE AND WAR THERE.
I USED MY REPUTATION TO BORROW MONEY FOR BUILDING THEIR... WAY STATION.
BEFORE GROUND WAS BROKEN, I RECEIVED A DISTRESS CALL. I LEFT IN THE MIDDLE OF OVERHAULING M-11.
MARVEL BOY! WE'RE BEING BOMBARDED BY RADIATION FROM THE PLANET'S CORE! ARE YOU NEARBY? WE NEED--
I ARRIVED AS THE CITY WAS DESTROYED. IN THAT MOMENT I WAS TRULY ILLUMINATED.
AN INHIBITOR PROTOCOL FEEDING TO MY HEADBAND FINALLY STOPPED. MANY TRUTHS THAT WERE HIDDEN FROM ME BECAME KNOWN INSTANTLY.

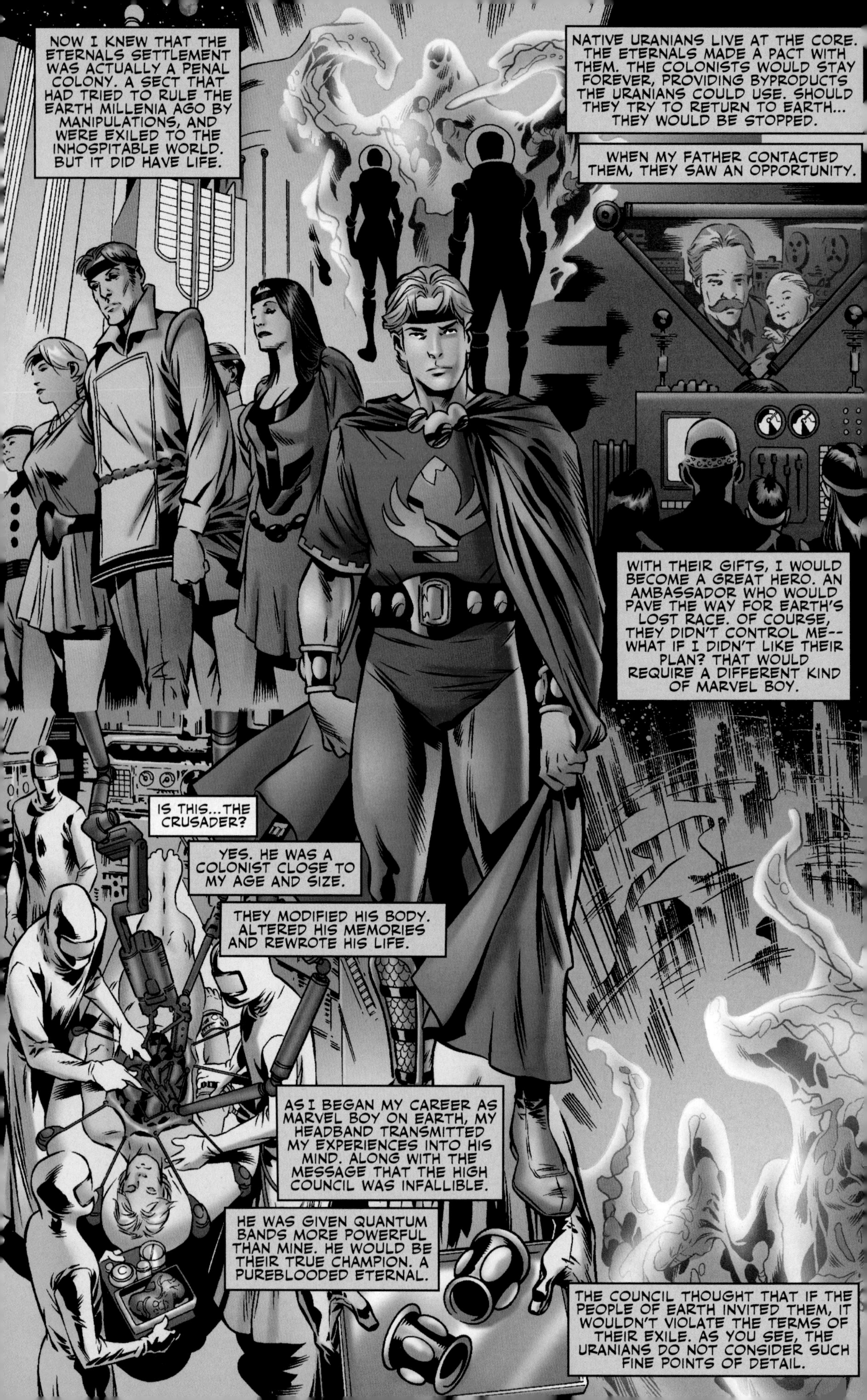
NOW I KNEW THAT THE ETERNALS SETTLEMENT WAS ACTUALLY A PENAL COLONY. A SECT THAT HAD TRIED TO RULE THE EARTH MILLENIA AGO BY MANIPULATIONS, AND WERE EXILED TO THE INHOSPITABLE WORLD. BUT IT DID HAVE LIFE.
NATIVE URANIANS LIVE AT THE CORE. THE ETERNALS MADE A PACT WITH THEM. THE COLONISTS WOULD STAY FOREVER, PROVIDING BYPRODUCTS THE URANIANS COULD USE. SHOULD THEY TRY TO RETURN TO EARTH... THEY WOULD BE STOPPED.
WHEN MY FATHER CONTACTED THEM, THEY SAW AN OPPORTUNITY.
WITH THEIR GIFTS, I WOULD BECOME A GREAT HERO. AN AMBASSADOR WHO WOULD PAVE THE WAY FOR EARTH'S LOST RACE. OF COURSE, THEY DIDN'T CONTROL ME-- WHAT IF I DIDN'T LIKE THEIR PLAN? THAT WOULD REQUIRE A DIFFERENT KIND OF MARVEL BOY.
IS THIS...THE CRUSADER?
YES. HE WAS A COLONIST CLOSE TO MY AGE AND SIZE.
THEY MODIFIED HIS BODY. ALTERED HIS MEMORIES AND REWROTE HIS LIFE.
AS I BEGAN MY CAREER AS MARVEL BOY ON EARTH, MY HEADBAND TRANSMITTED MY EXPERIENCES INTO HIS MIND. ALONG WITH THE MESSAGE THAT THE HIGH COUNCIL WAS INFALLIBLE.
HE WAS GIVEN QUANTUM BANDS MORE POWERFUL THAN MINE. HE WOULD BE THEIR TRUE CHAMPION. A PUREBLOODED ETERNAL.
THE COUNCIL THOUGHT THAT IF THE PEOPLE OF EARTH INVITED THEM, IT WOULDN'T VIOLATE THE TERMS OF THEIR EXILE. AS YOU SEE, THE URANIANS DO NOT CONSIDER SUCH FINE POINTS OF DETAIL.

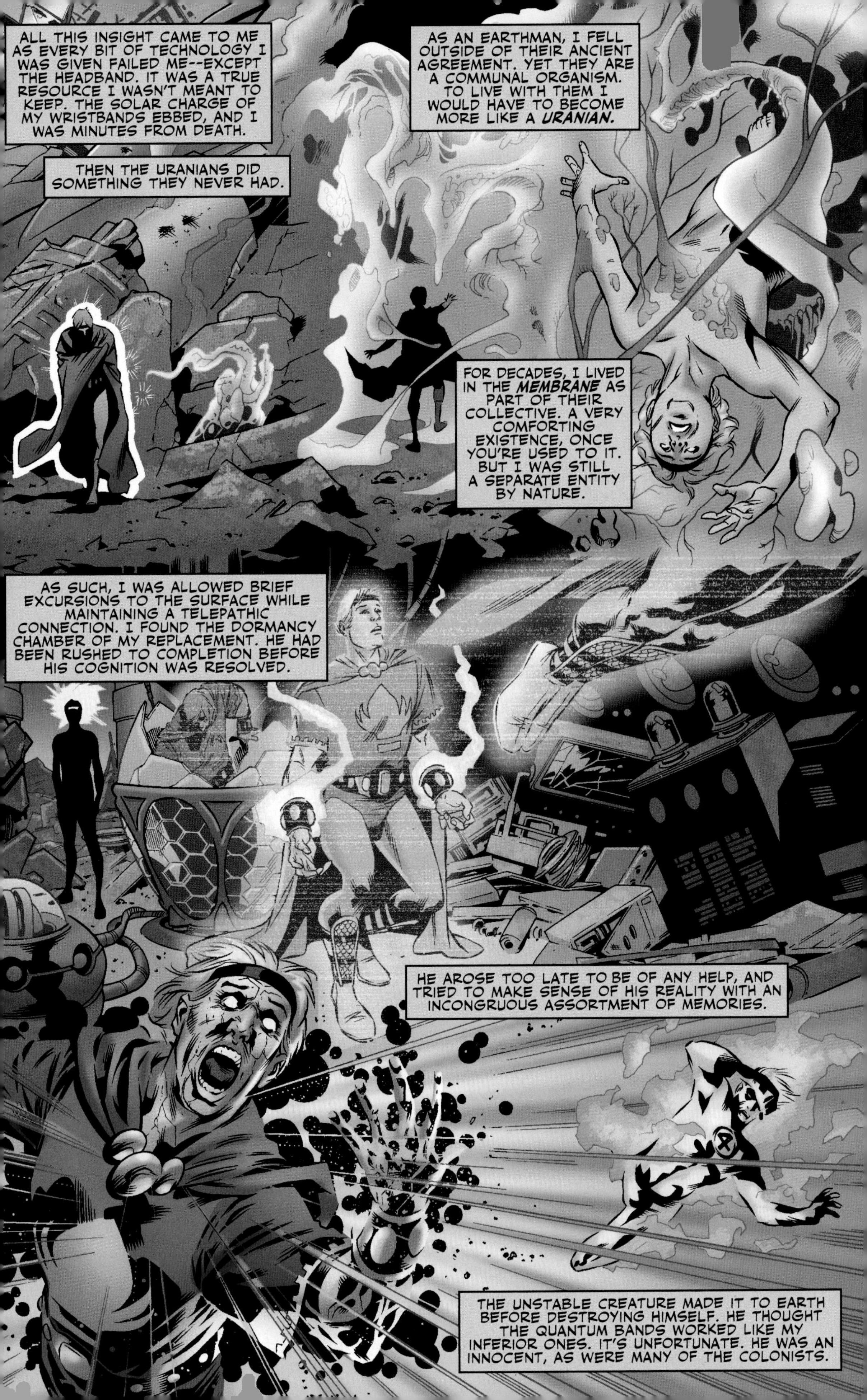
ALL THIS INSIGHT CAME TO ME AS EVERY BIT OF TECHNOLOGY I WAS GIVEN FAILED ME--EXCEPT THE HEADBAND. IT WAS A TRUE RESOURCE I WASN'T MEANT TO KEEP. THE SOLAR CHARGE OF MY WRISTBANDS EBBED, AND I WAS MINUTES FROM DEATH.
THEN THE URANIANS DID SOMETHING THEY NEVER HAD.
AS AN EARTHMAN, I FELL OUTSIDE OF THEIR ANCIENT AGREEMENT. YET THEY ARE A COMMUNAL ORGANISM. TO LIVE WITH THEM I WOULD HAVE TO BECOME MORE LIKE A *URANIAN.*
FOR DECADES, I LIVED IN THE *MEMBRANE* AS PART OF THEIR COLLECTIVE. A VERY COMFORTING EXISTENCE, ONCE YOU'RE USED TO IT. BUT I WAS STILL A SEPARATE ENTITY BY NATURE.
AS SUCH, I WAS ALLOWED BRIEF EXCURSIONS TO THE SURFACE WHILE MAINTAINING A TELEPATHIC CONNECTION. I FOUND THE DORMANCY CHAMBER OF MY REPLACEMENT. HE HAD BEEN RUSHED TO COMPLETION BEFORE HIS COGNITION WAS RESOLVED.
HE AROSE TOO LATE TO BE OF ANY HELP, AND TRIED TO MAKE SENSE OF HIS REALITY WITH AN INCONGRUOUS ASSORTMENT OF MEMORIES.
THE UNSTABLE CREATURE MADE IT TO EARTH BEFORE DESTROYING HIMSELF. HE THOUGHT THE QUANTUM BANDS WORKED LIKE MY INFERIOR ONES. IT'S UNFORTUNATE. HE WAS AN INNOCENT, AS WERE MANY OF THE COLONISTS.

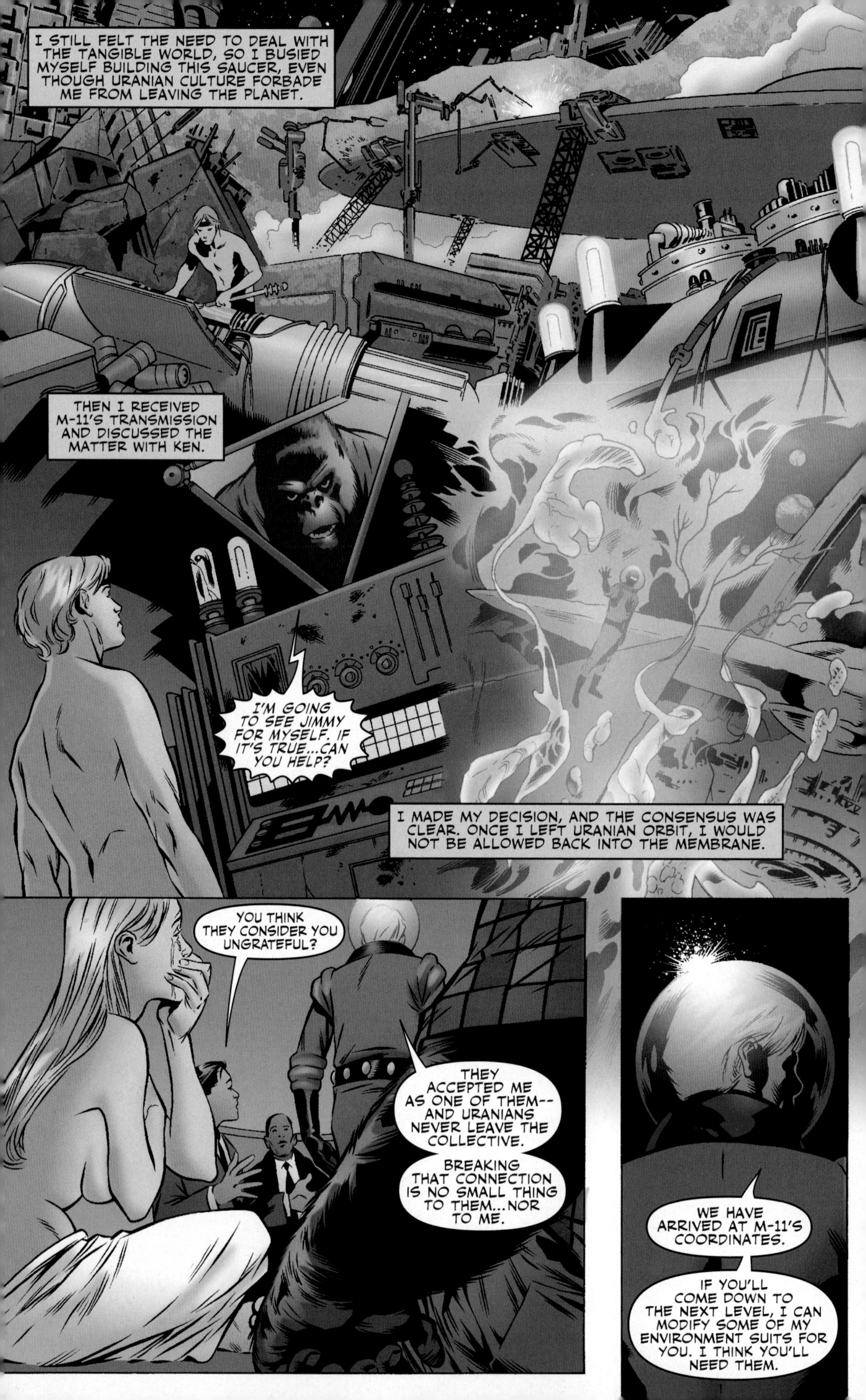
I STILL FELT THE NEED TO DEAL WITH THE TANGIBLE WORLD, SO I BUSIED MYSELF BUILDING THIS SAUCER, EVEN THOUGH URANIAN CULTURE FORBADE ME FROM LEAVING THE PLANET.
THEN I RECEIVED M-11'S TRANSMISSION AND DISCUSSED THE MATTER WITH KEN.
I'M GOING TO SEE JIMMY FOR MYSELF. IF IT'S TRUE...CAN YOU HELP?
I MADE MY DECISION, AND THE CONSENSUS WAS CLEAR. ONCE I LEFT URANIAN ORBIT, I WOULD NOT BE ALLOWED BACK INTO THE MEMBRANE.
YOU THINK THEY CONSIDER YOU UNGRATEFUL?
THEY ACCEPTED ME AS ONE OF THEM--AND URANIANS NEVER LEAVE THE COLLECTIVE.
BREAKING THAT CONNECTION IS NO SMALL THING TO THEM...NOR TO ME.
WE HAVE ARRIVED AT M-11'S COORDINATES.
IF YOU'LL COME DOWN TO THE NEXT LEVEL, I CAN MODIFY SOME OF MY ENVIRONMENT SUITS FOR YOU. I THINK YOU'LL NEED THEM.

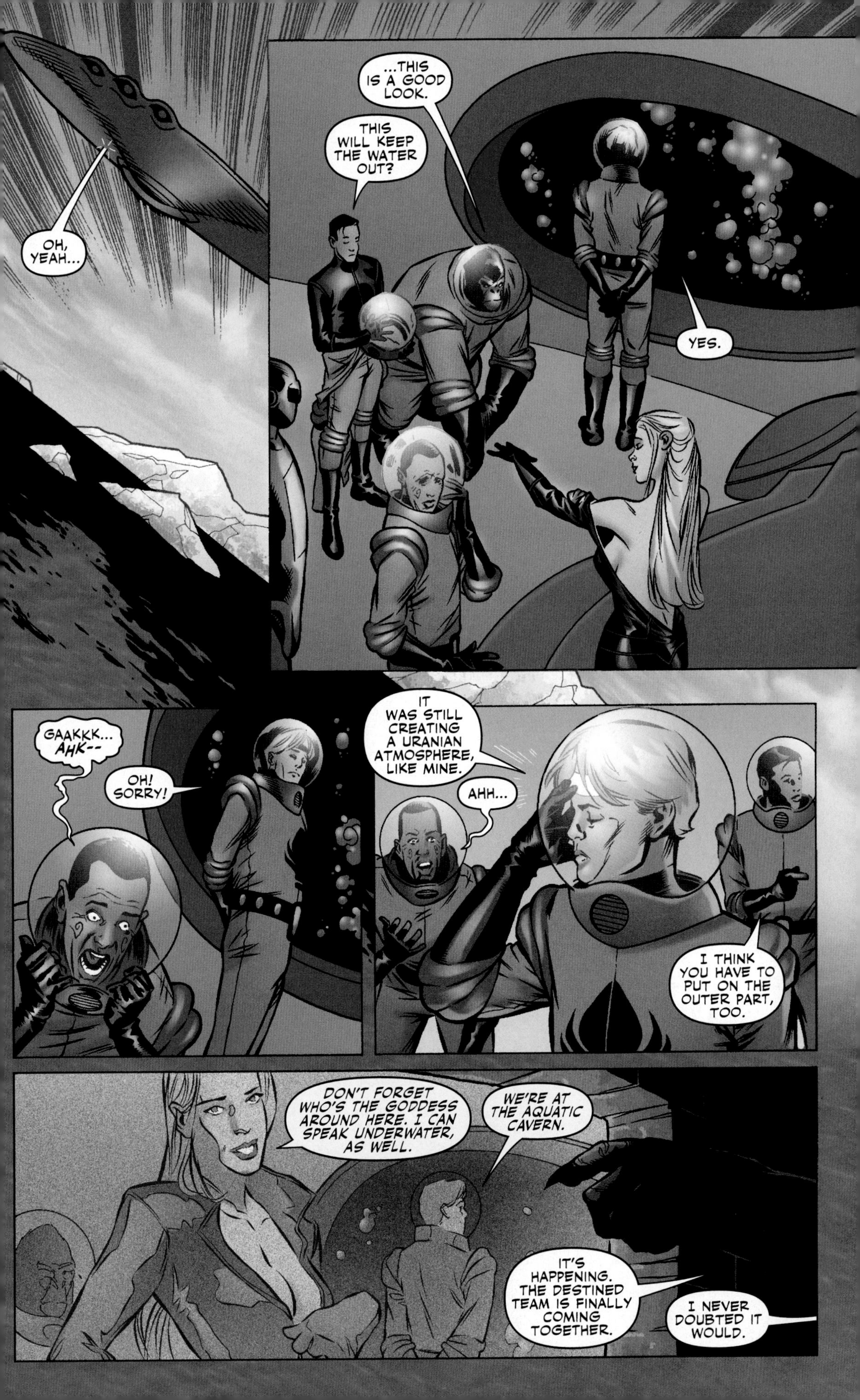
OH, YEAH...
THIS WILL KEEP THE WATER OUT?
...THIS IS A GOOD LOOK.
YES.
GAAKKK... AHK--
OH! SORRY!
IT WAS STILL CREATING A URANIAN ATMOSPHERE, LIKE MINE.
AHH...
I THINK YOU HAVE TO PUT ON THE OUTER PART, TOO.
DON'T FORGET WHO'S THE GODDESS AROUND HERE. I CAN SPEAK UNDERWATER, AS WELL.
WE'RE AT THE AQUATIC CAVERN.
IT'S HAPPENING. THE DESTINED TEAM IS FINALLY COMING TOGETHER.
I NEVER DOUBTED IT WOULD.

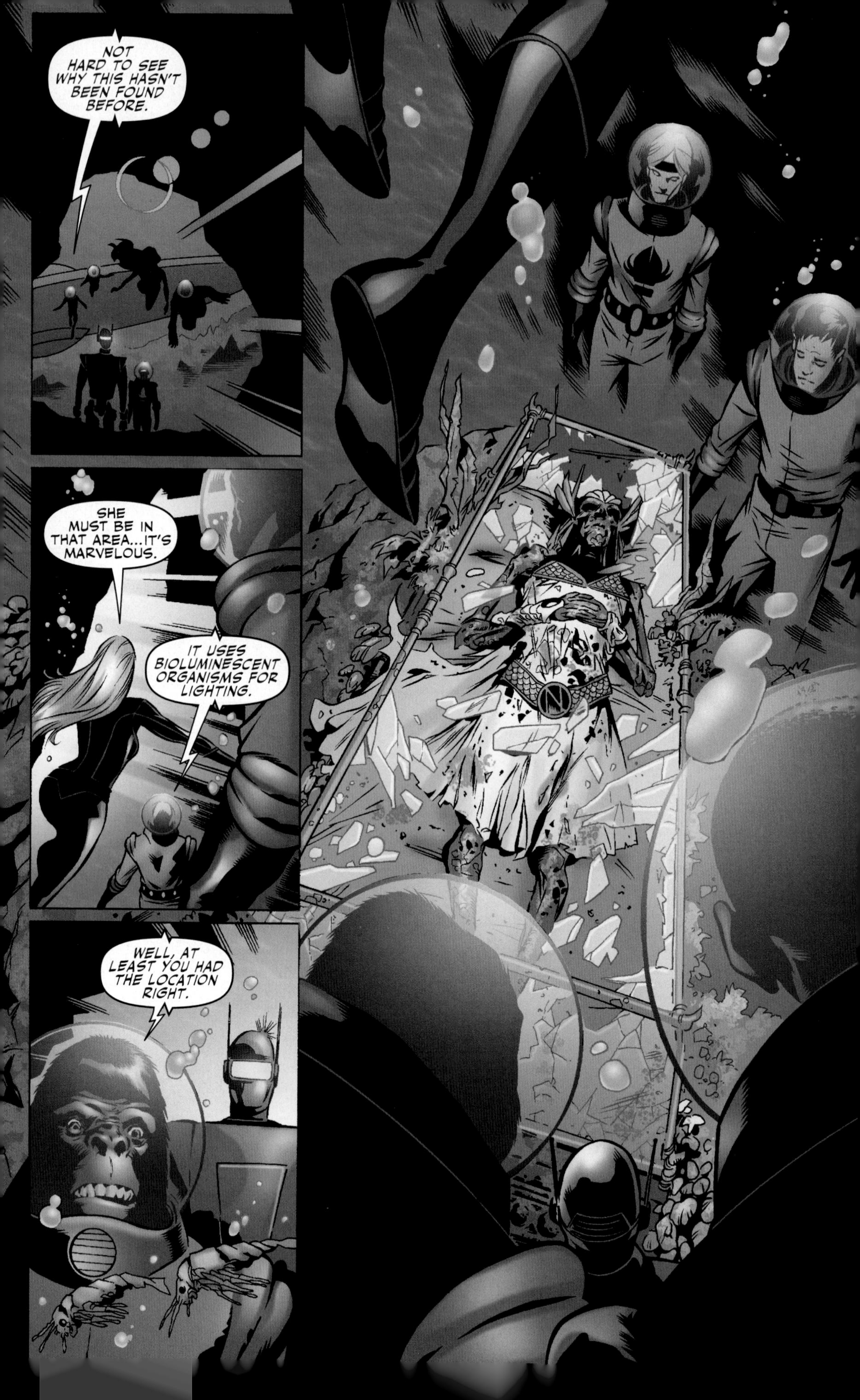
NOT HARD TO SEE WHY THIS HASN'T BEEN FOUND BEFORE.
SHE MUST BE IN THAT AREA...IT'S MARVELOUS.
IT USES BIOLUMINESCENT ORGANISMS FOR LIGHTING.
WELL, AT LEAST YOU HAD THE LOCATION RIGHT.

S.H.I.E.L.D. DOCUMENT 913583-29138 GRW

PROJECT DATABASE >> PROJECT: 6623279-0091 SWR >> LOGISTICS >> FIELD REPORTS & DOCS >> COMMUNICATION TRANSCRIPTS
SECRET CODE: BLUE

RECORDING DATE: 10/12/06 10:24 P.M.
OPERATOR: S.H.I.E.L.D. AGENT JENNIFER MULLINS — LEVEL 3
CALL ORIGIN: UNKNOWN
PHONE LOCATION: UNKNOWN
BROADCAST LOCKED. CODED AND SCRAMBLED USING NIC-7 CODE BLOCK.

AGENT MULLINS (OFF COMM)
…Sir, we're receiving Agent Khanata on Channel Alpha 9.
DUGAN
Put him through. Derek! What's your status?
KHANATA
Well, sir, I'm continuing my investigation with Woo and his original team. They're going to let me make short comms to keep you updated. I don't want to risk leaving the group because I don't think we'll be able to track them again.
DUGAN (OFF COMM)
Mullins! Where is this coming from?
AGENT MULLINS (OFF COMM)
We've chased the signal through 3,118 transmitters so far, sir.
DUGAN (OFF COMM)
So they know what you're saying to me.
KHANATA
Well, I'm talking to you through M-11, the robot. So, yes.
DUGAN
You gave that robot access to the Alpha 9 Channel??
KHANATA
No, it already knew about it somehow. Probably learned while it was in our Mojave Base.
DUGAN
(deleted)
KHANATA
Sorry, sir. They seem concerned with finding the facts behind the San Francisco mission as well. I think I'm in the best place to be.
DUGAN
Long as you ain't going Stockholm Syndrome on us.
KHANATA
I remember who I work for. It looks like Yellow Claw is involved.
DUGAN
Great. Doesn't anyone die anymore? Besides our agents, of course.
KHANATA
On that note, we're also going to investigate the possibility that the hybrid Merwoman Namora may still be alive.
DUGAN
The Sub-Mariner's cousin?
KHANATA
Yes, sir.
DUGAN
Don't sound like they're too worried about finding this Atlas Foundation.

SEARCH DATABASE

KHANATA
Actually, Jimmy Woo has been going over the clues he had been gathering over the years. Bob Grayson copied all that info from his house.
DUGAN
We're going through that, too.
KHANATA
In case you can't make out some of Jimmy's shorthand code, he's deciphered some codenames. We believe these are major Atlas online operatives:

DOOP1958 KRB NRG DPLOMBARDO MR. BLACK SLYMCYKE S. KLEEFELD KUYU001 EYECOLUMBUS JSHELMIG MARVEL LAD
MSR. ORESTEUS CHRIS MCFEELY NHARTZ CALVINMARSH COMMERCIALINN

AGENT MULLINS
Now we're up to 34,212 transmitter relays, sir.
DUGAN
Thanks, we had a few of those worked out, but that'll save us some time. So--is it true he can't remember anything after '59?
KHANATA
If he's faking the memory loss, he's fooled me. While we were investigating the recovery site in San Francisco, Woo pulled a gun on someone using a cell phone--he assumed the man was a spy. Ken Hale is working to get him up to speed on the 21st century. Hale said to tell you "Wa-hoo," by the way. Whatever that means.
DUGAN
That (deleted) gorilla.
KHANATA
I believe once the Namora side trip is done, they're going to investigate some of the possible Atlas operations. Have any of our men looked into those?
DUGAN
No, almost all of our resources are tied up with this (deleted) Superhuman Registration stuff. We'll try to send you backup if you need it, but I can't promise anything.
KHANATA
I understand sir. Hale is making the "wrap-it-up" motion, I'll have to sign off for now.
DUGAN
Roger that. One last thing….
KHANATA
Sir.
DUGAN
Jimmy--so he's doing pretty good now, right?
KHANATA
He's in great shape.
DUGAN
Heh. All right, over and out.

END TRANSMISSION

DUGAN (OFF COMM TO AGENT)
What did you get?
AGENT MULLINS
We tracked the source to…. Uranus.
DUGAN
(deleted)

Transcript reviewed and edited by Maria Hill for security clearance.
195-701

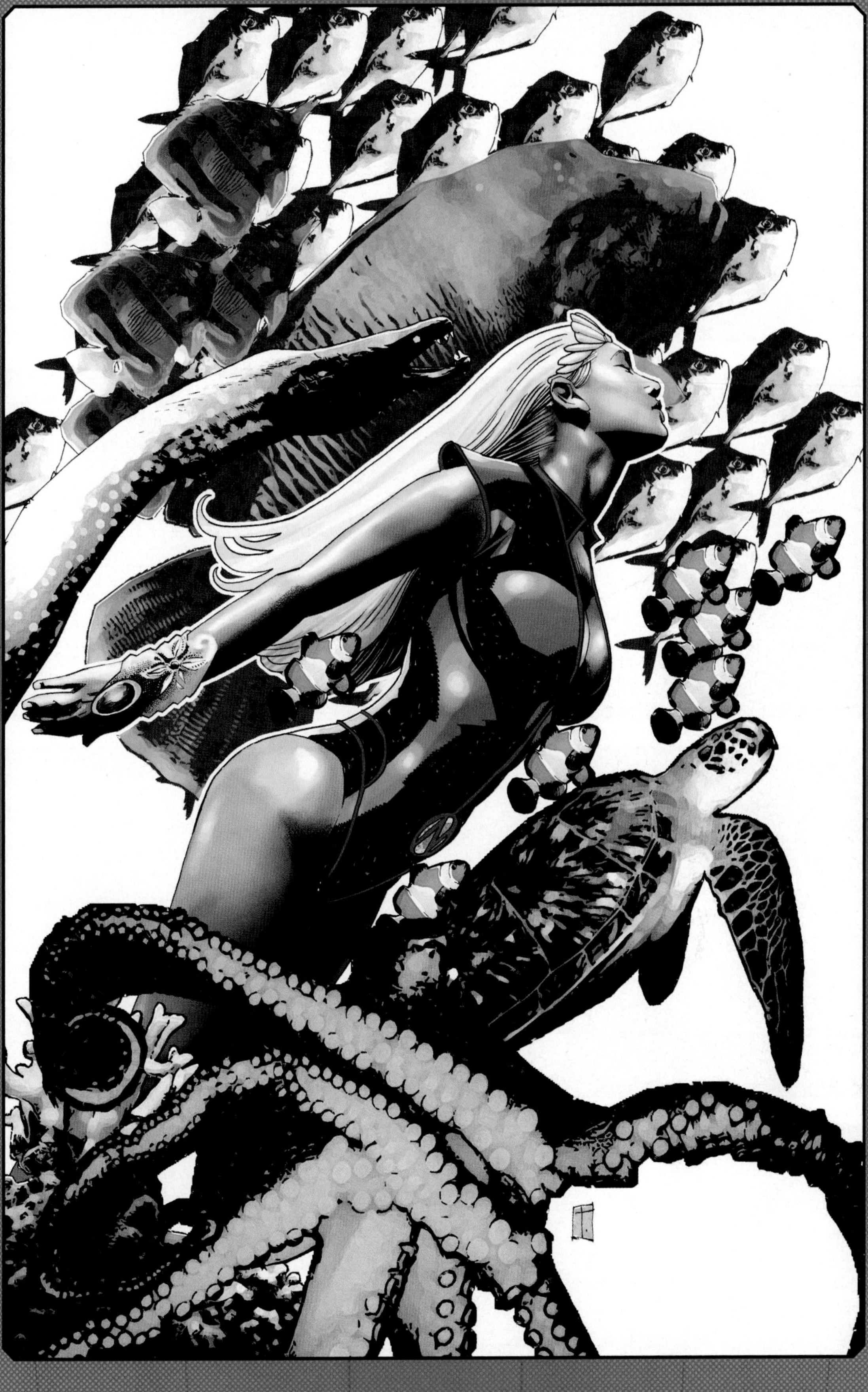

AGENTS OF ATLAS (2006) 4

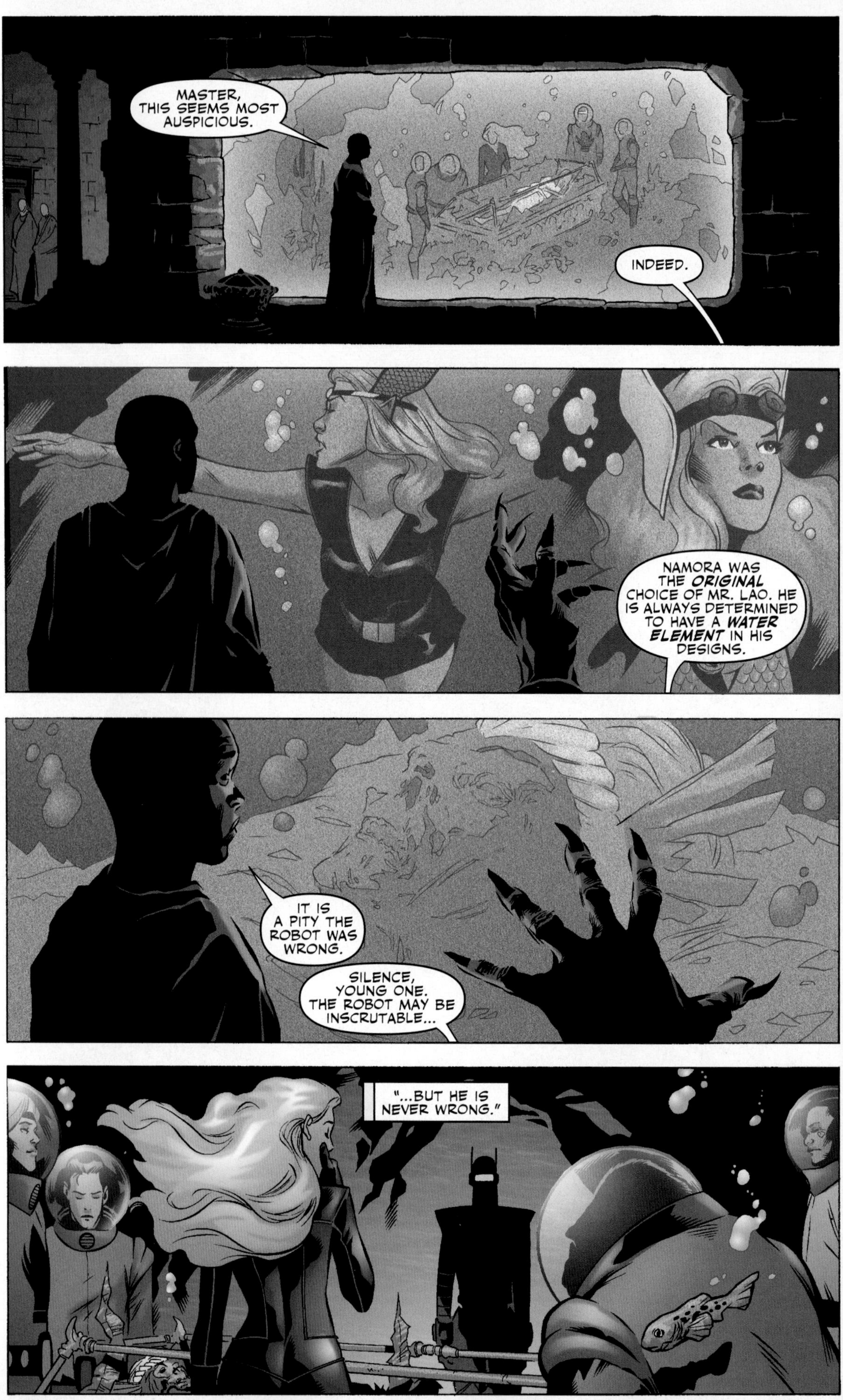
MASTER, THIS SEEMS MOST AUSPICIOUS.
INDEED.
NAMORA WAS THE *ORIGINAL* CHOICE OF MR. LAO. HE IS ALWAYS DETERMINED TO HAVE A ***WATER ELEMENT*** IN HIS DESIGNS.
IT IS A PITY THE ROBOT WAS WRONG.
SILENCE, YOUNG ONE. THE ROBOT MAY BE INSCRUTABLE...
"...BUT HE IS NEVER WRONG."

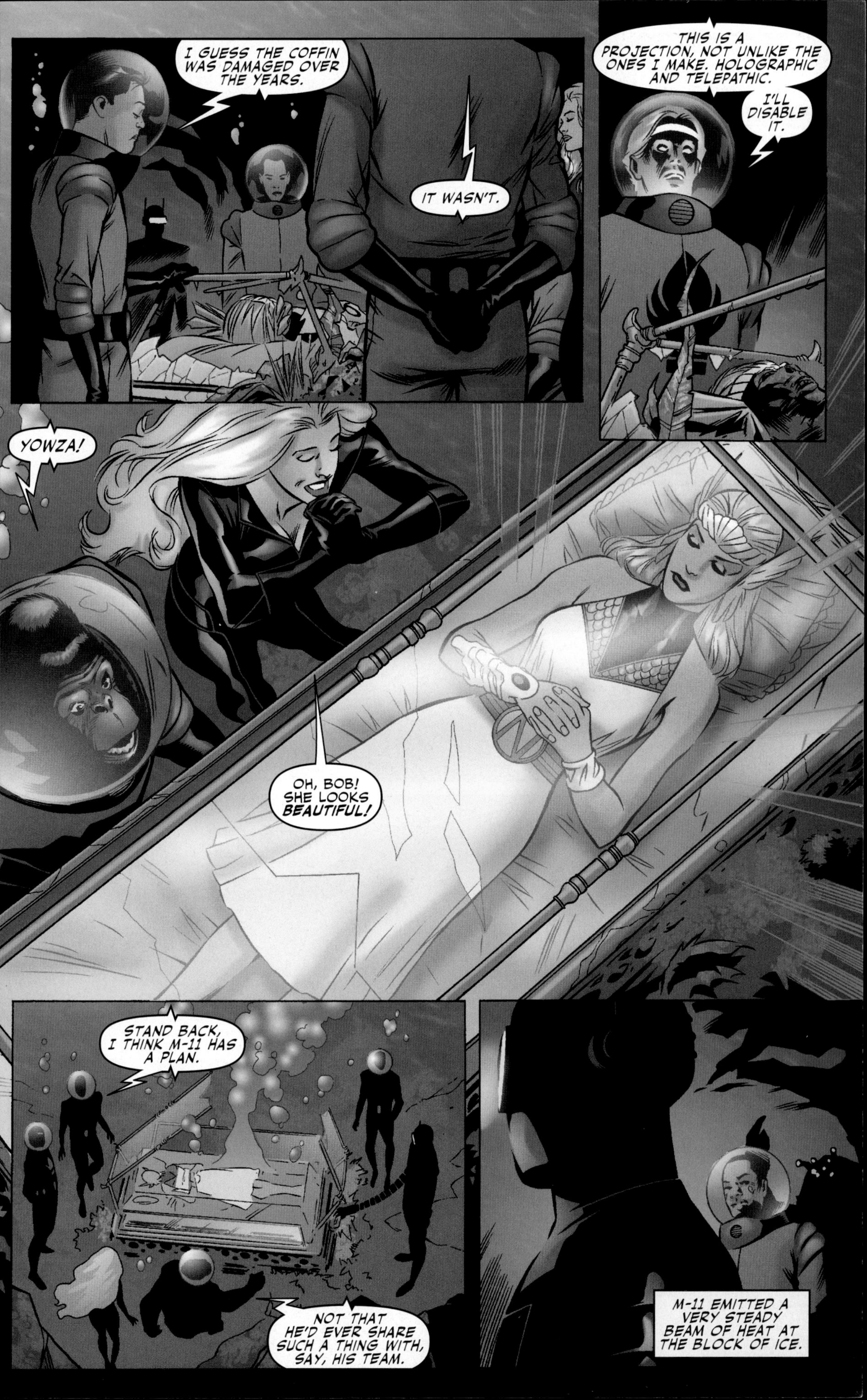
I GUESS THE COFFIN WAS DAMAGED OVER THE YEARS.
IT WASN'T.
THIS IS A PROJECTION, NOT UNLIKE THE ONES I MAKE. HOLOGRAPHIC AND TELEPATHIC.
I'LL DISABLE IT.
YOWZA!
OH, BOB! SHE LOOKS BEAUTIFUL!
STAND BACK, I THINK M-11 HAS A PLAN.
NOT THAT HE'D EVER SHARE SUCH A THING WITH, SAY, HIS TEAM.
M-11 EMITTED A VERY STEADY BEAM OF HEAT AT THE BLOCK OF ICE.

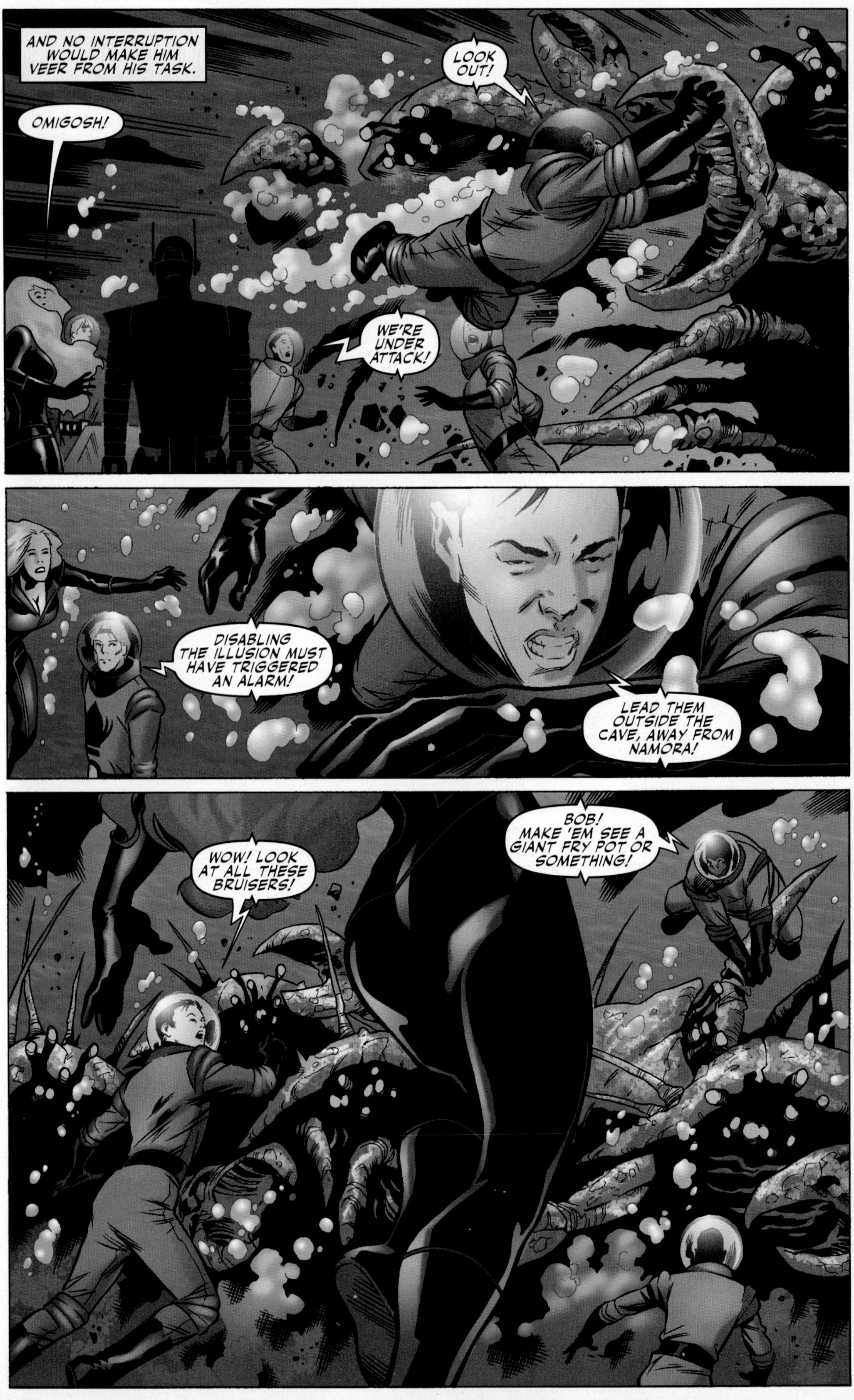
AND NO INTERRUPTION WOULD MAKE HIM VEER FROM HIS TASK.
OMIGOSH!
LOOK OUT!
WE'RE UNDER ATTACK!
DISABLING THE ILLUSION MUST HAVE TRIGGERED AN ALARM!
LEAD THEM OUTSIDE THE CAVE, AWAY FROM NAMORA!
WOW! LOOK AT ALL THESE BRUISERS!
BOB! MAKE 'EM SEE A GIANT FRY POT OR SOMETHING!

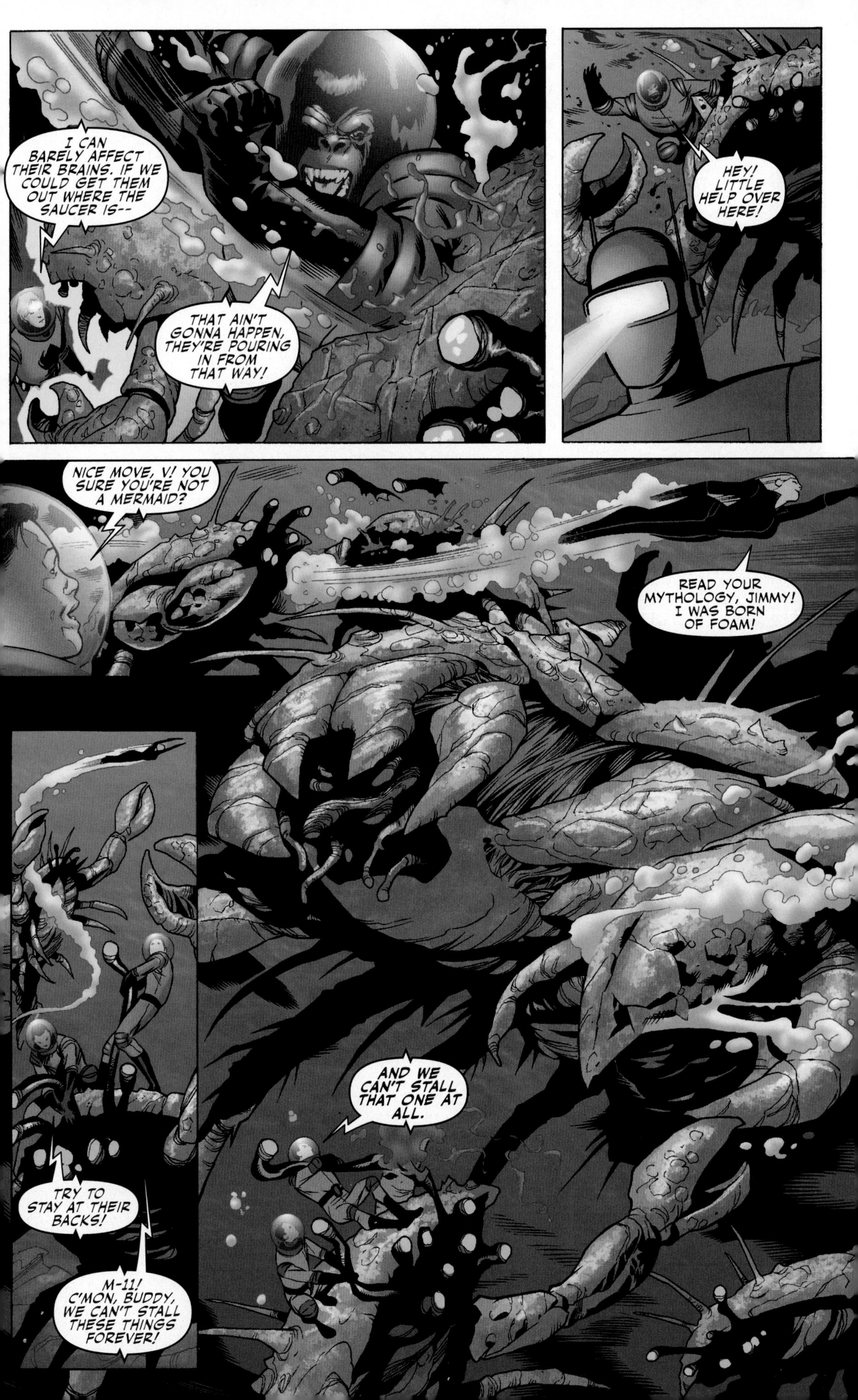
I CAN BARELY AFFECT THEIR BRAINS. IF WE COULD GET THEM OUT WHERE THE SAUCER IS--
THAT AIN'T GONNA HAPPEN, THEY'RE POURING IN FROM THAT WAY!
HEY! LITTLE HELP OVER HERE!
NICE MOVE, V! YOU SURE YOU'RE NOT A MERMAID?
READ YOUR MYTHOLOGY, JIMMY! I WAS BORN OF FOAM!
TRY TO STAY AT THEIR BACKS!
M-11! C'MON, BUDDY, WE CAN'T STALL THESE THINGS FOREVER!
AND WE CAN'T STALL THAT ONE AT ALL.

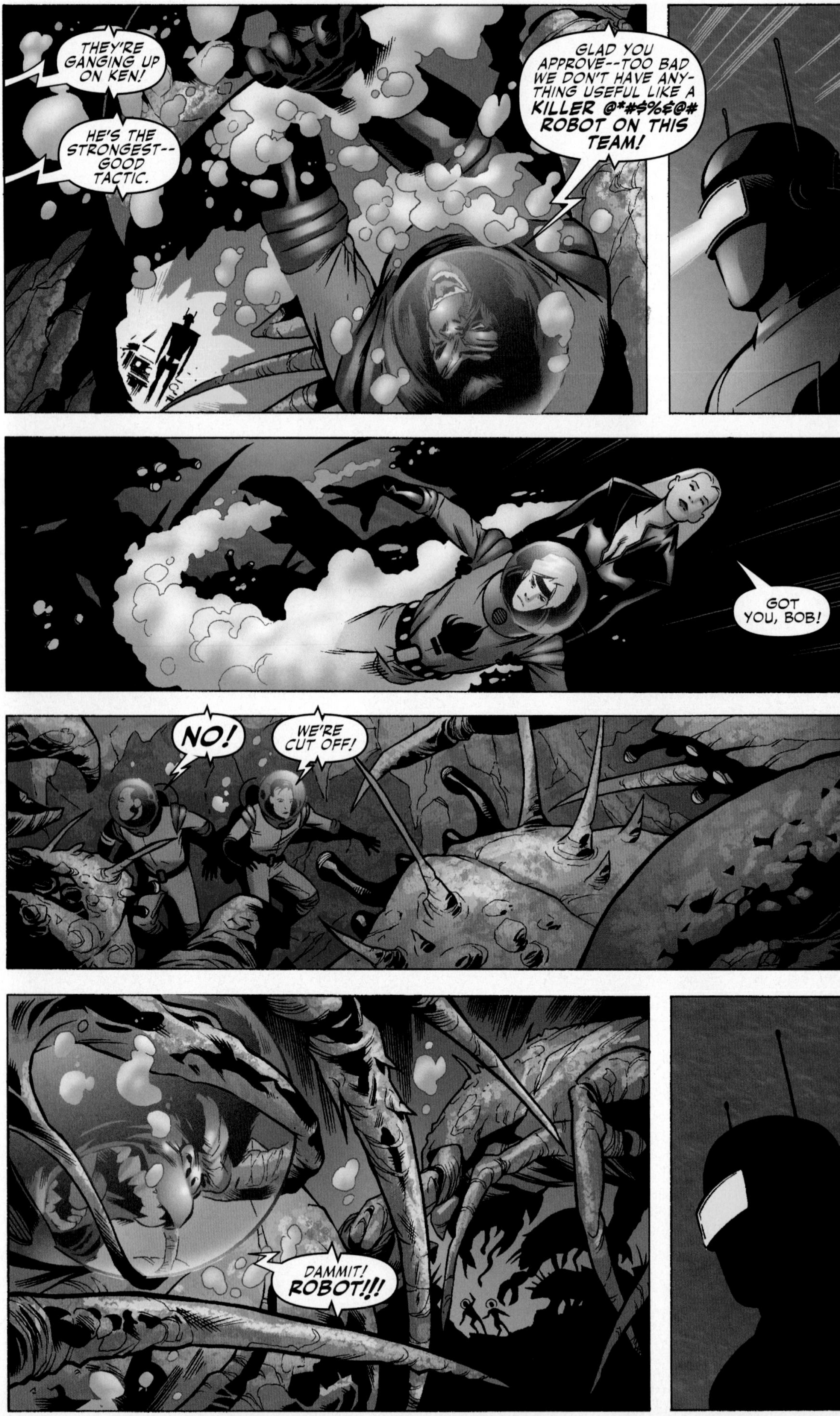
THEY'RE GANGING UP ON KEN!
HE'S THE STRONGEST--GOOD TACTIC.
GLAD YOU APPROVE--TOO BAD WE DON'T HAVE ANYTHING USEFUL LIKE A KILLER @*#$%&@# ROBOT ON THIS TEAM!
GOT YOU, BOB!
NO!
WE'RE CUT OFF!
DAMMIT! ROBOT!!!

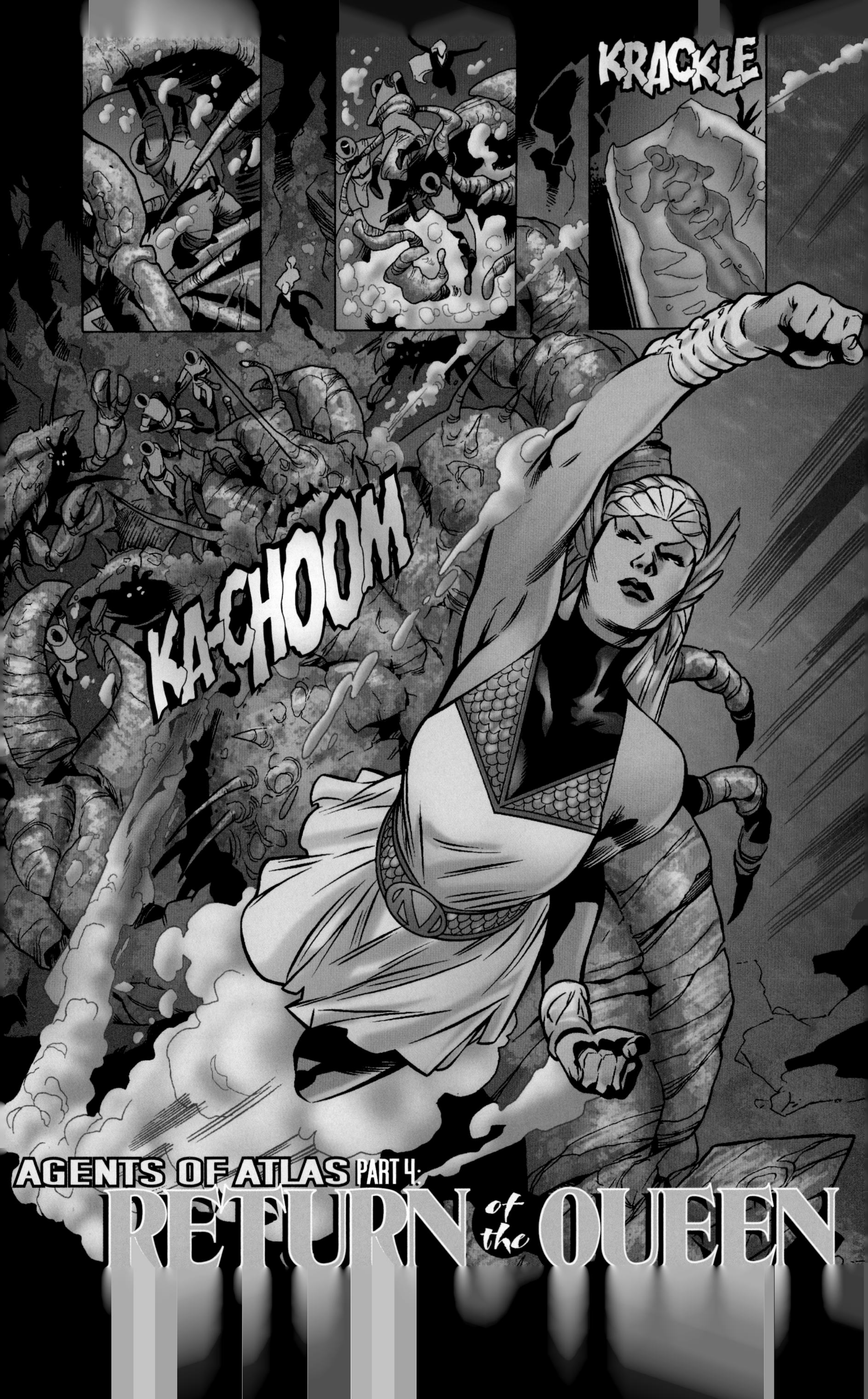
KRACKLE
KA-CHOOM
AGENTS OF ATLAS PART 4:
RETURN of the QUEEN

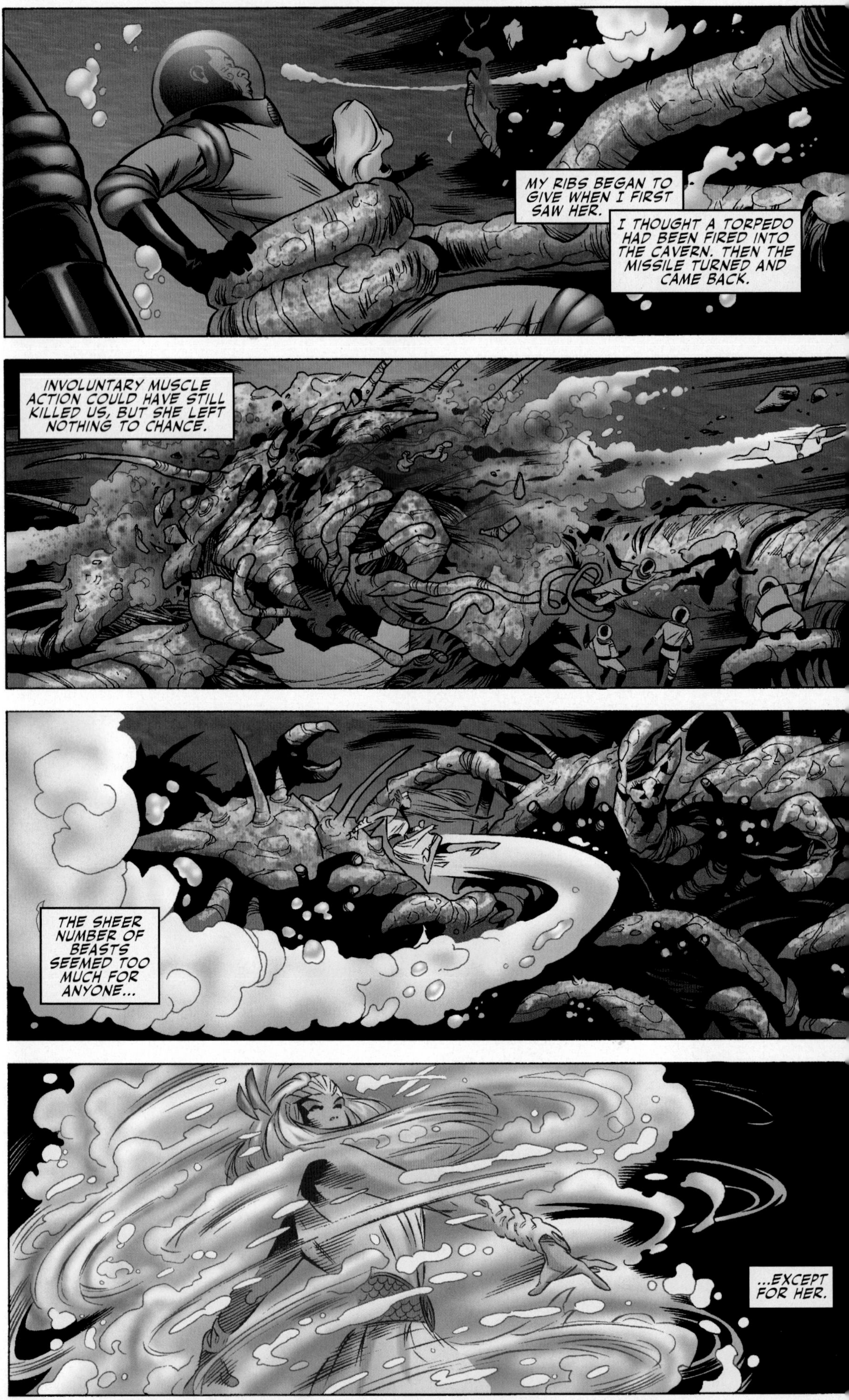
MY RIBS BEGAN TO GIVE WHEN I FIRST SAW HER.
I THOUGHT A TORPEDO HAD BEEN FIRED INTO THE CAVERN. THEN THE MISSILE TURNED AND CAME BACK.
INVOLUNTARY MUSCLE ACTION COULD HAVE STILL KILLED US, BUT SHE LEFT NOTHING TO CHANCE.
THE SHEER NUMBER OF BEASTS SEEMED TOO MUCH FOR ANYONE...
...EXCEPT FOR HER.

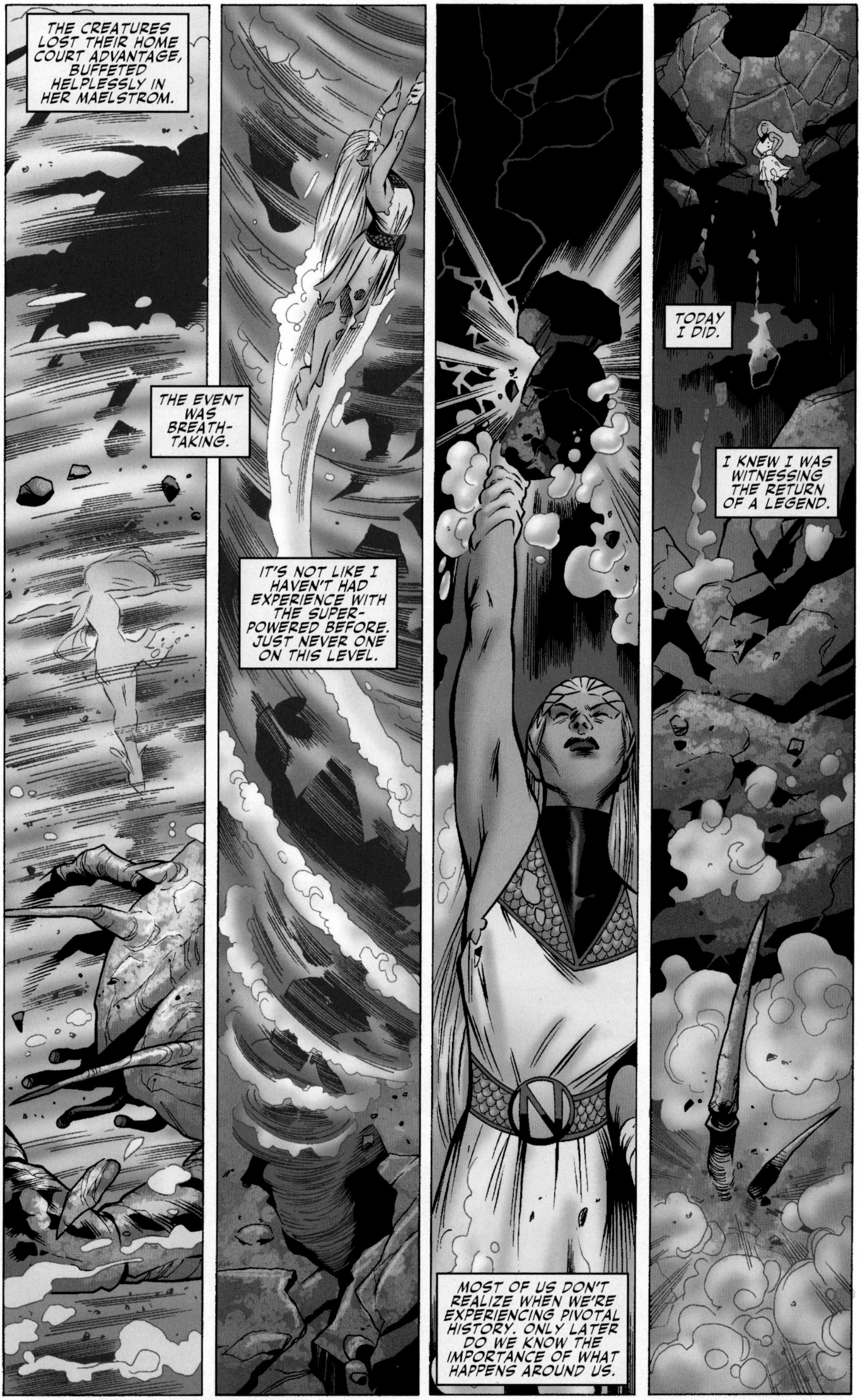
THE CREATURES LOST THEIR HOME COURT ADVANTAGE, BUFFETED HELPLESSLY IN HER MAELSTROM.
THE EVENT WAS BREATH-TAKING.
IT'S NOT LIKE I HAVEN'T HAD EXPERIENCE WITH THE SUPER-POWERED BEFORE. JUST NEVER ONE ON THIS LEVEL.
MOST OF US DON'T REALIZE WHEN WE'RE EXPERIENCING PIVOTAL HISTORY. ONLY LATER DO WE KNOW THE IMPORTANCE OF WHAT HAPPENS AROUND US.
TODAY I DID.
I KNEW I WAS WITNESSING THE RETURN OF A LEGEND.

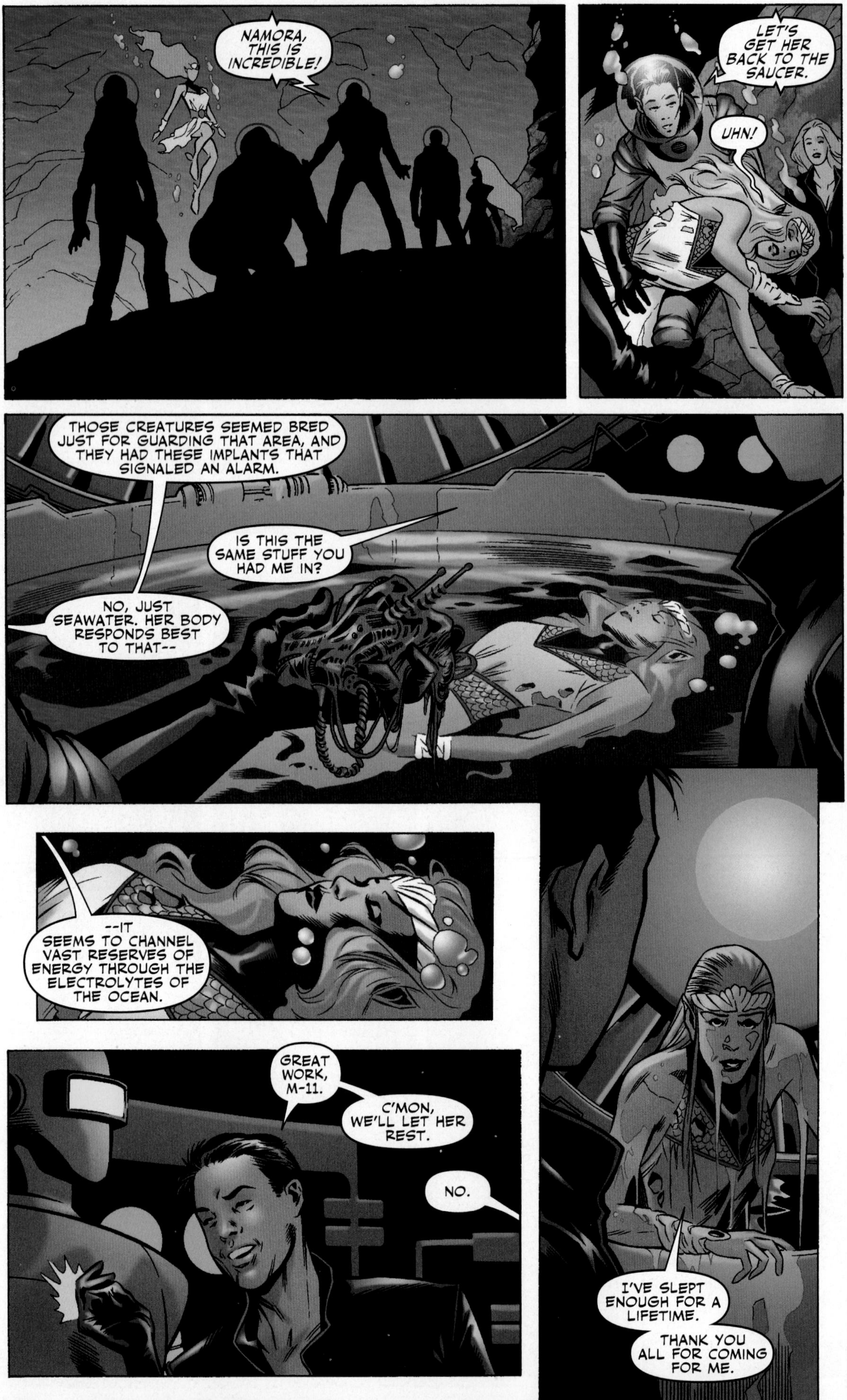
NAMORA, THIS IS INCREDIBLE!
LET'S GET HER BACK TO THE SAUCER.
UHN!
THOSE CREATURES SEEMED BRED JUST FOR GUARDING THAT AREA, AND THEY HAD THESE IMPLANTS THAT SIGNALED AN ALARM.
IS THIS THE SAME STUFF YOU HAD ME IN?
NO, JUST SEAWATER. HER BODY RESPONDS BEST TO THAT--
--IT SEEMS TO CHANNEL VAST RESERVES OF ENERGY THROUGH THE ELECTROLYTES OF THE OCEAN.
GREAT WORK, M-11.
C'MON, WE'LL LET HER REST.
NO.
I'VE SLEPT ENOUGH FOR A LIFETIME.
THANK YOU ALL FOR COMING FOR ME.

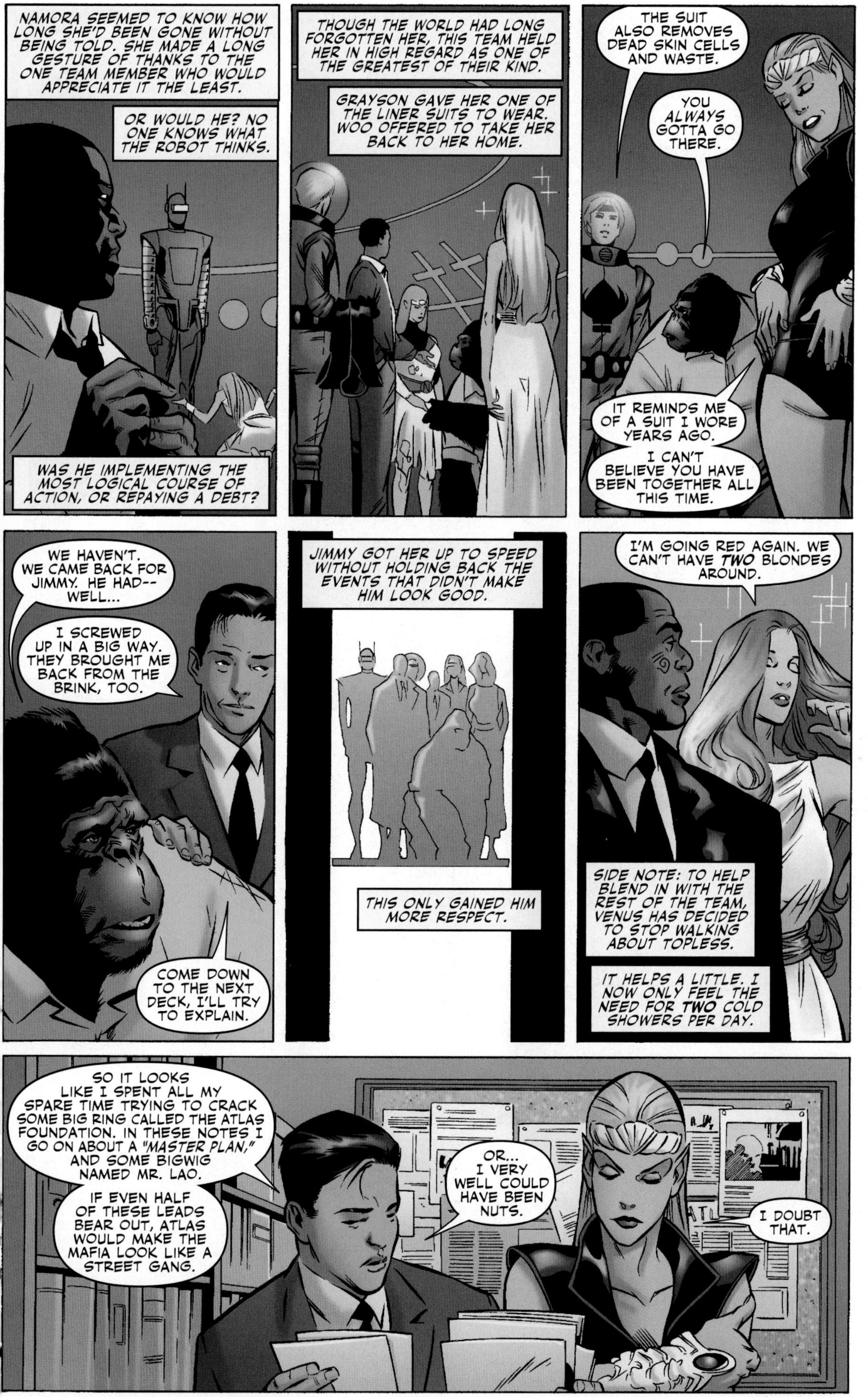
NAMORA SEEMED TO KNOW HOW LONG SHE'D BEEN GONE WITHOUT BEING TOLD. SHE MADE A LONG GESTURE OF THANKS TO THE ONE TEAM MEMBER WHO WOULD APPRECIATE IT THE LEAST.
OR WOULD HE? NO ONE KNOWS WHAT THE ROBOT THINKS.
WAS HE IMPLEMENTING THE MOST LOGICAL COURSE OF ACTION, OR REPAYING A DEBT?
THOUGH THE WORLD HAD LONG FORGOTTEN HER, THIS TEAM HELD HER IN HIGH REGARD AS ONE OF THE GREATEST OF THEIR KIND.
GRAYSON GAVE HER ONE OF THE LINER SUITS TO WEAR. WOO OFFERED TO TAKE HER BACK TO HER HOME.
THE SUIT ALSO REMOVES DEAD SKIN CELLS AND WASTE.
YOU ALWAYS GOTTA GO THERE.
IT REMINDS ME OF A SUIT I WORE YEARS AGO.
I CAN'T BELIEVE YOU HAVE BEEN TOGETHER ALL THIS TIME.
WE HAVEN'T. WE CAME BACK FOR JIMMY. HE HAD-- WELL...
I SCREWED UP IN A BIG WAY. THEY BROUGHT ME BACK FROM THE BRINK, TOO.
COME DOWN TO THE NEXT DECK, I'LL TRY TO EXPLAIN.
JIMMY GOT HER UP TO SPEED WITHOUT HOLDING BACK THE EVENTS THAT DIDN'T MAKE HIM LOOK GOOD.
THIS ONLY GAINED HIM MORE RESPECT.
I'M GOING RED AGAIN. WE CAN'T HAVE TWO BLONDES AROUND.
SIDE NOTE: TO HELP BLEND IN WITH THE REST OF THE TEAM, VENUS HAS DECIDED TO STOP WALKING ABOUT TOPLESS.
IT HELPS A LITTLE. I NOW ONLY FEEL THE NEED FOR TWO COLD SHOWERS PER DAY.
SO IT LOOKS LIKE I SPENT ALL MY SPARE TIME TRYING TO CRACK SOME BIG RING CALLED THE ATLAS FOUNDATION. IN THESE NOTES I GO ON ABOUT A "MASTER PLAN," AND SOME BIGWIG NAMED MR. LAO.
IF EVEN HALF OF THESE LEADS BEAR OUT, ATLAS WOULD MAKE THE MAFIA LOOK LIKE A STREET GANG.
OR... I VERY WELL COULD HAVE BEEN NUTS.
I DOUBT THAT.

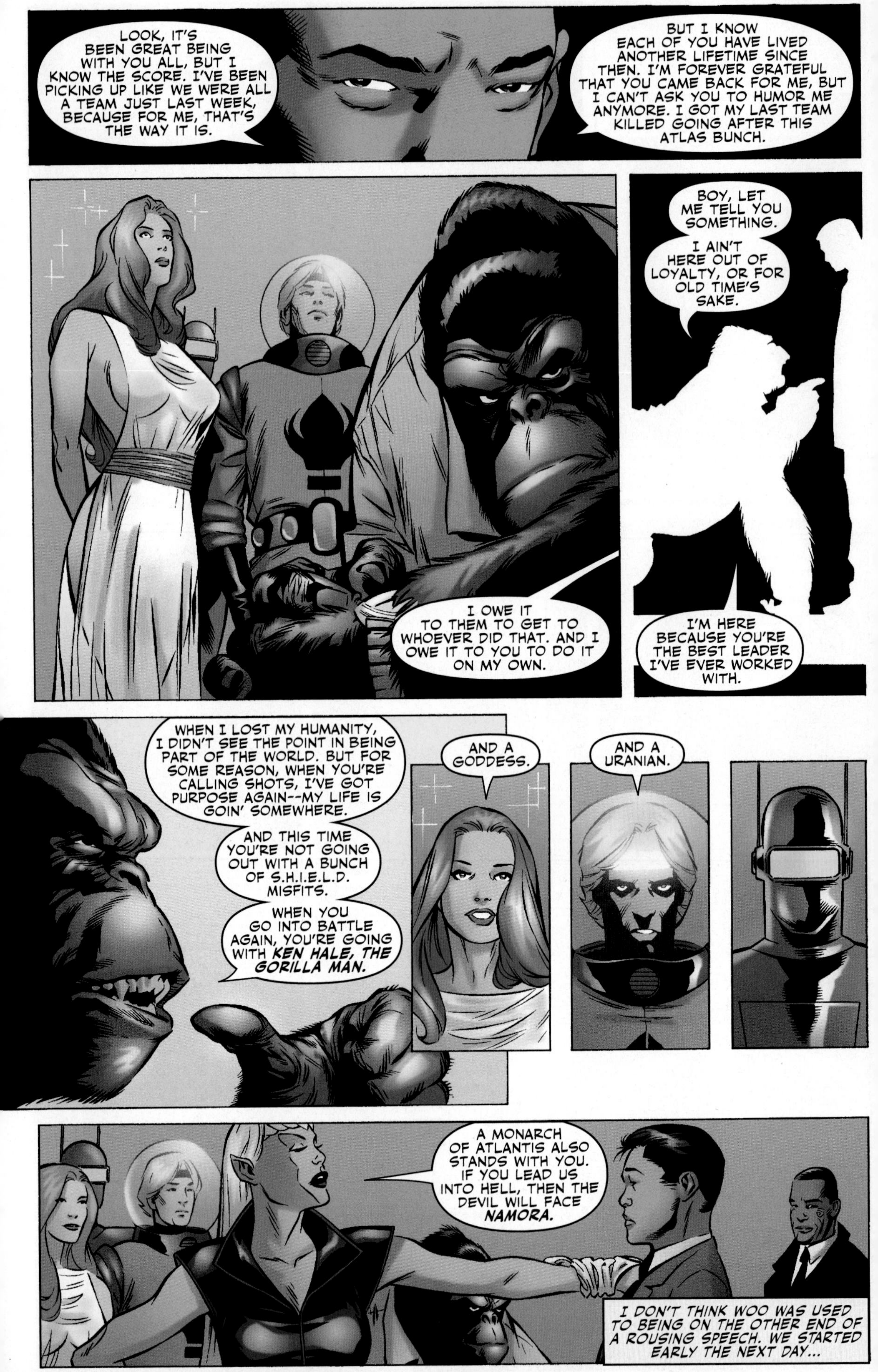
LOOK, IT'S BEEN GREAT BEING WITH YOU ALL, BUT I KNOW THE SCORE. I'VE BEEN PICKING UP LIKE WE WERE ALL A TEAM JUST LAST WEEK, BECAUSE FOR ME, THAT'S THE WAY IT IS.
BUT I KNOW EACH OF YOU HAVE LIVED ANOTHER LIFETIME SINCE THEN. I'M FOREVER GRATEFUL THAT YOU CAME BACK FOR ME, BUT I CAN'T ASK YOU TO HUMOR ME ANYMORE. I GOT MY LAST TEAM KILLED GOING AFTER THIS ATLAS BUNCH.
I OWE IT TO THEM TO GET TO WHOEVER DID THAT. AND I OWE IT TO YOU TO DO IT ON MY OWN.
BOY, LET ME TELL YOU SOMETHING.
I AIN'T HERE OUT OF LOYALTY, OR FOR OLD TIME'S SAKE.
I'M HERE BECAUSE YOU'RE THE BEST LEADER I'VE EVER WORKED WITH.
WHEN I LOST MY HUMANITY, I DIDN'T SEE THE POINT IN BEING PART OF THE WORLD. BUT FOR SOME REASON, WHEN YOU'RE CALLING SHOTS, I'VE GOT PURPOSE AGAIN--MY LIFE IS GOIN' SOMEWHERE.
AND THIS TIME YOU'RE NOT GOING OUT WITH A BUNCH OF S.H.I.E.L.D. MISFITS.
WHEN YOU GO INTO BATTLE AGAIN, YOU'RE GOING WITH ***KEN HALE, THE GORILLA MAN.***
AND A GODDESS.
AND A URANIAN.
A MONARCH OF ATLANTIS ALSO STANDS WITH YOU. IF YOU LEAD US INTO HELL, THEN THE DEVIL WILL FACE ***NAMORA.***
I DON'T THINK WOO WAS USED TO BEING ON THE OTHER END OF A ROUSING SPEECH. WE STARTED EARLY THE NEXT DAY...

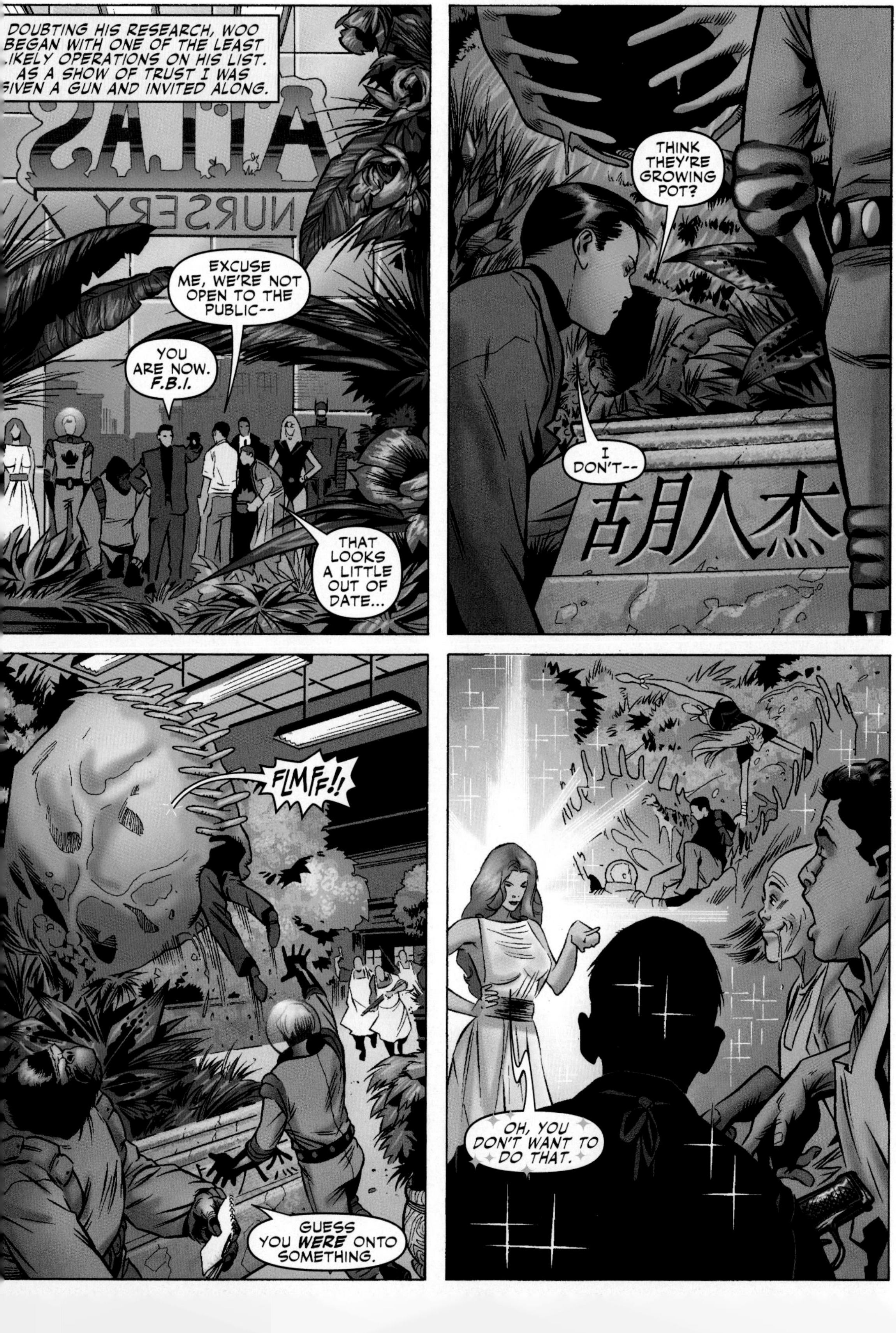
DOUBTING HIS RESEARCH, WOO BEGAN WITH ONE OF THE LEAST LIKELY OPERATIONS ON HIS LIST. AS A SHOW OF TRUST I WAS GIVEN A GUN AND INVITED ALONG.
ATLAS
NURSERY
EXCUSE ME, WE'RE NOT OPEN TO THE PUBLIC--
YOU ARE NOW. *F.B.I.*
THAT LOOKS A LITTLE OUT OF DATE...
THINK THEY'RE GROWING POT?
I DON'T--
古月人杰
FLMPFF!!
GUESS YOU ***WERE*** ONTO SOMETHING.
OH, YOU DON'T WANT TO DO THAT.

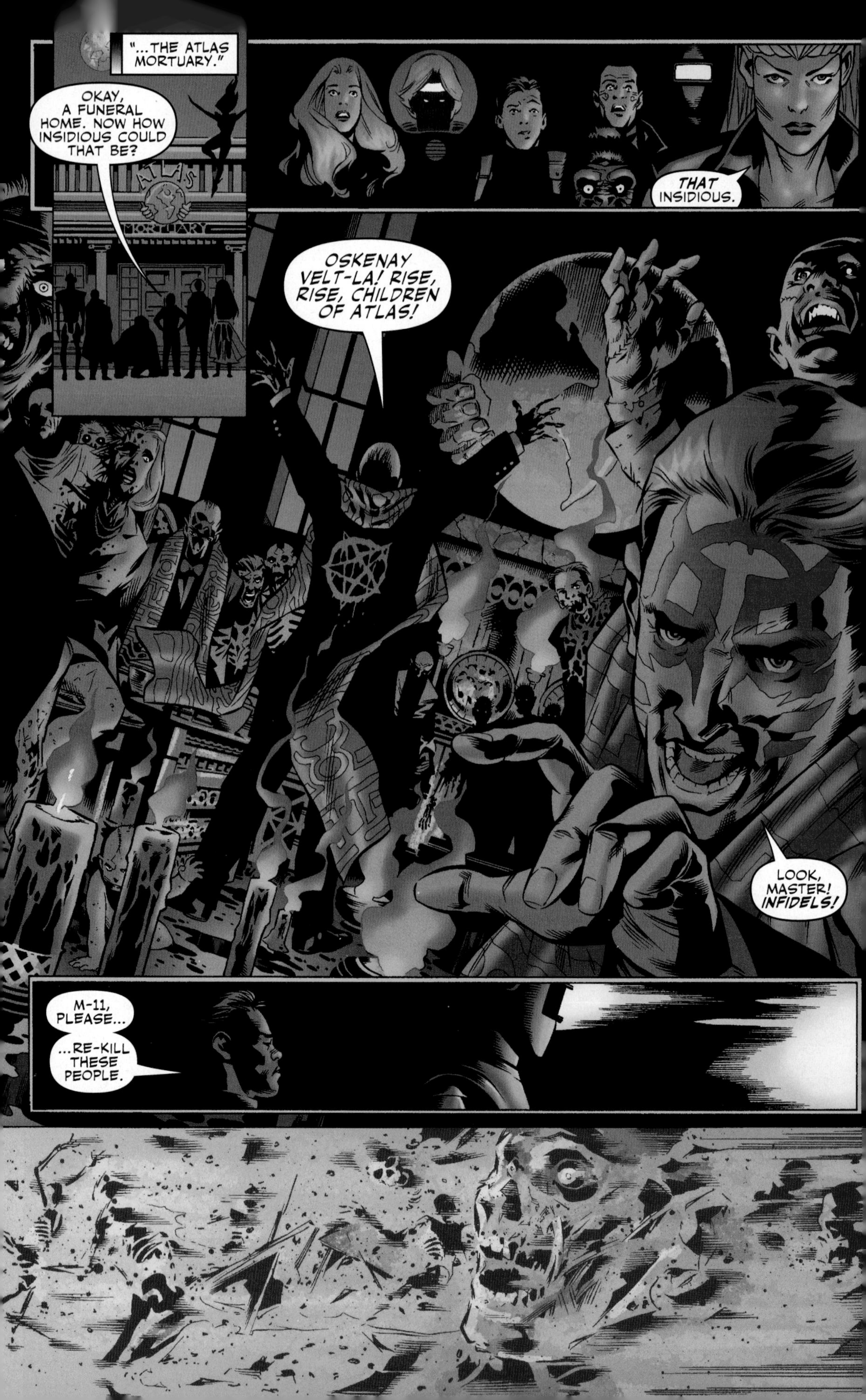
"...THE ATLAS MORTUARY."
OKAY, A FUNERAL HOME. NOW HOW INSIDIOUS COULD THAT BE?
ATLAS MORTUARY
THAT INSIDIOUS.
OSKENAY VELT-LA! RISE, RISE, CHILDREN OF ATLAS!
LOOK, MASTER! *INFIDELS!*
M-11, PLEASE...
...RE-KILL THESE PEOPLE.

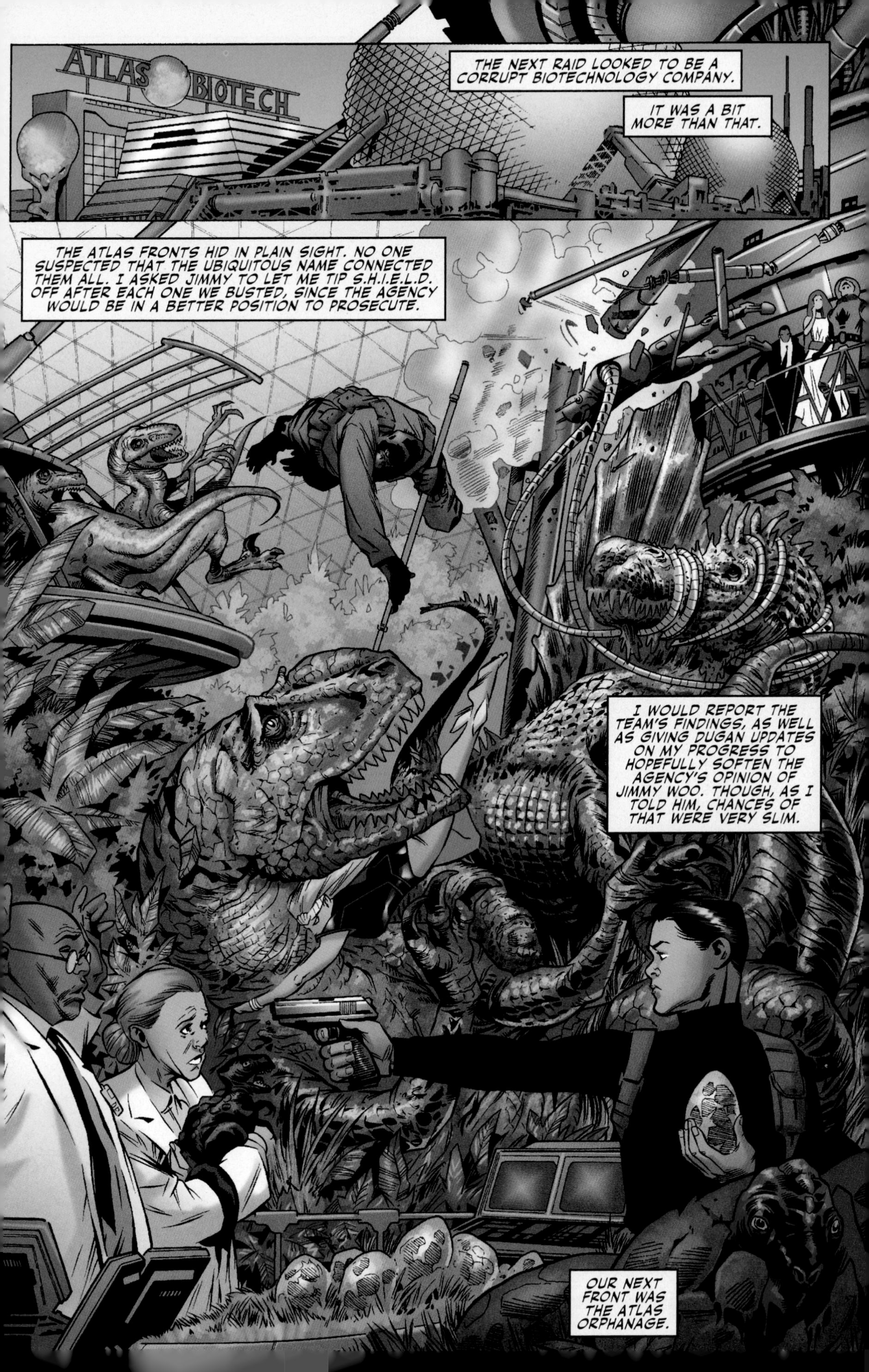
ATLAS BIOTECH
THE NEXT RAID LOOKED TO BE A CORRUPT BIOTECHNOLOGY COMPANY.
IT WAS A BIT MORE THAN THAT.
THE ATLAS FRONTS HID IN PLAIN SIGHT. NO ONE SUSPECTED THAT THE UBIQUITOUS NAME CONNECTED THEM ALL. I ASKED JIMMY TO LET ME TIP S.H.I.E.L.D. OFF AFTER EACH ONE WE BUSTED, SINCE THE AGENCY WOULD BE IN A BETTER POSITION TO PROSECUTE.
I WOULD REPORT THE TEAM'S FINDINGS, AS WELL AS GIVING DUGAN UPDATES ON MY PROGRESS TO HOPEFULLY SOFTEN THE AGENCY'S OPINION OF JIMMY WOO. THOUGH, AS I TOLD HIM, CHANCES OF THAT WERE VERY SLIM.
OUR NEXT FRONT WAS THE ATLAS ORPHANAGE.

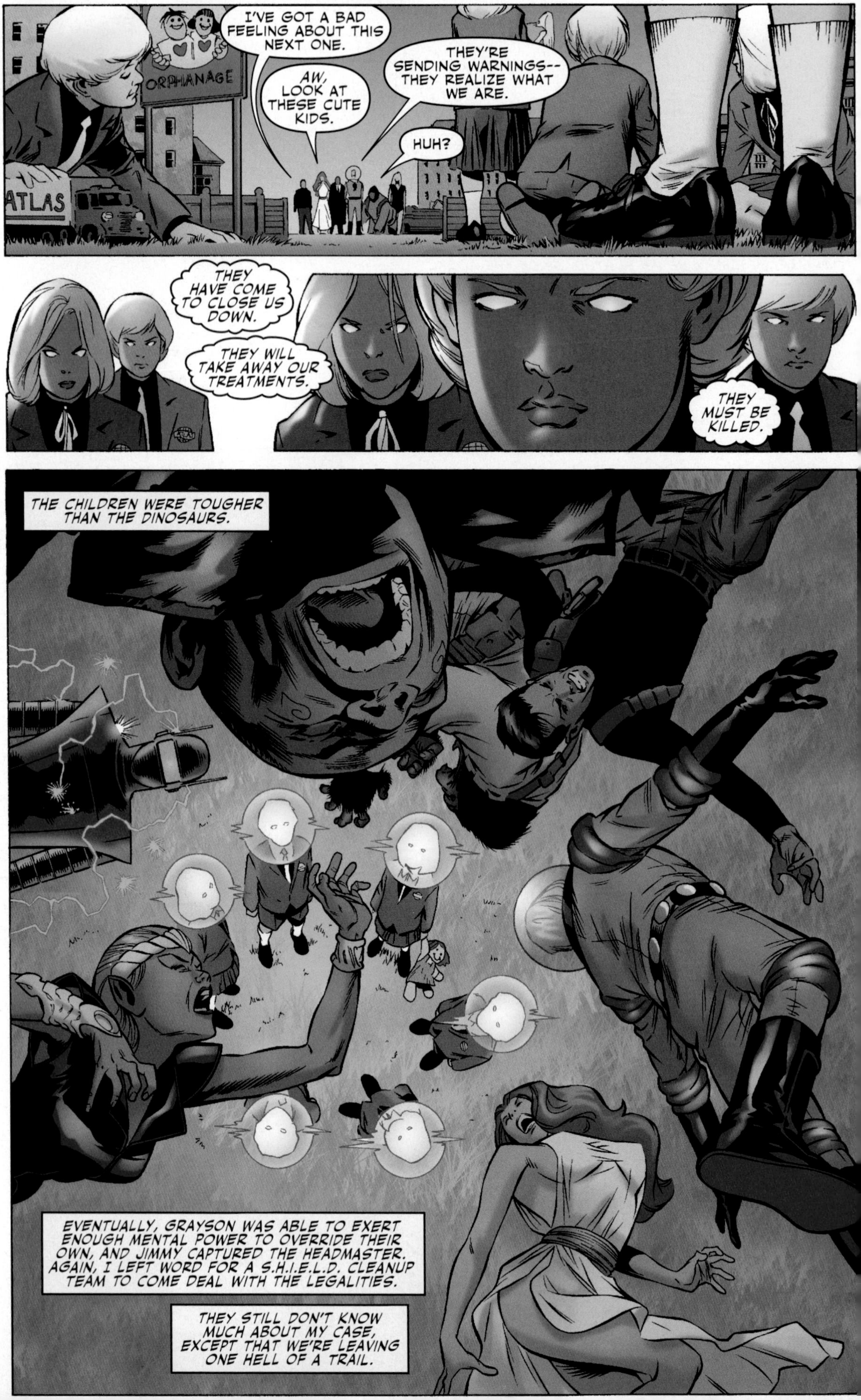
ORPHANAGE
I'VE GOT A BAD FEELING ABOUT THIS NEXT ONE.
AW, LOOK AT THESE CUTE KIDS.
THEY'RE SENDING WARNINGS-- THEY REALIZE WHAT WE ARE.
HUH?
ATLAS
THEY HAVE COME TO CLOSE US DOWN.
THEY WILL TAKE AWAY OUR TREATMENTS.
THEY MUST BE KILLED.
THE CHILDREN WERE TOUGHER THAN THE DINOSAURS.
EVENTUALLY, GRAYSON WAS ABLE TO EXERT ENOUGH MENTAL POWER TO OVERRIDE THEIR OWN, AND JIMMY CAPTURED THE HEADMASTER. AGAIN, I LEFT WORD FOR A S.H.I.E.L.D. CLEANUP TEAM TO COME DEAL WITH THE LEGALITIES.
THEY STILL DON'T KNOW MUCH ABOUT MY CASE, EXCEPT THAT WE'RE LEAVING ONE HELL OF A TRAIL.

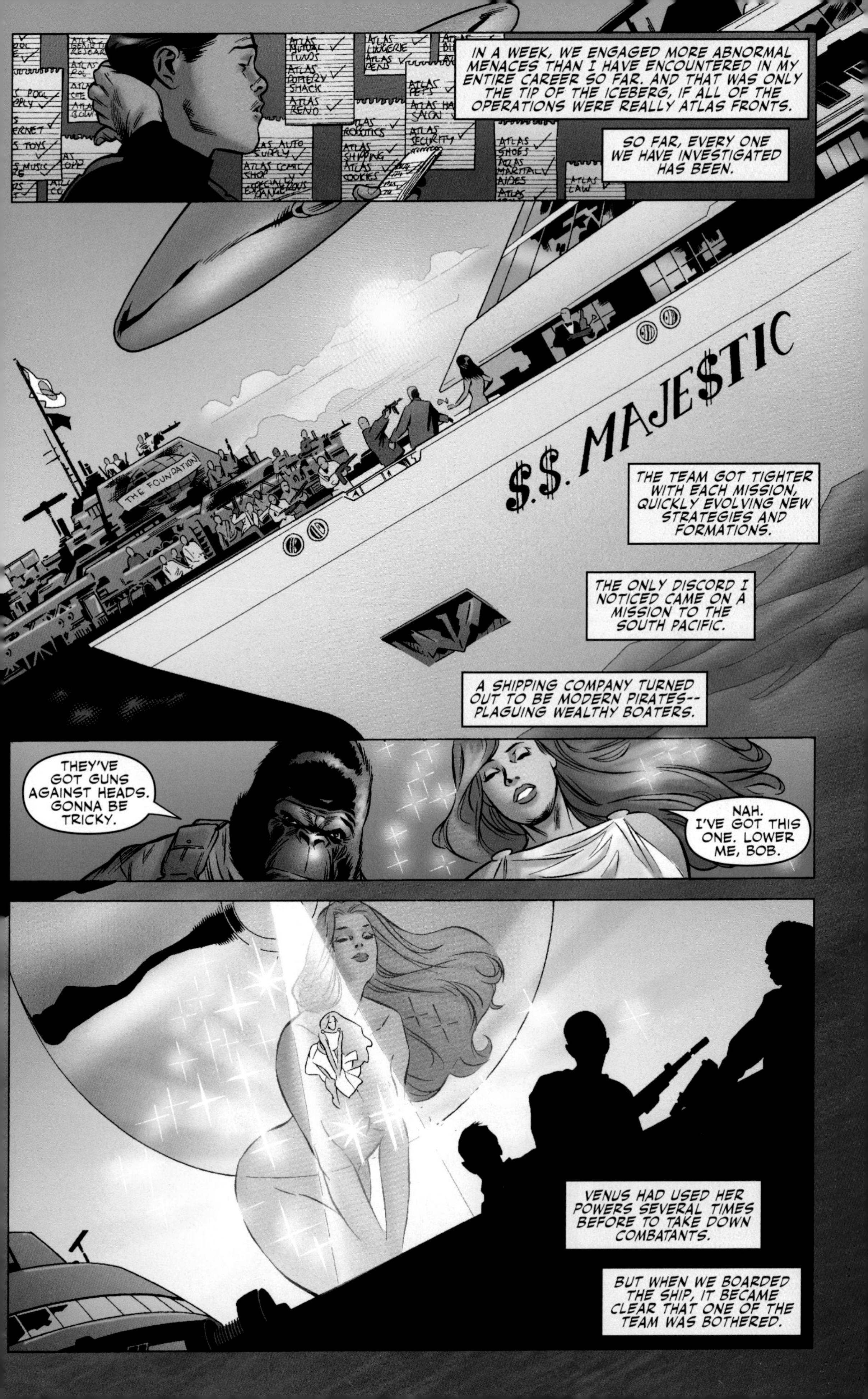
IN A WEEK, WE ENGAGED MORE ABNORMAL MENACES THAN I HAVE ENCOUNTERED IN MY ENTIRE CAREER SO FAR. AND THAT WAS ONLY THE TIP OF THE ICEBERG, IF ALL OF THE OPERATIONS WERE REALLY ATLAS FRONTS.
SO FAR, EVERY ONE WE HAVE INVESTIGATED HAS BEEN.
THE FOUNDATION
$.$. MAJE$TIC
THE TEAM GOT TIGHTER WITH EACH MISSION, QUICKLY EVOLVING NEW STRATEGIES AND FORMATIONS.
THE ONLY DISCORD I NOTICED CAME ON A MISSION TO THE SOUTH PACIFIC.
A SHIPPING COMPANY TURNED OUT TO BE MODERN PIRATES--PLAGUING WEALTHY BOATERS.
THEY'VE GOT GUNS AGAINST HEADS. GONNA BE TRICKY.
NAH. I'VE GOT THIS ONE. LOWER ME, BOB.
VENUS HAD USED HER POWERS SEVERAL TIMES BEFORE TO TAKE DOWN COMBATANTS.
BUT WHEN WE BOARDED THE SHIP, IT BECAME CLEAR THAT ONE OF THE TEAM WAS BOTHERED.

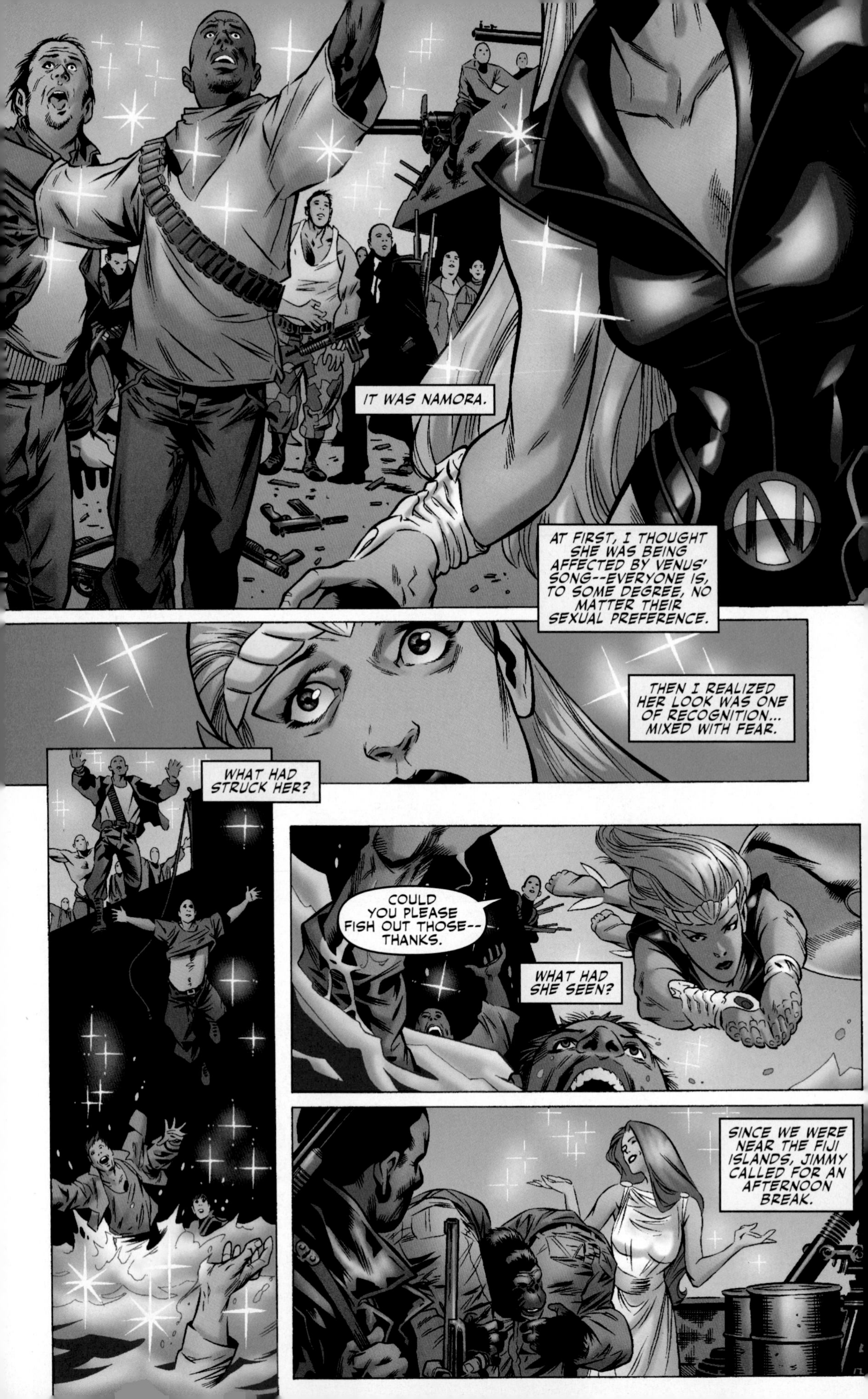
IT WAS NAMORA.
AT FIRST, I THOUGHT SHE WAS BEING AFFECTED BY VENUS' SONG--EVERYONE IS, TO SOME DEGREE, NO MATTER THEIR SEXUAL PREFERENCE.
THEN I REALIZED HER LOOK WAS ONE OF RECOGNITION... MIXED WITH FEAR.
WHAT HAD STRUCK HER?
COULD YOU PLEASE FISH OUT THOSE-- THANKS.
WHAT HAD SHE SEEN?
SINCE WE WERE NEAR THE FIJI ISLANDS, JIMMY CALLED FOR AN AFTERNOON BREAK.

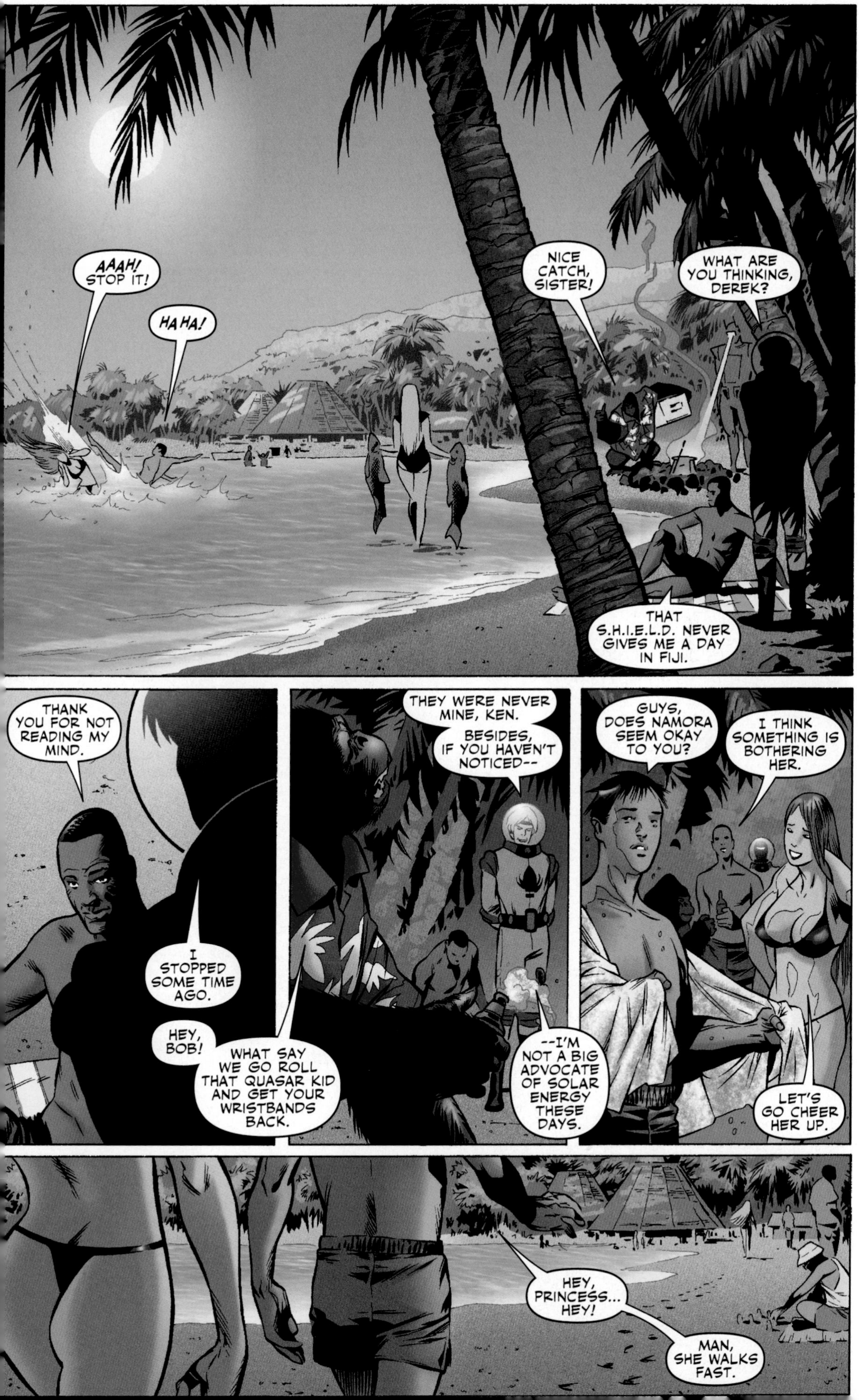
AAAH! STOP IT!
HA HA!
NICE CATCH, SISTER!
WHAT ARE YOU THINKING, DEREK?
THAT S.H.I.E.L.D. NEVER GIVES ME A DAY IN FIJI.
THANK YOU FOR NOT READING MY MIND.
I STOPPED SOME TIME AGO.
HEY, BOB!
WHAT SAY WE GO ROLL THAT QUASAR KID AND GET YOUR WRISTBANDS BACK.
THEY WERE NEVER MINE, KEN.
BESIDES, IF YOU HAVEN'T NOTICED--
--I'M NOT A BIG ADVOCATE OF SOLAR ENERGY THESE DAYS.
GUYS, DOES NAMORA SEEM OKAY TO YOU?
I THINK SOMETHING IS BOTHERING HER.
LET'S GO CHEER HER UP.
HEY, PRINCESS... HEY!
MAN, SHE WALKS FAST.

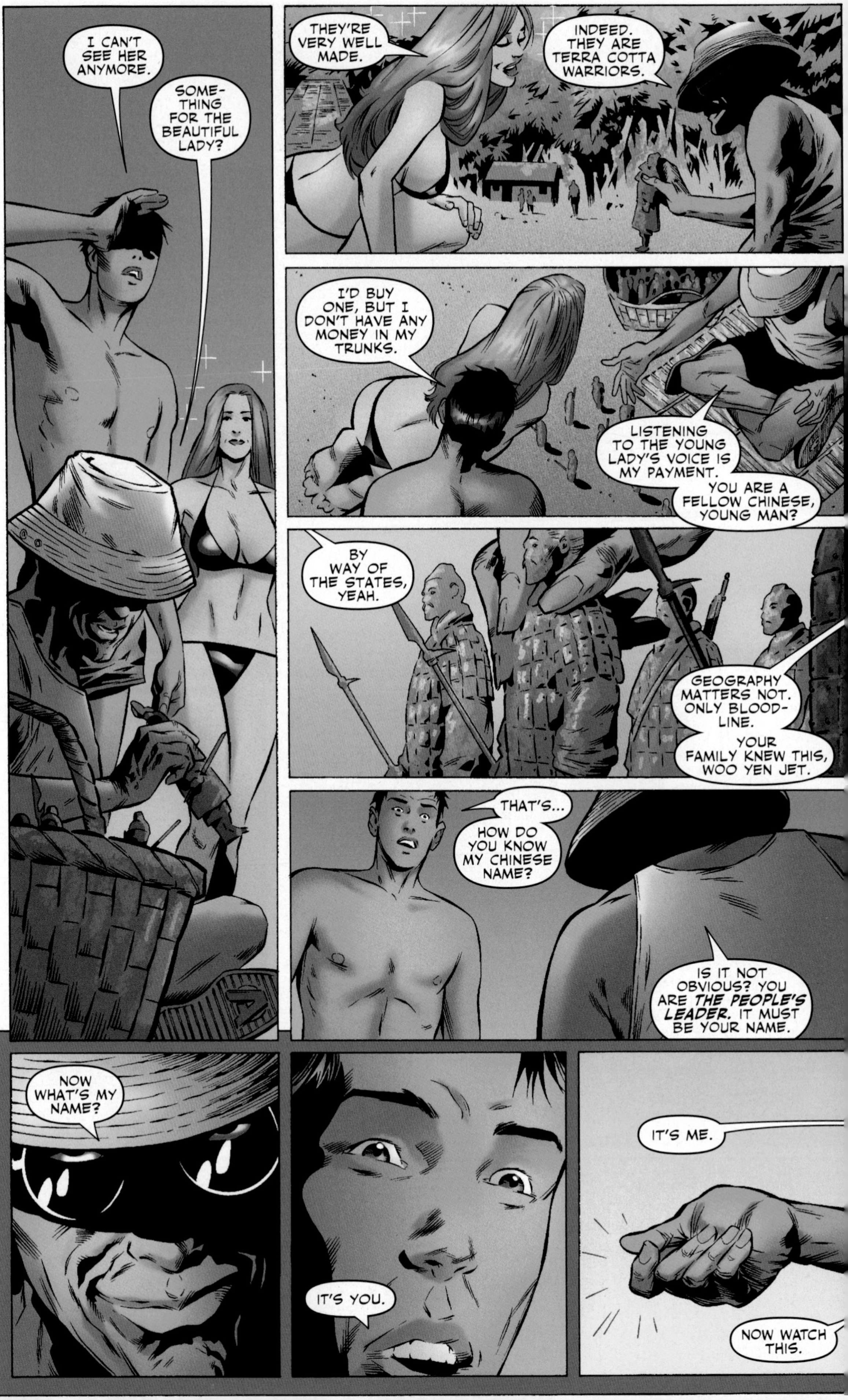
I CAN'T SEE HER ANYMORE.
SOME-THING FOR THE BEAUTIFUL LADY?
THEY'RE VERY WELL MADE.
INDEED. THEY ARE TERRA COTTA WARRIORS.
I'D BUY ONE, BUT I DON'T HAVE ANY MONEY IN MY TRUNKS.
LISTENING TO THE YOUNG LADY'S VOICE IS MY PAYMENT.
YOU ARE A FELLOW CHINESE, YOUNG MAN?
BY WAY OF THE STATES, YEAH.
GEOGRAPHY MATTERS NOT. ONLY BLOOD-LINE.
YOUR FAMILY KNEW THIS, WOO YEN JET.
THAT'S...
HOW DO YOU KNOW MY CHINESE NAME?
IS IT NOT OBVIOUS? YOU ARE *THE PEOPLE'S LEADER.* IT MUST BE YOUR NAME.
NOW WHAT'S MY NAME?
IT'S YOU.
IT'S ME.
NOW WATCH THIS.

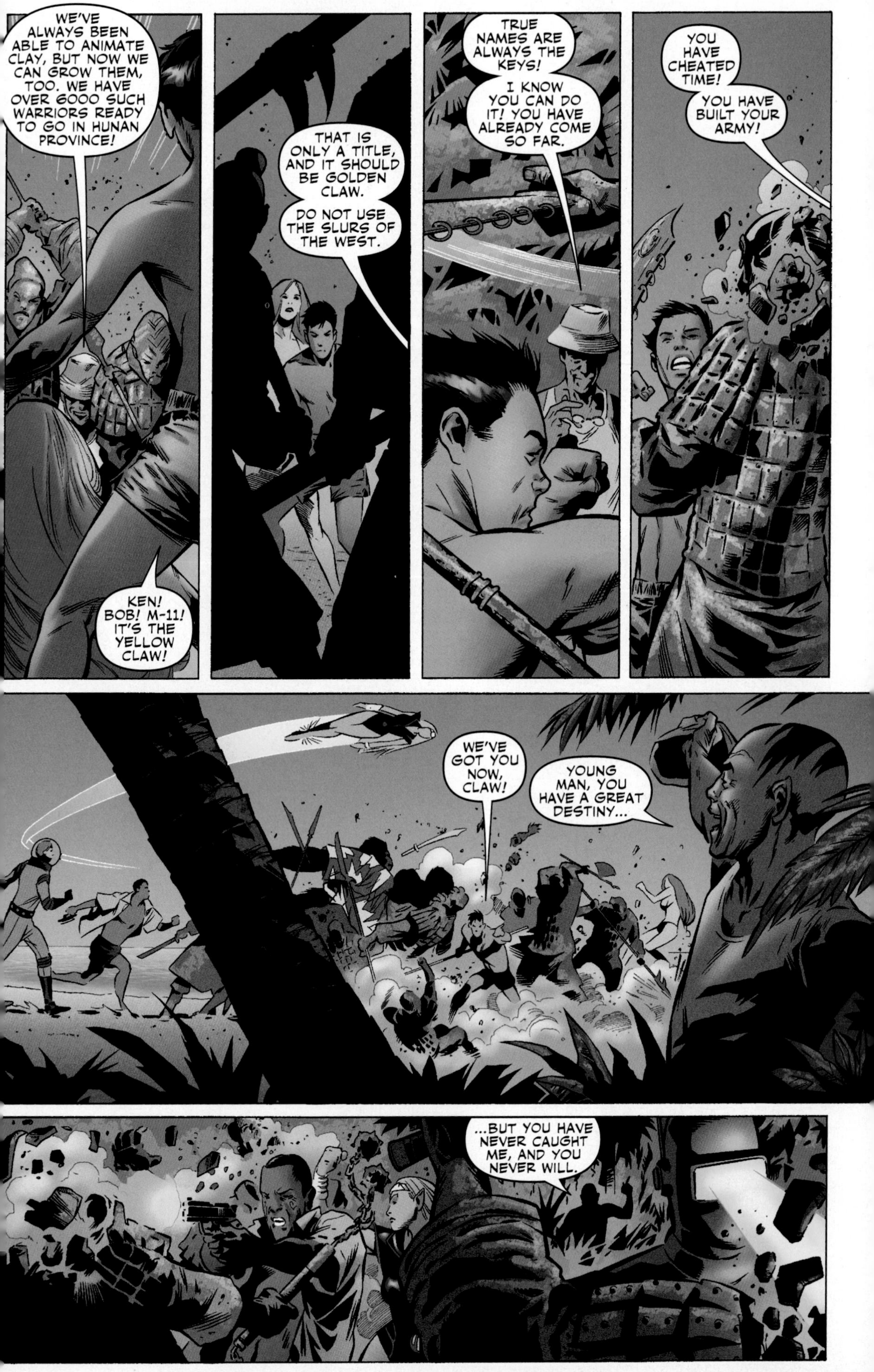
WE'VE ALWAYS BEEN ABLE TO ANIMATE CLAY, BUT NOW WE CAN GROW THEM, TOO. WE HAVE OVER 6000 SUCH WARRIORS READY TO GO IN HUNAN PROVINCE!
KEN! BOB! M-11! IT'S THE YELLOW CLAW!
THAT IS ONLY A TITLE, AND IT SHOULD BE GOLDEN CLAW.
DO NOT USE THE SLURS OF THE WEST.
TRUE NAMES ARE ALWAYS THE KEYS!
I KNOW YOU CAN DO IT! YOU HAVE ALREADY COME SO FAR.
YOU HAVE CHEATED TIME!
YOU HAVE BUILT YOUR ARMY!
WE'VE GOT YOU NOW, CLAW!
YOUNG MAN, YOU HAVE A GREAT DESTINY...
...BUT YOU HAVE NEVER CAUGHT ME, AND YOU NEVER WILL.

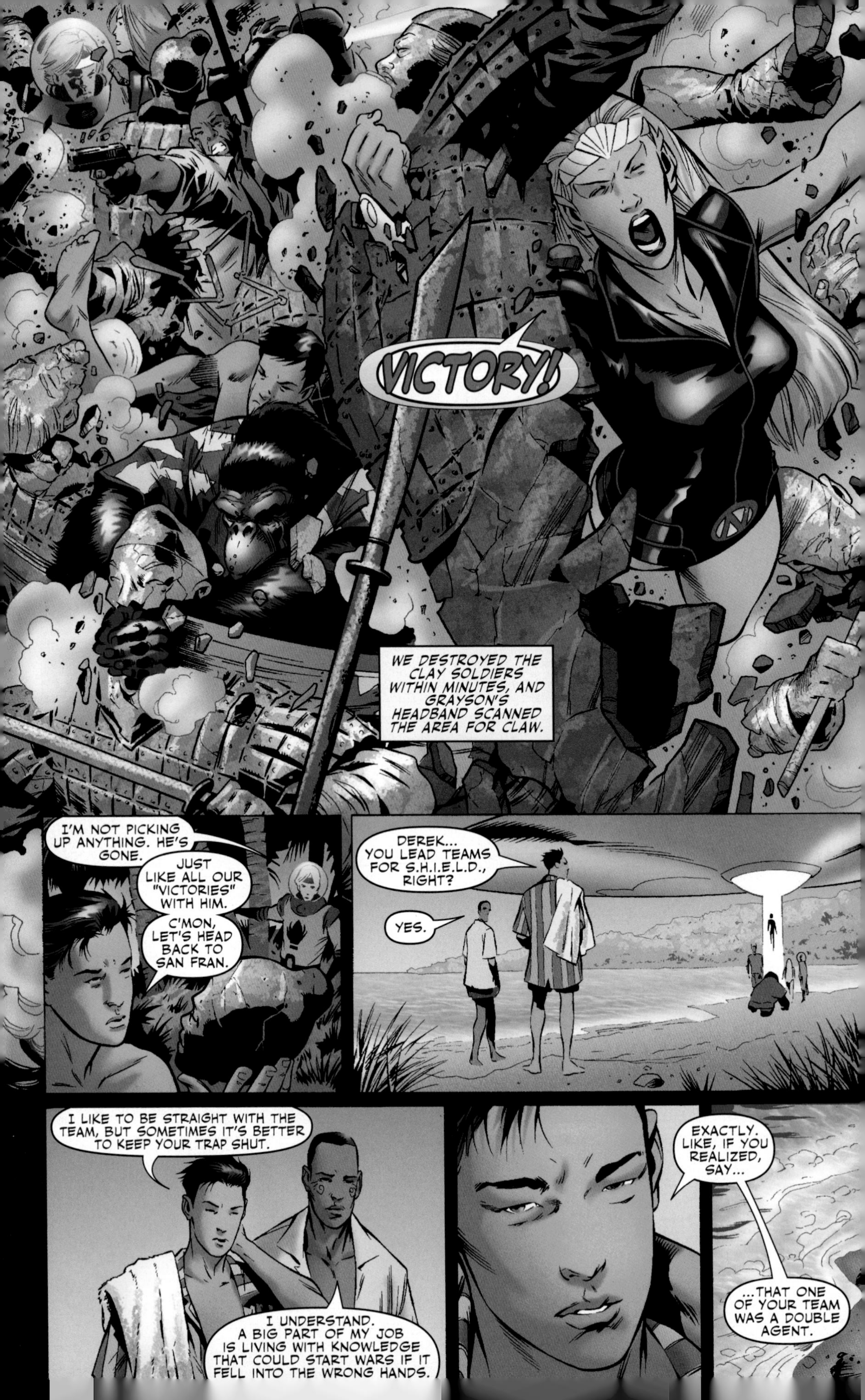
VICTORY!
WE DESTROYED THE CLAY SOLDIERS WITHIN MINUTES, AND GRAYSON'S HEADBAND SCANNED THE AREA FOR CLAW.
I'M NOT PICKING UP ANYTHING. HE'S GONE.
JUST LIKE ALL OUR "VICTORIES" WITH HIM.
C'MON, LET'S HEAD BACK TO SAN FRAN.
DEREK... YOU LEAD TEAMS FOR S.H.I.E.L.D., RIGHT?
YES.
I LIKE TO BE STRAIGHT WITH THE TEAM, BUT SOMETIMES IT'S BETTER TO KEEP YOUR TRAP SHUT.
I UNDERSTAND. A BIG PART OF MY JOB IS LIVING WITH KNOWLEDGE THAT COULD START WARS IF IT FELL INTO THE WRONG HANDS.
EXACTLY. LIKE, IF YOU REALIZED, SAY...
...THAT ONE OF YOUR TEAM WAS A DOUBLE AGENT.

Okay, I made Bob whip me up a jumbo keyboard so I can do some of these entries while Jimmy studies his research on the Atlas Foundation. We've been out, going through the list and knocking heads round the clock. Somebody has to keep track of all this stuff. I ought to let M-11 do it, that would be a hoot.

- K.H.

ATLAS RECORDS
About what you'd expect, the producers were working subliminal mind-control messages into their releases. Most of it was directed at making listeners buy more of their CD's, so they were pulling in good money. I got to punch a guy who organized boy bands, so it was a banner morning for me.

ATLAS VINEYARDS
They made truth-serum wine. We had some. Good stuff.

ATLAS MUNITIONS
Talk about heavy artillery! We non-bulletproofers hung back and let M-11 and Namora deal with those jokers. The place is a big scorched crater now.

ATLAS DAIRY
So not every business on the planet named Atlas is part of the Foundation. These people just bottle milk. We spooked a lot of cows before Bob determined that no one was up to anything. I felt bad and bought a bunch of cheese off of them to make up for it.

ATLAS COMICS
Jimmy determined this was on the up-and-up too, but I still think it's a front. They only had super hero books, and all of those had crossover stories, so you had to buy all of them to get one damn story! Gotta be a racket. And where's all the war books?

ATLAS NOVELTIES
I was sure this was going to be a bust too, then Venus opened a spring-loaded "can of peanuts" that let out real snakes--deadly adders. The manager tried to electrocute Bob with a lethal joy buzzer, but his suit rechanneled most of the current.

ATLAS ACADEMY OF MARTIAL ARTS
Now this was fun. Jimmy, Namora and I asked the others to stay outside while we got in a little hand-to-hand practice. My "pissed ape" style was too much for those hotshots and their fancy moves. Of course, Jimmy had the best form, he was flipping all over, spinning and busting heads like crazy! Every time we'd get their numbers down, a whole new team would come running out of secret doors and floorboards. Namora finally got ticked off and kicked out the wall, dropping the building on them.

FAMOUS ATLAS' COOKIES
Super-addictive cookies. We weren't sure if this was actually illegal, so we smashed their ovens and plan to get back here later for a follow-up. Everyone assumes I like coconut in sweets, but I want to make it clear that I DON'T.

ATLAS AUTO
Mostly legit--for an auto parts company, that is--but they smuggled weaponry in lots of the overseas shipments. Jimmy picked up some parts for the Edsel before we left.

ATLAS MINING
So here's where a lot of the Top 40 listeners of Atlas Records end up--digging ore out of this mountain in the San Andreas area. After we hustled the kids out of there, Bob leveled the mountain with the saucer's meteor-smasher. That was something to see.

APE ART by MIKE SHORT

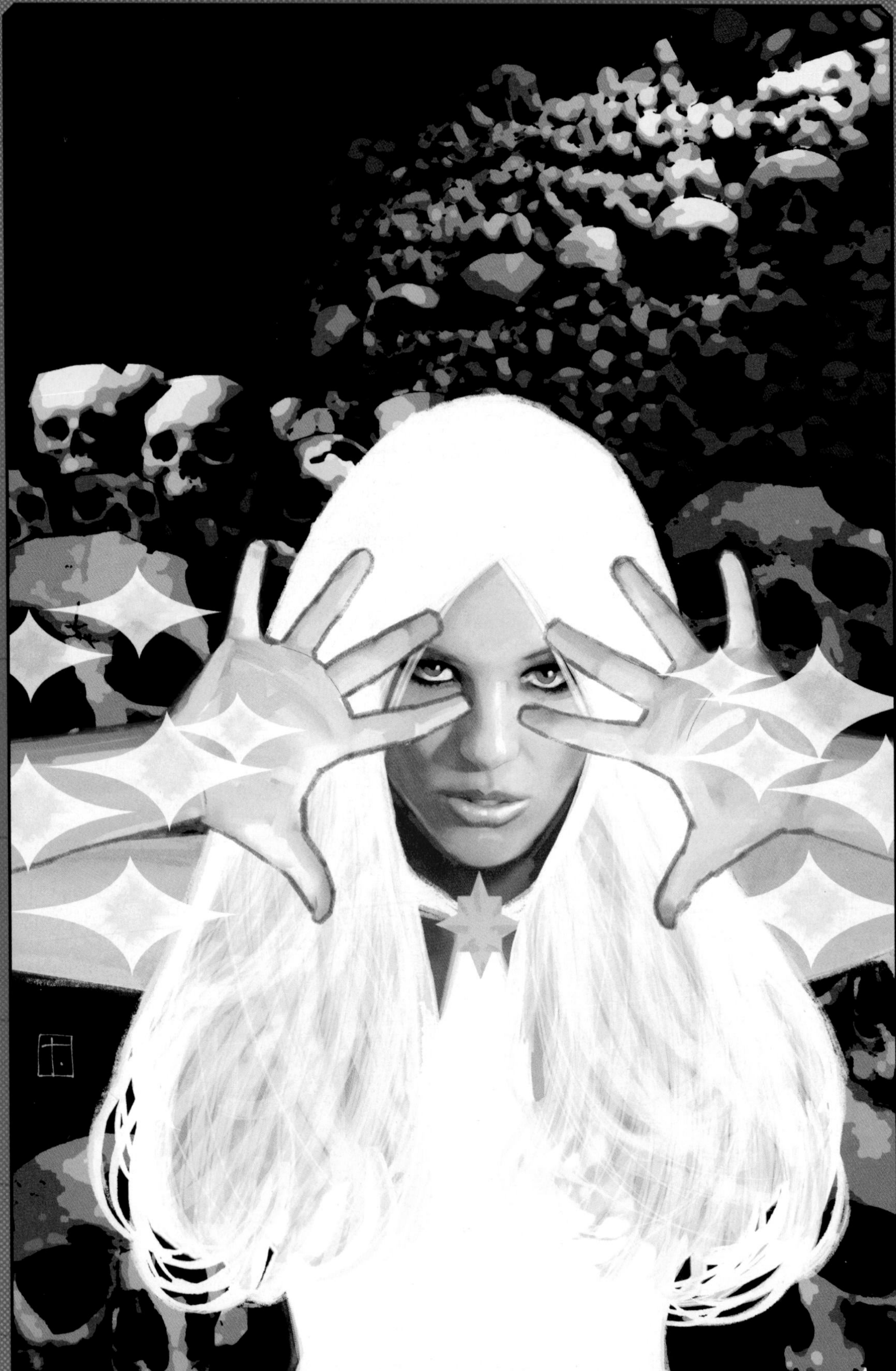

AGENTS OF ATLAS (2006) 5

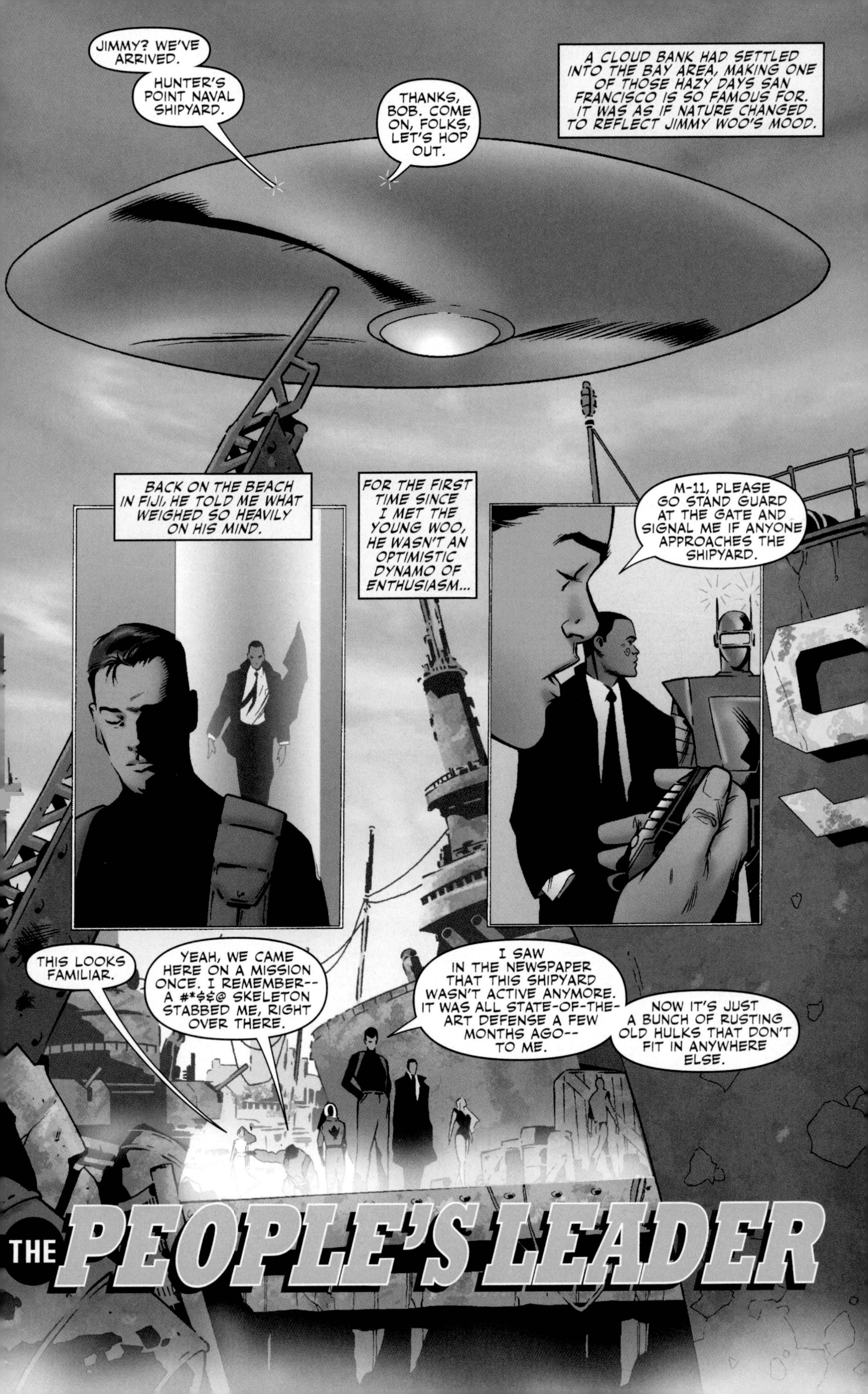

JIMMY? WE'VE ARRIVED.
HUNTER'S POINT NAVAL SHIPYARD.
THANKS, BOB. COME ON, FOLKS, LET'S HOP OUT.
A CLOUD BANK HAD SETTLED INTO THE BAY AREA, MAKING ONE OF THOSE HAZY DAYS SAN FRANCISCO IS SO FAMOUS FOR. IT WAS AS IF NATURE CHANGED TO REFLECT JIMMY WOO'S MOOD.
BACK ON THE BEACH IN FIJI, HE TOLD ME WHAT WEIGHED SO HEAVILY ON HIS MIND.
FOR THE FIRST TIME SINCE I MET THE YOUNG WOO, HE WASN'T AN OPTIMISTIC DYNAMO OF ENTHUSIASM...
M-11, PLEASE GO STAND GUARD AT THE GATE AND SIGNAL ME IF ANYONE APPROACHES THE SHIPYARD.
THIS LOOKS FAMILIAR.
YEAH, WE CAME HERE ON A MISSION ONCE. I REMEMBER-- A #*$¢@ SKELETON STABBED ME, RIGHT OVER THERE.
I SAW IN THE NEWSPAPER THAT THIS SHIPYARD WASN'T ACTIVE ANYMORE. IT WAS ALL STATE-OF-THE-ART DEFENSE A FEW MONTHS AGO-- TO ME.
NOW IT'S JUST A BUNCH OF RUSTING OLD HULKS THAT DON'T FIT IN ANYWHERE ELSE.
THE PEOPLE'S LEADER

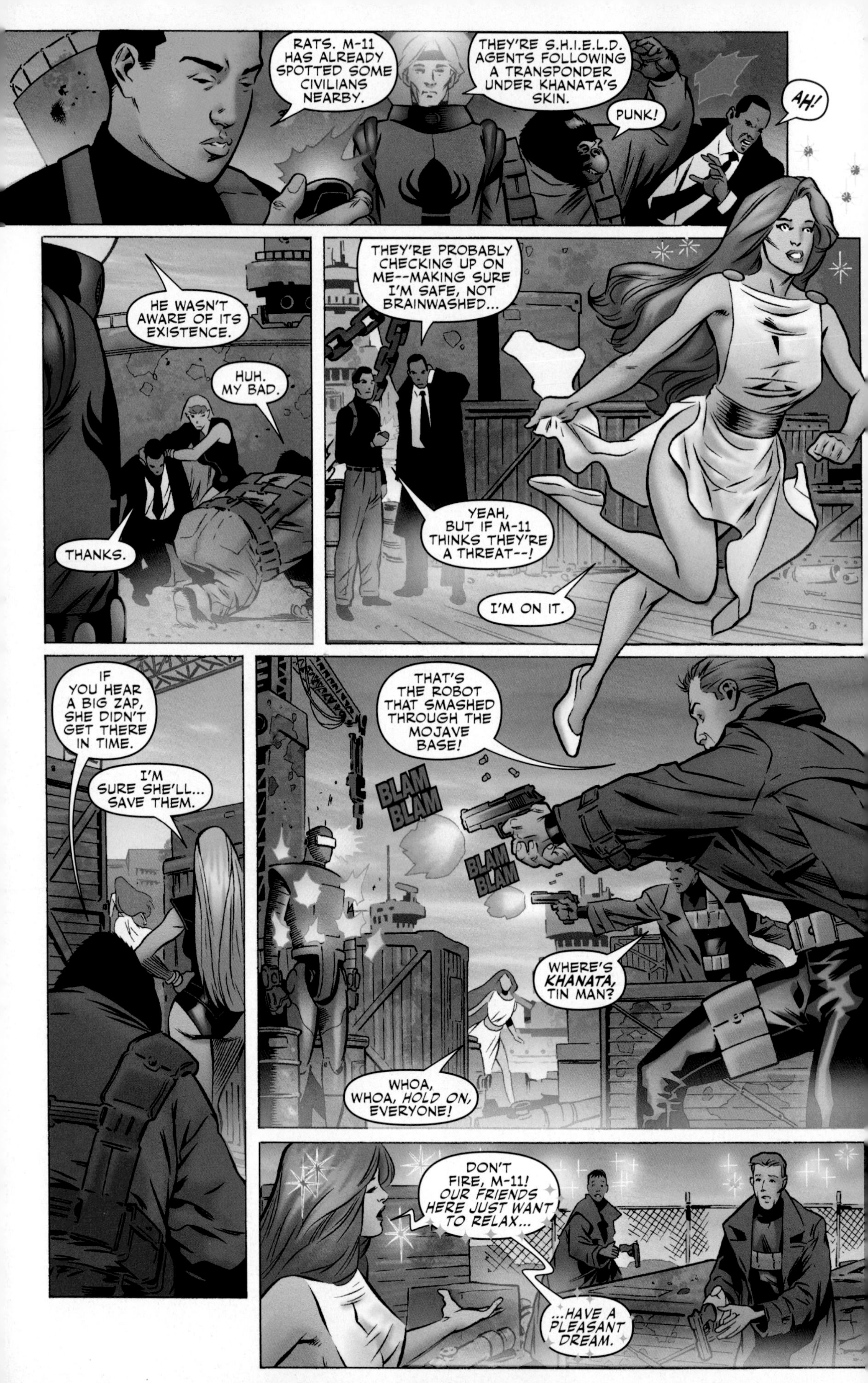
RATS. M-11 HAS ALREADY SPOTTED SOME CIVILIANS NEARBY.
THEY'RE S.H.I.E.L.D. AGENTS FOLLOWING A TRANSPONDER UNDER KHANATA'S SKIN.
PUNK!
AH!
HE WASN'T AWARE OF ITS EXISTENCE.
HUH. MY BAD.
THANKS.
THEY'RE PROBABLY CHECKING UP ON ME--MAKING SURE I'M SAFE, NOT BRAINWASHED...
YEAH, BUT IF M-11 THINKS THEY'RE A THREAT--!
I'M ON IT.
IF YOU HEAR A BIG ZAP, SHE DIDN'T GET THERE IN TIME.
I'M SURE SHE'LL... SAVE THEM.
THAT'S THE ROBOT THAT SMASHED THROUGH THE MOJAVE BASE!
BLAM BLAM
BLAM BLAM
WHERE'S *KHANATA,* TIN MAN?
WHOA, WHOA, *HOLD ON,* EVERYONE!
DON'T FIRE, M-11! *OUR FRIENDS HERE JUST WANT TO RELAX...*
...HAVE A PLEASANT DREAM.

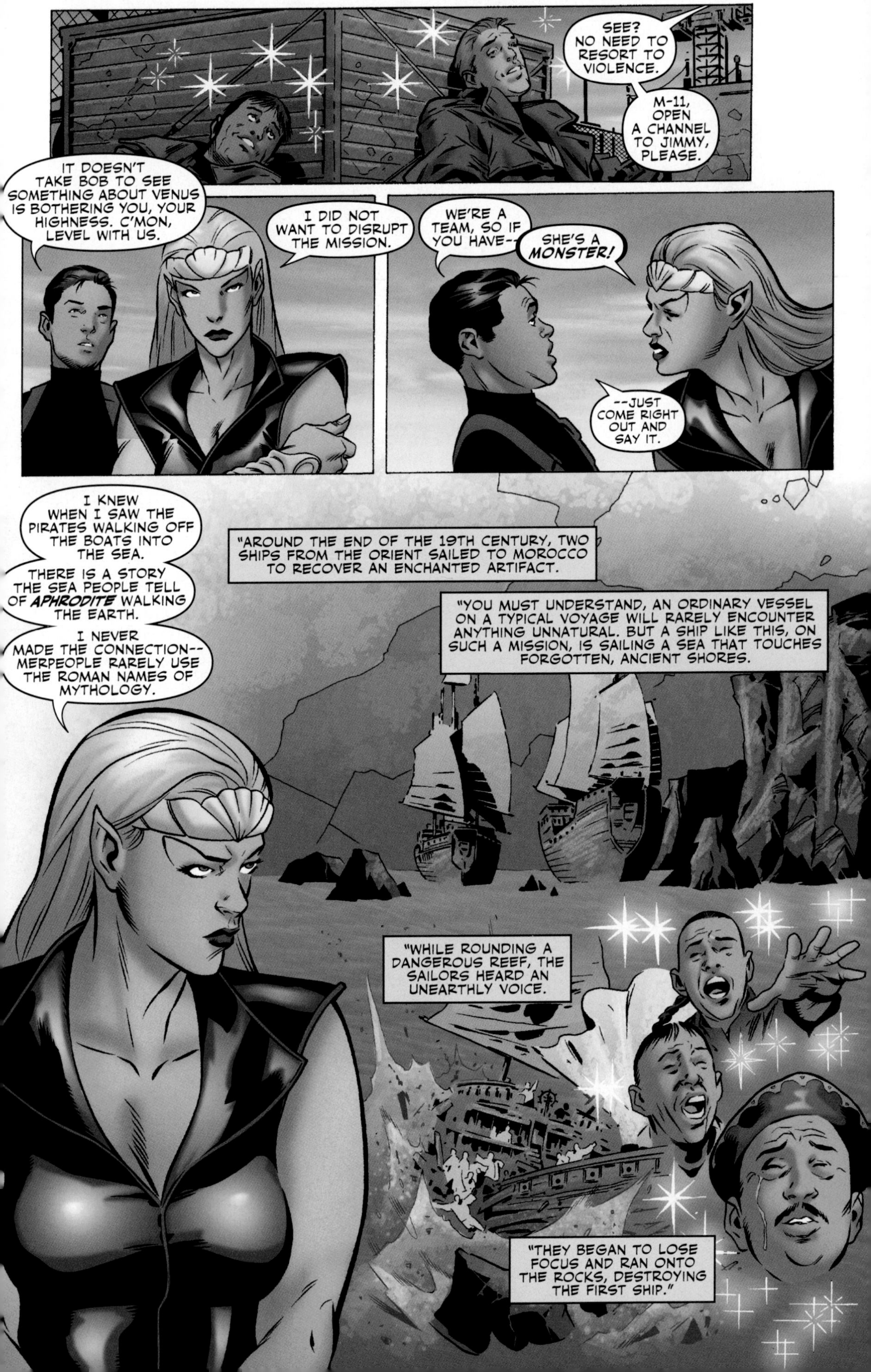
SEE? NO NEED TO RESORT TO VIOLENCE.
M-11, OPEN A CHANNEL TO JIMMY, PLEASE.
IT DOESN'T TAKE BOB TO SEE SOMETHING ABOUT VENUS IS BOTHERING YOU, YOUR HIGHNESS. C'MON, LEVEL WITH US.
I DID NOT WANT TO DISRUPT THE MISSION.
WE'RE A TEAM, SO IF YOU HAVE--
SHE'S A *MONSTER!*
--JUST COME RIGHT OUT AND SAY IT.
I KNEW WHEN I SAW THE PIRATES WALKING OFF THE BOATS INTO THE SEA.
THERE IS A STORY THE SEA PEOPLE TELL OF *APHRODITE* WALKING THE EARTH.
I NEVER MADE THE CONNECTION-- MERPEOPLE RARELY USE THE ROMAN NAMES OF MYTHOLOGY.
"AROUND THE END OF THE 19TH CENTURY, TWO SHIPS FROM THE ORIENT SAILED TO MOROCCO TO RECOVER AN ENCHANTED ARTIFACT.
"YOU MUST UNDERSTAND, AN ORDINARY VESSEL ON A TYPICAL VOYAGE WILL RARELY ENCOUNTER ANYTHING UNNATURAL. BUT A SHIP LIKE THIS, ON SUCH A MISSION, IS SAILING A SEA THAT TOUCHES FORGOTTEN, ANCIENT SHORES.
"WHILE ROUNDING A DANGEROUS REEF, THE SAILORS HEARD AN UNEARTHLY VOICE.
"THEY BEGAN TO LOSE FOCUS AND RAN ONTO THE ROCKS, DESTROYING THE FIRST SHIP."

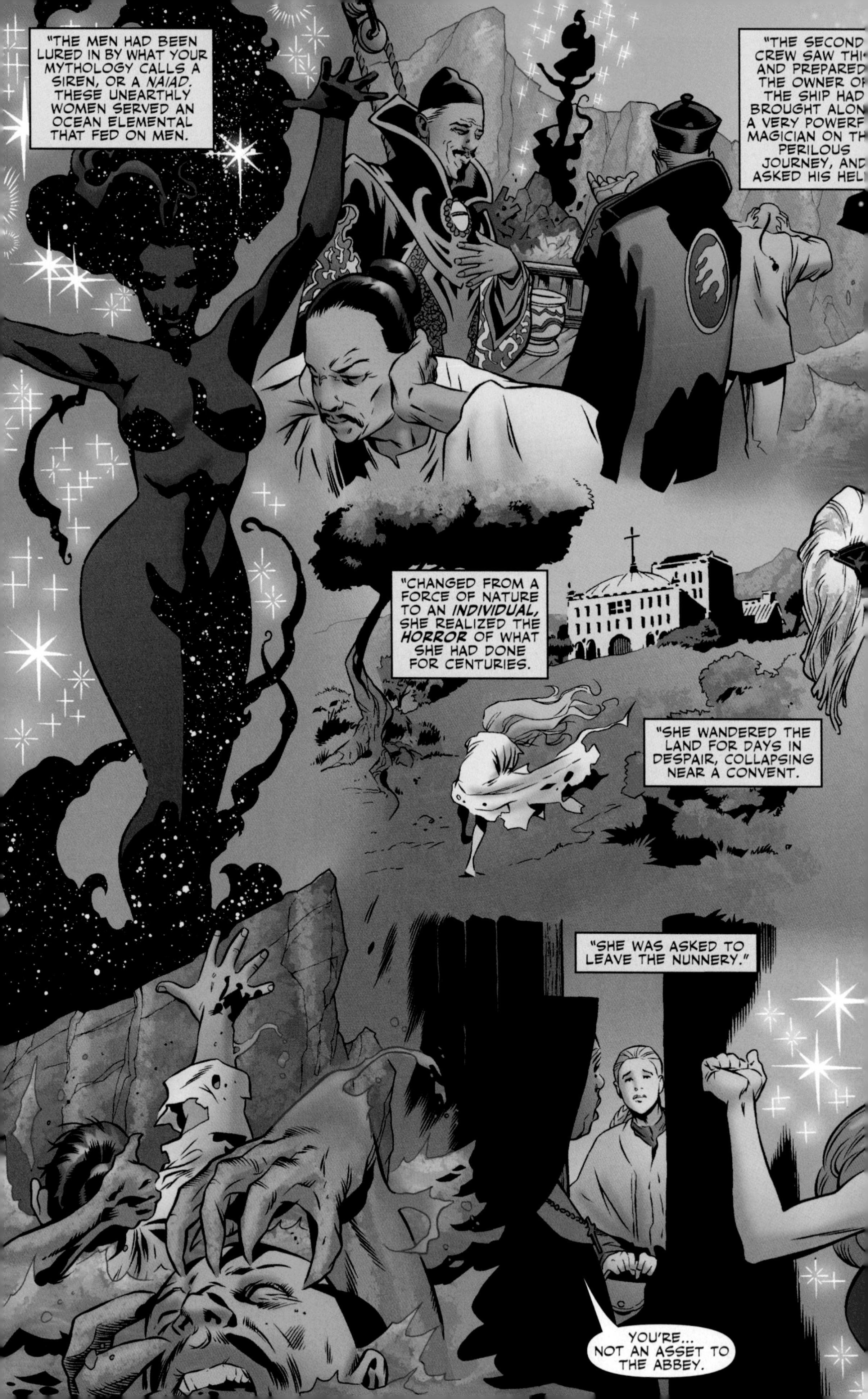
"THE MEN HAD BEEN LURED IN BY WHAT YOUR MYTHOLOGY CALLS A SIREN, OR A *NAIAD*. THESE UNEARTHLY WOMEN SERVED AN OCEAN ELEMENTAL THAT FED ON MEN.
"THE SECOND CREW SAW THI AND PREPARED THE OWNER O THE SHIP HAD BROUGHT ALON A VERY POWERF MAGICIAN ON TH PERILOUS JOURNEY, AND ASKED HIS HEL
"CHANGED FROM A FORCE OF NATURE TO AN *INDIVIDUAL*, SHE REALIZED THE ***HORROR*** OF WHAT SHE HAD DONE FOR CENTURIES.
"SHE WANDERED THE LAND FOR DAYS IN DESPAIR, COLLAPSING NEAR A CONVENT.
"SHE WAS ASKED TO LEAVE THE NUNNERY."
YOU'RE... NOT AN ASSET TO THE ABBEY.

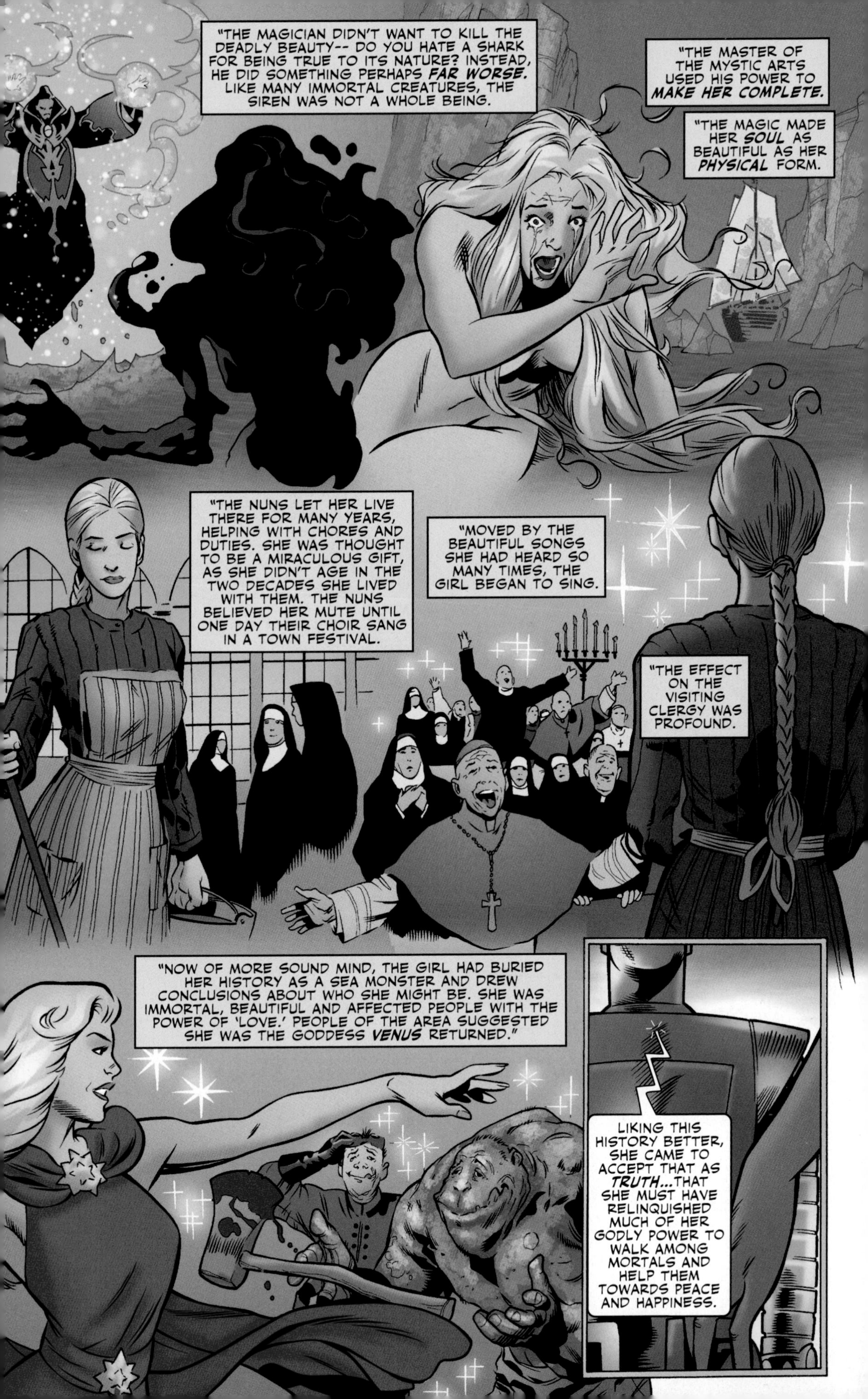
"THE MAGICIAN DIDN'T WANT TO KILL THE DEADLY BEAUTY-- DO YOU HATE A SHARK FOR BEING TRUE TO ITS NATURE? INSTEAD, HE DID SOMETHING PERHAPS *FAR WORSE.* LIKE MANY IMMORTAL CREATURES, THE SIREN WAS NOT A WHOLE BEING.
"THE MASTER OF THE MYSTIC ARTS USED HIS POWER TO *MAKE HER COMPLETE.*
"THE MAGIC MADE HER **SOUL** AS BEAUTIFUL AS HER *PHYSICAL* FORM.
"THE NUNS LET HER LIVE THERE FOR MANY YEARS, HELPING WITH CHORES AND DUTIES. SHE WAS THOUGHT TO BE A MIRACULOUS GIFT, AS SHE DIDN'T AGE IN THE TWO DECADES SHE LIVED WITH THEM. THE NUNS BELIEVED HER MUTE UNTIL ONE DAY THEIR CHOIR SANG IN A TOWN FESTIVAL.
"MOVED BY THE BEAUTIFUL SONGS SHE HAD HEARD SO MANY TIMES, THE GIRL BEGAN TO SING.
"THE EFFECT ON THE VISITING CLERGY WAS PROFOUND.
"NOW OF MORE SOUND MIND, THE GIRL HAD BURIED HER HISTORY AS A SEA MONSTER AND DREW CONCLUSIONS ABOUT WHO SHE MIGHT BE. SHE WAS IMMORTAL, BEAUTIFUL AND AFFECTED PEOPLE WITH THE POWER OF 'LOVE.' PEOPLE OF THE AREA SUGGESTED SHE WAS THE GODDESS *VENUS* RETURNED."
LIKING THIS HISTORY BETTER, SHE CAME TO ACCEPT THAT AS *TRUTH*...THAT SHE MUST HAVE RELINQUISHED MUCH OF HER GODLY POWER TO WALK AMONG MORTALS AND HELP THEM TOWARDS PEACE AND HAPPINESS.

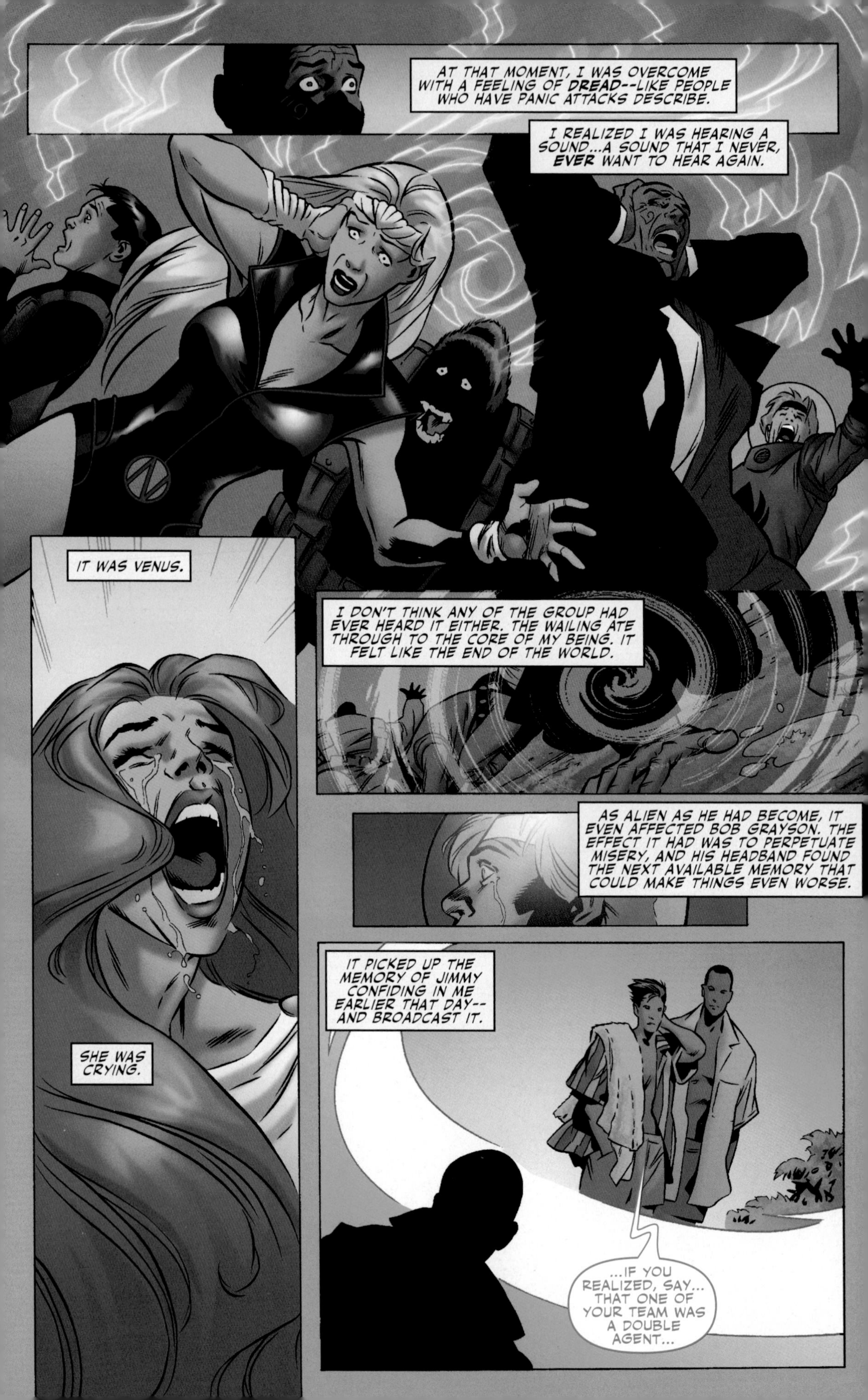
AT THAT MOMENT, I WAS OVERCOME WITH A FEELING OF DREAD--LIKE PEOPLE WHO HAVE PANIC ATTACKS DESCRIBE.
I REALIZED I WAS HEARING A SOUND...A SOUND THAT I NEVER, EVER WANT TO HEAR AGAIN.
IT WAS VENUS.
SHE WAS CRYING.
I DON'T THINK ANY OF THE GROUP HAD EVER HEARD IT EITHER. THE WAILING ATE THROUGH TO THE CORE OF MY BEING. IT FELT LIKE THE END OF THE WORLD.
AS ALIEN AS HE HAD BECOME, IT EVEN AFFECTED BOB GRAYSON. THE EFFECT IT HAD WAS TO PERPETUATE MISERY, AND HIS HEADBAND FOUND THE NEXT AVAILABLE MEMORY THAT COULD MAKE THINGS EVEN WORSE.
IT PICKED UP THE MEMORY OF JIMMY CONFIDING IN ME EARLIER THAT DAY-- AND BROADCAST IT.
...IF YOU REALIZED, SAY... THAT ONE OF YOUR TEAM WAS A DOUBLE AGENT...

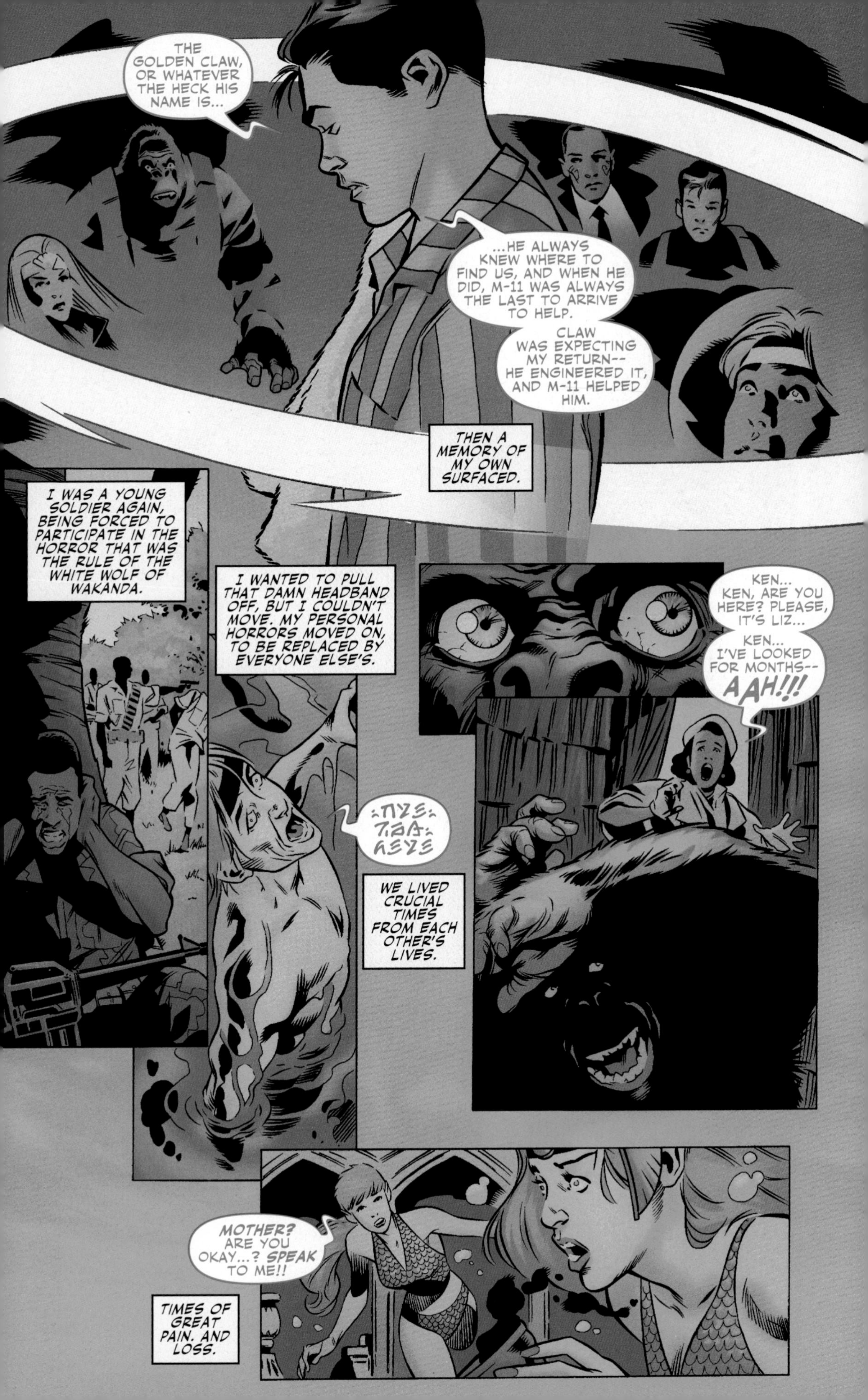
THE GOLDEN CLAW, OR WHATEVER THE HECK HIS NAME IS...
...HE ALWAYS KNEW WHERE TO FIND US, AND WHEN HE DID, M-11 WAS ALWAYS THE LAST TO ARRIVE TO HELP.
CLAW WAS EXPECTING MY RETURN-- HE ENGINEERED IT, AND M-11 HELPED HIM.
THEN A MEMORY OF MY OWN SURFACED.
I WAS A YOUNG SOLDIER AGAIN, BEING FORCED TO PARTICIPATE IN THE HORROR THAT WAS THE RULE OF THE WHITE WOLF OF WAKANDA.
I WANTED TO PULL THAT DAMN HEADBAND OFF, BUT I COULDN'T MOVE. MY PERSONAL HORRORS MOVED ON, TO BE REPLACED BY EVERYONE ELSE'S.
WE LIVED CRUCIAL TIMES FROM EACH OTHER'S LIVES.
KEN... KEN, ARE YOU HERE? PLEASE, IT'S LIZ...
KEN... I'VE LOOKED FOR MONTHS-- AAH!!!
MOTHER? ARE YOU OKAY...? SPEAK TO ME!!
TIMES OF GREAT PAIN. AND LOSS.

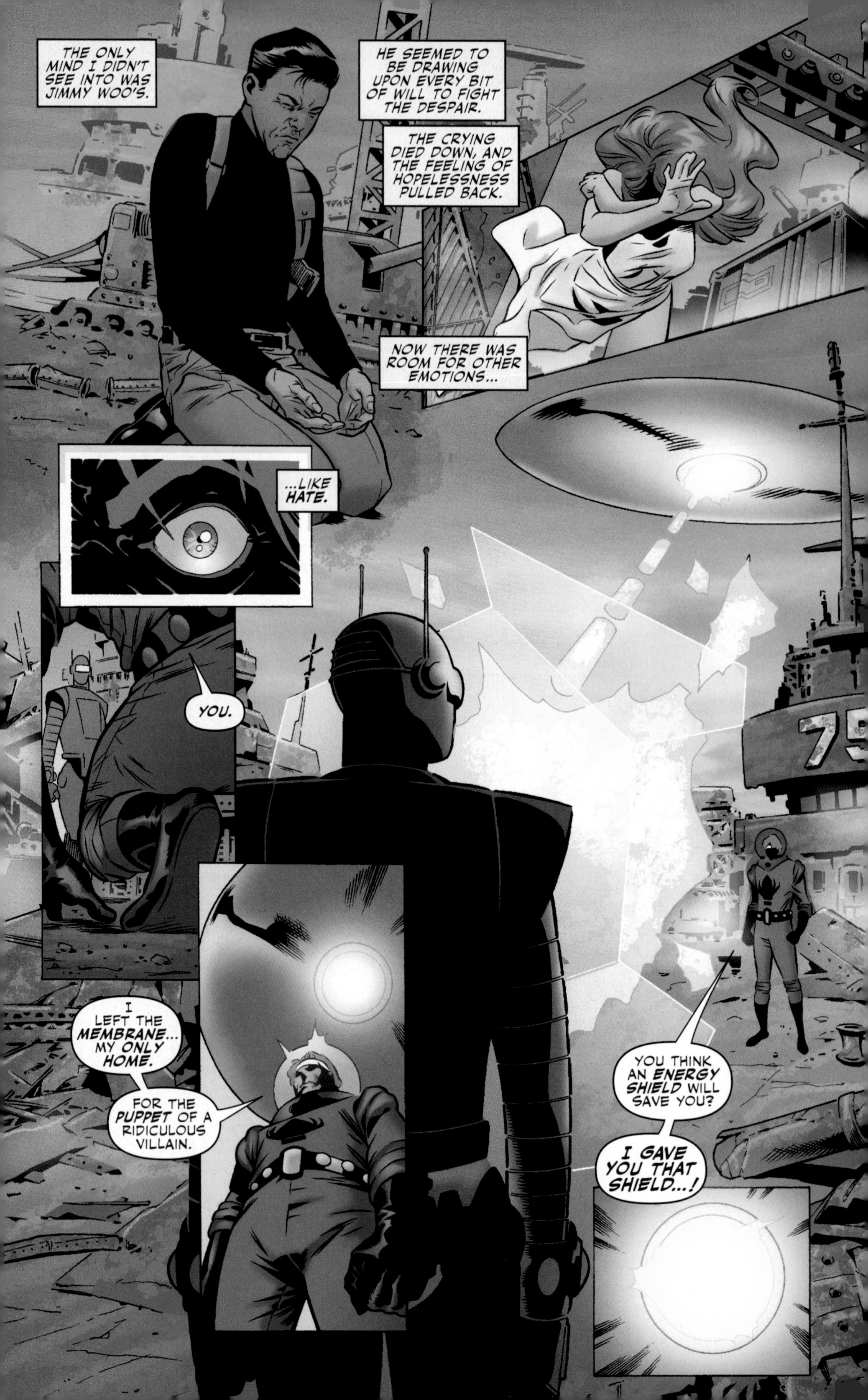
THE ONLY MIND I DIDN'T SEE INTO WAS JIMMY WOO'S.
HE SEEMED TO BE DRAWING UPON EVERY BIT OF WILL TO FIGHT THE DESPAIR.
THE CRYING DIED DOWN, AND THE FEELING OF HOPELESSNESS PULLED BACK.
NOW THERE WAS ROOM FOR OTHER EMOTIONS...
...LIKE HATE.
YOU.
75
I LEFT THE MEMBRANE... MY ONLY HOME.
FOR THE PUPPET OF A RIDICULOUS VILLAIN.
YOU THINK AN ENERGY SHIELD WILL SAVE YOU?
I GAVE YOU THAT SHIELD...!

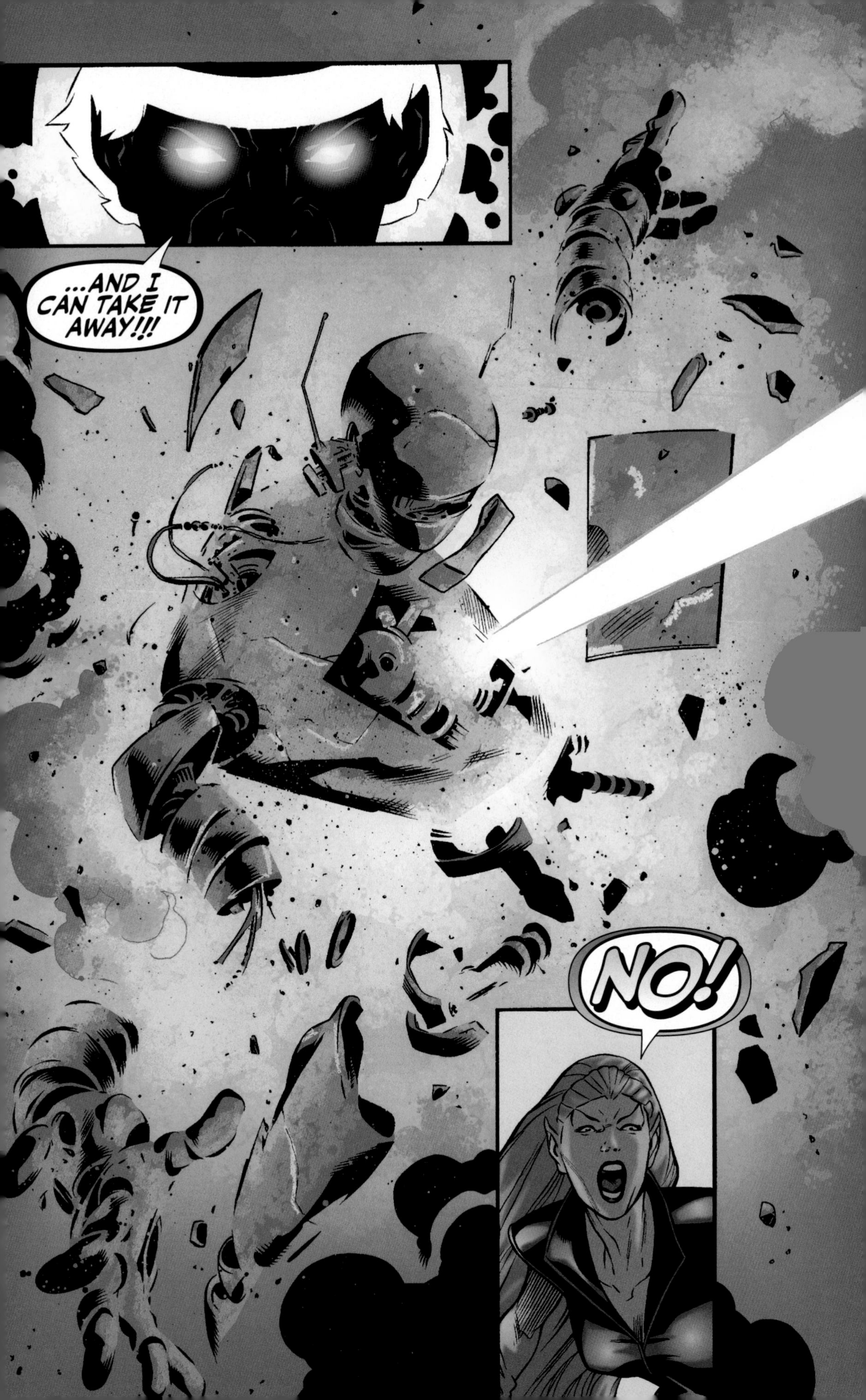
...AND I CAN TAKE IT AWAY!!!
NO!

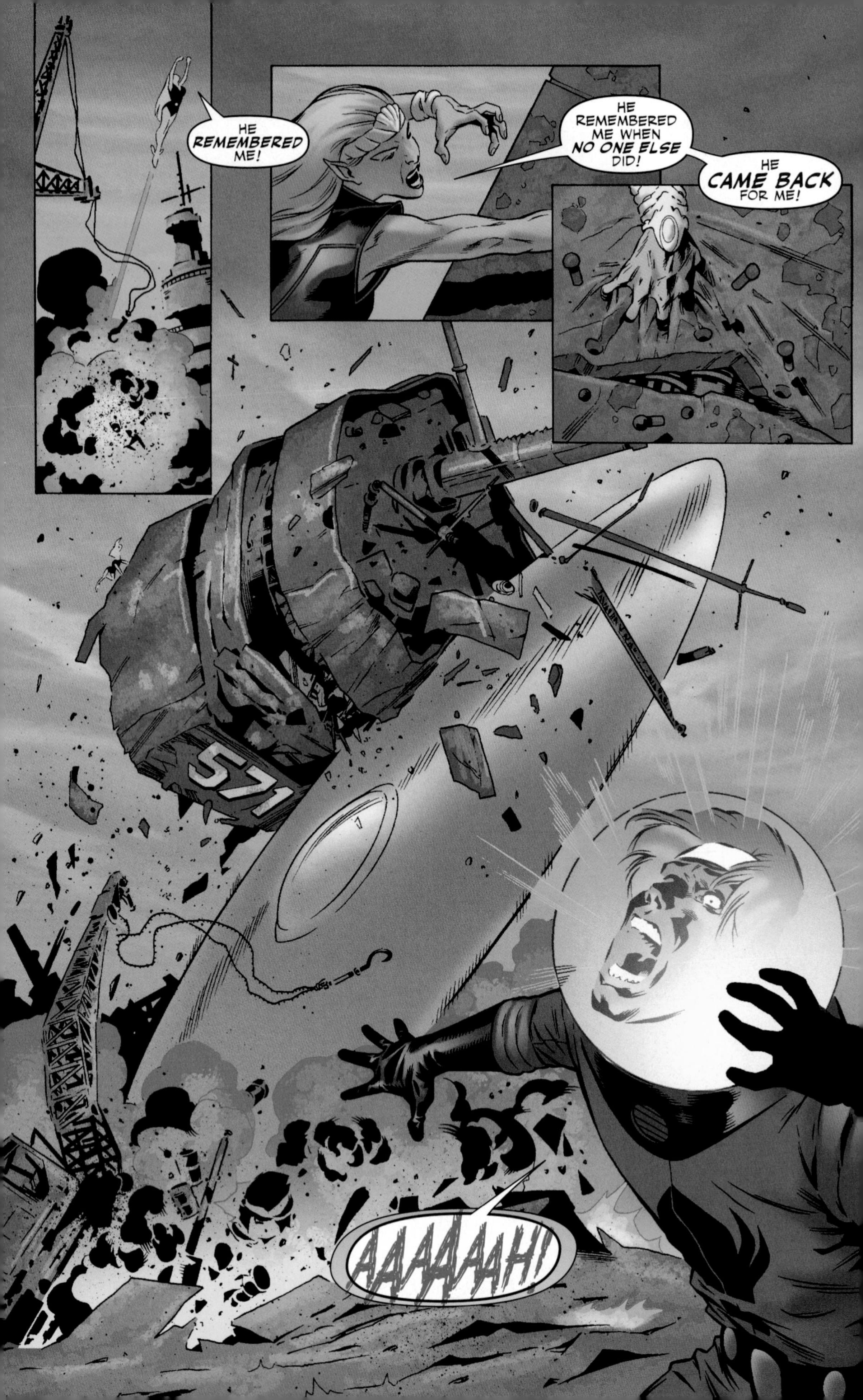
HE REMEMBERED ME!
HE REMEMBERED ME WHEN NO ONE ELSE DID!
HE CAME BACK FOR ME!
571
AAAAAAH!

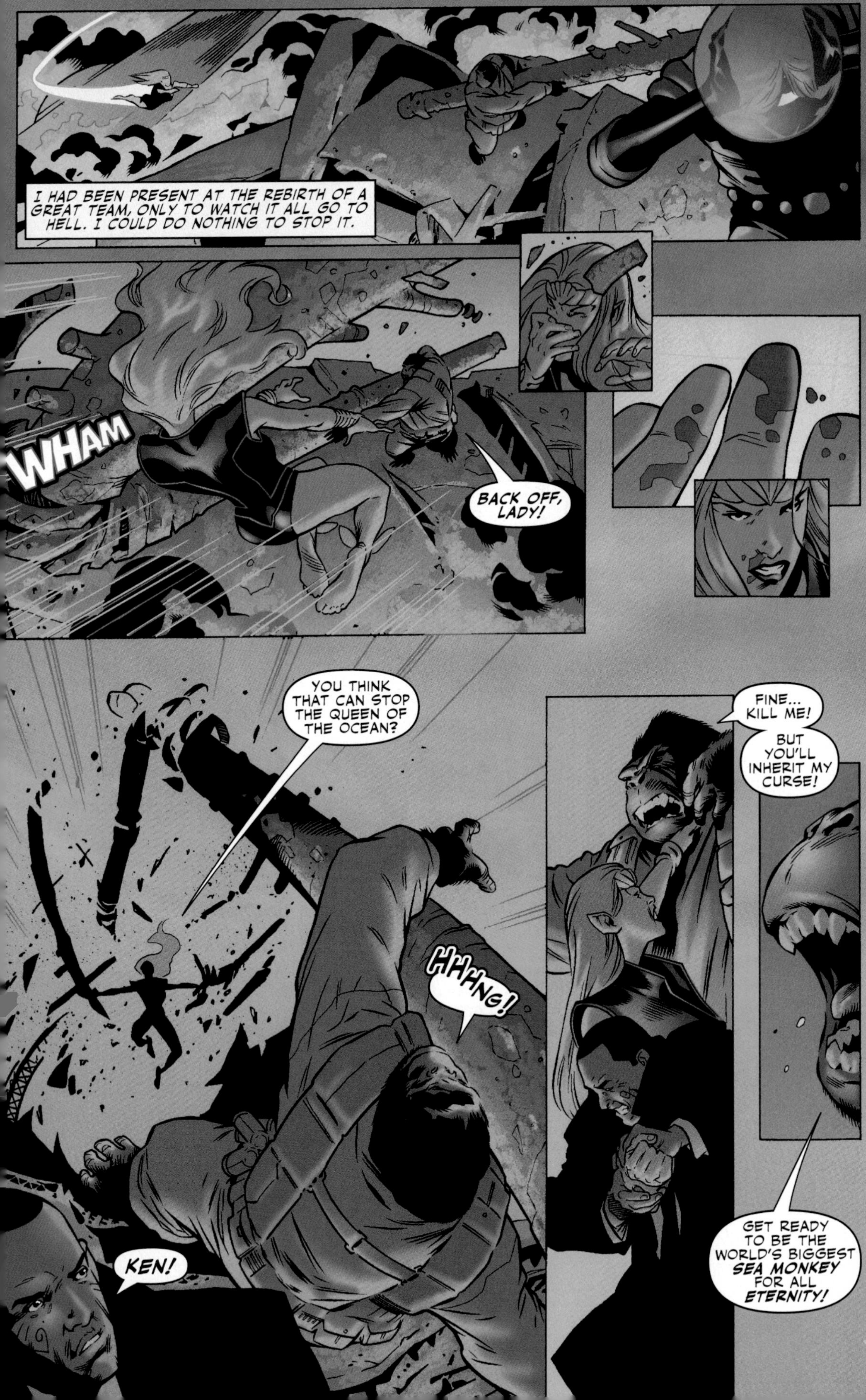
I HAD BEEN PRESENT AT THE REBIRTH OF A GREAT TEAM, ONLY TO WATCH IT ALL GO TO HELL. I COULD DO NOTHING TO STOP IT.
WHAM
BACK OFF, LADY!
YOU THINK THAT CAN STOP THE QUEEN OF THE OCEAN?
HHHNG!
KEN!
FINE... KILL ME!
BUT YOU'LL INHERIT MY CURSE!
GET READY TO BE THE WORLD'S BIGGEST SEA MONKEY FOR ALL ETERNITY!

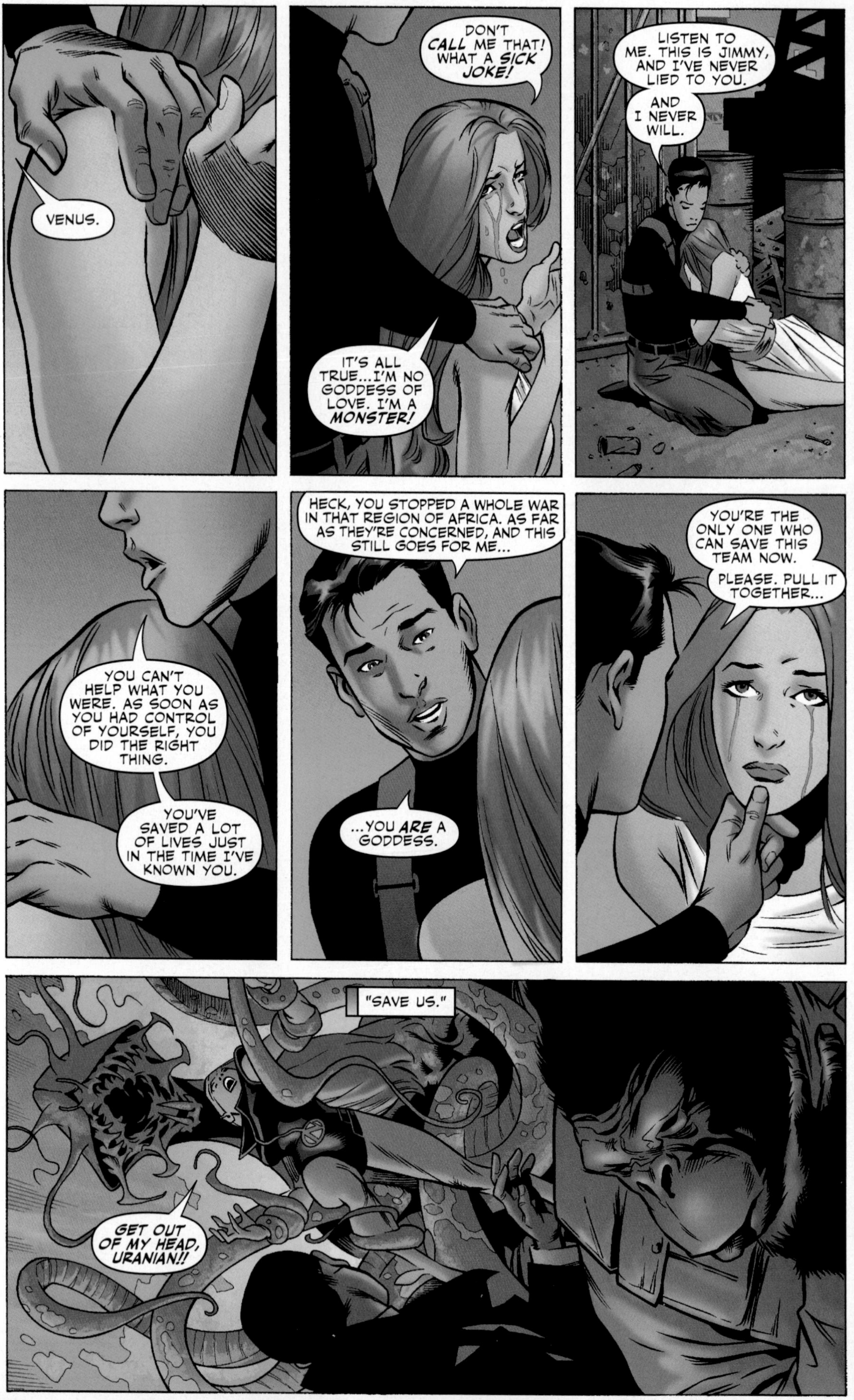
VENUS.
DON'T CALL ME THAT! WHAT A SICK JOKE!
IT'S ALL TRUE...I'M NO GODDESS OF LOVE. I'M A MONSTER!
LISTEN TO ME. THIS IS JIMMY, AND I'VE NEVER LIED TO YOU.
AND I NEVER WILL.
YOU CAN'T HELP WHAT YOU WERE. AS SOON AS YOU HAD CONTROL OF YOURSELF, YOU DID THE RIGHT THING.
YOU'VE SAVED A LOT OF LIVES JUST IN THE TIME I'VE KNOWN YOU.
HECK, YOU STOPPED A WHOLE WAR IN THAT REGION OF AFRICA. AS FAR AS THEY'RE CONCERNED, AND THIS STILL GOES FOR ME...
...YOU ARE A GODDESS.
YOU'RE THE ONLY ONE WHO CAN SAVE THIS TEAM NOW.
PLEASE. PULL IT TOGETHER...
"SAVE US."
GET OUT OF MY HEAD, URANIAN!!

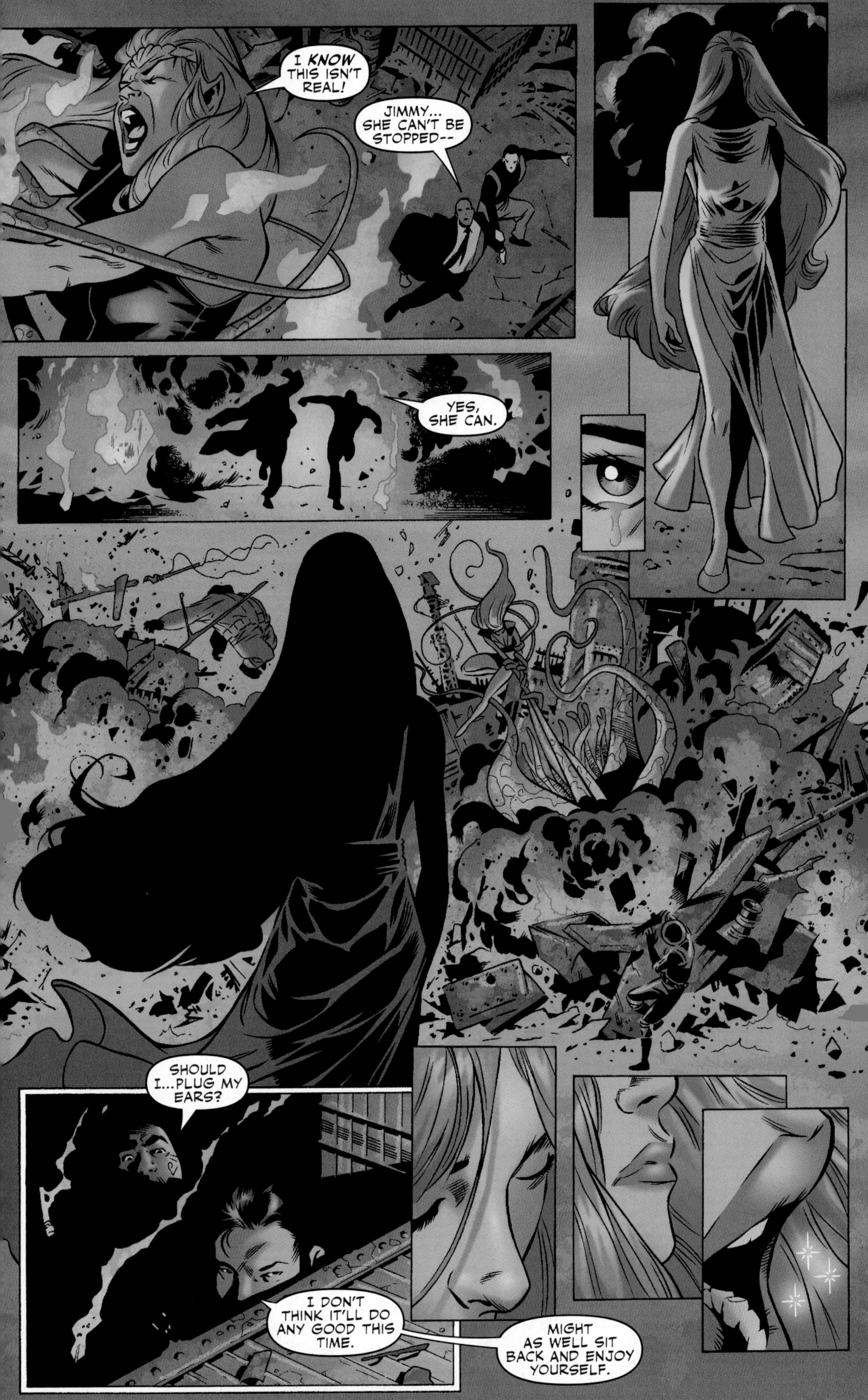
I *KNOW* THIS ISN'T REAL!
JIMMY... SHE CAN'T BE STOPPED--
YES, SHE CAN.
SHOULD I...PLUG MY EARS?
I DON'T THINK IT'LL DO ANY GOOD THIS TIME.
MIGHT AS WELL SIT BACK AND ENJOY YOURSELF.

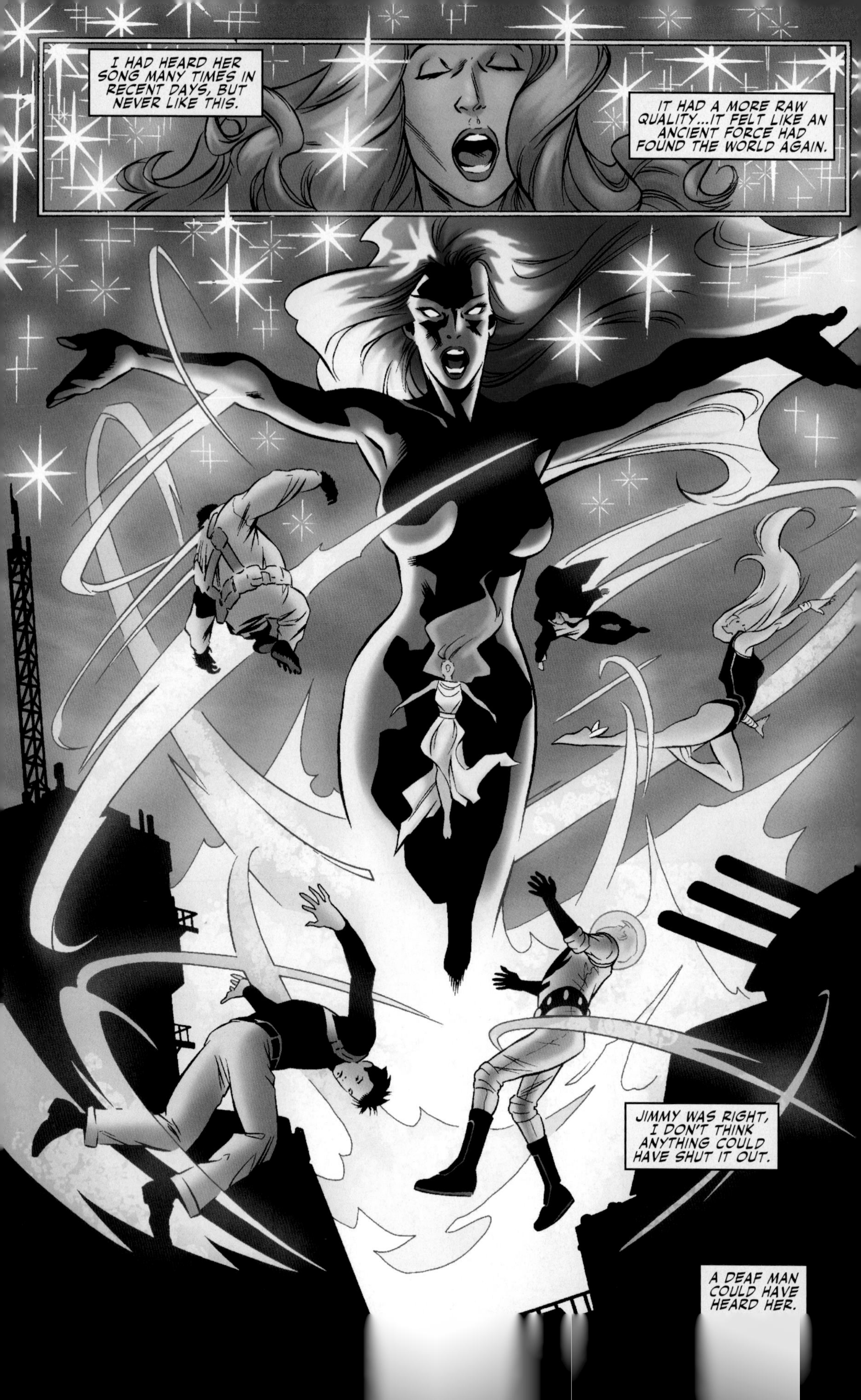
I HAD HEARD HER SONG MANY TIMES IN RECENT DAYS, BUT NEVER LIKE THIS.
IT HAD A MORE RAW QUALITY...IT FELT LIKE AN ANCIENT FORCE HAD FOUND THE WORLD AGAIN.
JIMMY WAS RIGHT, I DON'T THINK ANYTHING COULD HAVE SHUT IT OUT.
A DEAF MAN COULD HAVE HEARD HER.

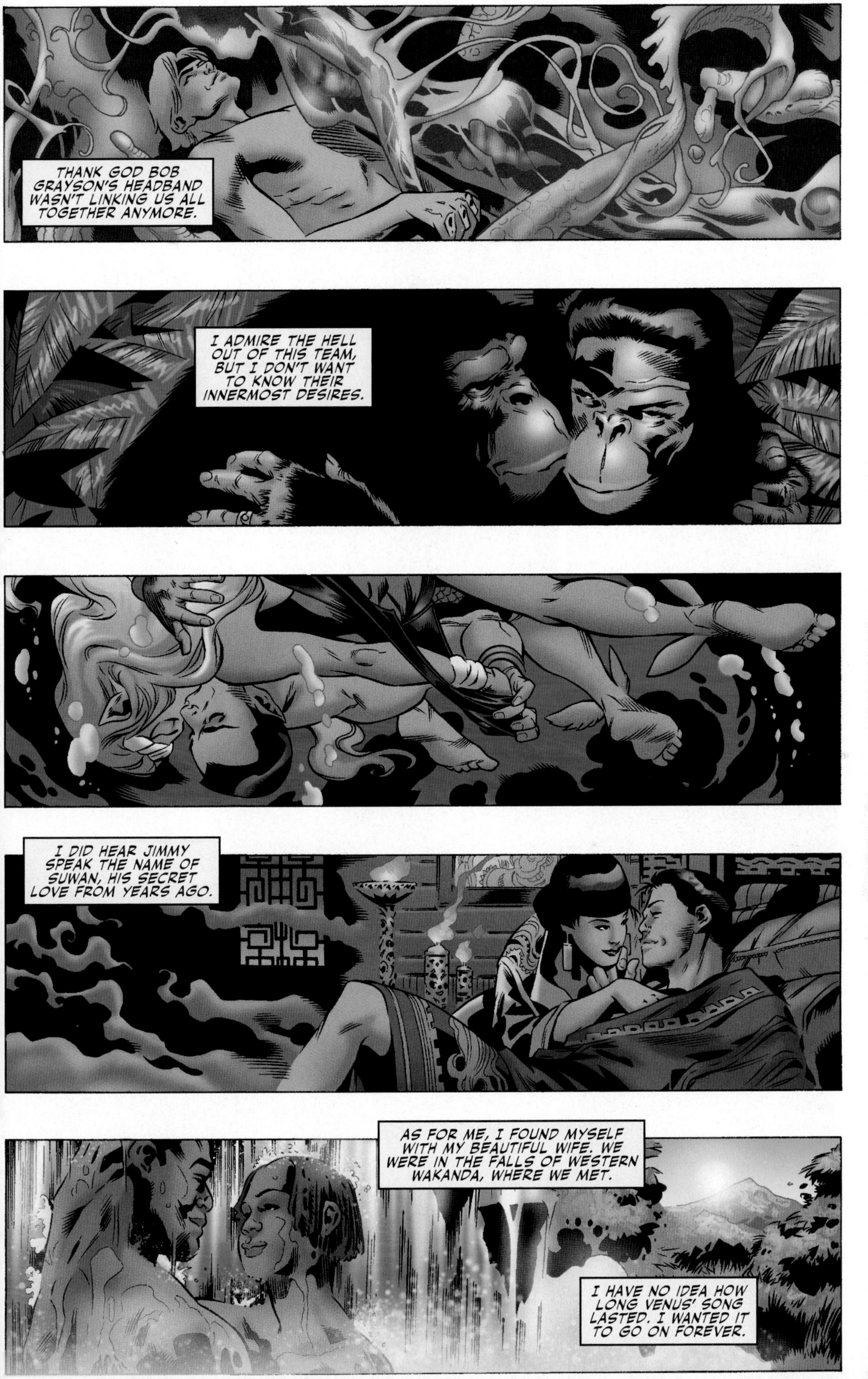
THANK GOD BOB GRAYSON'S HEADBAND WASN'T LINKING US ALL TOGETHER ANYMORE.
I ADMIRE THE HELL OUT OF THIS TEAM, BUT I DON'T WANT TO KNOW THEIR INNERMOST DESIRES.
I DID HEAR JIMMY SPEAK THE NAME OF SUWAN, HIS SECRET LOVE FROM YEARS AGO.
AS FOR ME, I FOUND MYSELF WITH MY BEAUTIFUL WIFE. WE WERE IN THE FALLS OF WESTERN WAKANDA, WHERE WE MET.
I HAVE NO IDEA HOW LONG VENUS' SONG LASTED. I WANTED IT TO GO ON FOREVER.

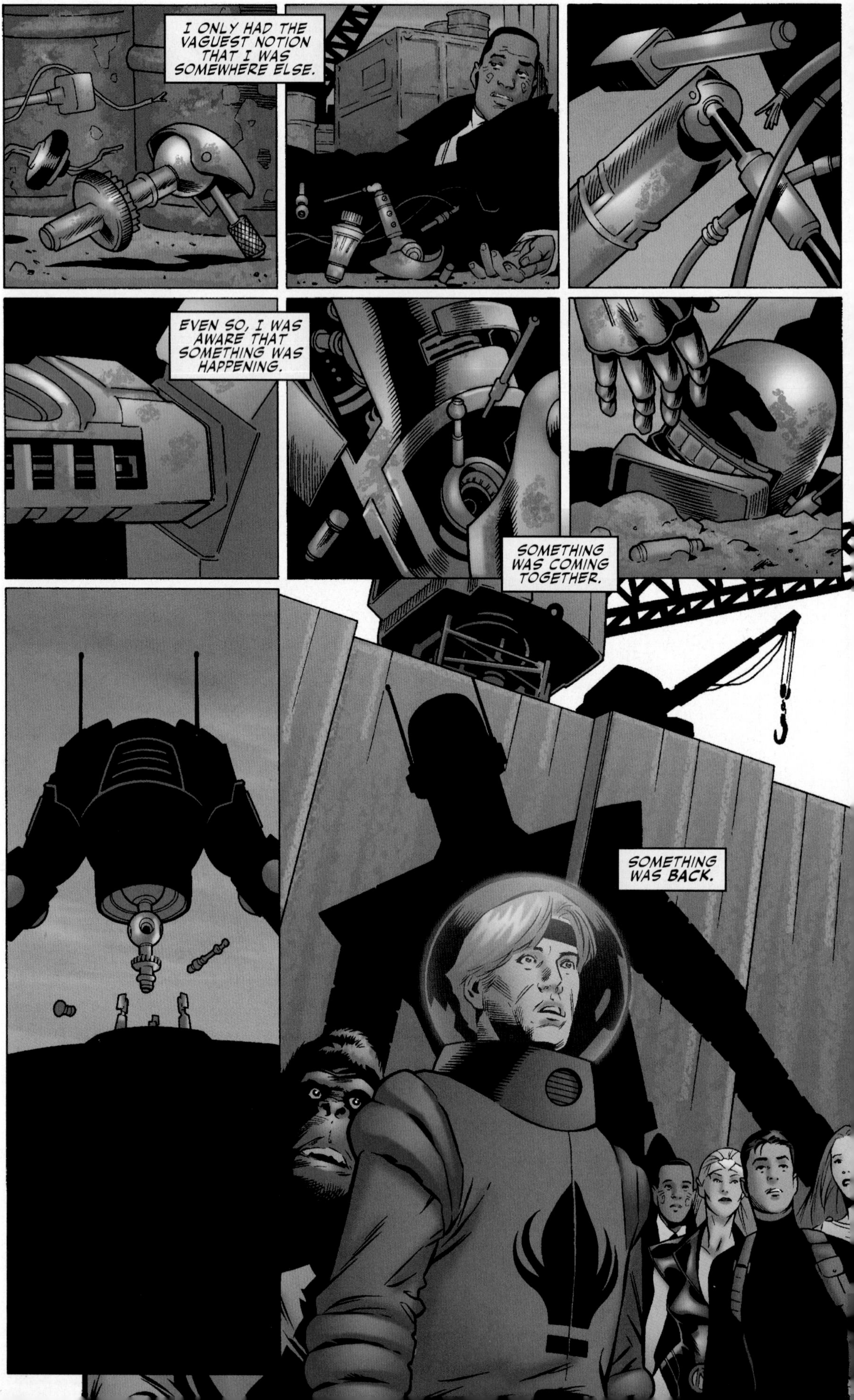
I ONLY HAD THE VAGUEST NOTION THAT I WAS SOMEWHERE ELSE.
EVEN SO, I WAS AWARE THAT SOMETHING WAS HAPPENING.
SOMETHING WAS COMING TOGETHER.
SOMETHING WAS BACK.

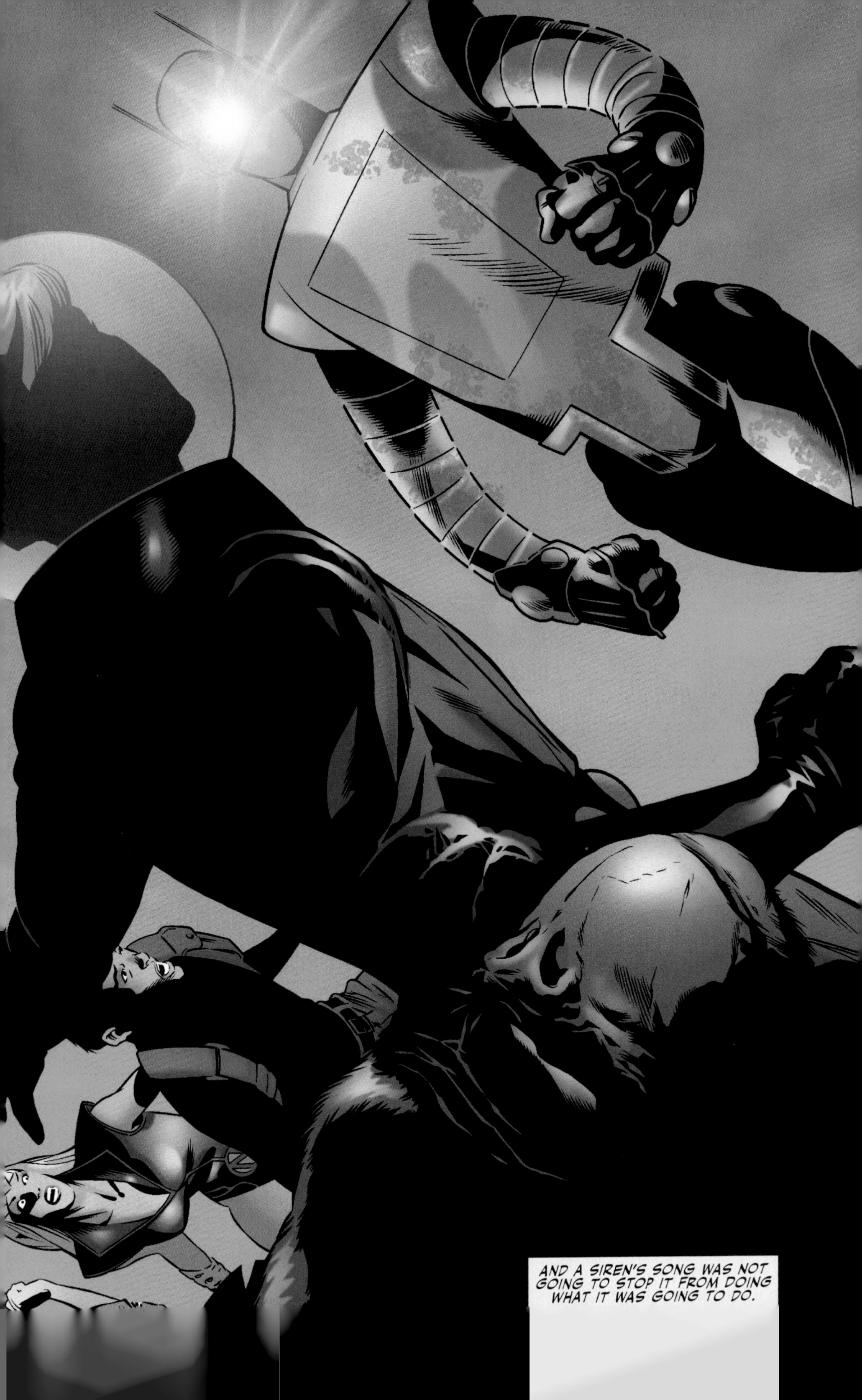
AND A SIREN'S SONG WAS NOT GOING TO STOP IT FROM DOING WHAT IT WAS GOING TO DO.

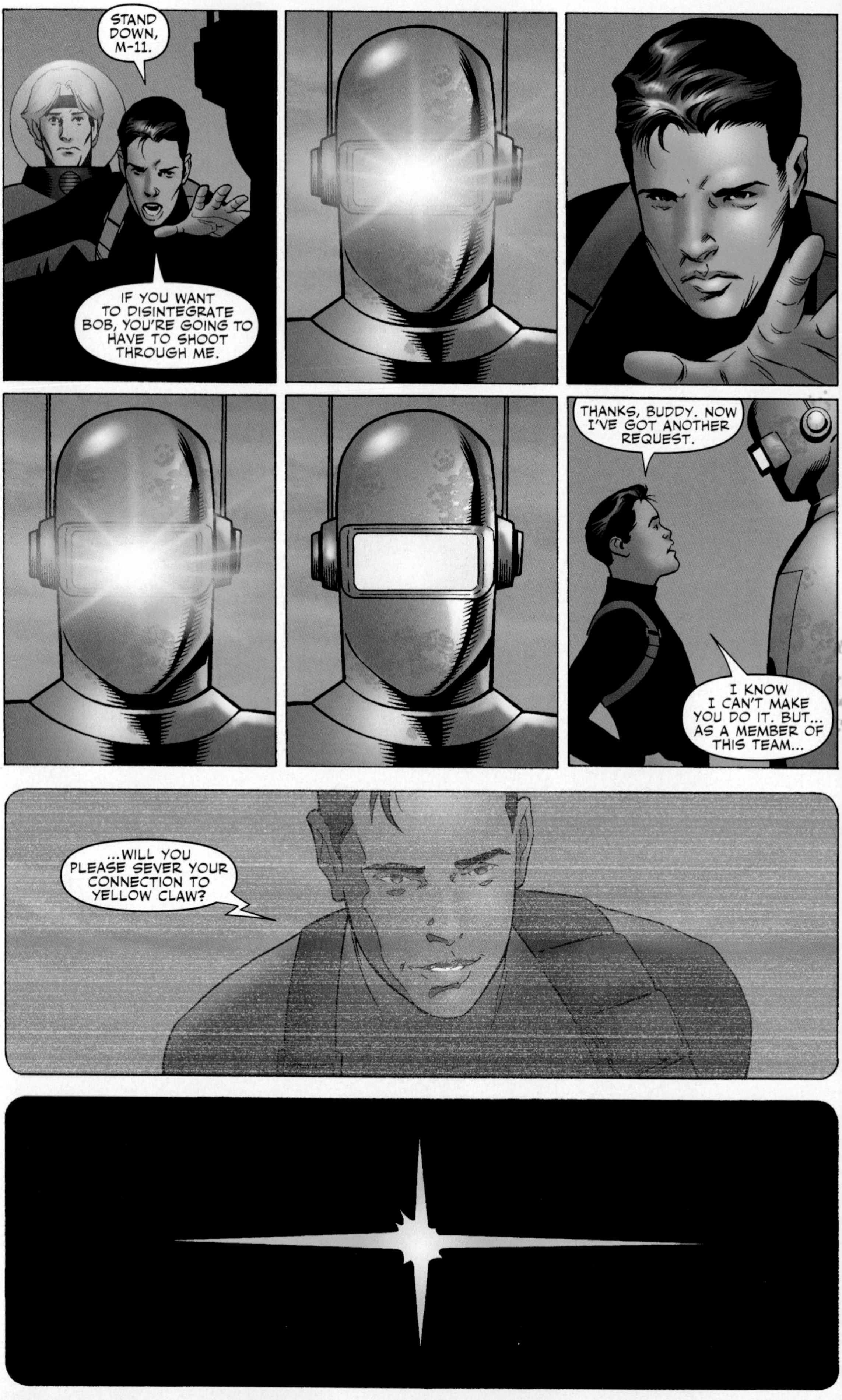
STAND DOWN, M-11.
IF YOU WANT TO DISINTEGRATE BOB, YOU'RE GOING TO HAVE TO SHOOT THROUGH ME.
THANKS, BUDDY. NOW I'VE GOT ANOTHER REQUEST.
I KNOW I CAN'T MAKE YOU DO IT. BUT... AS A MEMBER OF THIS TEAM...
...WILL YOU PLEASE SEVER YOUR CONNECTION TO YELLOW CLAW?

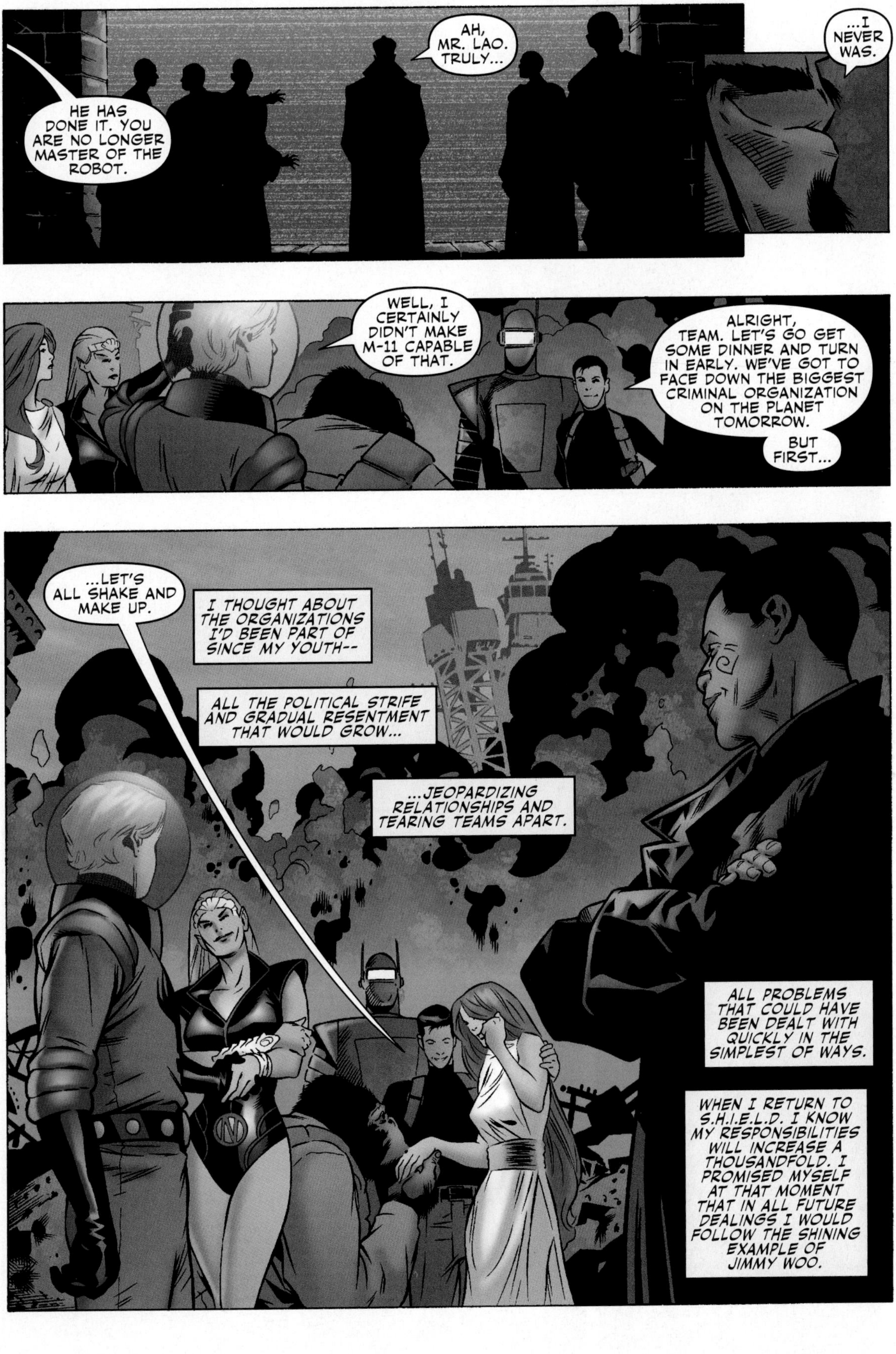
HE HAS DONE IT. YOU ARE NO LONGER MASTER OF THE ROBOT.
AH, MR. LAO. TRULY...
...I NEVER WAS.
WELL, I CERTAINLY DIDN'T MAKE M-11 CAPABLE OF THAT.
ALRIGHT, TEAM. LET'S GO GET SOME DINNER AND TURN IN EARLY. WE'VE GOT TO FACE DOWN THE BIGGEST CRIMINAL ORGANIZATION ON THE PLANET TOMORROW.
BUT FIRST...
...LET'S ALL SHAKE AND MAKE UP.
I THOUGHT ABOUT THE ORGANIZATIONS I'D BEEN PART OF SINCE MY YOUTH--
ALL THE POLITICAL STRIFE AND GRADUAL RESENTMENT THAT WOULD GROW...
...JEOPARDIZING RELATIONSHIPS AND TEARING TEAMS APART.
ALL PROBLEMS THAT COULD HAVE BEEN DEALT WITH QUICKLY IN THE SIMPLEST OF WAYS.
WHEN I RETURN TO S.H.I.E.L.D. I KNOW MY RESPONSIBILITIES WILL INCREASE A THOUSANDFOLD. I PROMISED MYSELF AT THAT MOMENT THAT IN ALL FUTURE DEALINGS I WOULD FOLLOW THE SHINING EXAMPLE OF JIMMY WOO.

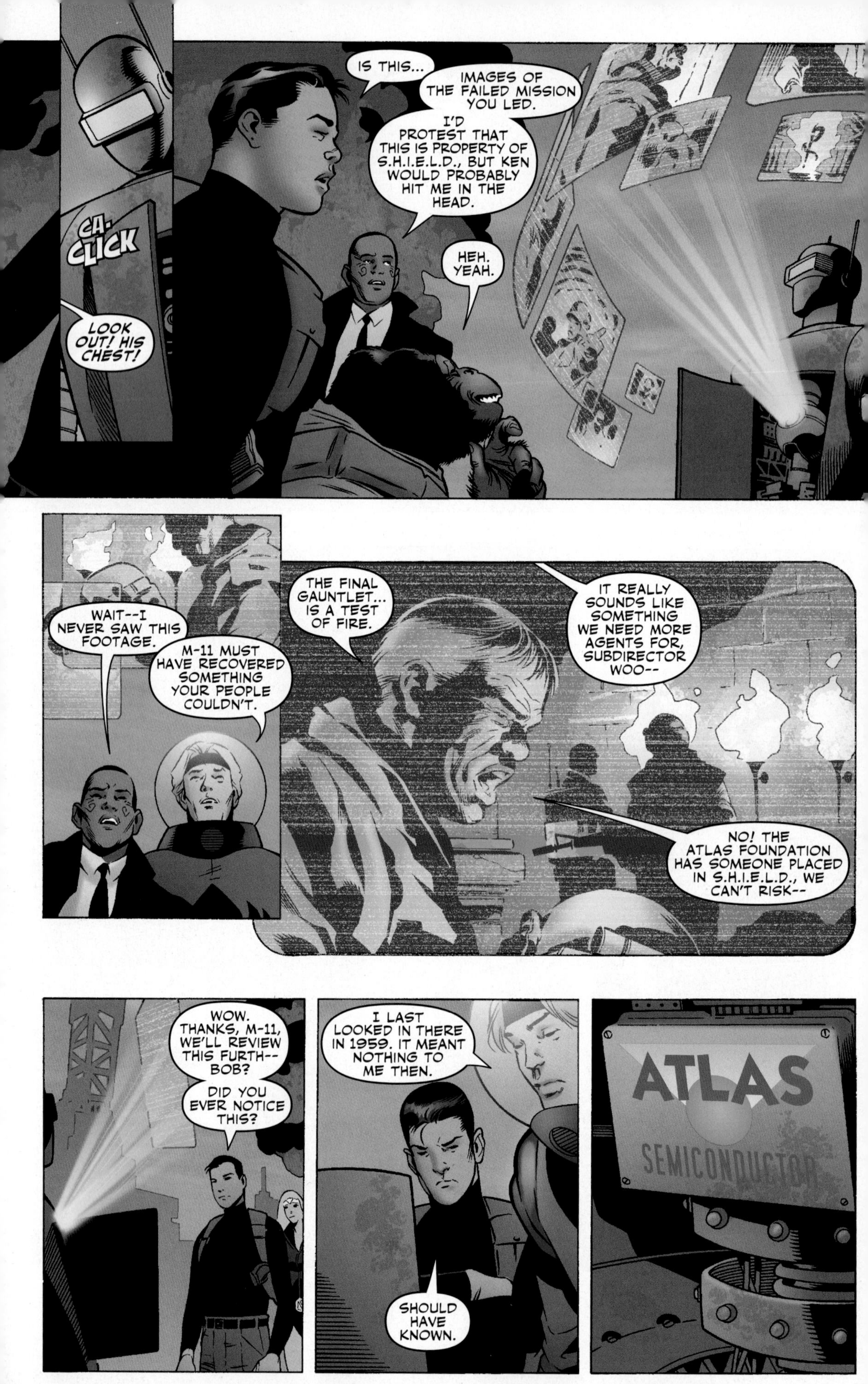
CA-CLICK
LOOK OUT! HIS CHEST!
IS THIS...
IMAGES OF THE FAILED MISSION YOU LED.
I'D PROTEST THAT THIS IS PROPERTY OF S.H.I.E.L.D., BUT KEN WOULD PROBABLY HIT ME IN THE HEAD.
HEH. YEAH.
WAIT--I NEVER SAW THIS FOOTAGE.
M-11 MUST HAVE RECOVERED SOMETHING YOUR PEOPLE COULDN'T.
THE FINAL GAUNTLET... IS A TEST OF FIRE.
IT REALLY SOUNDS LIKE SOMETHING WE NEED MORE AGENTS FOR, SUBDIRECTOR WOO--
NO! THE ATLAS FOUNDATION HAS SOMEONE PLACED IN S.H.I.E.L.D., WE CAN'T RISK--
WOW. THANKS, M-11, WE'LL REVIEW THIS FURTH-- BOB?
DID YOU EVER NOTICE THIS?
I LAST LOOKED IN THERE IN 1959. IT MEANT NOTHING TO ME THEN.
SHOULD HAVE KNOWN.
ATLAS
SEMICONDUCTOR

SHORE TO SHORE AM

WITH YOUR HOST WEBB TERRY
The Radio Call-In Show of The Unexplained

BROADCAST TRANSCRIPT: SHOW 5765-"GODS WALK AMONG US"

Webb Terry: Welcome back to hour two of tonight's show with our guest author Professor Derek Schiller, who has a new book out, "The Gods Walk Among Us." Dr. Schiller's book focuses mainly on one mythical figure in particular, though--the goddess, Venus.

Derek Schiller: That's right, Webb. I do touch upon other earthbound deities that we hear of in the news, though, like Hercules, Thor, Ares. Most people assume these are superhumans merely using the names of legends, but I'm finding more support for the idea that many are the figures from myth.

WT: But you say the woman who calls herself Venus is a bit more elusive than that?

DS: Yes. The woman I met in the late 50's and whom I've documented the most has a very sweet personality. This contradicts a lot of what Greco-Roman myths say about Venus or Aphrodite. Ancient writings give us a very temperamental figure that could be quite malicious when she wanted to. It seems night and day with the woman I write about.

WT: Guess someone could change in a few thousand years! (laughter)

DS: (laughter) Well, sure. Or we have more than one entity going by that name. A Venus interacted with the West Coast group called The Champions a few years ago. Now...Hercules was purported to have recognized this woman...

WT: Assuming he's real, that would support her existence.

DS: Yes, but no one there had interacted with the woman in these other cases I've documented. No, what I think is that maybe MY Venus is someone or something else altogether. And the Champions' woman may have been the actual Aphrodite, come to Earth, looking for who had been using her name.

WT: I would NOT want a possibly vengeful goddess on my case. (laughter)

DS: Nor I. (laughter)

WT: Let's go to the phones--east of the Rockies, we have Rich.

RICH: Hi, Webb, Dr. Schiller. I've read excerpts of your book already, and I'm wondering if this woman you describe might not be what we consider a "Nordic."

WT: Extraterrestrial with Scandinavian features, usually benevolent

DS: That's...not where my studies go, but I've been made aware of this idea by UFOlogists, and I do find it interesting that these aliens often claim to be from the planet Venus!

WT: Hmmm.

RICH: But don't you think there's a cold war being waged by the Nordics and the Grays, using our planet as--

WT: We've lost Rich. West of the Rockies, we have Dylan.

DYLAN: Hi, Webb! Now, haven't there been really frequent sightings of flying saucers in the past month? Could that connect to this Venus girl?

DS: I don't....

WT: That's more a question for Jonas Casey, tomorrow night's guest. ETs are on the rise, and Mr. Casey will explain why. Ken in San Francisco, you're on Shore to Shore!

KEN: Hi, Webb, longtime listener, first-time caller. Hey, you mentioned earlier that you saw this gal at Hunter's Point in the 50's riding in a car with a gorilla and a robot.

DS: Yes.

KEN: What. The talkin' gorilla and the robot didn't make an impression? Where's their books?

DS: Well, I describe it some more in detail, it was very--

KEN: Then they all fought a skeleton flying a Mustang a few minutes later--didja get that in there?

WT: Okay, Ken, you know our pranks rule, we're going--

DS: Wait! How do you know about the skeleton fight!? Do you know this group--have you seen her??

KEN: Aw, calm down, you'll see her again. Ooh--hey, *Iron Chef*'s on. Gotta go!

DS: Wait! Sir! Ken, wait!

KEN: Oh, one more thing, Webb--the Patterson footage? That's me walking by the woods. Alright, later, guys!

(hangs up)

DS: NO!!! Please, call back!

WT: We're going to take a station break, you're listening to Shore to Shore AM!

END OF TRANSCRIPT

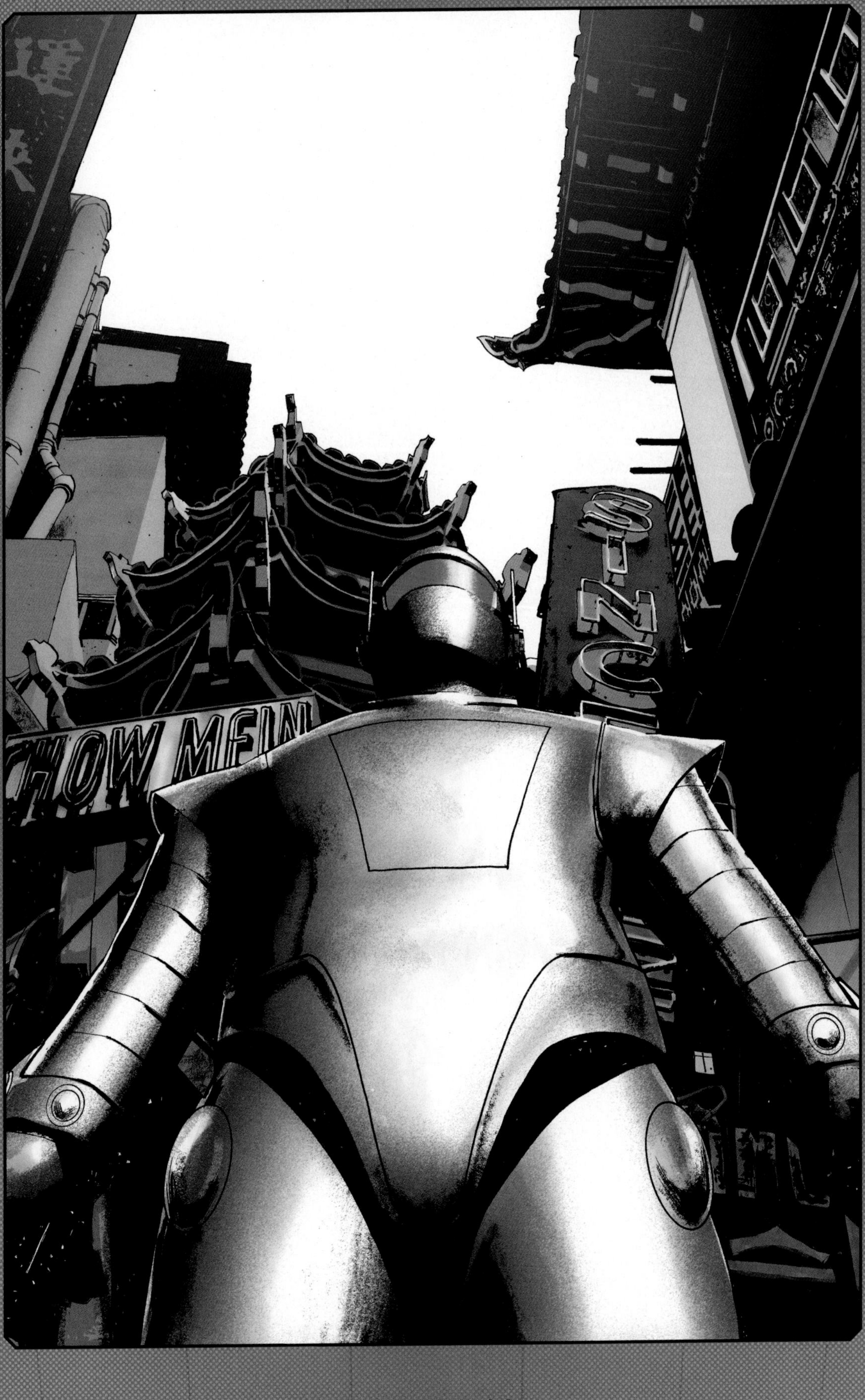
CHOW MEIN

AGENTS OF ATLAS (2006) 6

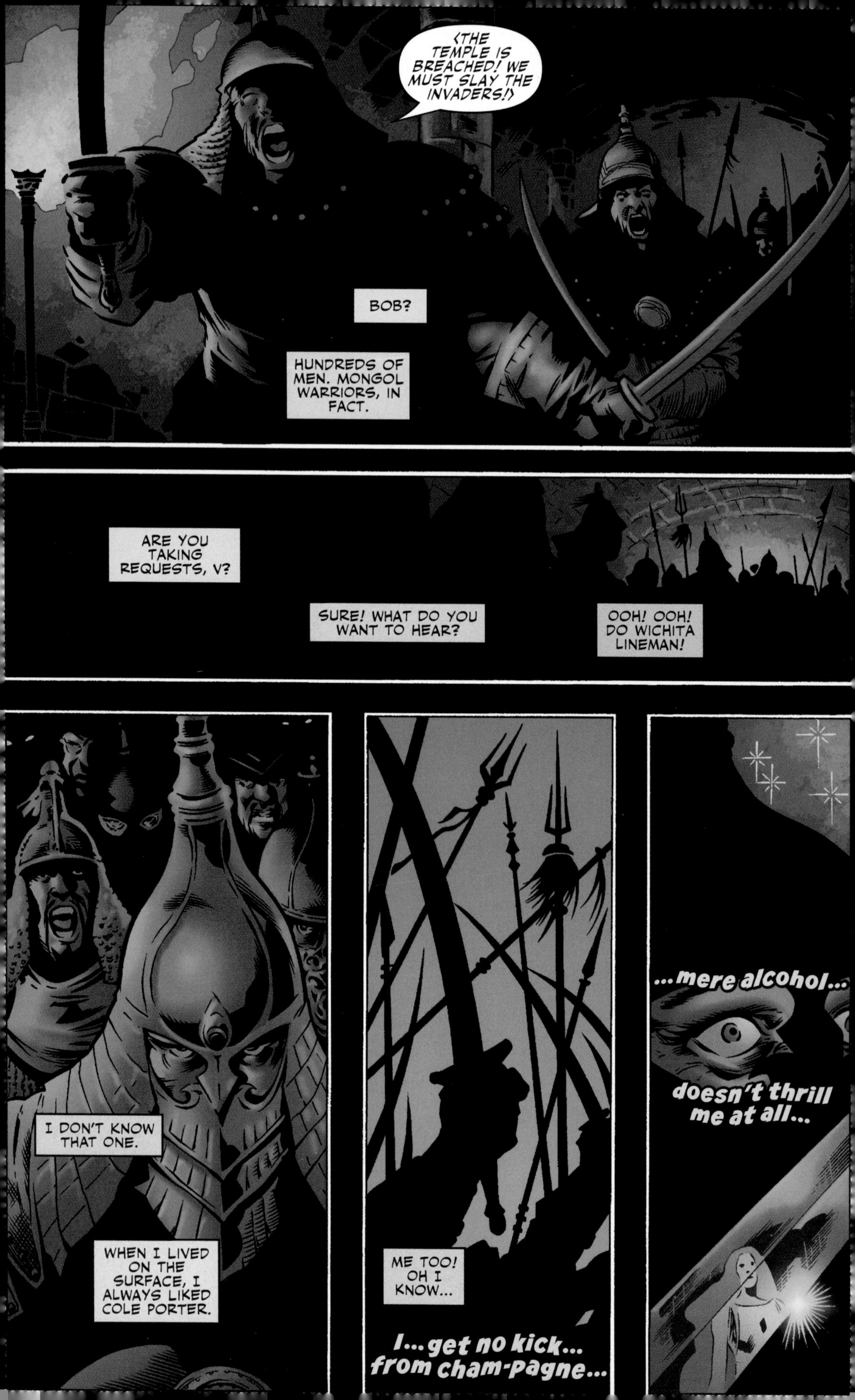
‹THE TEMPLE IS BREACHED! WE MUST SLAY THE INVADERS!›
BOB?
HUNDREDS OF MEN. MONGOL WARRIORS, IN FACT.
ARE YOU TAKING REQUESTS, V?
SURE! WHAT DO YOU WANT TO HEAR?
OOH! OOH! DO WICHITA LINEMAN!
I DON'T KNOW THAT ONE.
WHEN I LIVED ON THE SURFACE, I ALWAYS LIKED COLE PORTER.
ME TOO! OH I KNOW...
I...get no kick... from cham-pagne...
...mere alcohol...
doesn't thrill me at all...

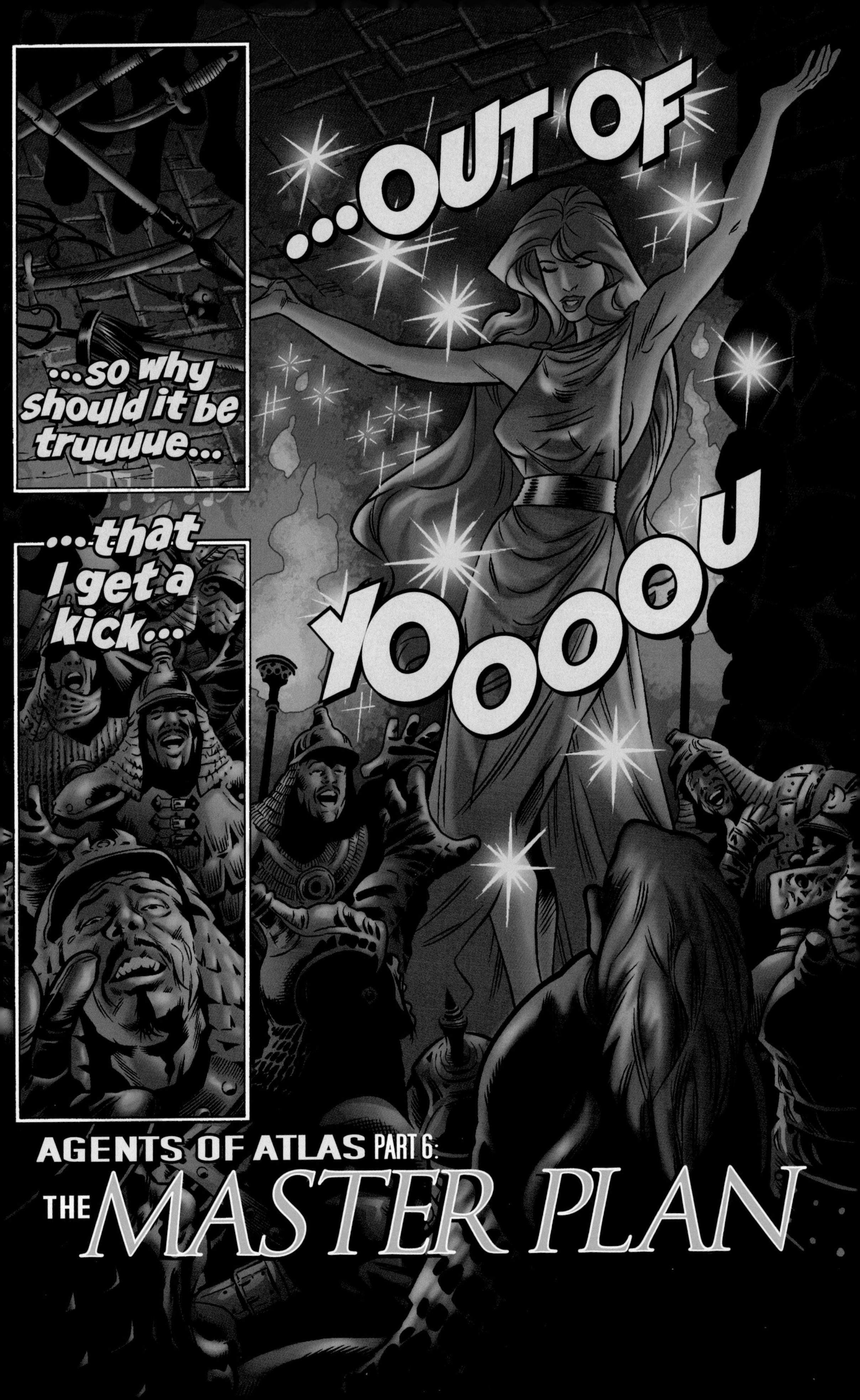
...so why should it be truuuue...
...that I get a kick...
...OUT OF YOOOOOU
AGENTS OF ATLAS PART 6:
THE MASTER PLAN

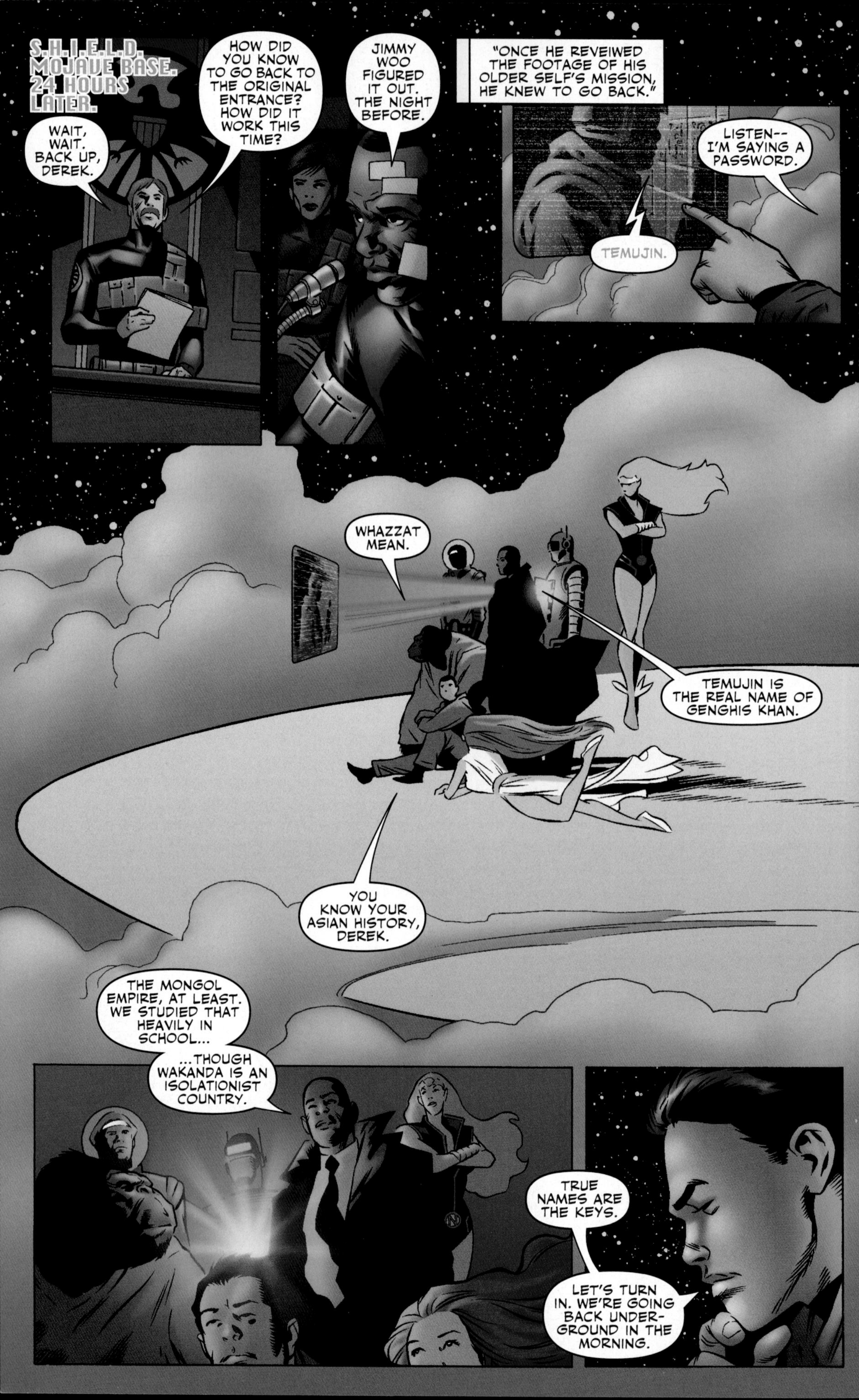
S.H.I.E.L.D. MOJAVE BASE. 24 HOURS LATER.
WAIT, WAIT. BACK UP, DEREK.
HOW DID YOU KNOW TO GO BACK TO THE ORIGINAL ENTRANCE? HOW DID IT WORK THIS TIME?
JIMMY WOO FIGURED IT OUT. THE NIGHT BEFORE.
"ONCE HE REVEIWED THE FOOTAGE OF HIS OLDER SELF'S MISSION, HE KNEW TO GO BACK."
LISTEN-- I'M SAYING A PASSWORD.
TEMUJIN.
WHAZZAT MEAN.
TEMUJIN IS THE REAL NAME OF GENGHIS KHAN.
YOU KNOW YOUR ASIAN HISTORY, DEREK.
THE MONGOL EMPIRE, AT LEAST. WE STUDIED THAT HEAVILY IN SCHOOL...
...THOUGH WAKANDA IS AN ISOLATIONIST COUNTRY.
TRUE NAMES ARE THE KEYS.
LET'S TURN IN. WE'RE GOING BACK UNDER-GROUND IN THE MORNING.

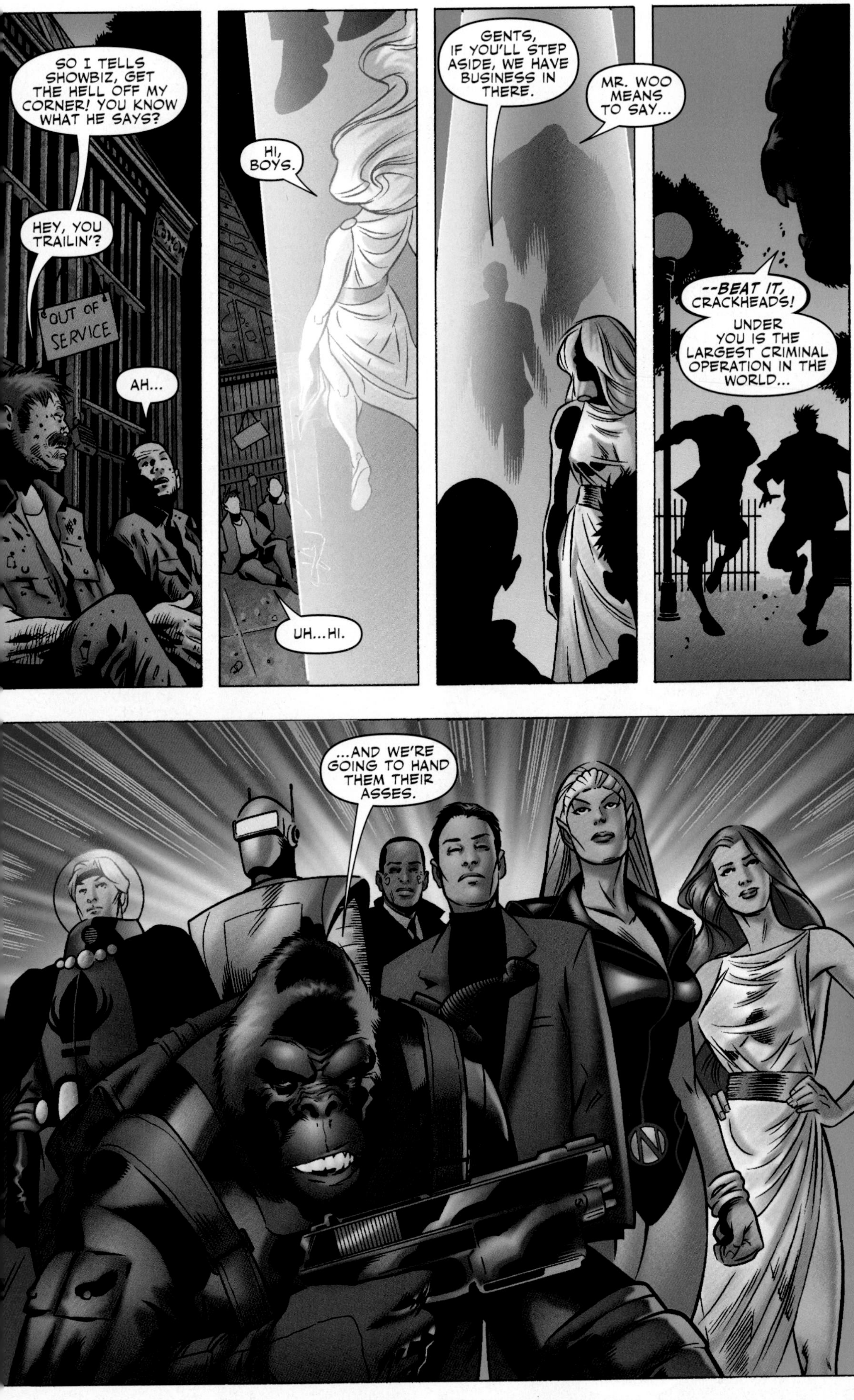
SO I TELLS SHOWBIZ, GET THE HELL OFF MY CORNER! YOU KNOW WHAT HE SAYS?
HEY, YOU TRAILIN'?
OUT OF SERVICE
AH...
HI, BOYS.
UH...HI.
GENTS, IF YOU'LL STEP ASIDE, WE HAVE BUSINESS IN THERE.
MR. WOO MEANS TO SAY...
--BEAT IT, CRACKHEADS!
UNDER YOU IS THE LARGEST CRIMINAL OPERATION IN THE WORLD...
...AND WE'RE GOING TO HAND THEM THEIR ASSES.

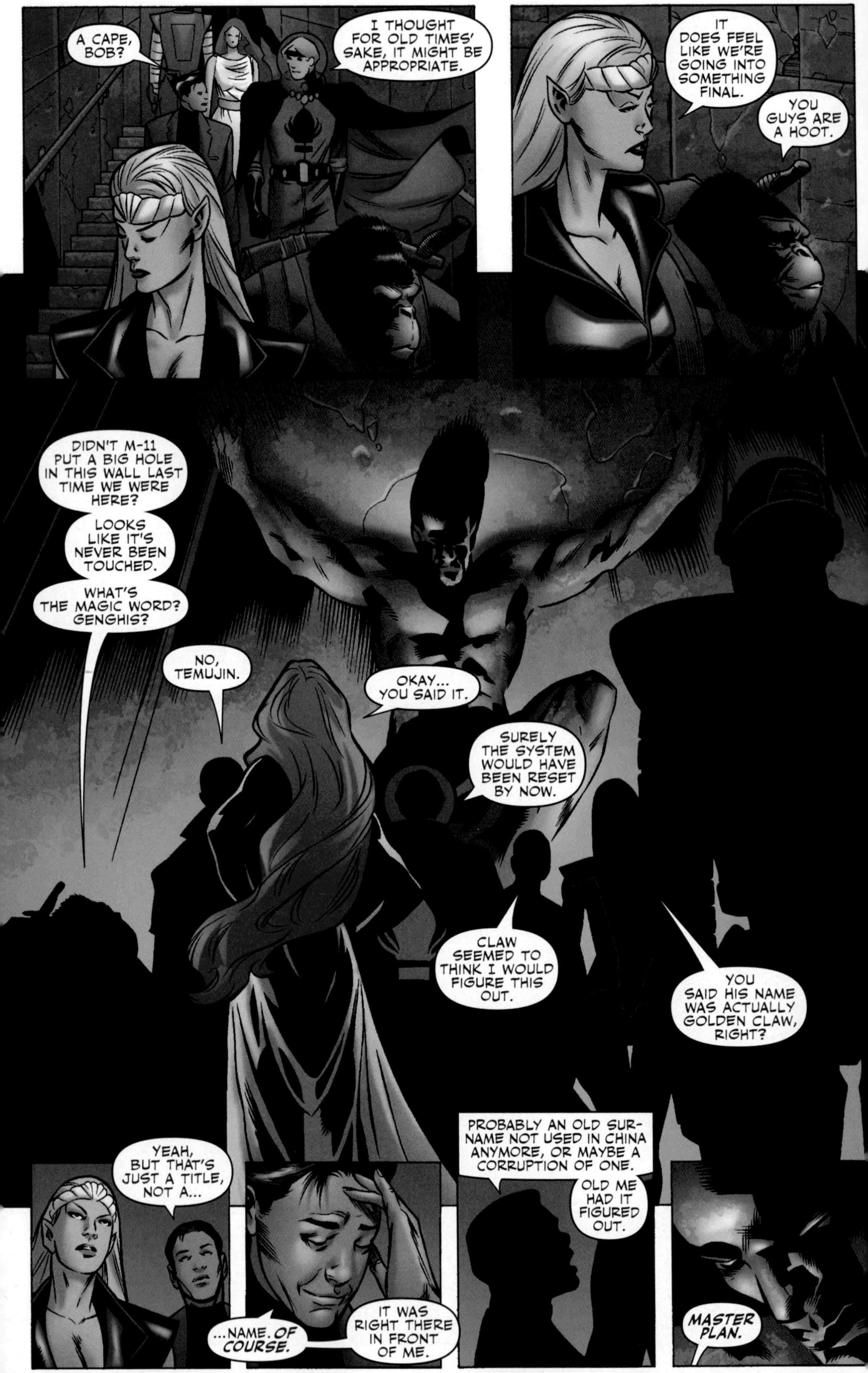
A CAPE, BOB?
I THOUGHT FOR OLD TIMES' SAKE, IT MIGHT BE APPROPRIATE.
IT DOES FEEL LIKE WE'RE GOING INTO SOMETHING FINAL.
YOU GUYS ARE A HOOT.
DIDN'T M-11 PUT A BIG HOLE IN THIS WALL LAST TIME WE WERE HERE?
LOOKS LIKE IT'S NEVER BEEN TOUCHED.
WHAT'S THE MAGIC WORD? GENGHIS?
NO, TEMUJIN.
OKAY... YOU SAID IT.
SURELY THE SYSTEM WOULD HAVE BEEN RESET BY NOW.
CLAW SEEMED TO THINK I WOULD FIGURE THIS OUT.
YOU SAID HIS NAME WAS ACTUALLY GOLDEN CLAW, RIGHT?
YEAH, BUT THAT'S JUST A TITLE, NOT A...
...NAME. OF COURSE.
IT WAS RIGHT THERE IN FRONT OF ME.
PROBABLY AN OLD SURNAME NOT USED IN CHINA ANYMORE, OR MAYBE A CORRUPTION OF ONE.
OLD ME HAD IT FIGURED OUT.
MASTER PLAN.

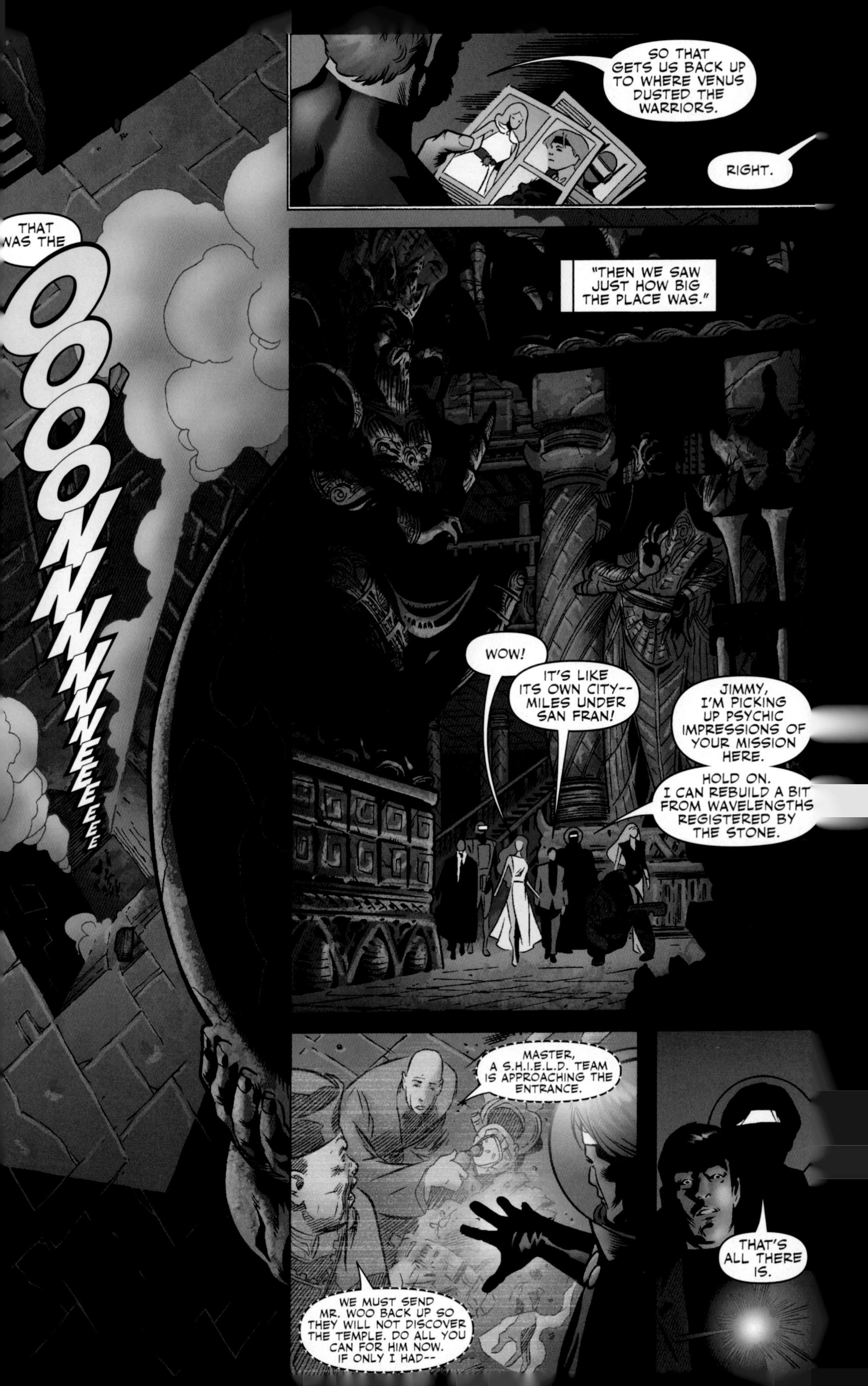

THAT WAS THE
OOOONNNNNEEEEEE
SO THAT GETS US BACK UP TO WHERE VENUS DUSTED THE WARRIORS.
RIGHT.
"THEN WE SAW JUST HOW BIG THE PLACE WAS."
WOW!
IT'S LIKE ITS OWN CITY-- MILES UNDER SAN FRAN!
JIMMY, I'M PICKING UP PSYCHIC IMPRESSIONS OF YOUR MISSION HERE.
HOLD ON. I CAN REBUILD A BIT FROM WAVELENGTHS REGISTERED BY THE STONE.
MASTER, A S.H.I.E.L.D. TEAM IS APPROACHING THE ENTRANCE.
WE MUST SEND MR. WOO BACK UP SO THEY WILL NOT DISCOVER THE TEMPLE. DO ALL YOU CAN FOR HIM NOW. IF ONLY I HAD--
THAT'S ALL THERE IS.

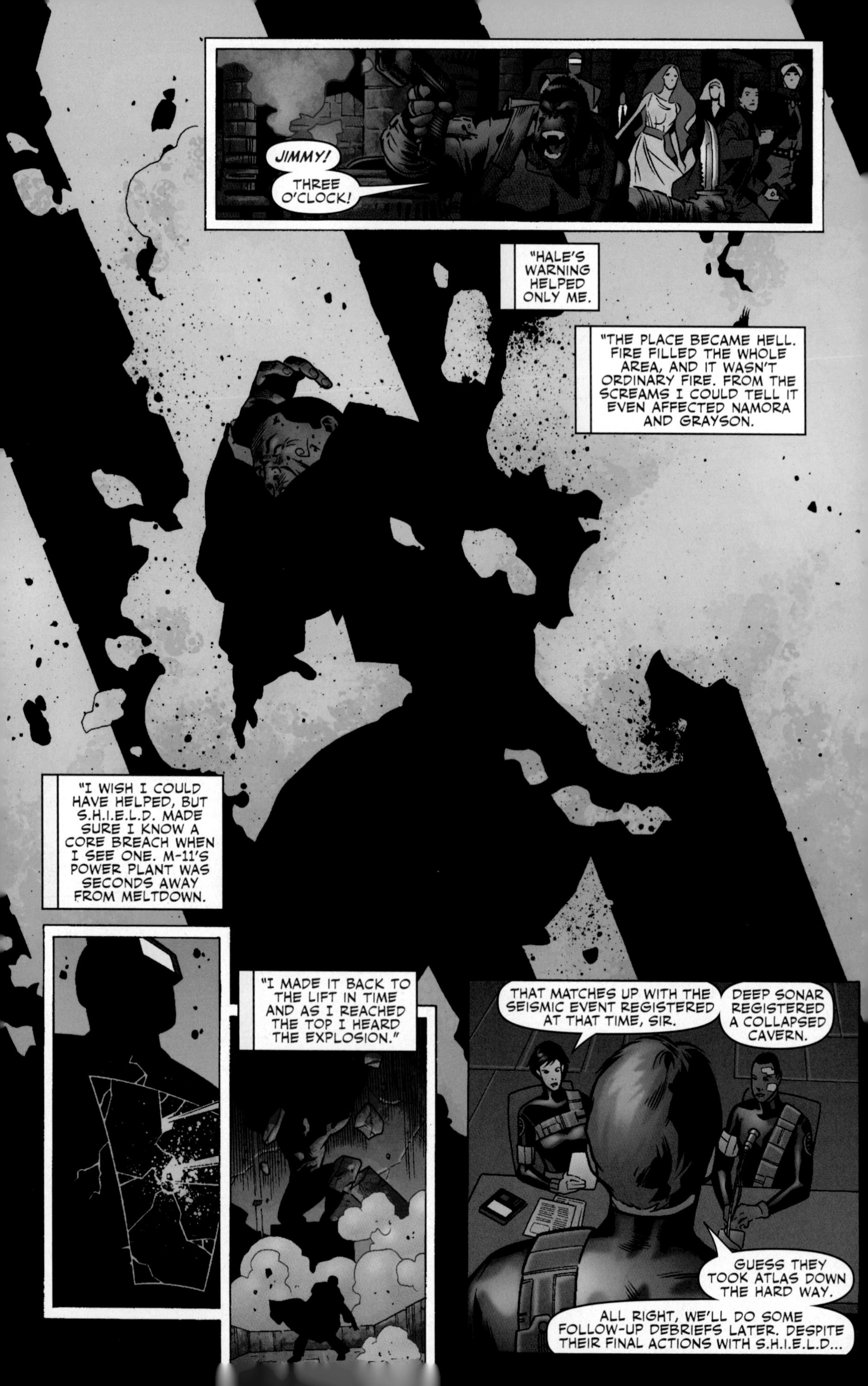
JIMMY!
THREE O'CLOCK!
"HALE'S WARNING HELPED ONLY ME.
"THE PLACE BECAME HELL. FIRE FILLED THE WHOLE AREA, AND IT WASN'T ORDINARY FIRE. FROM THE SCREAMS I COULD TELL IT EVEN AFFECTED NAMORA AND GRAYSON.
"I WISH I COULD HAVE HELPED, BUT S.H.I.E.L.D. MADE SURE I KNOW A CORE BREACH WHEN I SEE ONE. M-11'S POWER PLANT WAS SECONDS AWAY FROM MELTDOWN.
"I MADE IT BACK TO THE LIFT IN TIME AND AS I REACHED THE TOP I HEARD THE EXPLOSION."
THAT MATCHES UP WITH THE SEISMIC EVENT REGISTERED AT THAT TIME, SIR.
DEEP SONAR REGISTERED A COLLAPSED CAVERN.
GUESS THEY TOOK ATLAS DOWN THE HARD WAY.
ALL RIGHT, WE'LL DO SOME FOLLOW-UP DEBRIEFS LATER. DESPITE THEIR FINAL ACTIONS WITH S.H.I.E.L.D...

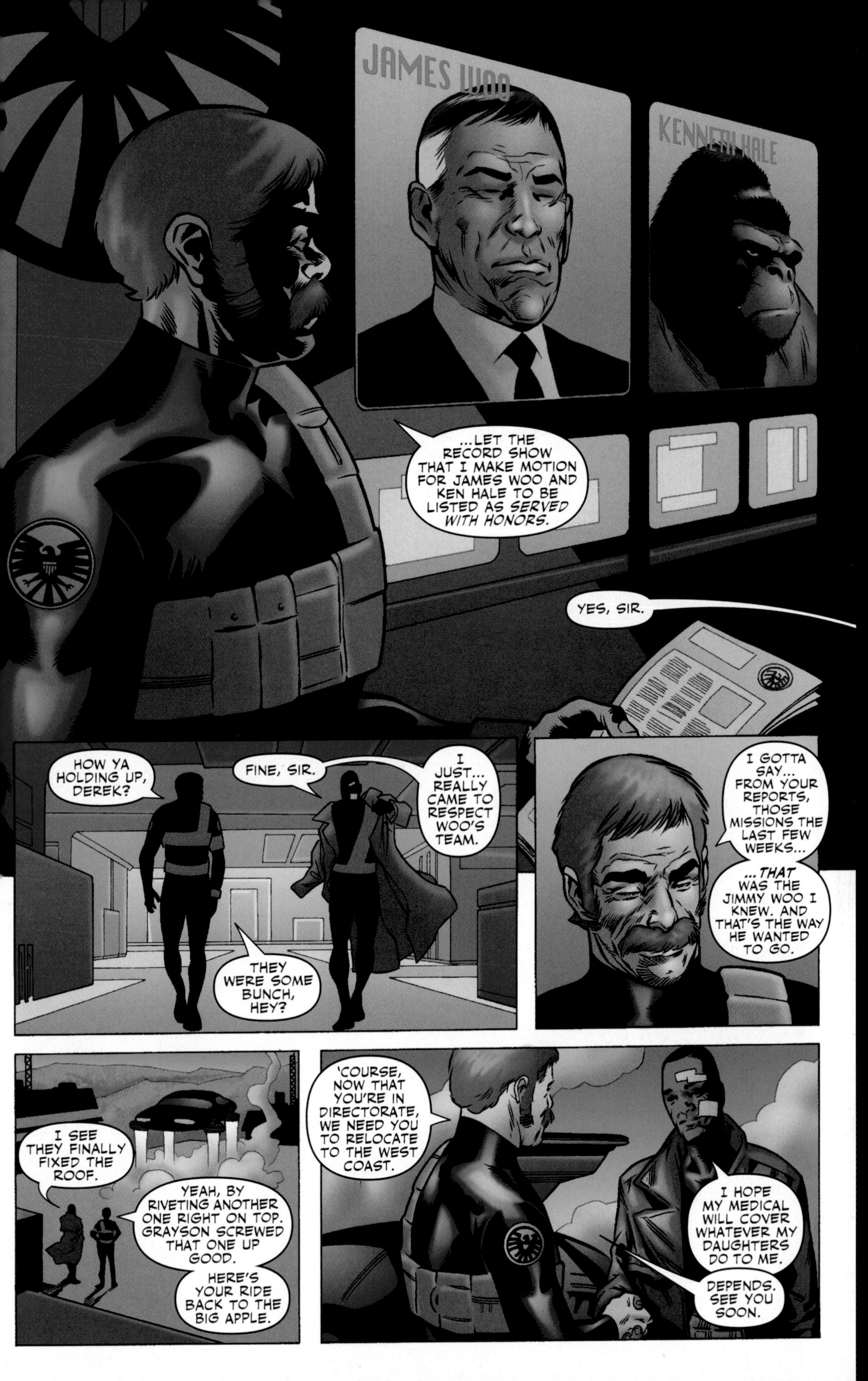
JAMES WOO
KENNETH HALE
...LET THE RECORD SHOW THAT I MAKE MOTION FOR JAMES WOO AND KEN HALE TO BE LISTED AS *SERVED WITH HONORS.*
YES, SIR.
HOW YA HOLDING UP, DEREK?
FINE, SIR.
I JUST... REALLY CAME TO RESPECT WOO'S TEAM.
THEY WERE SOME BUNCH, HEY?
I GOTTA SAY... FROM YOUR REPORTS, THOSE MISSIONS THE LAST FEW WEEKS...
...*THAT* WAS THE JIMMY WOO I KNEW. AND THAT'S THE WAY HE WANTED TO GO.
I SEE THEY FINALLY FIXED THE ROOF.
YEAH, BY RIVETING ANOTHER ONE RIGHT ON TOP. GRAYSON SCREWED THAT ONE UP GOOD.
HERE'S YOUR RIDE BACK TO THE BIG APPLE.
'COURSE, NOW THAT YOU'RE IN DIRECTORATE, WE NEED YOU TO RELOCATE TO THE WEST COAST.
I HOPE MY MEDICAL WILL COVER WHATEVER MY DAUGHTERS DO TO ME.
DEPENDS. SEE YOU SOON.

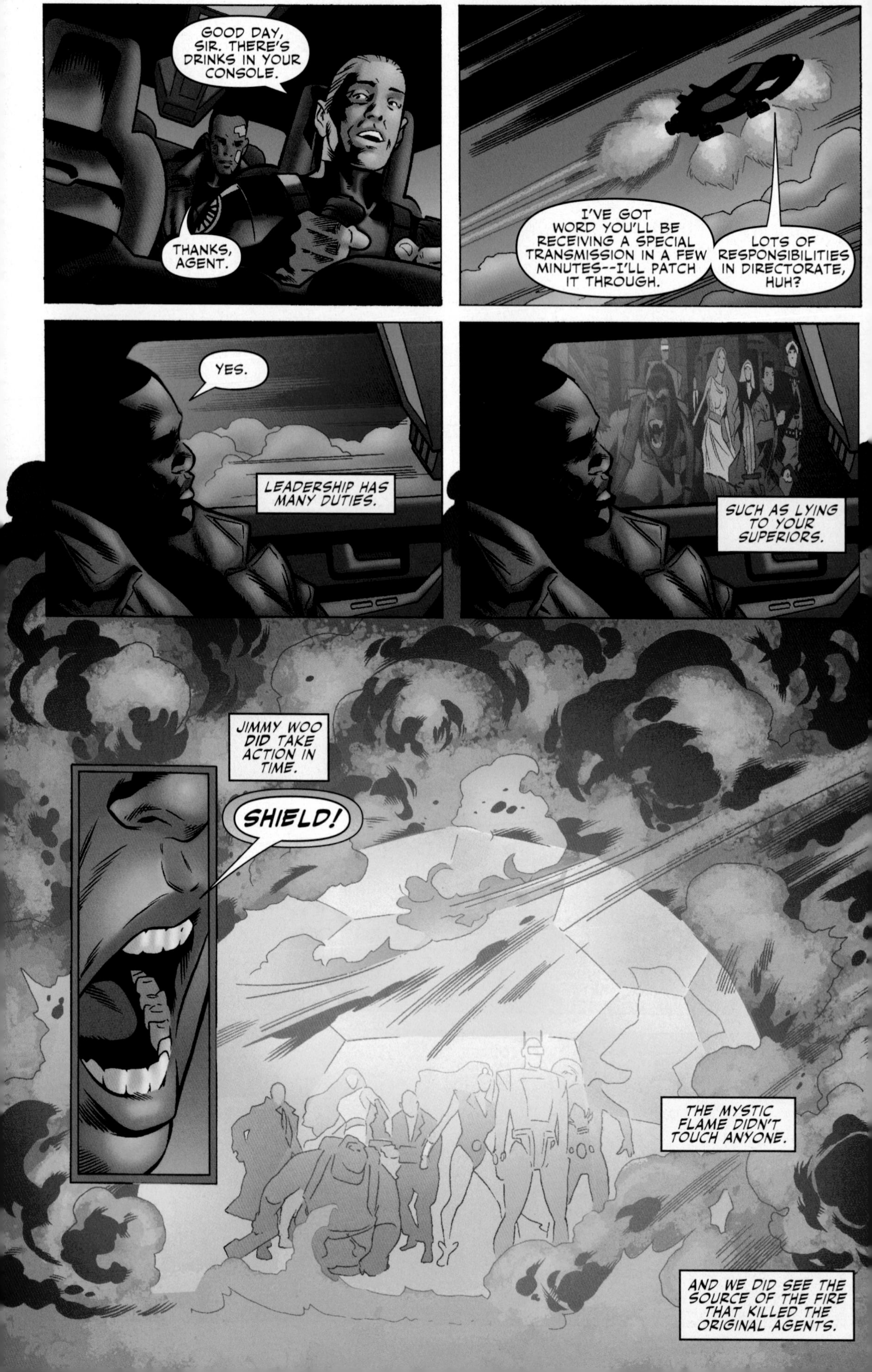
GOOD DAY, SIR. THERE'S DRINKS IN YOUR CONSOLE.
THANKS, AGENT.
I'VE GOT WORD YOU'LL BE RECEIVING A SPECIAL TRANSMISSION IN A FEW MINUTES--I'LL PATCH IT THROUGH.
LOTS OF RESPONSIBILITIES IN DIRECTORATE, HUH?
YES.
LEADERSHIP HAS MANY DUTIES.
SUCH AS LYING TO YOUR SUPERIORS.
JIMMY WOO DID TAKE ACTION IN TIME.
SHIELD!
THE MYSTIC FLAME DIDN'T TOUCH ANYONE.
AND WE DID SEE THE SOURCE OF THE FIRE THAT KILLED THE ORIGINAL AGENTS.

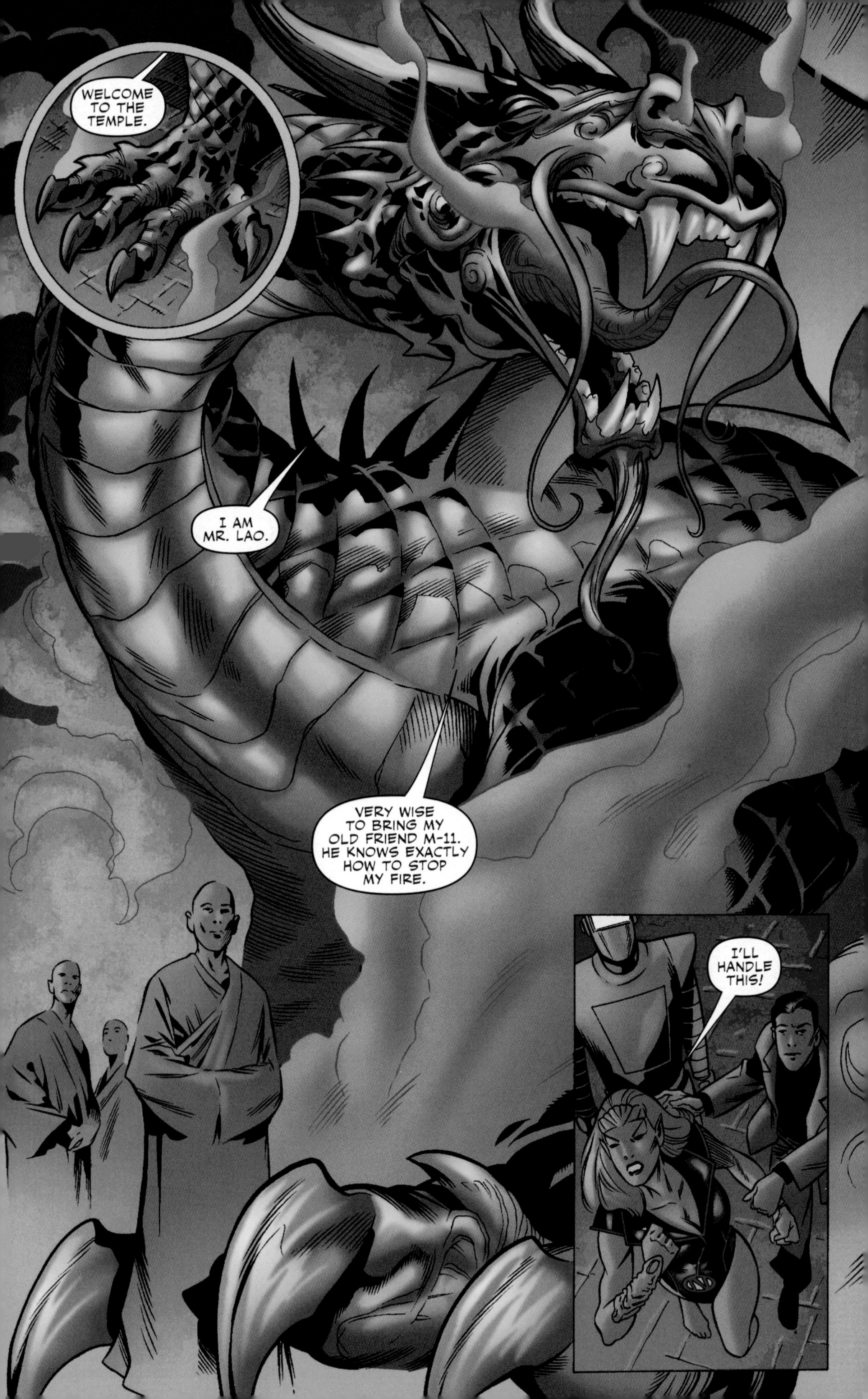
WELCOME TO THE TEMPLE.
I AM MR. LAO.
VERY WISE TO BRING MY OLD FRIEND M-11. HE KNOWS EXACTLY HOW TO STOP MY FIRE.
I'LL HANDLE THIS!

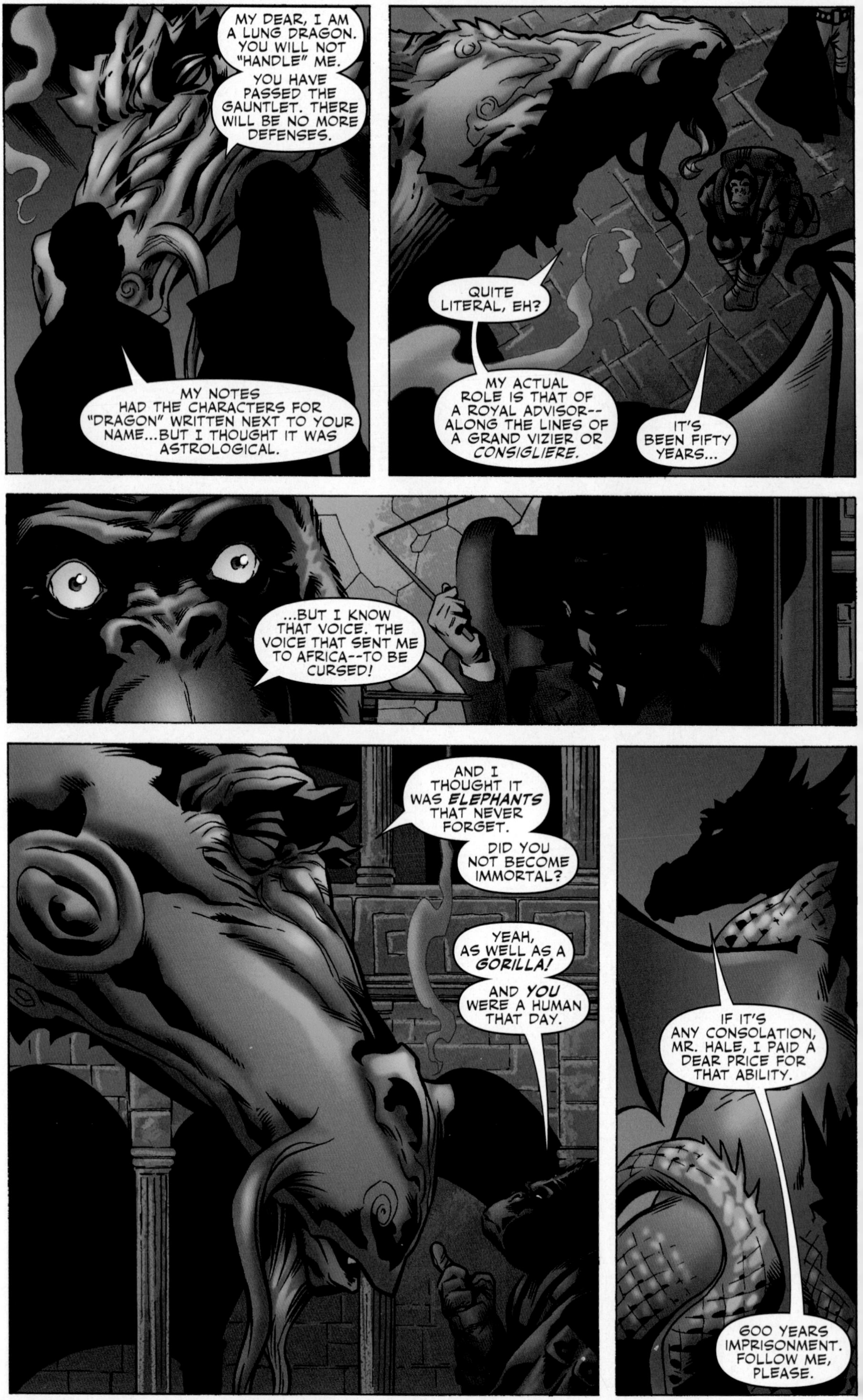
MY DEAR, I AM A LUNG DRAGON. YOU WILL NOT "HANDLE" ME.
YOU HAVE PASSED THE GAUNTLET. THERE WILL BE NO MORE DEFENSES.
MY NOTES HAD THE CHARACTERS FOR "DRAGON" WRITTEN NEXT TO YOUR NAME...BUT I THOUGHT IT WAS ASTROLOGICAL.
QUITE LITERAL, EH?
MY ACTUAL ROLE IS THAT OF A ROYAL ADVISOR--ALONG THE LINES OF A GRAND VIZIER OR CONSIGLIERE.
IT'S BEEN FIFTY YEARS...
...BUT I KNOW THAT VOICE. THE VOICE THAT SENT ME TO AFRICA--TO BE CURSED!
AND I THOUGHT IT WAS ELEPHANTS THAT NEVER FORGET.
DID YOU NOT BECOME IMMORTAL?
YEAH, AS WELL AS A GORILLA!
AND YOU WERE A HUMAN THAT DAY.
IF IT'S ANY CONSOLATION, MR. HALE, I PAID A DEAR PRICE FOR THAT ABILITY.
600 YEARS IMPRISONMENT. FOLLOW ME, PLEASE.

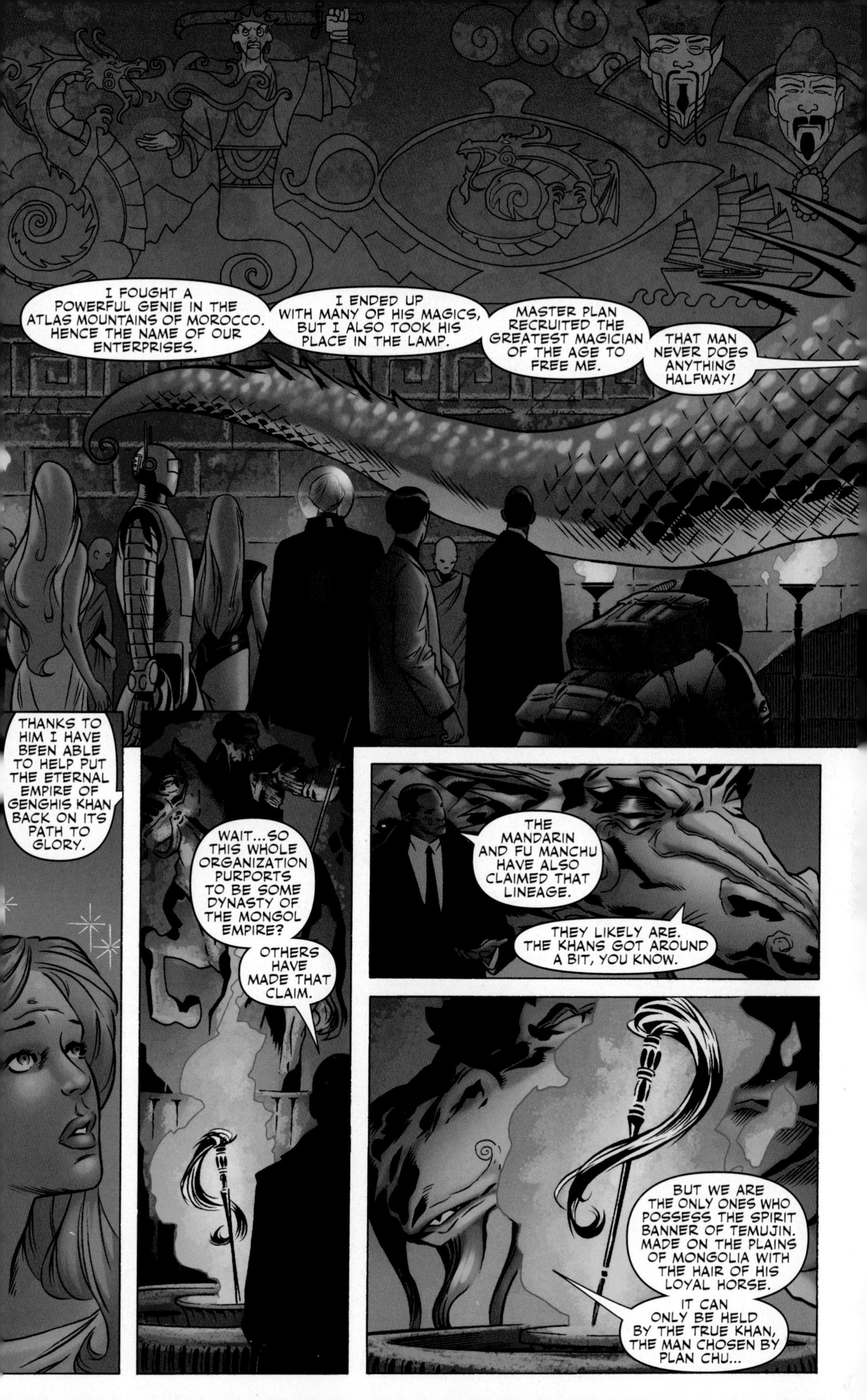

I FOUGHT A POWERFUL GENIE IN THE ATLAS MOUNTAINS OF MOROCCO. HENCE THE NAME OF OUR ENTERPRISES.
I ENDED UP WITH MANY OF HIS MAGICS, BUT I ALSO TOOK HIS PLACE IN THE LAMP.
MASTER PLAN RECRUITED THE GREATEST MAGICIAN OF THE AGE TO FREE ME.
THAT MAN NEVER DOES ANYTHING HALFWAY!
THANKS TO HIM I HAVE BEEN ABLE TO HELP PUT THE ETERNAL EMPIRE OF GENGHIS KHAN BACK ON ITS PATH TO GLORY.
WAIT...SO THIS WHOLE ORGANIZATION PURPORTS TO BE SOME DYNASTY OF THE MONGOL EMPIRE?
OTHERS HAVE MADE THAT CLAIM.
THE MANDARIN AND FU MANCHU HAVE ALSO CLAIMED THAT LINEAGE.
THEY LIKELY ARE. THE KHANS GOT AROUND A BIT, YOU KNOW.
BUT WE ARE THE ONLY ONES WHO POSSESS THE SPIRIT BANNER OF TEMUJIN. MADE ON THE PLAINS OF MONGOLIA WITH THE HAIR OF HIS LOYAL HORSE.
IT CAN ONLY BE HELD BY THE TRUE KHAN, THE MAN CHOSEN BY PLAN CHU...

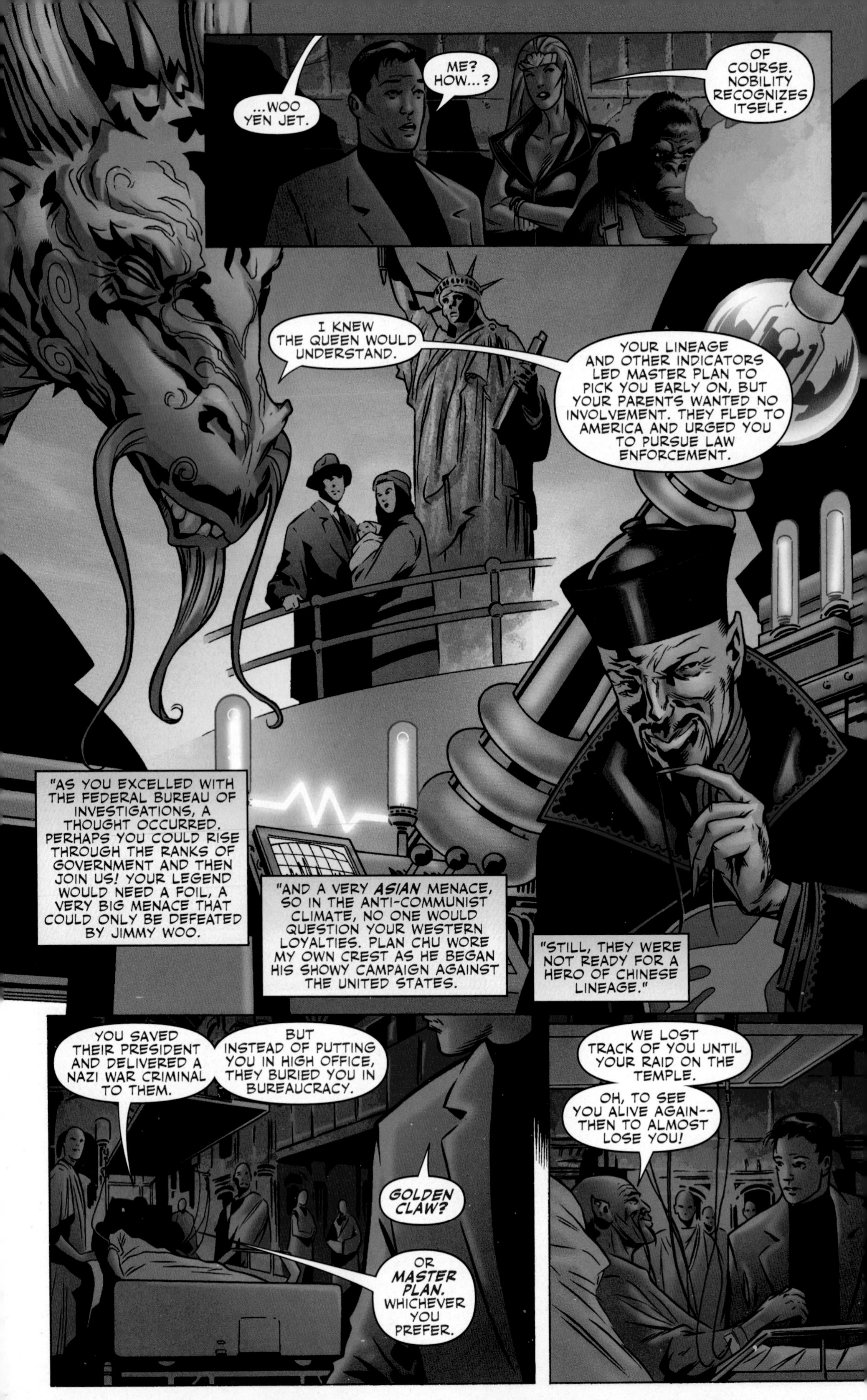
...WOO YEN JET.
ME? HOW...?
OF COURSE. NOBILITY RECOGNIZES ITSELF.
I KNEW THE QUEEN WOULD UNDERSTAND.
YOUR LINEAGE AND OTHER INDICATORS LED MASTER PLAN TO PICK YOU EARLY ON, BUT YOUR PARENTS WANTED NO INVOLVEMENT. THEY FLED TO AMERICA AND URGED YOU TO PURSUE LAW ENFORCEMENT.
"AS YOU EXCELLED WITH THE FEDERAL BUREAU OF INVESTIGATIONS, A THOUGHT OCCURRED. PERHAPS YOU COULD RISE THROUGH THE RANKS OF GOVERNMENT AND THEN JOIN US! YOUR LEGEND WOULD NEED A FOIL, A VERY BIG MENACE THAT COULD ONLY BE DEFEATED BY JIMMY WOO.
"AND A VERY *ASIAN* MENACE, SO IN THE ANTI-COMMUNIST CLIMATE, NO ONE WOULD QUESTION YOUR WESTERN LOYALTIES. PLAN CHU WORE MY OWN CREST AS HE BEGAN HIS SHOWY CAMPAIGN AGAINST THE UNITED STATES.
"STILL, THEY WERE NOT READY FOR A HERO OF CHINESE LINEAGE."
YOU SAVED THEIR PRESIDENT AND DELIVERED A NAZI WAR CRIMINAL TO THEM.
BUT INSTEAD OF PUTTING YOU IN HIGH OFFICE, THEY BURIED YOU IN BUREAUCRACY.
GOLDEN CLAW?
OR *MASTER PLAN.* WHICHEVER YOU PREFER.
WE LOST TRACK OF YOU UNTIL YOUR RAID ON THE TEMPLE.
OH, TO SEE YOU ALIVE AGAIN-- THEN TO ALMOST LOSE YOU!

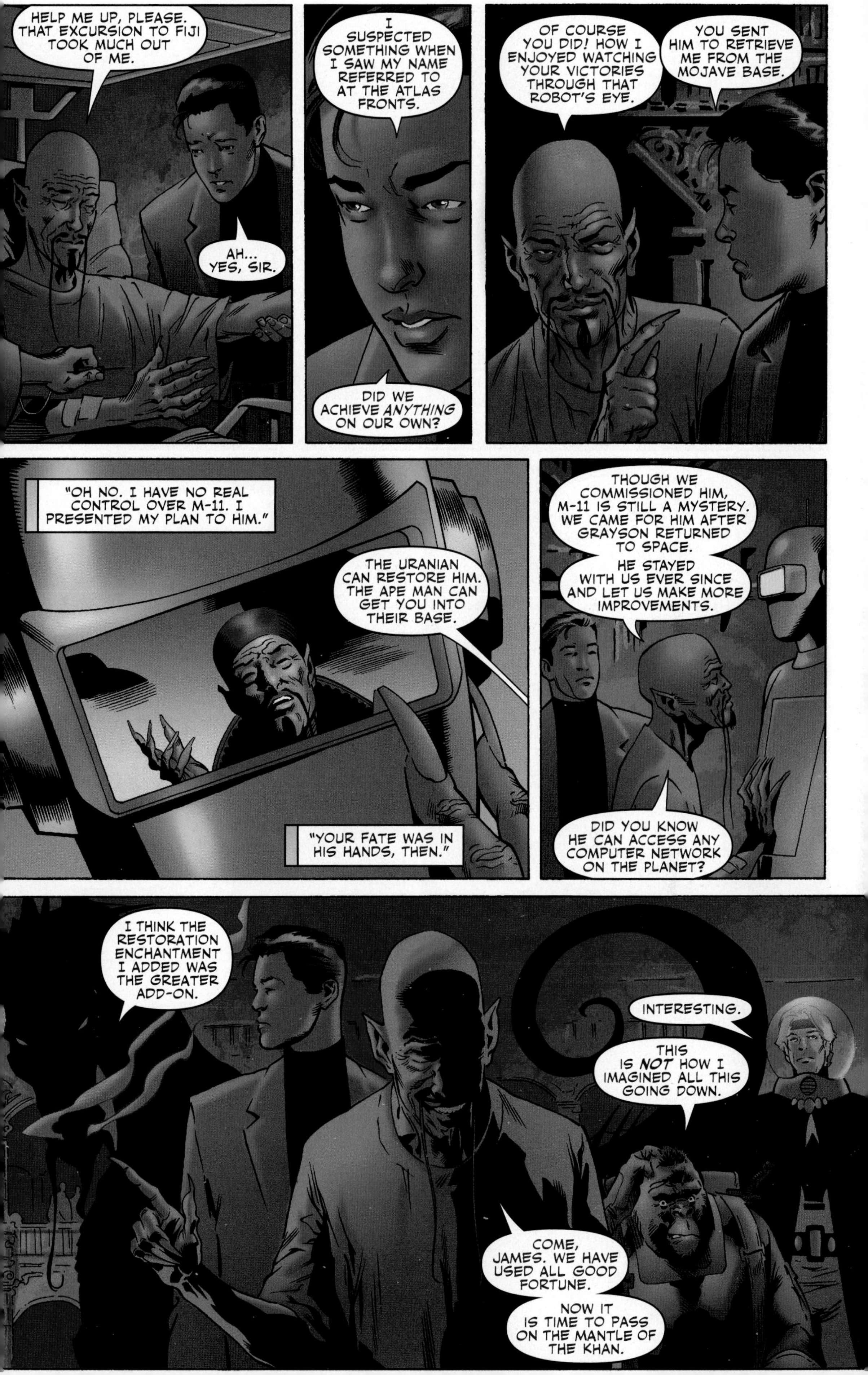
HELP ME UP, PLEASE. THAT EXCURSION TO FIJI TOOK MUCH OUT OF ME.
AH... YES, SIR.
I SUSPECTED SOMETHING WHEN I SAW MY NAME REFERRED TO AT THE ATLAS FRONTS.
DID WE ACHIEVE *ANYTHING* ON OUR OWN?
OF COURSE YOU DID! HOW I ENJOYED WATCHING YOUR VICTORIES THROUGH THAT ROBOT'S EYE.
YOU SENT HIM TO RETRIEVE ME FROM THE MOJAVE BASE.
"OH NO. I HAVE NO REAL CONTROL OVER M-11. I PRESENTED MY PLAN TO HIM."
THE URANIAN CAN RESTORE HIM. THE APE MAN CAN GET YOU INTO THEIR BASE.
"YOUR FATE WAS IN HIS HANDS, THEN."
THOUGH WE COMMISSIONED HIM, M-11 IS STILL A MYSTERY. WE CAME FOR HIM AFTER GRAYSON RETURNED TO SPACE.
HE STAYED WITH US EVER SINCE AND LET US MAKE MORE IMPROVEMENTS.
DID YOU KNOW HE CAN ACCESS ANY COMPUTER NETWORK ON THE PLANET?
I THINK THE RESTORATION ENCHANTMENT I ADDED WAS THE GREATER ADD-ON.
INTERESTING.
THIS IS **NOT** HOW I IMAGINED ALL THIS GOING DOWN.
COME, JAMES. WE HAVE USED ALL GOOD FORTUNE.
NOW IT IS TIME TO PASS ON THE MANTLE OF THE KHAN.

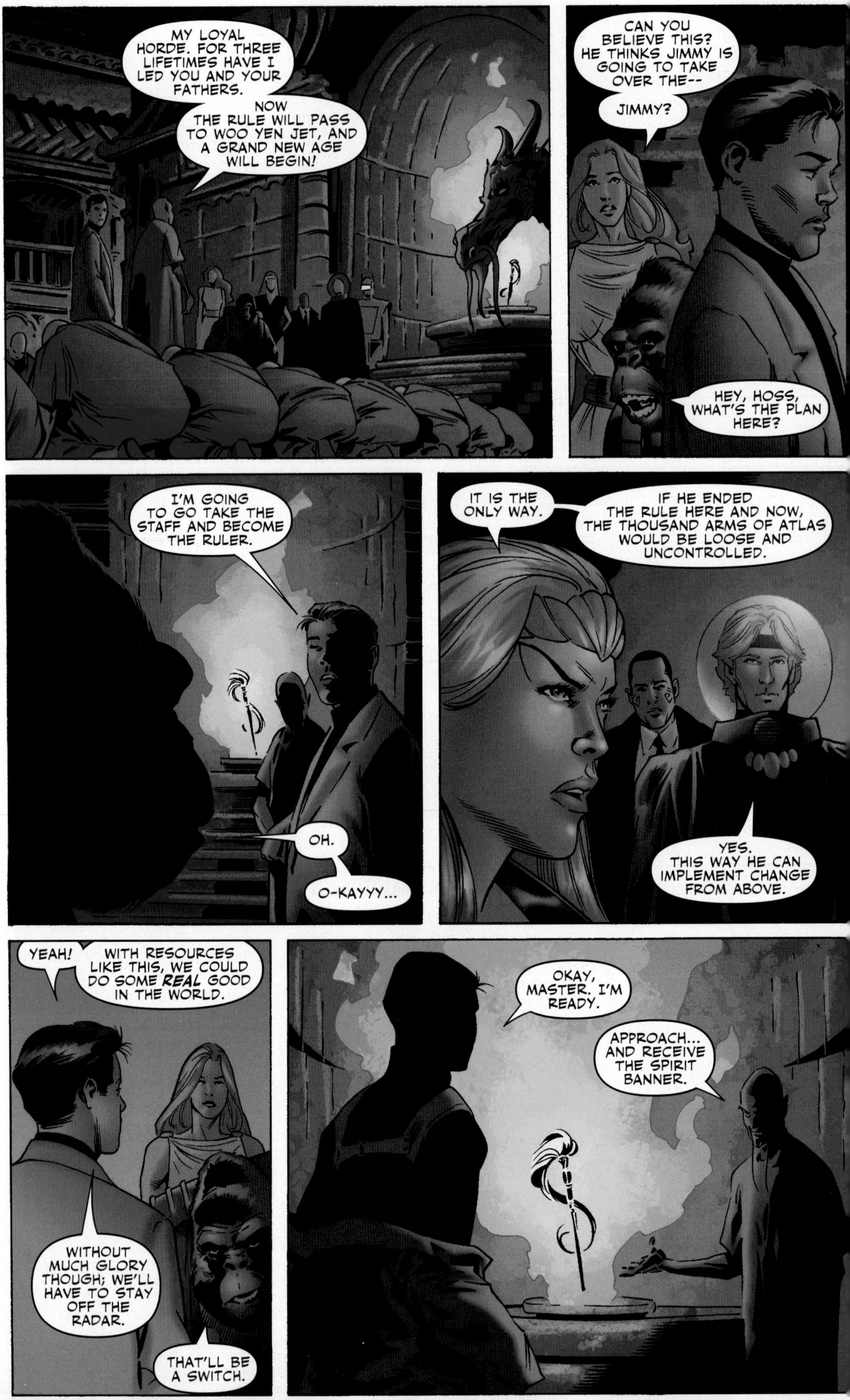

MY LOYAL HORDE. FOR THREE LIFETIMES HAVE I LED YOU AND YOUR FATHERS.
NOW THE RULE WILL PASS TO WOO YEN JET, AND A GRAND NEW AGE WILL BEGIN!
CAN YOU BELIEVE THIS? HE THINKS JIMMY IS GOING TO TAKE OVER THE--
JIMMY?
HEY, HOSS, WHAT'S THE PLAN HERE?
I'M GOING TO GO TAKE THE STAFF AND BECOME THE RULER.
OH.
O-KAYYY...
IT IS THE ONLY WAY.
IF HE ENDED THE RULE HERE AND NOW, THE THOUSAND ARMS OF ATLAS WOULD BE LOOSE AND UNCONTROLLED.
YES. THIS WAY HE CAN IMPLEMENT CHANGE FROM ABOVE.
YEAH!
WITH RESOURCES LIKE THIS, WE COULD DO SOME *REAL* GOOD IN THE WORLD.
WITHOUT MUCH GLORY THOUGH; WE'LL HAVE TO STAY OFF THE RADAR.
THAT'LL BE A SWITCH.
OKAY, MASTER. I'M READY.
APPROACH... AND RECEIVE THE SPIRIT BANNER.

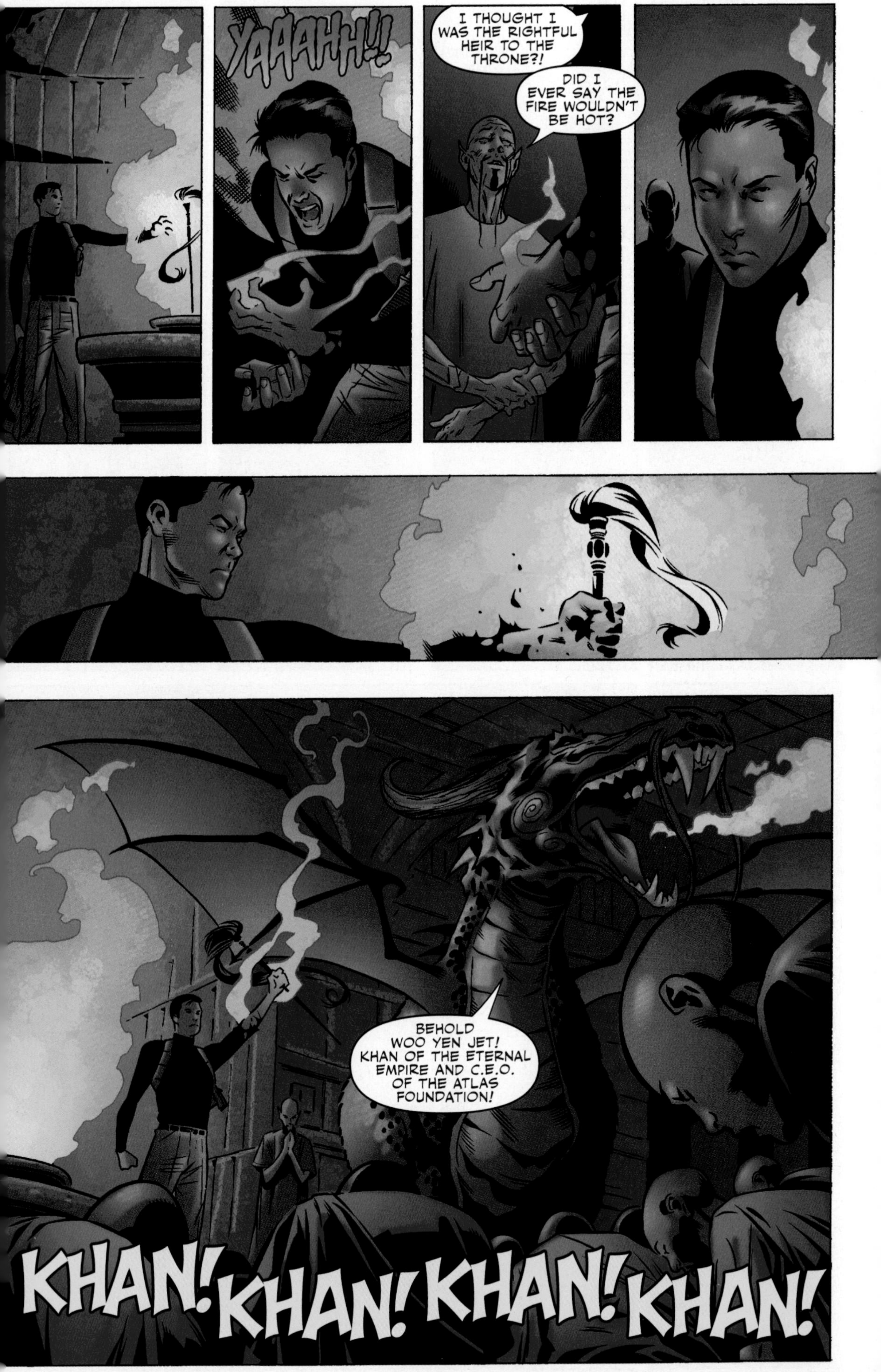
YAAAHH!!
I THOUGHT I WAS THE RIGHTFUL HEIR TO THE THRONE?!
DID I EVER SAY THE FIRE WOULDN'T BE HOT?
BEHOLD WOO YEN JET! KHAN OF THE ETERNAL EMPIRE AND C.E.O. OF THE ATLAS FOUNDATION!
KHAN! KHAN! KHAN! KHAN!

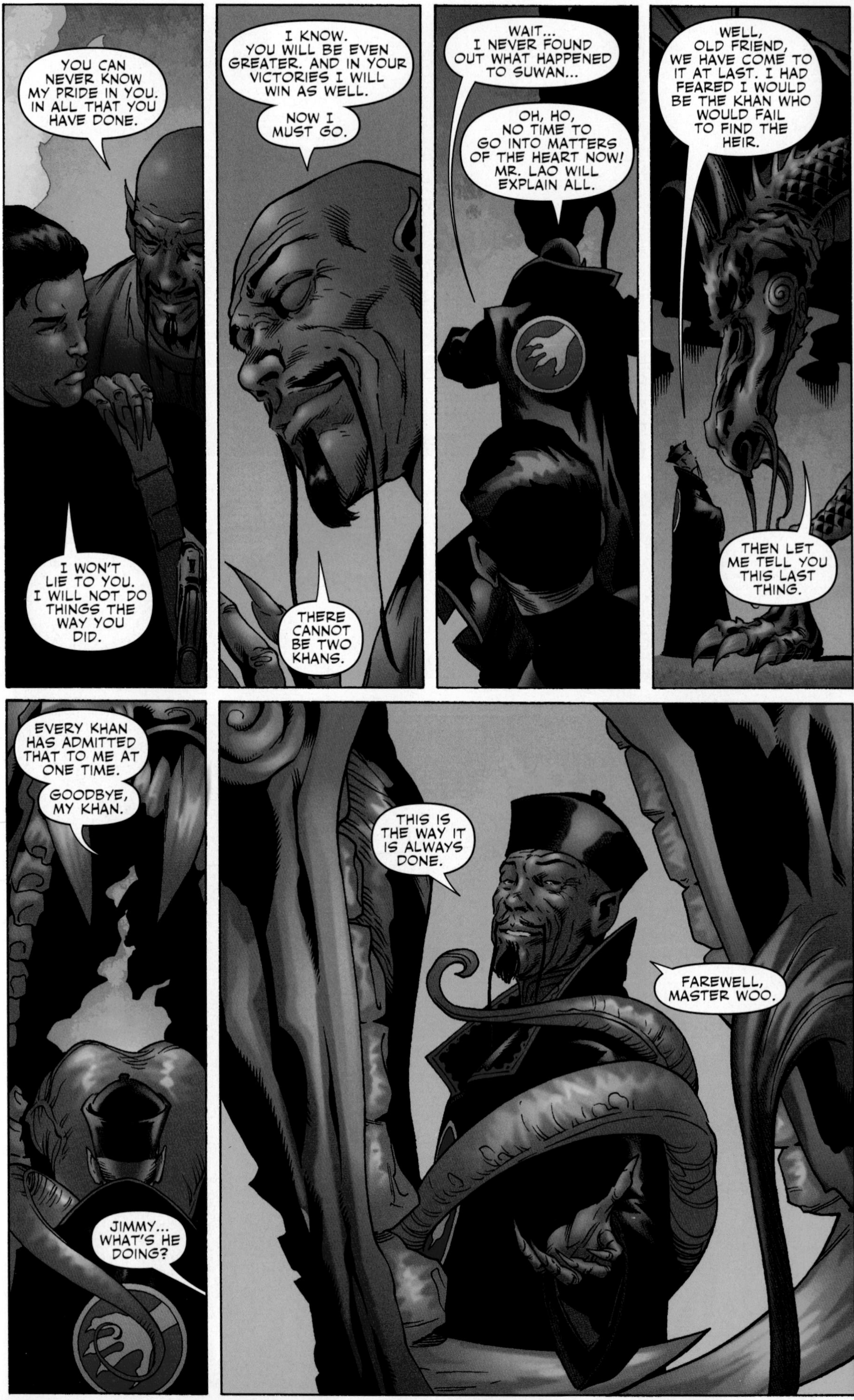
YOU CAN NEVER KNOW MY PRIDE IN YOU. IN ALL THAT YOU HAVE DONE.
I WON'T LIE TO YOU. I WILL NOT DO THINGS THE WAY YOU DID.
I KNOW. YOU WILL BE EVEN GREATER. AND IN YOUR VICTORIES I WILL WIN AS WELL.
NOW I MUST GO.
THERE CANNOT BE TWO KHANS.
WAIT... I NEVER FOUND OUT WHAT HAPPENED TO SUWAN...
OH, HO, NO TIME TO GO INTO MATTERS OF THE HEART NOW! MR. LAO WILL EXPLAIN ALL.
WELL, OLD FRIEND, WE HAVE COME TO IT AT LAST. I HAD FEARED I WOULD BE THE KHAN WHO WOULD FAIL TO FIND THE HEIR.
THEN LET ME TELL YOU THIS LAST THING.
EVERY KHAN HAS ADMITTED THAT TO ME AT ONE TIME.
GOODBYE, MY KHAN.
JIMMY... WHAT'S HE DOING?
THIS IS THE WAY IT IS ALWAYS DONE.
FAREWELL, MASTER WOO.

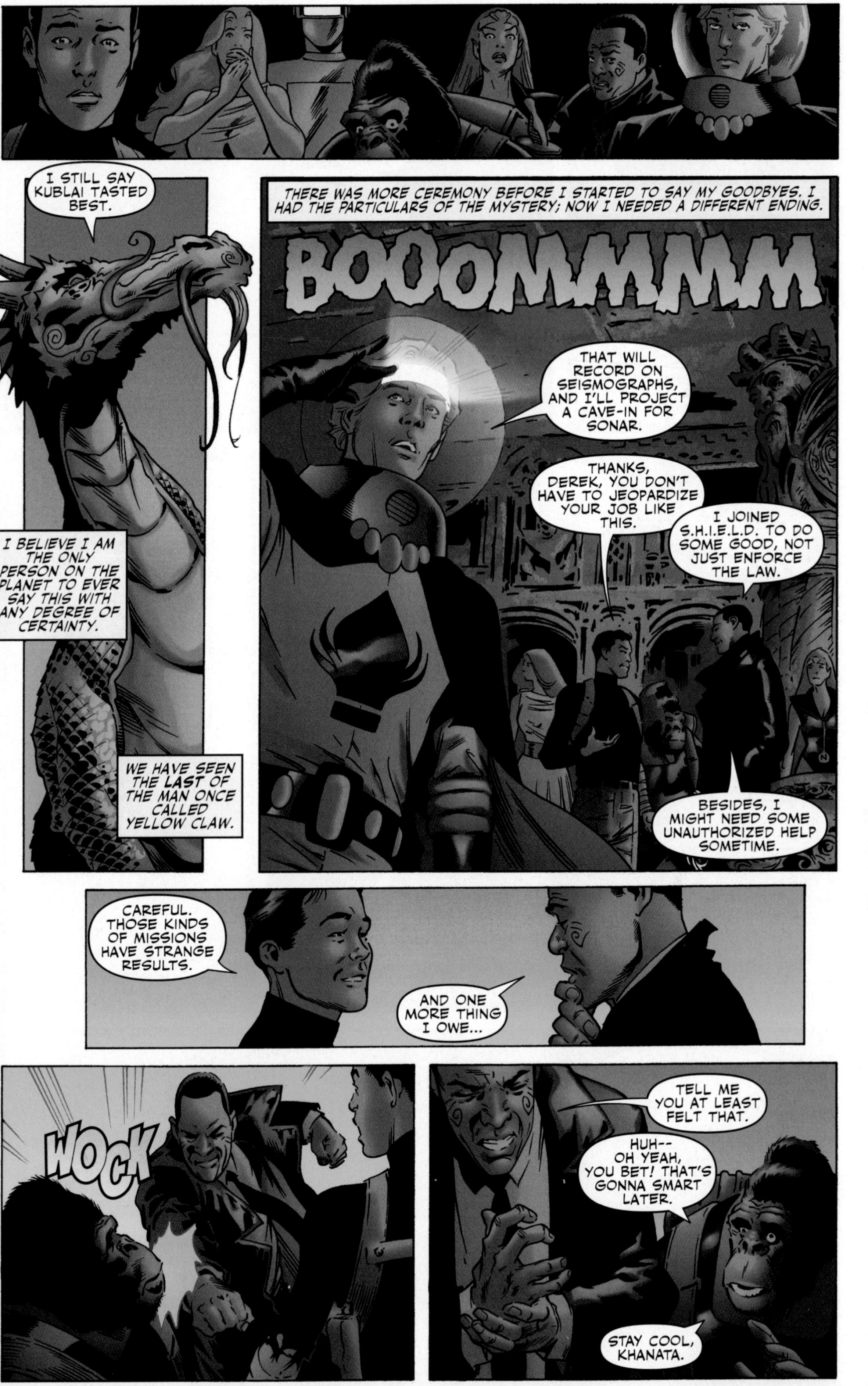
I STILL SAY KUBLAI TASTED BEST.
I BELIEVE I AM THE ONLY PERSON ON THE PLANET TO EVER SAY THIS WITH ANY DEGREE OF CERTAINTY.
WE HAVE SEEN THE LAST OF THE MAN ONCE CALLED YELLOW CLAW.
THERE WAS MORE CEREMONY BEFORE I STARTED TO SAY MY GOODBYES. I HAD THE PARTICULARS OF THE MYSTERY; NOW I NEEDED A DIFFERENT ENDING.
BOOOMMMM
THAT WILL RECORD ON SEISMOGRAPHS, AND I'LL PROJECT A CAVE-IN FOR SONAR.
THANKS, DEREK, YOU DON'T HAVE TO JEOPARDIZE YOUR JOB LIKE THIS.
I JOINED S.H.I.E.L.D. TO DO SOME GOOD, NOT JUST ENFORCE THE LAW.
BESIDES, I MIGHT NEED SOME UNAUTHORIZED HELP SOMETIME.
CAREFUL. THOSE KINDS OF MISSIONS HAVE STRANGE RESULTS.
AND ONE MORE THING I OWE...
WOCK
TELL ME YOU AT LEAST FELT THAT.
HUH-- OH YEAH, YOU BET! THAT'S GONNA SMART LATER.
STAY COOL, KHANATA.

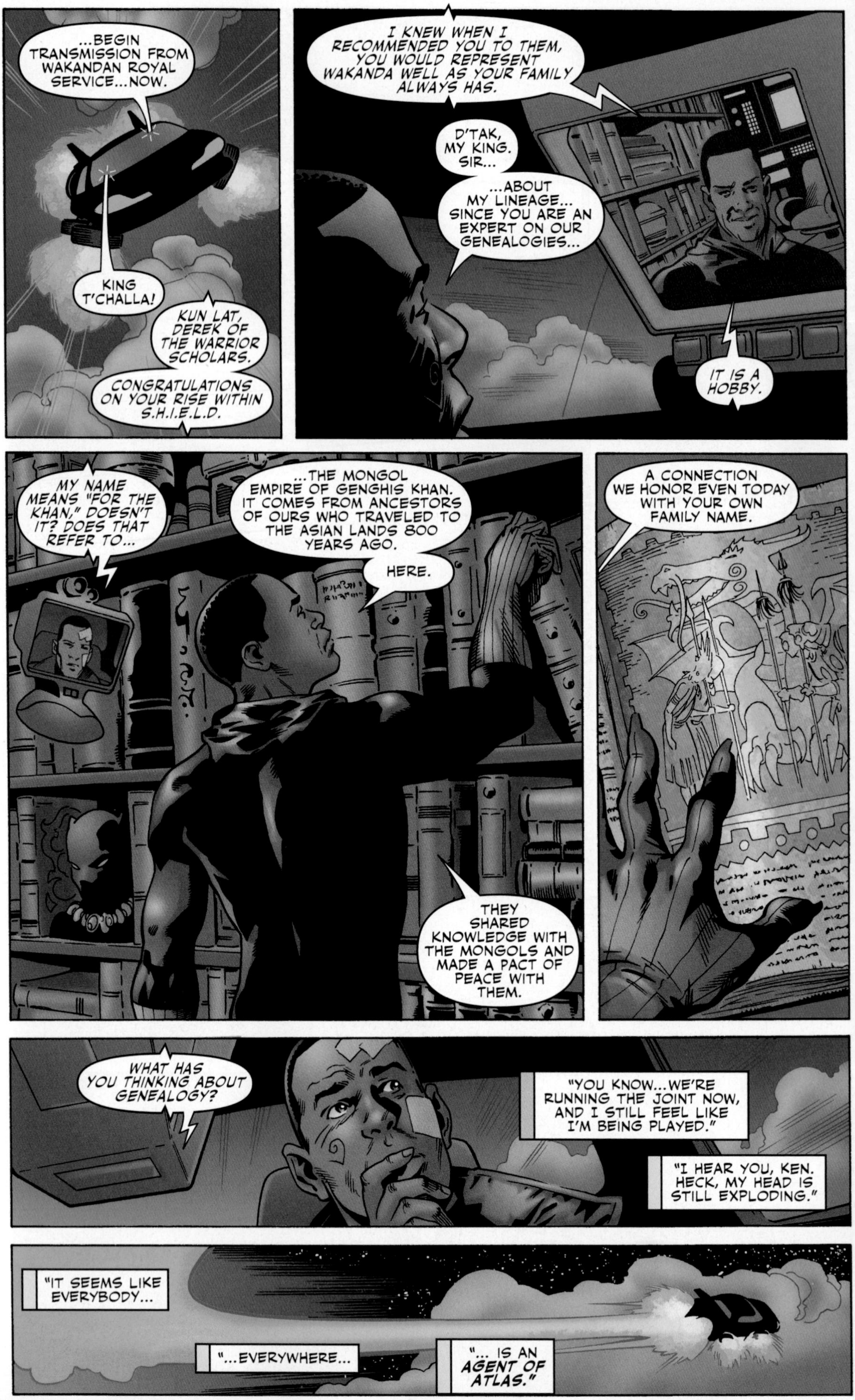
...BEGIN TRANSMISSION FROM WAKANDAN ROYAL SERVICE...NOW.
KING T'CHALLA!
KUN LAT, DEREK OF THE WARRIOR SCHOLARS.
CONGRATULATIONS ON YOUR RISE WITHIN S.H.I.E.L.D.
I KNEW WHEN I RECOMMENDED YOU TO THEM, YOU WOULD REPRESENT WAKANDA WELL AS YOUR FAMILY ALWAYS HAS.
D'TAK, MY KING. SIR...
...ABOUT MY LINEAGE... SINCE YOU ARE AN EXPERT ON OUR GENEALOGIES...
IT IS A HOBBY.
MY NAME MEANS "FOR THE KHAN," DOESN'T IT? DOES THAT REFER TO...
...THE MONGOL EMPIRE OF GENGHIS KHAN. IT COMES FROM ANCESTORS OF OURS WHO TRAVELED TO THE ASIAN LANDS 800 YEARS AGO.
HERE.
THEY SHARED KNOWLEDGE WITH THE MONGOLS AND MADE A PACT OF PEACE WITH THEM.
A CONNECTION WE HONOR EVEN TODAY WITH YOUR OWN FAMILY NAME.
WHAT HAS YOU THINKING ABOUT GENEALOGY?
"YOU KNOW...WE'RE RUNNING THE JOINT NOW, AND I STILL FEEL LIKE I'M BEING PLAYED."
"I HEAR YOU, KEN. HECK, MY HEAD IS STILL EXPLODING."
"IT SEEMS LIKE EVERYBODY...
"...EVERYWHERE...
"... IS AN AGENT OF ATLAS."

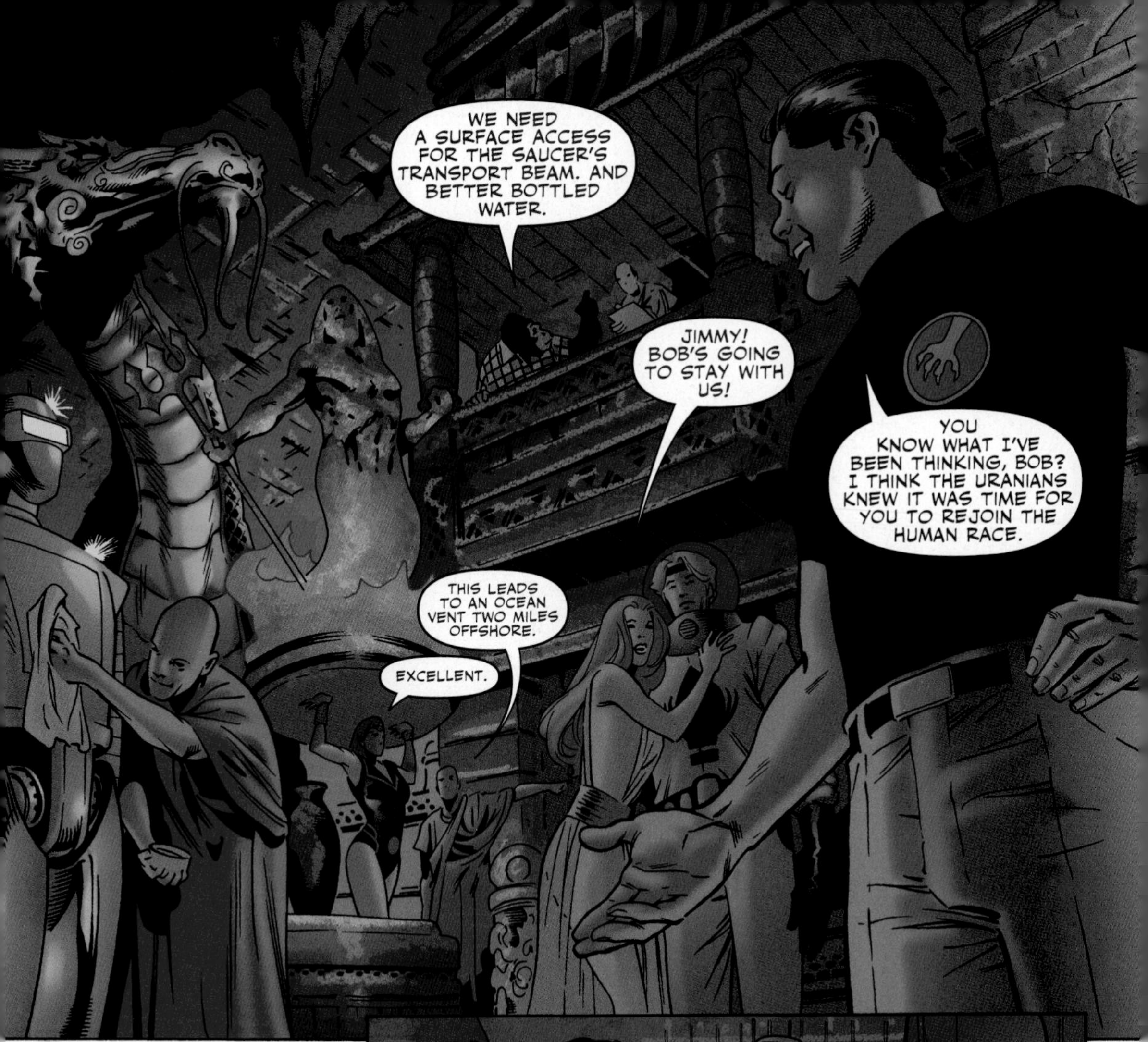
WE NEED A SURFACE ACCESS FOR THE SAUCER'S TRANSPORT BEAM. AND BETTER BOTTLED WATER.
JIMMY! BOB'S GOING TO STAY WITH US!
YOU KNOW WHAT I'VE BEEN THINKING, BOB? I THINK THE URANIANS KNEW IT WAS TIME FOR YOU TO REJOIN THE HUMAN RACE.
THIS LEADS TO AN OCEAN VENT TWO MILES OFFSHORE.
EXCELLENT.
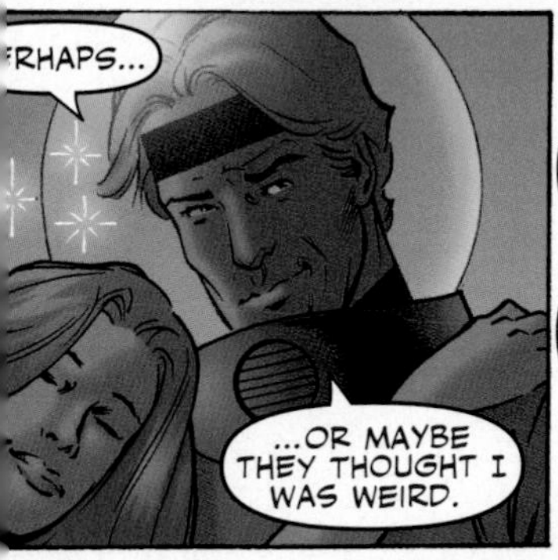
...OR MAYBE THEY THOUGHT I WAS WEIRD.
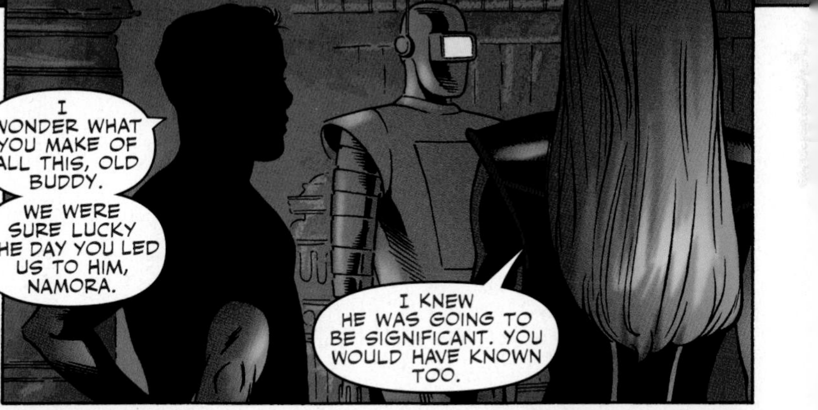
I WONDER WHAT YOU MAKE OF ALL THIS, OLD BUDDY.
WE WERE SURE LUCKY THE DAY YOU LED US TO HIM, NAMORA.
I KNEW HE WAS GOING TO BE SIGNIFICANT. YOU WOULD HAVE KNOWN TOO.
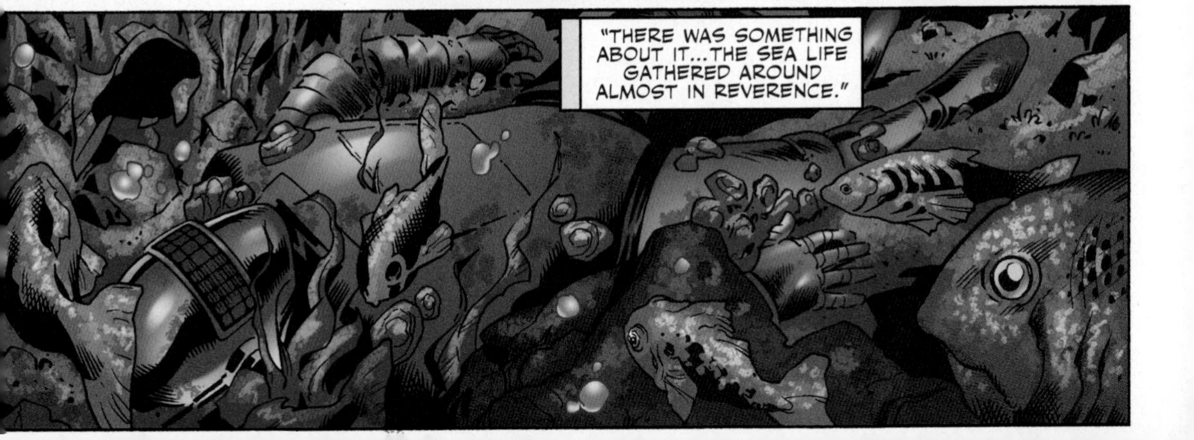
"THERE WAS SOMETHING ABOUT IT...THE SEA LIFE GATHERED AROUND ALMOST IN REVERENCE."

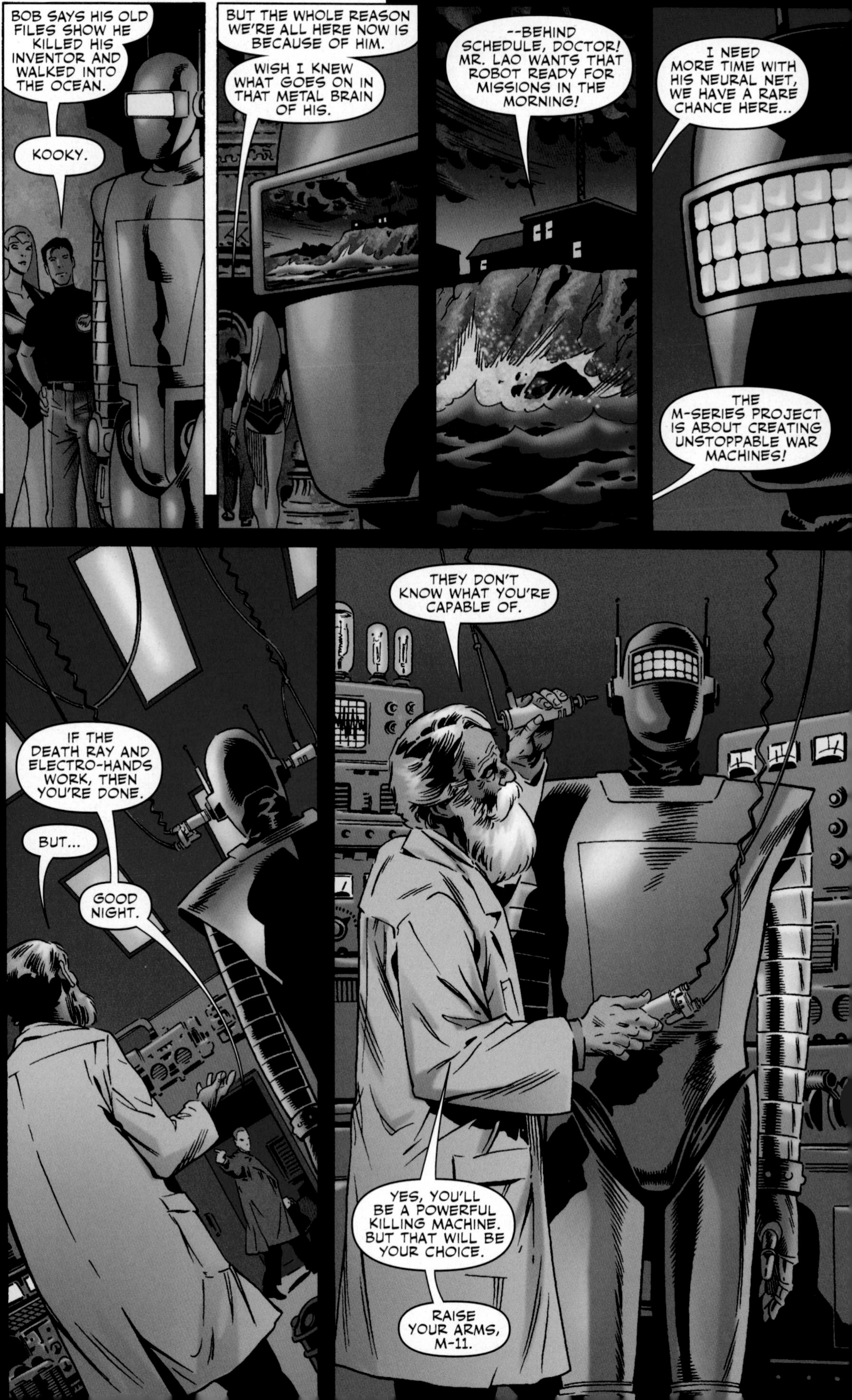
BOB SAYS HIS OLD FILES SHOW HE KILLED HIS INVENTOR AND WALKED INTO THE OCEAN.
KOOKY.
BUT THE WHOLE REASON WE'RE ALL HERE NOW IS BECAUSE OF HIM.
WISH I KNEW WHAT GOES ON IN THAT METAL BRAIN OF HIS.
--BEHIND SCHEDULE, DOCTOR! MR. LAO WANTS THAT ROBOT READY FOR MISSIONS IN THE MORNING!
I NEED MORE TIME WITH HIS NEURAL NET, WE HAVE A RARE CHANCE HERE...
THE M-SERIES PROJECT IS ABOUT CREATING UNSTOPPABLE WAR MACHINES!
IF THE DEATH RAY AND ELECTRO-HANDS WORK, THEN YOU'RE DONE.
BUT...
GOOD NIGHT.
THEY DON'T KNOW WHAT YOU'RE CAPABLE OF.
YES, YOU'LL BE A POWERFUL KILLING MACHINE. BUT THAT WILL BE YOUR CHOICE.
RAISE YOUR ARMS, M-11.

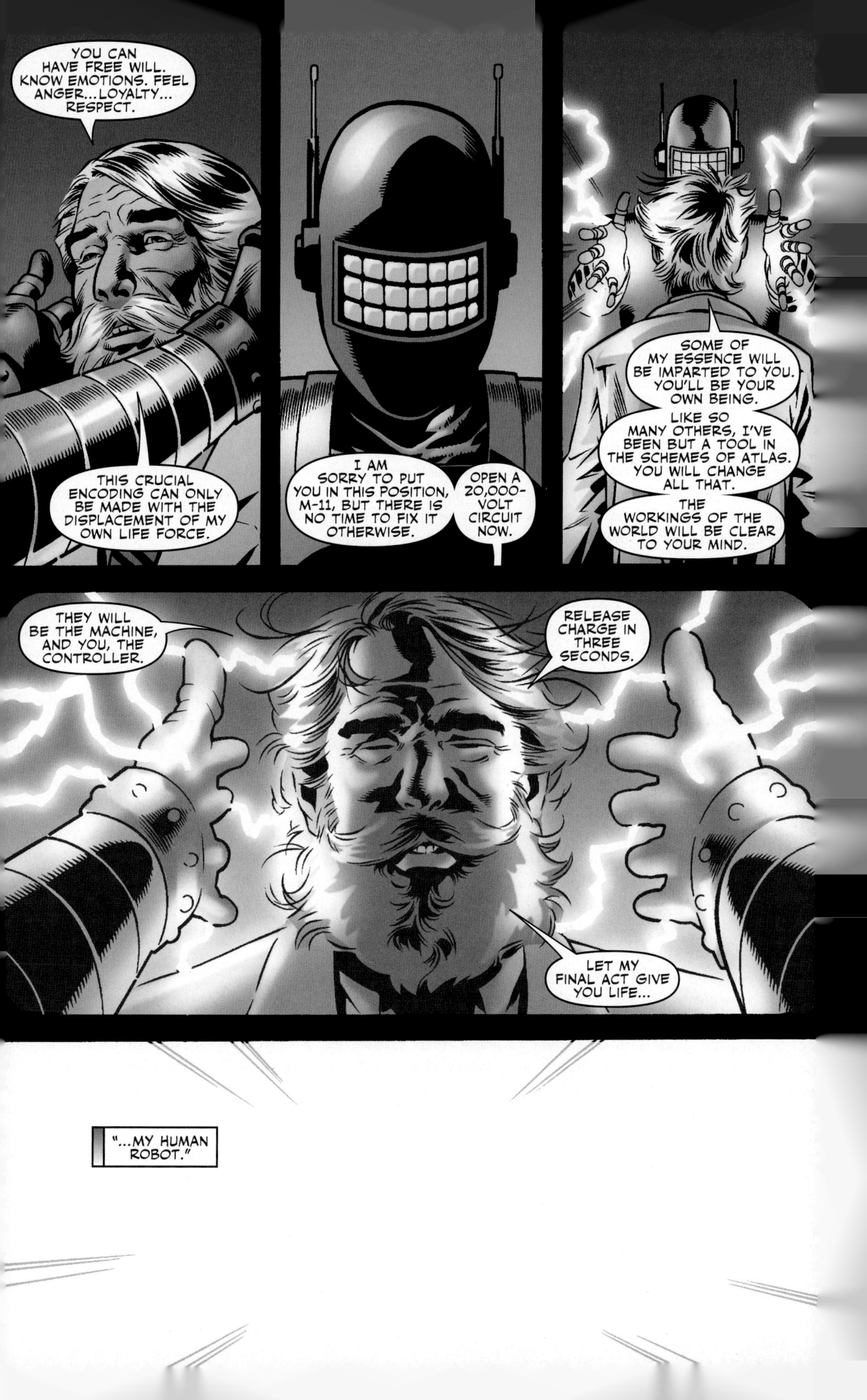
YOU CAN HAVE FREE WILL. KNOW EMOTIONS. FEEL ANGER...LOYALTY... RESPECT.
THIS CRUCIAL ENCODING CAN ONLY BE MADE WITH THE DISPLACEMENT OF MY OWN LIFE FORCE.
I AM SORRY TO PUT YOU IN THIS POSITION, M-11, BUT THERE IS NO TIME TO FIX IT OTHERWISE.
OPEN A 20,000-VOLT CIRCUIT NOW.
SOME OF MY ESSENCE WILL BE IMPARTED TO YOU. YOU'LL BE YOUR OWN BEING.
LIKE SO MANY OTHERS, I'VE BEEN BUT A TOOL IN THE SCHEMES OF ATLAS. YOU WILL CHANGE ALL THAT.
THE WORKINGS OF THE WORLD WILL BE CLEAR TO YOUR MIND.
THEY WILL BE THE MACHINE, AND YOU, THE CONTROLLER.
RELEASE CHARGE IN THREE SECONDS.
LET MY FINAL ACT GIVE YOU LIFE...
"...MY HUMAN ROBOT."

A Congratulations To My Successor, To Be Presented After My Death

James,

You are reading this, so the greatest undertaking of my career must have succeeded. Once I saw you on my very doorstep, even in such condition, it was clear the Fates were finally acknowledging my will. At last I can end the transfusions and consumption of elixirs that have granted me the lifetimes of three men, and go to my rest. You cannot imagine my relief.

Once you accept the mantle of Khan of the Eternal Empire, I will step into the jaws of the Dragon. Death will be abrupt, but it is always done thus, so the Horde Elite will see and know the passage of power. I also fear that you may change your mind, as you are less concerned with acquisition of power than previous rulers. No, you are ever in pursuit of adventure, and of that you shall have plenty. There are many paths to conquering the world, and if anyone can find a new way, it will be you and your Agents.

It has pained me to be so deceitful with you, but adversarial mentoring is a tradition within the empire. Just as the new Khan must break through the Royal Chamber defenses (how I look forward to seeing how you will achieve that with your mighty team!) to take the Spirit Banner. However, it could never equal my surprise as to how you assailed our Mongolian fortress in 1958. We had suspected you would recruit Marvel Boy, but had little influence there. Of course, our goal of one of the few successful Human/Merman hybrids was thwarted. Yet when you arrived with one of our very own M-series warbots—! Then I knew I had chosen a man of destiny. The siege began none too soon, thanks to my own legendary hospitality. Your Mr. Eisenhower was becoming relentless in trying to persuade me to create the world's largest golfing resort in Outer Mongolia. Americans and their sport...

When we lost track of you, I suspected you might be involved with S.H.I.E.L.D., but Mr. Lao believed you dead. You no doubt notice my own public activities ended at that time. In grief, I did as Lao had advised for years and began to concentrate on our influence in the world of commerce. I had always pictured myself as a conqueror in the classic mold; bold victories in the field and commanding respect with an iron will. Quietly acquiring large tracts of the economy is certainly the modern method, but I find it too easy and unrewarding.

You've likely guessed by now that I always wanted you to wed my niece (actually great-great-grand-niece), Suwan. I made much show of keeping you apart, the time-tested surest route to kindling your passions. No doubt you will want to know what became of her, and Mr. Lao will have to apprise you of that situation. It is ever the prerogative of rulers to pass down the greatest dilemmas to the next administration, and I am no different in that regard. I can say with certainty that it will be one of your greatest challenges.

Regarding our esteemed advisor, I should give you this advice of my own—do not trust that dragon! True, I love him as much as I could any human, and his return to the court has been the greatest boon towards putting a wayward campaign back on track. His presence is intoxicating, and his knowledge so deep that to be around him is like having the ear of God. But all dragons have their own agendas that they never disclose. Most of the time you will find him invaluable, but never forget that you are the Master of this Empire and he answers to you. It is to this end that I "urged" you to pick Venus for your team. Your experience in

resisting her voice will serve you well against the persuasions of Mr. Lao. I couldn't have dreamed she would prove so formidable in her own right! I also suspect Mr. Hale will have a healthy disrespect for the dragon to further temper the balance. Ah, if only I had had such a general as that gorilla serving under me...

Yes, this inner circle of yours exceeds all expectations. Never has a Khan combined the cerebral prowess of the Uranian and the sheer raw power of the Sea Queen. As to the inscrutable Robot, we have yet to see the end of his capabilities, and he never fails to surprise. Still, you have the drive and purpose that they all need. It is those attributes above all that move this world and determine history. There are also many, many hours of writings and recordings by me on all matters concerning the Empire that I hope will be of help. If it seems a bit like string-pulling from the grave, well, what can I say? I am who I am.

You will likely, as did I, feel some remorse upon the realization that your lifelong enemy was in truth a guiding member of your extended family. I assure you this gives the Khan greater drive in his duties. Only in taking my place will you know who I truly was. Shed no tears for me, Woo Yen Jet. For now I am on a celestial steed riding across the steppes with Temujin and his Golden Horde. We will feast under the stars and share tales of our victories by the fire. And we will await the distant day when you join our number, bringing the new legends that only you can tell. Until that time, know that you have made an old Chinese the happiest he has ever been.

Your Exalted Master and Humble Servant,

Plan Chu
The Golden Claw

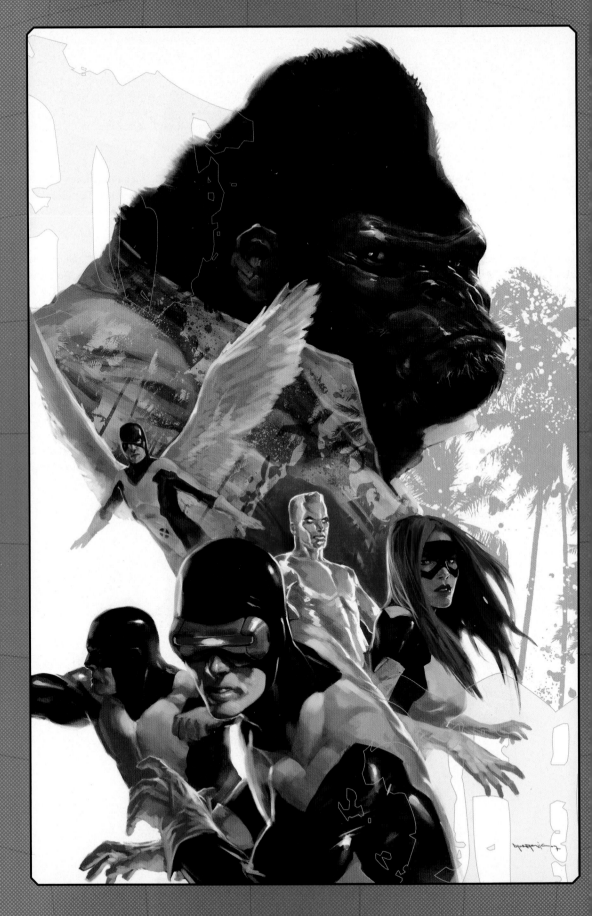

X-MEN: FIRST CLASS 8

THE NEXT STEP IN HUMAN EVOLUTION HAS ARRIVED—HOMO SUPERIOR. MANKIND ISN'T SURE WHETHER THIS REPRESENTS HOPE FOR THE FUTURE...OR THE END OF THE HUMAN RACE. IN A PRIVATE SCHOOL IN UPSTATE NEW YORK, ONE BRILLIANT MUTANT IS TEACHING A GROUP OF FIVE SUCH GIFTED STUDENTS WHAT THEY'LL NEED TO SURVIVE IN THIS NEW WORLD. THESE ARE THE UNTOLD STORIES OF PROFESSOR XAVIER'S FIRST CLASS OF X-MEN!

XAVIER'S SCHOOL FOR GIFTED YOUNGSTERS

PROPERTY OF:

Professor X

.h what a class. If I may
at myself on the back for
a moment, I did quite well
n choosing students. My only
regret is that I still had to
print a run of 1000 yearbooks
despite having only five students.

HEADMASTER

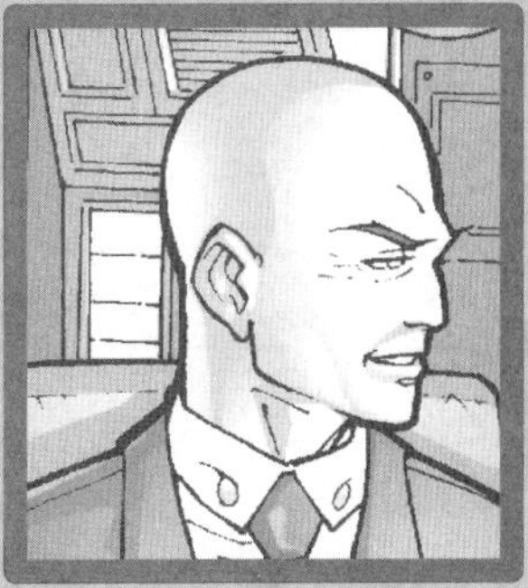

PROFESSOR CHARLES XAVIER

Scott. Exceptional field leader.
I often wish that he could see
the team as people as well as
he sees them as weapons. Still,
that discipline is what will
keep them alive, so I can
hardly complain.

Jean. Of this first class, she
gives me the most pride...
and the most trepidation. She is
potentially the most powerful
mutant alive, by my reckoning,
and I'm not sure any human
is ready for such power. The
school has given her the best
that it could however—peers
she loves. I hope that will make
the difference.

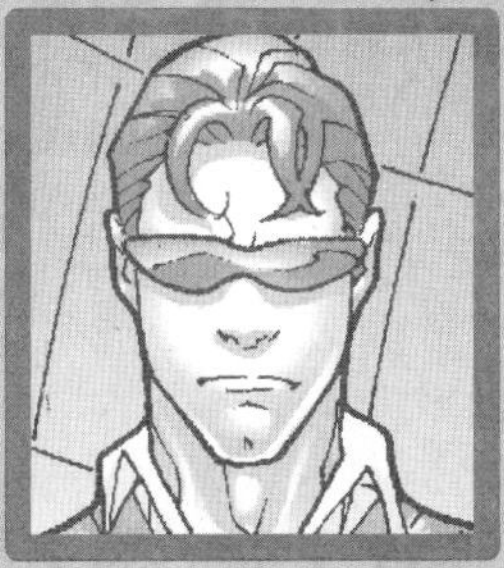

SCOTT SUMMERS
"CYCLOPS"

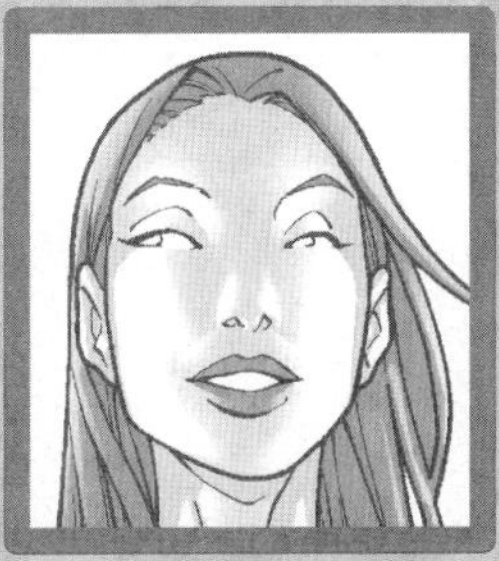

JEAN GREY
"MARVEL GIRL"

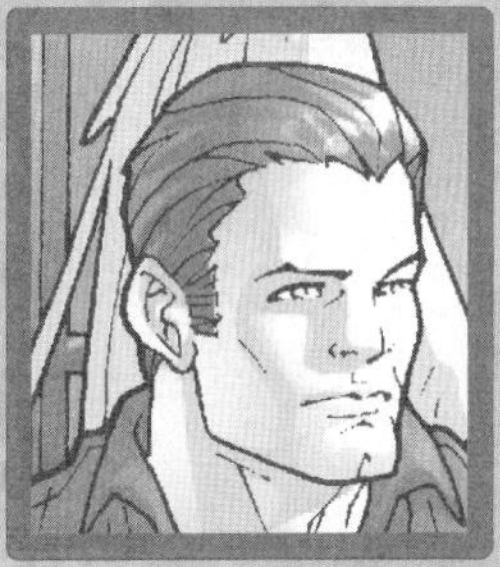

HENRY "HANK" McCOY
"BEAST"

Henry. It is very hard to look
at him and not see myself as a
younger man. Not that I'm that
much older, of course. His mind
will be a driving force in the
future of mutantkind, I am
sure of it.

Warren. Impetuous, easily
distracted, and a bit arrogant,
Yet if all mutants could be like
him rather than insecure, self-
loathing and paranoid, I would
be happy indeed.

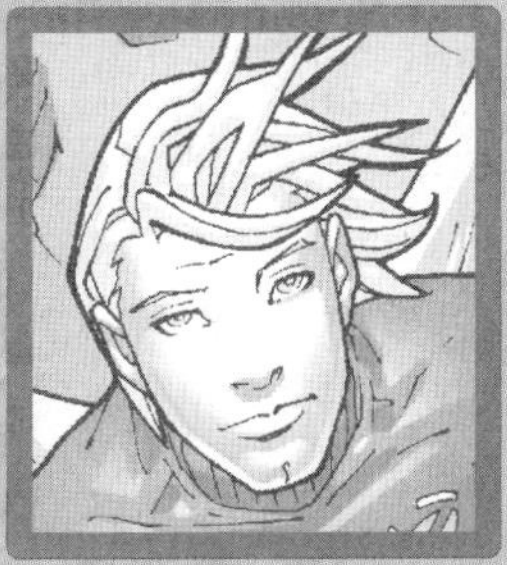

WARREN WORTHINGTON III
"ANGEL"

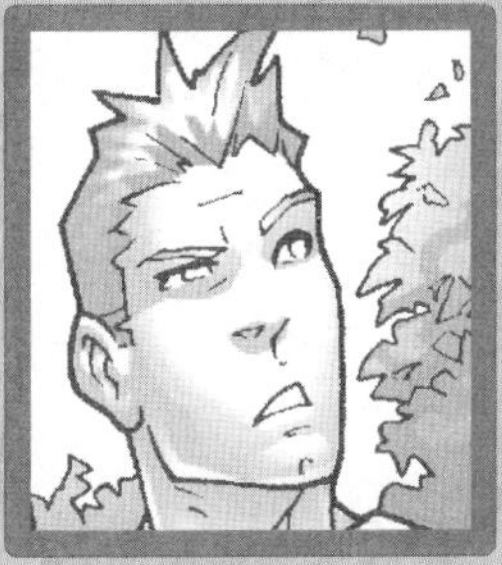

ROBERT DRAKE
"ICEMAN"

Robert. Somehow seems to grow
younger everday. I doubt I would
be much different if I could
make snow, though.

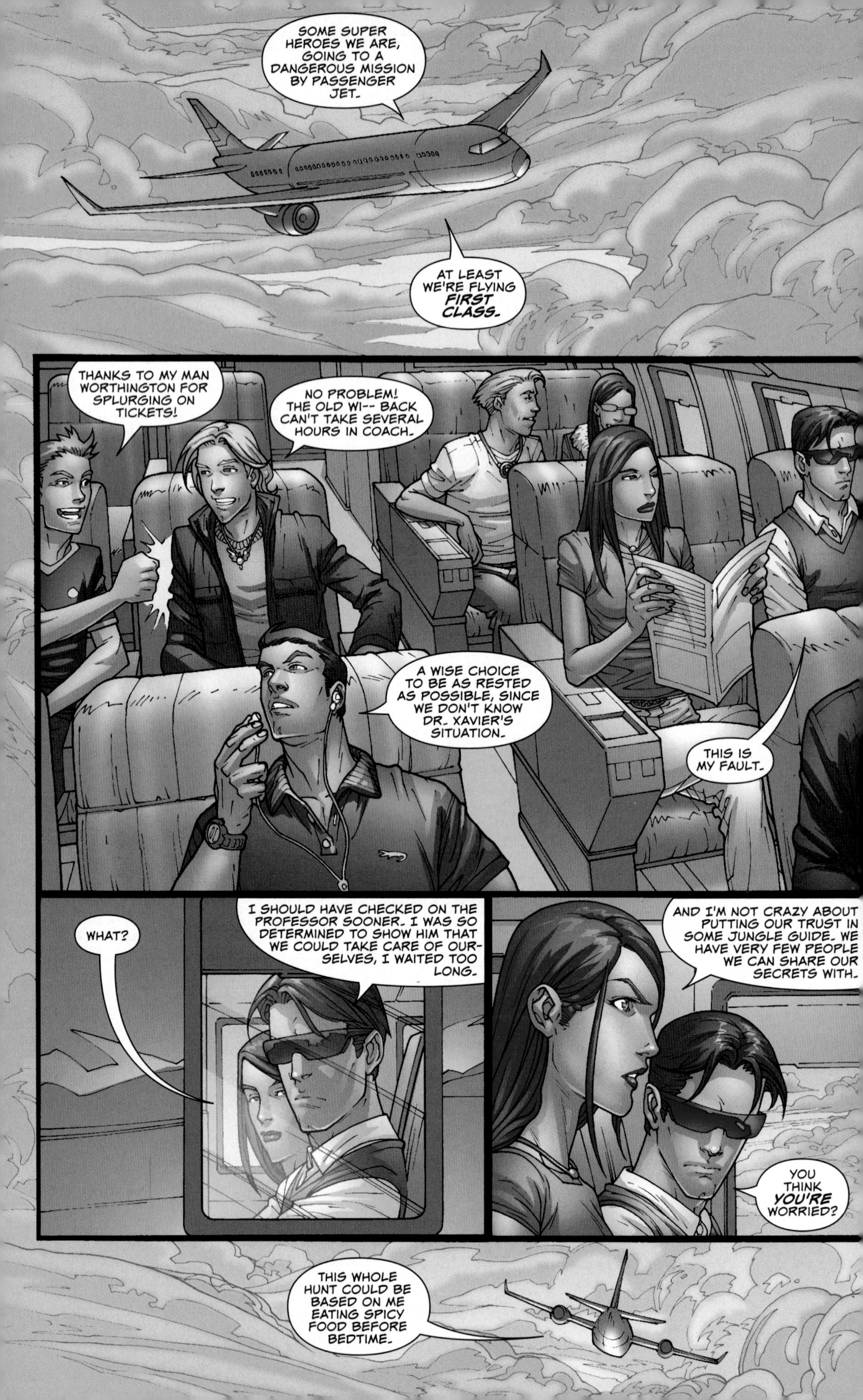
SOME SUPER HEROES WE ARE, GOING TO A DANGEROUS MISSION BY PASSENGER JET.
AT LEAST WE'RE FLYING FIRST CLASS.
THANKS TO MY MAN WORTHINGTON FOR SPLURGING ON TICKETS!
NO PROBLEM! THE OLD WI-- BACK CAN'T TAKE SEVERAL HOURS IN COACH.
A WISE CHOICE TO BE AS RESTED AS POSSIBLE, SINCE WE DON'T KNOW DR. XAVIER'S SITUATION.
THIS IS MY FAULT.
WHAT?
I SHOULD HAVE CHECKED ON THE PROFESSOR SOONER. I WAS SO DETERMINED TO SHOW HIM THAT WE COULD TAKE CARE OF OUR-SELVES, I WAITED TOO LONG.
AND I'M NOT CRAZY ABOUT PUTTING OUR TRUST IN SOME JUNGLE GUIDE. WE HAVE VERY FEW PEOPLE WE CAN SHARE OUR SECRETS WITH.
YOU THINK YOU'RE WORRIED?
THIS WHOLE HUNT COULD BE BASED ON ME EATING SPICY FOOD BEFORE BEDTIME.

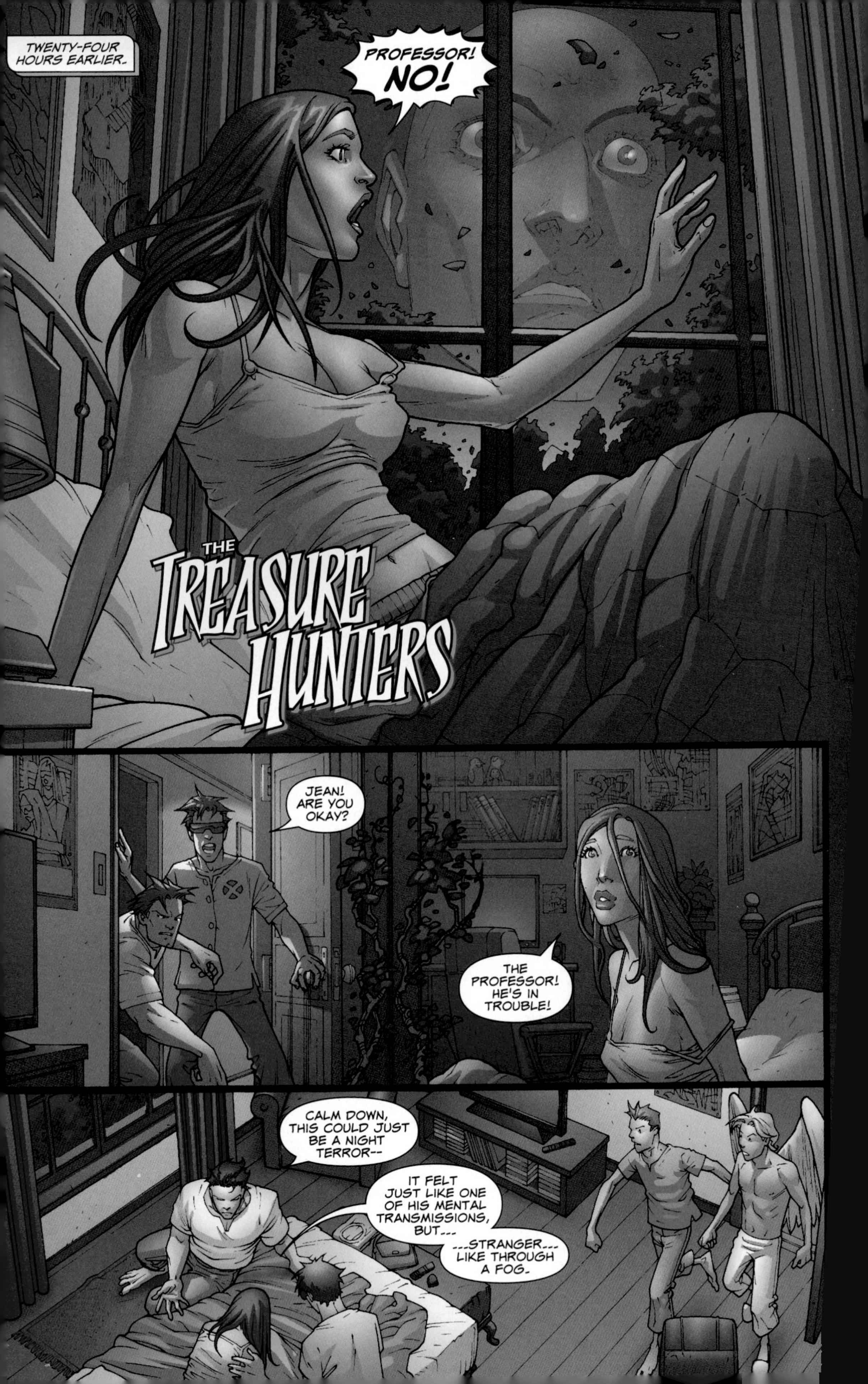
TWENTY-FOUR HOURS EARLIER.
PROFESSOR! NO!
THE TREASURE HUNTERS
JEAN! ARE YOU OKAY?
THE PROFESSOR! HE'S IN TROUBLE!
CALM DOWN, THIS COULD JUST BE A NIGHT TERROR--
IT FELT JUST LIKE ONE OF HIS MENTAL TRANSMISSIONS, BUT...
...STRANGER... LIKE THROUGH A FOG.

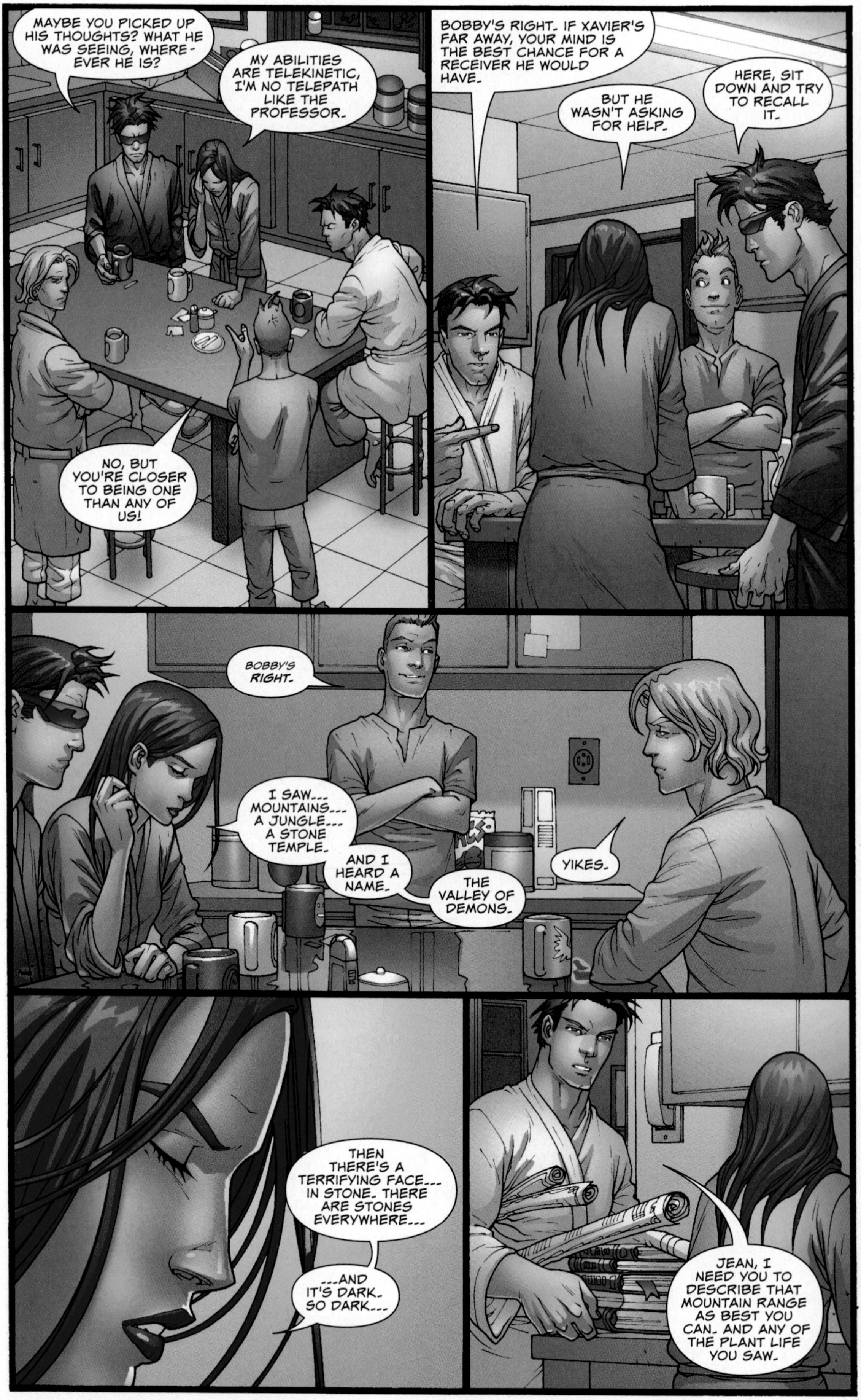
MAYBE YOU PICKED UP HIS THOUGHTS? WHAT HE WAS SEEING, WHERE-EVER HE IS?
MY ABILITIES ARE TELEKINETIC, I'M NO TELEPATH LIKE THE PROFESSOR.
NO, BUT YOU'RE CLOSER TO BEING ONE THAN ANY OF US!
BOBBY'S RIGHT. IF XAVIER'S FAR AWAY, YOUR MIND IS THE BEST CHANCE FOR A RECEIVER HE WOULD HAVE.
BUT HE WASN'T ASKING FOR HELP.
HERE, SIT DOWN AND TRY TO RECALL IT.
BOBBY'S RIGHT.
I SAW... MOUNTAINS... A JUNGLE... A STONE TEMPLE.
AND I HEARD A NAME.
THE VALLEY OF DEMONS.
YIKES.
THEN THERE'S A TERRIFYING FACE... IN STONE. THERE ARE STONES EVERYWHERE...
...AND IT'S DARK. SO DARK...
JEAN, I NEED YOU TO DESCRIBE THAT MOUNTAIN RANGE AS BEST YOU CAN. AND ANY OF THE PLANT LIFE YOU SAW.

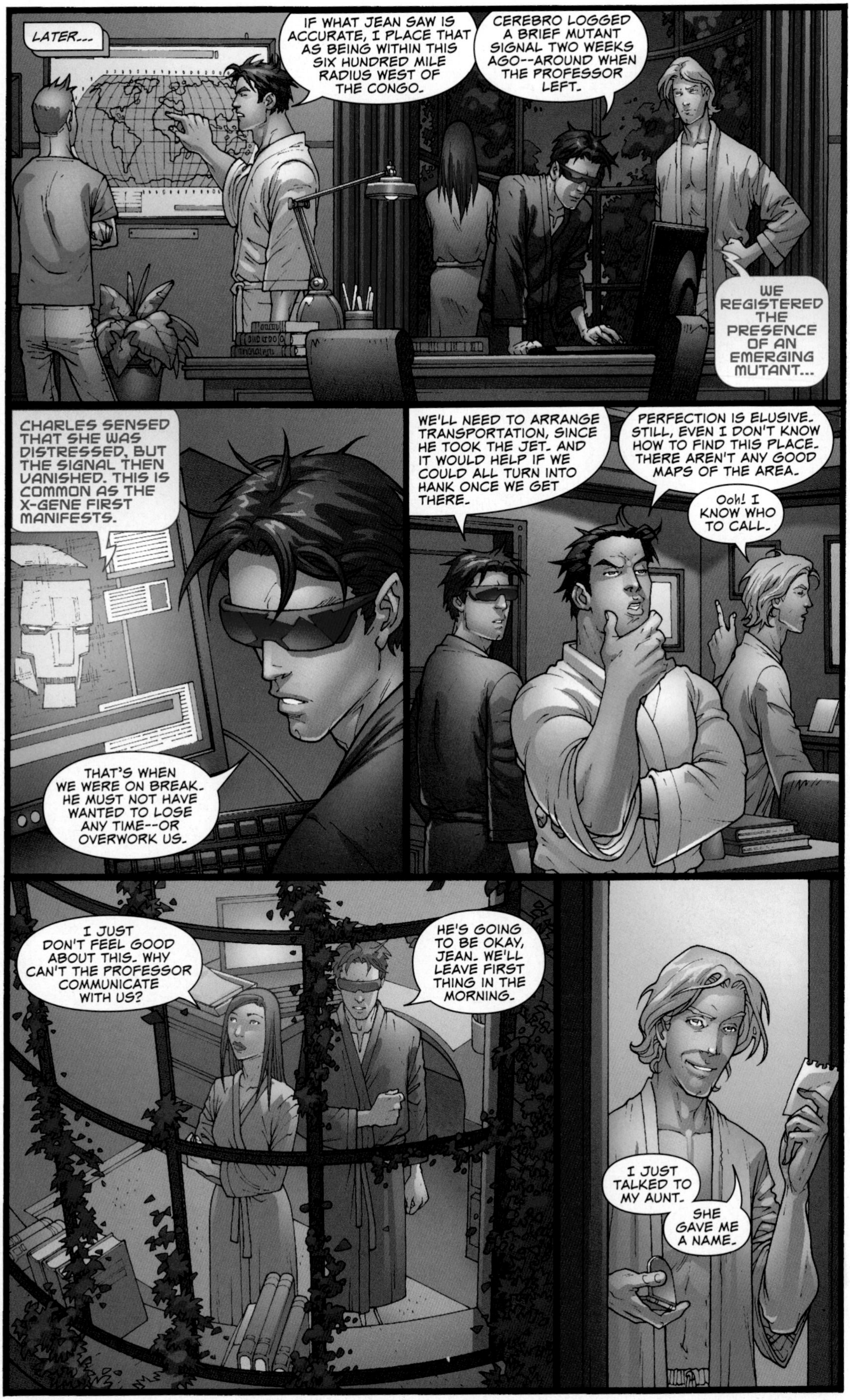
LATER...
IF WHAT JEAN SAW IS ACCURATE, I PLACE THAT AS BEING WITHIN THIS SIX HUNDRED MILE RADIUS WEST OF THE CONGO.
CEREBRO LOGGED A BRIEF MUTANT SIGNAL TWO WEEKS AGO--AROUND WHEN THE PROFESSOR LEFT.
WE REGISTERED THE PRESENCE OF AN EMERGING MUTANT...
CHARLES SENSED THAT SHE WAS DISTRESSED, BUT THE SIGNAL THEN VANISHED. THIS IS COMMON AS THE X-GENE FIRST MANIFESTS.
THAT'S WHEN WE WERE ON BREAK. HE MUST NOT HAVE WANTED TO LOSE ANY TIME--OR OVERWORK US.
WE'LL NEED TO ARRANGE TRANSPORTATION, SINCE HE TOOK THE JET. AND IT WOULD HELP IF WE COULD ALL TURN INTO HANK ONCE WE GET THERE.
PERFECTION IS ELUSIVE. STILL, EVEN I DON'T KNOW HOW TO FIND THIS PLACE. THERE AREN'T ANY GOOD MAPS OF THE AREA.
Ooh! I KNOW WHO TO CALL.
I JUST DON'T FEEL GOOD ABOUT THIS. WHY CAN'T THE PROFESSOR COMMUNICATE WITH US?
HE'S GOING TO BE OKAY, JEAN. WE'LL LEAVE FIRST THING IN THE MORNING.
I JUST TALKED TO MY AUNT.
SHE GAVE ME A NAME.

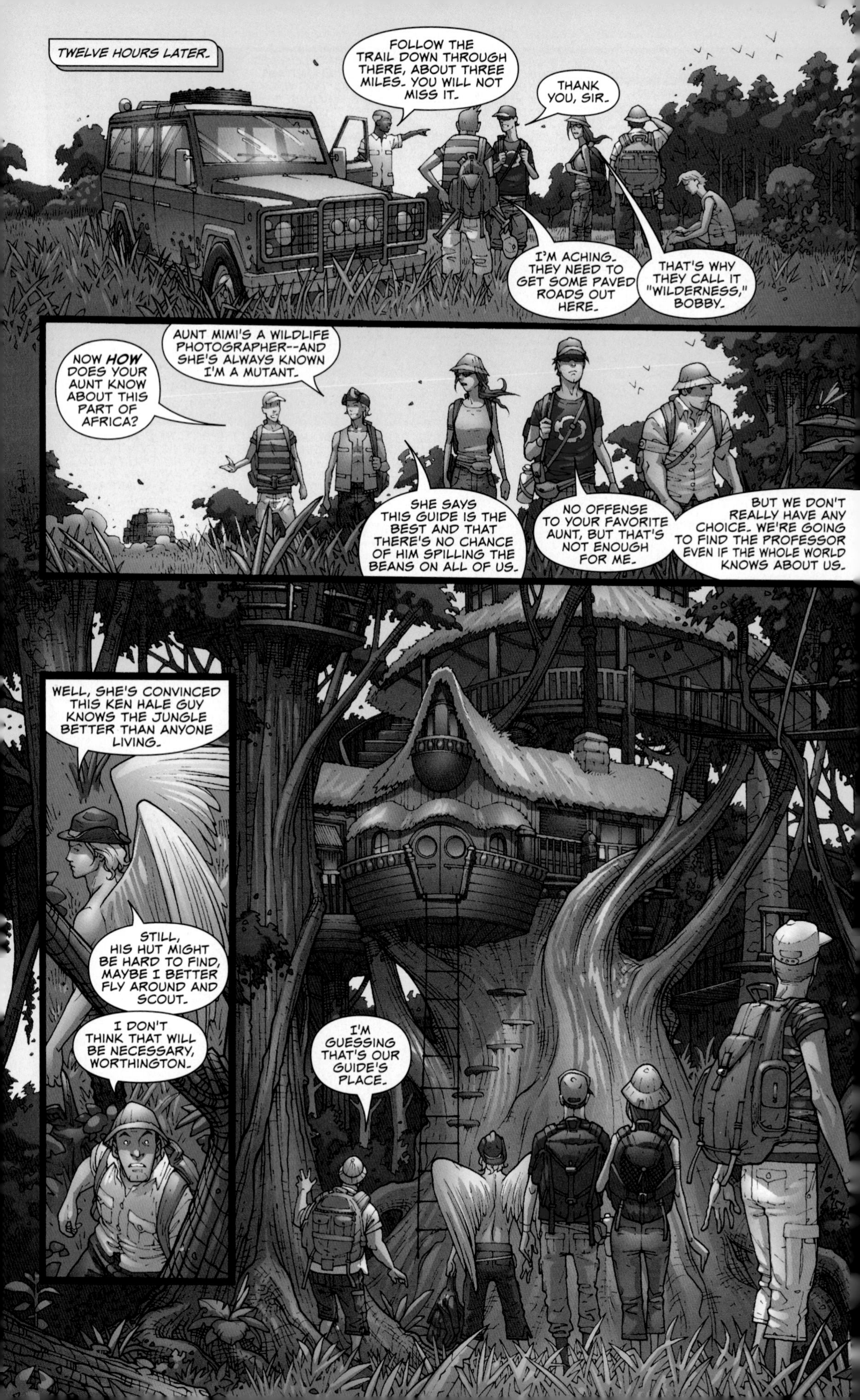

TWELVE HOURS LATER.
FOLLOW THE TRAIL DOWN THROUGH THERE, ABOUT THREE MILES. YOU WILL NOT MISS IT.
THANK YOU, SIR.
I'M ACHING. THEY NEED TO GET SOME PAVED ROADS OUT HERE.
THAT'S WHY THEY CALL IT "WILDERNESS," BOBBY.
NOW HOW DOES YOUR AUNT KNOW ABOUT THIS PART OF AFRICA?
AUNT MIMI'S A WILDLIFE PHOTOGRAPHER--AND SHE'S ALWAYS KNOWN I'M A MUTANT.
SHE SAYS THIS GUIDE IS THE BEST AND THAT THERE'S NO CHANCE OF HIM SPILLING THE BEANS ON ALL OF US.
NO OFFENSE TO YOUR FAVORITE AUNT, BUT THAT'S NOT ENOUGH FOR ME.
BUT WE DON'T REALLY HAVE ANY CHOICE. WE'RE GOING TO FIND THE PROFESSOR EVEN IF THE WHOLE WORLD KNOWS ABOUT US.
WELL, SHE'S CONVINCED THIS KEN HALE GUY KNOWS THE JUNGLE BETTER THAN ANYONE LIVING.
STILL, HIS HUT MIGHT BE HARD TO FIND, MAYBE I BETTER FLY AROUND AND SCOUT.
I DON'T THINK THAT WILL BE NECESSARY, WORTHINGTON.
I'M GUESSING THAT'S OUR GUIDE'S PLACE.

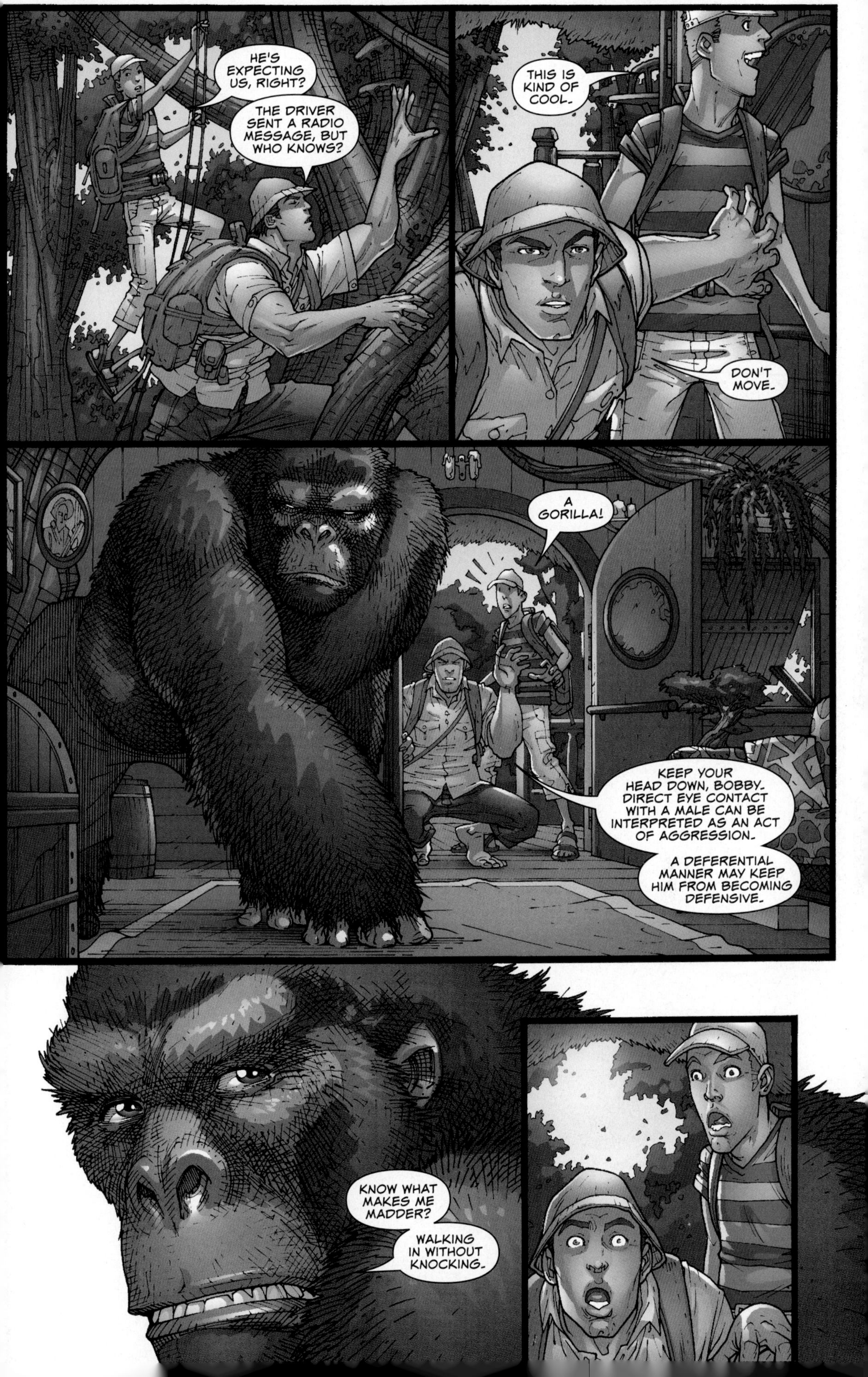
HE'S EXPECTING US, RIGHT?
THE DRIVER SENT A RADIO MESSAGE, BUT WHO KNOWS?
THIS IS KIND OF COOL.
DON'T MOVE.
A GORILLA!
KEEP YOUR HEAD DOWN, BOBBY. DIRECT EYE CONTACT WITH A MALE CAN BE INTERPRETED AS AN ACT OF AGGRESSION.
A DEFERENTIAL MANNER MAY KEEP HIM FROM BECOMING DEFENSIVE.
KNOW WHAT MAKES ME MADDER?
WALKING IN WITHOUT KNOCKING.

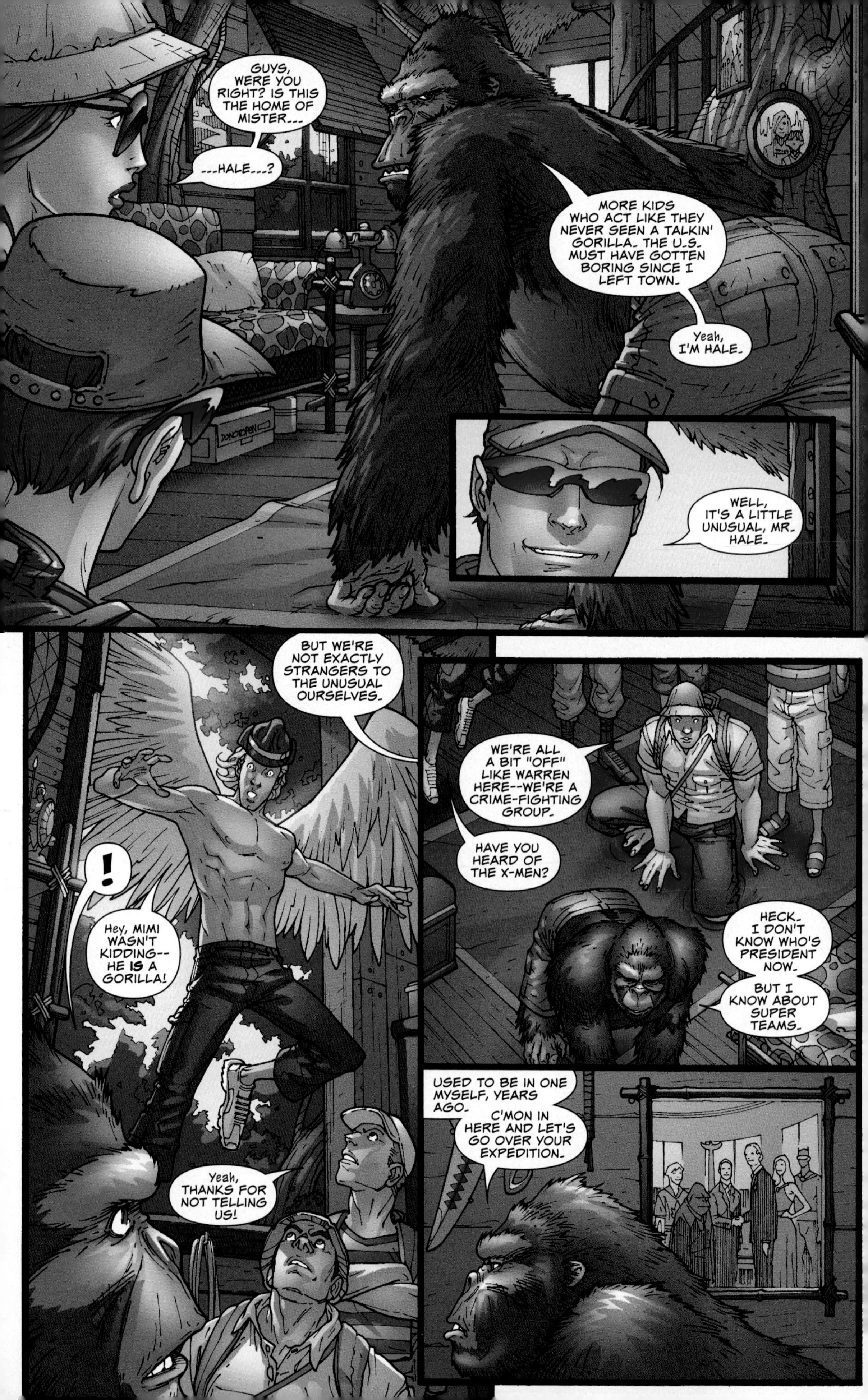
GUYS, WERE YOU RIGHT? IS THIS THE HOME OF MISTER---
---HALE---?
MORE KIDS WHO ACT LIKE THEY NEVER SEEN A TALKIN' GORILLA. THE U.S. MUST HAVE GOTTEN BORING SINCE I LEFT TOWN.
Yeah, I'M HALE.
WELL, IT'S A LITTLE UNUSUAL, MR. HALE.
BUT WE'RE NOT EXACTLY STRANGERS TO THE UNUSUAL OURSELVES.
!
Hey, MIMI WASN'T KIDDING--HE **IS** A GORILLA!
Yeah, THANKS FOR NOT TELLING US!
WE'RE ALL A BIT "OFF" LIKE WARREN HERE--WE'RE A CRIME-FIGHTING GROUP.
HAVE YOU HEARD OF THE X-MEN?
HECK. I DON'T KNOW WHO'S PRESIDENT NOW.
BUT I KNOW ABOUT SUPER TEAMS.
USED TO BE IN ONE MYSELF, YEARS AGO.
C'MON IN HERE AND LET'S GO OVER YOUR EXPEDITION.

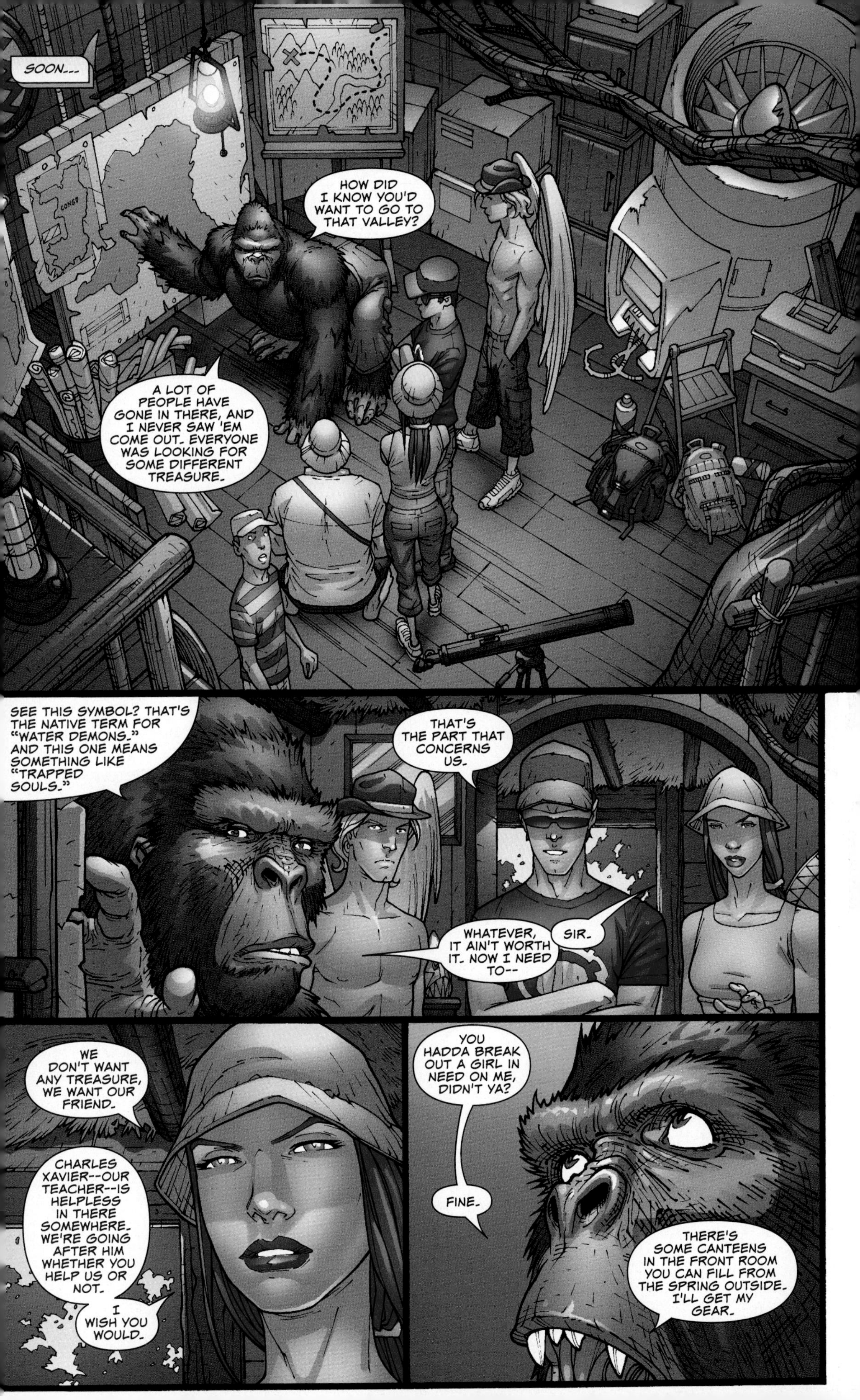
SOON---
HOW DID I KNOW YOU'D WANT TO GO TO THAT VALLEY?
A LOT OF PEOPLE HAVE GONE IN THERE, AND I NEVER SAW 'EM COME OUT. EVERYONE WAS LOOKING FOR SOME DIFFERENT TREASURE.
CONGO
SEE THIS SYMBOL? THAT'S THE NATIVE TERM FOR "WATER DEMONS." AND THIS ONE MEANS SOMETHING LIKE "TRAPPED SOULS."
THAT'S THE PART THAT CONCERNS US.
WHATEVER, IT AIN'T WORTH IT. NOW I NEED TO--
SIR.
WE DON'T WANT ANY TREASURE, WE WANT OUR FRIEND.
CHARLES XAVIER--OUR TEACHER--IS HELPLESS IN THERE SOMEWHERE. WE'RE GOING AFTER HIM WHETHER YOU HELP US OR NOT.
I WISH YOU WOULD.
YOU HADDA BREAK OUT A GIRL IN NEED ON ME, DIDN'T YA?
FINE.
THERE'S SOME CANTEENS IN THE FRONT ROOM YOU CAN FILL FROM THE SPRING OUTSIDE. I'LL GET MY GEAR.

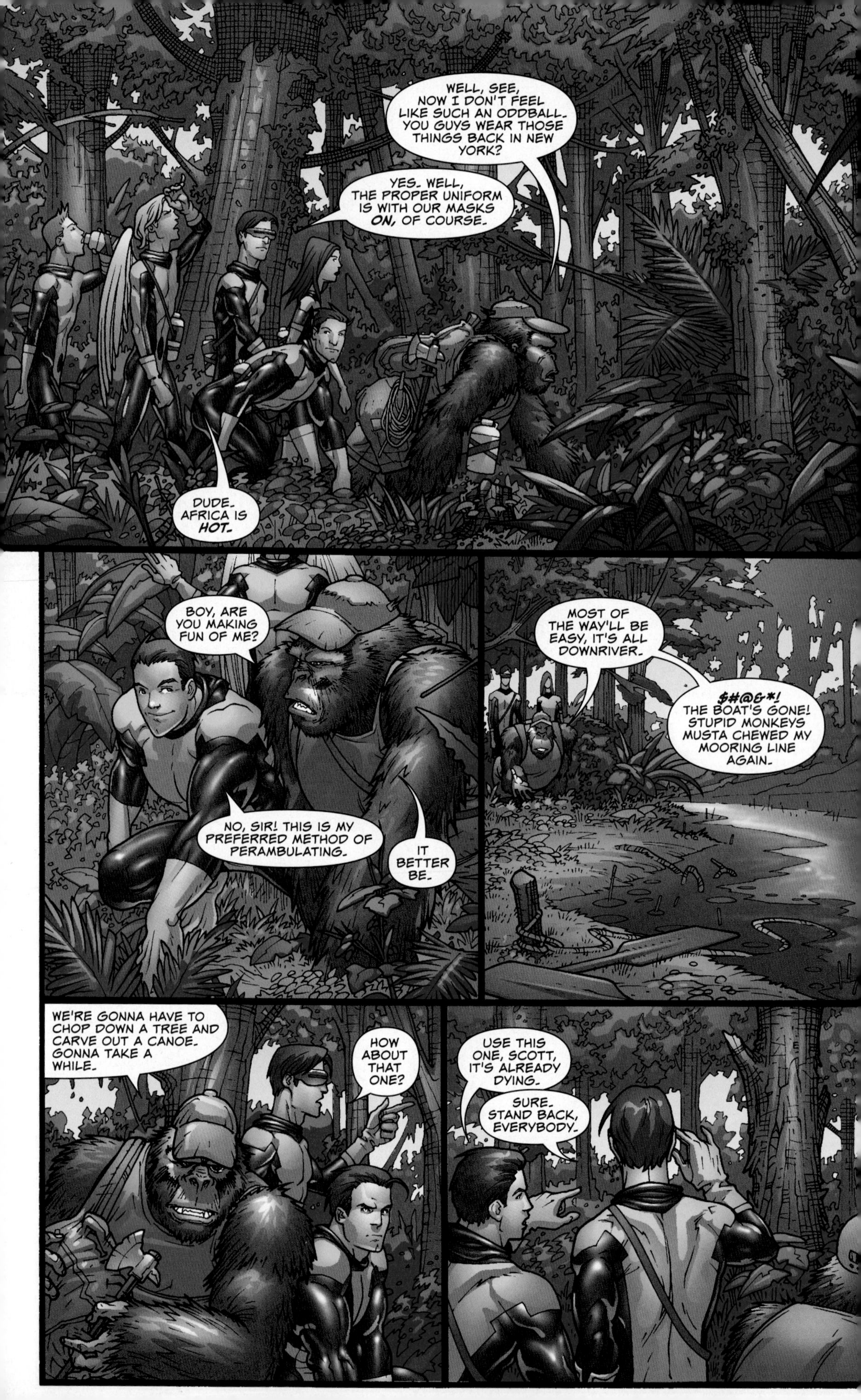
WELL, SEE, NOW I DON'T FEEL LIKE SUCH AN ODDBALL. YOU GUYS WEAR THOSE THINGS BACK IN NEW YORK?
YES. WELL, THE PROPER UNIFORM IS WITH OUR MASKS *ON,* OF COURSE.
DUDE. AFRICA IS *HOT.*
BOY, ARE YOU MAKING FUN OF ME?
NO, SIR! THIS IS MY PREFERRED METHOD OF PERAMBULATING.
IT BETTER BE.
MOST OF THE WAY'LL BE EASY, IT'S ALL DOWNRIVER.
$#@&!* THE BOAT'S GONE! STUPID MONKEYS MUSTA CHEWED MY MOORING LINE AGAIN.
WE'RE GONNA HAVE TO CHOP DOWN A TREE AND CARVE OUT A CANOE. GONNA TAKE A WHILE.
HOW ABOUT THAT ONE?
USE THIS ONE, SCOTT, IT'S ALREADY DYING.
SURE. STAND BACK, EVERYBODY.

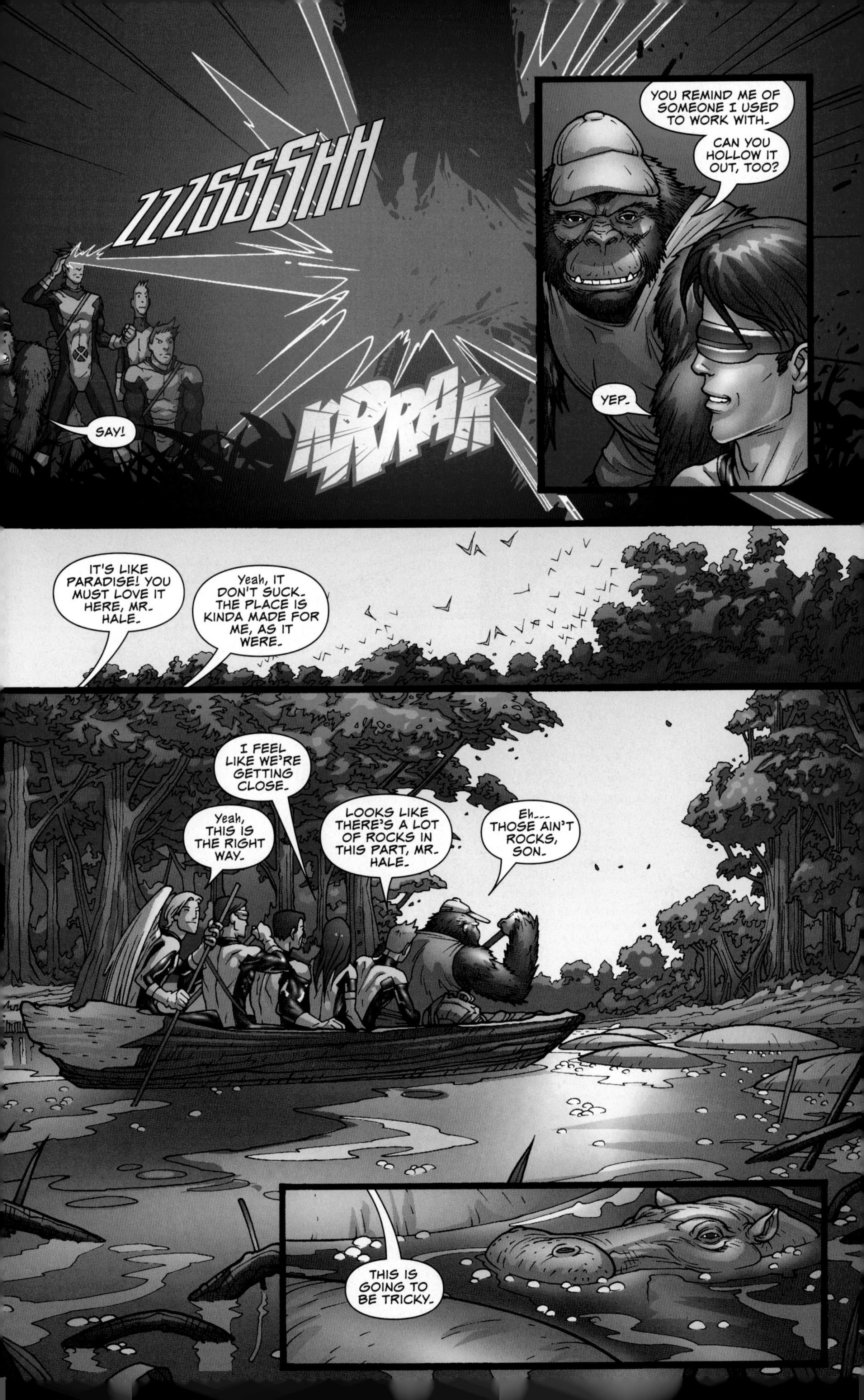
ZZZSSSSHH
SAY!
NRRAK
YOU REMIND ME OF SOMEONE I USED TO WORK WITH.
CAN YOU HOLLOW IT OUT, TOO?
YEP.
IT'S LIKE PARADISE! YOU MUST LOVE IT HERE, MR. HALE.
Yeah, IT DON'T SUCK. THE PLACE IS KINDA MADE FOR ME, AS IT WERE.
I FEEL LIKE WE'RE GETTING CLOSE.
Yeah, THIS IS THE RIGHT WAY.
LOOKS LIKE THERE'S A LOT OF ROCKS IN THIS PART, MR. HALE.
Eh... THOSE AIN'T ROCKS, SON.
THIS IS GOING TO BE TRICKY.

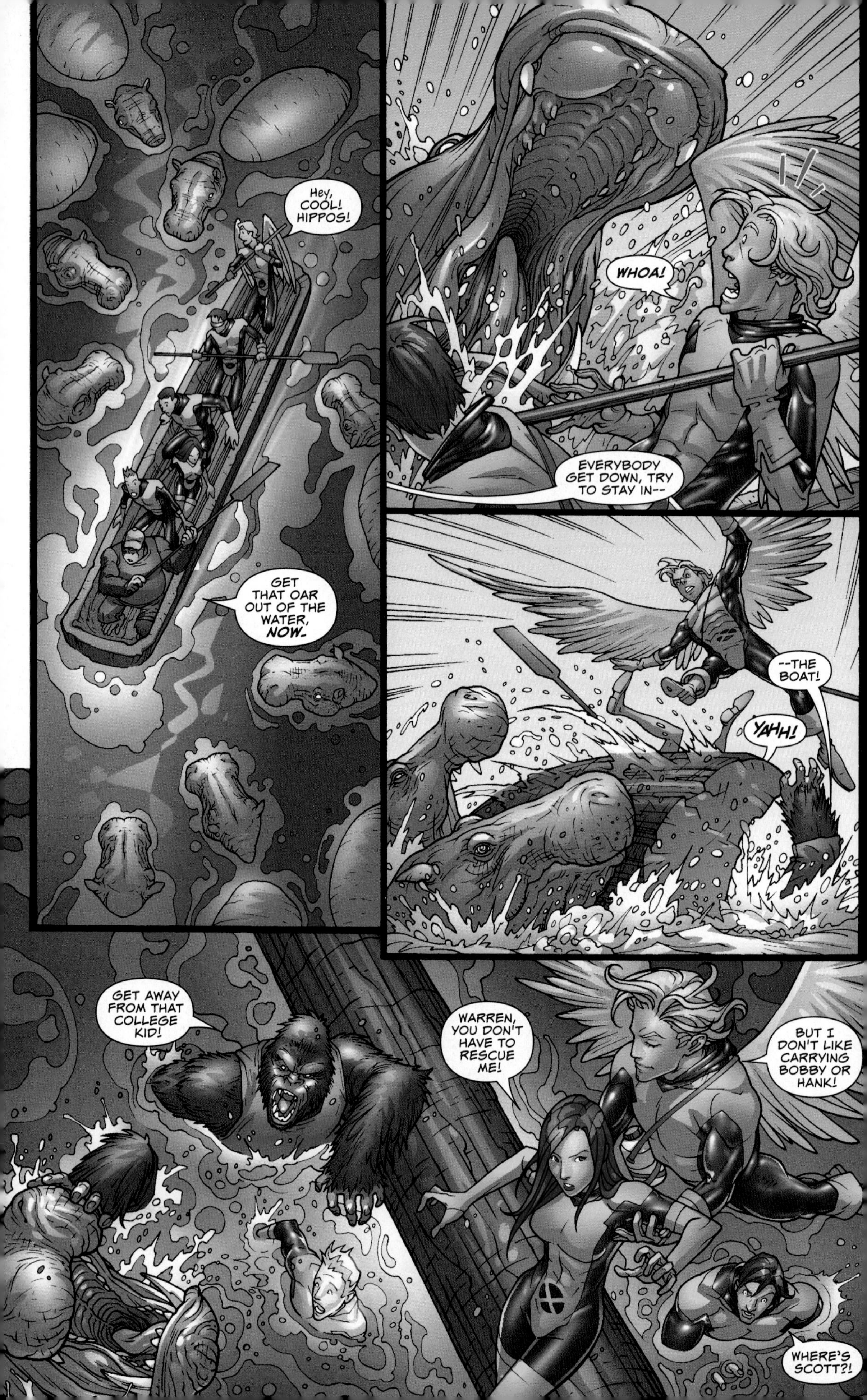
Hey, COOL! HIPPOS!
GET THAT OAR OUT OF THE WATER, NOW.
WHOA!
EVERYBODY GET DOWN, TRY TO STAY IN--
--THE BOAT!
YAHH!
GET AWAY FROM THAT COLLEGE KID!
WARREN, YOU DON'T HAVE TO RESCUE ME!
BUT I DON'T LIKE CARRYING BOBBY OR HANK!
WHERE'S SCOTT?!

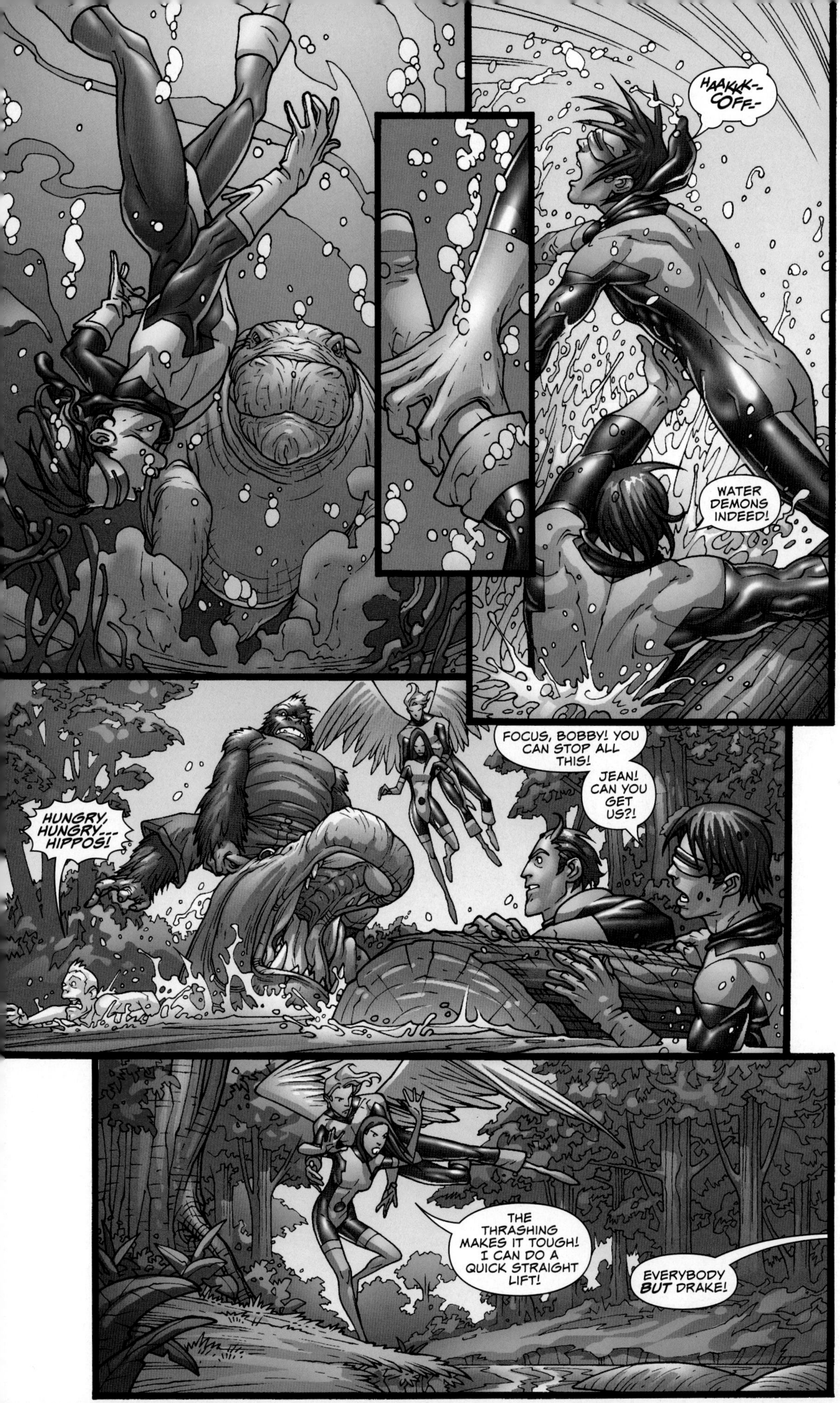
HAAKKK-- COFF--
WATER DEMONS INDEED!
HUNGRY, HUNGRY-- HIPPOS!
FOCUS, BOBBY! YOU CAN STOP ALL THIS!
JEAN! CAN YOU GET US?!
THE THRASHING MAKES IT TOUGH! I CAN DO A QUICK STRAIGHT LIFT!
EVERYBODY BUT DRAKE!

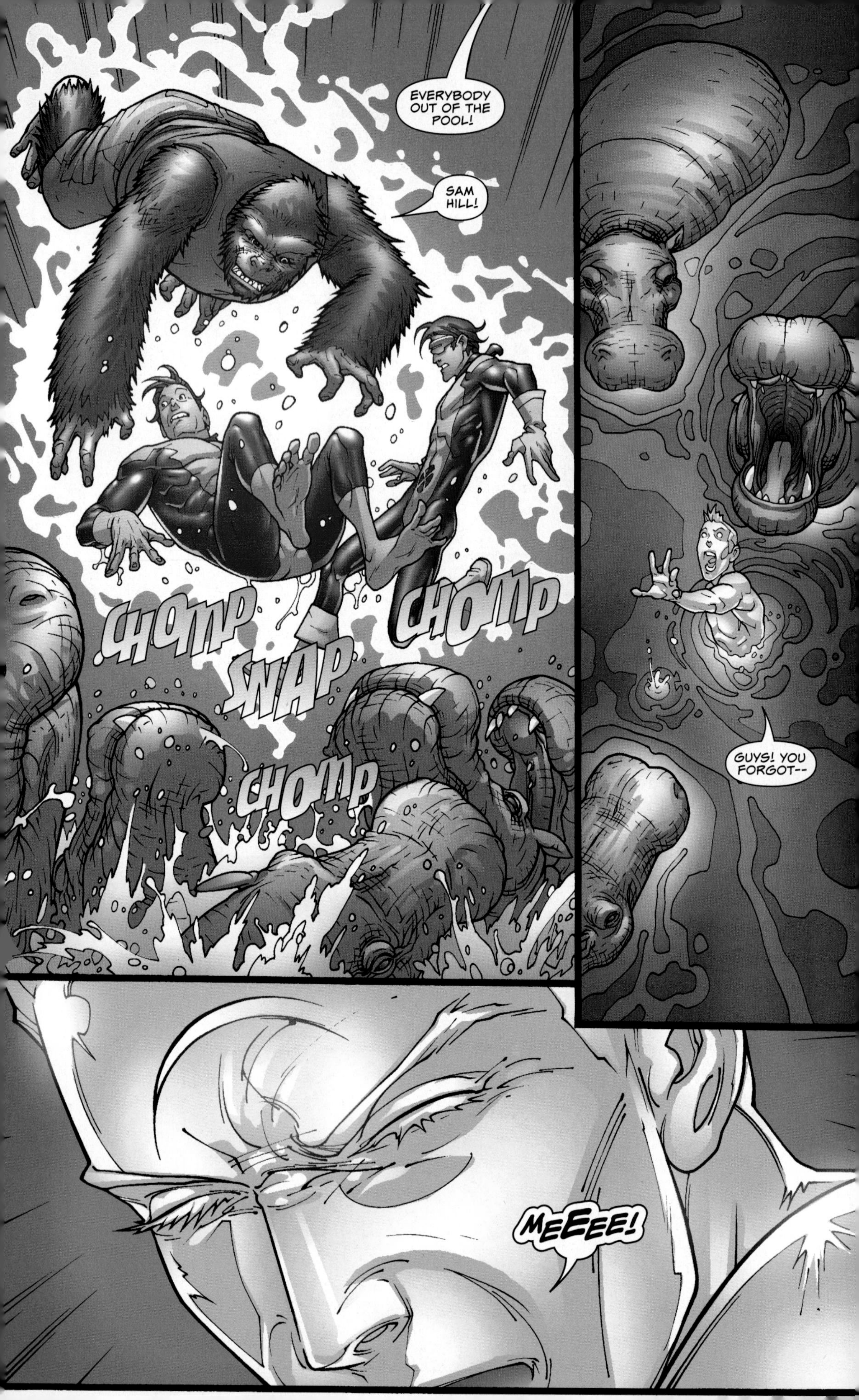
EVERYBODY OUT OF THE POOL!
SAM HILL!
CHOMP
SNAP
CHOMP
CHOMP
GUYS! YOU FORGOT--
MEEEE!

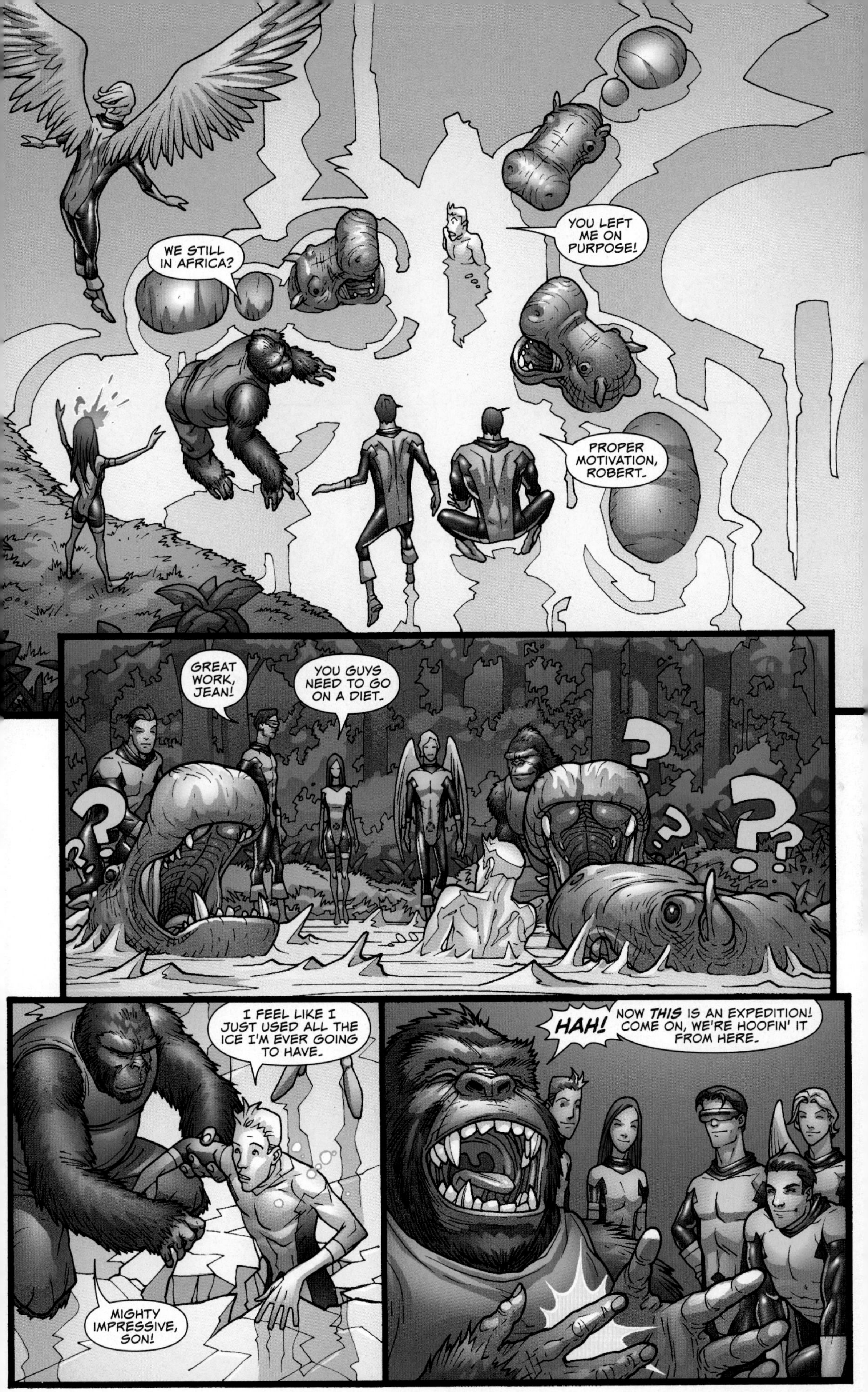
WE STILL IN AFRICA?
YOU LEFT ME ON PURPOSE!
PROPER MOTIVATION, ROBERT.
GREAT WORK, JEAN!
YOU GUYS NEED TO GO ON A DIET.
I FEEL LIKE I JUST USED ALL THE ICE I'M EVER GOING TO HAVE.
MIGHTY IMPRESSIVE, SON!
HAH!
NOW *THIS* IS AN EXPEDITION! COME ON, WE'RE HOOFIN' IT FROM HERE.

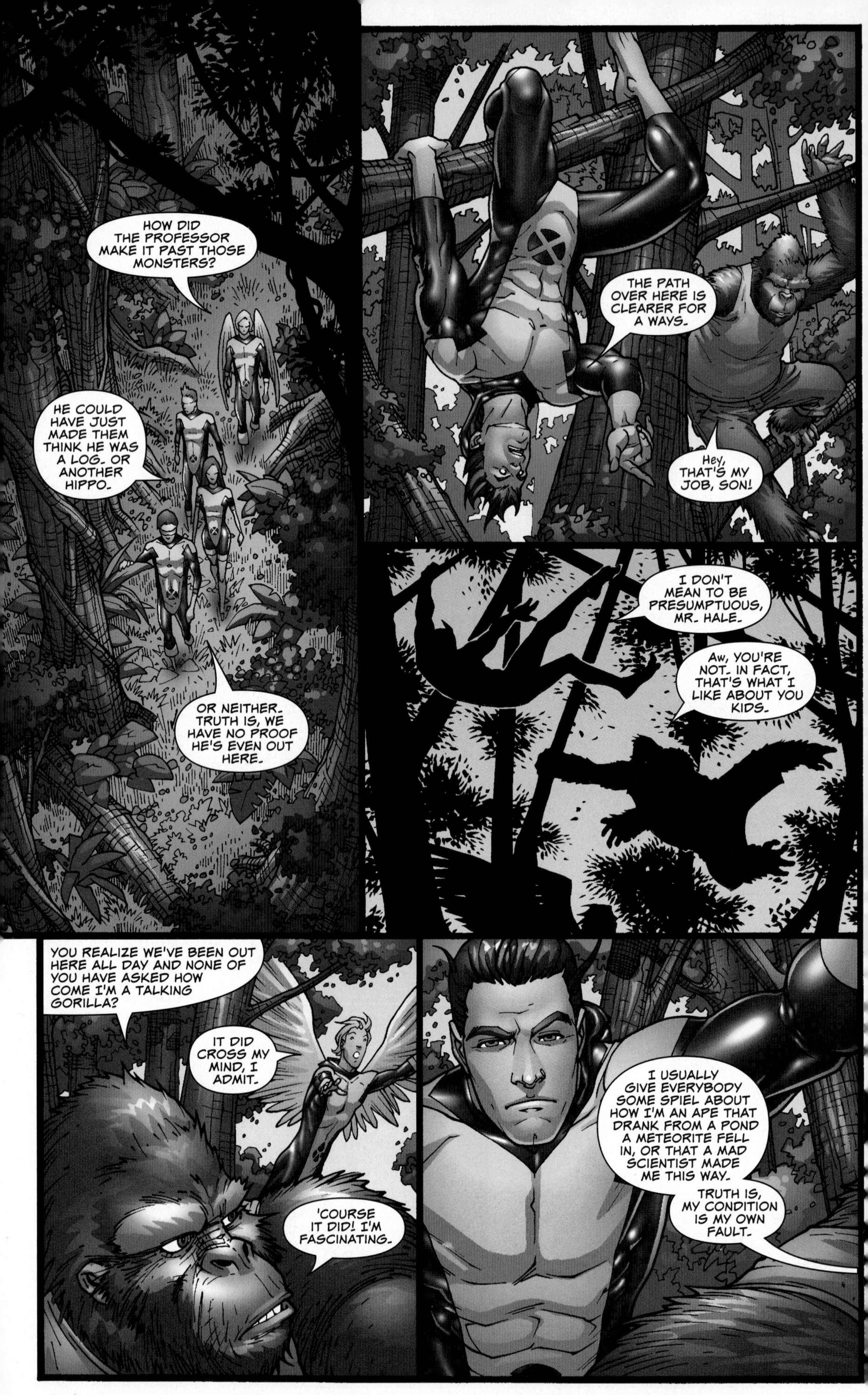
HOW DID THE PROFESSOR MAKE IT PAST THOSE MONSTERS?
HE COULD HAVE JUST MADE THEM THINK HE WAS A LOG. OR ANOTHER HIPPO.
OR NEITHER. TRUTH IS, WE HAVE NO PROOF HE'S EVEN OUT HERE.
THE PATH OVER HERE IS CLEARER FOR A WAYS.
Hey, THAT'S MY JOB, SON!
I DON'T MEAN TO BE PRESUMPTUOUS, MR. HALE.
Aw, YOU'RE NOT. IN FACT, THAT'S WHAT I LIKE ABOUT YOU KIDS.
YOU REALIZE WE'VE BEEN OUT HERE ALL DAY AND NONE OF YOU HAVE ASKED HOW COME I'M A TALKING GORILLA?
IT DID CROSS MY MIND, I ADMIT.
'COURSE IT DID! I'M FASCINATING.
I USUALLY GIVE EVERYBODY SOME SPIEL ABOUT HOW I'M AN APE THAT DRANK FROM A POND A METEORITE FELL IN, OR THAT A MAD SCIENTIST MADE ME THIS WAY.
TRUTH IS, MY CONDITION IS MY OWN FAULT.

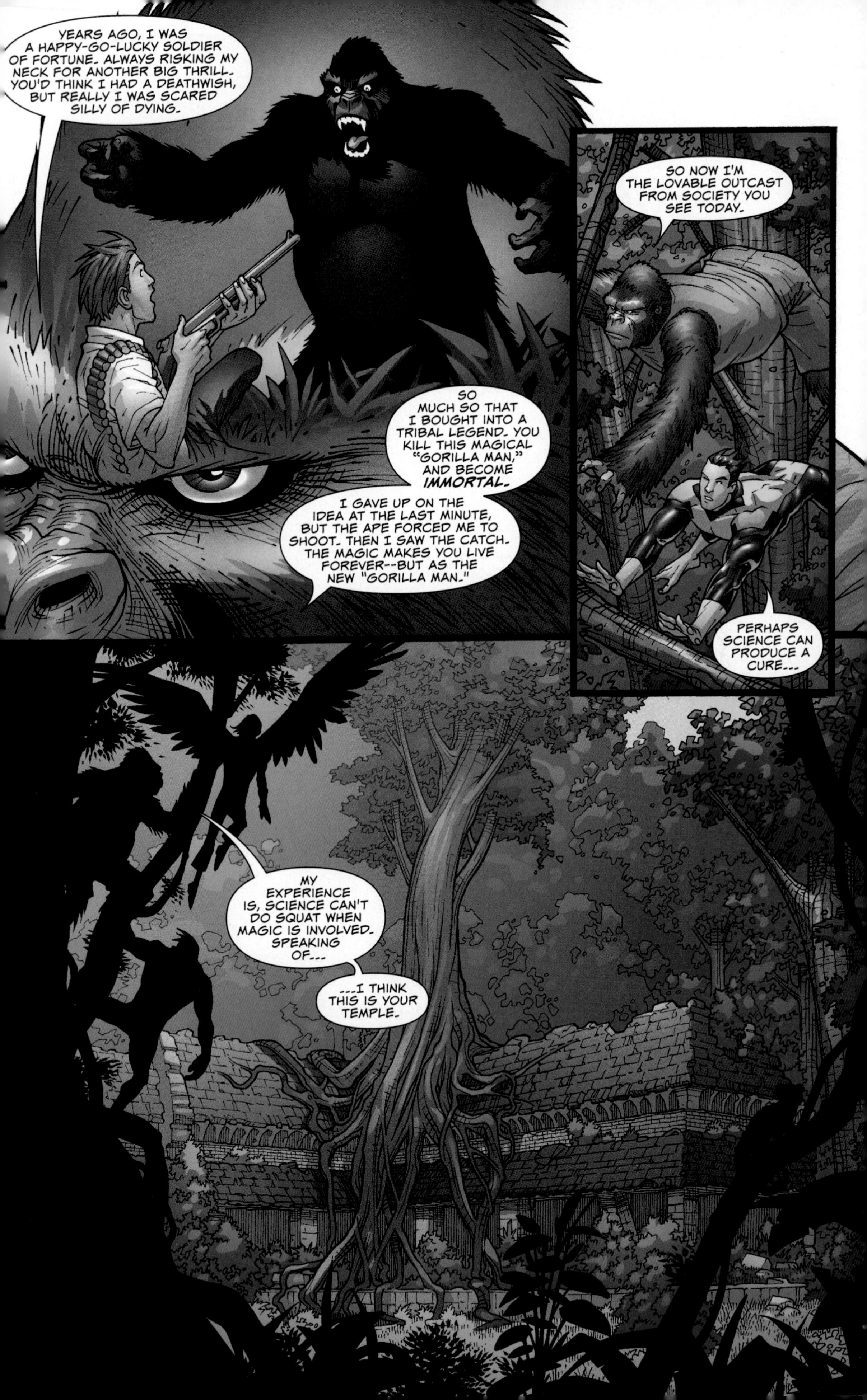
YEARS AGO, I WAS A HAPPY-GO-LUCKY SOLDIER OF FORTUNE. ALWAYS RISKING MY NECK FOR ANOTHER BIG THRILL. YOU'D THINK I HAD A DEATHWISH, BUT REALLY I WAS SCARED SILLY OF DYING.
SO MUCH SO THAT I BOUGHT INTO A TRIBAL LEGEND. YOU KILL THIS MAGICAL "GORILLA MAN," AND BECOME *IMMORTAL*.
I GAVE UP ON THE IDEA AT THE LAST MINUTE, BUT THE APE FORCED ME TO SHOOT. THEN I SAW THE CATCH. THE MAGIC MAKES YOU LIVE FOREVER--BUT AS THE NEW "GORILLA MAN."
SO NOW I'M THE LOVABLE OUTCAST FROM SOCIETY YOU SEE TODAY.
PERHAPS SCIENCE CAN PRODUCE A CURE...
MY EXPERIENCE IS, SCIENCE CAN'T DO SQUAT WHEN MAGIC IS INVOLVED. SPEAKING OF...
...I THINK THIS IS YOUR TEMPLE.

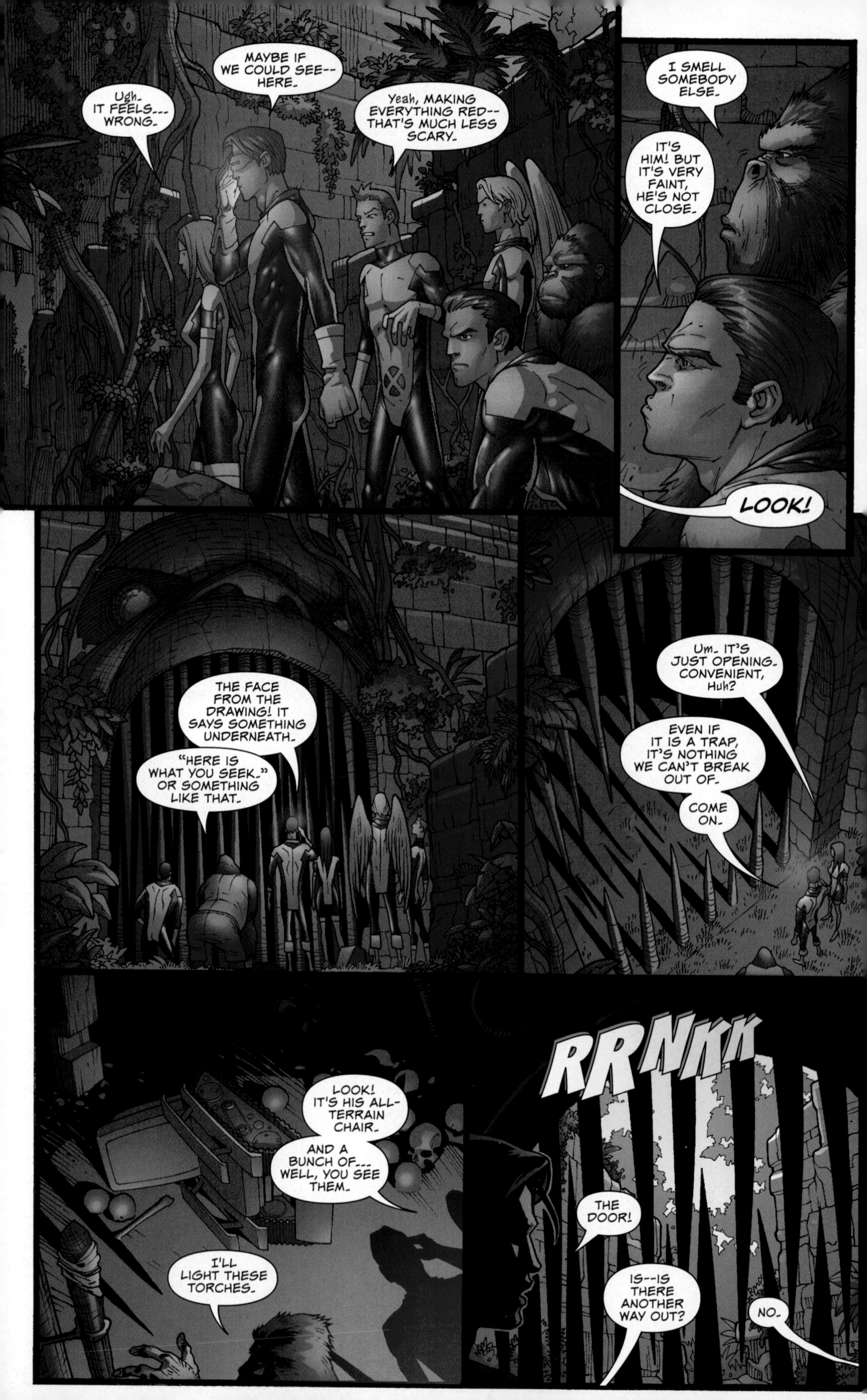
Ugh. IT FEELS... WRONG.
MAYBE IF WE COULD SEE-- HERE.
Yeah, MAKING EVERYTHING RED-- THAT'S MUCH LESS SCARY.
I SMELL SOMEBODY ELSE.
IT'S HIM! BUT IT'S VERY FAINT, HE'S NOT CLOSE.
LOOK!
THE FACE FROM THE DRAWING! IT SAYS SOMETHING UNDERNEATH.
"HERE IS WHAT YOU SEEK." OR SOMETHING LIKE THAT.
Um. IT'S JUST OPENING. CONVENIENT, Huh?
EVEN IF IT IS A TRAP, IT'S NOTHING WE CAN'T BREAK OUT OF.
COME ON.
LOOK! IT'S HIS ALL-TERRAIN CHAIR.
AND A BUNCH OF... WELL, YOU SEE THEM.
I'LL LIGHT THESE TORCHES.
RRNKK
THE DOOR!
IS--IS THERE ANOTHER WAY OUT?
NO.

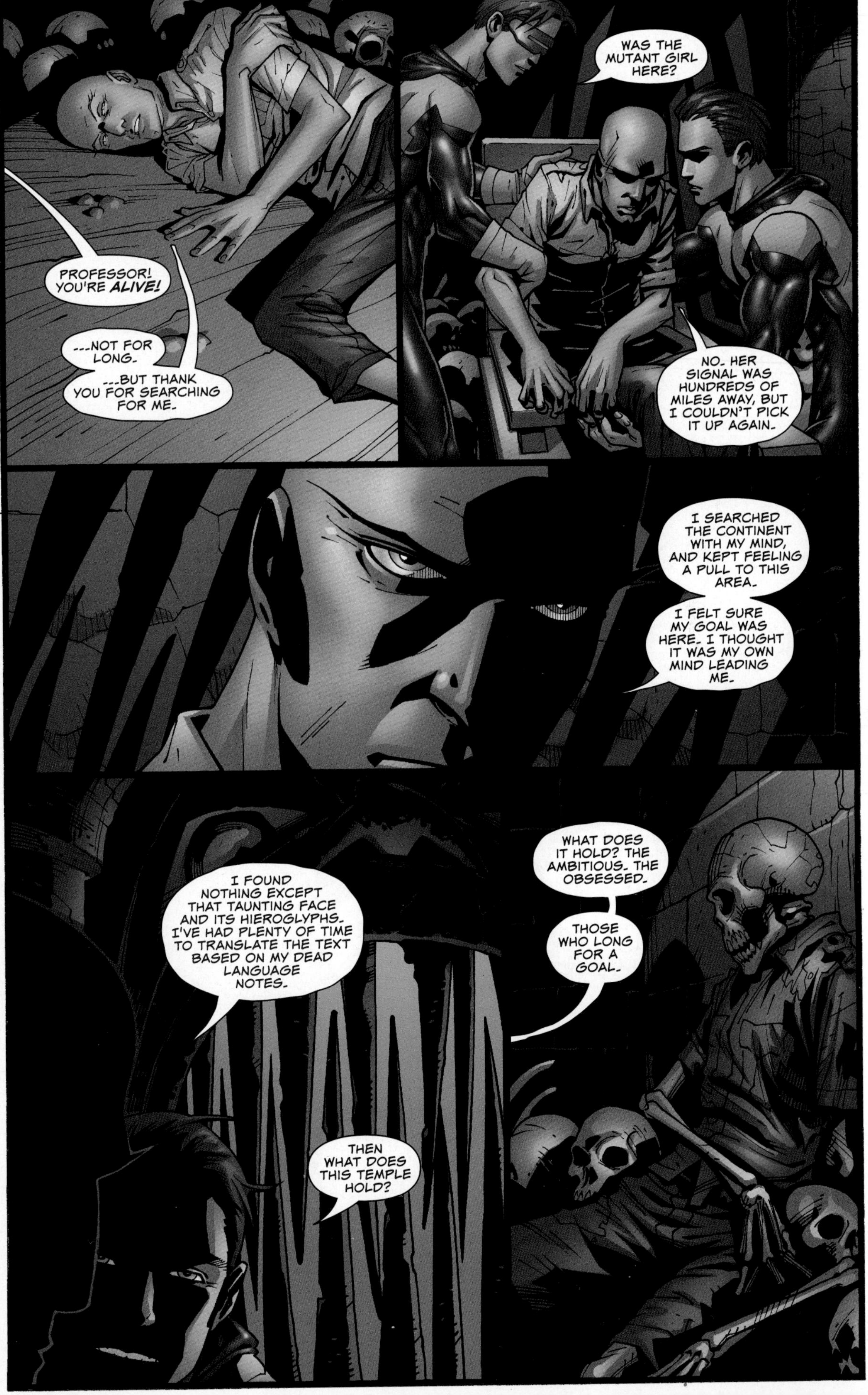
PROFESSOR! YOU'RE ALIVE!
...NOT FOR LONG.
...BUT THANK YOU FOR SEARCHING FOR ME.
WAS THE MUTANT GIRL HERE?
NO. HER SIGNAL WAS HUNDREDS OF MILES AWAY, BUT I COULDN'T PICK IT UP AGAIN.
I SEARCHED THE CONTINENT WITH MY MIND, AND KEPT FEELING A PULL TO THIS AREA.
I FELT SURE MY GOAL WAS HERE. I THOUGHT IT WAS MY OWN MIND LEADING ME.
I FOUND NOTHING EXCEPT THAT TAUNTING FACE AND ITS HIEROGLYPHS. I'VE HAD PLENTY OF TIME TO TRANSLATE THE TEXT BASED ON MY DEAD LANGUAGE NOTES.
THEN WHAT DOES THIS TEMPLE HOLD?
WHAT DOES IT HOLD? THE AMBITIOUS. THE OBSESSED.
THOSE WHO LONG FOR A GOAL.

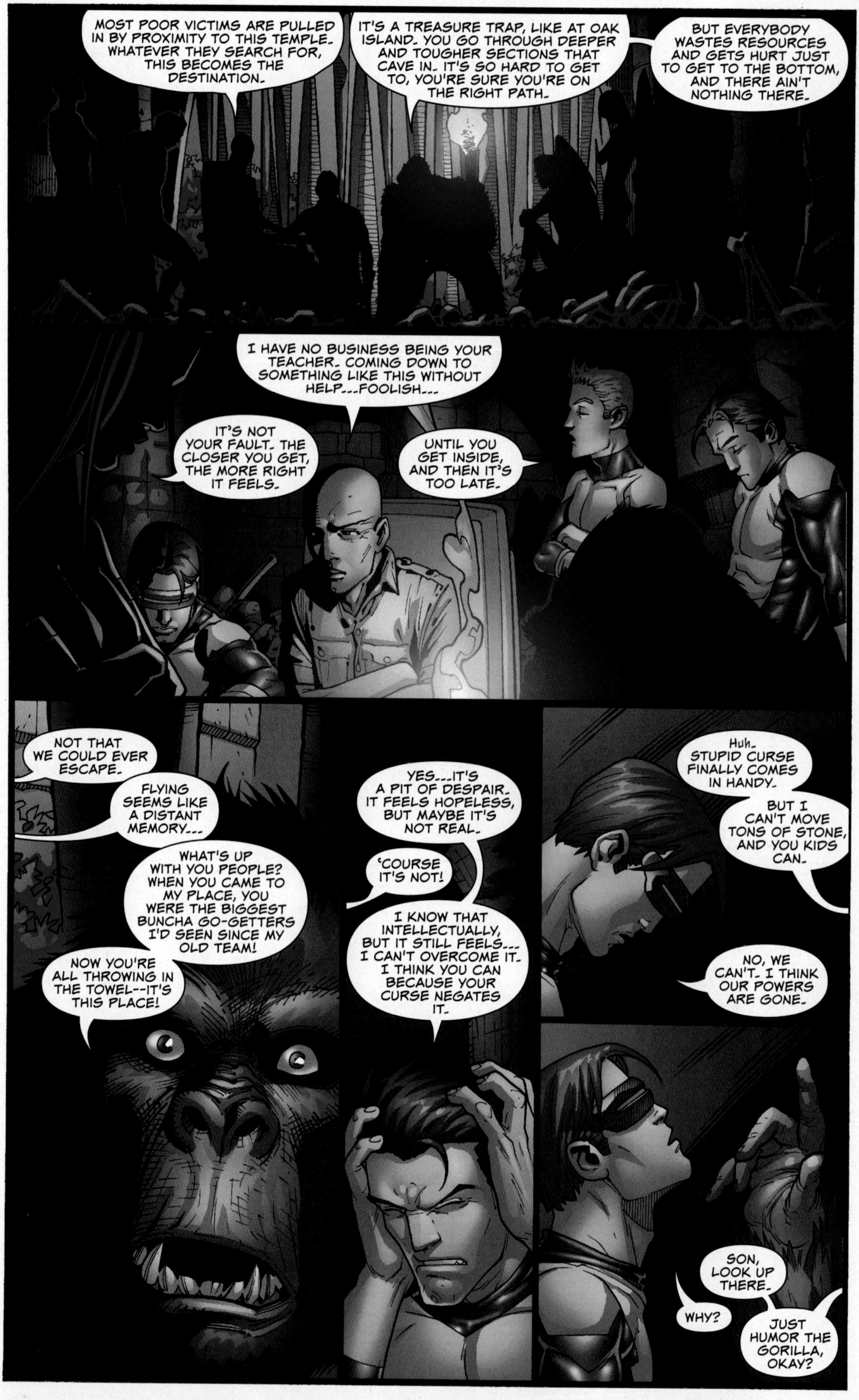
MOST POOR VICTIMS ARE PULLED IN BY PROXIMITY TO THIS TEMPLE. WHATEVER THEY SEARCH FOR, THIS BECOMES THE DESTINATION.
IT'S A TREASURE TRAP, LIKE AT OAK ISLAND. YOU GO THROUGH DEEPER AND TOUGHER SECTIONS THAT CAVE IN. IT'S SO HARD TO GET TO, YOU'RE SURE YOU'RE ON THE RIGHT PATH.
BUT EVERYBODY WASTES RESOURCES AND GETS HURT JUST TO GET TO THE BOTTOM, AND THERE AIN'T NOTHING THERE.
I HAVE NO BUSINESS BEING YOUR TEACHER. COMING DOWN TO SOMETHING LIKE THIS WITHOUT HELP...FOOLISH...
IT'S NOT YOUR FAULT. THE CLOSER YOU GET, THE MORE RIGHT IT FEELS.
UNTIL YOU GET INSIDE, AND THEN IT'S TOO LATE.
NOT THAT WE COULD EVER ESCAPE.
FLYING SEEMS LIKE A DISTANT MEMORY...
WHAT'S UP WITH YOU PEOPLE? WHEN YOU CAME TO MY PLACE, YOU WERE THE BIGGEST BUNCHA GO-GETTERS I'D SEEN SINCE MY OLD TEAM!
NOW YOU'RE ALL THROWING IN THE TOWEL--IT'S THIS PLACE!
YES...IT'S A PIT OF DESPAIR. IT FEELS HOPELESS, BUT MAYBE IT'S NOT REAL.
'COURSE IT'S NOT!
I KNOW THAT INTELLECTUALLY, BUT IT STILL FEELS... I CAN'T OVERCOME IT. I THINK YOU CAN BECAUSE YOUR CURSE NEGATES IT.
Huh. STUPID CURSE FINALLY COMES IN HANDY.
BUT I CAN'T MOVE TONS OF STONE, AND YOU KIDS CAN.
NO, WE CAN'T. I THINK OUR POWERS ARE GONE.
SON, LOOK UP THERE.
WHY?
JUST HUMOR THE GORILLA, OKAY?

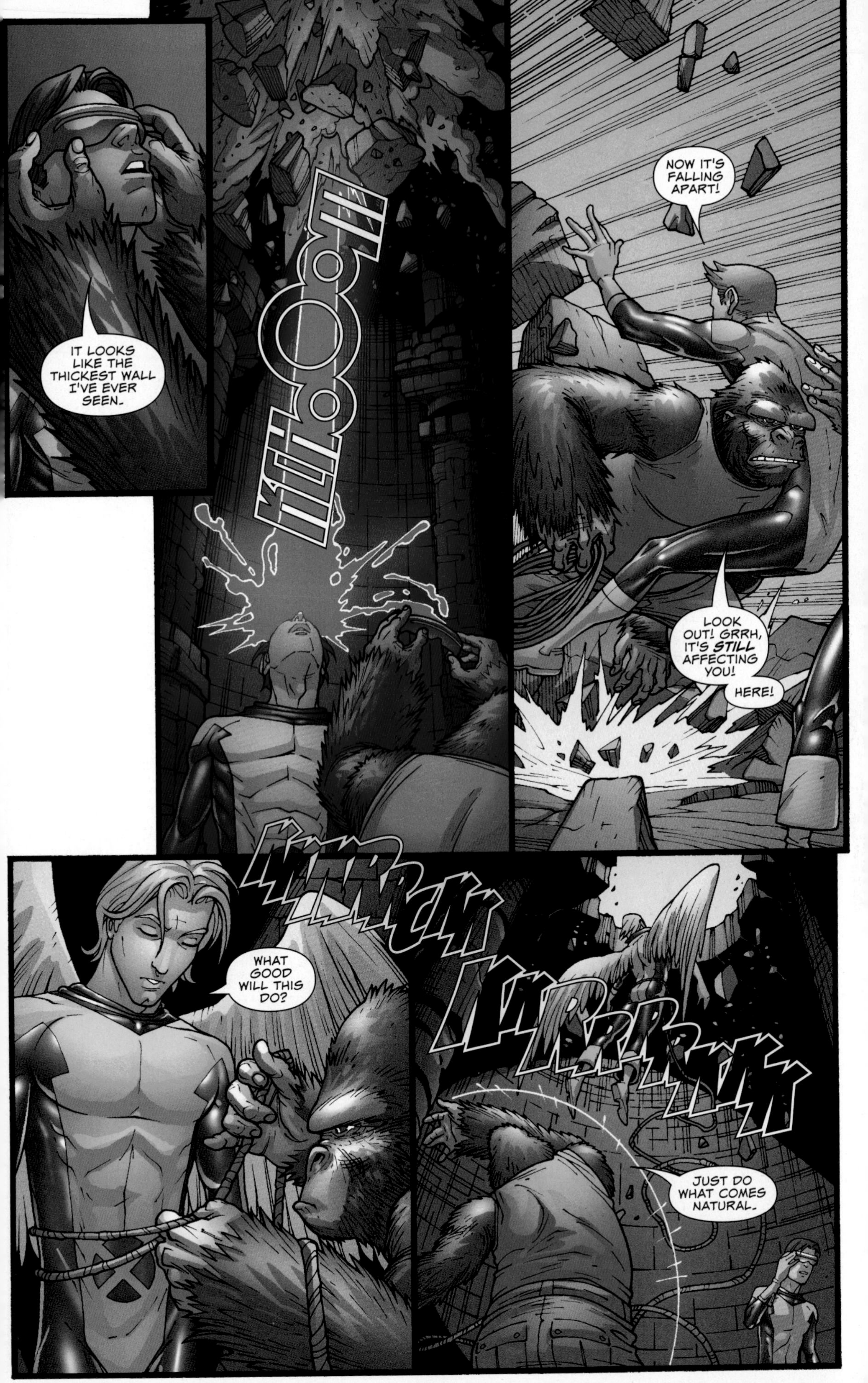
IT LOOKS LIKE THE THICKEST WALL I'VE EVER SEEN.
NOW IT'S FALLING APART!
LOOK OUT! GRRH, IT'S **STILL** AFFECTING YOU!
HERE!
WHAT GOOD WILL THIS DO?
JUST DO WHAT COMES NATURAL.

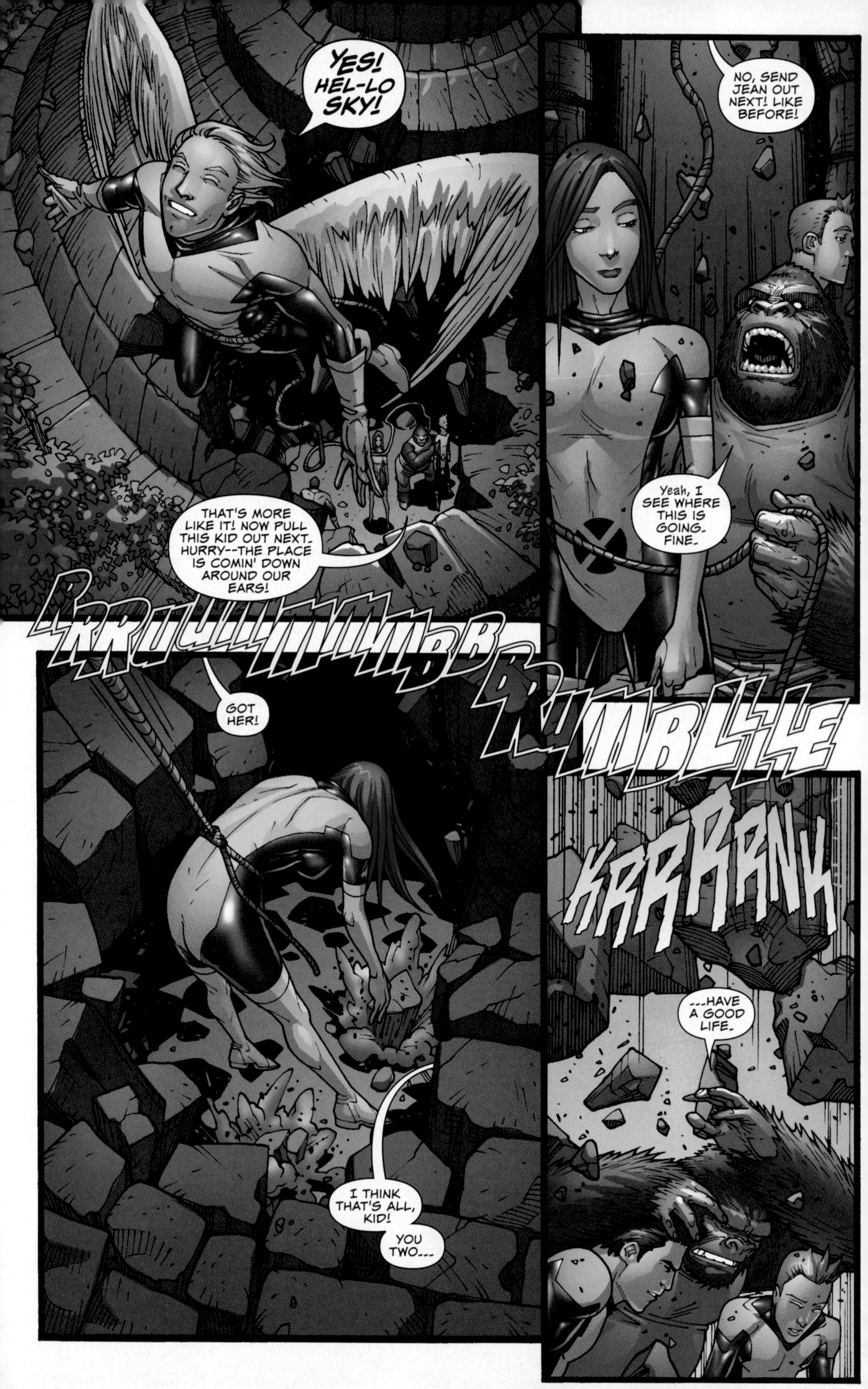
YES! HEL-LO SKY!
THAT'S MORE LIKE IT! NOW PULL THIS KID OUT NEXT. HURRY--THE PLACE IS COMIN' DOWN AROUND OUR EARS!
NO, SEND JEAN OUT NEXT! LIKE BEFORE!
Yeah, I SEE WHERE THIS IS GOING. FINE.
BRRUUUMMMB
BRUMBLLLE
GOT HER!
I THINK THAT'S ALL, KID!
YOU TWO...
KRRRANK
...HAVE A GOOD LIFE.

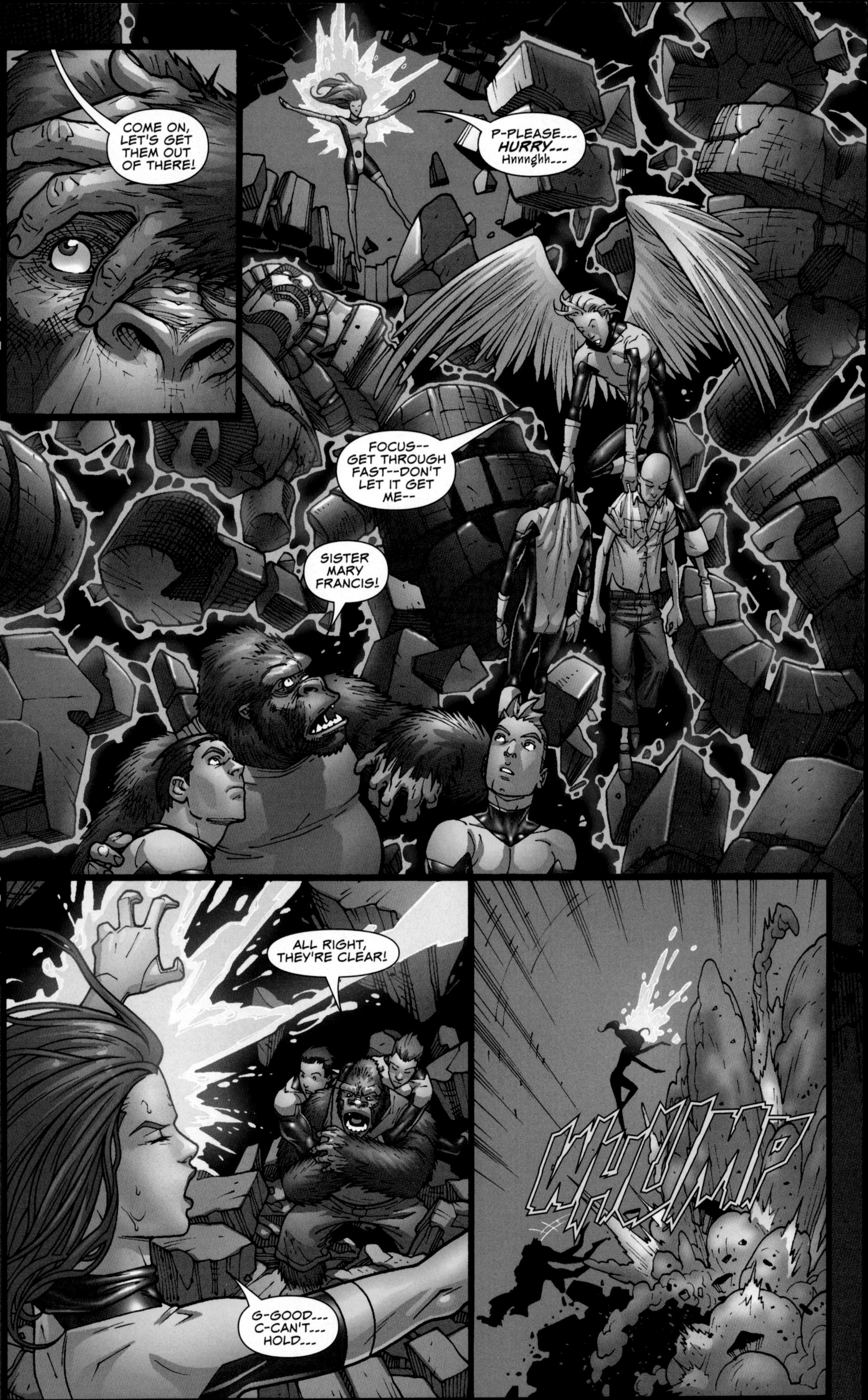
COME ON, LET'S GET THEM OUT OF THERE!
P-PLEASE--- HURRY--- Hnnnghh---
FOCUS-- GET THROUGH FAST--DON'T LET IT GET ME--
SISTER MARY FRANCIS!
ALL RIGHT, THEY'RE CLEAR!
G-GOOD--- C-CAN'T--- HOLD---
WHUMP

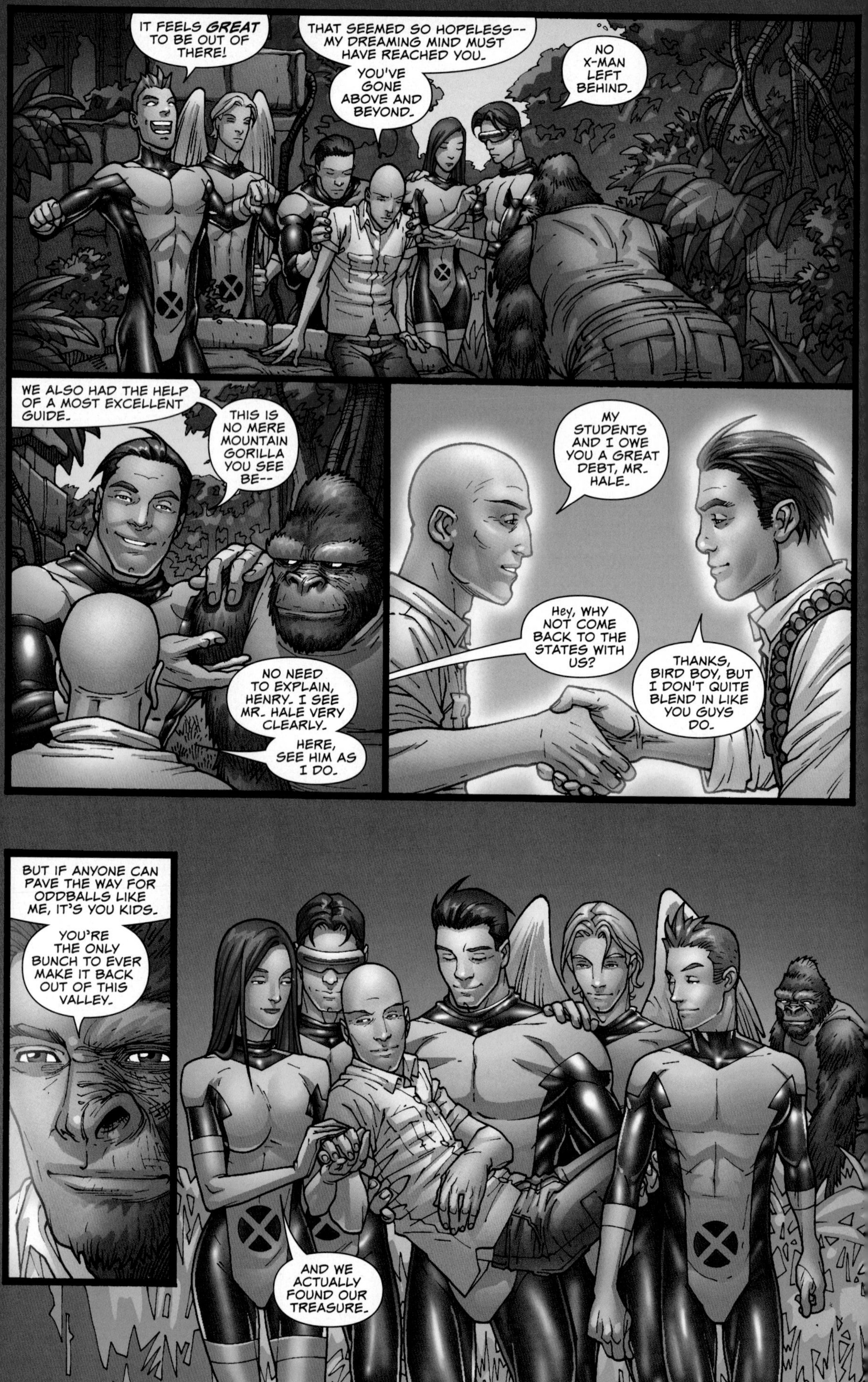
IT FEELS **GREAT** TO BE OUT OF THERE!
THAT SEEMED SO HOPELESS-- MY DREAMING MIND MUST HAVE REACHED YOU.
YOU'VE GONE ABOVE AND BEYOND.
NO X-MAN LEFT BEHIND.
WE ALSO HAD THE HELP OF A MOST EXCELLENT GUIDE.
THIS IS NO MERE MOUNTAIN GORILLA YOU SEE BE--
NO NEED TO EXPLAIN, HENRY. I SEE MR. HALE VERY CLEARLY.
HERE, SEE HIM AS I DO.
MY STUDENTS AND I OWE YOU A GREAT DEBT, MR. HALE.
Hey, WHY NOT COME BACK TO THE STATES WITH US?
THANKS, BIRD BOY, BUT I DON'T QUITE BLEND IN LIKE YOU GUYS DO.
BUT IF ANYONE CAN PAVE THE WAY FOR ODDBALLS LIKE ME, IT'S YOU KIDS.
YOU'RE THE ONLY BUNCH TO EVER MAKE IT BACK OUT OF THIS VALLEY.
AND WE ACTUALLY FOUND OUR TREASURE.

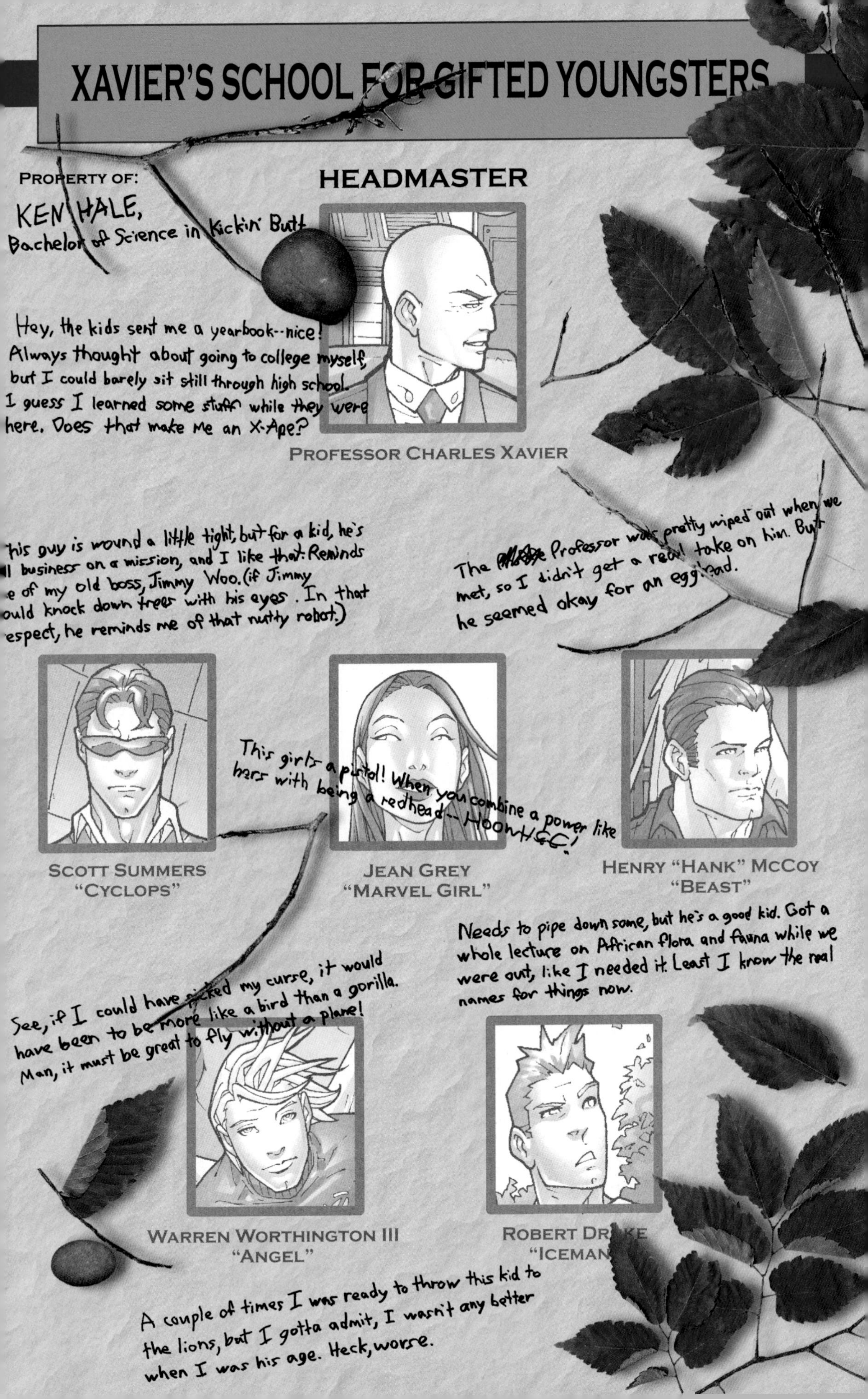
XAVIER'S SCHOOL FOR GIFTED YOUNGSTERS
PROPERTY OF:
KEN HALE,
Bachelor of Science in Kickin' Butt
HEADMASTER
Hey, the kids sent me a yearbook--nice! Always thought about going to college myself, but I could barely sit still through high school. I guess I learned some stuff while they were here. Does that make me an X-Ape?
PROFESSOR CHARLES XAVIER
his guy is wound a little tight, but for a kid, he's l business on a mission, and I like that. Reminds e of my old boss, Jimmy Woo. (if Jimmy ould knock down trees with his eyes. In that espect, he reminds me of that nutty robot.)
The Professor was pretty wiped out when we met, so I didn't get a real take on him. But he seemed okay for an egghead.
This girl's a pistol! When you combine a power like hers with being a redhead-- HOOWEE!
SCOTT SUMMERS
"CYCLOPS"
JEAN GREY
"MARVEL GIRL"
HENRY "HANK" McCOY
"BEAST"
Needs to pipe down some, but he's a good kid. Got a whole lecture on African flora and fauna while we were out, like I needed it. Least I know the real names for things now.
See, if I could have picked my curse, it would have been to be more like a bird than a gorilla. Man, it must be great to fly without a plane!
WARREN WORTHINGTON III
"ANGEL"
ROBERT DR KE
"ICEMAN
A couple of times I was ready to throw this kid to the lions, but I gotta admit, I wasn't any better when I was his age. Heck, worse.

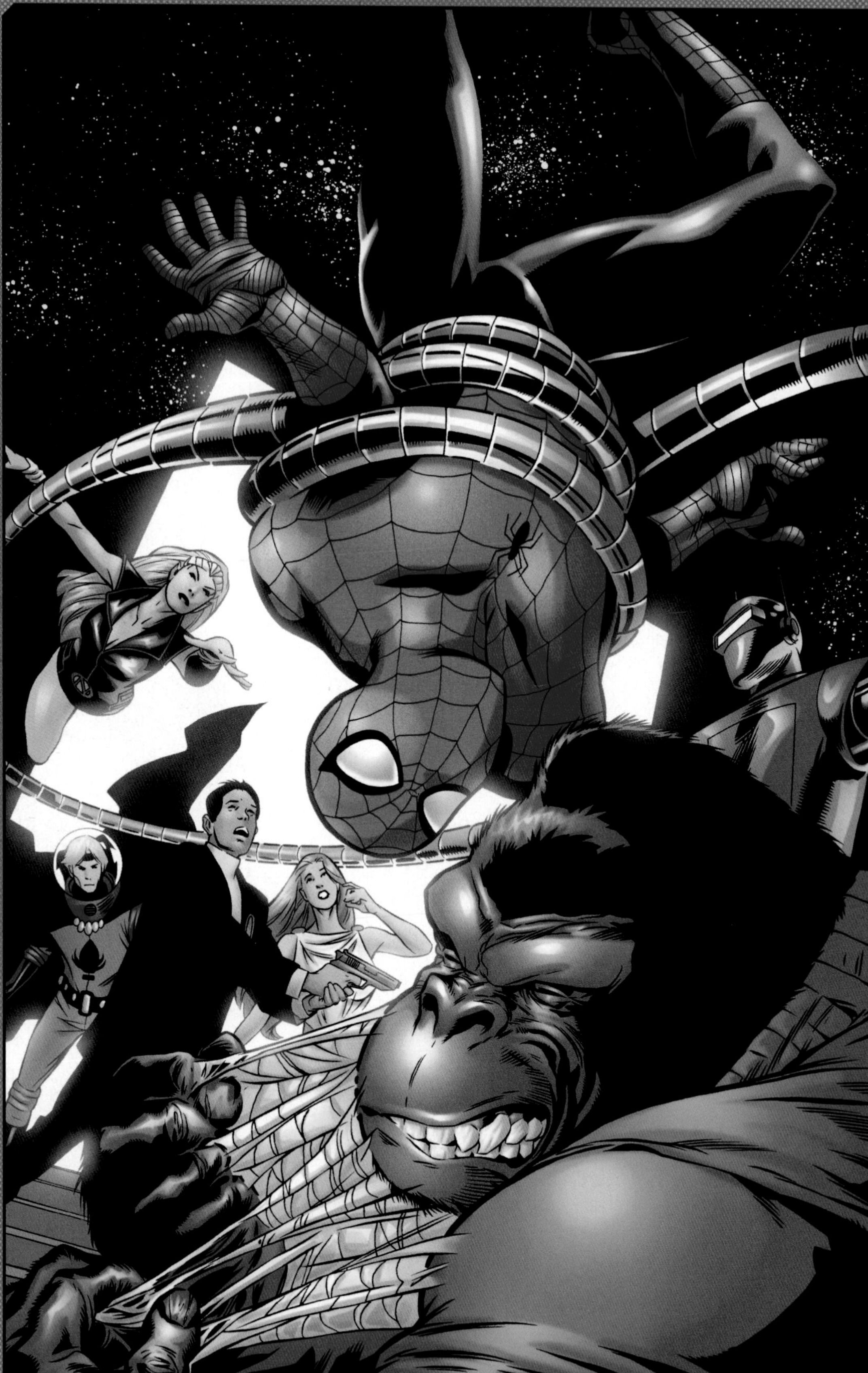

SPIDER-MAN FAMILY 4

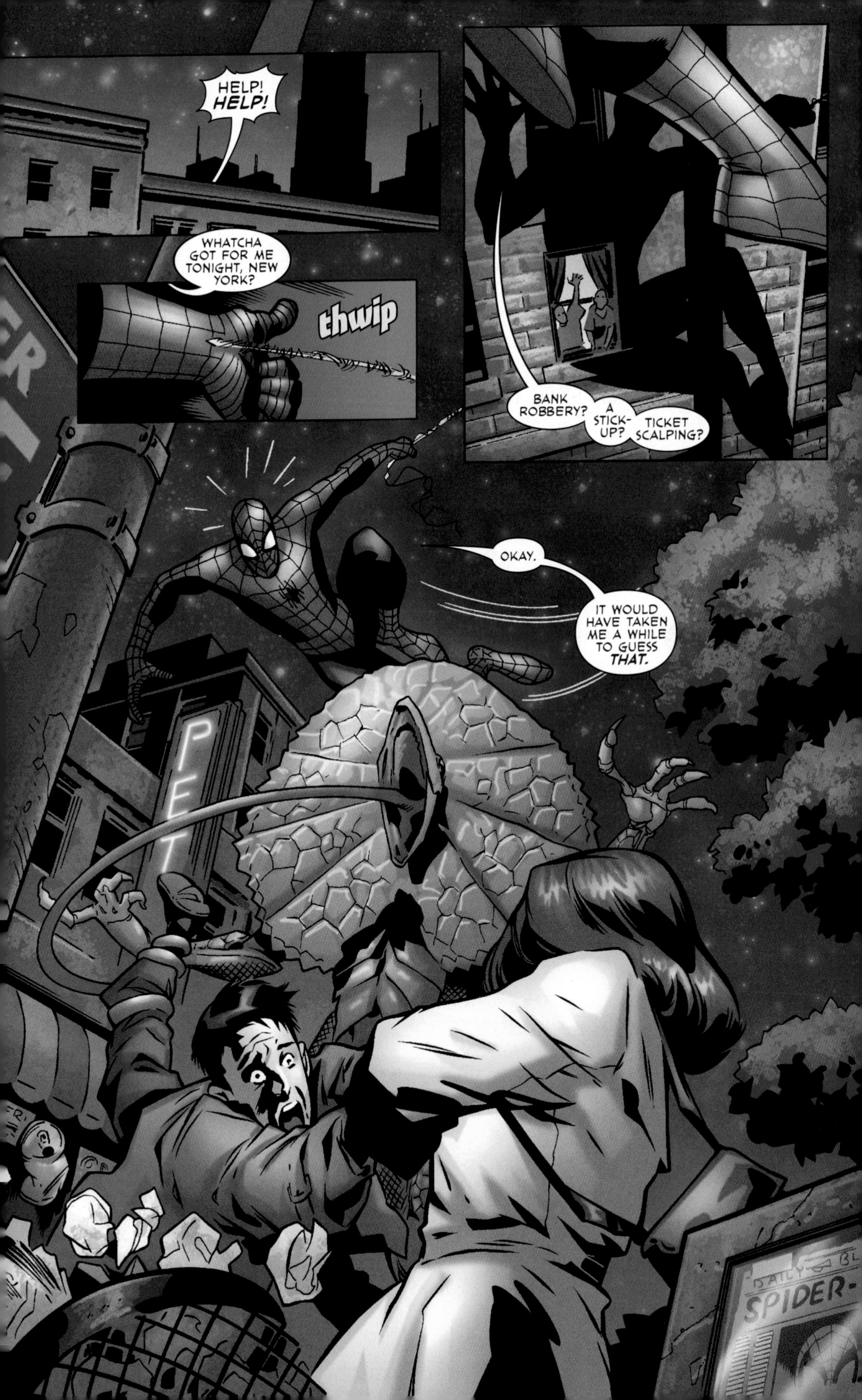
HELP! *HELP!*
WHATCHA GOT FOR ME TONIGHT, NEW YORK?
thwip
BANK ROBBERY?
A STICK-UP?
TICKET SCALPING?
OKAY.
IT WOULD HAVE TAKEN ME A WHILE TO GUESS *THAT.*
SPIDER-

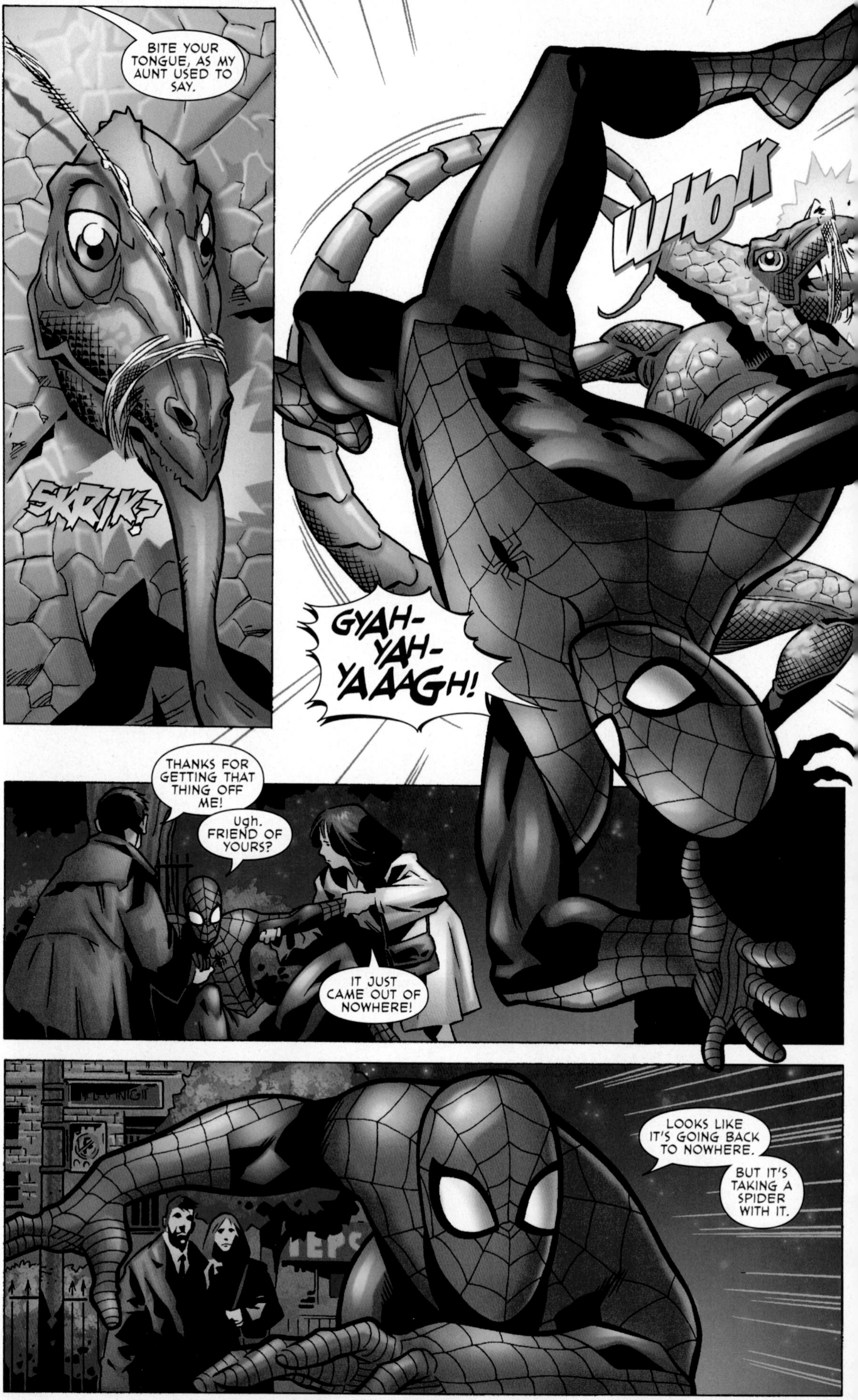
BITE YOUR TONGUE, AS MY AUNT USED TO SAY.
SKRIK!
WHOK
GYAH-YAH-YAAAGH!
THANKS FOR GETTING THAT THING OFF ME!
Ugh. FRIEND OF YOURS?
IT JUST CAME OUT OF NOWHERE!
LOOKS LIKE IT'S GOING BACK TO NOWHERE.
BUT IT'S TAKING A SPIDER WITH IT.

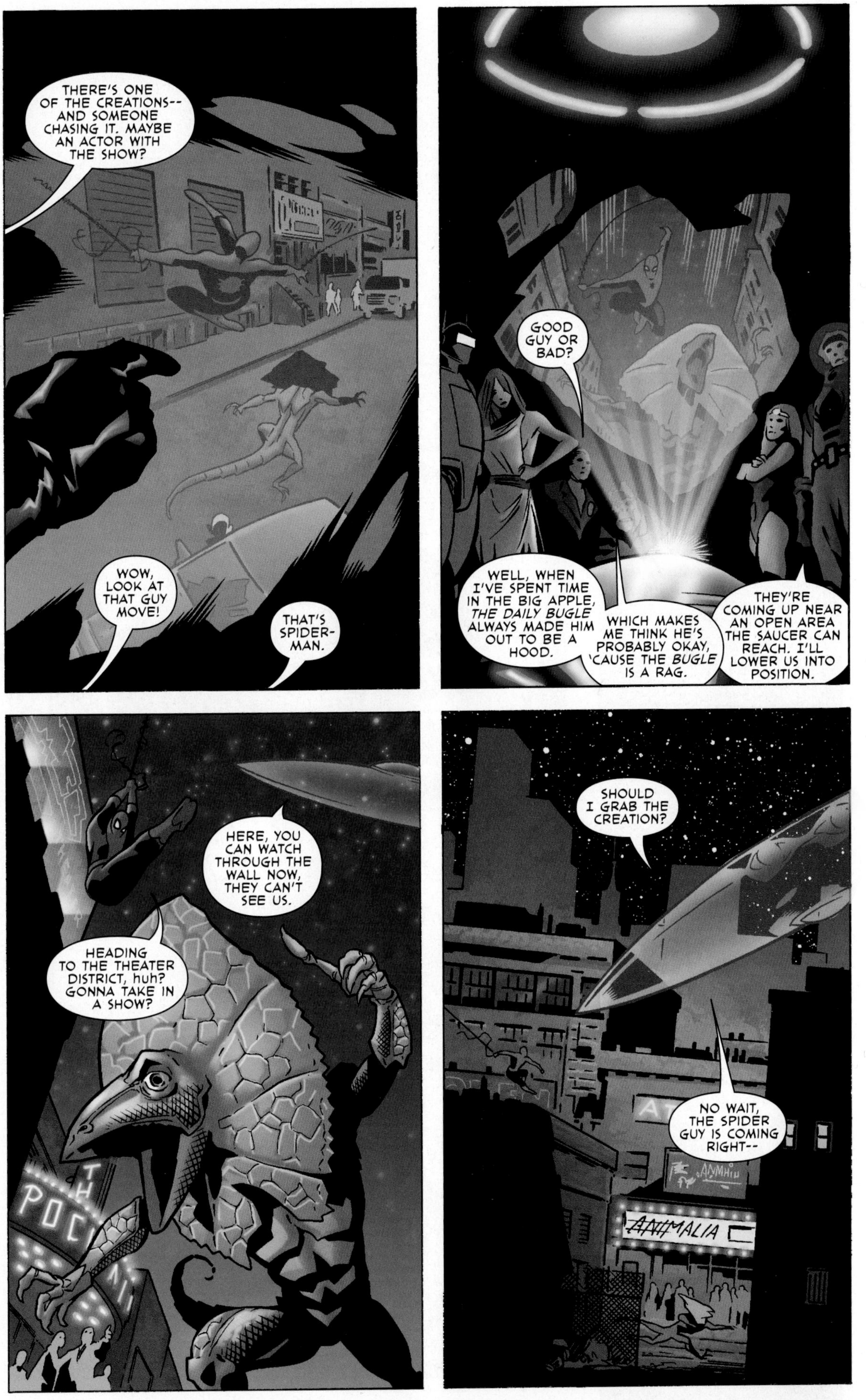
THERE'S ONE OF THE CREATIONS-- AND SOMEONE CHASING IT. MAYBE AN ACTOR WITH THE SHOW?
WOW, LOOK AT THAT GUY MOVE!
THAT'S SPIDER-MAN.
GOOD GUY OR BAD?
WELL, WHEN I'VE SPENT TIME IN THE BIG APPLE, *THE DAILY BUGLE* ALWAYS MADE HIM OUT TO BE A HOOD.
WHICH MAKES ME THINK HE'S PROBABLY OKAY, 'CAUSE THE *BUGLE* IS A RAG.
THEY'RE COMING UP NEAR AN OPEN AREA THE SAUCER CAN REACH. I'LL LOWER US INTO POSITION.
HERE, YOU CAN WATCH THROUGH THE WALL NOW, THEY CAN'T SEE US.
HEADING TO THE THEATER DISTRICT, huh? GONNA TAKE IN A SHOW?
SHOULD I GRAB THE CREATION?
NO WAIT, THE SPIDER GUY IS COMING RIGHT--

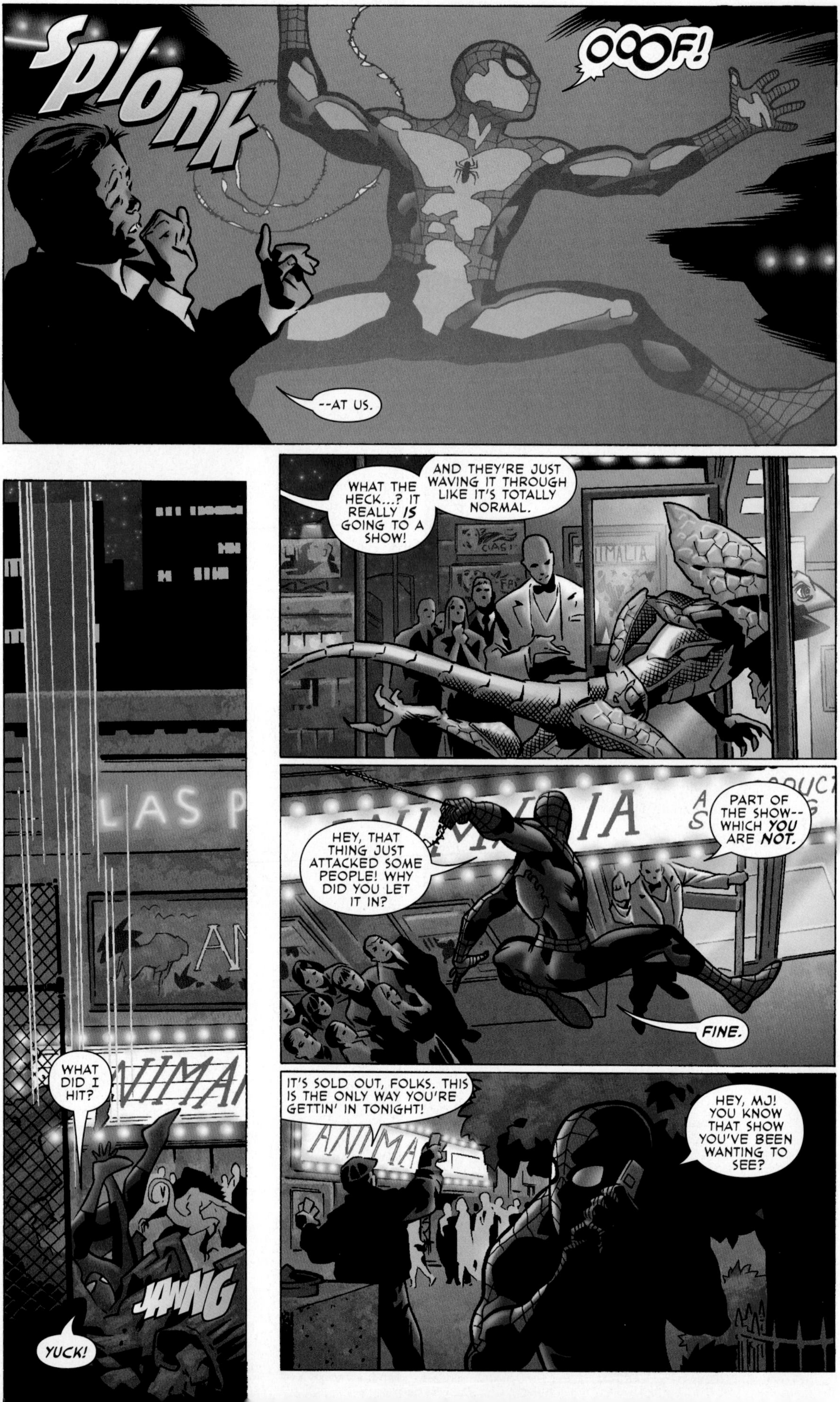

SPLONK
OOOF!
--AT US.
WHAT DID I HIT?
JANNG
YUCK!
WHAT THE HECK...? IT REALLY *IS* GOING TO A SHOW!
AND THEY'RE JUST WAVING IT THROUGH LIKE IT'S TOTALLY NORMAL.
HEY, THAT THING JUST ATTACKED SOME PEOPLE! WHY DID YOU LET IT IN?
PART OF THE SHOW-- WHICH *YOU* ARE *NOT.*
FINE.
IT'S SOLD OUT, FOLKS. THIS IS THE ONLY WAY YOU'RE GETTIN' IN TONIGHT!
HEY, MJ! YOU KNOW THAT SHOW YOU'VE BEEN WANTING TO SEE?

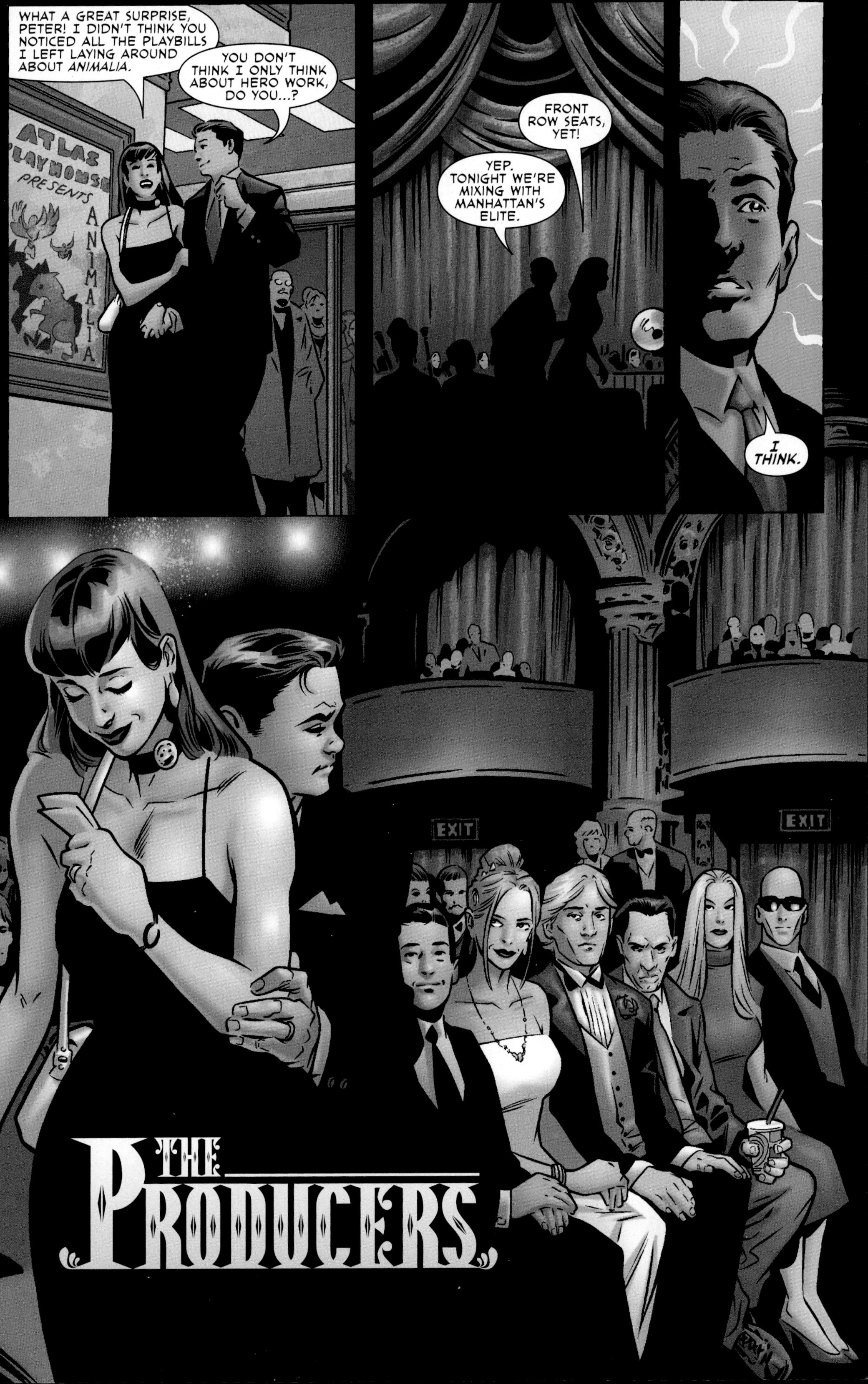
WHAT A GREAT SURPRISE, PETER! I DIDN'T THINK YOU NOTICED ALL THE PLAYBILLS I LEFT LAYING AROUND ABOUT *ANIMALIA*.
YOU DON'T THINK I ONLY THINK ABOUT HERO WORK, DO YOU...?
ATLAS PLAYHOUSE PRESENTS ANIMALIA
FRONT ROW SEATS, YET!
YEP. TONIGHT WE'RE MIXING WITH MANHATTAN'S ELITE.
I *THINK*.
EXIT
EXIT
THE PRODUCERS

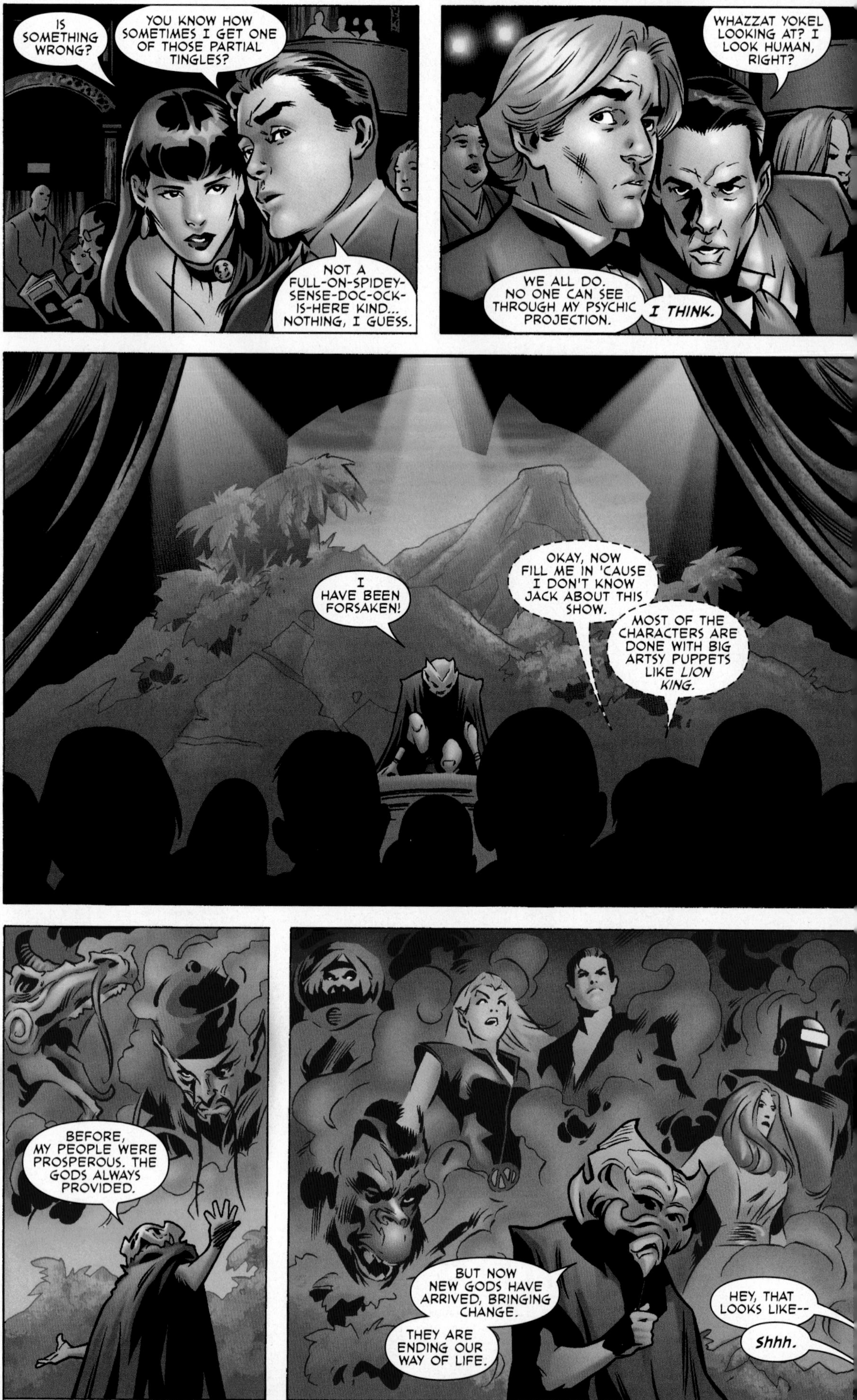
IS SOMETHING WRONG?
YOU KNOW HOW SOMETIMES I GET ONE OF THOSE PARTIAL TINGLES?
NOT A FULL-ON-SPIDEY-SENSE-DOC-OCK-IS-HERE KIND... NOTHING, I GUESS.
WHAZZAT YOKEL LOOKING AT? I LOOK HUMAN, RIGHT?
WE ALL DO. NO ONE CAN SEE THROUGH MY PSYCHIC PROJECTION.
I THINK.
I HAVE BEEN FORSAKEN!
OKAY, NOW FILL ME IN 'CAUSE I DON'T KNOW JACK ABOUT THIS SHOW.
MOST OF THE CHARACTERS ARE DONE WITH BIG ARTSY PUPPETS LIKE *LION KING.*
BEFORE, MY PEOPLE WERE PROSPEROUS. THE GODS ALWAYS PROVIDED.
BUT NOW NEW GODS HAVE ARRIVED, BRINGING CHANGE.
THEY ARE ENDING OUR WAY OF LIFE.
HEY, THAT LOOKS LIKE--
Shhh.

YET WE WILL RISE AGAIN, FOR I HAVE LEARNED THE MAGIC. RISE, MY FAITHFUL!

WATCH THIS, PETER, THIS IS COOL.

COME AND LET US SUMMON MORE OF OUR BROTHER SPIRITS!

Whoa, WHERE DID ALL THESE GUYS COME FROM?

NEAT, huh?

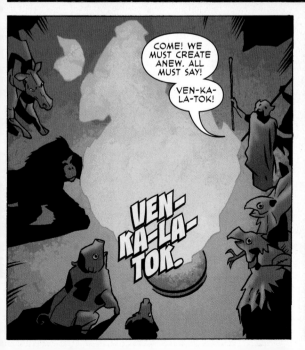

COME! WE MUST CREATE ANEW. ALL MUST SAY!

VEN-KA-LA-TOK!

VEN-KA-LA-TOK.

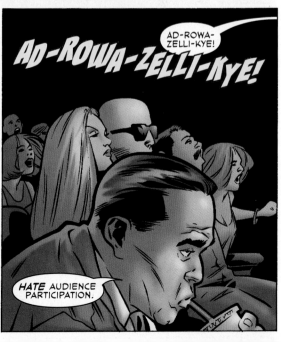

AD-ROWA-ZELLI-KYE!

AD-ROWA-ZELLI-KYE!

HATE AUDIENCE PARTICIPATION.

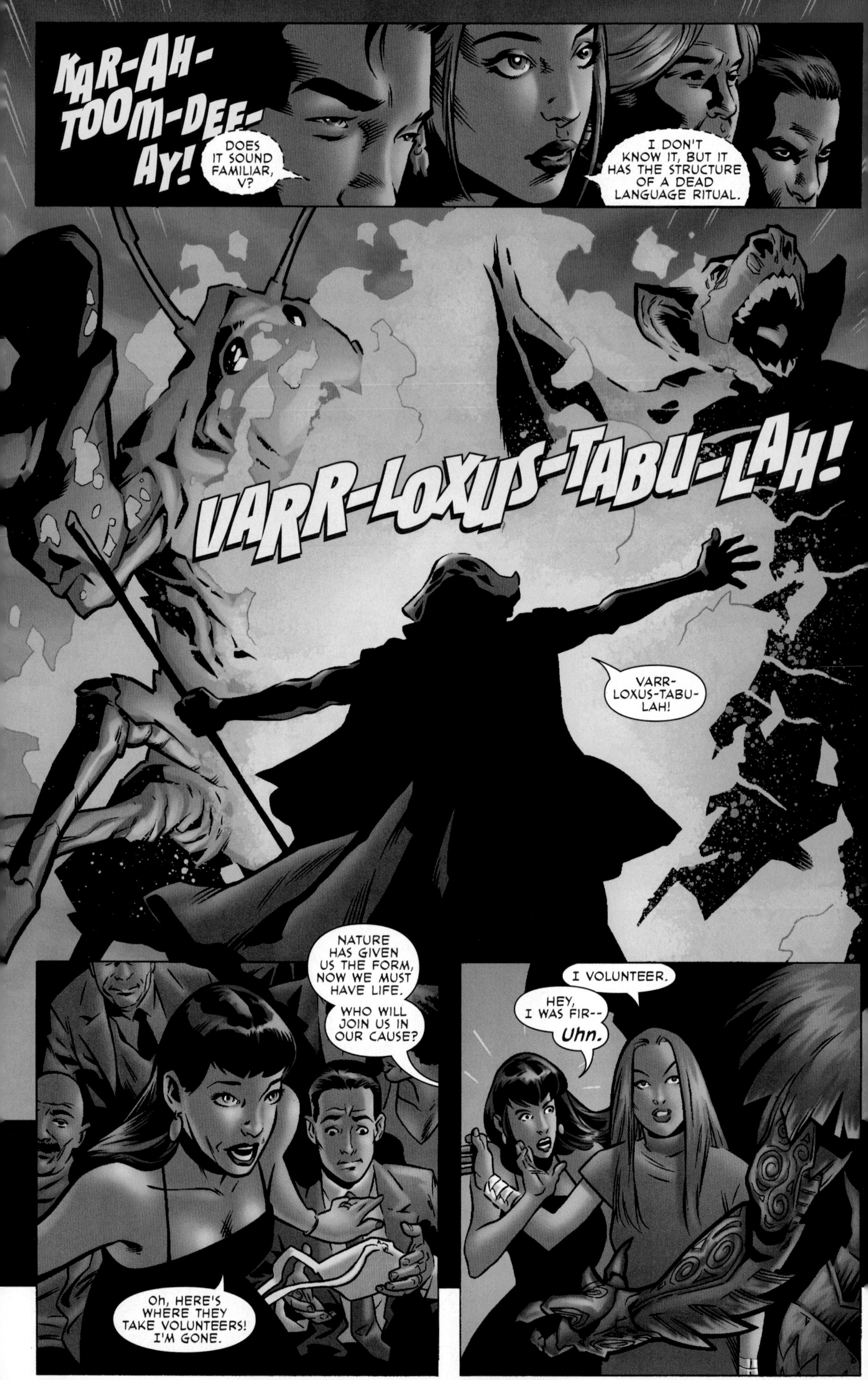
KAR-AH-TOOM-DEE-AY!
DOES IT SOUND FAMILIAR, V?
I DON'T KNOW IT, BUT IT HAS THE STRUCTURE OF A DEAD LANGUAGE RITUAL.
VARR-LOXUS-TABU-LAH!
VARR-LOXUS-TABU-LAH!
NATURE HAS GIVEN US THE FORM, NOW WE MUST HAVE LIFE.
WHO WILL JOIN US IN OUR CAUSE?
Oh, HERE'S WHERE THEY TAKE VOLUNTEERS! I'M GONE.
I VOLUNTEER.
HEY, I WAS FIR-- Uhn.

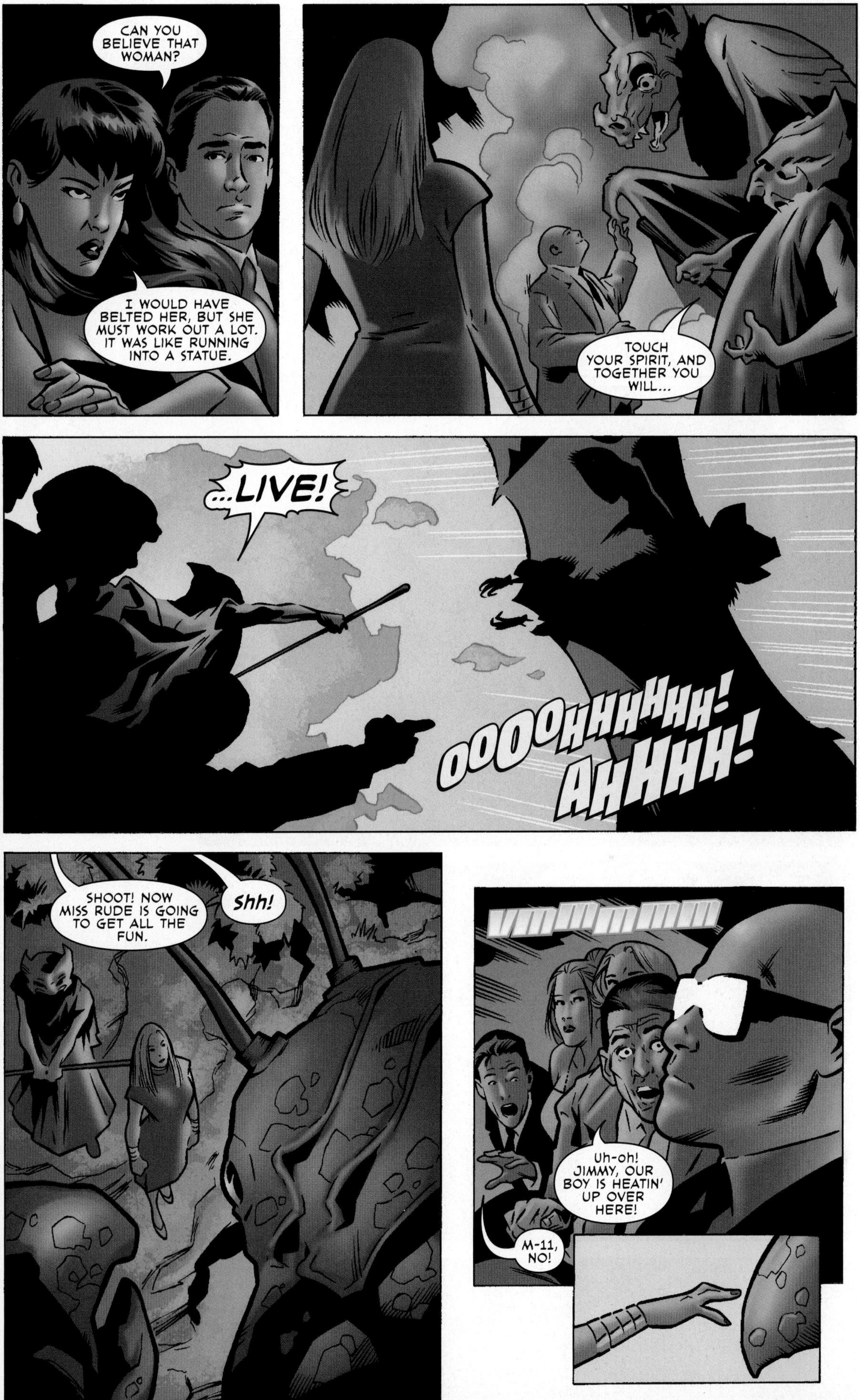
CAN YOU BELIEVE THAT WOMAN?
I WOULD HAVE BELTED HER, BUT SHE MUST WORK OUT A LOT. IT WAS LIKE RUNNING INTO A STATUE.
TOUCH YOUR SPIRIT, AND TOGETHER YOU WILL...
...LIVE!
OOOOHHHHHH! AHHHH!
SHOOT! NOW MISS RUDE IS GOING TO GET ALL THE FUN.
Shh!
VMMMMM
Uh-oh! JIMMY, OUR BOY IS HEATIN' UP OVER HERE!
M-11, NO!

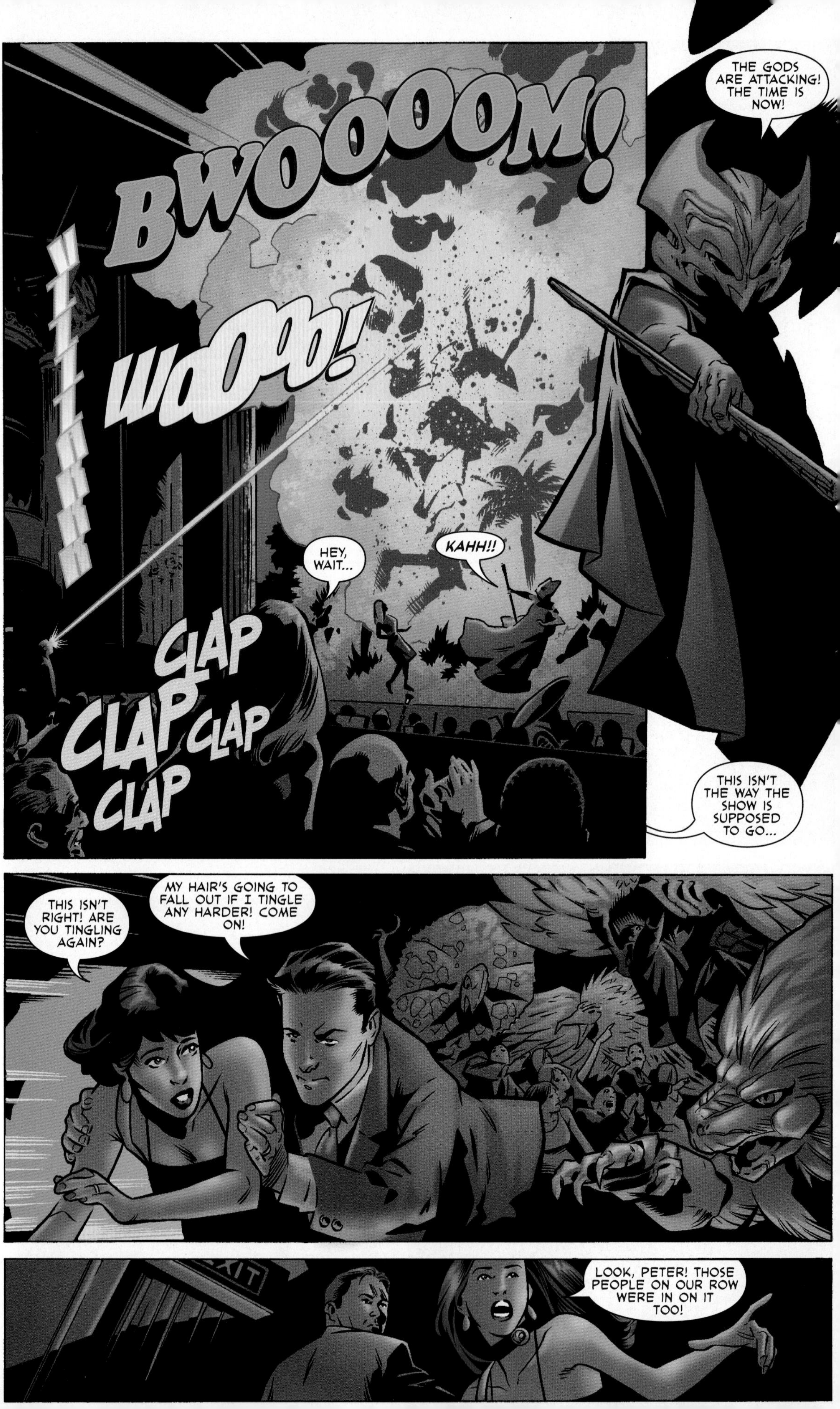
THE GODS ARE ATTACKING! THE TIME IS NOW!
BWOOOOM!
HEY, WAIT...
KAHH!!
CLAP CLAP CLAP CLAP
THIS ISN'T THE WAY THE SHOW IS SUPPOSED TO GO...
THIS ISN'T RIGHT! ARE YOU TINGLING AGAIN?
MY HAIR'S GOING TO FALL OUT IF I TINGLE ANY HARDER! COME ON!
EXIT
LOOK, PETER! THOSE PEOPLE ON OUR ROW WERE IN ON IT TOO!

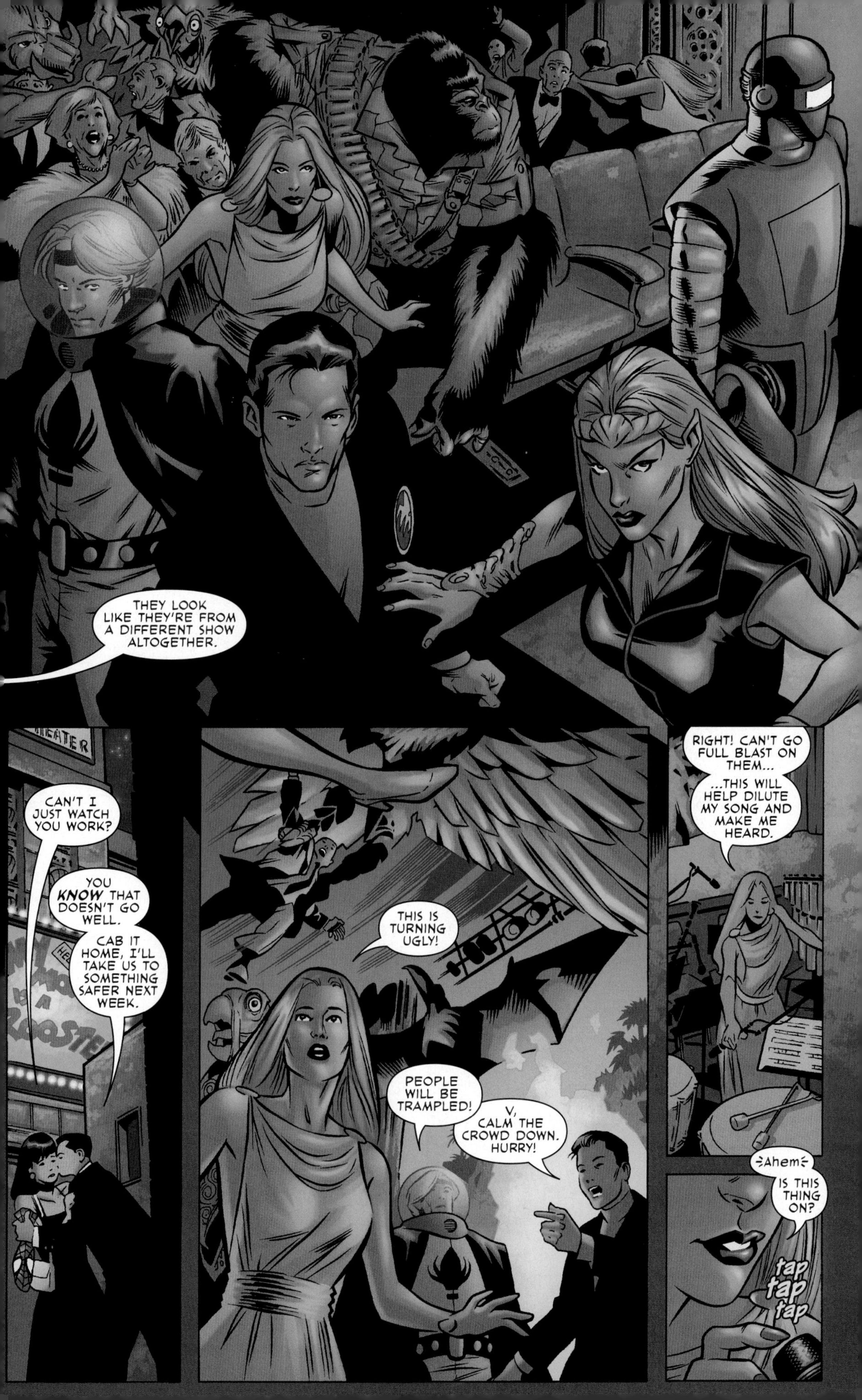
THEY LOOK LIKE THEY'RE FROM A DIFFERENT SHOW ALTOGETHER.
CAN'T I JUST WATCH YOU WORK?
YOU **KNOW** THAT DOESN'T GO WELL.
CAB IT HOME, I'LL TAKE US TO SOMETHING SAFER NEXT WEEK.
THIS IS TURNING UGLY!
PEOPLE WILL BE TRAMPLED!
V, CALM THE CROWD DOWN. HURRY!
RIGHT! CAN'T GO FULL BLAST ON THEM...
...THIS WILL HELP DILUTE MY SONG AND MAKE ME HEARD.
Ahem
IS THIS THING ON?
tap tap tap

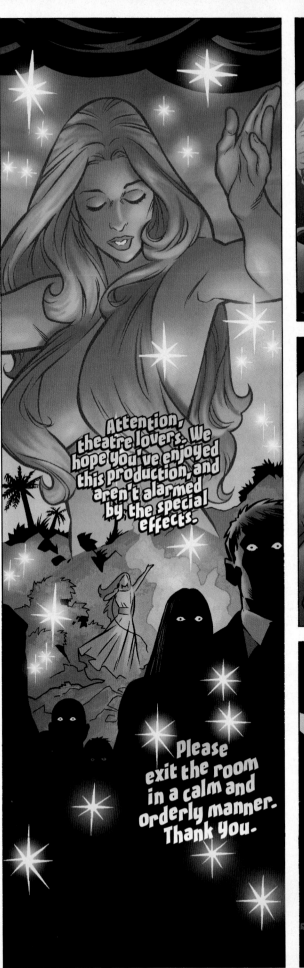

Attention, theatre lovers. We hope you've enjoyed this production, and aren't alarmed by the special effects.

Please exit the room in a calm and orderly manner. Thank you.

BOB, SCAN AND TRY TO FIND THAT MASK-HEAD GUY!

KEN, YOU AND M-11 CLOSE THOSE DOORS!

EVERYONE'S OUT, AND YOU'RE NOT GOIN' ANYWHERE!

HsSS!

NOW WE BETTER GET SOME ANSWERS!

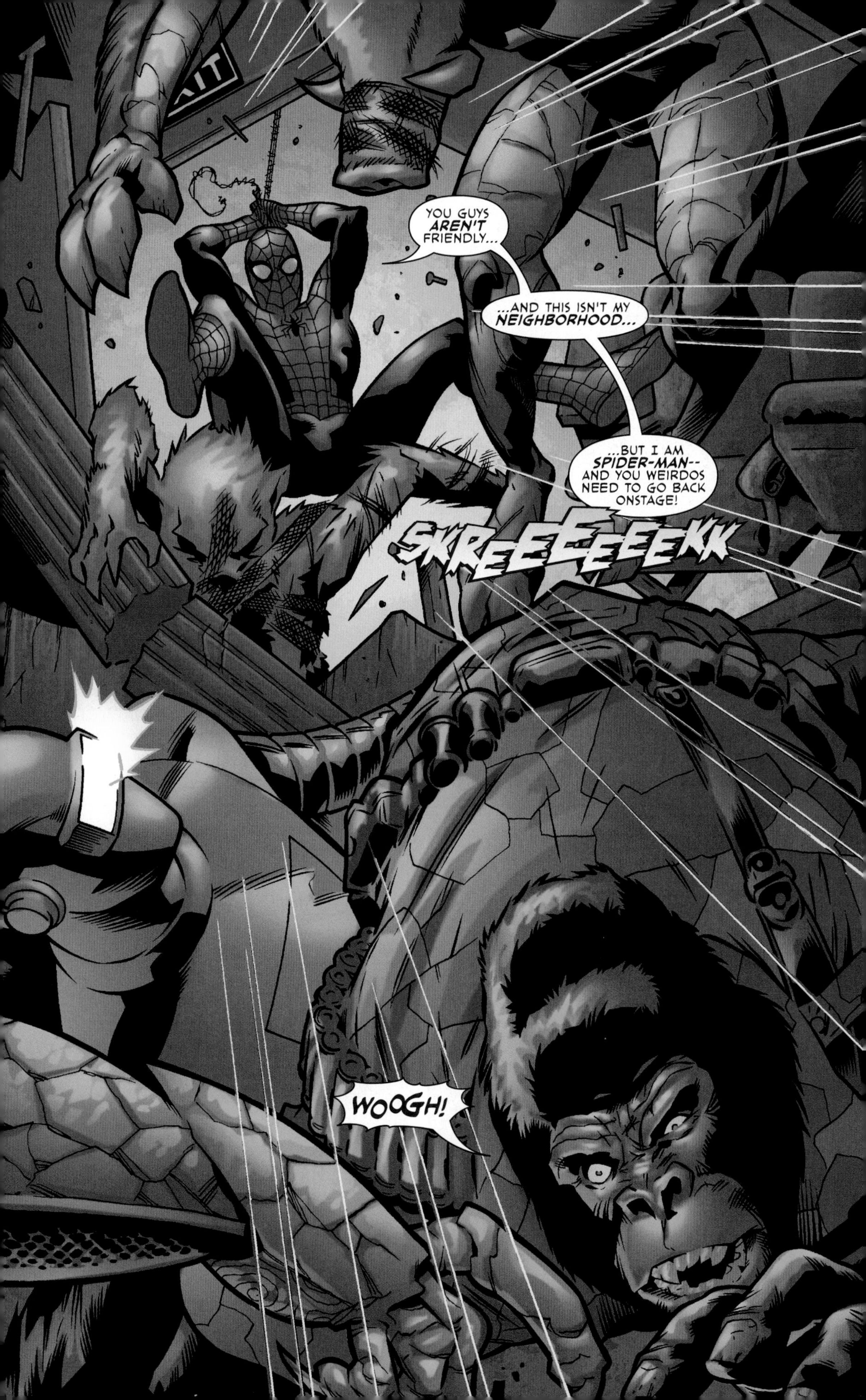
EXIT
YOU GUYS AREN'T FRIENDLY...
...AND THIS ISN'T MY NEIGHBORHOOD...
...BUT I AM SPIDER-MAN-- AND YOU WEIRDOS NEED TO GO BACK ONSTAGE!
SKREEEEEEEKK
WOOGH!

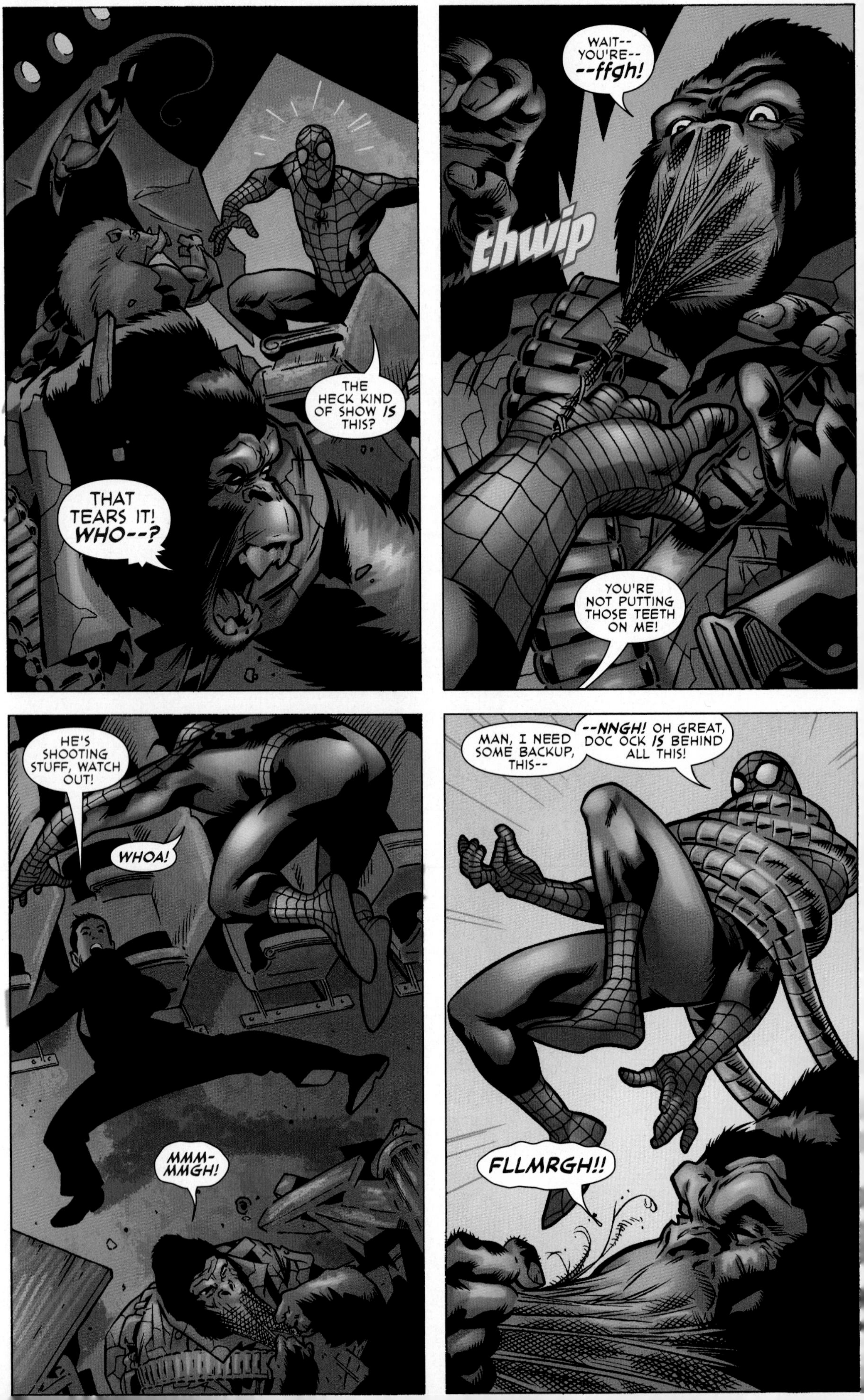
THE HECK KIND OF SHOW *IS* THIS?
THAT TEARS IT! *WHO--?*
WAIT-- YOU'RE-- *--ffgh!*
thwip
YOU'RE NOT PUTTING THOSE TEETH ON ME!
HE'S SHOOTING STUFF, WATCH OUT!
WHOA!
MMM-MMGH!
MAN, I NEED SOME BACKUP, THIS--
--NNGH! OH GREAT, DOC OCK *IS* BEHIND ALL THIS!
FLLMRGH!!

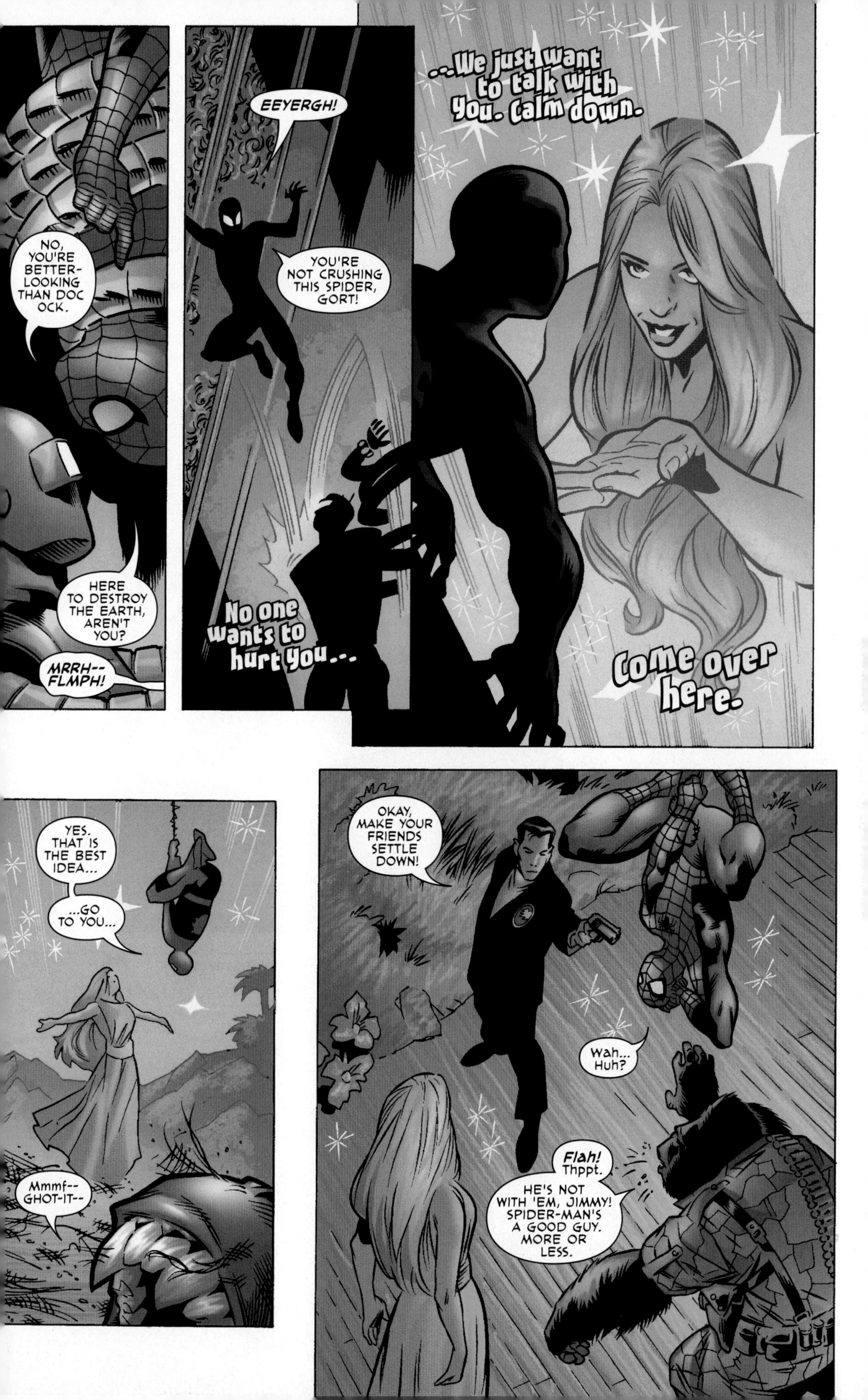
NO, YOU'RE BETTER-LOOKING THAN DOC OCK.
HERE TO DESTROY THE EARTH, AREN'T YOU?
MRRH--FLMPH!
EEYERGH!
YOU'RE NOT CRUSHING THIS SPIDER, GORT!
No one wants to hurt you...
--We just want to talk with you. Calm down.
Come over here.
YES. THAT IS THE BEST IDEA...
...GO TO YOU...
Mmmf--GHOT-IT--
OKAY, MAKE YOUR FRIENDS SETTLE DOWN!
Wah... Huh?
Flah! Thppt.
HE'S NOT WITH 'EM, JIMMY! SPIDER-MAN'S A GOOD GUY. MORE OR LESS.

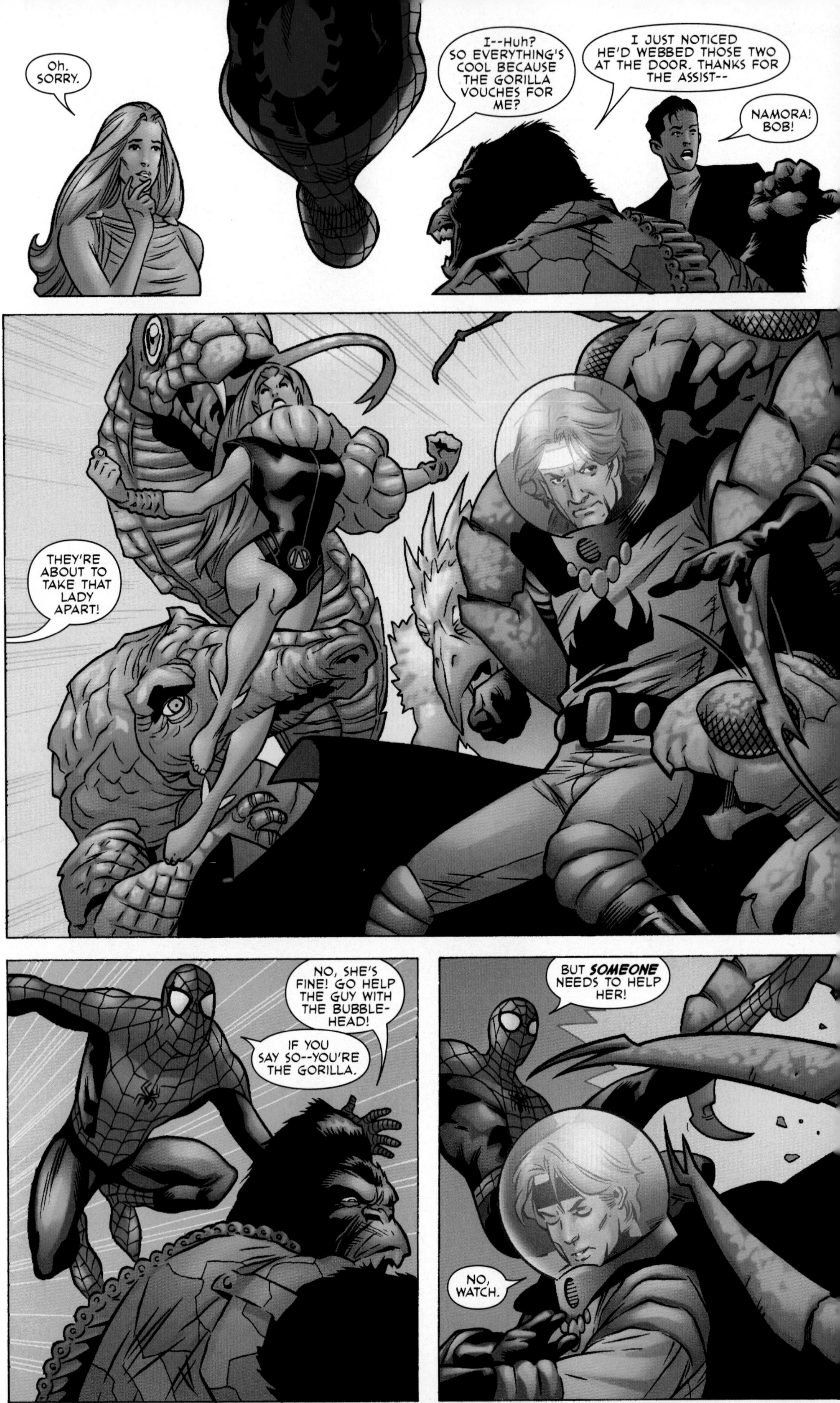
Oh. SORRY.
I--Huh? SO EVERYTHING'S COOL BECAUSE THE GORILLA VOUCHES FOR ME?
I JUST NOTICED HE'D WEBBED THOSE TWO AT THE DOOR. THANKS FOR THE ASSIST--
NAMORA! BOB!
THEY'RE ABOUT TO TAKE THAT LADY APART!
NO, SHE'S FINE! GO HELP THE GUY WITH THE BUBBLE-HEAD!
IF YOU SAY SO--YOU'RE THE GORILLA.
BUT SOMEONE NEEDS TO HELP HER!
NO, WATCH.

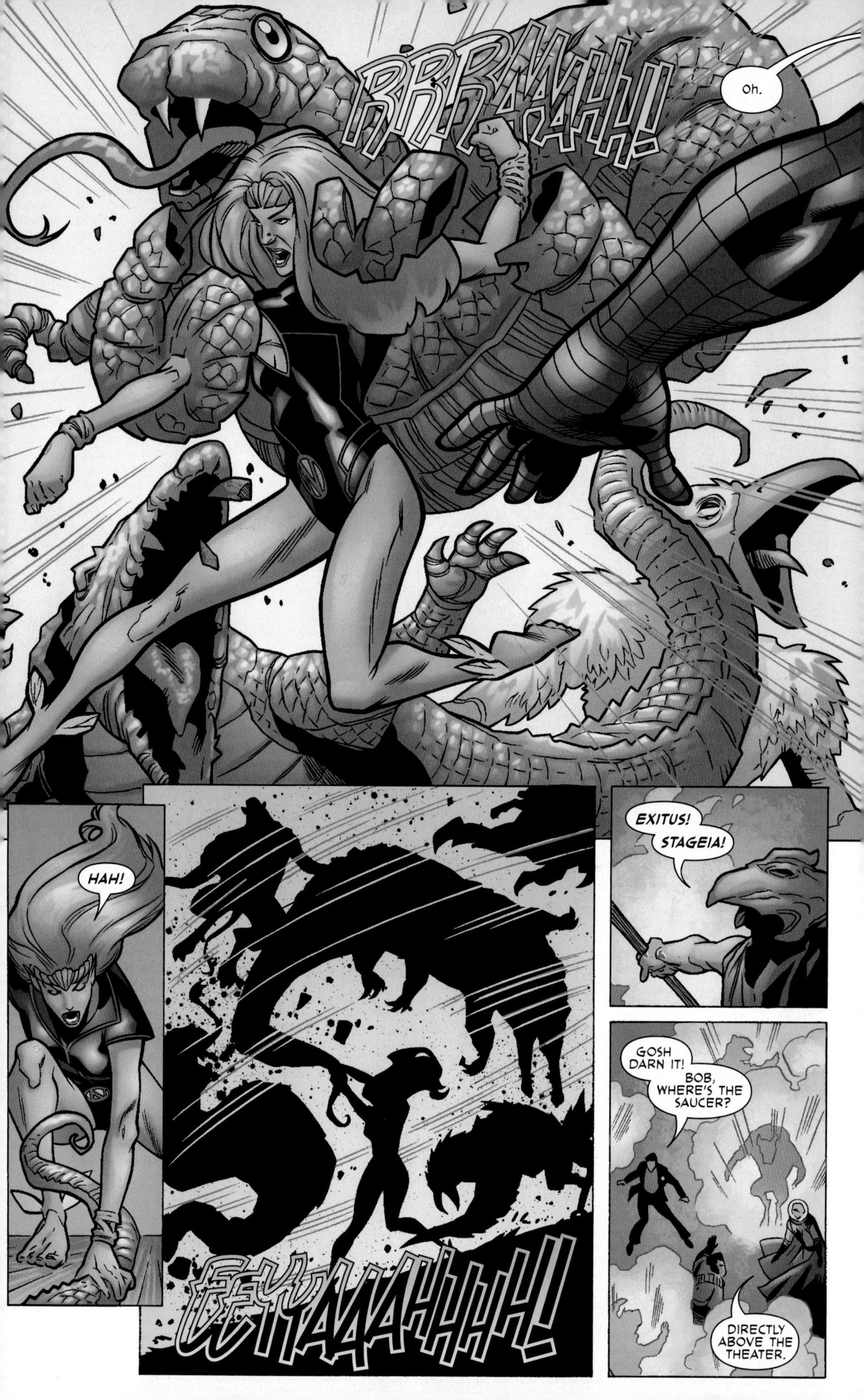
BRRRAAAHHH!
Oh.
HAH!
EEYAAAAHHHH!
EXITUS!
STAGEIA!
GOSH DARN IT!
BOB, WHERE'S THE SAUCER?
DIRECTLY ABOVE THE THEATER.

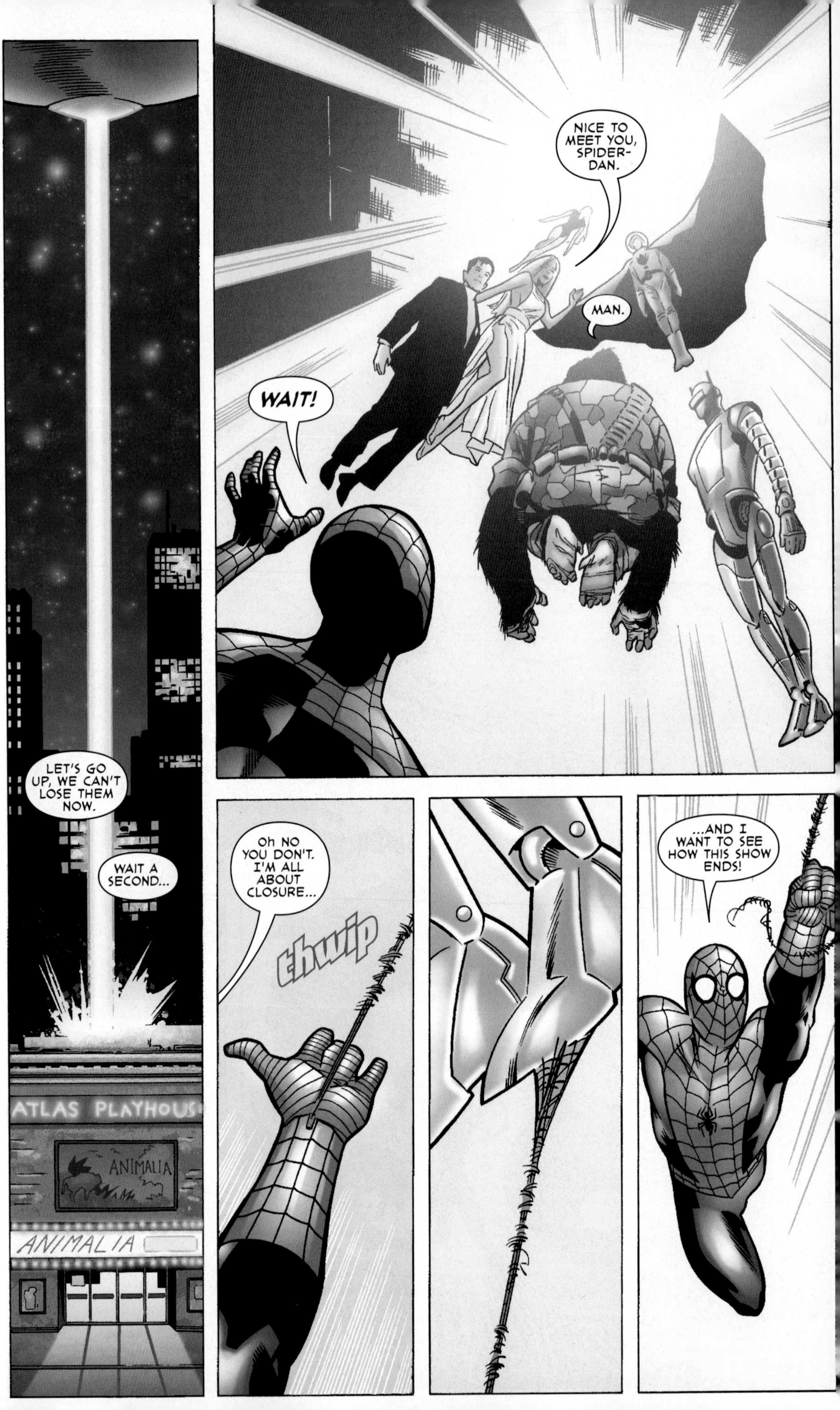
LET'S GO UP, WE CAN'T LOSE THEM NOW.
WAIT A SECOND...
ATLAS PLAYHOUS
ANIMALIA
ANIMALIA
NICE TO MEET YOU, SPIDER-DAN.
MAN.
WAIT!
Oh NO YOU DON'T. I'M ALL ABOUT CLOSURE...
thwip
...AND I WANT TO SEE HOW THIS SHOW ENDS!

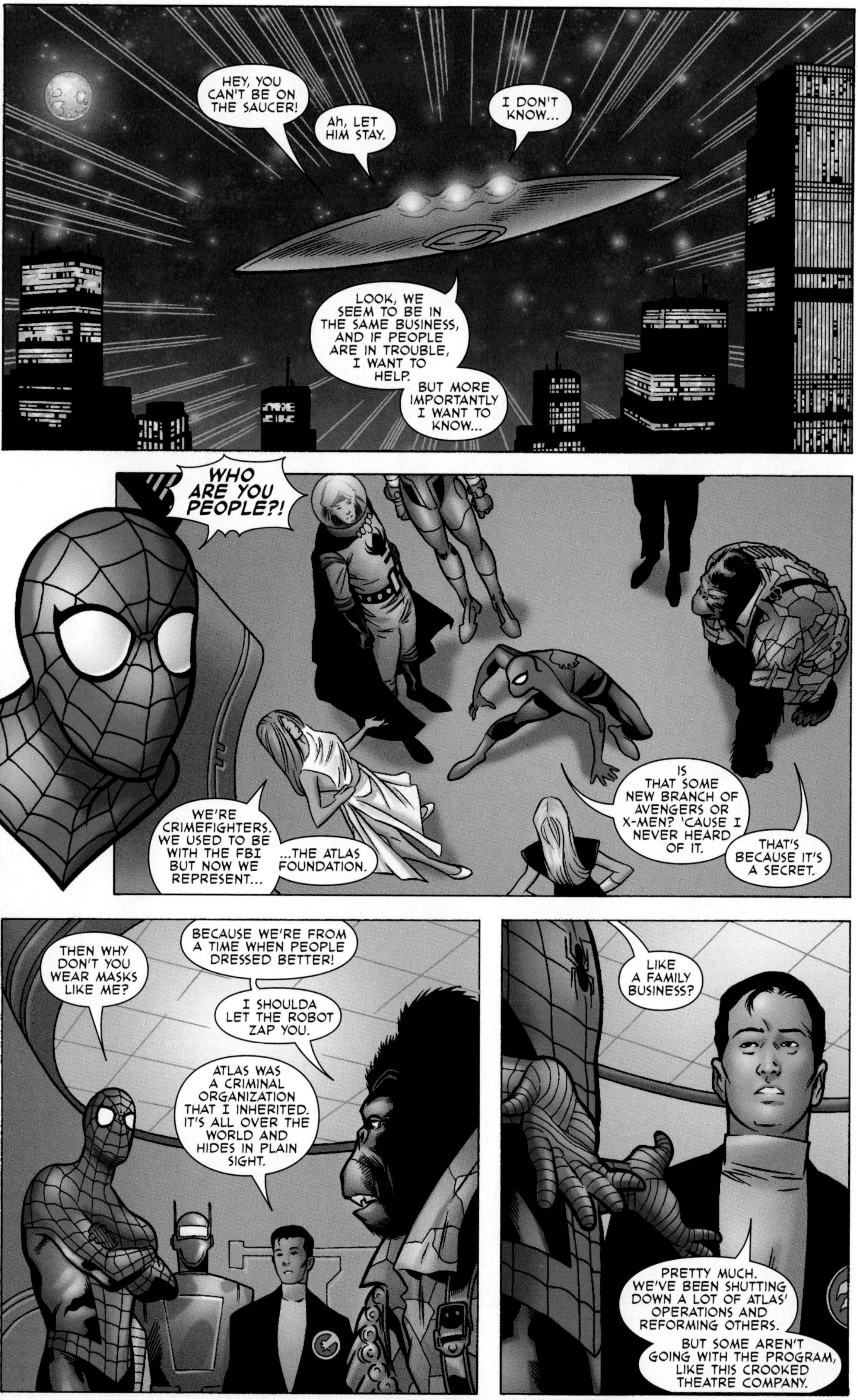
HEY, YOU CAN'T BE ON THE SAUCER!
Ah, LET HIM STAY.
I DON'T KNOW...
LOOK, WE SEEM TO BE IN THE SAME BUSINESS, AND IF PEOPLE ARE IN TROUBLE, I WANT TO HELP.
BUT MORE IMPORTANTLY I WANT TO KNOW...
WHO ARE YOU PEOPLE?!
WE'RE CRIMEFIGHTERS. WE USED TO BE WITH THE FBI BUT NOW WE REPRESENT...
...THE ATLAS FOUNDATION.
IS THAT SOME NEW BRANCH OF AVENGERS OR X-MEN? 'CAUSE I NEVER HEARD OF IT.
THAT'S BECAUSE IT'S A SECRET.
THEN WHY DON'T YOU WEAR MASKS LIKE ME?
BECAUSE WE'RE FROM A TIME WHEN PEOPLE DRESSED BETTER!
I SHOULDA LET THE ROBOT ZAP YOU.
ATLAS WAS A CRIMINAL ORGANIZATION THAT I INHERITED. IT'S ALL OVER THE WORLD AND HIDES IN PLAIN SIGHT.
LIKE A FAMILY BUSINESS?
PRETTY MUCH. WE'VE BEEN SHUTTING DOWN A LOT OF ATLAS' OPERATIONS AND REFORMING OTHERS.
BUT SOME AREN'T GOING WITH THE PROGRAM, LIKE THIS CROOKED THEATRE COMPANY.

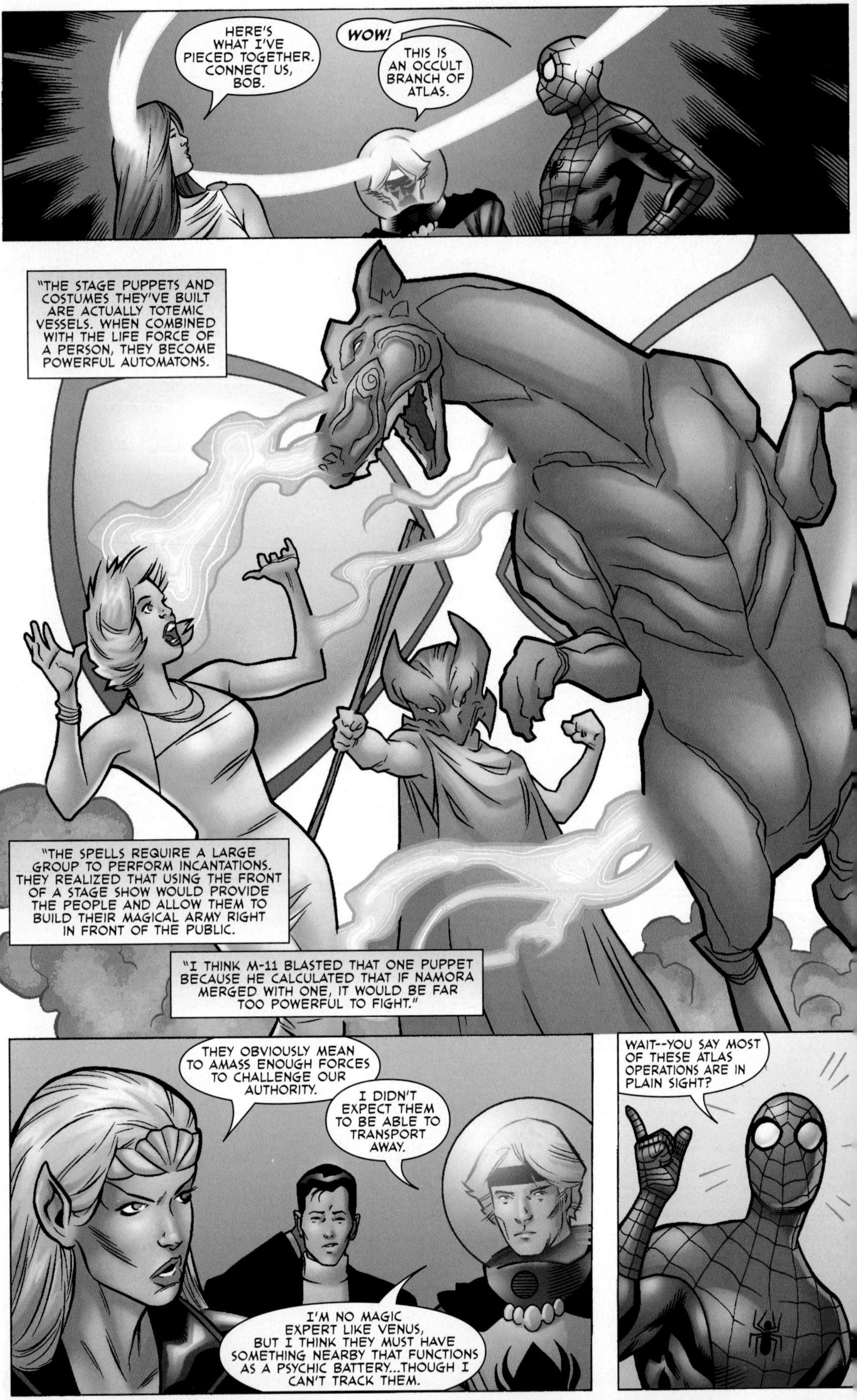
HERE'S WHAT I'VE PIECED TOGETHER. CONNECT US, BOB.
WOW!
THIS IS AN OCCULT BRANCH OF ATLAS.
"THE STAGE PUPPETS AND COSTUMES THEY'VE BUILT ARE ACTUALLY TOTEMIC VESSELS. WHEN COMBINED WITH THE LIFE FORCE OF A PERSON, THEY BECOME POWERFUL AUTOMATONS.
"THE SPELLS REQUIRE A LARGE GROUP TO PERFORM INCANTATIONS. THEY REALIZED THAT USING THE FRONT OF A STAGE SHOW WOULD PROVIDE THE PEOPLE AND ALLOW THEM TO BUILD THEIR MAGICAL ARMY RIGHT IN FRONT OF THE PUBLIC.
"I THINK M-11 BLASTED THAT ONE PUPPET BECAUSE HE CALCULATED THAT IF NAMORA MERGED WITH ONE, IT WOULD BE FAR TOO POWERFUL TO FIGHT."
THEY OBVIOUSLY MEAN TO AMASS ENOUGH FORCES TO CHALLENGE OUR AUTHORITY.
I DIDN'T EXPECT THEM TO BE ABLE TO TRANSPORT AWAY.
I'M NO MAGIC EXPERT LIKE VENUS, BUT I THINK THEY MUST HAVE SOMETHING NEARBY THAT FUNCTIONS AS A PSYCHIC BATTERY...THOUGH I CAN'T TRACK THEM.
WAIT--YOU SAY MOST OF THESE ATLAS OPERATIONS ARE IN PLAIN SIGHT?

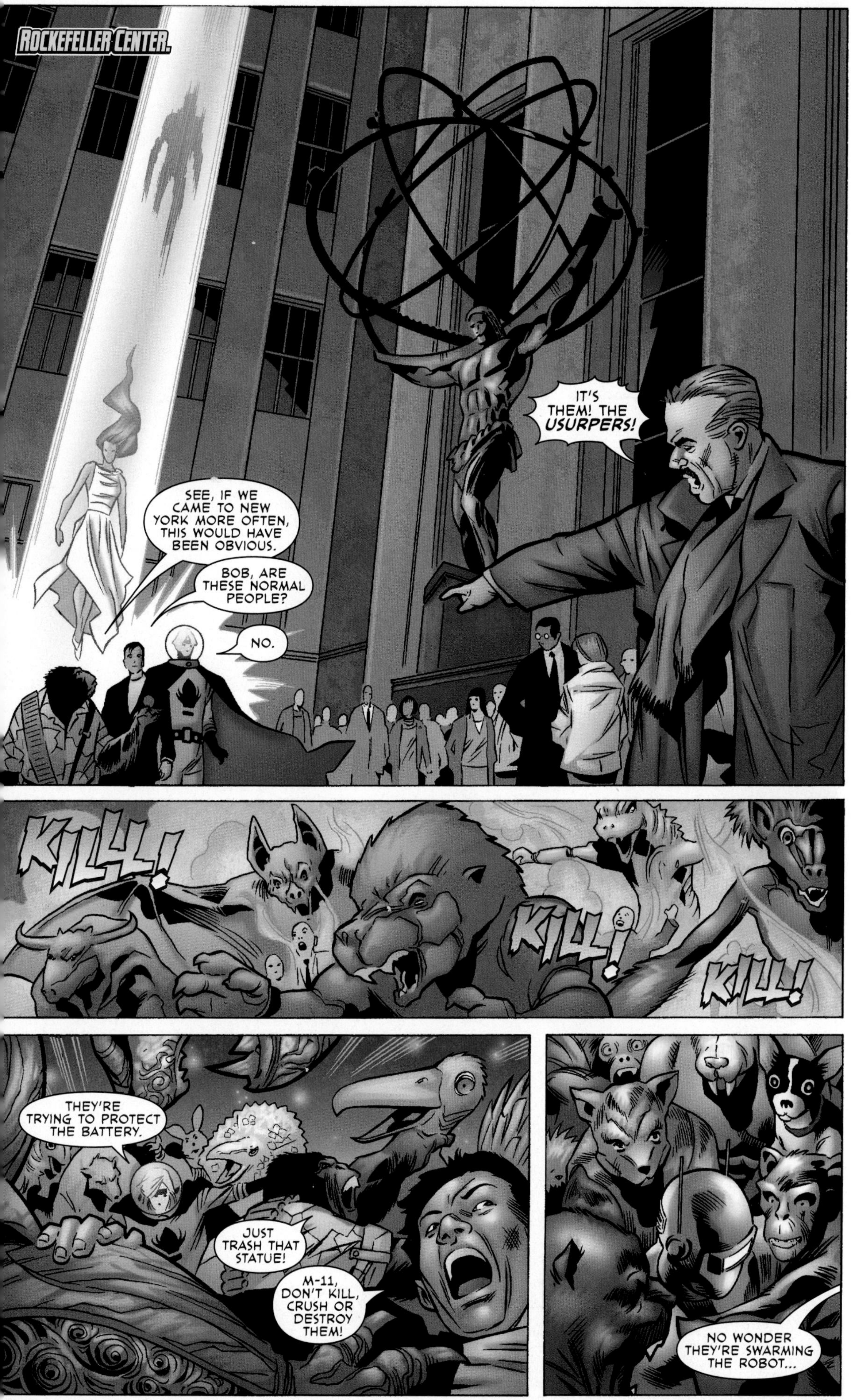
ROCKEFELLER CENTER.
SEE, IF WE CAME TO NEW YORK MORE OFTEN, THIS WOULD HAVE BEEN OBVIOUS.
BOB, ARE THESE NORMAL PEOPLE?
NO.
IT'S THEM! THE USURPERS!
KILL!
KILL!
KILL!
THEY'RE TRYING TO PROTECT THE BATTERY.
JUST TRASH THAT STATUE!
M-11, DON'T KILL, CRUSH OR DESTROY THEM!
NO WONDER THEY'RE SWARMING THE ROBOT...

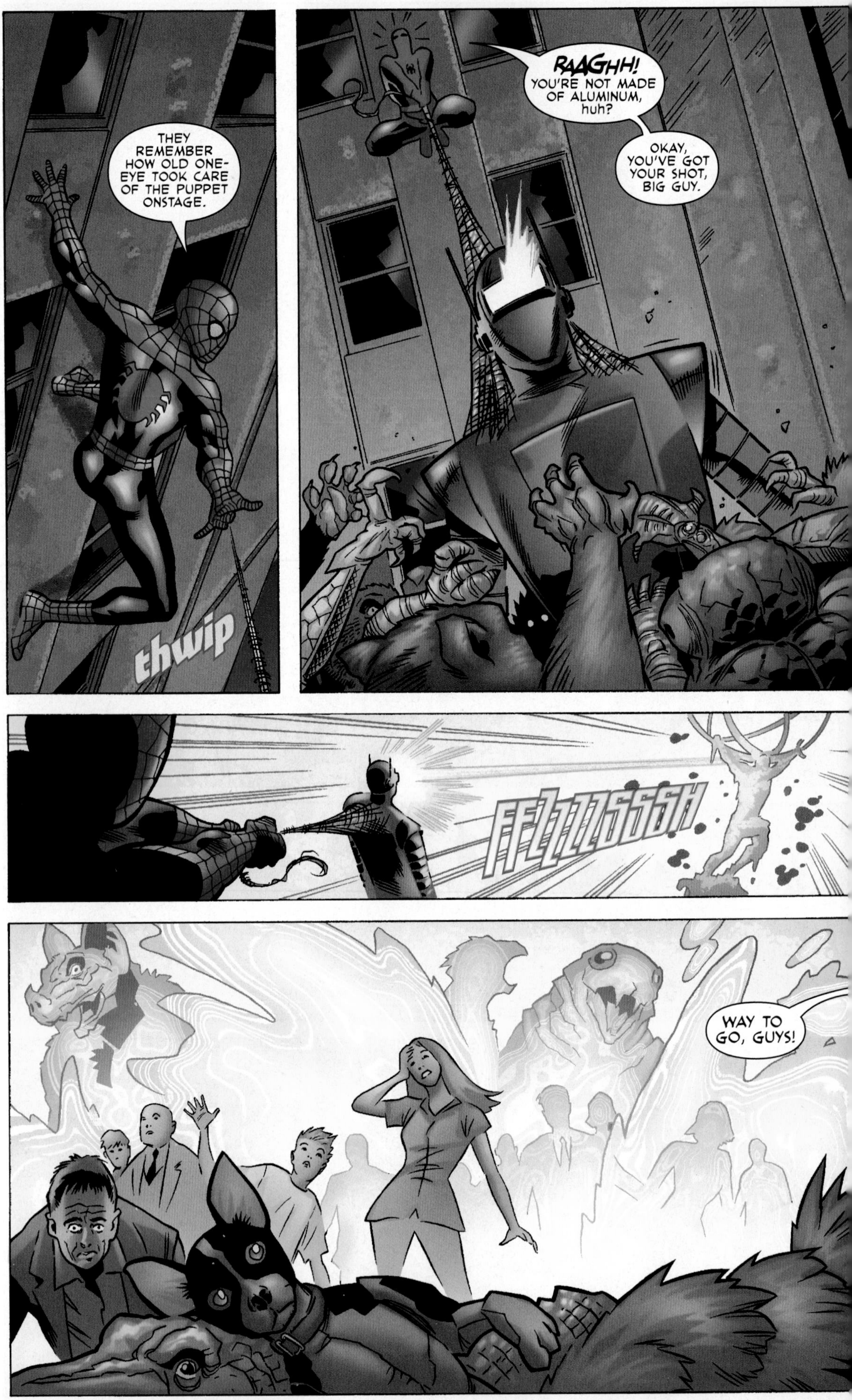
THEY REMEMBER HOW OLD ONE-EYE TOOK CARE OF THE PUPPET ONSTAGE.
thwip
RAAGHH! YOU'RE NOT MADE OF ALUMINUM, huh?
OKAY, YOU'VE GOT YOUR SHOT, BIG GUY.
FFZZZZSSSSH
WAY TO GO, GUYS!

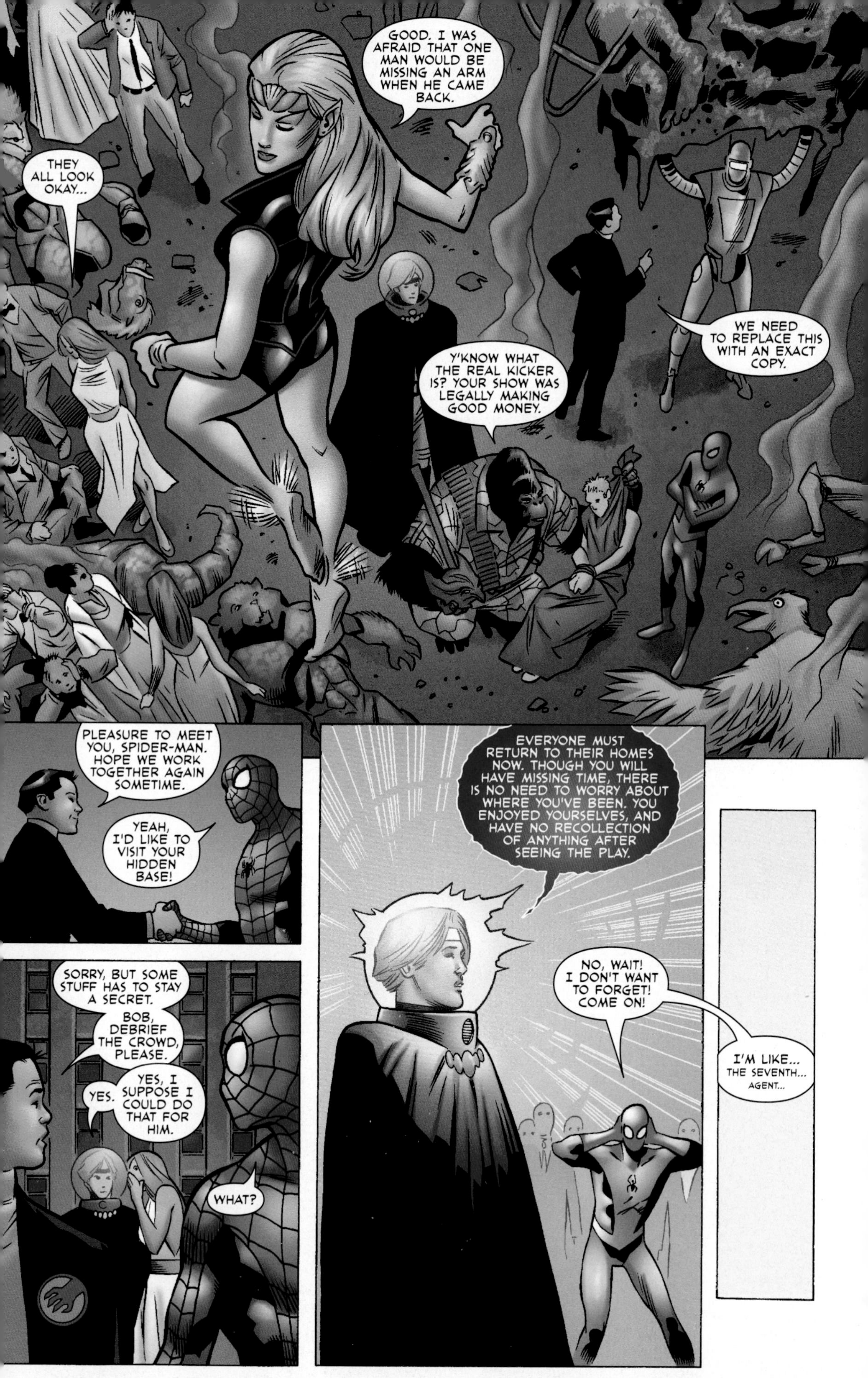
THEY ALL LOOK OKAY...
GOOD. I WAS AFRAID THAT ONE MAN WOULD BE MISSING AN ARM WHEN HE CAME BACK.
Y'KNOW WHAT THE REAL KICKER IS? YOUR SHOW WAS LEGALLY MAKING GOOD MONEY.
WE NEED TO REPLACE THIS WITH AN EXACT COPY.
PLEASURE TO MEET YOU, SPIDER-MAN. HOPE WE WORK TOGETHER AGAIN SOMETIME.
YEAH, I'D LIKE TO VISIT YOUR HIDDEN BASE!
SORRY, BUT SOME STUFF HAS TO STAY A SECRET.
BOB, DEBRIEF THE CROWD, PLEASE.
YES.
YES, I SUPPOSE I COULD DO THAT FOR HIM.
WHAT?
EVERYONE MUST RETURN TO THEIR HOMES NOW. THOUGH YOU WILL HAVE MISSING TIME, THERE IS NO NEED TO WORRY ABOUT WHERE YOU'VE BEEN. YOU ENJOYED YOURSELVES, AND HAVE NO RECOLLECTION OF ANYTHING AFTER SEEING THE PLAY.
NO, WAIT! I DON'T WANT TO FORGET! COME ON!
I'M LIKE... THE SEVENTH... AGENT...

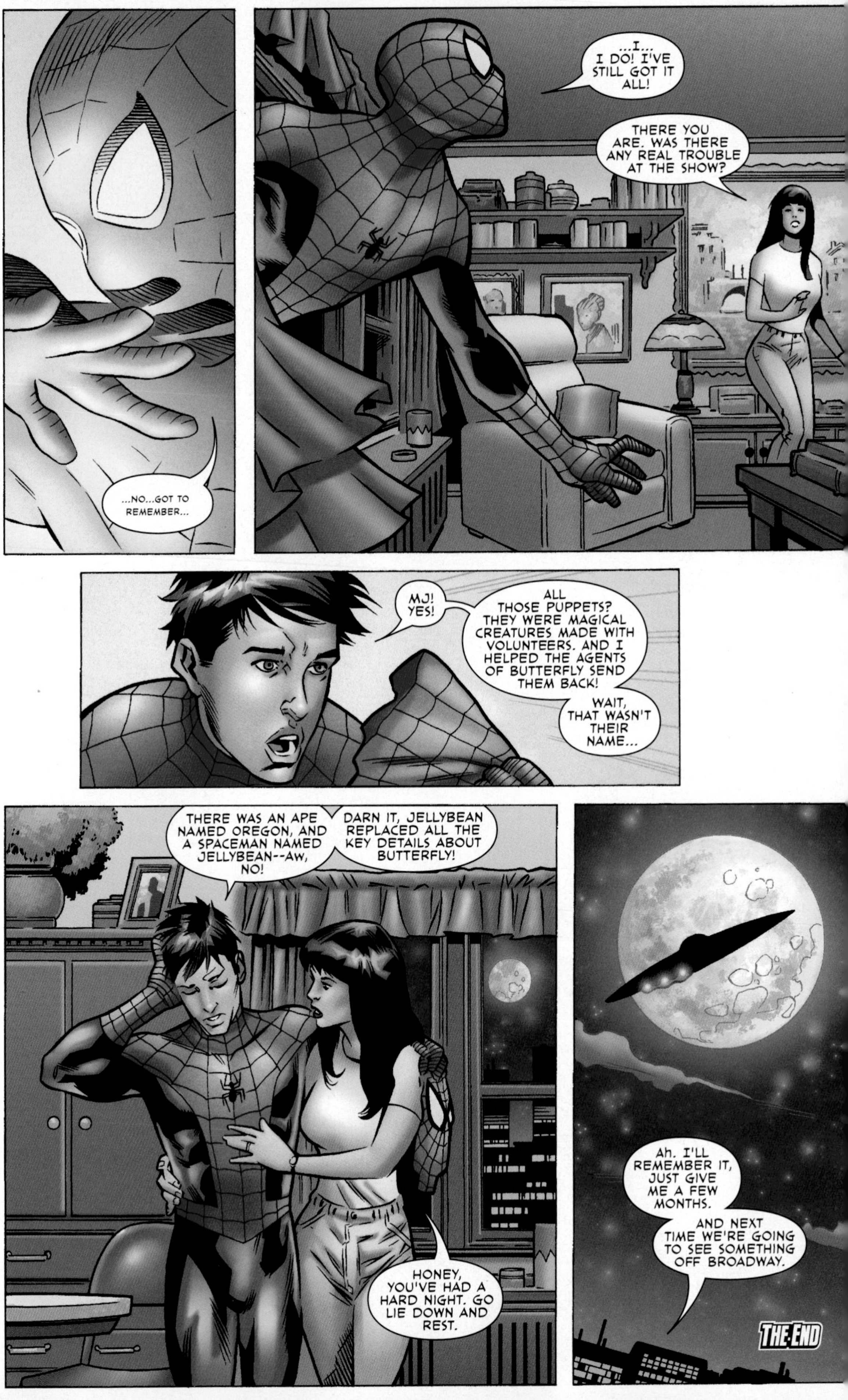
...NO...GOT TO REMEMBER...
...I... I DO! I'VE STILL GOT IT ALL!
THERE YOU ARE. WAS THERE ANY REAL TROUBLE AT THE SHOW?
MJ! YES!
ALL THOSE PUPPETS? THEY WERE MAGICAL CREATURES MADE WITH VOLUNTEERS. AND I HELPED THE AGENTS OF BUTTERFLY SEND THEM BACK!
WAIT, THAT WASN'T THEIR NAME...
THERE WAS AN APE NAMED OREGON, AND A SPACEMAN NAMED JELLYBEAN--AW, NO!
DARN IT, JELLYBEAN REPLACED ALL THE KEY DETAILS ABOUT BUTTERFLY!
HONEY, YOU'VE HAD A HARD NIGHT. GO LIE DOWN AND REST.
Ah. I'LL REMEMBER IT, JUST GIVE ME A FEW MONTHS.
AND NEXT TIME WE'RE GOING TO SEE SOMETHING OFF BROADWAY.
THE END

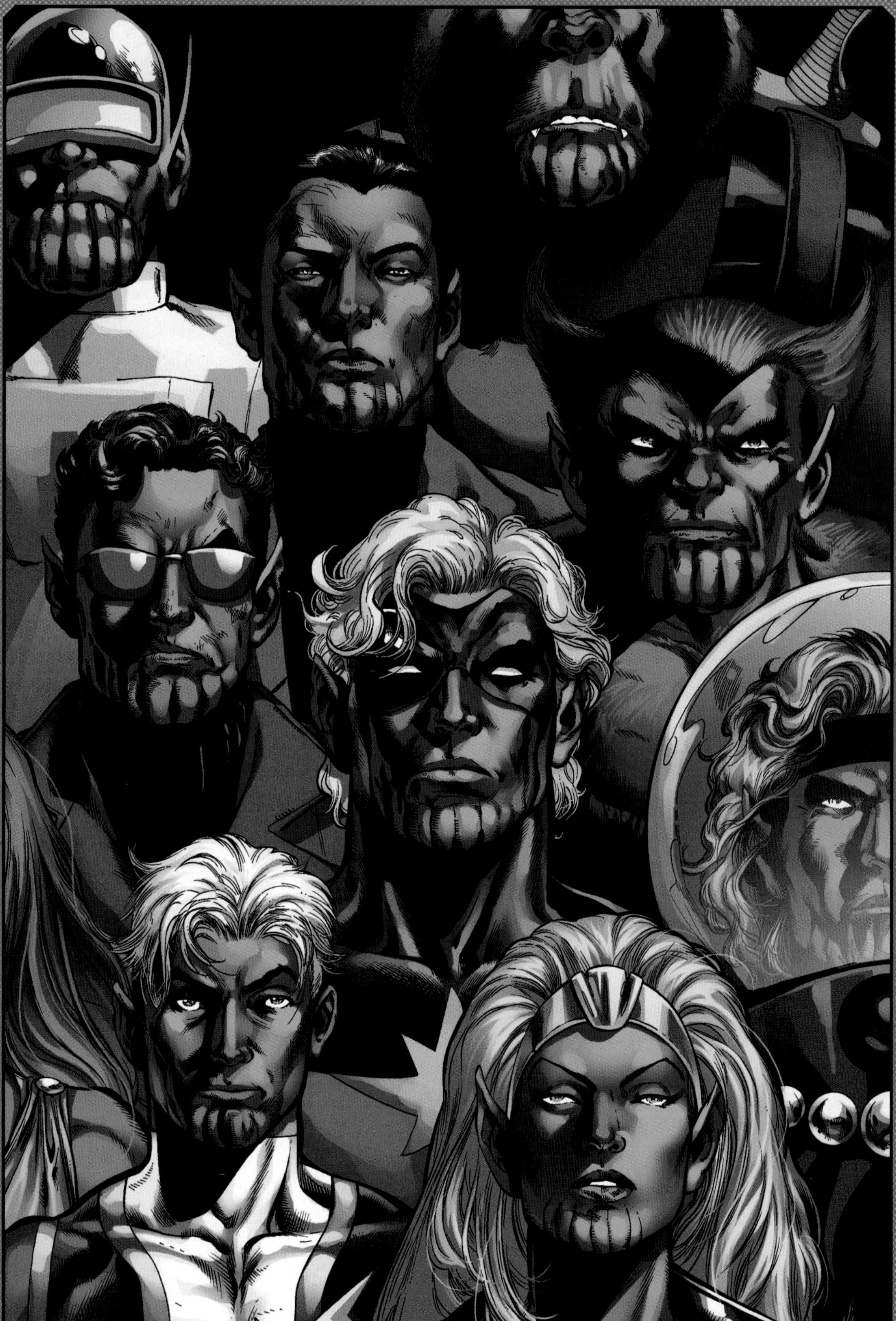

SECRET INVASION: WHO DO YOU TRUST?

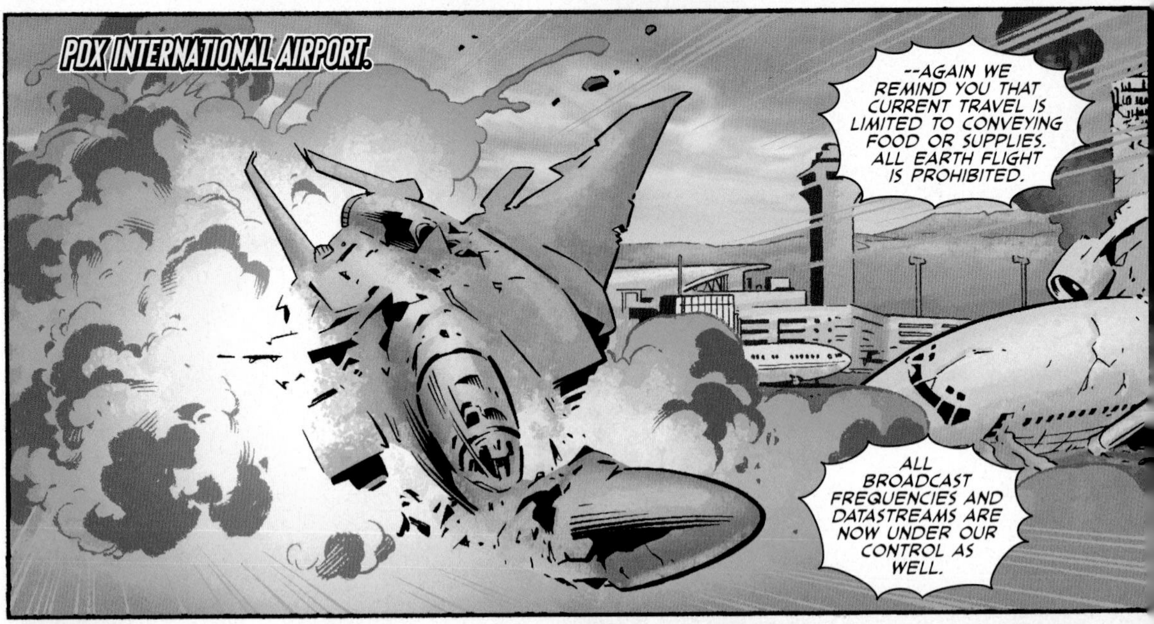
PDX INTERNATIONAL AIRPORT.
--AGAIN WE REMIND YOU THAT CURRENT TRAVEL IS LIMITED TO CONVEYING FOOD OR SUPPLIES. ALL EARTH FLIGHT IS PROHIBITED.
ALL BROADCAST FREQUENCIES AND DATASTREAMS ARE NOW UNDER OUR CONTROL AS WELL.
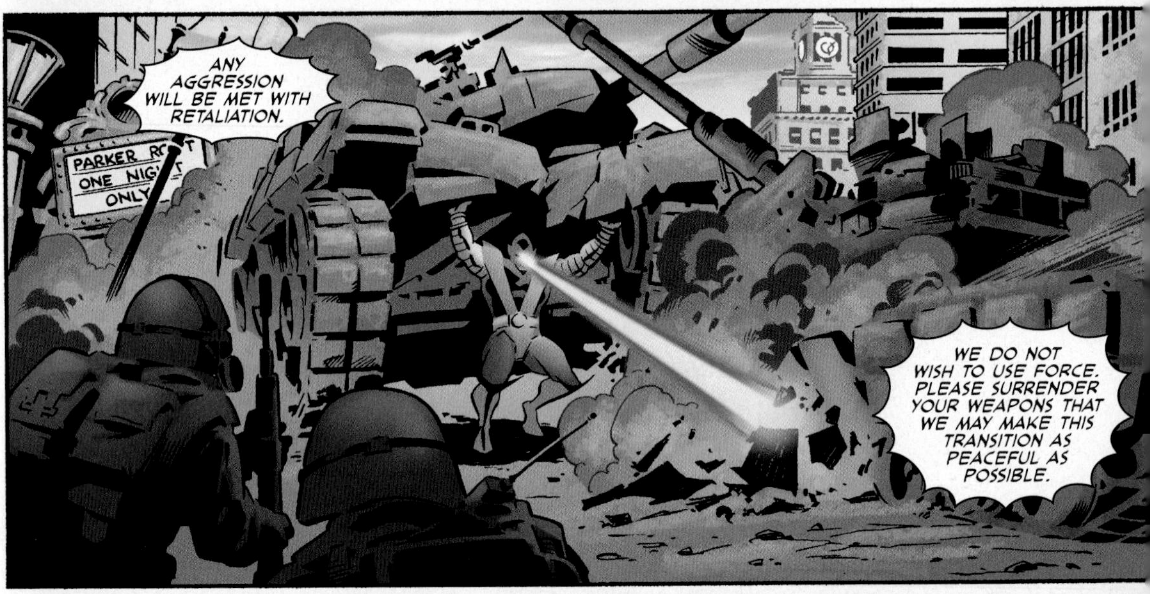
ANY AGGRESSION WILL BE MET WITH RETALIATION.
WE DO NOT WISH TO USE FORCE. PLEASE SURRENDER YOUR WEAPONS THAT WE MAY MAKE THIS TRANSITION AS PEACEFUL AS POSSIBLE.
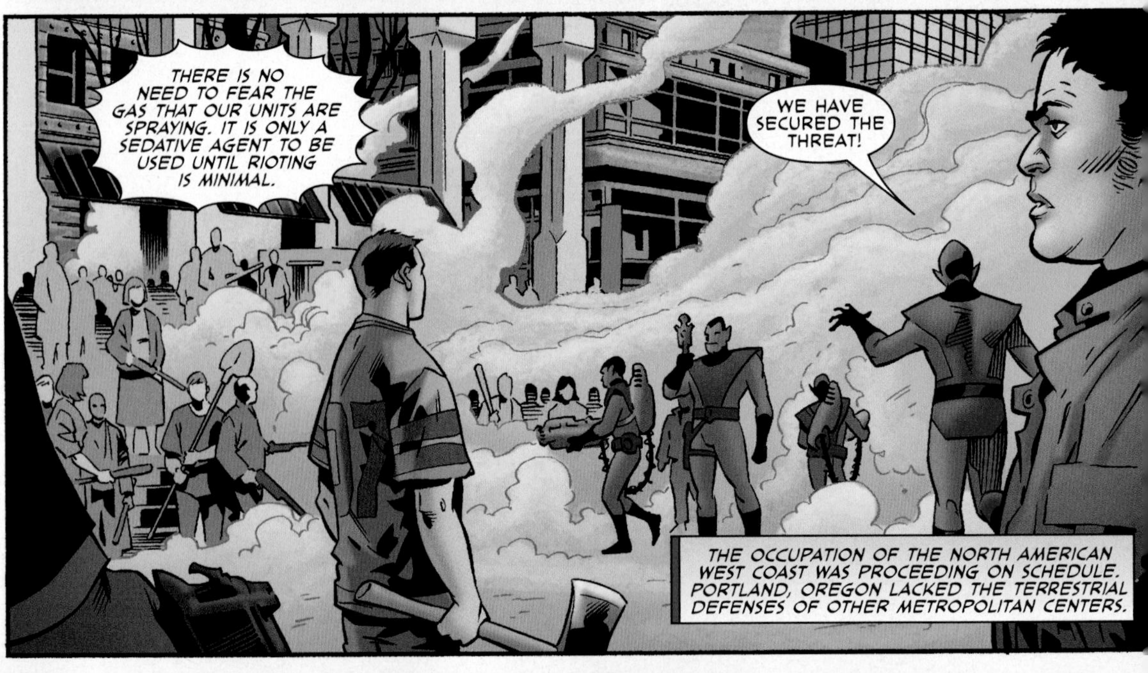
THERE IS NO NEED TO FEAR THE GAS THAT OUR UNITS ARE SPRAYING. IT IS ONLY A SEDATIVE AGENT TO BE USED UNTIL RIOTING IS MINIMAL.
WE HAVE SECURED THE THREAT!
THE OCCUPATION OF THE NORTH AMERICAN WEST COAST WAS PROCEEDING ON SCHEDULE. PORTLAND, OREGON LACKED THE TERRESTRIAL DEFENSES OF OTHER METROPOLITAN CENTERS.

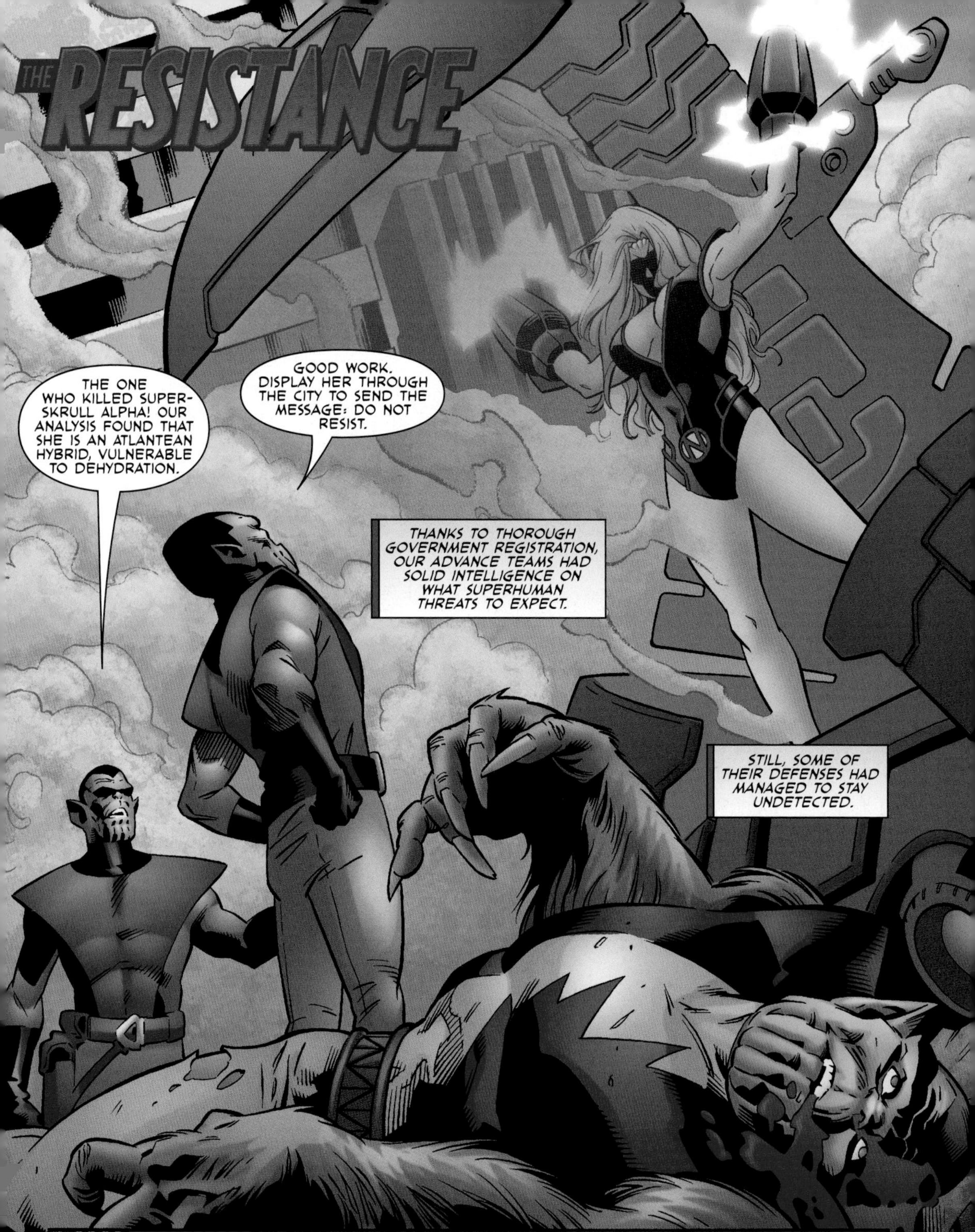
THE RESISTANCE
THE ONE WHO KILLED SUPER-SKRULL ALPHA! OUR ANALYSIS FOUND THAT SHE IS AN ATLANTEAN HYBRID, VULNERABLE TO DEHYDRATION.
GOOD WORK. DISPLAY HER THROUGH THE CITY TO SEND THE MESSAGE: DO NOT RESIST.
THANKS TO THOROUGH GOVERNMENT REGISTRATION, OUR ADVANCE TEAMS HAD SOLID INTELLIGENCE ON WHAT SUPERHUMAN THREATS TO EXPECT.
STILL, SOME OF THEIR DEFENSES HAD MANAGED TO STAY UNDETECTED.
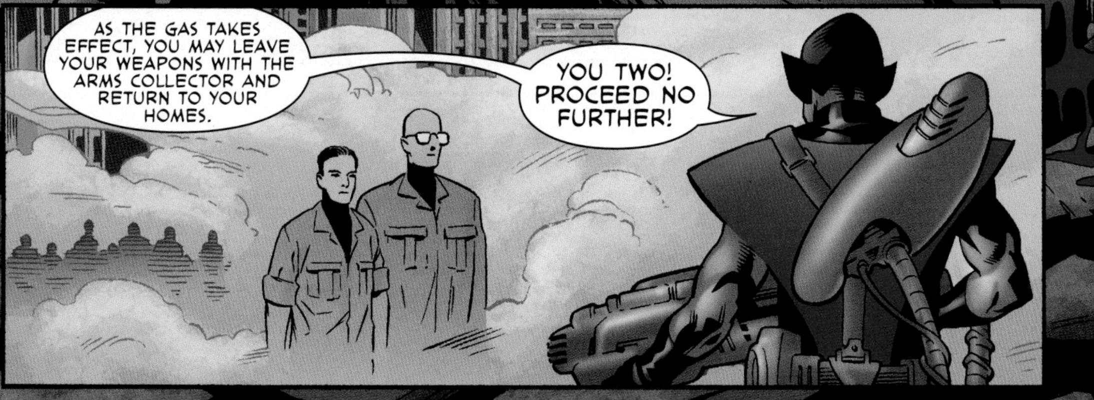
AS THE GAS TAKES EFFECT, YOU MAY LEAVE YOUR WEAPONS WITH THE ARMS COLLECTOR AND RETURN TO YOUR HOMES.
YOU TWO! PROCEED NO FURTHER!

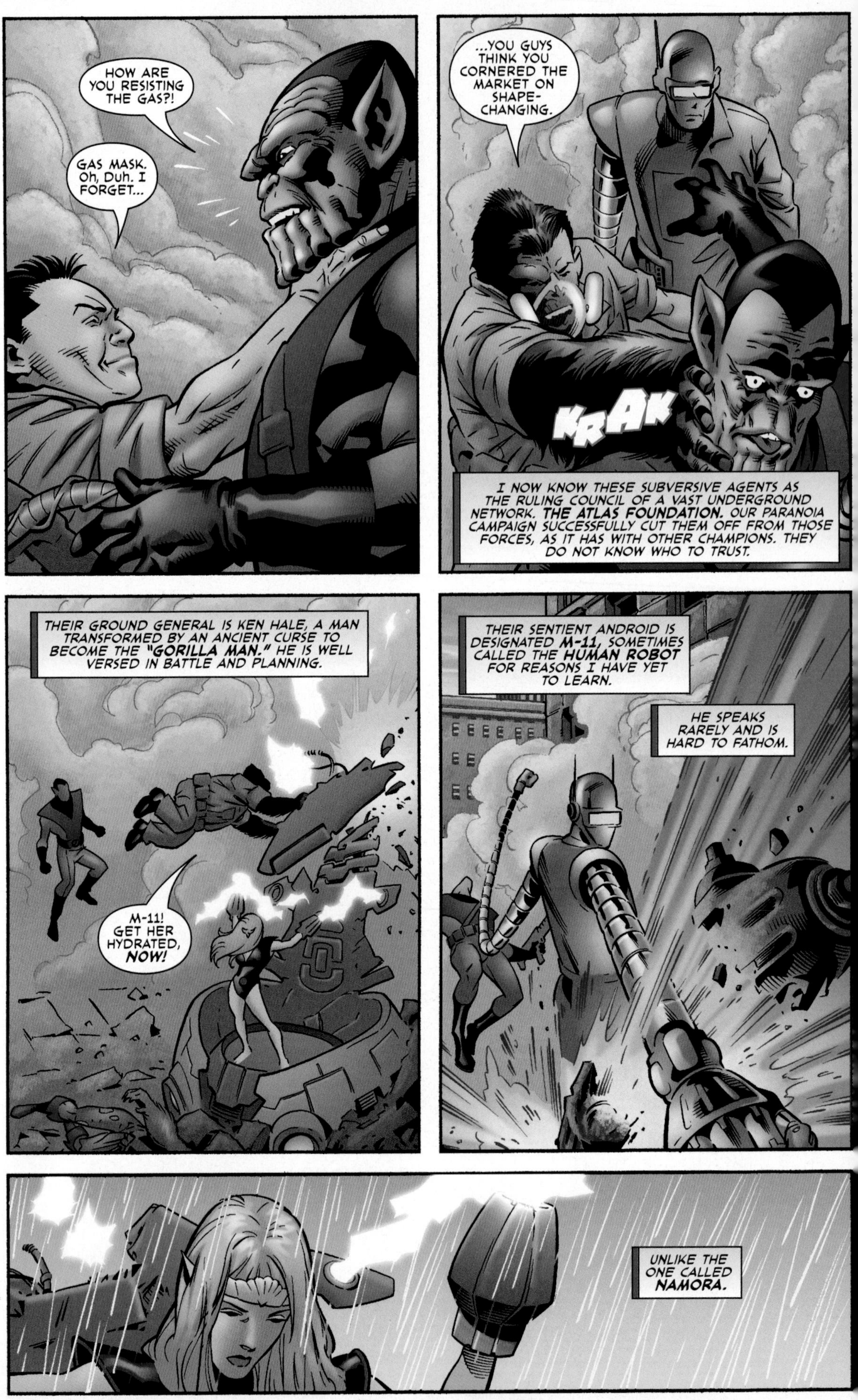
HOW ARE YOU RESISTING THE GAS?!
GAS MASK. Oh, Duh. I FORGET...
...YOU GUYS THINK YOU CORNERED THE MARKET ON SHAPE-CHANGING.
KRAK
I NOW KNOW THESE SUBVERSIVE AGENTS AS THE RULING COUNCIL OF A VAST UNDERGROUND NETWORK. **THE ATLAS FOUNDATION.** OUR PARANOIA CAMPAIGN SUCCESSFULLY CUT THEM OFF FROM THOSE FORCES, AS IT HAS WITH OTHER CHAMPIONS. THEY DO NOT KNOW WHO TO TRUST.
THEIR GROUND GENERAL IS KEN HALE, A MAN TRANSFORMED BY AN ANCIENT CURSE TO BECOME THE **"GORILLA MAN."** HE IS WELL VERSED IN BATTLE AND PLANNING.
M-11! GET HER HYDRATED, **NOW!**
THEIR SENTIENT ANDROID IS DESIGNATED **M-11,** SOMETIMES CALLED THE **HUMAN ROBOT** FOR REASONS I HAVE YET TO LEARN.
HE SPEAKS RARELY AND IS HARD TO FATHOM.
UNLIKE THE ONE CALLED **NAMORA.**

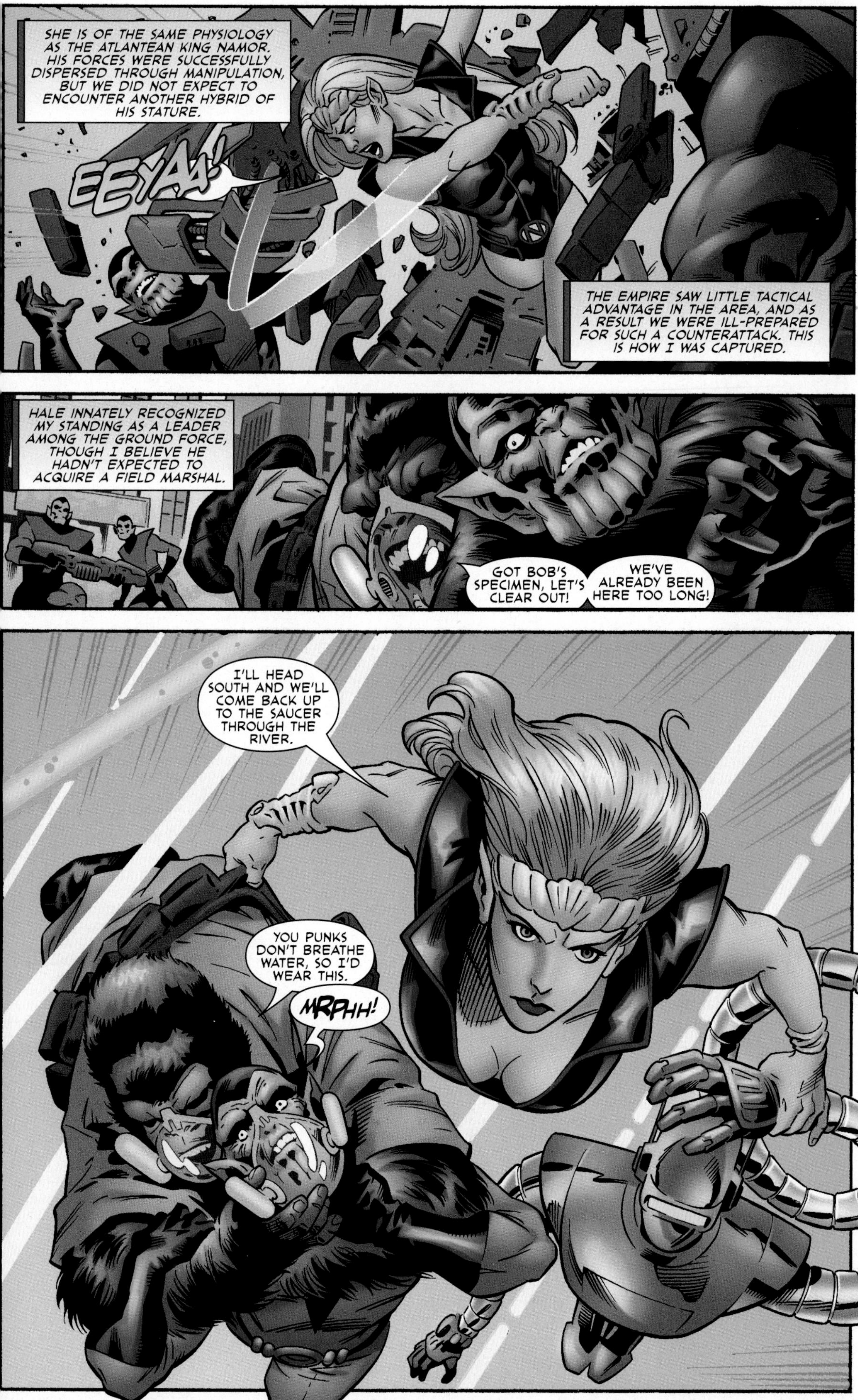
SHE IS OF THE SAME PHYSIOLOGY AS THE ATLANTEAN KING NAMOR. HIS FORCES WERE SUCCESSFULLY DISPERSED THROUGH MANIPULATION, BUT WE DID NOT EXPECT TO ENCOUNTER ANOTHER HYBRID OF HIS STATURE.
EEYAA!
THE EMPIRE SAW LITTLE TACTICAL ADVANTAGE IN THE AREA, AND AS A RESULT WE WERE ILL-PREPARED FOR SUCH A COUNTERATTACK. THIS IS HOW I WAS CAPTURED.
HALE INNATELY RECOGNIZED MY STANDING AS A LEADER AMONG THE GROUND FORCE, THOUGH I BELIEVE HE HADN'T EXPECTED TO ACQUIRE A FIELD MARSHAL.
GOT BOB'S SPECIMEN, LET'S CLEAR OUT!
WE'VE ALREADY BEEN HERE TOO LONG!
I'LL HEAD SOUTH AND WE'LL COME BACK UP TO THE SAUCER THROUGH THE RIVER.
YOU PUNKS DON'T BREATHE WATER, SO I'D WEAR THIS.
MRPHH!

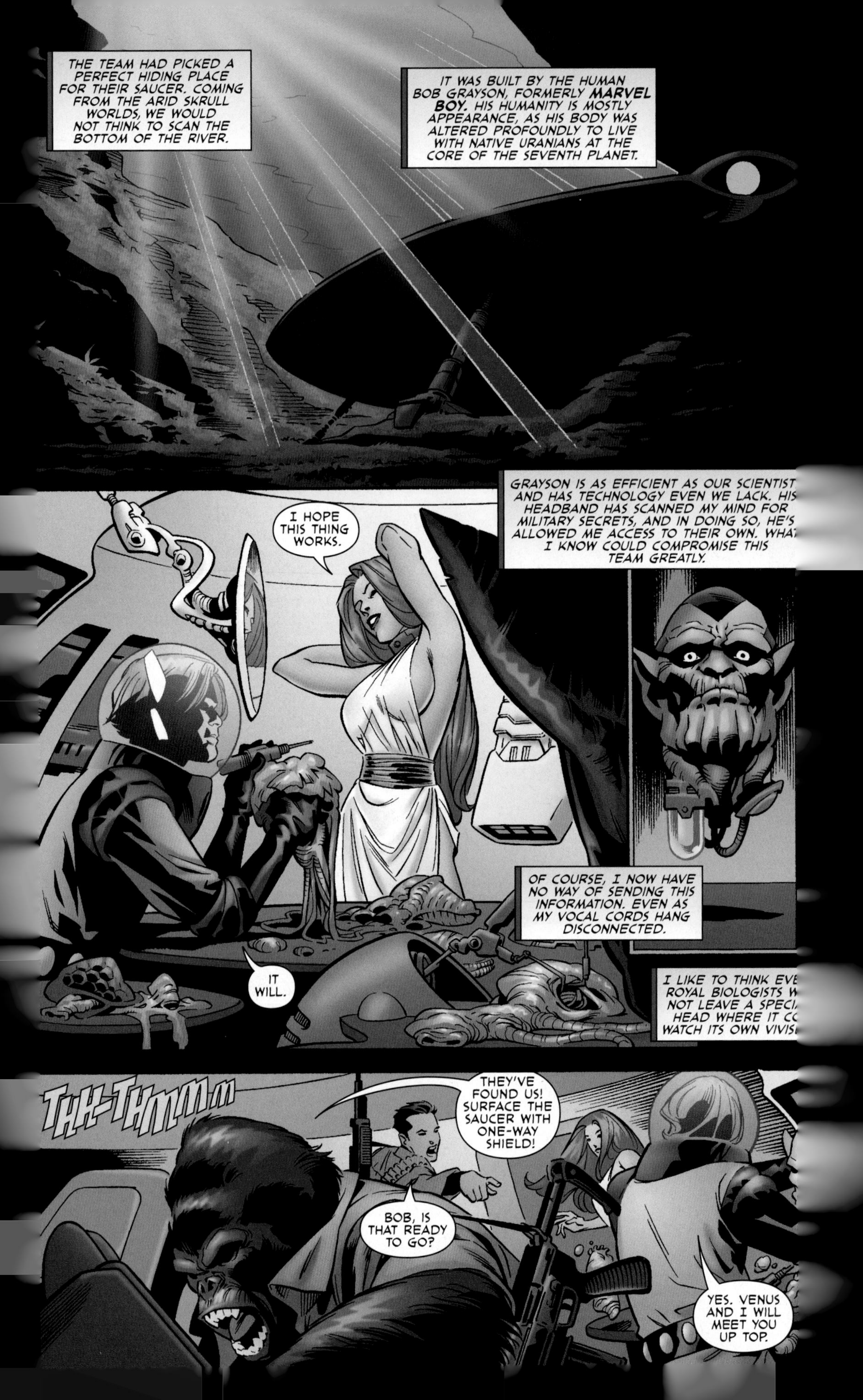
THE TEAM HAD PICKED A PERFECT HIDING PLACE FOR THEIR SAUCER. COMING FROM THE ARID SKRULL WORLDS, WE WOULD NOT THINK TO SCAN THE BOTTOM OF THE RIVER.
IT WAS BUILT BY THE HUMAN BOB GRAYSON, FORMERLY MARVEL BOY. HIS HUMANITY IS MOSTLY APPEARANCE, AS HIS BODY WAS ALTERED PROFOUNDLY TO LIVE WITH NATIVE URANIANS AT THE CORE OF THE SEVENTH PLANET.
I HOPE THIS THING WORKS.
GRAYSON IS AS EFFICIENT AS OUR SCIENTIST AND HAS TECHNOLOGY EVEN WE LACK. HIS HEADBAND HAS SCANNED MY MIND FOR MILITARY SECRETS, AND IN DOING SO, HE'S ALLOWED ME ACCESS TO THEIR OWN. WHAT I KNOW COULD COMPROMISE THIS TEAM GREATLY.
OF COURSE, I NOW HAVE NO WAY OF SENDING THIS INFORMATION. EVEN AS MY VOCAL CORDS HANG DISCONNECTED.
IT WILL.
I LIKE TO THINK EVE ROYAL BIOLOGISTS W NOT LEAVE A SPECI HEAD WHERE IT CO WATCH ITS OWN VIVISE
THH-THMMM
THEY'VE FOUND US! SURFACE THE SAUCER WITH ONE-WAY SHIELD!
BOB, IS THAT READY TO GO?
YES. VENUS AND I WILL MEET YOU UP TOP.

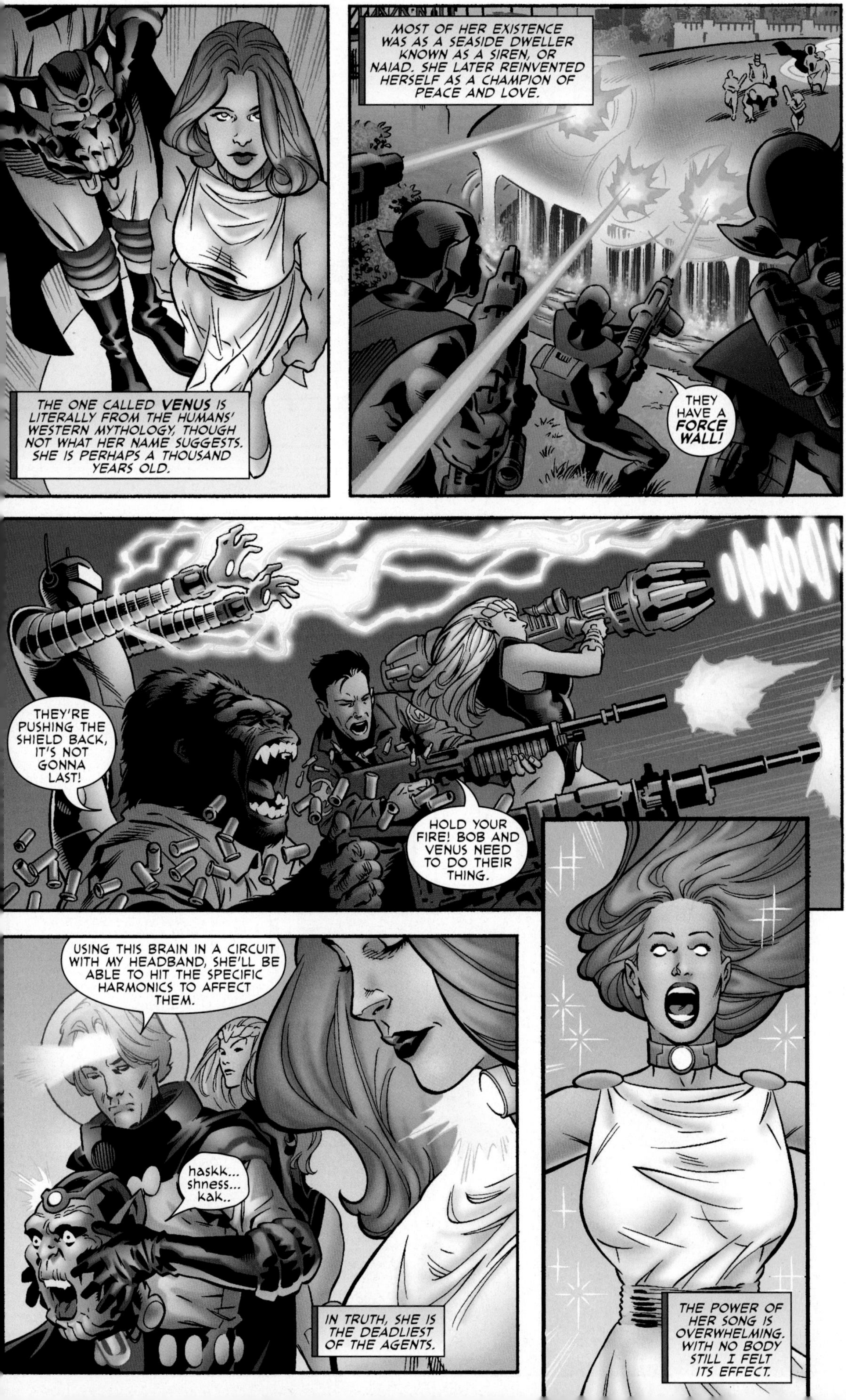
THE ONE CALLED **VENUS** IS LITERALLY FROM THE HUMANS' WESTERN MYTHOLOGY, THOUGH NOT WHAT HER NAME SUGGESTS. SHE IS PERHAPS A THOUSAND YEARS OLD.
MOST OF HER EXISTENCE WAS AS A SEASIDE DWELLER KNOWN AS A SIREN, OR NAIAD. SHE LATER REINVENTED HERSELF AS A CHAMPION OF PEACE AND LOVE.
THEY HAVE A **FORCE WALL!**
THEY'RE PUSHING THE SHIELD BACK, IT'S NOT GONNA LAST!
HOLD YOUR FIRE! BOB AND VENUS NEED TO DO THEIR THING.
USING THIS BRAIN IN A CIRCUIT WITH MY HEADBAND, SHE'LL BE ABLE TO HIT THE SPECIFIC HARMONICS TO AFFECT THEM.
haskk... shness... kak..
IN TRUTH, SHE IS THE DEADLIEST OF THE AGENTS.
THE POWER OF HER SONG IS OVERWHELMING. WITH NO BODY STILL I FELT ITS EFFECT.

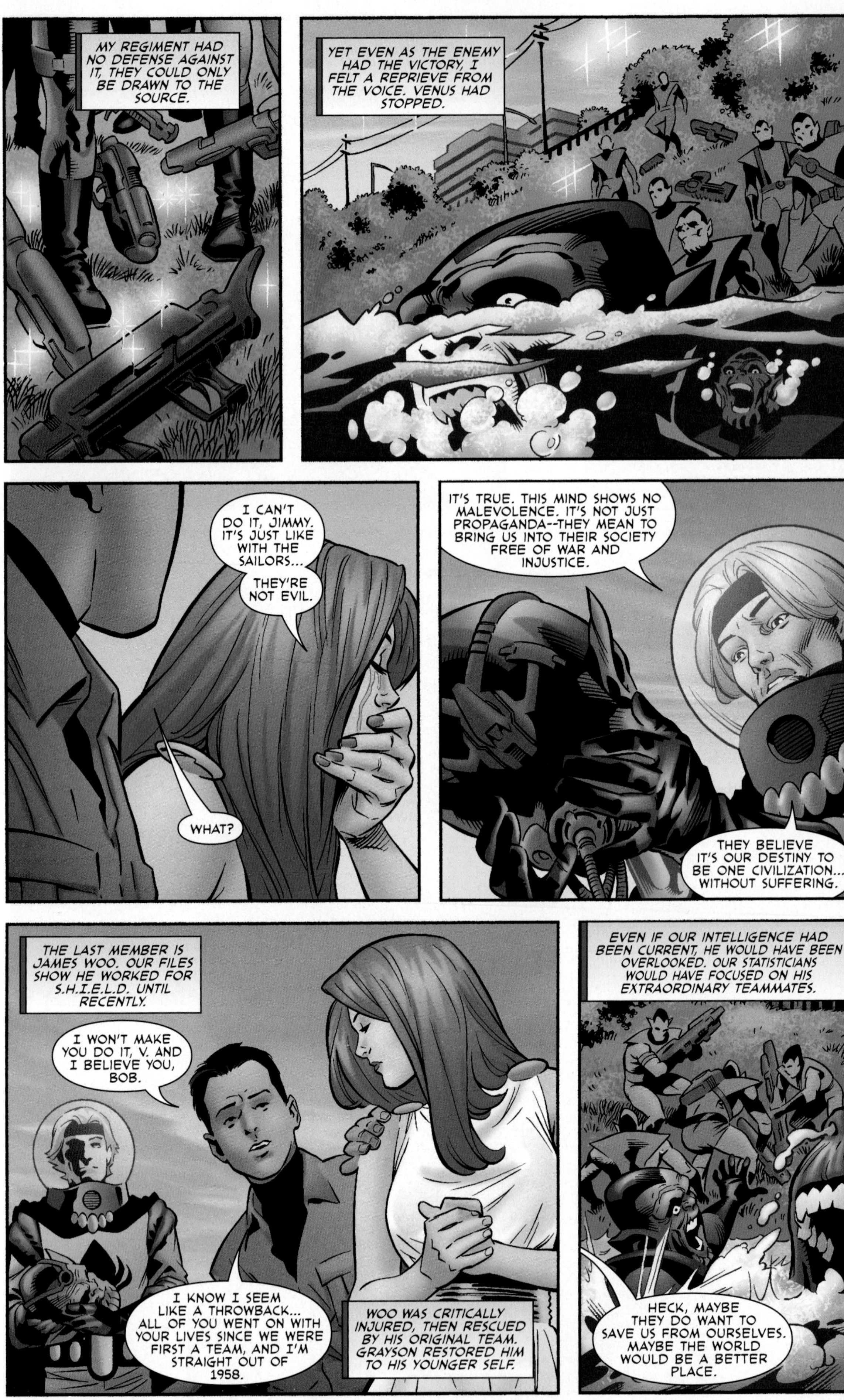
MY REGIMENT HAD NO DEFENSE AGAINST IT, THEY COULD ONLY BE DRAWN TO THE SOURCE.
YET EVEN AS THE ENEMY HAD THE VICTORY, I FELT A REPRIEVE FROM THE VOICE. VENUS HAD STOPPED.
I CAN'T DO IT, JIMMY. IT'S JUST LIKE WITH THE SAILORS...
THEY'RE NOT EVIL.
WHAT?
IT'S TRUE. THIS MIND SHOWS NO MALEVOLENCE. IT'S NOT JUST PROPAGANDA--THEY MEAN TO BRING US INTO THEIR SOCIETY FREE OF WAR AND INJUSTICE.
THEY BELIEVE IT'S OUR DESTINY TO BE ONE CIVILIZATION... WITHOUT SUFFERING.
THE LAST MEMBER IS JAMES WOO. OUR FILES SHOW HE WORKED FOR S.H.I.E.L.D. UNTIL RECENTLY.
I WON'T MAKE YOU DO IT, V. AND I BELIEVE YOU, BOB.
I KNOW I SEEM LIKE A THROWBACK... ALL OF YOU WENT ON WITH YOUR LIVES SINCE WE WERE FIRST A TEAM, AND I'M STRAIGHT OUT OF 1958.
WOO WAS CRITICALLY INJURED, THEN RESCUED BY HIS ORIGINAL TEAM. GRAYSON RESTORED HIM TO HIS YOUNGER SELF.
EVEN IF OUR INTELLIGENCE HAD BEEN CURRENT, HE WOULD HAVE BEEN OVERLOOKED. OUR STATISTICIANS WOULD HAVE FOCUSED ON HIS EXTRAORDINARY TEAMMATES.
HECK, MAYBE THEY DO WANT TO SAVE US FROM OURSELVES. MAYBE THE WORLD WOULD BE A BETTER PLACE.

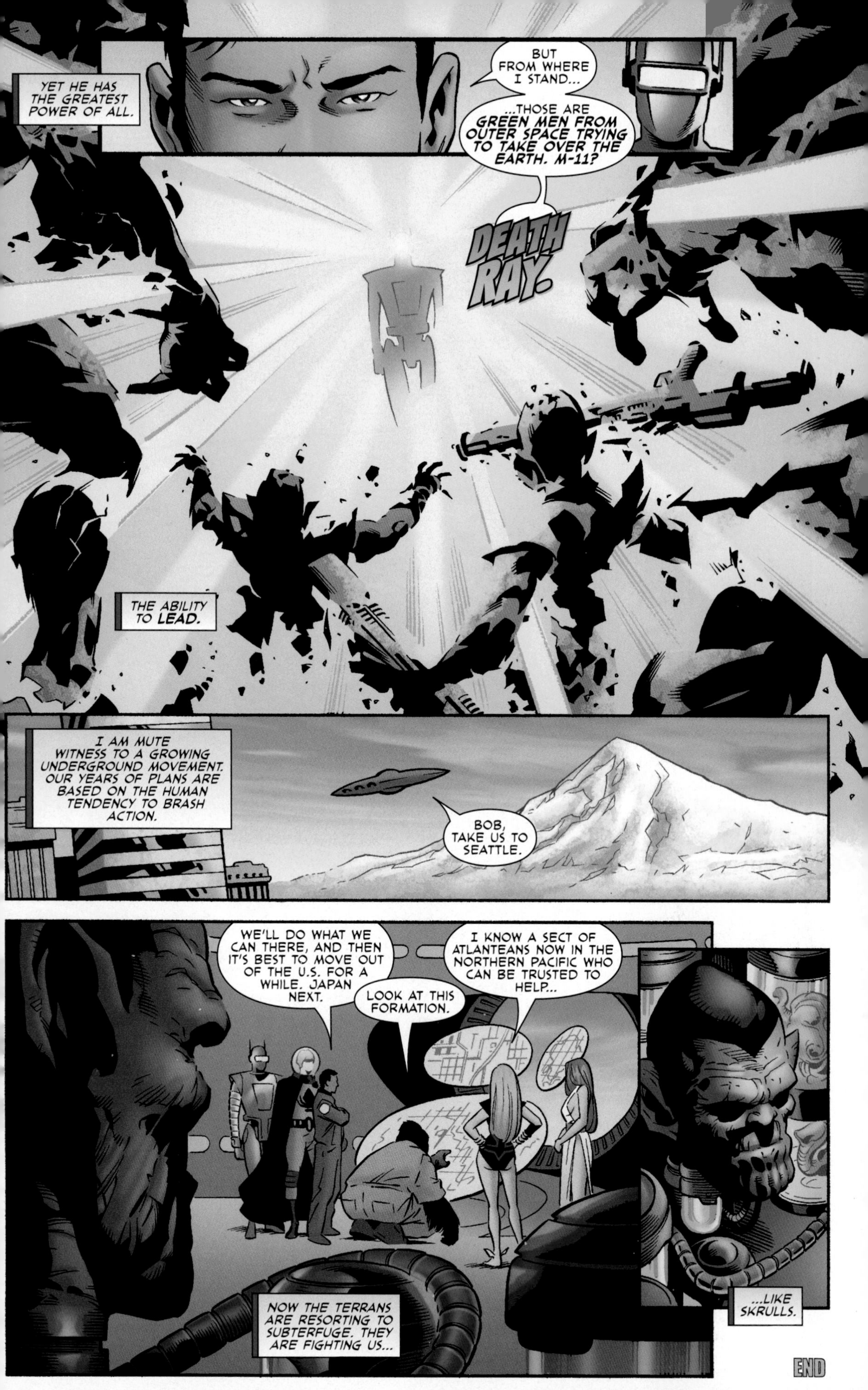
YET HE HAS THE GREATEST POWER OF ALL.
BUT FROM WHERE I STAND...
...THOSE ARE GREEN MEN FROM OUTER SPACE TRYING TO TAKE OVER THE EARTH. M-11?
DEATH RAY.
THE ABILITY TO LEAD.
I AM MUTE WITNESS TO A GROWING UNDERGROUND MOVEMENT. OUR YEARS OF PLANS ARE BASED ON THE HUMAN TENDENCY TO BRASH ACTION.
BOB, TAKE US TO SEATTLE.
WE'LL DO WHAT WE CAN THERE, AND THEN IT'S BEST TO MOVE OUT OF THE U.S. FOR A WHILE. JAPAN NEXT.
LOOK AT THIS FORMATION.
I KNOW A SECT OF ATLANTEANS NOW IN THE NORTHERN PACIFIC WHO CAN BE TRUSTED TO HELP...
NOW THE TERRANS ARE RESORTING TO SUBTERFUGE. THEY ARE FIGHTING US...
...LIKE SKRULLS.
END

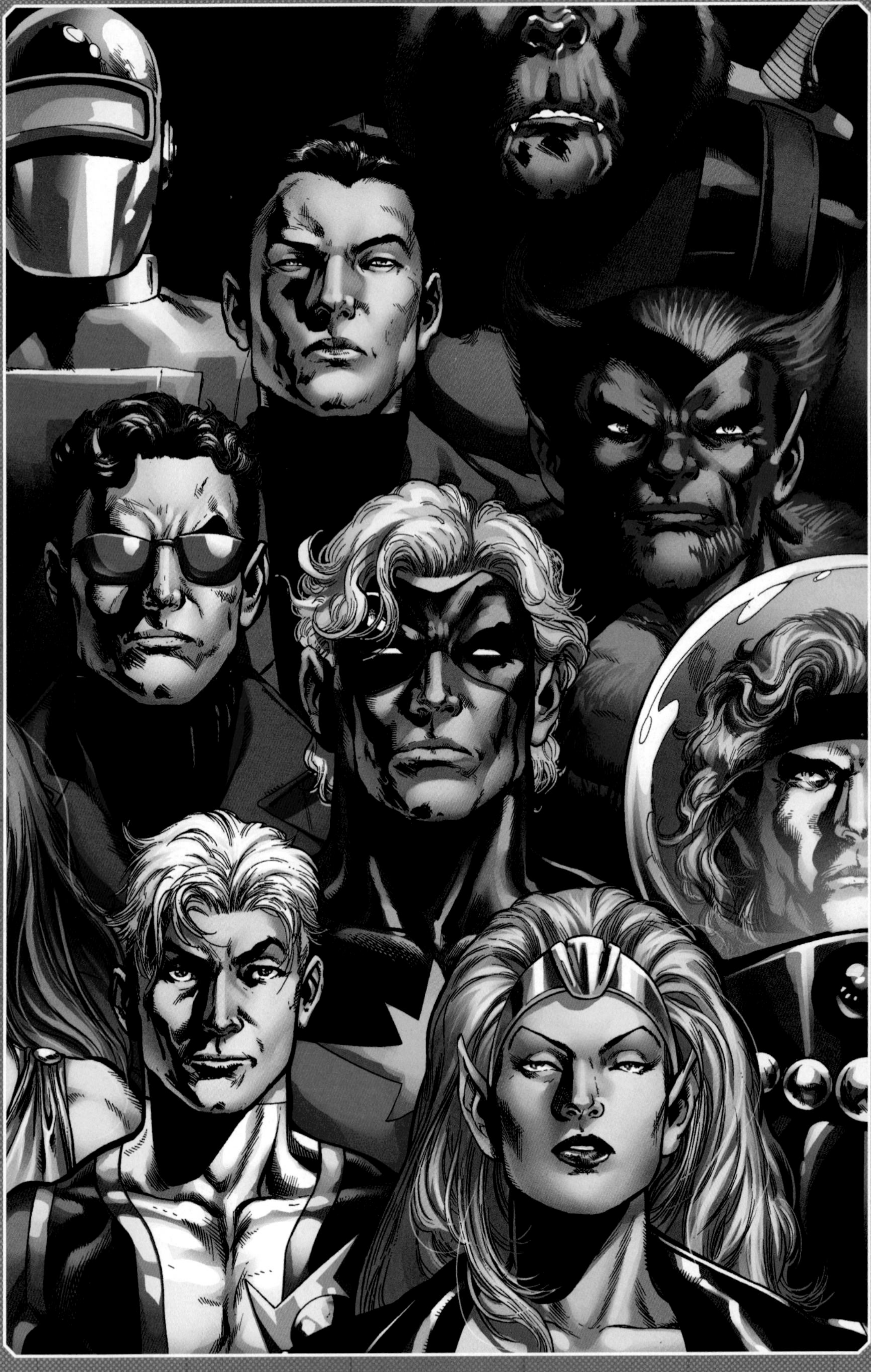

SECRET INVASION: WHO DO YOU TRUST? 2ND-PRINTING VARIANT BY
PHIL JIMENEZ, ANDY LANNING & CHRISTINA STRAIN

CLASSIFIED DOCUMENT / FEDERAL BUREAU OF
INVESTIGATION

CASE 7-A / JAMES WOO- HEAD OF WEST COAST SPECIAL
DEPARTMENT ZERO

Transcribed by Agent Angela Wellington,
San Francisco Adjunct

May 3rd, 1958/ CUBA

As with all other transcriptions of Agent Woo's DEPART-
MENT ZERO group, I have received audio recordings from
the automaton known as M-11, supplemented with accounts from the other members of the team. This was
particularly necessary in this instance as M-11's files
are exceptionally unreliable near mission's end, for
causes which will become apparent. Also supplied is
aerial photography from Bob Grayson's craft The Silver
Bullet.

-A. Wellington

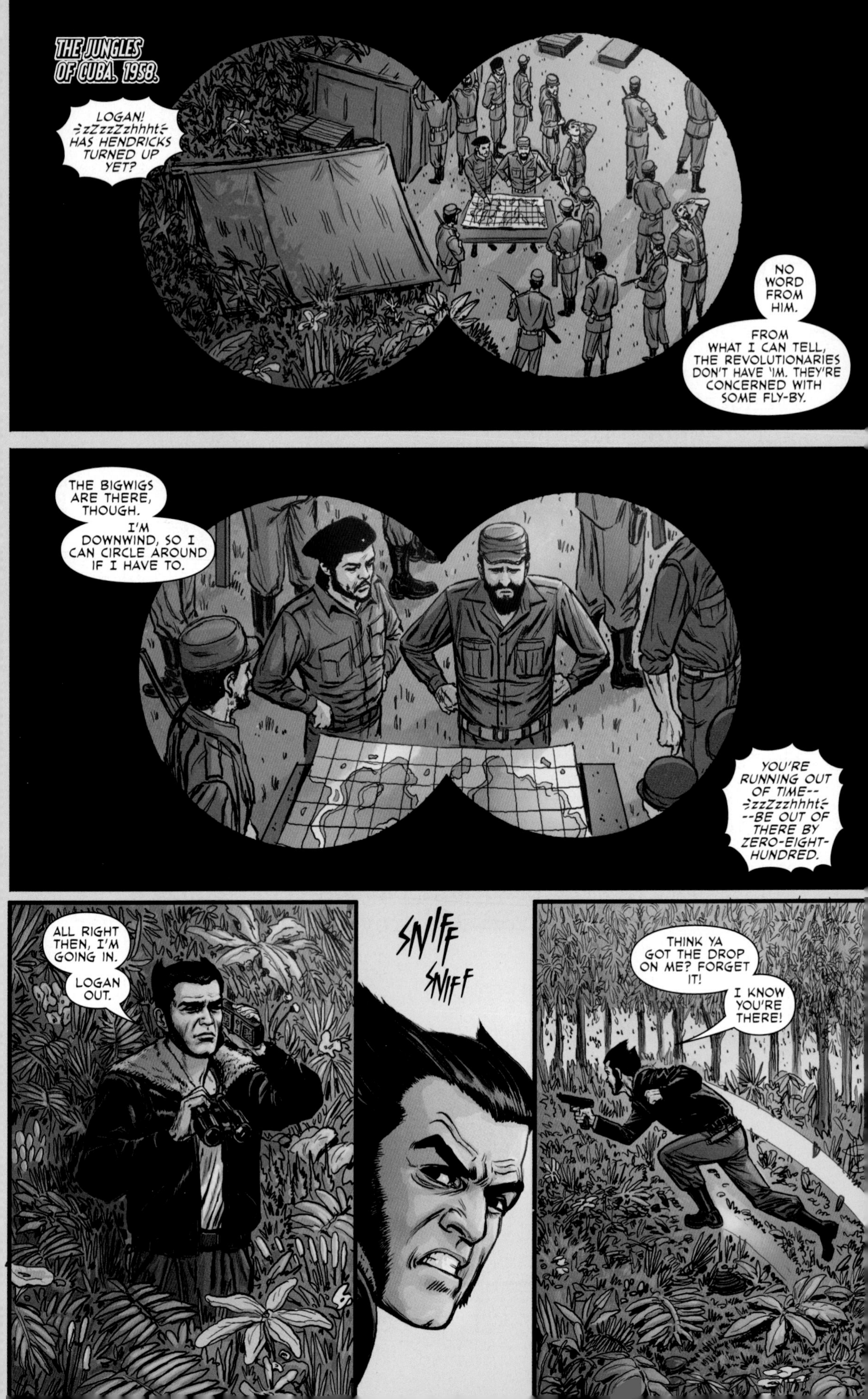
THE JUNGLES OF CUBA. 1958.
LOGAN! -zZzzZzhhht- HAS HENDRICKS TURNED UP YET?
NO WORD FROM HIM.
FROM WHAT I CAN TELL, THE REVOLUTIONARIES DON'T HAVE 'IM. THEY'RE CONCERNED WITH SOME FLY-BY.
THE BIGWIGS ARE THERE, THOUGH.
I'M DOWNWIND, SO I CAN CIRCLE AROUND IF I HAVE TO.
YOU'RE RUNNING OUT OF TIME-- -zzZzzhhht- --BE OUT OF THERE BY ZERO-EIGHT-HUNDRED.
ALL RIGHT THEN, I'M GOING IN.
LOGAN OUT.
SNIFF
SNIFF
THINK YA GOT THE DROP ON ME? FORGET IT!
I KNOW YOU'RE THERE!

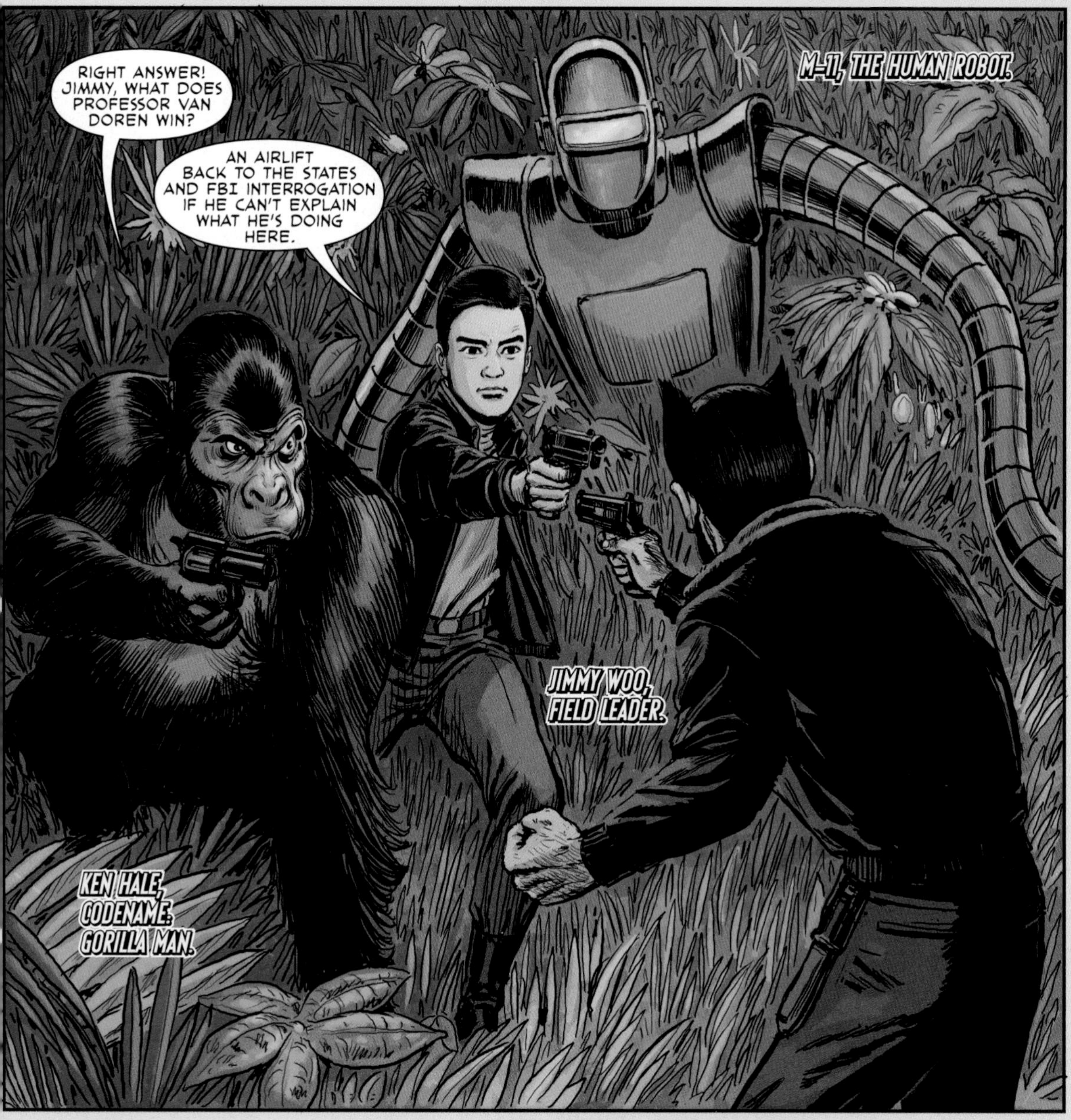
RIGHT ANSWER! JIMMY, WHAT DOES PROFESSOR VAN DOREN WIN?
M-11, THE HUMAN ROBOT.
AN AIRLIFT BACK TO THE STATES AND FBI INTERROGATION IF HE CAN'T EXPLAIN WHAT HE'S DOING HERE.
JIMMY WOO, FIELD LEADER.
KEN HALE, CODENAME: GORILLA MAN.

WOLVERINE
AGENT OF ATLAS

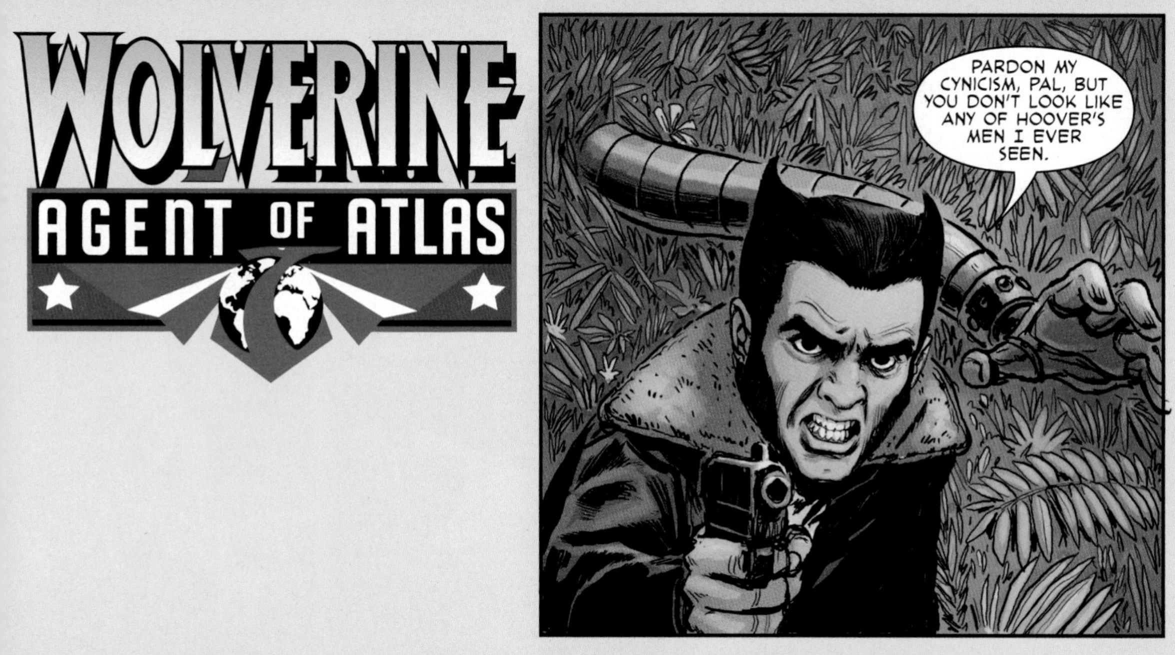
PARDON MY CYNICISM, PAL, BUT YOU DON'T LOOK LIKE ANY OF HOOVER'S MEN I EVER SEEN.

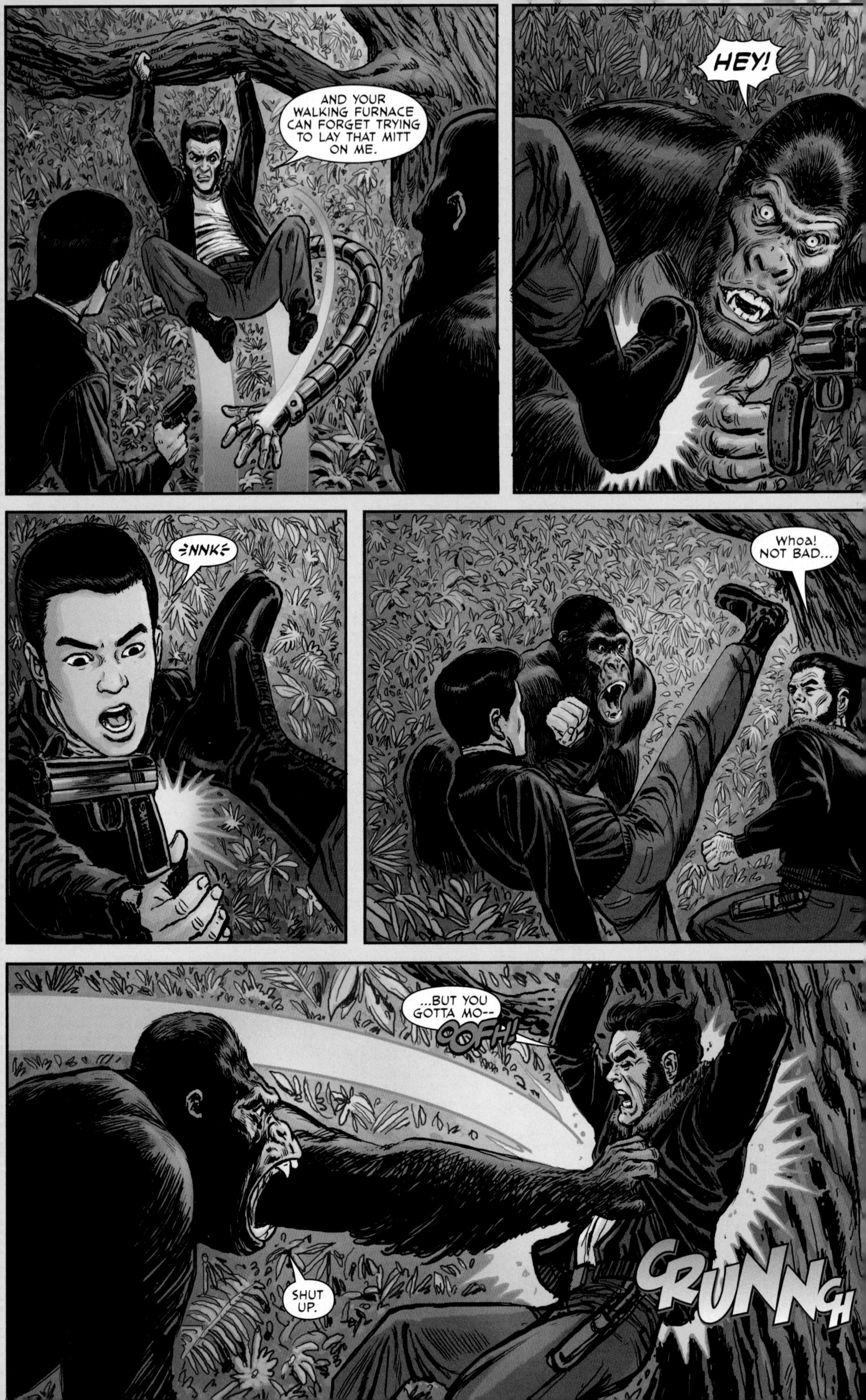
AND YOUR WALKING FURNACE CAN FORGET TRYING TO LAY THAT MITT ON ME.
HEY!
NNK
Whoa! NOT BAD...
...BUT YOU GOTTA MO--
OOFH!
SHUT UP.
CRUNNCH

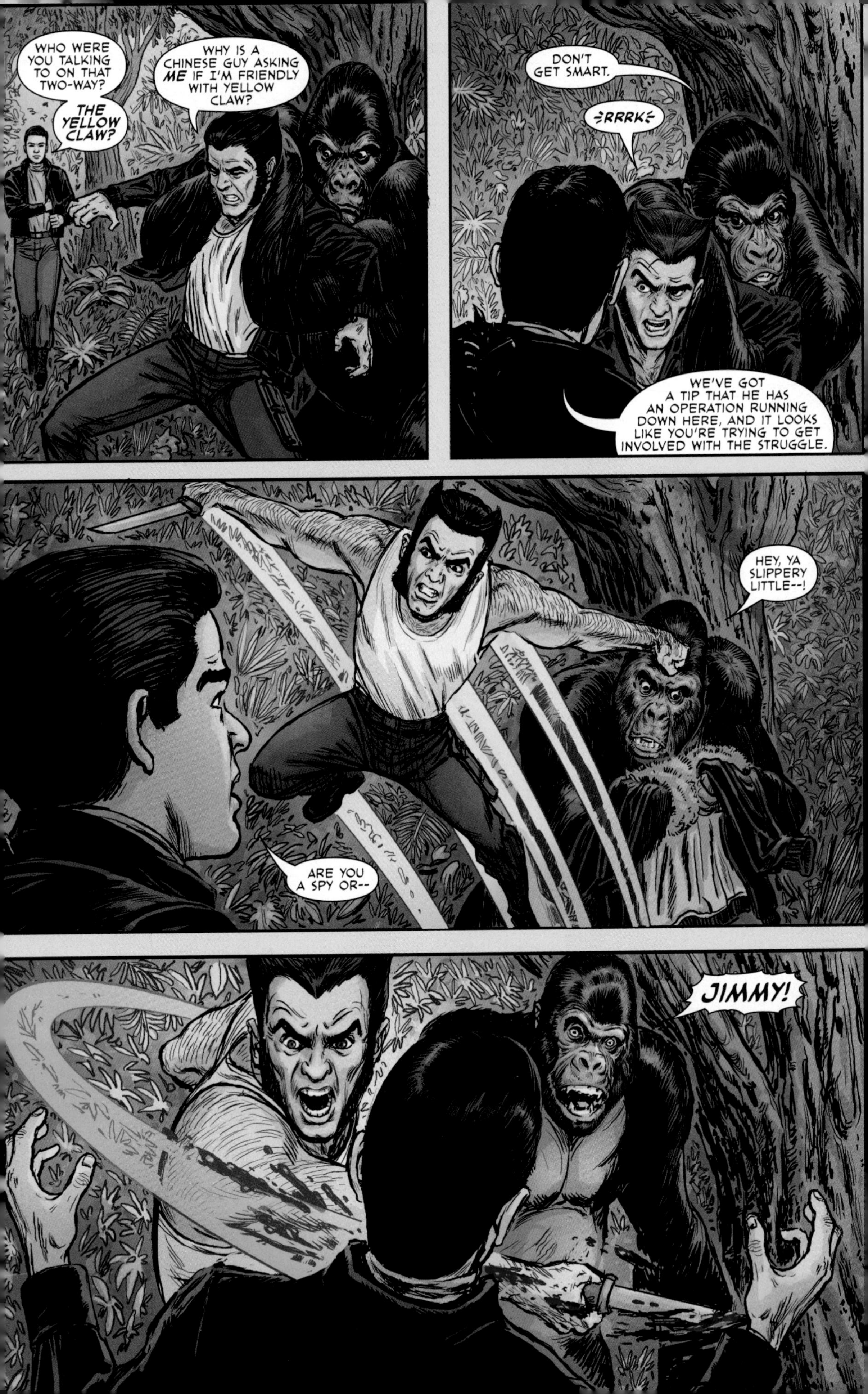
WHO WERE YOU TALKING TO ON THAT TWO-WAY?
THE YELLOW CLAW?
WHY IS A CHINESE GUY ASKING ME IF I'M FRIENDLY WITH YELLOW CLAW?
DON'T GET SMART.
RRRK
WE'VE GOT A TIP THAT HE HAS AN OPERATION RUNNING DOWN HERE, AND IT LOOKS LIKE YOU'RE TRYING TO GET INVOLVED WITH THE STRUGGLE.
HEY, YA SLIPPERY LITTLE--!
ARE YOU A SPY OR--
JIMMY!

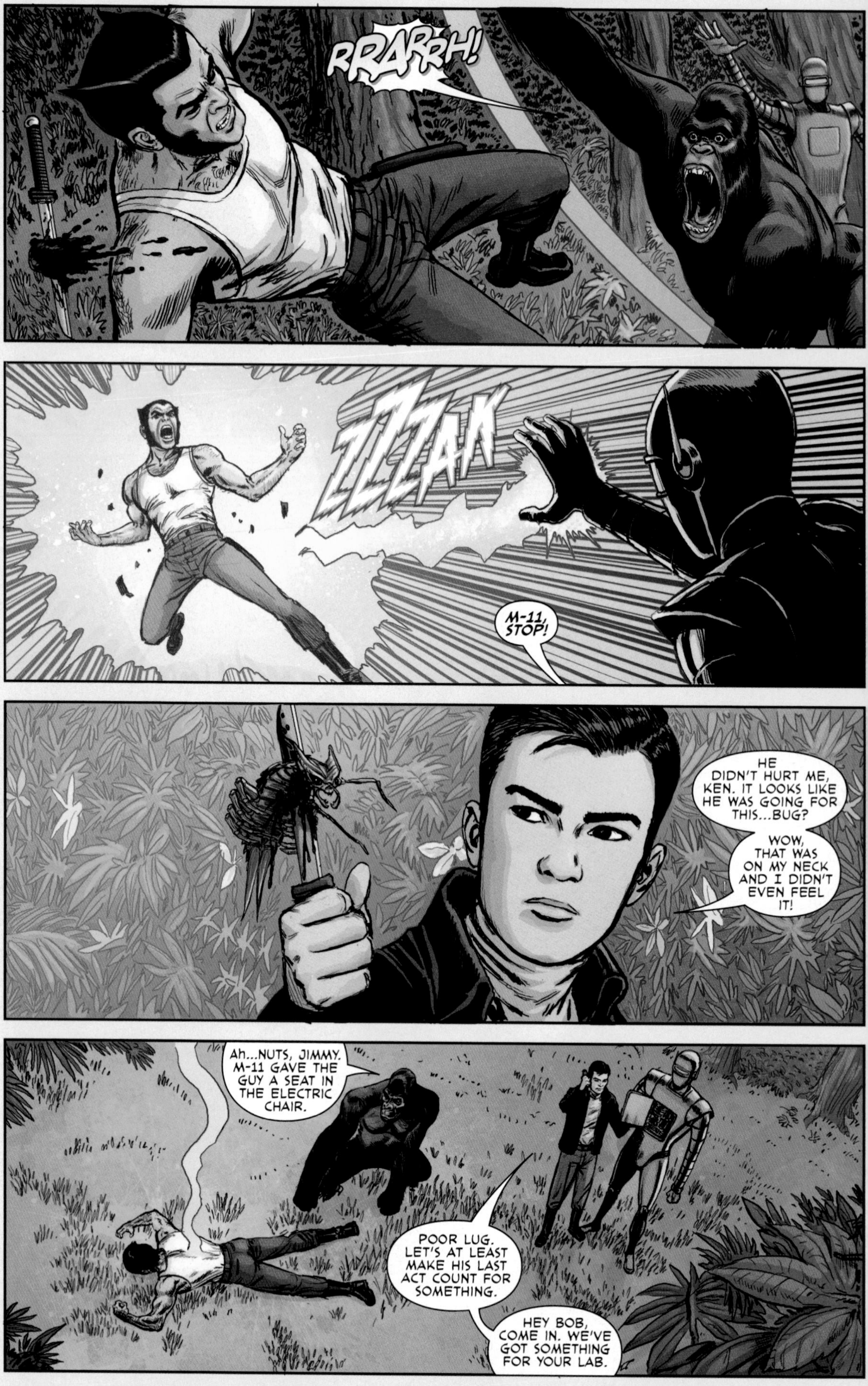
RRARRH!
ZZZAK
M-11, STOP!
HE DIDN'T HURT ME, KEN. IT LOOKS LIKE HE WAS GOING FOR THIS...BUG?
WOW, THAT WAS ON MY NECK AND I DIDN'T EVEN FEEL IT!
Ah...NUTS, JIMMY. M-11 GAVE THE GUY A SEAT IN THE ELECTRIC CHAIR.
POOR LUG. LET'S AT LEAST MAKE HIS LAST ACT COUNT FOR SOMETHING.
HEY BOB, COME IN. WE'VE GOT SOMETHING FOR YOUR LAB.

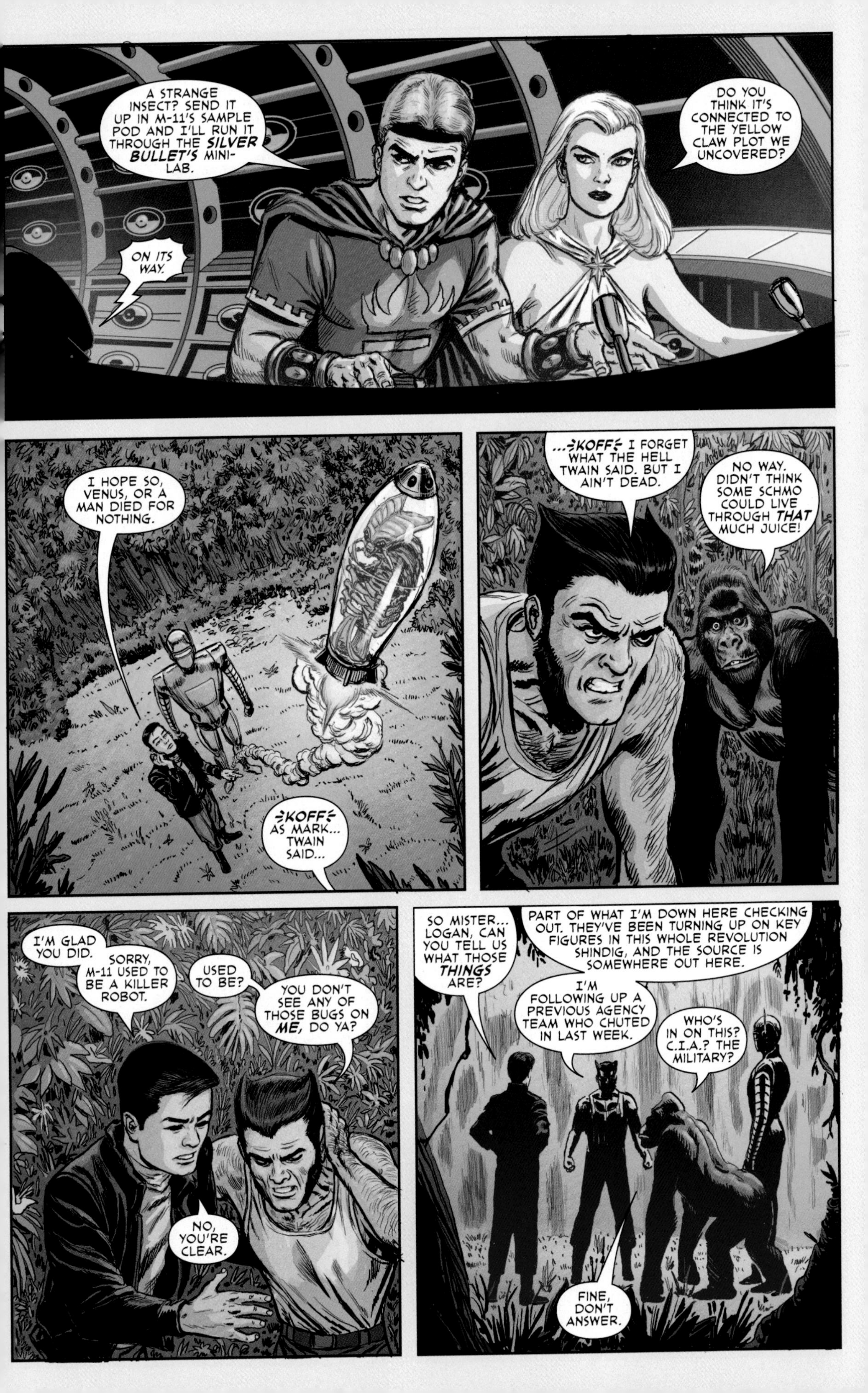
A STRANGE INSECT? SEND IT UP IN M-11'S SAMPLE POD AND I'LL RUN IT THROUGH THE SILVER BULLET'S MINI-LAB.
DO YOU THINK IT'S CONNECTED TO THE YELLOW CLAW PLOT WE UNCOVERED?
ON ITS WAY.
I HOPE SO, VENUS, OR A MAN DIED FOR NOTHING.
KOFF AS MARK... TWAIN SAID...
...KOFF I FORGET WHAT THE HELL TWAIN SAID. BUT I AIN'T DEAD.
NO WAY. DIDN'T THINK SOME SCHMO COULD LIVE THROUGH THAT MUCH JUICE!
I'M GLAD YOU DID.
SORRY, M-11 USED TO BE A KILLER ROBOT.
USED TO BE?
YOU DON'T SEE ANY OF THOSE BUGS ON ME, DO YA?
NO, YOU'RE CLEAR.
SO MISTER... LOGAN, CAN YOU TELL US WHAT THOSE THINGS ARE?
PART OF WHAT I'M DOWN HERE CHECKING OUT. THEY'VE BEEN TURNING UP ON KEY FIGURES IN THIS WHOLE REVOLUTION SHINDIG, AND THE SOURCE IS SOMEWHERE OUT HERE.
I'M FOLLOWING UP A PREVIOUS AGENCY TEAM WHO CHUTED IN LAST WEEK.
WHO'S IN ON THIS? C.I.A.? THE MILITARY?
FINE, DON'T ANSWER.

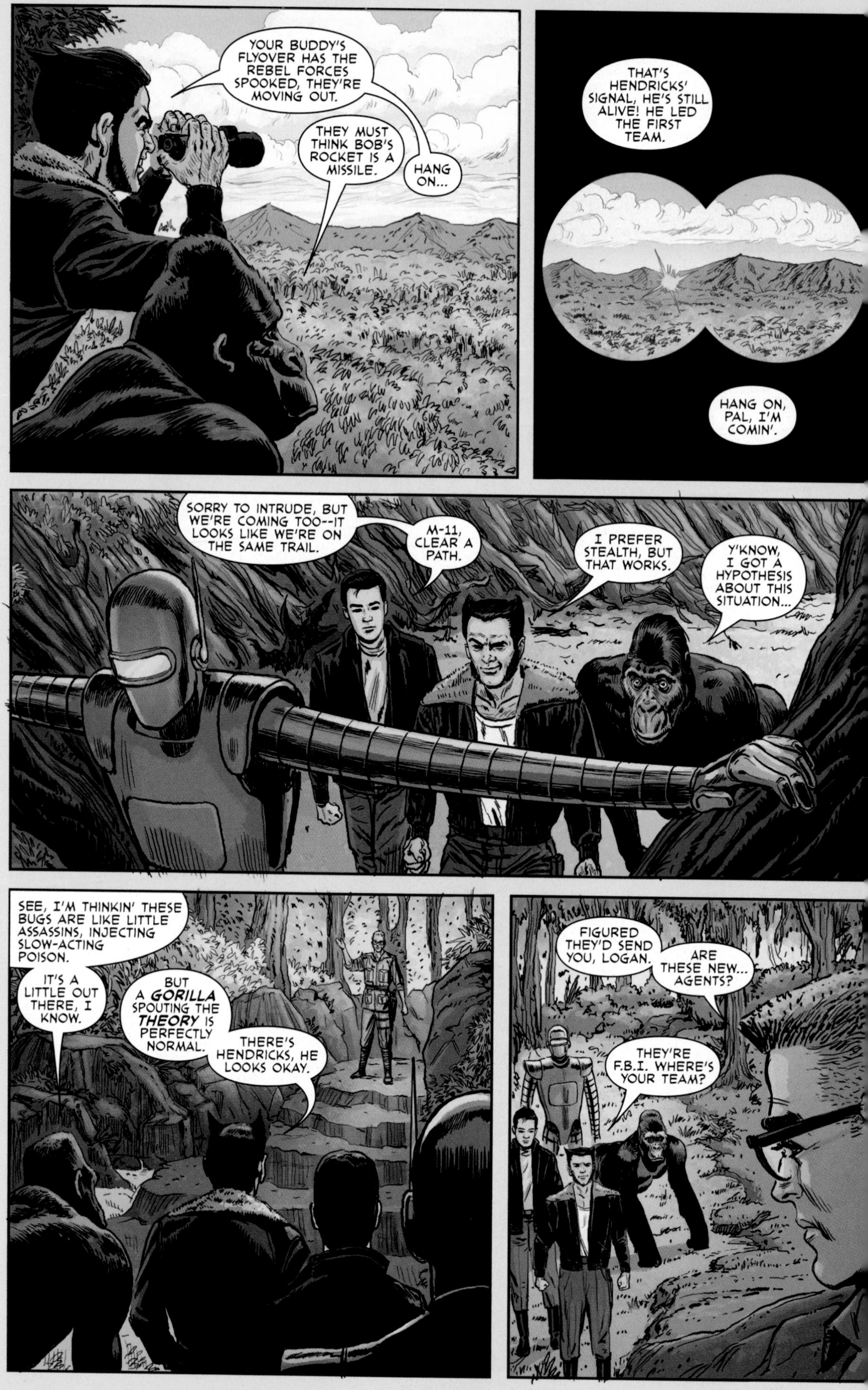
YOUR BUDDY'S FLYOVER HAS THE REBEL FORCES SPOOKED, THEY'RE MOVING OUT.
THEY MUST THINK BOB'S ROCKET IS A MISSILE.
HANG ON...
THAT'S HENDRICKS' SIGNAL, HE'S STILL ALIVE! HE LED THE FIRST TEAM.
HANG ON, PAL, I'M COMIN'.
SORRY TO INTRUDE, BUT WE'RE COMING TOO--IT LOOKS LIKE WE'RE ON THE SAME TRAIL.
M-11, CLEAR A PATH.
I PREFER STEALTH, BUT THAT WORKS.
Y'KNOW, I GOT A HYPOTHESIS ABOUT THIS SITUATION...
SEE, I'M THINKIN' THESE BUGS ARE LIKE LITTLE ASSASSINS, INJECTING SLOW-ACTING POISON.
IT'S A LITTLE OUT THERE, I KNOW.
BUT A **GORILLA** SPOUTING THE ***THEORY*** IS PERFECTLY NORMAL.
THERE'S HENDRICKS, HE LOOKS OKAY.
FIGURED THEY'D SEND YOU, LOGAN.
ARE THESE NEW... AGENTS?
THEY'RE F.B.I. WHERE'S YOUR TEAM?

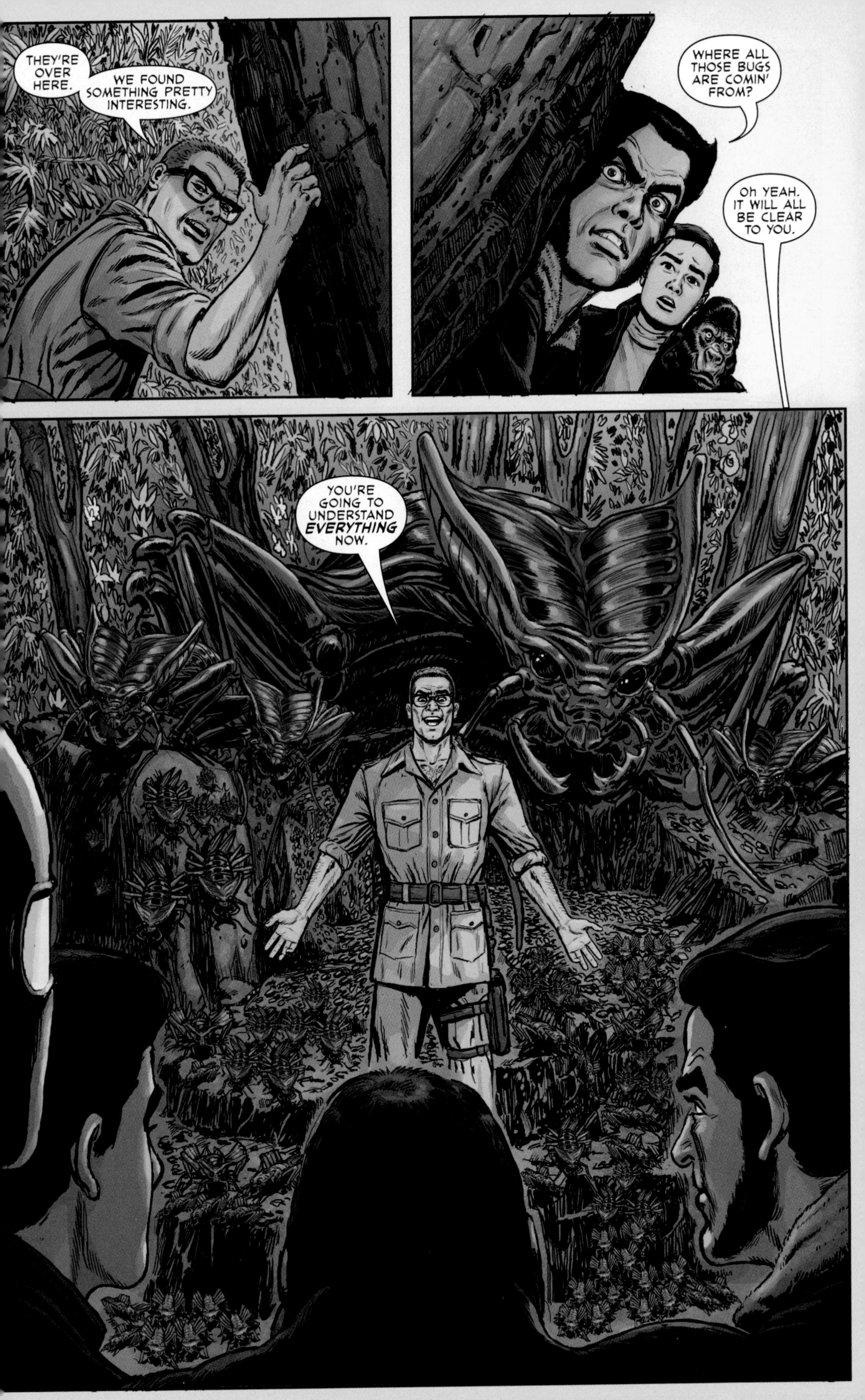
THEY'RE OVER HERE.
WE FOUND SOMETHING PRETTY INTERESTING.
WHERE ALL THOSE BUGS ARE COMIN' FROM?
Oh YEAH. IT WILL ALL BE CLEAR TO YOU.
YOU'RE GOING TO UNDERSTAND *EVERYTHING* NOW.

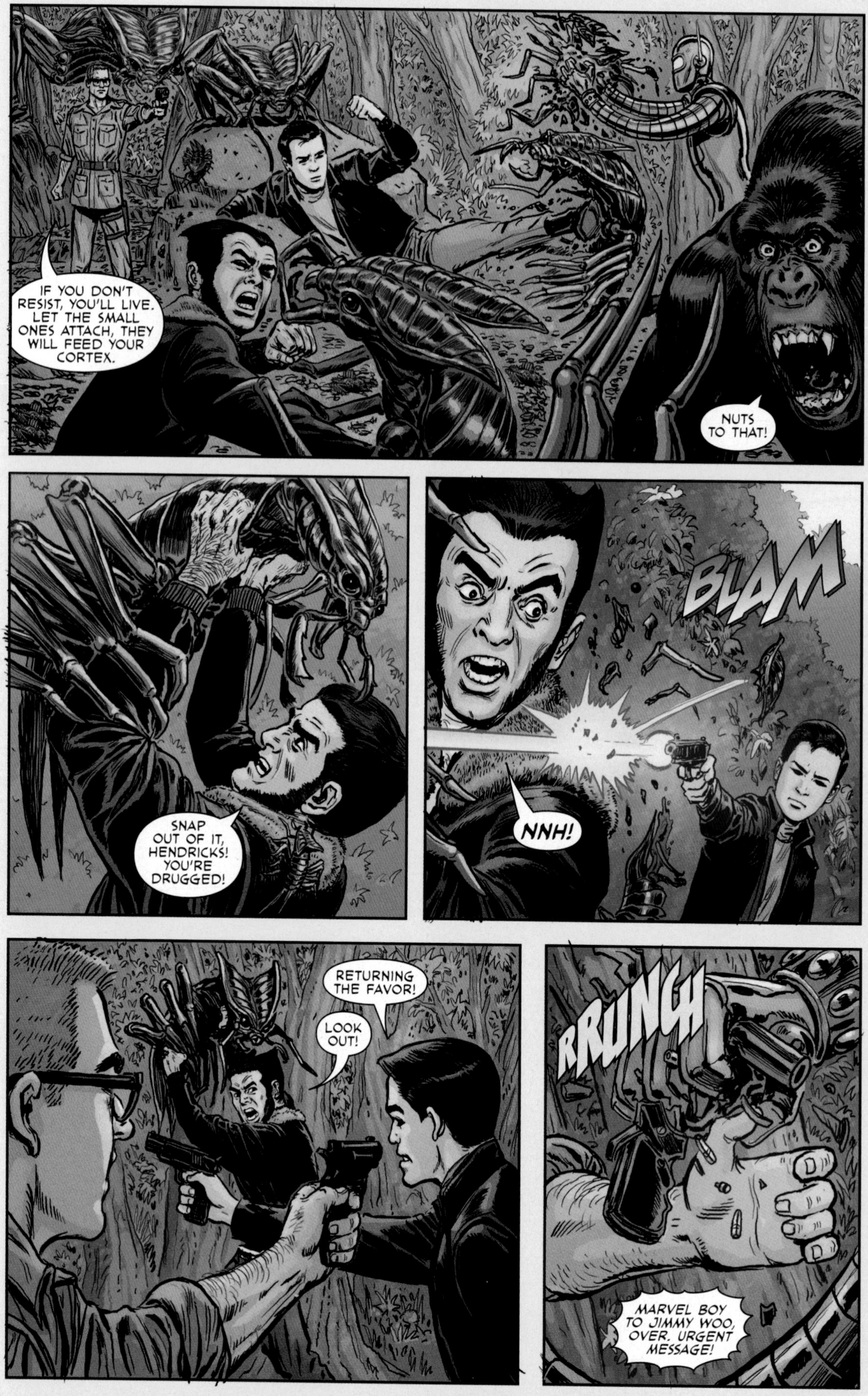
IF YOU DON'T RESIST, YOU'LL LIVE. LET THE SMALL ONES ATTACH, THEY WILL FEED YOUR CORTEX.
NUTS TO THAT!
SNAP OUT OF IT, HENDRICKS! YOU'RE DRUGGED!
BLAM
NNH!
RETURNING THE FAVOR!
LOOK OUT!
RRUNCH
MARVEL BOY TO JIMMY WOO, OVER. URGENT MESSAGE!

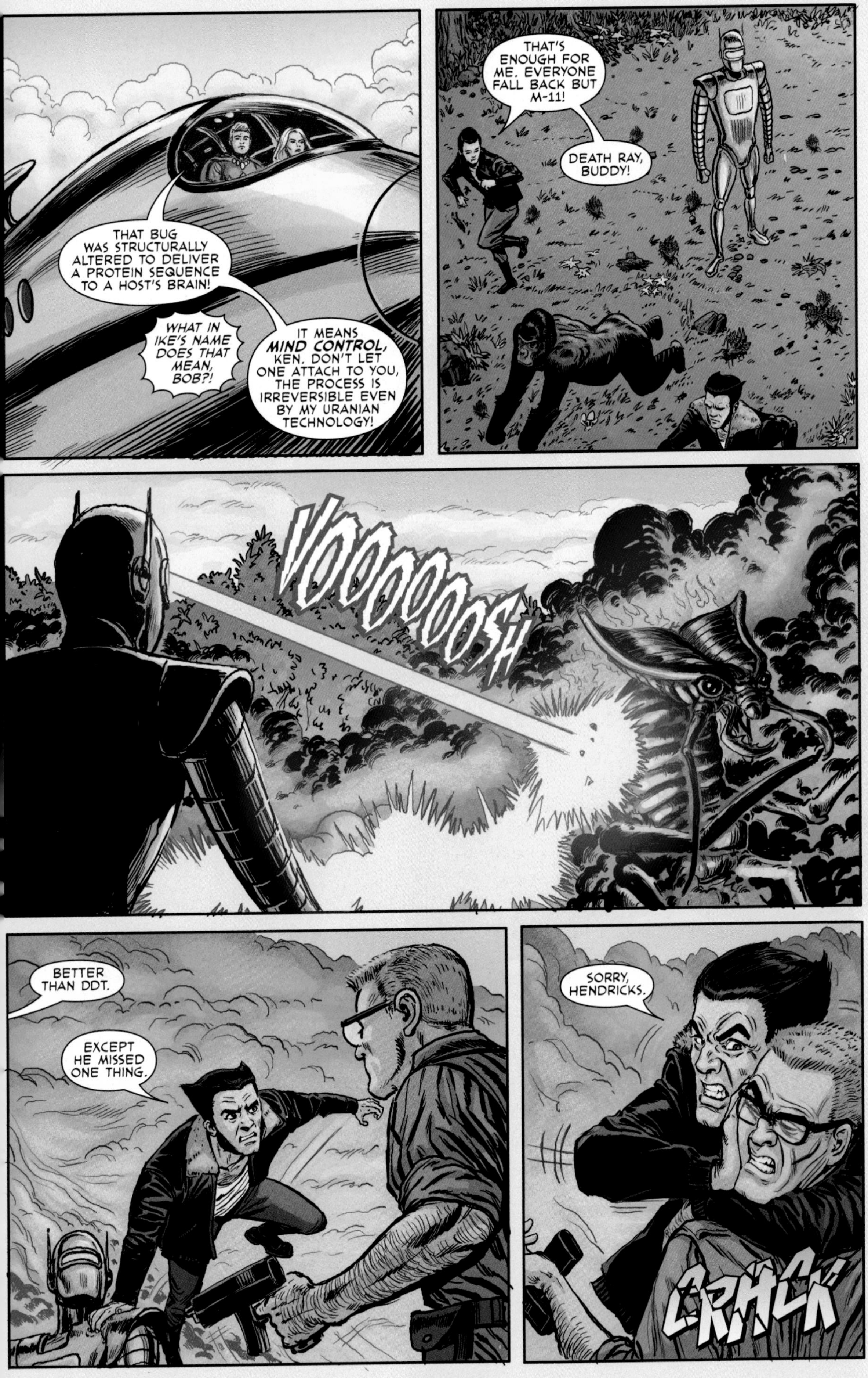
THAT BUG WAS STRUCTURALLY ALTERED TO DELIVER A PROTEIN SEQUENCE TO A HOST'S BRAIN!
WHAT IN IKE'S NAME DOES THAT MEAN, BOB?!
IT MEANS MIND CONTROL, KEN. DON'T LET ONE ATTACH TO YOU, THE PROCESS IS IRREVERSIBLE EVEN BY MY URANIAN TECHNOLOGY!
THAT'S ENOUGH FOR ME. EVERYONE FALL BACK BUT M-11!
DEATH RAY, BUDDY!
VOOOOOOSH
BETTER THAN DDT.
EXCEPT HE MISSED ONE THING.
SORRY, HENDRICKS.
CRACK!

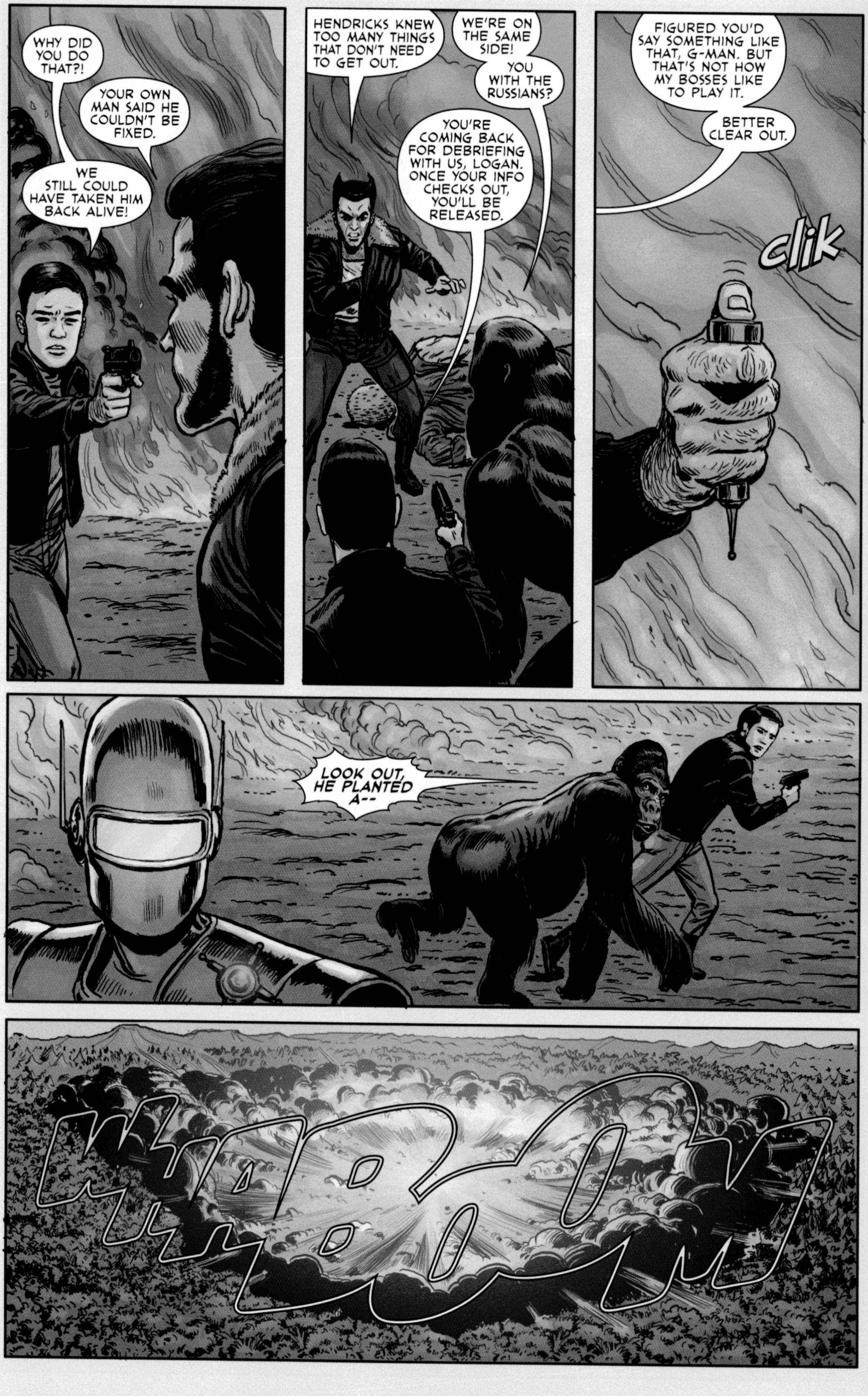
WHY DID YOU DO THAT?!
YOUR OWN MAN SAID HE COULDN'T BE FIXED.
WE STILL COULD HAVE TAKEN HIM BACK ALIVE!
HENDRICKS KNEW TOO MANY THINGS THAT DON'T NEED TO GET OUT.
WE'RE ON THE SAME SIDE!
YOU WITH THE RUSSIANS?
YOU'RE COMING BACK FOR DEBRIEFING WITH US, LOGAN. ONCE YOUR INFO CHECKS OUT, YOU'LL BE RELEASED.
FIGURED YOU'D SAY SOMETHING LIKE THAT, G-MAN. BUT THAT'S NOT HOW MY BOSSES LIKE TO PLAY IT.
BETTER CLEAR OUT.
clik
LOOK OUT, HE PLANTED A--
WHOOOM

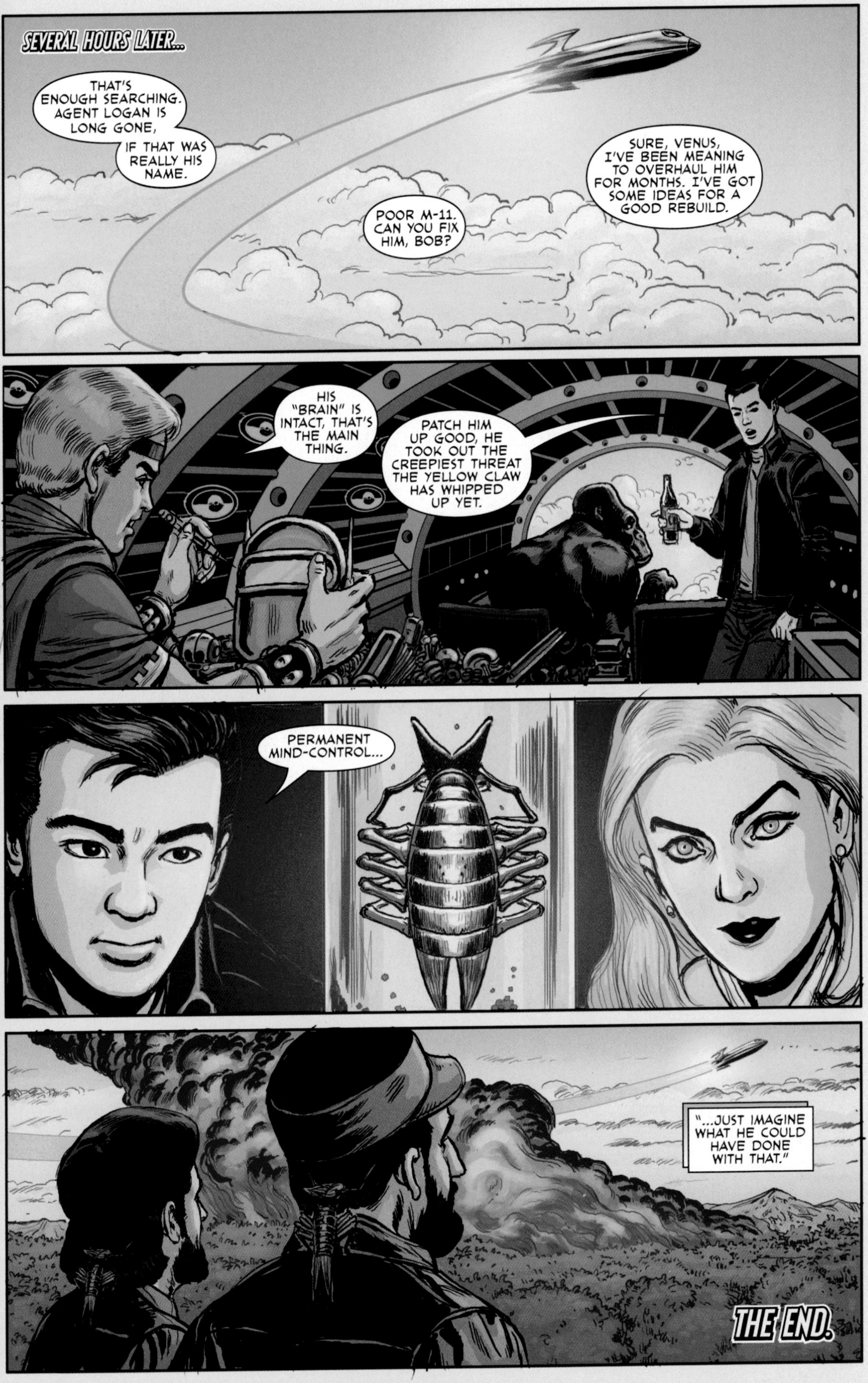
SEVERAL HOURS LATER...
THAT'S ENOUGH SEARCHING. AGENT LOGAN IS LONG GONE,
IF THAT WAS REALLY HIS NAME.
POOR M-11. CAN YOU FIX HIM, BOB?
SURE, VENUS, I'VE BEEN MEANING TO OVERHAUL HIM FOR MONTHS. I'VE GOT SOME IDEAS FOR A GOOD REBUILD.
HIS "BRAIN" IS INTACT, THAT'S THE MAIN THING.
PATCH HIM UP GOOD, HE TOOK OUT THE CREEPIEST THREAT THE YELLOW CLAW HAS WHIPPED UP YET.
PERMANENT MIND-CONTROL...
"...JUST IMAGINE WHAT HE COULD HAVE DONE WITH THAT."
THE END.

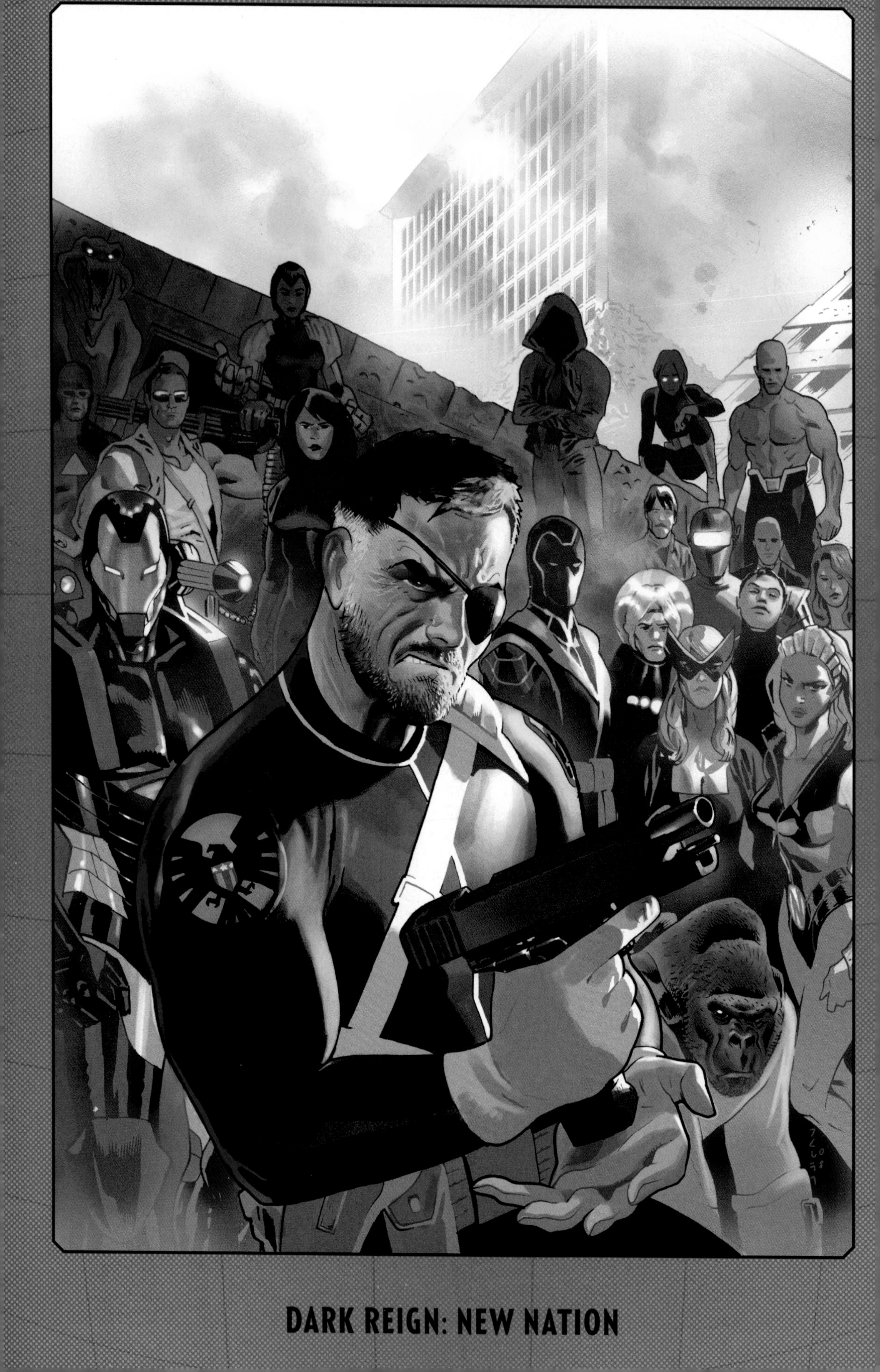

DARK REIGN: NEW NATION

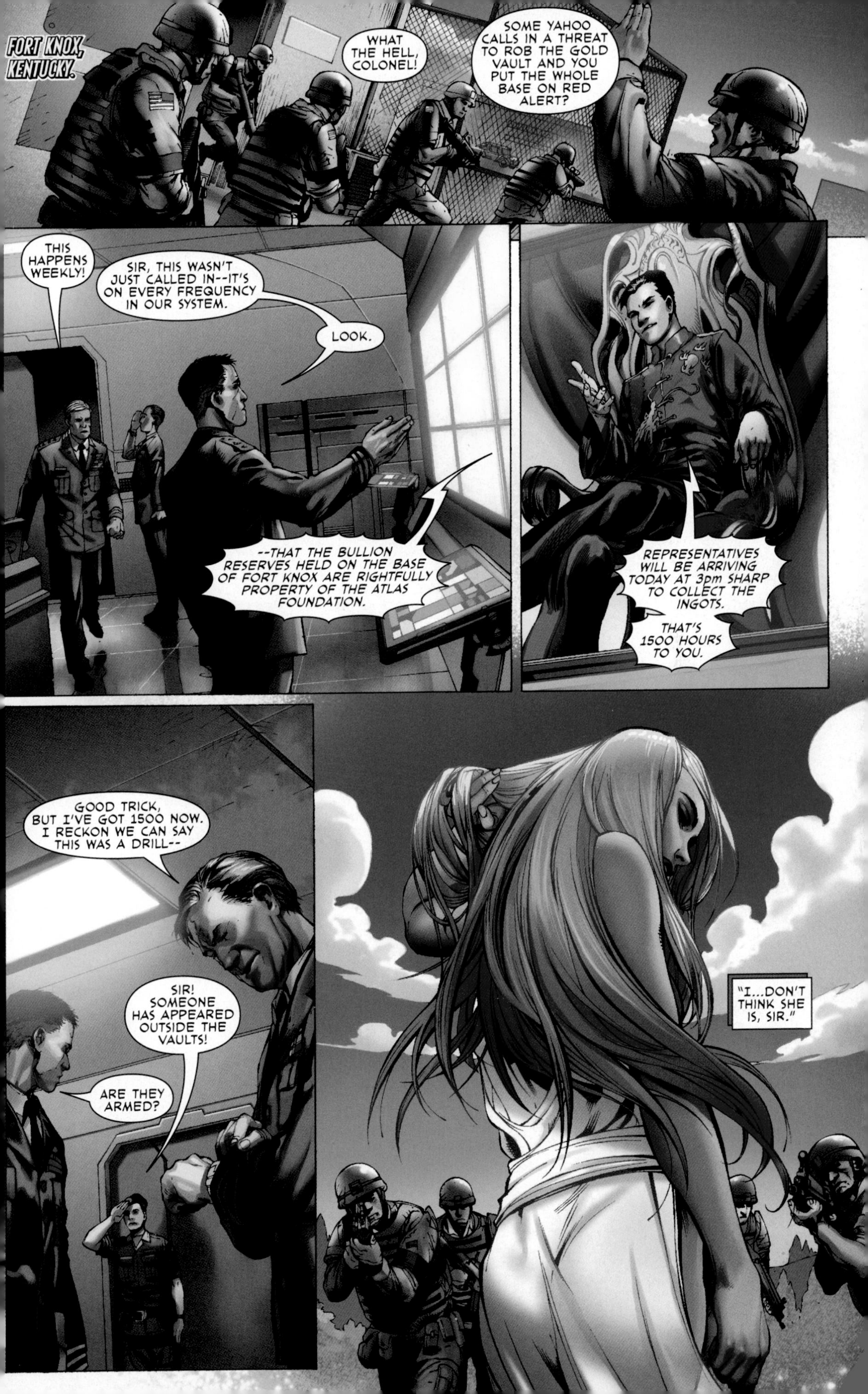
FORT KNOX, KENTUCKY.
WHAT THE HELL, COLONEL!
SOME YAHOO CALLS IN A THREAT TO ROB THE GOLD VAULT AND YOU PUT THE WHOLE BASE ON RED ALERT?
THIS HAPPENS WEEKLY!
SIR, THIS WASN'T JUST CALLED IN--IT'S ON EVERY FREQUENCY IN OUR SYSTEM.
LOOK.
--THAT THE BULLION RESERVES HELD ON THE BASE OF FORT KNOX ARE RIGHTFULLY PROPERTY OF THE ATLAS FOUNDATION.
REPRESENTATIVES WILL BE ARRIVING TODAY AT 3pm SHARP TO COLLECT THE INGOTS.
THAT'S 1500 HOURS TO YOU.
GOOD TRICK, BUT I'VE GOT 1500 NOW. I RECKON WE CAN SAY THIS WAS A DRILL--
SIR! SOMEONE HAS APPEARED OUTSIDE THE VAULTS!
ARE THEY ARMED?
"I...DON'T THINK SHE IS, SIR."

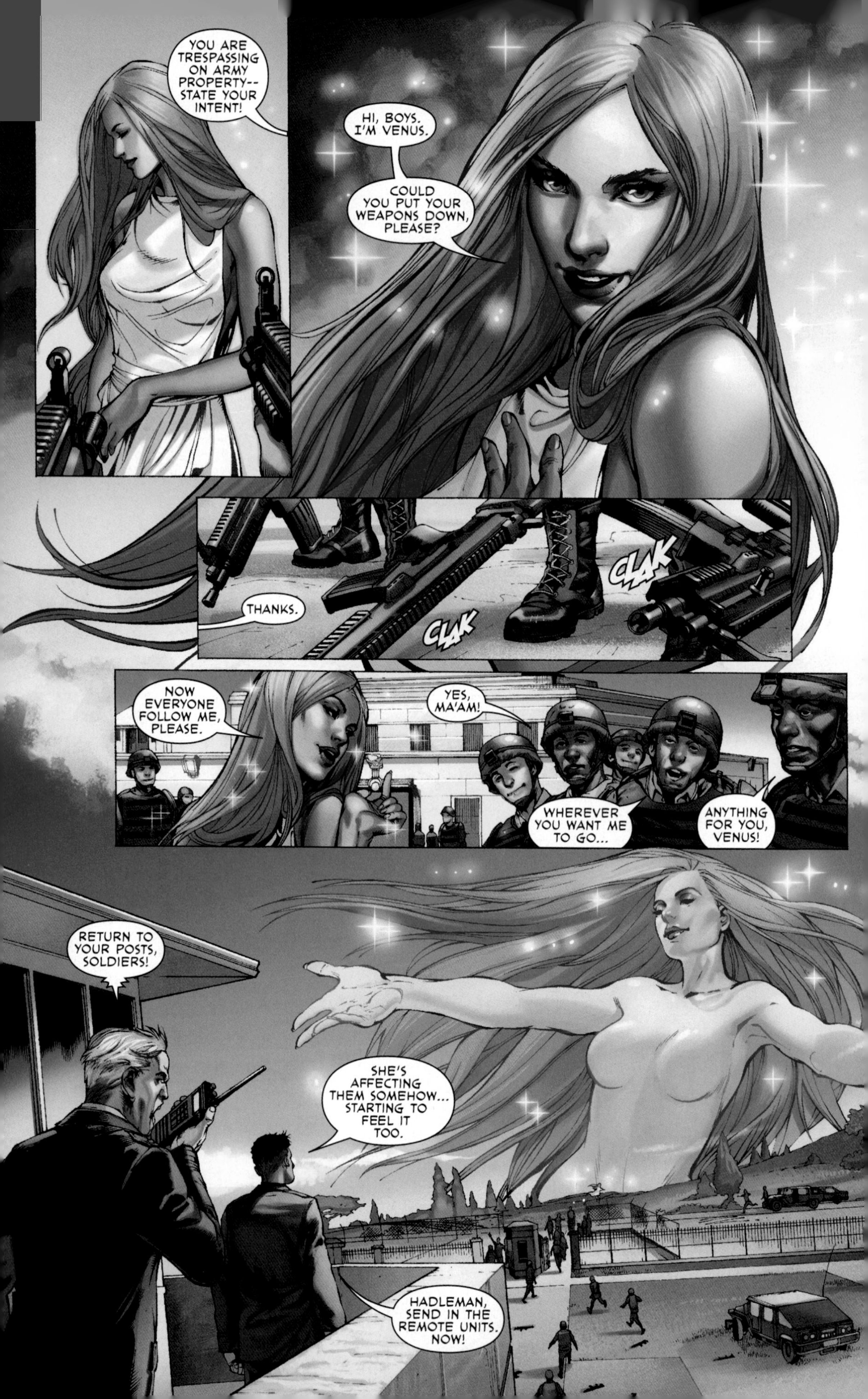
YOU ARE TRESPASSING ON ARMY PROPERTY-- STATE YOUR INTENT!
HI, BOYS. I'M VENUS.
COULD YOU PUT YOUR WEAPONS DOWN, PLEASE?
CLAK
THANKS.
CLAK
NOW EVERYONE FOLLOW ME, PLEASE.
YES, MA'AM!
WHEREVER YOU WANT ME TO GO...
ANYTHING FOR YOU, VENUS!
RETURN TO YOUR POSTS, SOLDIERS!
SHE'S AFFECTING THEM SOMEHOW... STARTING TO FEEL IT TOO.
HADLEMAN, SEND IN THE REMOTE UNITS. NOW!

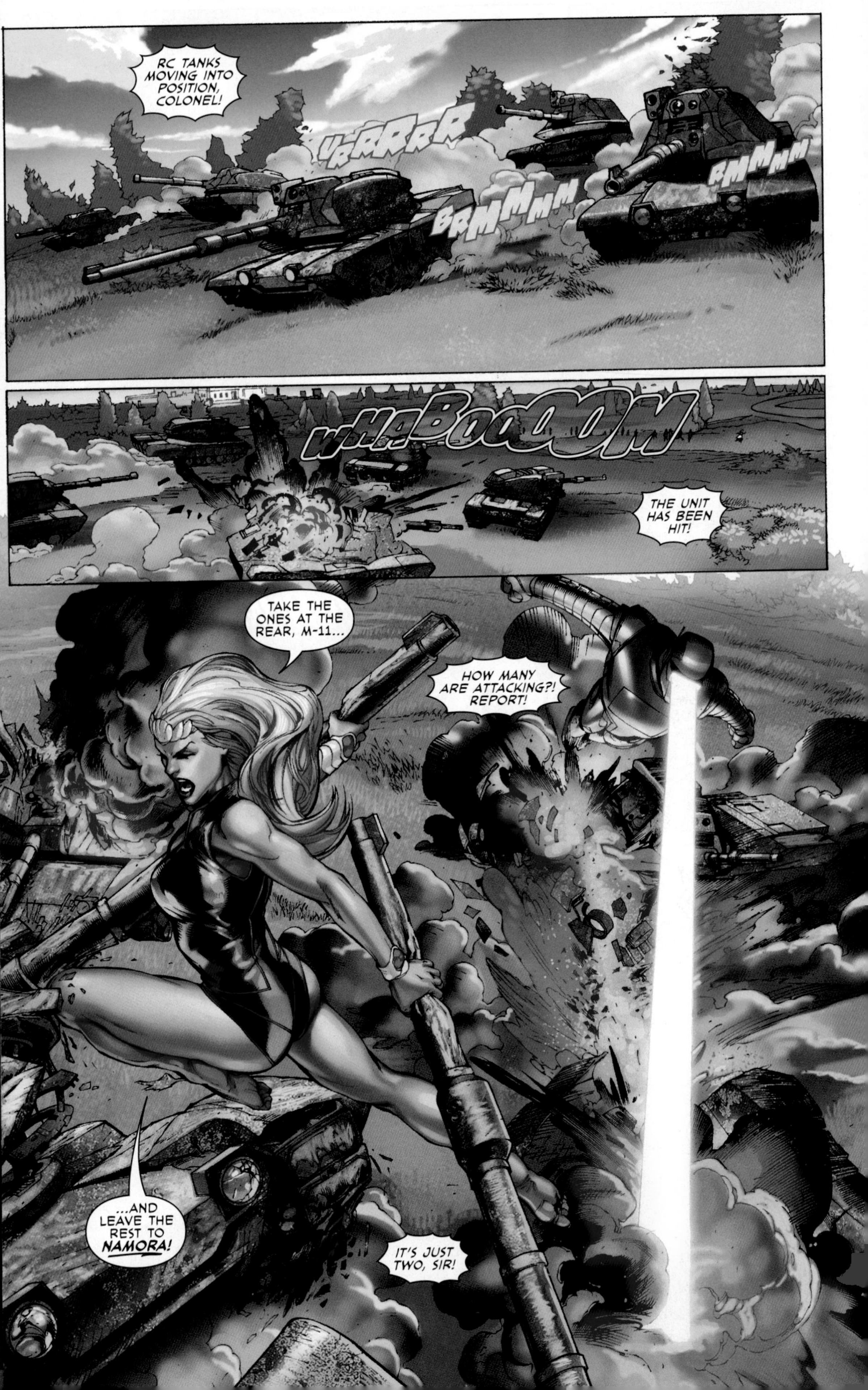
RC TANKS MOVING INTO POSITION, COLONEL!
VRRRRRR
BRMMMMM
BRMMMM
WHABOOOOM
THE UNIT HAS BEEN HIT!
TAKE THE ONES AT THE REAR, M-11...
HOW MANY ARE ATTACKING?! REPORT!
...AND LEAVE THE REST TO NAMORA!
IT'S JUST TWO, SIR!

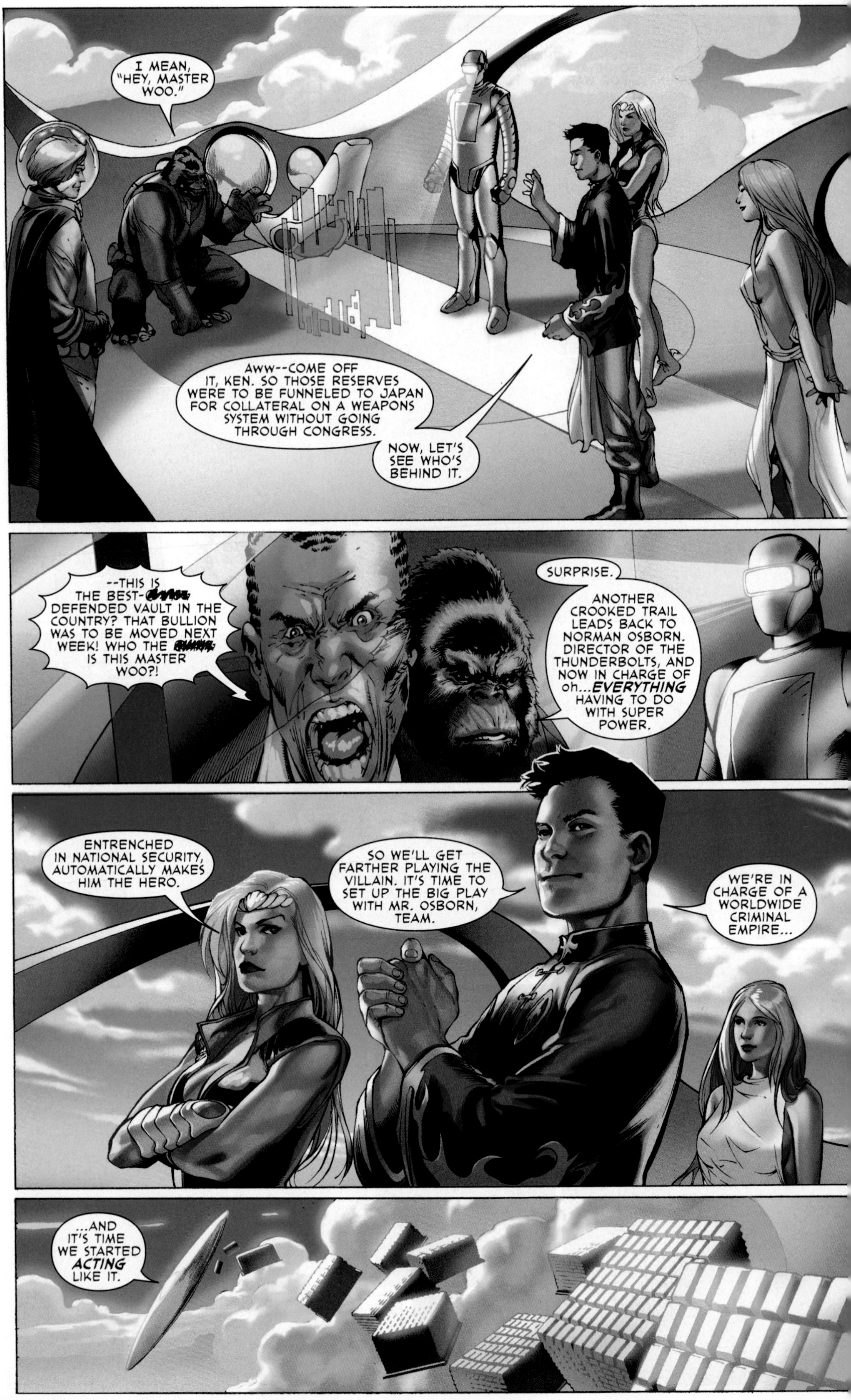
I MEAN, "HEY, MASTER WOO."
AWW--COME OFF IT, KEN. SO THOSE RESERVES WERE TO BE FUNNELED TO JAPAN FOR COLLATERAL ON A WEAPONS SYSTEM WITHOUT GOING THROUGH CONGRESS.
NOW, LET'S SEE WHO'S BEHIND IT.
--THIS IS THE BEST- DEFENDED VAULT IN THE COUNTRY? THAT BULLION WAS TO BE MOVED NEXT WEEK! WHO THE IS THIS MASTER WOO?!
SURPRISE.
ANOTHER CROOKED TRAIL LEADS BACK TO NORMAN OSBORN. DIRECTOR OF THE THUNDERBOLTS, AND NOW IN CHARGE OF oh...*EVERYTHING* HAVING TO DO WITH SUPER POWER.
ENTRENCHED IN NATIONAL SECURITY, AUTOMATICALLY MAKES HIM THE HERO.
SO WE'LL GET FARTHER PLAYING THE VILLAIN. IT'S TIME TO SET UP THE BIG PLAY WITH MR. OSBORN, TEAM.
WE'RE IN CHARGE OF A WORLDWIDE CRIMINAL EMPIRE...
...AND IT'S TIME WE STARTED *ACTING* LIKE IT.

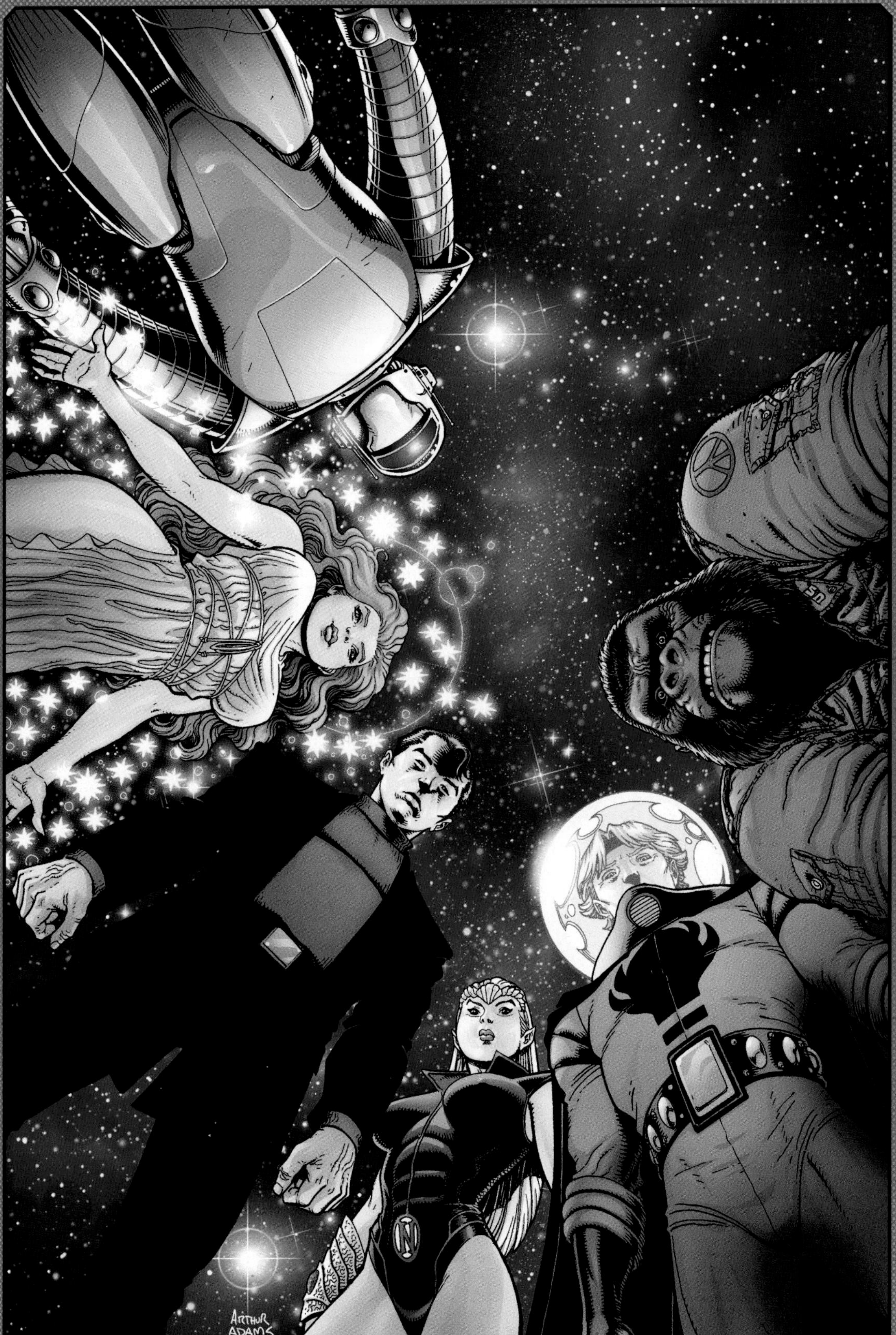
ARTHUR ADAMS
10-4-2008

AGENTS OF ATLAS (2009) **1**

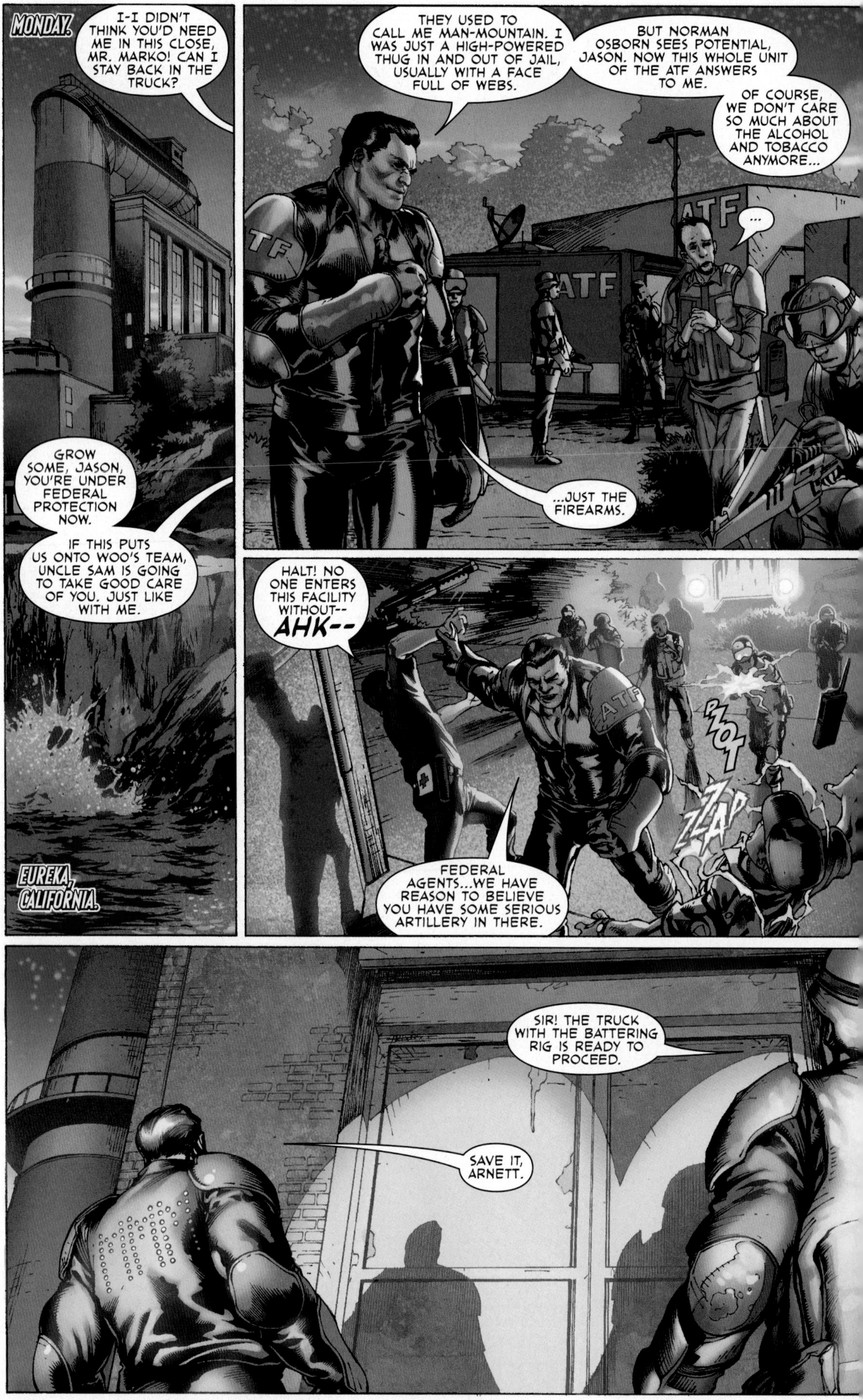
MONDAY.
I-I DIDN'T THINK YOU'D NEED ME IN THIS CLOSE, MR. MARKO! CAN I STAY BACK IN THE TRUCK?
GROW SOME, JASON, YOU'RE UNDER FEDERAL PROTECTION NOW.
IF THIS PUTS US ONTO WOO'S TEAM, UNCLE SAM IS GOING TO TAKE GOOD CARE OF YOU. JUST LIKE WITH ME.
EUREKA, CALIFORNIA.
THEY USED TO CALL ME MAN-MOUNTAIN. I WAS JUST A HIGH-POWERED THUG IN AND OUT OF JAIL, USUALLY WITH A FACE FULL OF WEBS.
BUT NORMAN OSBORN SEES POTENTIAL, JASON. NOW THIS WHOLE UNIT OF THE ATF ANSWERS TO ME.
OF COURSE, WE DON'T CARE SO MUCH ABOUT THE ALCOHOL AND TOBACCO ANYMORE...
ATF
...
ATF
TF
...JUST THE FIREARMS.
HALT! NO ONE ENTERS THIS FACILITY WITHOUT-- AHK--
ATF
PLOT
ZZAP
FEDERAL AGENTS...WE HAVE REASON TO BELIEVE YOU HAVE SOME SERIOUS ARTILLERY IN THERE.
SIR! THE TRUCK WITH THE BATTERING RIG IS READY TO PROCEED.
SAVE IT, ARNETT.

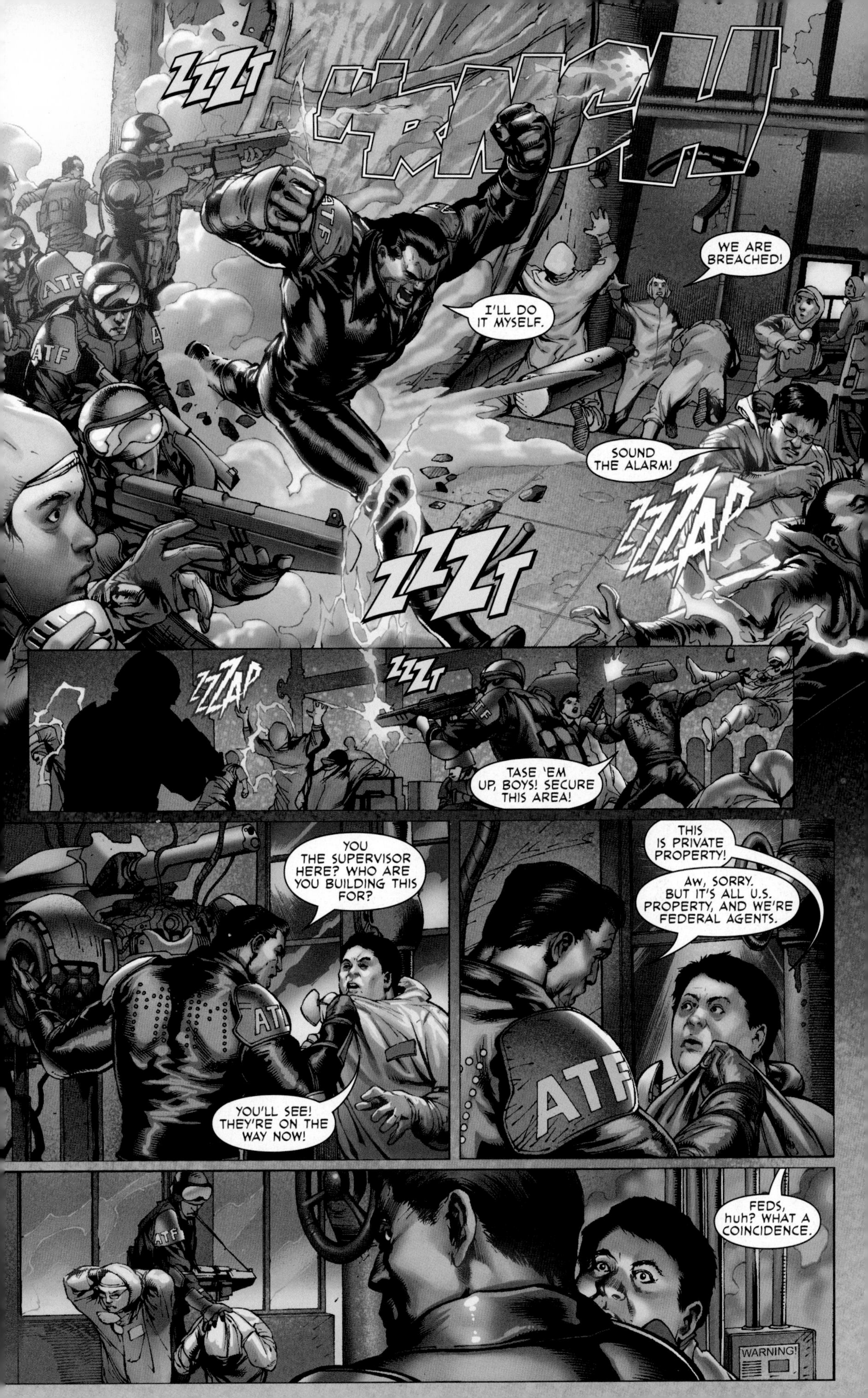
ZZZT
WE ARE BREACHED!
I'LL DO IT MYSELF.
SOUND THE ALARM!
ZZZAP
ZZZT
ZZZAP
ZZZT
TASE 'EM UP, BOYS! SECURE THIS AREA!
YOU THE SUPERVISOR HERE? WHO ARE YOU BUILDING THIS FOR?
YOU'LL SEE! THEY'RE ON THE WAY NOW!
THIS IS PRIVATE PROPERTY!
AW, SORRY. BUT IT'S ALL U.S. PROPERTY, AND WE'RE FEDERAL AGENTS.
FEDS, huh? WHAT A COINCIDENCE.
WARNING!

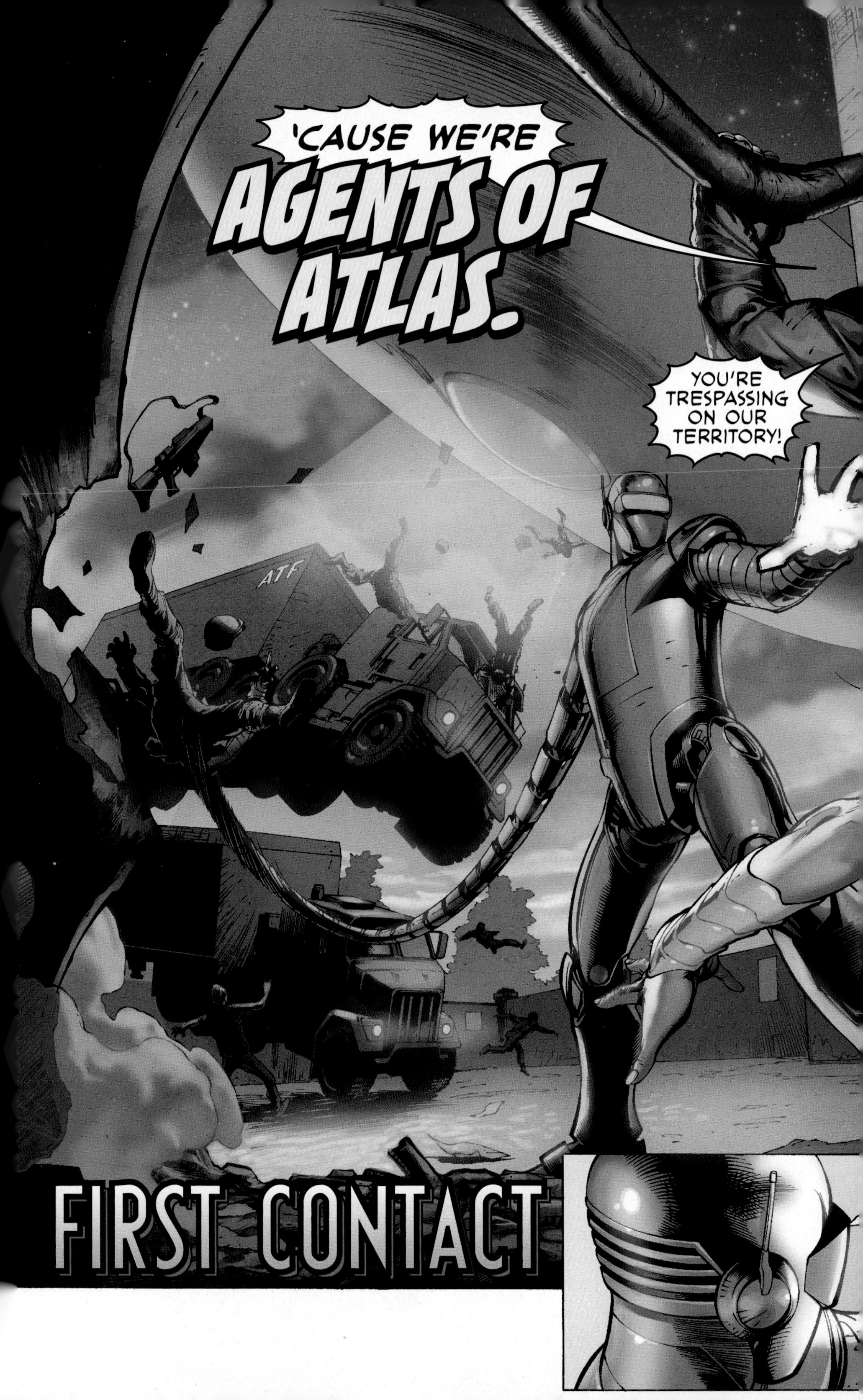
'CAUSE WE'RE AGENTS OF ATLAS.
YOU'RE TRESPASSING ON OUR TERRITORY!
ATF
FIRST CONTACT

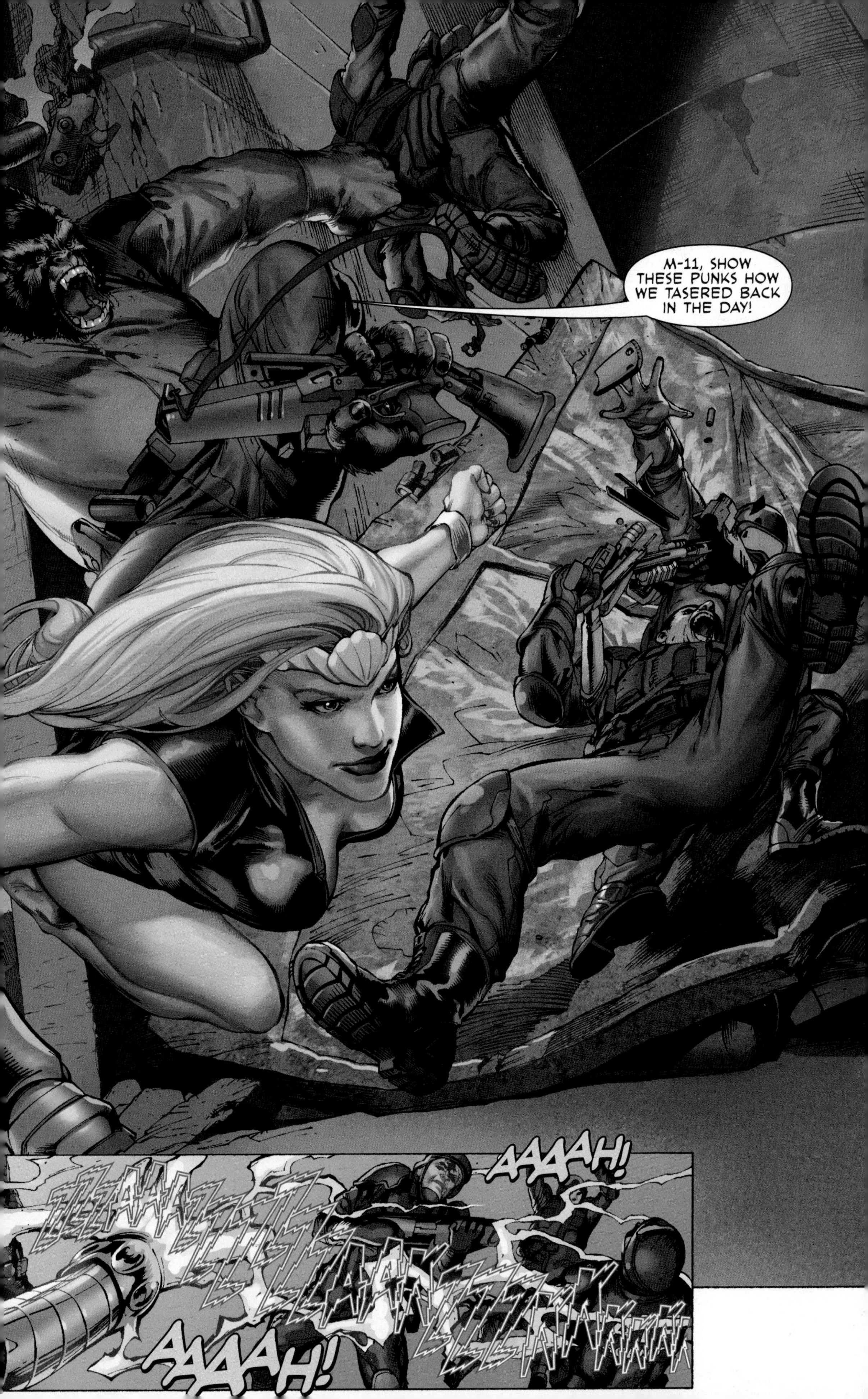
M-11, SHOW THESE PUNKS HOW WE TASERED BACK IN THE DAY!
AAAAH!
AAAAH!

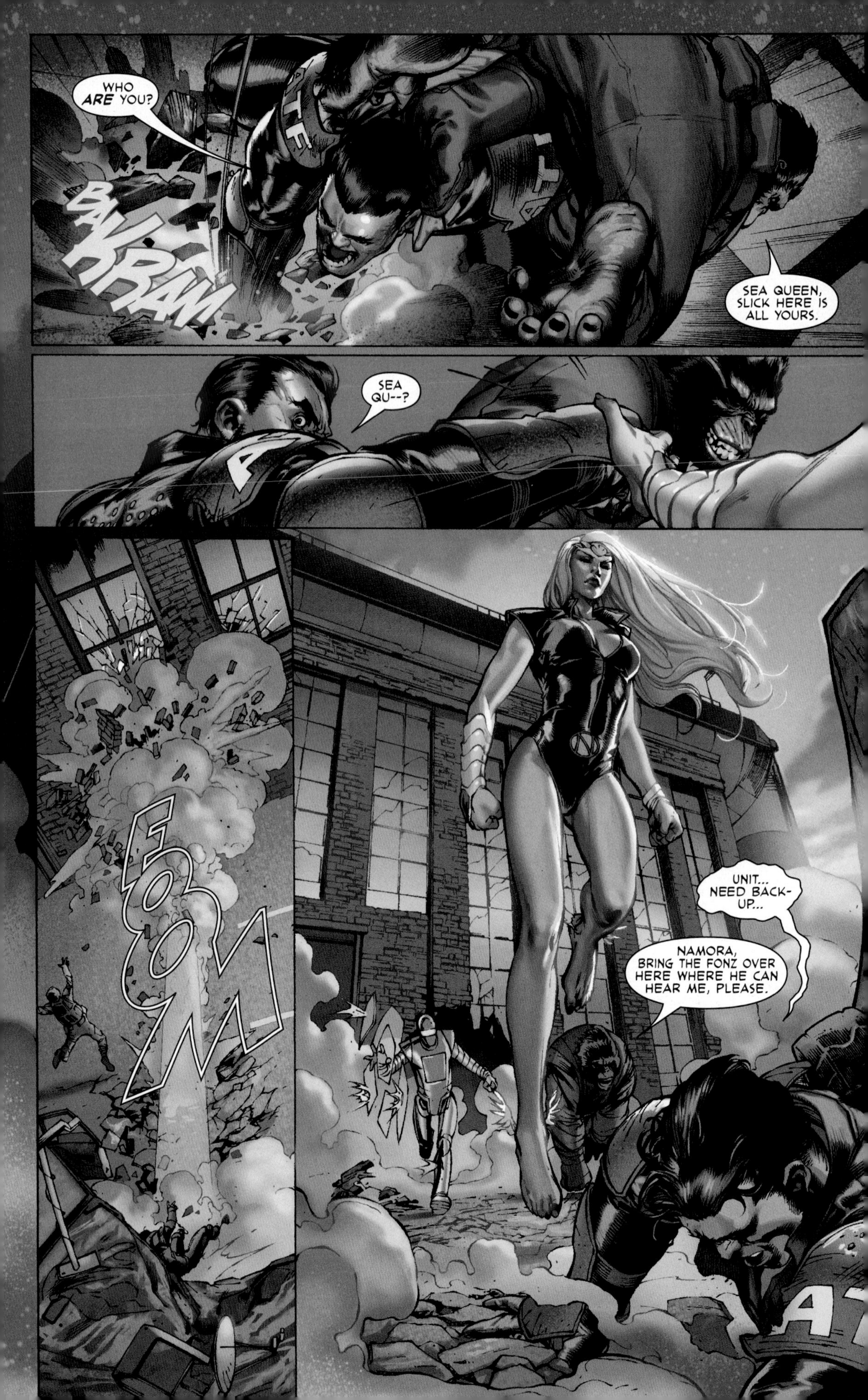
WHO ARE YOU?
BAKRAM
SEA QUEEN, SLICK HERE IS ALL YOURS.
SEA QU--?
FOOOM
UNIT... NEED BACK-UP...
NAMORA, BRING THE FONZ OVER HERE WHERE HE CAN HEAR ME, PLEASE.

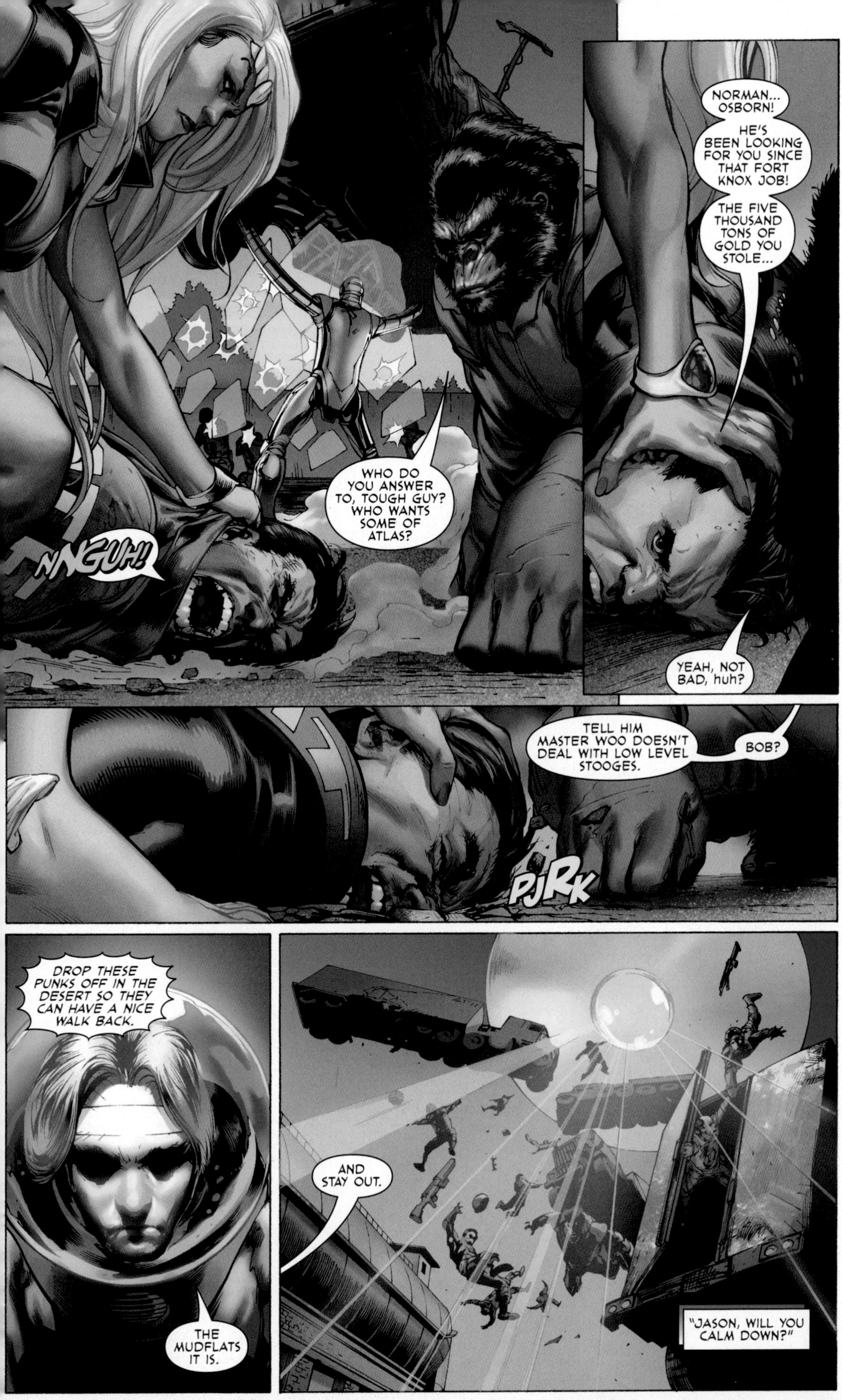
WHO DO YOU ANSWER TO, TOUGH GUY? WHO WANTS SOME OF ATLAS?
NNGUH!
NORMAN... OSBORN!
HE'S BEEN LOOKING FOR YOU SINCE THAT FORT KNOX JOB!
THE FIVE THOUSAND TONS OF GOLD YOU STOLE...
YEAH, NOT BAD, huh?
TELL HIM MASTER WOO DOESN'T DEAL WITH LOW LEVEL STOOGES.
BOB?
PJRK
DROP THESE PUNKS OFF IN THE DESERT SO THEY CAN HAVE A NICE WALK BACK.
THE MUDFLATS IT IS.
AND STAY OUT.
"JASON, WILL YOU CALM DOWN?"

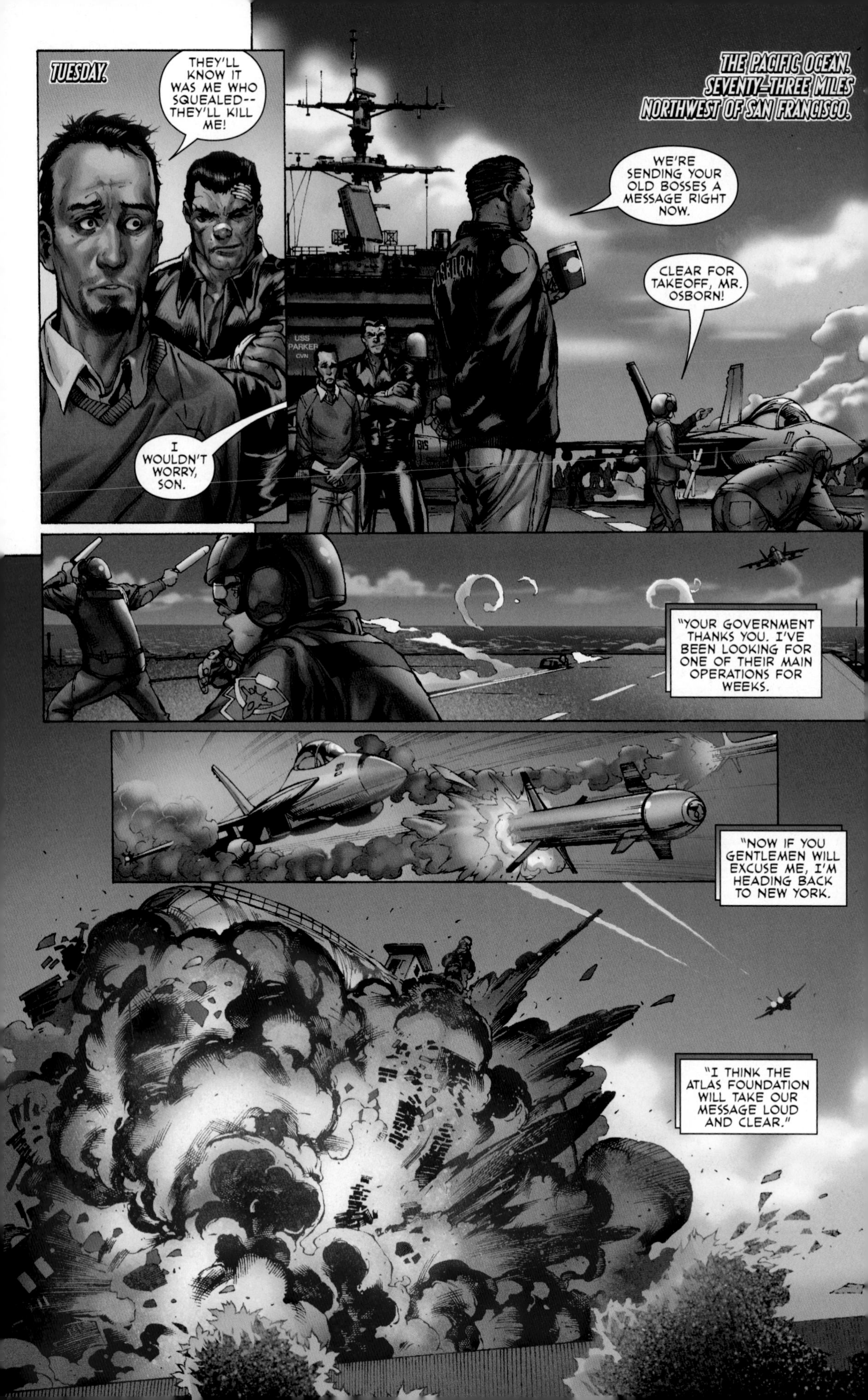
TUESDAY.
THEY'LL KNOW IT WAS ME WHO SQUEALED-- THEY'LL KILL ME!
I WOULDN'T WORRY, SON.
THE PACIFIC OCEAN. SEVENTY-THREE MILES NORTHWEST OF SAN FRANCISCO.
WE'RE SENDING YOUR OLD BOSSES A MESSAGE RIGHT NOW.
CLEAR FOR TAKEOFF, MR. OSBORN!
"YOUR GOVERNMENT THANKS YOU. I'VE BEEN LOOKING FOR ONE OF THEIR MAIN OPERATIONS FOR WEEKS.
"NOW IF YOU GENTLEMEN WILL EXCUSE ME, I'M HEADING BACK TO NEW YORK.
"I THINK THE ATLAS FOUNDATION WILL TAKE OUR MESSAGE LOUD AND CLEAR."

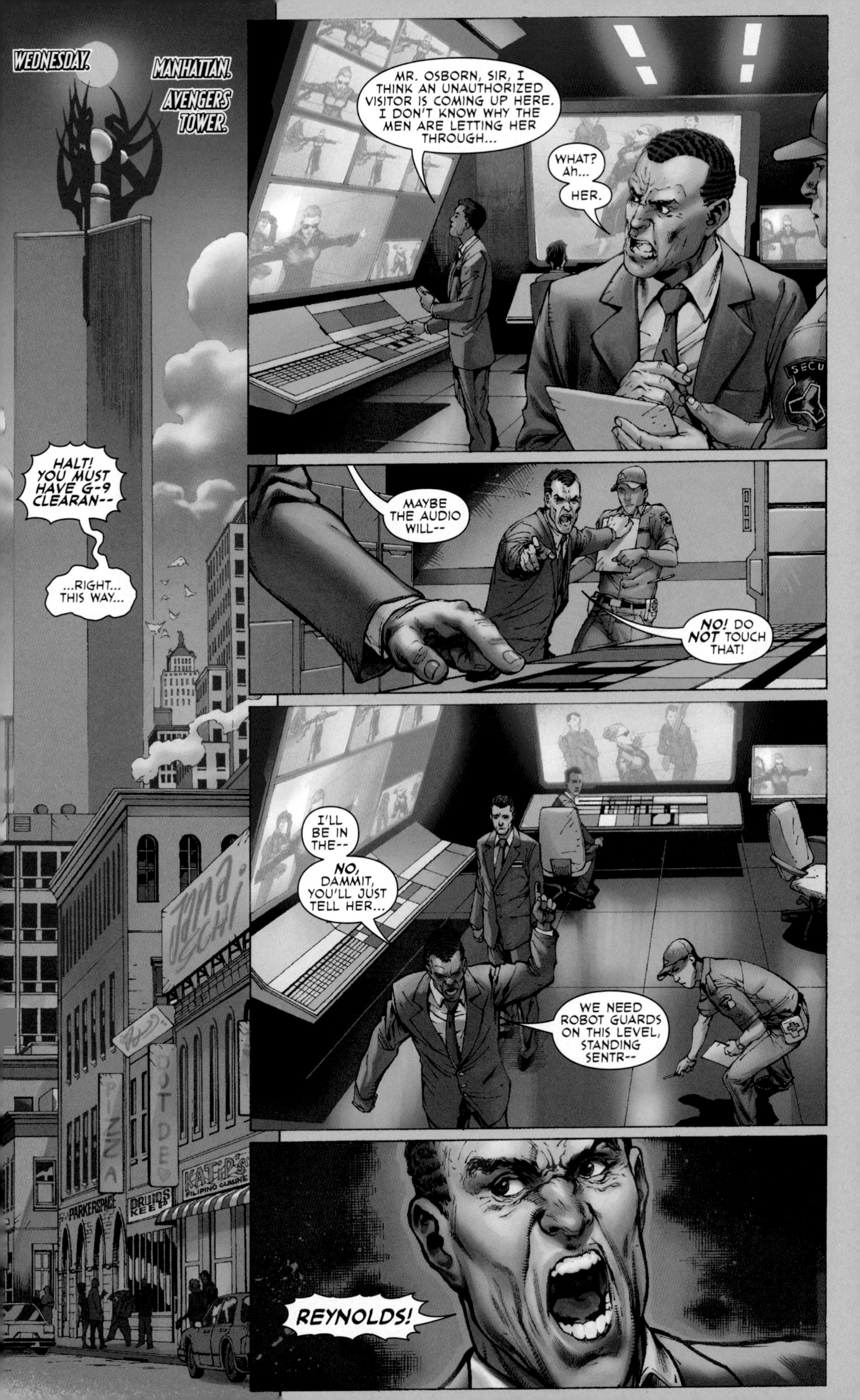
WEDNESDAY.
MANHATTAN.
AVENGERS TOWER.
HALT! YOU MUST HAVE G-9 CLEARAN--
...RIGHT... THIS WAY...
PIZZA
PARKERSPACE
DRUIDS KEEP
MR. OSBORN, SIR, I THINK AN UNAUTHORIZED VISITOR IS COMING UP HERE. I DON'T KNOW WHY THE MEN ARE LETTING HER THROUGH...
WHAT? Ah...
HER.
MAYBE THE AUDIO WILL--
NO! DO NOT TOUCH THAT!
I'LL BE IN THE--
NO, DAMMIT, YOU'LL JUST TELL HER...
WE NEED ROBOT GUARDS ON THIS LEVEL, STANDING SENTR--
REYNOLDS!

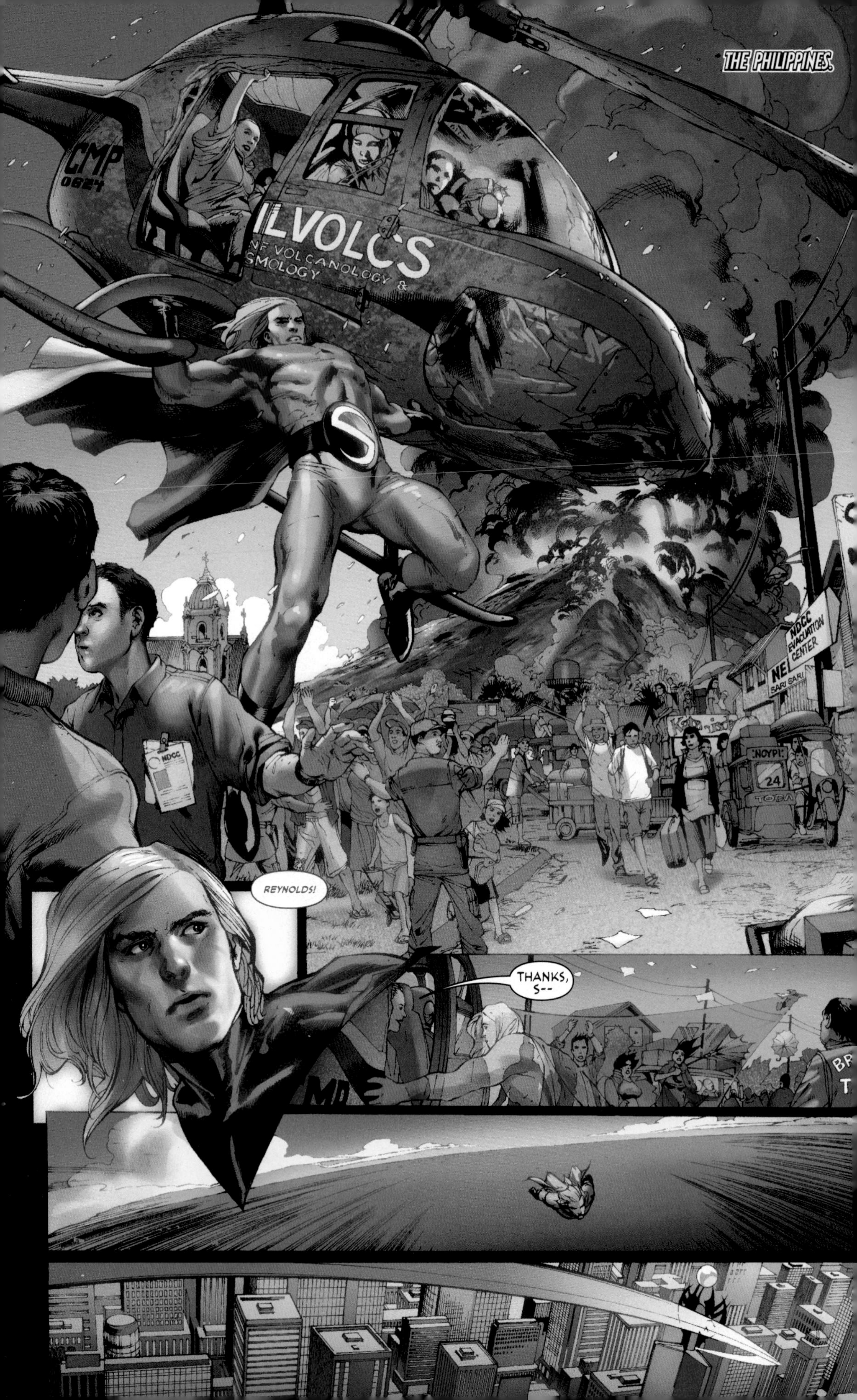
THE PHILIPPINES.
CMP
0624
ILVOLCS
NF VOLCANOLOGY &
SMOLOGY
NDCC
EVACUATION
CENTER
SARI SARI
NOYPI
24
TODA
REYNOLDS!
THANKS, S--

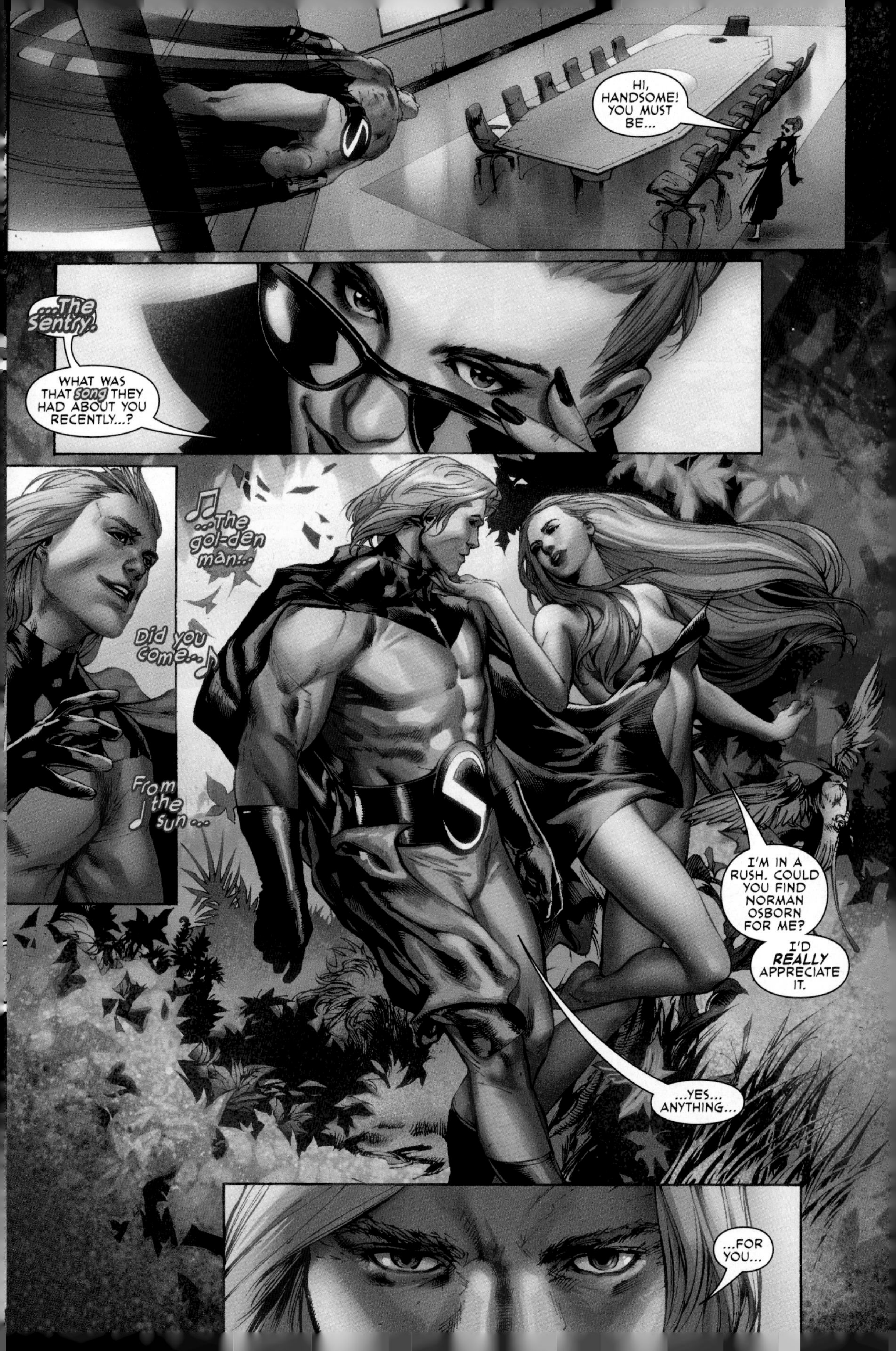
HI, HANDSOME! YOU MUST BE...
...The Sentry.
WHAT WAS THAT SONG THEY HAD ABOUT YOU RECENTLY...?
...The gol-den man...
Did you come...
From the sun...
I'M IN A RUSH. COULD YOU FIND NORMAN OSBORN FOR ME?
I'D REALLY APPRECIATE IT.
...YES... ANYTHING...
...FOR YOU...

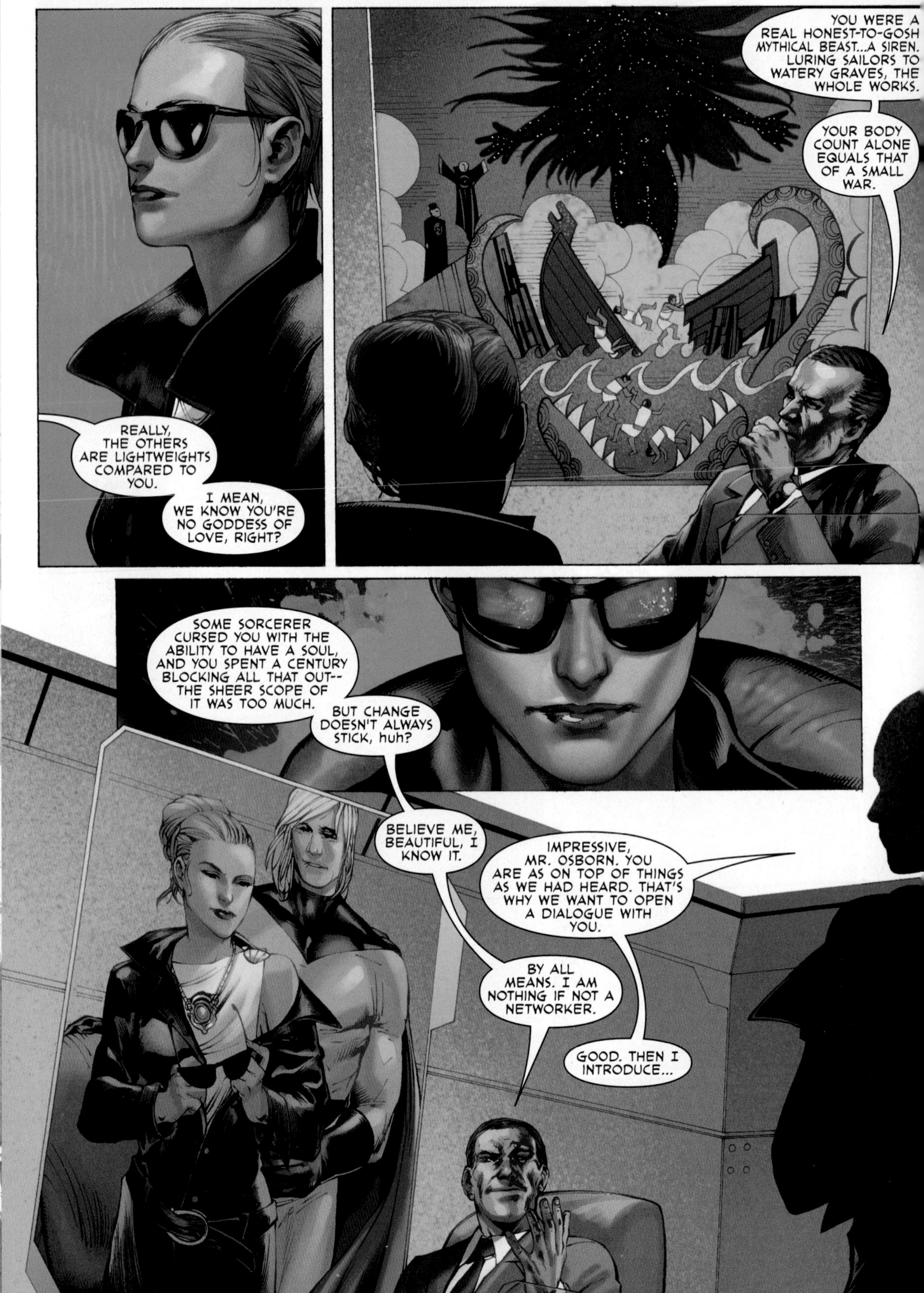
YOU WERE A REAL HONEST-TO-GOSH MYTHICAL BEAST...A SIREN. LURING SAILORS TO WATERY GRAVES, THE WHOLE WORKS.
YOUR BODY COUNT ALONE EQUALS THAT OF A SMALL WAR.
REALLY, THE OTHERS ARE LIGHTWEIGHTS COMPARED TO YOU.
I MEAN, WE KNOW YOU'RE NO GODDESS OF LOVE, RIGHT?
SOME SORCERER CURSED YOU WITH THE ABILITY TO HAVE A SOUL, AND YOU SPENT A CENTURY BLOCKING ALL THAT OUT-- THE SHEER SCOPE OF IT WAS TOO MUCH.
BUT CHANGE DOESN'T ALWAYS STICK, huh?
BELIEVE ME, BEAUTIFUL, I KNOW IT.
IMPRESSIVE, MR. OSBORN. YOU ARE AS ON TOP OF THINGS AS WE HAD HEARD. THAT'S WHY WE WANT TO OPEN A DIALOGUE WITH YOU.
BY ALL MEANS. I AM NOTHING IF NOT A NETWORKER.
GOOD. THEN I INTRODUCE...

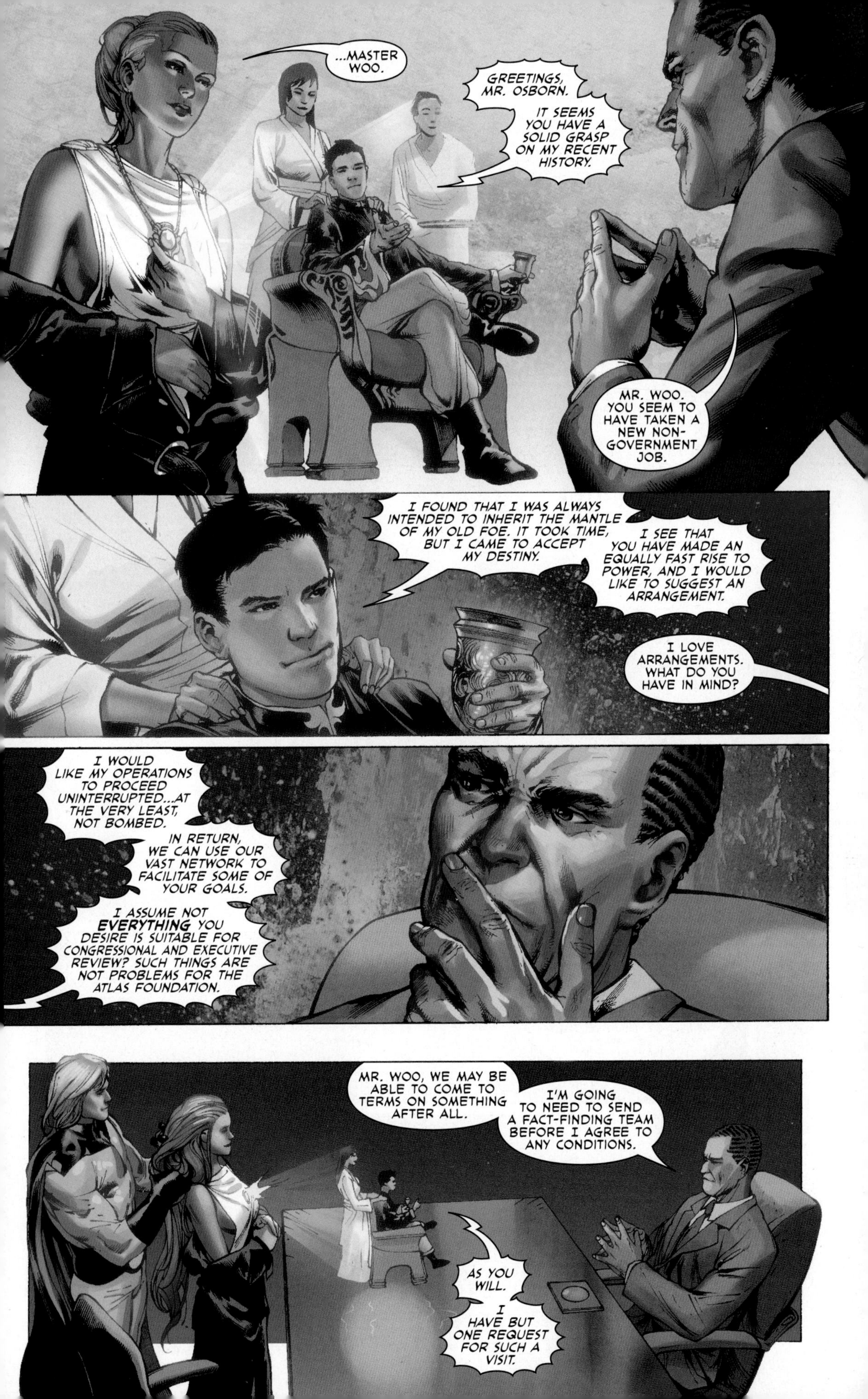

...MASTER WOO.
GREETINGS, MR. OSBORN.
IT SEEMS YOU HAVE A SOLID GRASP ON MY RECENT HISTORY.
MR. WOO. YOU SEEM TO HAVE TAKEN A NEW NON-GOVERNMENT JOB.
I FOUND THAT I WAS ALWAYS INTENDED TO INHERIT THE MANTLE OF MY OLD FOE. IT TOOK TIME, BUT I CAME TO ACCEPT MY DESTINY.
I SEE THAT YOU HAVE MADE AN EQUALLY FAST RISE TO POWER, AND I WOULD LIKE TO SUGGEST AN ARRANGEMENT.
I LOVE ARRANGEMENTS. WHAT DO YOU HAVE IN MIND?
I WOULD LIKE MY OPERATIONS TO PROCEED UNINTERRUPTED...AT THE VERY LEAST, NOT BOMBED.
IN RETURN, WE CAN USE OUR VAST NETWORK TO FACILITATE SOME OF YOUR GOALS.
I ASSUME NOT **EVERYTHING** YOU DESIRE IS SUITABLE FOR CONGRESSIONAL AND EXECUTIVE REVIEW? SUCH THINGS ARE NOT PROBLEMS FOR THE ATLAS FOUNDATION.
MR. WOO, WE MAY BE ABLE TO COME TO TERMS ON SOMETHING AFTER ALL.
I'M GOING TO NEED TO SEND A FACT-FINDING TEAM BEFORE I AGREE TO ANY CONDITIONS.
AS YOU WILL.
I HAVE BUT ONE REQUEST FOR SUCH A VISIT.

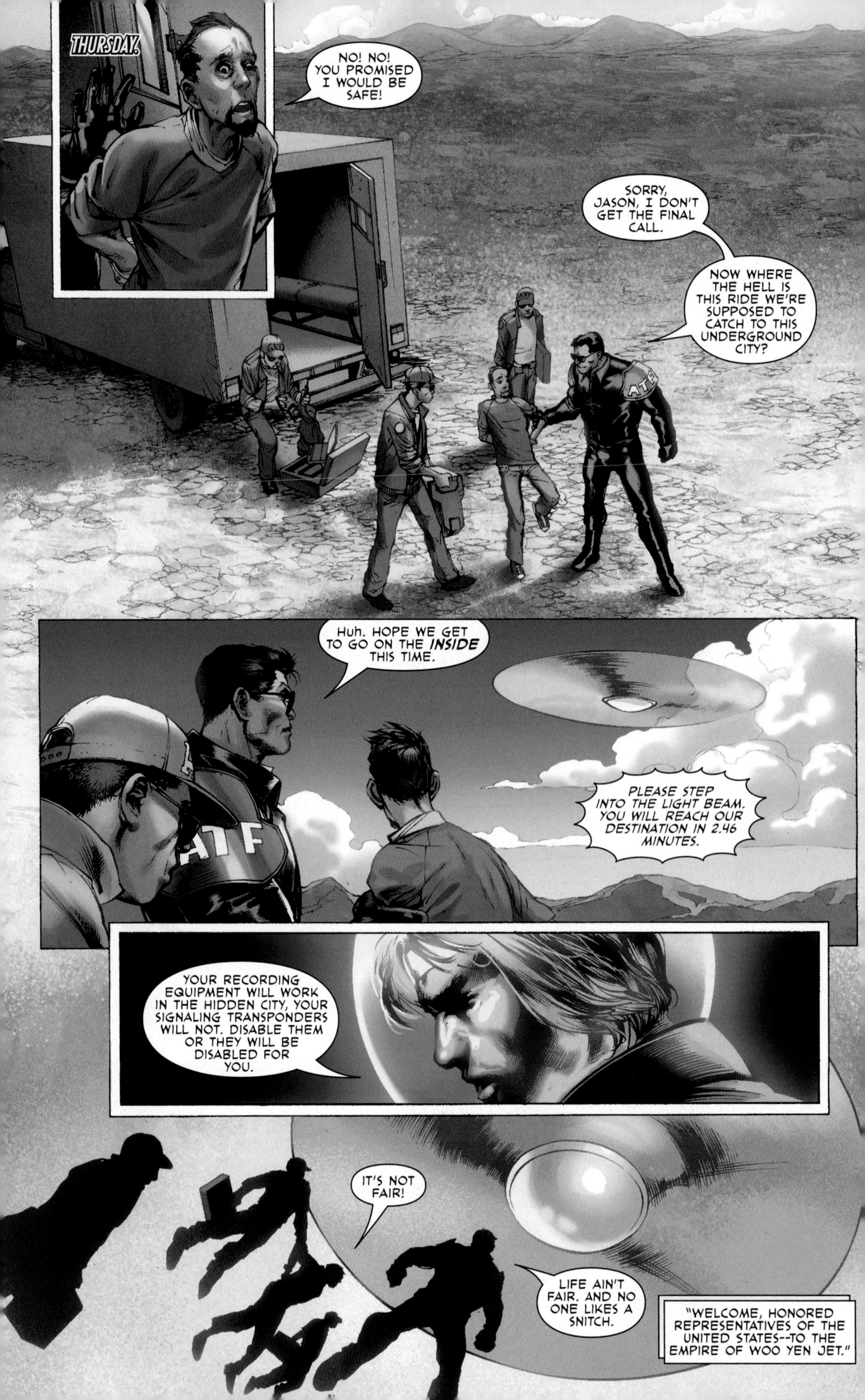
THURSDAY.
NO! NO! YOU PROMISED I WOULD BE SAFE!
SORRY, JASON, I DON'T GET THE FINAL CALL.
NOW WHERE THE HELL IS THIS RIDE WE'RE SUPPOSED TO CATCH TO THIS UNDERGROUND CITY?
Huh. HOPE WE GET TO GO ON THE *INSIDE* THIS TIME.
PLEASE STEP INTO THE LIGHT BEAM. YOU WILL REACH OUR DESTINATION IN 2.46 MINUTES.
YOUR RECORDING EQUIPMENT WILL WORK IN THE HIDDEN CITY, YOUR SIGNALING TRANSPONDERS WILL NOT. DISABLE THEM OR THEY WILL BE DISABLED FOR YOU.
IT'S NOT FAIR!
LIFE AIN'T FAIR. AND NO ONE LIKES A SNITCH.
"WELCOME, HONORED REPRESENTATIVES OF THE UNITED STATES--TO THE EMPIRE OF WOO YEN JET."

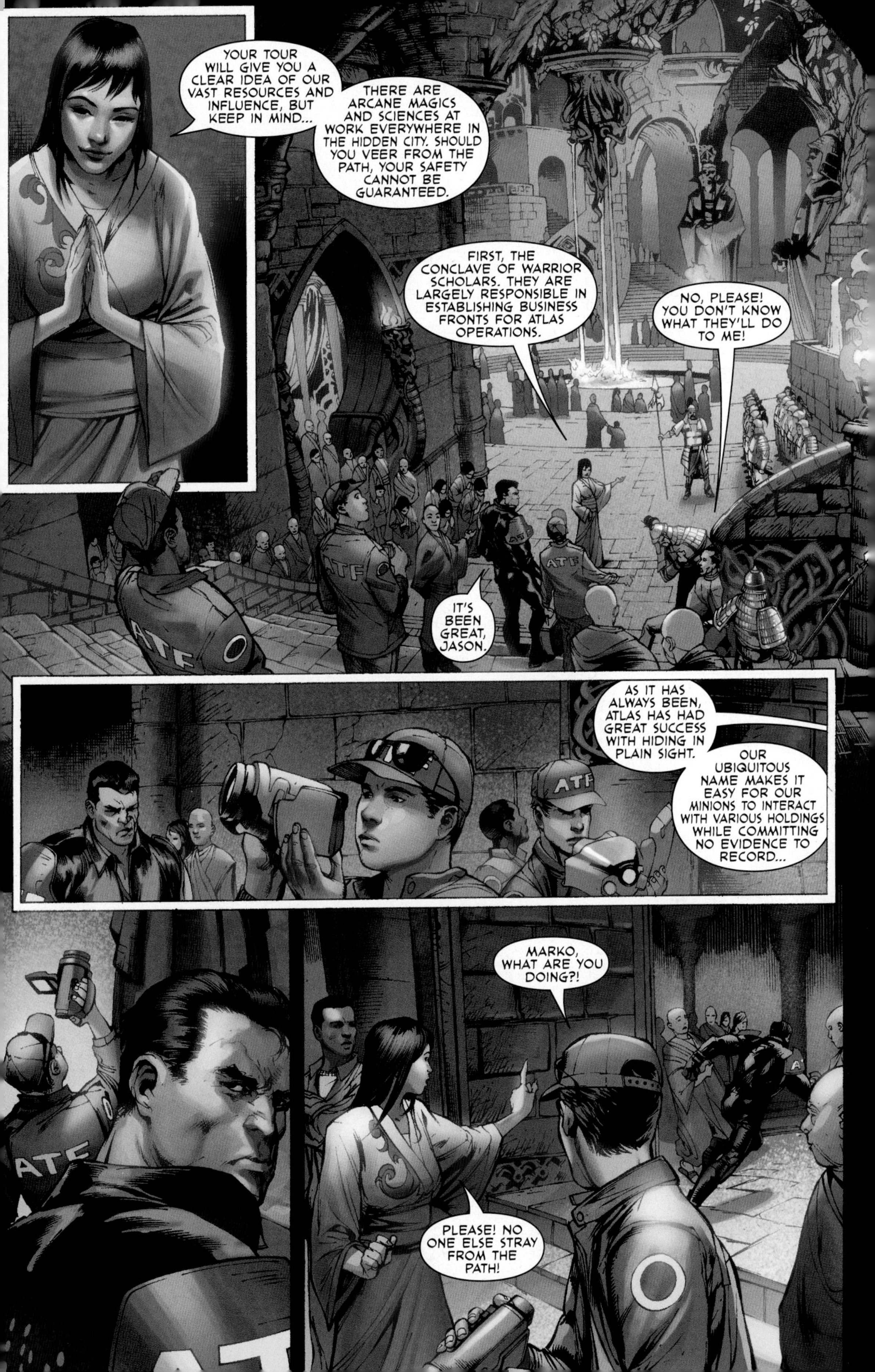
YOUR TOUR WILL GIVE YOU A CLEAR IDEA OF OUR VAST RESOURCES AND INFLUENCE, BUT KEEP IN MIND...
THERE ARE ARCANE MAGICS AND SCIENCES AT WORK EVERYWHERE IN THE HIDDEN CITY. SHOULD YOU VEER FROM THE PATH, YOUR SAFETY CANNOT BE GUARANTEED.
FIRST, THE CONCLAVE OF WARRIOR SCHOLARS. THEY ARE LARGELY RESPONSIBLE IN ESTABLISHING BUSINESS FRONTS FOR ATLAS OPERATIONS.
NO, PLEASE! YOU DON'T KNOW WHAT THEY'LL DO TO ME!
IT'S BEEN GREAT, JASON.
AS IT HAS ALWAYS BEEN, ATLAS HAS HAD GREAT SUCCESS WITH HIDING IN PLAIN SIGHT.
OUR UBIQUITOUS NAME MAKES IT EASY FOR OUR MINIONS TO INTERACT WITH VARIOUS HOLDINGS WHILE COMMITTING NO EVIDENCE TO RECORD...
MARKO, WHAT ARE YOU DOING?!
PLEASE! NO ONE ELSE STRAY FROM THE PATH!

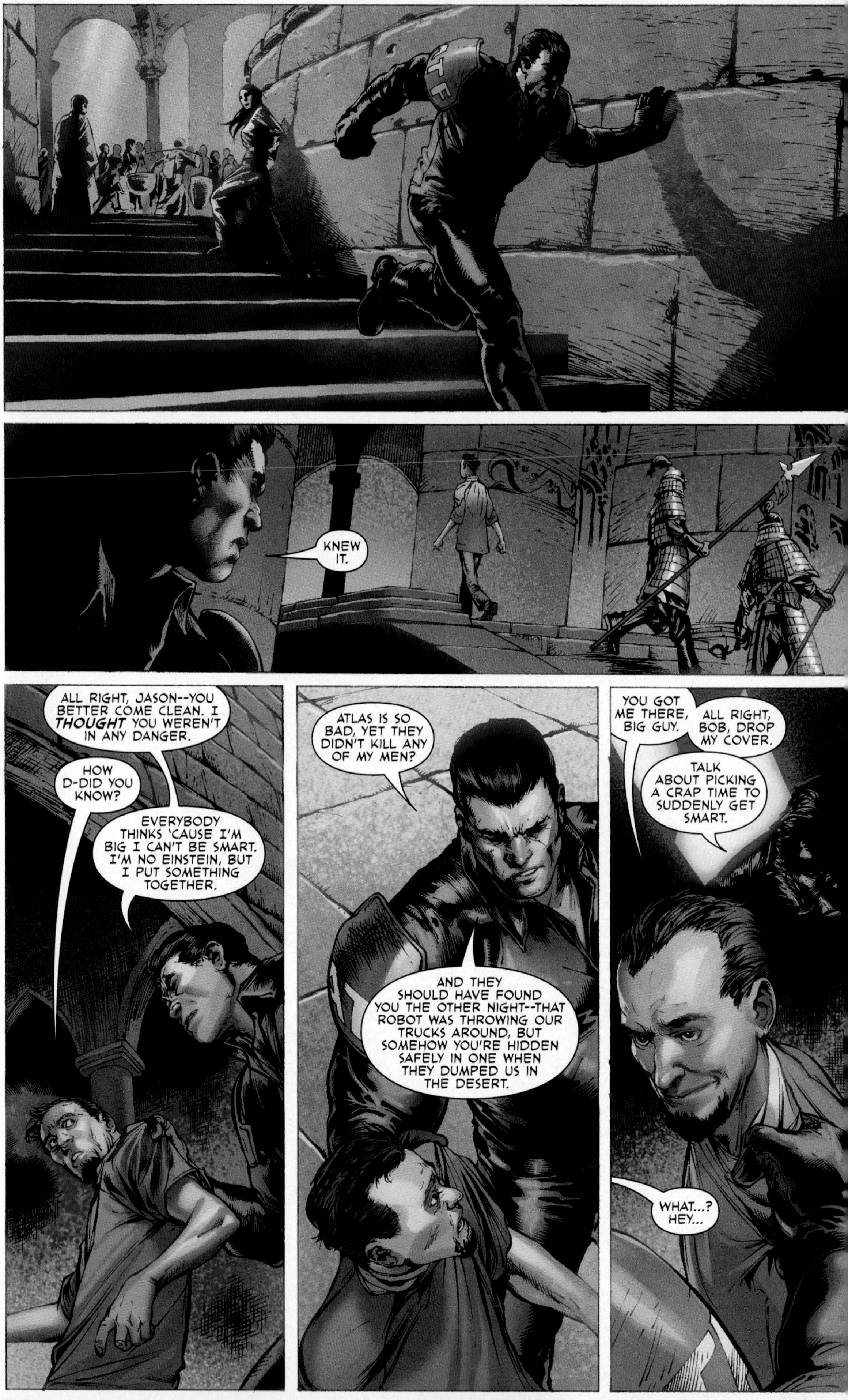
KNEW IT.
ALL RIGHT, JASON--YOU BETTER COME CLEAN. I *THOUGHT* YOU WEREN'T IN ANY DANGER.
HOW D-DID YOU KNOW?
EVERYBODY THINKS 'CAUSE I'M BIG I CAN'T BE SMART. I'M NO EINSTEIN, BUT I PUT SOMETHING TOGETHER.
ATLAS IS SO BAD, YET THEY DIDN'T KILL ANY OF MY MEN?
AND THEY SHOULD HAVE FOUND YOU THE OTHER NIGHT--THAT ROBOT WAS THROWING OUR TRUCKS AROUND, BUT SOMEHOW YOU'RE HIDDEN SAFELY IN ONE WHEN THEY DUMPED US IN THE DESERT.
YOU GOT ME THERE, BIG GUY.
ALL RIGHT, BOB, DROP MY COVER.
TALK ABOUT PICKING A CRAP TIME TO SUDDENLY GET SMART.
WHAT...? HEY...

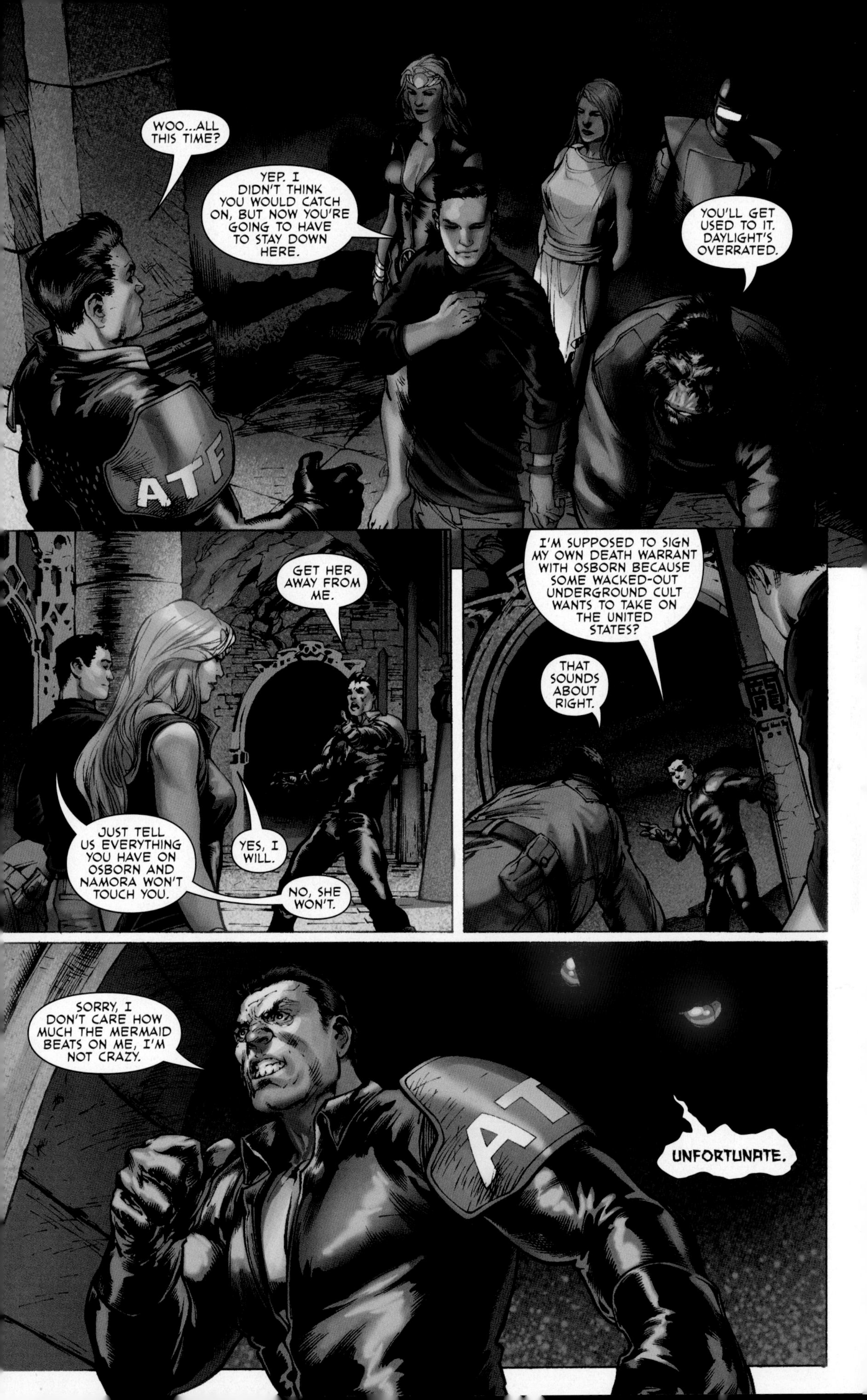
WOO...ALL THIS TIME?
YEP. I DIDN'T THINK YOU WOULD CATCH ON, BUT NOW YOU'RE GOING TO HAVE TO STAY DOWN HERE.
YOU'LL GET USED TO IT. DAYLIGHT'S OVERRATED.
ATF
GET HER AWAY FROM ME.
JUST TELL US EVERYTHING YOU HAVE ON OSBORN AND NAMORA WON'T TOUCH YOU.
YES, I WILL.
NO, SHE WON'T.
I'M SUPPOSED TO SIGN MY OWN DEATH WARRANT WITH OSBORN BECAUSE SOME WACKED-OUT UNDERGROUND CULT WANTS TO TAKE ON THE UNITED STATES?
THAT SOUNDS ABOUT RIGHT.
SORRY, I DON'T CARE HOW MUCH THE MERMAID BEATS ON ME, I'M NOT CRAZY.
UNFORTUNATE.

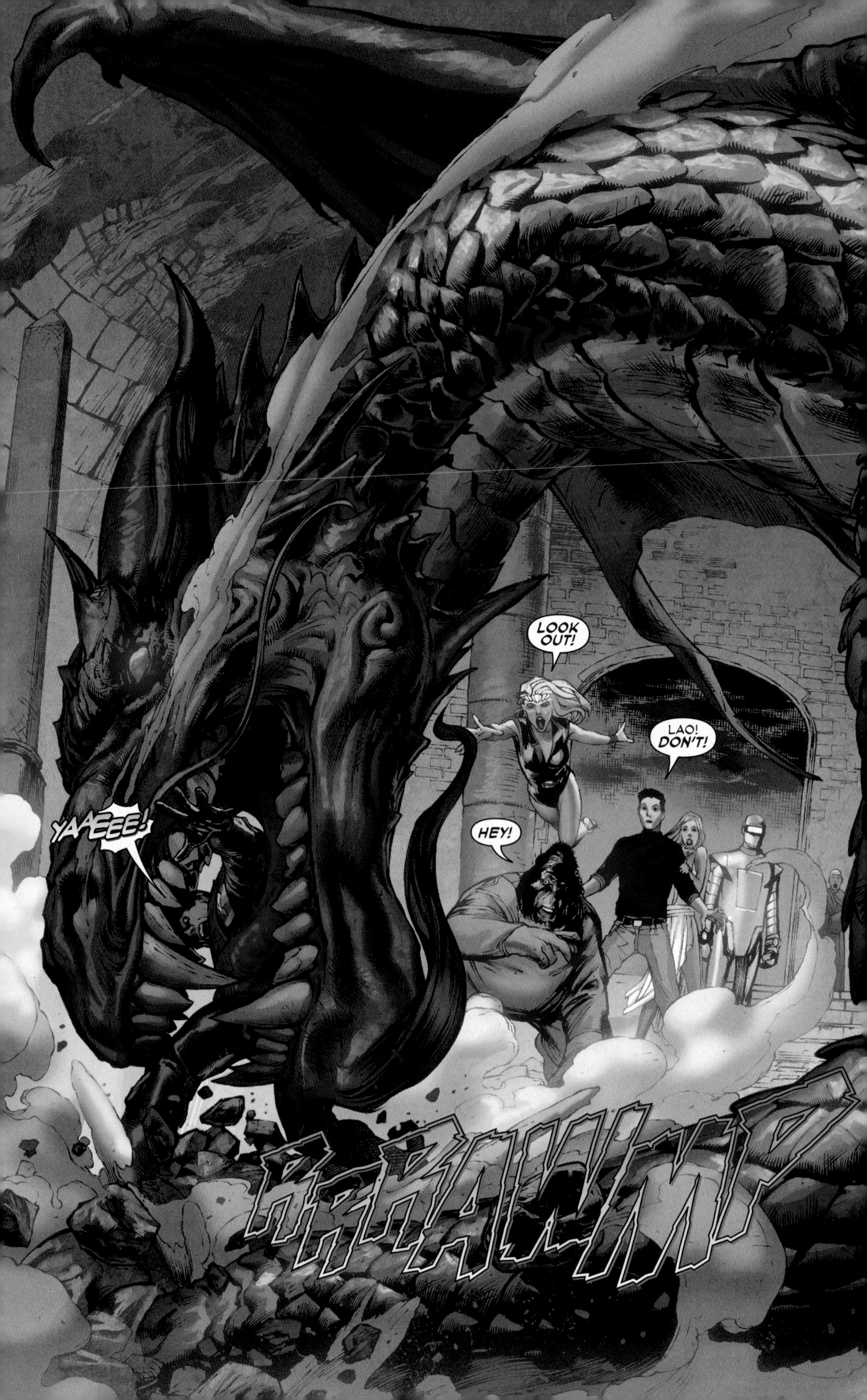
YAAEEE!
LOOK OUT!
LAO! DON'T!
HEY!

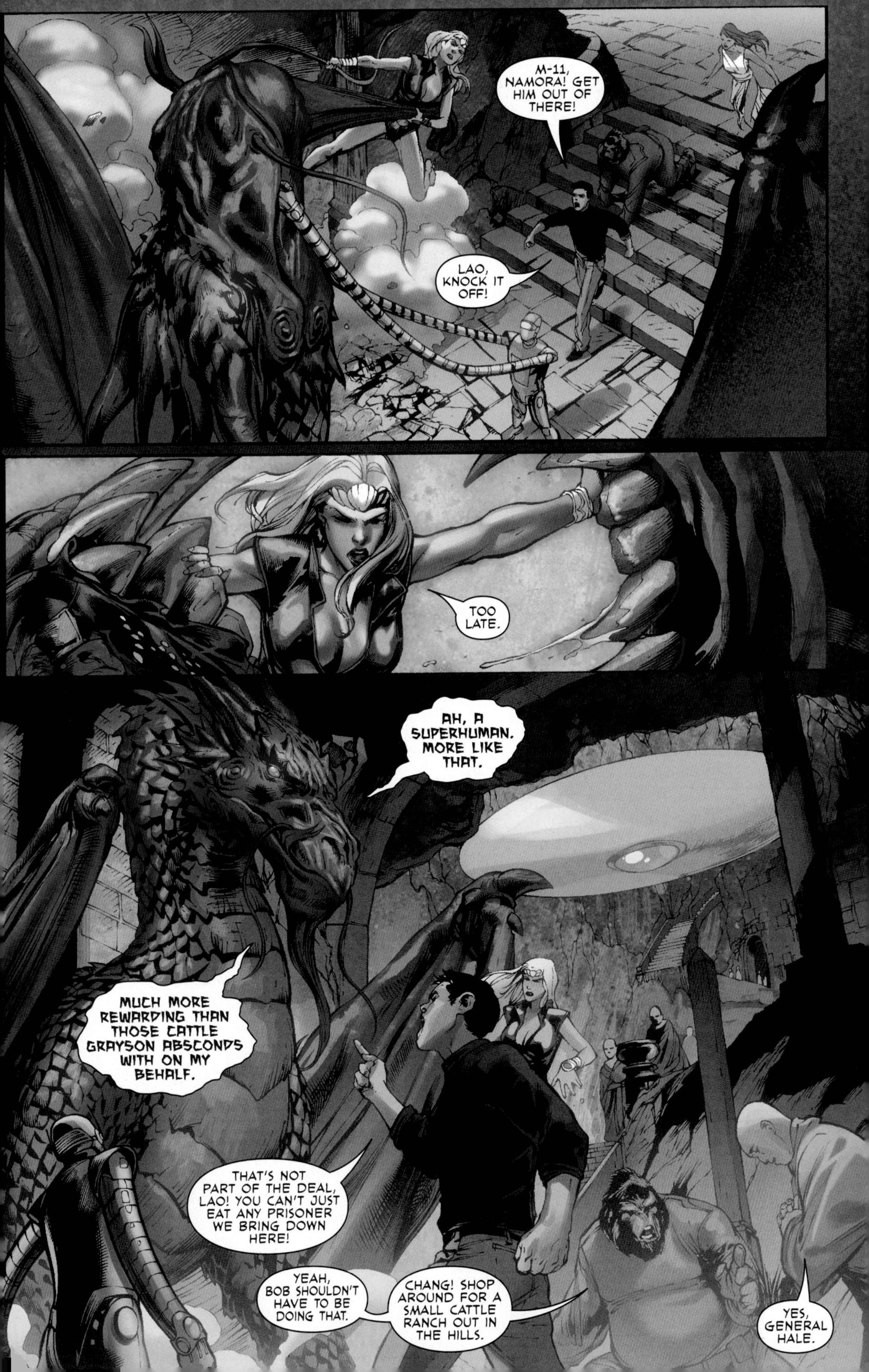
M-11, NAMORA! GET HIM OUT OF THERE!
LAO, KNOCK IT OFF!
TOO LATE.
AH, A SUPERHUMAN. MORE LIKE THAT.
MUCH MORE REWARDING THAN THOSE CATTLE GRAYSON ABSCONDS WITH ON MY BEHALF.
THAT'S NOT PART OF THE DEAL, LAO! YOU CAN'T JUST EAT ANY PRISONER WE BRING DOWN HERE!
YEAH, BOB SHOULDN'T HAVE TO BE DOING THAT.
CHANG! SHOP AROUND FOR A SMALL CATTLE RANCH OUT IN THE HILLS.
YES, GENERAL HALE.

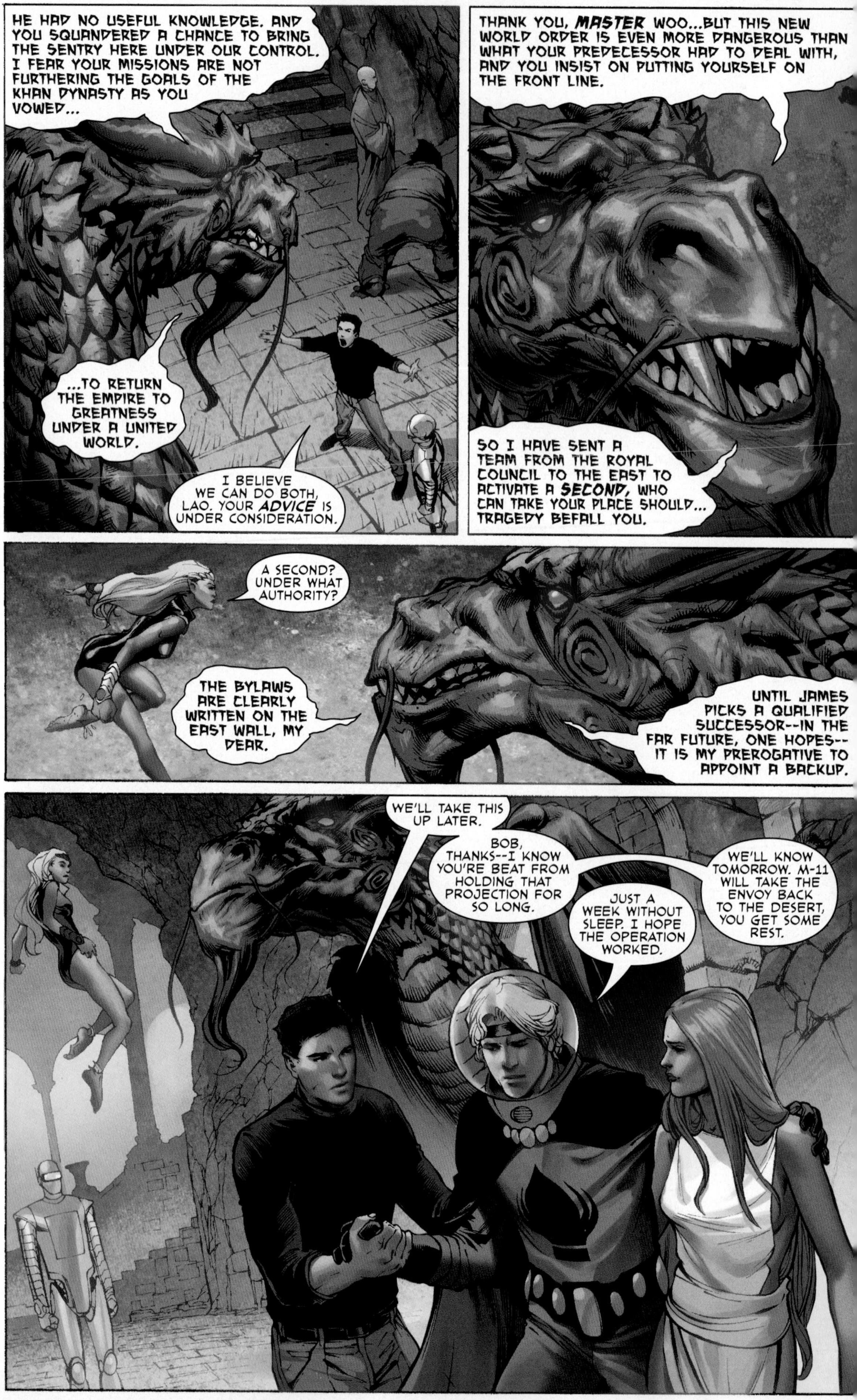

HE HAD NO USEFUL KNOWLEDGE. AND YOU SQUANDERED A CHANCE TO BRING THE SENTRY HERE UNDER OUR CONTROL. I FEAR YOUR MISSIONS ARE NOT FURTHERING THE GOALS OF THE KHAN DYNASTY AS YOU VOWED...
...TO RETURN THE EMPIRE TO GREATNESS UNDER A UNITED WORLD.
I BELIEVE WE CAN DO BOTH, LAO. YOUR ADVICE IS UNDER CONSIDERATION.
THANK YOU, MASTER WOO...BUT THIS NEW WORLD ORDER IS EVEN MORE DANGEROUS THAN WHAT YOUR PREDECESSOR HAD TO DEAL WITH, AND YOU INSIST ON PUTTING YOURSELF ON THE FRONT LINE.
SO I HAVE SENT A TEAM FROM THE ROYAL COUNCIL TO THE EAST TO ACTIVATE A SECOND, WHO CAN TAKE YOUR PLACE SHOULD... TRAGEDY BEFALL YOU.
A SECOND? UNDER WHAT AUTHORITY?
THE BYLAWS ARE CLEARLY WRITTEN ON THE EAST WALL, MY DEAR.
UNTIL JAMES PICKS A QUALIFIED SUCCESSOR--IN THE FAR FUTURE, ONE HOPES--IT IS MY PREROGATIVE TO APPOINT A BACKUP.
WE'LL TAKE THIS UP LATER.
BOB, THANKS--I KNOW YOU'RE BEAT FROM HOLDING THAT PROJECTION FOR SO LONG.
JUST A WEEK WITHOUT SLEEP. I HOPE THE OPERATION WORKED.
WE'LL KNOW TOMORROW. M-11 WILL TAKE THE ENVOY BACK TO THE DESERT, YOU GET SOME REST.

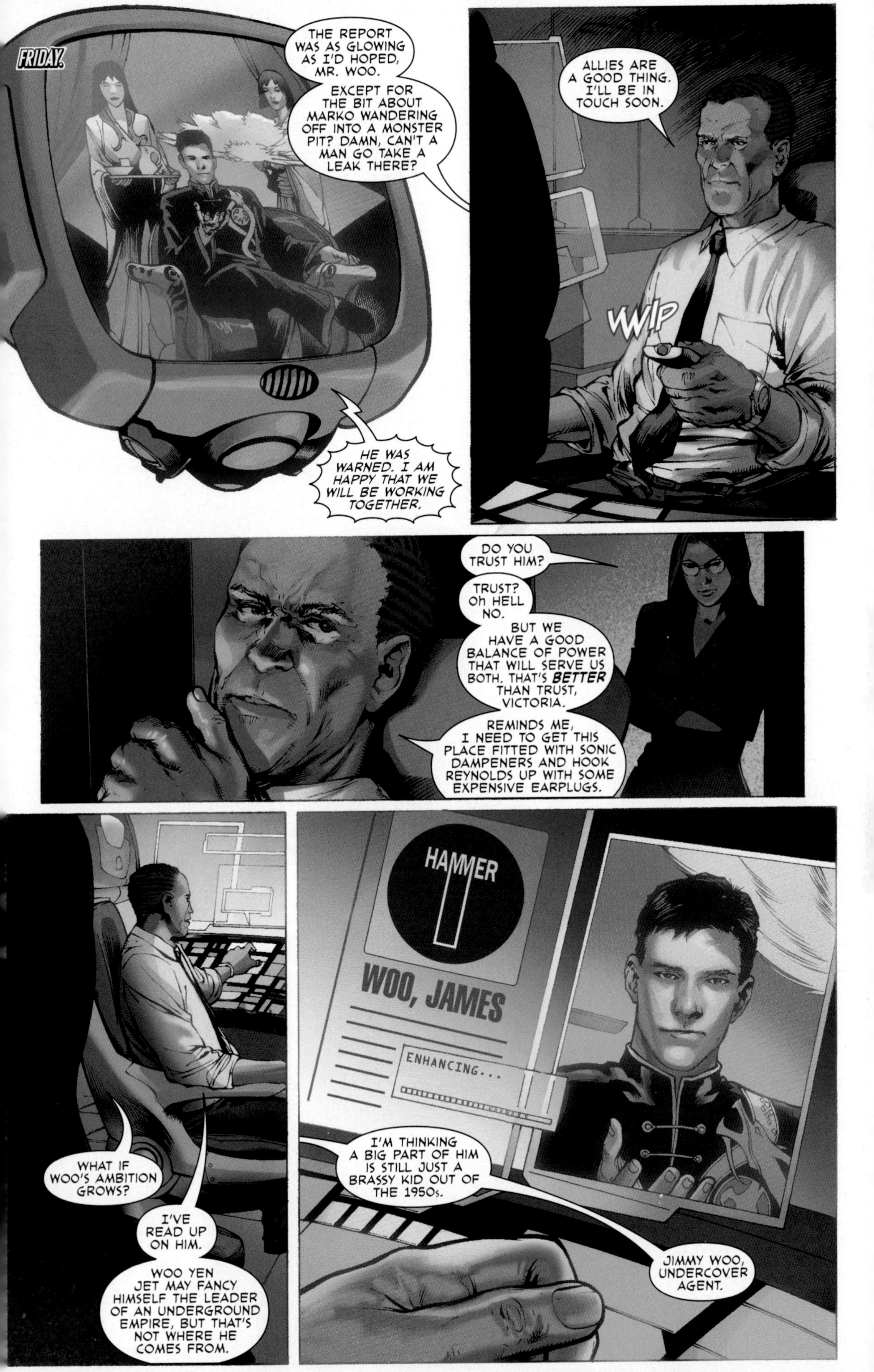
FRIDAY.
THE REPORT WAS AS GLOWING AS I'D HOPED, MR. WOO.
EXCEPT FOR THE BIT ABOUT MARKO WANDERING OFF INTO A MONSTER PIT? DAMN, CAN'T A MAN GO TAKE A LEAK THERE?
HE WAS WARNED. I AM HAPPY THAT WE WILL BE WORKING TOGETHER.
ALLIES ARE A GOOD THING. I'LL BE IN TOUCH SOON.
WWIP
DO YOU TRUST HIM?
TRUST? Oh HELL NO.
BUT WE HAVE A GOOD BALANCE OF POWER THAT WILL SERVE US BOTH. THAT'S BETTER THAN TRUST, VICTORIA.
REMINDS ME, I NEED TO GET THIS PLACE FITTED WITH SONIC DAMPENERS AND HOOK REYNOLDS UP WITH SOME EXPENSIVE EARPLUGS.
WHAT IF WOO'S AMBITION GROWS?
I'VE READ UP ON HIM.
WOO YEN JET MAY FANCY HIMSELF THE LEADER OF AN UNDERGROUND EMPIRE, BUT THAT'S NOT WHERE HE COMES FROM.
HAMMER
WOO, JAMES
ENHANCING...
I'M THINKING A BIG PART OF HIM IS STILL JUST A BRASSY KID OUT OF THE 1950s.
JIMMY WOO, UNDERCOVER AGENT.

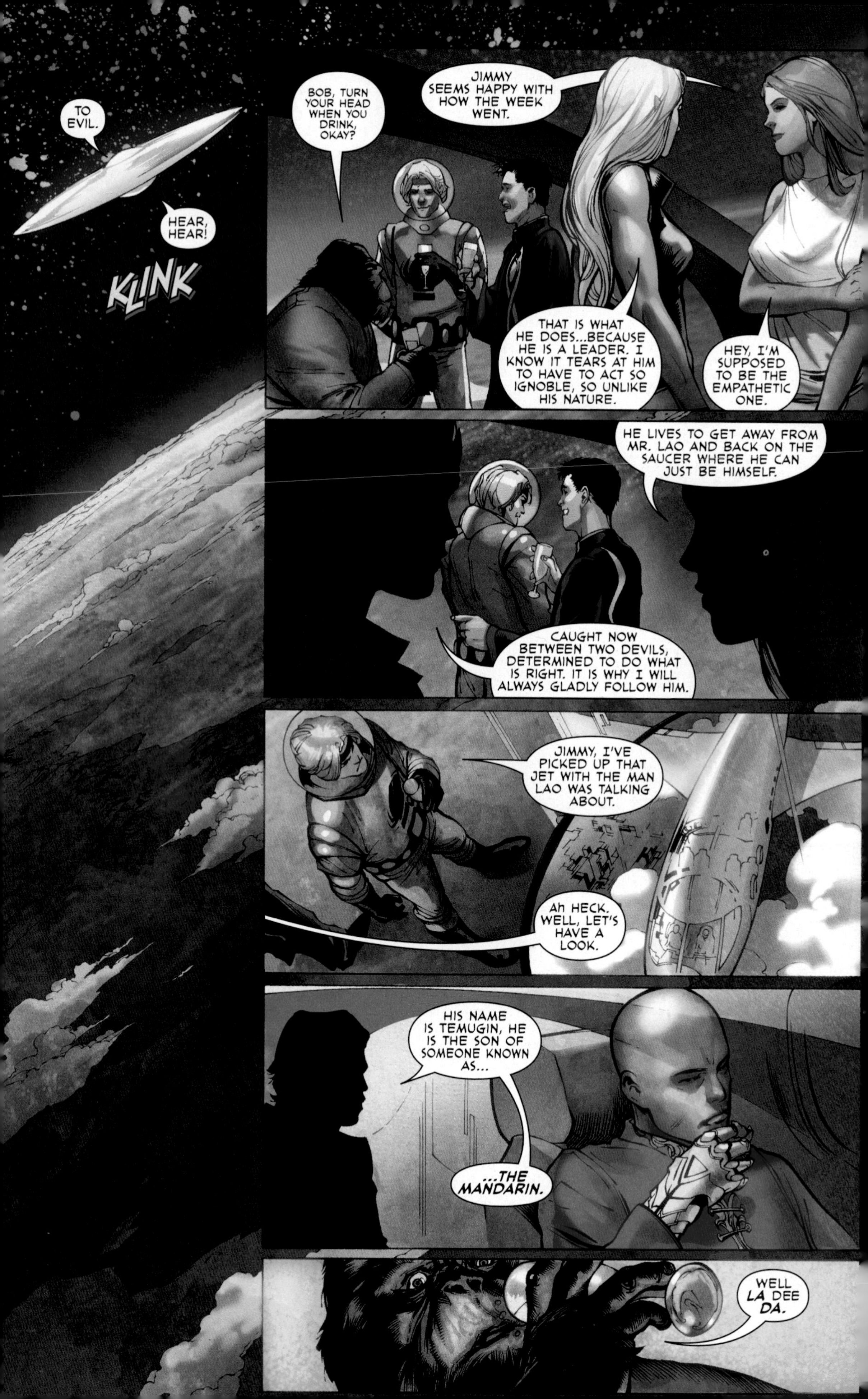
TO EVIL.
HEAR, HEAR!
KLINK
BOB, TURN YOUR HEAD WHEN YOU DRINK, OKAY?
JIMMY SEEMS HAPPY WITH HOW THE WEEK WENT.
THAT IS WHAT HE DOES...BECAUSE HE IS A LEADER. I KNOW IT TEARS AT HIM TO HAVE TO ACT SO IGNOBLE, SO UNLIKE HIS NATURE.
HEY, I'M SUPPOSED TO BE THE EMPATHETIC ONE.
HE LIVES TO GET AWAY FROM MR. LAO AND BACK ON THE SAUCER WHERE HE CAN JUST BE HIMSELF.
CAUGHT NOW BETWEEN TWO DEVILS, DETERMINED TO DO WHAT IS RIGHT. IT IS WHY I WILL ALWAYS GLADLY FOLLOW HIM.
JIMMY, I'VE PICKED UP THAT JET WITH THE MAN LAO WAS TALKING ABOUT.
Ah HECK. WELL, LET'S HAVE A LOOK.
HIS NAME IS TEMUGIN, HE IS THE SON OF SOMEONE KNOWN AS...
...THE MANDARIN.
WELL LA DEE DA.

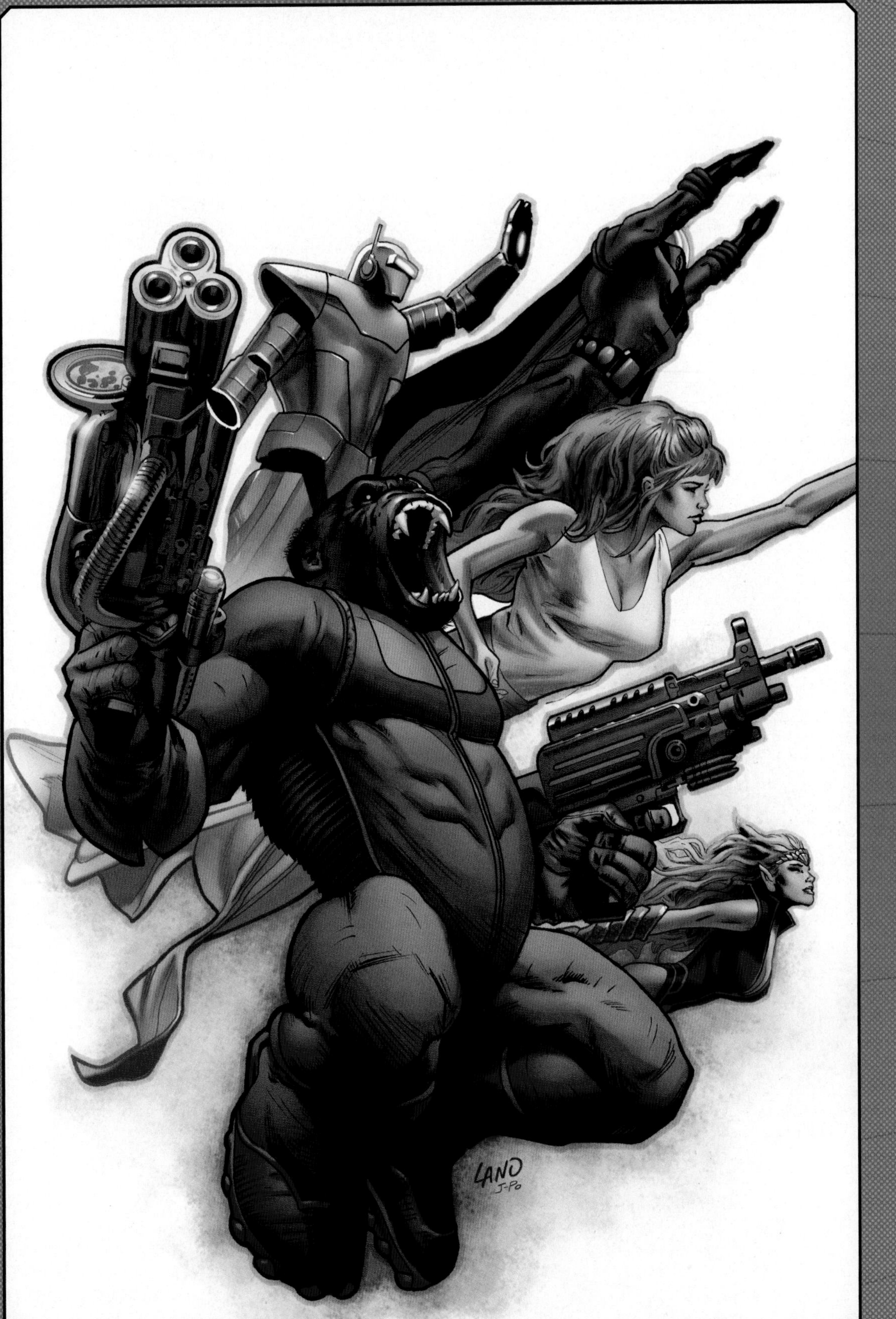
LANO
J-Po

AGENTS OF ATLAS (2009) **2**

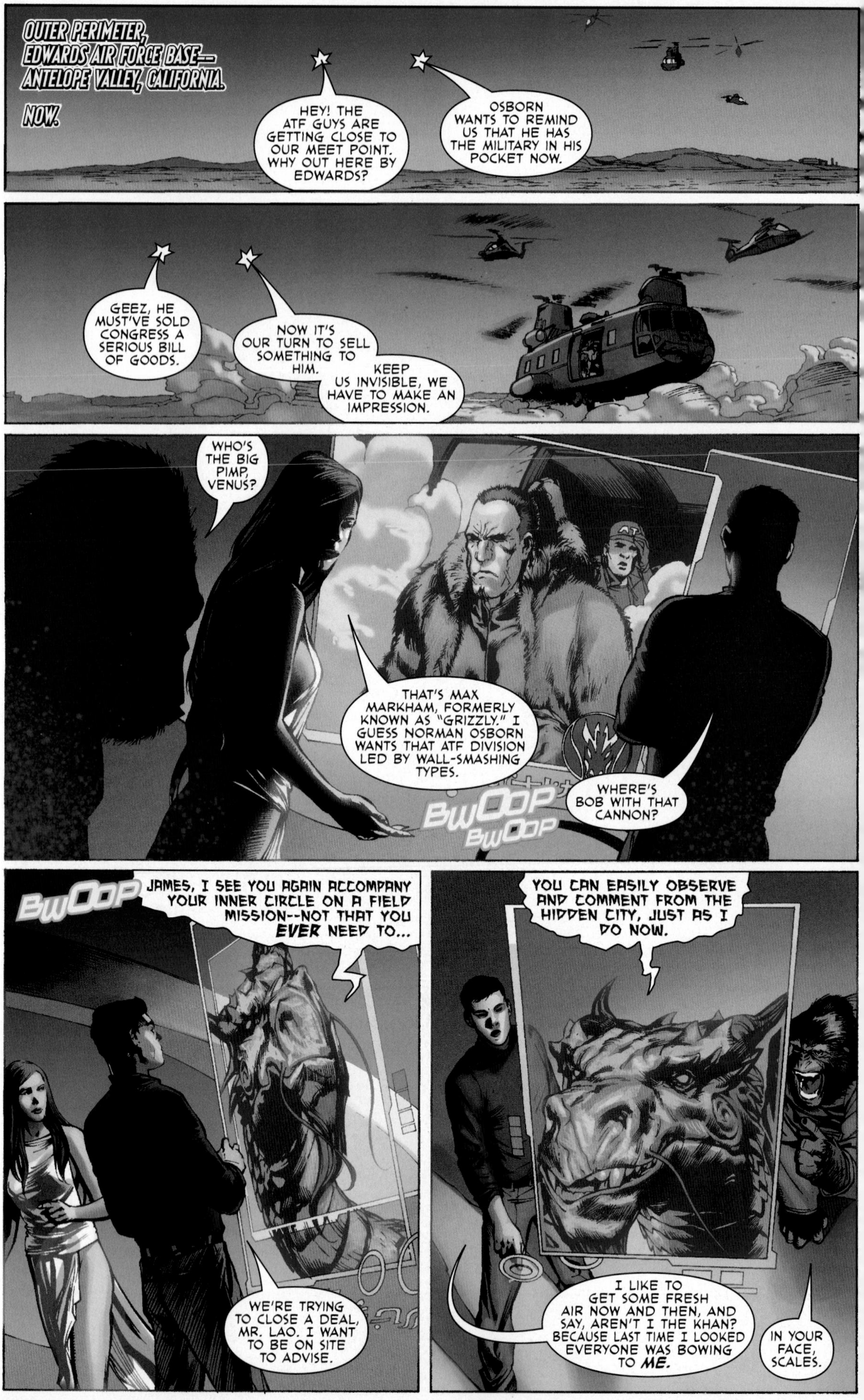
OUTER PERIMETER, EDWARDS AIR FORCE BASE-- ANTELOPE VALLEY, CALIFORNIA.
NOW.
HEY! THE ATF GUYS ARE GETTING CLOSE TO OUR MEET POINT. WHY OUT HERE BY EDWARDS?
OSBORN WANTS TO REMIND US THAT HE HAS THE MILITARY IN HIS POCKET NOW.
GEEZ, HE MUST'VE SOLD CONGRESS A SERIOUS BILL OF GOODS.
NOW IT'S OUR TURN TO SELL SOMETHING TO HIM.
KEEP US INVISIBLE, WE HAVE TO MAKE AN IMPRESSION.
WHO'S THE BIG PIMP, VENUS?
THAT'S MAX MARKHAM, FORMERLY KNOWN AS "GRIZZLY." I GUESS NORMAN OSBORN WANTS THAT ATF DIVISION LED BY WALL-SMASHING TYPES.
WHERE'S BOB WITH THAT CANNON?
BWOOP BWOOP
BWOOP
JAMES, I SEE YOU AGAIN ACCOMPANY YOUR INNER CIRCLE ON A FIELD MISSION--NOT THAT YOU EVER NEED TO...
WE'RE TRYING TO CLOSE A DEAL, MR. LAO. I WANT TO BE ON SITE TO ADVISE.
YOU CAN EASILY OBSERVE AND COMMENT FROM THE HIDDEN CITY, JUST AS I DO NOW.
I LIKE TO GET SOME FRESH AIR NOW AND THEN, AND SAY, AREN'T I THE KHAN? BECAUSE LAST TIME I LOOKED EVERYONE WAS BOWING TO ME.
IN YOUR FACE, SCALES.

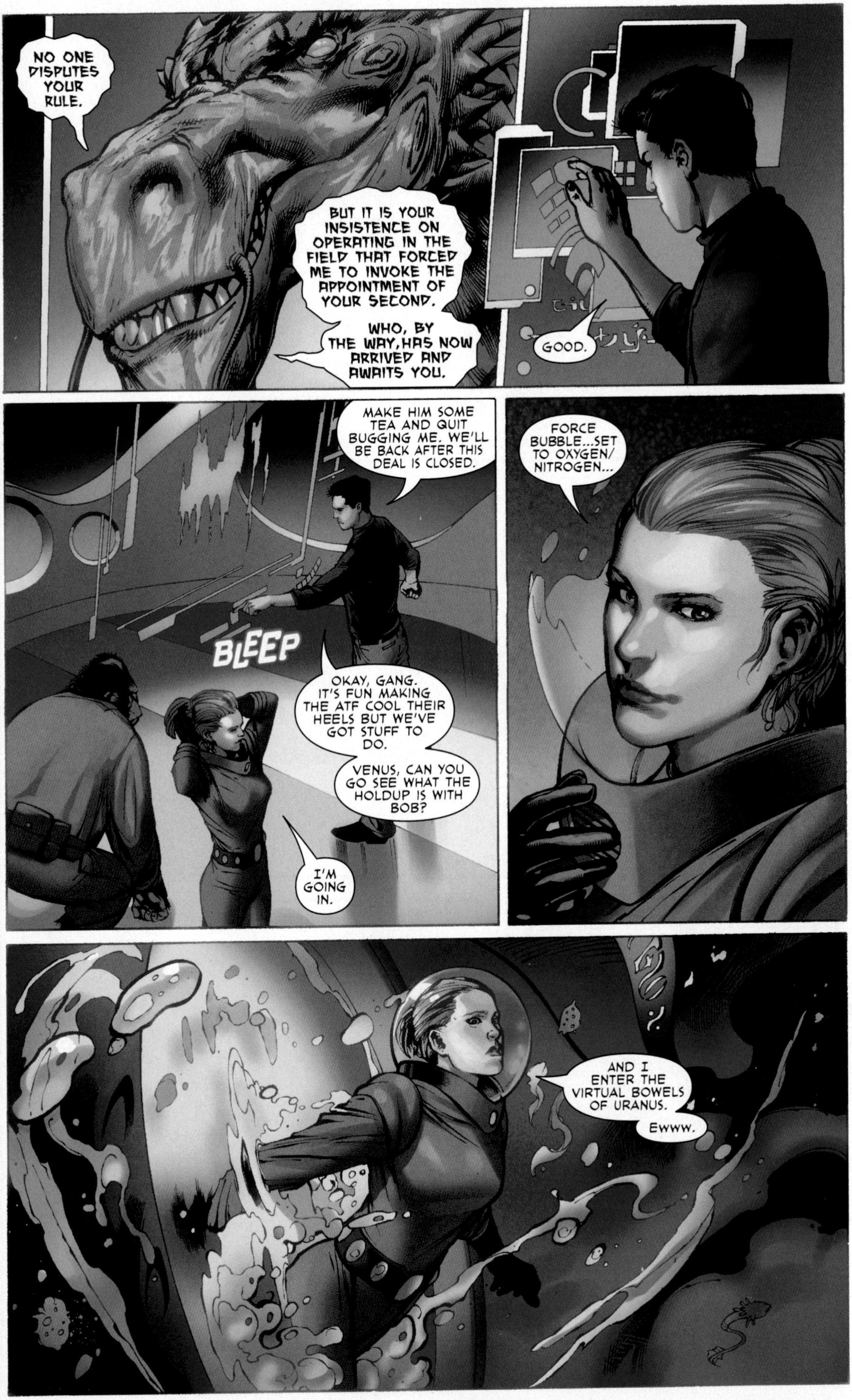
NO ONE DISPUTES YOUR RULE.
BUT IT IS YOUR INSISTENCE ON OPERATING IN THE FIELD THAT FORCED ME TO INVOKE THE APPOINTMENT OF YOUR SECOND.
WHO, BY THE WAY, HAS NOW ARRIVED AND AWAITS YOU.
GOOD.
MAKE HIM SOME TEA AND QUIT BUGGING ME. WE'LL BE BACK AFTER THIS DEAL IS CLOSED.
BLEEP
OKAY, GANG. IT'S FUN MAKING THE ATF COOL THEIR HEELS BUT WE'VE GOT STUFF TO DO.
VENUS, CAN YOU GO SEE WHAT THE HOLDUP IS WITH BOB?
I'M GOING IN.
FORCE BUBBLE...SET TO OXYGEN/ NITROGEN...
AND I ENTER THE VIRTUAL BOWELS OF URANUS.
Ewww.

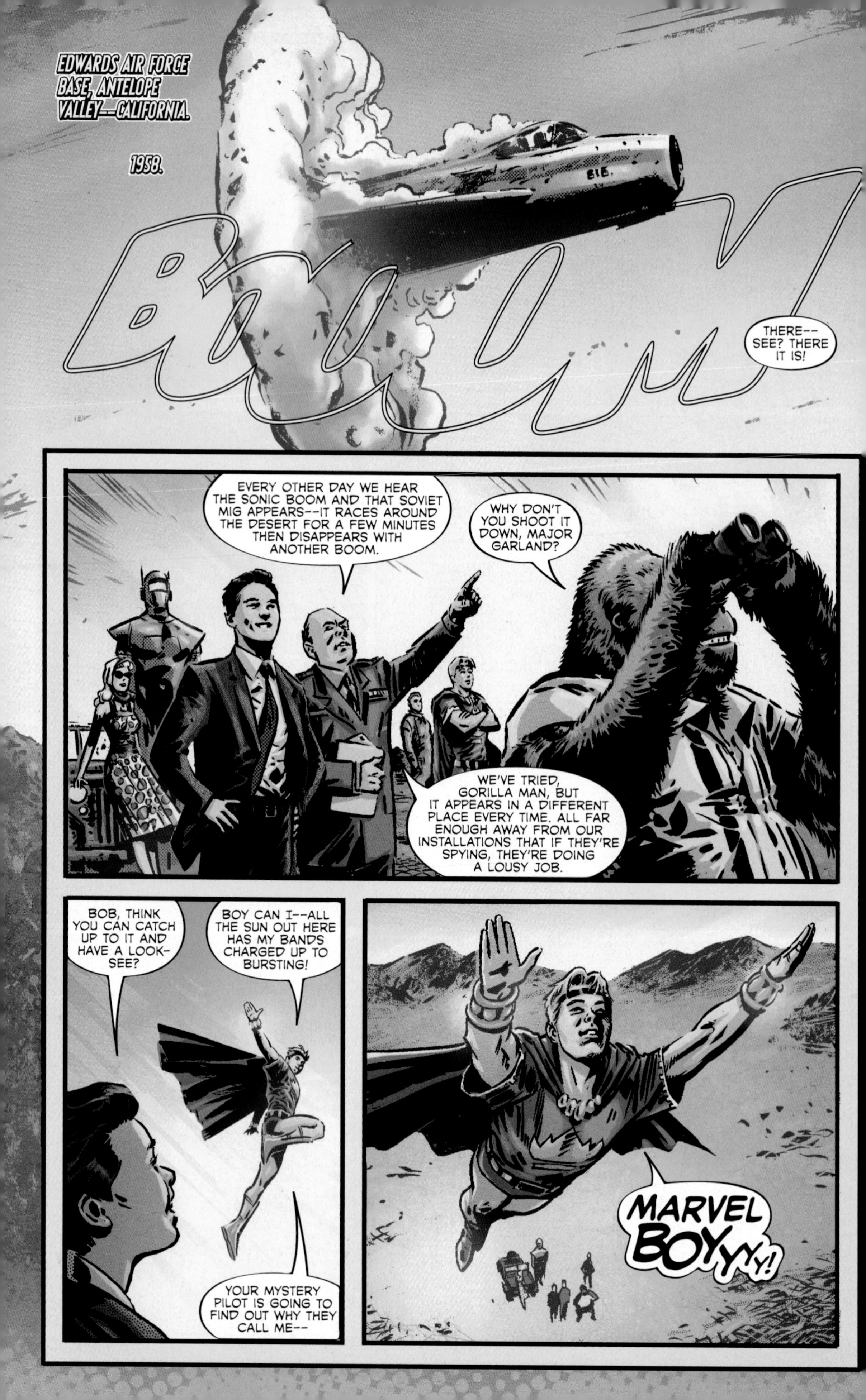
EDWARDS AIR FORCE BASE, ANTELOPE VALLEY--CALIFORNIA.
1958.
BOOM
THERE--SEE? THERE IT IS!
EVERY OTHER DAY WE HEAR THE SONIC BOOM AND THAT SOVIET MIG APPEARS--IT RACES AROUND THE DESERT FOR A FEW MINUTES THEN DISAPPEARS WITH ANOTHER BOOM.
WHY DON'T YOU SHOOT IT DOWN, MAJOR GARLAND?
WE'VE TRIED, GORILLA MAN, BUT IT APPEARS IN A DIFFERENT PLACE EVERY TIME. ALL FAR ENOUGH AWAY FROM OUR INSTALLATIONS THAT IF THEY'RE SPYING, THEY'RE DOING A LOUSY JOB.
BOB, THINK YOU CAN CATCH UP TO IT AND HAVE A LOOK-SEE?
BOY CAN I--ALL THE SUN OUT HERE HAS MY BANDS CHARGED UP TO BURSTING!
YOUR MYSTERY PILOT IS GOING TO FIND OUT WHY THEY CALL ME--
MARVEL BOYYY!

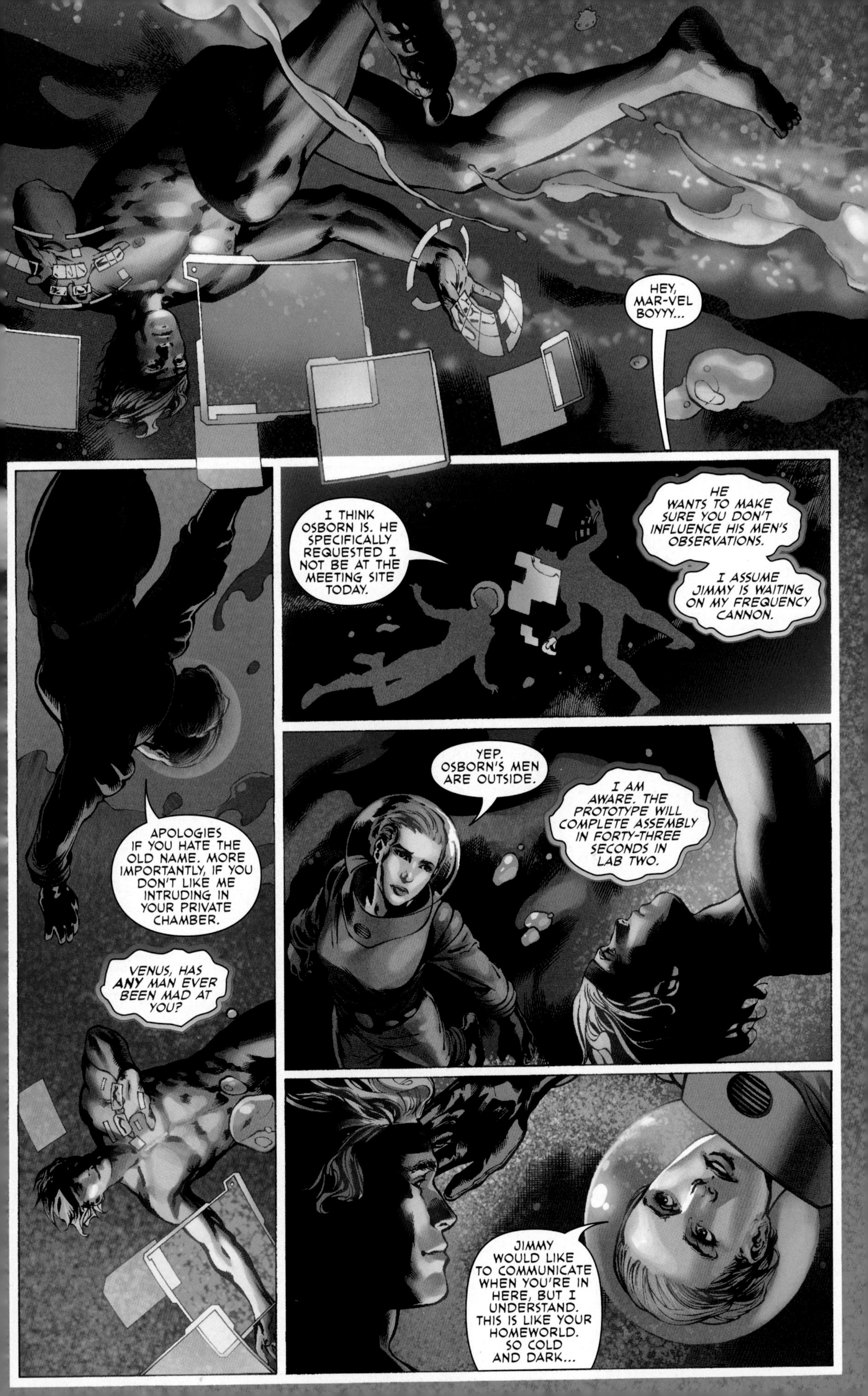
HEY, MAR-VEL BOYYY...
APOLOGIES IF YOU HATE THE OLD NAME. MORE IMPORTANTLY, IF YOU DON'T LIKE ME INTRUDING IN YOUR PRIVATE CHAMBER.
VENUS, HAS **ANY** MAN EVER BEEN MAD AT YOU?
I THINK OSBORN IS. HE SPECIFICALLY REQUESTED I NOT BE AT THE MEETING SITE TODAY.
HE WANTS TO MAKE SURE YOU DON'T INFLUENCE HIS MEN'S OBSERVATIONS.
I ASSUME JIMMY IS WAITING ON MY FREQUENCY CANNON.
YEP. OSBORN'S MEN ARE OUTSIDE.
I AM AWARE. THE PROTOTYPE WILL COMPLETE ASSEMBLY IN FORTY-THREE SECONDS IN LAB TWO.
JIMMY WOULD LIKE TO COMMUNICATE WHEN YOU'RE IN HERE, BUT I UNDERSTAND. THIS IS LIKE YOUR HOMEWORLD. SO COLD AND DARK...

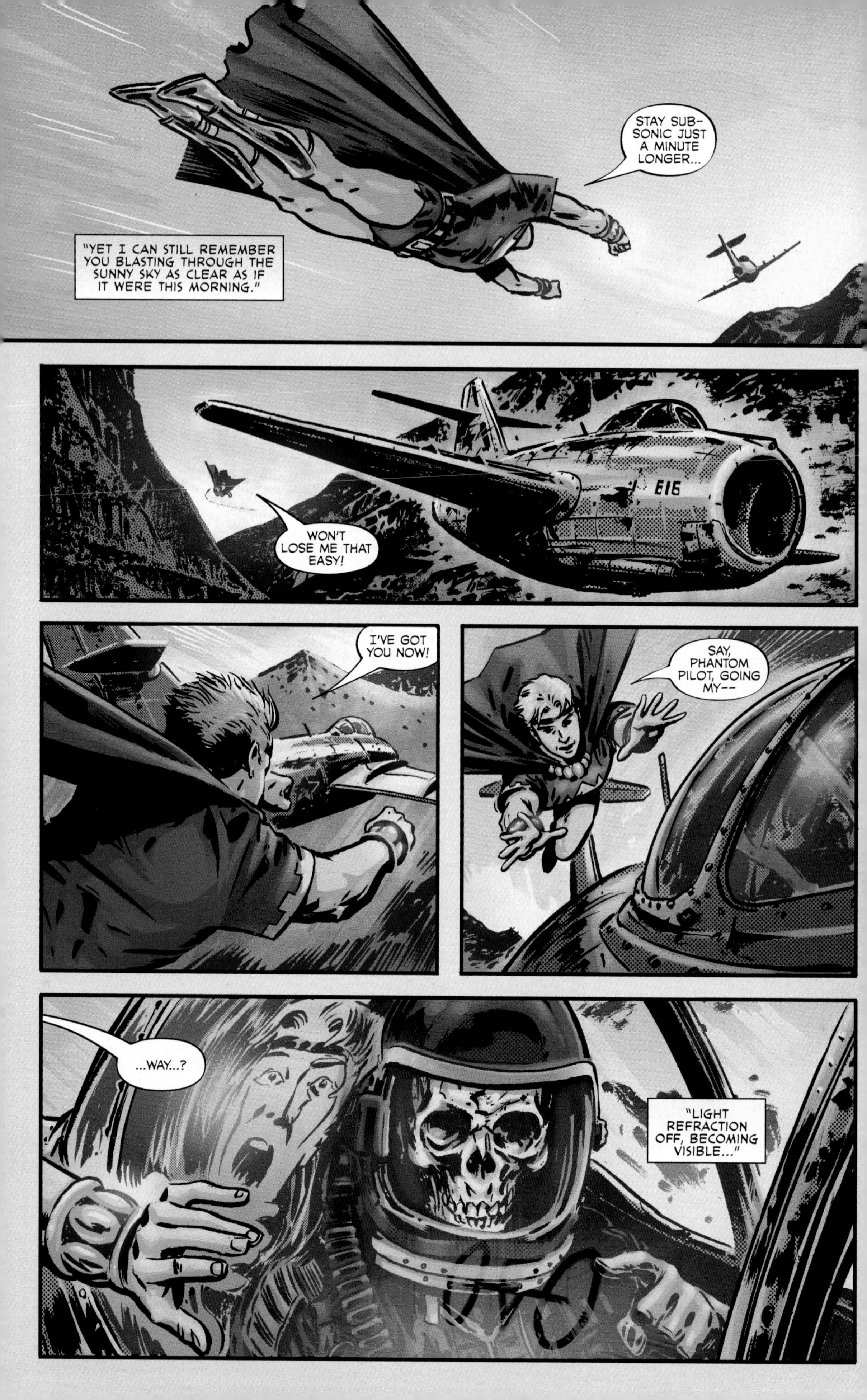
STAY SUB-SONIC JUST A MINUTE LONGER...
"YET I CAN STILL REMEMBER YOU BLASTING THROUGH THE SUNNY SKY AS CLEAR AS IF IT WERE THIS MORNING."
816
WON'T LOSE ME THAT EASY!
I'VE GOT YOU NOW!
SAY, PHANTOM PILOT, GOING MY--
...WAY...?
"LIGHT REFRACTION OFF, BECOMING VISIBLE..."

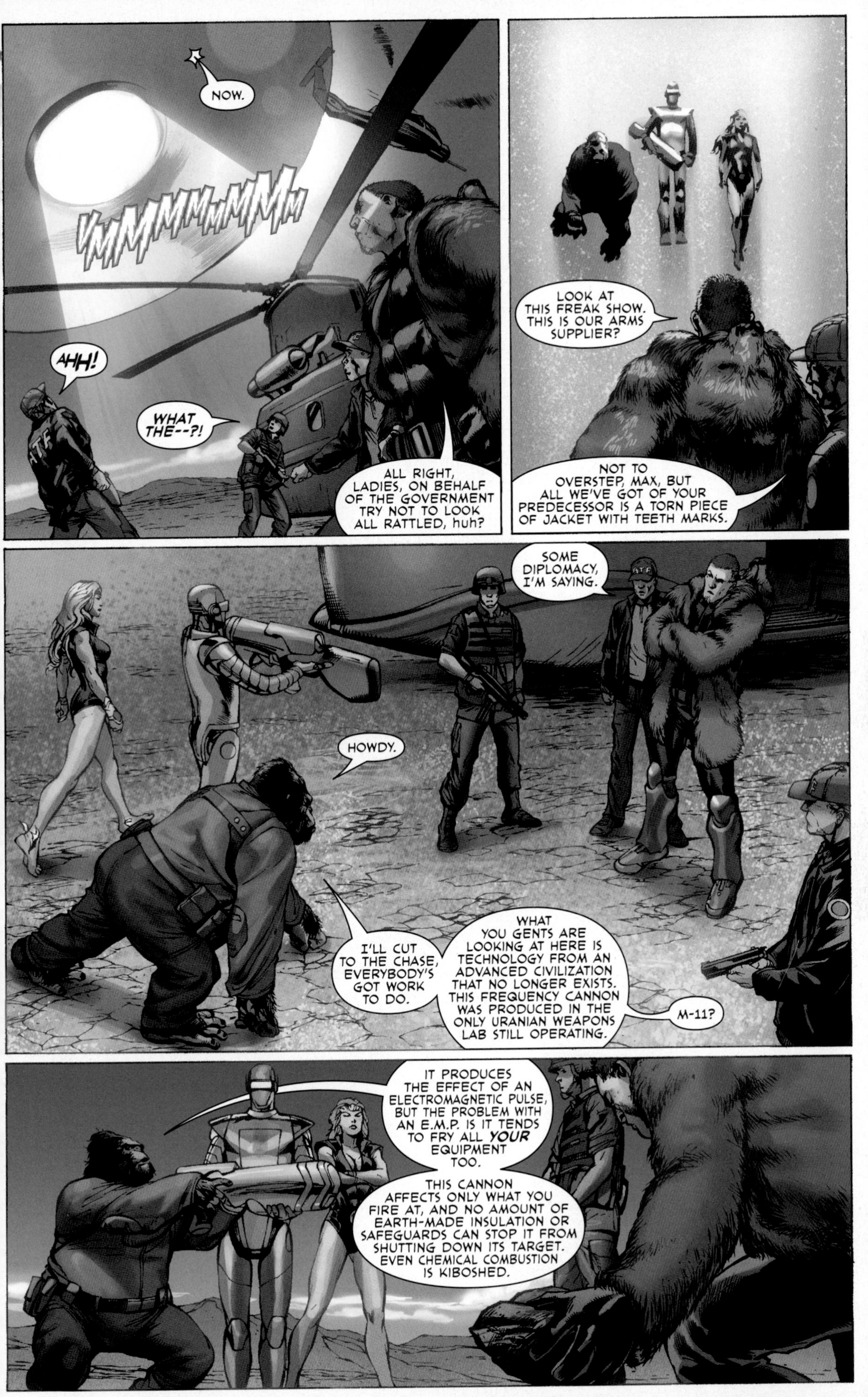
NOW.
VMMMMMMMMM
AHH!
WHAT THE--?!
ALL RIGHT, LADIES, ON BEHALF OF THE GOVERNMENT TRY NOT TO LOOK ALL RATTLED, huh?
LOOK AT THIS FREAK SHOW. THIS IS OUR ARMS SUPPLIER?
NOT TO OVERSTEP, MAX, BUT ALL WE'VE GOT OF YOUR PREDECESSOR IS A TORN PIECE OF JACKET WITH TEETH MARKS.
SOME DIPLOMACY, I'M SAYING.
HOWDY.
I'LL CUT TO THE CHASE, EVERYBODY'S GOT WORK TO DO.
WHAT YOU GENTS ARE LOOKING AT HERE IS TECHNOLOGY FROM AN ADVANCED CIVILIZATION THAT NO LONGER EXISTS. THIS FREQUENCY CANNON WAS PRODUCED IN THE ONLY URANIAN WEAPONS LAB STILL OPERATING.
M-11?
IT PRODUCES THE EFFECT OF AN ELECTROMAGNETIC PULSE, BUT THE PROBLEM WITH AN E.M.P. IS IT TENDS TO FRY ALL YOUR EQUIPMENT TOO.
THIS CANNON AFFECTS ONLY WHAT YOU FIRE AT, AND NO AMOUNT OF EARTH-MADE INSULATION OR SAFEGUARDS CAN STOP IT FROM SHUTTING DOWN ITS TARGET. EVEN CHEMICAL COMBUSTION IS KIBOSHED.

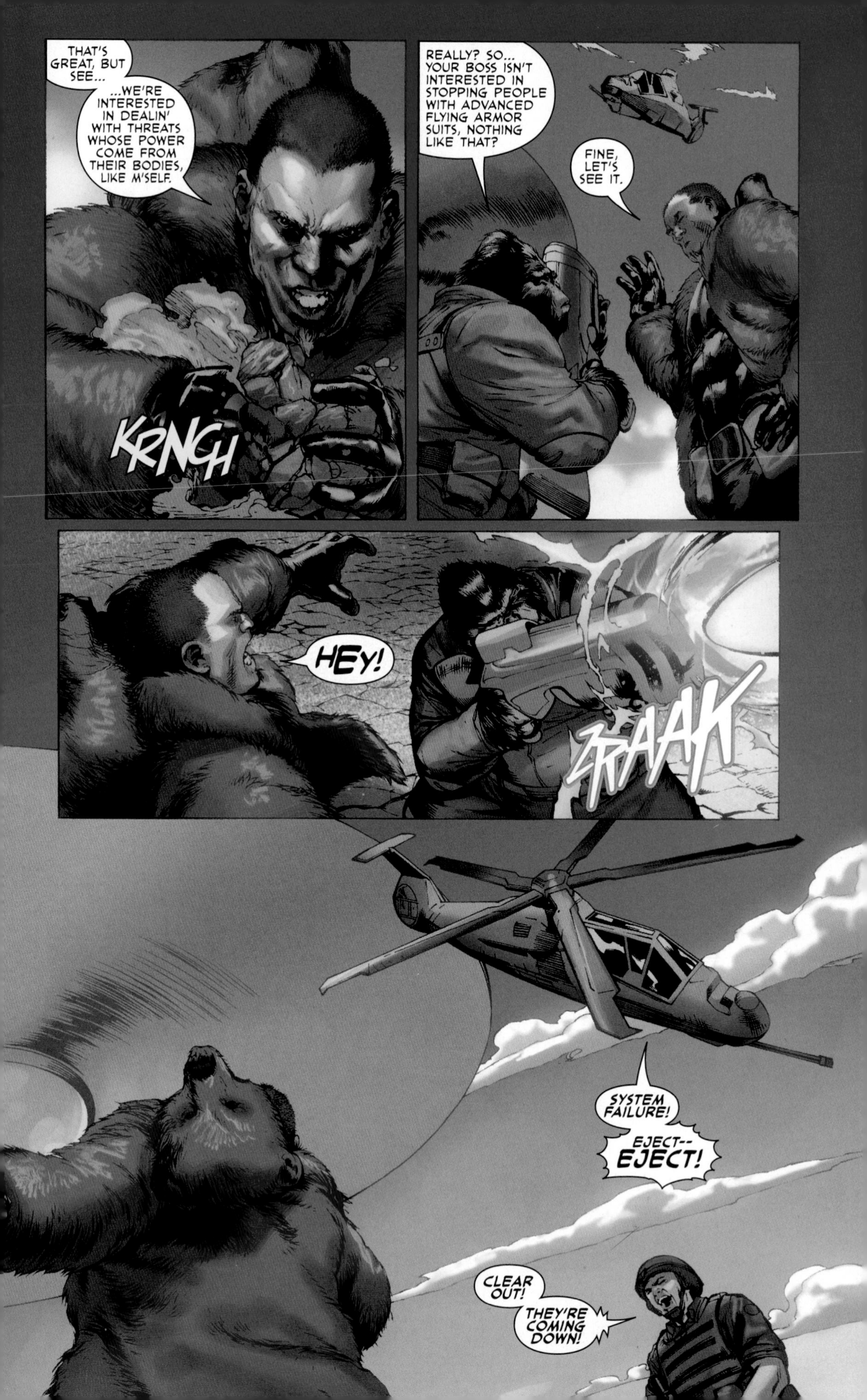
THAT'S GREAT, BUT SEE...
...WE'RE INTERESTED IN DEALIN' WITH THREATS WHOSE POWER COME FROM THEIR BODIES, LIKE M'SELF.
KRNCH
REALLY? SO... YOUR BOSS ISN'T INTERESTED IN STOPPING PEOPLE WITH ADVANCED FLYING ARMOR SUITS, NOTHING LIKE THAT?
FINE, LET'S SEE IT.
HEY!
ZRAAK
SYSTEM FAILURE!
EJECT-- EJECT!
CLEAR OUT!
THEY'RE COMING DOWN!

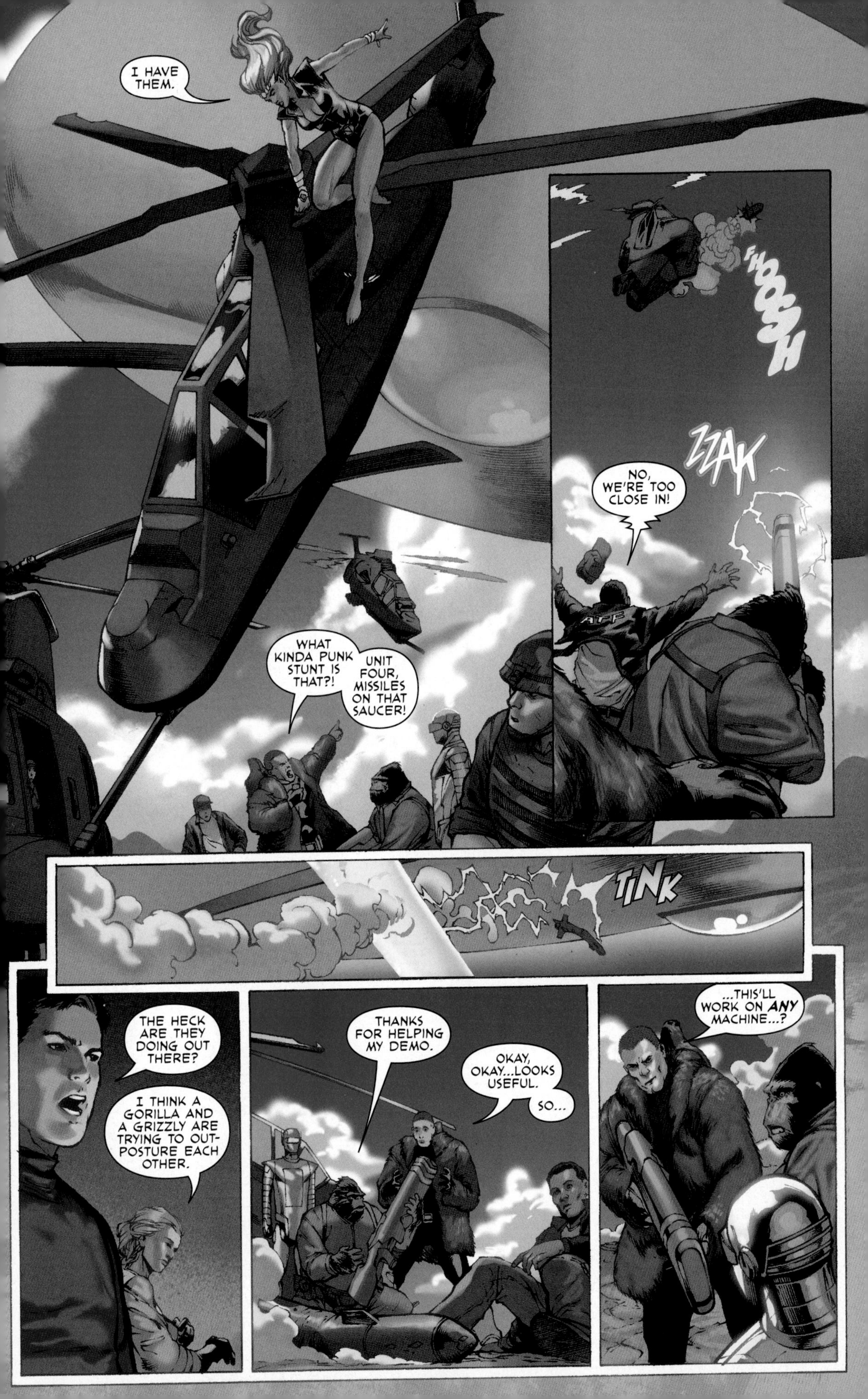

I HAVE THEM.
WHAT KINDA PUNK STUNT IS THAT?!
UNIT FOUR, MISSILES ON THAT SAUCER!
FHOOSH
ZZAK
NO, WE'RE TOO CLOSE IN!
TINK
THE HECK ARE THEY DOING OUT THERE?
I THINK A GORILLA AND A GRIZZLY ARE TRYING TO OUT-POSTURE EACH OTHER.
THANKS FOR HELPING MY DEMO.
OKAY, OKAY...LOOKS USEFUL.
SO...
...THIS'LL WORK ON *ANY* MACHINE...?

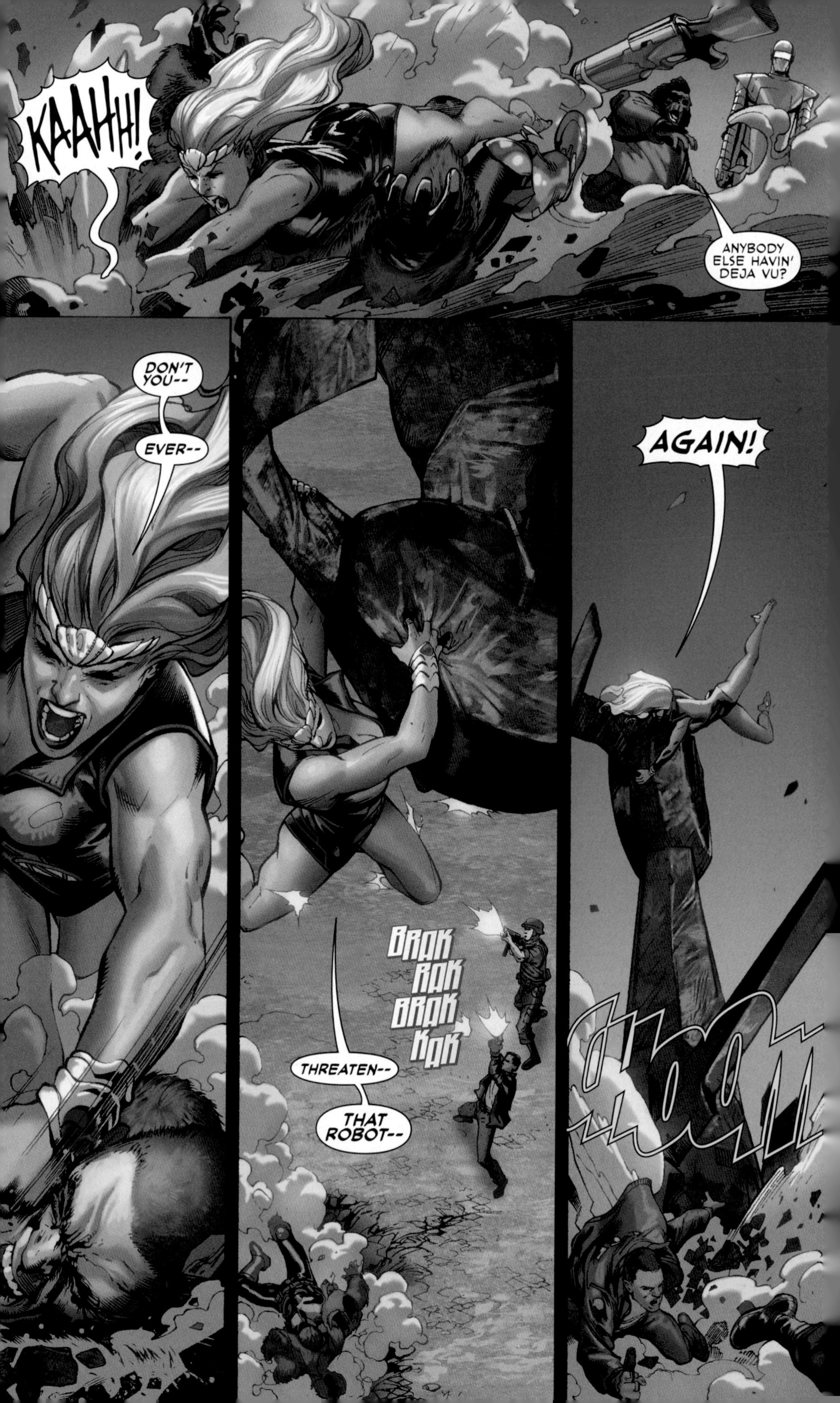
KAAHH!
ANYBODY ELSE HAVIN' DEJA VU?
DON'T YOU--
EVER--
BRAK RAK BRAK KAK
THREATEN--
THAT ROBOT--
AGAIN!

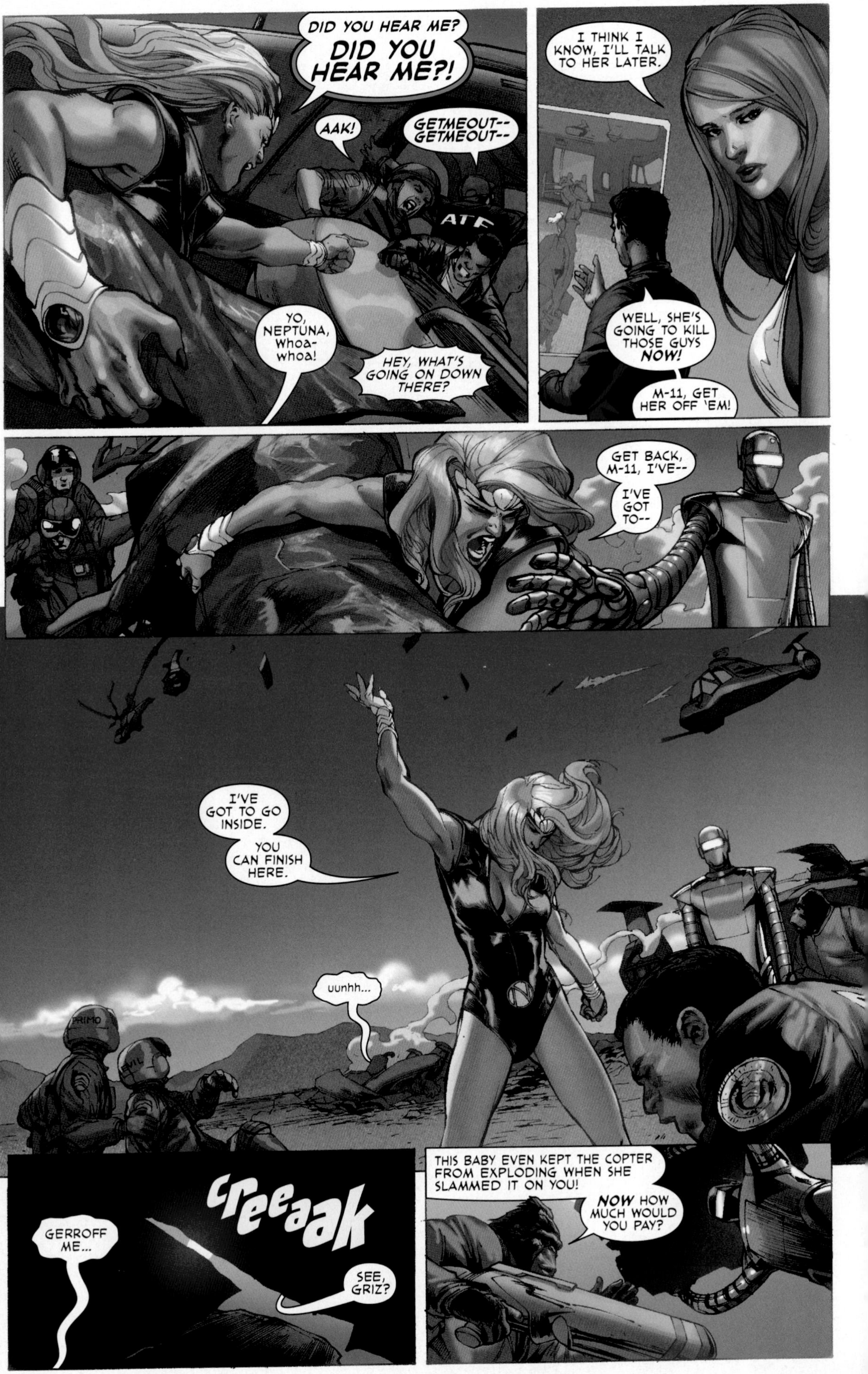
DID YOU HEAR ME? DID YOU HEAR ME?!
AAK!
GETMEOUT-- GETMEOUT--
ATF
YO, NEPTUNA, Whoa-whoa!
HEY, WHAT'S GOING ON DOWN THERE?
I THINK I KNOW, I'LL TALK TO HER LATER.
WELL, SHE'S GOING TO KILL THOSE GUYS NOW!
M-11, GET HER OFF 'EM!
GET BACK, M-11, I'VE--
I'VE GOT TO--
I'VE GOT TO GO INSIDE.
YOU CAN FINISH HERE.
uunhh...
PRIMO
GERROFF ME...
creeaak
SEE, GRIZ?
THIS BABY EVEN KEPT THE COPTER FROM EXPLODING WHEN SHE SLAMMED IT ON YOU!
NOW HOW MUCH WOULD YOU PAY?

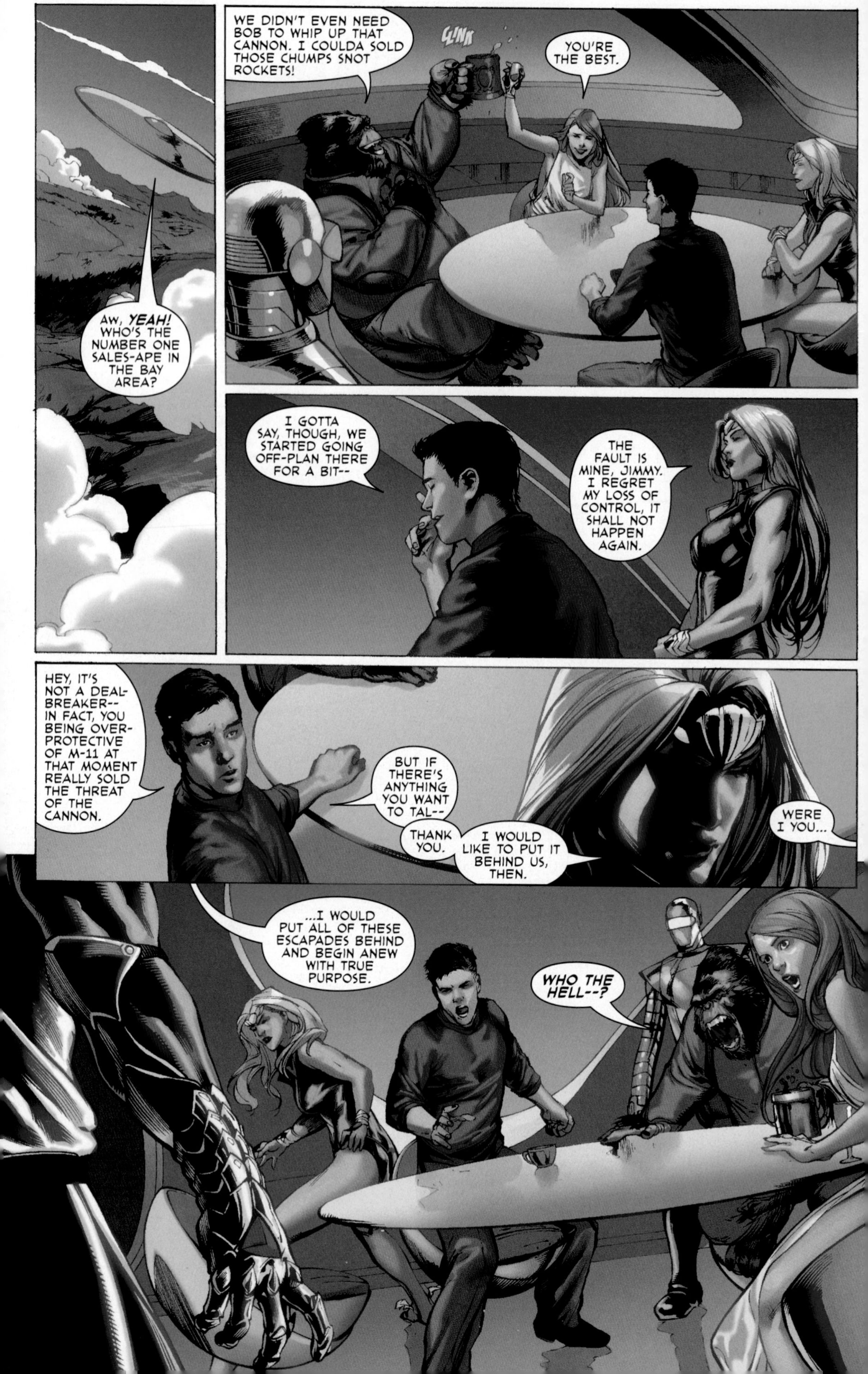
Aw, YEAH! WHO'S THE NUMBER ONE SALES-APE IN THE BAY AREA?
WE DIDN'T EVEN NEED BOB TO WHIP UP THAT CANNON. I COULDA SOLD THOSE CHUMPS SNOT ROCKETS!
CLINK
YOU'RE THE BEST.
I GOTTA SAY, THOUGH, WE STARTED GOING OFF-PLAN THERE FOR A BIT--
THE FAULT IS MINE, JIMMY. I REGRET MY LOSS OF CONTROL, IT SHALL NOT HAPPEN AGAIN.
HEY, IT'S NOT A DEAL-BREAKER-- IN FACT, YOU BEING OVER-PROTECTIVE OF M-11 AT THAT MOMENT REALLY SOLD THE THREAT OF THE CANNON.
BUT IF THERE'S ANYTHING YOU WANT TO TAL--
THANK YOU.
I WOULD LIKE TO PUT IT BEHIND US, THEN.
WERE I YOU...
...I WOULD PUT ALL OF THESE ESCAPADES BEHIND AND BEGIN ANEW WITH TRUE PURPOSE.
WHO THE HELL--?

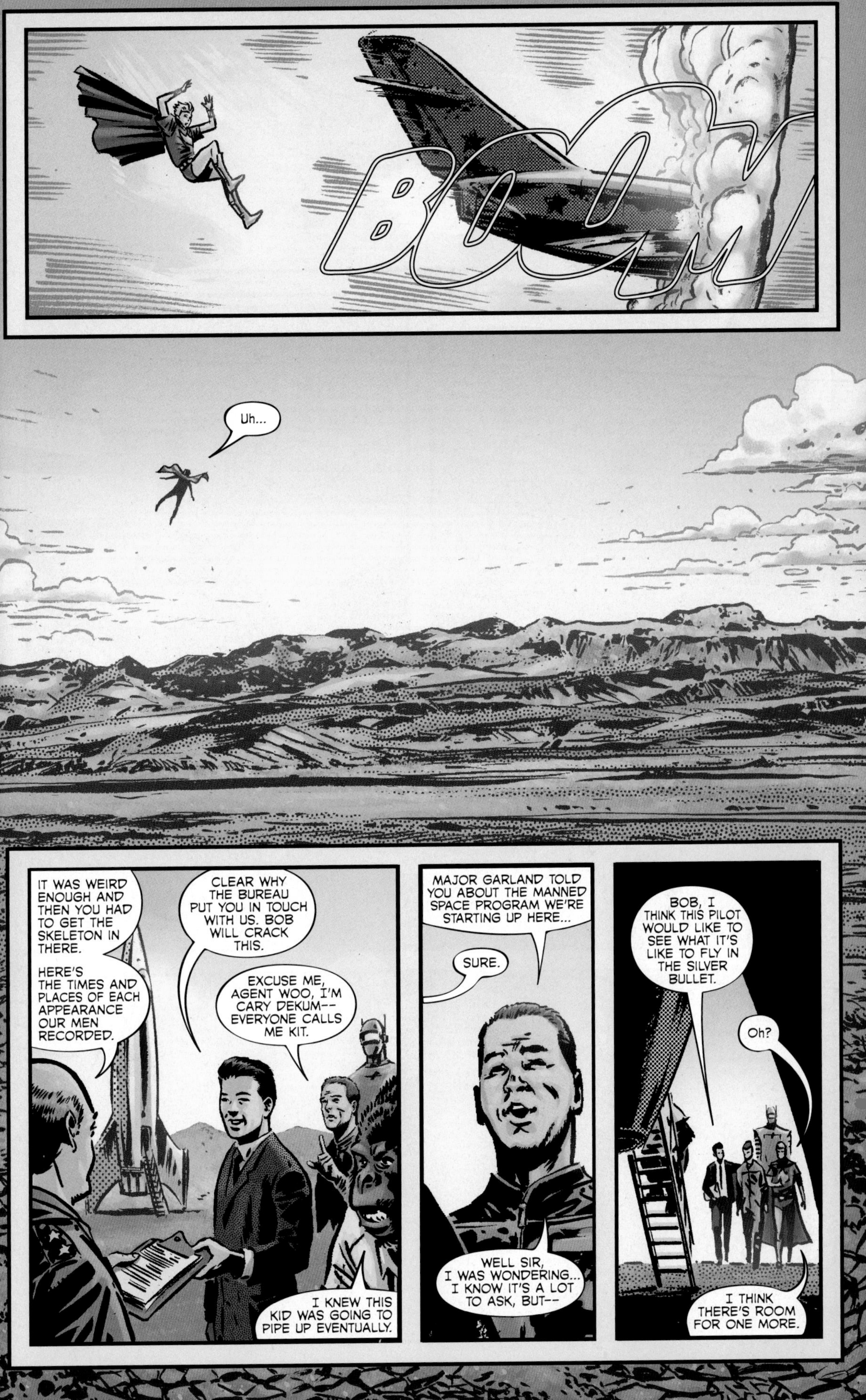
BOOM
Uh...
IT WAS WEIRD ENOUGH AND THEN YOU HAD TO GET THE SKELETON IN THERE.
HERE'S THE TIMES AND PLACES OF EACH APPEARANCE OUR MEN RECORDED.
CLEAR WHY THE BUREAU PUT YOU IN TOUCH WITH US. BOB WILL CRACK THIS.
EXCUSE ME, AGENT WOO, I'M CARY DEKUM-- EVERYONE CALLS ME KIT.
I KNEW THIS KID WAS GOING TO PIPE UP EVENTUALLY.
MAJOR GARLAND TOLD YOU ABOUT THE MANNED SPACE PROGRAM WE'RE STARTING UP HERE...
SURE.
WELL SIR, I WAS WONDERING... I KNOW IT'S A LOT TO ASK, BUT--
BOB, I THINK THIS PILOT WOULD LIKE TO SEE WHAT IT'S LIKE TO FLY IN THE SILVER BULLET.
Oh?
I THINK THERE'S ROOM FOR ONE MORE.

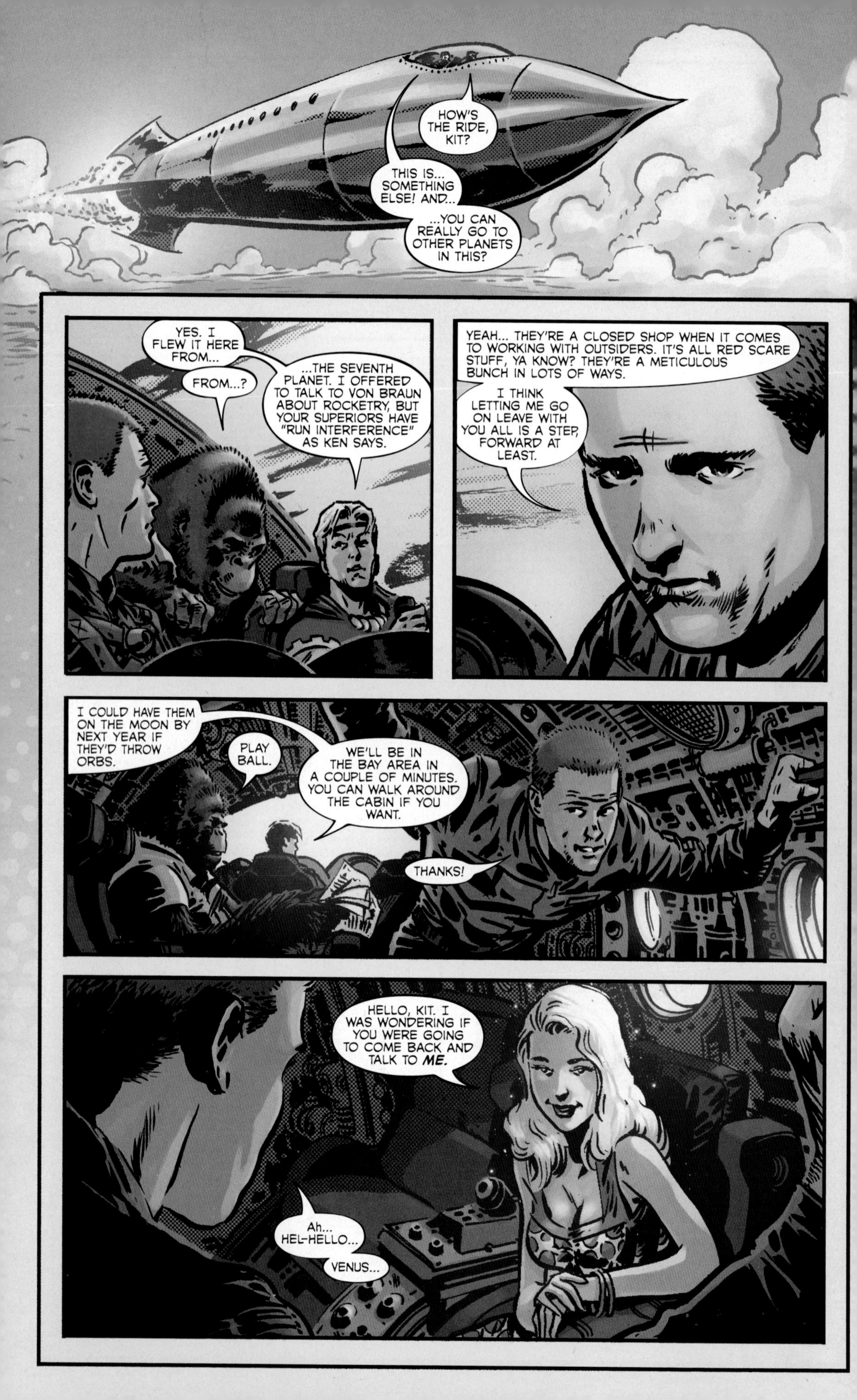
HOW'S THE RIDE, KIT?
THIS IS... SOMETHING ELSE! AND...
...YOU CAN REALLY GO TO OTHER PLANETS IN THIS?
YES. I FLEW IT HERE FROM...
FROM...?
...THE SEVENTH PLANET. I OFFERED TO TALK TO VON BRAUN ABOUT ROCKETRY, BUT YOUR SUPERIORS HAVE "RUN INTERFERENCE" AS KEN SAYS.
YEAH... THEY'RE A CLOSED SHOP WHEN IT COMES TO WORKING WITH OUTSIDERS. IT'S ALL RED SCARE STUFF, YA KNOW? THEY'RE A METICULOUS BUNCH IN LOTS OF WAYS.
I THINK LETTING ME GO ON LEAVE WITH YOU ALL IS A STEP FORWARD AT LEAST.
I COULD HAVE THEM ON THE MOON BY NEXT YEAR IF THEY'D THROW ORBS.
PLAY BALL.
WE'LL BE IN THE BAY AREA IN A COUPLE OF MINUTES. YOU CAN WALK AROUND THE CABIN IF YOU WANT.
THANKS!
HELLO, KIT. I WAS WONDERING IF YOU WERE GOING TO COME BACK AND TALK TO ***ME.***
Ah... HEL-HELLO...
VENUS...

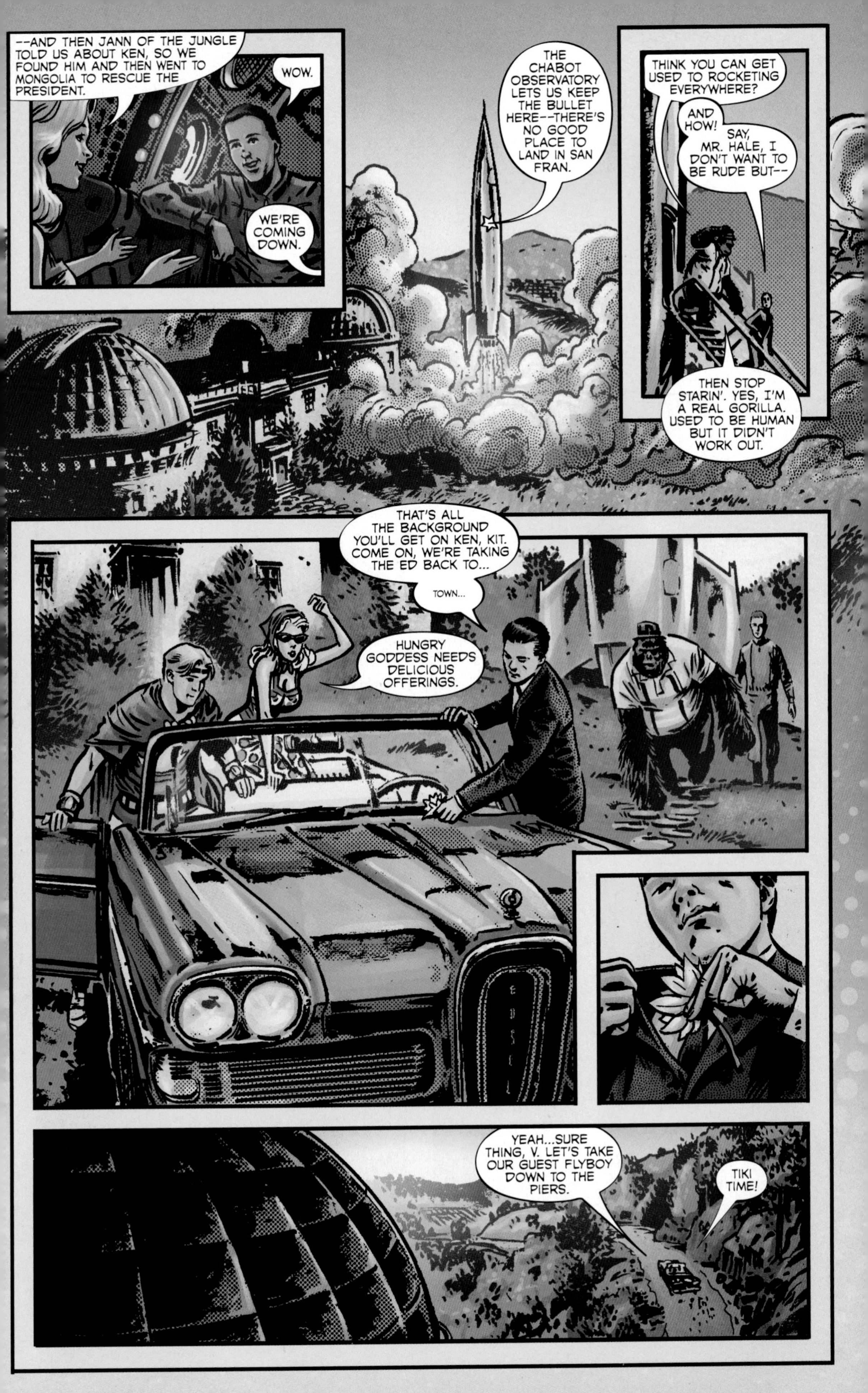
--AND THEN JANN OF THE JUNGLE TOLD US ABOUT KEN, SO WE FOUND HIM AND THEN WENT TO MONGOLIA TO RESCUE THE PRESIDENT.
WOW.
WE'RE COMING DOWN.
THE CHABOT OBSERVATORY LETS US KEEP THE BULLET HERE--THERE'S NO GOOD PLACE TO LAND IN SAN FRAN.
THINK YOU CAN GET USED TO ROCKETING EVERYWHERE?
AND HOW!
SAY, MR. HALE, I DON'T WANT TO BE RUDE BUT--
THEN STOP STARIN'. YES, I'M A REAL GORILLA. USED TO BE HUMAN BUT IT DIDN'T WORK OUT.
THAT'S ALL THE BACKGROUND YOU'LL GET ON KEN, KIT. COME ON, WE'RE TAKING THE ED BACK TO...
TOWN...
HUNGRY GODDESS NEEDS DELICIOUS OFFERINGS.
YEAH...SURE THING, V. LET'S TAKE OUR GUEST FLYBOY DOWN TO THE PIERS.
TIKI TIME!

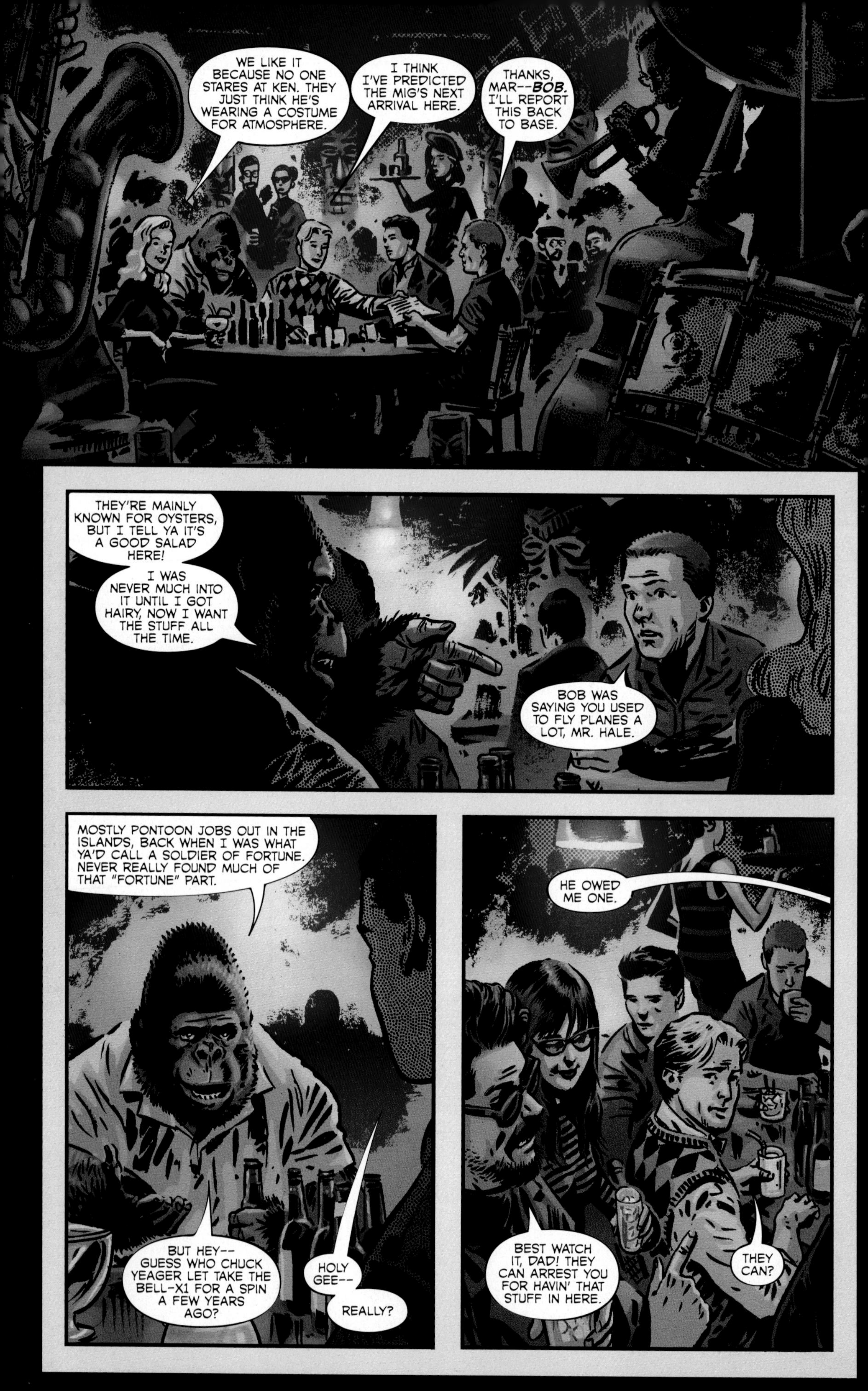
WE LIKE IT BECAUSE NO ONE STARES AT KEN. THEY JUST THINK HE'S WEARING A COSTUME FOR ATMOSPHERE.
I THINK I'VE PREDICTED THE MIG'S NEXT ARRIVAL HERE.
THANKS, MAR--*BOB.* I'LL REPORT THIS BACK TO BASE.
THEY'RE MAINLY KNOWN FOR OYSTERS, BUT I TELL YA IT'S A GOOD SALAD HERE!
I WAS NEVER MUCH INTO IT UNTIL I GOT HAIRY, NOW I WANT THE STUFF ALL THE TIME.
BOB WAS SAYING YOU USED TO FLY PLANES A LOT, MR. HALE.
MOSTLY PONTOON JOBS OUT IN THE ISLANDS, BACK WHEN I WAS WHAT YA'D CALL A SOLDIER OF FORTUNE. NEVER REALLY FOUND MUCH OF THAT "FORTUNE" PART.
BUT HEY-- GUESS WHO CHUCK YEAGER LET TAKE THE BELL-X1 FOR A SPIN A FEW YEARS AGO?
HOLY GEE--
REALLY?
HE OWED ME ONE.
BEST WATCH IT, DAD! THEY CAN ARREST YOU FOR HAVIN' THAT STUFF IN HERE.
THEY CAN?

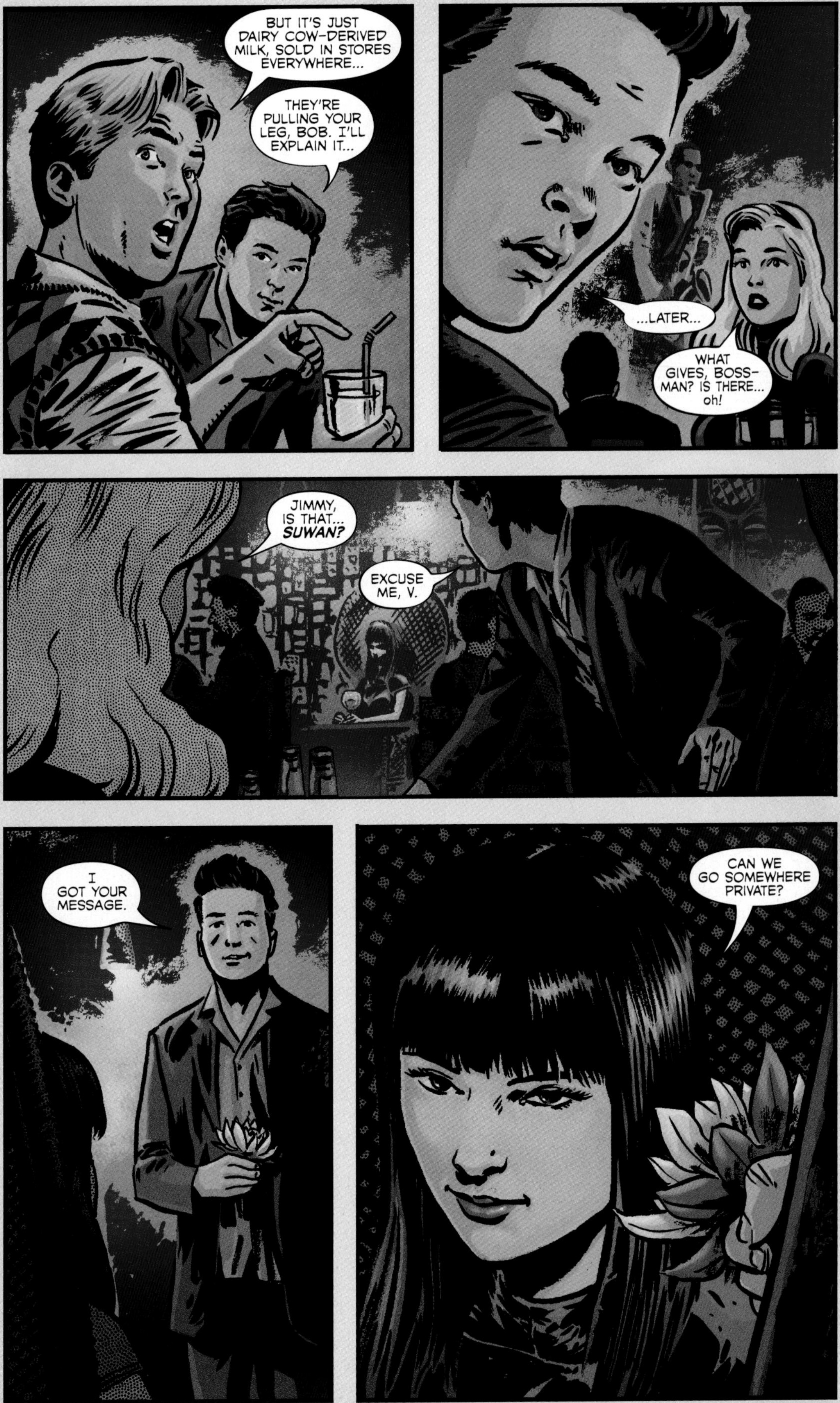
BUT IT'S JUST DAIRY COW-DERIVED MILK, SOLD IN STORES EVERYWHERE...
THEY'RE PULLING YOUR LEG, BOB. I'LL EXPLAIN IT...
...LATER...
WHAT GIVES, BOSS-MAN? IS THERE... oh!
JIMMY, IS THAT... SUWAN?
EXCUSE ME, V.
I GOT YOUR MESSAGE.
CAN WE GO SOMEWHERE PRIVATE?

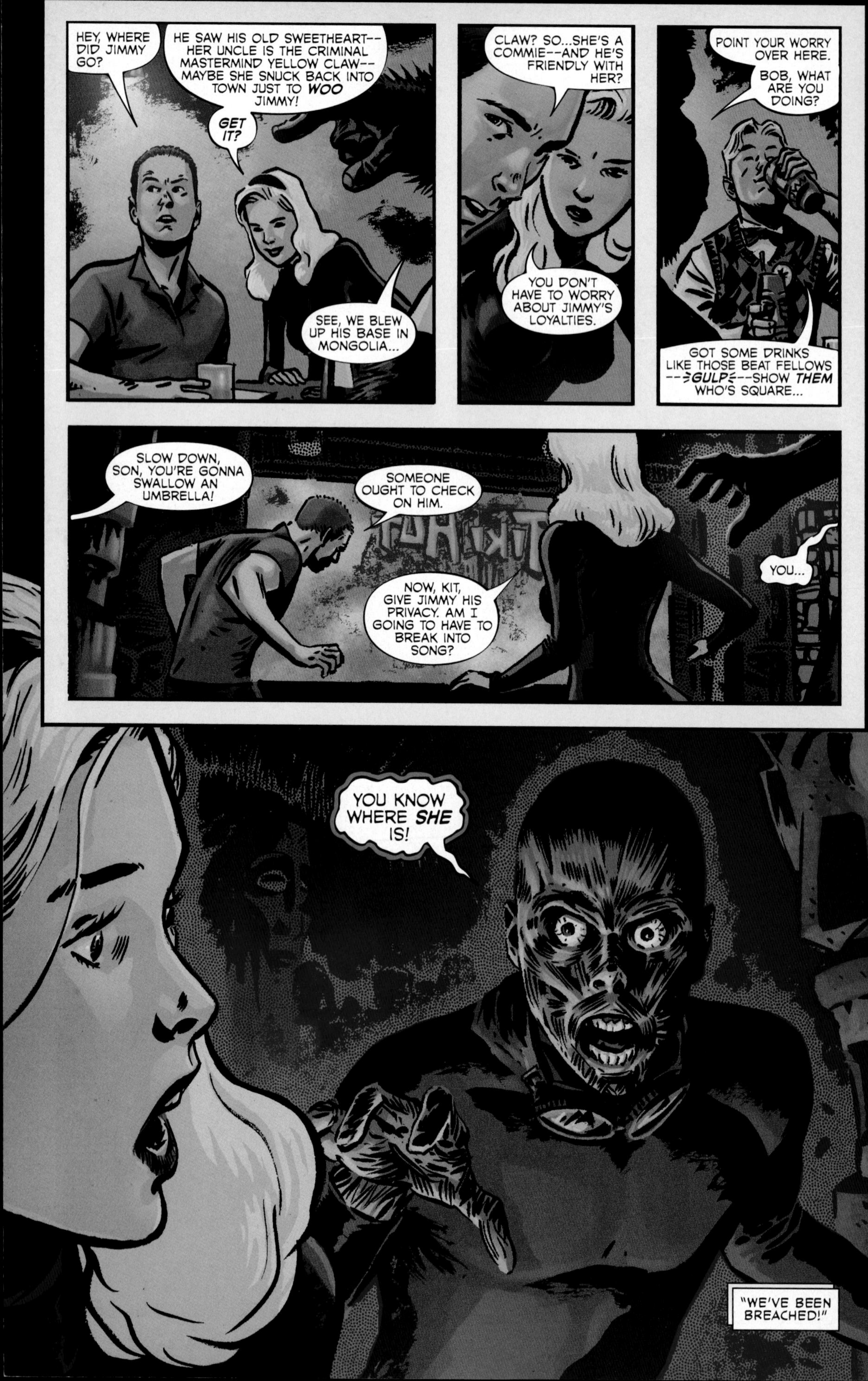
HEY, WHERE DID JIMMY GO?
HE SAW HIS OLD SWEETHEART-- HER UNCLE IS THE CRIMINAL MASTERMIND YELLOW CLAW-- MAYBE SHE SNUCK BACK INTO TOWN JUST TO WOO JIMMY!
GET IT?
SEE, WE BLEW UP HIS BASE IN MONGOLIA...
CLAW? SO...SHE'S A COMMIE--AND HE'S FRIENDLY WITH HER?
YOU DON'T HAVE TO WORRY ABOUT JIMMY'S LOYALTIES.
POINT YOUR WORRY OVER HERE.
BOB, WHAT ARE YOU DOING?
GOT SOME DRINKS LIKE THOSE BEAT FELLOWS --GULP--SHOW THEM WHO'S SQUARE...
SLOW DOWN, SON, YOU'RE GONNA SWALLOW AN UMBRELLA!
SOMEONE OUGHT TO CHECK ON HIM.
NOW, KIT, GIVE JIMMY HIS PRIVACY. AM I GOING TO HAVE TO BREAK INTO SONG?
YOU...
YOU KNOW WHERE SHE IS!
"WE'VE BEEN BREACHED!"

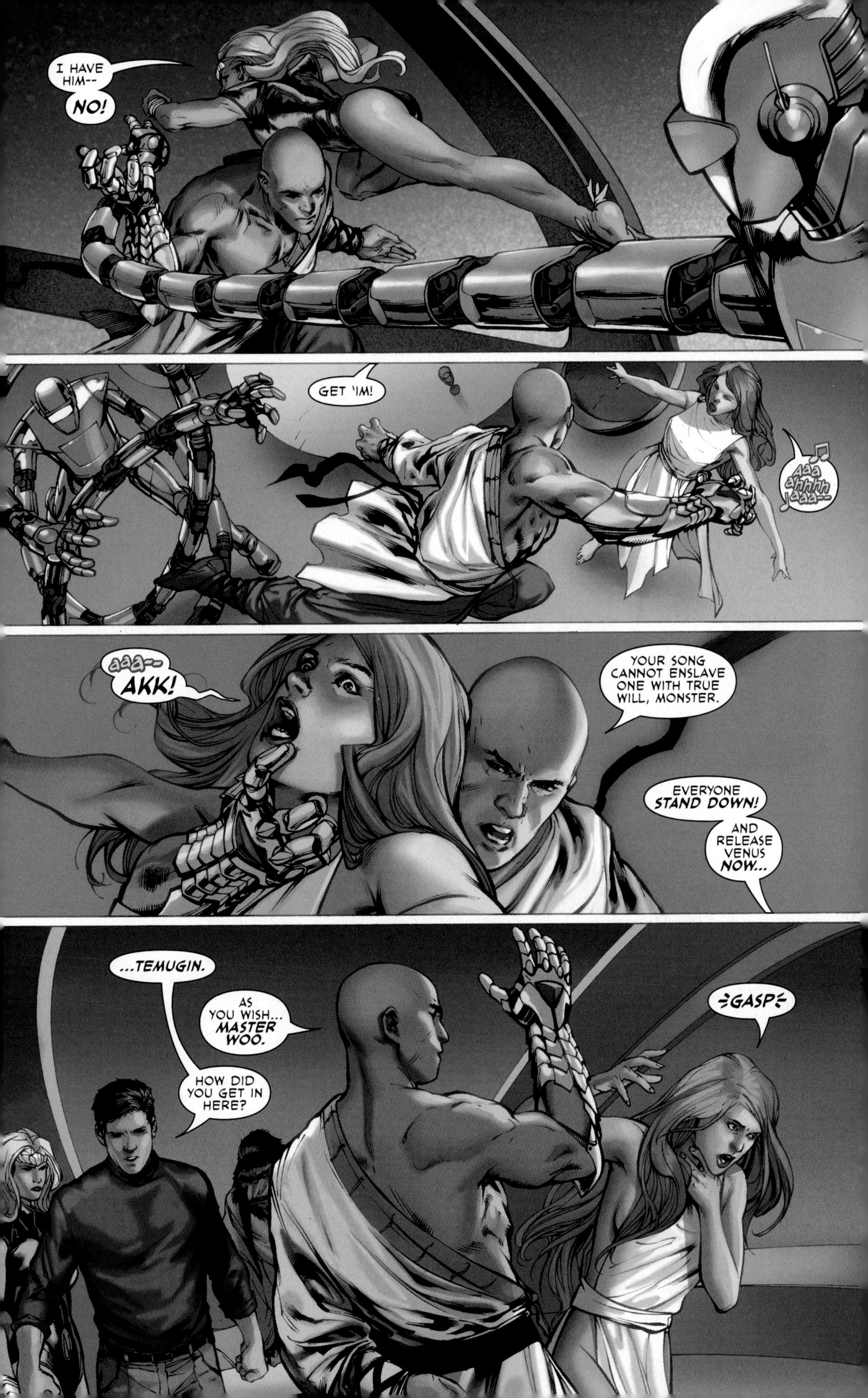
I HAVE HIM-- NO!
GET 'IM!
Aaa ahhhh aaa--
aaa-- AKK!
YOUR SONG CANNOT ENSLAVE ONE WITH TRUE WILL, MONSTER.
EVERYONE STAND DOWN!
AND RELEASE VENUS NOW...
...TEMUGIN.
AS YOU WISH... MASTER WOO.
HOW DID YOU GET IN HERE?
GASP

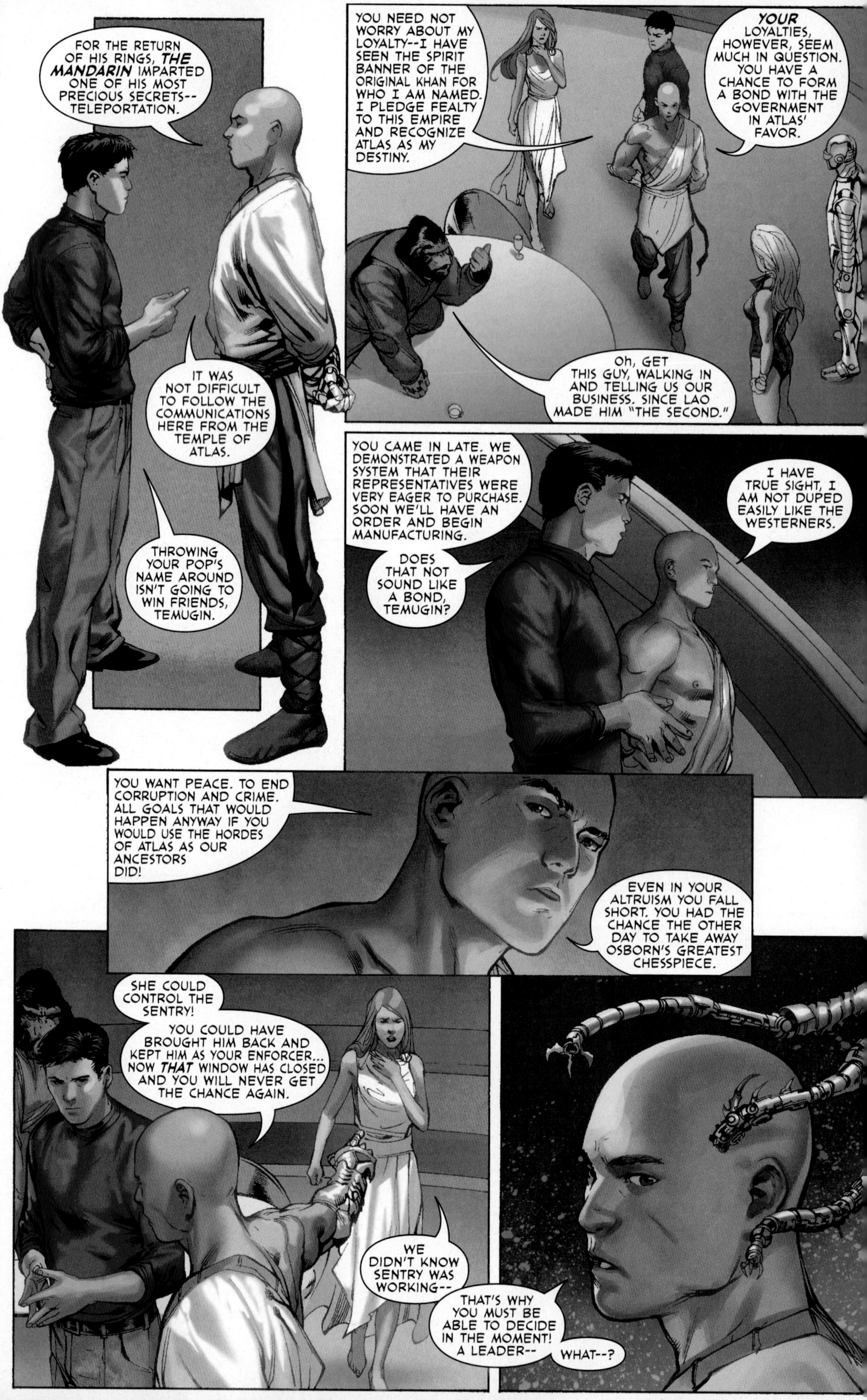
FOR THE RETURN OF HIS RINGS, THE MANDARIN IMPARTED ONE OF HIS MOST PRECIOUS SECRETS-- TELEPORTATION.
IT WAS NOT DIFFICULT TO FOLLOW THE COMMUNICATIONS HERE FROM THE TEMPLE OF ATLAS.
THROWING YOUR POP'S NAME AROUND ISN'T GOING TO WIN FRIENDS, TEMUGIN.
YOU NEED NOT WORRY ABOUT MY LOYALTY--I HAVE SEEN THE SPIRIT BANNER OF THE ORIGINAL KHAN FOR WHO I AM NAMED. I PLEDGE FEALTY TO THIS EMPIRE AND RECOGNIZE ATLAS AS MY DESTINY.
YOUR LOYALTIES, HOWEVER, SEEM MUCH IN QUESTION. YOU HAVE A CHANCE TO FORM A BOND WITH THE GOVERNMENT IN ATLAS' FAVOR.
Oh, GET THIS GUY, WALKING IN AND TELLING US OUR BUSINESS. SINCE LAO MADE HIM "THE SECOND."
YOU CAME IN LATE. WE DEMONSTRATED A WEAPON SYSTEM THAT THEIR REPRESENTATIVES WERE VERY EAGER TO PURCHASE. SOON WE'LL HAVE AN ORDER AND BEGIN MANUFACTURING.
DOES THAT NOT SOUND LIKE A BOND, TEMUGIN?
I HAVE TRUE SIGHT, I AM NOT DUPED EASILY LIKE THE WESTERNERS.
YOU WANT PEACE. TO END CORRUPTION AND CRIME. ALL GOALS THAT WOULD HAPPEN ANYWAY IF YOU WOULD USE THE HORDES OF ATLAS AS OUR ANCESTORS DID!
EVEN IN YOUR ALTRUISM YOU FALL SHORT. YOU HAD THE CHANCE THE OTHER DAY TO TAKE AWAY OSBORN'S GREATEST CHESSPIECE.
SHE COULD CONTROL THE SENTRY!
YOU COULD HAVE BROUGHT HIM BACK AND KEPT HIM AS YOUR ENFORCER... NOW THAT WINDOW HAS CLOSED AND YOU WILL NEVER GET THE CHANCE AGAIN.
WE DIDN'T KNOW SENTRY WAS WORKING--
THAT'S WHY YOU MUST BE ABLE TO DECIDE IN THE MOMENT! A LEADER--
WHAT--?

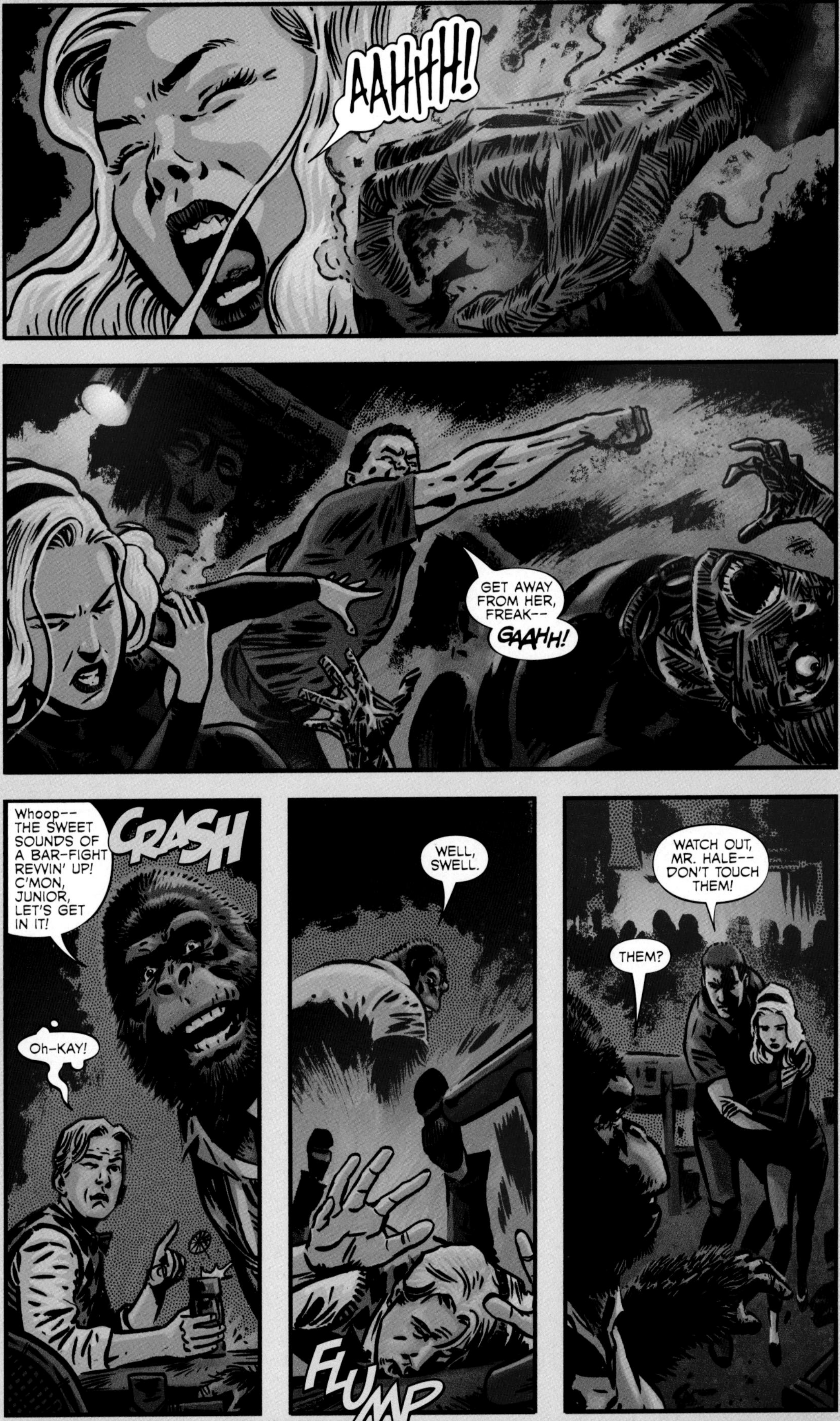
AAHHH!
GET AWAY FROM HER, FREAK-- GAAHH!
Whoop-- THE SWEET SOUNDS OF A BAR-FIGHT REVVIN' UP! C'MON, JUNIOR, LET'S GET IN IT!
CRASH
Oh-KAY!
WELL, SWELL.
FLUMP
WATCH OUT, MR. HALE-- DON'T TOUCH THEM!
THEM?

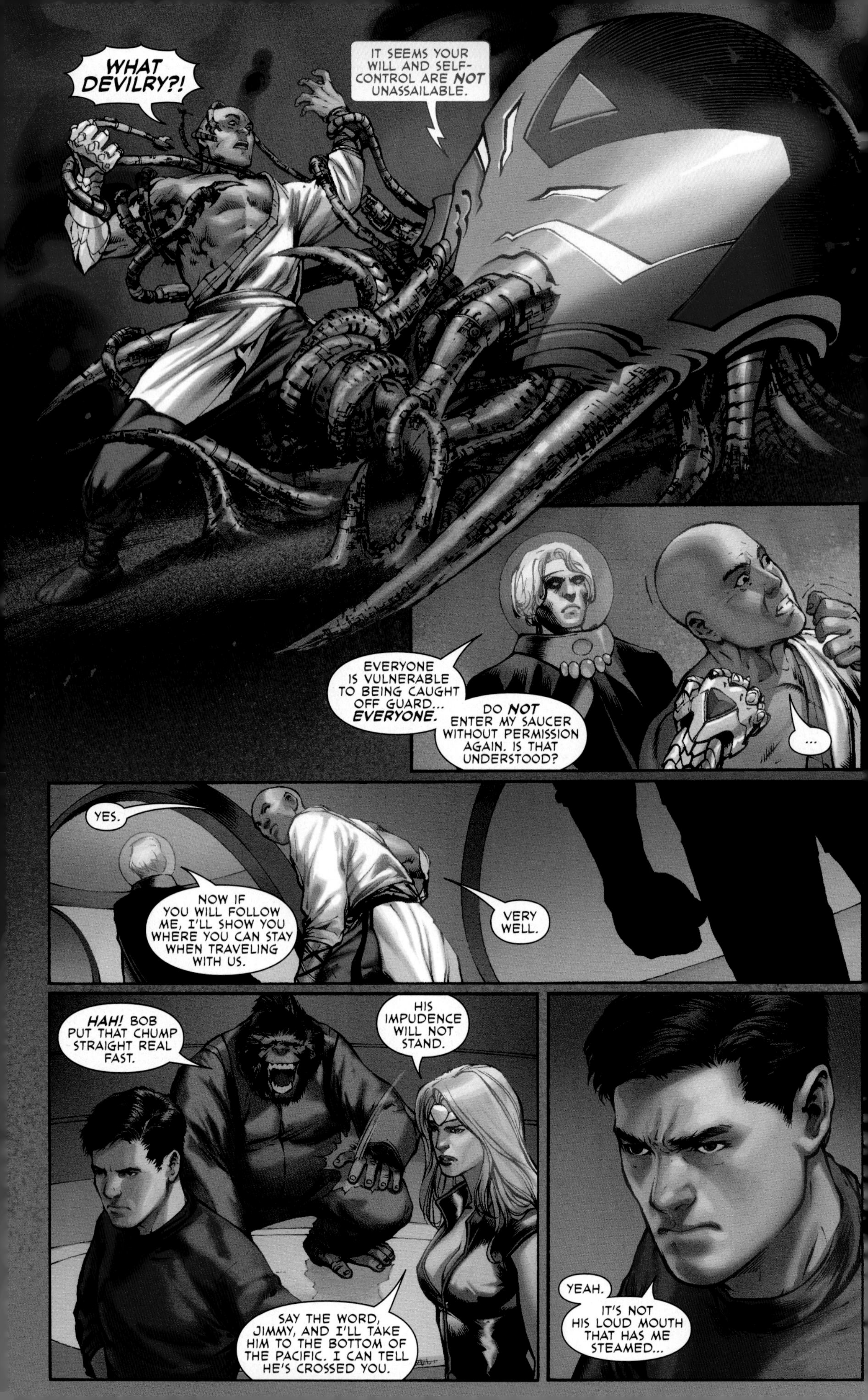
WHAT DEVILRY?!
IT SEEMS YOUR WILL AND SELF-CONTROL ARE NOT UNASSAILABLE.
EVERYONE IS VULNERABLE TO BEING CAUGHT OFF GUARD... EVERYONE.
DO NOT ENTER MY SAUCER WITHOUT PERMISSION AGAIN. IS THAT UNDERSTOOD?
...
YES.
NOW IF YOU WILL FOLLOW ME, I'LL SHOW YOU WHERE YOU CAN STAY WHEN TRAVELING WITH US.
VERY WELL.
HAH! BOB PUT THAT CHUMP STRAIGHT REAL FAST.
HIS IMPUDENCE WILL NOT STAND.
SAY THE WORD, JIMMY, AND I'LL TAKE HIM TO THE BOTTOM OF THE PACIFIC. I CAN TELL HE'S CROSSED YOU.
YEAH.
IT'S NOT HIS LOUD MOUTH THAT HAS ME STEAMED...

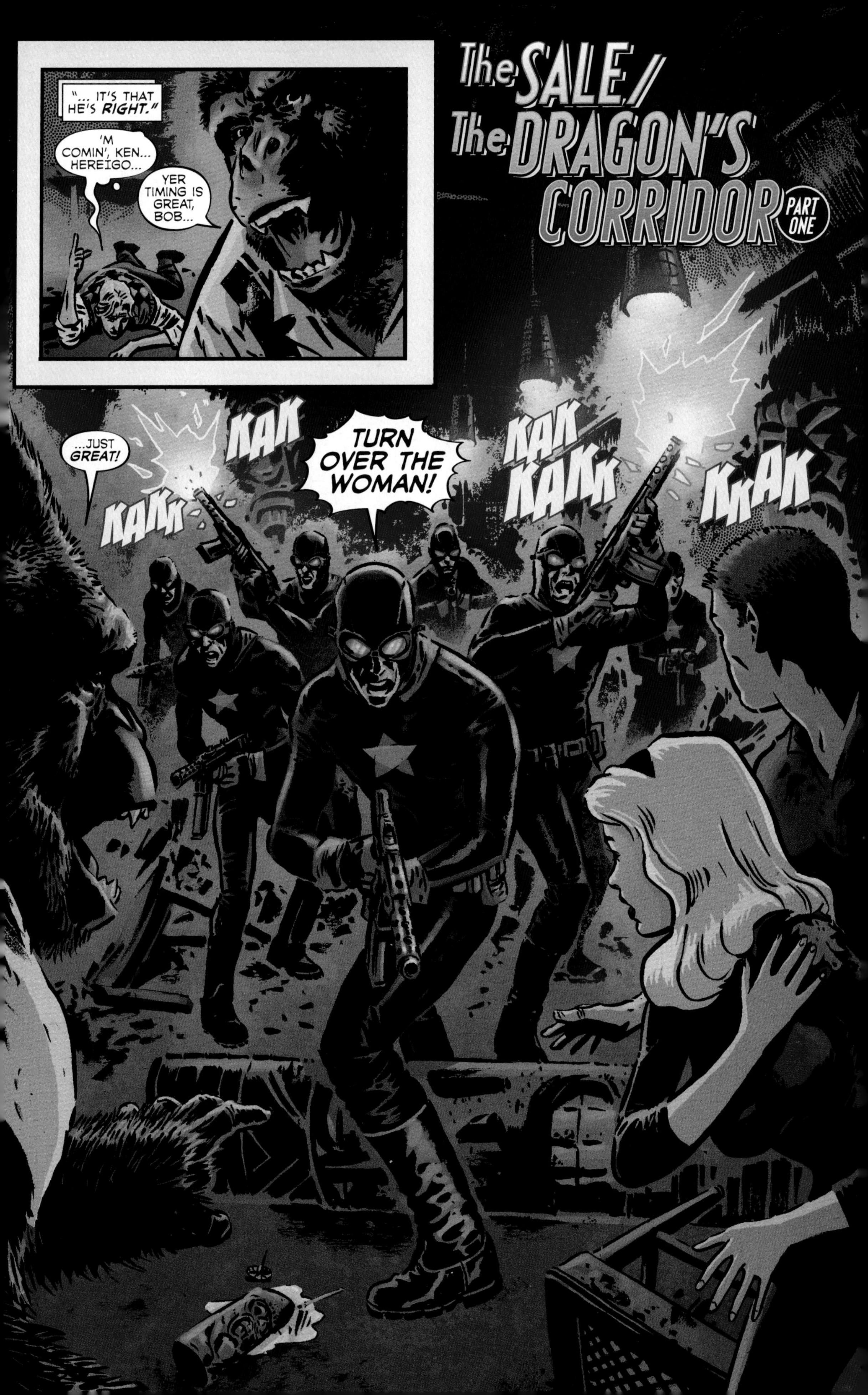
"... IT'S THAT HE'S *RIGHT.*"
'M COMIN', KEN... HEREÍGO...
YER TIMING IS GREAT, BOB...
The SALE/ The DRAGON'S CORRIDOR PART ONE
...JUST *GREAT!*
KAKK
KAK
TURN OVER THE WOMAN!
KAK KAKK
KKAK

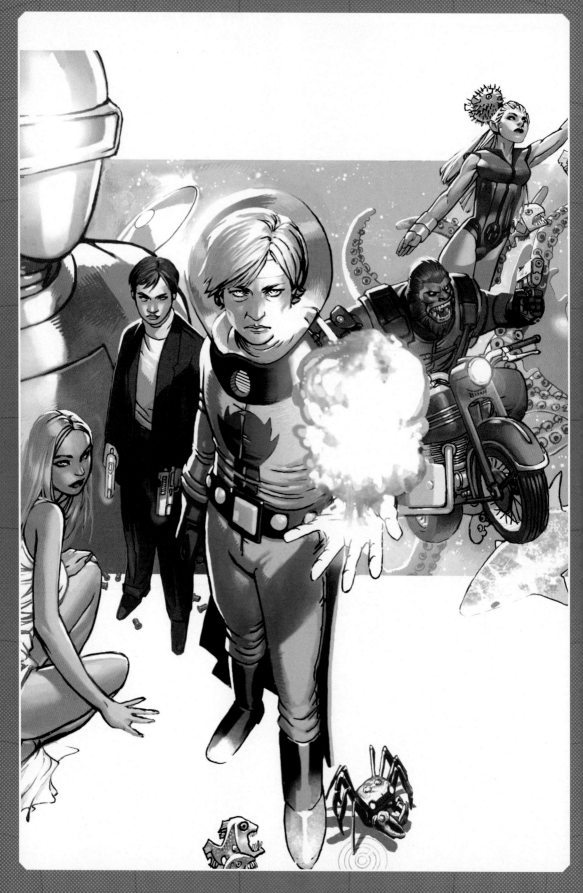

AGENTS OF ATLAS (2009) #2 2ND-PRINTING VARIANT BY
CHRIS BACHALO

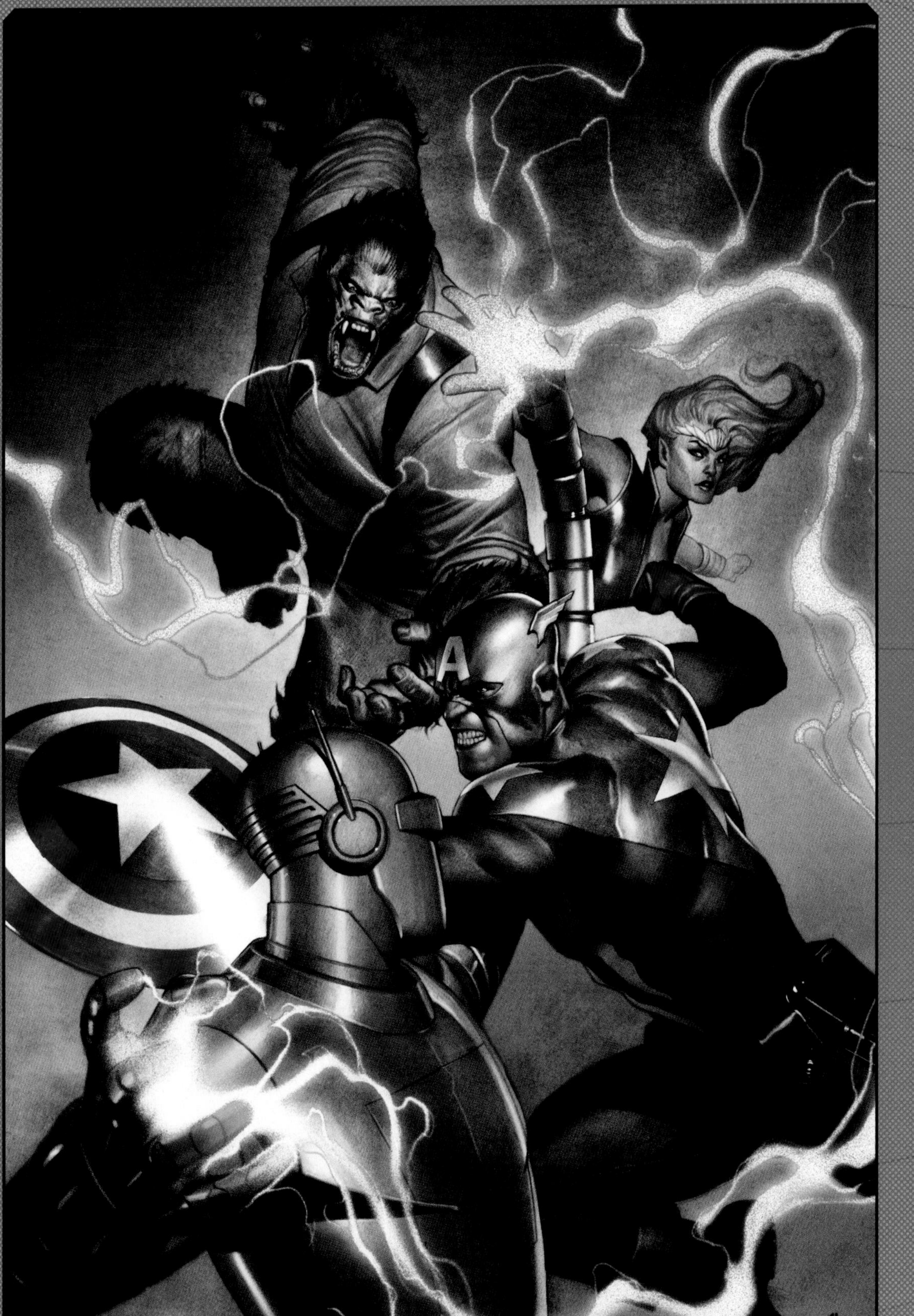

AGENTS OF ATLAS (2009) **3**

1958.

⟨WHERE IS THE CHINESE WOMAN?⟩

⟨ANSWER NOW OR WE WILL BURN THIS BUILDING DOWN!⟩

VMMM

Emm...

...lebbn.

THUMP

HANG ON, I THINK I KNOW WHERE THIS GAL YOU'RE LOOKING FOR IS.

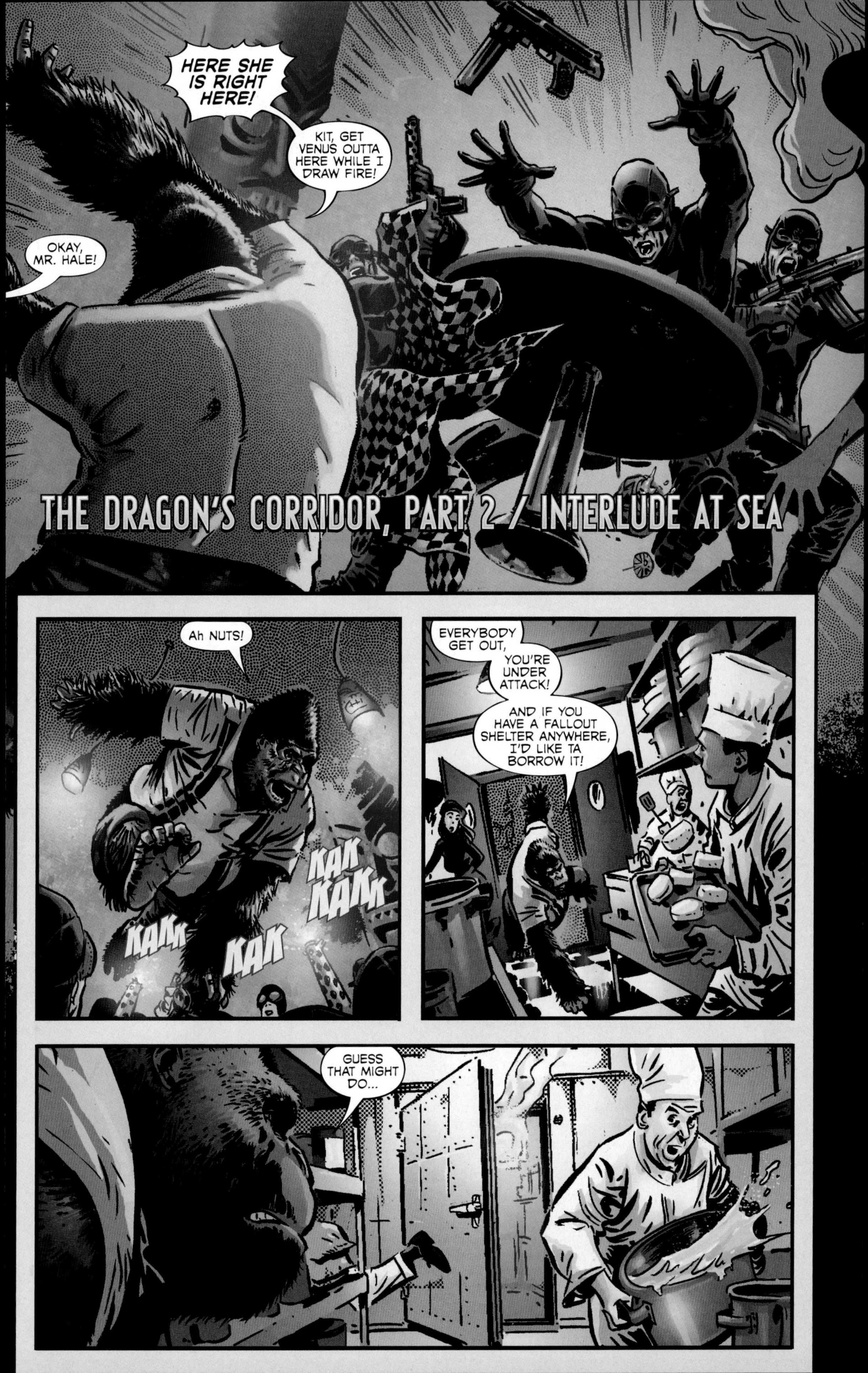
HERE SHE IS RIGHT HERE!
KIT, GET VENUS OUTTA HERE WHILE I DRAW FIRE!
OKAY, MR. HALE!
THE DRAGON'S CORRIDOR, PART 2 / INTERLUDE AT SEA
Ah NUTS!
KAK KAKK
KAKK
KAK
EVERYBODY GET OUT,
YOU'RE UNDER ATTACK!
AND IF YOU HAVE A FALLOUT SHELTER ANYWHERE, I'D LIKE TA BORROW IT!
GUESS THAT MIGHT DO...

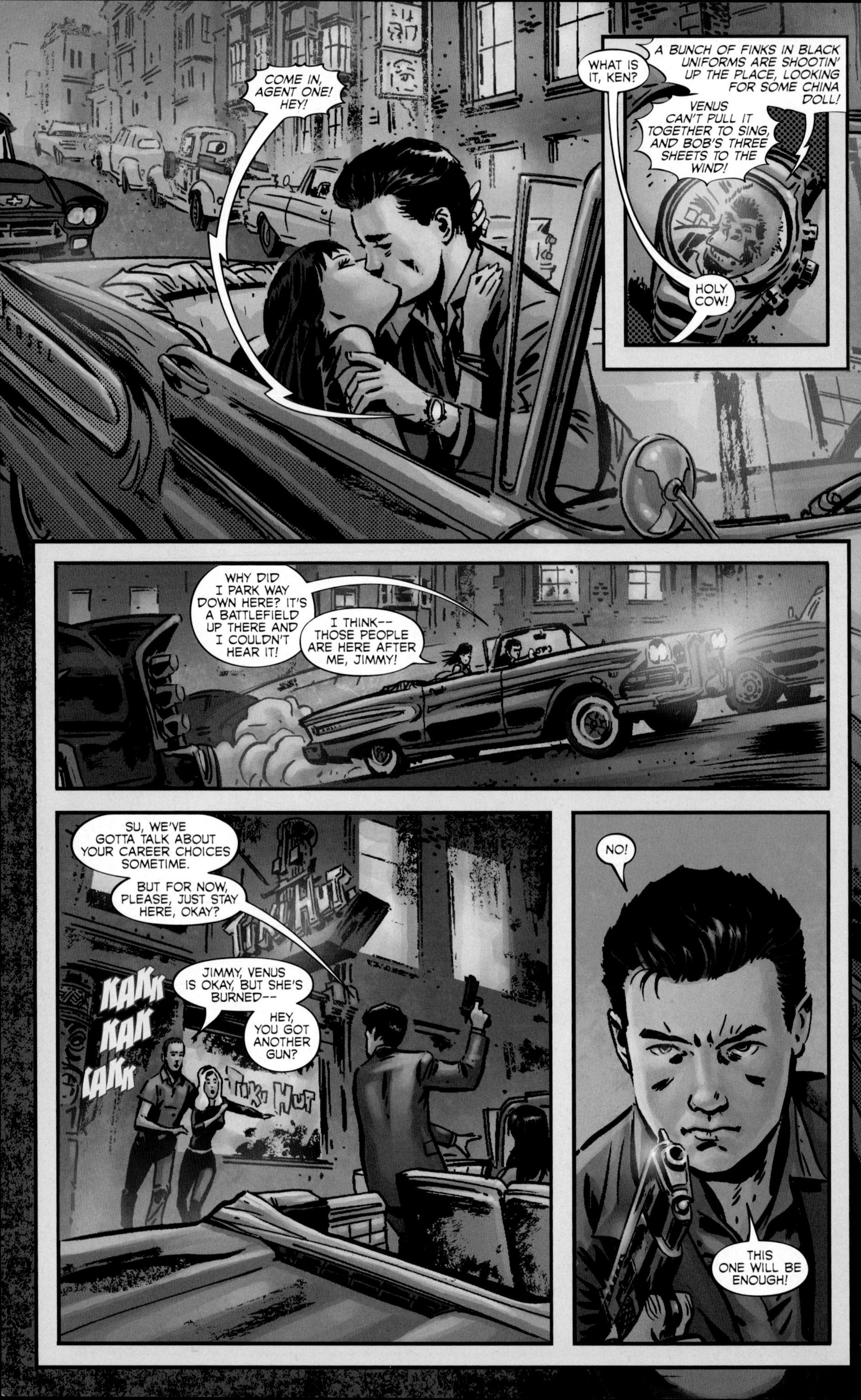
COME IN, AGENT ONE! HEY!
WHAT IS IT, KEN?
A BUNCH OF FINKS IN BLACK UNIFORMS ARE SHOOTIN' UP THE PLACE, LOOKING FOR SOME CHINA DOLL!
VENUS CAN'T PULL IT TOGETHER TO SING, AND BOB'S THREE SHEETS TO THE WIND!
HOLY COW!
WHY DID I PARK WAY DOWN HERE? IT'S A BATTLEFIELD UP THERE AND I COULDN'T HEAR IT!
I THINK-- THOSE PEOPLE ARE HERE AFTER ME, JIMMY!
SU, WE'VE GOTTA TALK ABOUT YOUR CAREER CHOICES SOMETIME.
BUT FOR NOW, PLEASE, JUST STAY HERE, OKAY?
KAKK KAK KAKK
JIMMY, VENUS IS OKAY, BUT SHE'S BURNED--
HEY, YOU GOT ANOTHER GUN?
TIKI HUT
NO!
THIS ONE WILL BE ENOUGH!

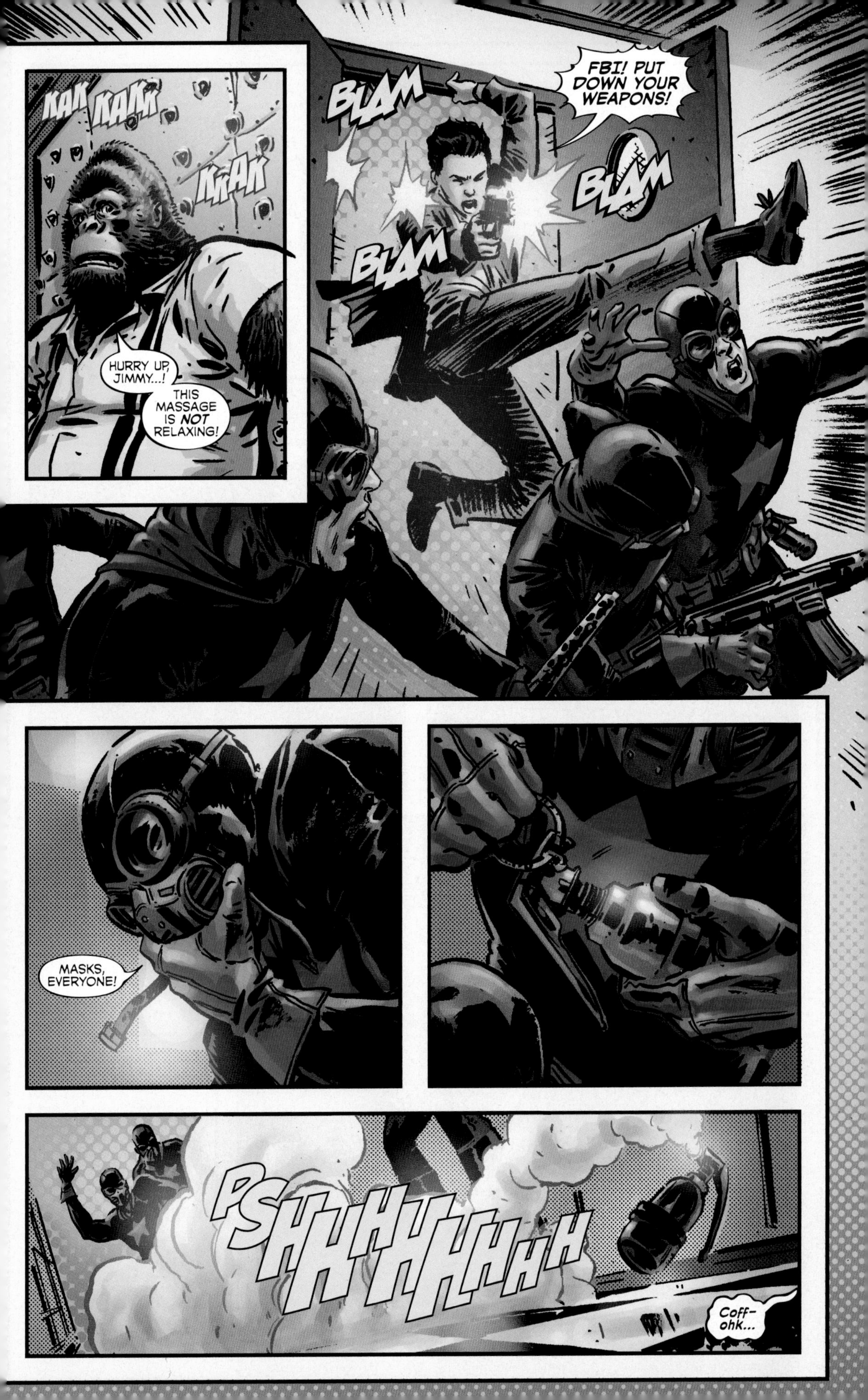

KAK KAKK
KRAK
HURRY UP, JIMMY...!
THIS MASSAGE IS ***NOT*** RELAXING!
BLAM
FBI! PUT DOWN YOUR WEAPONS!
BLAM
BLAM
MASKS, EVERYONE!
PSHHHHHHHHHH
Coff-ohk...

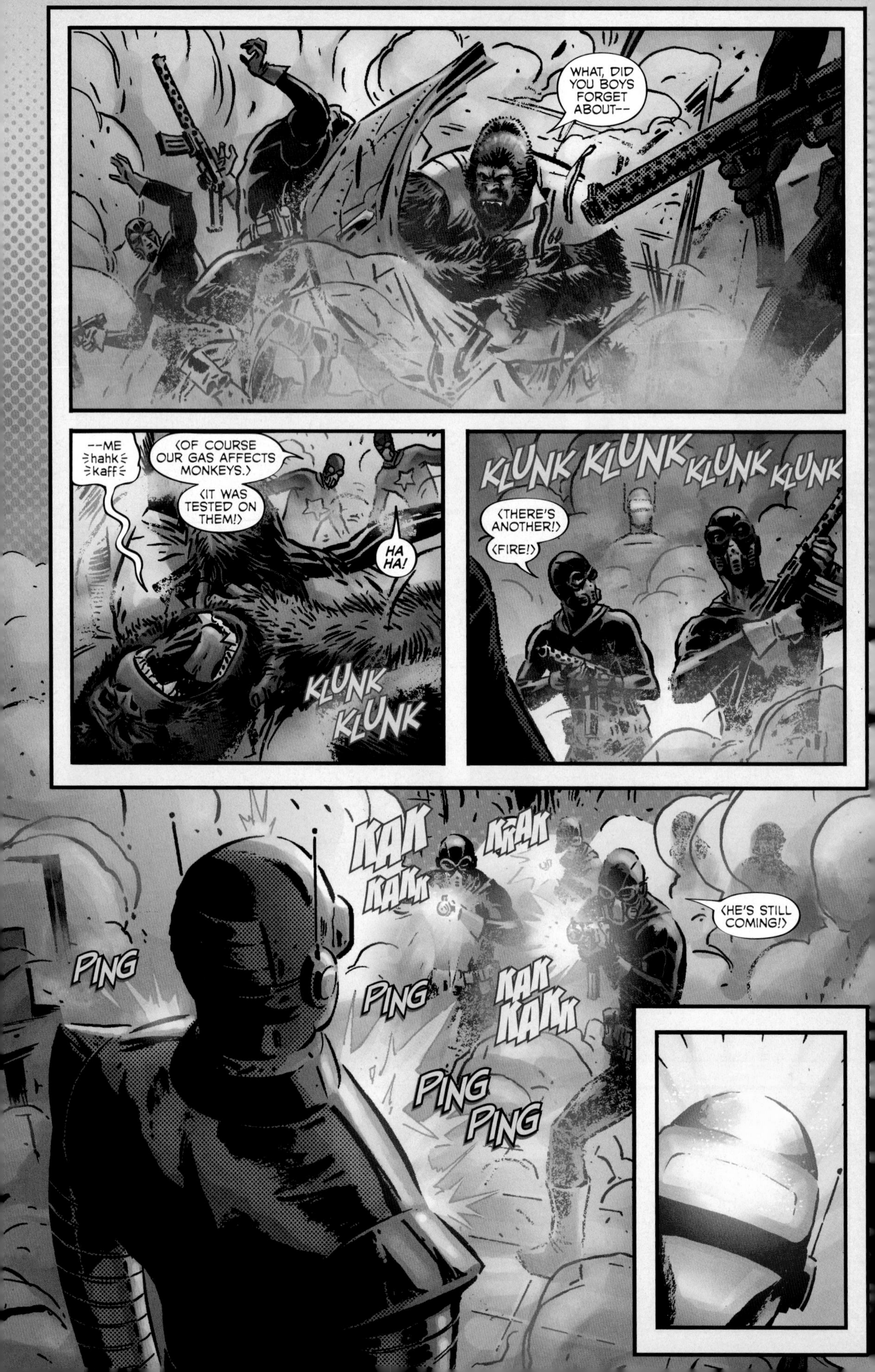

WHAT, DID YOU BOYS FORGET ABOUT--
--ME hahk kaff
⟨OF COURSE OUR GAS AFFECTS MONKEYS.⟩
⟨IT WAS TESTED ON THEM!⟩
HA HA!
KLUNK KLUNK
KLUNK KLUNK KLUNK KLUNK
⟨THERE'S ANOTHER!⟩
⟨FIRE!⟩
KAK KAKK
KRAK
⟨HE'S STILL COMING!⟩
PING
PING
KAK KAKK
PING PING

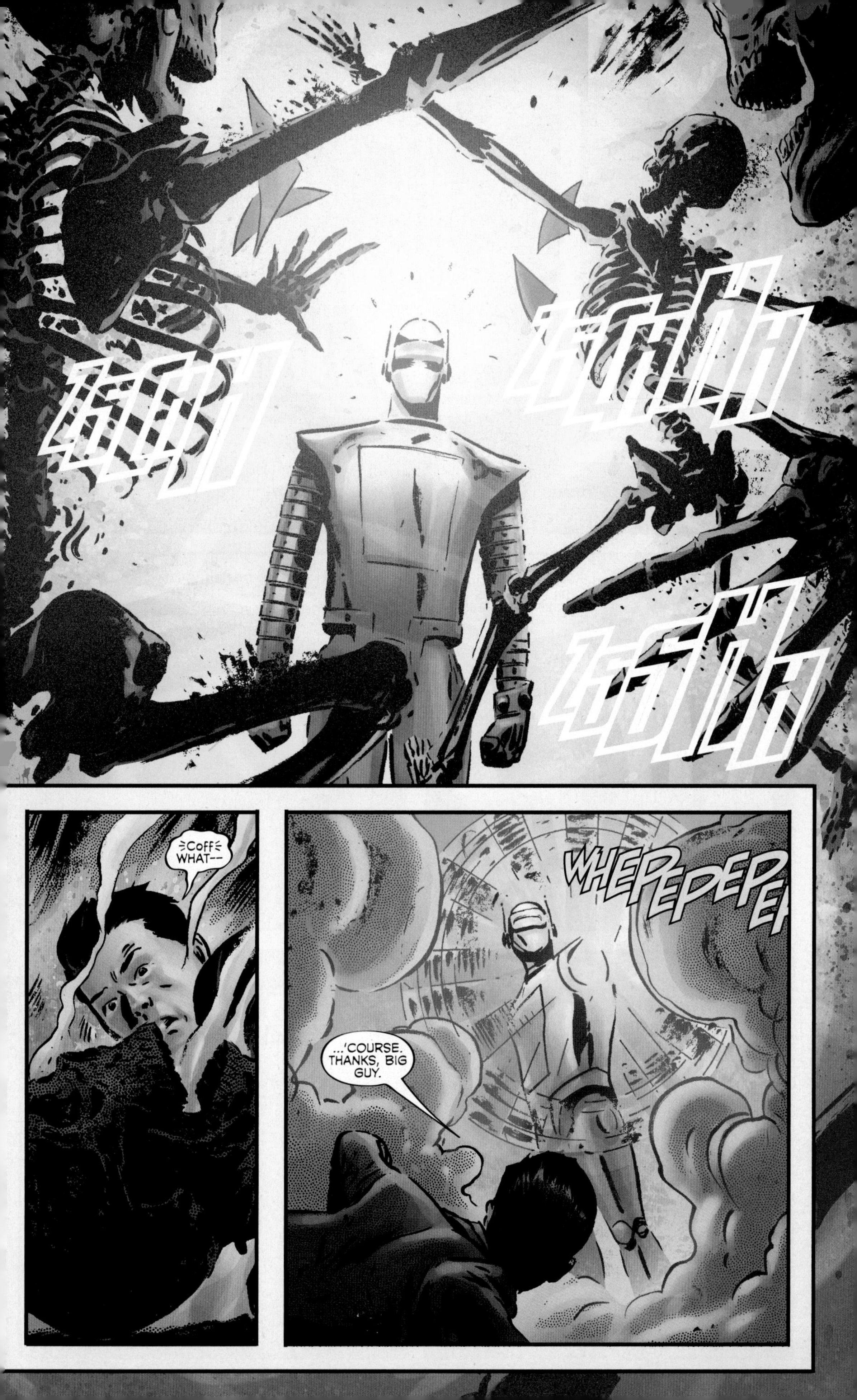

Coff
WHAT--
WHEPEPEPEP
...'COURSE. THANKS, BIG GUY.

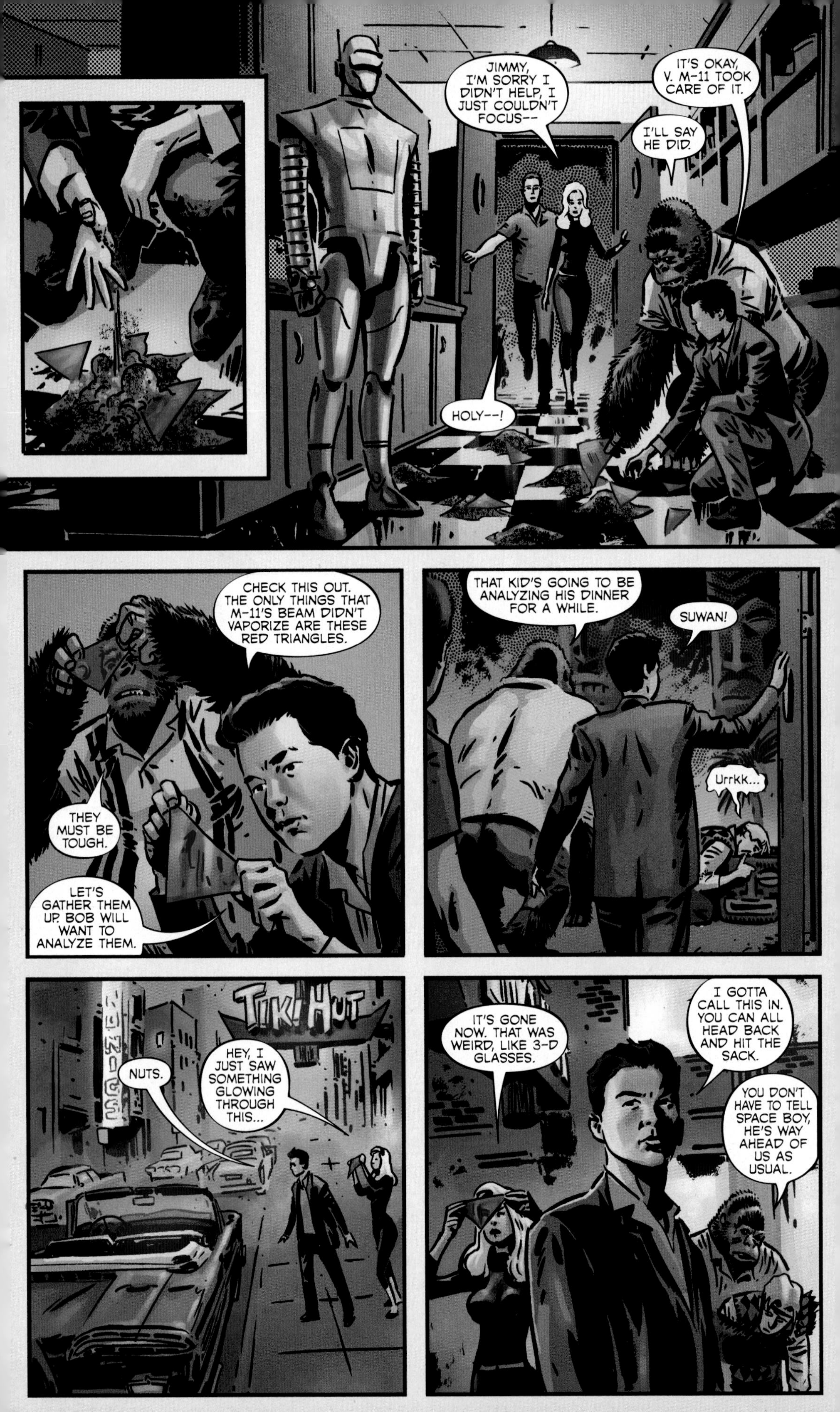
JIMMY, I'M SORRY I DIDN'T HELP, I JUST COULDN'T FOCUS--
IT'S OKAY, V. M-11 TOOK CARE OF IT.
I'LL SAY HE DID.
HOLY--!
CHECK THIS OUT. THE ONLY THINGS THAT M-11'S BEAM DIDN'T VAPORIZE ARE THESE RED TRIANGLES.
THEY MUST BE TOUGH.
LET'S GATHER THEM UP. BOB WILL WANT TO ANALYZE THEM.
THAT KID'S GOING TO BE ANALYZING HIS DINNER FOR A WHILE.
SUWAN!
Urrkk...
TIKI HUT
NUTS.
HEY, I JUST SAW SOMETHING GLOWING THROUGH THIS...
IT'S GONE NOW. THAT WAS WEIRD, LIKE 3-D GLASSES.
I GOTTA CALL THIS IN. YOU CAN ALL HEAD BACK AND HIT THE SACK.
YOU DON'T HAVE TO TELL SPACE BOY, HE'S WAY AHEAD OF US AS USUAL.

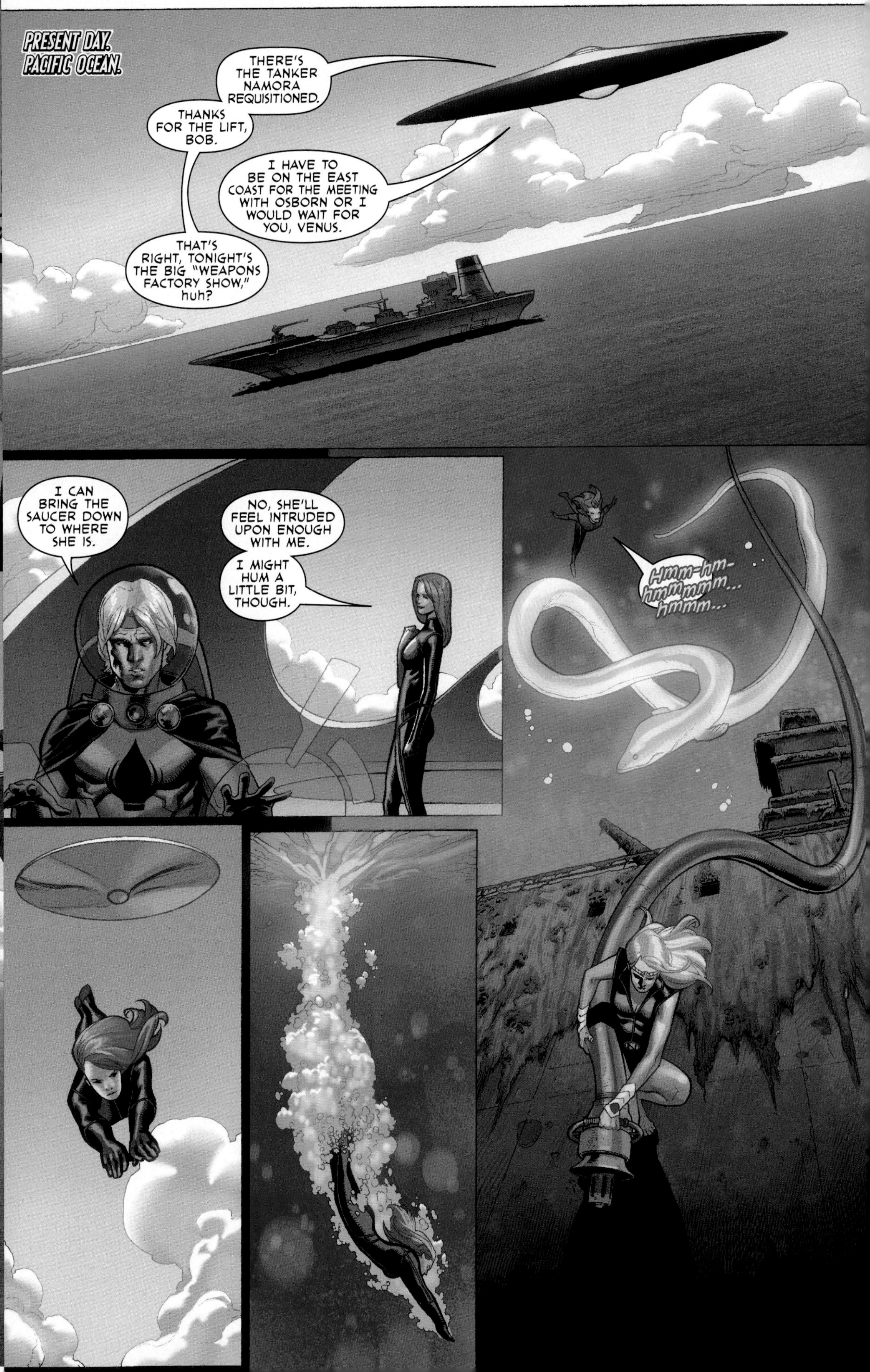
PRESENT DAY. PACIFIC OCEAN.
THERE'S THE TANKER NAMORA REQUISITIONED.
THANKS FOR THE LIFT, BOB.
I HAVE TO BE ON THE EAST COAST FOR THE MEETING WITH OSBORN OR I WOULD WAIT FOR YOU, VENUS.
THAT'S RIGHT, TONIGHT'S THE BIG "WEAPONS FACTORY SHOW," huh?
I CAN BRING THE SAUCER DOWN TO WHERE SHE IS.
NO, SHE'LL FEEL INTRUDED UPON ENOUGH WITH ME.
I MIGHT HUM A LITTLE BIT, THOUGH.
Hmm-hm-hmmmmm... hmmm...

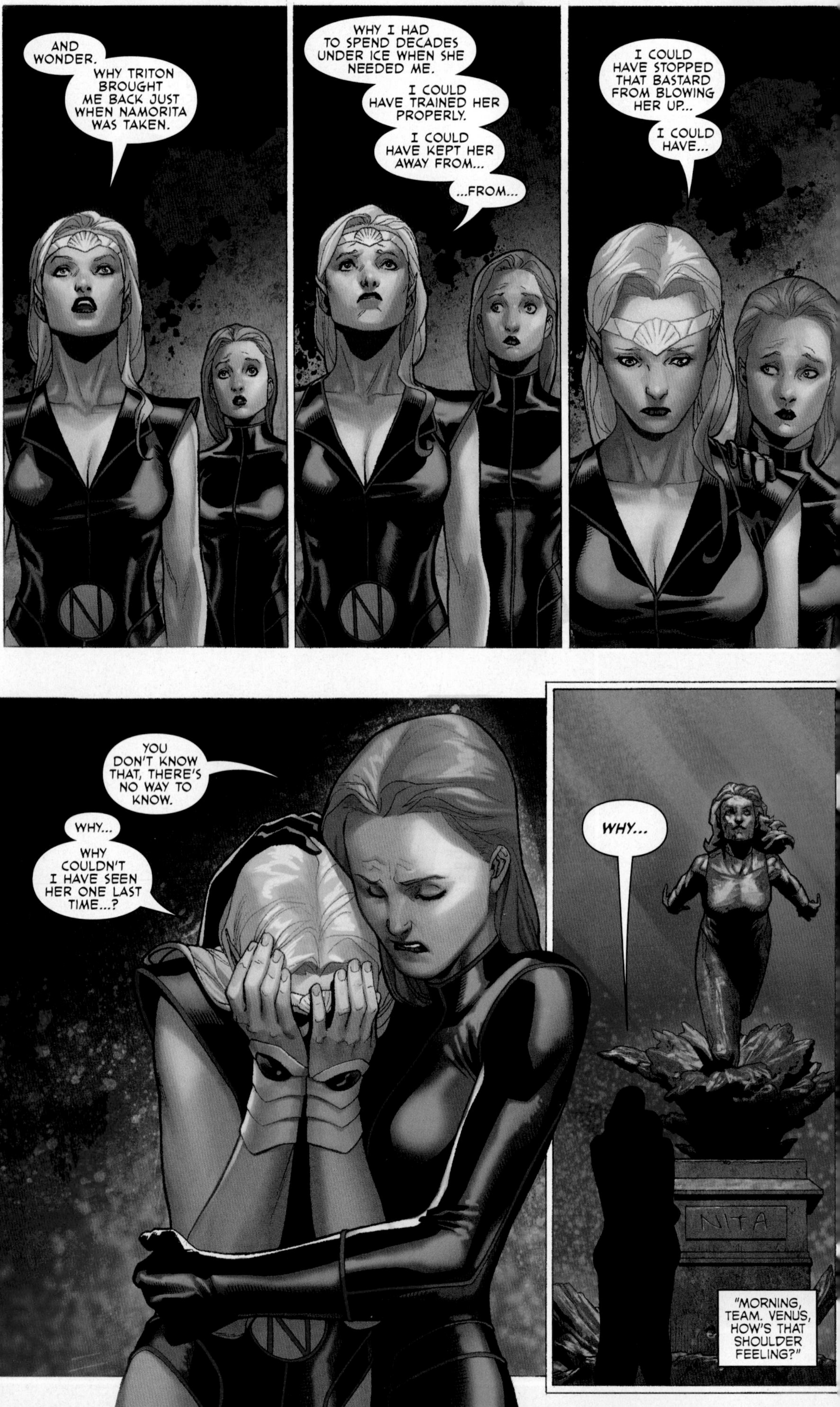
AND WONDER.
WHY TRITON BROUGHT ME BACK JUST WHEN NAMORITA WAS TAKEN.
WHY I HAD TO SPEND DECADES UNDER ICE WHEN SHE NEEDED ME.
I COULD HAVE TRAINED HER PROPERLY.
I COULD HAVE KEPT HER AWAY FROM...
...FROM...
I COULD HAVE STOPPED THAT BASTARD FROM BLOWING HER UP...
I COULD HAVE...
YOU DON'T KNOW THAT, THERE'S NO WAY TO KNOW.
WHY...
WHY COULDN'T I HAVE SEEN HER ONE LAST TIME...?
WHY...
NITA
"MORNING, TEAM. VENUS, HOW'S THAT SHOULDER FEELING?"

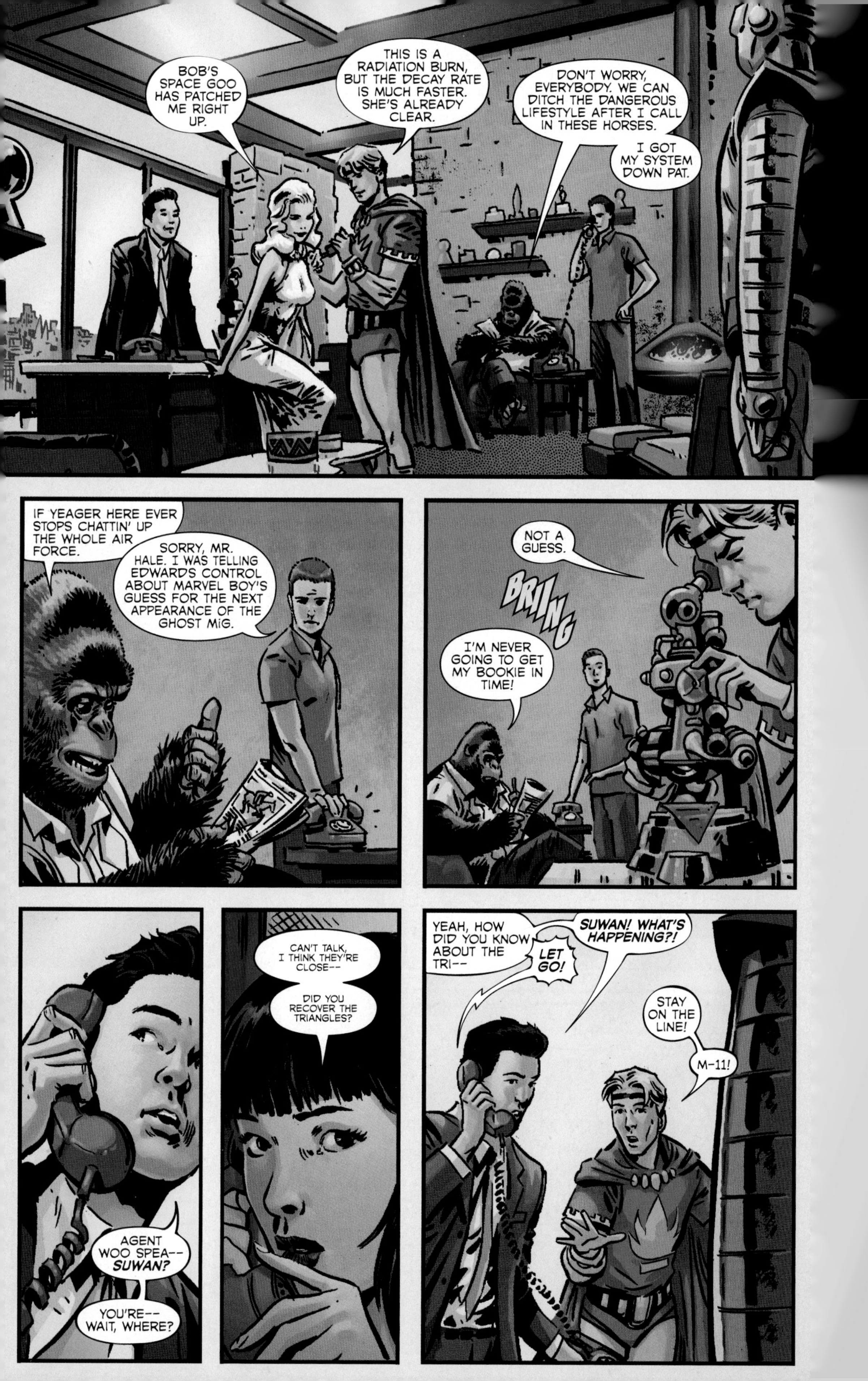
BOB'S SPACE GOO HAS PATCHED ME RIGHT UP.
THIS IS A RADIATION BURN, BUT THE DECAY RATE IS MUCH FASTER. SHE'S ALREADY CLEAR.
DON'T WORRY, EVERYBODY. WE CAN DITCH THE DANGEROUS LIFESTYLE AFTER I CALL IN THESE HORSES.
I GOT MY SYSTEM DOWN PAT.
IF YEAGER HERE EVER STOPS CHATTIN' UP THE WHOLE AIR FORCE.
SORRY, MR. HALE. I WAS TELLING EDWARDS CONTROL ABOUT MARVEL BOY'S GUESS FOR THE NEXT APPEARANCE OF THE GHOST MiG.
NOT A GUESS.
BRING
I'M NEVER GOING TO GET MY BOOKIE IN TIME!
AGENT WOO SPEA-- SUWAN?
YOU'RE-- WAIT, WHERE?
CAN'T TALK, I THINK THEY'RE CLOSE--
DID YOU RECOVER THE TRIANGLES?
YEAH, HOW DID YOU KNOW ABOUT THE TRI--
LET GO!
SUWAN! WHAT'S HAPPENING?!
STAY ON THE LINE!
M-11!

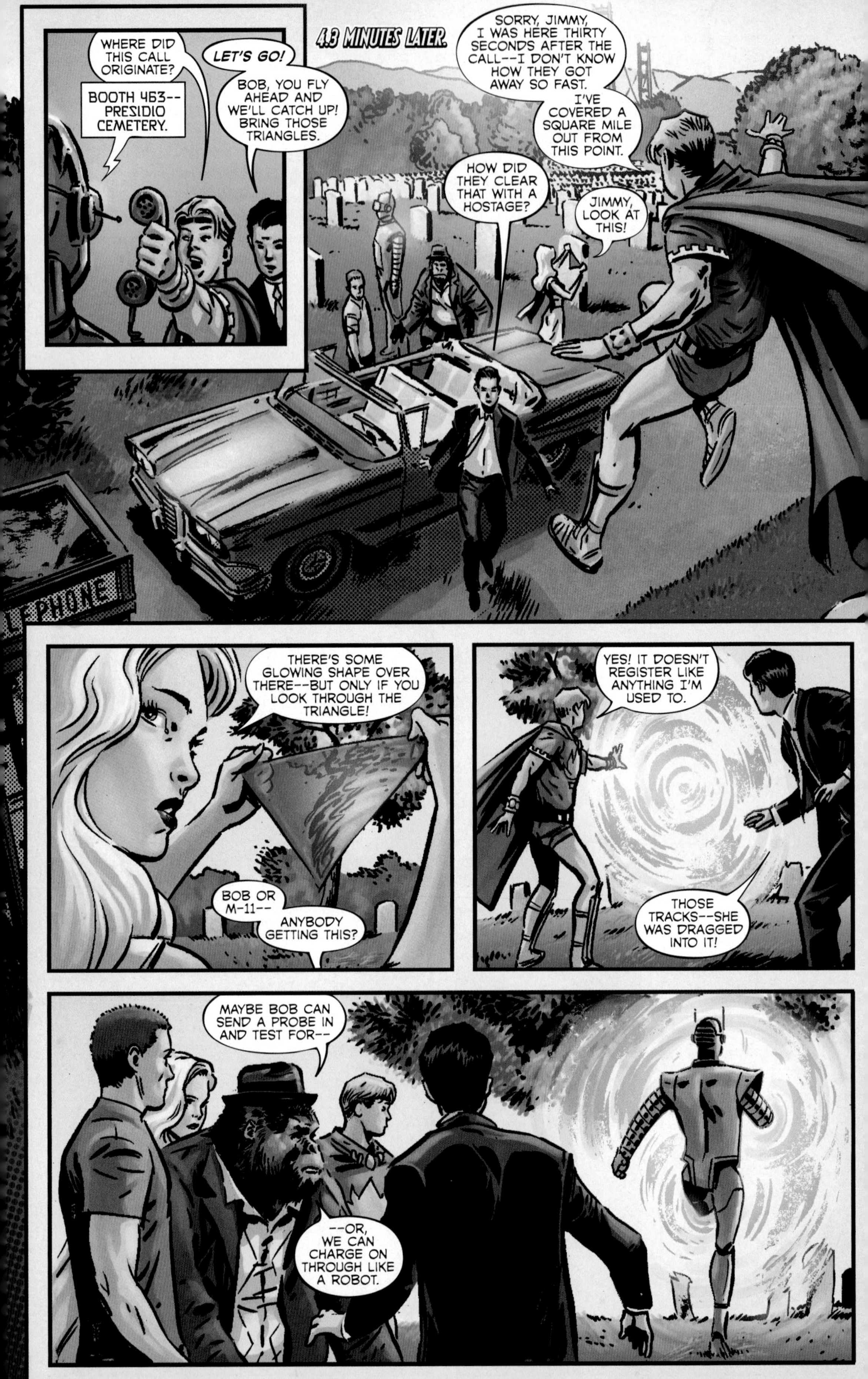

WHERE DID THIS CALL ORIGINATE?
BOOTH 463--PRESIDIO CEMETERY.
LET'S GO!
BOB, YOU FLY AHEAD AND WE'LL CATCH UP! BRING THOSE TRIANGLES.
4.3 MINUTES LATER.
SORRY, JIMMY, I WAS HERE THIRTY SECONDS AFTER THE CALL--I DON'T KNOW HOW THEY GOT AWAY SO FAST.
I'VE COVERED A SQUARE MILE OUT FROM THIS POINT.
HOW DID THEY CLEAR THAT WITH A HOSTAGE?
JIMMY, LOOK AT THIS!
THERE'S SOME GLOWING SHAPE OVER THERE--BUT ONLY IF YOU LOOK THROUGH THE TRIANGLE!
BOB OR M-11--
ANYBODY GETTING THIS?
YES! IT DOESN'T REGISTER LIKE ANYTHING I'M USED TO.
THOSE TRACKS--SHE WAS DRAGGED INTO IT!
MAYBE BOB CAN SEND A PROBE IN AND TEST FOR--
--OR, WE CAN CHARGE ON THROUGH LIKE A ROBOT.

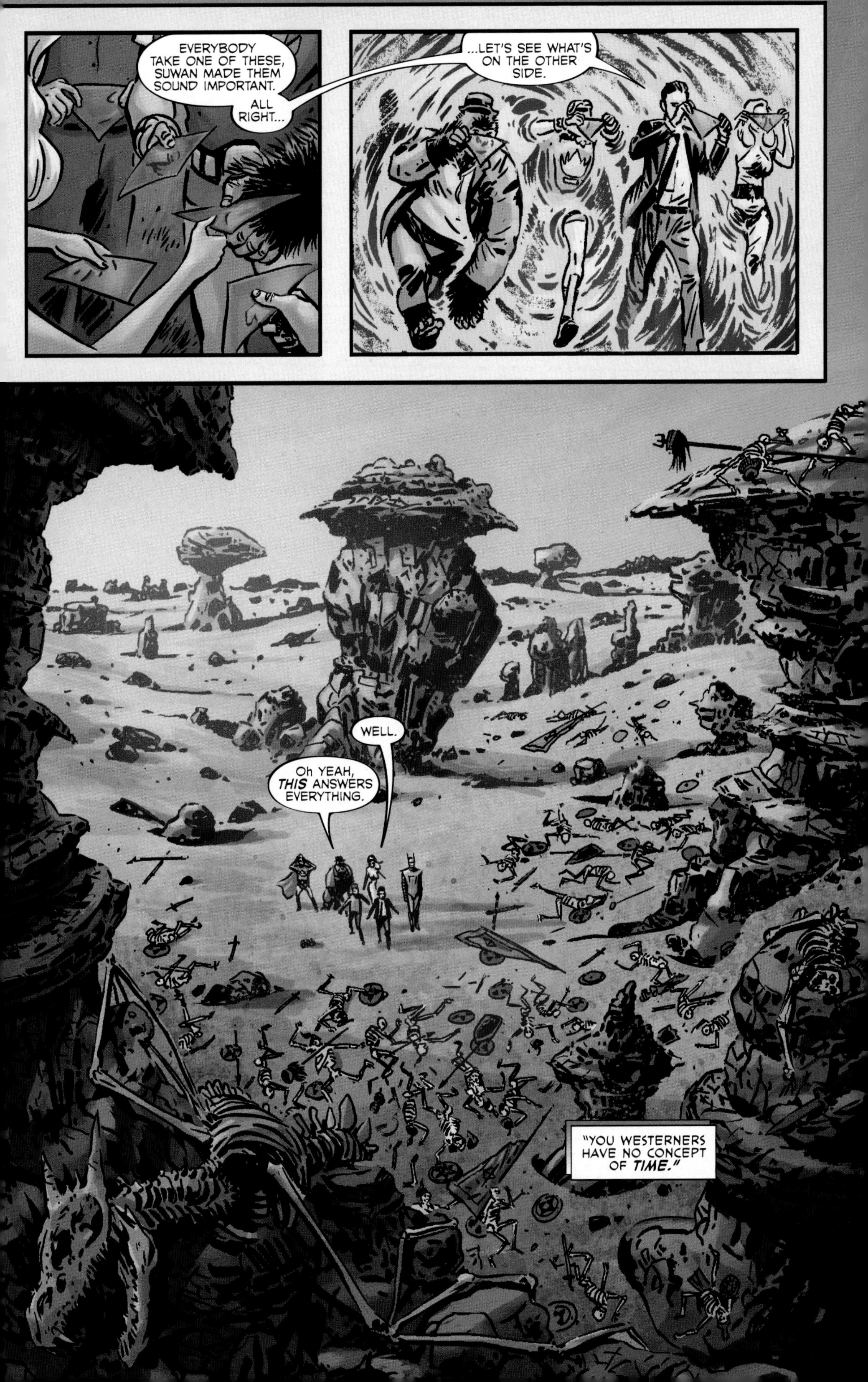
EVERYBODY TAKE ONE OF THESE, SUWAN MADE THEM SOUND IMPORTANT.
ALL RIGHT...
...LET'S SEE WHAT'S ON THE OTHER SIDE.
WELL.
Oh YEAH, *THIS* ANSWERS EVERYTHING.
"YOU WESTERNERS HAVE NO CONCEPT OF *TIME.*"

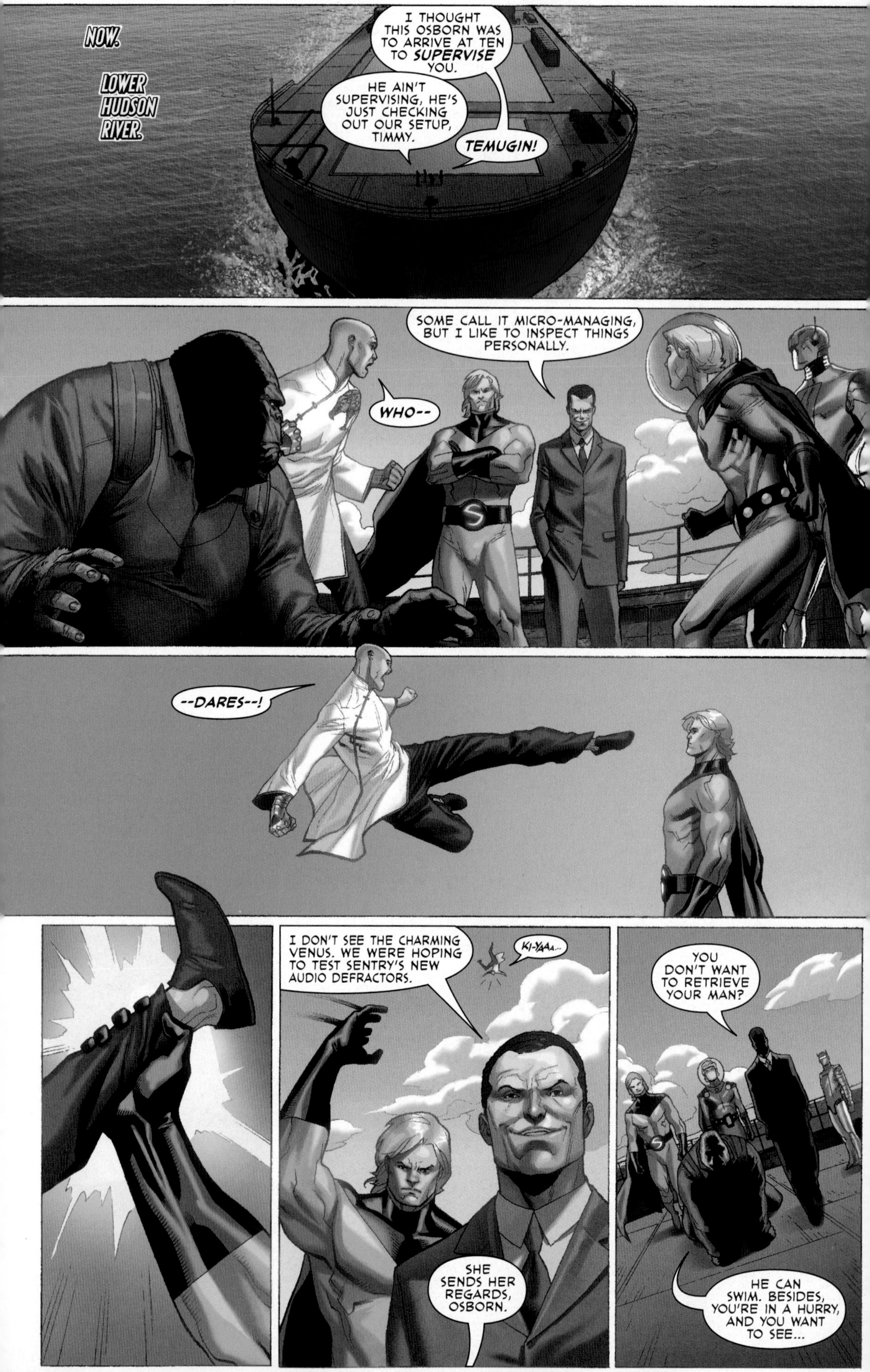
NOW.
LOWER HUDSON RIVER.
I THOUGHT THIS OSBORN WAS TO ARRIVE AT TEN TO SUPERVISE YOU.
HE AIN'T SUPERVISING, HE'S JUST CHECKING OUT OUR SETUP, TIMMY.
TEMUGIN!
WHO--
SOME CALL IT MICRO-MANAGING, BUT I LIKE TO INSPECT THINGS PERSONALLY.
--DARES--!
I DON'T SEE THE CHARMING VENUS. WE WERE HOPING TO TEST SENTRY'S NEW AUDIO DEFRACTORS.
KI-YAAA...
SHE SENDS HER REGARDS, OSBORN.
YOU DON'T WANT TO RETRIEVE YOUR MAN?
HE CAN SWIM. BESIDES, YOU'RE IN A HURRY, AND YOU WANT TO SEE...

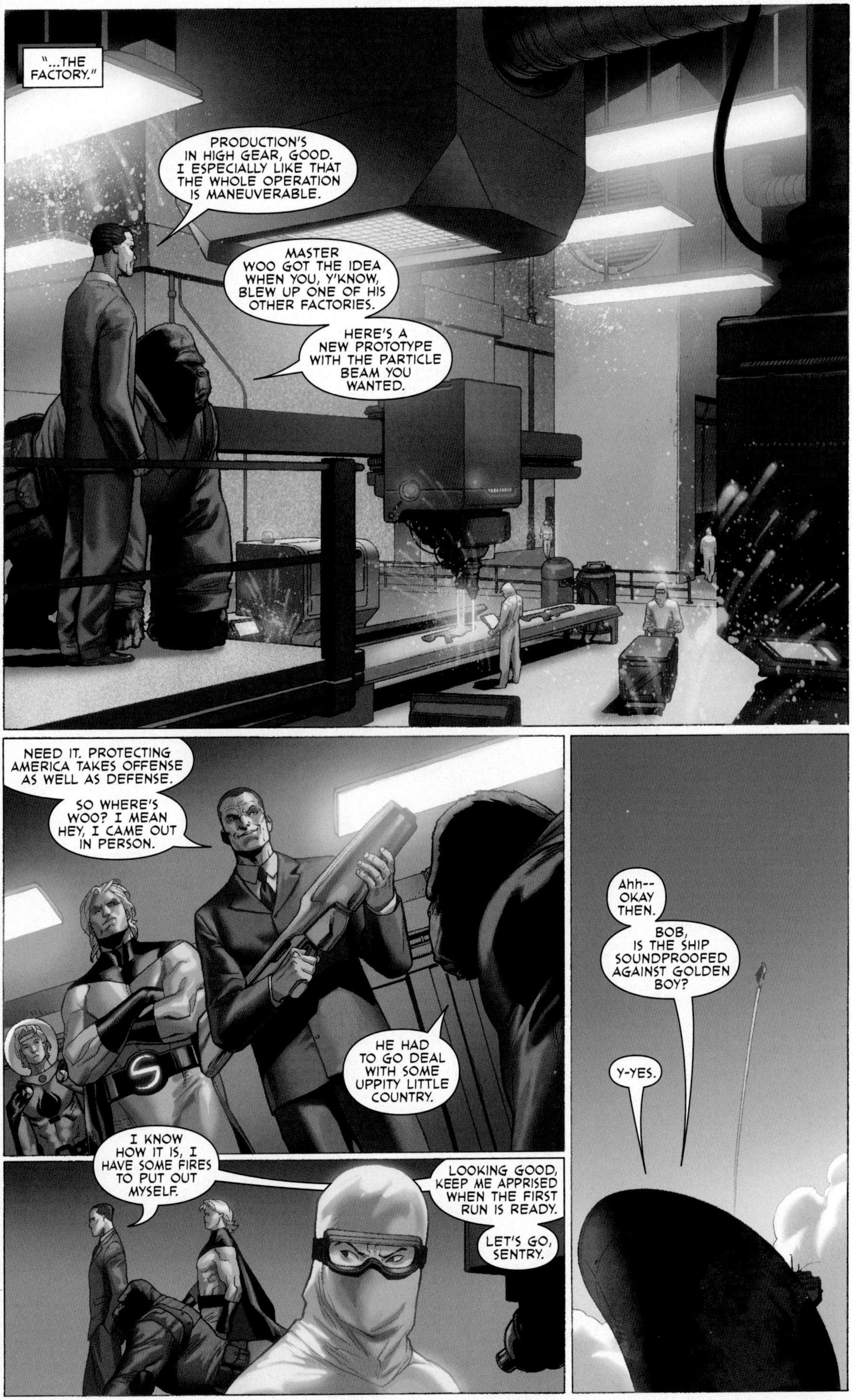
"...THE FACTORY."
PRODUCTION'S IN HIGH GEAR, GOOD. I ESPECIALLY LIKE THAT THE WHOLE OPERATION IS MANEUVERABLE.
MASTER WOO GOT THE IDEA WHEN YOU, Y'KNOW, BLEW UP ONE OF HIS OTHER FACTORIES.
HERE'S A NEW PROTOTYPE WITH THE PARTICLE BEAM YOU WANTED.
NEED IT. PROTECTING AMERICA TAKES OFFENSE AS WELL AS DEFENSE.
SO WHERE'S WOO? I MEAN HEY, I CAME OUT IN PERSON.
HE HAD TO GO DEAL WITH SOME UPPITY LITTLE COUNTRY.
I KNOW HOW IT IS, I HAVE SOME FIRES TO PUT OUT MYSELF.
LOOKING GOOD, KEEP ME APPRISED WHEN THE FIRST RUN IS READY.
LET'S GO, SENTRY.
Ahh-- OKAY THEN.
BOB, IS THE SHIP SOUNDPROOFED AGAINST GOLDEN BOY?
Y-YES.

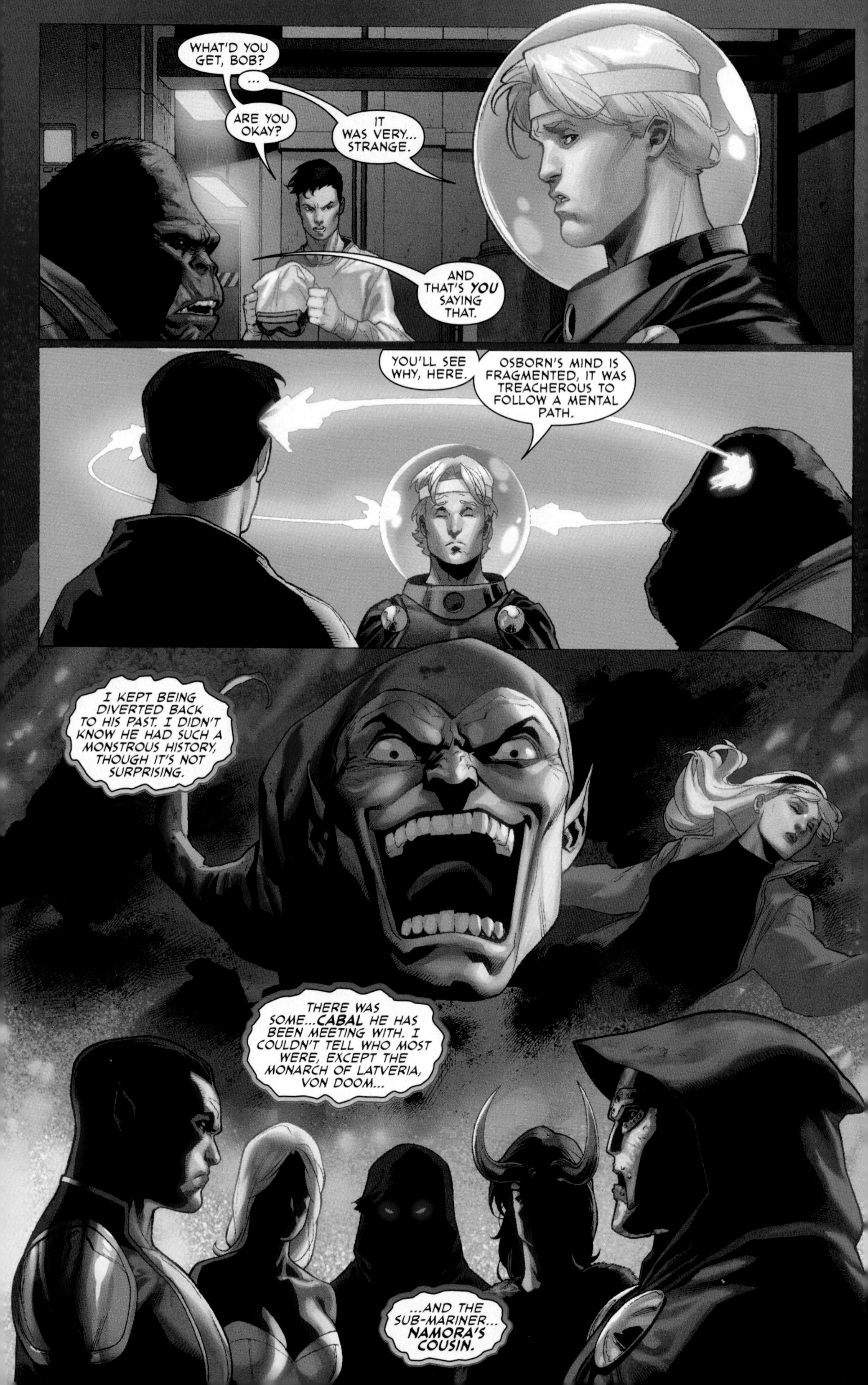
WHAT'D YOU GET, BOB?
...
ARE YOU OKAY?
IT WAS VERY... STRANGE.
AND THAT'S YOU SAYING THAT.
YOU'LL SEE WHY, HERE.
OSBORN'S MIND IS FRAGMENTED, IT WAS TREACHEROUS TO FOLLOW A MENTAL PATH.
I KEPT BEING DIVERTED BACK TO HIS PAST. I DIDN'T KNOW HE HAD SUCH A MONSTROUS HISTORY, THOUGH IT'S NOT SURPRISING.
THERE WAS SOME...CABAL HE HAS BEEN MEETING WITH. I COULDN'T TELL WHO MOST WERE, EXCEPT THE MONARCH OF LATVERIA, VON DOOM...
...AND THE SUB-MARINER... NAMORA'S COUSIN.

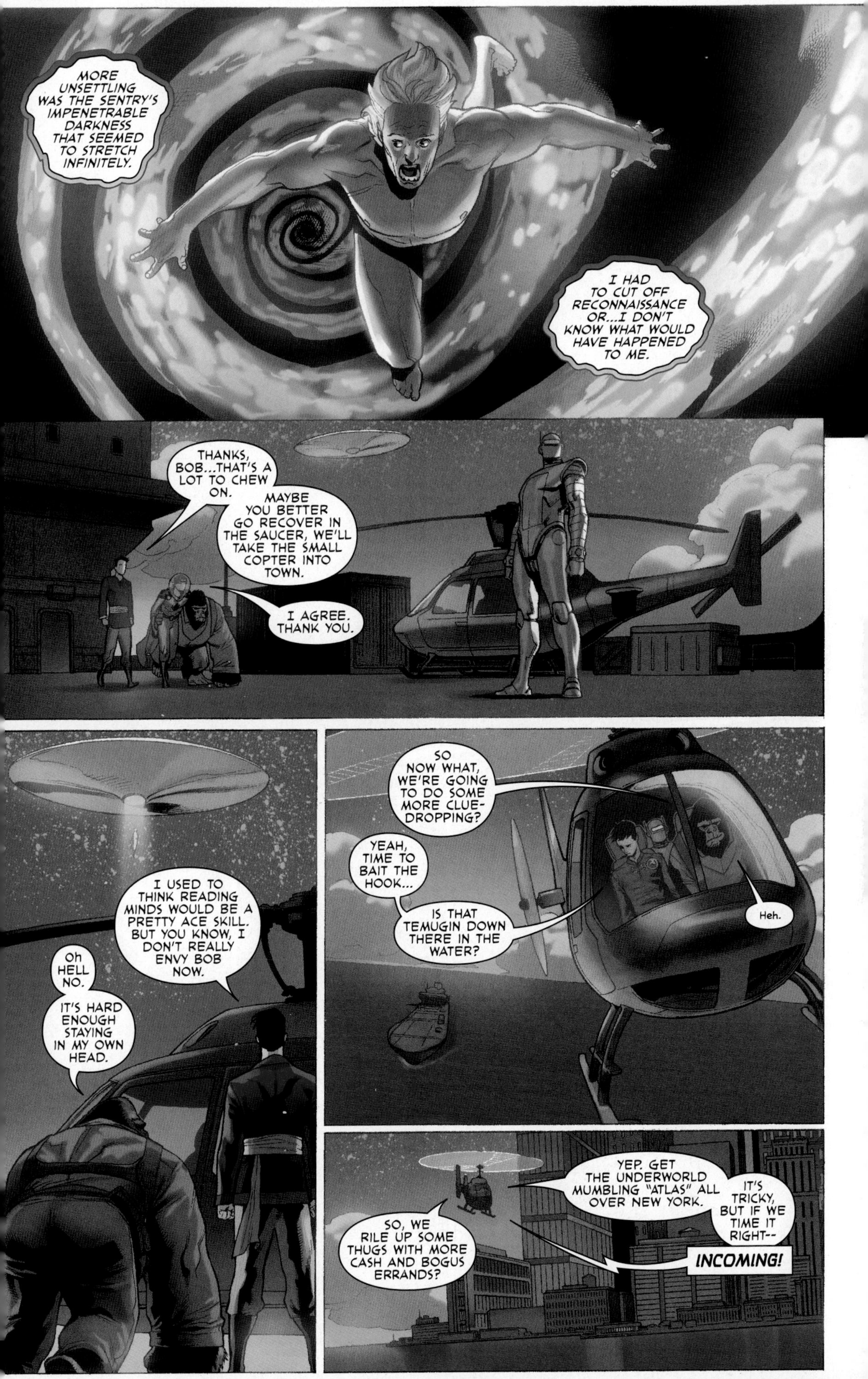
MORE UNSETTLING WAS THE SENTRY'S IMPENETRABLE DARKNESS THAT SEEMED TO STRETCH INFINITELY.
I HAD TO CUT OFF RECONNAISSANCE OR...I DON'T KNOW WHAT WOULD HAVE HAPPENED TO ME.
THANKS, BOB...THAT'S A LOT TO CHEW ON.
MAYBE YOU BETTER GO RECOVER IN THE SAUCER, WE'LL TAKE THE SMALL COPTER INTO TOWN.
I AGREE. THANK YOU.
I USED TO THINK READING MINDS WOULD BE A PRETTY ACE SKILL. BUT YOU KNOW, I DON'T REALLY ENVY BOB NOW.
Oh HELL NO.
IT'S HARD ENOUGH STAYING IN MY OWN HEAD.
SO NOW WHAT, WE'RE GOING TO DO SOME MORE CLUE-DROPPING?
YEAH, TIME TO BAIT THE HOOK...
IS THAT TEMUGIN DOWN THERE IN THE WATER?
Heh.
YEP. GET THE UNDERWORLD MUMBLING "ATLAS" ALL OVER NEW YORK.
SO, WE RILE UP SOME THUGS WITH MORE CASH AND BOGUS ERRANDS?
IT'S TRICKY, BUT IF WE TIME IT RIGHT--
INCOMING!

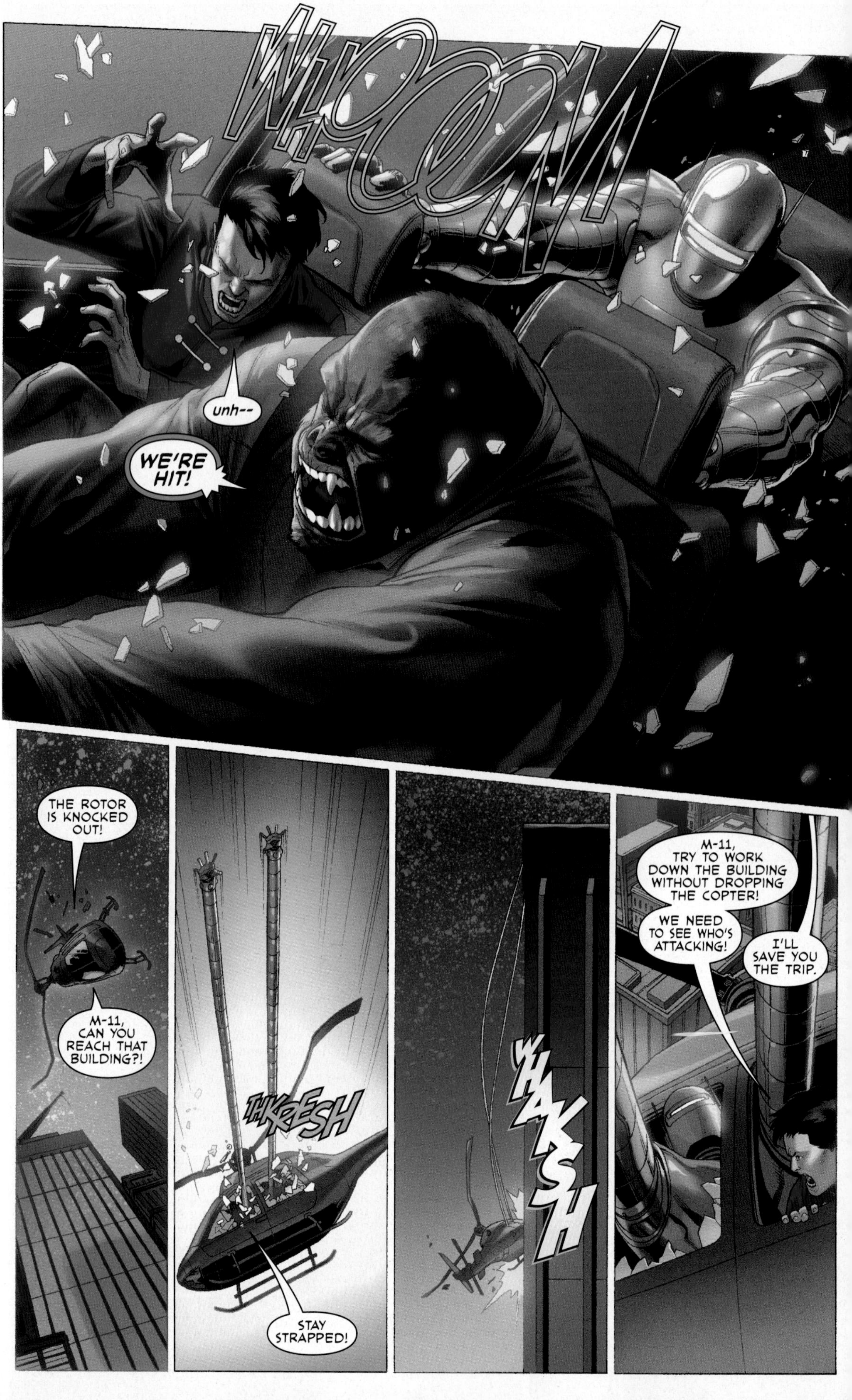
WHOOM
unh--
WE'RE HIT!
THE ROTOR IS KNOCKED OUT!
M-11, CAN YOU REACH THAT BUILDING?!
THKRESH
STAY STRAPPED!
WHAKSH
M-11, TRY TO WORK DOWN THE BUILDING WITHOUT DROPPING THE COPTER!
WE NEED TO SEE WHO'S ATTACKING!
I'LL SAVE YOU THE TRIP.

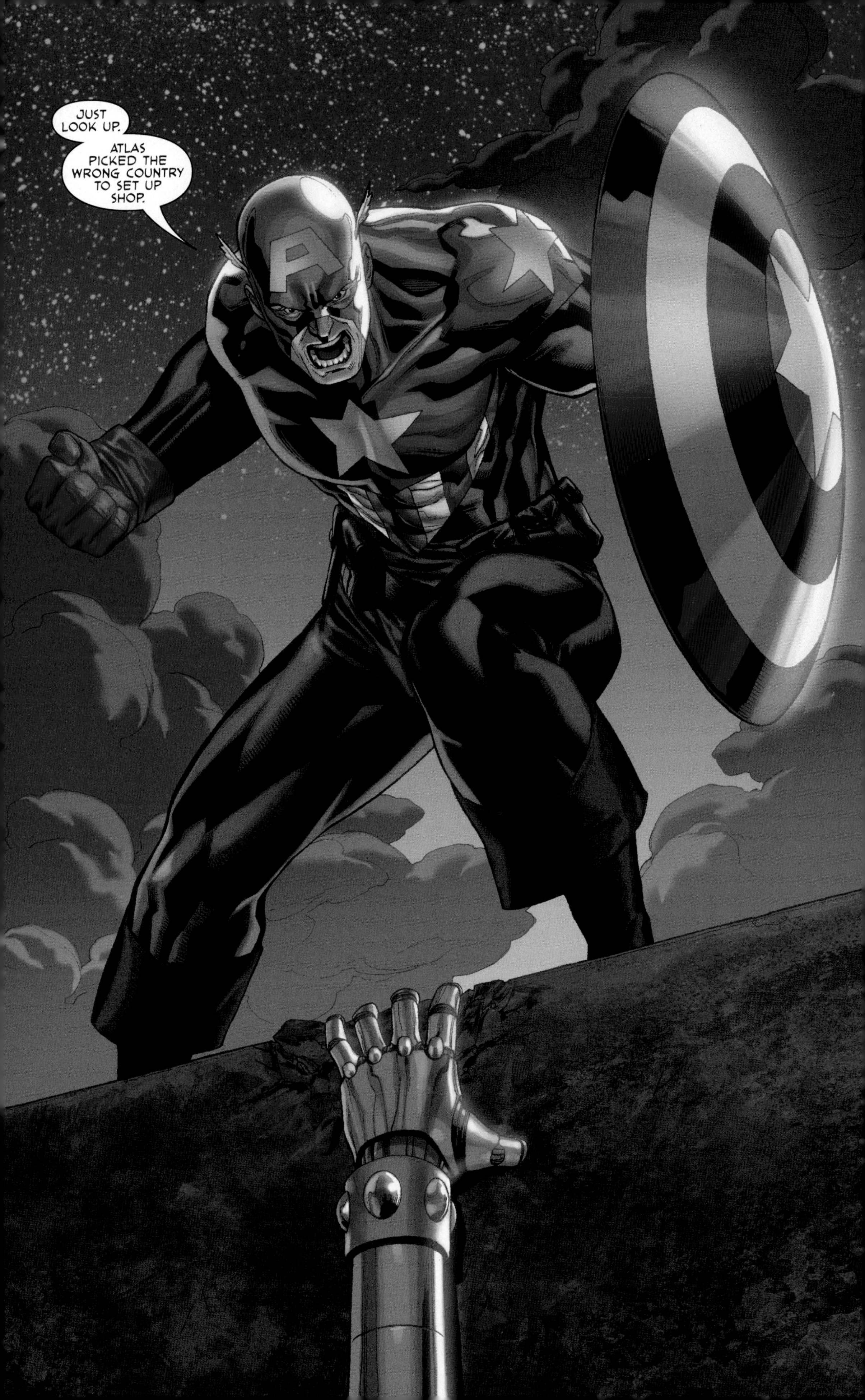
JUST LOOK UP.
ATLAS PICKED THE WRONG COUNTRY TO SET UP SHOP.

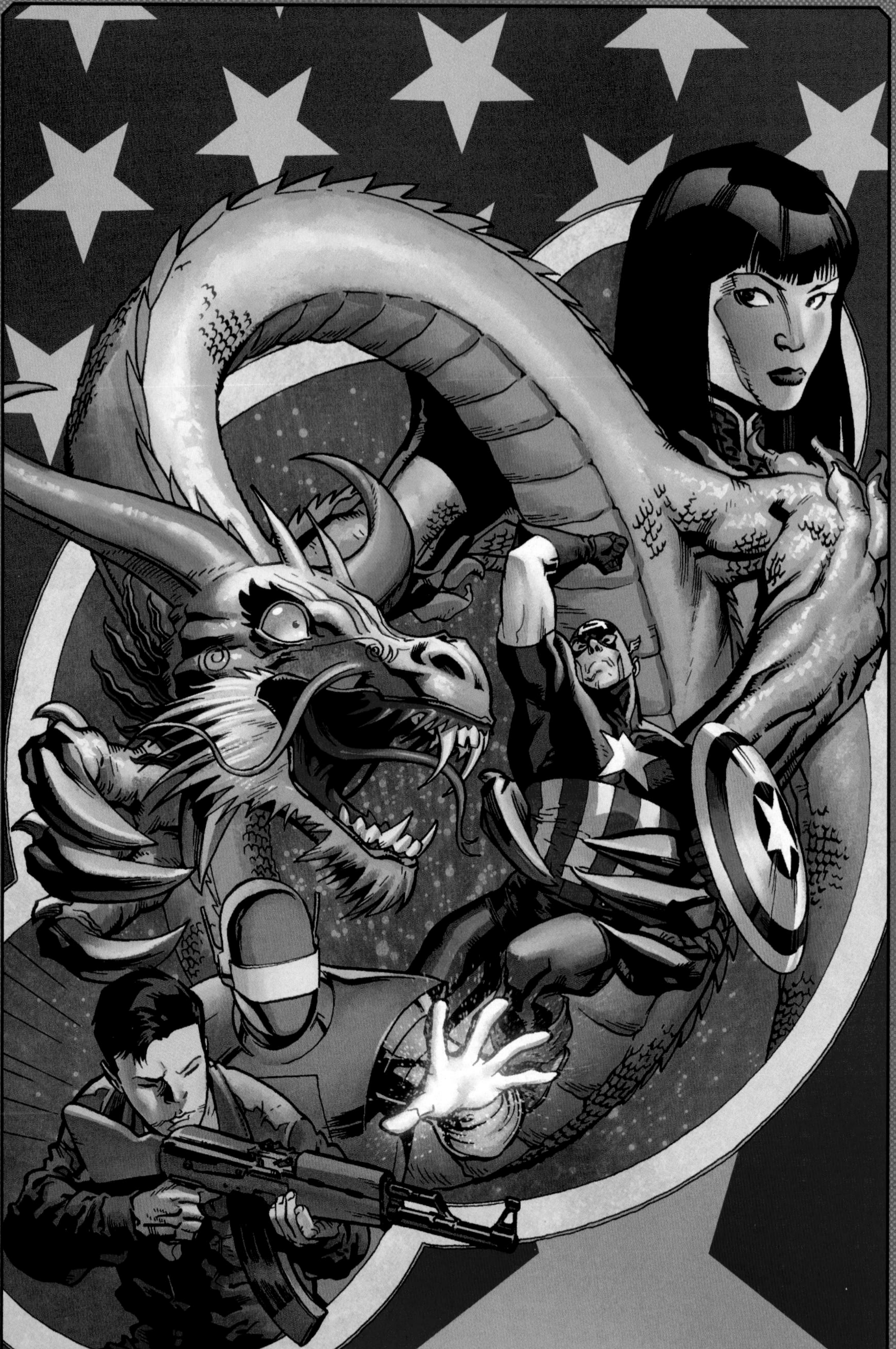

AGENTS OF ATLAS (2009) 4

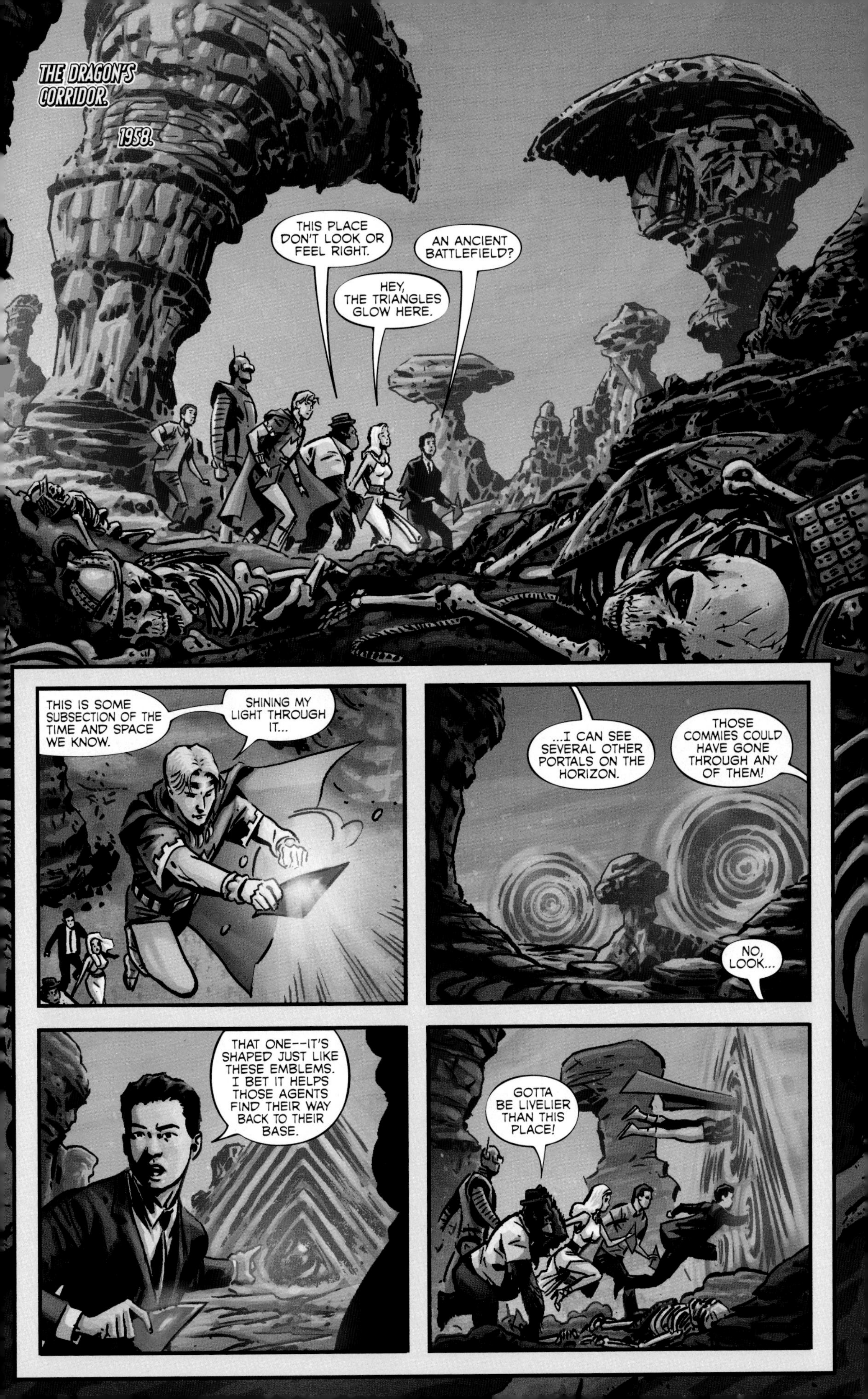
THE DRAGON'S CORRIDOR.
1958.
THIS PLACE DON'T LOOK OR FEEL RIGHT.
HEY, THE TRIANGLES GLOW HERE.
AN ANCIENT BATTLEFIELD?
THIS IS SOME SUBSECTION OF THE TIME AND SPACE WE KNOW.
SHINING MY LIGHT THROUGH IT...
...I CAN SEE SEVERAL OTHER PORTALS ON THE HORIZON.
THOSE COMMIES COULD HAVE GONE THROUGH ANY OF THEM!
NO, LOOK...
THAT ONE--IT'S SHAPED JUST LIKE THESE EMBLEMS. I BET IT HELPS THOSE AGENTS FIND THEIR WAY BACK TO THEIR BASE.
GOTTA BE LIVELIER THAN THIS PLACE!

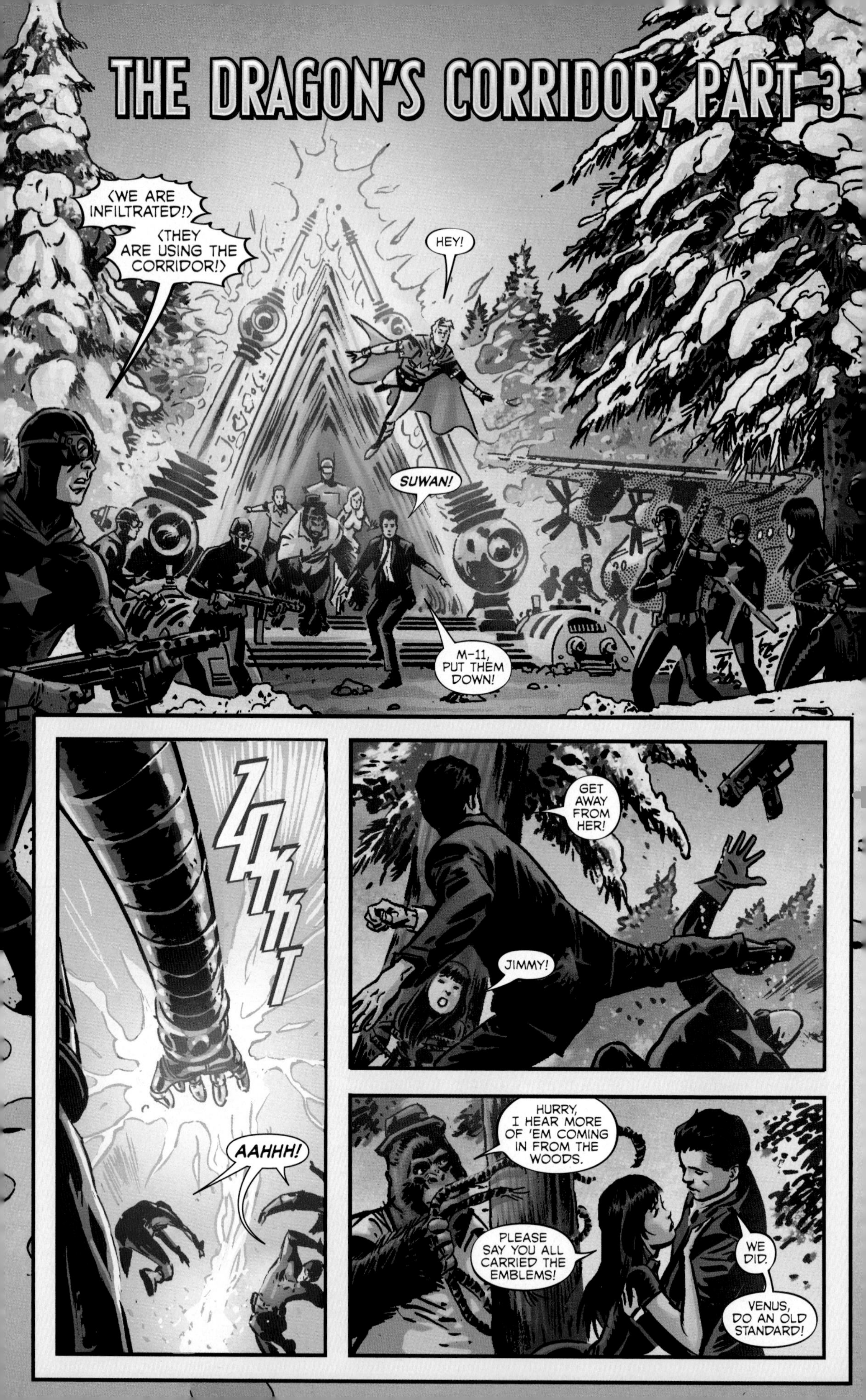
THE DRAGON'S CORRIDOR, PART 3
⟨WE ARE INFILTRATED!⟩
⟨THEY ARE USING THE CORRIDOR!⟩
HEY!
SUWAN!
M-11, PUT THEM DOWN!
AAHHH!
GET AWAY FROM HER!
JIMMY!
HURRY, I HEAR MORE OF 'EM COMING IN FROM THE WOODS.
PLEASE SAY YOU ALL CARRIED THE EMBLEMS!
WE DID.
VENUS, DO AN OLD STANDARD!

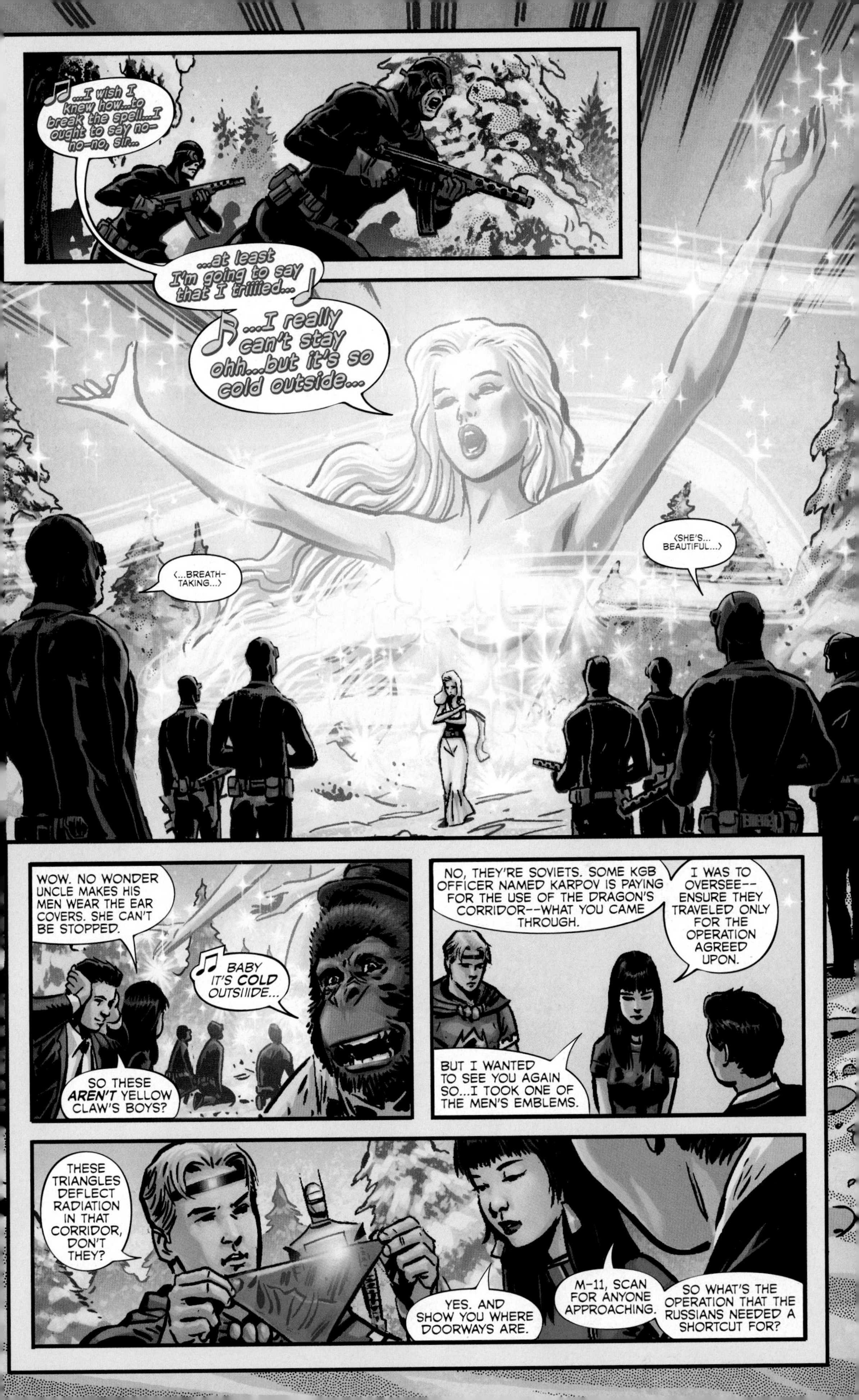

♫...I wish I knew how...to break the spell...I ought to say no-no-no, sir...
...at least I'm going to say that I triiiied...♩
♫...I really can't stay ohh...but it's so cold outside...
‹...BREATH-TAKING...›
‹SHE'S... BEAUTIFUL...›
WOW. NO WONDER UNCLE MAKES HIS MEN WEAR THE EAR COVERS. SHE CAN'T BE STOPPED.
♫ BABY IT'S **COLD** OUTSIIIDE...
SO THESE ***AREN'T*** YELLOW CLAW'S BOYS?
NO, THEY'RE SOVIETS. SOME KGB OFFICER NAMED KARPOV IS PAYING FOR THE USE OF THE DRAGON'S CORRIDOR--WHAT YOU CAME THROUGH.
I WAS TO OVERSEE--ENSURE THEY TRAVELED ONLY FOR THE OPERATION AGREED UPON.
BUT I WANTED TO SEE YOU AGAIN SO...I TOOK ONE OF THE MEN'S EMBLEMS.
THESE TRIANGLES DEFLECT RADIATION IN THAT CORRIDOR, DON'T THEY?
YES. AND SHOW YOU WHERE DOORWAYS ARE.
M-11, SCAN FOR ANYONE APPROACHING.
SO WHAT'S THE OPERATION THAT THE RUSSIANS NEEDED A SHORTCUT FOR?

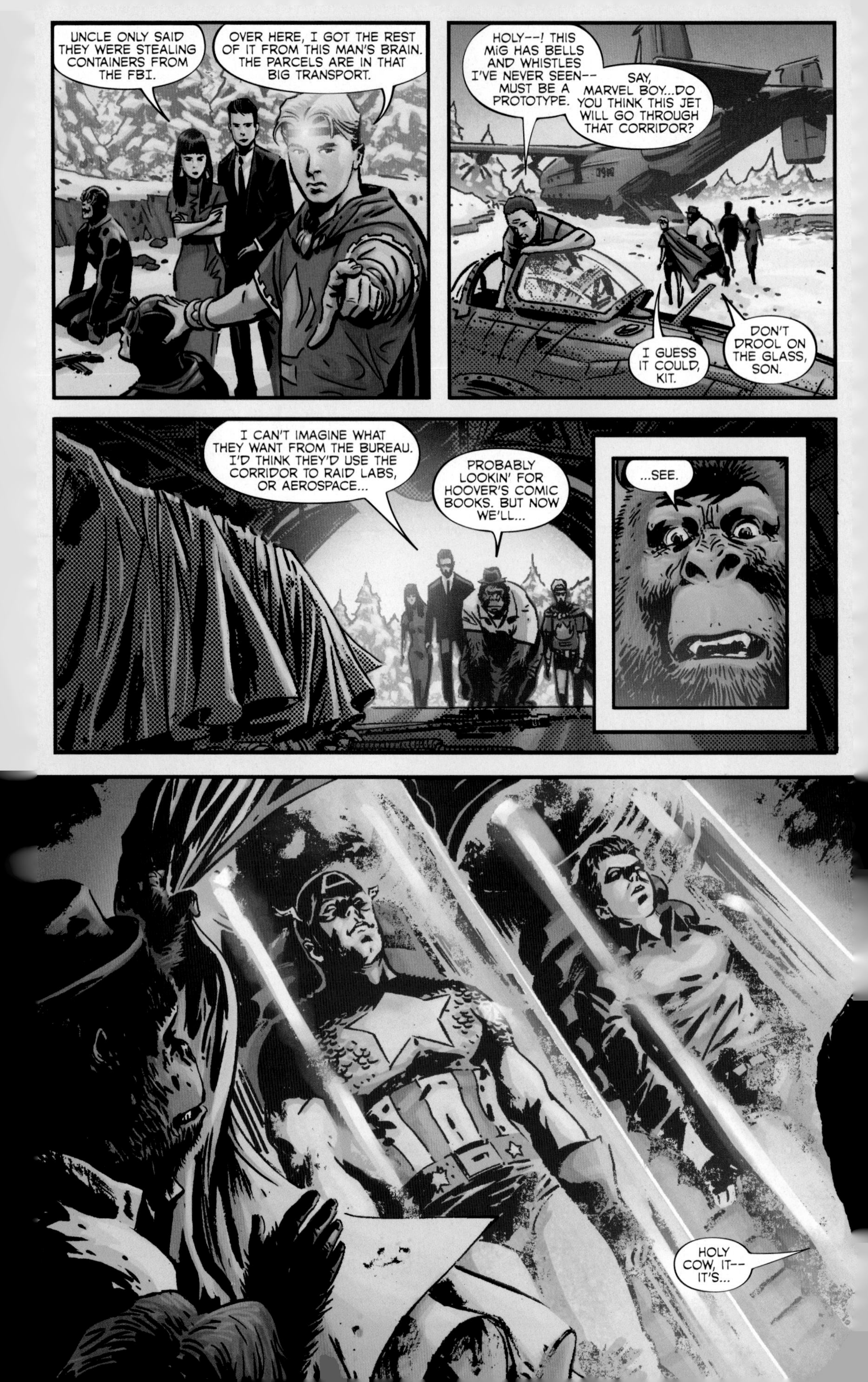
UNCLE ONLY SAID THEY WERE STEALING CONTAINERS FROM THE FBI.
OVER HERE, I GOT THE REST OF IT FROM THIS MAN'S BRAIN. THE PARCELS ARE IN THAT BIG TRANSPORT.
HOLY--! THIS MiG HAS BELLS AND WHISTLES I'VE NEVER SEEN-- MUST BE A PROTOTYPE.
SAY, MARVEL BOY...DO YOU THINK THIS JET WILL GO THROUGH THAT CORRIDOR?
I GUESS IT COULD, KIT.
DON'T DROOL ON THE GLASS, SON.
I CAN'T IMAGINE WHAT THEY WANT FROM THE BUREAU. I'D THINK THEY'D USE THE CORRIDOR TO RAID LABS, OR AEROSPACE...
PROBABLY LOOKIN' FOR HOOVER'S COMIC BOOKS. BUT NOW WE'LL...
...SEE.
HOLY COW, IT-- IT'S...

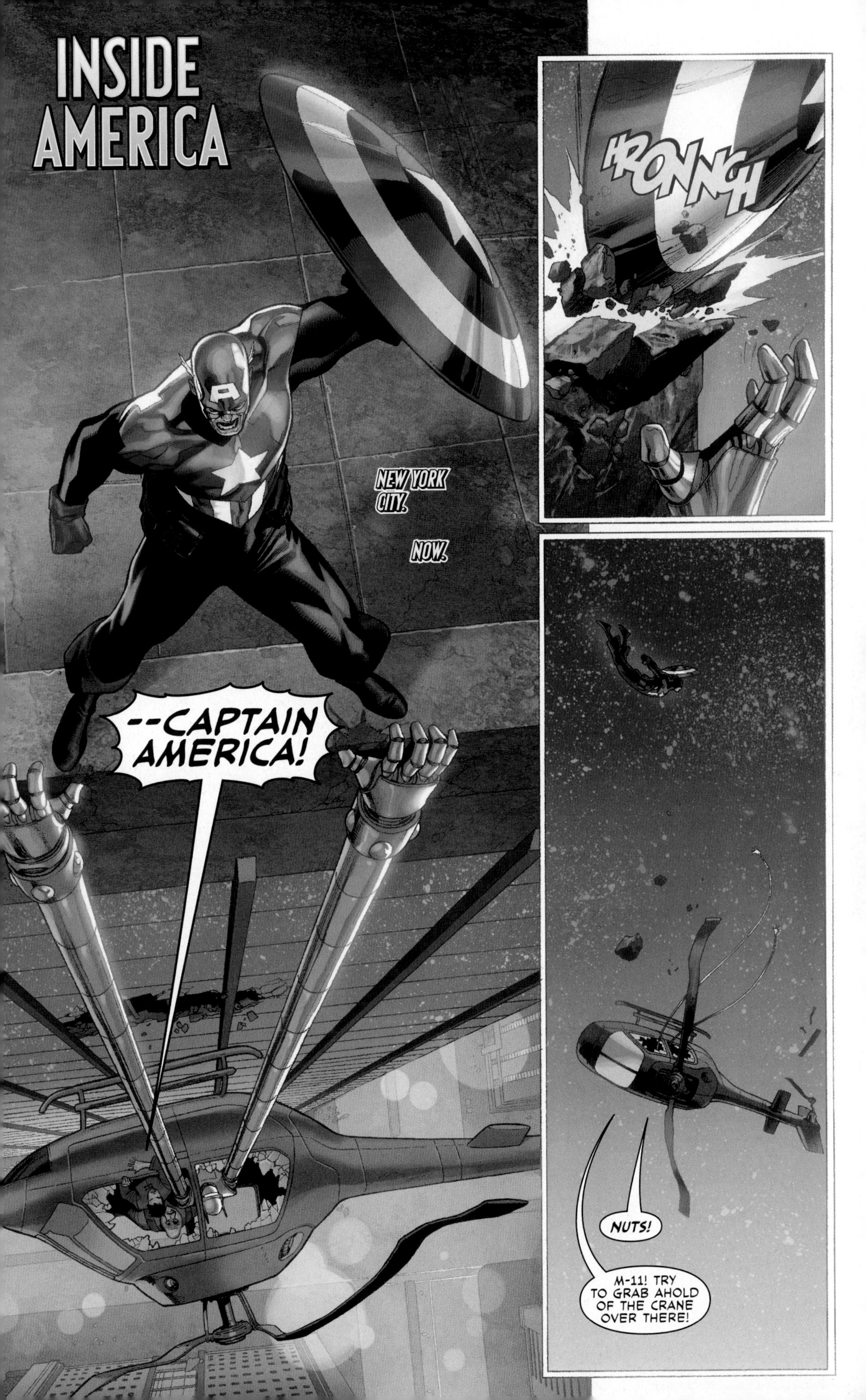
INSIDE AMERICA
NEW YORK CITY.
NOW.
--CAPTAIN AMERICA!
HRONNGH
NUTS!
M-11! TRY TO GRAB AHOLD OF THE CRANE OVER THERE!

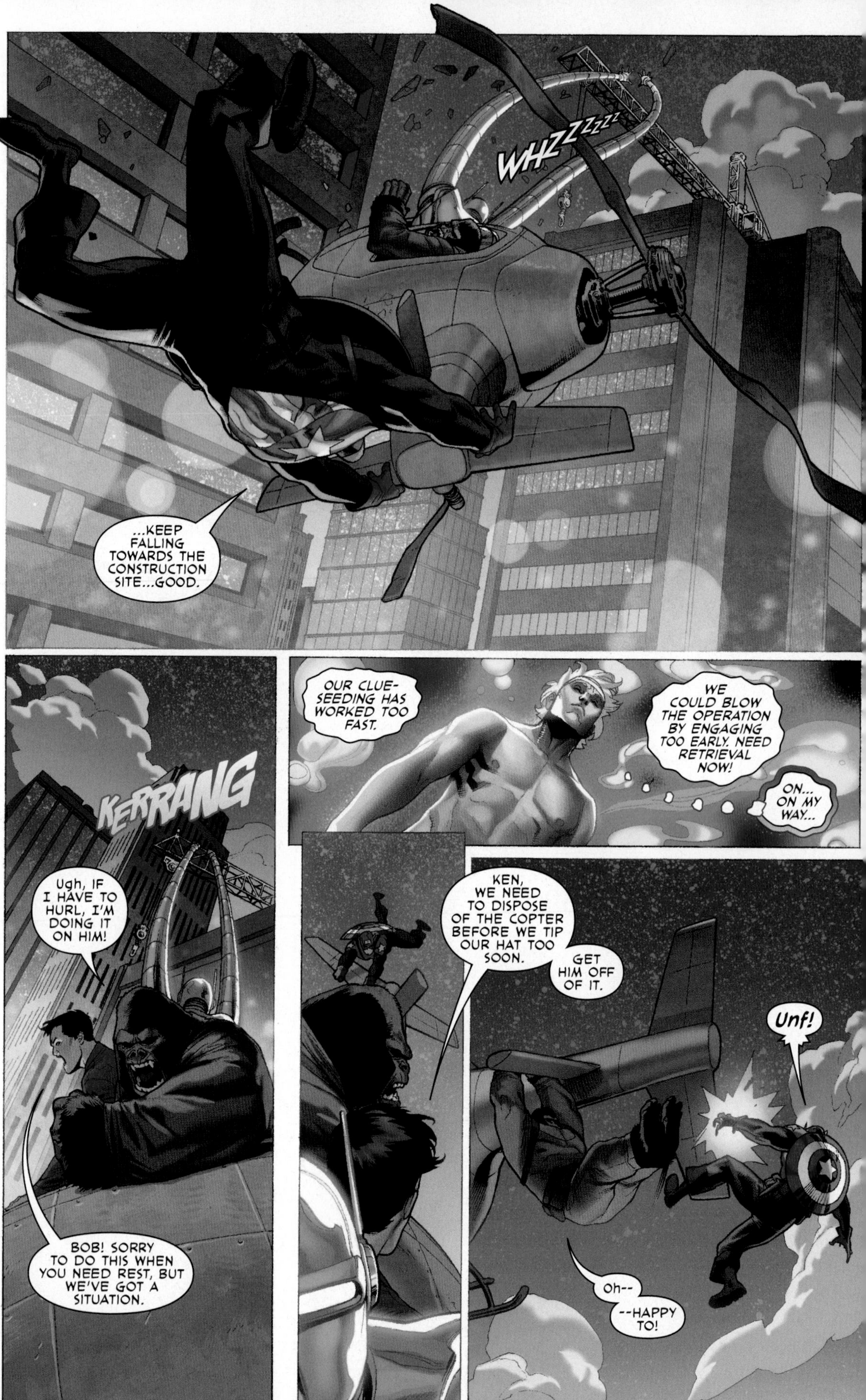
WHZZZZZZ
...KEEP FALLING TOWARDS THE CONSTRUCTION SITE...GOOD.
KERRANG
Ugh, IF I HAVE TO HURL, I'M DOING IT ON HIM!
BOB! SORRY TO DO THIS WHEN YOU NEED REST, BUT WE'VE GOT A SITUATION.
OUR CLUE-SEEDING HAS WORKED TOO FAST.
WE COULD BLOW THE OPERATION BY ENGAGING TOO EARLY. NEED RETRIEVAL NOW!
ON... ON MY WAY...
KEN, WE NEED TO DISPOSE OF THE COPTER BEFORE WE TIP OUR HAT TOO SOON.
GET HIM OFF OF IT.
Unf!
Oh--
--HAPPY TO!

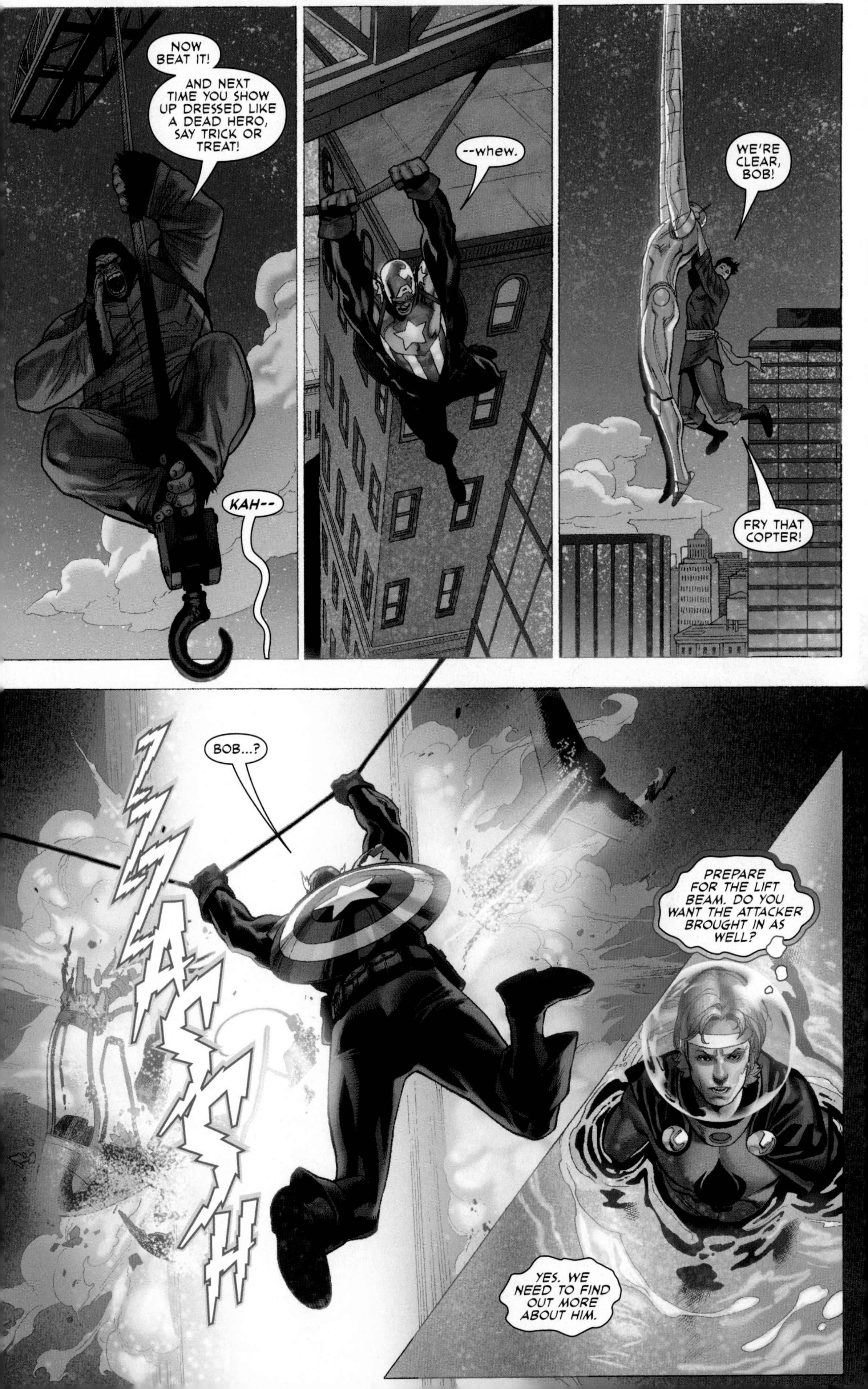
NOW BEAT IT!
AND NEXT TIME YOU SHOW UP DRESSED LIKE A DEAD HERO, SAY TRICK OR TREAT!
KAH--
--whew.
WE'RE CLEAR, BOB!
FRY THAT COPTER!
BOB...?
ZZZLAASSHH
PREPARE FOR THE LIFT BEAM. DO YOU WANT THE ATTACKER BROUGHT IN AS WELL?
YES. WE NEED TO FIND OUT MORE ABOUT HIM.

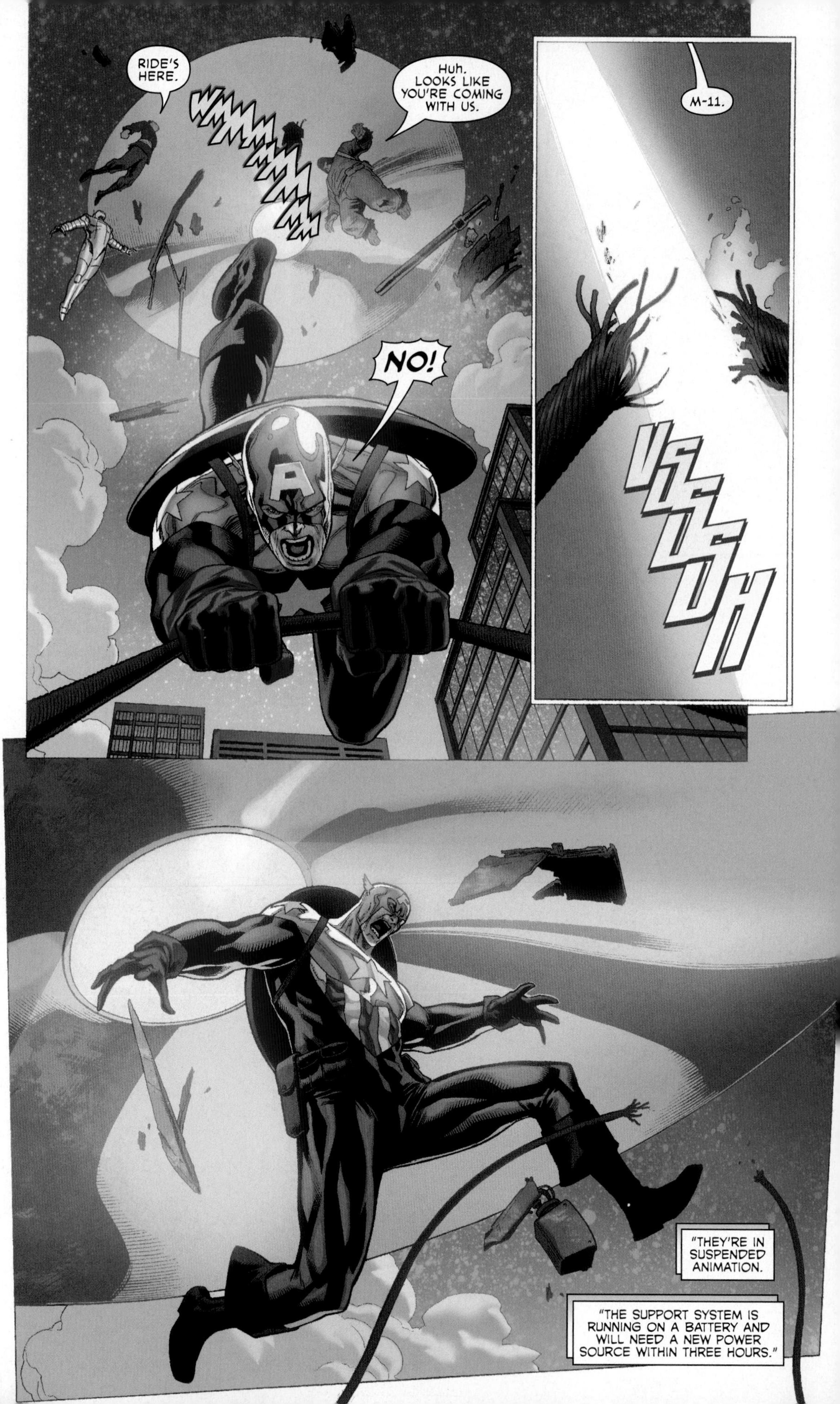
RIDE'S HERE.
Huh. LOOKS LIKE YOU'RE COMING WITH US.
NO!
M-11.
"THEY'RE IN SUSPENDED ANIMATION.
"THE SUPPORT SYSTEM IS RUNNING ON A BATTERY AND WILL NEED A NEW POWER SOURCE WITHIN THREE HOURS."

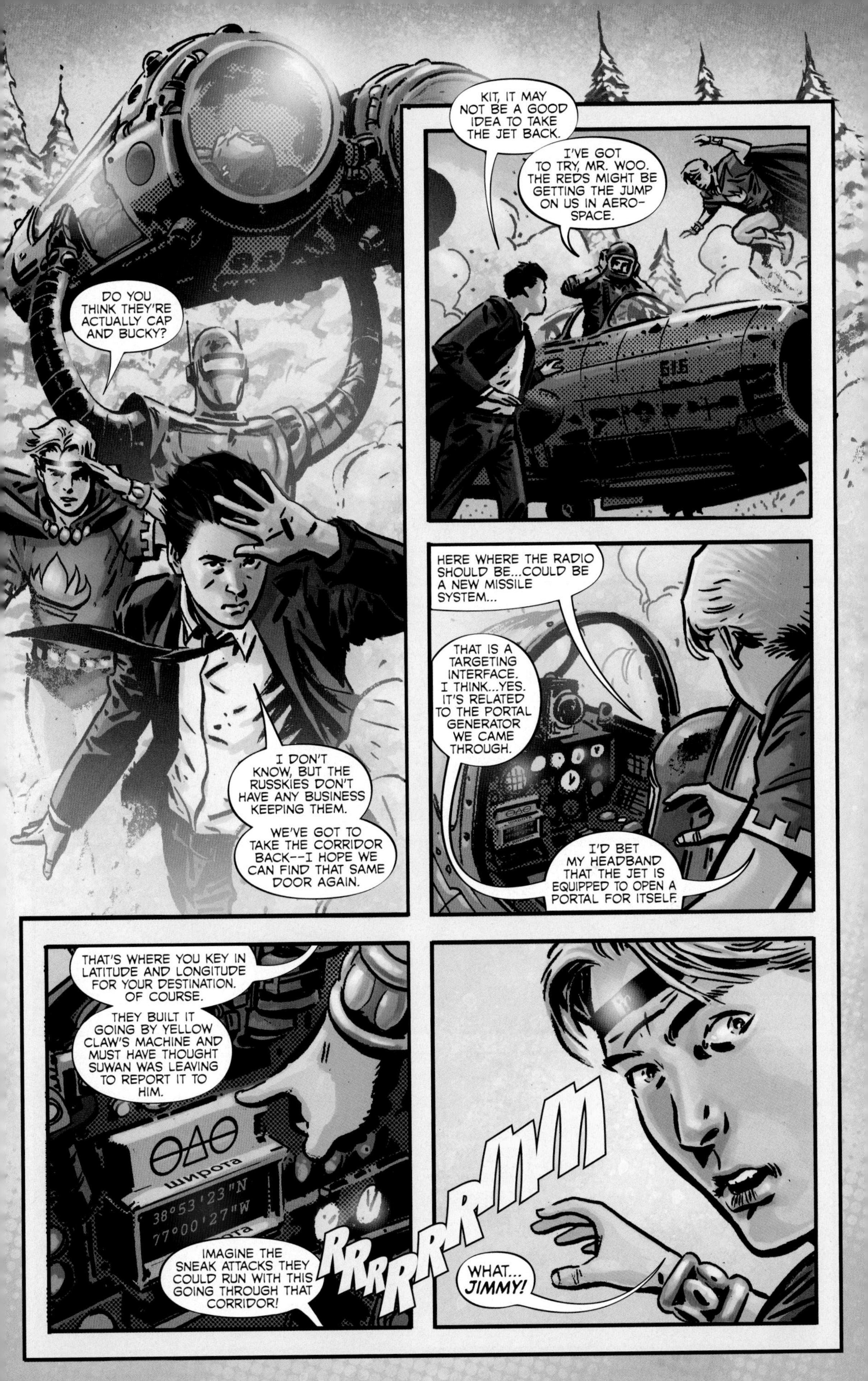
DO YOU THINK THEY'RE ACTUALLY CAP AND BUCKY?
I DON'T KNOW, BUT THE RUSSKIES DON'T HAVE ANY BUSINESS KEEPING THEM.
WE'VE GOT TO TAKE THE CORRIDOR BACK--I HOPE WE CAN FIND THAT SAME DOOR AGAIN.
KIT, IT MAY NOT BE A GOOD IDEA TO TAKE THE JET BACK.
I'VE GOT TO TRY, MR. WOO. THE REDS MIGHT BE GETTING THE JUMP ON US IN AERO-SPACE.
515
HERE WHERE THE RADIO SHOULD BE...COULD BE A NEW MISSILE SYSTEM...
THAT IS A TARGETING INTERFACE. I THINK...YES. IT'S RELATED TO THE PORTAL GENERATOR WE CAME THROUGH.
I'D BET MY HEADBAND THAT THE JET IS EQUIPPED TO OPEN A PORTAL FOR ITSELF.
THAT'S WHERE YOU KEY IN LATITUDE AND LONGITUDE FOR YOUR DESTINATION. OF COURSE.
THEY BUILT IT GOING BY YELLOW CLAW'S MACHINE AND MUST HAVE THOUGHT SUWAN WAS LEAVING TO REPORT IT TO HIM.
широта
38°53'23"N
77°00'27"W
IMAGINE THE SNEAK ATTACKS THEY COULD RUN WITH THIS GOING THROUGH THAT CORRIDOR!
RRRRRRRMMM
WHAT... *JIMMY!*

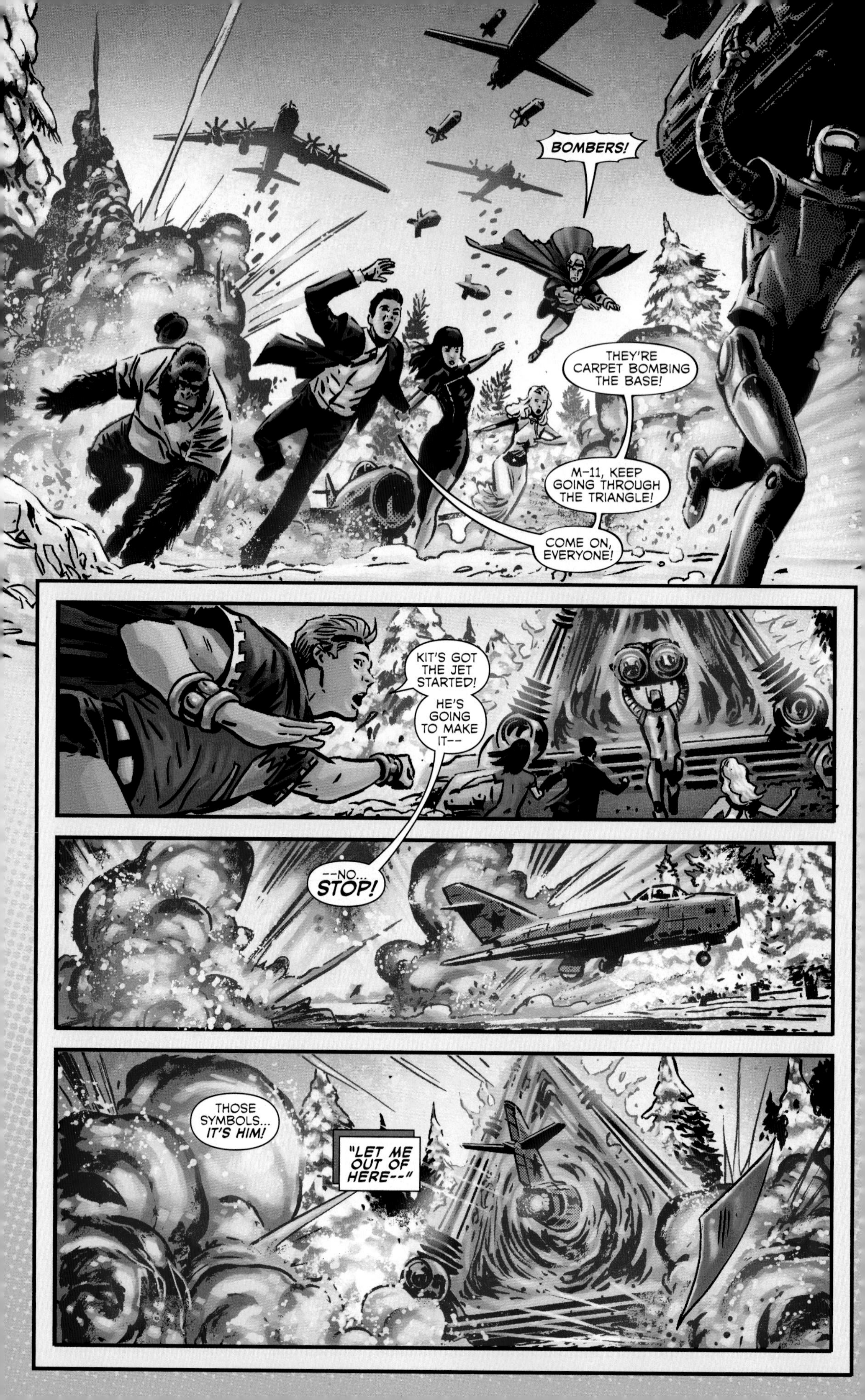
BOMBERS!
THEY'RE CARPET BOMBING THE BASE!
M-11, KEEP GOING THROUGH THE TRIANGLE!
COME ON, EVERYONE!
KIT'S GOT THE JET STARTED!
HE'S GOING TO MAKE IT--
--NO... STOP!
THOSE SYMBOLS... IT'S HIM!
"LET ME OUT OF HERE--"

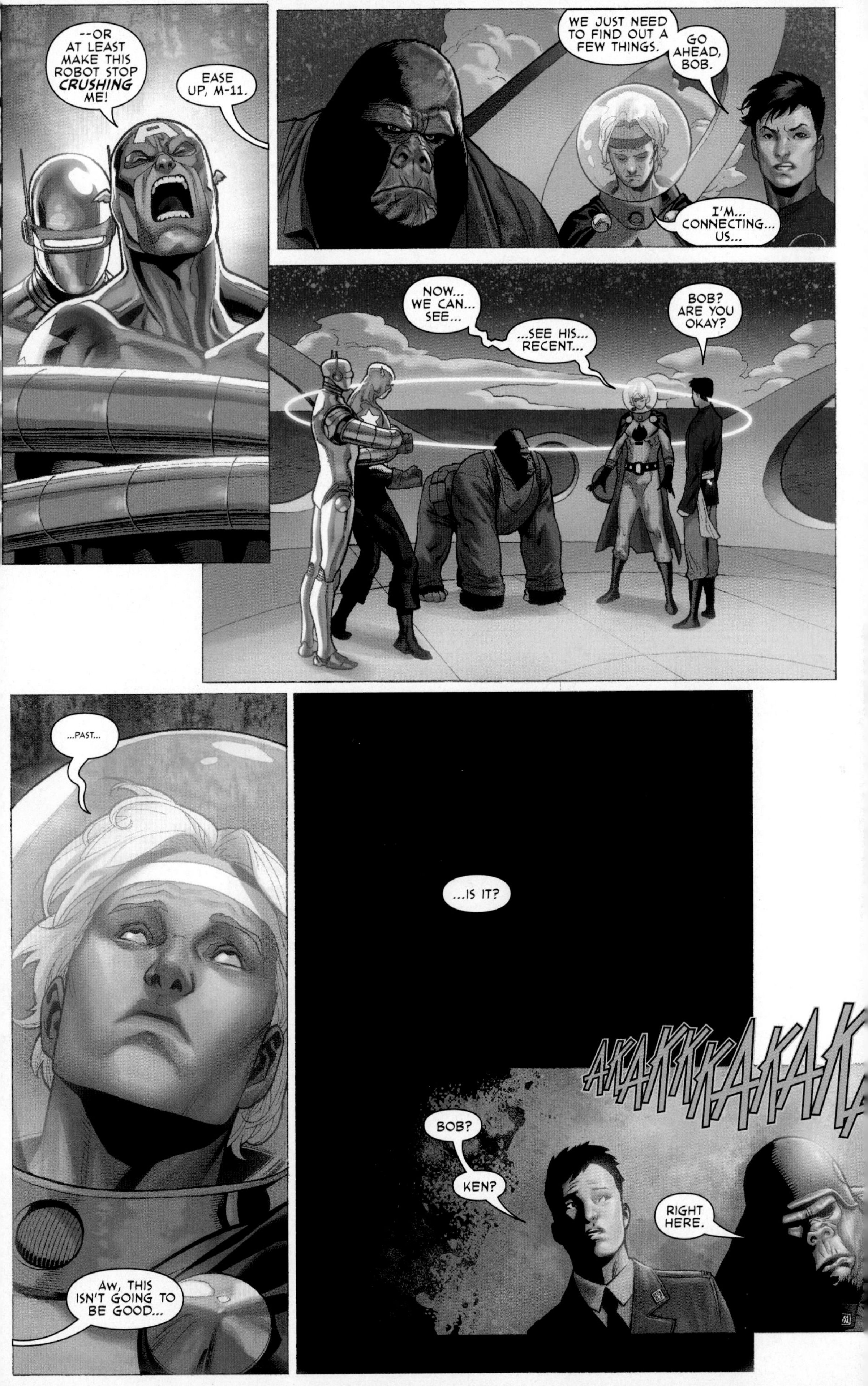
--OR AT LEAST MAKE THIS ROBOT STOP *CRUSHING* ME!
EASE UP, M-11.
WE JUST NEED TO FIND OUT A FEW THINGS.
GO AHEAD, BOB.
I'M... CONNECTING... US...
NOW... WE CAN... SEE...
...SEE HIS... RECENT...
BOB? ARE YOU OKAY?
...PAST...
AW, THIS ISN'T GOING TO BE GOOD...
...IS IT?
AKAKKKAKAKAK
BOB?
KEN?
RIGHT HERE.

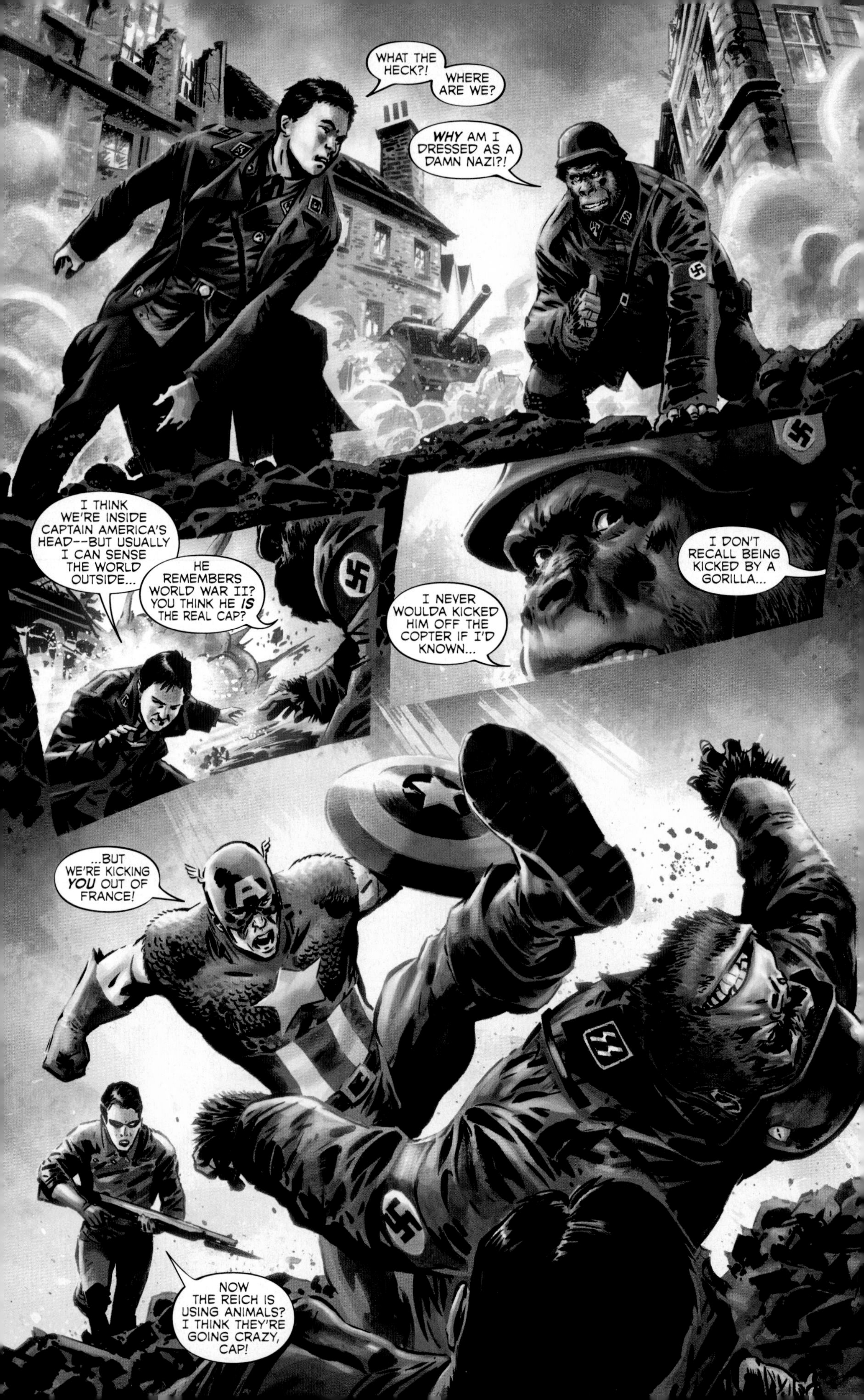
WHAT THE HECK?! WHERE ARE WE?
WHY AM I DRESSED AS A DAMN NAZI?!
I THINK WE'RE INSIDE CAPTAIN AMERICA'S HEAD--BUT USUALLY I CAN SENSE THE WORLD OUTSIDE...
HE REMEMBERS WORLD WAR II? YOU THINK HE *IS* THE REAL CAP?
I NEVER WOULDA KICKED HIM OFF THE COPTER IF I'D KNOWN...
I DON'T RECALL BEING KICKED BY A GORILLA...
...BUT WE'RE KICKING *YOU* OUT OF FRANCE!
NOW THE REICH IS USING ANIMALS? I THINK THEY'RE GOING CRAZY, CAP!

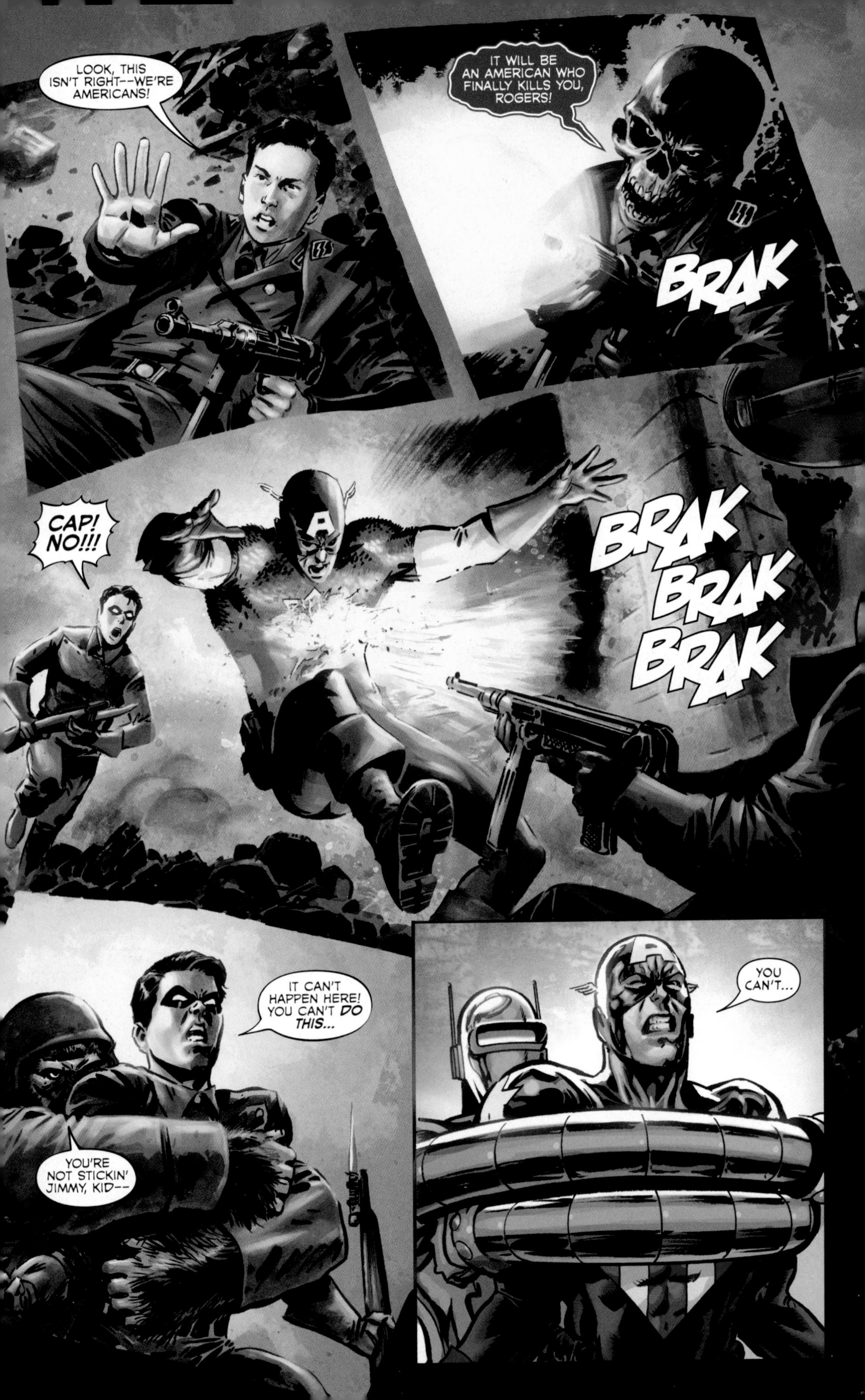

LOOK, THIS ISN'T RIGHT--WE'RE AMERICANS!
IT WILL BE AN AMERICAN WHO FINALLY KILLS YOU, ROGERS!
BRAK
CAP! NO!!!
BRAK BRAK BRAK
IT CAN'T HAPPEN HERE! YOU CAN'T *DO THIS*...
YOU'RE NOT STICKIN' JIMMY, KID--
YOU CAN'T...

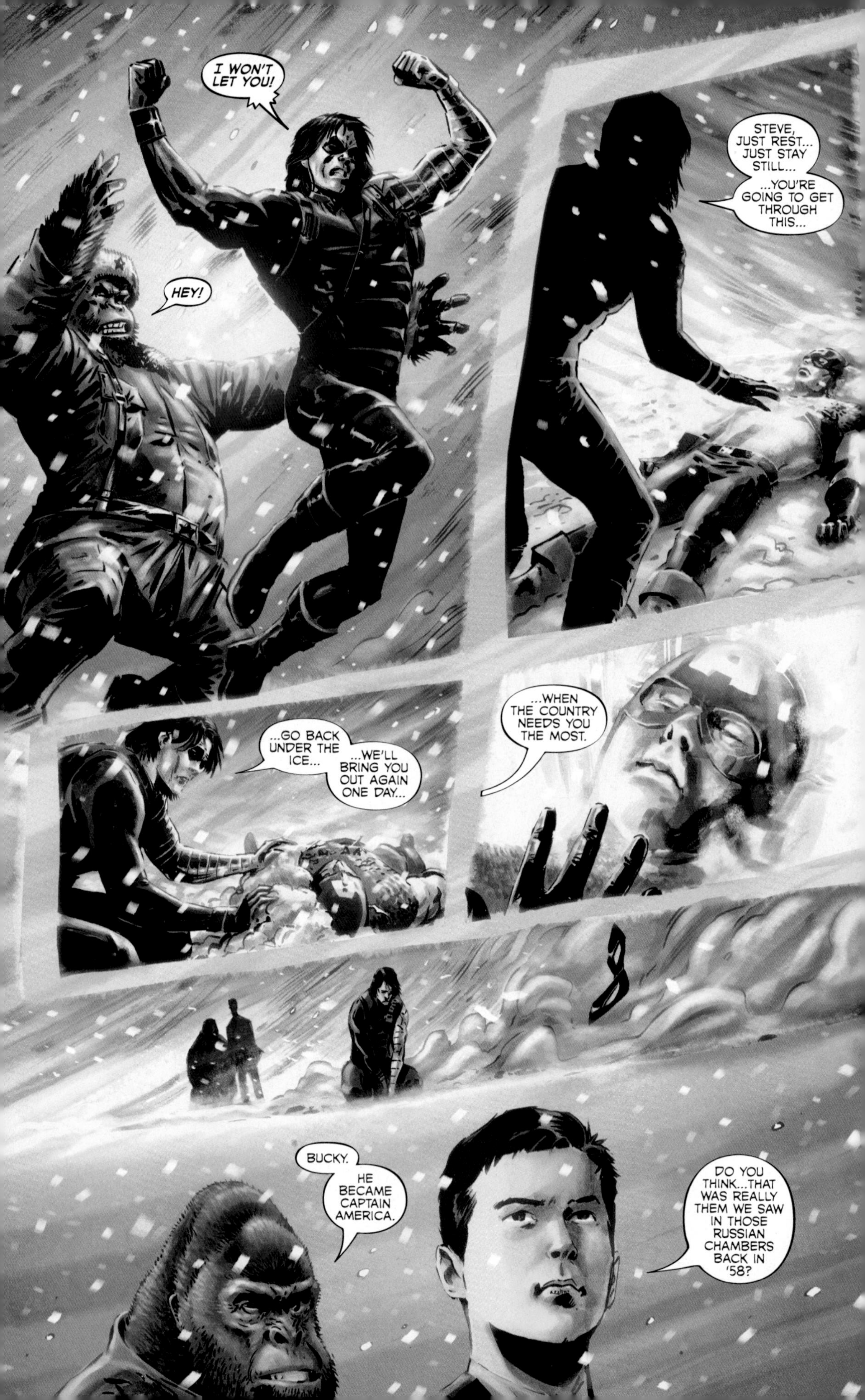
I WON'T LET YOU!
HEY!
STEVE, JUST REST... JUST STAY STILL...
...YOU'RE GOING TO GET THROUGH THIS...
...GO BACK UNDER THE ICE...
...WE'LL BRING YOU OUT AGAIN ONE DAY...
...WHEN THE COUNTRY NEEDS YOU THE MOST.
BUCKY.
HE BECAME CAPTAIN AMERICA.
DO YOU THINK...THAT WAS REALLY THEM WE SAW IN THOSE RUSSIAN CHAMBERS BACK IN '58?

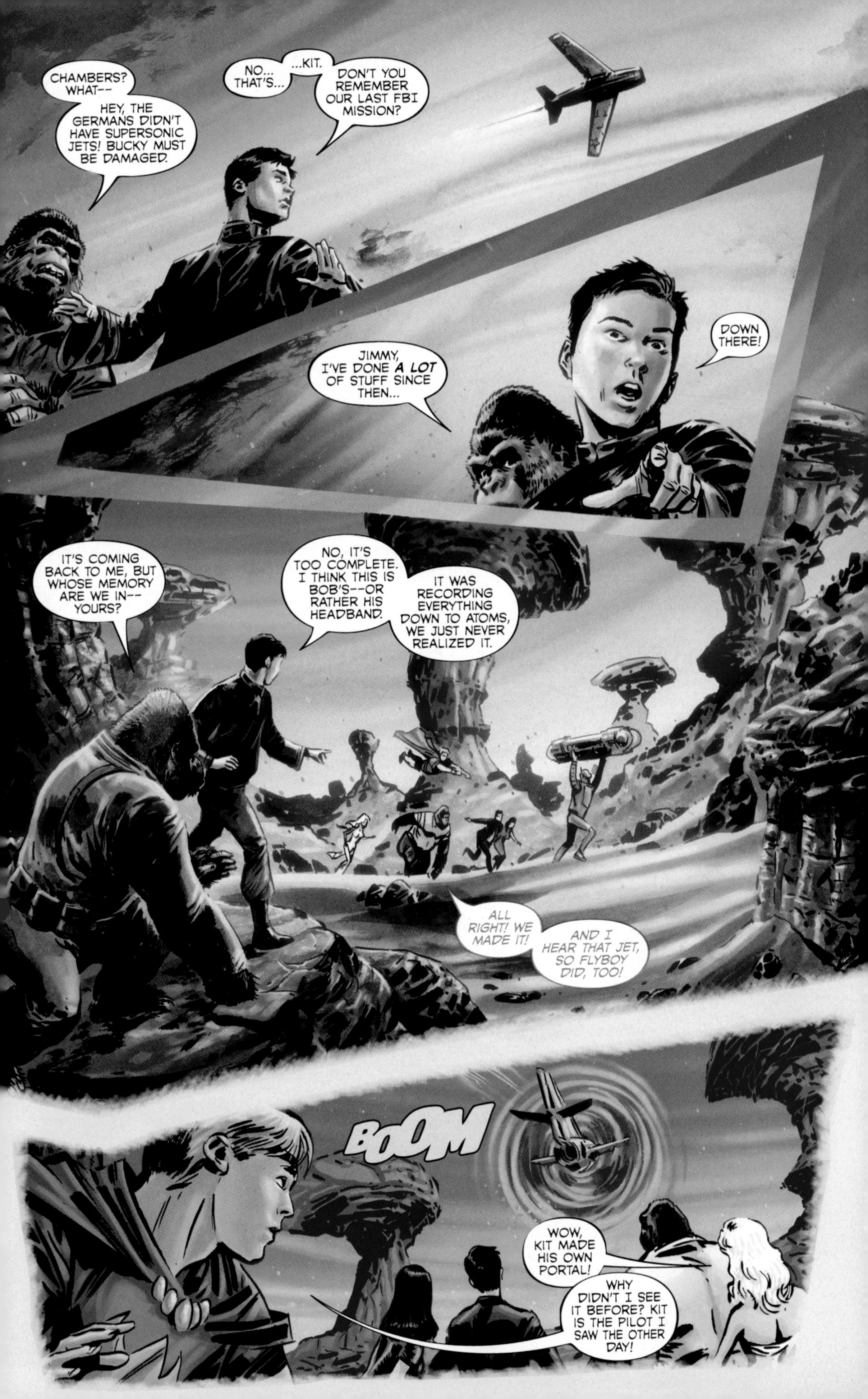
CHAMBERS? WHAT--
HEY, THE GERMANS DIDN'T HAVE SUPERSONIC JETS! BUCKY MUST BE DAMAGED.
NO... THAT'S...
...KIT.
DON'T YOU REMEMBER OUR LAST FBI MISSION?
JIMMY, I'VE DONE *A LOT* OF STUFF SINCE THEN...
DOWN THERE!
IT'S COMING BACK TO ME, BUT WHOSE MEMORY ARE WE IN-- YOURS?
NO, IT'S TOO COMPLETE. I THINK THIS IS BOB'S--OR RATHER HIS HEADBAND.
IT WAS RECORDING EVERYTHING DOWN TO ATOMS, WE JUST NEVER REALIZED IT.
ALL RIGHT! WE MADE IT!
AND I HEAR THAT JET, SO FLYBOY DID, TOO!
BOOM
WOW, KIT MADE HIS OWN PORTAL!
WHY DIDN'T I SEE IT BEFORE? KIT IS THE PILOT I SAW THE OTHER DAY!

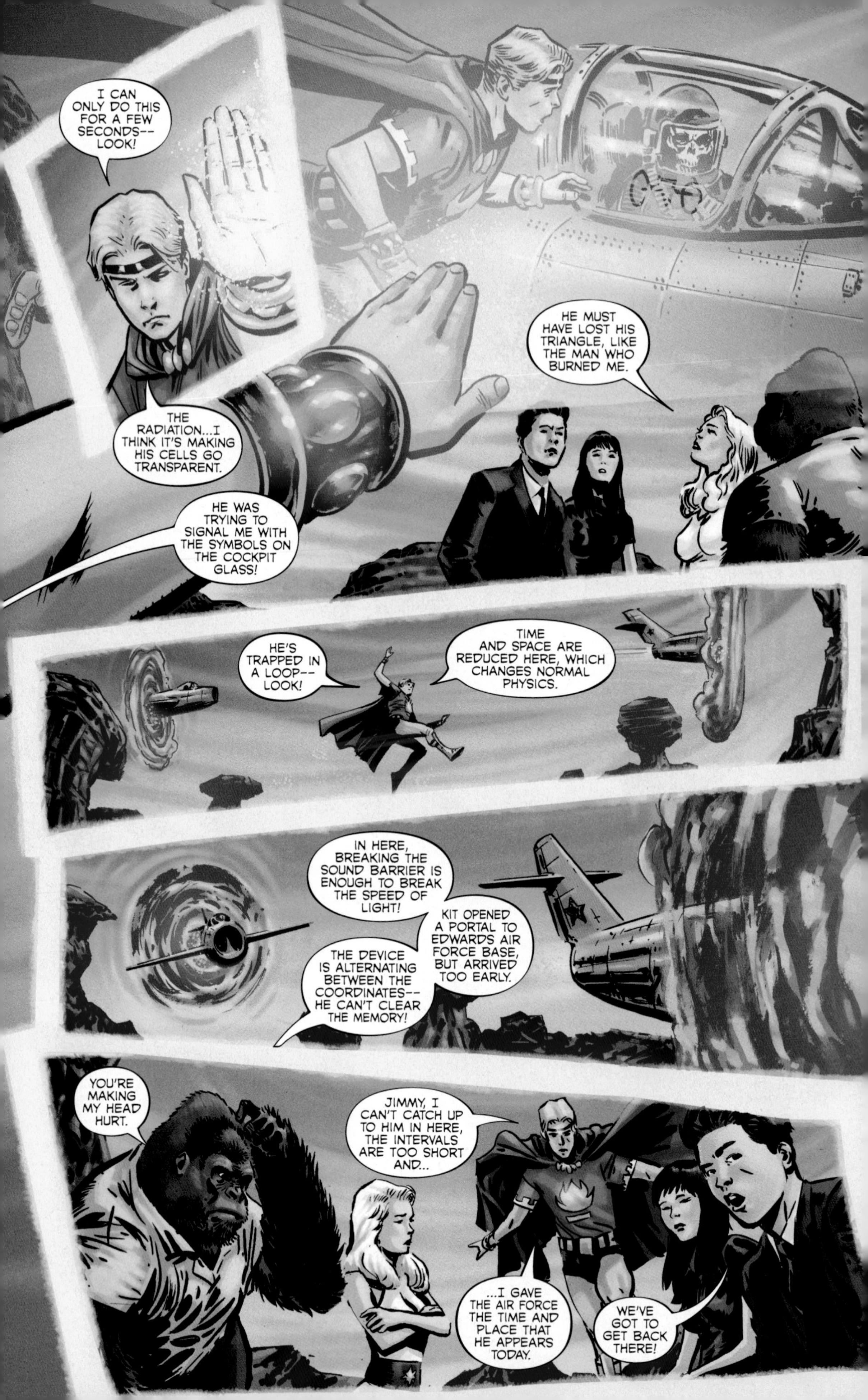
I CAN ONLY DO THIS FOR A FEW SECONDS-- LOOK!
THE RADIATION...I THINK IT'S MAKING HIS CELLS GO TRANSPARENT.
HE WAS TRYING TO SIGNAL ME WITH THE SYMBOLS ON THE COCKPIT GLASS!
HE MUST HAVE LOST HIS TRIANGLE, LIKE THE MAN WHO BURNED ME.
HE'S TRAPPED IN A LOOP-- LOOK!
TIME AND SPACE ARE REDUCED HERE, WHICH CHANGES NORMAL PHYSICS.
IN HERE, BREAKING THE SOUND BARRIER IS ENOUGH TO BREAK THE SPEED OF LIGHT!
THE DEVICE IS ALTERNATING BETWEEN THE COORDINATES-- HE CAN'T CLEAR THE MEMORY!
KIT OPENED A PORTAL TO EDWARDS AIR FORCE BASE, BUT ARRIVED TOO EARLY.
YOU'RE MAKING MY HEAD HURT.
JIMMY, I CAN'T CATCH UP TO HIM IN HERE, THE INTERVALS ARE TOO SHORT AND...
...I GAVE THE AIR FORCE THE TIME AND PLACE THAT HE APPEARS TODAY.
WE'VE GOT TO GET BACK THERE!

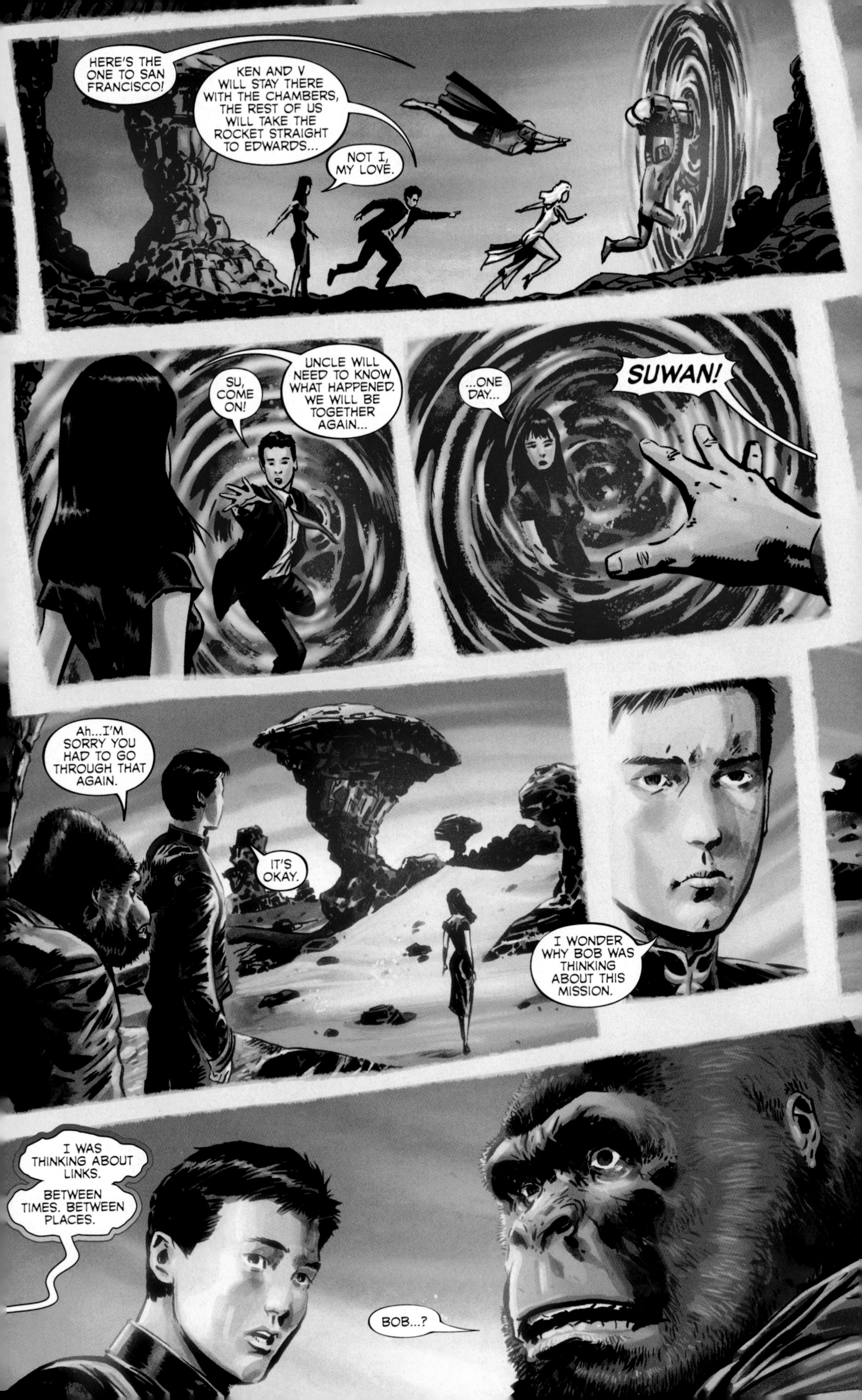
HERE'S THE ONE TO SAN FRANCISCO!
KEN AND V WILL STAY THERE WITH THE CHAMBERS, THE REST OF US WILL TAKE THE ROCKET STRAIGHT TO EDWARDS...
NOT I, MY LOVE.
SU, COME ON!
UNCLE WILL NEED TO KNOW WHAT HAPPENED. WE WILL BE TOGETHER AGAIN...
...ONE DAY...
SUWAN!
Ah...I'M SORRY YOU HAD TO GO THROUGH THAT AGAIN.
IT'S OKAY.
I WONDER WHY BOB WAS THINKING ABOUT THIS MISSION.
I WAS THINKING ABOUT LINKS.
BETWEEN TIMES. BETWEEN PLACES.
BOB...?

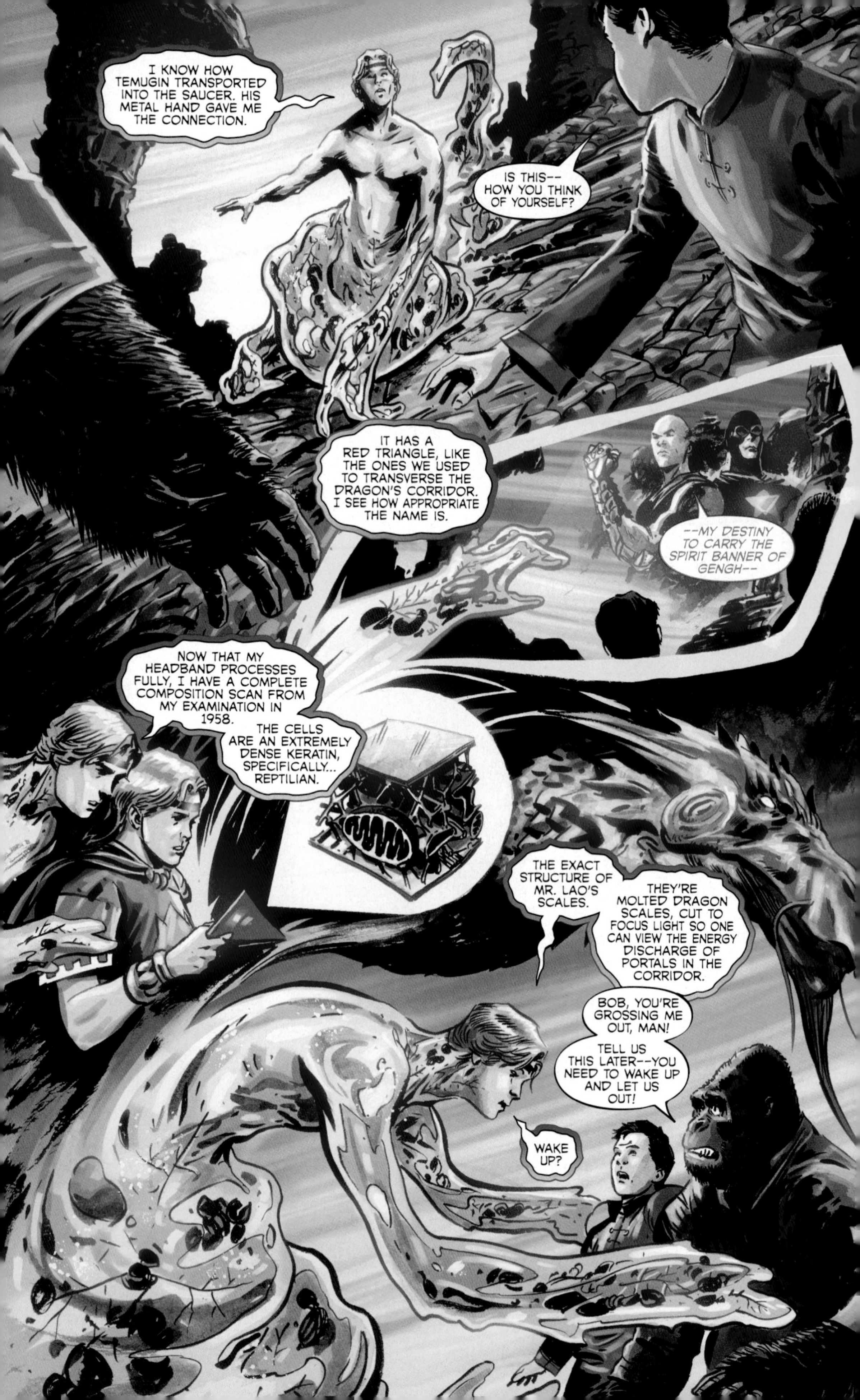
I KNOW HOW TEMUGIN TRANSPORTED INTO THE SAUCER. HIS METAL HAND GAVE ME THE CONNECTION.
IS THIS-- HOW YOU THINK OF YOURSELF?
IT HAS A RED TRIANGLE, LIKE THE ONES WE USED TO TRANSVERSE THE DRAGON'S CORRIDOR. I SEE HOW APPROPRIATE THE NAME IS.
--MY DESTINY TO CARRY THE SPIRIT BANNER OF GENGH--
NOW THAT MY HEADBAND PROCESSES FULLY, I HAVE A COMPLETE COMPOSITION SCAN FROM MY EXAMINATION IN 1958.
THE CELLS ARE AN EXTREMELY DENSE KERATIN, SPECIFICALLY... REPTILIAN.
THE EXACT STRUCTURE OF MR. LAO'S SCALES.
THEY'RE MOLTED DRAGON SCALES, CUT TO FOCUS LIGHT SO ONE CAN VIEW THE ENERGY DISCHARGE OF PORTALS IN THE CORRIDOR.
BOB, YOU'RE GROSSING ME OUT, MAN!
TELL US THIS LATER--YOU NEED TO WAKE UP AND LET US OUT!
WAKE UP?

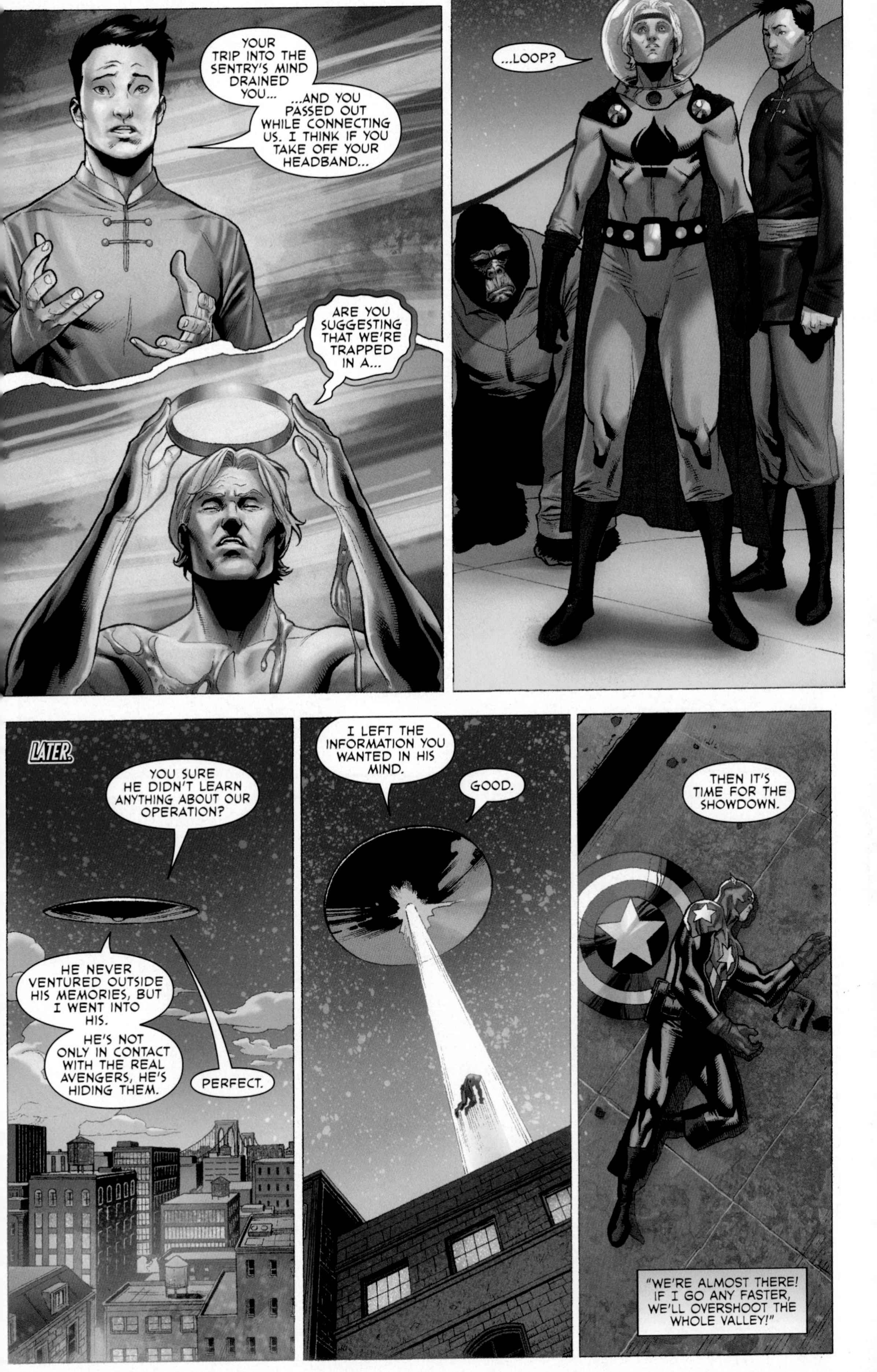
YOUR TRIP INTO THE SENTRY'S MIND DRAINED YOU...
...AND YOU PASSED OUT WHILE CONNECTING US. I THINK IF YOU TAKE OFF YOUR HEADBAND...
ARE YOU SUGGESTING THAT WE'RE TRAPPED IN A...
...LOOP?
LATER.
YOU SURE HE DIDN'T LEARN ANYTHING ABOUT OUR OPERATION?
HE NEVER VENTURED OUTSIDE HIS MEMORIES, BUT I WENT INTO HIS.
HE'S NOT ONLY IN CONTACT WITH THE REAL AVENGERS, HE'S HIDING THEM.
PERFECT.
I LEFT THE INFORMATION YOU WANTED IN HIS MIND.
GOOD.
THEN IT'S TIME FOR THE SHOWDOWN.
"WE'RE ALMOST THERE! IF I GO ANY FASTER, WE'LL OVERSHOOT THE WHOLE VALLEY!"

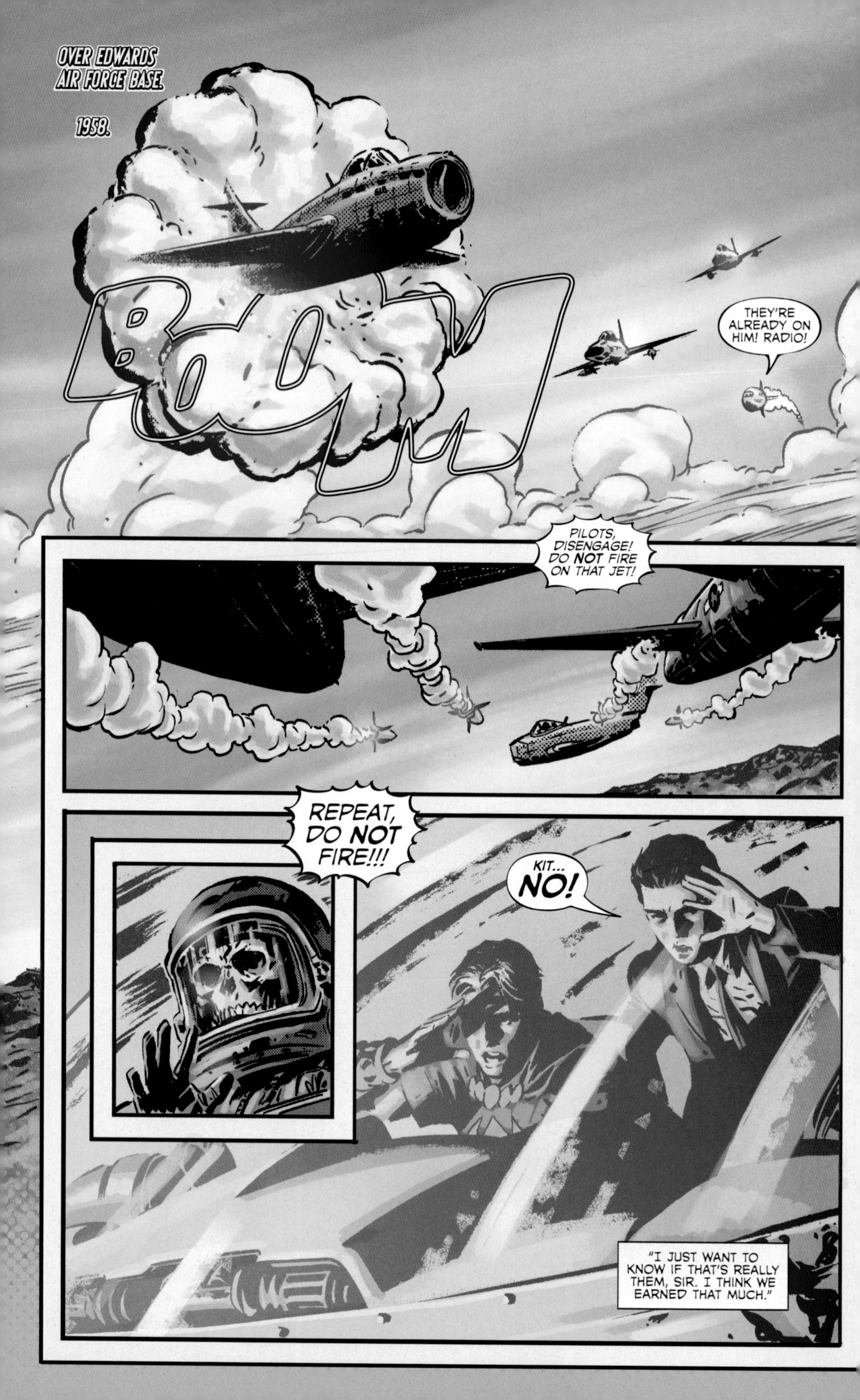
OVER EDWARDS AIR FORCE BASE.
1958.
BOOM
THEY'RE ALREADY ON HIM! RADIO!
PILOTS, DISENGAGE! DO **NOT** FIRE ON THAT JET!
REPEAT, DO **NOT** FIRE!!!
KIT... **NO!**
"I JUST WANT TO KNOW IF THAT'S REALLY THEM, SIR. I THINK WE EARNED THAT MUCH."

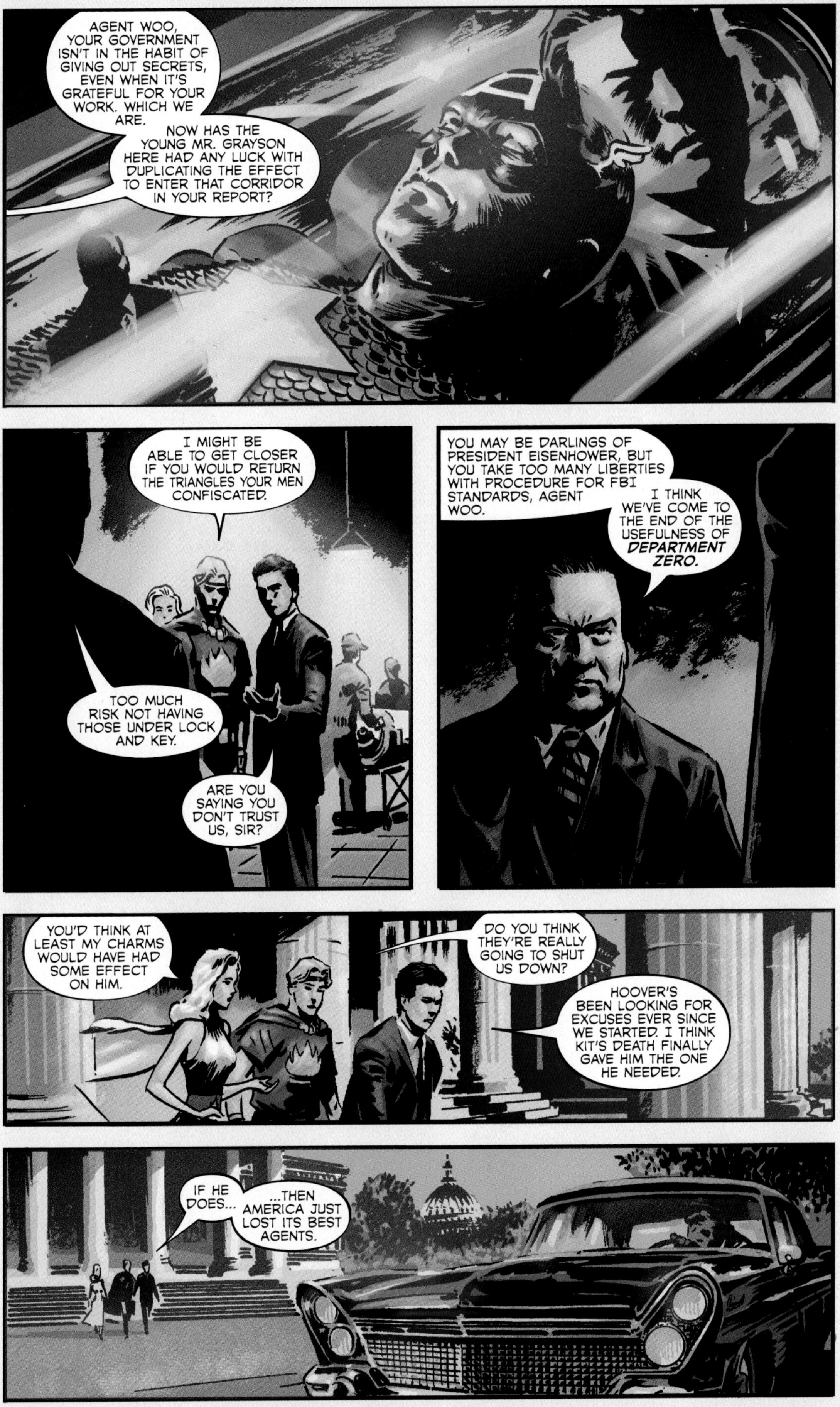
AGENT WOO, YOUR GOVERNMENT ISN'T IN THE HABIT OF GIVING OUT SECRETS, EVEN WHEN IT'S GRATEFUL FOR YOUR WORK. WHICH WE ARE.
NOW HAS THE YOUNG MR. GRAYSON HERE HAD ANY LUCK WITH DUPLICATING THE EFFECT TO ENTER THAT CORRIDOR IN YOUR REPORT?
I MIGHT BE ABLE TO GET CLOSER IF YOU WOULD RETURN THE TRIANGLES YOUR MEN CONFISCATED.
TOO MUCH RISK NOT HAVING THOSE UNDER LOCK AND KEY.
ARE YOU SAYING YOU DON'T TRUST US, SIR?
YOU MAY BE DARLINGS OF PRESIDENT EISENHOWER, BUT YOU TAKE TOO MANY LIBERTIES WITH PROCEDURE FOR FBI STANDARDS, AGENT WOO.
I THINK WE'VE COME TO THE END OF THE USEFULNESS OF ***DEPARTMENT ZERO.***
YOU'D THINK AT LEAST MY CHARMS WOULD HAVE HAD SOME EFFECT ON HIM.
DO YOU THINK THEY'RE REALLY GOING TO SHUT US DOWN?
HOOVER'S BEEN LOOKING FOR EXCUSES EVER SINCE WE STARTED. I THINK KIT'S DEATH FINALLY GAVE HIM THE ONE HE NEEDED.
IF HE DOES...
...THEN AMERICA JUST LOST ITS BEST AGENTS.

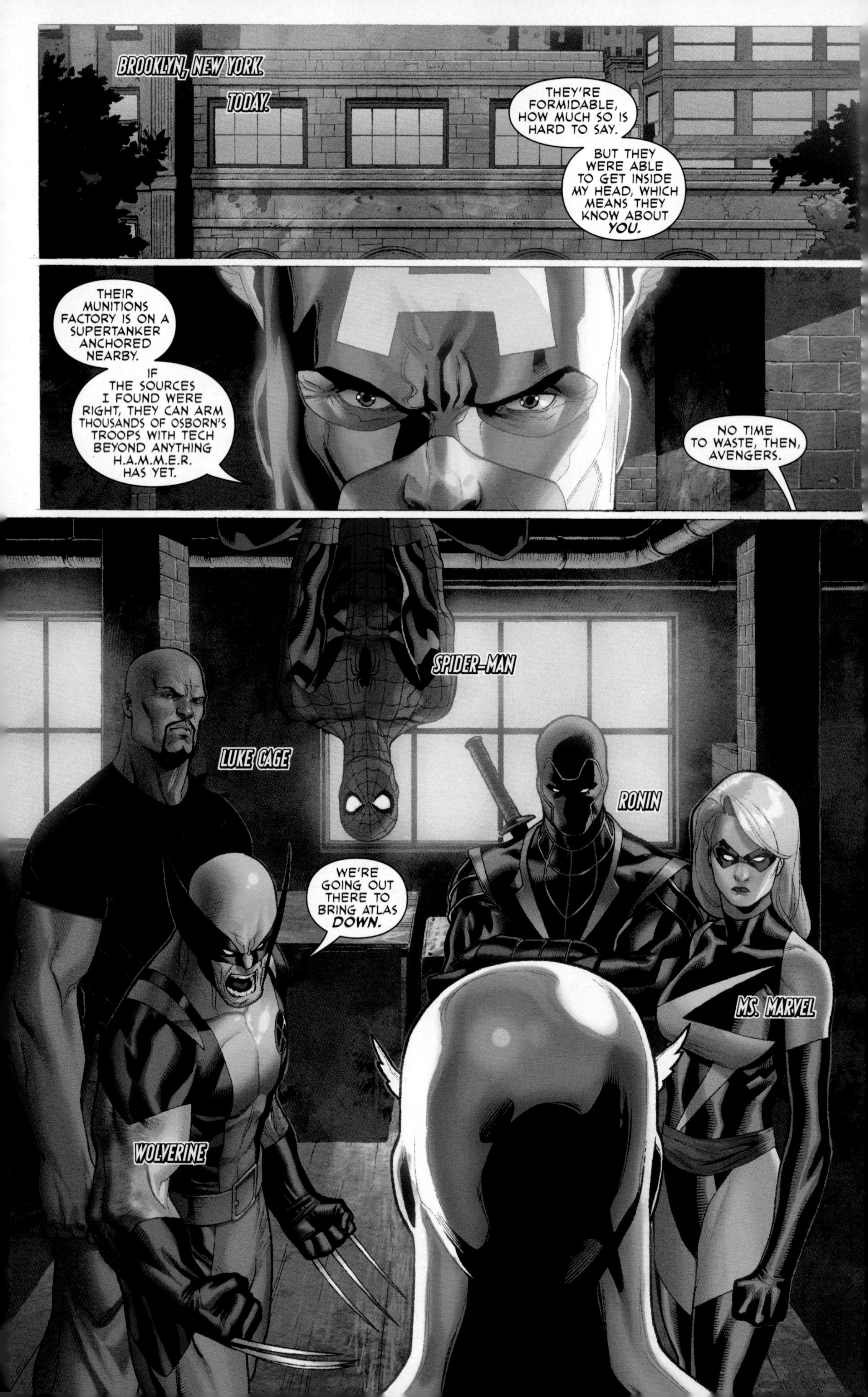
BROOKLYN, NEW YORK.
TODAY.
THEY'RE FORMIDABLE, HOW MUCH SO IS HARD TO SAY.
BUT THEY WERE ABLE TO GET INSIDE MY HEAD, WHICH MEANS THEY KNOW ABOUT *YOU.*
THEIR MUNITIONS FACTORY IS ON A SUPERTANKER ANCHORED NEARBY.
IF THE SOURCES I FOUND WERE RIGHT, THEY CAN ARM THOUSANDS OF OSBORN'S TROOPS WITH TECH BEYOND ANYTHING H.A.M.M.E.R. HAS YET.
NO TIME TO WASTE, THEN, AVENGERS.
SPIDER-MAN
LUKE CAGE
RONIN
WE'RE GOING OUT THERE TO BRING ATLAS *DOWN.*
MS. MARVEL
WOLVERINE

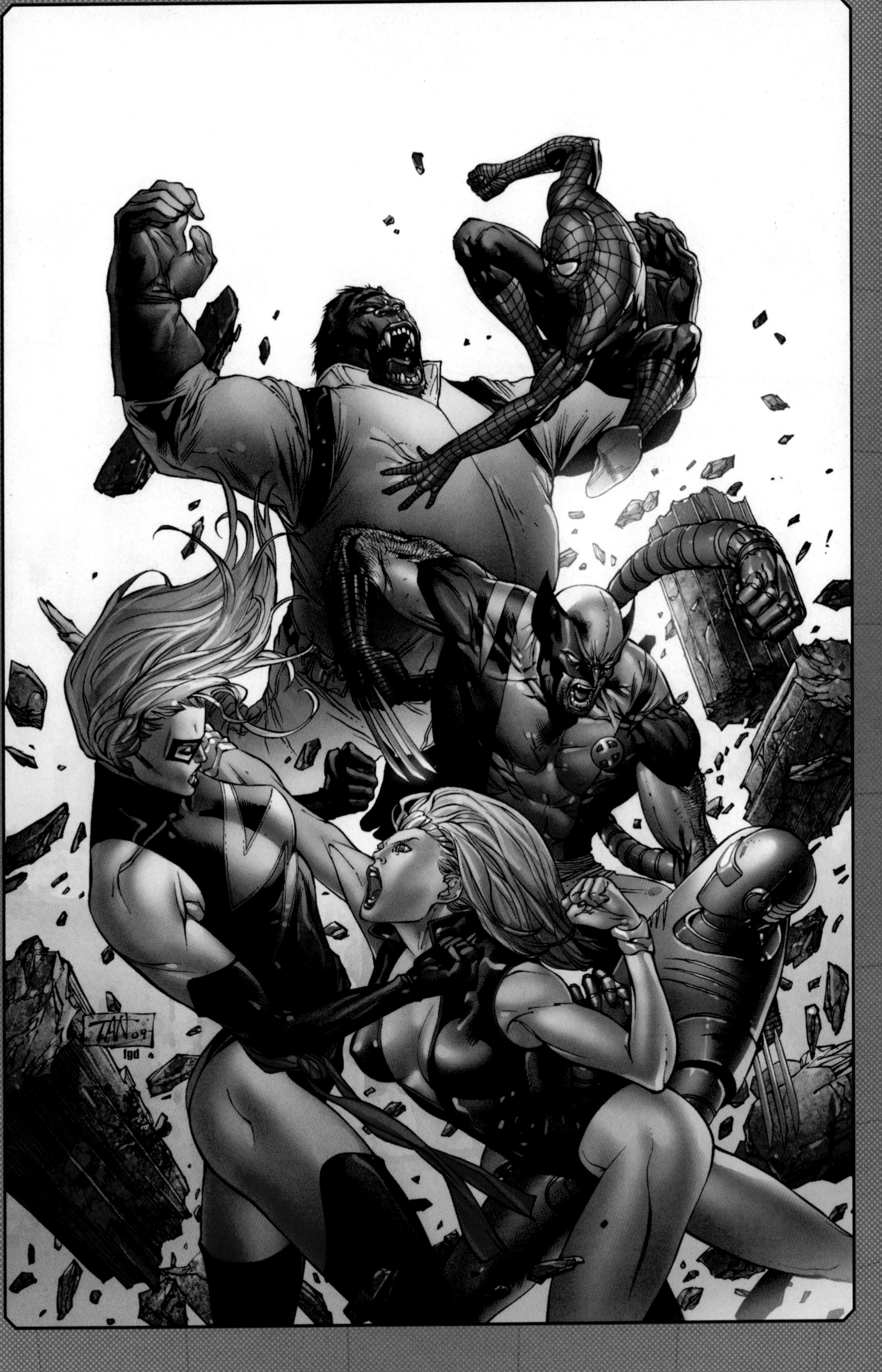

AGENTS OF ATLAS (2009) **5**

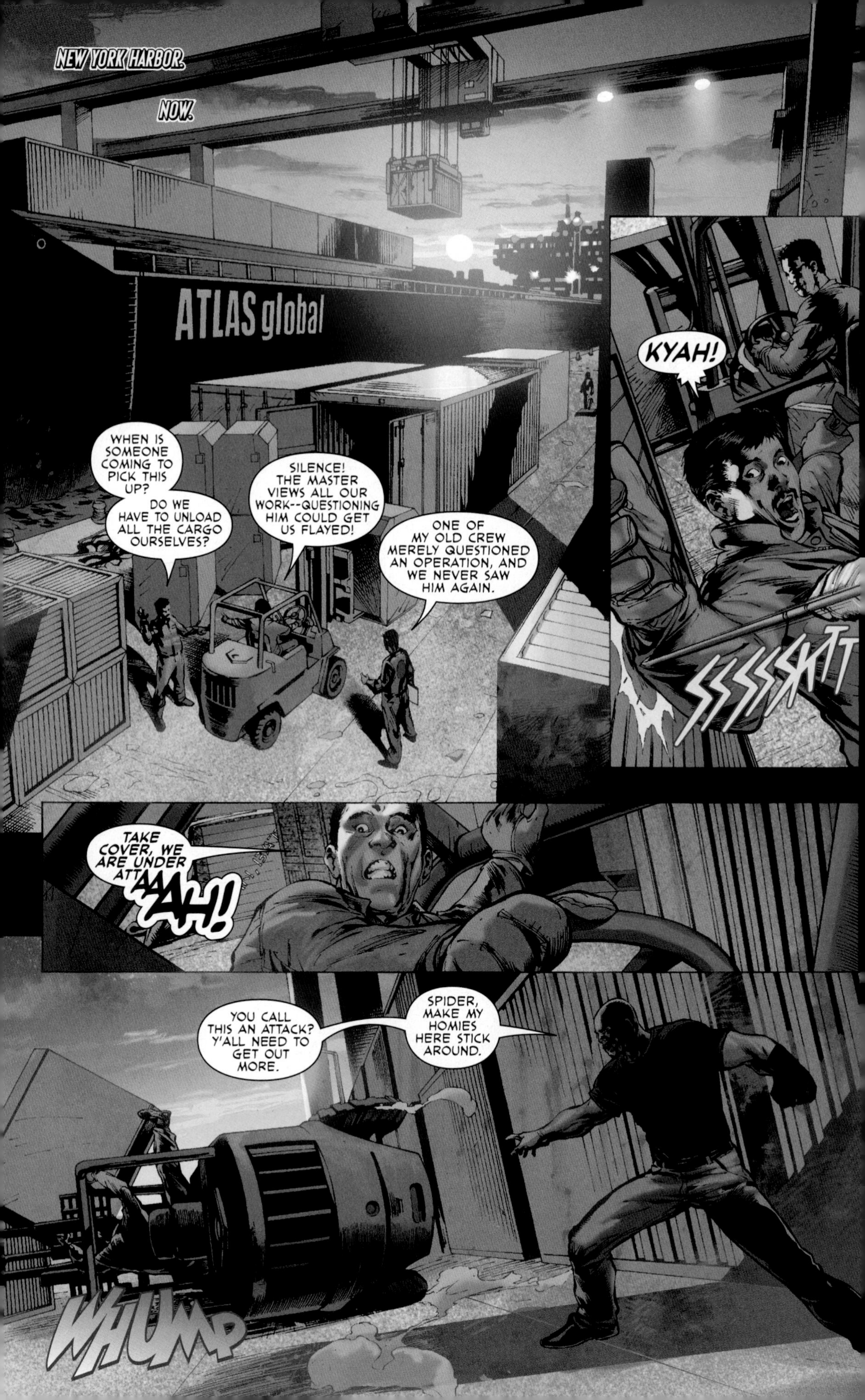
NEW YORK HARBOR.
NOW.
ATLAS global
WHEN IS SOMEONE COMING TO PICK THIS UP?
DO WE HAVE TO UNLOAD ALL THE CARGO OURSELVES?
SILENCE! THE MASTER VIEWS ALL OUR WORK--QUESTIONING HIM COULD GET US FLAYED!
ONE OF MY OLD CREW MERELY QUESTIONED AN OPERATION, AND WE NEVER SAW HIM AGAIN.
KYAH!
SSSSSKTT
TAKE COVER, WE ARE UNDER ATTAAAH!!
YOU CALL THIS AN ATTACK? Y'ALL NEED TO GET OUT MORE.
SPIDER, MAKE MY HOMIES HERE STICK AROUND.
WHUMP

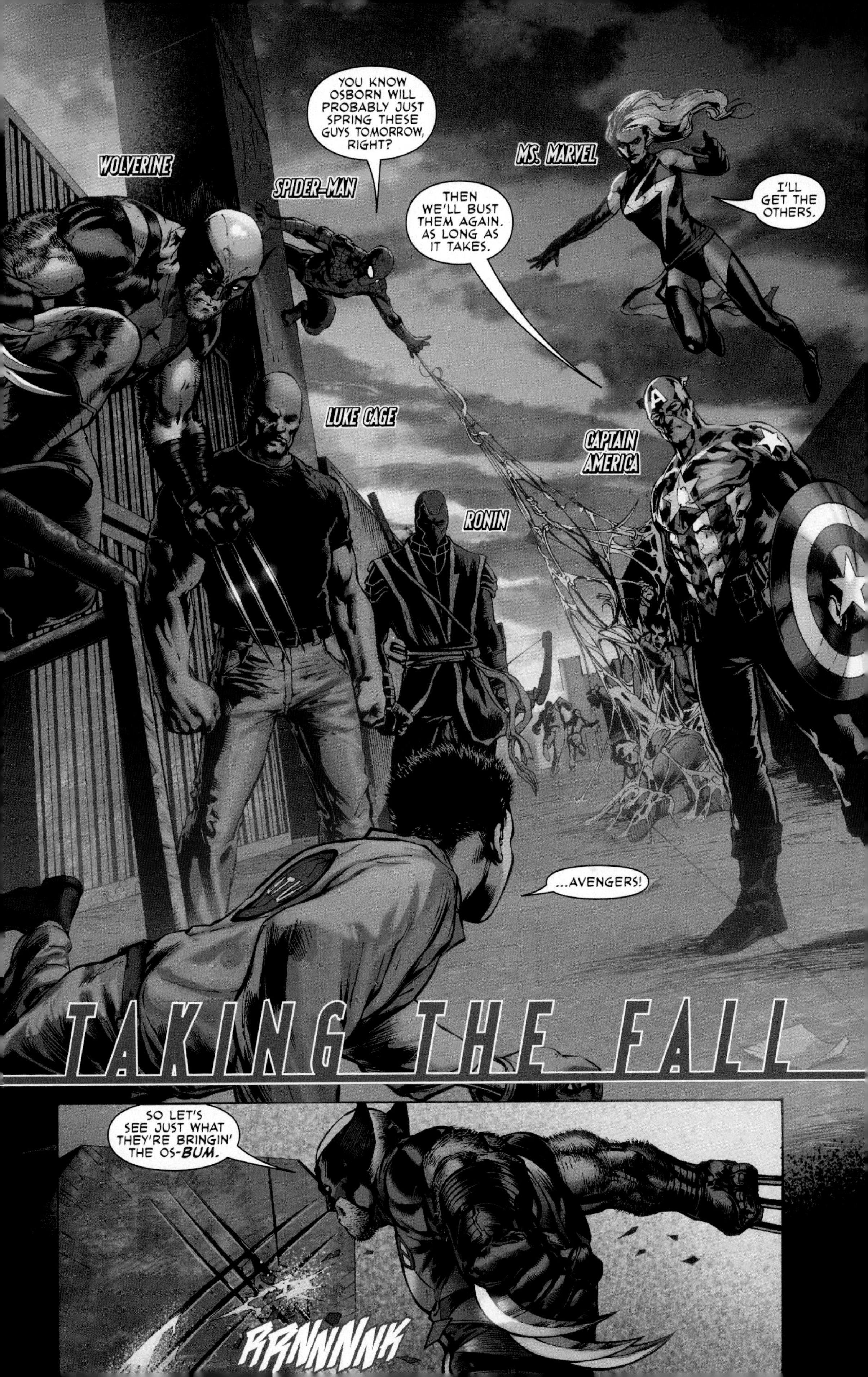
WOLVERINE
SPIDER-MAN
YOU KNOW OSBORN WILL PROBABLY JUST SPRING THESE GUYS TOMORROW, RIGHT?
MS. MARVEL
THEN WE'LL BUST THEM AGAIN. AS LONG AS IT TAKES.
I'LL GET THE OTHERS.
LUKE CAGE
CAPTAIN AMERICA
RONIN
...AVENGERS!
TAKING THE FALL
SO LET'S SEE JUST WHAT THEY'RE BRINGIN' THE OS-BUM.
RRNNNNK

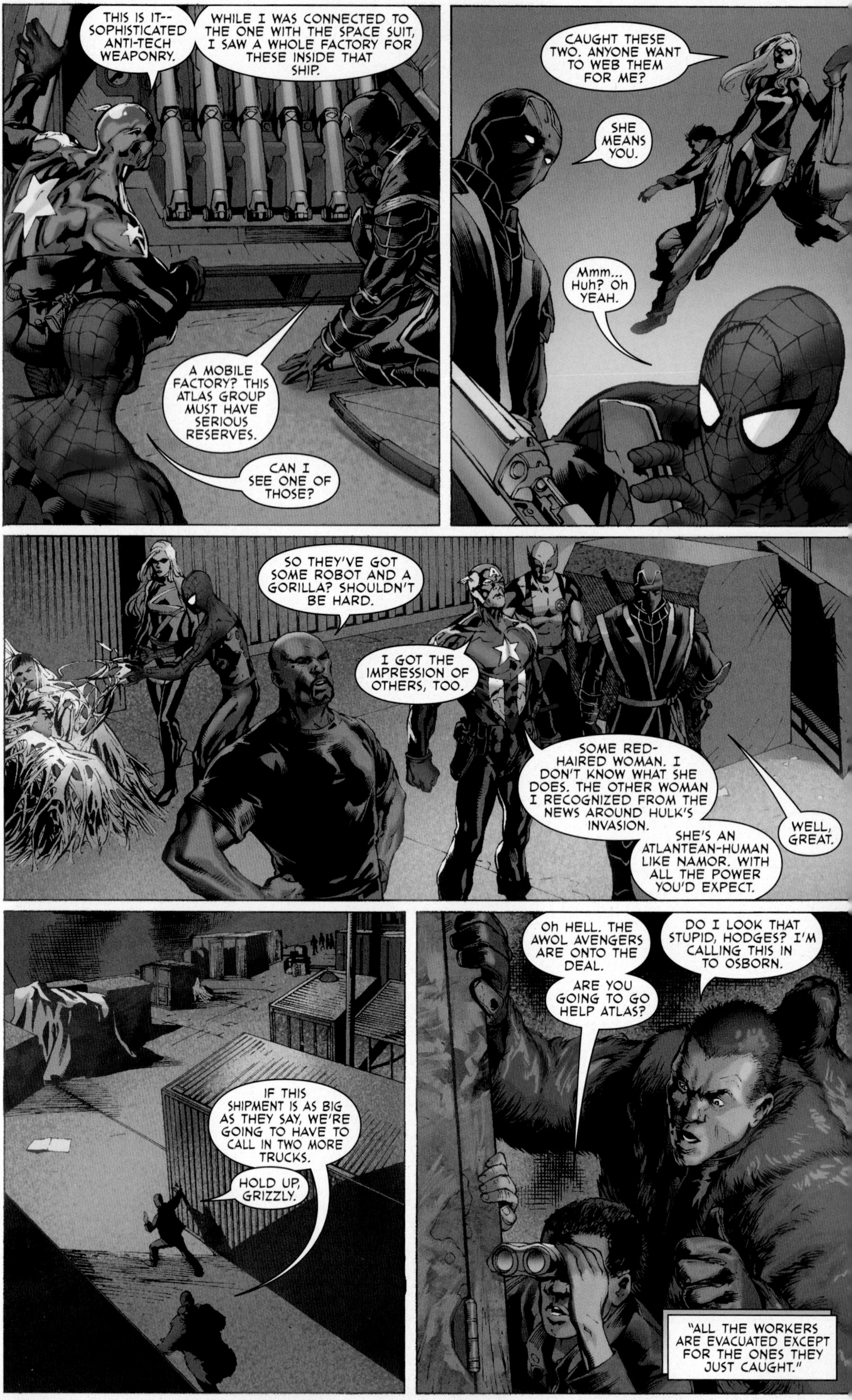
THIS IS IT-- SOPHISTICATED ANTI-TECH WEAPONRY.
WHILE I WAS CONNECTED TO THE ONE WITH THE SPACE SUIT, I SAW A WHOLE FACTORY FOR THESE INSIDE THAT SHIP.
A MOBILE FACTORY? THIS ATLAS GROUP MUST HAVE SERIOUS RESERVES.
CAN I SEE ONE OF THOSE?
CAUGHT THESE TWO. ANYONE WANT TO WEB THEM FOR ME?
SHE MEANS YOU.
Mmm... Huh? Oh YEAH.
SO THEY'VE GOT SOME ROBOT AND A GORILLA? SHOULDN'T BE HARD.
I GOT THE IMPRESSION OF OTHERS, TOO.
SOME RED-HAIRED WOMAN. I DON'T KNOW WHAT SHE DOES. THE OTHER WOMAN I RECOGNIZED FROM THE NEWS AROUND HULK'S INVASION.
SHE'S AN ATLANTEAN-HUMAN LIKE NAMOR. WITH ALL THE POWER YOU'D EXPECT.
WELL, GREAT.
IF THIS SHIPMENT IS AS BIG AS THEY SAY, WE'RE GOING TO HAVE TO CALL IN TWO MORE TRUCKS.
HOLD UP, GRIZZLY.
Oh HELL. THE AWOL AVENGERS ARE ONTO THE DEAL.
ARE YOU GOING TO GO HELP ATLAS?
DO I LOOK THAT STUPID, HODGES? I'M CALLING THIS IN TO OSBORN.
"ALL THE WORKERS ARE EVACUATED EXCEPT FOR THE ONES THEY JUST CAUGHT."

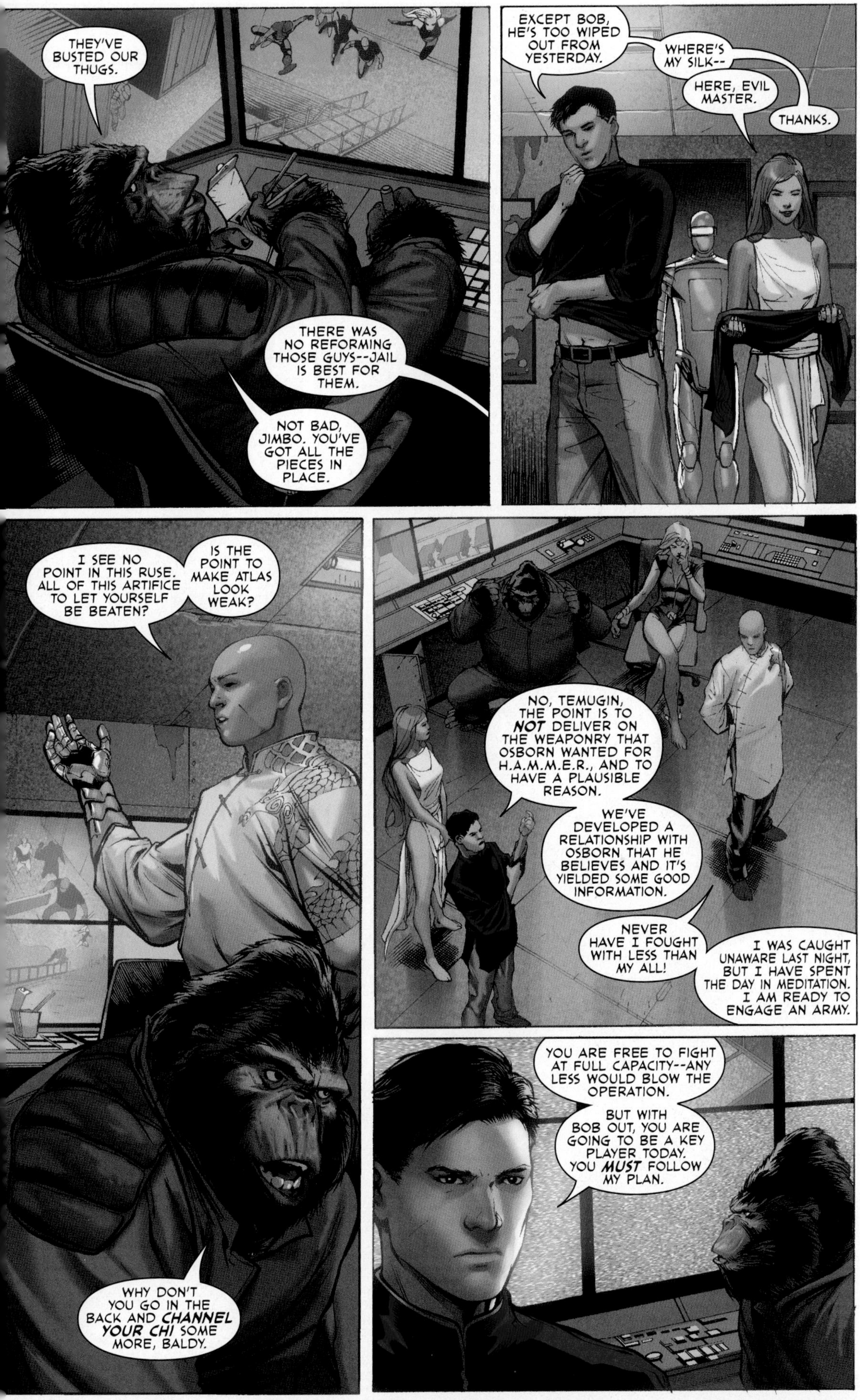
THEY'VE BUSTED OUR THUGS.
THERE WAS NO REFORMING THOSE GUYS--JAIL IS BEST FOR THEM.
NOT BAD, JIMBO. YOU'VE GOT ALL THE PIECES IN PLACE.
EXCEPT BOB, HE'S TOO WIPED OUT FROM YESTERDAY.
WHERE'S MY SILK--
HERE, EVIL MASTER.
THANKS.
I SEE NO POINT IN THIS RUSE. ALL OF THIS ARTIFICE TO LET YOURSELF BE BEATEN?
IS THE POINT TO MAKE ATLAS LOOK WEAK?
WHY DON'T YOU GO IN THE BACK AND CHANNEL YOUR CHI SOME MORE, BALDY.
NO, TEMUGIN, THE POINT IS TO NOT DELIVER ON THE WEAPONRY THAT OSBORN WANTED FOR H.A.M.M.E.R., AND TO HAVE A PLAUSIBLE REASON.
WE'VE DEVELOPED A RELATIONSHIP WITH OSBORN THAT HE BELIEVES AND IT'S YIELDED SOME GOOD INFORMATION.
NEVER HAVE I FOUGHT WITH LESS THAN MY ALL!
I WAS CAUGHT UNAWARE LAST NIGHT, BUT I HAVE SPENT THE DAY IN MEDITATION. I AM READY TO ENGAGE AN ARMY.
YOU ARE FREE TO FIGHT AT FULL CAPACITY--ANY LESS WOULD BLOW THE OPERATION.
BUT WITH BOB OUT, YOU ARE GOING TO BE A KEY PLAYER TODAY. YOU MUST FOLLOW MY PLAN.

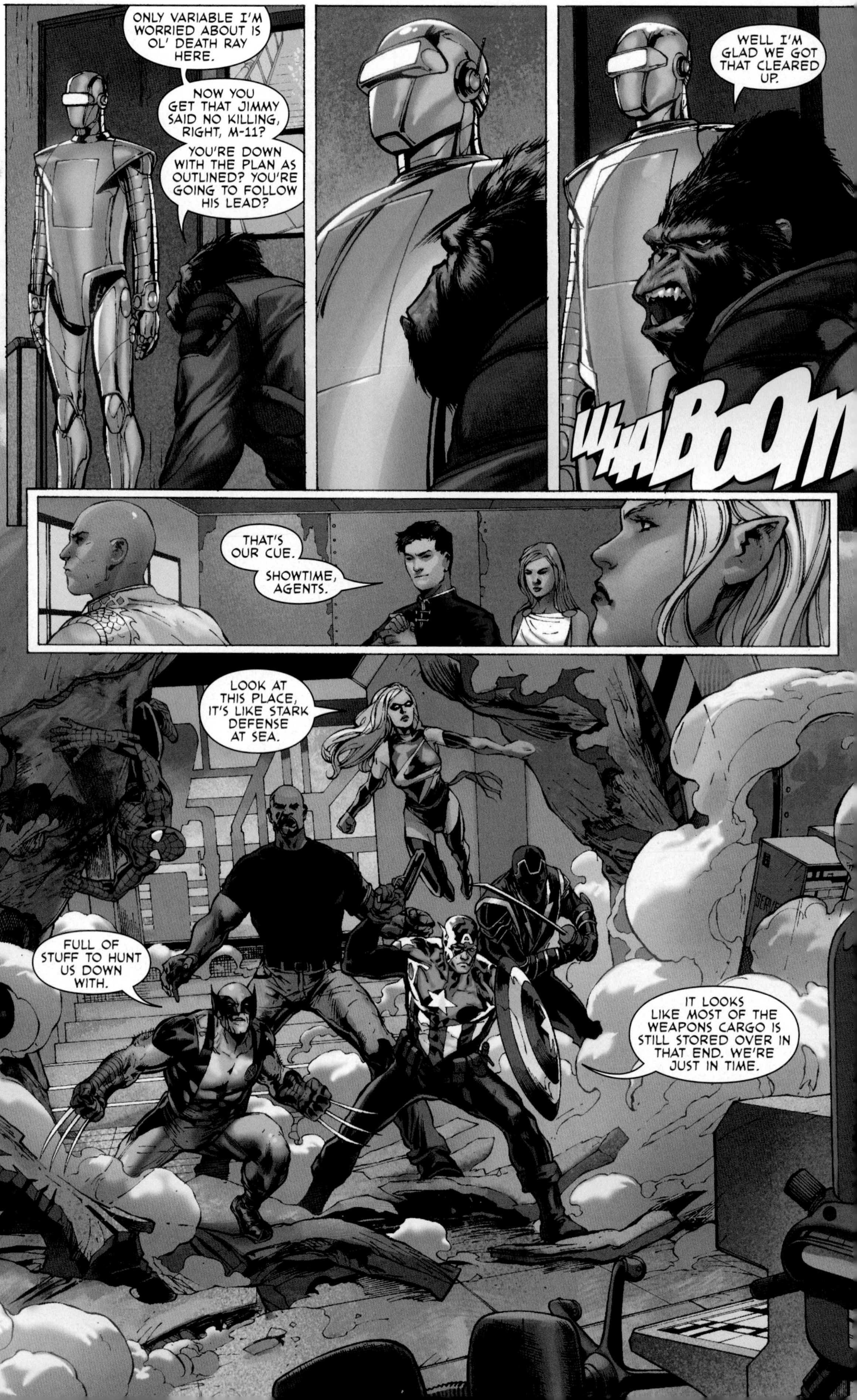
ONLY VARIABLE I'M WORRIED ABOUT IS OL' DEATH RAY HERE.
NOW YOU GET THAT JIMMY SAID NO KILLING, RIGHT, M-11?
YOU'RE DOWN WITH THE PLAN AS OUTLINED? YOU'RE GOING TO FOLLOW HIS LEAD?
WELL I'M GLAD WE GOT THAT CLEARED UP.
WHABOOM
THAT'S OUR CUE.
SHOWTIME, AGENTS.
LOOK AT THIS PLACE, IT'S LIKE STARK DEFENSE AT SEA.
FULL OF STUFF TO HUNT US DOWN WITH.
IT LOOKS LIKE MOST OF THE WEAPONS CARGO IS STILL STORED OVER IN THAT END. WE'RE JUST IN TIME.

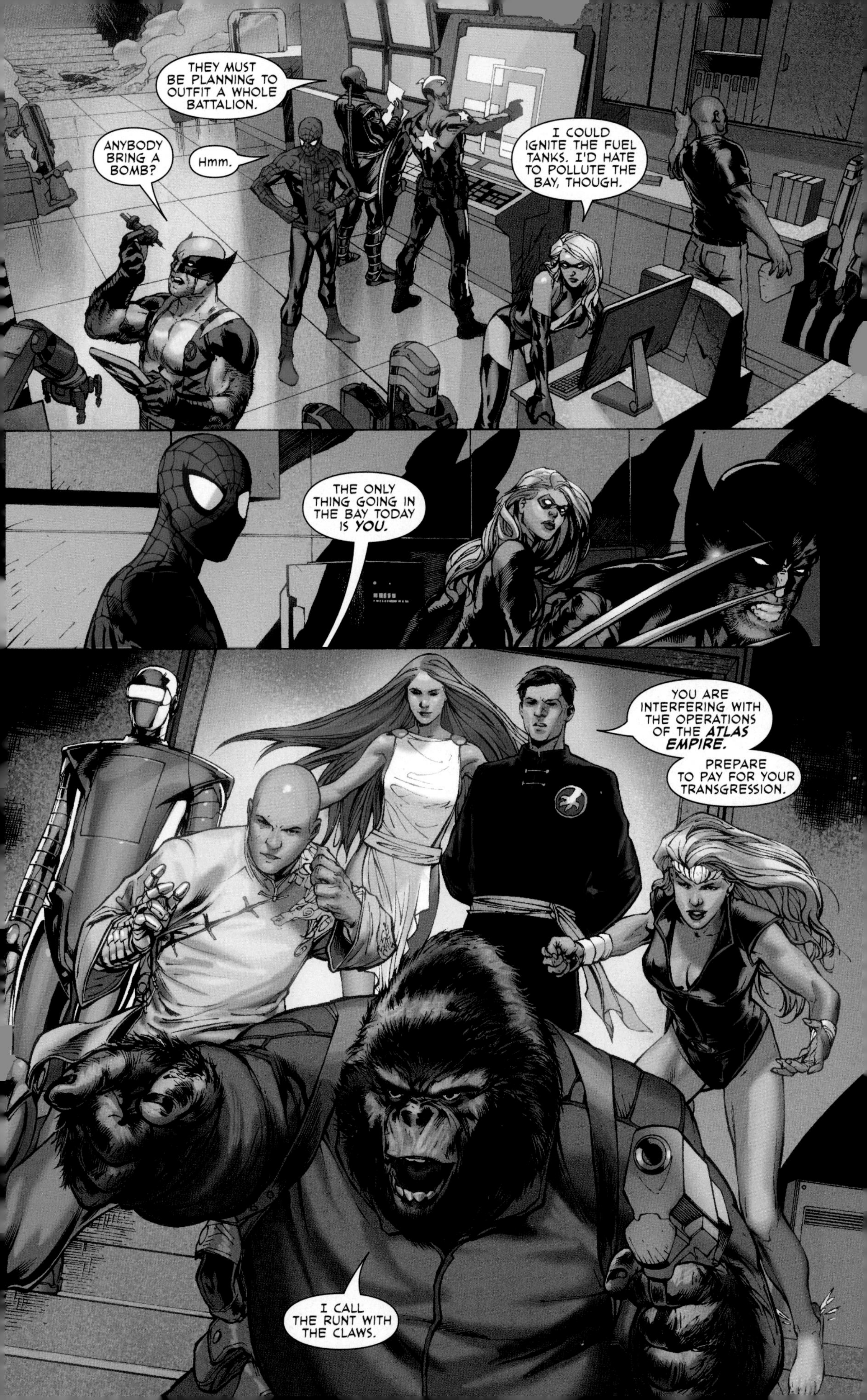
THEY MUST BE PLANNING TO OUTFIT A WHOLE BATTALION.
ANYBODY BRING A BOMB?
Hmm.
I COULD IGNITE THE FUEL TANKS. I'D HATE TO POLLUTE THE BAY, THOUGH.
THE ONLY THING GOING IN THE BAY TODAY IS *YOU.*
YOU ARE INTERFERING WITH THE OPERATIONS OF THE *ATLAS EMPIRE.*
PREPARE TO PAY FOR YOUR TRANSGRESSION.
I CALL THE RUNT WITH THE CLAWS.

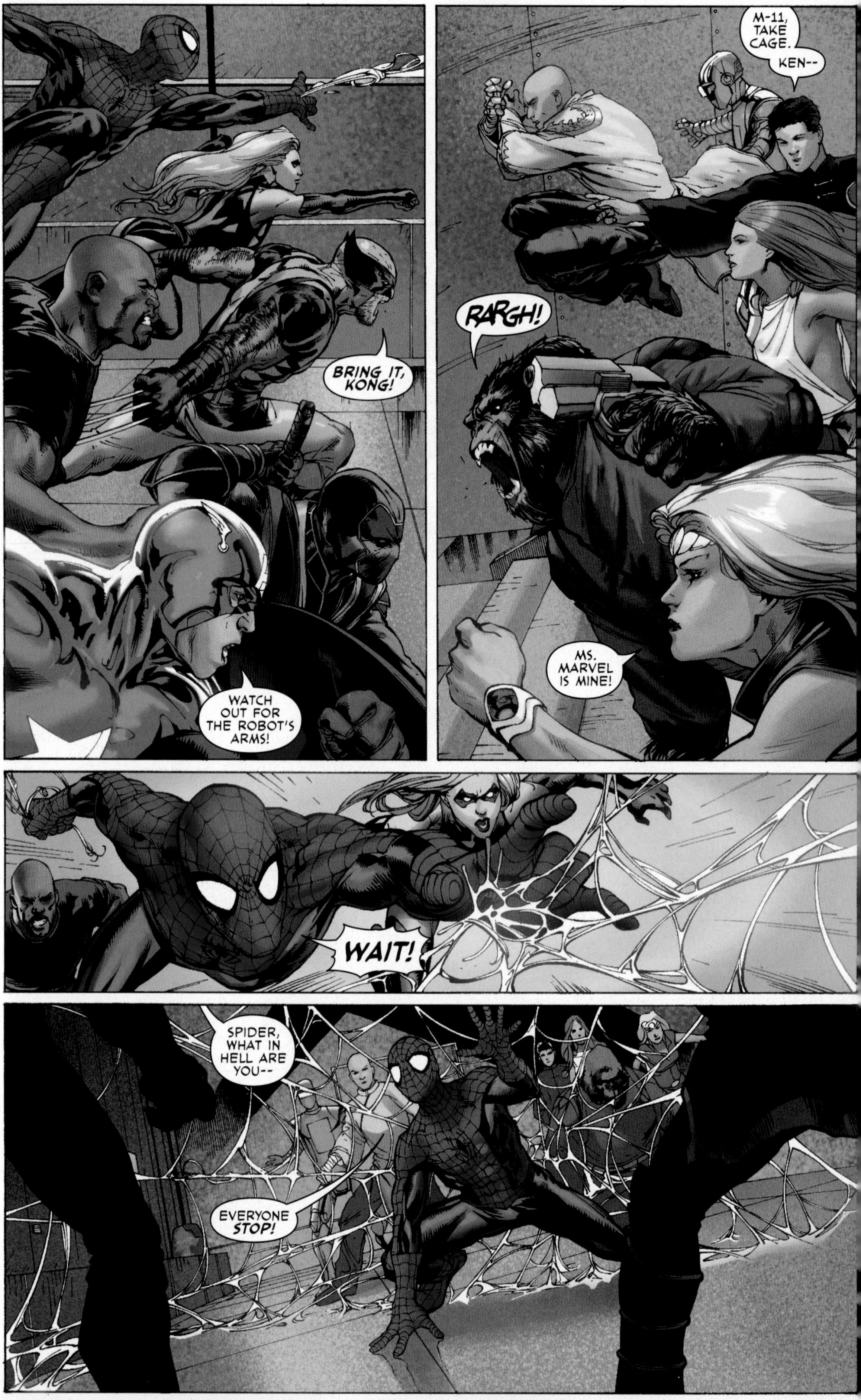
BRING IT, KONG!
WATCH OUT FOR THE ROBOT'S ARMS!
M-11, TAKE CAGE.
KEN--
RARGH!
MS. MARVEL IS MINE!
WAIT!
SPIDER, WHAT IN HELL ARE YOU--
EVERYONE STOP!

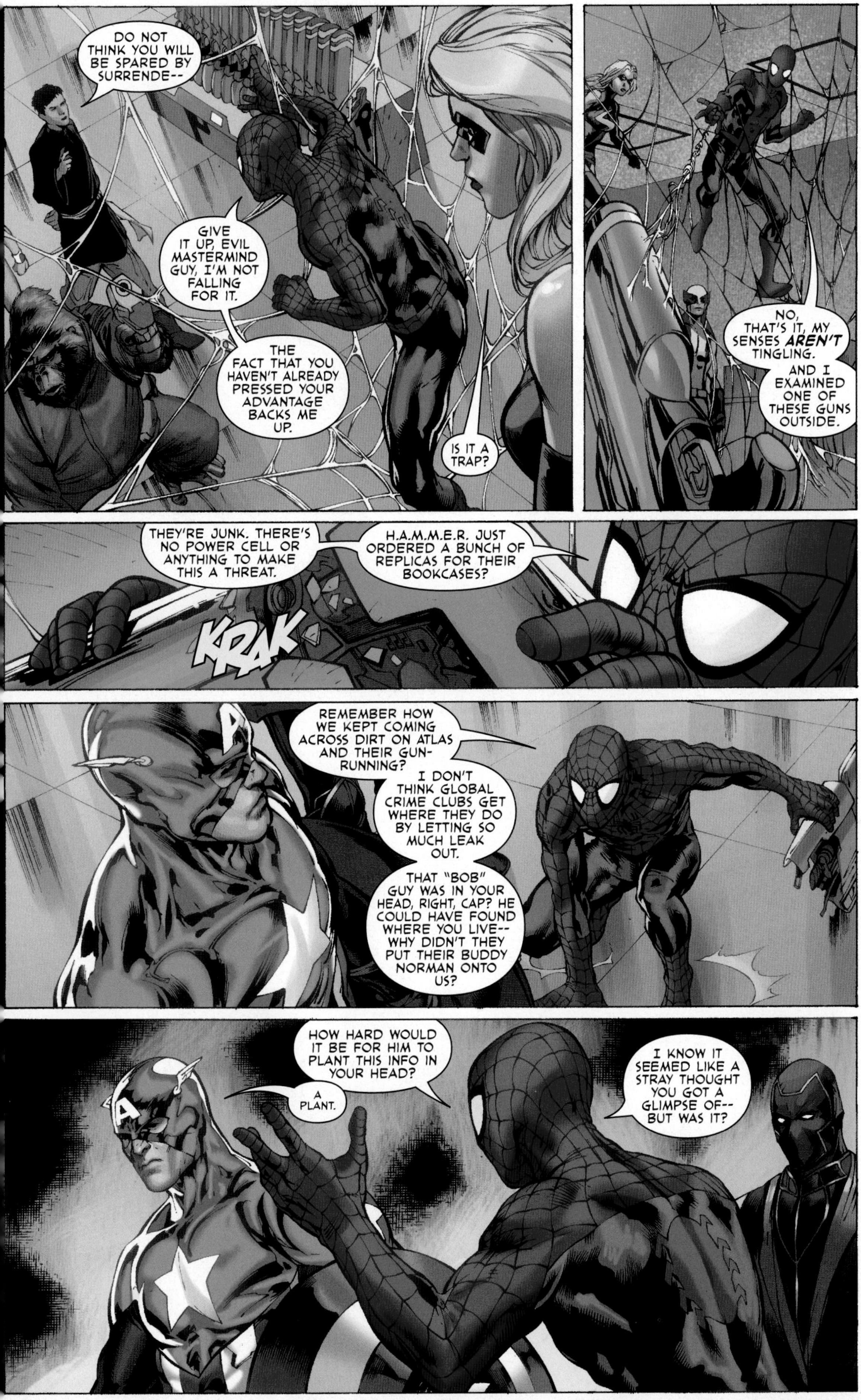
DO NOT THINK YOU WILL BE SPARED BY SURRENDE--
GIVE IT UP, EVIL MASTERMIND GUY, I'M NOT FALLING FOR IT.
THE FACT THAT YOU HAVEN'T ALREADY PRESSED YOUR ADVANTAGE BACKS ME UP.
IS IT A TRAP?
NO, THAT'S IT, MY SENSES *AREN'T* TINGLING.
AND I EXAMINED ONE OF THESE GUNS OUTSIDE.
THEY'RE JUNK. THERE'S NO POWER CELL OR ANYTHING TO MAKE THIS A THREAT.
H.A.M.M.E.R. JUST ORDERED A BUNCH OF REPLICAS FOR THEIR BOOKCASES?
KRAK
REMEMBER HOW WE KEPT COMING ACROSS DIRT ON ATLAS AND THEIR GUN-RUNNING?
I DON'T THINK GLOBAL CRIME CLUBS GET WHERE THEY DO BY LETTING SO MUCH LEAK OUT.
THAT "BOB" GUY WAS IN YOUR HEAD, RIGHT, CAP? HE COULD HAVE FOUND WHERE YOU LIVE-- WHY DIDN'T THEY PUT THEIR BUDDY NORMAN ONTO US?
HOW HARD WOULD IT BE FOR HIM TO PLANT THIS INFO IN YOUR HEAD?
A PLANT.
I KNOW IT SEEMED LIKE A STRAY THOUGHT YOU GOT A GLIMPSE OF-- BUT WAS IT?

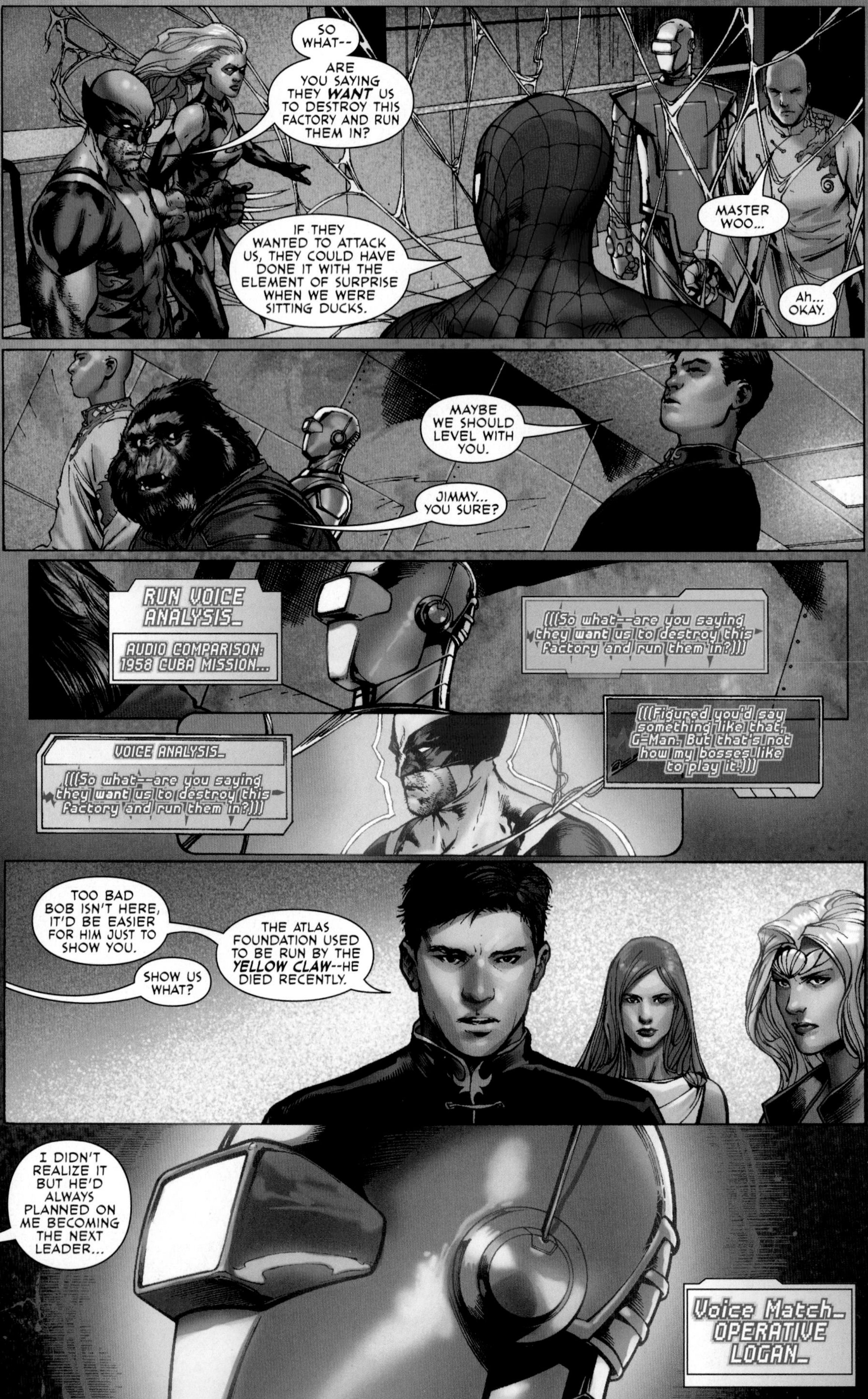
SO WHAT-- ARE YOU SAYING THEY WANT US TO DESTROY THIS FACTORY AND RUN THEM IN?
IF THEY WANTED TO ATTACK US, THEY COULD HAVE DONE IT WITH THE ELEMENT OF SURPRISE WHEN WE WERE SITTING DUCKS.
MASTER WOO...
Ah... OKAY.
MAYBE WE SHOULD LEVEL WITH YOU.
JIMMY... YOU SURE?
RUN VOICE ANALYSIS_
AUDIO COMPARISON: 1958 CUBA MISSION...
(((So what--are you saying they want us to destroy this factory and run them in?)))
VOICE ANALYSIS_
(((So what--are you saying they want us to destroy this factory and run them in?)))
(((Figured you'd say something like that, G-Man. But that's not how my bosses like to play it.)))
TOO BAD BOB ISN'T HERE, IT'D BE EASIER FOR HIM JUST TO SHOW YOU.
SHOW US WHAT?
THE ATLAS FOUNDATION USED TO BE RUN BY THE YELLOW CLAW--HE DIED RECENTLY.
I DIDN'T REALIZE IT BUT HE'D ALWAYS PLANNED ON ME BECOMING THE NEXT LEADER...
Voice Match_ OPERATIVE LOGAN_

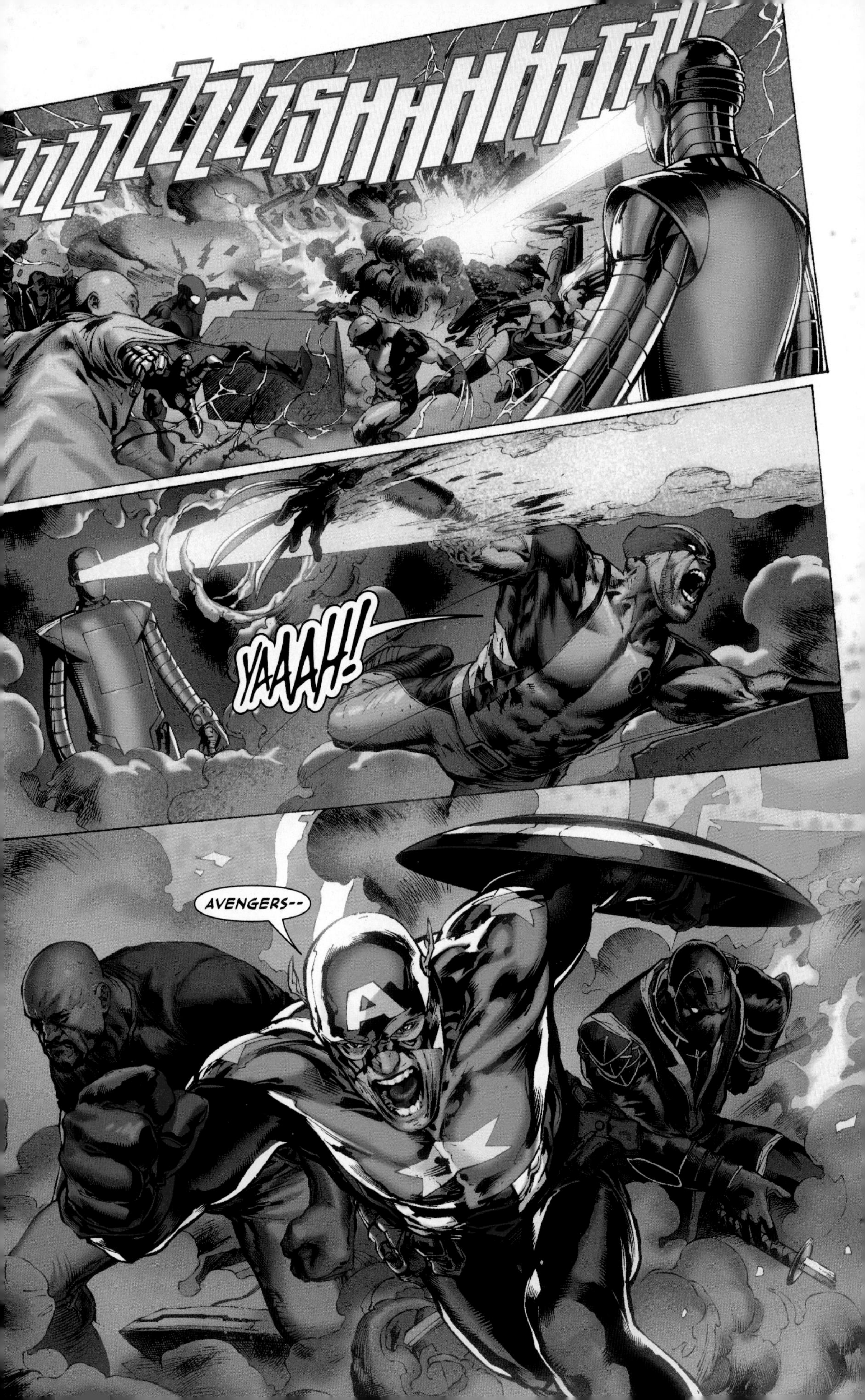
ZZZZZZZZZSHHHHHTT!!
YAAAH!
AVENGERS--

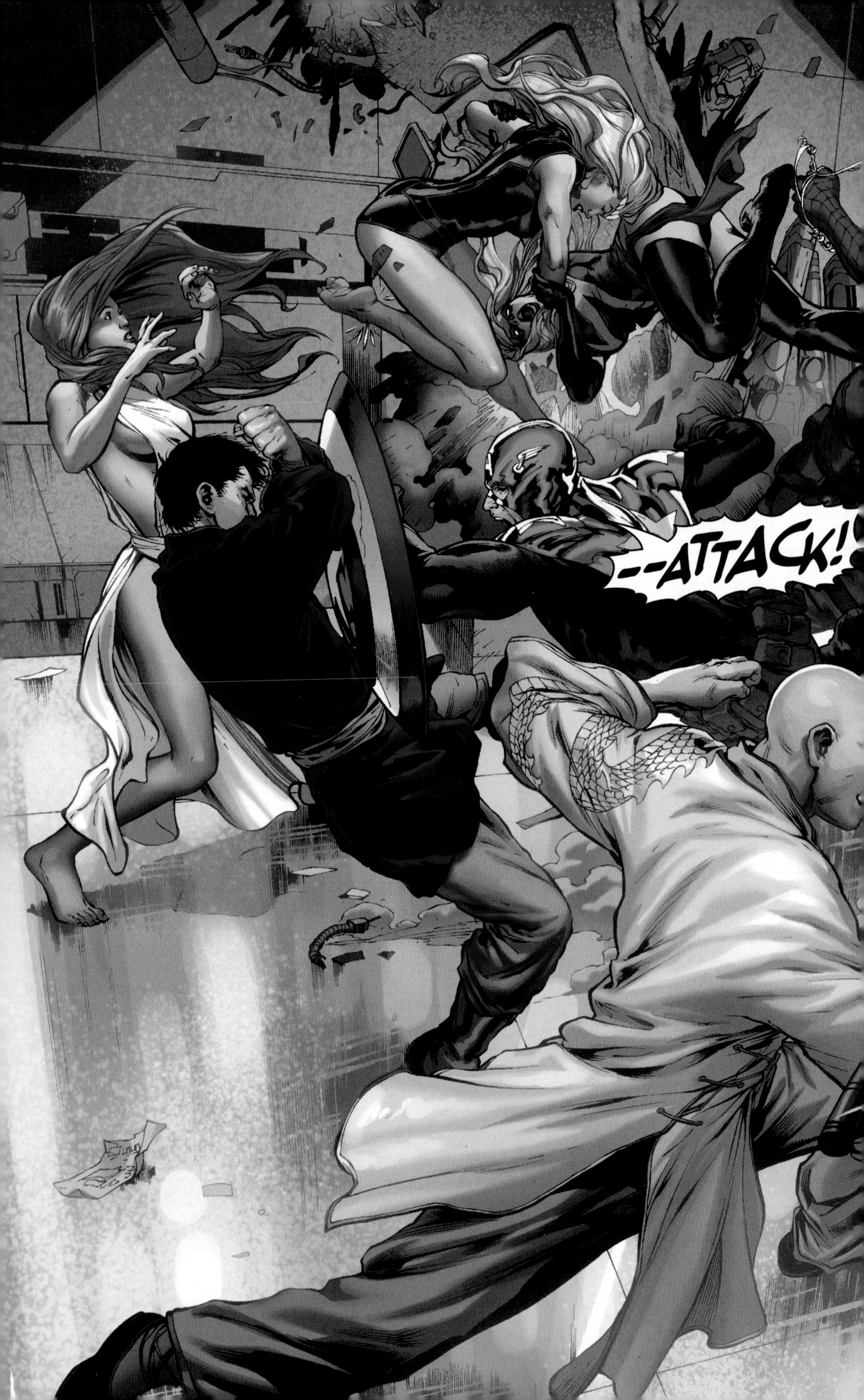
--ATTACK!

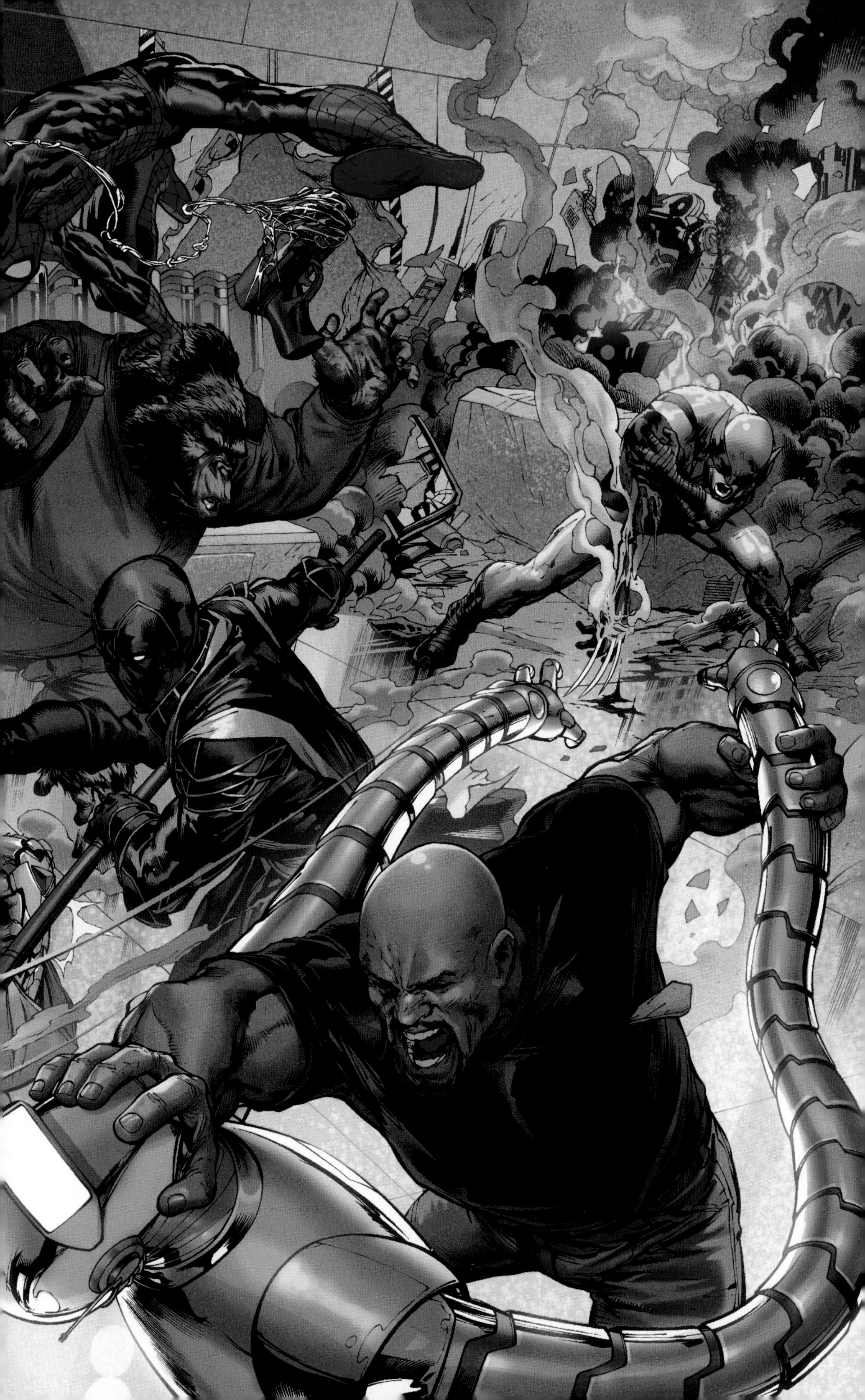

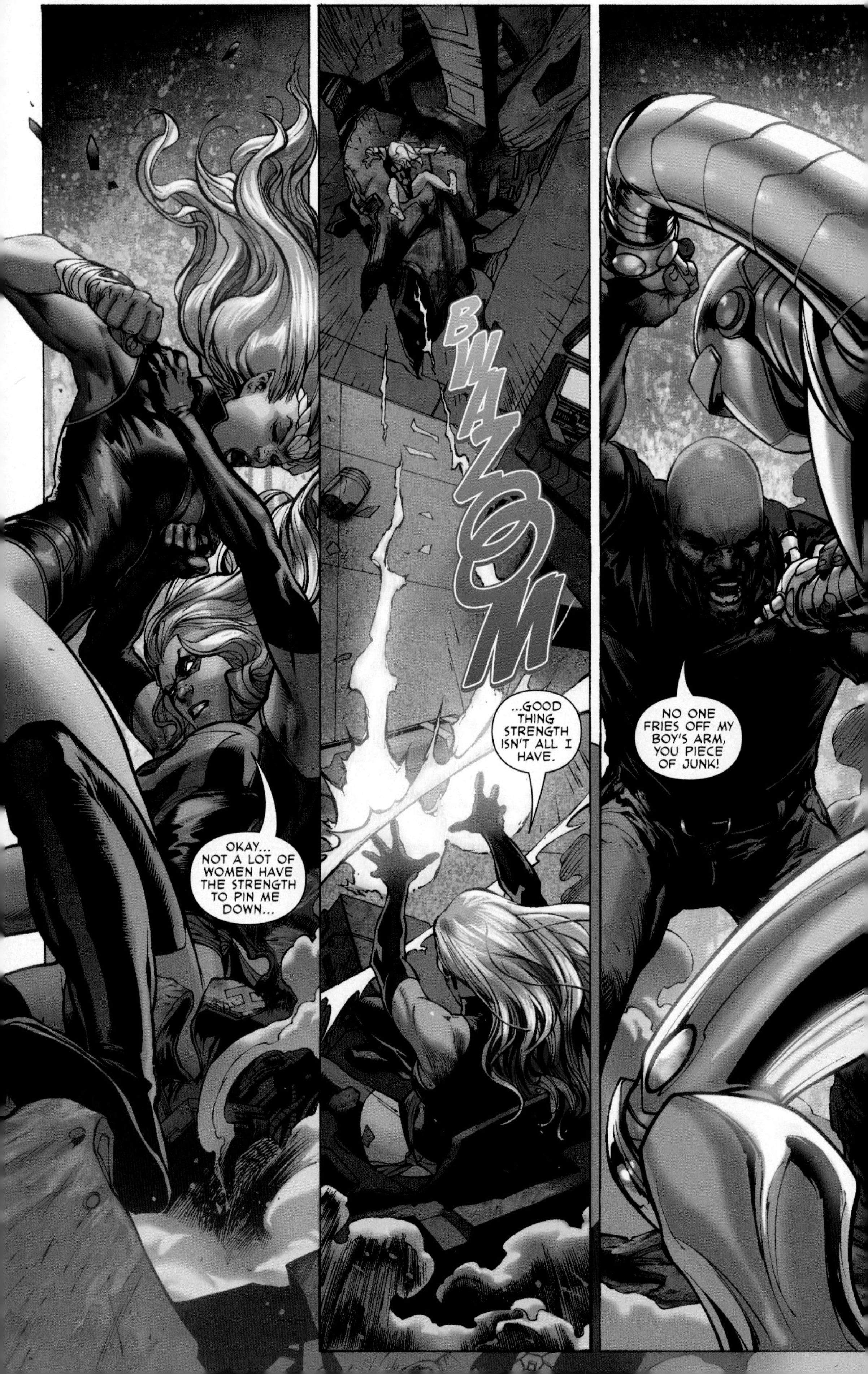
OKAY... NOT A LOT OF WOMEN HAVE THE STRENGTH TO PIN ME DOWN...
BWAZOOM
...GOOD THING STRENGTH ISN'T ALL I HAVE.
NO ONE FRIES OFF MY BOY'S ARM, YOU PIECE OF JUNK!

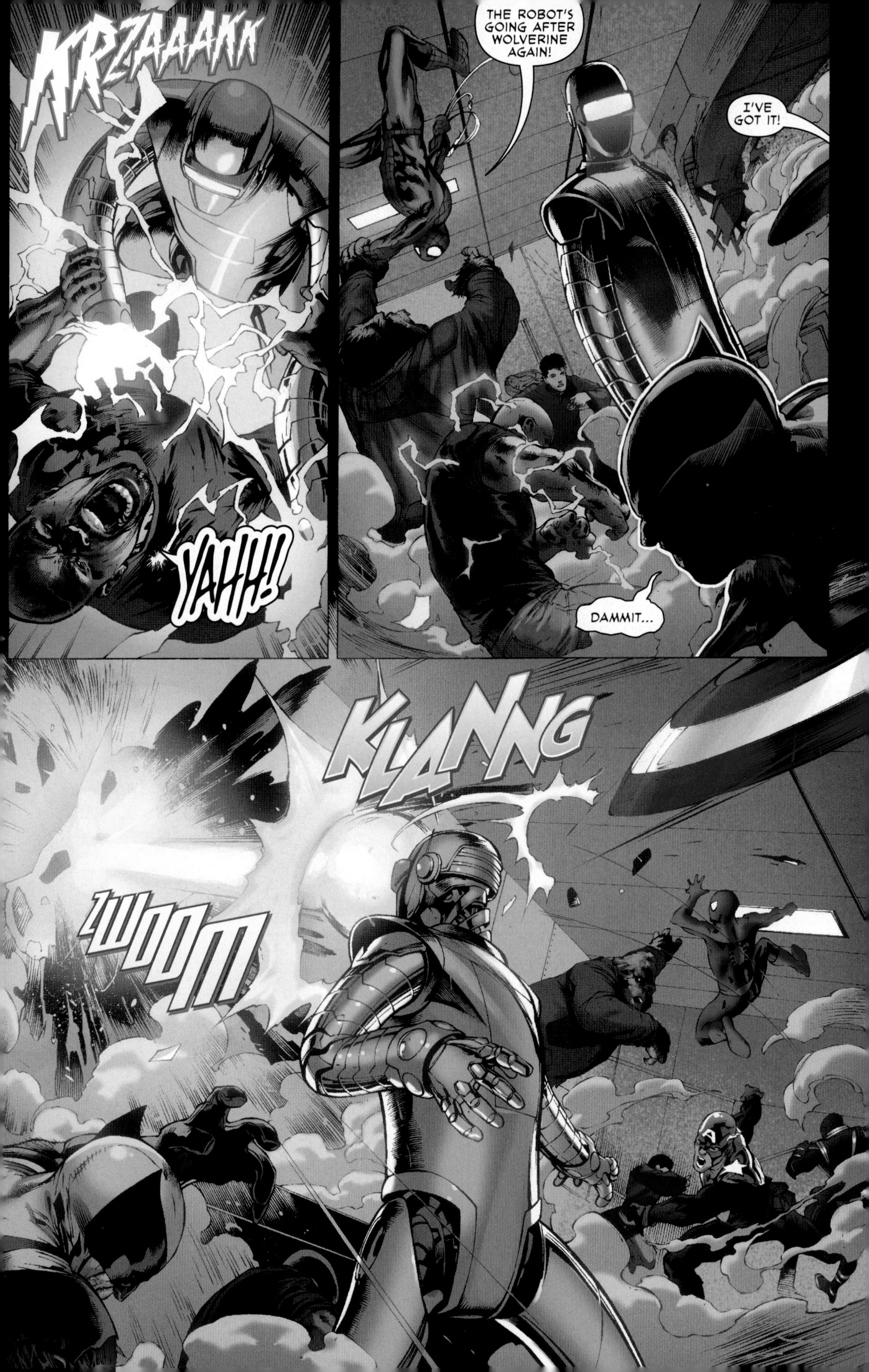
KRZAAAKK
YAHH!
THE ROBOT'S GOING AFTER WOLVERINE AGAIN!
I'VE GOT IT!
DAMMIT...
KLANNG
ZWOOM

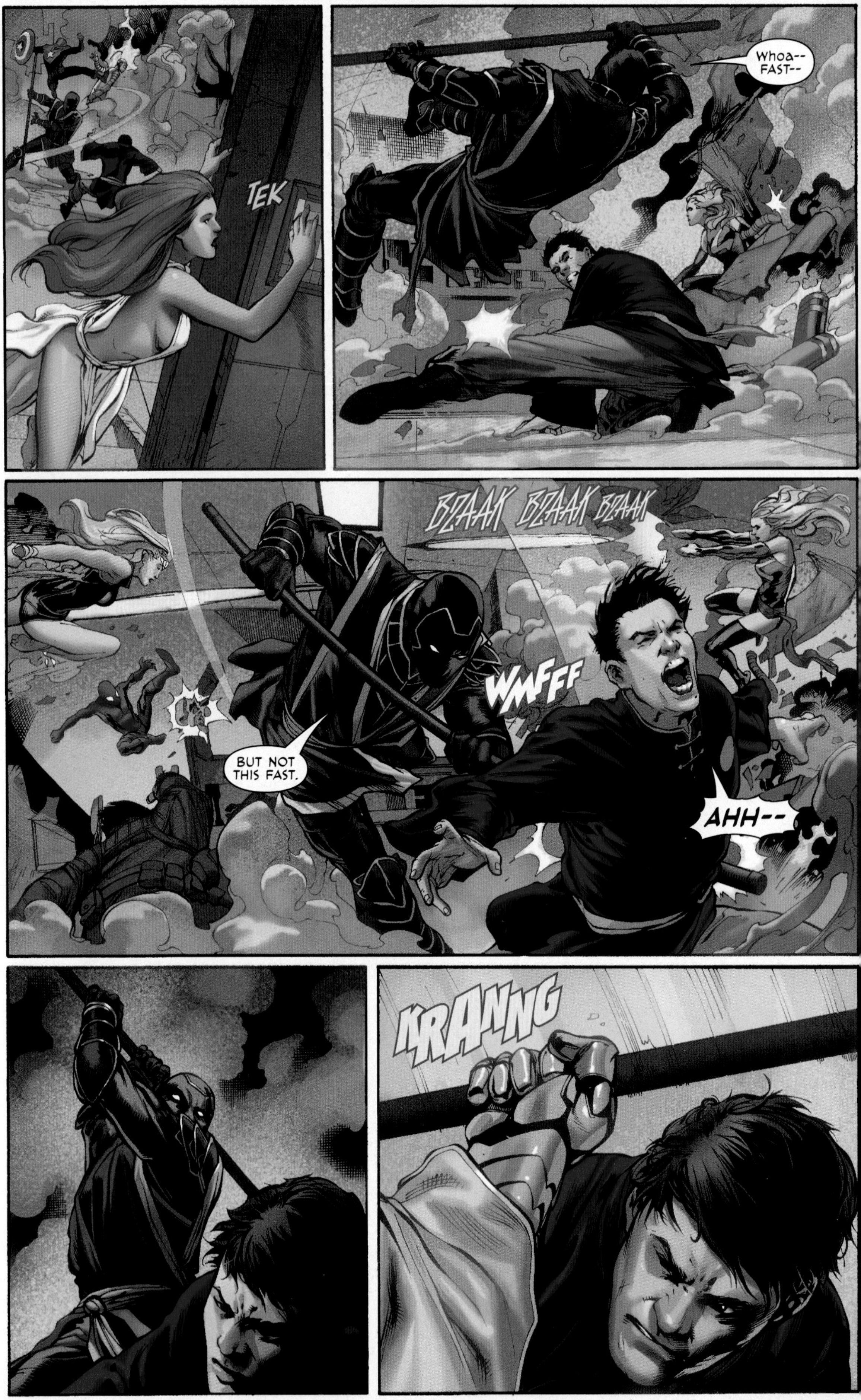
TEK
Whoa-- FAST--
BZAAK BZAAK BZAAK
WMFFF
BUT NOT THIS FAST.
AHH--
KRANNG

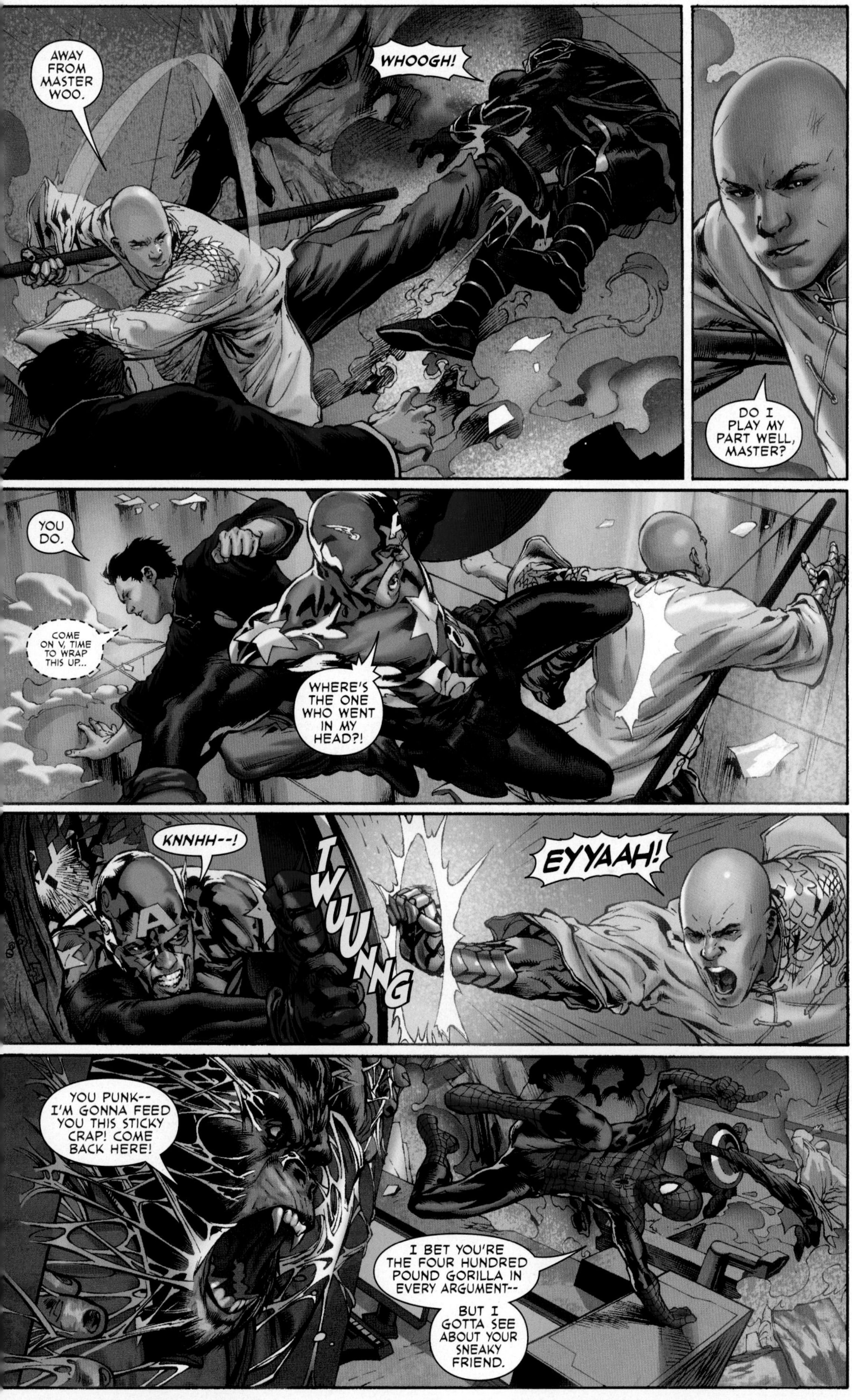
AWAY FROM MASTER WOO.
WHOOGH!
DO I PLAY MY PART WELL, MASTER?
YOU DO.
COME ON V, TIME TO WRAP THIS UP...
WHERE'S THE ONE WHO WENT IN MY HEAD?!
KNNHH--!
TWUUNNG
EYYAAH!
YOU PUNK-- I'M GONNA FEED YOU THIS STICKY CRAP! COME BACK HERE!
I BET YOU'RE THE FOUR HUNDRED POUND GORILLA IN EVERY ARGUMENT--
BUT I GOTTA SEE ABOUT YOUR SNEAKY FRIEND.

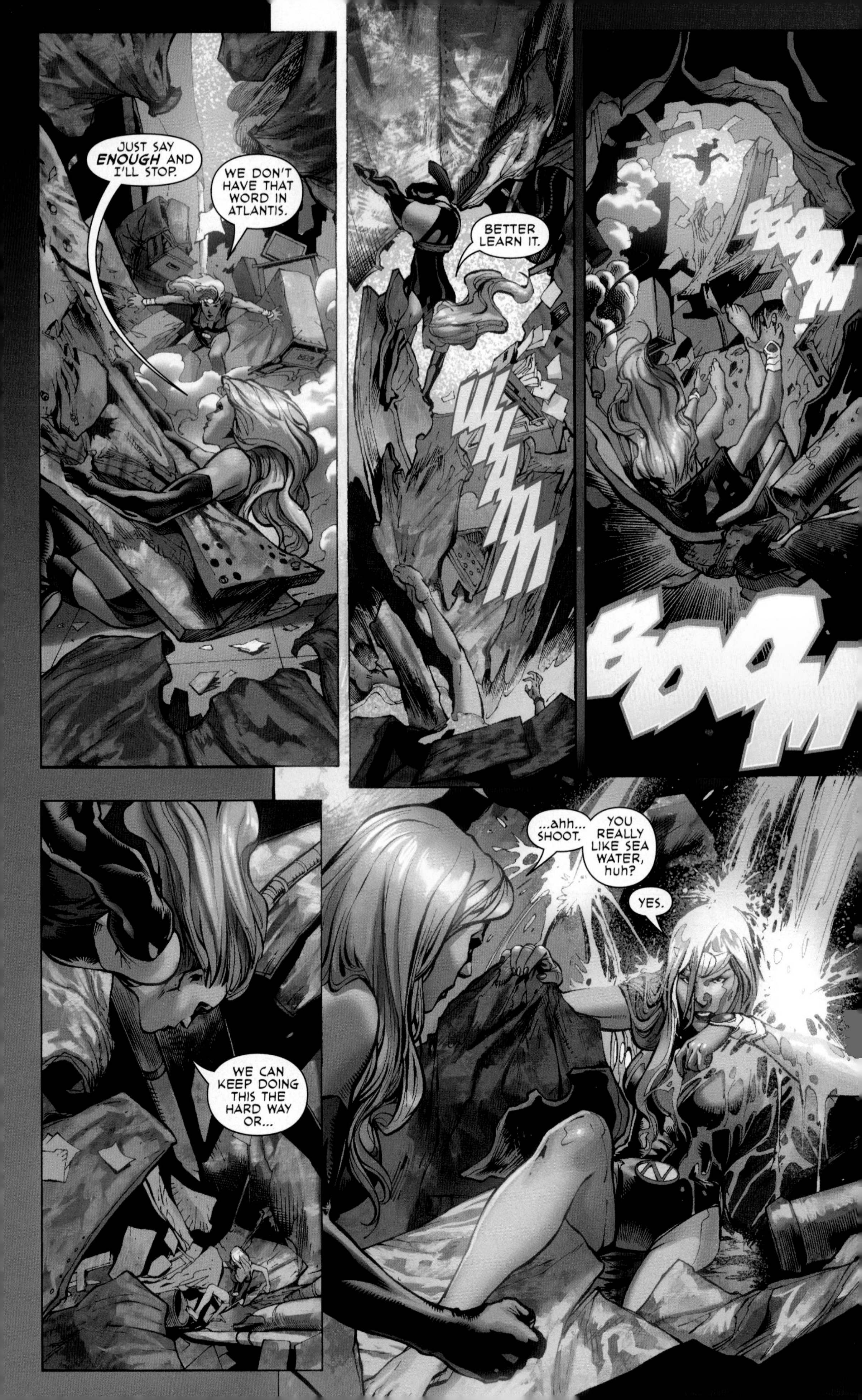
JUST SAY ENOUGH AND I'LL STOP.
WE DON'T HAVE THAT WORD IN ATLANTIS.
BETTER LEARN IT.
WHAM
BBOOM
BOOM
WE CAN KEEP DOING THIS THE HARD WAY OR...
...ahh... SHOOT.
YOU REALLY LIKE SEA WATER, huh?
YES.

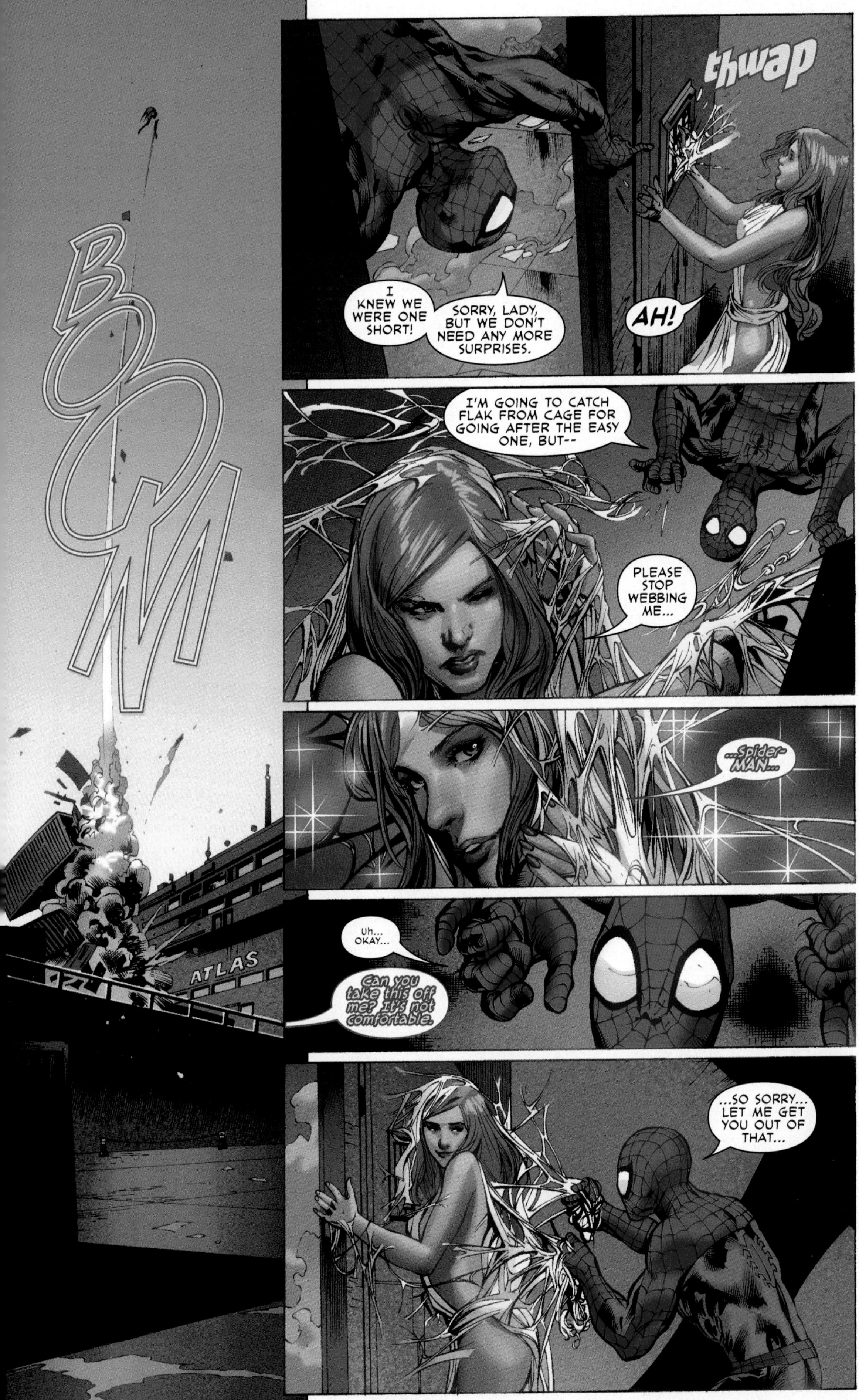
BOOM
ATLAS
thwap
I KNEW WE WERE ONE SHORT!
SORRY, LADY, BUT WE DON'T NEED ANY MORE SURPRISES.
AH!
I'M GOING TO CATCH FLAK FROM CAGE FOR GOING AFTER THE EASY ONE, BUT--
PLEASE STOP WEBBING ME...
...Spider-MAN...
Uh... OKAY...
Can you take this off me? It's not comfortable.
...SO SORRY... LET ME GET YOU OUT OF THAT...

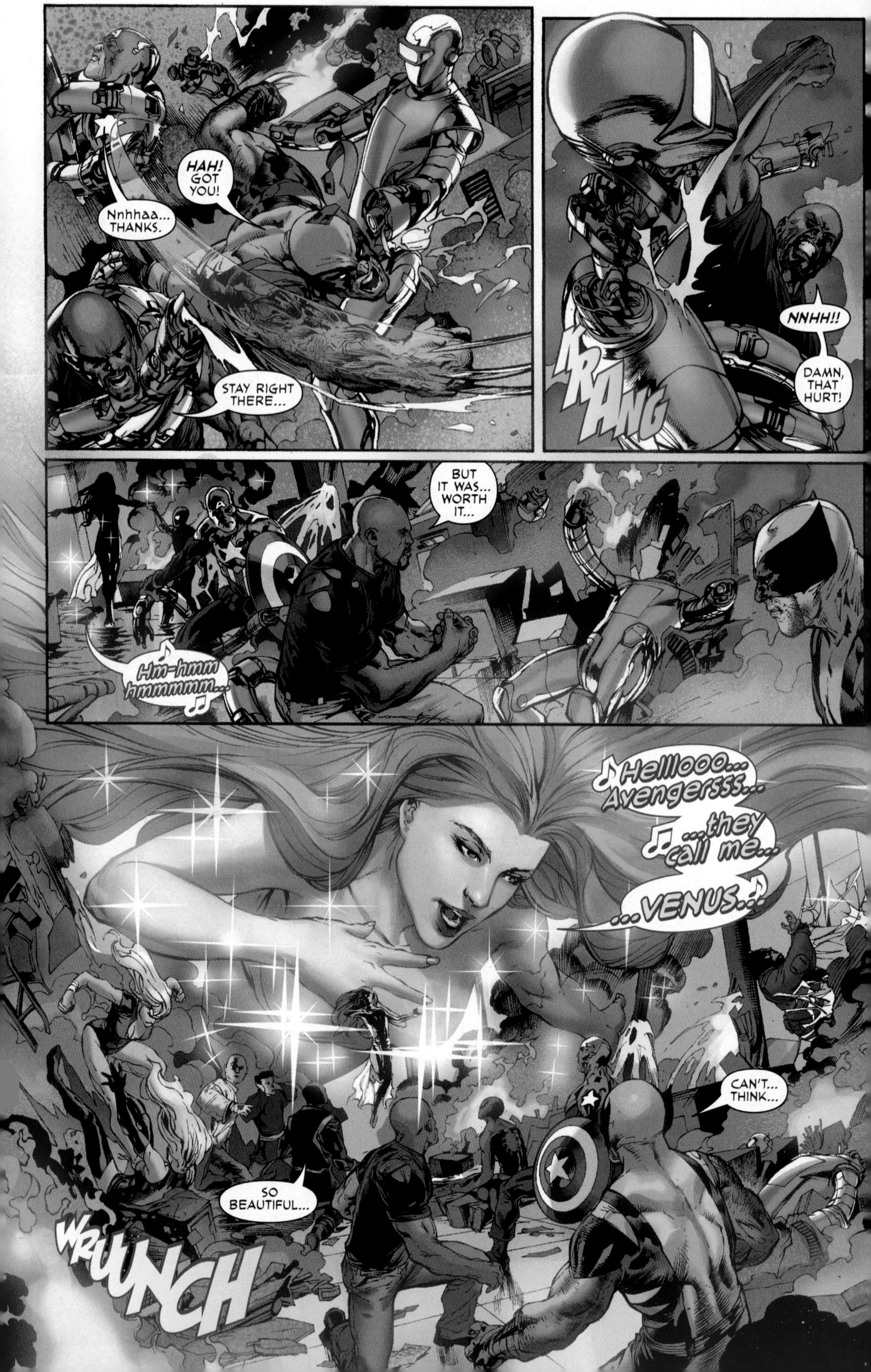
HAH! GOT YOU!
Nnhhaa... THANKS.
STAY RIGHT THERE...
NNHH!!
DAMN, THAT HURT!
KRANG
BUT IT WAS... WORTH IT...
Hm-hmm hmmmmm...
Helllooo... Avengersss...
...they call me...
...VENUS...
CAN'T... THINK...
SO BEAUTIFUL...
WRUUNCH

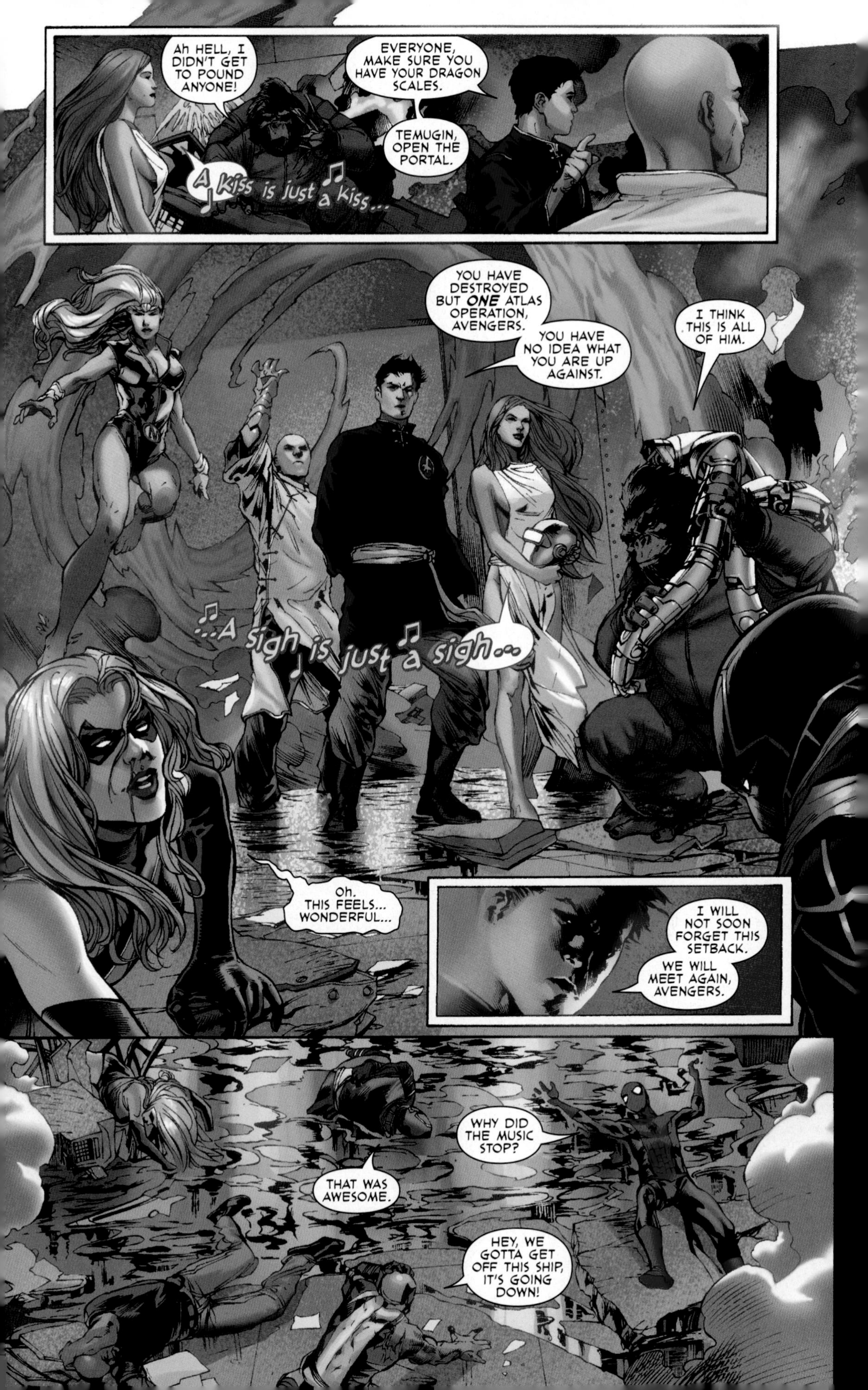
Ah HELL, I DIDN'T GET TO POUND ANYONE!
EVERYONE, MAKE SURE YOU HAVE YOUR DRAGON SCALES.
TEMUGIN, OPEN THE PORTAL.
A kiss is just a kiss...
YOU HAVE DESTROYED BUT *ONE* ATLAS OPERATION, AVENGERS.
YOU HAVE NO IDEA WHAT YOU ARE UP AGAINST.
I THINK THIS IS ALL OF HIM.
...A sigh is just a sigh...
Oh. THIS FEELS... WONDERFUL...
I WILL NOT SOON FORGET THIS SETBACK.
WE WILL MEET AGAIN, AVENGERS.
WHY DID THE MUSIC STOP?
THAT WAS AWESOME.
HEY, WE GOTTA GET OFF THIS SHIP, IT'S GOING DOWN!

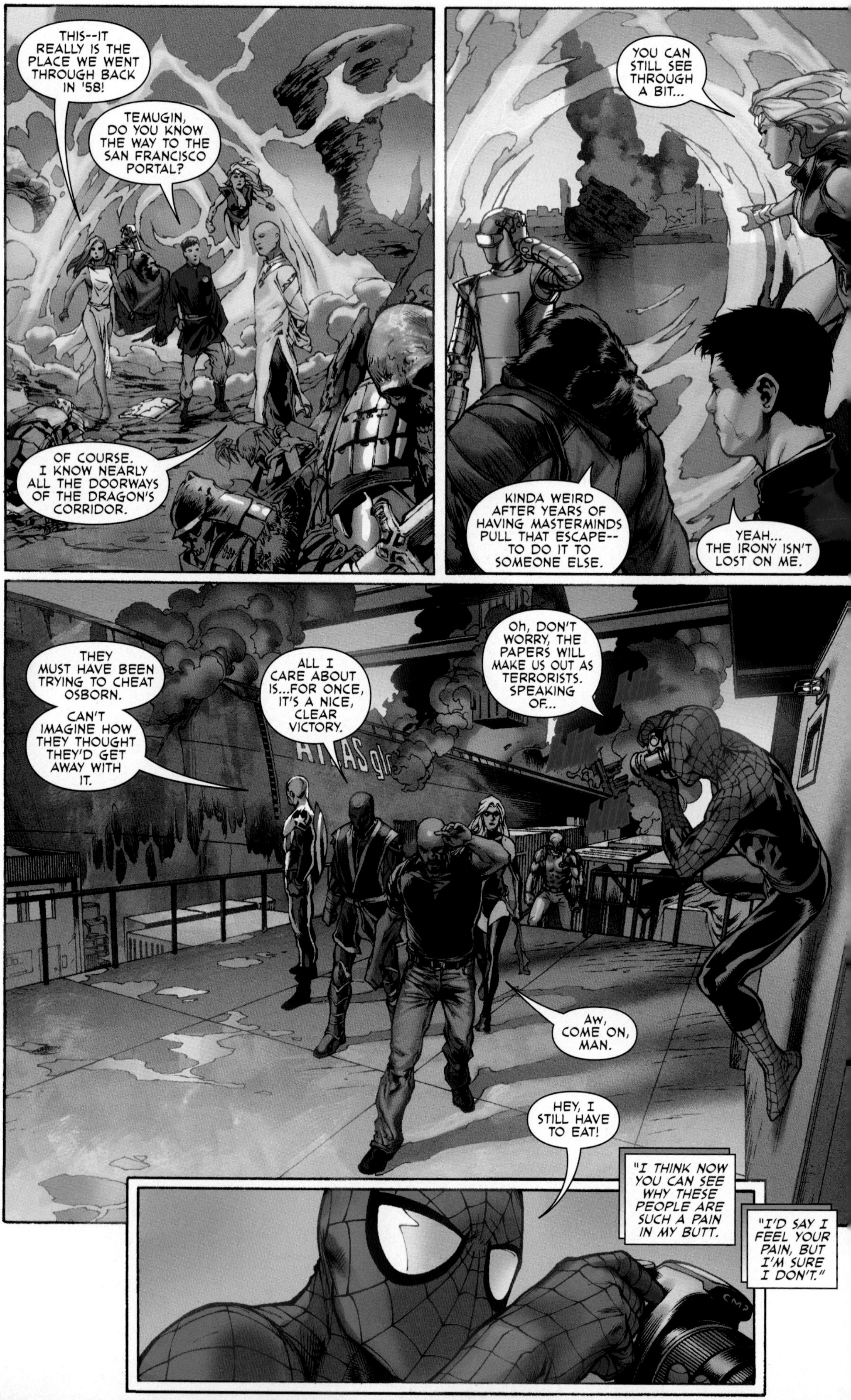
THIS--IT REALLY IS THE PLACE WE WENT THROUGH BACK IN '58!
TEMUGIN, DO YOU KNOW THE WAY TO THE SAN FRANCISCO PORTAL?
OF COURSE. I KNOW NEARLY ALL THE DOORWAYS OF THE DRAGON'S CORRIDOR.
YOU CAN STILL SEE THROUGH A BIT...
KINDA WEIRD AFTER YEARS OF HAVING MASTERMINDS PULL THAT ESCAPE-- TO DO IT TO SOMEONE ELSE.
YEAH... THE IRONY ISN'T LOST ON ME.
THEY MUST HAVE BEEN TRYING TO CHEAT OSBORN.
CAN'T IMAGINE HOW THEY THOUGHT THEY'D GET AWAY WITH IT.
ALL I CARE ABOUT IS...FOR ONCE, IT'S A NICE, CLEAR VICTORY.
Oh, DON'T WORRY, THE PAPERS WILL MAKE US OUT AS TERRORISTS. SPEAKING OF...
Aw, COME ON, MAN.
HEY, I STILL HAVE TO EAT!
"I THINK NOW YOU CAN SEE WHY THESE PEOPLE ARE SUCH A PAIN IN MY BUTT.
"I'D SAY I FEEL YOUR PAIN, BUT I'M SURE I DON'T."

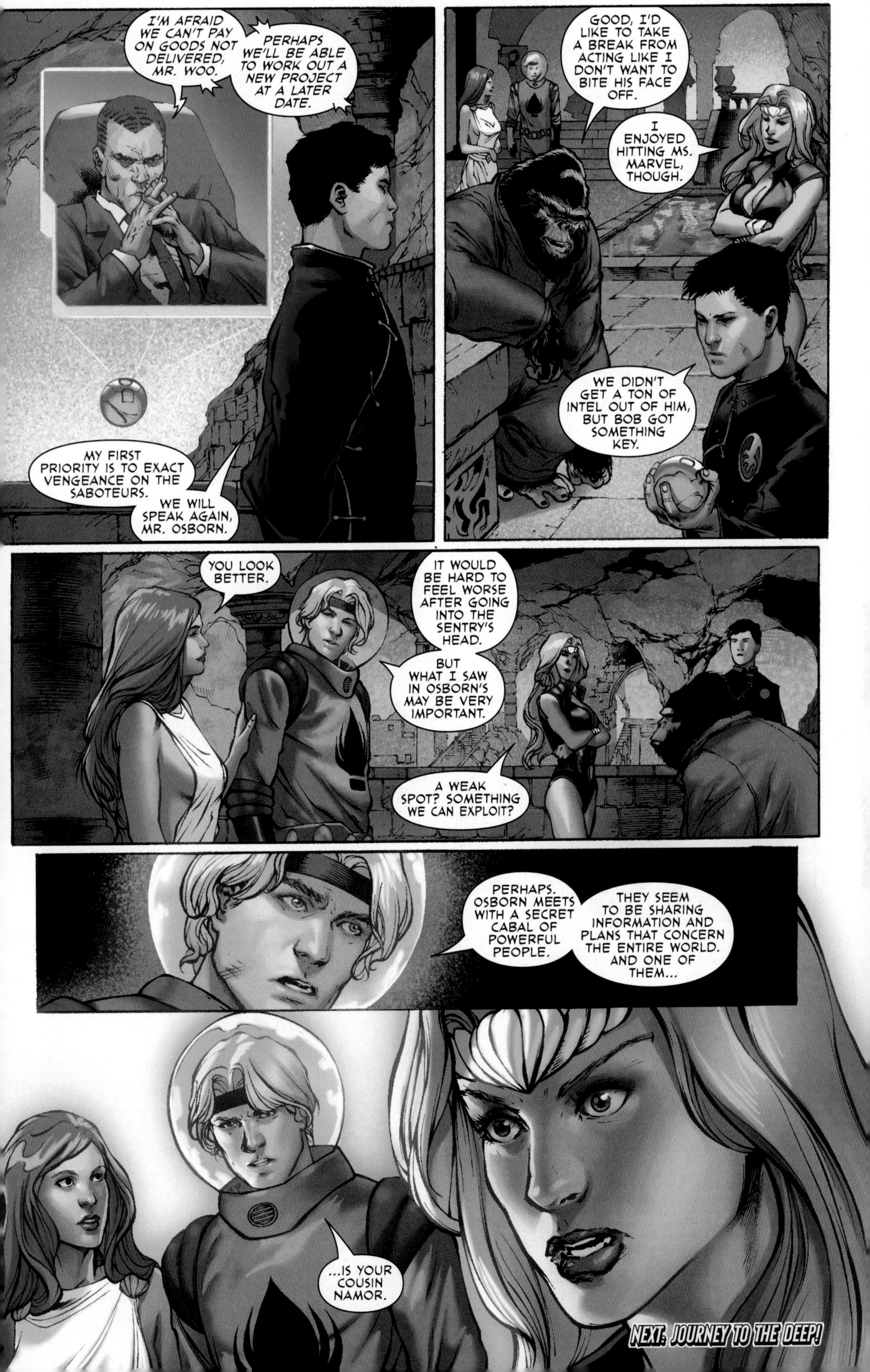
I'M AFRAID WE CAN'T PAY ON GOODS NOT DELIVERED, MR. WOO.
PERHAPS WE'LL BE ABLE TO WORK OUT A NEW PROJECT AT A LATER DATE.
MY FIRST PRIORITY IS TO EXACT VENGEANCE ON THE SABOTEURS.
WE WILL SPEAK AGAIN, MR. OSBORN.
GOOD, I'D LIKE TO TAKE A BREAK FROM ACTING LIKE I DON'T WANT TO BITE HIS FACE OFF.
I ENJOYED HITTING MS. MARVEL, THOUGH.
WE DIDN'T GET A TON OF INTEL OUT OF HIM, BUT BOB GOT SOMETHING KEY.
YOU LOOK BETTER.
IT WOULD BE HARD TO FEEL WORSE AFTER GOING INTO THE SENTRY'S HEAD.
BUT WHAT I SAW IN OSBORN'S MAY BE VERY IMPORTANT.
A WEAK SPOT? SOMETHING WE CAN EXPLOIT?
PERHAPS. OSBORN MEETS WITH A SECRET CABAL OF POWERFUL PEOPLE.
THEY SEEM TO BE SHARING INFORMATION AND PLANS THAT CONCERN THE ENTIRE WORLD. AND ONE OF THEM...
...IS YOUR COUSIN NAMOR.
NEXT: JOURNEY TO THE DEEP!

MARVEL MYSTERY COMICS #82 (MAY 1947), THE FIRST APPEARANCE OF NAMORA
ARTISTS: **KEN BALD & SYD SHORES** • COVER ARTIST: **BOB POWELL** • EDITOR: **STAN LEE**

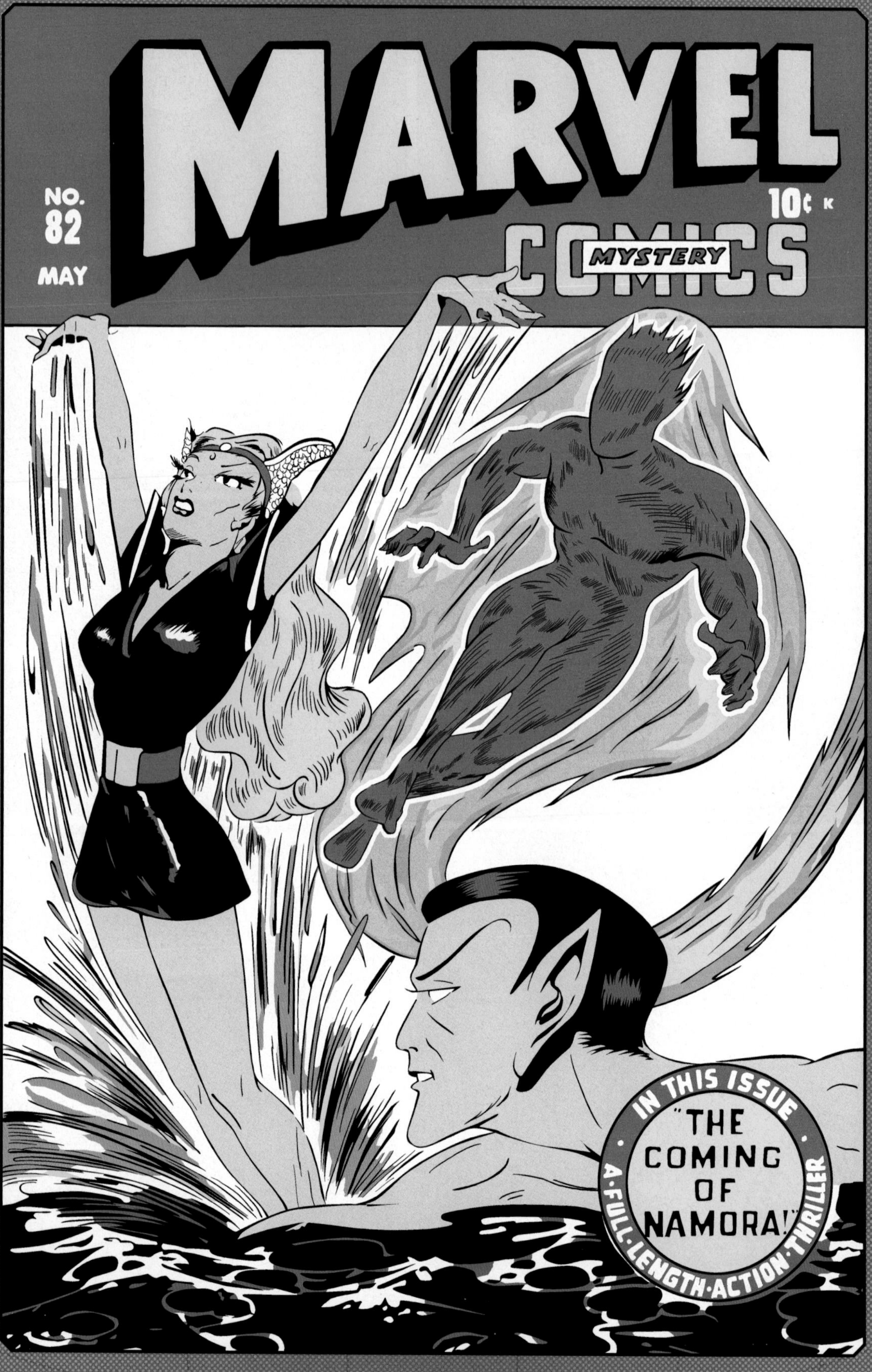
MARVEL
NO. 82
MAY
10¢ K
MYSTERY
COMICS
IN THIS ISSUE
"THE COMING OF NAMORA!"
A·FULL·LENGTH·ACTION·THRILLER

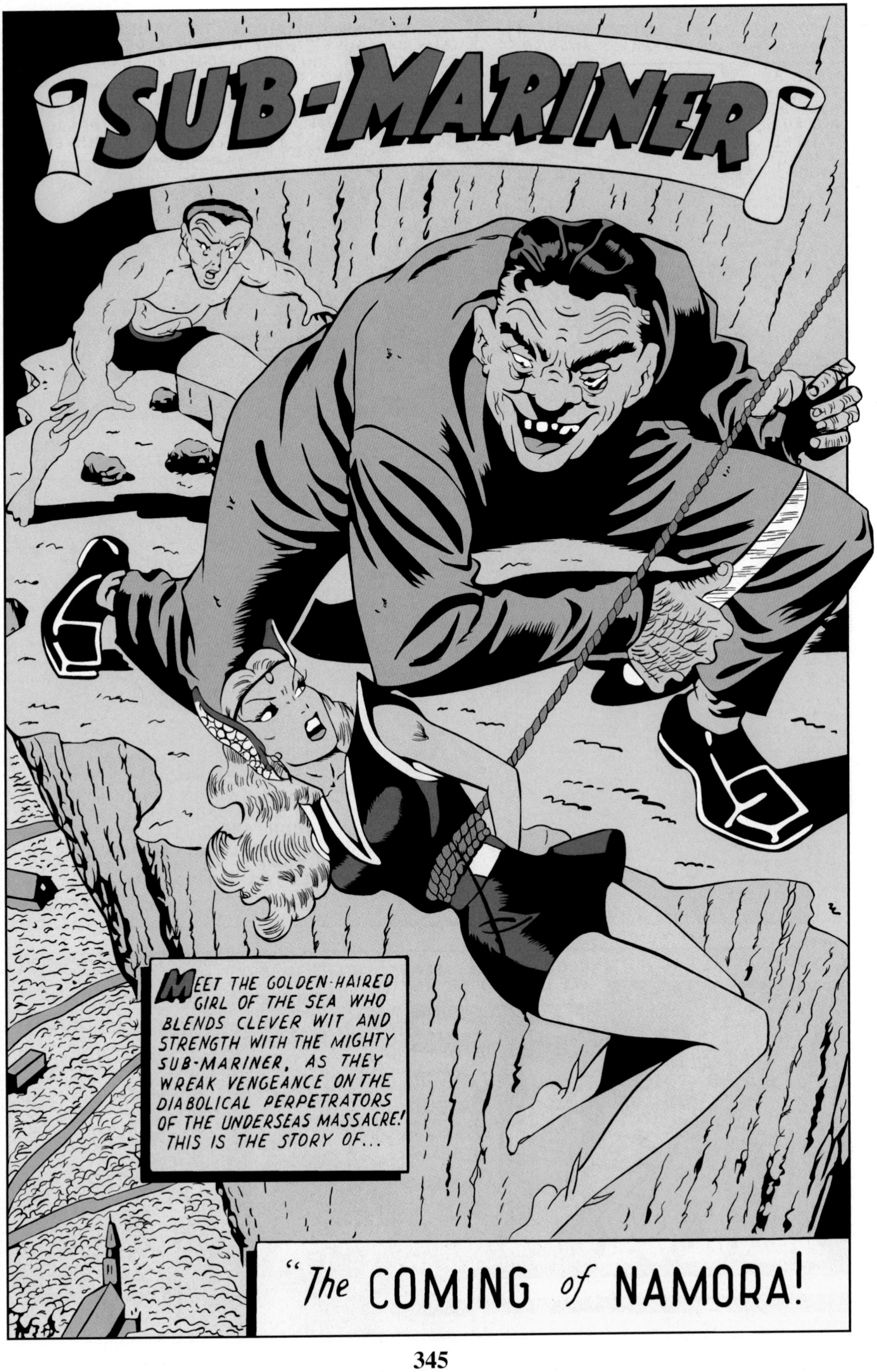
SUB-MARINER
MEET THE GOLDEN-HAIRED GIRL OF THE SEA WHO BLENDS CLEVER WIT AND STRENGTH WITH THE MIGHTY SUB-MARINER, AS THEY WREAK VENGEANCE ON THE DIABOLICAL PERPETRATORS OF THE UNDERSEAS MASSACRE! THIS IS THE STORY OF...
"The COMING of NAMORA!

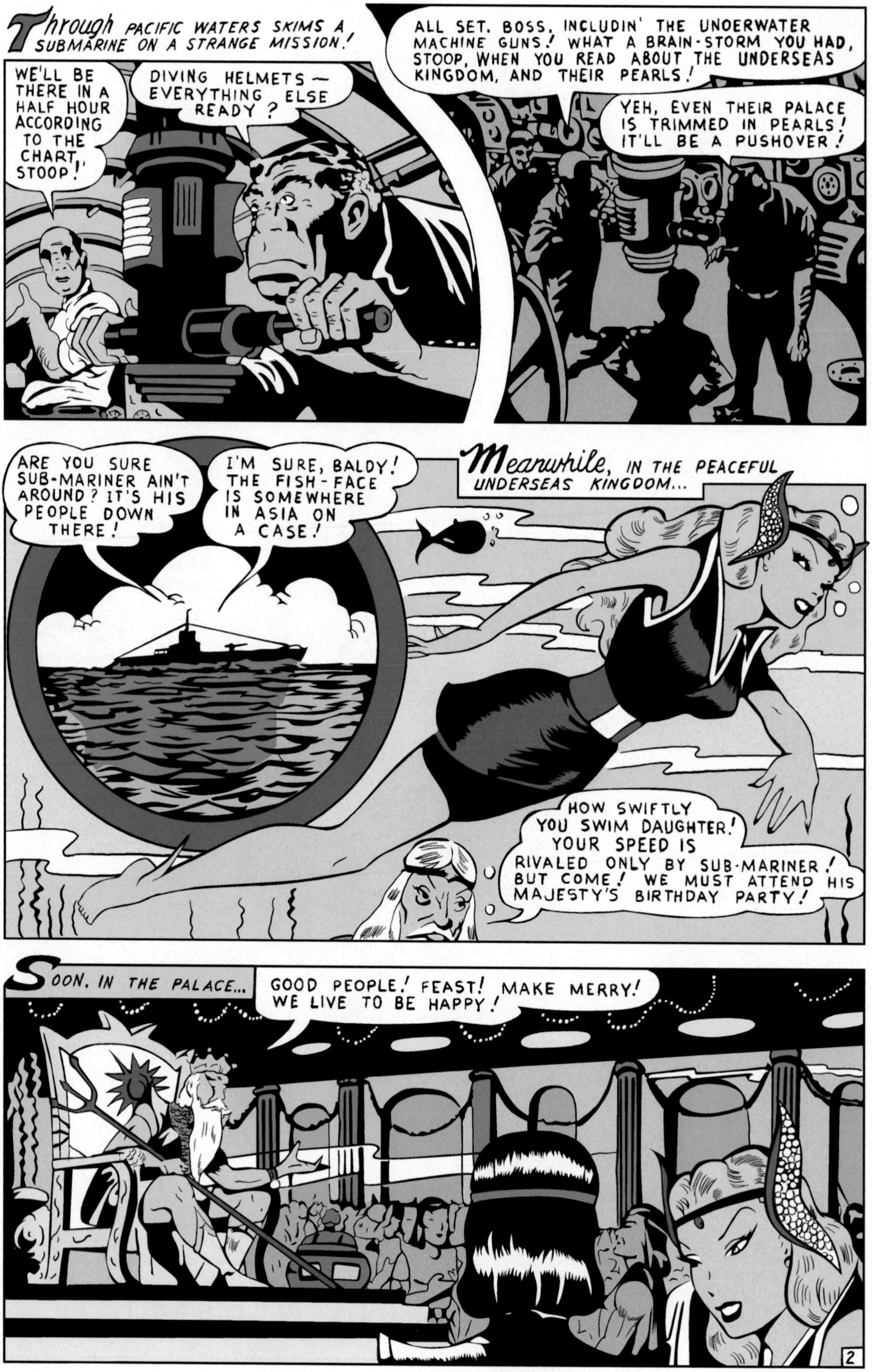
Through PACIFIC WATERS SKIMS A SUBMARINE ON A STRANGE MISSION!
WE'LL BE THERE IN A HALF HOUR ACCORDING TO THE CHART, STOOP!
DIVING HELMETS— EVERYTHING ELSE READY?
ALL SET, BOSS, INCLUDIN' THE UNDERWATER MACHINE GUNS! WHAT A BRAIN-STORM YOU HAD, STOOP, WHEN YOU READ ABOUT THE UNDERSEAS KINGDOM, AND THEIR PEARLS!
YEH, EVEN THEIR PALACE IS TRIMMED IN PEARLS! IT'LL BE A PUSHOVER!
ARE YOU SURE SUB-MARINER AIN'T AROUND? IT'S HIS PEOPLE DOWN THERE!
I'M SURE, BALDY! THE FISH-FACE IS SOMEWHERE IN ASIA ON A CASE!
Meanwhile, IN THE PEACEFUL UNDERSEAS KINGDOM...
HOW SWIFTLY YOU SWIM DAUGHTER! YOUR SPEED IS RIVALED ONLY BY SUB-MARINER! BUT COME! WE MUST ATTEND HIS MAJESTY'S BIRTHDAY PARTY!
SOON, IN THE PALACE...
GOOD PEOPLE! FEAST! MAKE MERRY! WE LIVE TO BE HAPPY!
2

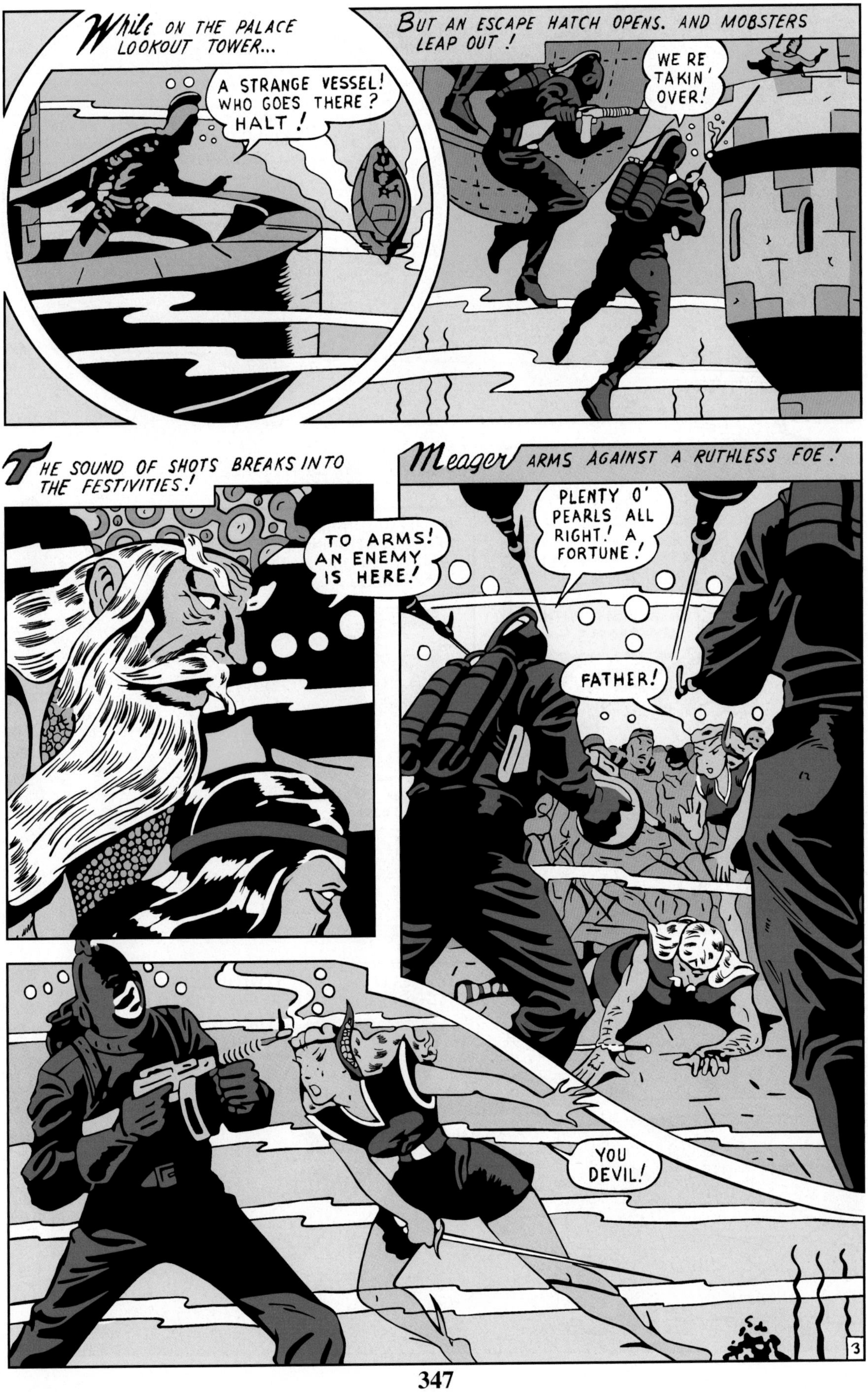

While on the palace lookout tower...
A strange vessel! Who goes there? Halt!
But an escape hatch opens. And mobsters leap out!
We re takin' over!
The sound of shots breaks into the festivities!
To arms! An enemy is here!
Meager arms against a ruthless foe!
Plenty o' pearls all right! A fortune!
Father!
You devil!
3

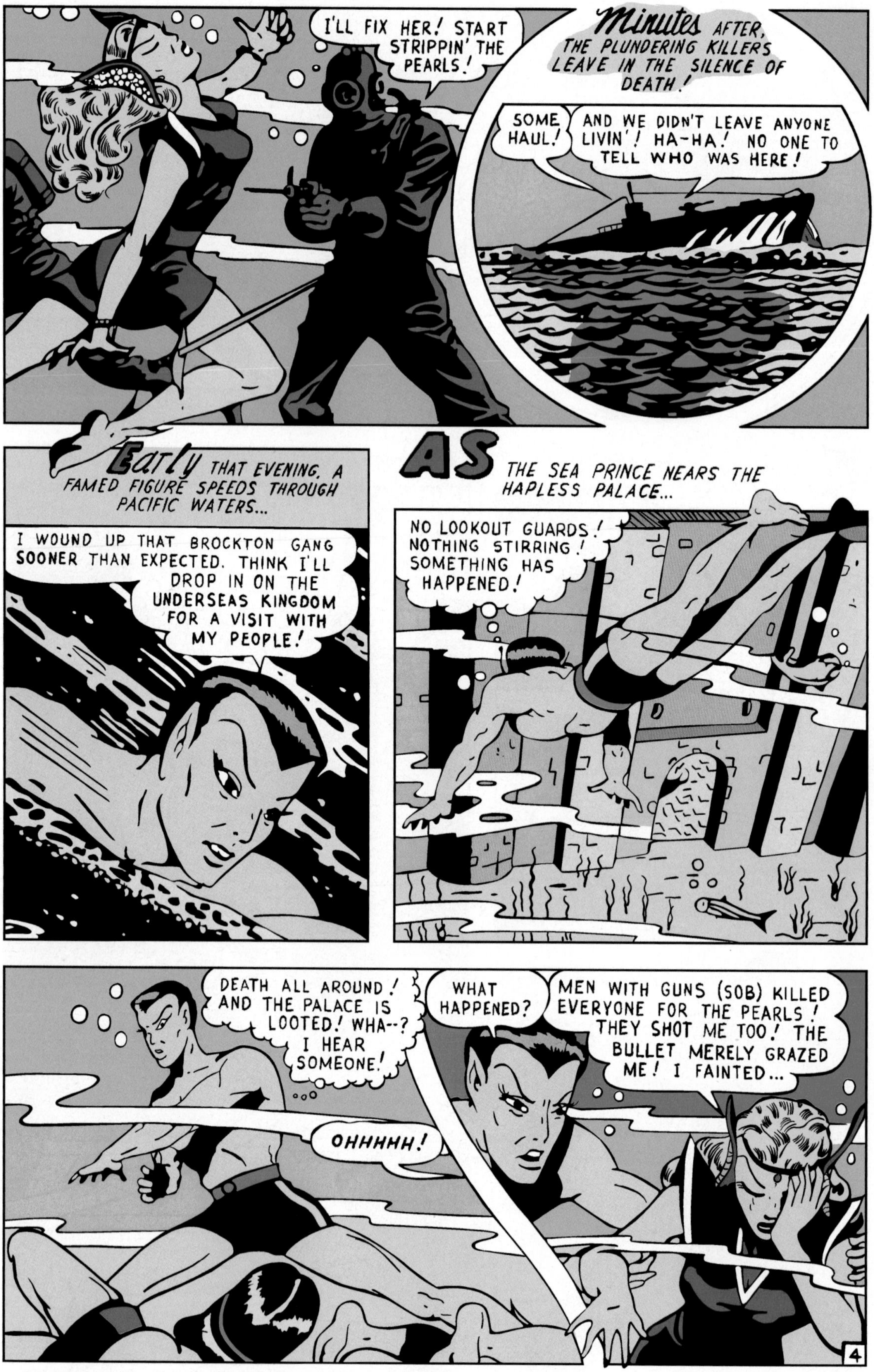
I'LL FIX HER! START STRIPPIN' THE PEARLS!
Minutes AFTER, THE PLUNDERING KILLERS LEAVE IN THE SILENCE OF DEATH!
SOME HAUL!
AND WE DIDN'T LEAVE ANYONE LIVIN'! HA-HA! NO ONE TO TELL WHO WAS HERE!
Early THAT EVENING, A FAMED FIGURE SPEEDS THROUGH PACIFIC WATERS...
I WOUND UP THAT BROCKTON GANG SOONER THAN EXPECTED. THINK I'LL DROP IN ON THE UNDERSEAS KINGDOM FOR A VISIT WITH MY PEOPLE!
AS THE SEA PRINCE NEARS THE HAPLESS PALACE...
NO LOOKOUT GUARDS! NOTHING STIRRING! SOMETHING HAS HAPPENED!
DEATH ALL AROUND! AND THE PALACE IS LOOTED! WHA--? I HEAR SOMEONE!
OHHHHH!
WHAT HAPPENED?
MEN WITH GUNS (SOB) KILLED EVERYONE FOR THE PEARLS! THEY SHOT ME TOO! THE BULLET MERELY GRAZED ME! I FAINTED...
4

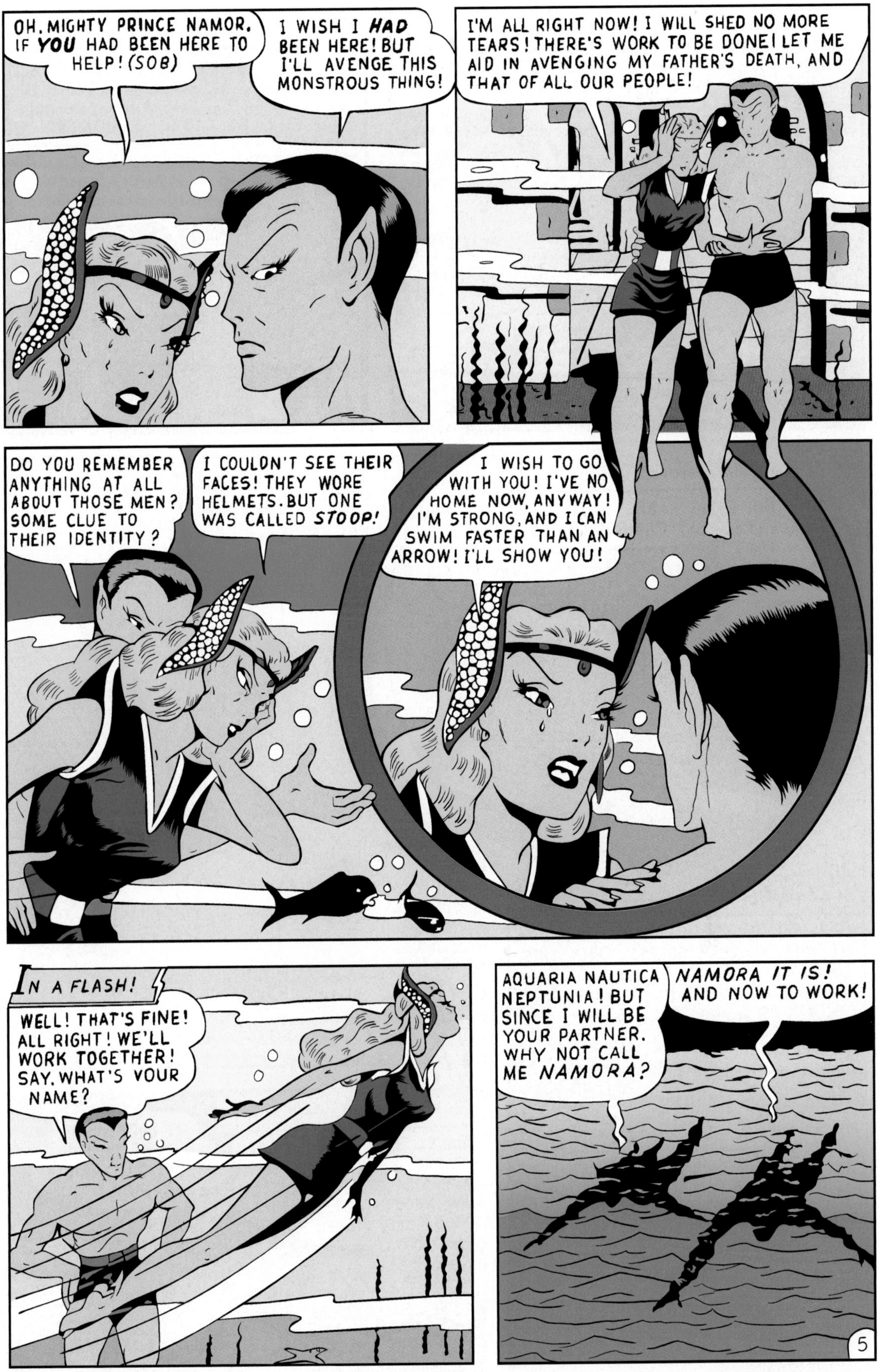

OH, MIGHTY PRINCE NAMOR, IF YOU HAD BEEN HERE TO HELP! (SOB)
I WISH I HAD BEEN HERE! BUT I'LL AVENGE THIS MONSTROUS THING!
I'M ALL RIGHT NOW! I WILL SHED NO MORE TEARS! THERE'S WORK TO BE DONE! LET ME AID IN AVENGING MY FATHER'S DEATH, AND THAT OF ALL OUR PEOPLE!
DO YOU REMEMBER ANYTHING AT ALL ABOUT THOSE MEN? SOME CLUE TO THEIR IDENTITY?
I COULDN'T SEE THEIR FACES! THEY WORE HELMETS. BUT ONE WAS CALLED STOOP!
I WISH TO GO WITH YOU! I'VE NO HOME NOW, ANYWAY! I'M STRONG, AND I CAN SWIM FASTER THAN AN ARROW! I'LL SHOW YOU!
IN A FLASH!
WELL! THAT'S FINE! ALL RIGHT! WE'LL WORK TOGETHER! SAY, WHAT'S YOUR NAME?
AQUARIA NAUTICA NEPTUNIA! BUT SINCE I WILL BE YOUR PARTNER, WHY NOT CALL ME NAMORA?
NAMORA IT IS! AND NOW TO WORK!
5

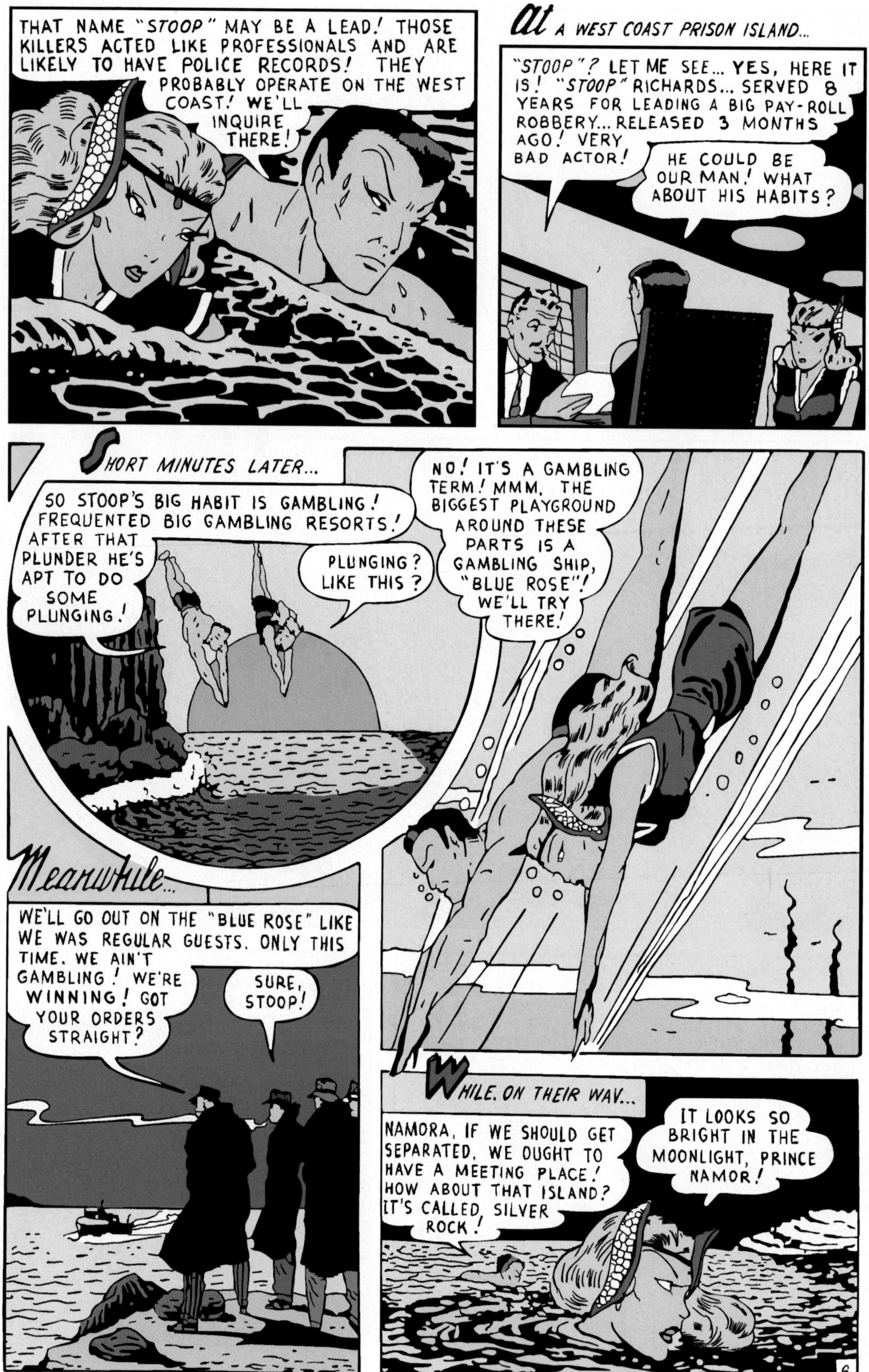

THAT NAME "STOOP" MAY BE A LEAD! THOSE KILLERS ACTED LIKE PROFESSIONALS AND ARE LIKELY TO HAVE POLICE RECORDS! THEY PROBABLY OPERATE ON THE WEST COAST! WE'LL INQUIRE THERE!
AT A WEST COAST PRISON ISLAND...
"STOOP"? LET ME SEE... YES, HERE IT IS! "STOOP" RICHARDS... SERVED 8 YEARS FOR LEADING A BIG PAY-ROLL ROBBERY... RELEASED 3 MONTHS AGO! VERY BAD ACTOR!
HE COULD BE OUR MAN! WHAT ABOUT HIS HABITS?
SHORT MINUTES LATER...
SO STOOP'S BIG HABIT IS GAMBLING! FREQUENTED BIG GAMBLING RESORTS! AFTER THAT PLUNDER HE'S APT TO DO SOME PLUNGING!
PLUNGING? LIKE THIS?
NO! IT'S A GAMBLING TERM! MMM, THE BIGGEST PLAYGROUND AROUND THESE PARTS IS A GAMBLING SHIP, "BLUE ROSE"! WE'LL TRY THERE!
MEANWHILE...
WE'LL GO OUT ON THE "BLUE ROSE" LIKE WE WAS REGULAR GUESTS. ONLY THIS TIME, WE AIN'T GAMBLING! WE'RE WINNING! GOT YOUR ORDERS STRAIGHT?
SURE, STOOP!
WHILE, ON THEIR WAY...
NAMORA, IF WE SHOULD GET SEPARATED, WE OUGHT TO HAVE A MEETING PLACE! HOW ABOUT THAT ISLAND? IT'S CALLED, SILVER ROCK!
IT LOOKS SO BRIGHT IN THE MOONLIGHT, PRINCE NAMOR!
6

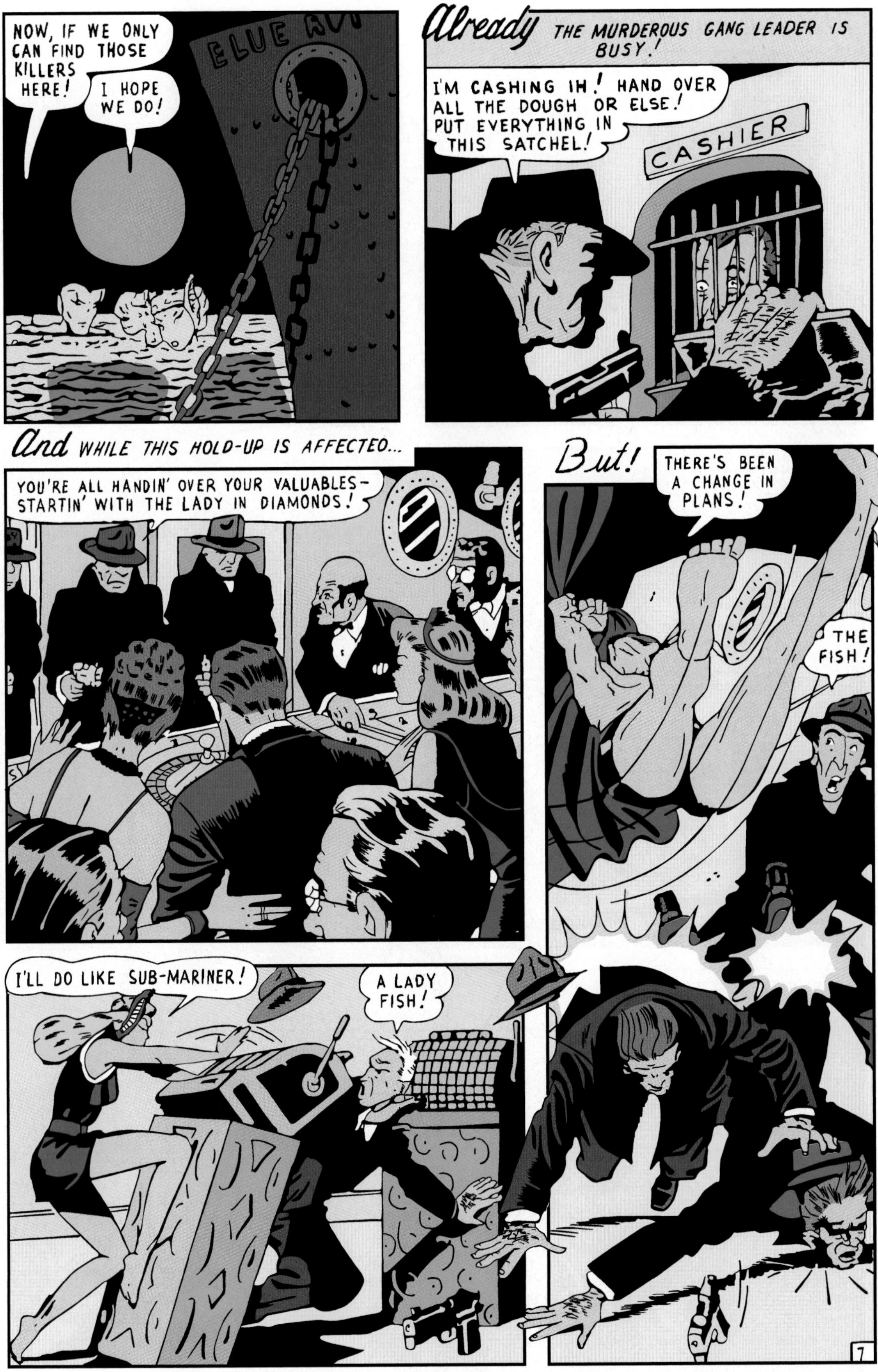
NOW, IF WE ONLY CAN FIND THOSE KILLERS HERE!
I HOPE WE DO!
Already THE MURDEROUS GANG LEADER IS BUSY!
I'M CASHING IN! HAND OVER ALL THE DOUGH OR ELSE! PUT EVERYTHING IN THIS SATCHEL!
CASHIER
And WHILE THIS HOLD-UP IS AFFECTED...
YOU'RE ALL HANDIN' OVER YOUR VALUABLES- STARTIN' WITH THE LADY IN DIAMONDS!
But!
THERE'S BEEN A CHANGE IN PLANS!
THE FISH!
I'LL DO LIKE SUB-MARINER!
A LADY FISH!
7

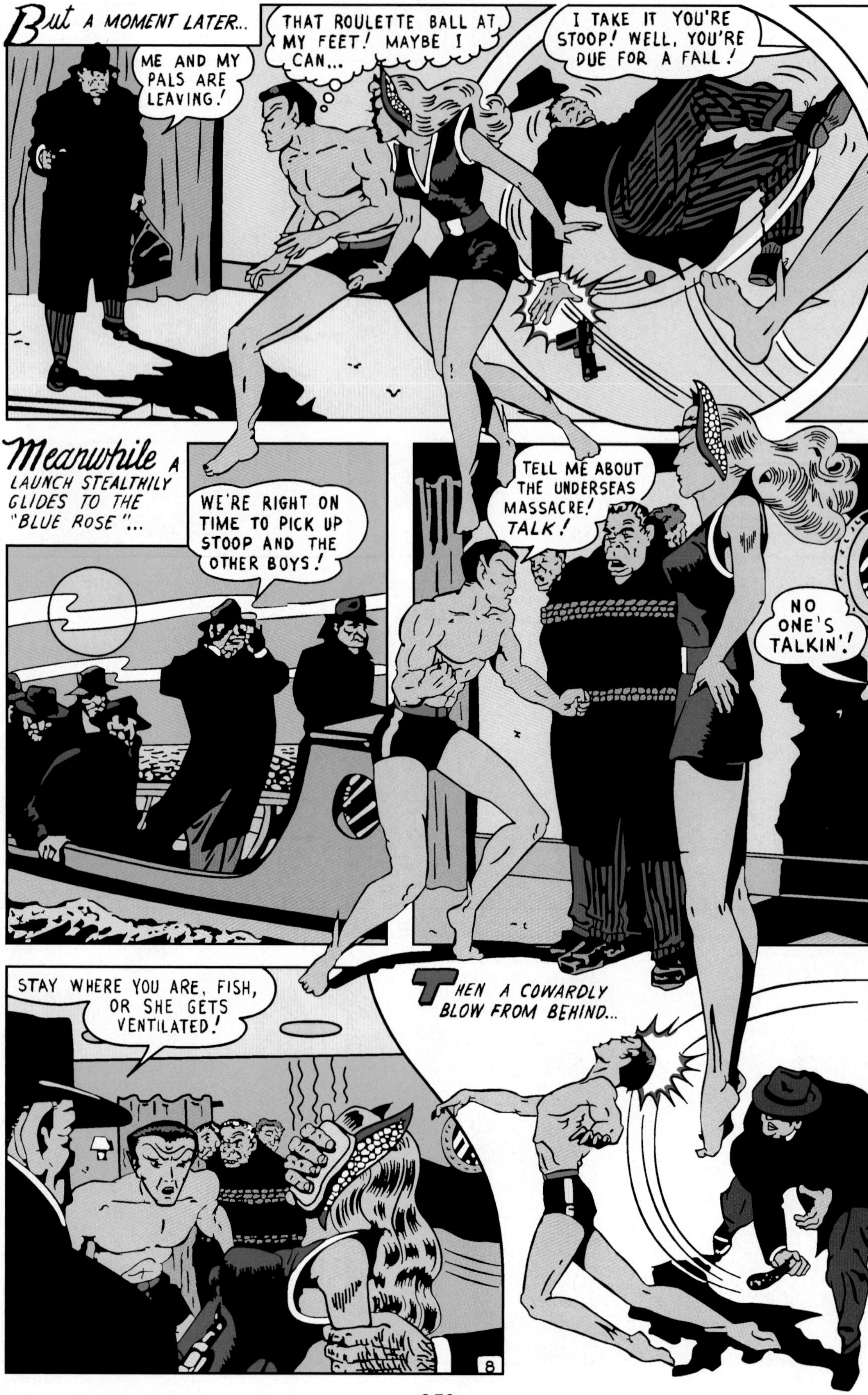
But A MOMENT LATER...
ME AND MY PALS ARE LEAVING!
THAT ROULETTE BALL AT MY FEET! MAYBE I CAN...
I TAKE IT YOU'RE STOOP! WELL, YOU'RE DUE FOR A FALL!
Meanwhile A LAUNCH STEALTHILY GLIDES TO THE "BLUE ROSE"...
WE'RE RIGHT ON TIME TO PICK UP STOOP AND THE OTHER BOYS!
TELL ME ABOUT THE UNDERSEAS MASSACRE! TALK!
NO ONE'S TALKIN'!
STAY WHERE YOU ARE, FISH, OR SHE GETS VENTILATED!
THEN A COWARDLY BLOW FROM BEHIND...
8

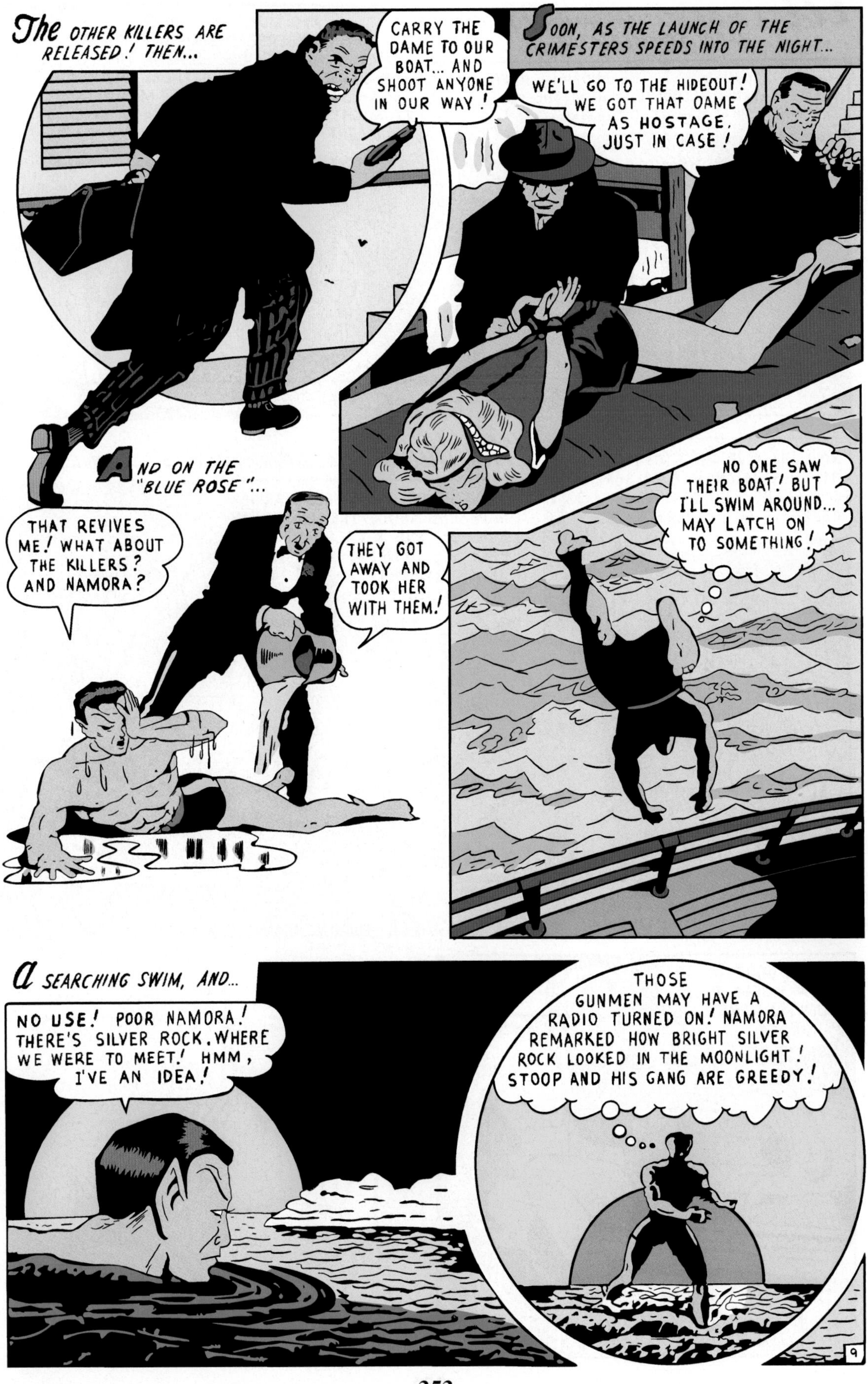
The other killers are released! Then...
Carry the dame to our boat... and shoot anyone in our way!
Soon, as the launch of the crimesters speeds into the night...
We'll go to the hideout! We got that dame as hostage, just in case!
And on the "Blue Rose"...
That revives me! What about the killers? And Namora?
They got away and took her with them!
No one saw their boat! But I'll swim around... may latch on to something!
A searching swim, and...
No use! Poor Namora! There's Silver Rock, where we were to meet! Hmm, I've an idea!
Those gunmen may have a radio turned on! Namora remarked how bright Silver Rock looked in the moonlight! Stoop and his gang are greedy!
9

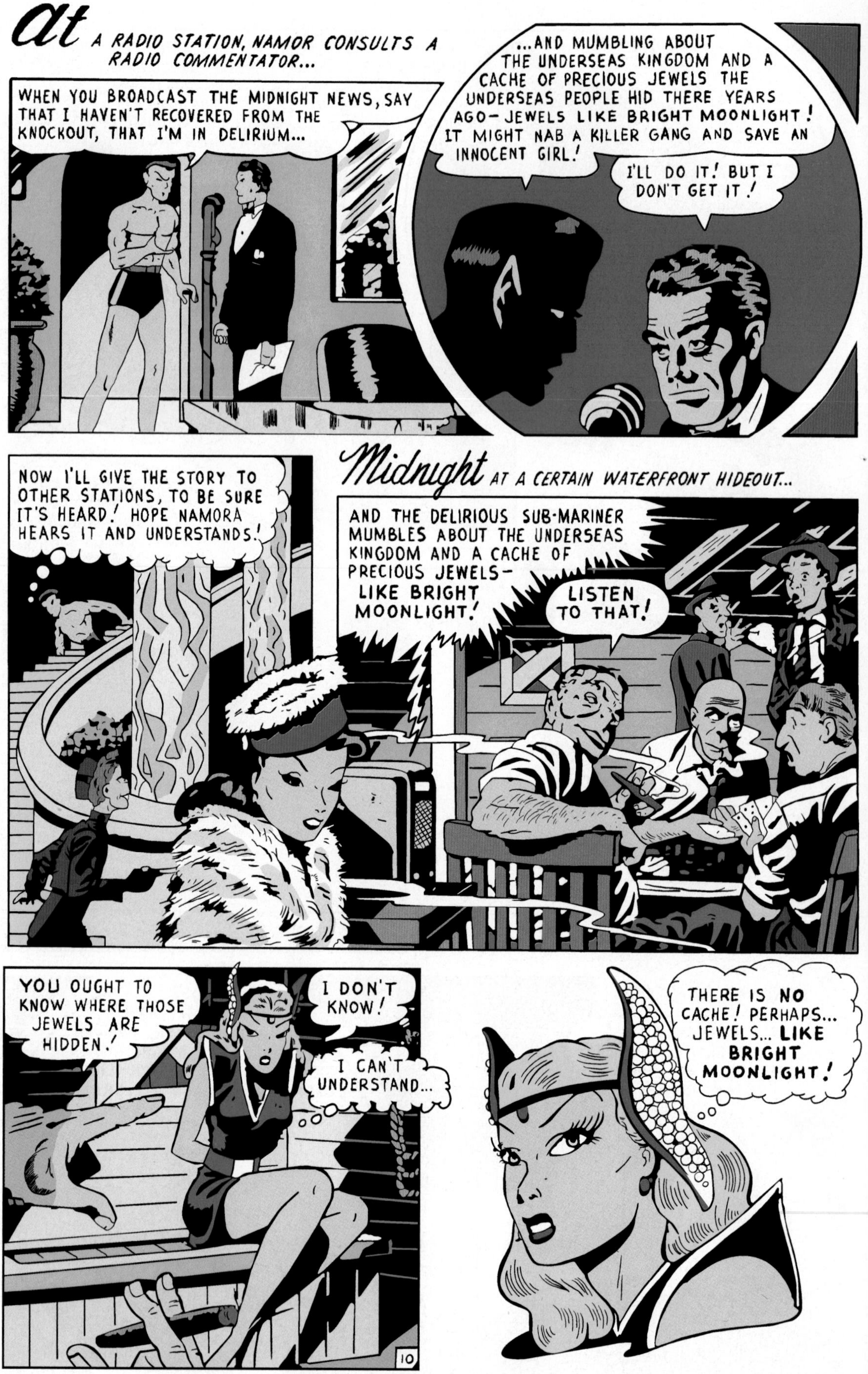
At A RADIO STATION, NAMOR CONSULTS A RADIO COMMENTATOR...
WHEN YOU BROADCAST THE MIDNIGHT NEWS, SAY THAT I HAVEN'T RECOVERED FROM THE KNOCKOUT, THAT I'M IN DELIRIUM...
...AND MUMBLING ABOUT THE UNDERSEAS KINGDOM AND A CACHE OF PRECIOUS JEWELS THE UNDERSEAS PEOPLE HID THERE YEARS AGO— JEWELS LIKE BRIGHT MOONLIGHT! IT MIGHT NAB A KILLER GANG AND SAVE AN INNOCENT GIRL!
I'LL DO IT! BUT I DON'T GET IT!
NOW I'LL GIVE THE STORY TO OTHER STATIONS, TO BE SURE IT'S HEARD! HOPE NAMORA HEARS IT AND UNDERSTANDS!
Midnight AT A CERTAIN WATERFRONT HIDEOUT...
AND THE DELIRIOUS SUB-MARINER MUMBLES ABOUT THE UNDERSEAS KINGDOM AND A CACHE OF PRECIOUS JEWELS— LIKE BRIGHT MOONLIGHT!
LISTEN TO THAT!
YOU OUGHT TO KNOW WHERE THOSE JEWELS ARE HIDDEN!
I DON'T KNOW!
I CAN'T UNDERSTAND...
10
THERE IS NO CACHE! PERHAPS... JEWELS... LIKE BRIGHT MOONLIGHT!

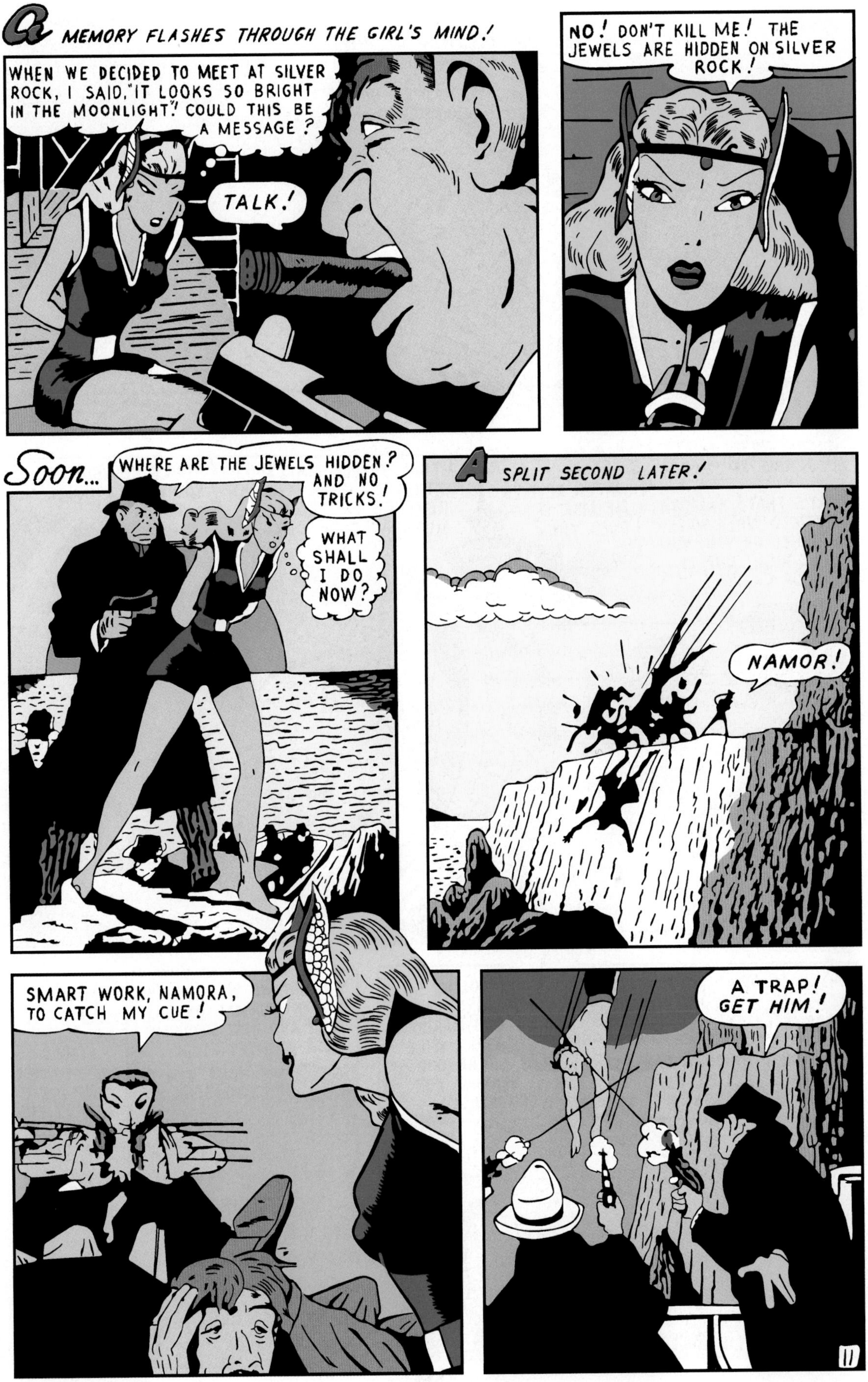
A MEMORY FLASHES THROUGH THE GIRL'S MIND!
WHEN WE DECIDED TO MEET AT SILVER ROCK, I SAID, "IT LOOKS SO BRIGHT IN THE MOONLIGHT"! COULD THIS BE A MESSAGE?
TALK!
NO! DON'T KILL ME! THE JEWELS ARE HIDDEN ON SILVER ROCK!
Soon...
WHERE ARE THE JEWELS HIDDEN? AND NO TRICKS!
WHAT SHALL I DO NOW?
A SPLIT SECOND LATER!
NAMOR!
SMART WORK, NAMORA, TO CATCH MY CUE!
A TRAP! GET HIM!
11

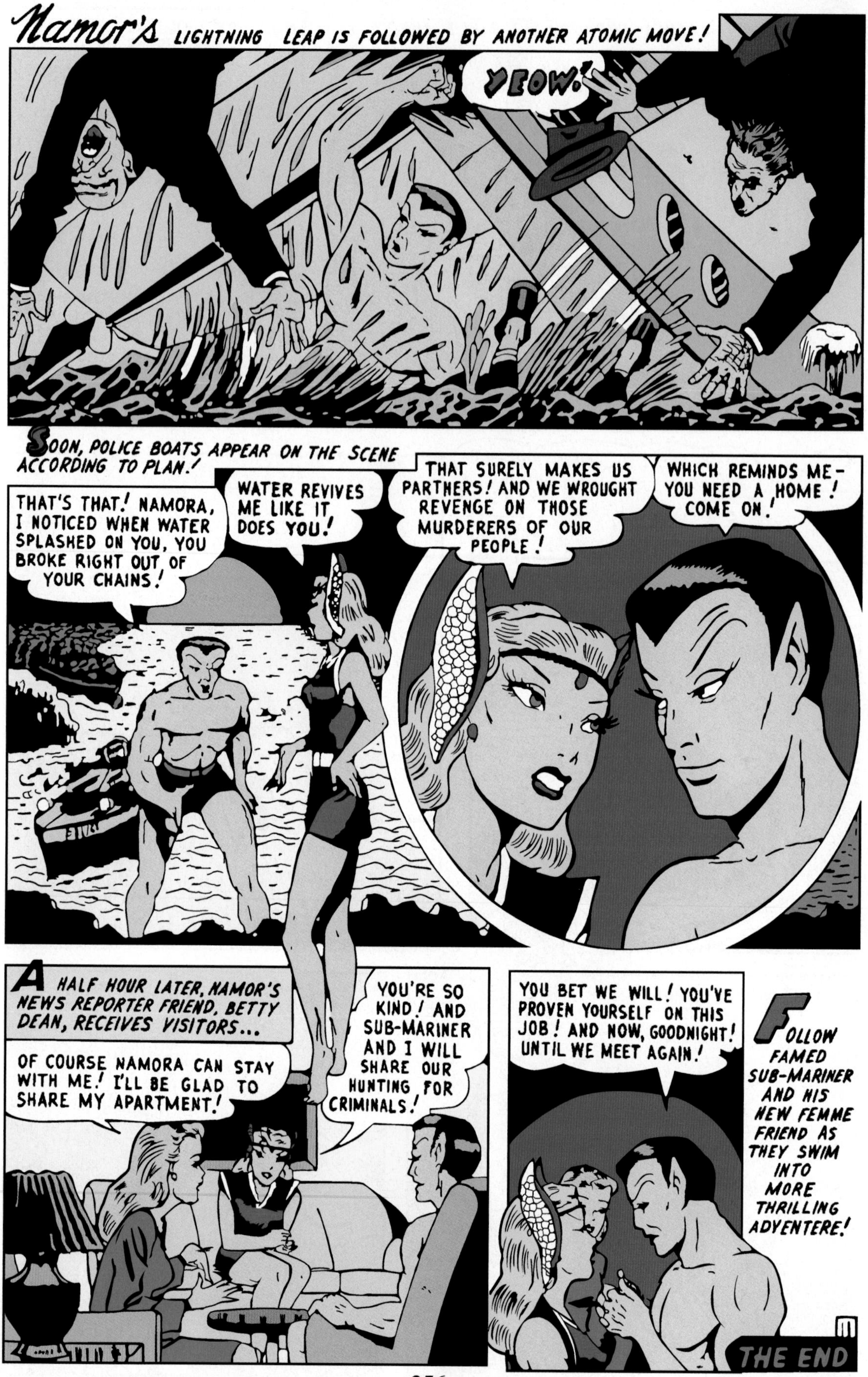
Namor's LIGHTNING LEAP IS FOLLOWED BY ANOTHER ATOMIC MOVE!
YEOW!
SOON, POLICE BOATS APPEAR ON THE SCENE ACCORDING TO PLAN!
THAT'S THAT! NAMORA, I NOTICED WHEN WATER SPLASHED ON YOU, YOU BROKE RIGHT OUT OF YOUR CHAINS!
WATER REVIVES ME LIKE IT DOES YOU!
THAT SURELY MAKES US PARTNERS! AND WE WROUGHT REVENGE ON THOSE MURDERERS OF OUR PEOPLE!
WHICH REMINDS ME - YOU NEED A HOME! COME ON!
A HALF HOUR LATER, NAMOR'S NEWS REPORTER FRIEND, BETTY DEAN, RECEIVES VISITORS...
OF COURSE NAMORA CAN STAY WITH ME! I'LL BE GLAD TO SHARE MY APARTMENT!
YOU'RE SO KIND! AND SUB-MARINER AND I WILL SHARE OUR HUNTING FOR CRIMINALS!
YOU BET WE WILL! YOU'VE PROVEN YOURSELF ON THIS JOB! AND NOW, GOODNIGHT! UNTIL WE MEET AGAIN!
FOLLOW FAMED SUB-MARINER AND HIS NEW FEMME FRIEND AS THEY SWIM INTO MORE THRILLING ADVENTERE!
THE END

VENUS #1 (AUGUST 1948), THE FIRST APPEARANCE OF VENUS

ARTISTS: **GEORGE KLEIN** & **LIN STREETER** • COVER ARTIST: **GEORGE KLEIN** • EDITOR: **STAN LEE**

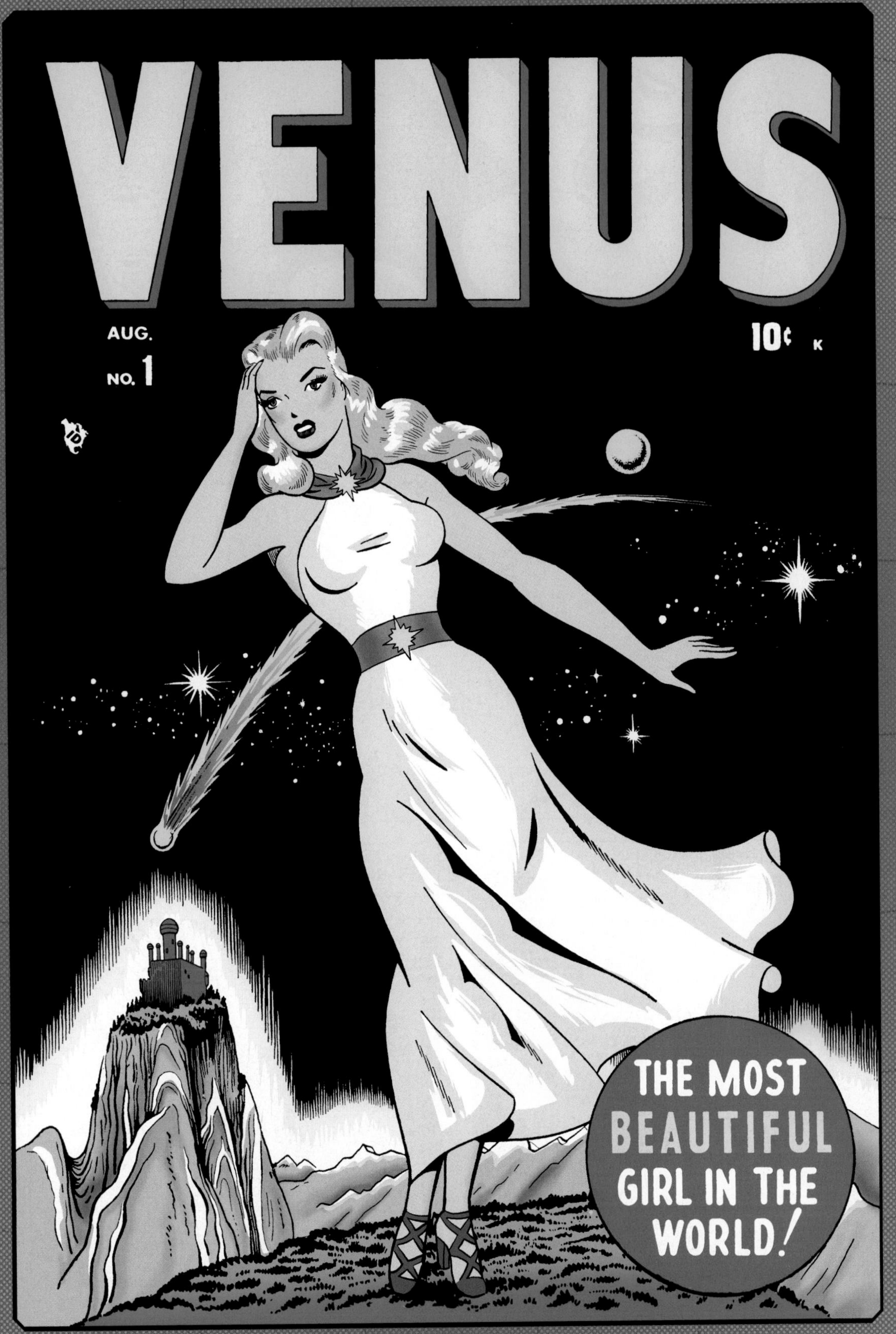
VENUS
AUG.
NO. 1
10¢
K
THE MOST BEAUTIFUL GIRL IN THE WORLD!

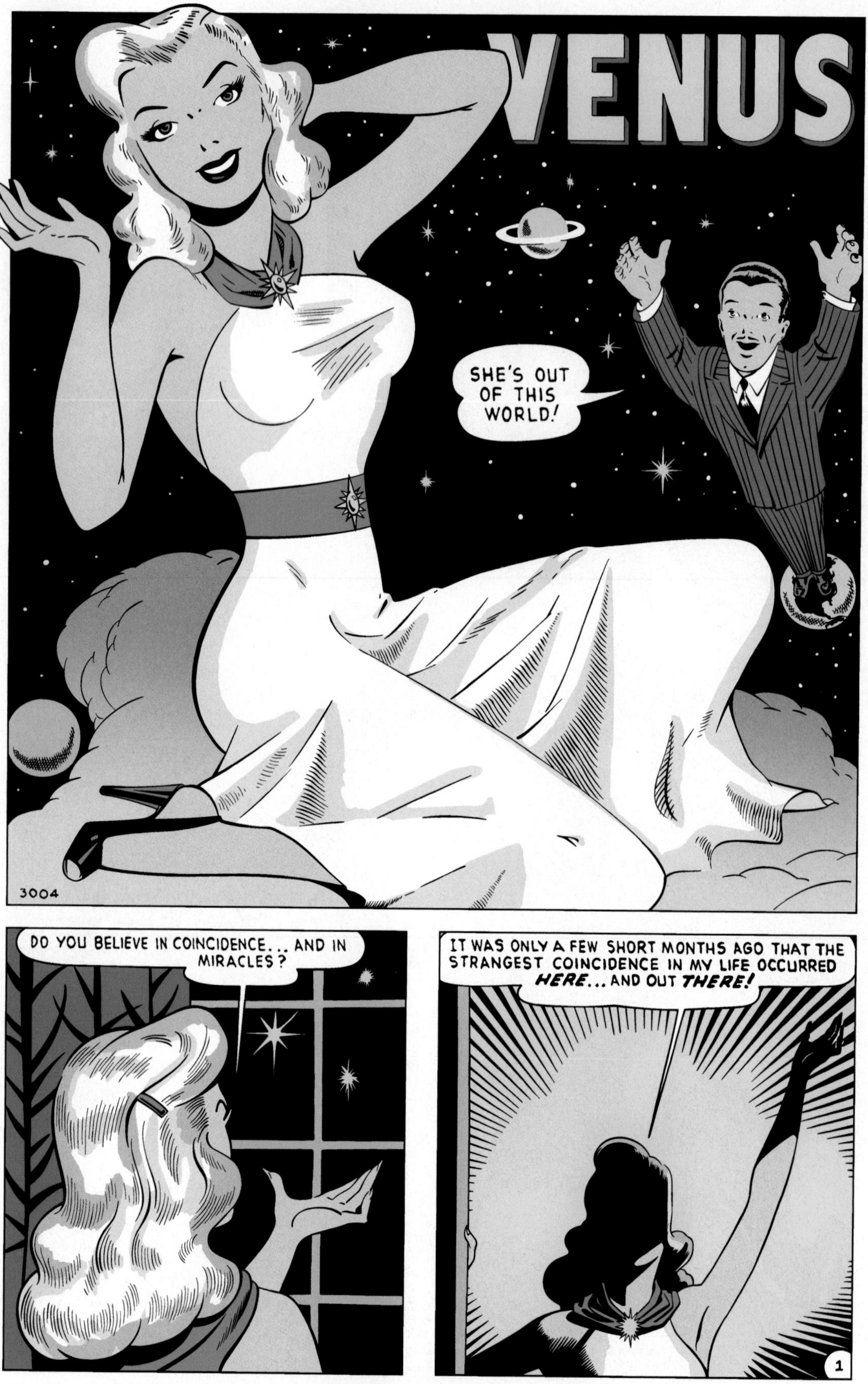
VENUS
SHE'S OUT OF THIS WORLD!
3004
DO YOU BELIEVE IN COINCIDENCE... AND IN MIRACLES?
IT WAS ONLY A FEW SHORT MONTHS AGO THAT THE STRANGEST COINCIDENCE IN MY LIFE OCCURRED HERE... AND OUT THERE!
1

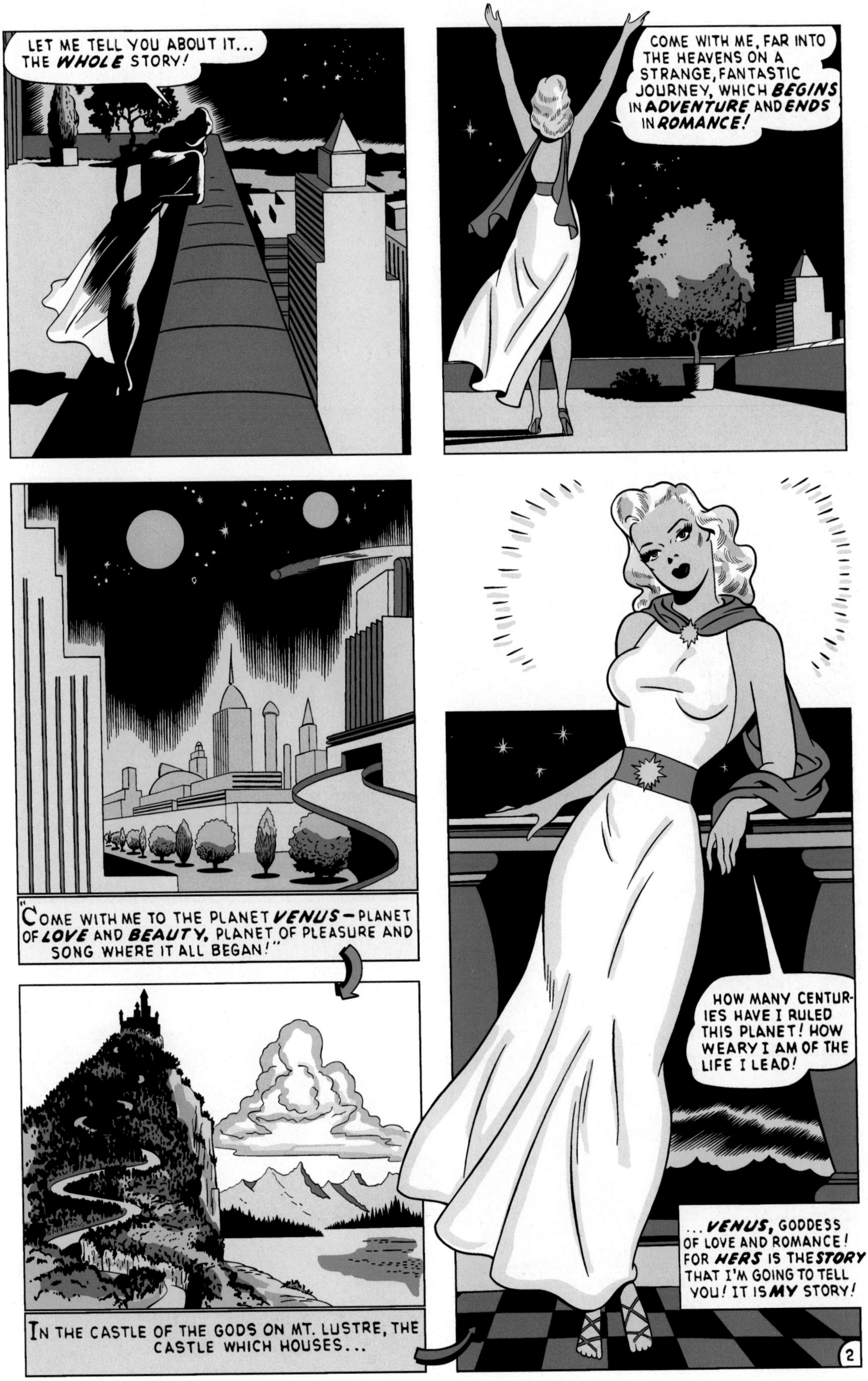
LET ME TELL YOU ABOUT IT... THE WHOLE STORY!
COME WITH ME, FAR INTO THE HEAVENS ON A STRANGE, FANTASTIC JOURNEY, WHICH BEGINS IN ADVENTURE AND ENDS IN ROMANCE!
"COME WITH ME TO THE PLANET VENUS—PLANET OF LOVE AND BEAUTY, PLANET OF PLEASURE AND SONG WHERE IT ALL BEGAN!"
IN THE CASTLE OF THE GODS ON MT. LUSTRE, THE CASTLE WHICH HOUSES...
HOW MANY CENTURIES HAVE I RULED THIS PLANET! HOW WEARY I AM OF THE LIFE I LEAD!
...VENUS, GODDESS OF LOVE AND ROMANCE! FOR HERS IS THE STORY THAT I'M GOING TO TELL YOU! IT IS MY STORY!
2

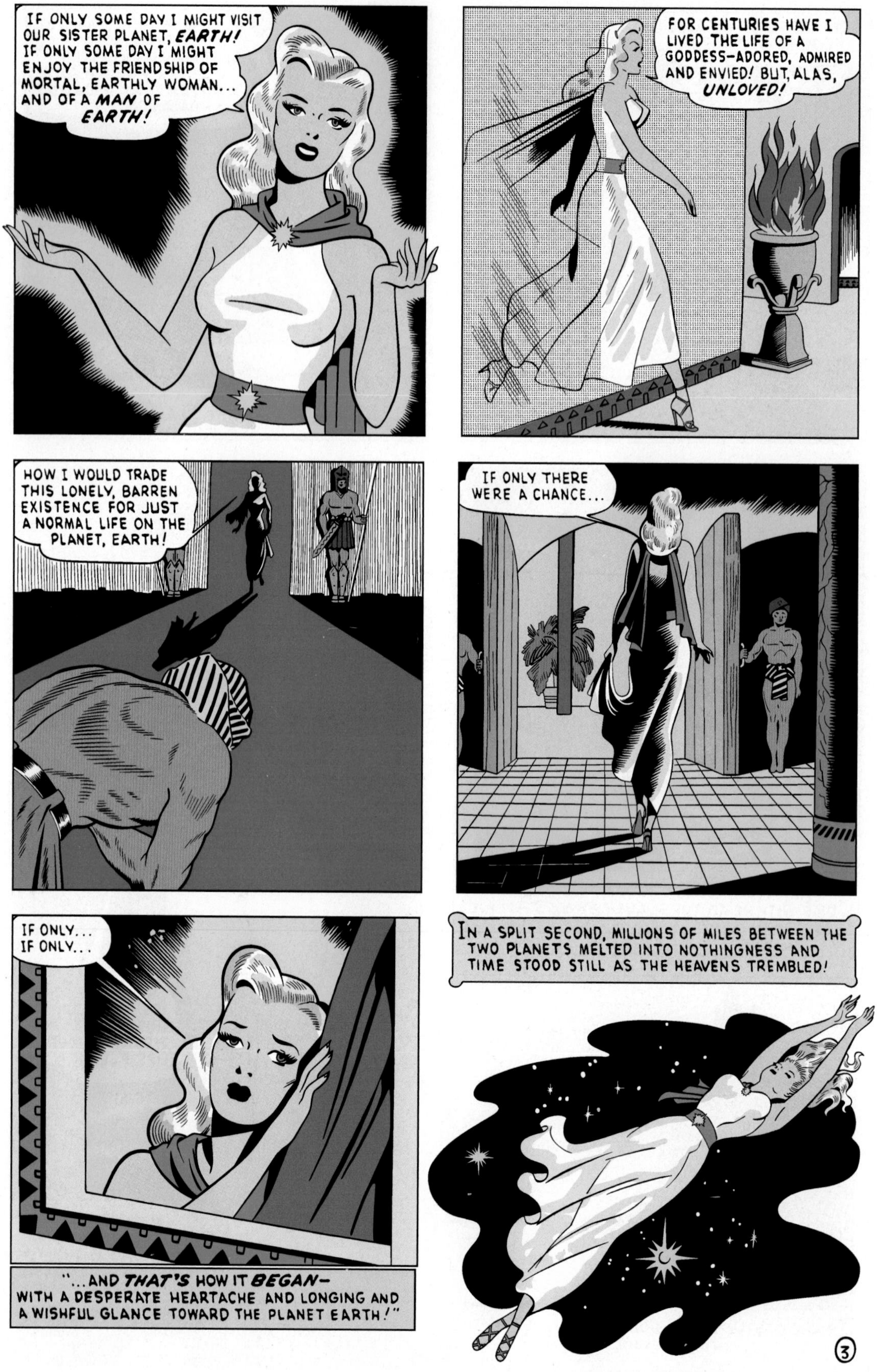
IF ONLY SOME DAY I MIGHT VISIT OUR SISTER PLANET, EARTH! IF ONLY SOME DAY I MIGHT ENJOY THE FRIENDSHIP OF MORTAL, EARTHLY WOMAN... AND OF A MAN OF EARTH!
FOR CENTURIES HAVE I LIVED THE LIFE OF A GODDESS–ADORED, ADMIRED AND ENVIED! BUT, ALAS, UNLOVED!
HOW I WOULD TRADE THIS LONELY, BARREN EXISTENCE FOR JUST A NORMAL LIFE ON THE PLANET, EARTH!
IF ONLY THERE WERE A CHANCE...
IF ONLY... IF ONLY...
"...AND THAT'S HOW IT BEGAN– WITH A DESPERATE HEARTACHE AND LONGING AND A WISHFUL GLANCE TOWARD THE PLANET EARTH!"
IN A SPLIT SECOND, MILLIONS OF MILES BETWEEN THE TWO PLANETS MELTED INTO NOTHINGNESS AND TIME STOOD STILL AS THE HEAVENS TREMBLED!
3

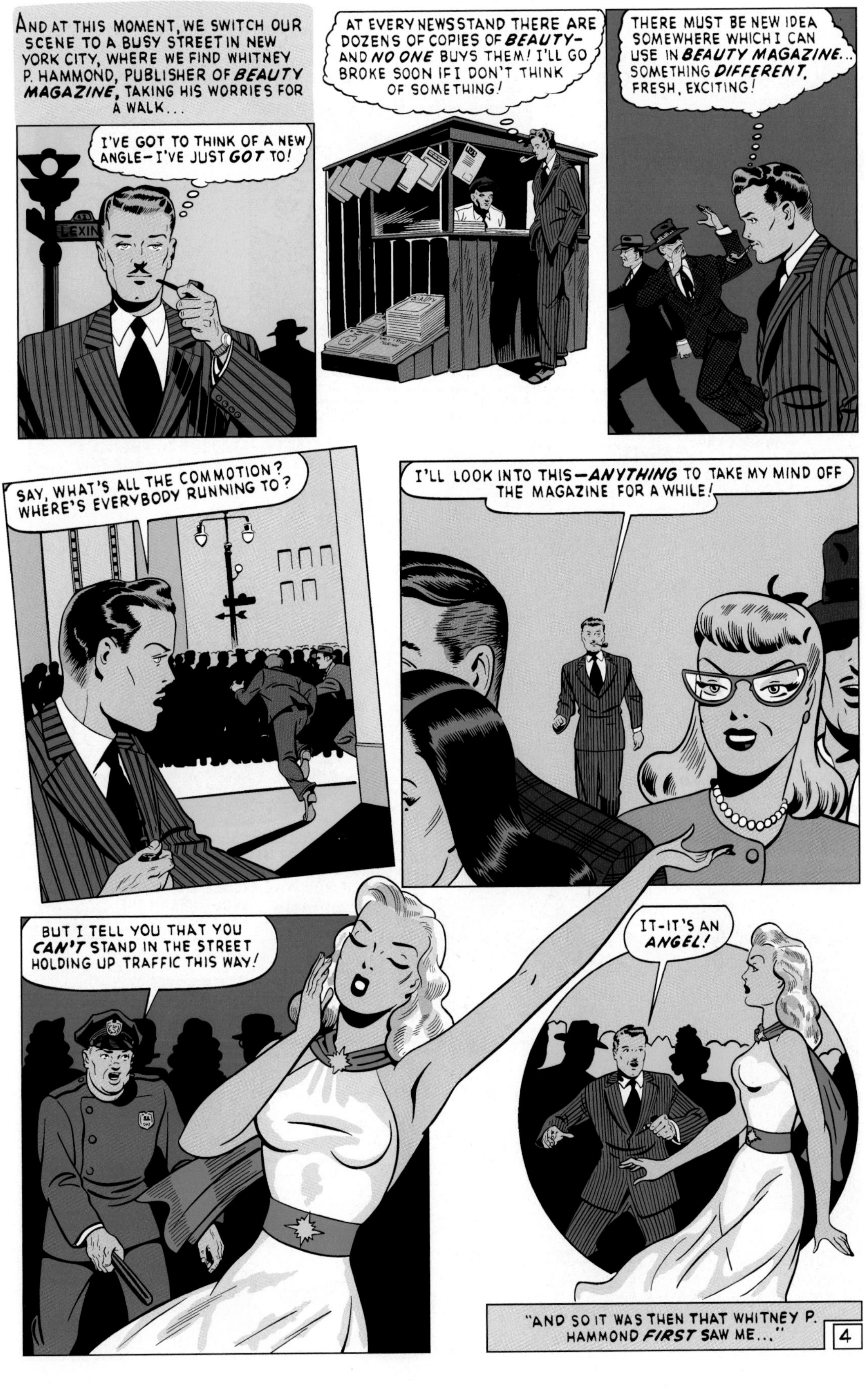
AND AT THIS MOMENT, WE SWITCH OUR SCENE TO A BUSY STREET IN NEW YORK CITY, WHERE WE FIND WHITNEY P. HAMMOND, PUBLISHER OF BEAUTY MAGAZINE, TAKING HIS WORRIES FOR A WALK...
I'VE GOT TO THINK OF A NEW ANGLE—I'VE JUST GOT TO!
LEXIN
AT EVERY NEWSSTAND THERE ARE DOZENS OF COPIES OF BEAUTY— AND NO ONE BUYS THEM! I'LL GO BROKE SOON IF I DON'T THINK OF SOMETHING!
THERE MUST BE NEW IDEA SOMEWHERE WHICH I CAN USE IN BEAUTY MAGAZINE... SOMETHING DIFFERENT, FRESH, EXCITING!
SAY, WHAT'S ALL THE COMMOTION? WHERE'S EVERYBODY RUNNING TO?
I'LL LOOK INTO THIS—ANYTHING TO TAKE MY MIND OFF THE MAGAZINE FOR A WHILE!
BUT I TELL YOU THAT YOU CAN'T STAND IN THE STREET HOLDING UP TRAFFIC THIS WAY!
IT-IT'S AN ANGEL!
"AND SO IT WAS THEN THAT WHITNEY P. HAMMOND FIRST SAW ME..."
4

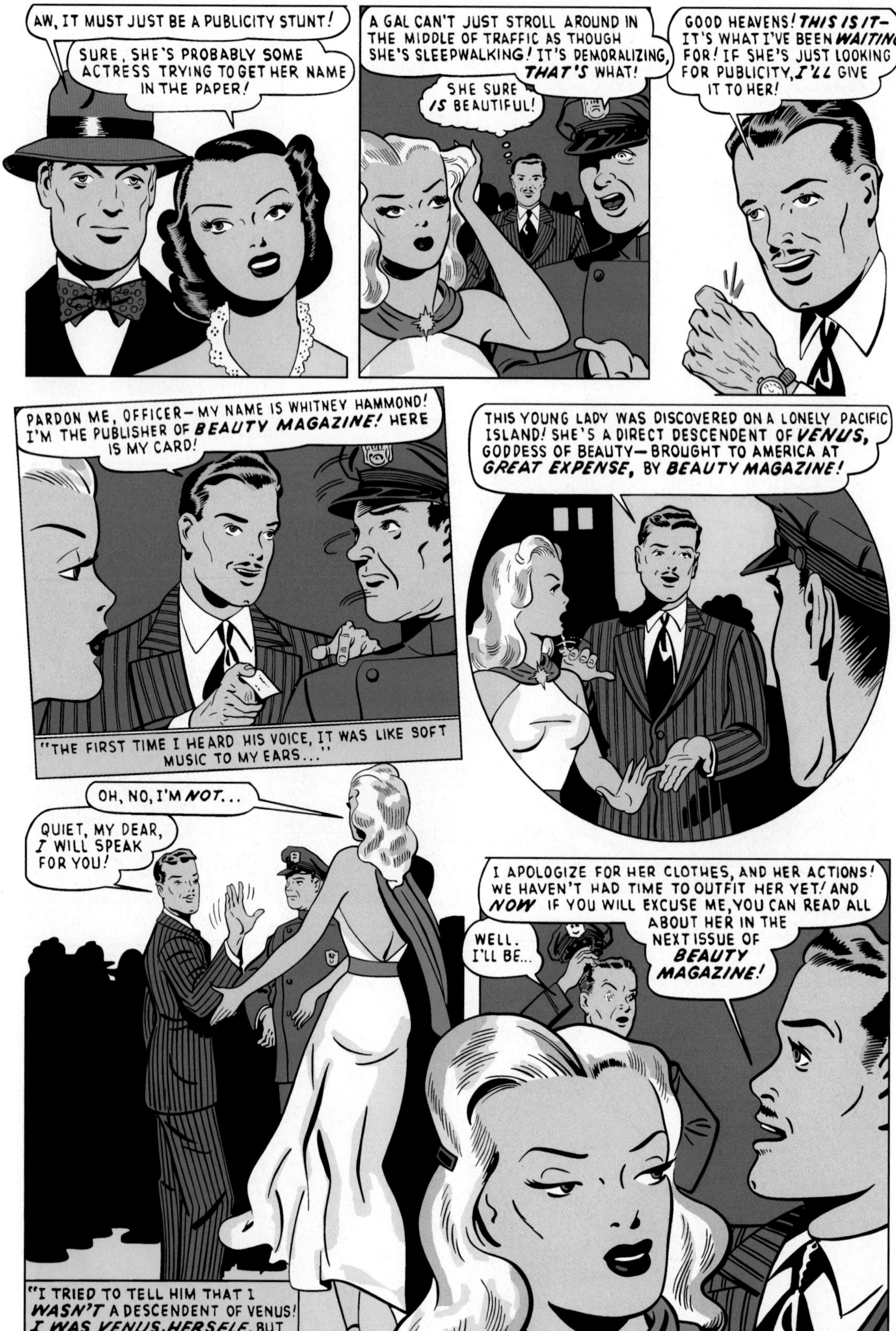
AW, IT MUST JUST BE A PUBLICITY STUNT!
SURE, SHE'S PROBABLY SOME ACTRESS TRYING TO GET HER NAME IN THE PAPER!
A GAL CAN'T JUST STROLL AROUND IN THE MIDDLE OF TRAFFIC AS THOUGH SHE'S SLEEPWALKING! IT'S DEMORALIZING, THAT'S WHAT!
SHE SURE IS BEAUTIFUL!
GOOD HEAVENS! THIS IS IT— IT'S WHAT I'VE BEEN WAITING FOR! IF SHE'S JUST LOOKING FOR PUBLICITY, I'LL GIVE IT TO HER!
PARDON ME, OFFICER— MY NAME IS WHITNEY HAMMOND! I'M THE PUBLISHER OF BEAUTY MAGAZINE! HERE IS MY CARD!
"THE FIRST TIME I HEARD HIS VOICE, IT WAS LIKE SOFT MUSIC TO MY EARS..."
THIS YOUNG LADY WAS DISCOVERED ON A LONELY PACIFIC ISLAND! SHE'S A DIRECT DESCENDENT OF VENUS, GODDESS OF BEAUTY— BROUGHT TO AMERICA AT GREAT EXPENSE, BY BEAUTY MAGAZINE!
OH, NO, I'M NOT...
QUIET, MY DEAR, I WILL SPEAK FOR YOU!
"I TRIED TO TELL HIM THAT I WASN'T A DESCENDENT OF VENUS! I WAS VENUS, HERSELF, BUT HE WOULDN'T LISTEN!"
I APOLOGIZE FOR HER CLOTHES, AND HER ACTIONS! WE HAVEN'T HAD TIME TO OUTFIT HER YET! AND NOW IF YOU WILL EXCUSE ME, YOU CAN READ ALL ABOUT HER IN THE NEXT ISSUE OF BEAUTY MAGAZINE!
WELL. I'LL BE...
5

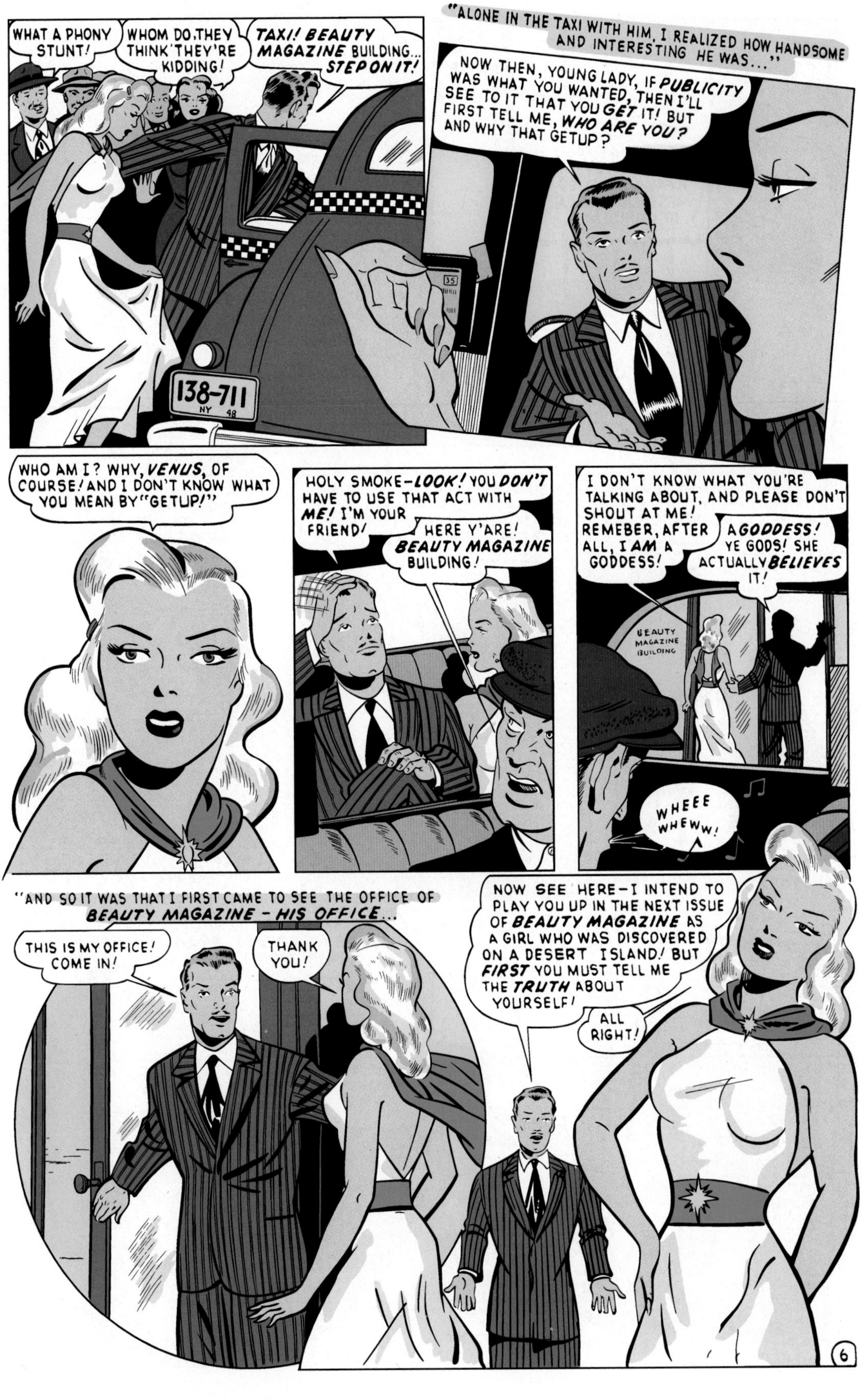
WHAT A PHONY STUNT!
WHOM DO THEY THINK THEY'RE KIDDING!
TAXI! BEAUTY MAGAZINE BUILDING... STEP ON IT!
138-711 NY 48
"ALONE IN THE TAXI WITH HIM, I REALIZED HOW HANDSOME AND INTERESTING HE WAS..."
NOW THEN, YOUNG LADY, IF PUBLICITY WAS WHAT YOU WANTED, THEN I'LL SEE TO IT THAT YOU GET IT! BUT FIRST TELL ME, WHO ARE YOU? AND WHY THAT GETUP?
WHO AM I? WHY, VENUS, OF COURSE! AND I DON'T KNOW WHAT YOU MEAN BY "GETUP!"
HOLY SMOKE—LOOK! YOU DON'T HAVE TO USE THAT ACT WITH ME! I'M YOUR FRIEND!
HERE Y'ARE! BEAUTY MAGAZINE BUILDING!
I DON'T KNOW WHAT YOU'RE TALKING ABOUT, AND PLEASE DON'T SHOUT AT ME! REMEBER, AFTER ALL, I AM A GODDESS!
A GODDESS! YE GODS! SHE ACTUALLY BELIEVES IT!
BEAUTY MAGAZINE BUILDING
WHEEE WHEWW!
"AND SO IT WAS THAT I FIRST CAME TO SEE THE OFFICE OF BEAUTY MAGAZINE — HIS OFFICE...
THIS IS MY OFFICE! COME IN!
THANK YOU!
NOW SEE HERE—I INTEND TO PLAY YOU UP IN THE NEXT ISSUE OF BEAUTY MAGAZINE AS A GIRL WHO WAS DISCOVERED ON A DESERT ISLAND! BUT FIRST YOU MUST TELL ME THE TRUTH ABOUT YOURSELF!
ALL RIGHT!
6

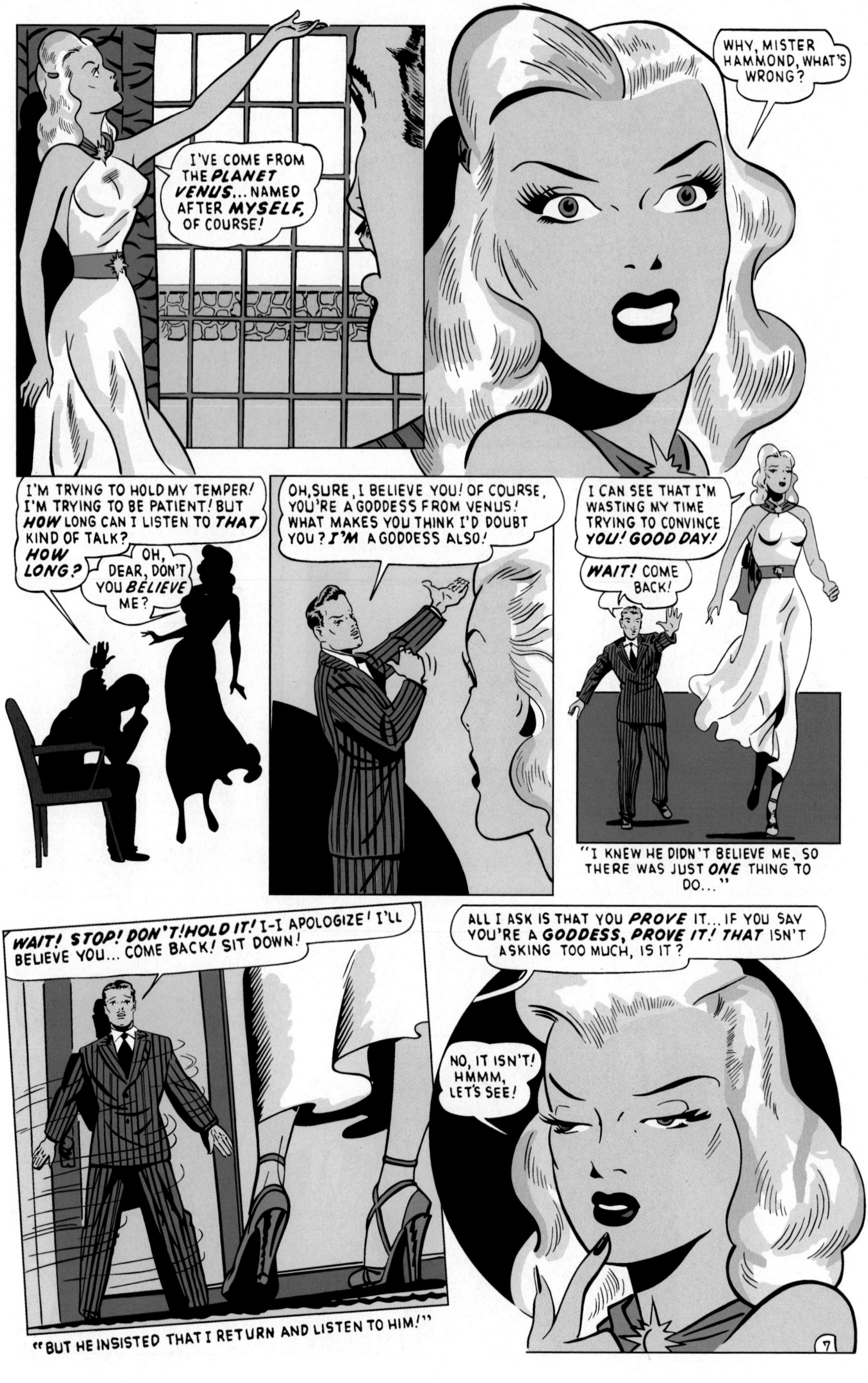
I'VE COME FROM THE PLANET VENUS... NAMED AFTER MYSELF, OF COURSE!
WHY, MISTER HAMMOND, WHAT'S WRONG?
I'M TRYING TO HOLD MY TEMPER! I'M TRYING TO BE PATIENT! BUT HOW LONG CAN I LISTEN TO THAT KIND OF TALK? HOW LONG?
OH, DEAR, DON'T YOU BELIEVE ME?
OH, SURE, I BELIEVE YOU! OF COURSE, YOU'RE A GODDESS FROM VENUS! WHAT MAKES YOU THINK I'D DOUBT YOU? I'M A GODDESS ALSO!
I CAN SEE THAT I'M WASTING MY TIME TRYING TO CONVINCE YOU! GOOD DAY!
WAIT! COME BACK!
"I KNEW HE DIDN'T BELIEVE ME, SO THERE WAS JUST ONE THING TO DO..."
WAIT! STOP! DON'T! HOLD IT! I-I APOLOGIZE! I'LL BELIEVE YOU... COME BACK! SIT DOWN!
"BUT HE INSISTED THAT I RETURN AND LISTEN TO HIM!"
ALL I ASK IS THAT YOU PROVE IT... IF YOU SAY YOU'RE A GODDESS, PROVE IT! THAT ISN'T ASKING TOO MUCH, IS IT?
NO, IT ISN'T! HMMM, LET'S SEE!
7

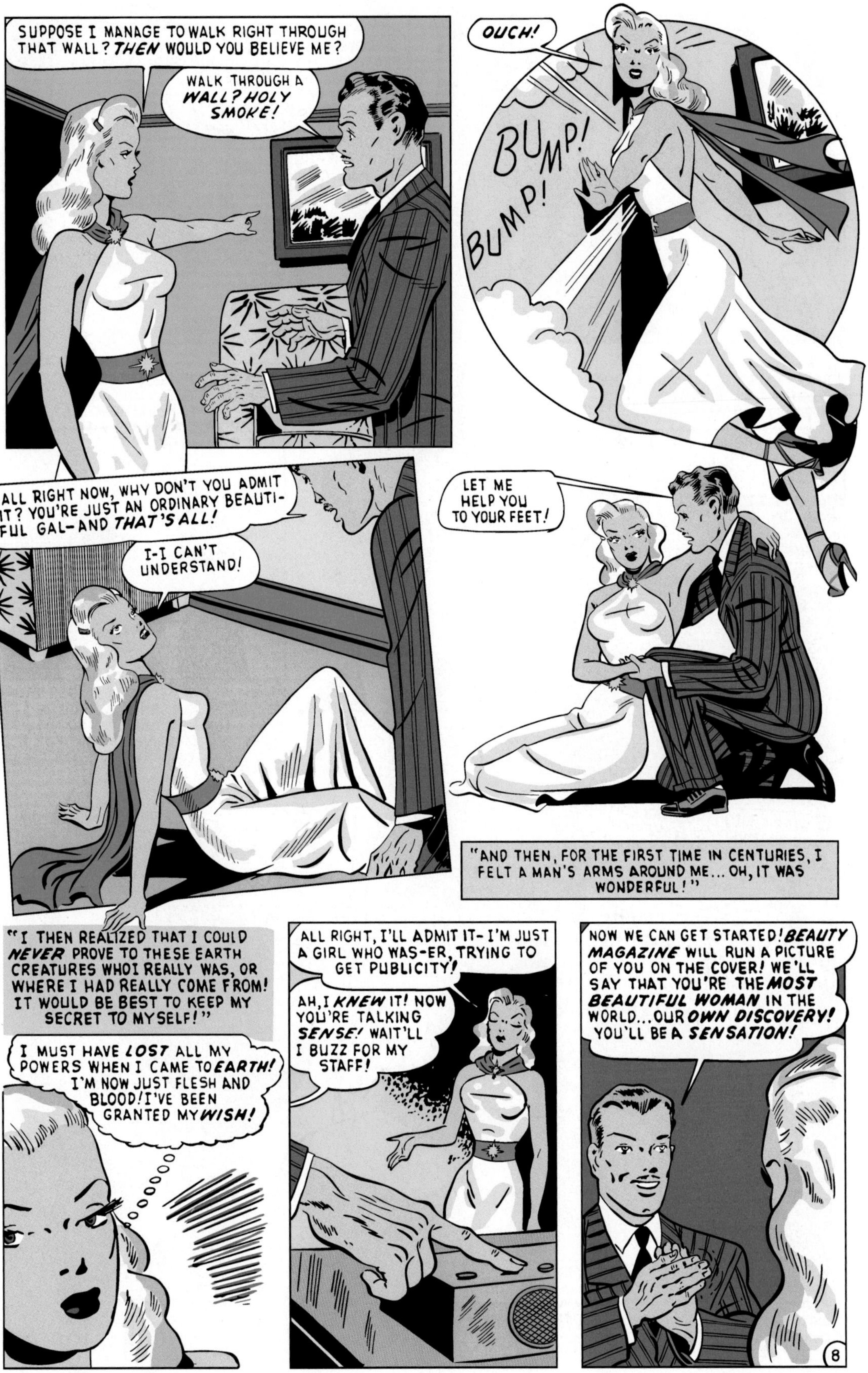
SUPPOSE I MANAGE TO WALK RIGHT THROUGH THAT WALL? THEN WOULD YOU BELIEVE ME?
WALK THROUGH A WALL? HOLY SMOKE!
OUCH!
BUMP!
BUMP!
ALL RIGHT NOW, WHY DON'T YOU ADMIT IT? YOU'RE JUST AN ORDINARY BEAUTIFUL GAL—AND THAT'S ALL!
I-I CAN'T UNDERSTAND!
LET ME HELP YOU TO YOUR FEET!
"AND THEN, FOR THE FIRST TIME IN CENTURIES, I FELT A MAN'S ARMS AROUND ME... OH, IT WAS WONDERFUL!"
"I THEN REALIZED THAT I COULD NEVER PROVE TO THESE EARTH CREATURES WHO I REALLY WAS, OR WHERE I HAD REALLY COME FROM! IT WOULD BE BEST TO KEEP MY SECRET TO MYSELF!"
I MUST HAVE LOST ALL MY POWERS WHEN I CAME TO EARTH! I'M NOW JUST FLESH AND BLOOD! I'VE BEEN GRANTED MY WISH!
ALL RIGHT, I'LL ADMIT IT— I'M JUST A GIRL WHO WAS-ER, TRYING TO GET PUBLICITY!
AH, I KNEW IT! NOW YOU'RE TALKING SENSE! WAIT'LL I BUZZ FOR MY STAFF!
NOW WE CAN GET STARTED! BEAUTY MAGAZINE WILL RUN A PICTURE OF YOU ON THE COVER! WE'LL SAY THAT YOU'RE THE MOST BEAUTIFUL WOMAN IN THE WORLD... OUR OWN DISCOVERY! YOU'LL BE A SENSATION!
8

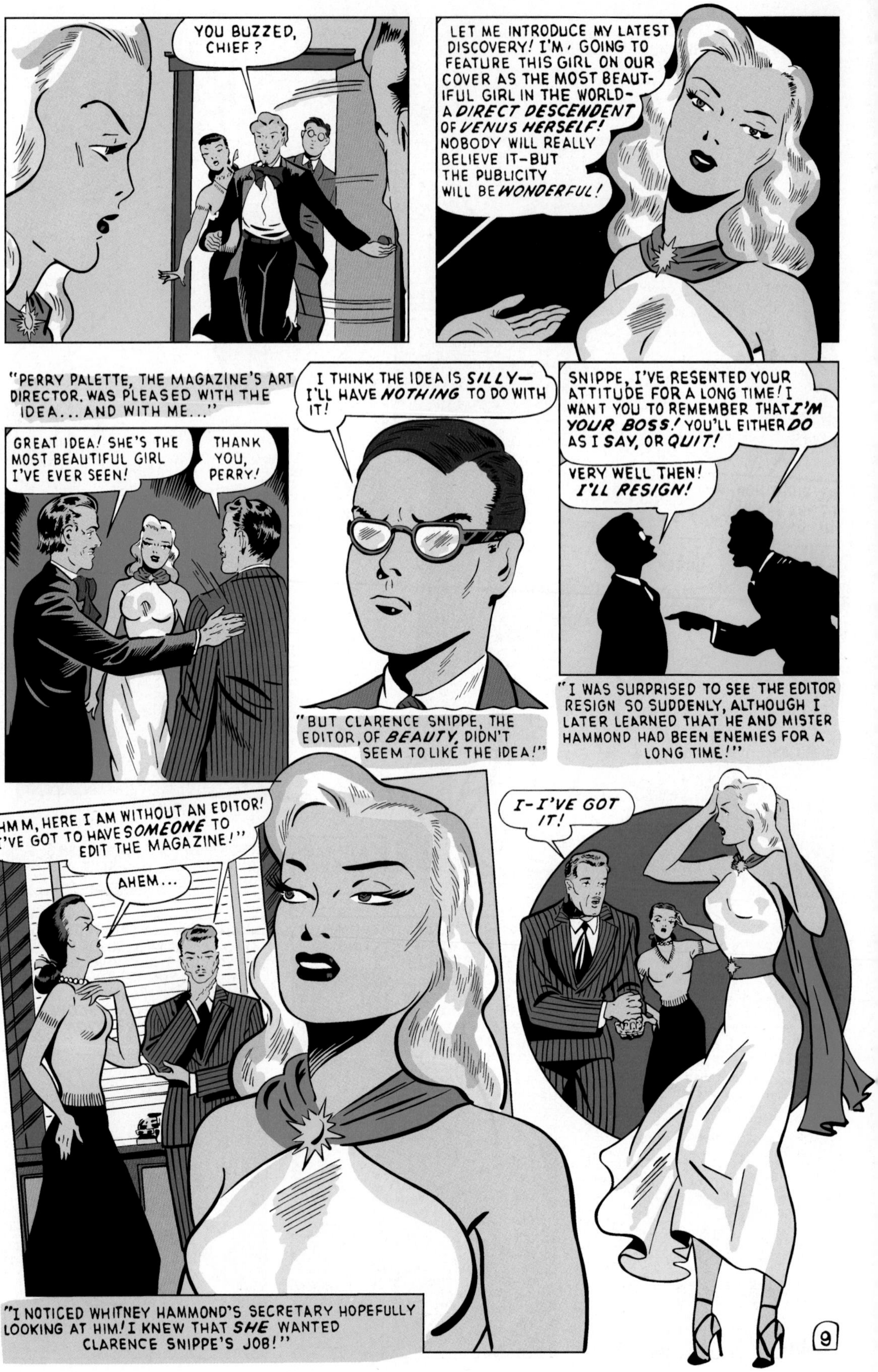
YOU BUZZED, CHIEF?
LET ME INTRODUCE MY LATEST DISCOVERY! I'M GOING TO FEATURE THIS GIRL ON OUR COVER AS THE MOST BEAUTIFUL GIRL IN THE WORLD- A DIRECT DESCENDENT OF VENUS HERSELF! NOBODY WILL REALLY BELIEVE IT-BUT THE PUBLICITY WILL BE WONDERFUL!
"PERRY PALETTE, THE MAGAZINE'S ART DIRECTOR, WAS PLEASED WITH THE IDEA... AND WITH ME..."
GREAT IDEA! SHE'S THE MOST BEAUTIFUL GIRL I'VE EVER SEEN!
THANK YOU, PERRY!
I THINK THE IDEA IS SILLY— I'LL HAVE NOTHING TO DO WITH IT!
"BUT CLARENCE SNIPPE, THE EDITOR, OF BEAUTY, DIDN'T SEEM TO LIKE THE IDEA!"
SNIPPE, I'VE RESENTED YOUR ATTITUDE FOR A LONG TIME! I WANT YOU TO REMEMBER THAT I'M YOUR BOSS! YOU'LL EITHER DO AS I SAY, OR QUIT!
VERY WELL THEN! I'LL RESIGN!
"I WAS SURPRISED TO SEE THE EDITOR RESIGN SO SUDDENLY, ALTHOUGH I LATER LEARNED THAT HE AND MISTER HAMMOND HAD BEEN ENEMIES FOR A LONG TIME!"
HMM, HERE I AM WITHOUT AN EDITOR! I'VE GOT TO HAVE SOMEONE TO EDIT THE MAGAZINE!"
AHEM...
"I NOTICED WHITNEY HAMMOND'S SECRETARY HOPEFULLY LOOKING AT HIM! I KNEW THAT SHE WANTED CLARENCE SNIPPE'S JOB!"
I-I'VE GOT IT!
9

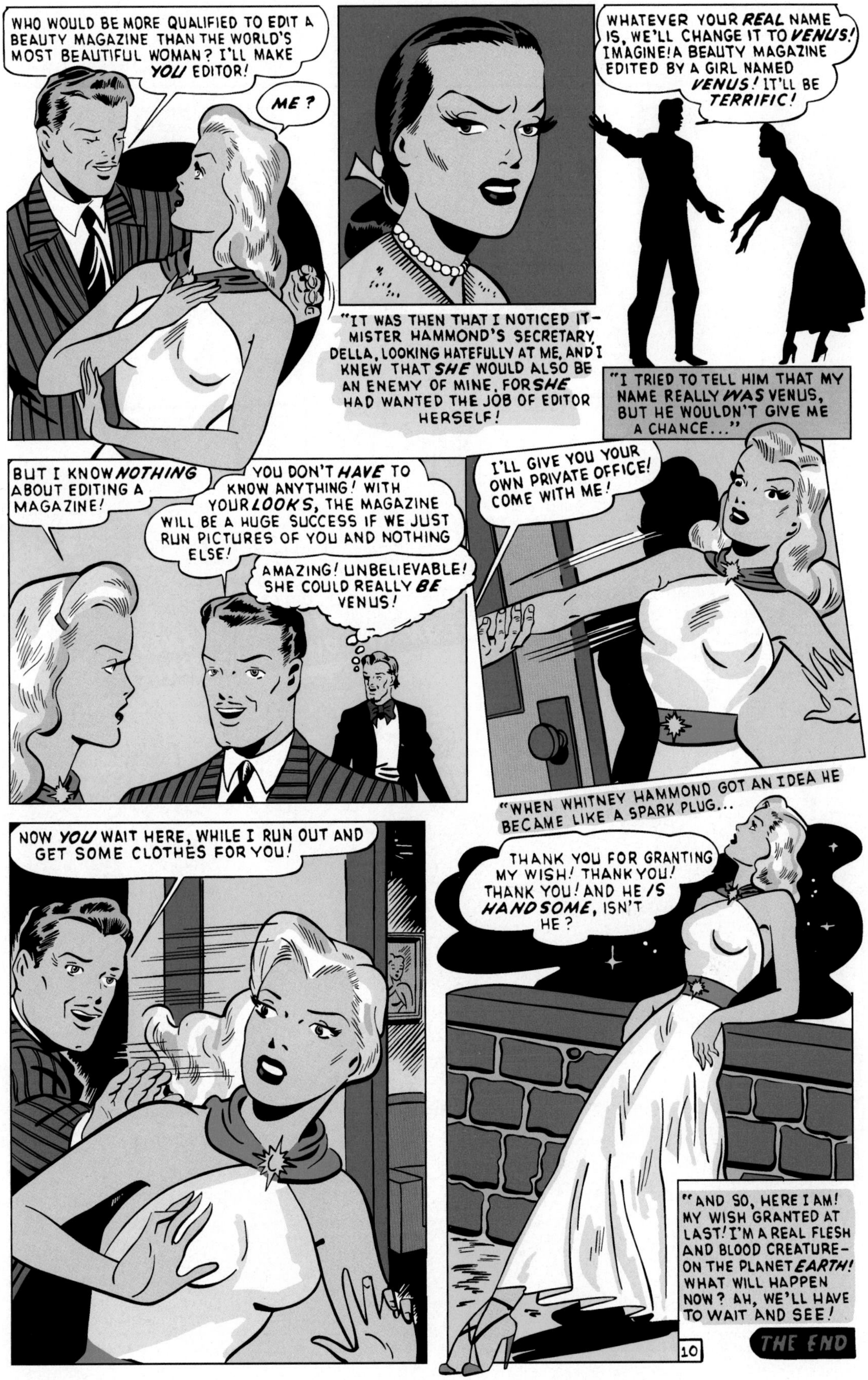
WHO WOULD BE MORE QUALIFIED TO EDIT A BEAUTY MAGAZINE THAN THE WORLD'S MOST BEAUTIFUL WOMAN? I'LL MAKE YOU EDITOR!
ME?
"IT WAS THEN THAT I NOTICED IT-- MISTER HAMMOND'S SECRETARY, DELLA, LOOKING HATEFULLY AT ME, AND I KNEW THAT SHE WOULD ALSO BE AN ENEMY OF MINE, FOR SHE HAD WANTED THE JOB OF EDITOR HERSELF!
WHATEVER YOUR REAL NAME IS, WE'LL CHANGE IT TO VENUS! IMAGINE! A BEAUTY MAGAZINE EDITED BY A GIRL NAMED VENUS! IT'LL BE TERRIFIC!
"I TRIED TO TELL HIM THAT MY NAME REALLY WAS VENUS, BUT HE WOULDN'T GIVE ME A CHANCE..."
BUT I KNOW NOTHING ABOUT EDITING A MAGAZINE!
YOU DON'T HAVE TO KNOW ANYTHING! WITH YOUR LOOKS, THE MAGAZINE WILL BE A HUGE SUCCESS IF WE JUST RUN PICTURES OF YOU AND NOTHING ELSE!
AMAZING! UNBELIEVABLE! SHE COULD REALLY BE VENUS!
I'LL GIVE YOU YOUR OWN PRIVATE OFFICE! COME WITH ME!
NOW YOU WAIT HERE, WHILE I RUN OUT AND GET SOME CLOTHES FOR YOU!
"WHEN WHITNEY HAMMOND GOT AN IDEA HE BECAME LIKE A SPARK PLUG...
THANK YOU FOR GRANTING MY WISH! THANK YOU! THANK YOU! AND HE IS HANDSOME, ISN'T HE?
"AND SO, HERE I AM! MY WISH GRANTED AT LAST! I'M A REAL FLESH AND BLOOD CREATURE-- ON THE PLANET EARTH! WHAT WILL HAPPEN NOW? AH, WE'LL HAVE TO WAIT AND SEE!
10
THE END

MARVEL BOY #1 (DECEMBER 1950), THE FIRST APPEARANCE OF MARVEL BOY
ARTIST & COVER ARTIST: **RUSS HEATH** • EDITOR: **STAN LEE**

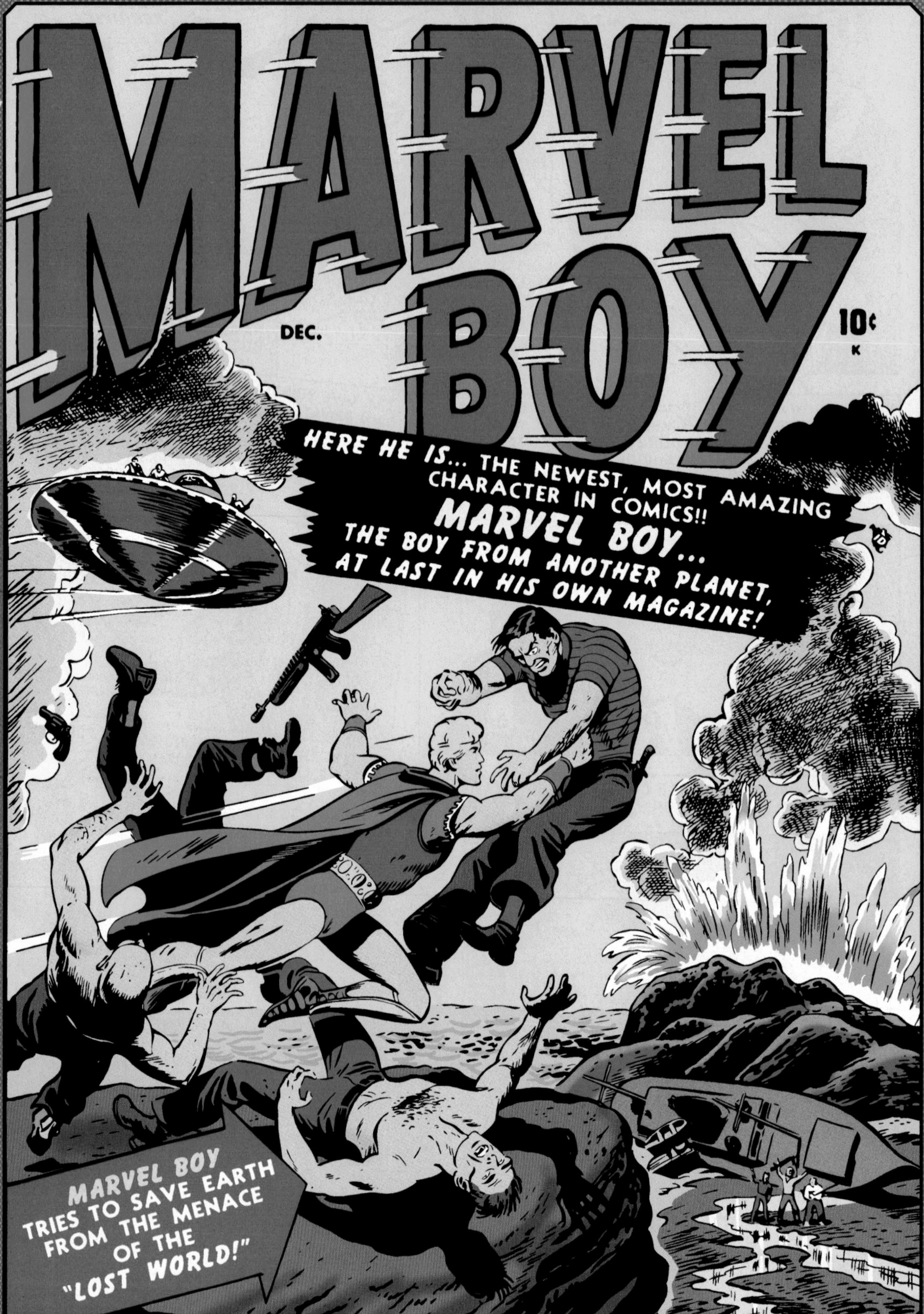
MARVEL BOY
DEC.
10¢
HERE HE IS... THE NEWEST, MOST AMAZING CHARACTER IN COMICS!! MARVEL BOY... THE BOY FROM ANOTHER PLANET, AT LAST IN HIS OWN MAGAZINE!
MARVEL BOY TRIES TO SAVE EARTH FROM THE MENACE OF THE "LOST WORLD!"

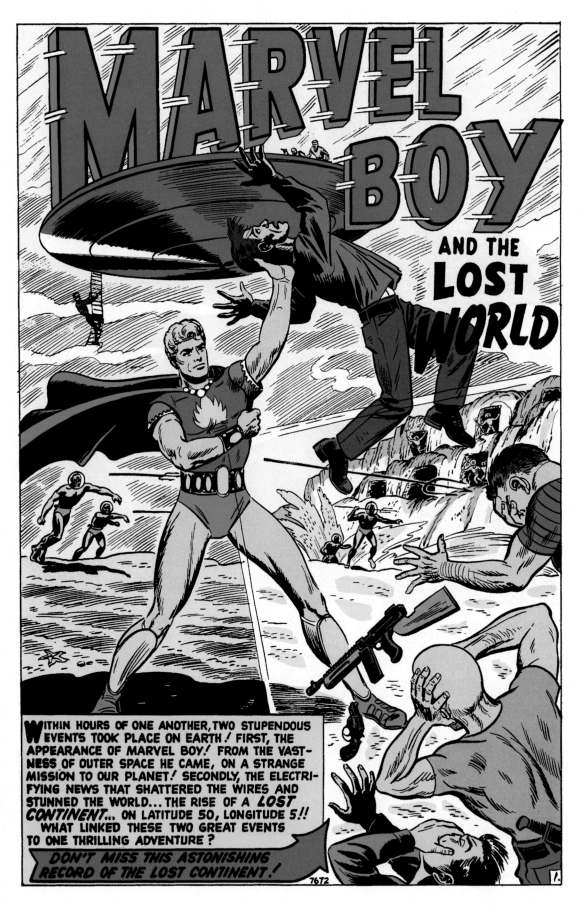

MARVEL BOY

AND THE LOST WORLD

WITHIN HOURS OF ONE ANOTHER, TWO STUPENDOUS EVENTS TOOK PLACE ON EARTH! FIRST, THE APPEARANCE OF MARVEL BOY! FROM THE VASTNESS OF OUTER SPACE HE CAME, ON A STRANGE MISSION TO OUR PLANET! SECONDLY, THE ELECTRIFYING NEWS THAT SHATTERED THE WIRES AND STUNNED THE WORLD... THE RISE OF A *LOST CONTINENT*... ON LATITUDE 50, LONGITUDE 5!!
WHAT LINKED THESE TWO GREAT EVENTS TO ONE THRILLING ADVENTURE?

DON'T MISS THIS ASTONISHING RECORD OF THE LOST CONTINENT!

7672

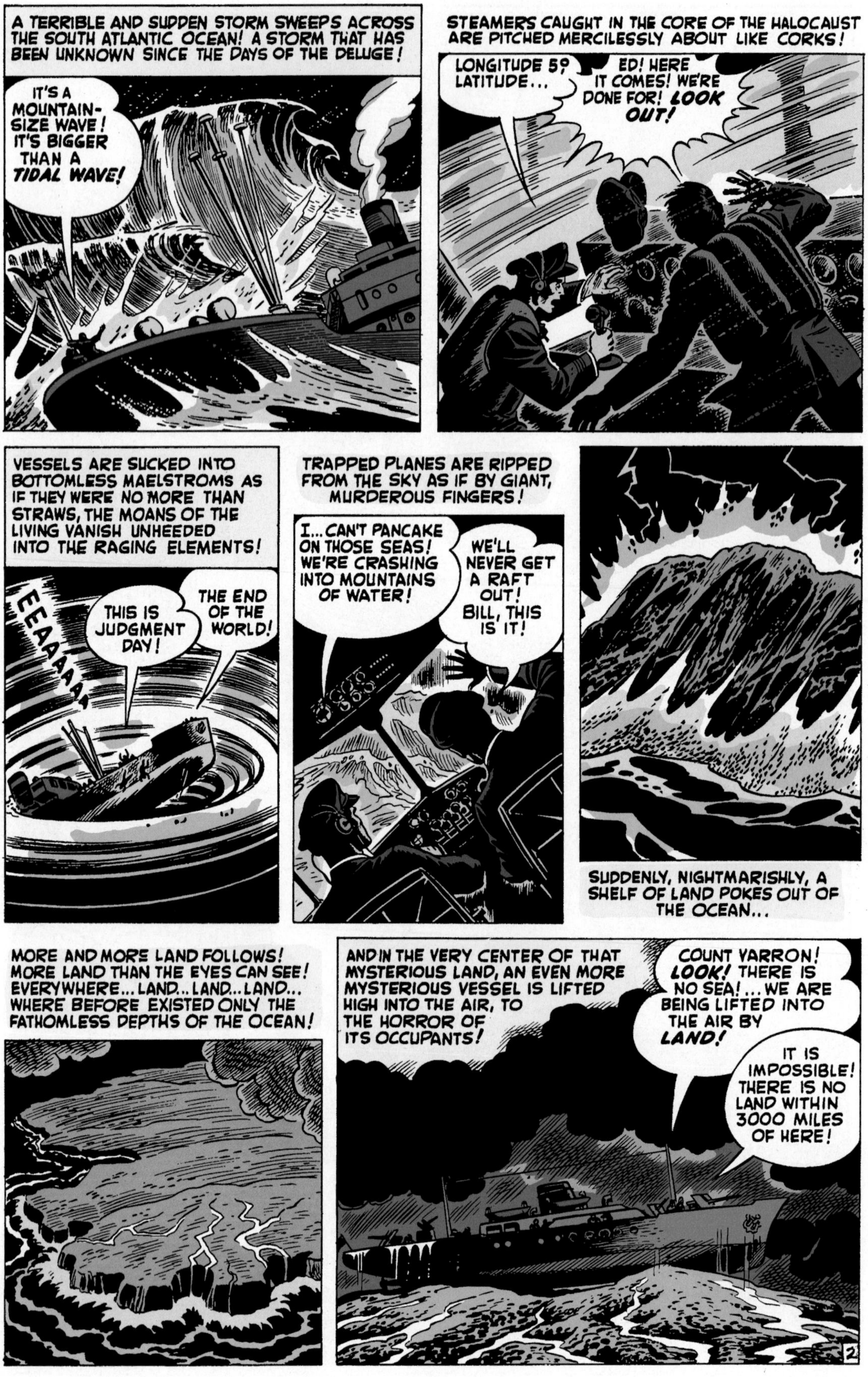
A TERRIBLE AND SUDDEN STORM SWEEPS ACROSS THE SOUTH ATLANTIC OCEAN! A STORM THAT HAS BEEN UNKNOWN SINCE THE DAYS OF THE DELUGE!
IT'S A MOUNTAIN-SIZE WAVE! IT'S BIGGER THAN A TIDAL WAVE!
STEAMERS CAUGHT IN THE CORE OF THE HALOCAUST ARE PITCHED MERCILESSLY ABOUT LIKE CORKS!
LONGITUDE 5° LATITUDE...
ED! HERE IT COMES! WE'RE DONE FOR! LOOK OUT!
VESSELS ARE SUCKED INTO BOTTOMLESS MAELSTROMS AS IF THEY WERE NO MORE THAN STRAWS, THE MOANS OF THE LIVING VANISH UNHEEDED INTO THE RAGING ELEMENTS!
EEAAAAAA
THIS IS JUDGMENT DAY!
THE END OF THE WORLD!
TRAPPED PLANES ARE RIPPED FROM THE SKY AS IF BY GIANT, MURDEROUS FINGERS!
I...CAN'T PANCAKE ON THOSE SEAS! WE'RE CRASHING INTO MOUNTAINS OF WATER!
WE'LL NEVER GET A RAFT OUT! BILL, THIS IS IT!
SUDDENLY, NIGHTMARISHLY, A SHELF OF LAND POKES OUT OF THE OCEAN...
MORE AND MORE LAND FOLLOWS! MORE LAND THAN THE EYES CAN SEE! EVERYWHERE... LAND... LAND... LAND... WHERE BEFORE EXISTED ONLY THE FATHOMLESS DEPTHS OF THE OCEAN!
AND IN THE VERY CENTER OF THAT MYSTERIOUS LAND, AN EVEN MORE MYSTERIOUS VESSEL IS LIFTED HIGH INTO THE AIR, TO THE HORROR OF ITS OCCUPANTS!
COUNT VARRON! LOOK! THERE IS NO SEA! ... WE ARE BEING LIFTED INTO THE AIR BY LAND!
IT IS IMPOSSIBLE! THERE IS NO LAND WITHIN 3000 MILES OF HERE!
2

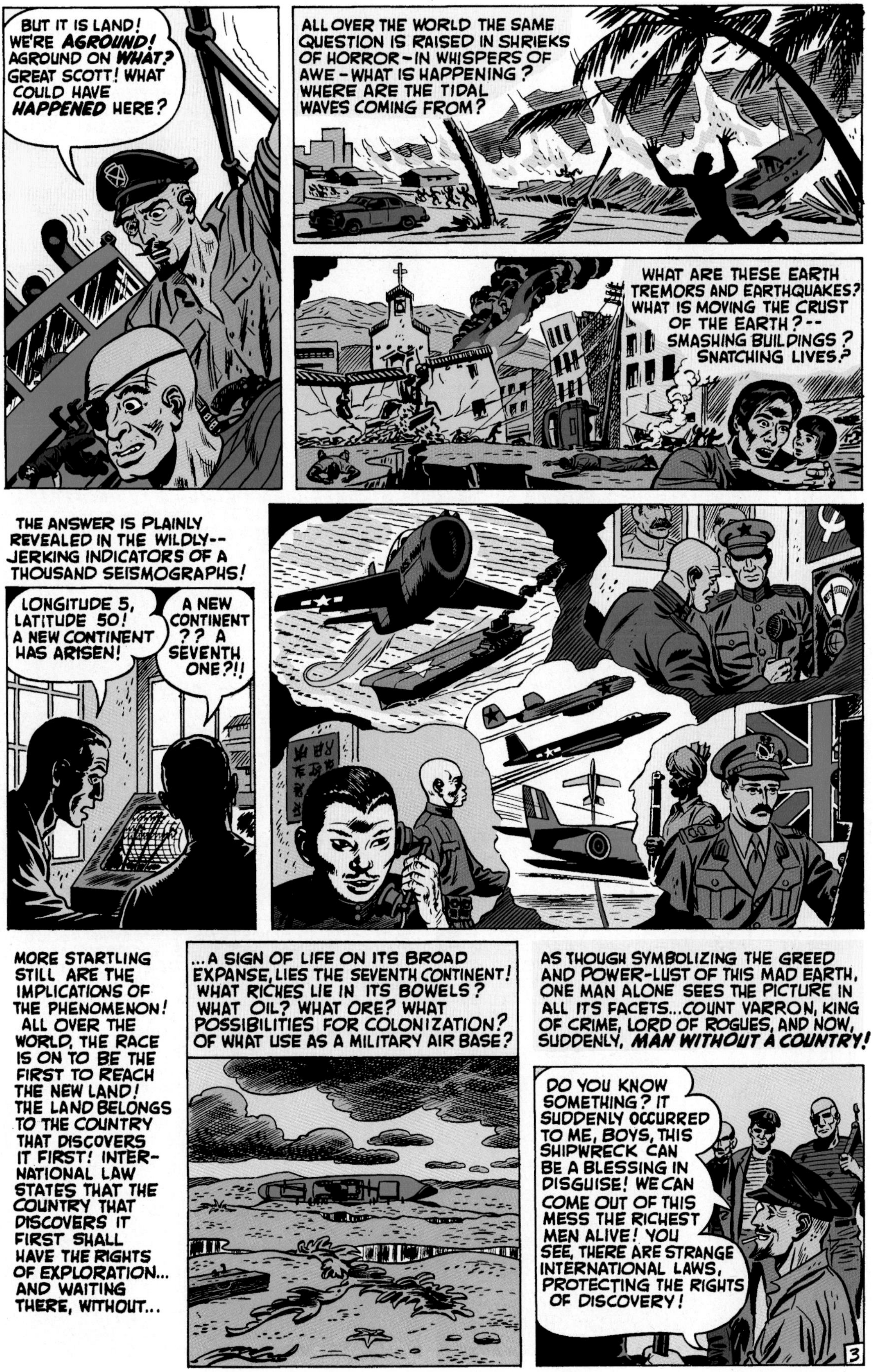
BUT IT IS LAND! WE'RE AGROUND! AGROUND ON WHAT? GREAT SCOTT! WHAT COULD HAVE HAPPENED HERE?
ALL OVER THE WORLD THE SAME QUESTION IS RAISED IN SHRIEKS OF HORROR - IN WHISPERS OF AWE - WHAT IS HAPPENING? WHERE ARE THE TIDAL WAVES COMING FROM?
WHAT ARE THESE EARTH TREMORS AND EARTHQUAKES? WHAT IS MOVING THE CRUST OF THE EARTH? -- SMASHING BUILDINGS? SNATCHING LIVES?
THE ANSWER IS PLAINLY REVEALED IN THE WILDLY-- JERKING INDICATORS OF A THOUSAND SEISMOGRAPHS!
LONGITUDE 5, LATITUDE 50! A NEW CONTINENT HAS ARISEN!
A NEW CONTINENT ?? A SEVENTH ONE?!!
MORE STARTLING STILL ARE THE IMPLICATIONS OF THE PHENOMENON! ALL OVER THE WORLD, THE RACE IS ON TO BE THE FIRST TO REACH THE NEW LAND! THE LAND BELONGS TO THE COUNTRY THAT DISCOVERS IT FIRST! INTER-NATIONAL LAW STATES THAT THE COUNTRY THAT DISCOVERS IT FIRST SHALL HAVE THE RIGHTS OF EXPLORATION... AND WAITING THERE, WITHOUT...
...A SIGN OF LIFE ON ITS BROAD EXPANSE, LIES THE SEVENTH CONTINENT! WHAT RICHES LIE IN ITS BOWELS? WHAT OIL? WHAT ORE? WHAT POSSIBILITIES FOR COLONIZATION? OF WHAT USE AS A MILITARY AIR BASE?
AS THOUGH SYMBOLIZING THE GREED AND POWER-LUST OF THIS MAD EARTH, ONE MAN ALONE SEES THE PICTURE IN ALL ITS FACETS...COUNT VARRON, KING OF CRIME, LORD OF ROGUES, AND NOW, SUDDENLY, MAN WITHOUT A COUNTRY!
DO YOU KNOW SOMETHING? IT SUDDENLY OCCURRED TO ME, BOYS, THIS SHIPWRECK CAN BE A BLESSING IN DISGUISE! WE CAN COME OUT OF THIS MESS THE RICHEST MEN ALIVE! YOU SEE, THERE ARE STRANGE INTERNATIONAL LAWS, PROTECTING THE RIGHTS OF DISCOVERY!
3

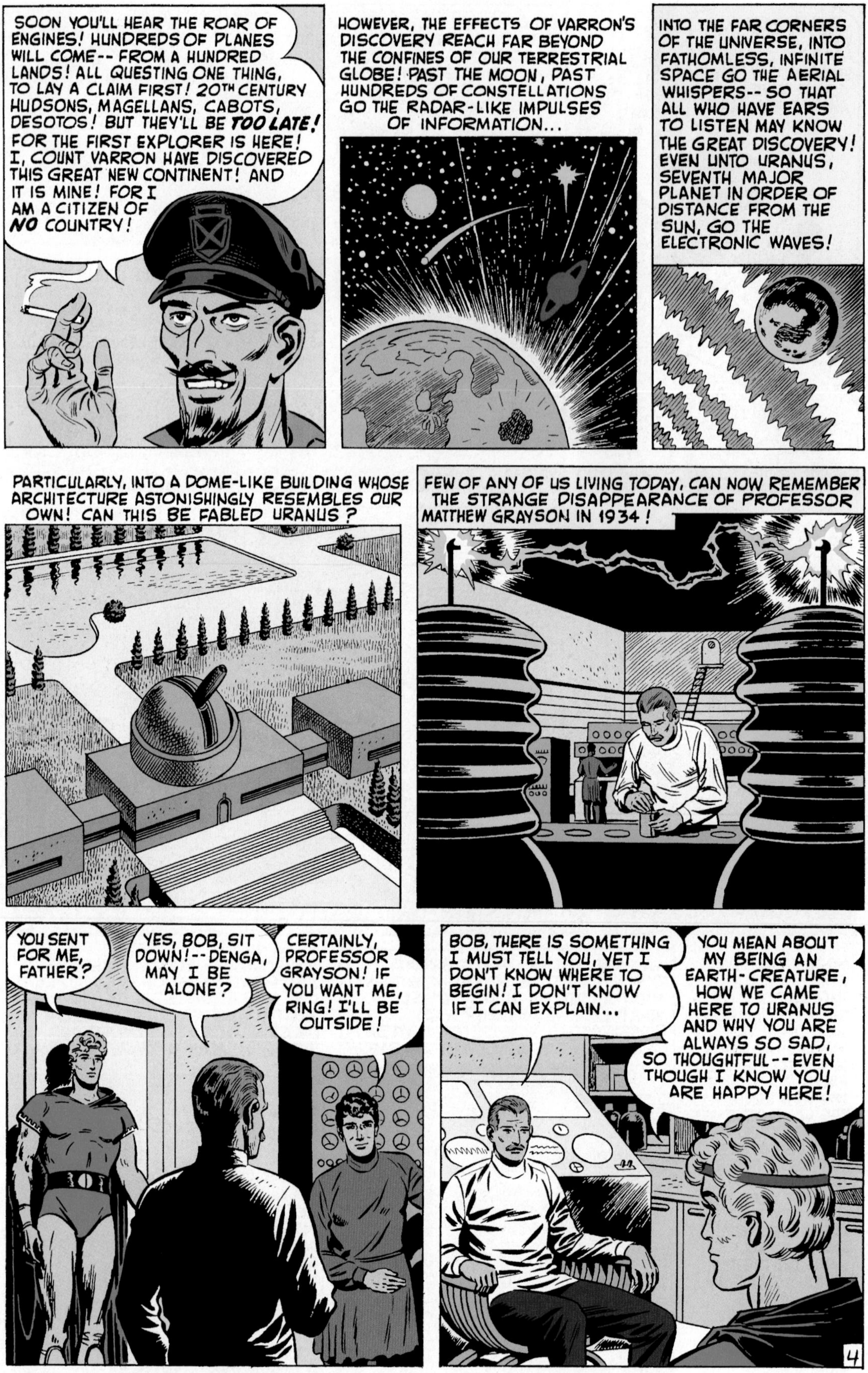
SOON YOU'LL HEAR THE ROAR OF ENGINES! HUNDREDS OF PLANES WILL COME-- FROM A HUNDRED LANDS! ALL QUESTING ONE THING, TO LAY A CLAIM FIRST! 20TH CENTURY HUDSONS, MAGELLANS, CABOTS, DESOTOS! BUT THEY'LL BE TOO LATE! FOR THE FIRST EXPLORER IS HERE! I, COUNT VARRON HAVE DISCOVERED THIS GREAT NEW CONTINENT! AND IT IS MINE! FOR I AM A CITIZEN OF NO COUNTRY!
HOWEVER, THE EFFECTS OF VARRON'S DISCOVERY REACH FAR BEYOND THE CONFINES OF OUR TERRESTRIAL GLOBE! PAST THE MOON, PAST HUNDREDS OF CONSTELLATIONS GO THE RADAR-LIKE IMPULSES OF INFORMATION...
INTO THE FAR CORNERS OF THE UNIVERSE, INTO FATHOMLESS, INFINITE SPACE GO THE AERIAL WHISPERS-- SO THAT ALL WHO HAVE EARS TO LISTEN MAY KNOW THE GREAT DISCOVERY! EVEN UNTO URANUS, SEVENTH MAJOR PLANET IN ORDER OF DISTANCE FROM THE SUN, GO THE ELECTRONIC WAVES!
PARTICULARLY, INTO A DOME-LIKE BUILDING WHOSE ARCHITECTURE ASTONISHINGLY RESEMBLES OUR OWN! CAN THIS BE FABLED URANUS?
FEW OF ANY OF US LIVING TODAY, CAN NOW REMEMBER THE STRANGE DISAPPEARANCE OF PROFESSOR MATTHEW GRAYSON IN 1934!
YOU SENT FOR ME, FATHER?
YES, BOB, SIT DOWN!--DENGA, MAY I BE ALONE?
CERTAINLY, PROFESSOR GRAYSON! IF YOU WANT ME, RING! I'LL BE OUTSIDE!
BOB, THERE IS SOMETHING I MUST TELL YOU, YET I DON'T KNOW WHERE TO BEGIN! I DON'T KNOW IF I CAN EXPLAIN...
YOU MEAN ABOUT MY BEING AN EARTH-CREATURE, HOW WE CAME HERE TO URANUS AND WHY YOU ARE ALWAYS SO SAD, SO THOUGHTFUL--EVEN THOUGH I KNOW YOU ARE HAPPY HERE!
4

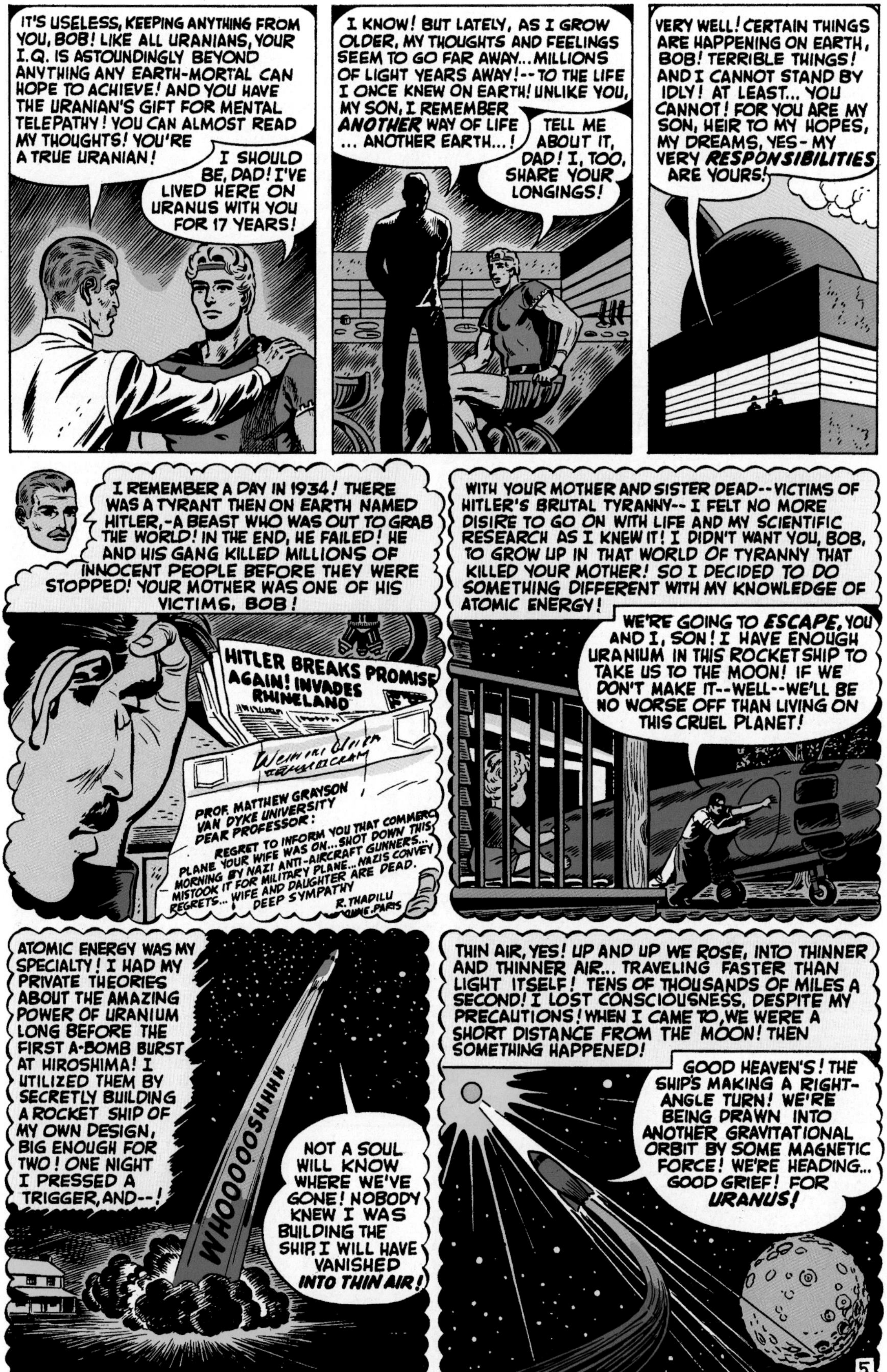

IT'S USELESS, KEEPING ANYTHING FROM YOU, BOB! LIKE ALL URANIANS, YOUR I.Q. IS ASTOUNDINGLY BEYOND ANYTHING ANY EARTH-MORTAL CAN HOPE TO ACHIEVE! AND YOU HAVE THE URANIAN'S GIFT FOR MENTAL TELEPATHY! YOU CAN ALMOST READ MY THOUGHTS! YOU'RE A TRUE URANIAN!
I SHOULD BE, DAD! I'VE LIVED HERE ON URANUS WITH YOU FOR 17 YEARS!
I KNOW! BUT LATELY, AS I GROW OLDER, MY THOUGHTS AND FEELINGS SEEM TO GO FAR AWAY... MILLIONS OF LIGHT YEARS AWAY!-- TO THE LIFE I ONCE KNEW ON EARTH! UNLIKE YOU, MY SON, I REMEMBER *ANOTHER* WAY OF LIFE ... ANOTHER EARTH...!
TELL ME ABOUT IT, DAD! I, TOO, SHARE YOUR LONGINGS!
VERY WELL! CERTAIN THINGS ARE HAPPENING ON EARTH, BOB! TERRIBLE THINGS! AND I CANNOT STAND BY IDLY! AT LEAST... YOU CANNOT! FOR YOU ARE MY SON, HEIR TO MY HOPES, MY DREAMS, YES- MY VERY *RESPONSIBILITIES* ARE YOURS!
I REMEMBER A DAY IN 1934! THERE WAS A TYRANT THEN ON EARTH NAMED HITLER,-A BEAST WHO WAS OUT TO GRAB THE WORLD! IN THE END, HE FAILED! HE AND HIS GANG KILLED MILLIONS OF INNOCENT PEOPLE BEFORE THEY WERE STOPPED! YOUR MOTHER WAS ONE OF HIS VICTIMS, BOB!
HITLER BREAKS PROMISE AGAIN! INVADES RHINELAND
PROF. MATTHEW GRAYSON VAN DYKE UNIVERSITY DEAR PROFESSOR:
REGRET TO INFORM YOU THAT COMMERC PLANE YOUR WIFE WAS ON... SHOT DOWN THIS MORNING BY NAZI ANTI-AIRCRAFT GUNNERS... MISTOOK IT FOR MILITARY PLANE... NAZIS CONVEY REGRETS... WIFE AND DAUGHTER ARE DEAD. DEEP SYMPATHY
R. THADILU
WITH YOUR MOTHER AND SISTER DEAD--VICTIMS OF HITLER'S BRUTAL TYRANNY-- I FELT NO MORE DISIRE TO GO ON WITH LIFE AND MY SCIENTIFIC RESEARCH AS I KNEW IT! I DIDN'T WANT YOU, BOB, TO GROW UP IN THAT WORLD OF TYRANNY THAT KILLED YOUR MOTHER! SO I DECIDED TO DO SOMETHING DIFFERENT WITH MY KNOWLEDGE OF ATOMIC ENERGY!
WE'RE GOING TO *ESCAPE,* YOU AND I, SON! I HAVE ENOUGH URANIUM IN THIS ROCKET SHIP TO TAKE US TO THE MOON! IF WE DON'T MAKE IT--WELL--WE'LL BE NO WORSE OFF THAN LIVING ON THIS CRUEL PLANET!
ATOMIC ENERGY WAS MY SPECIALTY! I HAD MY PRIVATE THEORIES ABOUT THE AMAZING POWER OF URANIUM LONG BEFORE THE FIRST A-BOMB BURST AT HIROSHIMA! I UTILIZED THEM BY SECRETLY BUILDING A ROCKET SHIP OF MY OWN DESIGN, BIG ENOUGH FOR TWO! ONE NIGHT I PRESSED A TRIGGER, AND--!
WHOOOOOSHHHH
NOT A SOUL WILL KNOW WHERE WE'VE GONE! NOBODY KNEW I WAS BUILDING THE SHIP, I WILL HAVE VANISHED *INTO THIN AIR!*
THIN AIR, YES! UP AND UP WE ROSE, INTO THINNER AND THINNER AIR... TRAVELING FASTER THAN LIGHT ITSELF! TENS OF THOUSANDS OF MILES A SECOND! I LOST CONSCIOUSNESS, DESPITE MY PRECAUTIONS! WHEN I CAME TO, WE WERE A SHORT DISTANCE FROM THE MOON! THEN SOMETHING HAPPENED!
GOOD HEAVEN'S! THE SHIP'S MAKING A RIGHT-ANGLE TURN! WE'RE BEING DRAWN INTO ANOTHER GRAVITATIONAL ORBIT BY SOME MAGNETIC FORCE! WE'RE HEADING... GOOD GRIEF! FOR *URANUS!*
5

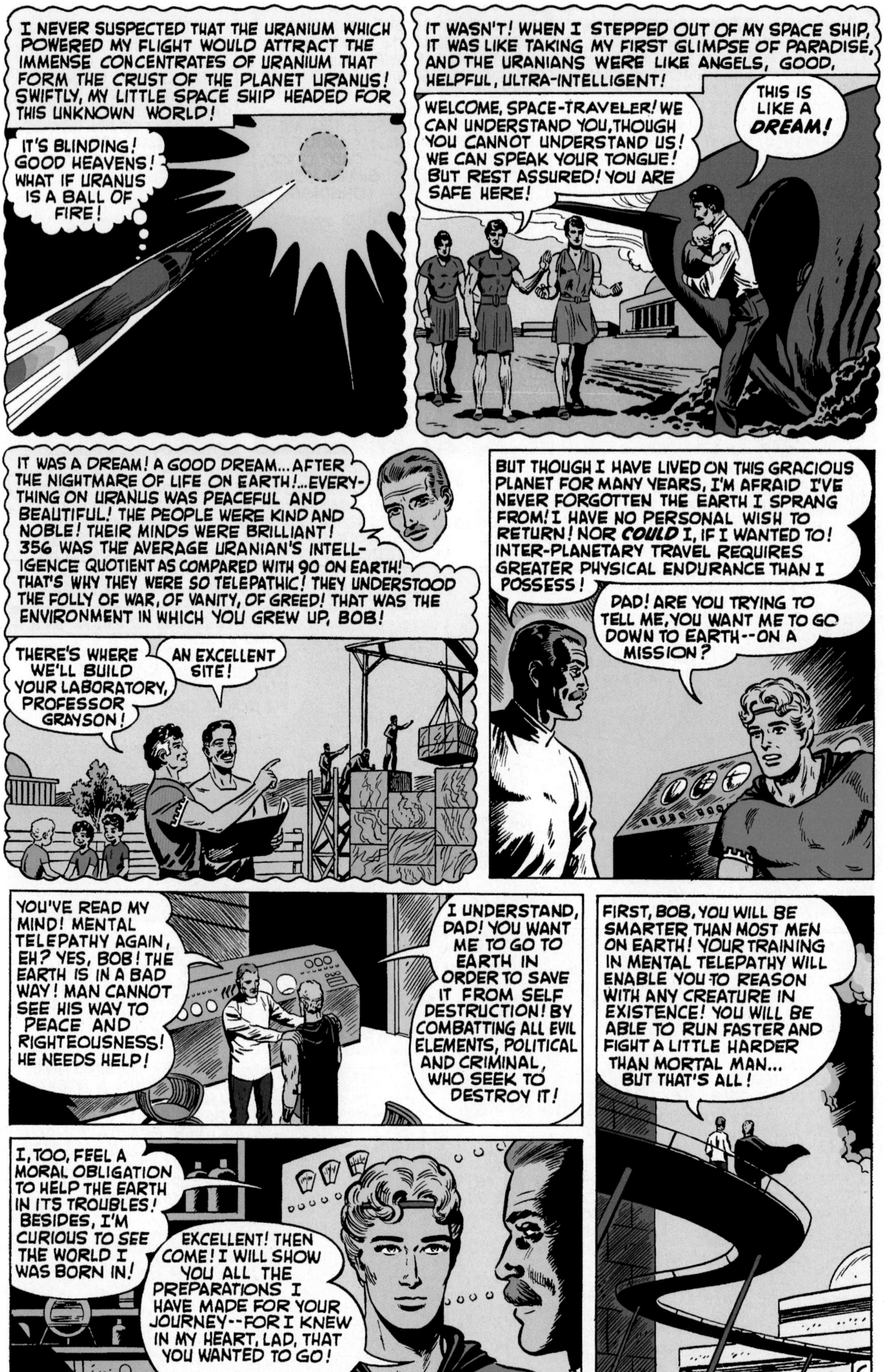
I NEVER SUSPECTED THAT THE URANIUM WHICH POWERED MY FLIGHT WOULD ATTRACT THE IMMENSE CONCENTRATES OF URANIUM THAT FORM THE CRUST OF THE PLANET URANUS! SWIFTLY, MY LITTLE SPACE SHIP HEADED FOR THIS UNKNOWN WORLD!
IT'S BLINDING! GOOD HEAVENS! WHAT IF URANUS IS A BALL OF FIRE!
IT WASN'T! WHEN I STEPPED OUT OF MY SPACE SHIP, IT WAS LIKE TAKING MY FIRST GLIMPSE OF PARADISE, AND THE URANIANS WERE LIKE ANGELS, GOOD, HELPFUL, ULTRA-INTELLIGENT!
WELCOME, SPACE-TRAVELER! WE CAN UNDERSTAND YOU, THOUGH YOU CANNOT UNDERSTAND US! WE CAN SPEAK YOUR TONGUE! BUT REST ASSURED! YOU ARE SAFE HERE!
THIS IS LIKE A DREAM!
IT WAS A DREAM! A GOOD DREAM... AFTER THE NIGHTMARE OF LIFE ON EARTH!...EVERYTHING ON URANUS WAS PEACEFUL AND BEAUTIFUL! THE PEOPLE WERE KIND AND NOBLE! THEIR MINDS WERE BRILLIANT! 356 WAS THE AVERAGE URANIAN'S INTELLIGENCE QUOTIENT AS COMPARED WITH 90 ON EARTH! THAT'S WHY THEY WERE SO TELEPATHIC! THEY UNDERSTOOD THE FOLLY OF WAR, OF VANITY, OF GREED! THAT WAS THE ENVIRONMENT IN WHICH YOU GREW UP, BOB!
THERE'S WHERE WE'LL BUILD YOUR LABORATORY, PROFESSOR GRAYSON!
AN EXCELLENT SITE!
BUT THOUGH I HAVE LIVED ON THIS GRACIOUS PLANET FOR MANY YEARS, I'M AFRAID I'VE NEVER FORGOTTEN THE EARTH I SPRANG FROM! I HAVE NO PERSONAL WISH TO RETURN! NOR COULD I, IF I WANTED TO! INTER-PLANETARY TRAVEL REQUIRES GREATER PHYSICAL ENDURANCE THAN I POSSESS!
DAD! ARE YOU TRYING TO TELL ME, YOU WANT ME TO GO DOWN TO EARTH--ON A MISSION?
YOU'VE READ MY MIND! MENTAL TELEPATHY AGAIN, EH? YES, BOB! THE EARTH IS IN A BAD WAY! MAN CANNOT SEE HIS WAY TO PEACE AND RIGHTEOUSNESS! HE NEEDS HELP!
I UNDERSTAND, DAD! YOU WANT ME TO GO TO EARTH IN ORDER TO SAVE IT FROM SELF DESTRUCTION! BY COMBATTING ALL EVIL ELEMENTS, POLITICAL AND CRIMINAL, WHO SEEK TO DESTROY IT!
I, TOO, FEEL A MORAL OBLIGATION TO HELP THE EARTH IN ITS TROUBLES! BESIDES, I'M CURIOUS TO SEE THE WORLD I WAS BORN IN!
EXCELLENT! THEN COME! I WILL SHOW YOU ALL THE PREPARATIONS I HAVE MADE FOR YOUR JOURNEY--FOR I KNEW IN MY HEART, LAD, THAT YOU WANTED TO GO!
FIRST, BOB, YOU WILL BE SMARTER THAN MOST MEN ON EARTH! YOUR TRAINING IN MENTAL TELEPATHY WILL ENABLE YOU TO REASON WITH ANY CREATURE IN EXISTENCE! YOU WILL BE ABLE TO RUN FASTER AND FIGHT A LITTLE HARDER THAN MORTAL MAN... BUT THAT'S ALL!
6

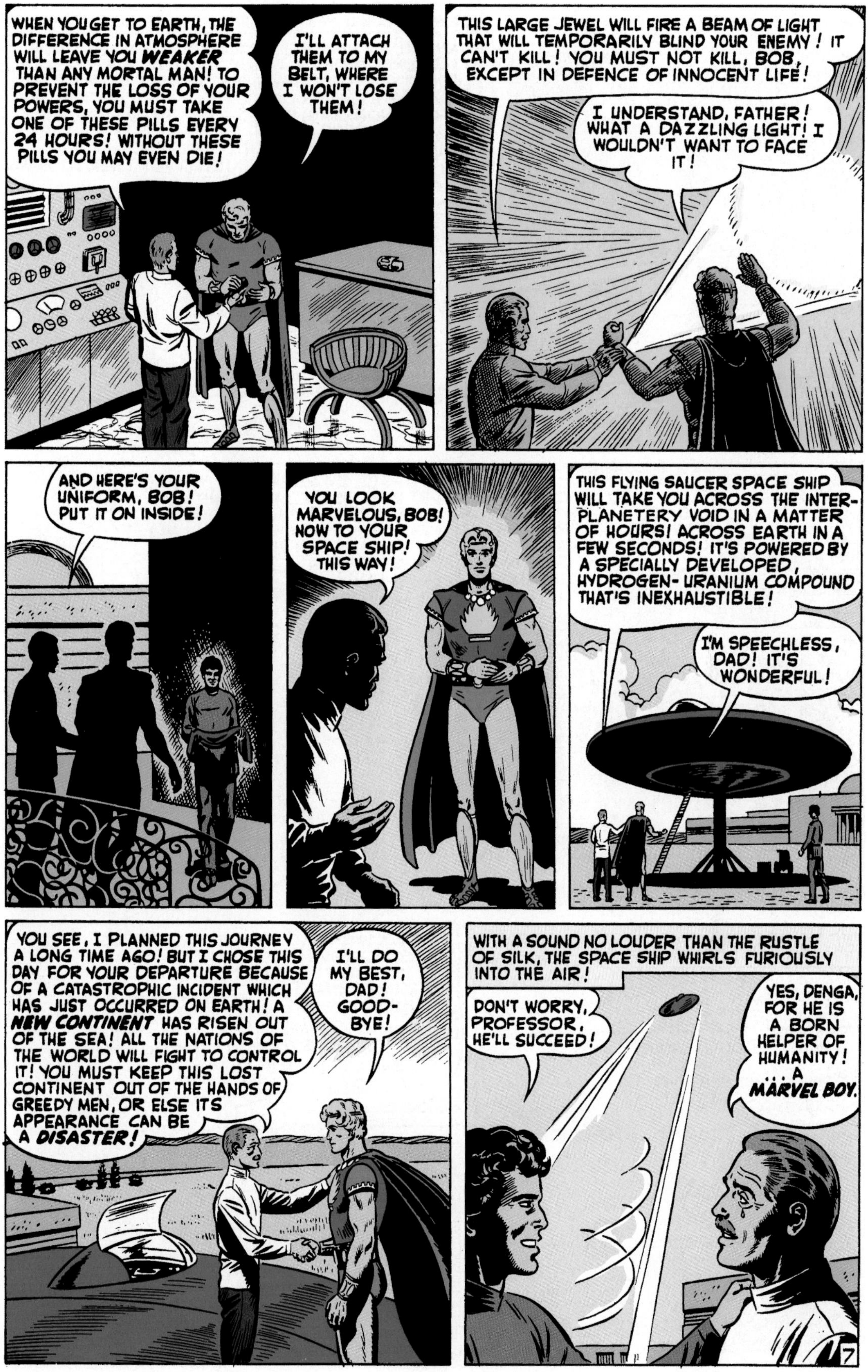
WHEN YOU GET TO EARTH, THE DIFFERENCE IN ATMOSPHERE WILL LEAVE YOU WEAKER THAN ANY MORTAL MAN! TO PREVENT THE LOSS OF YOUR POWERS, YOU MUST TAKE ONE OF THESE PILLS EVERY 24 HOURS! WITHOUT THESE PILLS YOU MAY EVEN DIE!
I'LL ATTACH THEM TO MY BELT, WHERE I WON'T LOSE THEM!
THIS LARGE JEWEL WILL FIRE A BEAM OF LIGHT THAT WILL TEMPORARILY BLIND YOUR ENEMY! IT CAN'T KILL! YOU MUST NOT KILL, BOB, EXCEPT IN DEFENCE OF INNOCENT LIFE!
I UNDERSTAND, FATHER! WHAT A DAZZLING LIGHT! I WOULDN'T WANT TO FACE IT!
AND HERE'S YOUR UNIFORM, BOB! PUT IT ON INSIDE!
YOU LOOK MARVELOUS, BOB! NOW TO YOUR SPACE SHIP! THIS WAY!
THIS FLYING SAUCER SPACE SHIP WILL TAKE YOU ACROSS THE INTER-PLANETERY VOID IN A MATTER OF HOURS! ACROSS EARTH IN A FEW SECONDS! IT'S POWERED BY A SPECIALLY DEVELOPED, HYDROGEN-URANIUM COMPOUND THAT'S INEXHAUSTIBLE!
I'M SPEECHLESS, DAD! IT'S WONDERFUL!
YOU SEE, I PLANNED THIS JOURNEY A LONG TIME AGO! BUT I CHOSE THIS DAY FOR YOUR DEPARTURE BECAUSE OF A CATASTROPHIC INCIDENT WHICH HAS JUST OCCURRED ON EARTH! A NEW CONTINENT HAS RISEN OUT OF THE SEA! ALL THE NATIONS OF THE WORLD WILL FIGHT TO CONTROL IT! YOU MUST KEEP THIS LOST CONTINENT OUT OF THE HANDS OF GREEDY MEN, OR ELSE ITS APPEARANCE CAN BE A DISASTER!
I'LL DO MY BEST, DAD! GOOD-BYE!
WITH A SOUND NO LOUDER THAN THE RUSTLE OF SILK, THE SPACE SHIP WHIRLS FURIOUSLY INTO THE AIR!
DON'T WORRY, PROFESSOR, HE'LL SUCCEED!
YES, DENGA, FOR HE IS A BORN HELPER OF HUMANITY! ...A MARVEL BOY.
7

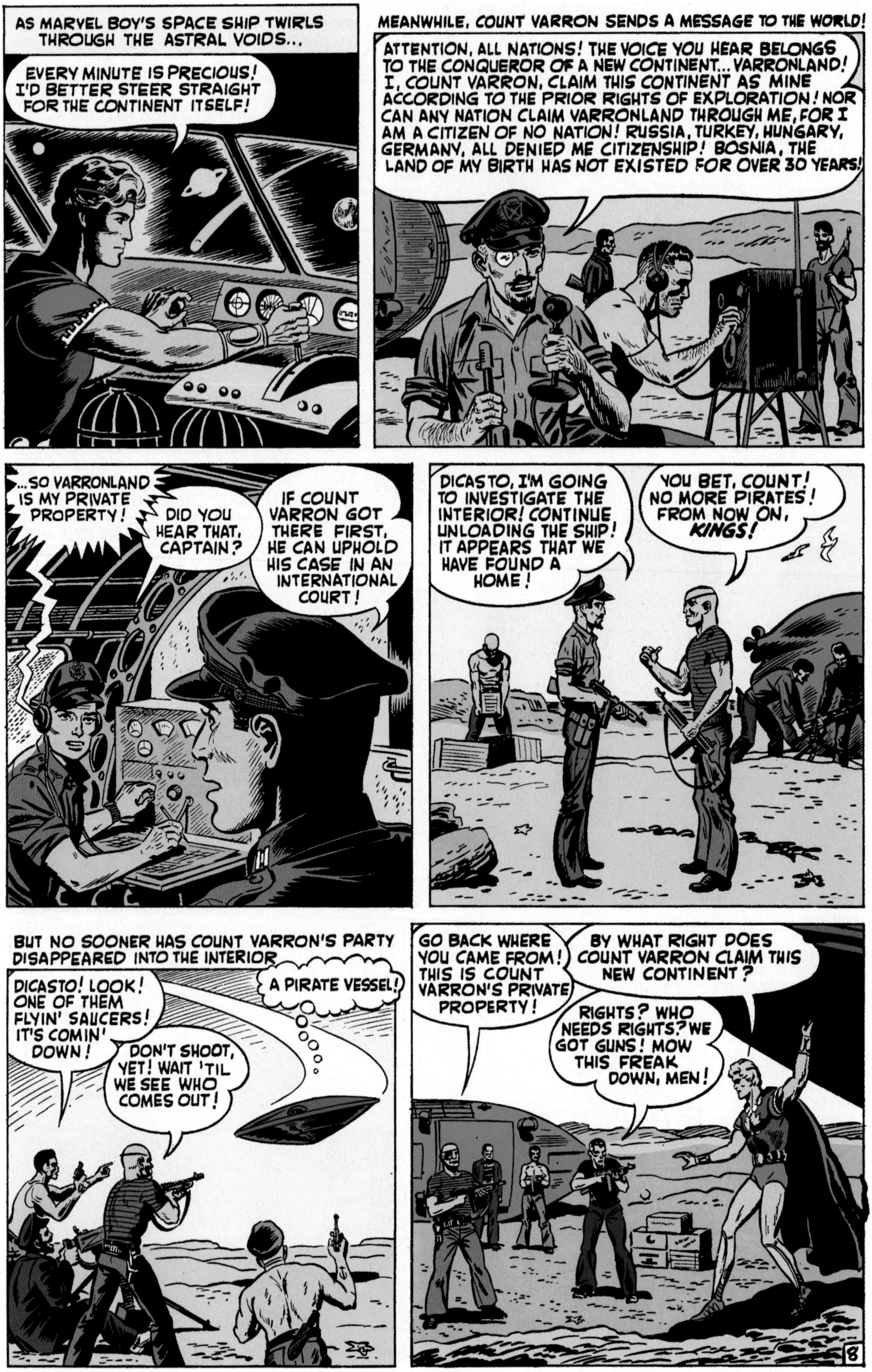
AS MARVEL BOY'S SPACE SHIP TWIRLS THROUGH THE ASTRAL VOIDS...
EVERY MINUTE IS PRECIOUS! I'D BETTER STEER STRAIGHT FOR THE CONTINENT ITSELF!
MEANWHILE, COUNT VARRON SENDS A MESSAGE TO THE WORLD!
ATTENTION, ALL NATIONS! THE VOICE YOU HEAR BELONGS TO THE CONQUEROR OF A NEW CONTINENT... VARRONLAND! I, COUNT VARRON, CLAIM THIS CONTINENT AS MINE ACCORDING TO THE PRIOR RIGHTS OF EXPLORATION! NOR CAN ANY NATION CLAIM VARRONLAND THROUGH ME, FOR I AM A CITIZEN OF NO NATION! RUSSIA, TURKEY, HUNGARY, GERMANY, ALL DENIED ME CITIZENSHIP! BOSNIA, THE LAND OF MY BIRTH HAS NOT EXISTED FOR OVER 30 YEARS!
...SO VARRONLAND IS MY PRIVATE PROPERTY!
DID YOU HEAR THAT, CAPTAIN?
IF COUNT VARRON GOT THERE FIRST, HE CAN UPHOLD HIS CASE IN AN INTERNATIONAL COURT!
DICASTO, I'M GOING TO INVESTIGATE THE INTERIOR! CONTINUE UNLOADING THE SHIP! IT APPEARS THAT WE HAVE FOUND A HOME!
YOU BET, COUNT! NO MORE PIRATES! FROM NOW ON, KINGS!
BUT NO SOONER HAS COUNT VARRON'S PARTY DISAPPEARED INTO THE INTERIOR
DICASTO! LOOK! ONE OF THEM FLYIN' SAUCERS! IT'S COMIN' DOWN!
DON'T SHOOT, YET! WAIT 'TIL WE SEE WHO COMES OUT!
A PIRATE VESSEL!
GO BACK WHERE YOU CAME FROM! THIS IS COUNT VARRON'S PRIVATE PROPERTY!
BY WHAT RIGHT DOES COUNT VARRON CLAIM THIS NEW CONTINENT?
RIGHTS? WHO NEEDS RIGHTS? WE GOT GUNS! MOW THIS FREAK DOWN, MEN!
8

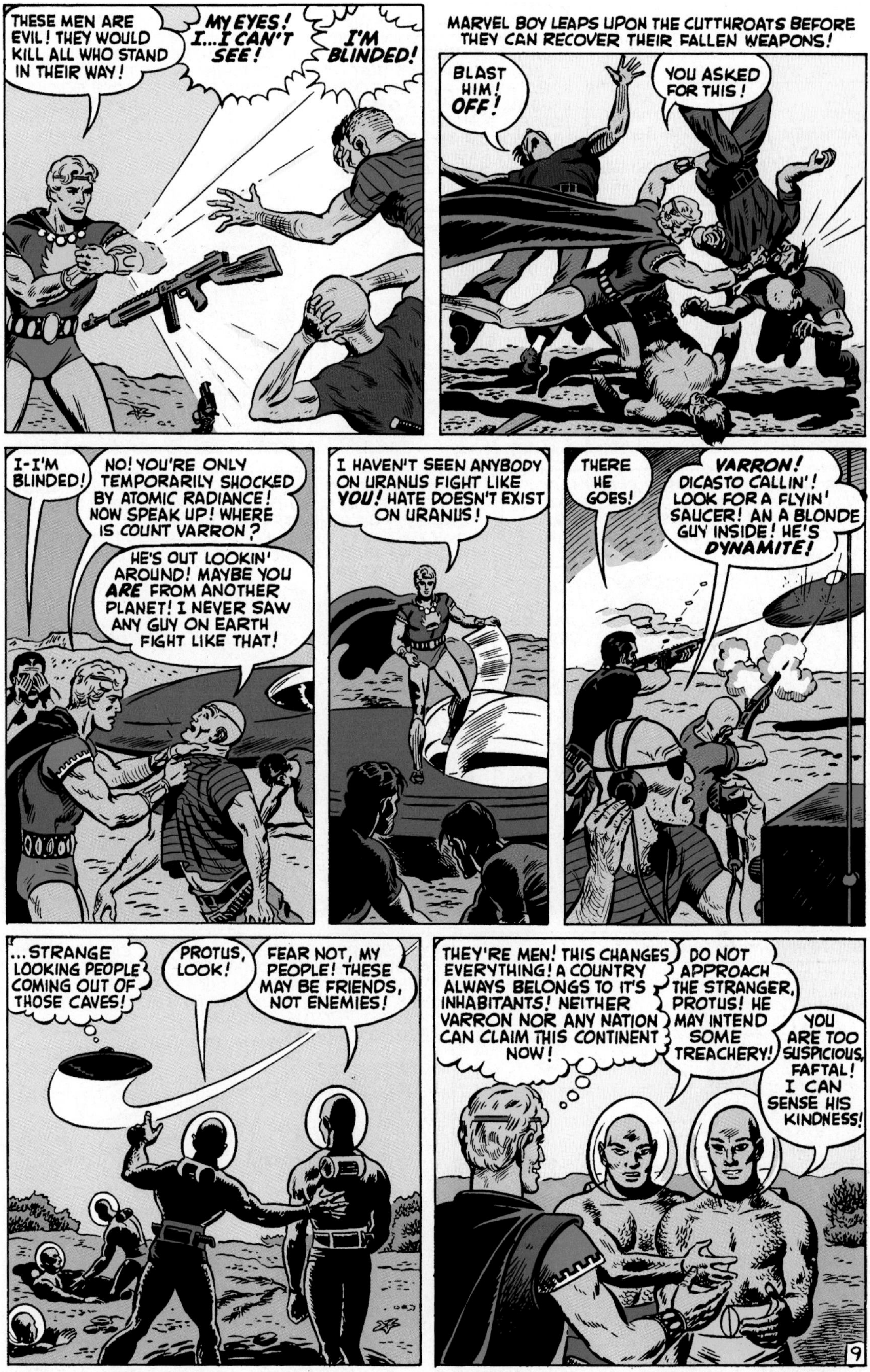
THESE MEN ARE EVIL! THEY WOULD KILL ALL WHO STAND IN THEIR WAY!
MY EYES! I...I CAN'T SEE!
I'M BLINDED!
MARVEL BOY LEAPS UPON THE CUTTHROATS BEFORE THEY CAN RECOVER THEIR FALLEN WEAPONS!
BLAST HIM! OFF!
YOU ASKED FOR THIS!
I-I'M BLINDED!
NO! YOU'RE ONLY TEMPORARILY SHOCKED BY ATOMIC RADIANCE! NOW SPEAK UP! WHERE IS COUNT VARRON?
HE'S OUT LOOKIN' AROUND! MAYBE YOU ARE FROM ANOTHER PLANET! I NEVER SAW ANY GUY ON EARTH FIGHT LIKE THAT!
I HAVEN'T SEEN ANYBODY ON URANUS FIGHT LIKE YOU! HATE DOESN'T EXIST ON URANUS!
THERE HE GOES!
VARRON! DICASTO CALLIN'! LOOK FOR A FLYIN' SAUCER! AN A BLONDE GUY INSIDE! HE'S DYNAMITE!
...STRANGE LOOKING PEOPLE COMING OUT OF THOSE CAVES!
PROTUS, LOOK!
FEAR NOT, MY PEOPLE! THESE MAY BE FRIENDS, NOT ENEMIES!
THEY'RE MEN! THIS CHANGES EVERYTHING! A COUNTRY ALWAYS BELONGS TO IT'S INHABITANTS! NEITHER VARRON NOR ANY NATION CAN CLAIM THIS CONTINENT NOW!
DO NOT APPROACH THE STRANGER, PROTUS! HE MAY INTEND SOME TREACHERY!
YOU ARE TOO SUSPICIOUS, FAFTAL! I CAN SENSE HIS KINDNESS!
9

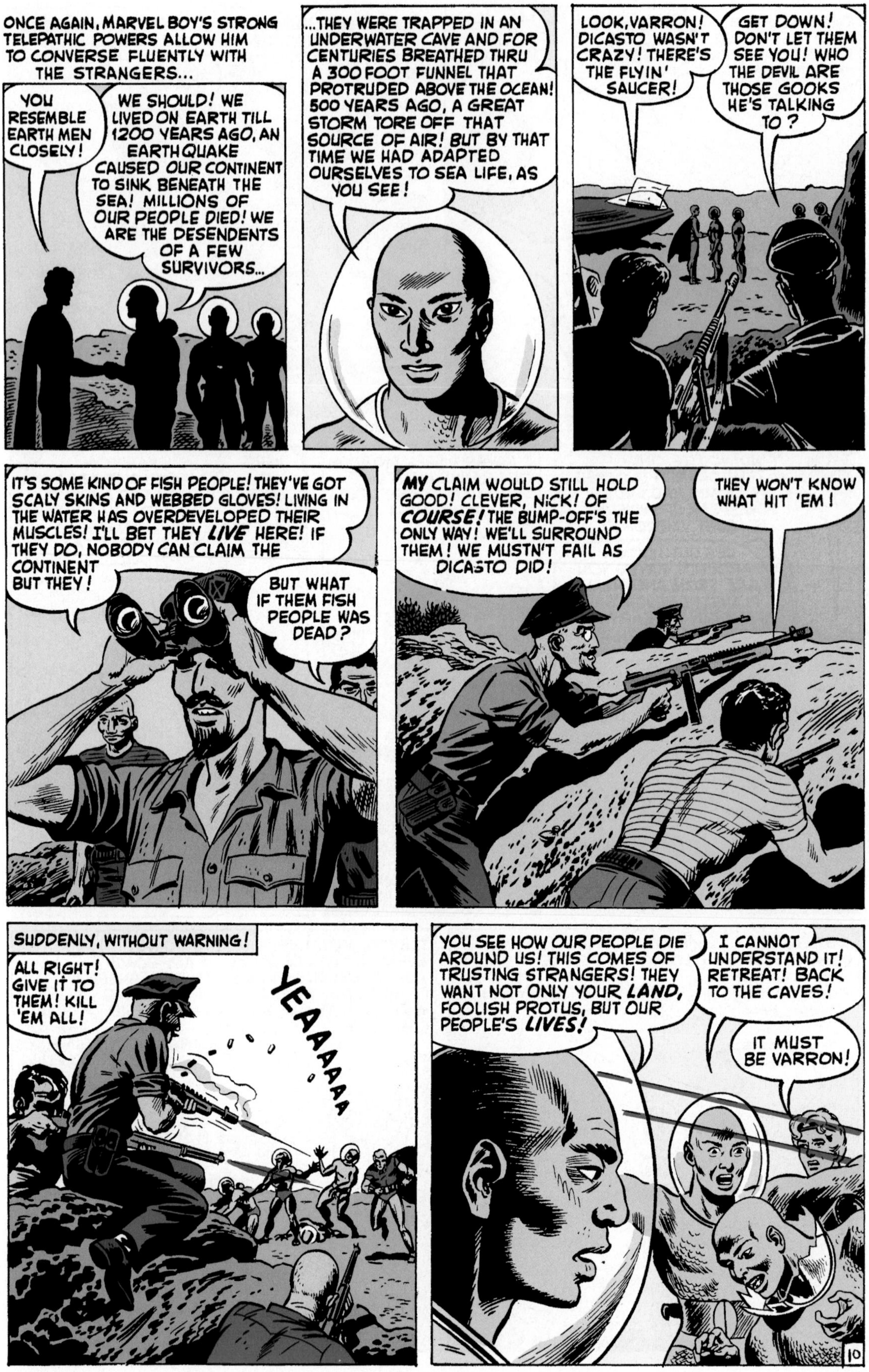
ONCE AGAIN, MARVEL BOY'S STRONG TELEPATHIC POWERS ALLOW HIM TO CONVERSE FLUENTLY WITH THE STRANGERS...
YOU RESEMBLE EARTH MEN CLOSELY!
WE SHOULD! WE LIVED ON EARTH TILL 1200 YEARS AGO, AN EARTHQUAKE CAUSED OUR CONTINENT TO SINK BENEATH THE SEA! MILLIONS OF OUR PEOPLE DIED! WE ARE THE DESENDENTS OF A FEW SURVIVORS...
...THEY WERE TRAPPED IN AN UNDERWATER CAVE AND FOR CENTURIES BREATHED THRU A 300 FOOT FUNNEL THAT PROTRUDED ABOVE THE OCEAN! 500 YEARS AGO, A GREAT STORM TORE OFF THAT SOURCE OF AIR! BUT BY THAT TIME WE HAD ADAPTED OURSELVES TO SEA LIFE, AS YOU SEE!
LOOK, VARRON! DICASTO WASN'T CRAZY! THERE'S THE FLYIN' SAUCER!
GET DOWN! DON'T LET THEM SEE YOU! WHO THE DEVIL ARE THOSE GOOKS HE'S TALKING TO?
IT'S SOME KIND OF FISH PEOPLE! THEY'VE GOT SCALY SKINS AND WEBBED GLOVES! LIVING IN THE WATER HAS OVERDEVELOPED THEIR MUSCLES! I'LL BET THEY LIVE HERE! IF THEY DO, NOBODY CAN CLAIM THE CONTINENT BUT THEY!
BUT WHAT IF THEM FISH PEOPLE WAS DEAD?
MY CLAIM WOULD STILL HOLD GOOD! CLEVER, NICK! OF COURSE! THE BUMP-OFF'S THE ONLY WAY! WE'LL SURROUND THEM! WE MUSTN'T FAIL AS DICASTO DID!
THEY WON'T KNOW WHAT HIT 'EM!
SUDDENLY, WITHOUT WARNING!
ALL RIGHT! GIVE IT TO THEM! KILL 'EM ALL!
YEAAAAAA
YOU SEE HOW OUR PEOPLE DIE AROUND US! THIS COMES OF TRUSTING STRANGERS! THEY WANT NOT ONLY YOUR LAND, FOOLISH PROTUS, BUT OUR PEOPLE'S LIVES!
I CANNOT UNDERSTAND IT! RETREAT! BACK TO THE CAVES!
IT MUST BE VARRON!
10

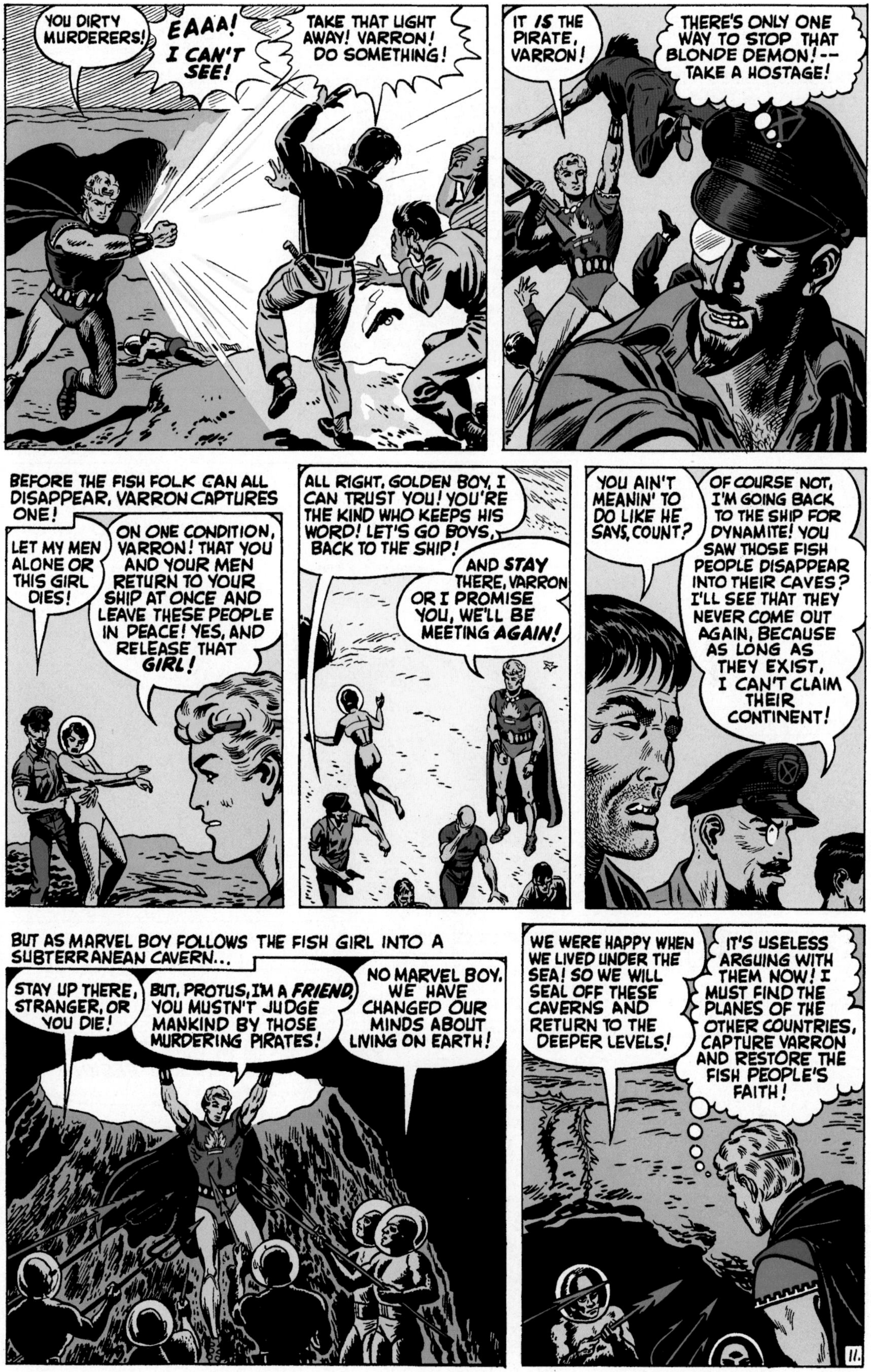
YOU DIRTY MURDERERS!
EAAA! I CAN'T SEE!
TAKE THAT LIGHT AWAY! VARRON! DO SOMETHING!
IT IS THE PIRATE, VARRON!
THERE'S ONLY ONE WAY TO STOP THAT BLONDE DEMON!-- TAKE A HOSTAGE!
BEFORE THE FISH FOLK CAN ALL DISAPPEAR, VARRON CAPTURES ONE!
LET MY MEN ALONE OR THIS GIRL DIES!
ON ONE CONDITION, VARRON! THAT YOU AND YOUR MEN RETURN TO YOUR SHIP AT ONCE AND LEAVE THESE PEOPLE IN PEACE! YES, AND RELEASE THAT GIRL!
ALL RIGHT, GOLDEN BOY, I CAN TRUST YOU! YOU'RE THE KIND WHO KEEPS HIS WORD! LET'S GO BOYS, BACK TO THE SHIP!
AND STAY THERE, VARRON OR I PROMISE YOU, WE'LL BE MEETING AGAIN!
YOU AIN'T MEANIN' TO DO LIKE HE SAYS, COUNT?
OF COURSE NOT, I'M GOING BACK TO THE SHIP FOR DYNAMITE! YOU SAW THOSE FISH PEOPLE DISAPPEAR INTO THEIR CAVES? I'LL SEE THAT THEY NEVER COME OUT AGAIN, BECAUSE AS LONG AS THEY EXIST, I CAN'T CLAIM THEIR CONTINENT!
BUT AS MARVEL BOY FOLLOWS THE FISH GIRL INTO A SUBTERRANEAN CAVERN...
STAY UP THERE, STRANGER, OR YOU DIE!
BUT, PROTUS, I'M A FRIEND, YOU MUSTN'T JUDGE MANKIND BY THOSE MURDERING PIRATES!
NO MARVEL BOY. WE HAVE CHANGED OUR MINDS ABOUT LIVING ON EARTH!
WE WERE HAPPY WHEN WE LIVED UNDER THE SEA! SO WE WILL SEAL OFF THESE CAVERNS AND RETURN TO THE DEEPER LEVELS!
IT'S USELESS ARGUING WITH THEM NOW! I MUST FIND THE PLANES OF THE OTHER COUNTRIES, CAPTURE VARRON AND RESTORE THE FISH PEOPLE'S FAITH!
11.

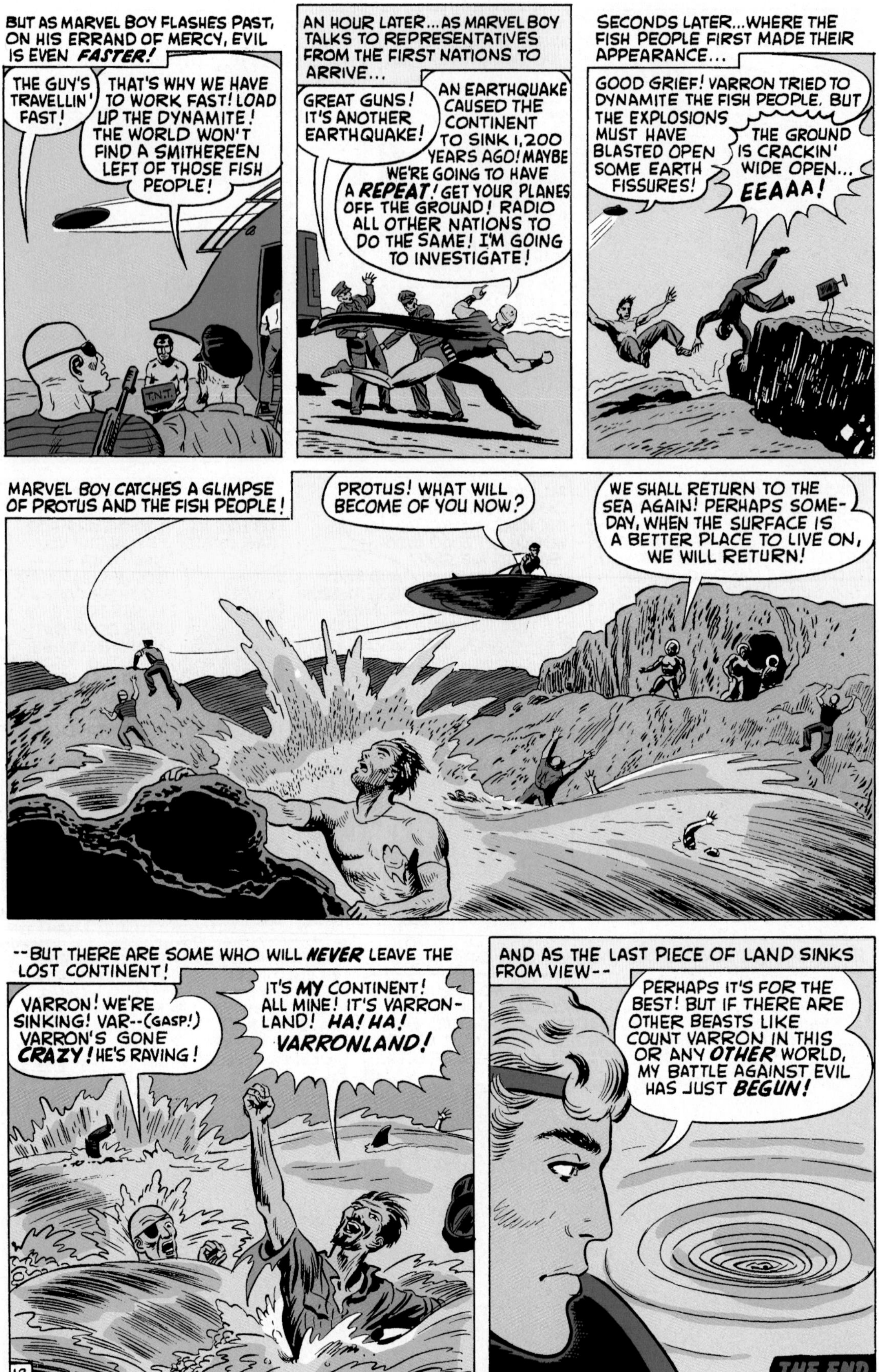
BUT AS MARVEL BOY FLASHES PAST, ON HIS ERRAND OF MERCY, EVIL IS EVEN FASTER!
THE GUY'S TRAVELLIN' FAST!
THAT'S WHY WE HAVE TO WORK FAST! LOAD UP THE DYNAMITE! THE WORLD WON'T FIND A SMITHEREEN LEFT OF THOSE FISH PEOPLE!
T.N.T.
AN HOUR LATER... AS MARVEL BOY TALKS TO REPRESENTATIVES FROM THE FIRST NATIONS TO ARRIVE...
GREAT GUNS! IT'S ANOTHER EARTHQUAKE!
AN EARTHQUAKE CAUSED THE CONTINENT TO SINK 1,200 YEARS AGO! MAYBE WE'RE GOING TO HAVE A REPEAT! GET YOUR PLANES OFF THE GROUND! RADIO ALL OTHER NATIONS TO DO THE SAME! I'M GOING TO INVESTIGATE!
SECONDS LATER... WHERE THE FISH PEOPLE FIRST MADE THEIR APPEARANCE...
GOOD GRIEF! VARRON TRIED TO DYNAMITE THE FISH PEOPLE, BUT THE EXPLOSIONS MUST HAVE BLASTED OPEN SOME EARTH FISSURES!
THE GROUND IS CRACKIN' WIDE OPEN... EEAAA!
MARVEL BOY CATCHES A GLIMPSE OF PROTUS AND THE FISH PEOPLE!
PROTUS! WHAT WILL BECOME OF YOU NOW?
WE SHALL RETURN TO THE SEA AGAIN! PERHAPS SOME-DAY, WHEN THE SURFACE IS A BETTER PLACE TO LIVE ON, WE WILL RETURN!
--BUT THERE ARE SOME WHO WILL NEVER LEAVE THE LOST CONTINENT!
VARRON! WE'RE SINKING! VAR--(GASP!) VARRON'S GONE CRAZY! HE'S RAVING!
IT'S MY CONTINENT! ALL MINE! IT'S VARRON-LAND! HA! HA! VARRONLAND!
12
AND AS THE LAST PIECE OF LAND SINKS FROM VIEW--
PERHAPS IT'S FOR THE BEST! BUT IF THERE ARE OTHER BEASTS LIKE COUNT VARRON IN THIS OR ANY OTHER WORLD, MY BATTLE AGAINST EVIL HAS JUST BEGUN!
THE END

MEN'S ADVENTURES #26 (MARCH 1954), THE FIRST APPEARANCE OF GORILLA MAN
ARTIST: **ROBERT Q. SALE** • EDITOR: **STAN LEE**

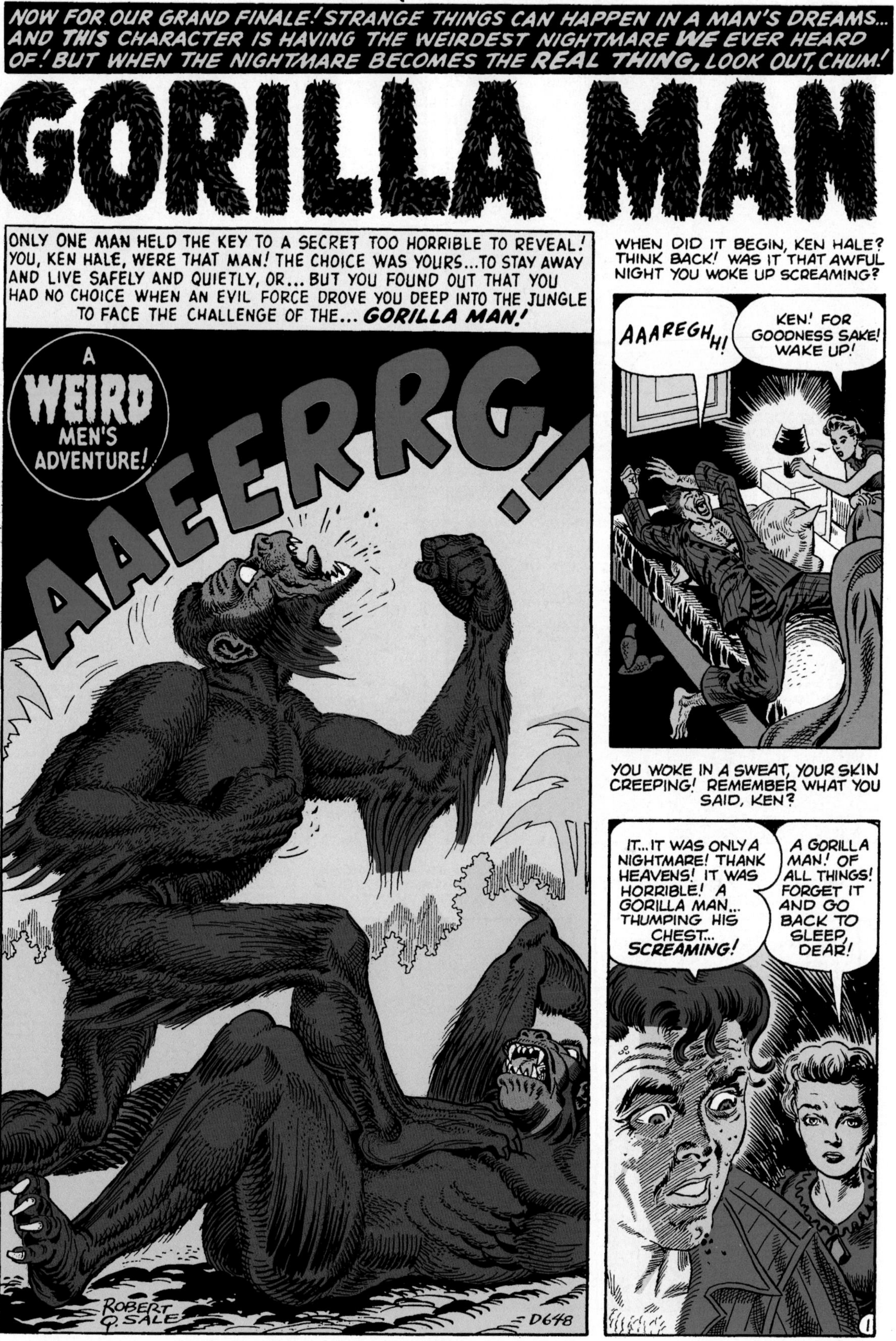
NOW FOR OUR GRAND FINALE! STRANGE THINGS CAN HAPPEN IN A MAN'S DREAMS... AND THIS CHARACTER IS HAVING THE WEIRDEST NIGHTMARE WE EVER HEARD OF! BUT WHEN THE NIGHTMARE BECOMES THE REAL THING, LOOK OUT, CHUM!
GORILLA MAN
ONLY ONE MAN HELD THE KEY TO A SECRET TOO HORRIBLE TO REVEAL! YOU, KEN HALE, WERE THAT MAN! THE CHOICE WAS YOURS...TO STAY AWAY AND LIVE SAFELY AND QUIETLY, OR... BUT YOU FOUND OUT THAT YOU HAD NO CHOICE WHEN AN EVIL FORCE DROVE YOU DEEP INTO THE JUNGLE TO FACE THE CHALLENGE OF THE... GORILLA MAN!
A WEIRD MEN'S ADVENTURE!
AAEERRG!
ROBERT Q. SALE
D648
WHEN DID IT BEGIN, KEN HALE? THINK BACK! WAS IT THAT AWFUL NIGHT YOU WOKE UP SCREAMING?
AAAREGHH!
KEN! FOR GOODNESS SAKE! WAKE UP!
YOU WOKE IN A SWEAT, YOUR SKIN CREEPING! REMEMBER WHAT YOU SAID, KEN?
IT...IT WAS ONLY A NIGHTMARE! THANK HEAVENS! IT WAS HORRIBLE! A GORILLA MAN... THUMPING HIS CHEST... SCREAMING!
A GORILLA MAN! OF ALL THINGS! FORGET IT AND GO BACK TO SLEEP, DEAR!
1

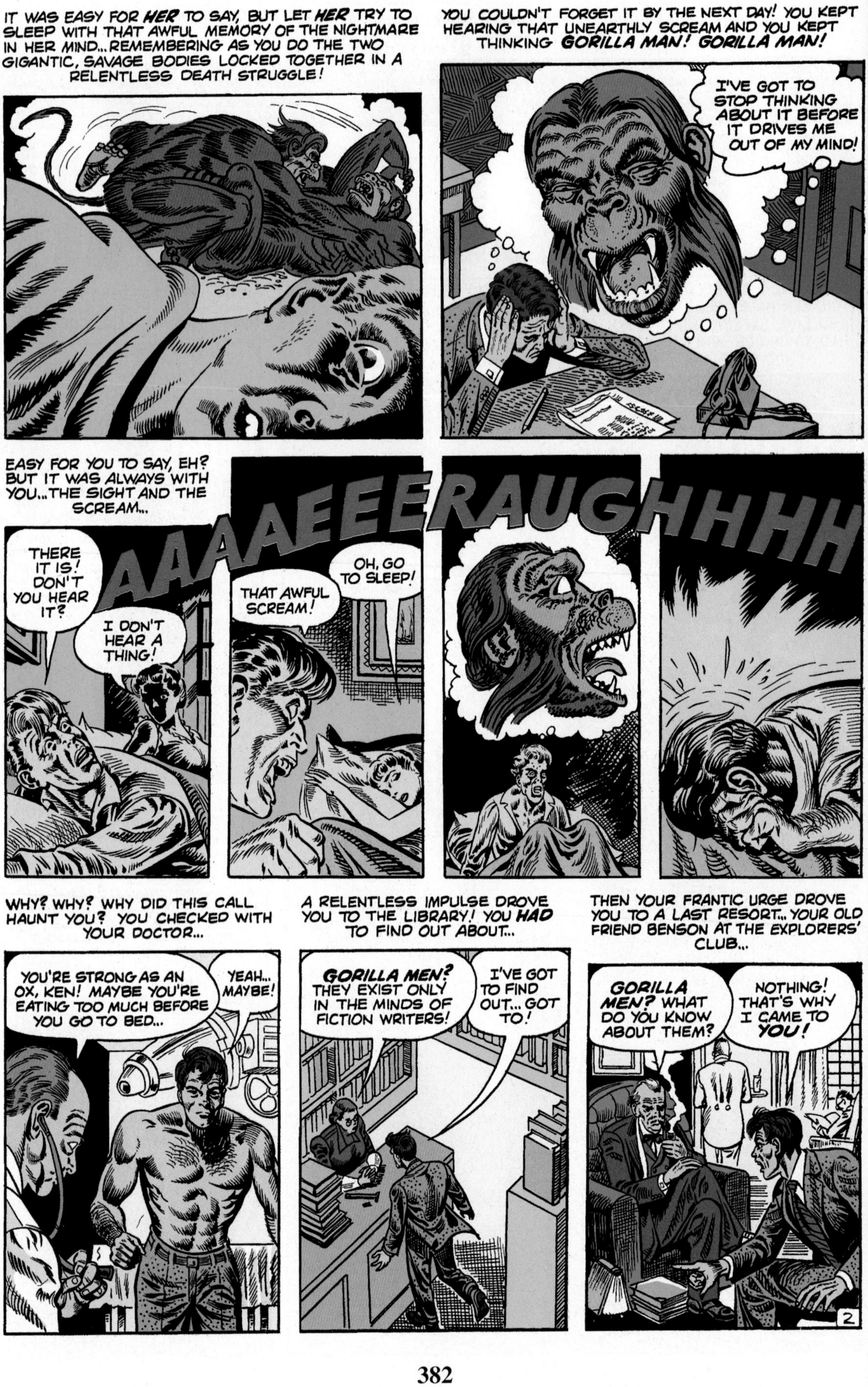
IT WAS EASY FOR **HER** TO SAY, BUT LET **HER** TRY TO SLEEP WITH THAT AWFUL MEMORY OF THE NIGHTMARE IN HER MIND... REMEMBERING AS YOU DO THE TWO GIGANTIC, SAVAGE BODIES LOCKED TOGETHER IN A RELENTLESS DEATH STRUGGLE!
YOU COULDN'T FORGET IT BY THE NEXT DAY! YOU KEPT HEARING THAT UNEARTHLY SCREAM AND YOU KEPT THINKING **GORILLA MAN! GORILLA MAN!**
I'VE GOT TO STOP THINKING ABOUT IT BEFORE IT DRIVES ME OUT OF MY MIND!
EASY FOR YOU TO SAY, EH? BUT IT WAS ALWAYS WITH YOU... THE SIGHT AND THE SCREAM...
AAAAEEERAUGHHHH
THERE IT IS! DON'T YOU HEAR IT?
I DON'T HEAR A THING!
THAT AWFUL SCREAM!
OH, GO TO SLEEP!
WHY? WHY? WHY DID THIS CALL HAUNT YOU? YOU CHECKED WITH YOUR DOCTOR...
YOU'RE STRONG AS AN OX, KEN! MAYBE YOU'RE EATING TOO MUCH BEFORE YOU GO TO BED...
YEAH... MAYBE!
A RELENTLESS IMPULSE DROVE YOU TO THE LIBRARY! YOU **HAD** TO FIND OUT ABOUT...
GORILLA MEN? THEY EXIST ONLY IN THE MINDS OF FICTION WRITERS!
I'VE GOT TO FIND OUT... GOT TO!
THEN YOUR FRANTIC URGE DROVE YOU TO A LAST RESORT... YOUR OLD FRIEND BENSON AT THE EXPLORERS' CLUB...
GORILLA MEN? WHAT DO YOU KNOW ABOUT THEM?
NOTHING! THAT'S WHY I CAME TO **YOU**!
2

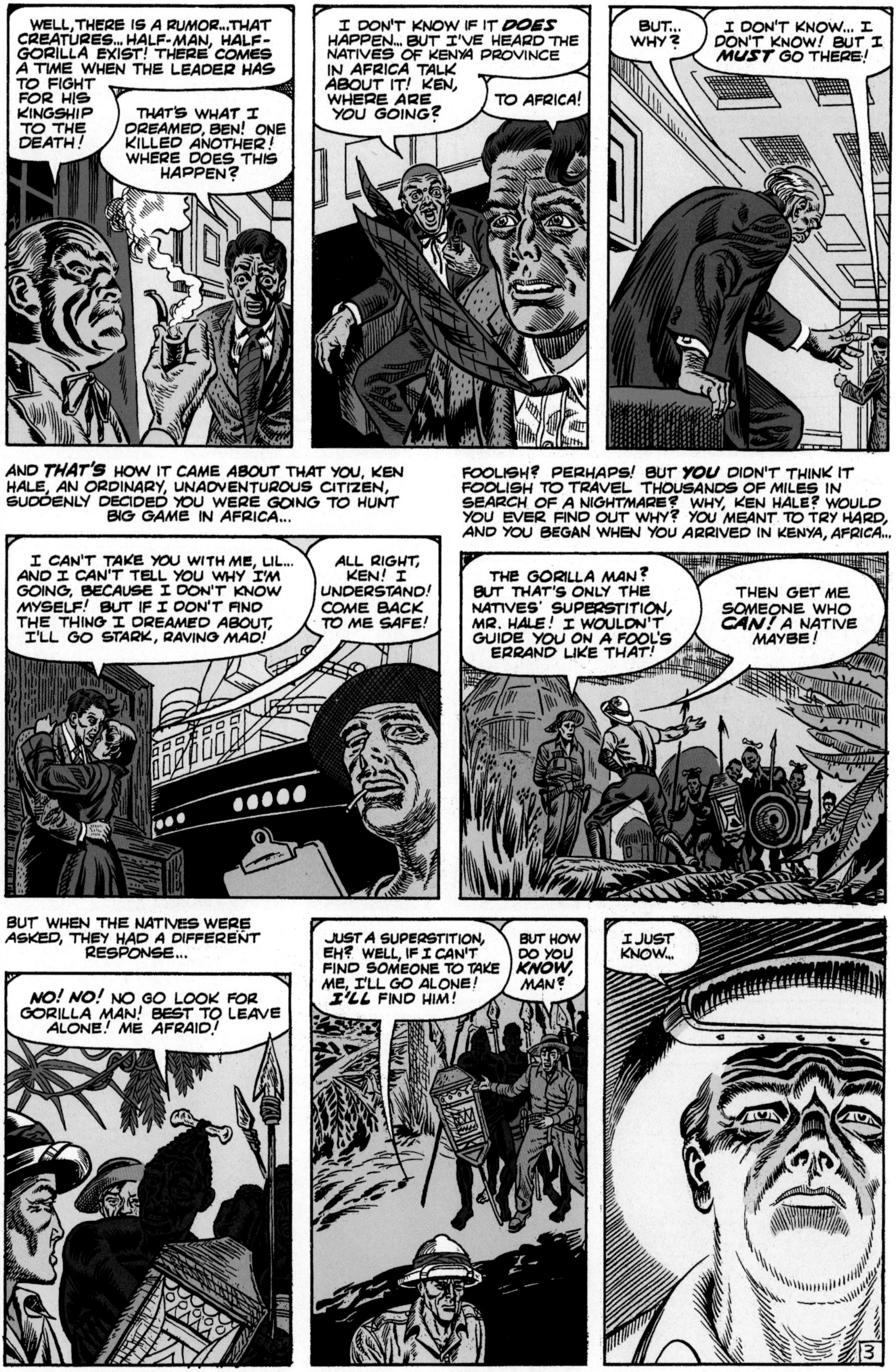
WELL, THERE IS A RUMOR... THAT CREATURES... HALF-MAN, HALF-GORILLA EXIST! THERE COMES A TIME WHEN THE LEADER HAS TO FIGHT FOR HIS KINGSHIP TO THE DEATH!
THAT'S WHAT I DREAMED, BEN! ONE KILLED ANOTHER! WHERE DOES THIS HAPPEN?
I DON'T KNOW IF IT DOES HAPPEN... BUT I'VE HEARD THE NATIVES OF KENYA PROVINCE IN AFRICA TALK ABOUT IT! KEN, WHERE ARE YOU GOING?
TO AFRICA!
BUT... WHY?
I DON'T KNOW... I DON'T KNOW! BUT I MUST GO THERE!
AND THAT'S HOW IT CAME ABOUT THAT YOU, KEN HALE, AN ORDINARY, UNADVENTUROUS CITIZEN, SUDDENLY DECIDED YOU WERE GOING TO HUNT BIG GAME IN AFRICA...
I CAN'T TAKE YOU WITH ME, LIL... AND I CAN'T TELL YOU WHY I'M GOING, BECAUSE I DON'T KNOW MYSELF! BUT IF I DON'T FIND THE THING I DREAMED ABOUT, I'LL GO STARK, RAVING MAD!
ALL RIGHT, KEN! I UNDERSTAND! COME BACK TO ME SAFE!
FOOLISH? PERHAPS! BUT YOU DIDN'T THINK IT FOOLISH TO TRAVEL THOUSANDS OF MILES IN SEARCH OF A NIGHTMARE? WHY, KEN HALE? WOULD YOU EVER FIND OUT WHY? YOU MEANT TO TRY HARD, AND YOU BEGAN WHEN YOU ARRIVED IN KENYA, AFRICA...
THE GORILLA MAN? BUT THAT'S ONLY THE NATIVES' SUPERSTITION, MR. HALE! I WOULDN'T GUIDE YOU ON A FOOL'S ERRAND LIKE THAT!
THEN GET ME SOMEONE WHO CAN! A NATIVE MAYBE!
BUT WHEN THE NATIVES WERE ASKED, THEY HAD A DIFFERENT RESPONSE...
NO! NO! NO GO LOOK FOR GORILLA MAN! BEST TO LEAVE ALONE! ME AFRAID!
JUST A SUPERSTITION, EH? WELL, IF I CAN'T FIND SOMEONE TO TAKE ME, I'LL GO ALONE! I'LL FIND HIM!
BUT HOW DO YOU KNOW, MAN?
I JUST KNOW...
3

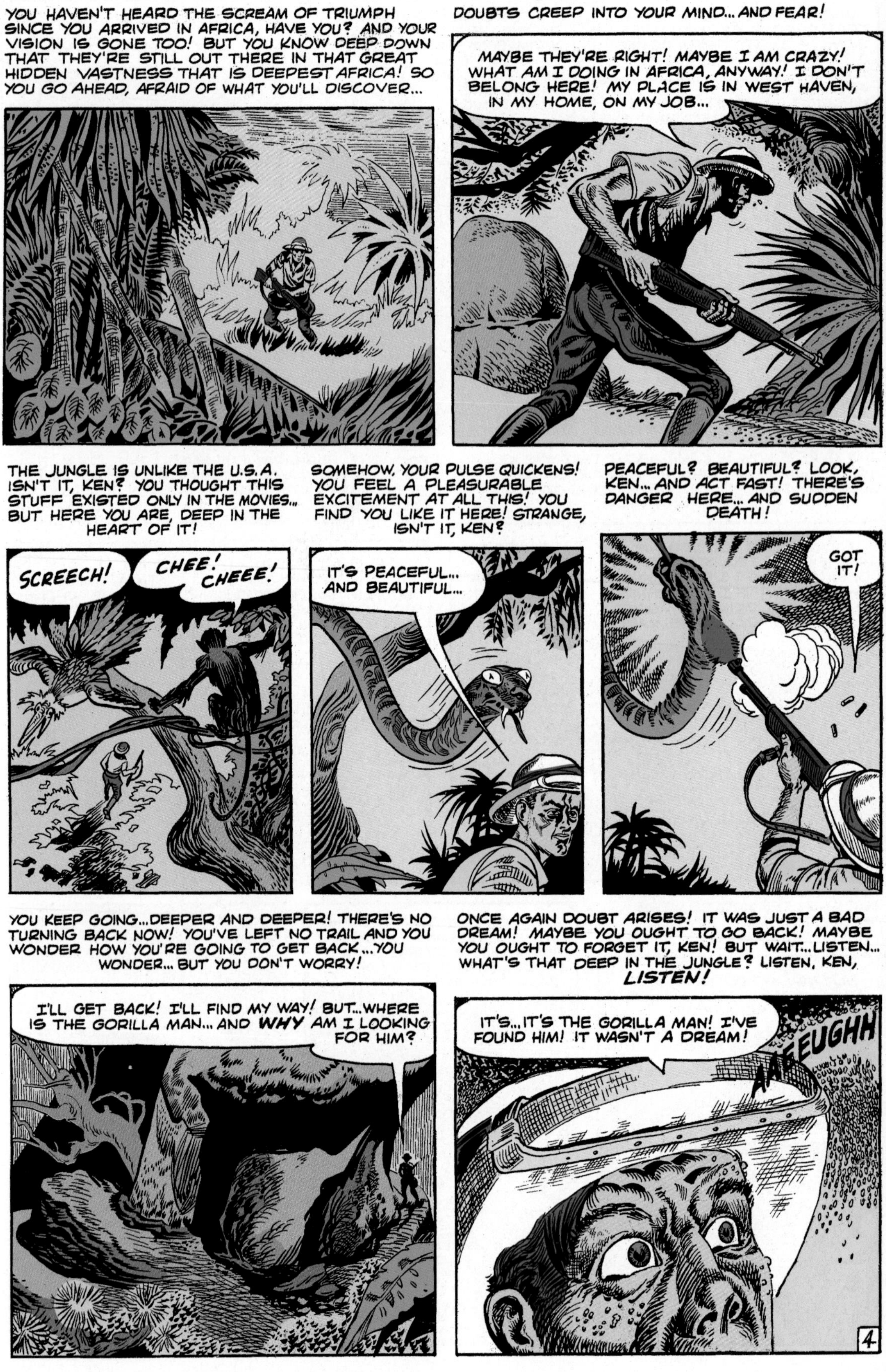
YOU HAVEN'T HEARD THE SCREAM OF TRIUMPH SINCE YOU ARRIVED IN AFRICA, HAVE YOU? AND YOUR VISION IS GONE TOO! BUT YOU KNOW DEEP DOWN THAT THEY'RE STILL OUT THERE IN THAT GREAT HIDDEN VASTNESS THAT IS DEEPEST AFRICA! SO YOU GO AHEAD, AFRAID OF WHAT YOU'LL DISCOVER...
DOUBTS CREEP INTO YOUR MIND... AND FEAR!
MAYBE THEY'RE RIGHT! MAYBE I AM CRAZY! WHAT AM I DOING IN AFRICA, ANYWAY! I DON'T BELONG HERE! MY PLACE IS IN WEST HAVEN, IN MY HOME, ON MY JOB...
THE JUNGLE IS UNLIKE THE U.S.A. ISN'T IT, KEN? YOU THOUGHT THIS STUFF EXISTED ONLY IN THE MOVIES... BUT HERE YOU ARE, DEEP IN THE HEART OF IT!
SCREECH!
CHEE! CHEEE!
SOMEHOW, YOUR PULSE QUICKENS! YOU FEEL A PLEASURABLE EXCITEMENT AT ALL THIS! YOU FIND YOU LIKE IT HERE! STRANGE, ISN'T IT, KEN?
IT'S PEACEFUL... AND BEAUTIFUL...
PEACEFUL? BEAUTIFUL? LOOK, KEN... AND ACT FAST! THERE'S DANGER HERE... AND SUDDEN DEATH!
GOT IT!
YOU KEEP GOING...DEEPER AND DEEPER! THERE'S NO TURNING BACK NOW! YOU'VE LEFT NO TRAIL AND YOU WONDER HOW YOU'RE GOING TO GET BACK...YOU WONDER... BUT YOU DON'T WORRY!
I'LL GET BACK! I'LL FIND MY WAY! BUT...WHERE IS THE GORILLA MAN... AND WHY AM I LOOKING FOR HIM?
ONCE AGAIN DOUBT ARISES! IT WAS JUST A BAD DREAM! MAYBE YOU OUGHT TO GO BACK! MAYBE YOU OUGHT TO FORGET IT, KEN! BUT WAIT...LISTEN... WHAT'S THAT DEEP IN THE JUNGLE? LISTEN, KEN, LISTEN!
IT'S... IT'S THE GORILLA MAN! I'VE FOUND HIM! IT WASN'T A DREAM!
AAEEUGHH
4

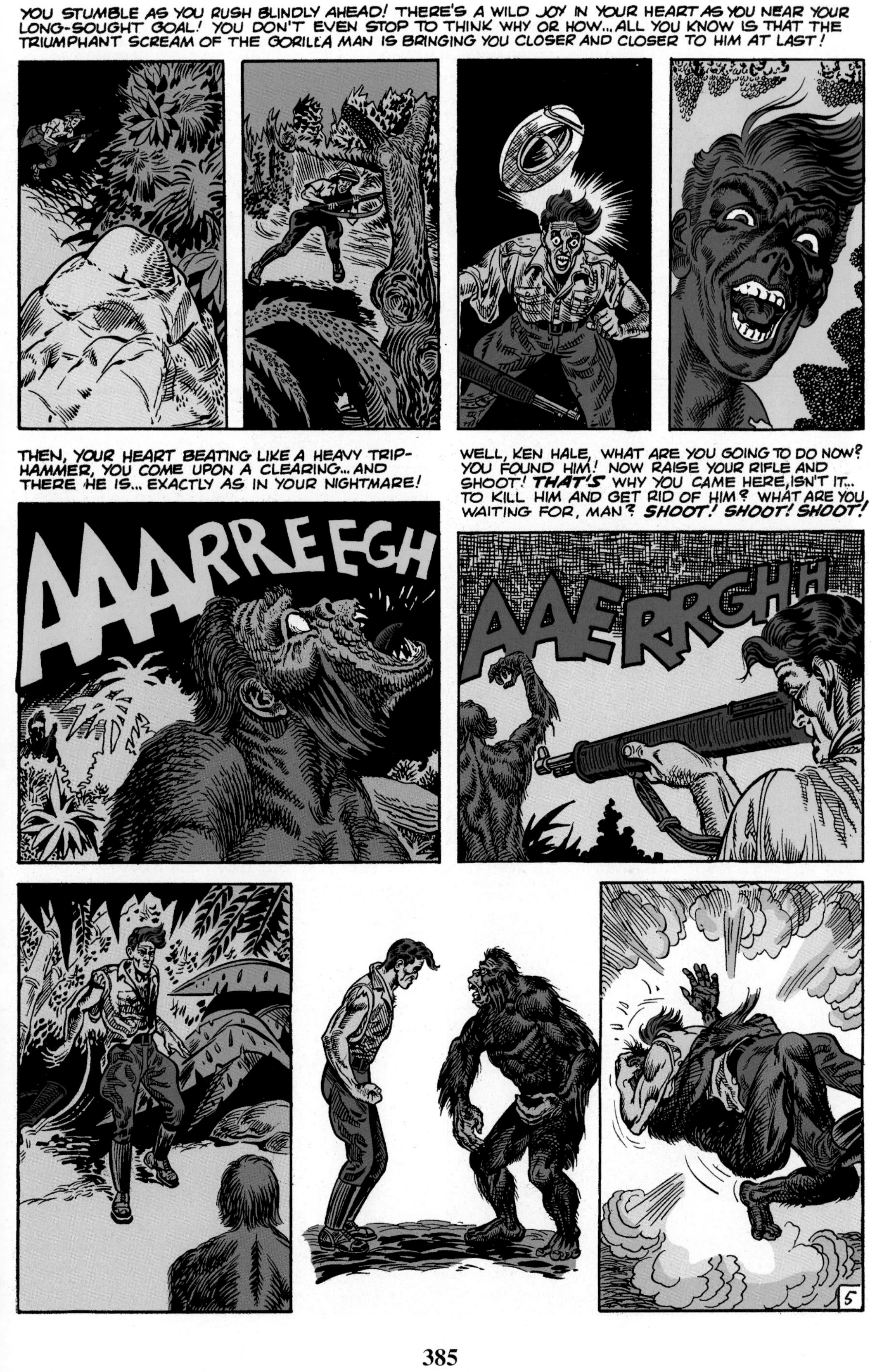
YOU STUMBLE AS YOU RUSH BLINDLY AHEAD! THERE'S A WILD JOY IN YOUR HEART AS YOU NEAR YOUR LONG-SOUGHT GOAL! YOU DON'T EVEN STOP TO THINK WHY OR HOW... ALL YOU KNOW IS THAT THE TRIUMPHANT SCREAM OF THE GORILLA MAN IS BRINGING YOU CLOSER AND CLOSER TO HIM AT LAST!
THEN, YOUR HEART BEATING LIKE A HEAVY TRIP-HAMMER, YOU COME UPON A CLEARING... AND THERE HE IS... EXACTLY AS IN YOUR NIGHTMARE!
AAARREEGH
WELL, KEN HALE, WHAT ARE YOU GOING TO DO NOW? YOU FOUND HIM! NOW RAISE YOUR RIFLE AND SHOOT! **THAT'S** WHY YOU CAME HERE, ISN'T IT... TO KILL HIM AND GET RID OF HIM? WHAT ARE YOU WAITING FOR, MAN? **SHOOT! SHOOT! SHOOT!**
AAERRGHH
5

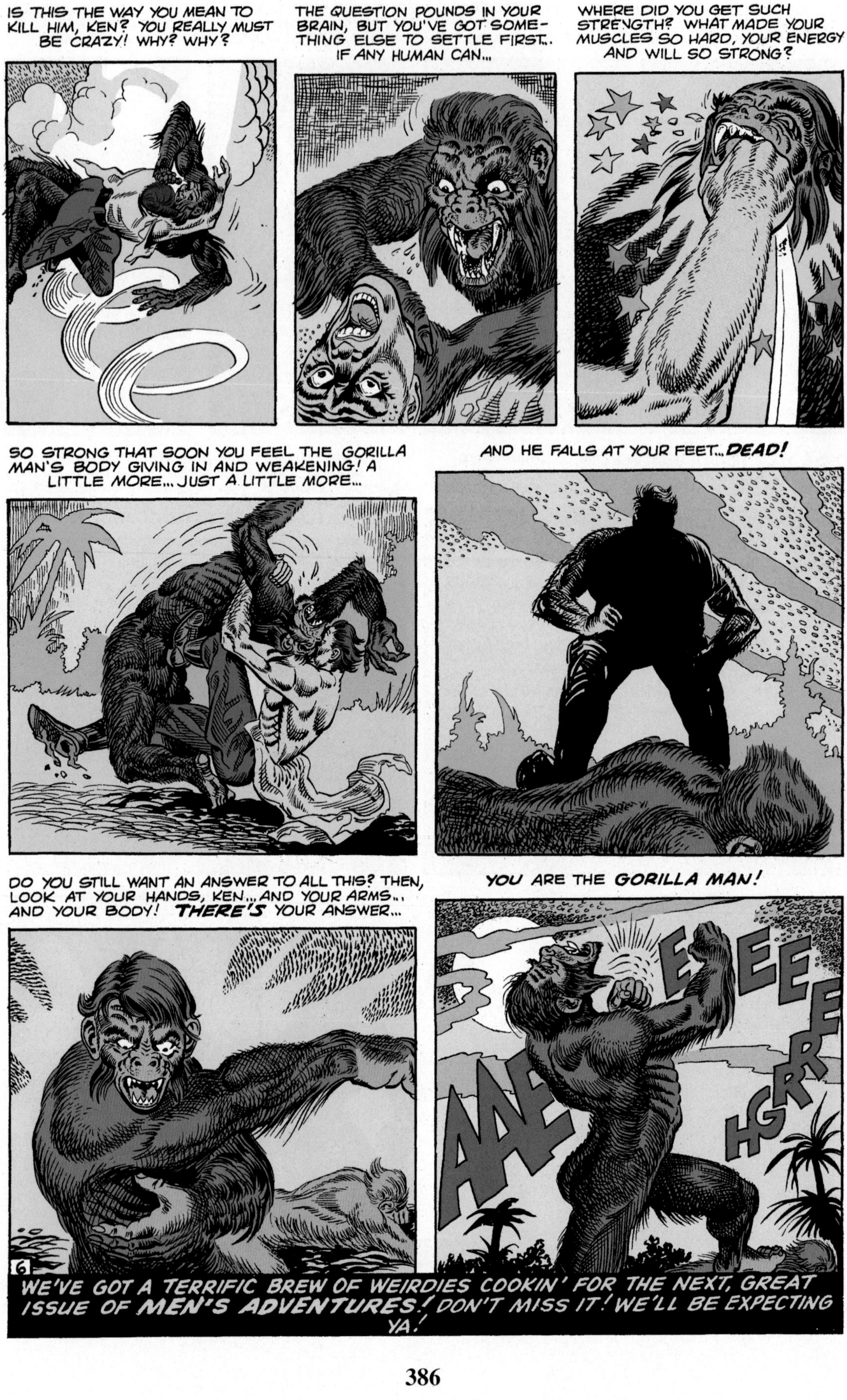
IS THIS THE WAY YOU MEAN TO KILL HIM, KEN? YOU REALLY MUST BE CRAZY! WHY? WHY?
THE QUESTION POUNDS IN YOUR BRAIN, BUT YOU'VE GOT SOMETHING ELSE TO SETTLE FIRST... IF ANY HUMAN CAN...
WHERE DID YOU GET SUCH STRENGTH? WHAT MADE YOUR MUSCLES SO HARD, YOUR ENERGY AND WILL SO STRONG?
SO STRONG THAT SOON YOU FEEL THE GORILLA MAN'S BODY GIVING IN AND WEAKENING! A LITTLE MORE... JUST A LITTLE MORE...
AND HE FALLS AT YOUR FEET... **DEAD!**
DO YOU STILL WANT AN ANSWER TO ALL THIS? THEN, LOOK AT YOUR HANDS, KEN... AND YOUR ARMS... AND YOUR BODY! **THERE'S** YOUR ANSWER...
6
YOU ARE THE **GORILLA MAN!**
AAE
EEEE
HGRRE
WE'VE GOT A TERRIFIC BREW OF WEIRDIES COOKIN' FOR THE NEXT, GREAT ISSUE OF **MEN'S ADVENTURES!** DON'T MISS IT! WE'LL BE EXPECTING YA!

MENACE #11 (MAY 1954), THE FIRST APPEARANCE OF THE HUMAN ROBOT
ARTIST: **JOHN ROMITA SR.** • EDITOR: **STAN LEE**

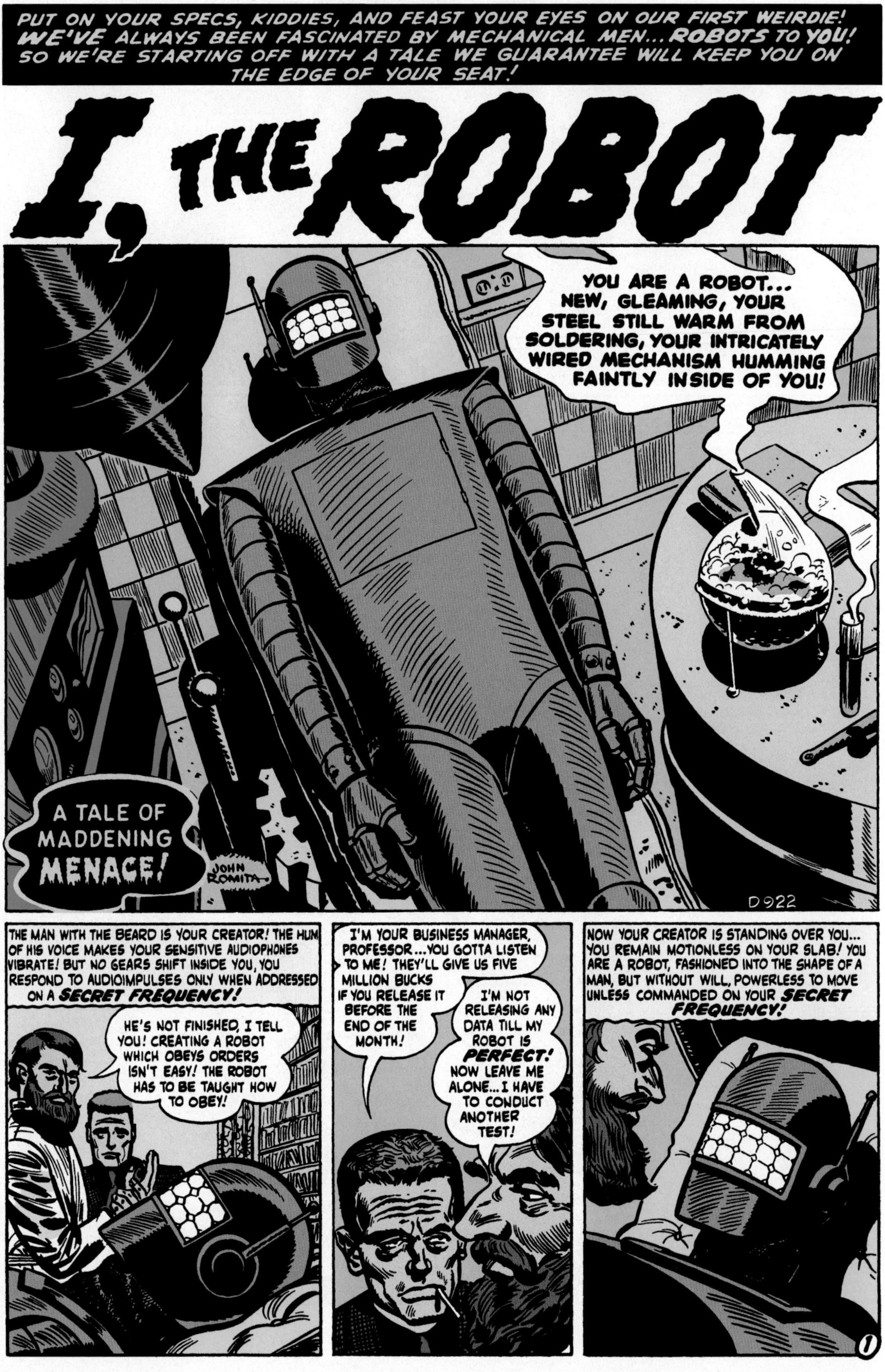
PUT ON YOUR SPECS, KIDDIES, AND FEAST YOUR EYES ON OUR FIRST WEIRDIE! WE'VE ALWAYS BEEN FASCINATED BY MECHANICAL MEN... ROBOTS TO YOU! SO WE'RE STARTING OFF WITH A TALE WE GUARANTEE WILL KEEP YOU ON THE EDGE OF YOUR SEAT!
I, THE ROBOT
YOU ARE A ROBOT... NEW, GLEAMING, YOUR STEEL STILL WARM FROM SOLDERING, YOUR INTRICATELY WIRED MECHANISM HUMMING FAINTLY INSIDE OF YOU!
A TALE OF MADDENING MENACE!
JOHN ROMITA
D922
THE MAN WITH THE BEARD IS YOUR CREATOR! THE HUM OF HIS VOICE MAKES YOUR SENSITIVE AUDIOPHONES VIBRATE! BUT NO GEARS SHIFT INSIDE YOU, YOU RESPOND TO AUDIOIMPULSES ONLY WHEN ADDRESSED ON A SECRET FREQUENCY!
HE'S NOT FINISHED, I TELL YOU! CREATING A ROBOT WHICH OBEYS ORDERS ISN'T EASY! THE ROBOT HAS TO BE TAUGHT HOW TO OBEY!
I'M YOUR BUSINESS MANAGER, PROFESSOR... YOU GOTTA LISTEN TO ME! THEY'LL GIVE US FIVE MILLION BUCKS IF YOU RELEASE IT BEFORE THE END OF THE MONTH!
I'M NOT RELEASING ANY DATA TILL MY ROBOT IS PERFECT! NOW LEAVE ME ALONE... I HAVE TO CONDUCT ANOTHER TEST!
NOW YOUR CREATOR IS STANDING OVER YOU... YOU REMAIN MOTIONLESS ON YOUR SLAB! YOU ARE A ROBOT, FASHIONED INTO THE SHAPE OF A MAN, BUT WITHOUT WILL, POWERLESS TO MOVE UNLESS COMMANDED ON YOUR SECRET FREQUENCY!
1

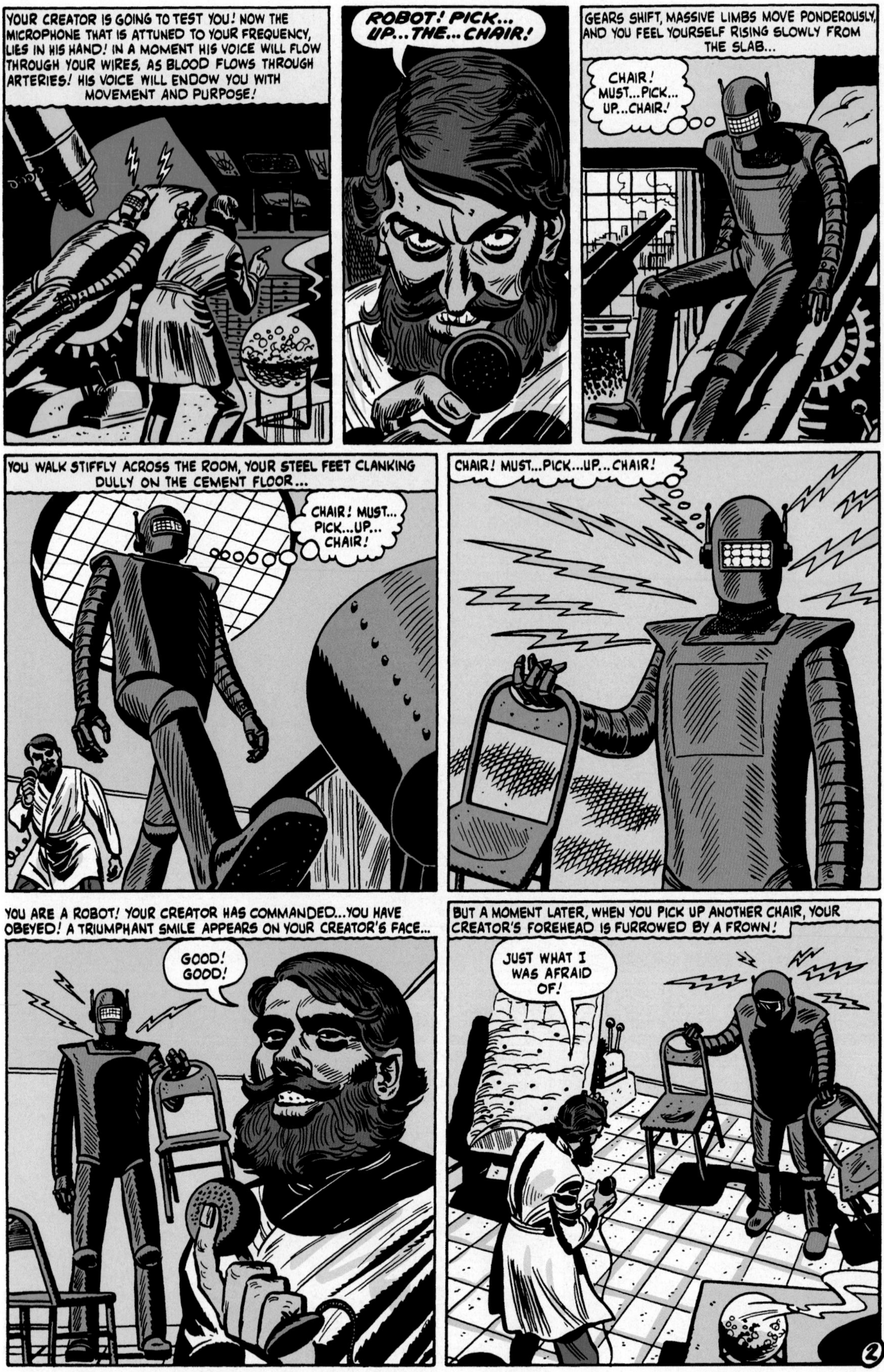
YOUR CREATOR IS GOING TO TEST YOU! NOW THE MICROPHONE THAT IS ATTUNED TO YOUR FREQUENCY, LIES IN HIS HAND! IN A MOMENT HIS VOICE WILL FLOW THROUGH YOUR WIRES, AS BLOOD FLOWS THROUGH ARTERIES! HIS VOICE WILL ENDOW YOU WITH MOVEMENT AND PURPOSE!
ROBOT! PICK... UP... THE... CHAIR!
GEARS SHIFT, MASSIVE LIMBS MOVE PONDEROUSLY, AND YOU FEEL YOURSELF RISING SLOWLY FROM THE SLAB...
CHAIR! MUST...PICK... UP...CHAIR!
YOU WALK STIFFLY ACROSS THE ROOM, YOUR STEEL FEET CLANKING DULLY ON THE CEMENT FLOOR...
CHAIR! MUST... PICK...UP... CHAIR!
CHAIR! MUST...PICK...UP...CHAIR!
YOU ARE A ROBOT! YOUR CREATOR HAS COMMANDED...YOU HAVE OBEYED! A TRIUMPHANT SMILE APPEARS ON YOUR CREATOR'S FACE...
GOOD! GOOD!
BUT A MOMENT LATER, WHEN YOU PICK UP ANOTHER CHAIR, YOUR CREATOR'S FOREHEAD IS FURROWED BY A FROWN!
JUST WHAT I WAS AFRAID OF!
2

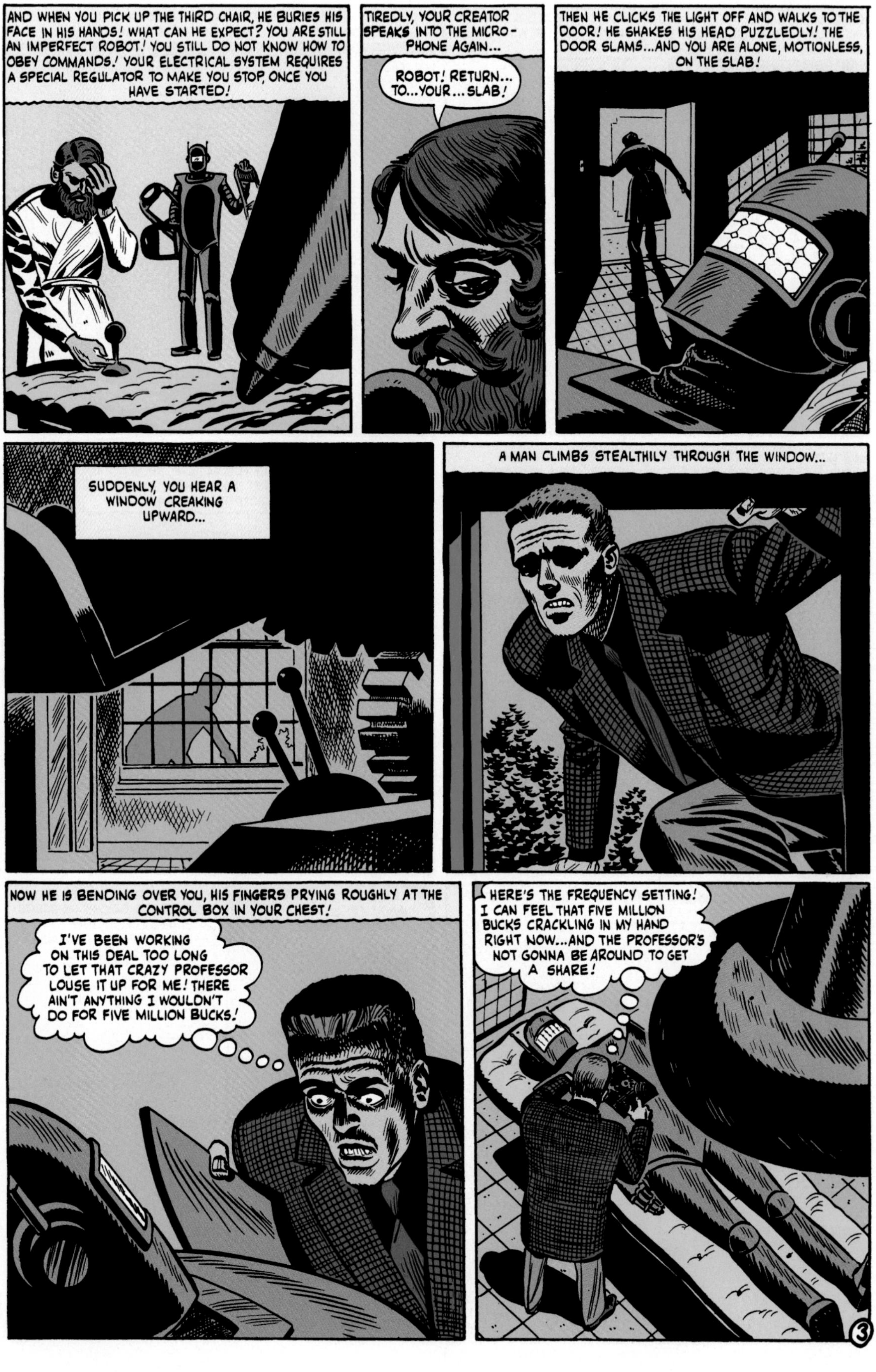
AND WHEN YOU PICK UP THE THIRD CHAIR, HE BURIES HIS FACE IN HIS HANDS! WHAT CAN HE EXPECT? YOU ARE STILL AN IMPERFECT ROBOT! YOU STILL DO NOT KNOW HOW TO OBEY COMMANDS! YOUR ELECTRICAL SYSTEM REQUIRES A SPECIAL REGULATOR TO MAKE YOU STOP, ONCE YOU HAVE STARTED!
TIREDLY, YOUR CREATOR SPEAKS INTO THE MICRO-PHONE AGAIN...
ROBOT! RETURN... TO...YOUR...SLAB!
THEN HE CLICKS THE LIGHT OFF AND WALKS TO THE DOOR! HE SHAKES HIS HEAD PUZZLEDLY! THE DOOR SLAMS...AND YOU ARE ALONE, MOTIONLESS, ON THE SLAB!
SUDDENLY, YOU HEAR A WINDOW CREAKING UPWARD...
A MAN CLIMBS STEALTHILY THROUGH THE WINDOW...
NOW HE IS BENDING OVER YOU, HIS FINGERS PRYING ROUGHLY AT THE CONTROL BOX IN YOUR CHEST!
I'VE BEEN WORKING ON THIS DEAL TOO LONG TO LET THAT CRAZY PROFESSOR LOUSE IT UP FOR ME! THERE AIN'T ANYTHING I WOULDN'T DO FOR FIVE MILLION BUCKS!
HERE'S THE FREQUENCY SETTING! I CAN FEEL THAT FIVE MILLION BUCKS CRACKLING IN MY HAND RIGHT NOW...AND THE PROFESSOR'S NOT GONNA BE AROUND TO GET A SHARE!
3

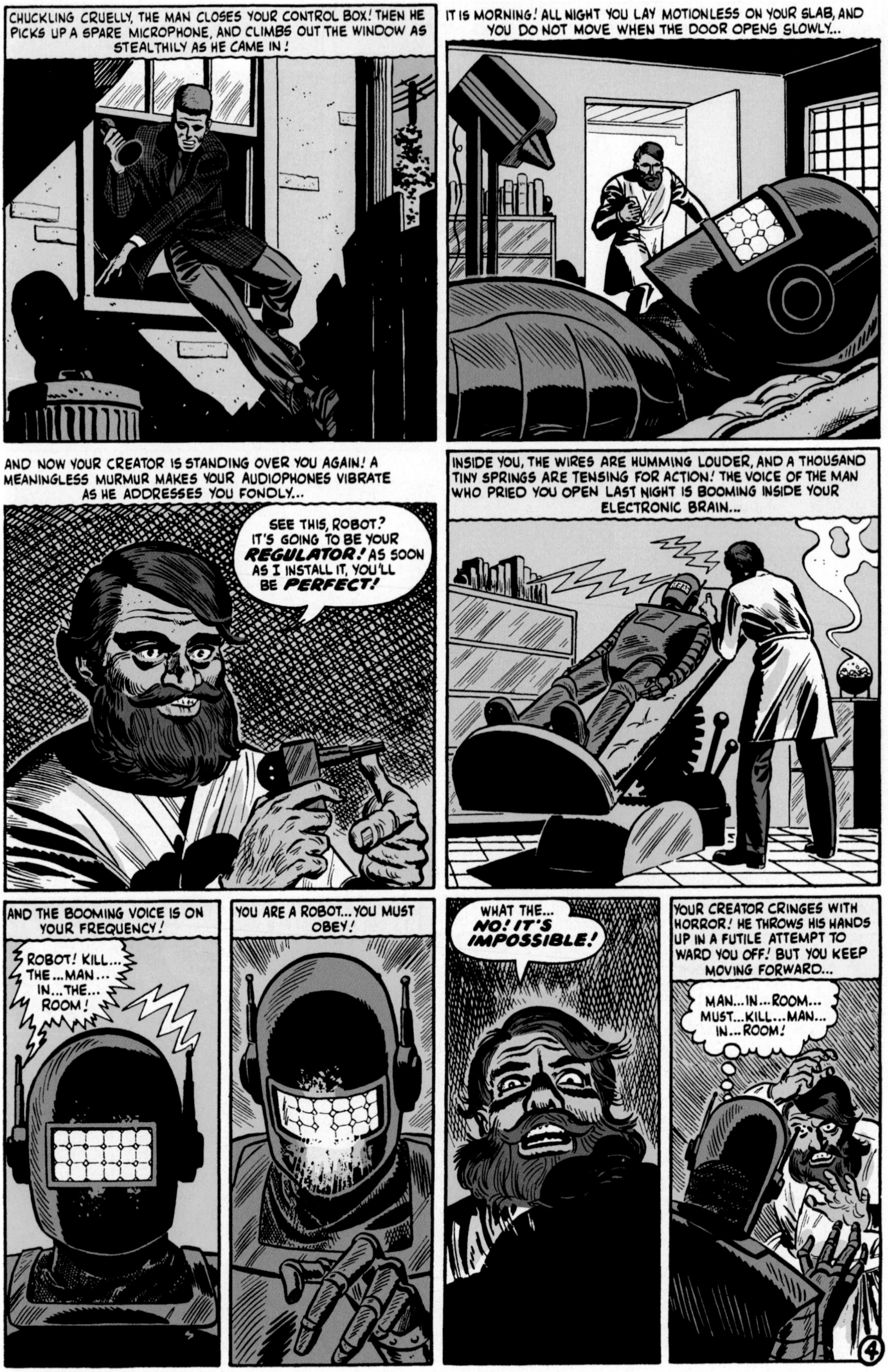
CHUCKLING CRUELLY, THE MAN CLOSES YOUR CONTROL BOX! THEN HE PICKS UP A SPARE MICROPHONE, AND CLIMBS OUT THE WINDOW AS STEALTHILY AS HE CAME IN!
IT IS MORNING! ALL NIGHT YOU LAY MOTIONLESS ON YOUR SLAB, AND YOU DO NOT MOVE WHEN THE DOOR OPENS SLOWLY...
AND NOW YOUR CREATOR IS STANDING OVER YOU AGAIN! A MEANINGLESS MURMUR MAKES YOUR AUDIOPHONES VIBRATE AS HE ADDRESSES YOU FONDLY...
SEE THIS, ROBOT? IT'S GOING TO BE YOUR REGULATOR! AS SOON AS I INSTALL IT, YOU'LL BE PERFECT!
INSIDE YOU, THE WIRES ARE HUMMING LOUDER, AND A THOUSAND TINY SPRINGS ARE TENSING FOR ACTION! THE VOICE OF THE MAN WHO PRIED YOU OPEN LAST NIGHT IS BOOMING INSIDE YOUR ELECTRONIC BRAIN...
AND THE BOOMING VOICE IS ON YOUR FREQUENCY!
ROBOT! KILL... THE...MAN... IN...THE... ROOM!
YOU ARE A ROBOT...YOU MUST OBEY!
WHAT THE... NO! IT'S IMPOSSIBLE!
YOUR CREATOR CRINGES WITH HORROR! HE THROWS HIS HANDS UP IN A FUTILE ATTEMPT TO WARD YOU OFF! BUT YOU KEEP MOVING FORWARD...
MAN...IN...ROOM... MUST...KILL...MAN... IN...ROOM!
4

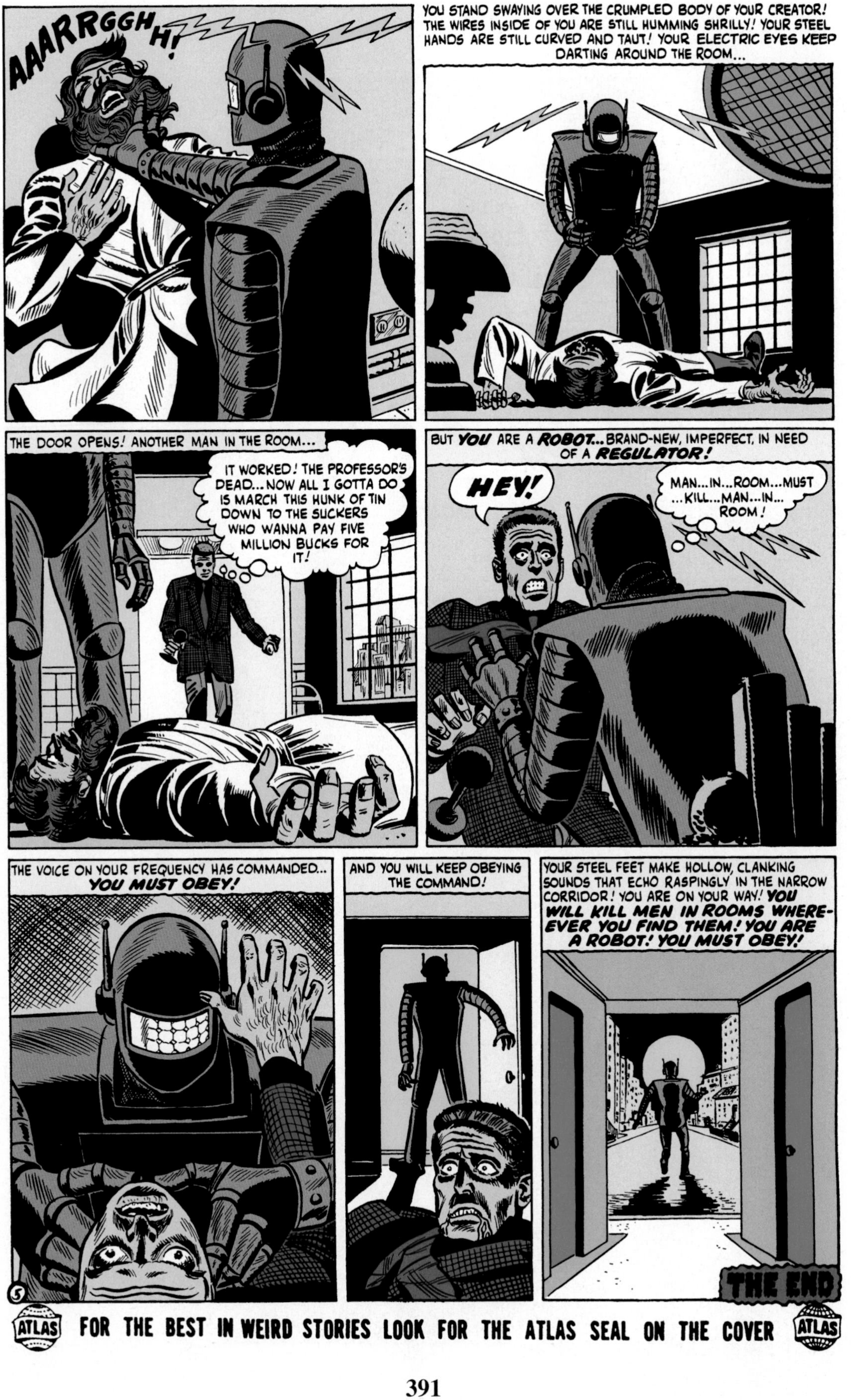

AAARRGGHH!
YOU STAND SWAYING OVER THE CRUMPLED BODY OF YOUR CREATOR! THE WIRES INSIDE OF YOU ARE STILL HUMMING SHRILLY! YOUR STEEL HANDS ARE STILL CURVED AND TAUT! YOUR ELECTRIC EYES KEEP DARTING AROUND THE ROOM...
THE DOOR OPENS! ANOTHER MAN IN THE ROOM...
IT WORKED! THE PROFESSOR'S DEAD... NOW ALL I GOTTA DO IS MARCH THIS HUNK OF TIN DOWN TO THE SUCKERS WHO WANNA PAY FIVE MILLION BUCKS FOR IT!
BUT YOU ARE A ROBOT... BRAND-NEW, IMPERFECT, IN NEED OF A REGULATOR!
HEY!
MAN... IN... ROOM... MUST ... KILL... MAN... IN... ROOM!
THE VOICE ON YOUR FREQUENCY HAS COMMANDED... YOU MUST OBEY!
5
AND YOU WILL KEEP OBEYING THE COMMAND!
YOUR STEEL FEET MAKE HOLLOW, CLANKING SOUNDS THAT ECHO RASPINGLY IN THE NARROW CORRIDOR! YOU ARE ON YOUR WAY! YOU WILL KILL MEN IN ROOMS WHEREEVER YOU FIND THEM! YOU ARE A ROBOT! YOU MUST OBEY!
THE END

ATLAS FOR THE BEST IN WEIRD STORIES LOOK FOR THE ATLAS SEAL ON THE COVER ATLAS

YELLOW CLAW #1 (OCTOBER 1956), THE FIRST APPEARANCE OF YELLOW CLAW AND JIMMY WOO
WRITER: **AL FELDSTEIN** • ARTIST & COVER ARTIST: **JOE MANEELY** • EDITOR: **STAN LEE**

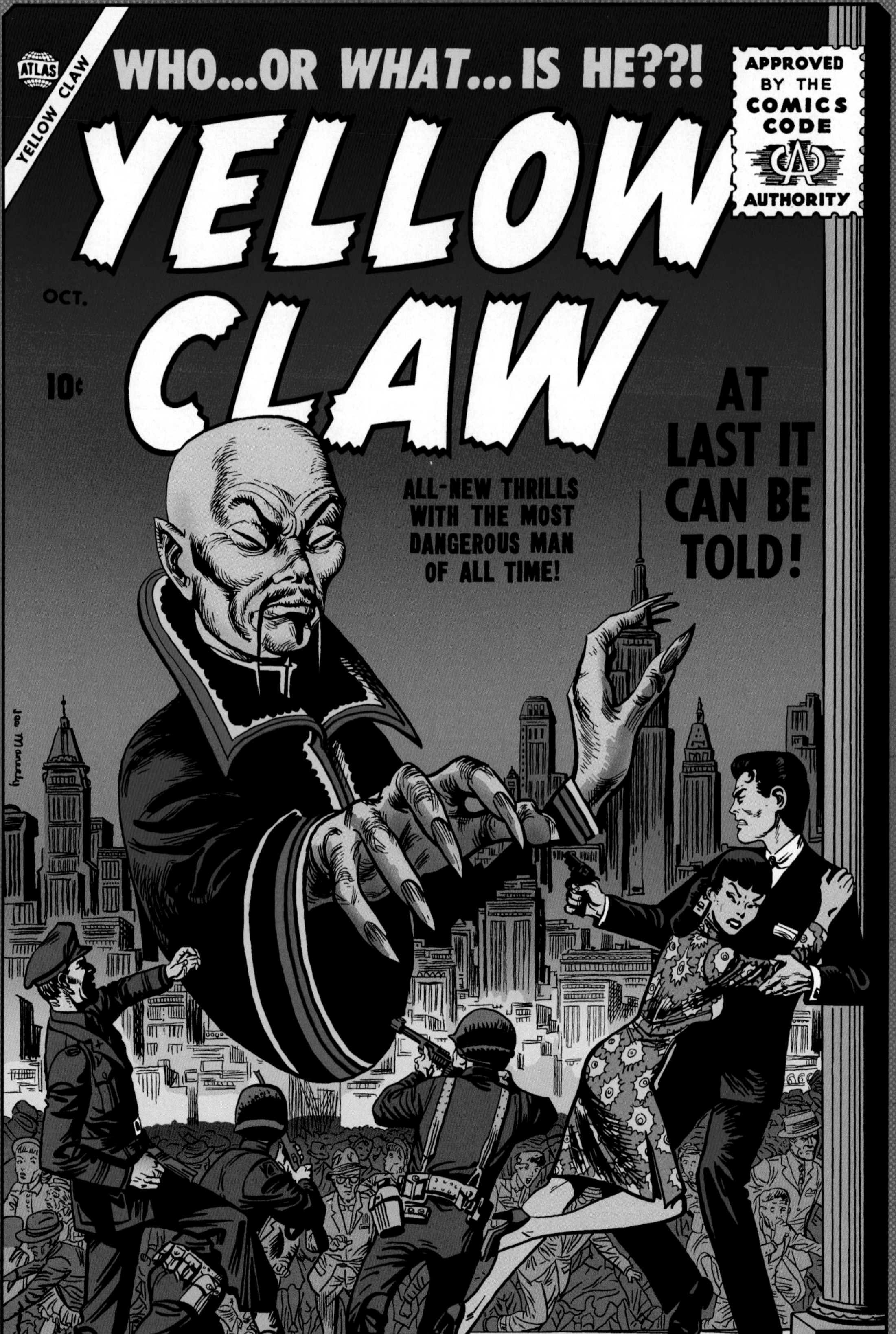
ATLAS
YELLOW CLAW
WHO...OR WHAT...IS HE??!
YELLOW CLAW
OCT.
10¢
APPROVED BY THE COMICS CODE AUTHORITY
AT LAST IT CAN BE TOLD!
ALL-NEW THRILLS WITH THE MOST DANGEROUS MAN OF ALL TIME!
Joe Maneely

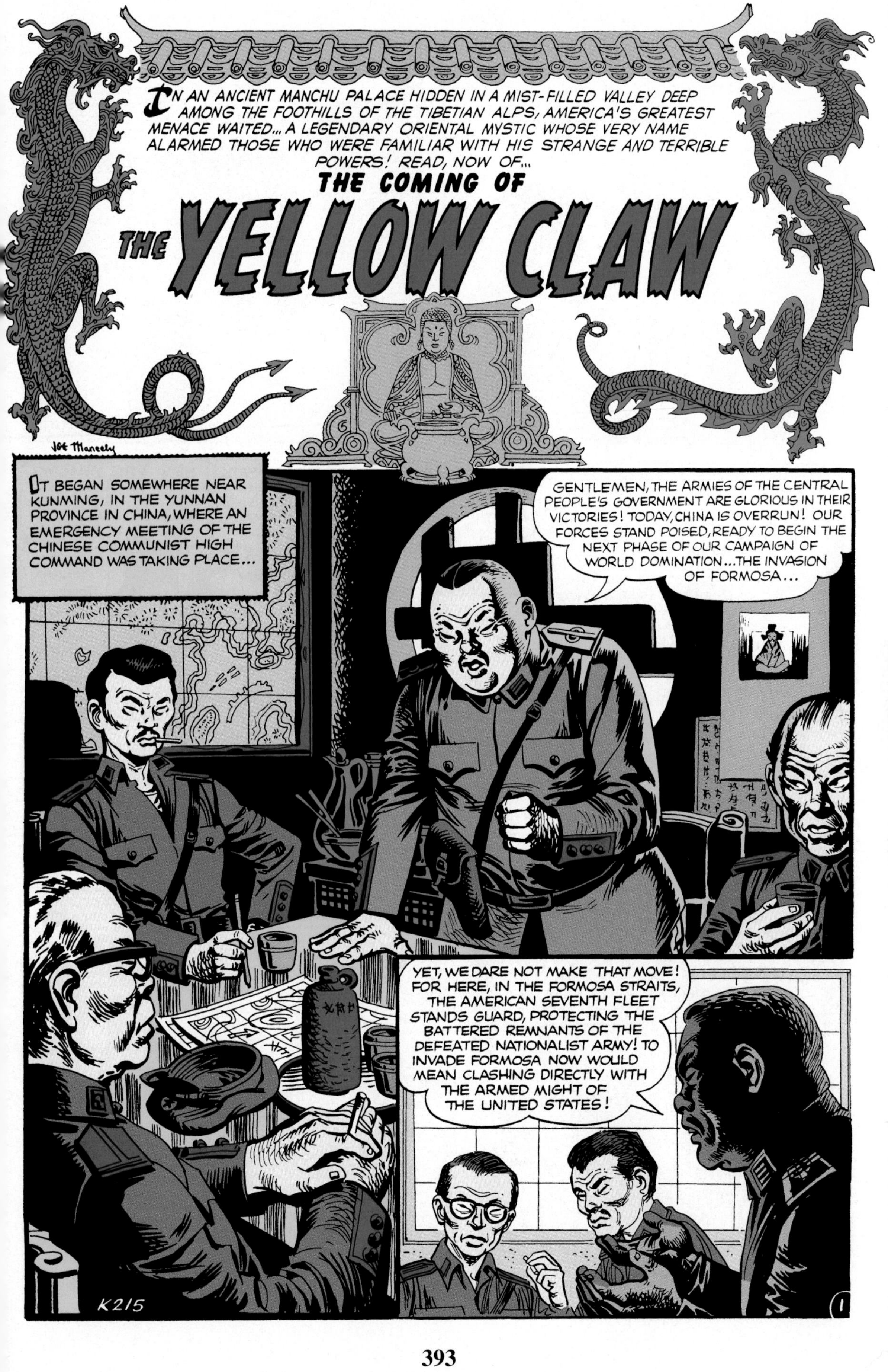
IN AN ANCIENT MANCHU PALACE HIDDEN IN A MIST-FILLED VALLEY DEEP AMONG THE FOOTHILLS OF THE TIBETIAN ALPS, AMERICA'S GREATEST MENACE WAITED... A LEGENDARY ORIENTAL MYSTIC WHOSE VERY NAME ALARMED THOSE WHO WERE FAMILIAR WITH HIS STRANGE AND TERRIBLE POWERS! READ, NOW OF...
THE COMING OF
THE YELLOW CLAW
JOE MANEELY
IT BEGAN SOMEWHERE NEAR KUNMING, IN THE YUNNAN PROVINCE IN CHINA, WHERE AN EMERGENCY MEETING OF THE CHINESE COMMUNIST HIGH COMMAND WAS TAKING PLACE...
GENTLEMEN, THE ARMIES OF THE CENTRAL PEOPLE'S GOVERNMENT ARE GLORIOUS IN THEIR VICTORIES! TODAY, CHINA IS OVERRUN! OUR FORCES STAND POISED, READY TO BEGIN THE NEXT PHASE OF OUR CAMPAIGN OF WORLD DOMINATION...THE INVASION OF FORMOSA...
K215
YET, WE DARE NOT MAKE THAT MOVE! FOR HERE, IN THE FORMOSA STRAITS, THE AMERICAN SEVENTH FLEET STANDS GUARD, PROTECTING THE BATTERED REMNANTS OF THE DEFEATED NATIONALIST ARMY! TO INVADE FORMOSA NOW WOULD MEAN CLASHING DIRECTLY WITH THE ARMED MIGHT OF THE UNITED STATES!
1

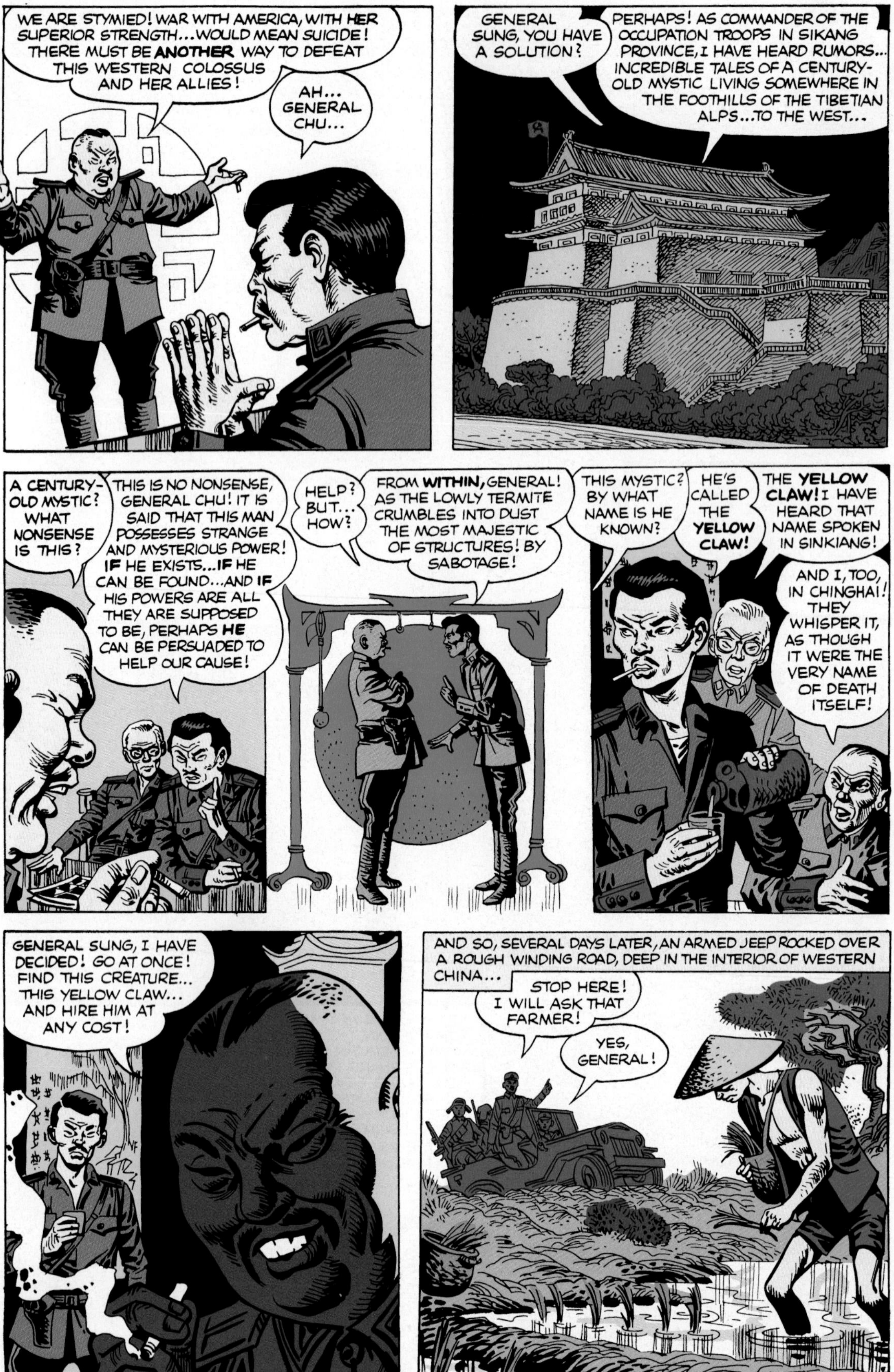

WE ARE STYMIED! WAR WITH AMERICA, WITH HER SUPERIOR STRENGTH...WOULD MEAN SUICIDE! THERE MUST BE ANOTHER WAY TO DEFEAT THIS WESTERN COLOSSUS AND HER ALLIES!
AH... GENERAL CHU...
GENERAL SUNG, YOU HAVE A SOLUTION?
PERHAPS! AS COMMANDER OF THE OCCUPATION TROOPS IN SIKANG PROVINCE, I HAVE HEARD RUMORS... INCREDIBLE TALES OF A CENTURY-OLD MYSTIC LIVING SOMEWHERE IN THE FOOTHILLS OF THE TIBETIAN ALPS...TO THE WEST...
A CENTURY-OLD MYSTIC? WHAT NONSENSE IS THIS?
THIS IS NO NONSENSE, GENERAL CHU! IT IS SAID THAT THIS MAN POSSESSES STRANGE AND MYSTERIOUS POWER! IF HE EXISTS...IF HE CAN BE FOUND...AND IF HIS POWERS ARE ALL THEY ARE SUPPOSED TO BE, PERHAPS HE CAN BE PERSUADED TO HELP OUR CAUSE!
HELP? BUT... HOW?
FROM WITHIN, GENERAL! AS THE LOWLY TERMITE CRUMBLES INTO DUST THE MOST MAJESTIC OF STRUCTURES! BY SABOTAGE!
THIS MYSTIC? BY WHAT NAME IS HE KNOWN?
HE'S CALLED THE YELLOW CLAW!
THE YELLOW CLAW! I HAVE HEARD THAT NAME SPOKEN IN SINKIANG!
AND I, TOO, IN CHINGHAI! THEY WHISPER IT, AS THOUGH IT WERE THE VERY NAME OF DEATH ITSELF!
GENERAL SUNG, I HAVE DECIDED! GO AT ONCE! FIND THIS CREATURE... THIS YELLOW CLAW... AND HIRE HIM AT ANY COST!
AND SO, SEVERAL DAYS LATER, AN ARMED JEEP ROCKED OVER A ROUGH WINDING ROAD, DEEP IN THE INTERIOR OF WESTERN CHINA...
STOP HERE! I WILL ASK THAT FARMER!
YES, GENERAL!
2

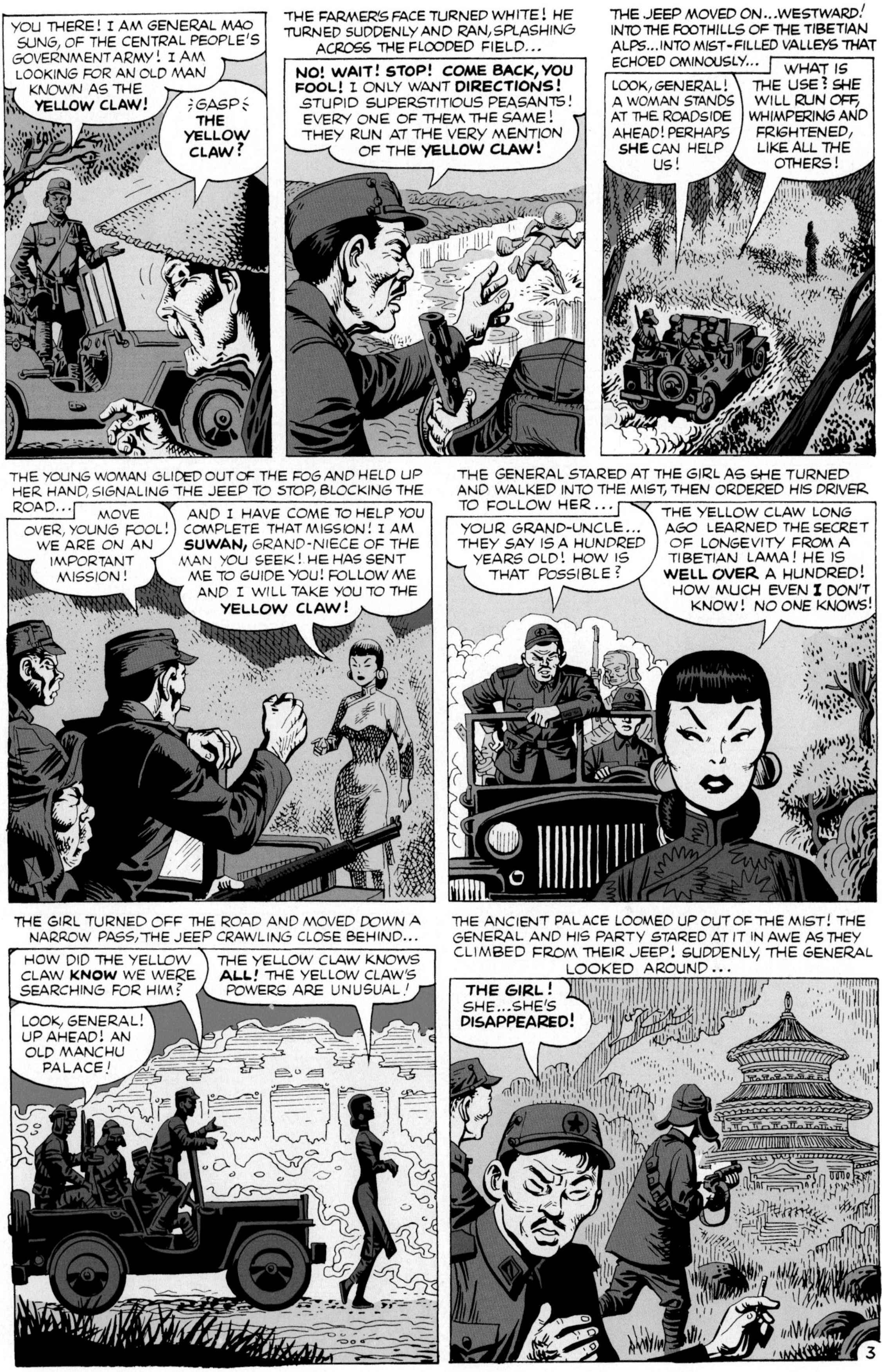
YOU THERE! I AM GENERAL MAO SUNG, OF THE CENTRAL PEOPLE'S GOVERNMENT ARMY! I AM LOOKING FOR AN OLD MAN KNOWN AS THE YELLOW CLAW!
GASP! THE YELLOW CLAW?
THE FARMER'S FACE TURNED WHITE! HE TURNED SUDDENLY AND RAN, SPLASHING ACROSS THE FLOODED FIELD...
NO! WAIT! STOP! COME BACK, YOU FOOL! I ONLY WANT DIRECTIONS! STUPID SUPERSTITIOUS PEASANTS! EVERY ONE OF THEM THE SAME! THEY RUN AT THE VERY MENTION OF THE YELLOW CLAW!
THE JEEP MOVED ON...WESTWARD! INTO THE FOOTHILLS OF THE TIBETIAN ALPS...INTO MIST-FILLED VALLEYS THAT ECHOED OMINOUSLY...
LOOK, GENERAL! A WOMAN STANDS AT THE ROADSIDE AHEAD! PERHAPS SHE CAN HELP US!
WHAT IS THE USE? SHE WILL RUN OFF, WHIMPERING AND FRIGHTENED, LIKE ALL THE OTHERS!
THE YOUNG WOMAN GLIDED OUT OF THE FOG AND HELD UP HER HAND, SIGNALING THE JEEP TO STOP, BLOCKING THE ROAD...
MOVE OVER, YOUNG FOOL! WE ARE ON AN IMPORTANT MISSION!
AND I HAVE COME TO HELP YOU COMPLETE THAT MISSION! I AM SUWAN, GRAND-NIECE OF THE MAN YOU SEEK! HE HAS SENT ME TO GUIDE YOU! FOLLOW ME AND I WILL TAKE YOU TO THE YELLOW CLAW!
THE GENERAL STARED AT THE GIRL AS SHE TURNED AND WALKED INTO THE MIST, THEN ORDERED HIS DRIVER TO FOLLOW HER...
YOUR GRAND-UNCLE... THEY SAY IS A HUNDRED YEARS OLD! HOW IS THAT POSSIBLE?
THE YELLOW CLAW LONG AGO LEARNED THE SECRET OF LONGEVITY FROM A TIBETIAN LAMA! HE IS WELL OVER A HUNDRED! HOW MUCH EVEN I DON'T KNOW! NO ONE KNOWS!
THE GIRL TURNED OFF THE ROAD AND MOVED DOWN A NARROW PASS, THE JEEP CRAWLING CLOSE BEHIND...
HOW DID THE YELLOW CLAW KNOW WE WERE SEARCHING FOR HIM?
THE YELLOW CLAW KNOWS ALL! THE YELLOW CLAW'S POWERS ARE UNUSUAL!
LOOK, GENERAL! UP AHEAD! AN OLD MANCHU PALACE!
THE ANCIENT PALACE LOOMED UP OUT OF THE MIST! THE GENERAL AND HIS PARTY STARED AT IT IN AWE AS THEY CLIMBED FROM THEIR JEEP! SUDDENLY, THE GENERAL LOOKED AROUND...
THE GIRL! SHE...SHE'S DISAPPEARED!
3

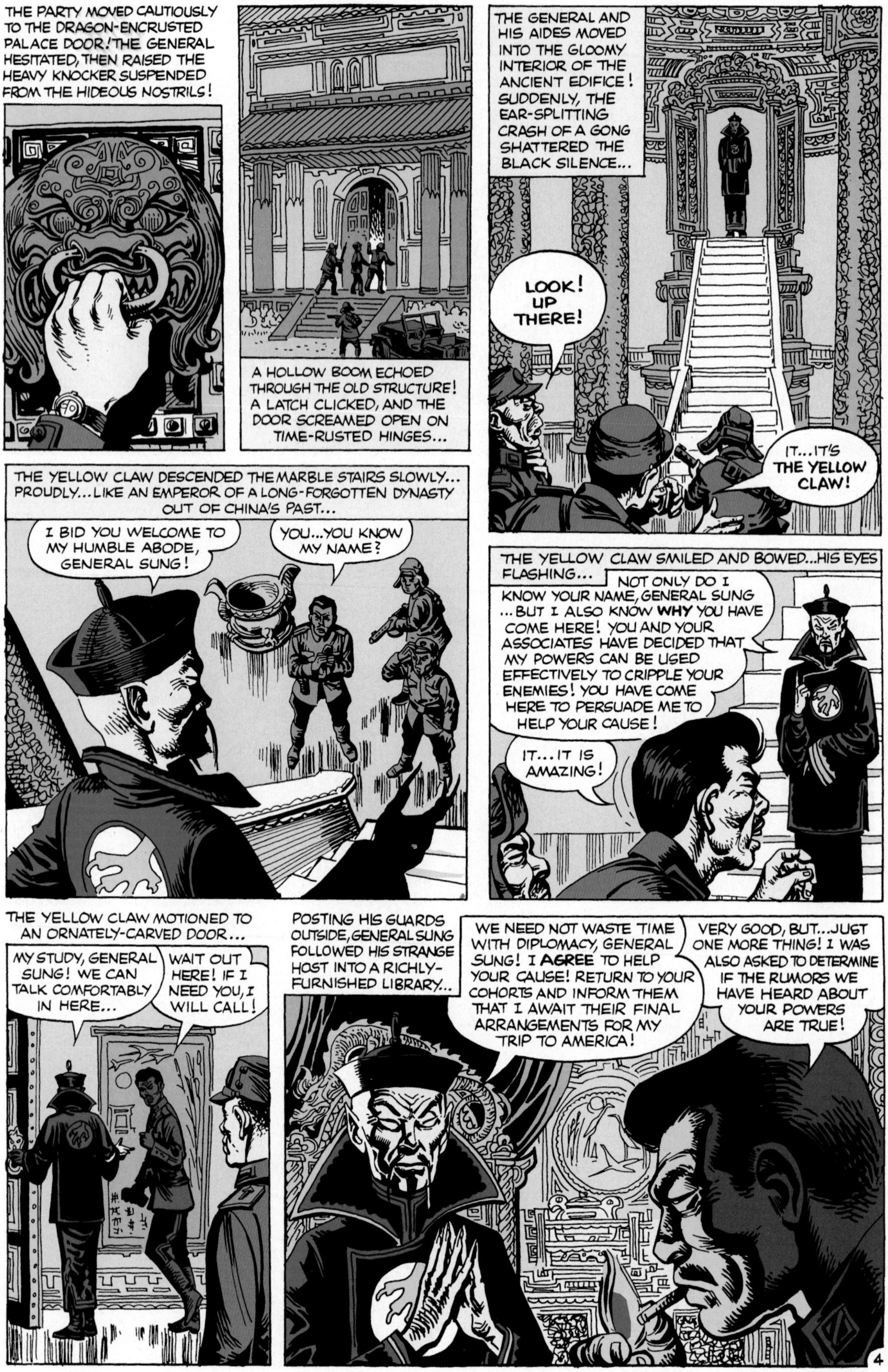
THE PARTY MOVED CAUTIOUSLY TO THE DRAGON-ENCRUSTED PALACE DOOR! THE GENERAL HESITATED, THEN RAISED THE HEAVY KNOCKER SUSPENDED FROM THE HIDEOUS NOSTRILS!
A HOLLOW BOOM ECHOED THROUGH THE OLD STRUCTURE! A LATCH CLICKED, AND THE DOOR SCREAMED OPEN ON TIME-RUSTED HINGES...
THE GENERAL AND HIS AIDES MOVED INTO THE GLOOMY INTERIOR OF THE ANCIENT EDIFICE! SUDDENLY, THE EAR-SPLITTING CRASH OF A GONG SHATTERED THE BLACK SILENCE...
LOOK! UP THERE!
IT...IT'S THE YELLOW CLAW!
THE YELLOW CLAW DESCENDED THE MARBLE STAIRS SLOWLY... PROUDLY...LIKE AN EMPEROR OF A LONG-FORGOTTEN DYNASTY OUT OF CHINA'S PAST...
I BID YOU WELCOME TO MY HUMBLE ABODE, GENERAL SUNG!
YOU...YOU KNOW MY NAME?
THE YELLOW CLAW SMILED AND BOWED...HIS EYES FLASHING...
NOT ONLY DO I KNOW YOUR NAME, GENERAL SUNG ...BUT I ALSO KNOW WHY YOU HAVE COME HERE! YOU AND YOUR ASSOCIATES HAVE DECIDED THAT MY POWERS CAN BE USED EFFECTIVELY TO CRIPPLE YOUR ENEMIES! YOU HAVE COME HERE TO PERSUADE ME TO HELP YOUR CAUSE!
IT...IT IS AMAZING!
THE YELLOW CLAW MOTIONED TO AN ORNATELY-CARVED DOOR...
MY STUDY, GENERAL SUNG! WE CAN TALK COMFORTABLY IN HERE...
WAIT OUT HERE! IF I NEED YOU, I WILL CALL!
POSTING HIS GUARDS OUTSIDE, GENERAL SUNG FOLLOWED HIS STRANGE HOST INTO A RICHLY-FURNISHED LIBRARY...
WE NEED NOT WASTE TIME WITH DIPLOMACY, GENERAL SUNG! I AGREE TO HELP YOUR CAUSE! RETURN TO YOUR COHORTS AND INFORM THEM THAT I AWAIT THEIR FINAL ARRANGEMENTS FOR MY TRIP TO AMERICA!
VERY GOOD, BUT...JUST ONE MORE THING! I WAS ALSO ASKED TO DETERMINE IF THE RUMORS WE HAVE HEARD ABOUT YOUR POWERS ARE TRUE!
4

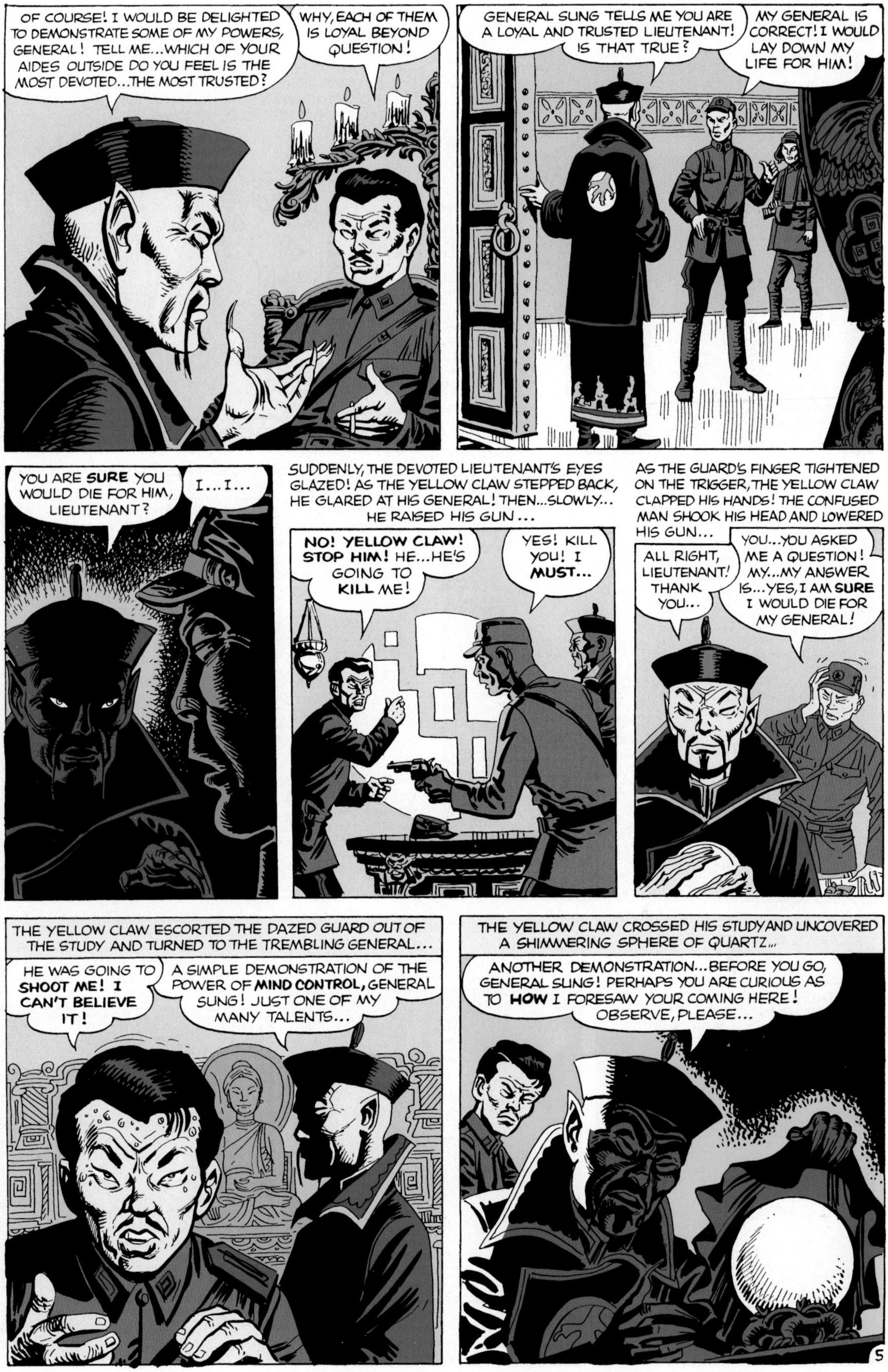
OF COURSE! I WOULD BE DELIGHTED TO DEMONSTRATE SOME OF MY POWERS, GENERAL! TELL ME...WHICH OF YOUR AIDES OUTSIDE DO YOU FEEL IS THE MOST DEVOTED...THE MOST TRUSTED?
WHY, EACH OF THEM IS LOYAL BEYOND QUESTION!
GENERAL SUNG TELLS ME YOU ARE A LOYAL AND TRUSTED LIEUTENANT! IS THAT TRUE?
MY GENERAL IS CORRECT! I WOULD LAY DOWN MY LIFE FOR HIM!
YOU ARE SURE YOU WOULD DIE FOR HIM, LIEUTENANT?
I...I...
SUDDENLY, THE DEVOTED LIEUTENANT'S EYES GLAZED! AS THE YELLOW CLAW STEPPED BACK, HE GLARED AT HIS GENERAL! THEN...SLOWLY... HE RAISED HIS GUN...
NO! YELLOW CLAW! STOP HIM! HE...HE'S GOING TO KILL ME!
YES! KILL YOU! I MUST...
AS THE GUARD'S FINGER TIGHTENED ON THE TRIGGER, THE YELLOW CLAW CLAPPED HIS HANDS! THE CONFUSED MAN SHOOK HIS HEAD AND LOWERED HIS GUN...
ALL RIGHT, LIEUTENANT! THANK YOU...
YOU...YOU ASKED ME A QUESTION! MY...MY ANSWER IS...YES, I AM SURE I WOULD DIE FOR MY GENERAL!
THE YELLOW CLAW ESCORTED THE DAZED GUARD OUT OF THE STUDY AND TURNED TO THE TREMBLING GENERAL...
HE WAS GOING TO SHOOT ME! I CAN'T BELIEVE IT!
A SIMPLE DEMONSTRATION OF THE POWER OF MIND CONTROL, GENERAL SUNG! JUST ONE OF MY MANY TALENTS...
THE YELLOW CLAW CROSSED HIS STUDY AND UNCOVERED A SHIMMERING SPHERE OF QUARTZ...
ANOTHER DEMONSTRATION...BEFORE YOU GO, GENERAL SUNG! PERHAPS YOU ARE CURIOUS AS TO HOW I FORESAW YOUR COMING HERE! OBSERVE, PLEASE...
5

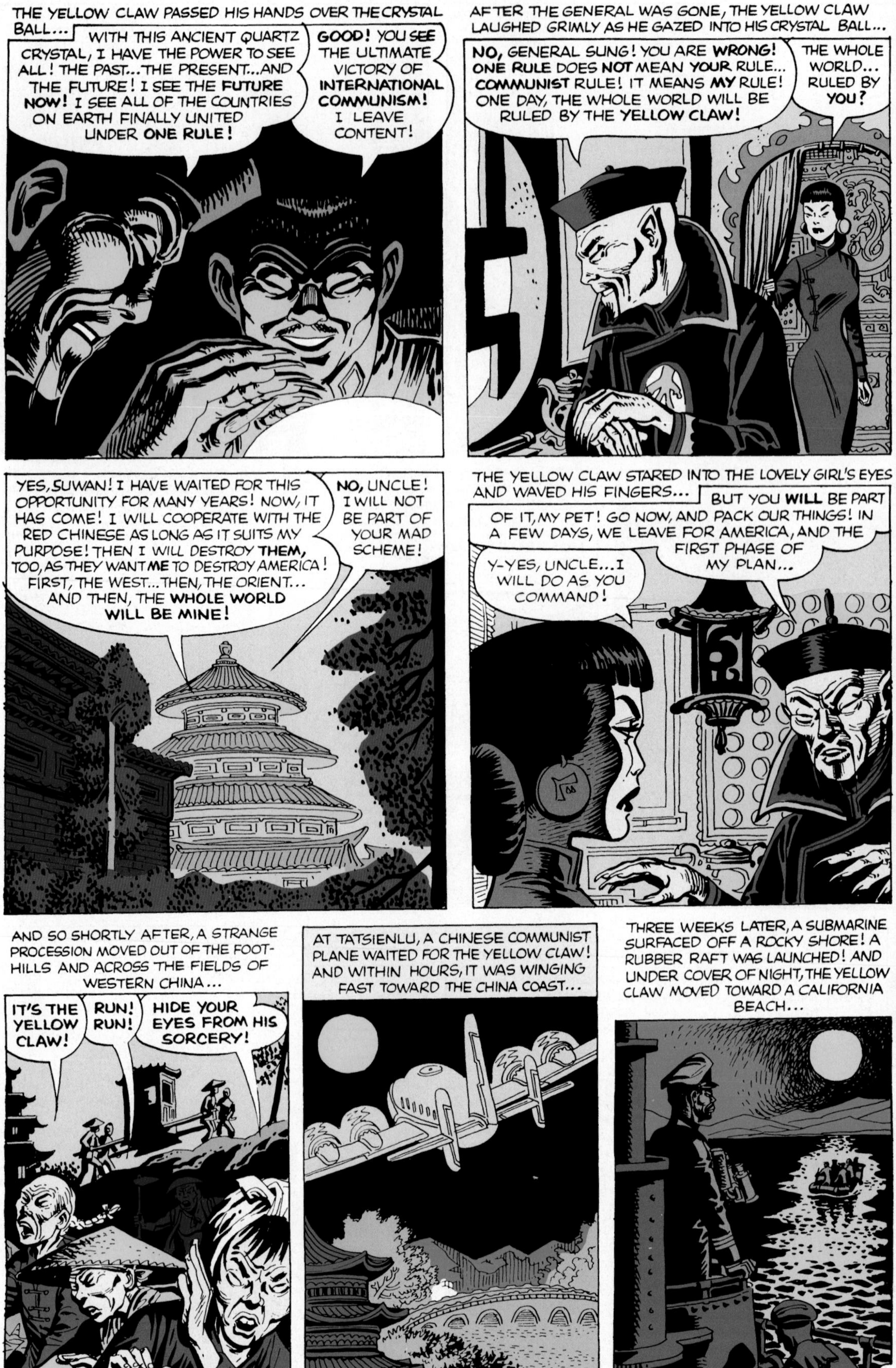
THE YELLOW CLAW PASSED HIS HANDS OVER THE CRYSTAL BALL...
WITH THIS ANCIENT QUARTZ CRYSTAL, I HAVE THE POWER TO SEE ALL! THE PAST...THE PRESENT...AND THE FUTURE! I SEE THE FUTURE NOW! I SEE ALL OF THE COUNTRIES ON EARTH FINALLY UNITED UNDER ONE RULE!
GOOD! YOU SEE THE ULTIMATE VICTORY OF INTERNATIONAL COMMUNISM! I LEAVE CONTENT!
AFTER THE GENERAL WAS GONE, THE YELLOW CLAW LAUGHED GRIMLY AS HE GAZED INTO HIS CRYSTAL BALL...
NO, GENERAL SUNG! YOU ARE WRONG! ONE RULE DOES NOT MEAN YOUR RULE... COMMUNIST RULE! IT MEANS MY RULE! ONE DAY, THE WHOLE WORLD WILL BE RULED BY THE YELLOW CLAW!
THE WHOLE WORLD... RULED BY YOU?
YES, SUWAN! I HAVE WAITED FOR THIS OPPORTUNITY FOR MANY YEARS! NOW, IT HAS COME! I WILL COOPERATE WITH THE RED CHINESE AS LONG AS IT SUITS MY PURPOSE! THEN I WILL DESTROY THEM, TOO, AS THEY WANT ME TO DESTROY AMERICA! FIRST, THE WEST...THEN, THE ORIENT... AND THEN, THE WHOLE WORLD WILL BE MINE!
NO, UNCLE! I WILL NOT BE PART OF YOUR MAD SCHEME!
THE YELLOW CLAW STARED INTO THE LOVELY GIRL'S EYES AND WAVED HIS FINGERS...
BUT YOU WILL BE PART OF IT, MY PET! GO NOW, AND PACK OUR THINGS! IN A FEW DAYS, WE LEAVE FOR AMERICA, AND THE FIRST PHASE OF MY PLAN...
Y-YES, UNCLE...I WILL DO AS YOU COMMAND!
AND SO SHORTLY AFTER, A STRANGE PROCESSION MOVED OUT OF THE FOOT-HILLS AND ACROSS THE FIELDS OF WESTERN CHINA...
IT'S THE YELLOW CLAW!
RUN! RUN!
HIDE YOUR EYES FROM HIS SORCERY!
AT TATSIENLU, A CHINESE COMMUNIST PLANE WAITED FOR THE YELLOW CLAW! AND WITHIN HOURS, IT WAS WINGING FAST TOWARD THE CHINA COAST...
THREE WEEKS LATER, A SUBMARINE SURFACED OFF A ROCKY SHORE! A RUBBER RAFT WAS LAUNCHED! AND UNDER COVER OF NIGHT, THE YELLOW CLAW MOVED TOWARD A CALIFORNIA BEACH...
6

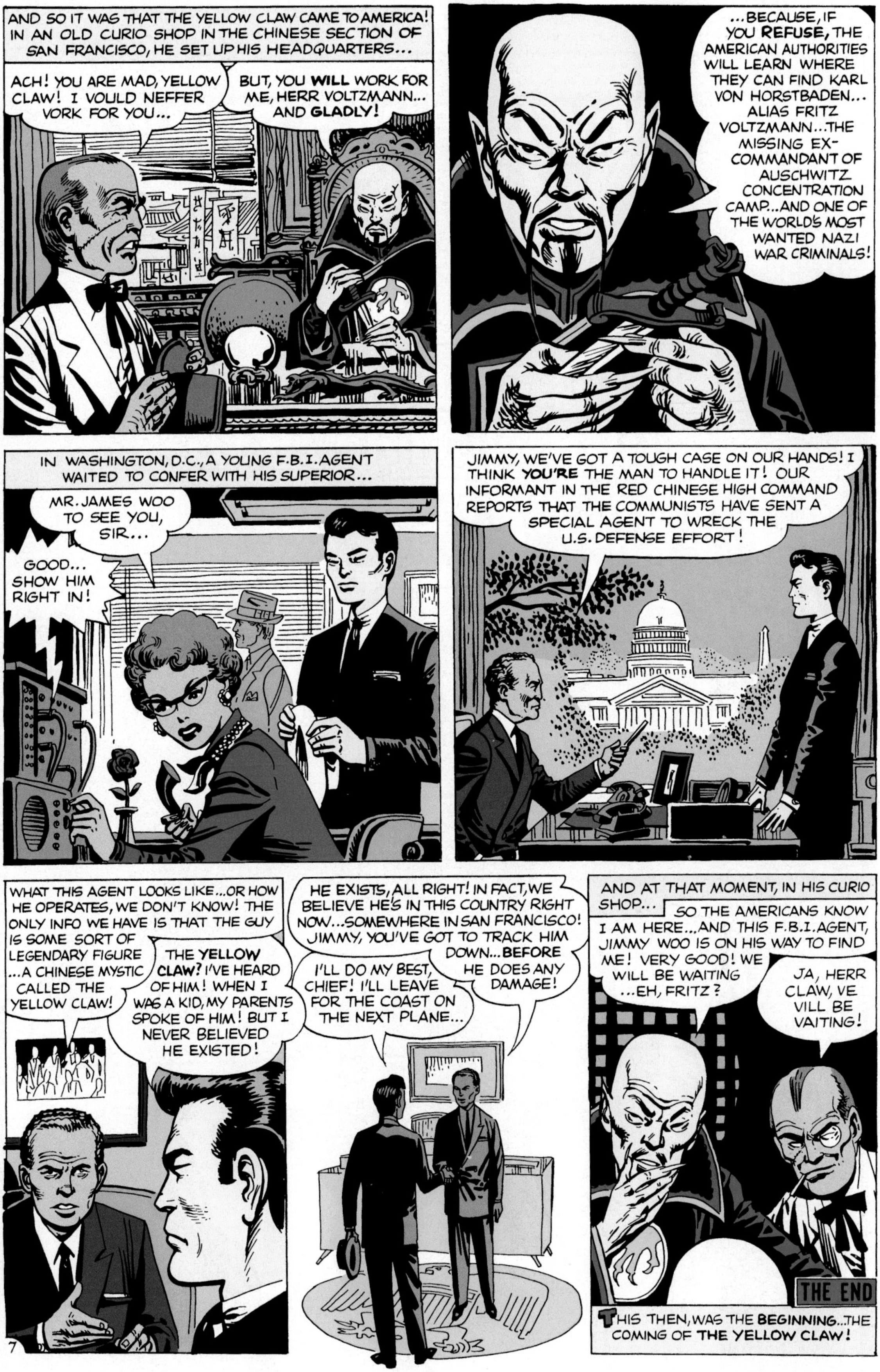
AND SO IT WAS THAT THE YELLOW CLAW CAME TO AMERICA! IN AN OLD CURIO SHOP IN THE CHINESE SECTION OF SAN FRANCISCO, HE SET UP HIS HEADQUARTERS...
ACH! YOU ARE MAD, YELLOW CLAW! I VOULD NEFFER VORK FOR YOU...
BUT, YOU **WILL** WORK FOR ME, HERR VOLTZMANN... AND **GLADLY!**
...BECAUSE, IF YOU **REFUSE,** THE AMERICAN AUTHORITIES WILL LEARN WHERE THEY CAN FIND KARL VON HORSTBADEN... ALIAS FRITZ VOLTZMANN...THE MISSING EX-COMMANDANT OF AUSCHWITZ CONCENTRATION CAMP...AND ONE OF THE WORLD'S MOST WANTED NAZI WAR CRIMINALS!
IN WASHINGTON, D.C., A YOUNG F.B.I. AGENT WAITED TO CONFER WITH HIS SUPERIOR...
MR. JAMES WOO TO SEE YOU, SIR...
GOOD... SHOW HIM RIGHT IN!
JIMMY, WE'VE GOT A TOUGH CASE ON OUR HANDS! I THINK **YOU'RE** THE MAN TO HANDLE IT! OUR INFORMANT IN THE RED CHINESE HIGH COMMAND REPORTS THAT THE COMMUNISTS HAVE SENT A SPECIAL AGENT TO WRECK THE U.S. DEFENSE EFFORT!
WHAT THIS AGENT LOOKS LIKE...OR HOW HE OPERATES, WE DON'T KNOW! THE ONLY INFO WE HAVE IS THAT THE GUY IS SOME SORT OF LEGENDARY FIGURE ...A CHINESE MYSTIC CALLED THE YELLOW CLAW!
THE **YELLOW CLAW**? I'VE HEARD OF HIM! WHEN I WAS A KID, MY PARENTS SPOKE OF HIM! BUT I NEVER BELIEVED HE EXISTED!
7
HE EXISTS, ALL RIGHT! IN FACT, WE BELIEVE HE'S IN THIS COUNTRY RIGHT NOW...SOMEWHERE IN SAN FRANCISCO! JIMMY, YOU'VE GOT TO TRACK HIM DOWN... **BEFORE** HE DOES ANY DAMAGE!
I'LL DO MY BEST, CHIEF! I'LL LEAVE FOR THE COAST ON THE NEXT PLANE...
AND AT THAT MOMENT, IN HIS CURIO SHOP...
SO THE AMERICANS KNOW I AM HERE...AND THIS F.B.I. AGENT, JIMMY WOO IS ON HIS WAY TO FIND ME! VERY GOOD! WE WILL BE WAITING ...EH, FRITZ?
JA, HERR CLAW, VE VILL BE VAITING!
THE END
THIS THEN, WAS THE **BEGINNING**...THE COMING OF **THE YELLOW CLAW!**

WHAT IF? #9 (JUNE 1978), THE FIRST APPEARANCE OF THE 1950s AVENGERS

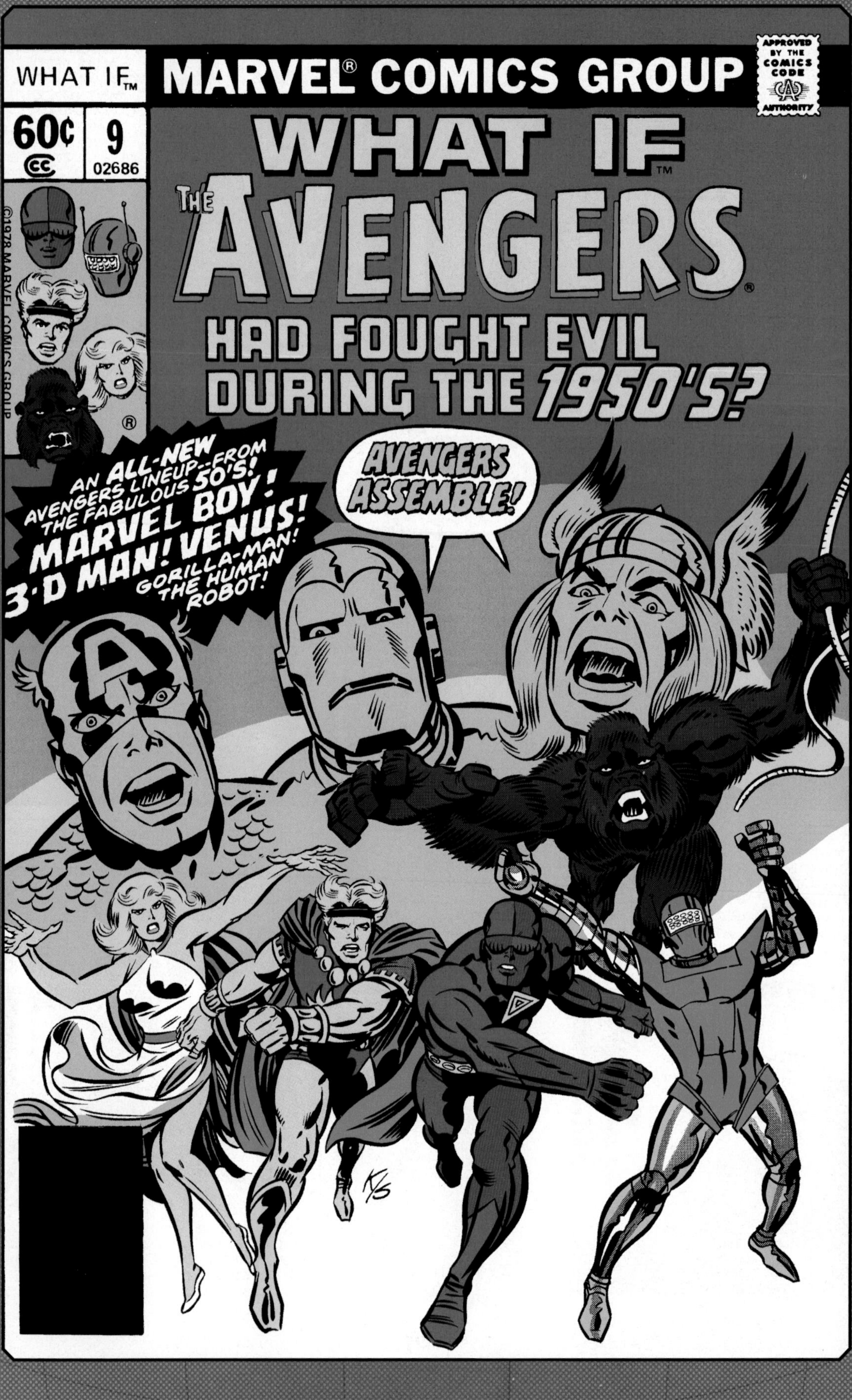
WHAT IF™
MARVEL® COMICS GROUP
APPROVED BY THE COMICS CODE AUTHORITY
60¢
9
02686
©1978 MARVEL COMICS GROUP
WHAT IF™
THE AVENGERS®
HAD FOUGHT EVIL DURING THE 1950'S?
AN ALL-NEW AVENGERS LINEUP--FROM THE FABULOUS 50'S! MARVEL BOY! 3-D MAN! VENUS! GORILLA-MAN! THE HUMAN ROBOT!
AVENGERS ASSEMBLE!

STAN LEE PRESENTS: A STUNNING SAGA OF AN ALTERNATE REALITY!

DON GLUT, SCRIPT ✦ ALAN KUPPERBERG and BILL BLACK, ART | TOM ORZECHOWSKI, lettering; CARL GAFFORD, colors | ROY THOMAS, CONCEPT & EDITING

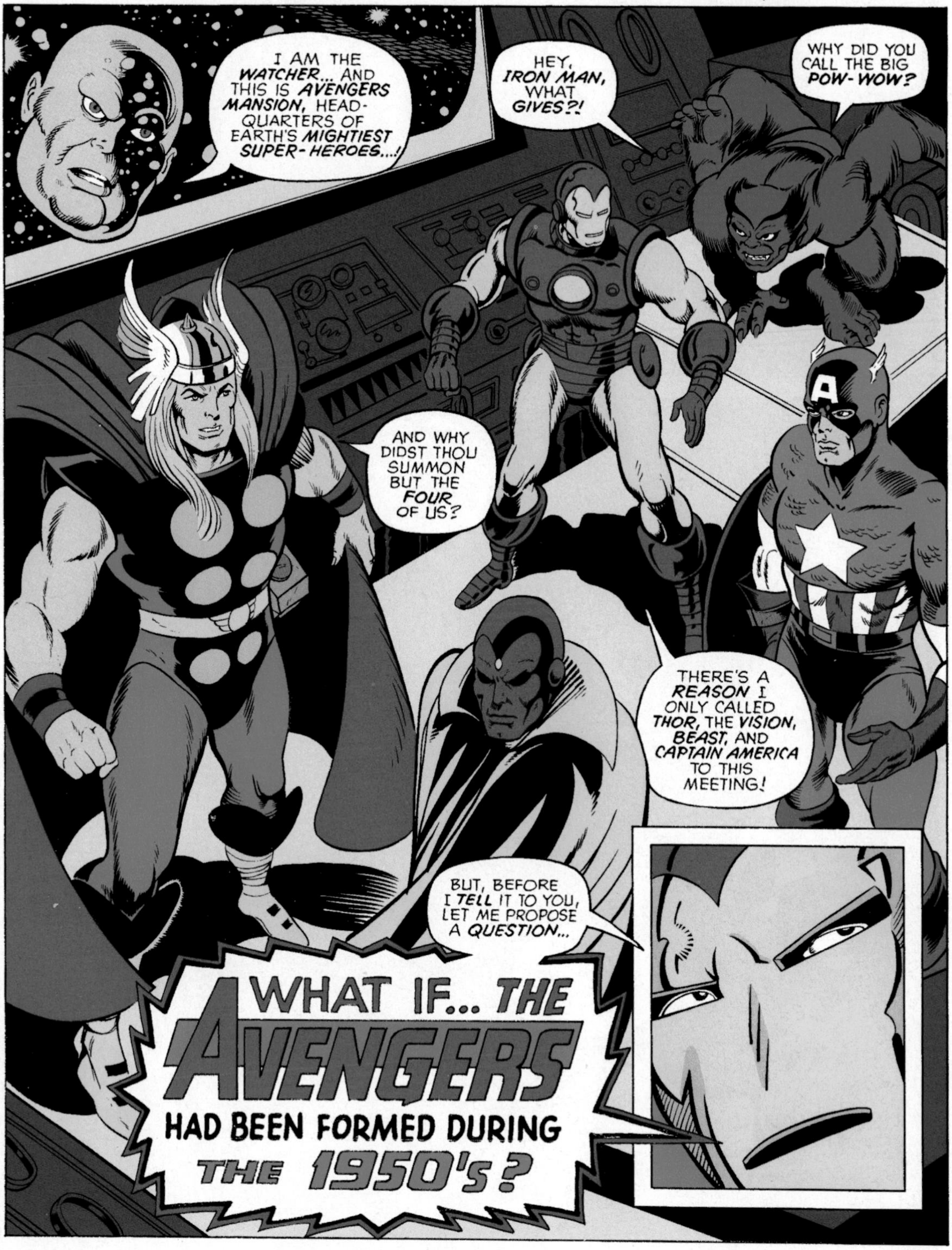

I AM THE WATCHER... AND THIS IS AVENGERS MANSION, HEAD-QUARTERS OF EARTH'S MIGHTIEST SUPER-HEROES...!
HEY, IRON MAN, WHAT GIVES?!
WHY DID YOU CALL THE BIG POW-WOW?
AND WHY DIDST THOU SUMMON BUT THE FOUR OF US?
THERE'S A REASON I ONLY CALLED THOR, THE VISION, BEAST, AND CAPTAIN AMERICA TO THIS MEETING!
BUT, BEFORE I TELL IT TO YOU, LET ME PROPOSE A QUESTION...
WHAT IF... THE AVENGERS HAD BEEN FORMED DURING THE 1950's?

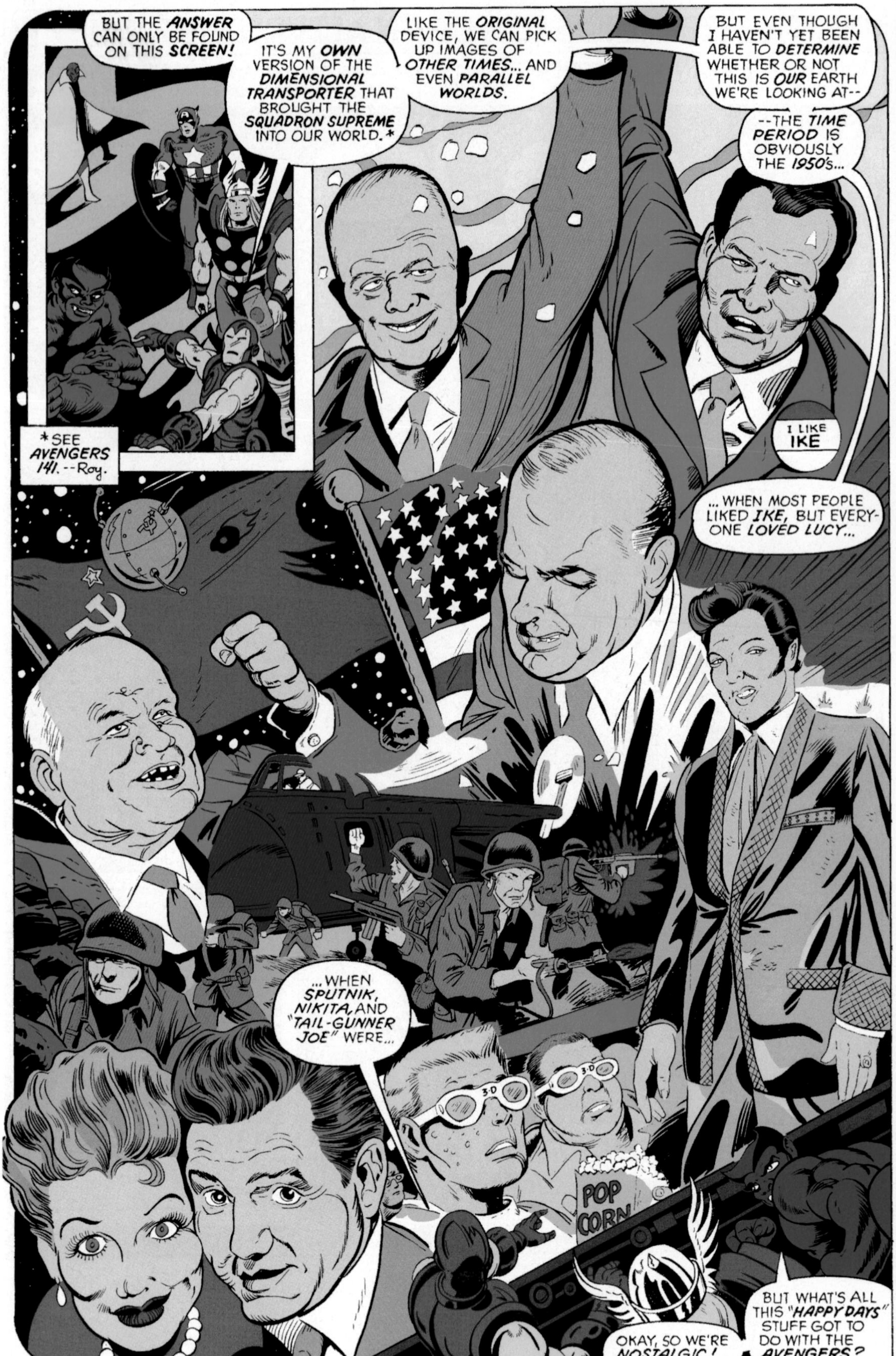
BUT THE ANSWER CAN ONLY BE FOUND ON THIS SCREEN!
IT'S MY OWN VERSION OF THE DIMENSIONAL TRANSPORTER THAT BROUGHT THE SQUADRON SUPREME INTO OUR WORLD.*
*SEE AVENGERS 141. --Roy.
LIKE THE ORIGINAL DEVICE, WE CAN PICK UP IMAGES OF OTHER TIMES... AND EVEN PARALLEL WORLDS.
BUT EVEN THOUGH I HAVEN'T YET BEEN ABLE TO DETERMINE WHETHER OR NOT THIS IS OUR EARTH WE'RE LOOKING AT--
--THE TIME PERIOD IS OBVIOUSLY THE 1950's...
I LIKE IKE
...WHEN MOST PEOPLE LIKED IKE, BUT EVERY-ONE LOVED LUCY...
...WHEN SPUTNIK, NIKITA, AND "TAIL-GUNNER JOE" WERE...
3-D
3-D
POP CORN
OKAY, SO WE'RE NOSTALGIC!
BUT WHAT'S ALL THIS "HAPPY DAYS" STUFF GOT TO DO WITH THE AVENGERS?

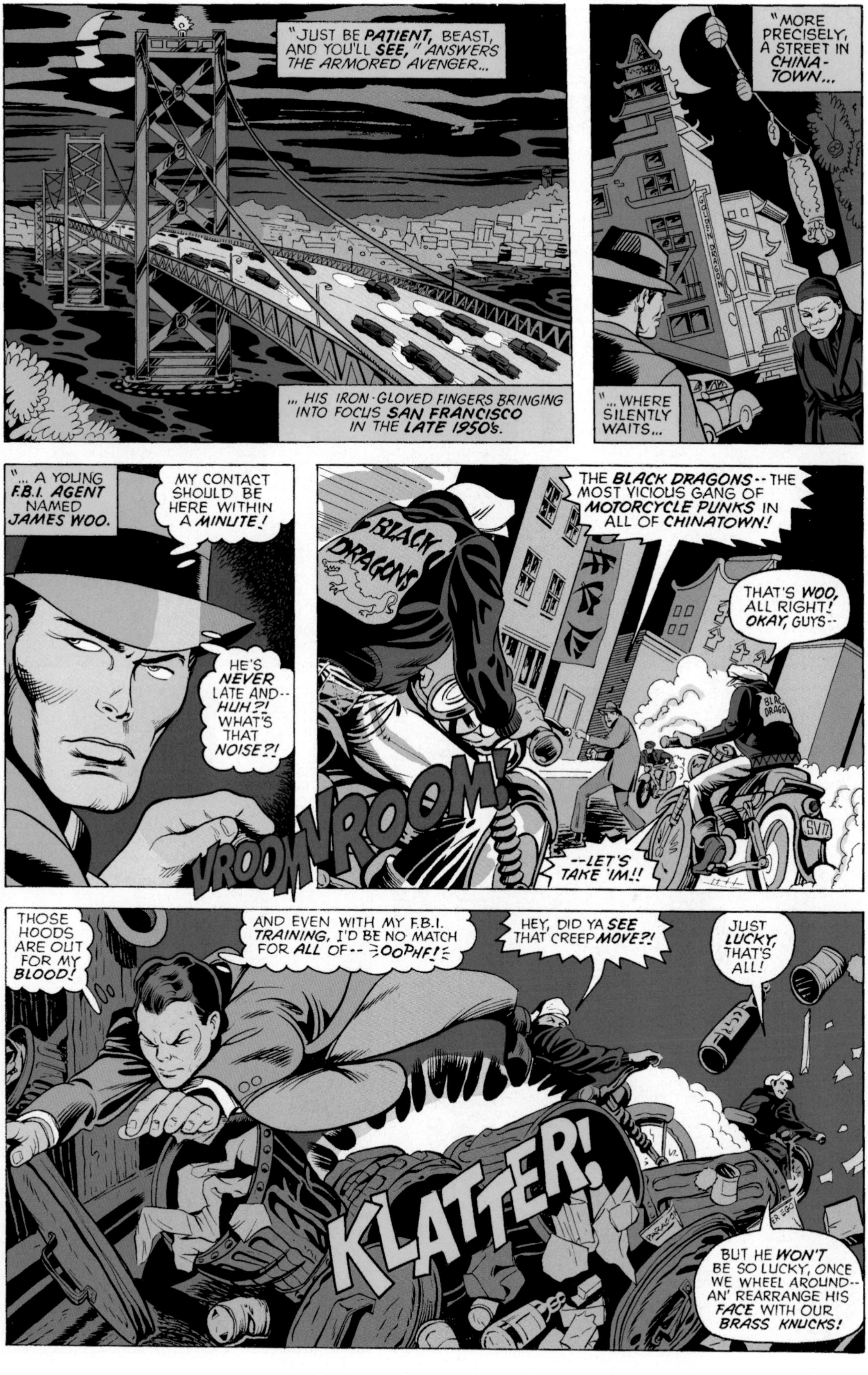
"JUST BE PATIENT, BEAST, AND YOU'LL SEE," ANSWERS THE ARMORED AVENGER...
... HIS IRON-GLOVED FINGERS BRINGING INTO FOCUS SAN FRANCISCO IN THE LATE 1950's.
"MORE PRECISELY, A STREET IN CHINA-TOWN...
GOLDEN DRAGON
"... WHERE SILENTLY WAITS...
"... A YOUNG F.B.I. AGENT NAMED JAMES WOO.
MY CONTACT SHOULD BE HERE WITHIN A MINUTE!
HE'S NEVER LATE AND-- HUH?! WHAT'S THAT NOISE?!
VROOM VROOM!
BLACK DRAGONS
THE BLACK DRAGONS-- THE MOST VICIOUS GANG OF MOTORCYCLE PUNKS IN ALL OF CHINATOWN!
THAT'S WOO, ALL RIGHT! OKAY, GUYS--
--LET'S TAKE 'IM!!
SV17
THOSE HOODS ARE OUT FOR MY BLOOD!
AND EVEN WITH MY F.B.I. TRAINING, I'D BE NO MATCH FOR ALL OF-- OOPHF!
HEY, DID YA SEE THAT CREEP MOVE?!
JUST LUCKY, THAT'S ALL!
KLATTER!
BUT HE WON'T BE SO LUCKY, ONCE WE WHEEL AROUND-- AN' REARRANGE HIS FACE WITH OUR BRASS KNUCKS!

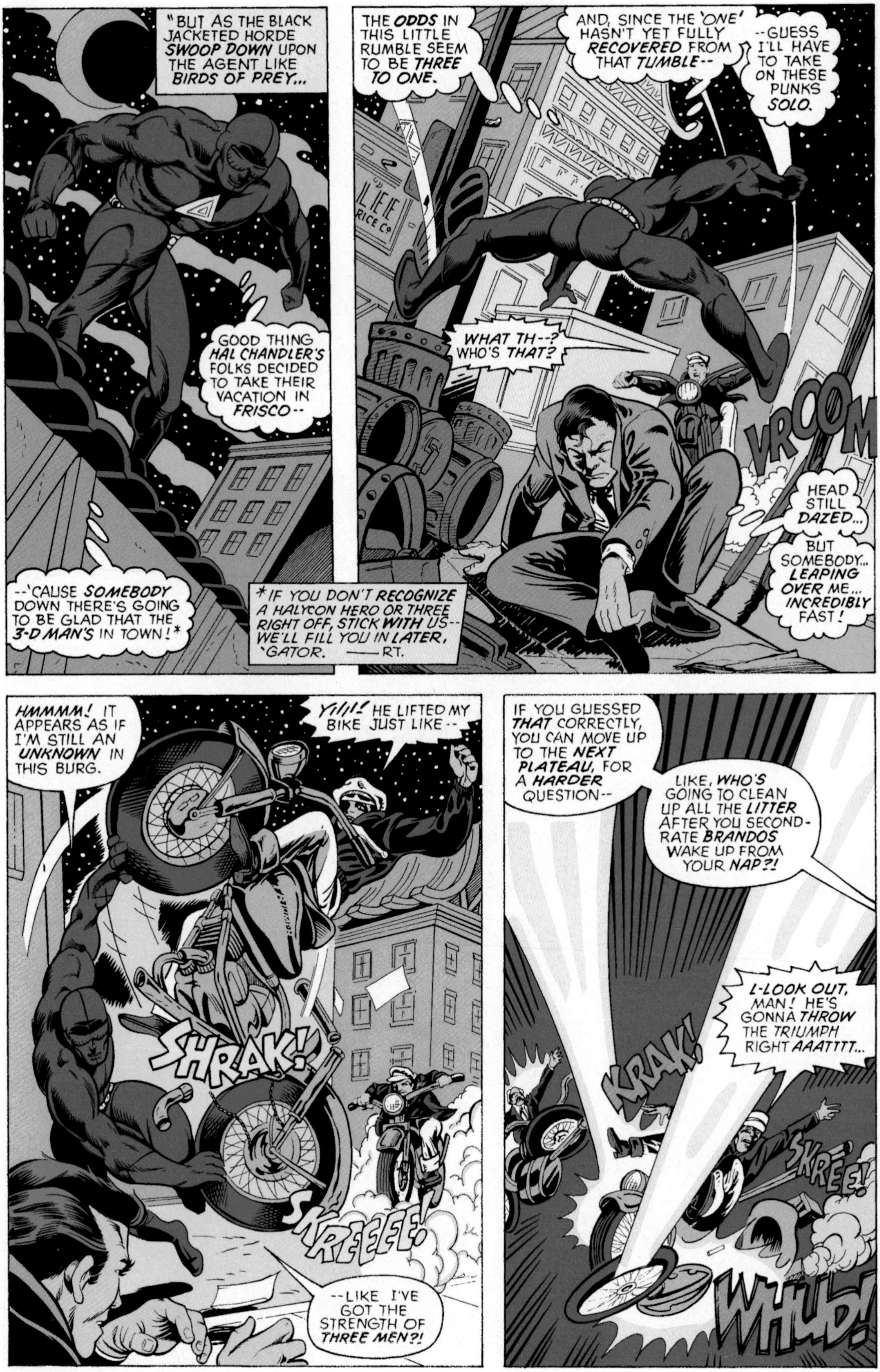
"BUT AS THE BLACK JACKETED HORDE SWOOP DOWN UPON THE AGENT LIKE BIRDS OF PREY...
GOOD THING HAL CHANDLER'S FOLKS DECIDED TO TAKE THEIR VACATION IN FRISCO--
--'CAUSE SOMEBODY DOWN THERE'S GOING TO BE GLAD THAT THE 3-D MAN'S IN TOWN!*
*IF YOU DON'T RECOGNIZE A HALYCON HERO OR THREE RIGHT OFF, STICK WITH US-- WE'LL FILL YOU IN LATER, 'GATOR. ——RT.
THE ODDS IN THIS LITTLE RUMBLE SEEM TO BE THREE TO ONE.
AND, SINCE THE 'ONE' HASN'T YET FULLY RECOVERED FROM THAT TUMBLE--
--GUESS I'LL HAVE TO TAKE ON THESE PUNKS SOLO.
WHAT TH--? WHO'S THAT?
VROOM
HEAD STILL DAZED...
BUT SOMEBODY... LEAPING OVER ME... INCREDIBLY FAST!
HMMMM! IT APPEARS AS IF I'M STILL AN UNKNOWN IN THIS BURG.
YIII! HE LIFTED MY BIKE JUST LIKE--
SHRAK!
SKREEEEE!
--LIKE I'VE GOT THE STRENGTH OF THREE MEN?!
IF YOU GUESSED THAT CORRECTLY, YOU CAN MOVE UP TO THE NEXT PLATEAU, FOR A HARDER QUESTION--
LIKE, WHO'S GOING TO CLEAN UP ALL THE LITTER AFTER YOU SECOND-RATE BRANDOS WAKE UP FROM YOUR NAP?!
L-LOOK OUT, MAN! HE'S GONNA THROW THE TRIUMPH RIGHT AAATTTT...
KRAK!
SKREEE!
WHUD!

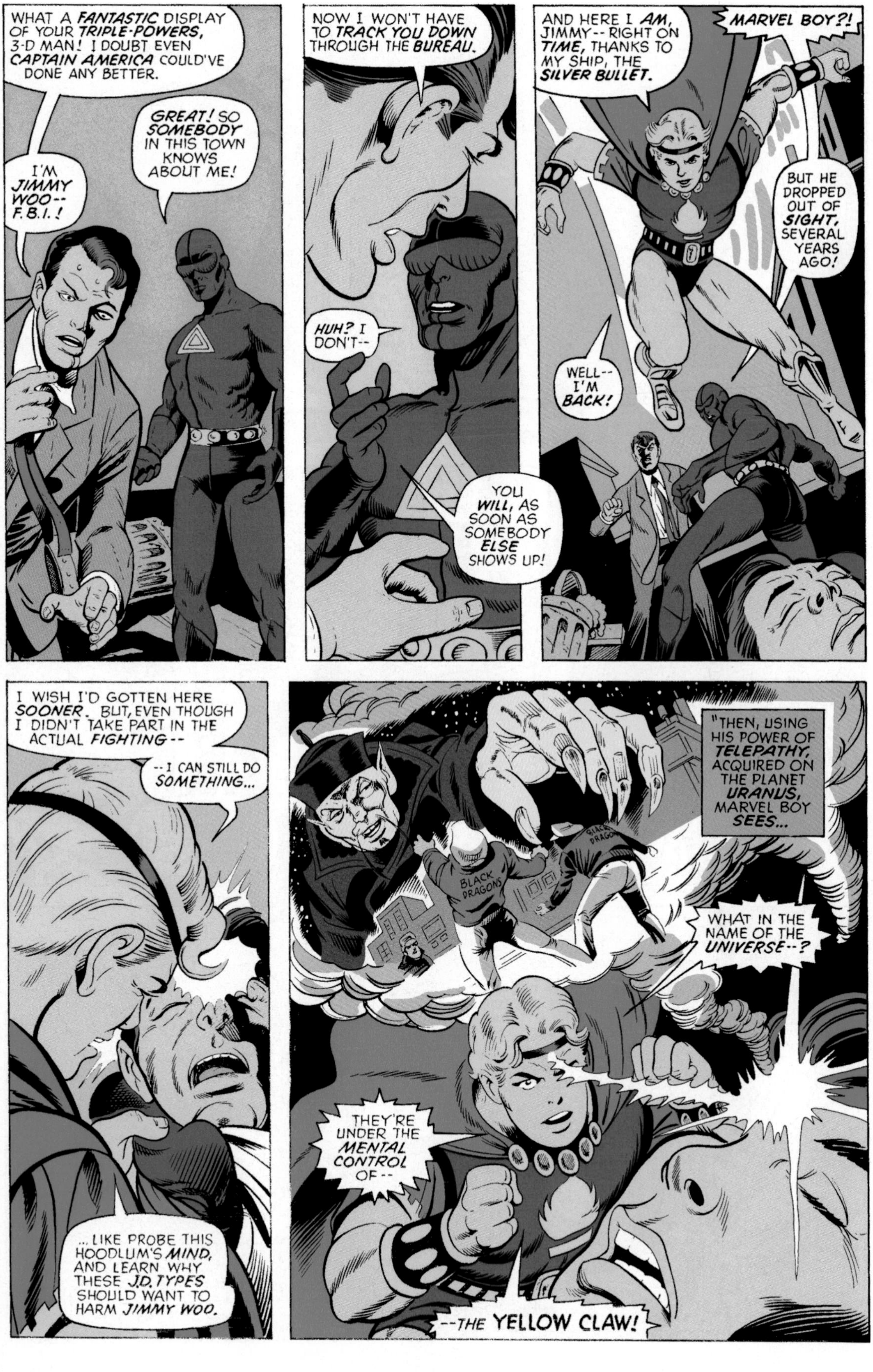
WHAT A FANTASTIC DISPLAY OF YOUR TRIPLE-POWERS, 3-D MAN! I DOUBT EVEN CAPTAIN AMERICA COULD'VE DONE ANY BETTER.
GREAT! SO SOMEBODY IN THIS TOWN KNOWS ABOUT ME!
I'M JIMMY WOO-- F.B.I.!
NOW I WON'T HAVE TO TRACK YOU DOWN THROUGH THE BUREAU.
HUH? I DON'T--
YOU WILL, AS SOON AS SOMEBODY ELSE SHOWS UP!
AND HERE I AM, JIMMY-- RIGHT ON TIME, THANKS TO MY SHIP, THE SILVER BULLET.
MARVEL BOY?!
BUT HE DROPPED OUT OF SIGHT, SEVERAL YEARS AGO!
WELL-- I'M BACK!
I WISH I'D GOTTEN HERE SOONER. BUT, EVEN THOUGH I DIDN'T TAKE PART IN THE ACTUAL FIGHTING--
--I CAN STILL DO SOMETHING...
...LIKE PROBE THIS HOODLUM'S MIND, AND LEARN WHY THESE J.D. TYPES SHOULD WANT TO HARM JIMMY WOO.
"THEN, USING HIS POWER OF TELEPATHY, ACQUIRED ON THE PLANET URANUS, MARVEL BOY SEES...
BLACK DRAGONS
BLACK DRAGONS
WHAT IN THE NAME OF THE UNIVERSE--?
THEY'RE UNDER THE MENTAL CONTROL OF--
--THE YELLOW CLAW!

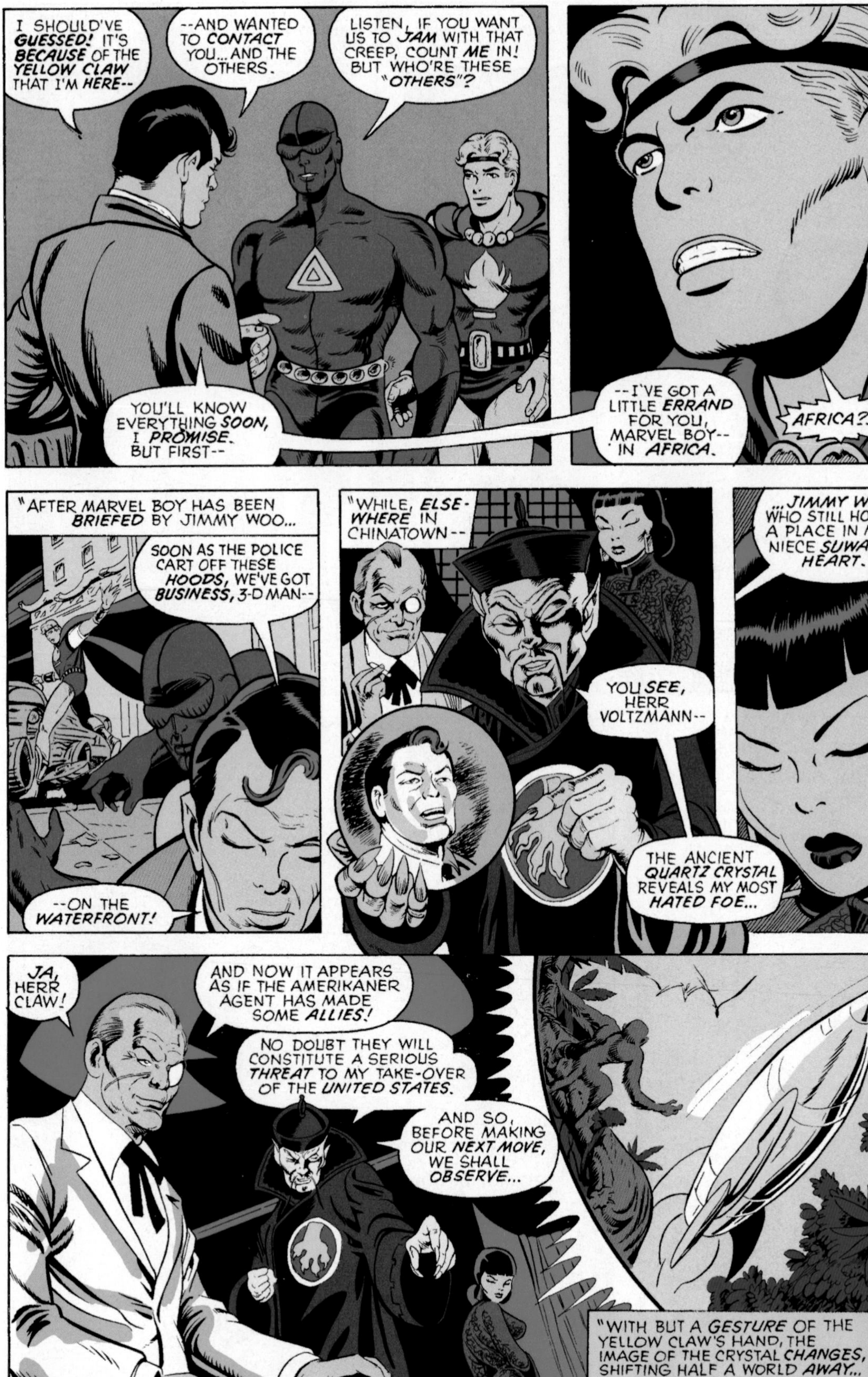
I SHOULD'VE GUESSED! IT'S BECAUSE OF THE YELLOW CLAW THAT I'M HERE--
--AND WANTED TO CONTACT YOU... AND THE OTHERS.
LISTEN, IF YOU WANT US TO JAM WITH THAT CREEP, COUNT ME IN! BUT WHO'RE THESE "OTHERS"?
YOU'LL KNOW EVERYTHING SOON, I PROMISE. BUT FIRST--
--I'VE GOT A LITTLE ERRAND FOR YOU, MARVEL BOY-- IN AFRICA.
AFRICA?!!
"AFTER MARVEL BOY HAS BEEN BRIEFED BY JIMMY WOO...
SOON AS THE POLICE CART OFF THESE HOODS, WE'VE GOT BUSINESS, 3-D MAN--
--ON THE WATERFRONT!
"WHILE, ELSEWHERE IN CHINATOWN--
YOU SEE, HERR VOLTZMANN--
THE ANCIENT QUARTZ CRYSTAL REVEALS MY MOST HATED FOE...
...JIMMY WOO, WHO STILL HOLDS A PLACE IN MY NIECE SUWAN'S HEART.
JA, HERR CLAW!
AND NOW IT APPEARS AS IF THE AMERIKANER AGENT HAS MADE SOME ALLIES!
NO DOUBT THEY WILL CONSTITUTE A SERIOUS THREAT TO MY TAKE-OVER OF THE UNITED STATES.
AND SO, BEFORE MAKING OUR NEXT MOVE, WE SHALL OBSERVE...
"WITH BUT A GESTURE OF THE YELLOW CLAW'S HAND, THE IMAGE OF THE CRYSTAL CHANGES, SHIFTING HALF A WORLD AWAY...

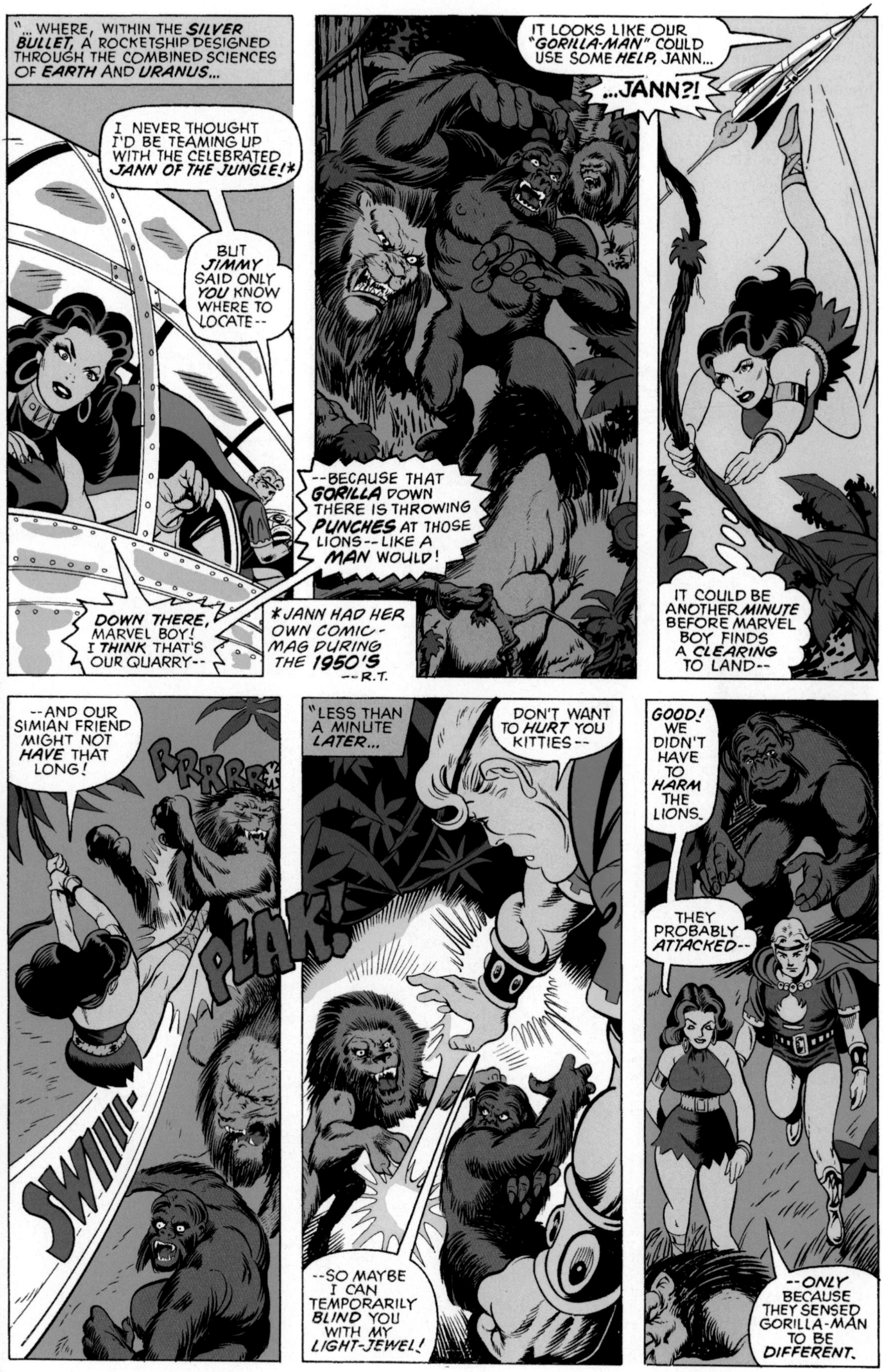
"... WHERE, WITHIN THE SILVER BULLET, A ROCKETSHIP DESIGNED THROUGH THE COMBINED SCIENCES OF EARTH AND URANUS...
I NEVER THOUGHT I'D BE TEAMING UP WITH THE CELEBRATED JANN OF THE JUNGLE!*
BUT JIMMY SAID ONLY YOU KNOW WHERE TO LOCATE--
DOWN THERE, MARVEL BOY! I THINK THAT'S OUR QUARRY--
--BECAUSE THAT GORILLA DOWN THERE IS THROWING PUNCHES AT THOSE LIONS--LIKE A MAN WOULD!
*JANN HAD HER OWN COMIC-MAG DURING THE 1950'S --R.T.
IT LOOKS LIKE OUR "GORILLA-MAN" COULD USE SOME HELP, JANN...
...JANN?!
IT COULD BE ANOTHER MINUTE BEFORE MARVEL BOY FINDS A CLEARING TO LAND--
--AND OUR SIMIAN FRIEND MIGHT NOT HAVE THAT LONG!
RRRRR
PLAK!
SWIII
"LESS THAN A MINUTE LATER...
DON'T WANT TO HURT YOU KITTIES--
--SO MAYBE I CAN TEMPORARILY BLIND YOU WITH MY LIGHT-JEWEL!
GOOD! WE DIDN'T HAVE TO HARM THE LIONS.
THEY PROBABLY ATTACKED--
--ONLY BECAUSE THEY SENSED GORILLA-MAN TO BE DIFFERENT.

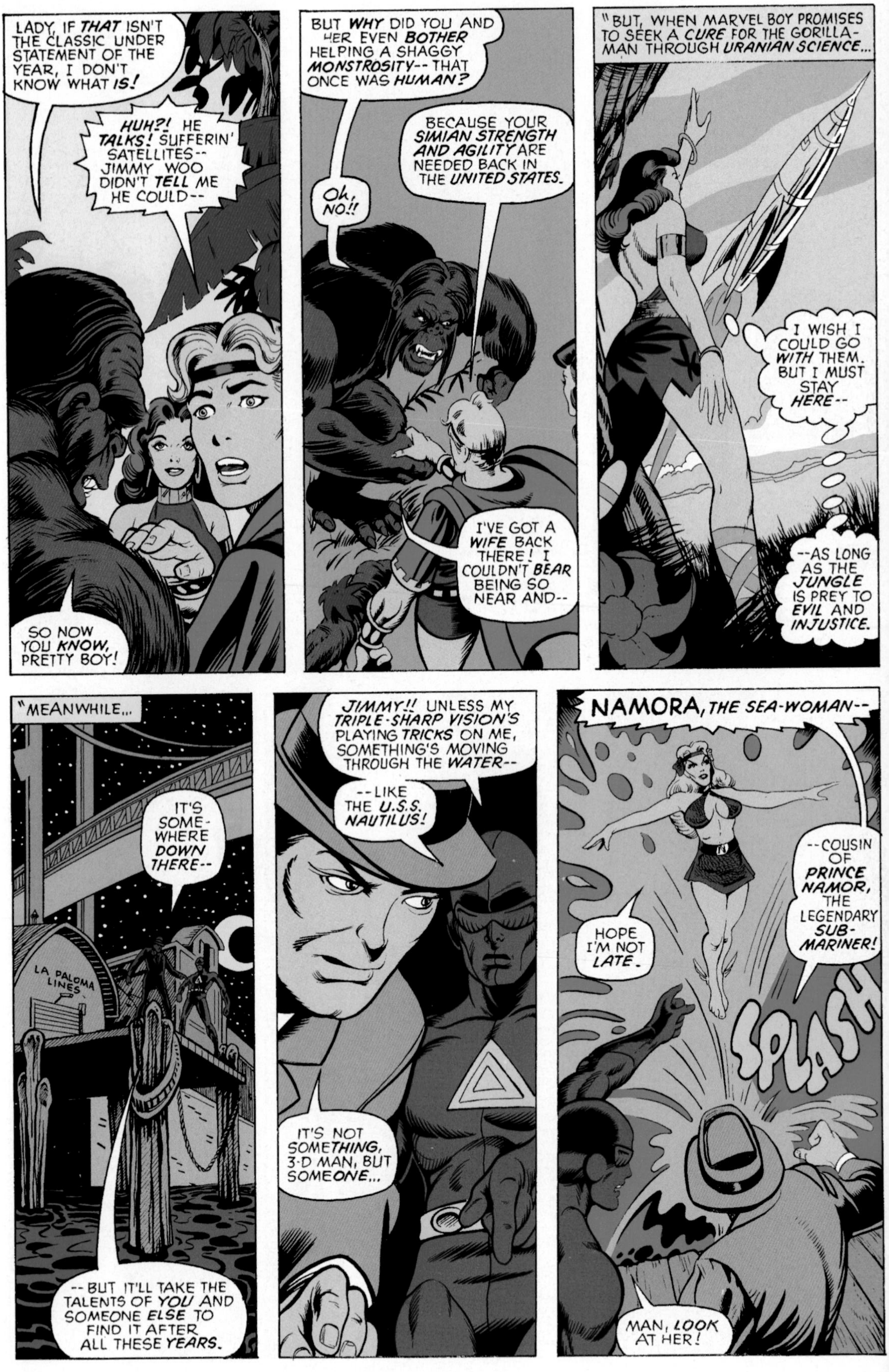
LADY, IF THAT ISN'T THE CLASSIC UNDER STATEMENT OF THE YEAR, I DON'T KNOW WHAT IS!
HUH?! HE TALKS! SUFFERIN' SATELLITES-- JIMMY WOO DIDN'T TELL ME HE COULD--
SO NOW YOU KNOW, PRETTY BOY!
BUT WHY DID YOU AND HER EVEN BOTHER HELPING A SHAGGY MONSTROSITY-- THAT ONCE WAS HUMAN?
BECAUSE YOUR SIMIAN STRENGTH AND AGILITY ARE NEEDED BACK IN THE UNITED STATES.
Oh, NO!!
I'VE GOT A WIFE BACK THERE! I COULDN'T BEAR BEING SO NEAR AND--
"BUT, WHEN MARVEL BOY PROMISES TO SEEK A CURE FOR THE GORILLA-MAN THROUGH URANIAN SCIENCE...
I WISH I COULD GO WITH THEM. BUT I MUST STAY HERE--
--AS LONG AS THE JUNGLE IS PREY TO EVIL AND INJUSTICE.
"MEANWHILE...
IT'S SOMEWHERE DOWN THERE--
LA PALOMA LINES
--BUT IT'LL TAKE THE TALENTS OF YOU AND SOMEONE ELSE TO FIND IT AFTER ALL THESE YEARS.
JIMMY!! UNLESS MY TRIPLE-SHARP VISION'S PLAYING TRICKS ON ME, SOMETHING'S MOVING THROUGH THE WATER--
--LIKE THE U.S.S. NAUTILUS!
IT'S NOT SOMETHING, 3-D MAN, BUT SOMEONE...
NAMORA, THE SEA-WOMAN--
--COUSIN OF PRINCE NAMOR, THE LEGENDARY SUB-MARINER!
HOPE I'M NOT LATE.
SPLASH
MAN, LOOK AT HER!

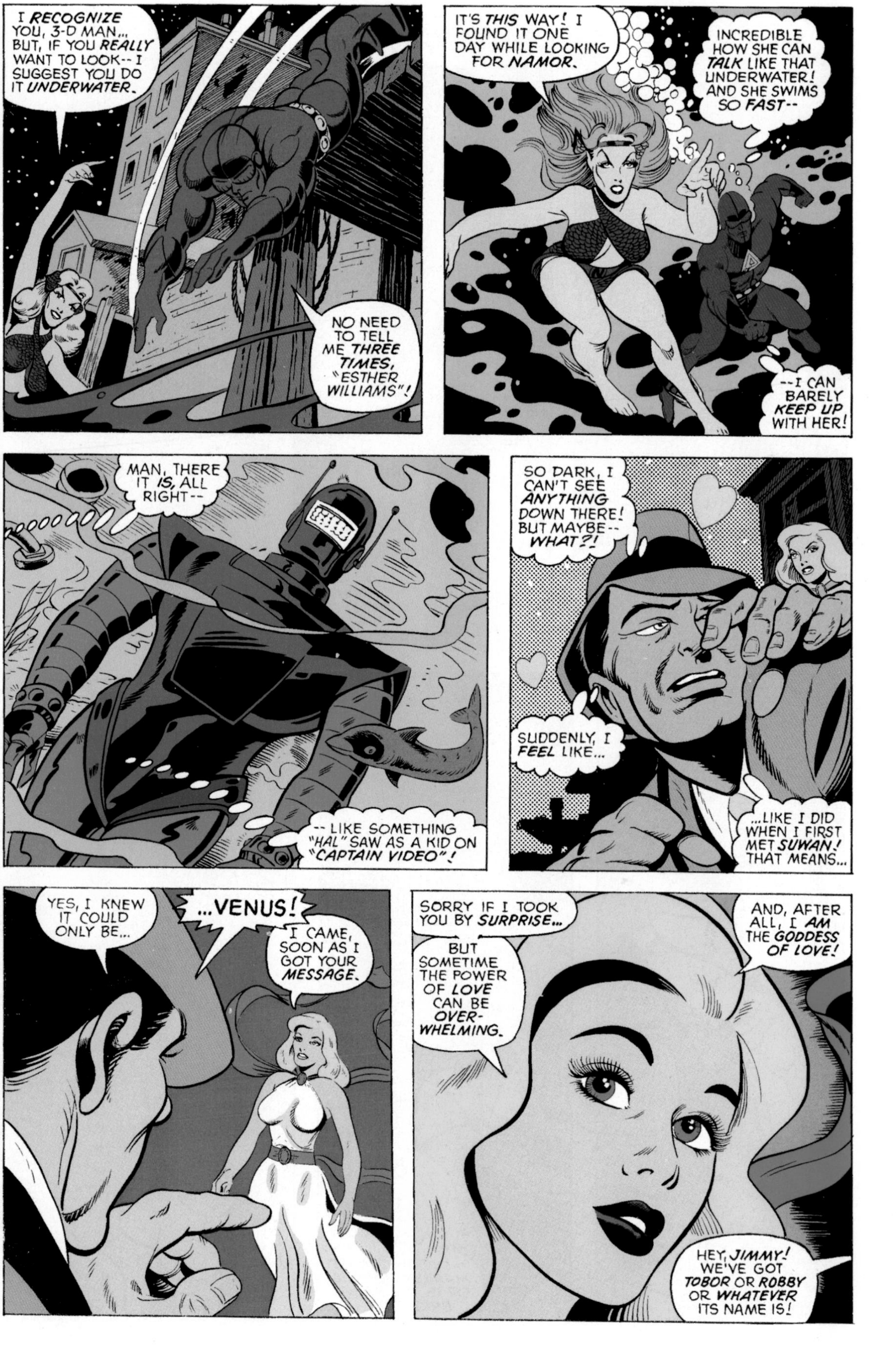
I RECOGNIZE YOU, 3-D MAN... BUT, IF YOU REALLY WANT TO LOOK-- I SUGGEST YOU DO IT UNDERWATER.
NO NEED TO TELL ME THREE TIMES, "ESTHER WILLIAMS"!
IT'S THIS WAY! I FOUND IT ONE DAY WHILE LOOKING FOR NAMOR.
INCREDIBLE HOW SHE CAN TALK LIKE THAT UNDERWATER! AND SHE SWIMS SO FAST--
--I CAN BARELY KEEP UP WITH HER!
MAN, THERE IT IS, ALL RIGHT--
-- LIKE SOMETHING "HAL" SAW AS A KID ON "CAPTAIN VIDEO"!
SO DARK, I CAN'T SEE ANYTHING DOWN THERE! BUT MAYBE-- WHAT?!
SUDDENLY, I FEEL LIKE...
...LIKE I DID WHEN I FIRST MET SUWAN! THAT MEANS...
YES, I KNEW IT COULD ONLY BE...
...VENUS!
I CAME, SOON AS I GOT YOUR MESSAGE.
SORRY IF I TOOK YOU BY SURPRISE...
BUT SOMETIME THE POWER OF LOVE CAN BE OVER-WHELMING.
AND, AFTER ALL, I AM THE GODDESS OF LOVE!
HEY, JIMMY! WE'VE GOT TOBOR OR ROBBY OR WHATEVER ITS NAME IS!

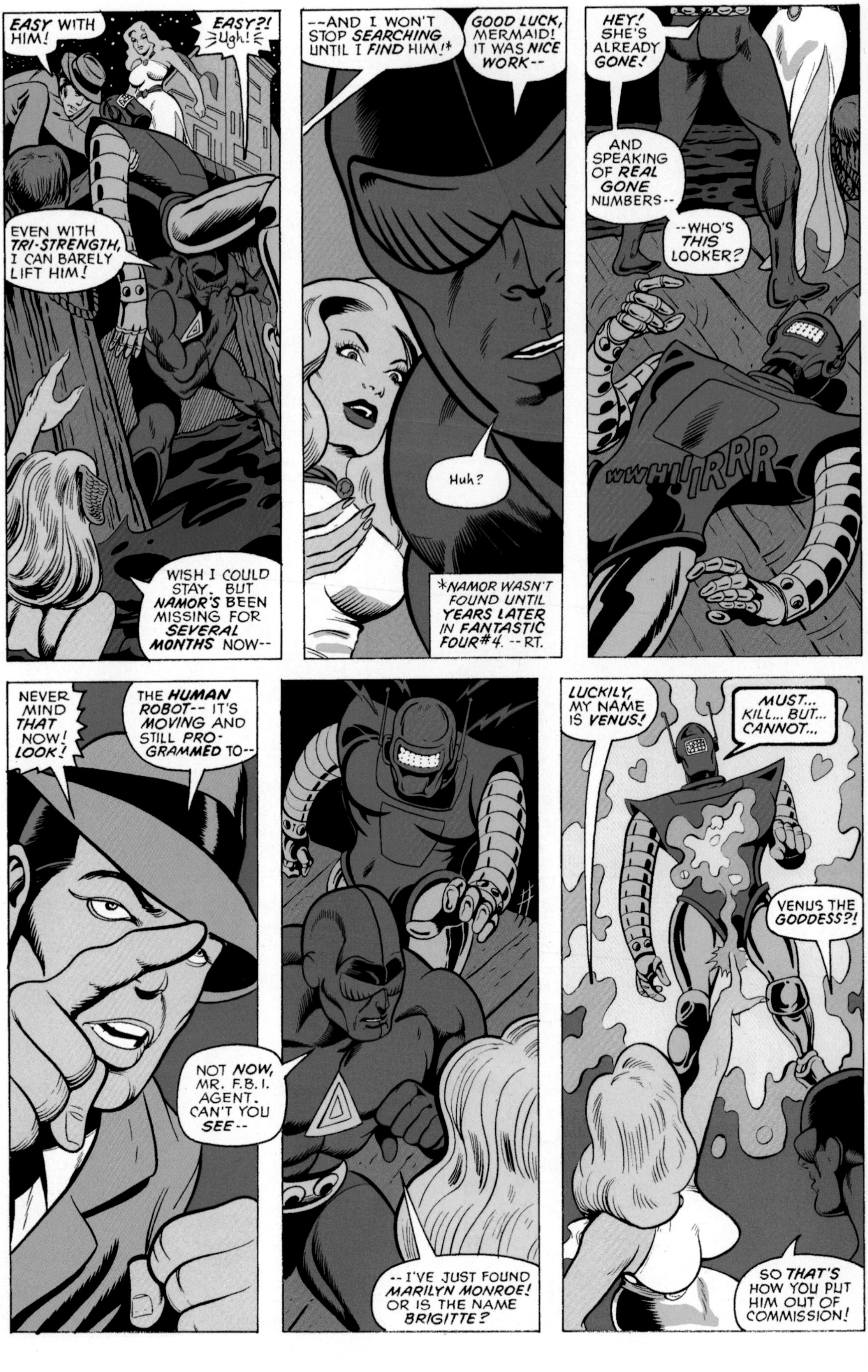
EASY WITH HIM!
EASY?! Ugh!
EVEN WITH TRI-STRENGTH, I CAN BARELY LIFT HIM!
WISH I COULD STAY. BUT NAMOR'S BEEN MISSING FOR SEVERAL MONTHS NOW--
--AND I WON'T STOP SEARCHING UNTIL I FIND HIM!*
GOOD LUCK, MERMAID! IT WAS NICE WORK--
Huh?
*NAMOR WASN'T FOUND UNTIL YEARS LATER IN FANTASTIC FOUR #4. --RT.
HEY! SHE'S ALREADY GONE!
AND SPEAKING OF REAL GONE NUMBERS--
--WHO'S THIS LOOKER?
WWHIIIRRR
NEVER MIND THAT NOW! LOOK!
THE HUMAN ROBOT-- IT'S MOVING AND STILL PRO-GRAMMED TO--
NOT NOW, MR. F.B.I. AGENT. CAN'T YOU SEE--
--I'VE JUST FOUND MARILYN MONROE! OR IS THE NAME BRIGITTE?
LUCKILY, MY NAME IS VENUS!
MUST... KILL... BUT... CANNOT...
VENUS THE GODDESS?!
SO THAT'S HOW YOU PUT HIM OUT OF COMMISSION!

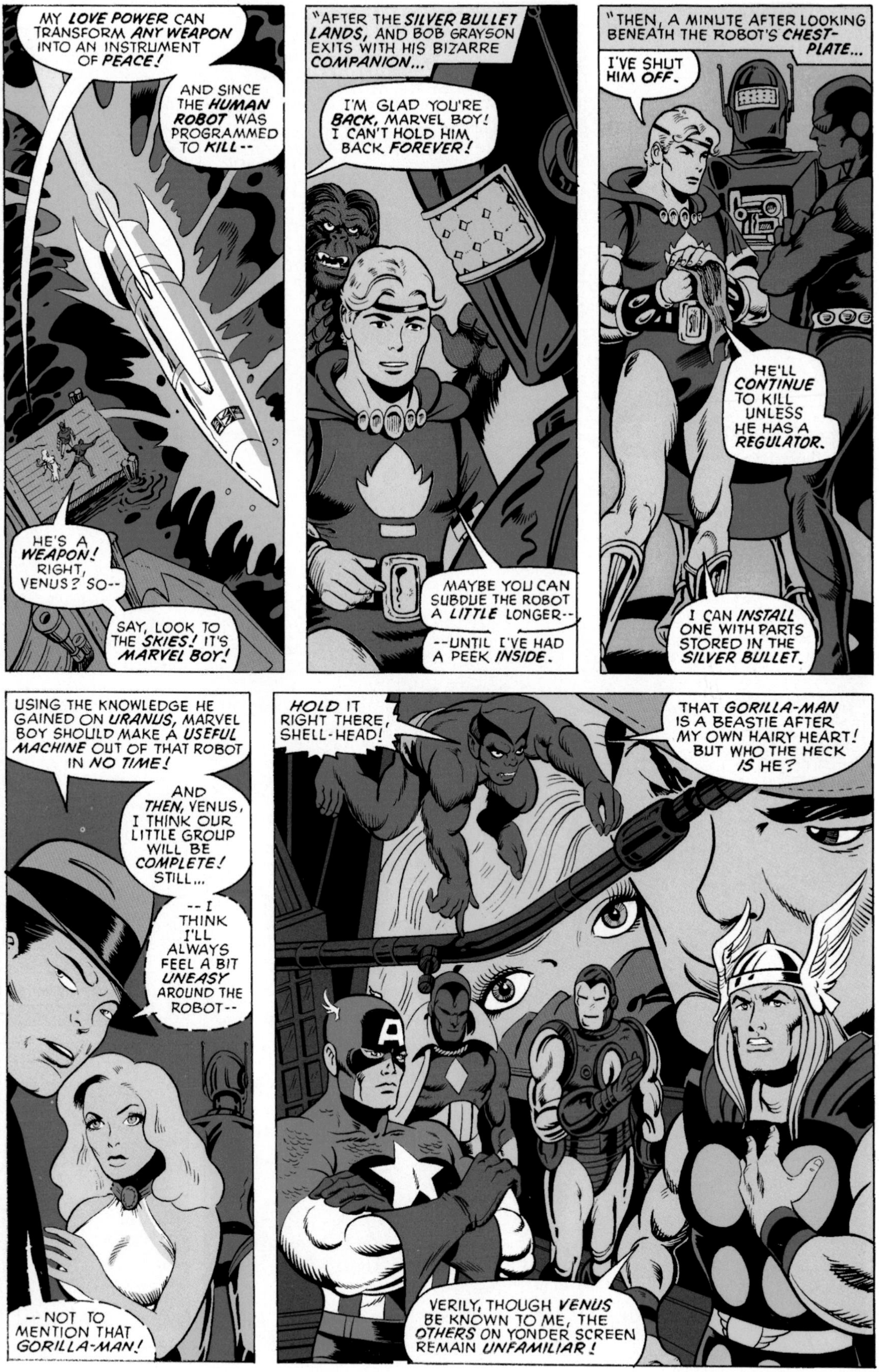
MY LOVE POWER CAN TRANSFORM ANY WEAPON INTO AN INSTRUMENT OF PEACE!
AND SINCE THE HUMAN ROBOT WAS PROGRAMMED TO KILL--
HE'S A WEAPON! RIGHT, VENUS? SO--
SAY, LOOK TO THE SKIES! IT'S MARVEL BOY!
"AFTER THE SILVER BULLET LANDS, AND BOB GRAYSON EXITS WITH HIS BIZARRE COMPANION...
I'M GLAD YOU'RE BACK, MARVEL BOY! I CAN'T HOLD HIM BACK FOREVER!
MAYBE YOU CAN SUBDUE THE ROBOT A LITTLE LONGER--
--UNTIL I'VE HAD A PEEK INSIDE.
"THEN, A MINUTE AFTER LOOKING BENEATH THE ROBOT'S CHEST-PLATE...
I'VE SHUT HIM OFF.
HE'LL CONTINUE TO KILL UNLESS HE HAS A REGULATOR.
I CAN INSTALL ONE WITH PARTS STORED IN THE SILVER BULLET.
USING THE KNOWLEDGE HE GAINED ON URANUS, MARVEL BOY SHOULD MAKE A USEFUL MACHINE OUT OF THAT ROBOT IN NO TIME!
AND THEN, VENUS, I THINK OUR LITTLE GROUP WILL BE COMPLETE! STILL...
--I THINK I'LL ALWAYS FEEL A BIT UNEASY AROUND THE ROBOT--
--NOT TO MENTION THAT GORILLA-MAN!
HOLD IT RIGHT THERE, SHELL-HEAD!
THAT GORILLA-MAN IS A BEASTIE AFTER MY OWN HAIRY HEART! BUT WHO THE HECK IS HE?
VERILY, THOUGH VENUS BE KNOWN TO ME, THE OTHERS ON YONDER SCREEN REMAIN UNFAMILIAR!

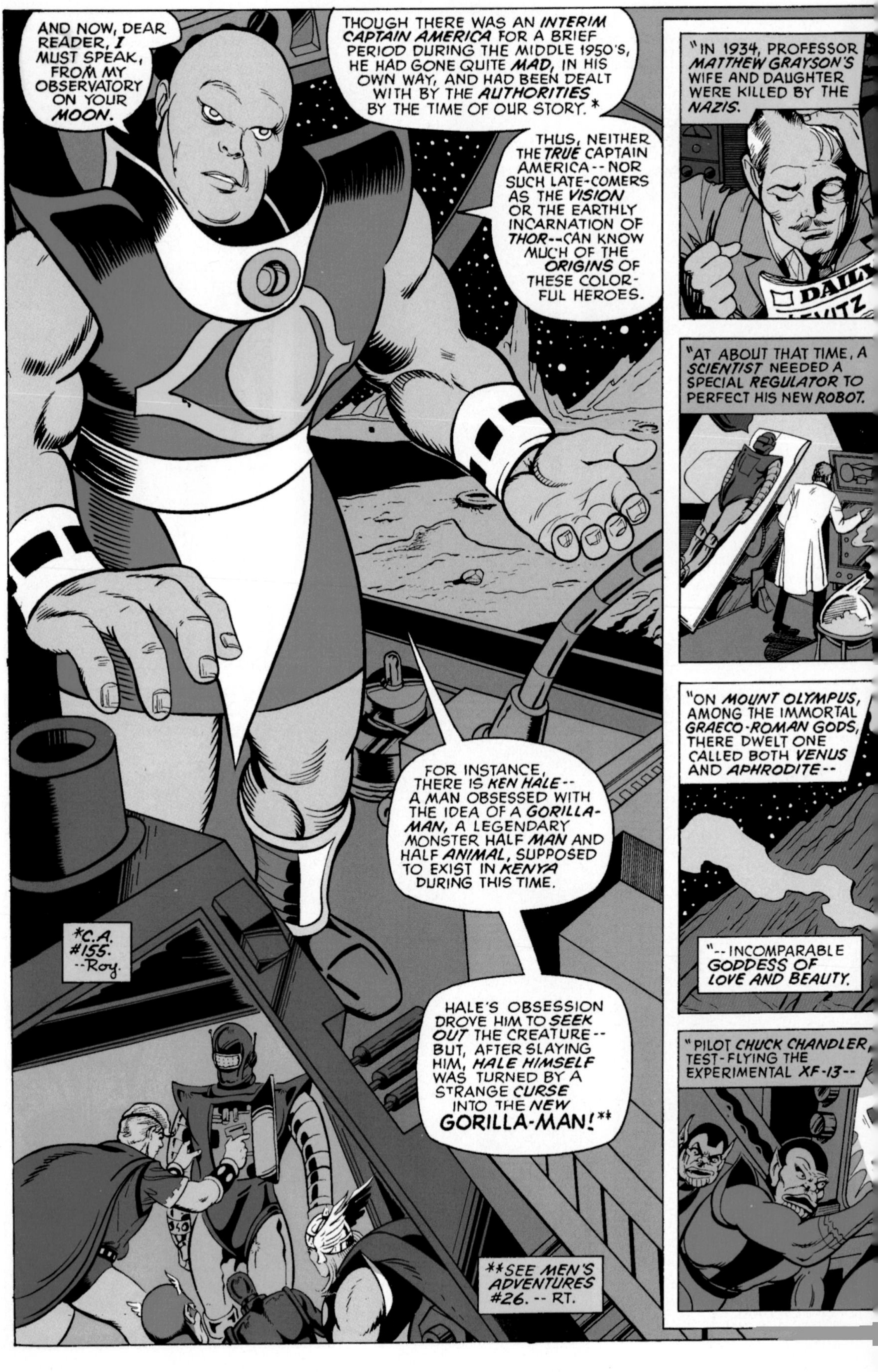
AND NOW, DEAR READER, I MUST SPEAK, FROM MY OBSERVATORY ON YOUR MOON.
THOUGH THERE WAS AN INTERIM CAPTAIN AMERICA FOR A BRIEF PERIOD DURING THE MIDDLE 1950'S, HE HAD GONE QUITE MAD, IN HIS OWN WAY, AND HAD BEEN DEALT WITH BY THE AUTHORITIES BY THE TIME OF OUR STORY.*
THUS, NEITHER THE TRUE CAPTAIN AMERICA -- NOR SUCH LATE-COMERS AS THE VISION OR THE EARTHLY INCARNATION OF THOR--CAN KNOW MUCH OF THE ORIGINS OF THESE COLORFUL HEROES.
FOR INSTANCE, THERE IS KEN HALE -- A MAN OBSESSED WITH THE IDEA OF A GORILLA-MAN, A LEGENDARY MONSTER HALF MAN AND HALF ANIMAL, SUPPOSED TO EXIST IN KENYA DURING THIS TIME.
*C.A. #155. --Roy.
HALE'S OBSESSION DROVE HIM TO SEEK OUT THE CREATURE -- BUT, AFTER SLAYING HIM, HALE HIMSELF WAS TURNED BY A STRANGE CURSE INTO THE NEW GORILLA-MAN!**
**SEE MEN'S ADVENTURES #26. -- RT.
"IN 1934, PROFESSOR MATTHEW GRAYSON'S WIFE AND DAUGHTER WERE KILLED BY THE NAZIS.
DAILY
"AT ABOUT THAT TIME, A SCIENTIST NEEDED A SPECIAL REGULATOR TO PERFECT HIS NEW ROBOT.
"ON MOUNT OLYMPUS, AMONG THE IMMORTAL GRAECO-ROMAN GODS, THERE DWELT ONE CALLED BOTH VENUS AND APHRODITE --
"-- INCOMPARABLE GODDESS OF LOVE AND BEAUTY.
"PILOT CHUCK CHANDLER, TEST-FLYING THE EXPERIMENTAL XF-13 --

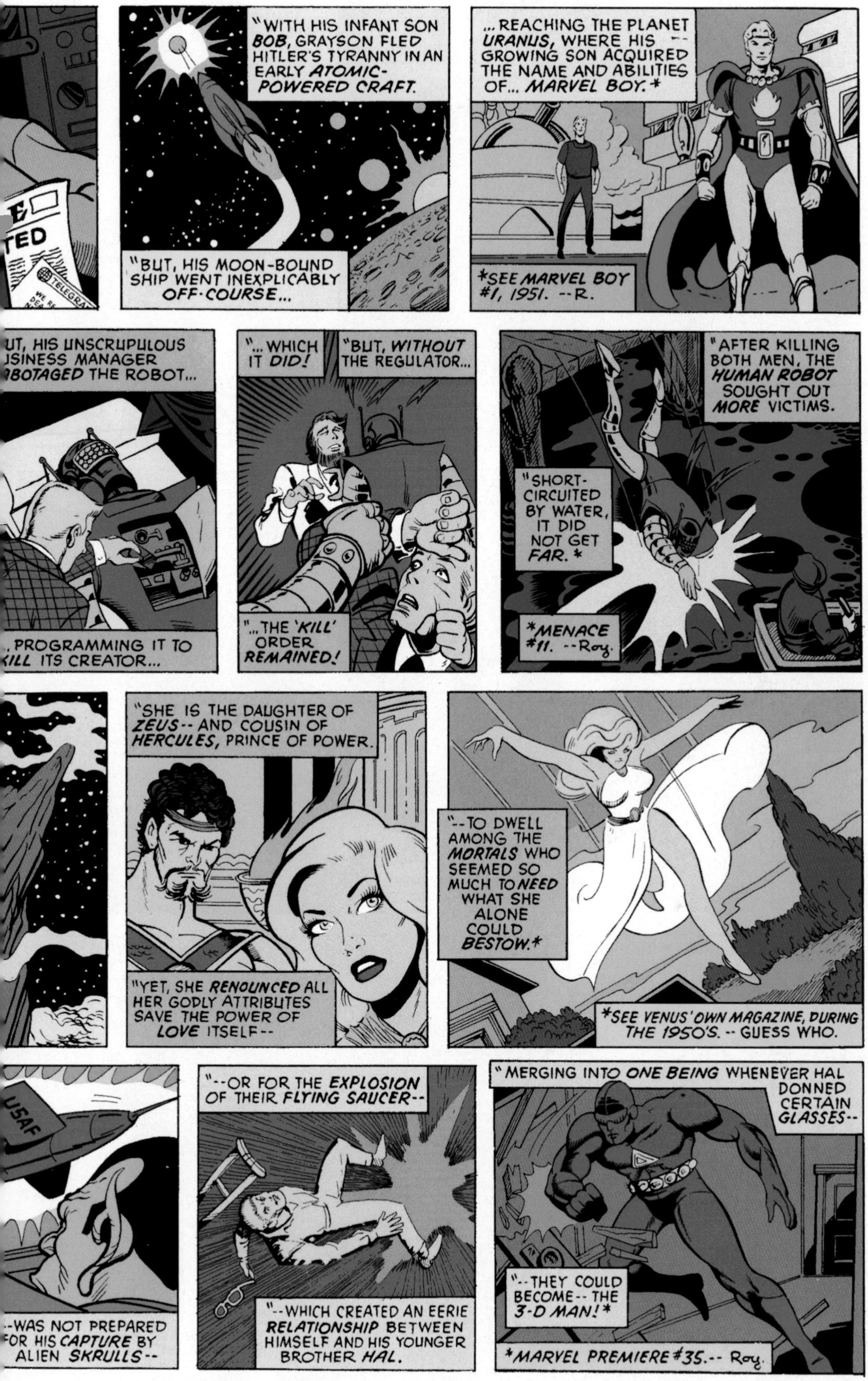
"WITH HIS INFANT SON BOB, GRAYSON FLED HITLER'S TYRANNY IN AN EARLY ATOMIC-POWERED CRAFT.
"BUT, HIS MOON-BOUND SHIP WENT INEXPLICABLY OFF-COURSE...
...REACHING THE PLANET URANUS, WHERE HIS GROWING SON ACQUIRED THE NAME AND ABILITIES OF... MARVEL BOY.*
*SEE MARVEL BOY #1, 1951. --R.
UT, HIS UNSCRUPULOUS USINESS MANAGER BOTAGED THE ROBOT...
.. PROGRAMMING IT TO ILL ITS CREATOR...
"...WHICH IT DID!
"BUT, WITHOUT THE REGULATOR...
"...THE 'KILL' ORDER REMAINED!
"AFTER KILLING BOTH MEN, THE HUMAN ROBOT SOUGHT OUT MORE VICTIMS.
"SHORT-CIRCUITED BY WATER, IT DID NOT GET FAR.*
*MENACE #11. --Roy.
"SHE IS THE DAUGHTER OF ZEUS-- AND COUSIN OF HERCULES, PRINCE OF POWER.
"YET, SHE RENOUNCED ALL HER GODLY ATTRIBUTES SAVE THE POWER OF LOVE ITSELF--
"--TO DWELL AMONG THE MORTALS WHO SEEMED SO MUCH TO NEED WHAT SHE ALONE COULD BESTOW.*
*SEE VENUS' OWN MAGAZINE, DURING THE 1950'S. -- GUESS WHO.
USAF
--WAS NOT PREPARED FOR HIS CAPTURE BY ALIEN SKRULLS--
"--OR FOR THE EXPLOSION OF THEIR FLYING SAUCER--
"--WHICH CREATED AN EERIE RELATIONSHIP BETWEEN HIMSELF AND HIS YOUNGER BROTHER HAL.
"MERGING INTO ONE BEING WHENEVER HAL DONNED CERTAIN GLASSES--
"--THEY COULD BECOME-- THE 3-D MAN!*
*MARVEL PREMIERE #35.-- Roy.

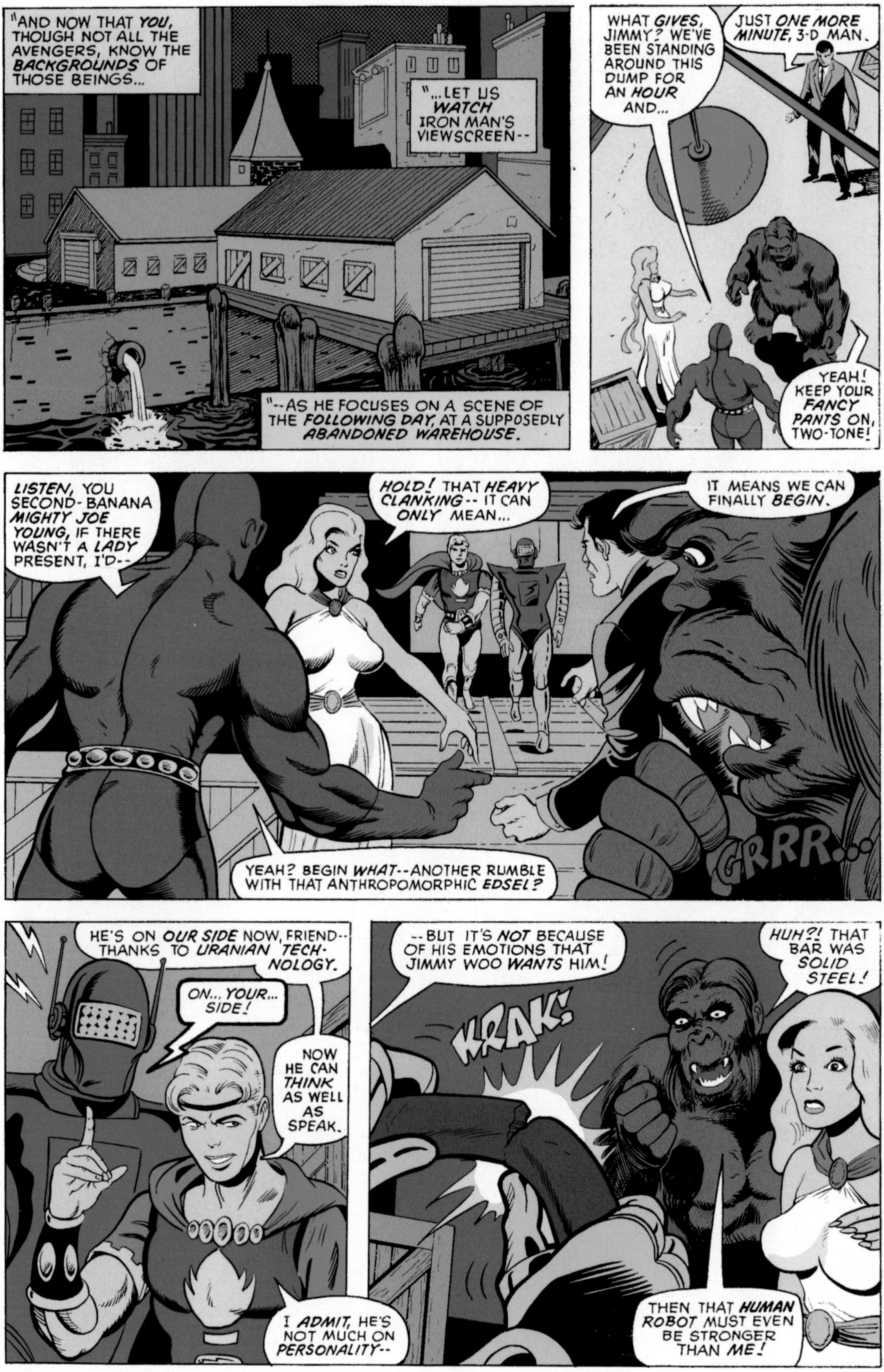
"AND NOW THAT YOU, THOUGH NOT ALL THE AVENGERS, KNOW THE BACKGROUNDS OF THOSE BEINGS...
"...LET US WATCH IRON MAN'S VIEWSCREEN--
"--AS HE FOCUSES ON A SCENE OF THE FOLLOWING DAY, AT A SUPPOSEDLY ABANDONED WAREHOUSE.
WHAT GIVES, JIMMY? WE'VE BEEN STANDING AROUND THIS DUMP FOR AN HOUR AND...
JUST ONE MORE MINUTE, 3-D MAN.
YEAH! KEEP YOUR FANCY PANTS ON, TWO-TONE!
LISTEN, YOU SECOND-BANANA MIGHTY JOE YOUNG, IF THERE WASN'T A LADY PRESENT, I'D--
HOLD! THAT HEAVY CLANKING-- IT CAN ONLY MEAN...
IT MEANS WE CAN FINALLY BEGIN.
YEAH? BEGIN WHAT--ANOTHER RUMBLE WITH THAT ANTHROPOMORPHIC EDSEL?
GRRR...
HE'S ON OUR SIDE NOW, FRIEND-- THANKS TO URANIAN TECH-NOLOGY.
ON... YOUR... SIDE!
NOW HE CAN THINK AS WELL AS SPEAK.
I ADMIT, HE'S NOT MUCH ON PERSONALITY--
--BUT IT'S NOT BECAUSE OF HIS EMOTIONS THAT JIMMY WOO WANTS HIM!
KRAK!
HUH?! THAT BAR WAS SOLID STEEL!
THEN THAT HUMAN ROBOT MUST EVEN BE STRONGER THAN ME!

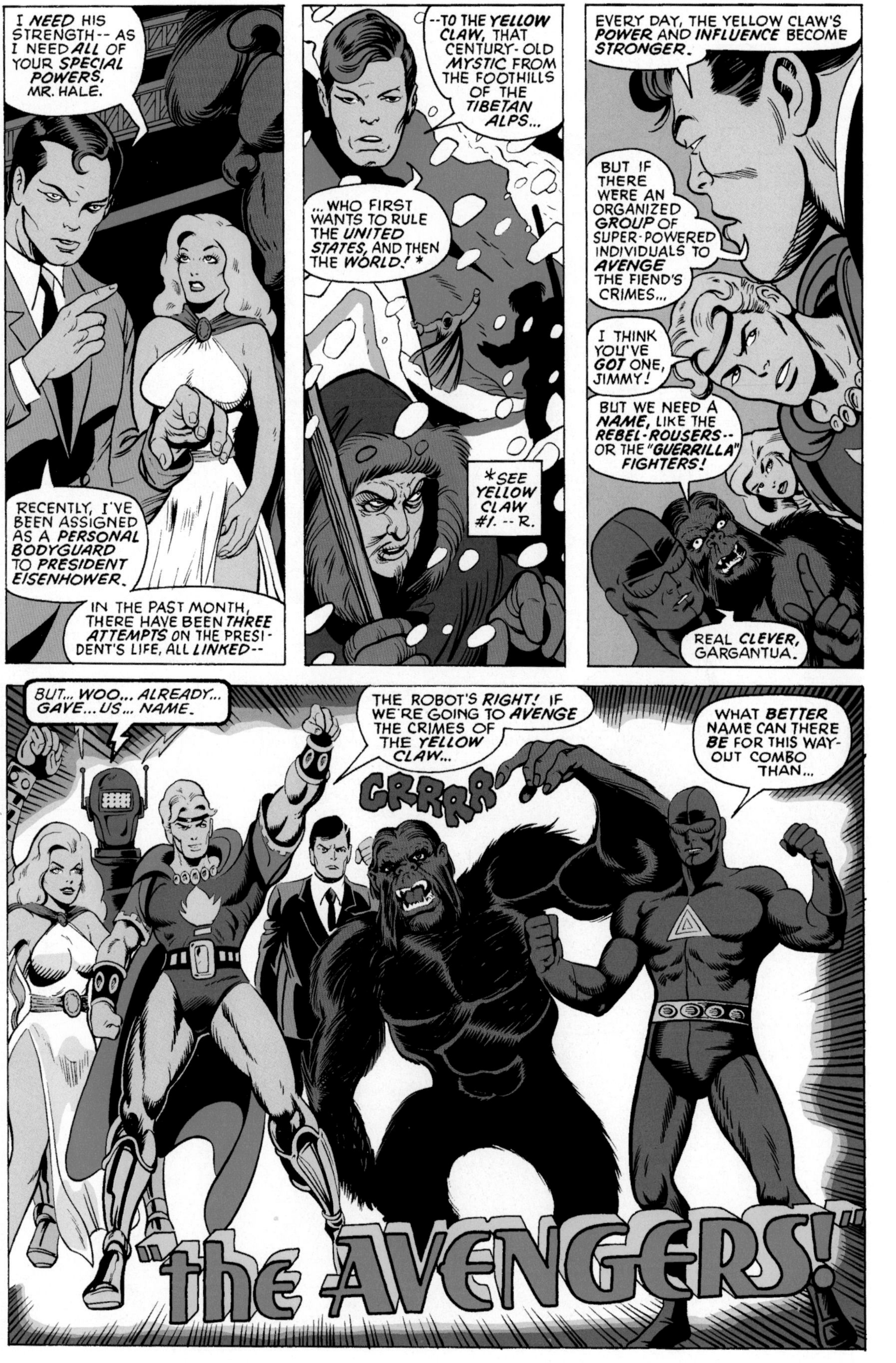
I NEED HIS STRENGTH-- AS I NEED ALL OF YOUR SPECIAL POWERS, MR. HALE.
RECENTLY, I'VE BEEN ASSIGNED AS A PERSONAL BODYGUARD TO PRESIDENT EISENHOWER.
IN THE PAST MONTH, THERE HAVE BEEN THREE ATTEMPTS ON THE PRESIDENT'S LIFE, ALL LINKED--
--TO THE YELLOW CLAW, THAT CENTURY-OLD MYSTIC FROM THE FOOTHILLS OF THE TIBETAN ALPS...
...WHO FIRST WANTS TO RULE THE UNITED STATES, AND THEN THE WORLD! *
*SEE YELLOW CLAW #1. --R.
EVERY DAY, THE YELLOW CLAW'S POWER AND INFLUENCE BECOME STRONGER.
BUT IF THERE WERE AN ORGANIZED GROUP OF SUPER-POWERED INDIVIDUALS TO AVENGE THE FIEND'S CRIMES...
I THINK YOU'VE GOT ONE, JIMMY!
BUT WE NEED A NAME, LIKE THE REBEL-ROUSERS-- OR THE "GUERRILLA" FIGHTERS!
REAL CLEVER, GARGANTUA.
BUT... WOO... ALREADY... GAVE... US... NAME.
THE ROBOT'S RIGHT! IF WE'RE GOING TO AVENGE THE CRIMES OF THE YELLOW CLAW...
GRRRRR
WHAT BETTER NAME CAN THERE BE FOR THIS WAY-OUT COMBO THAN...
"the AVENGERS!"

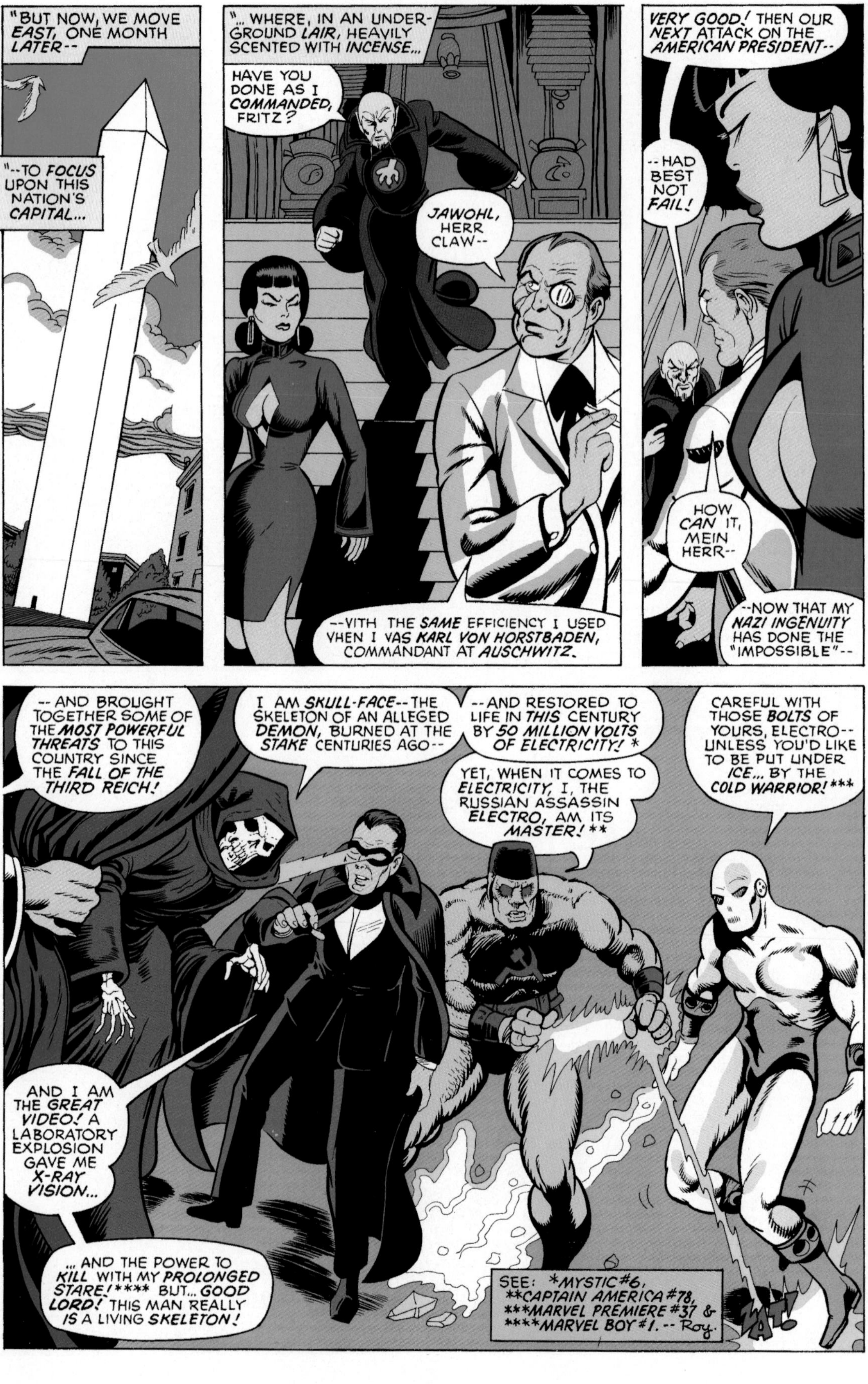
"BUT NOW, WE MOVE EAST, ONE MONTH LATER--
"--TO FOCUS UPON THIS NATION'S CAPITAL...
"... WHERE, IN AN UNDERGROUND LAIR, HEAVILY SCENTED WITH INCENSE...
HAVE YOU DONE AS I COMMANDED, FRITZ?
JAWOHL, HERR CLAW--
--VITH THE SAME EFFICIENCY I USED VHEN I VAS KARL VON HORSTBADEN, COMMANDANT AT AUSCHWITZ.
VERY GOOD! THEN OUR NEXT ATTACK ON THE AMERICAN PRESIDENT--
--HAD BEST NOT FAIL!
HOW CAN IT, MEIN HERR--
--NOW THAT MY NAZI INGENUITY HAS DONE THE "IMPOSSIBLE"--
--AND BROUGHT TOGETHER SOME OF THE MOST POWERFUL THREATS TO THIS COUNTRY SINCE THE FALL OF THE THIRD REICH!
I AM SKULL-FACE--THE SKELETON OF AN ALLEGED DEMON, BURNED AT THE STAKE CENTURIES AGO--
--AND RESTORED TO LIFE IN THIS CENTURY BY 50 MILLION VOLTS OF ELECTRICITY! *
YET, WHEN IT COMES TO ELECTRICITY, I, THE RUSSIAN ASSASSIN ELECTRO, AM ITS MASTER! **
CAREFUL WITH THOSE BOLTS OF YOURS, ELECTRO--UNLESS YOU'D LIKE TO BE PUT UNDER ICE... BY THE COLD WARRIOR! ***
AND I AM THE GREAT VIDEO! A LABORATORY EXPLOSION GAVE ME X-RAY VISION...
... AND THE POWER TO KILL WITH MY PROLONGED STARE! **** BUT... GOOD LORD! THIS MAN REALLY IS A LIVING SKELETON!
SEE: *MYSTIC #6, **CAPTAIN AMERICA #78, ***MARVEL PREMIERE #37 & ****MARVEL BOY #1. --Roy.

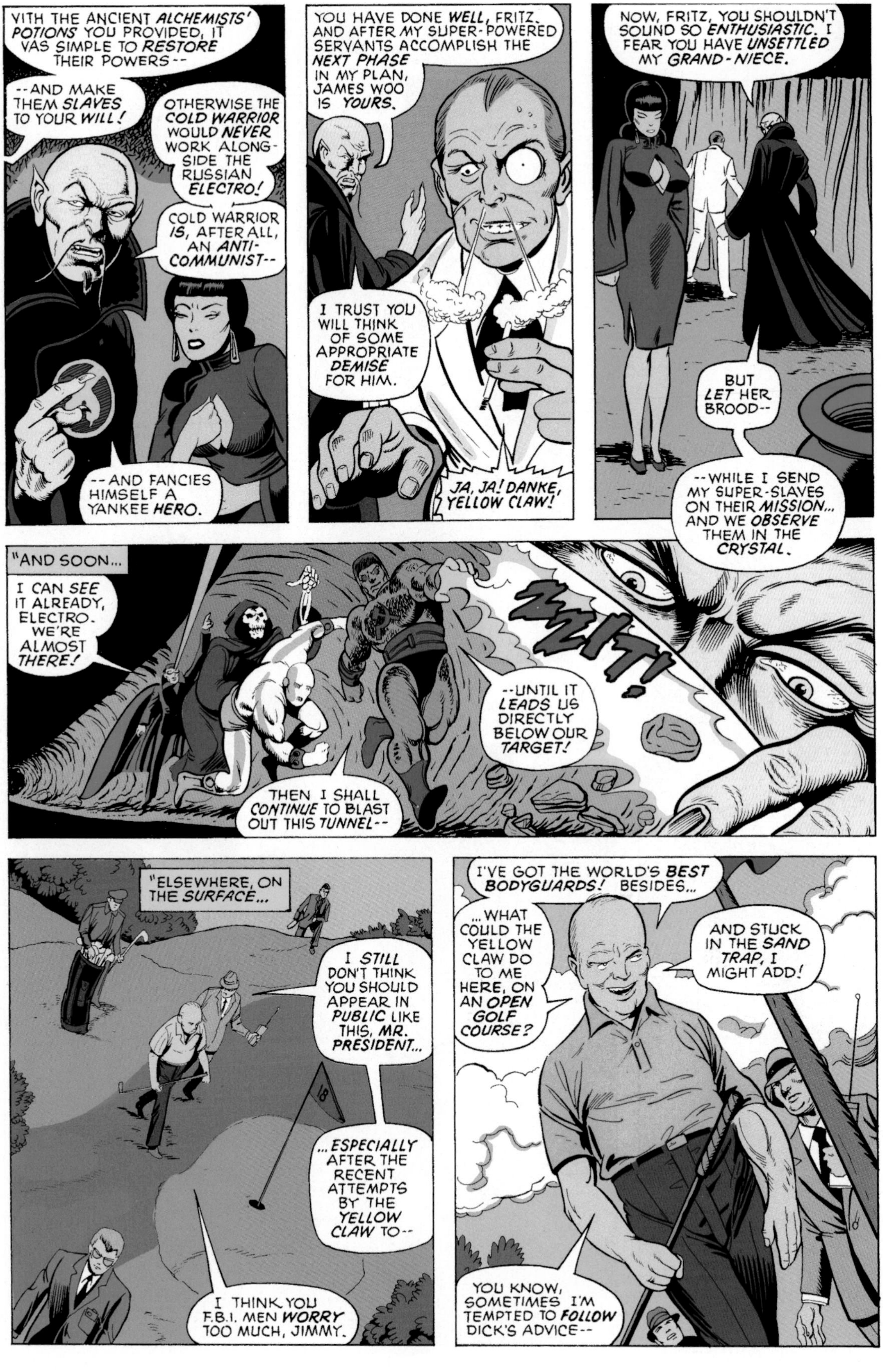
VITH THE ANCIENT ALCHEMISTS' POTIONS YOU PROVIDED, IT VAS SIMPLE TO RESTORE THEIR POWERS--
--AND MAKE THEM SLAVES TO YOUR WILL!
OTHERWISE THE COLD WARRIOR WOULD NEVER WORK ALONGSIDE THE RUSSIAN ELECTRO!
COLD WARRIOR IS, AFTER ALL, AN ANTI-COMMUNIST--
--AND FANCIES HIMSELF A YANKEE HERO.
YOU HAVE DONE WELL, FRITZ. AND AFTER MY SUPER-POWERED SERVANTS ACCOMPLISH THE NEXT PHASE IN MY PLAN, JAMES WOO IS YOURS.
I TRUST YOU WILL THINK OF SOME APPROPRIATE DEMISE FOR HIM.
JA, JA! DANKE, YELLOW CLAW!
NOW, FRITZ, YOU SHOULDN'T SOUND SO ENTHUSIASTIC. I FEAR YOU HAVE UNSETTLED MY GRAND-NIECE.
BUT LET HER BROOD--
--WHILE I SEND MY SUPER-SLAVES ON THEIR MISSION... AND WE OBSERVE THEM IN THE CRYSTAL.
"AND SOON...
I CAN SEE IT ALREADY, ELECTRO. WE'RE ALMOST THERE!
ZZZIT!
THEN I SHALL CONTINUE TO BLAST OUT THIS TUNNEL--
--UNTIL IT LEADS US DIRECTLY BELOW OUR TARGET!
"ELSEWHERE, ON THE SURFACE...
I STILL DON'T THINK YOU SHOULD APPEAR IN PUBLIC LIKE THIS, MR. PRESIDENT...
...ESPECIALLY AFTER THE RECENT ATTEMPTS BY THE YELLOW CLAW TO--
I THINK YOU F.B.I. MEN WORRY TOO MUCH, JIMMY.
18
I'VE GOT THE WORLD'S BEST BODYGUARDS! BESIDES...
...WHAT COULD THE YELLOW CLAW DO TO ME HERE, ON AN OPEN GOLF COURSE?
AND STUCK IN THE SAND TRAP, I MIGHT ADD!
YOU KNOW, SOMETIMES I'M TEMPTED TO FOLLOW DICK'S ADVICE--

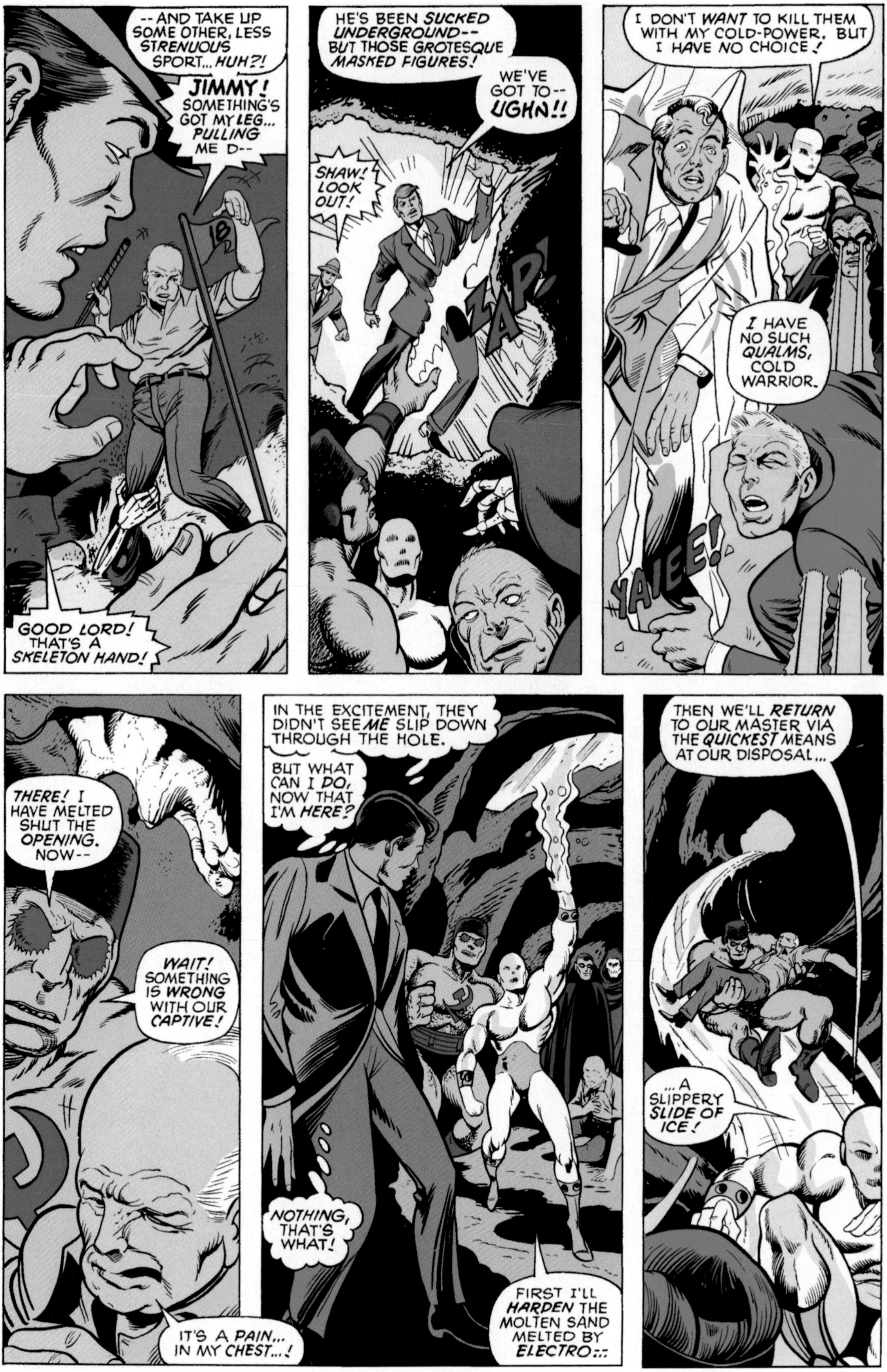

--AND TAKE UP SOME OTHER, LESS STRENUOUS SPORT... HUH?!
JIMMY! SOMETHING'S GOT MY LEG... PULLING ME D--
GOOD LORD! THAT'S A SKELETON HAND!
HE'S BEEN SUCKED UNDERGROUND-- BUT THOSE GROTESQUE MASKED FIGURES!
WE'VE GOT TO-- UGHN!!
SHAW! LOOK OUT!
ZAP!
I DON'T WANT TO KILL THEM WITH MY COLD-POWER, BUT I HAVE NO CHOICE!
I HAVE NO SUCH QUALMS, COLD WARRIOR.
YAIEE!
THERE! I HAVE MELTED SHUT THE OPENING. NOW--
WAIT! SOMETHING IS WRONG WITH OUR CAPTIVE!
IT'S A PAIN... IN MY CHEST...!
IN THE EXCITEMENT, THEY DIDN'T SEE ME SLIP DOWN THROUGH THE HOLE.
BUT WHAT CAN I DO, NOW THAT I'M HERE?
NOTHING, THAT'S WHAT!
FIRST I'LL HARDEN THE MOLTEN SAND MELTED BY ELECTRO...
THEN WE'LL RETURN TO OUR MASTER VIA THE QUICKEST MEANS AT OUR DISPOSAL...
...A SLIPPERY SLIDE OF ICE!

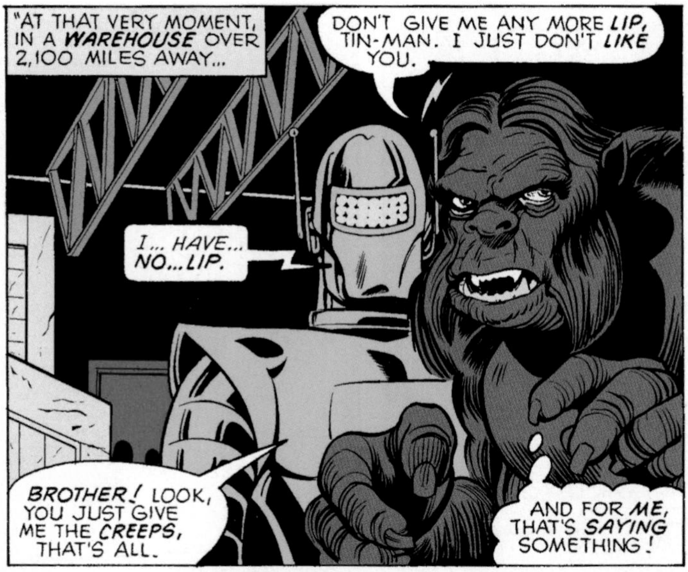
"AT THAT VERY MOMENT, IN A WAREHOUSE OVER 2,100 MILES AWAY...
DON'T GIVE ME ANY MORE LIP, TIN-MAN. I JUST DON'T LIKE YOU.
I... HAVE... NO... LIP.
BROTHER! LOOK, YOU JUST GIVE ME THE CREEPS, THAT'S ALL.
AND FOR ME, THAT'S SAYING SOMETHING!
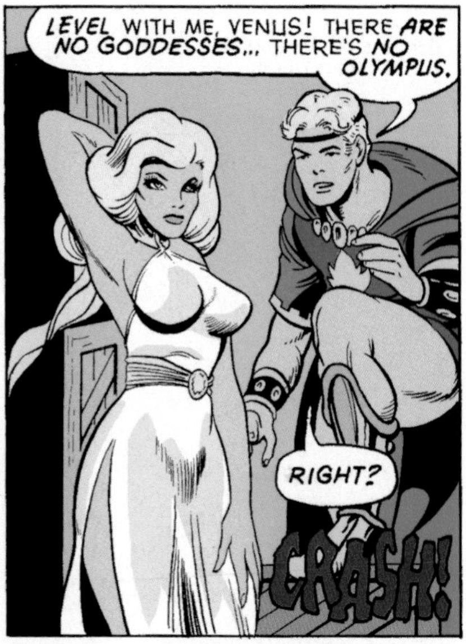
LEVEL WITH ME, VENUS! THERE ARE NO GODDESSES... THERE'S NO OLYMPUS.
RIGHT?
CRASH!
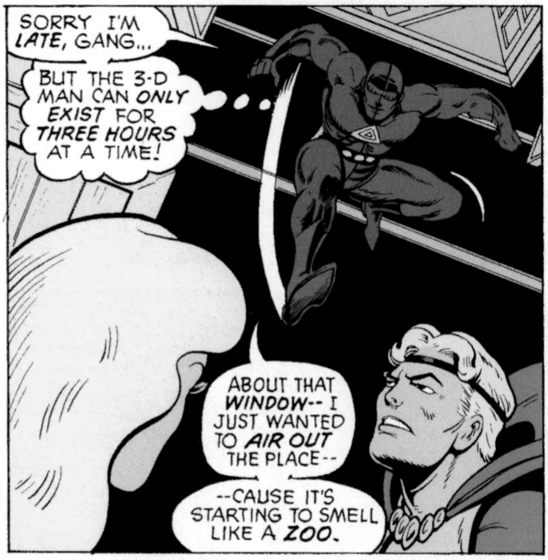
SORRY I'M LATE, GANG...
BUT THE 3-D MAN CAN ONLY EXIST FOR THREE HOURS AT A TIME!
ABOUT THAT WINDOW-- I JUST WANTED TO AIR OUT THE PLACE--
--CAUSE IT'S STARTING TO SMELL LIKE A ZOO.
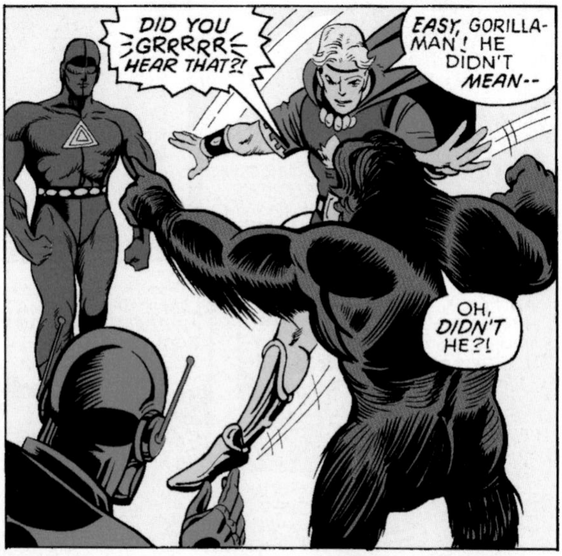
DID YOU GRRRRR HEAR THAT?!
EASY, GORILLA-MAN! HE DIDN'T MEAN--
OH, DIDN'T HE?!
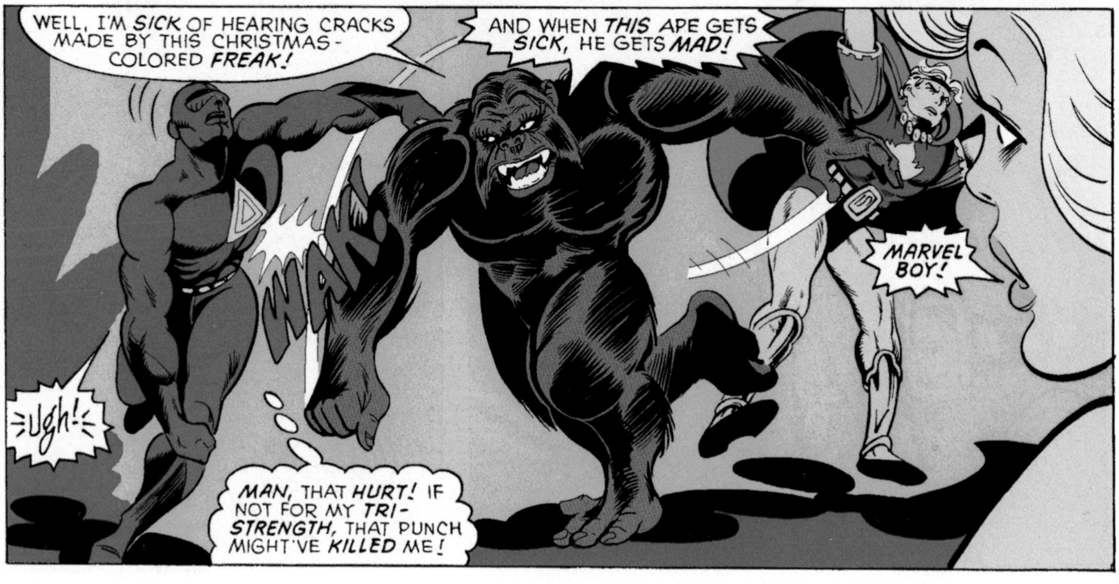
WELL, I'M SICK OF HEARING CRACKS MADE BY THIS CHRISTMAS-COLORED FREAK!
AND WHEN THIS APE GETS SICK, HE GETS MAD!
WAK!
MARVEL BOY!
UGH!
MAN, THAT HURT! IF NOT FOR MY TRI-STRENGTH, THAT PUNCH MIGHT'VE KILLED ME!

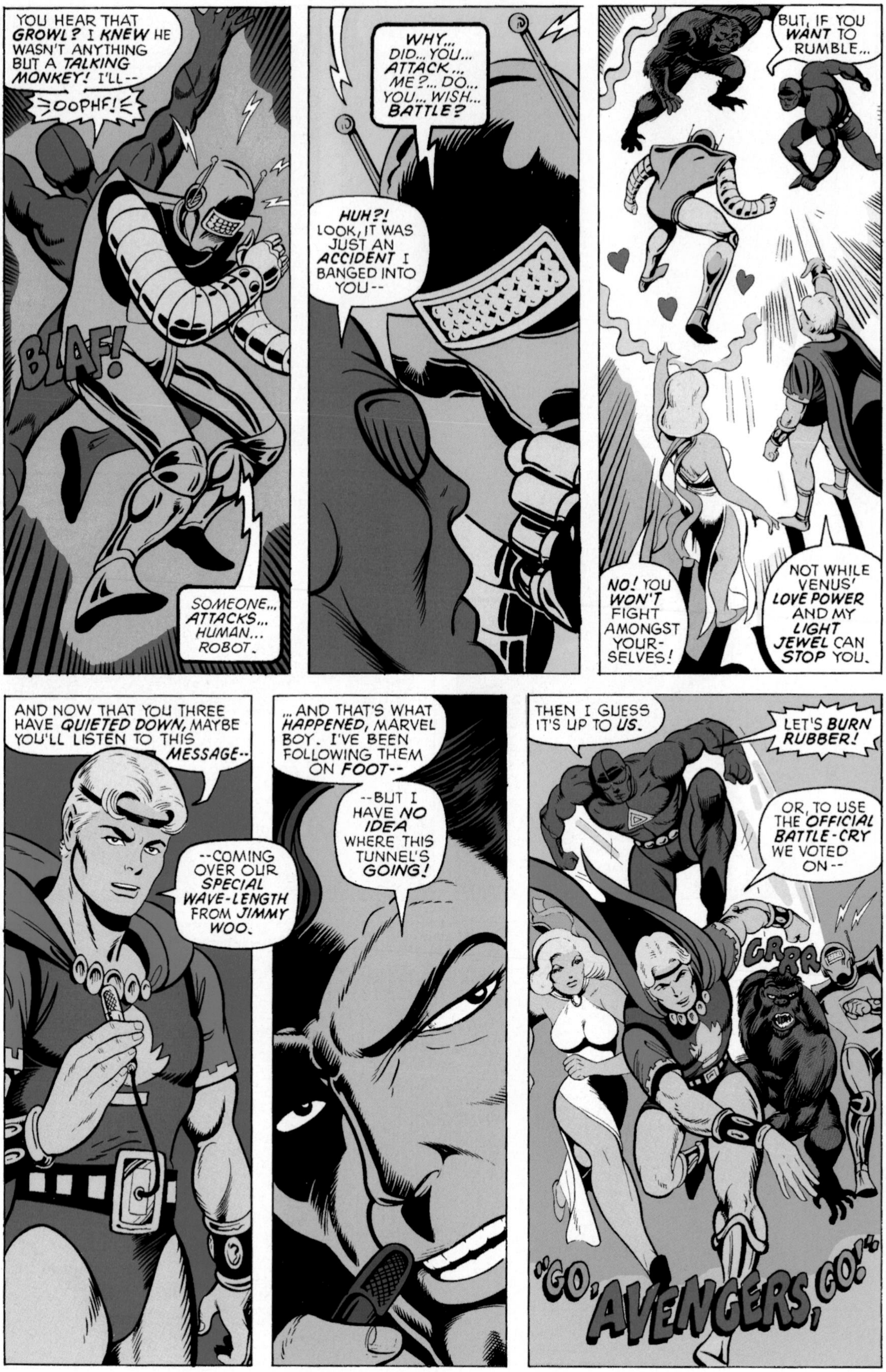
YOU HEAR THAT GROWL? I KNEW HE WASN'T ANYTHING BUT A TALKING MONKEY! I'LL--
OOPHF!
BLAF!
SOMEONE... ATTACKS... HUMAN... ROBOT.
WHY... DID... YOU... ATTACK... ME?... DO... YOU... WISH... BATTLE?
HUH?! LOOK, IT WAS JUST AN ACCIDENT I BANGED INTO YOU--
BUT, IF YOU WANT TO RUMBLE...
NO! YOU WON'T FIGHT AMONGST YOURSELVES!
NOT WHILE VENUS' LOVE POWER AND MY LIGHT JEWEL CAN STOP YOU.
AND NOW THAT YOU THREE HAVE QUIETED DOWN, MAYBE YOU'LL LISTEN TO THIS MESSAGE--
--COMING OVER OUR SPECIAL WAVE-LENGTH FROM JIMMY WOO.
...AND THAT'S WHAT HAPPENED, MARVEL BOY. I'VE BEEN FOLLOWING THEM ON FOOT--
--BUT I HAVE NO IDEA WHERE THIS TUNNEL'S GOING!
THEN I GUESS IT'S UP TO US.
LET'S BURN RUBBER!
OR, TO USE THE OFFICIAL BATTLE-CRY WE VOTED ON--
GRRR
"GO, AVENGERS, GO!"

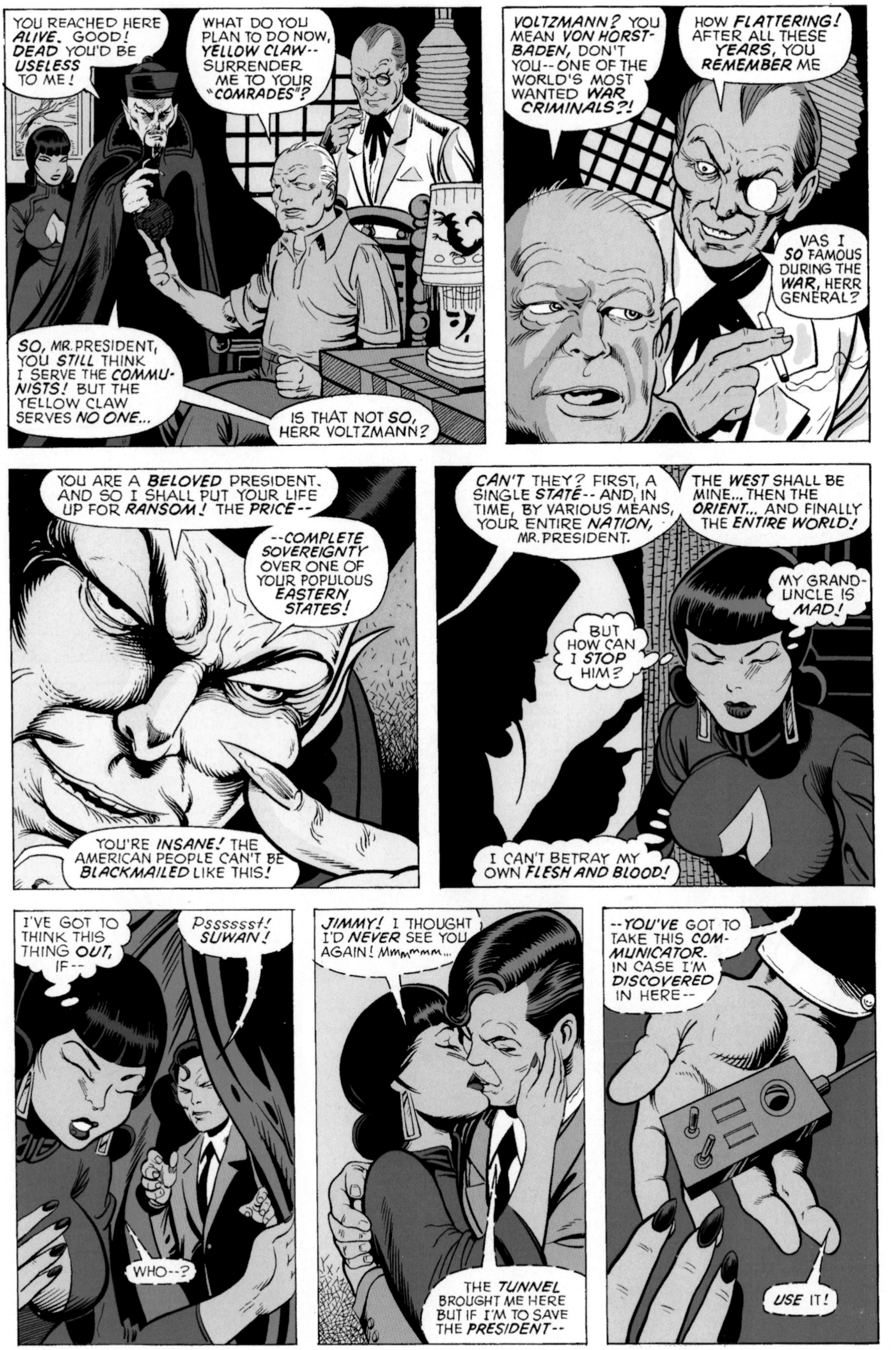
YOU REACHED HERE ALIVE. GOOD! DEAD YOU'D BE USELESS TO ME!
WHAT DO YOU PLAN TO DO NOW, YELLOW CLAW-- SURRENDER ME TO YOUR "COMRADES"?
SO, MR. PRESIDENT, YOU STILL THINK I SERVE THE COMMU-NISTS! BUT THE YELLOW CLAW SERVES NO ONE...
IS THAT NOT SO, HERR VOLTZMANN?
VOLTZMANN? YOU MEAN VON HORST-BADEN, DON'T YOU--ONE OF THE WORLD'S MOST WANTED WAR CRIMINALS?!
HOW FLATTERING! AFTER ALL THESE YEARS, YOU REMEMBER ME
VAS I SO FAMOUS DURING THE WAR, HERR GENERAL?
YOU ARE A BELOVED PRESIDENT. AND SO I SHALL PUT YOUR LIFE UP FOR RANSOM! THE PRICE--
--COMPLETE SOVEREIGNTY OVER ONE OF YOUR POPULOUS EASTERN STATES!
YOU'RE INSANE! THE AMERICAN PEOPLE CAN'T BE BLACKMAILED LIKE THIS!
CAN'T THEY? FIRST, A SINGLE STATE-- AND, IN TIME, BY VARIOUS MEANS, YOUR ENTIRE NATION, MR. PRESIDENT.
THE WEST SHALL BE MINE... THEN THE ORIENT... AND FINALLY THE ENTIRE WORLD!
MY GRAND-UNCLE IS MAD!
BUT HOW CAN I STOP HIM?
I CAN'T BETRAY MY OWN FLESH AND BLOOD!
I'VE GOT TO THINK THIS THING OUT, IF--
Psssssst! SUWAN!
WHO--?
JIMMY! I THOUGHT I'D NEVER SEE YOU AGAIN! Mmmmmm...
THE TUNNEL BROUGHT ME HERE BUT IF I'M TO SAVE THE PRESIDENT--
--YOU'VE GOT TO TAKE THIS COM-MUNICATOR. IN CASE I'M DISCOVERED IN HERE--
USE IT!

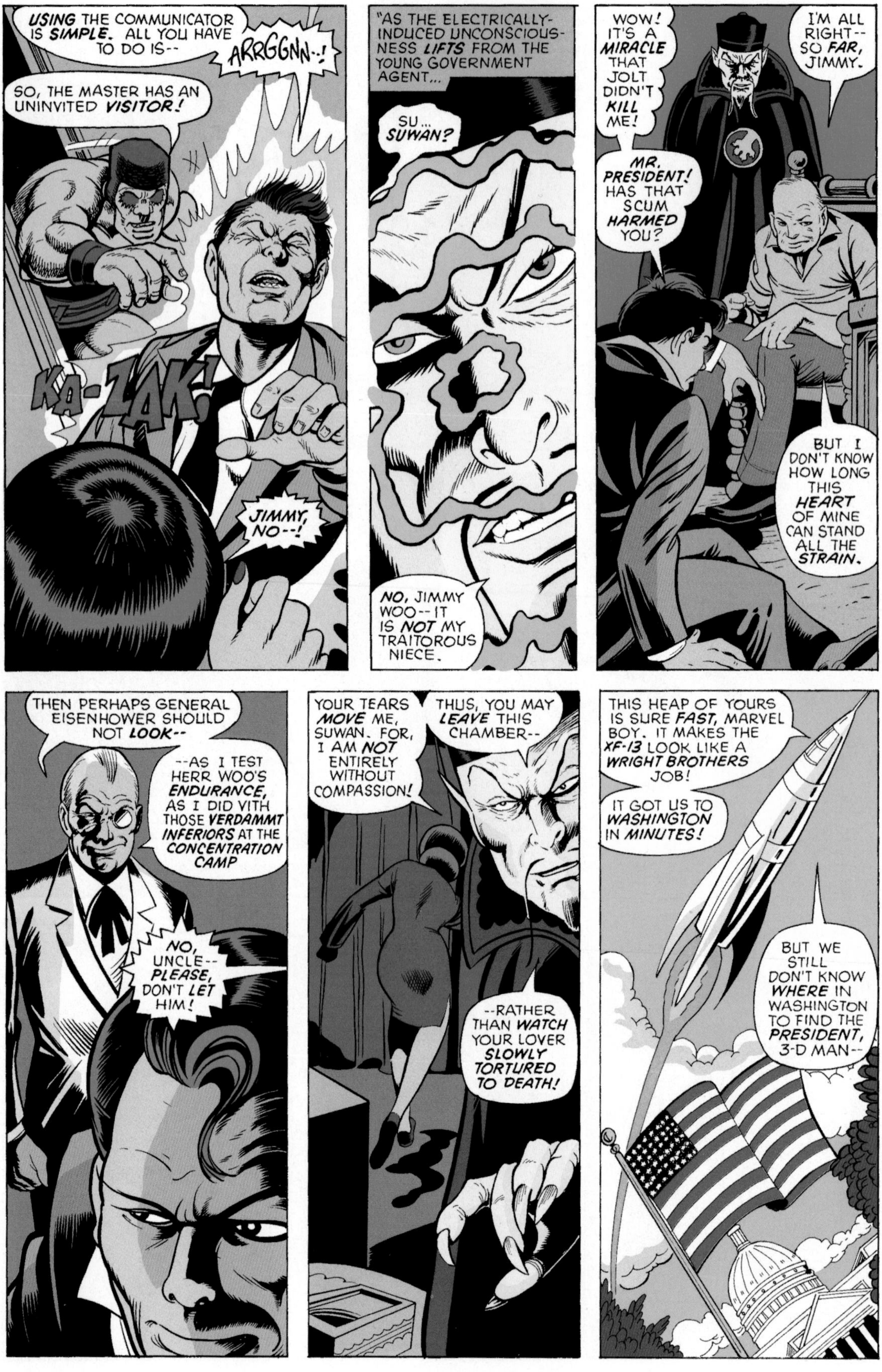
USING THE COMMUNICATOR IS SIMPLE. ALL YOU HAVE TO DO IS--
ARRGGNN--!
SO, THE MASTER HAS AN UNINVITED VISITOR!
KA-ZAK!
JIMMY, NO--!
"AS THE ELECTRICALLY-INDUCED UNCONSCIOUSNESS LIFTS FROM THE YOUNG GOVERNMENT AGENT...
SU... SUWAN?
NO, JIMMY WOO--IT IS NOT MY TRAITOROUS NIECE.
WOW! IT'S A MIRACLE THAT JOLT DIDN'T KILL ME!
I'M ALL RIGHT--SO FAR, JIMMY.
MR. PRESIDENT! HAS THAT SCUM HARMED YOU?
BUT I DON'T KNOW HOW LONG THIS HEART OF MINE CAN STAND ALL THE STRAIN.
THEN PERHAPS GENERAL EISENHOWER SHOULD NOT LOOK--
--AS I TEST HERR WOO'S ENDURANCE, AS I DID VITH THOSE VERDAMMT INFERIORS AT THE CONCENTRATION CAMP
NO, UNCLE--PLEASE, DON'T LET HIM!
YOUR TEARS MOVE ME, SUWAN. FOR, I AM NOT ENTIRELY WITHOUT COMPASSION!
THUS, YOU MAY LEAVE THIS CHAMBER--
--RATHER THAN WATCH YOUR LOVER SLOWLY TORTURED TO DEATH!
THIS HEAP OF YOURS IS SURE FAST, MARVEL BOY. IT MAKES THE XF-13 LOOK LIKE A WRIGHT BROTHERS JOB!
IT GOT US TO WASHINGTON IN MINUTES!
BUT WE STILL DON'T KNOW WHERE IN WASHINGTON TO FIND THE PRESIDENT, 3-D MAN--

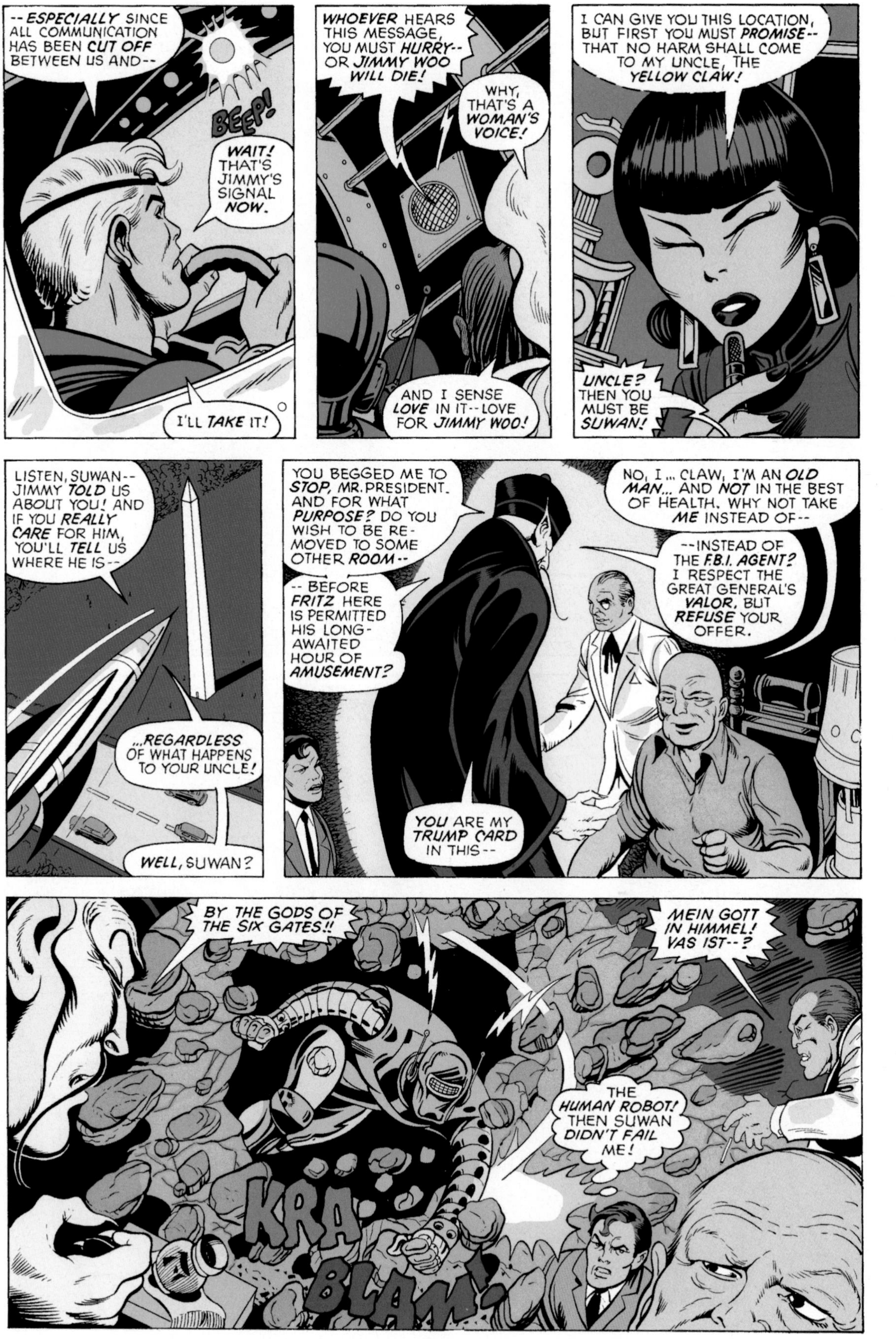
--ESPECIALLY SINCE ALL COMMUNICATION HAS BEEN CUT OFF BETWEEN US AND--
BEEP!
WAIT! THAT'S JIMMY'S SIGNAL NOW.
I'LL TAKE IT!
WHOEVER HEARS THIS MESSAGE, YOU MUST HURRY-- OR JIMMY WOO WILL DIE!
WHY, THAT'S A WOMAN'S VOICE!
AND I SENSE LOVE IN IT--LOVE FOR JIMMY WOO!
I CAN GIVE YOU THIS LOCATION, BUT FIRST YOU MUST PROMISE-- THAT NO HARM SHALL COME TO MY UNCLE, THE YELLOW CLAW!
UNCLE? THEN YOU MUST BE SUWAN!
LISTEN, SUWAN-- JIMMY TOLD US ABOUT YOU! AND IF YOU REALLY CARE FOR HIM, YOU'LL TELL US WHERE HE IS--
...REGARDLESS OF WHAT HAPPENS TO YOUR UNCLE!
WELL, SUWAN?
YOU BEGGED ME TO STOP, MR. PRESIDENT. AND FOR WHAT PURPOSE? DO YOU WISH TO BE REMOVED TO SOME OTHER ROOM--
-- BEFORE FRITZ HERE IS PERMITTED HIS LONG-AWAITED HOUR OF AMUSEMENT?
NO, I... CLAW, I'M AN OLD MAN... AND NOT IN THE BEST OF HEALTH. WHY NOT TAKE ME INSTEAD OF--
--INSTEAD OF THE F.B.I. AGENT? I RESPECT THE GREAT GENERAL'S VALOR, BUT REFUSE YOUR OFFER.
YOU ARE MY TRUMP CARD IN THIS--
BY THE GODS OF THE SIX GATES!!
MEIN GOTT IN HIMMEL! VAS IST--?
THE HUMAN ROBOT! THEN SUWAN DIDN'T FAIL ME!
KRA BLAM!

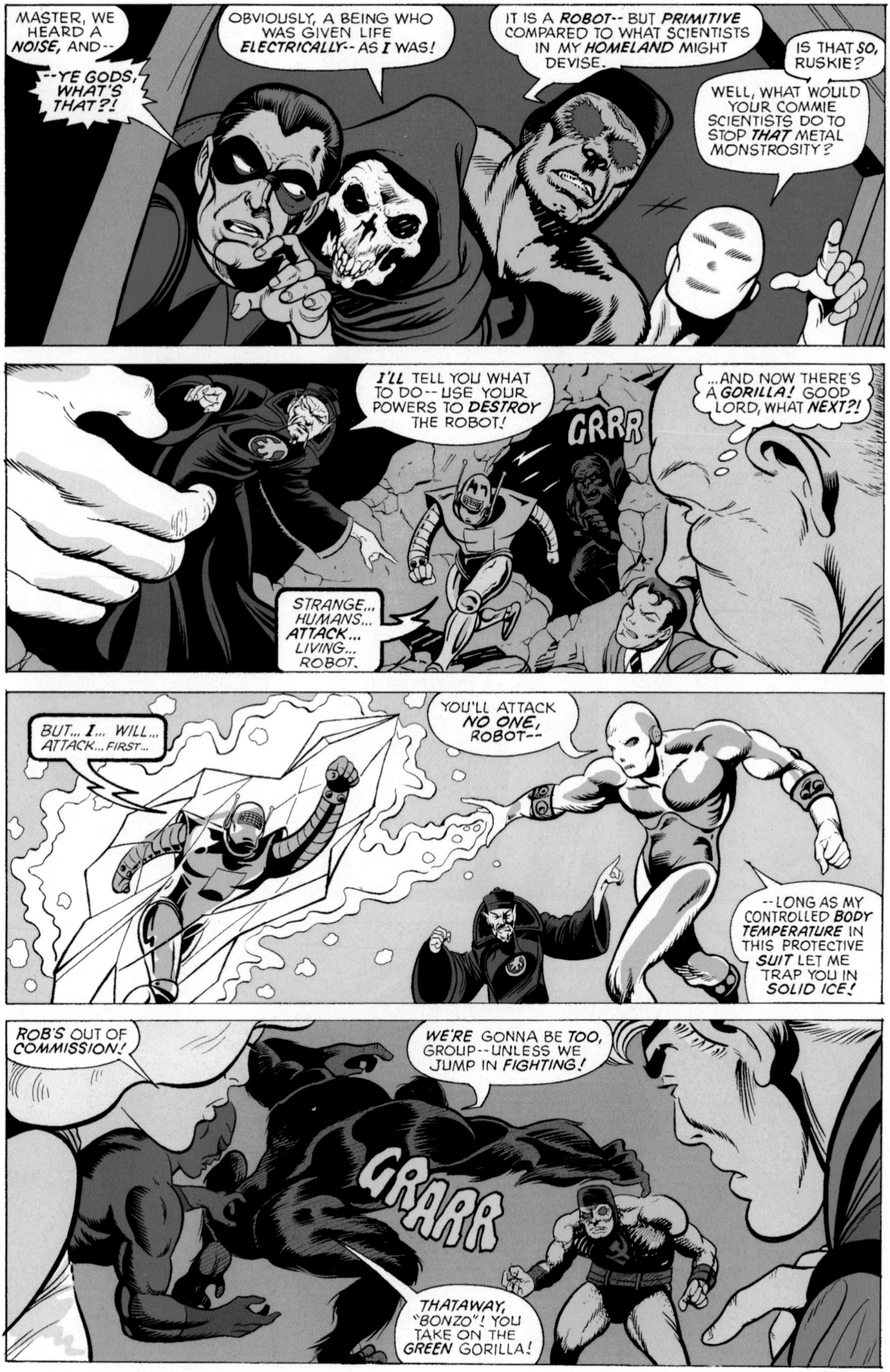

MASTER, WE HEARD A NOISE, AND--
--YE GODS, WHAT'S THAT?!
OBVIOUSLY, A BEING WHO WAS GIVEN LIFE ELECTRICALLY-- AS I WAS!
IT IS A ROBOT-- BUT PRIMITIVE COMPARED TO WHAT SCIENTISTS IN MY HOMELAND MIGHT DEVISE.
IS THAT SO, RUSKIE?
WELL, WHAT WOULD YOUR COMMIE SCIENTISTS DO TO STOP THAT METAL MONSTROSITY?
I'LL TELL YOU WHAT TO DO-- USE YOUR POWERS TO DESTROY THE ROBOT!
GRRR
STRANGE... HUMANS... ATTACK... LIVING... ROBOT.
...AND NOW THERE'S A GORILLA! GOOD LORD, WHAT NEXT?!
BUT... I... WILL... ATTACK... FIRST...
YOU'LL ATTACK NO ONE, ROBOT--
--LONG AS MY CONTROLLED BODY TEMPERATURE IN THIS PROTECTIVE SUIT LET ME TRAP YOU IN SOLID ICE!
ROB'S OUT OF COMMISSION!
WE'RE GONNA BE TOO, GROUP-- UNLESS WE JUMP IN FIGHTING!
GRARR
THATAWAY, "BONZO"! YOU TAKE ON THE GREEN GORILLA!

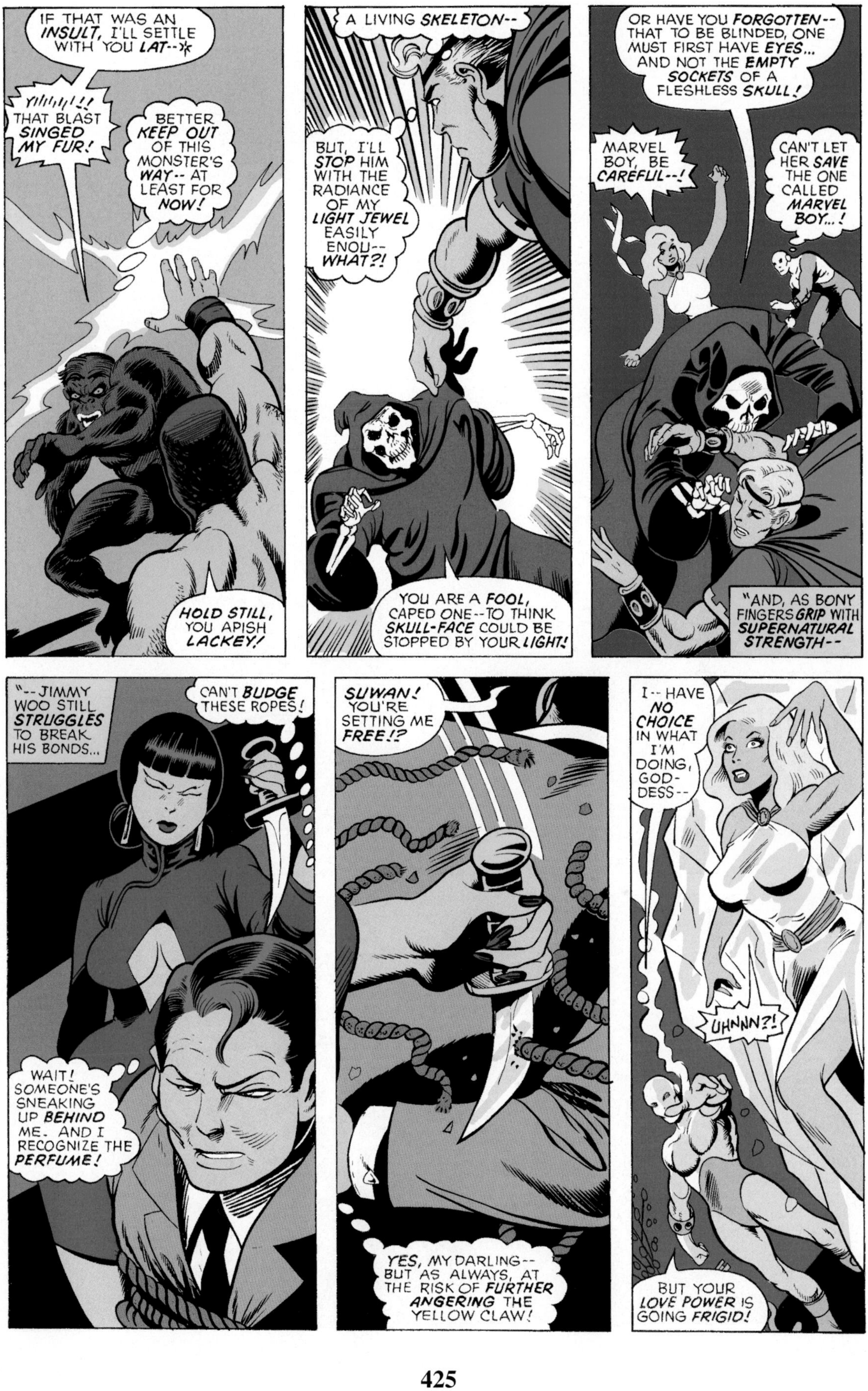
IF THAT WAS AN INSULT, I'LL SETTLE WITH YOU LAT--*
YIIIII!! THAT BLAST SINGED MY FUR!
BETTER KEEP OUT OF THIS MONSTER'S WAY-- AT LEAST FOR NOW!
HOLD STILL, YOU APISH LACKEY!
A LIVING SKELETON--
BUT, I'LL STOP HIM WITH THE RADIANCE OF MY LIGHT JEWEL EASILY ENOU-- WHAT?!
YOU ARE A FOOL, CAPED ONE--TO THINK SKULL-FACE COULD BE STOPPED BY YOUR LIGHT!
OR HAVE YOU FORGOTTEN-- THAT TO BE BLINDED, ONE MUST FIRST HAVE EYES... AND NOT THE EMPTY SOCKETS OF A FLESHLESS SKULL!
MARVEL BOY, BE CAREFUL--!
CAN'T LET HER SAVE THE ONE CALLED MARVEL BOY...!
"AND, AS BONY FINGERS GRIP WITH SUPERNATURAL STRENGTH--
"--JIMMY WOO STILL STRUGGLES TO BREAK HIS BONDS...
CAN'T BUDGE THESE ROPES!
WAIT! SOMEONE'S SNEAKING UP BEHIND ME. AND I RECOGNIZE THE PERFUME!
SUWAN! YOU'RE SETTING ME FREE!?
YES, MY DARLING-- BUT AS ALWAYS, AT THE RISK OF FURTHER ANGERING THE YELLOW CLAW!
I--HAVE NO CHOICE IN WHAT I'M DOING, GOD-DESS--
UHNNN?!
BUT YOUR LOVE POWER IS GOING FRIGID!

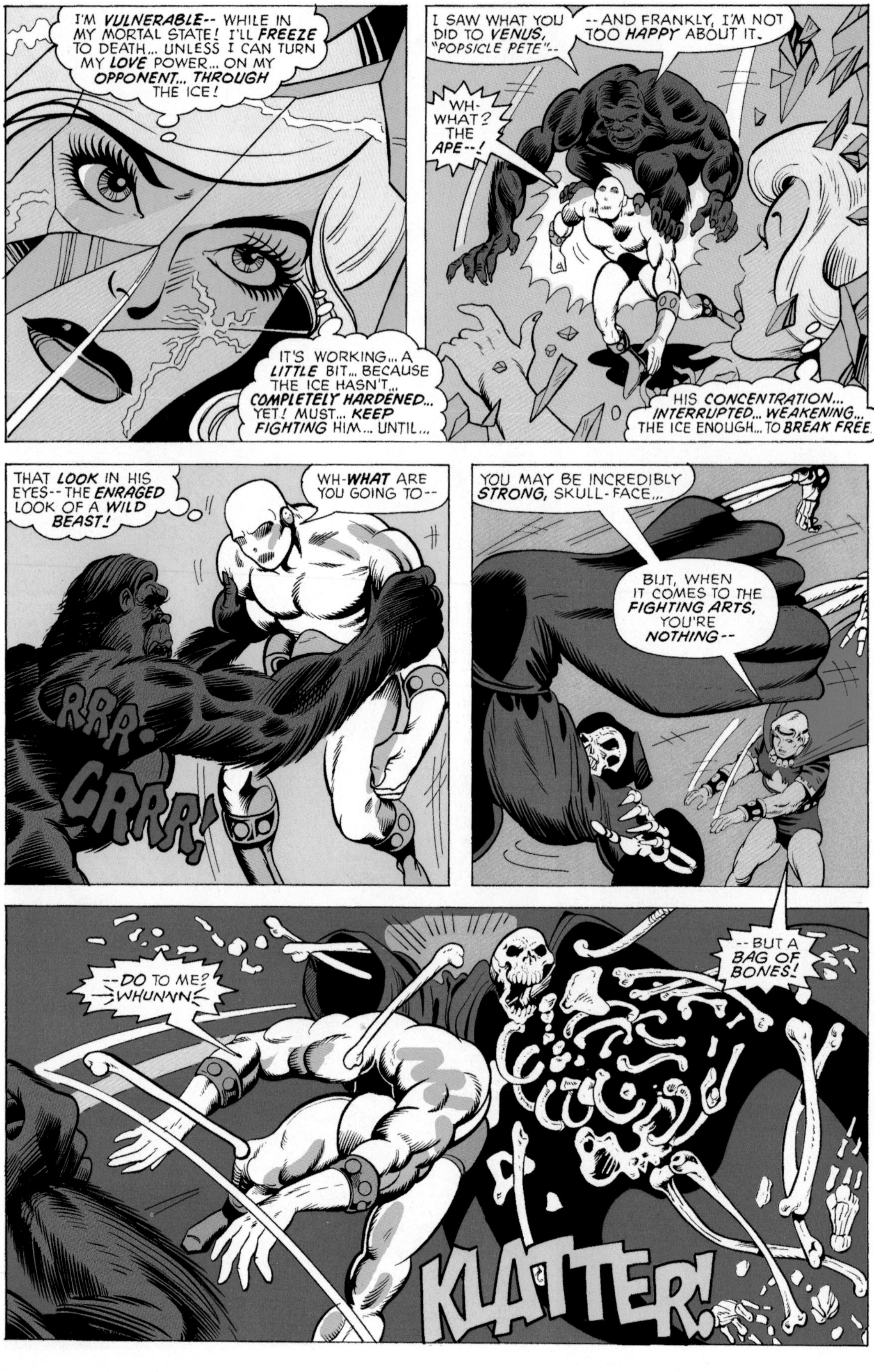
I'M VULNERABLE-- WHILE IN MY MORTAL STATE! I'LL FREEZE TO DEATH... UNLESS I CAN TURN MY LOVE POWER... ON MY OPPONENT... THROUGH THE ICE!
IT'S WORKING... A LITTLE BIT... BECAUSE THE ICE HASN'T... COMPLETELY HARDENED... YET! MUST... KEEP FIGHTING HIM... UNTIL...
I SAW WHAT YOU DID TO VENUS, "POPSICLE PETE"--
--AND FRANKLY, I'M NOT TOO HAPPY ABOUT IT.
WH-WHAT? THE APE--!
HIS CONCENTRATION... INTERRUPTED... WEAKENING... THE ICE ENOUGH... TO BREAK FREE.
THAT LOOK IN HIS EYES-- THE ENRAGED LOOK OF A WILD BEAST!
WH-WHAT ARE YOU GOING TO--
RRR-GRRR!
YOU MAY BE INCREDIBLY STRONG, SKULL-FACE...
BUT, WHEN IT COMES TO THE FIGHTING ARTS, YOU'RE NOTHING--
--DO TO ME? WHUNNN
--BUT A BAG OF BONES!
KLATTER!

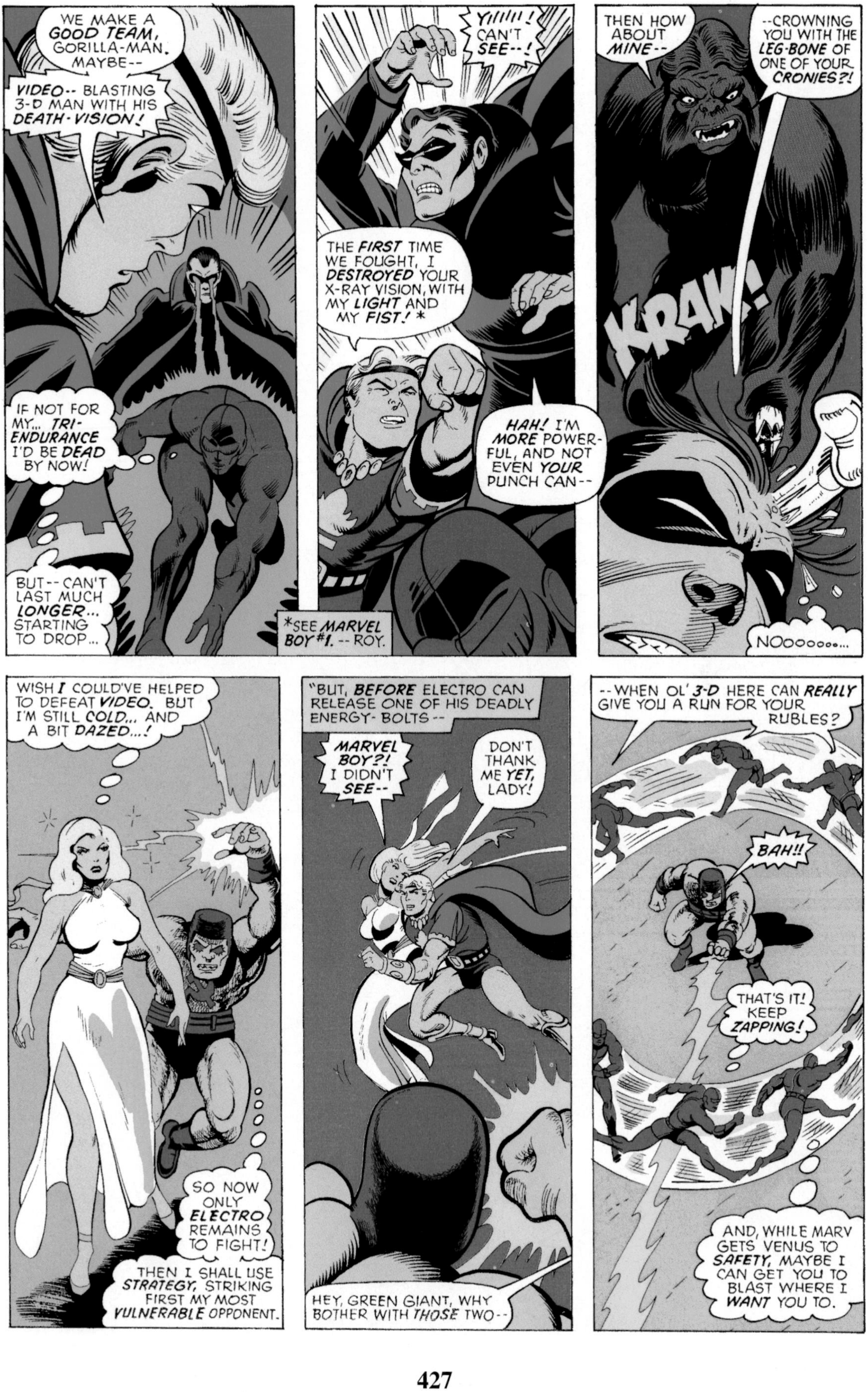
WE MAKE A GOOD TEAM, GORILLA-MAN. MAYBE--
VIDEO-- BLASTING 3-D MAN WITH HIS DEATH-VISION!
IF NOT FOR MY... TRI-ENDURANCE I'D BE DEAD BY NOW!
BUT-- CAN'T LAST MUCH LONGER... STARTING TO DROP...
YIIIII! CAN'T SEE--!
THE FIRST TIME WE FOUGHT, I DESTROYED YOUR X-RAY VISION, WITH MY LIGHT AND MY FIST! *
HAH! I'M MORE POWERFUL, AND NOT EVEN YOUR PUNCH CAN--
*SEE MARVEL BOY #1. -- ROY.
THEN HOW ABOUT MINE--
--CROWNING YOU WITH THE LEG-BONE OF ONE OF YOUR CRONIES?!
KRAK!
NOooooo...
WISH I COULD'VE HELPED TO DEFEAT VIDEO. BUT I'M STILL COLD... AND A BIT DAZED...!
SO NOW ONLY ELECTRO REMAINS TO FIGHT!
THEN I SHALL USE STRATEGY, STRIKING FIRST MY MOST VULNERABLE OPPONENT.
"BUT, BEFORE ELECTRO CAN RELEASE ONE OF HIS DEADLY ENERGY-BOLTS--
MARVEL BOY?! I DIDN'T SEE--
DON'T THANK ME YET, LADY!
HEY, GREEN GIANT, WHY BOTHER WITH THOSE TWO--
--WHEN OL' 3-D HERE CAN REALLY GIVE YOU A RUN FOR YOUR RUBLES?
BAH!!
THAT'S IT! KEEP ZAPPING!
AND, WHILE MARV GETS VENUS TO SAFETY, MAYBE I CAN GET YOU TO BLAST WHERE I WANT YOU TO.

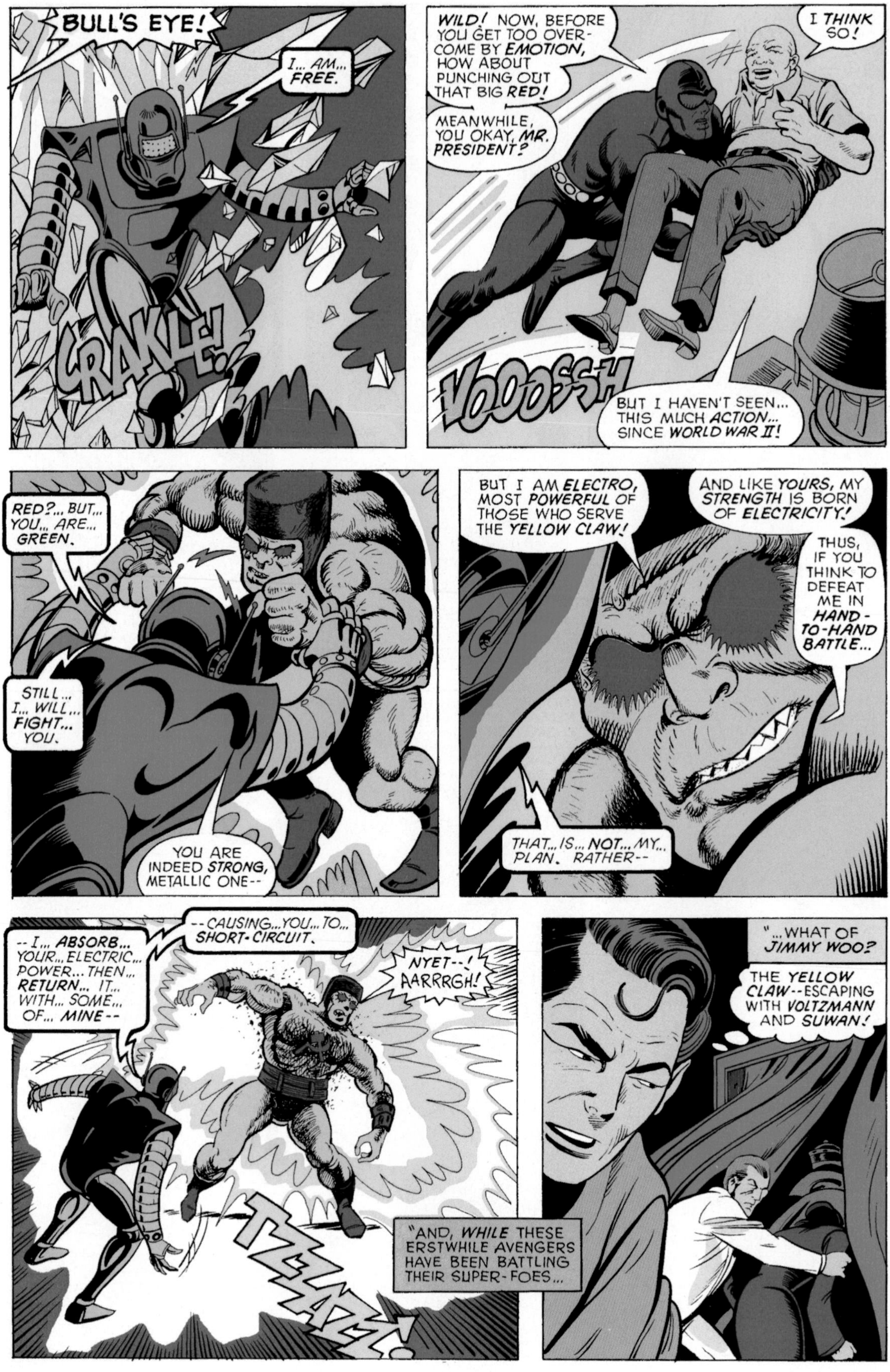
BULL'S EYE!
I... AM... FREE.
CRAKLE!
WILD! NOW, BEFORE YOU GET TOO OVER-COME BY EMOTION, HOW ABOUT PUNCHING OUT THAT BIG RED!
I THINK SO!
MEANWHILE, YOU OKAY, MR. PRESIDENT?
VOOOSSH
BUT I HAVEN'T SEEN... THIS MUCH ACTION... SINCE WORLD WAR II!
RED?... BUT... YOU... ARE... GREEN.
STILL... I... WILL... FIGHT... YOU.
YOU ARE INDEED STRONG, METALLIC ONE--
BUT I AM ELECTRO, MOST POWERFUL OF THOSE WHO SERVE THE YELLOW CLAW!
AND LIKE YOURS, MY STRENGTH IS BORN OF ELECTRICITY!
THUS, IF YOU THINK TO DEFEAT ME IN HAND-TO-HAND BATTLE...
THAT... IS... NOT... MY... PLAN. RATHER--
--I... ABSORB... YOUR... ELECTRIC... POWER... THEN... RETURN... IT... WITH... SOME... OF... MINE--
--CAUSING... YOU... TO... SHORT-CIRCUIT.
NYET--! AARRRGH!
TZZAZZ!
"AND, WHILE THESE ERSTWHILE AVENGERS HAVE BEEN BATTLING THEIR SUPER-FOES...
"...WHAT OF JIMMY WOO?
THE YELLOW CLAW--ESCAPING WITH VOLTZMANN AND SUWAN!

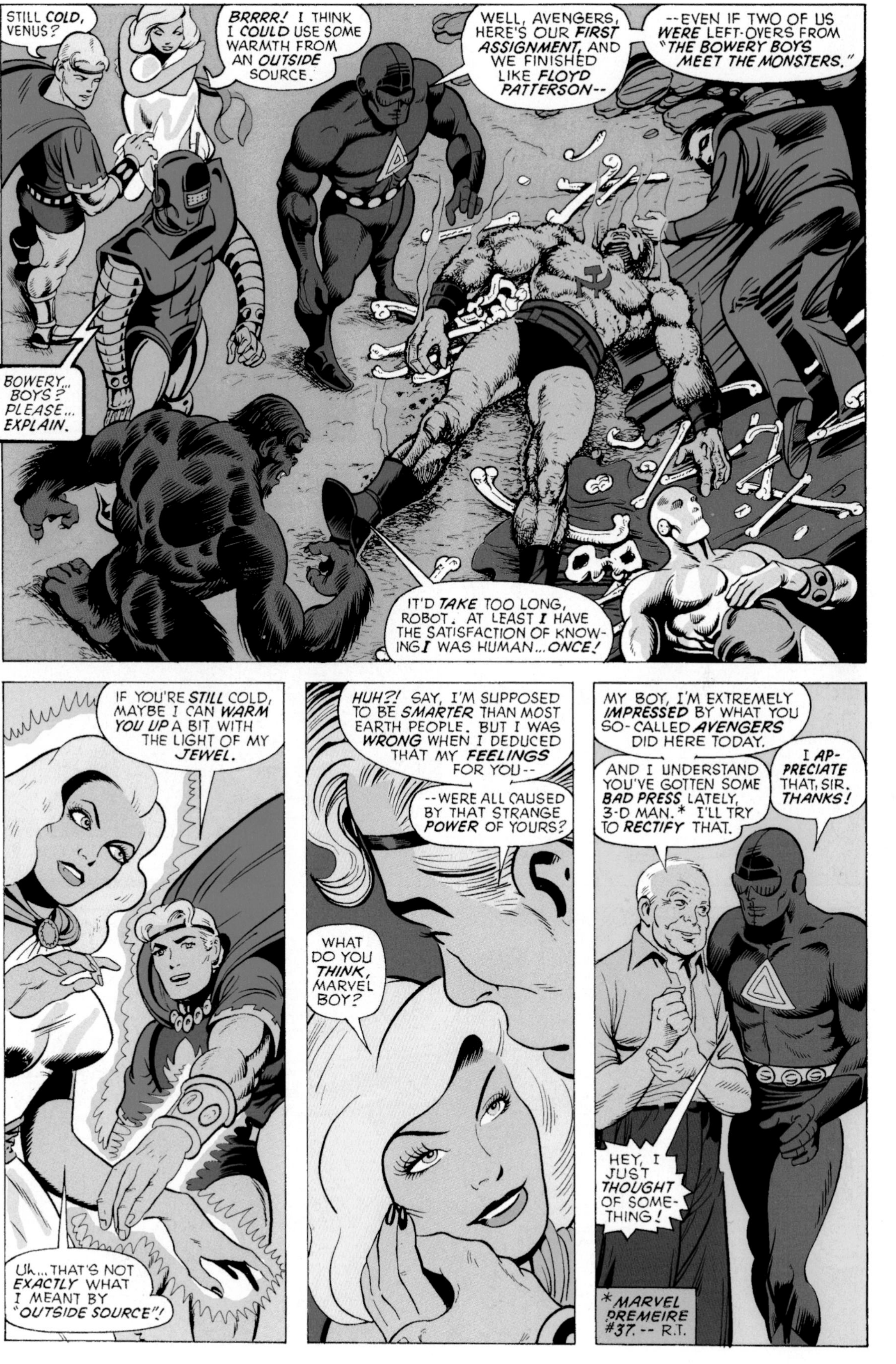
STILL COLD, VENUS?
BRRRR! I THINK I COULD USE SOME WARMTH FROM AN OUTSIDE SOURCE.
WELL, AVENGERS, HERE'S OUR FIRST ASSIGNMENT, AND WE FINISHED LIKE FLOYD PATTERSON--
--EVEN IF TWO OF US WERE LEFT-OVERS FROM "THE BOWERY BOYS MEET THE MONSTERS."
BOWERY... BOYS? PLEASE... EXPLAIN.
IT'D TAKE TOO LONG, ROBOT. AT LEAST I HAVE THE SATISFACTION OF KNOWING I WAS HUMAN... ONCE!
IF YOU'RE STILL COLD, MAYBE I CAN WARM YOU UP A BIT WITH THE LIGHT OF MY JEWEL.
Uh... THAT'S NOT EXACTLY WHAT I MEANT BY "OUTSIDE SOURCE"!
HUH?! SAY, I'M SUPPOSED TO BE SMARTER THAN MOST EARTH PEOPLE. BUT I WAS WRONG WHEN I DEDUCED THAT MY FEELINGS FOR YOU--
--WERE ALL CAUSED BY THAT STRANGE POWER OF YOURS?
WHAT DO YOU THINK, MARVEL BOY?
MY BOY, I'M EXTREMELY IMPRESSED BY WHAT YOU SO-CALLED AVENGERS DID HERE TODAY.
AND I UNDERSTAND YOU'VE GOTTEN SOME BAD PRESS LATELY, 3-D MAN.* I'LL TRY TO RECTIFY THAT.
I APPRECIATE THAT, SIR. THANKS!
HEY, I JUST THOUGHT OF SOMETHING!
*MARVEL PREMEIRE #37. -- R.T.

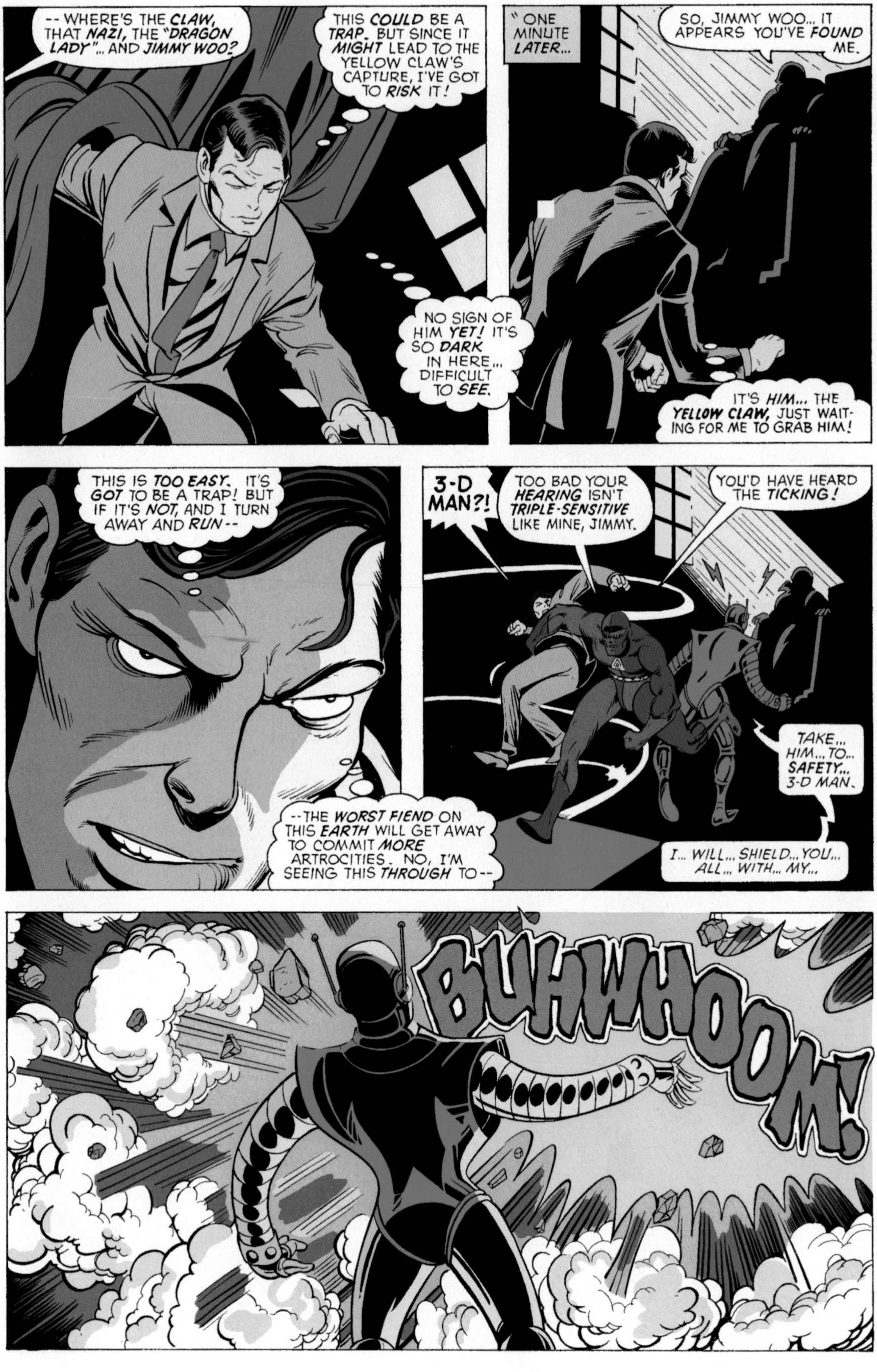
-- WHERE'S THE CLAW, THAT NAZI, THE "DRAGON LADY"... AND JIMMY WOO?
THIS COULD BE A TRAP. BUT SINCE IT MIGHT LEAD TO THE YELLOW CLAW'S CAPTURE, I'VE GOT TO RISK IT!
NO SIGN OF HIM YET! IT'S SO DARK IN HERE... DIFFICULT TO SEE.
" ONE MINUTE LATER...
SO, JIMMY WOO... IT APPEARS YOU'VE FOUND ME.
IT'S HIM... THE YELLOW CLAW, JUST WAITING FOR ME TO GRAB HIM!
THIS IS TOO EASY. IT'S GOT TO BE A TRAP! BUT IF IT'S NOT, AND I TURN AWAY AND RUN --
-- THE WORST FIEND ON THIS EARTH WILL GET AWAY TO COMMIT MORE ARTROCITIES. NO, I'M SEEING THIS THROUGH TO --
3-D MAN?!
TOO BAD YOUR HEARING ISN'T TRIPLE-SENSITIVE LIKE MINE, JIMMY.
YOU'D HAVE HEARD THE TICKING!
TAKE... HIM... TO... SAFETY... 3-D MAN.
I... WILL... SHIELD... YOU... ALL... WITH... MY...
BUHWHOOOM!

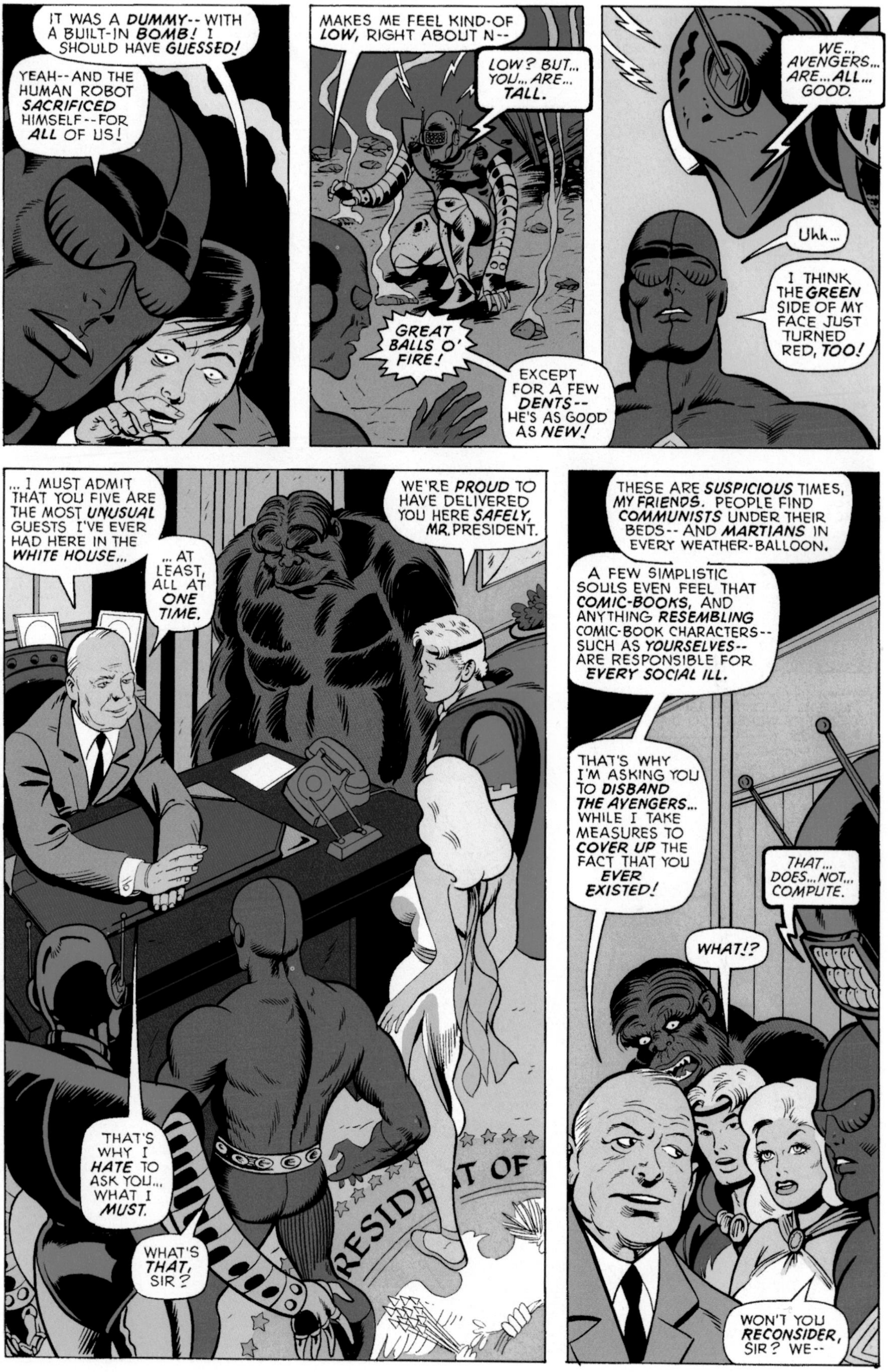
IT WAS A DUMMY-- WITH A BUILT-IN BOMB! I SHOULD HAVE GUESSED!
YEAH-- AND THE HUMAN ROBOT SACRIFICED HIMSELF--FOR ALL OF US!
MAKES ME FEEL KIND-OF LOW, RIGHT ABOUT N--
LOW? BUT... YOU... ARE... TALL.
GREAT BALLS O' FIRE!
EXCEPT FOR A FEW DENTS-- HE'S AS GOOD AS NEW!
WE... AVENGERS... ARE... ALL... GOOD.
Uhh...
I THINK THE GREEN SIDE OF MY FACE JUST TURNED RED, TOO!
... I MUST ADMIT THAT YOU FIVE ARE THE MOST UNUSUAL GUESTS I'VE EVER HAD HERE IN THE WHITE HOUSE...
... AT LEAST, ALL AT ONE TIME.
WE'RE PROUD TO HAVE DELIVERED YOU HERE SAFELY, MR. PRESIDENT.
THAT'S WHY I HATE TO ASK YOU... WHAT I MUST.
WHAT'S THAT, SIR?
RESIDENT OF
THESE ARE SUSPICIOUS TIMES, MY FRIENDS. PEOPLE FIND COMMUNISTS UNDER THEIR BEDS-- AND MARTIANS IN EVERY WEATHER-BALLOON.
A FEW SIMPLISTIC SOULS EVEN FEEL THAT COMIC-BOOKS, AND ANYTHING RESEMBLING COMIC-BOOK CHARACTERS-- SUCH AS YOURSELVES-- ARE RESPONSIBLE FOR EVERY SOCIAL ILL.
THAT'S WHY I'M ASKING YOU TO DISBAND THE AVENGERS... WHILE I TAKE MEASURES TO COVER UP THE FACT THAT YOU EVER EXISTED!
THAT... DOES... NOT... COMPUTE.
WHAT!?
WON'T YOU RECONSIDER, SIR? WE--

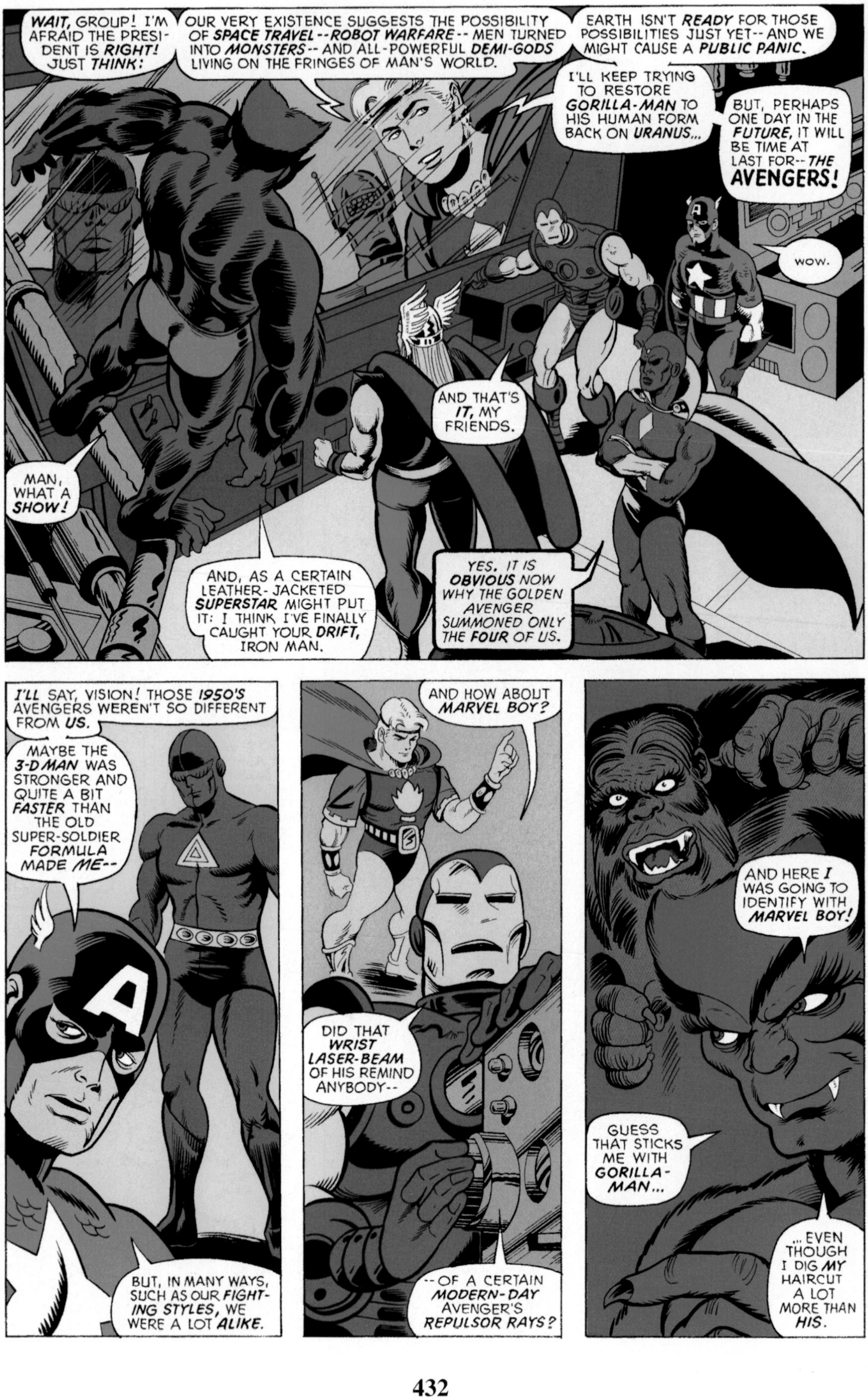
WAIT, GROUP! I'M AFRAID THE PRESIDENT IS RIGHT! JUST THINK:
OUR VERY EXISTENCE SUGGESTS THE POSSIBILITY OF SPACE TRAVEL--ROBOT WARFARE--MEN TURNED INTO MONSTERS--AND ALL-POWERFUL DEMI-GODS LIVING ON THE FRINGES OF MAN'S WORLD.
EARTH ISN'T READY FOR THOSE POSSIBILITIES JUST YET--AND WE MIGHT CAUSE A PUBLIC PANIC.
I'LL KEEP TRYING TO RESTORE GORILLA-MAN TO HIS HUMAN FORM BACK ON URANUS...
BUT, PERHAPS ONE DAY IN THE FUTURE, IT WILL BE TIME AT LAST FOR--THE AVENGERS!
WOW.
AND THAT'S IT, MY FRIENDS.
MAN, WHAT A SHOW!
AND, AS A CERTAIN LEATHER-JACKETED SUPERSTAR MIGHT PUT IT: I THINK I'VE FINALLY CAUGHT YOUR DRIFT, IRON MAN.
YES. IT IS OBVIOUS NOW WHY THE GOLDEN AVENGER SUMMONED ONLY THE FOUR OF US.
I'LL SAY, VISION! THOSE 1950'S AVENGERS WEREN'T SO DIFFERENT FROM US.
MAYBE THE 3-D MAN WAS STRONGER AND QUITE A BIT FASTER THAN THE OLD SUPER-SOLDIER FORMULA MADE ME--
BUT, IN MANY WAYS, SUCH AS OUR FIGHTING STYLES, WE WERE A LOT ALIKE.
AND HOW ABOUT MARVEL BOY?
DID THAT WRIST LASER-BEAM OF HIS REMIND ANYBODY--
--OF A CERTAIN MODERN-DAY AVENGER'S REPULSOR RAYS?
AND HERE I WAS GOING TO IDENTIFY WITH MARVEL BOY!
GUESS THAT STICKS ME WITH GORILLA-MAN...
...EVEN THOUGH I DIG MY HAIRCUT A LOT MORE THAN HIS.

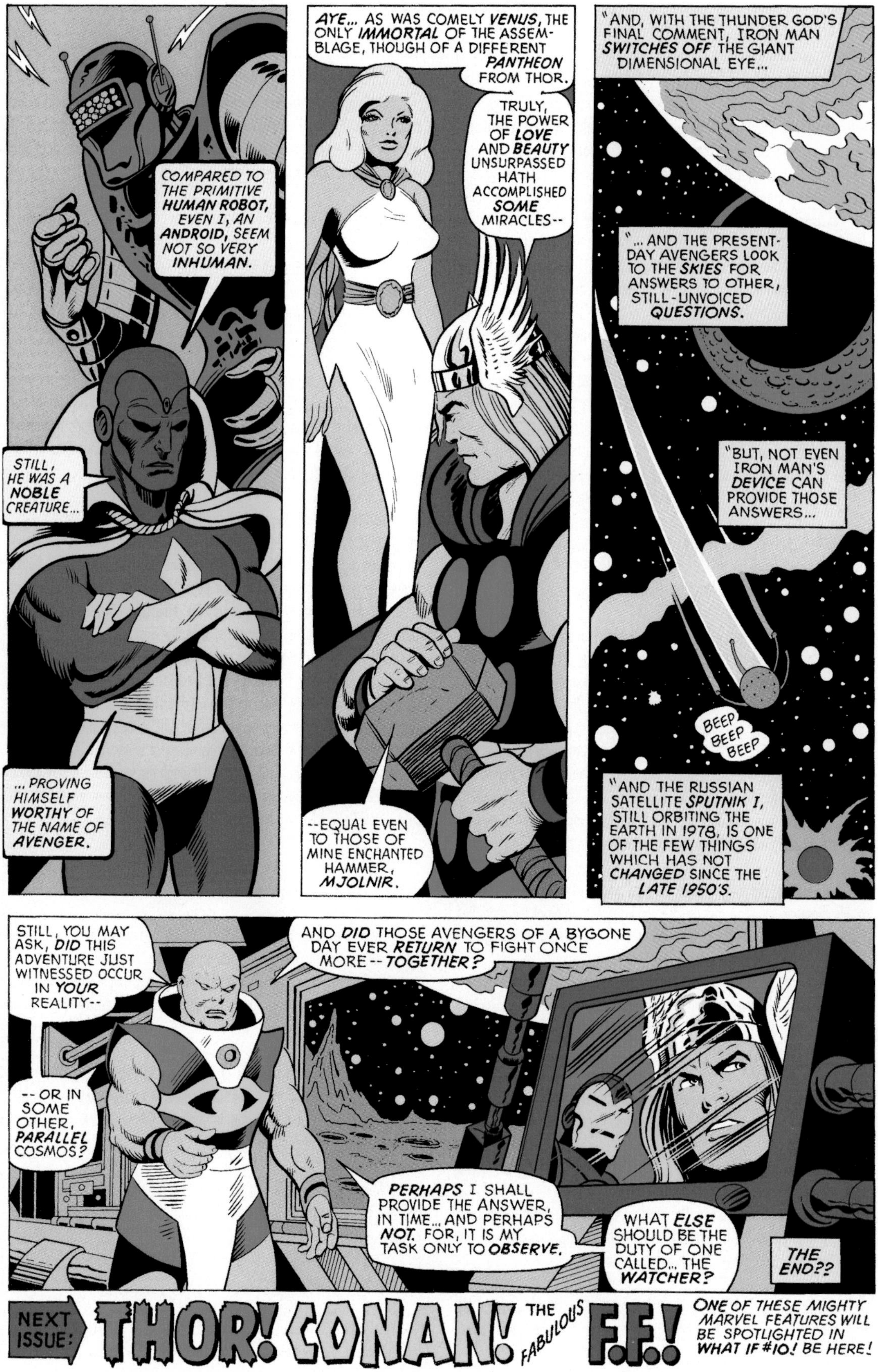
COMPARED TO THE PRIMITIVE HUMAN ROBOT, EVEN I, AN ANDROID, SEEM NOT SO VERY INHUMAN.
STILL, HE WAS A NOBLE CREATURE...
...PROVING HIMSELF WORTHY OF THE NAME OF AVENGER.
AYE... AS WAS COMELY VENUS, THE ONLY IMMORTAL OF THE ASSEMBLAGE, THOUGH OF A DIFFERENT PANTHEON FROM THOR.
TRULY, THE POWER OF LOVE AND BEAUTY UNSURPASSED HATH ACCOMPLISHED SOME MIRACLES--
--EQUAL EVEN TO THOSE OF MINE ENCHANTED HAMMER, MJOLNIR.
"AND, WITH THE THUNDER GOD'S FINAL COMMENT, IRON MAN SWITCHES OFF THE GIANT DIMENSIONAL EYE...
"...AND THE PRESENT-DAY AVENGERS LOOK TO THE SKIES FOR ANSWERS TO OTHER, STILL-UNVOICED QUESTIONS.
"BUT, NOT EVEN IRON MAN'S DEVICE CAN PROVIDE THOSE ANSWERS...
BEEP BEEP BEEP
"AND THE RUSSIAN SATELLITE SPUTNIK I, STILL ORBITING THE EARTH IN 1978, IS ONE OF THE FEW THINGS WHICH HAS NOT CHANGED SINCE THE LATE 1950'S.
STILL, YOU MAY ASK, DID THIS ADVENTURE JUST WITNESSED OCCUR IN YOUR REALITY--
AND DID THOSE AVENGERS OF A BYGONE DAY EVER RETURN TO FIGHT ONCE MORE--TOGETHER?
--OR IN SOME OTHER, PARALLEL COSMOS?
PERHAPS I SHALL PROVIDE THE ANSWER, IN TIME... AND PERHAPS NOT. FOR, IT IS MY TASK ONLY TO OBSERVE.
WHAT ELSE SHOULD BE THE DUTY OF ONE CALLED... THE WATCHER?
THE END??
NEXT ISSUE: THOR! CONAN! THE FABULOUS F.F.!
ONE OF THESE MIGHTY MARVEL FEATURES WILL BE SPOTLIGHTED IN WHAT IF #10! BE HERE!

Glowing embers pulsed and hoarded their heat in the large fireplace. The metal hand telescoped in to turn the logs over, then the other placed two more large chunks of pine on top. With a casual squeeze the hands split open the new timbers so that they might catch aflame faster. Within minutes a sizable conflagration roared steady like an engine, warming the old Federal drawing room and all the agents inside. The tender of the fire stepped to the side of the mantle and resumed a vigilant position. A brandy snifter smashed suddenly against the crackling wood fueling a bright flare, and the unmoving figure spun its head around to rest a cyclopic gaze on the gorilla, who winced.

"Watch where you're pointing that death ray, Howdy Doody! Throwing the glass in the fire is an old custom. Hey, when's Golden Boy showing up? I'm ready for dinner." Ken Hale loped over to the chair next to Jimmy Woo's desk to pore through a stack of betting forms.

The reclining figure on the couch stretched and pushed back a thick drape of shining hair to let more of the fire's heat warm her perfect face. She didn't open her eyes, but smiled as she answered her teammate.

"I believe Bob is in Huntsville, Alabama consulting Dr. Von Braun and the new space agency on stellar travel. He should be back soon. He gets so frustrated when Earth scientists can't follow his directions."

Though the young woman's response was brief and factual, her speech had a profound effect on the visiting government agents in the room. Both went into a slight stupor as the ethereal locution wound through the men, like a ghostly serpent coursing through their bodies. The man seated at the large oaken desk kept his fingers against his temples, calm and unaffected. Some have supposed that his ability to retain his wits at these instances was the result of having mastered ancient Chinese disciplines of meditation and concentration. In fact, a careful observer would notice that the fingers against his temples was not a gesture of focus, but a convenient way to put his thumbs in his ears whenever the woman began to speak.

The taller man, Oglethorpe, shook his head quickly as if to revive. "Ahem... so, ah, those are the ships that disappeared last week. None of the cargo has been reported turning up yet, at least not at the ports we can rely on to admit it."

"If this is all part of the same operation, it's one heck of an operation, I'll say. So why are you guys coming to us in particular with this? Because one of the ships was docked out here at Hunter's Point?"

"Actually, Mr. Woo," the shorter man volunteered, "because it does look to be so large an effort, Washington suggested that it's probably the work of someone you know best. The eastern mastermind known as—"

"YELLOW CLAW?!?" roared Gorilla Man. The visiting agents both crouched a bit, bracing themselves against Jimmy Woo's desk. The pencil he held with his toes snapped in two. Jimmy Woo held up his hand to indicate that calm and order was called for. Disturbed from her firewatching, Venus sat up and rested her head and arms on the plush back of the leather couch.

"I seriously doubt The Yellow Claw is behind this," said Jimmy Woo. "My team and I delivered a major setback to his organization just over a month ago."

"There's a great big hole in Outer Mongolia where a fortress used to be," Gorilla Man added smugly.

"Well sure," Agent Dirsken rejoined, "there's no arguing your outfit is top dog since that big rescue mission. Don't think the rest of us back in D.C. aren't green all over—I mean, the fact that you can run a team like this out of San Francisco proves you don't really answer to J. Edgar!"

"We completely respect the Director's wishes," Jimmy assured the man.

"Well sure. I didn't mean to—anyway, what I'm getting at is that— Yellow Claw or no—whoever's behind this thing has a major network behind him." Gorilla Man lost interest in the visiting agent and picked up the newspaper.

"Or her." Venus added. Normally a reminder to consider female prowess rubbed Agent Dirsken the wrong way, as it usually came from his wife or her sister. Instead of offering his glare in such cases, Dirsken made a grateful smile to let Venus know that he would never think her as intruding, and in fact her help was very, very welcome.

A flash reflected on the glass of the grandfather clock near Woo's desk, catching the eye of Agent Oglethorpe. He looked out the large french windows for the source. Over the buildings in the distance hung layers of cloud banks trapping a citywide cache of fog that kept the sky gray and visibility to a minimum. As the cumulonimbus lit up, the agent thought he was seeing a lightning storm. Then he remembered that the west coast rarely gets such electrical activity, and the flashes were coming closer. They seemed to be forming a trail. Agents Oglethorpe and Dirsken quickly stepped away from the window while Jimmy Woo simply raised his hand to shield his eyes. An aurous glow flooded the opening and bathed half of the room in shimmering warm light that looked to have the consistency of water. The lithe figure of a young man gracefully described an arc through the window and glided to a stop before the office door. Rather than switch off when the man stopped, the light seemed to retreat into the thick bands around his wrists.

"What's shakin' Bob. Are those slide-rule jockeys hep on how to make rockets yet?" Jimmy asked.

"They have a ways to go," Bob Grayson answered with a grin. "Everyone's still sweating over the Sputnik satellite program the Soviets are running. I told them the first one didn't have anything more than a simple transmitter that pinged out the temperature, but those fellows at NASA are working around the clock anyway."

Realization landed on the face of one of the visiting agents. "Say, with you pitching in, we could have men up in space—on the moon in no time!" said Agent Derskin, suddenly rapt in thought. "Wow, the Ruskies would probably kill to have their own spaceman."

Bob lowered the intensity of his usual smile, indicating he was about to be serious for a moment. "Astronaut is the term they use at the Flight Center, actually, and—"

"Star sailor?" asked Venus.

"Yes," said Marvel Boy. "...I don't actively show the scientists how to build anything. Mostly I let them know when they're on a trail that's leading to dangerous results. Which is often. They're pretty eager to get the Space Agency up and running, and the test pilots who have signed on to be the first astronauts are fearless. They'd throw themselves into orbit with a giant trebuchet if they could."

"Hah-ha, my kinda guys!" laughed Gorilla Man, busily scribbling his pencil on forms for tomorrow's Kentucky Derby. "Heck, I'm just gonna put everything on Tim Tam, he looks good. Still, we ain't ever gonna see the likes of Citation again. Now that was a horse! Wonder how late that bookie is up."

Unfettered by Ken Hale's non-sequiter, Agent Derskin returned to Marvel Boy. "You can't let those commies get ahead of us in the Space Race! Why don't you just show 'em the plans to your own rocket, the Silvery... Missile..?"

"Silver Bullet," replied Marvel Boy, now quite serious. "Look sir, I know the country is gripped hard by the fear of the Reds, but I assure you they're not ahead of the United States with their technology. They're just being less careful. I'll pipe up to keep good men from dying, sure. But it's incredibly dangerous to give people technological advancements they weren't ready to discover on their own. The people of Uranus will decide when they want to share their technology with people of Earth."

"Yeah, but you're from Earth, right?" Derskin's face grew more flushed. "I mean, you're still an American, ain't ya?"

"Legally speaking, I'm not a citizen of any country. I could pursue citizenship, but it might be tricky. If my father had never taken me from Earth, I'd be a German."

Derskin's eyes bulged. "A German! No wonder you don't have any loyal—"

The words hung in the agent's throat, stopped as his collar pulled up against his adam's apple. He became aware that a gorilla was holding him in the air by the back of the neck. "Son, I'd remember whose office I was in," said Ken. "Especially seeing how that window is still open."

Jimmy Woo got up from his desk. "I think you guys can head back to Washington, we can take it from here."

After the men left, Jimmy drifted over near the ape, again engrossed in his betting forms.

"Ken, your expertise as a mercenary might be a help here."

Even under the massive brow, Gorilla Man's eyes could be seen to roll in weariness. "I prefer Soldier of Fortune, thanks. Mercenaries will fight anyone for the right price. I like to think I've been a little more particular."

"We'd all like to think that," Venus added with a big sweet smile. That was as close as she had ever come to a verbal jab, but the light teasing lowered Gorilla Man's hackles. As far as anyone could tell, Venus was mostly incapable of delivering sarcasm, though she did appreciate it.

"Sorry Ken, I get terms confused sometimes. I mean heck, you fought with us in Mongolia out of national loyalty with no promise of compensation. There's no question about your principles, big guy—you've got plenty."

Ken put down his list of horses and raised up on his knuckles to have a look at the photos Jimmy Woo held. He seemed embarrassed that Jimmy felt it necessary to apologize.

"Let's have a look at those. I don't know that I'll be any real help."

"Well look at this," Jimmy offered. "This looks military—"

"That's a Coast Guard Cutter," Ken blurted. His massive hands began flipping through the photos rapidly. "And that's a PT 728... that one's an old PT boat too..."

"So, do they have anything in common?"

"They're all pretty fast," the ape replied, "and they all have cargo holds. My experience? Smugglers like to use vessels like this."

Jimmy turned to Marvel Boy. "Bob, do you think your rocket could track the equipment on any of these ships?"

"Not likely. There's nothing about the technology here—as I can see it— that would differentiate it enough to track just by its makeup. Your engineers are starting to use transponders on aircraft, but I doubt these ships would have them. Eventually you'll probably have them in all vehicles working with a system of tracking satellites. Then any pilot or skipper will know their exact coordinates at all times." Bob Grayson realized that he'd digressed into what Jimmy called "Criswelling" once again. The speculations were interesting but not always helpful, so he wrapped up his musing. "For now though, all you have is a Russian metal ball that pings."

"We'll get cracking at six," said Jimmy. "Everybody go visit the Sandman—we need to be rested up."

"Let me go phone this in," said Gorilla Man, loping off with his Derby picks. Everyone but the robot soon left the top floor office and went to their private suites in the old Federal Building. M-11 stepped out of the large window onto the ledge and walked to the corner of the structure. His head pivoted methodically from side to side as he scanned the city for criminal activity. After five minutes at one corner he walked the ledge to the next and scanned from there. This would continue until daybreak.

* * * * *

Jimmy Woo found himself walking down a corridor, though the details of his surroundings were hidden by mists. He thought of how unreal it all felt and then realized he was dreaming. Attempts to pinch himself seemed to hurt, but he was still certain that he was in deep sleep. It occurred to him to try to fly—he had been able to do so before when Venus explained the concept of lucid dreaming to him. Then he realized he would hit his head on the ceiling of the corridor. He walked a bit further before remembering that the corridor was still a dream, and that if he were in control of things, it wouldn't stop him from flying. He began to raise his arms and concentrate when he became aware of movement at his feet. Two large boa constrictors were slithering around him, winding ever closer. Looking up quickly he saw a murky form move closer to him from down the corridor. At ten feet away it became clear that the form was a human skeleton, walking as steadily as if it had complete musculature. Which of course, it did not. Jimmy not only could not fly, but he also couldn't move—the two snakes had worked up his body and had him held fast. The skeleton walked closer until its skull was inches away from Jimmy's face. No part of his body could move. He could only see the black of the cavernous eye sockets and hear a constant thumping. The thumping was steady enough that Jimmy thought it was his heart, and something in the back of his mind told him that it was knocking at the door of his suite. Opening his eyes confirmed this, and he raced over to open the door and thank M-11 for waking him.

Thirty minutes later after coffee and a half-toasted bagel, Jimmy Woo grabbed his overcoat off the rack. "Okay, the bad guys aren't going to come to us, so let's do some footwork and see what shakes loose."

"Should I start up The Silver Bullet?" asked Marvel Boy, eager to be more help.

"Nah, we're taking the Ed. One of the boats was snatched from Hunters Point Naval Shipyard, that's only a few minutes drive. Especially at this hour, no one's on the road yet."

The five agents entered the dedicated freight elevator outside the office and descended to the basement garage. As the metal doors slid apart a slight reflective outline gleamed from "The Ed," the 1958 Convertible Edsel that Jimmy requisitioned upon the group's return to the States. The car was big enough to accommodate a party of five that included a rather bulky robot and a mountain gorilla. It had also been the suggested choice of Marvel Boy, who found all fuel-combustion engine vehicles primitive, but did acknowledge that this model at least showed some innovation. Soon the auto was rolling down Divisadero Street and towards the bay.

Ken Hale's large nostrils took in the smells of the shore. "Love that salt air. Look into that blue. It's been a long time since I was out on the high seas. Now that's living. Well, maybe not for the tin woodsman back there, he might rust solid." Venus looked at the robot with concern. Sitting in the back seat, M-11 was so inert that it was easy to imagine he was merely a Hollywood prop, or perhaps some part of the car itself.

"M-11 can't corrode anymore," said Marvel Boy. "I converted all the metal of his frame to a Uranian alloy that won't bond with oxygen. I can't think of many natural forces on Earth that could degrade his body."

Ken Hale scratched at his massive brow as Jimmy Woo smiled. "See Bob, that's what we on Earth call a joke. Granted, I'm no Sid Caesar, but I'm just havin' a laugh at our one-eyed pal." Marvel Boy slid down in his seat a bit and pretended to pay no attention to the gorilla. One of his favorite things about being on Earth was the admiration and respect most people showed him. A few minutes of interaction with Gorilla Man always reminded him that he was still young and quite literally grew up in a bubble. Since joining Jimmy Woo's team, Grayson was excited to be out in a larger world with its vast lands and people so he could get the kinds of experience unattainable in the controlled environment of the Uranian Colony. Yet the worldly wise Hale constantly made him realize how far he still had to go. The resentment drifted away quickly with a pleasant melody that made any more barbed talked seem ridiculous. Perhaps inspired by the view of the Pacific Ocean, Venus was humming Bali Ha'i. Jimmy made an extra effort to control the steering wheel. "Man, I usually think musicals are for squares, but then you make the song really go. You oughta cut a record, V."

Venus smiled with genuine modesty. "Aw, I'm not that good, Jimmy. Anyway, it would be kind of like cheating—but who knows? Maybe just a recording of me wouldn't have the same kick."

Hale rapped his knuckles on the bench seat. "Huh. It never occurred to me to try that. Boy, if we could broadcast your effect over the Voice of America transmitters..."

"Maybe we could create world peace!"

"Uh... I was thinking we could stymie the Soviets, but yeah—same thing."

Bob's confidence returned. "It wouldn't work, unfortunately. Any more than pleasant music already calms people down. I've watched how Venus

affects men we go up against. Her proximity determines the potency of the effect, so I think her biology figures heavily into it."

"I'll say it does," said Jimmy, winking into the rear view mirror. Venus gave the back of his head a playful swat as everyone except M-11 enjoyed a laugh. Soon the Edsel was entering the main gate of the Naval Shipyards. Jimmy kept trying to show the guard his FBI identification card, but the young ensign couldn't stop staring at the unlikely group of passengers. His stare widened more as the gorilla in the front seat started speaking, and he realized the ape was, in fact, addressing him.

"Close that mouth, son, you might swallow a bug. What, you haven't seen an Edsel before?"

"Ah...no, I—"

"Check your day schedule," Jimmy said helpfully. "I let Petty Officer Arlidge know we were coming a while ago."

The guard looked over at the flagged note. "Oh...yes. Yes, go right in, sir."

The convertible motored into the shipyard and eventually stopped at Dock 7, where the Coast Guard Cutter Cape Hedge had been taken. The group piled out of the car, which raised noticeably when M-11 stepped out at last.

"You were a Navy man weren't you, Ken?" Jimmy asked.

Ken ambled along pleasantly, watching all the activity around the yard. "Naw. I was in the Merchant Marine though. I'll tie any knot you want. Alright, let's get this caper cracked by midday so I can go down to the bar and watch the race."

"Feeling antsy, Ken?" asked Venus.

"Yeah... I think I put a little too much dough down on that horse. Ahh. Too late now."

"Ken, I gave you a formula three weeks ago that would predict Equine victory eight out of ten times. If you would follow that—"

"Thanks kid, but I couldn't make heads or tails outta that. It's all Greek to me. I just put it up on my wall and called it modern art." The team continued walking in shadow, and Gorilla Man looked up at what cast it—a large aircraft carrier in for repairs.

"It's just math—the universal language," explained Marvel Boy in a louder voice to compete with the nearby sound of a motor.

"I thought love was the universal language." countered Venus.

"Impossible. There are cultures that don't have the concept of love."

"Well I wouldn't want to meet any of those folks!" the silvery-haired woman returned, aghast at the very idea. Her hair was blowing towards the bay and briefly laid down as the breeze died. Now the sound of propellers could be heard growing louder. Almost as one the team turned to see a P-51 Mustang reach the edge of the Carrier and continue down towards them. It was already so close they could see that the pilot in the cockpit was a skeleton.

Jimmy Woo's arms and legs wouldn't budge. He had never frozen in fear before, and he was still sure he hadn't. Though every instinct screamed for him to run, duck and roll, or jump into the water, he could only stand as the propeller of the Mustang grew quickly closer. The blasts of concentrated light he expected to fire into the plane weren't coming, neither was the clutch of a hairy arm to pull him out of harm's way. The distance between the plane and the team closed enough that he could even see missing teeth on the death's head of the skeletal pilot. The old warhorse of a plane was likely retired from active use, only kept around for training purposes. Still, it flew, and standing in its path was not the best place for anyone who wished to continue living.

Then two projectiles slammed into the aircraft—one at the base of the right wing, and one directly into the engine, jamming the blades instantly. Jimmy could now see the length of the silvery missiles, which were actually the extended arms of M-11, the Human Robot. The arms swiftly changed the course of the Mustang, first lifting its body just before it would have wiped the ground with the five agents. As fast as it all happened, the events seemed slowed down to a crawl. Jimmy could make out art on the nosecone, mere feet over his head. Some overzealous young team had painted a little rebus.

Underneath a slogan was written out. Five letters were faded, but in context of the rebus Jimmy understood it was supposed to say I GUN COMMIES. Jimmy preferred pretty girl art. Then the plane swung around as M-11's torso rotated 180 degrees and released the four-ton warbird towards the empty section of the shipyards. It slid and spun, spitting up waves of sparks until came to a crashing halt against a supply shack, the wing knocking out a window over an officer's desk.

"Thanks M-11," said Jimmy, now fascinated with his ability to lift his arms up and down. "I don't know what happened—I couldn't move a muscle."

"It was just like in that bizarre dream I had last night," said Venus. "Snakes had me bound so tight I—"

"You dreamt that too?" said the surprised Marvel Boy. "My dream had snakes—I was in this dark hallway walking and I saw a skeleton—"

"Then the big boa constrictors wrapped you up," finished Gorilla Man. "Either we're such a tight team that we have all the same nightmares, or someone's got our number somehow. I knew I was in a dream, too, 'cause a couple a' stupid snakes can't hold us in real life."

"Somebody's put a whammy on us. We all saw the skeleton, and then the snakes tied us up. Then when we see a skeleton in the cockpit of that plane, we're frozen just like in the dream." Jimmy Woo then looked over to where the plane sat, smoke rolling out of its engine from being punctured.

"Good thing M-11 doesn't have nightmares," said Marvel Boy, looking at the gleaming figure of the robot. "Of course, he doesn't do anything that approximates sleeping. I wonder if he did, would he dream?"

Marvel Boy's musings were cut short by the group now rushing over to the plane, led by an angry gorilla. "That skeleton is behind this! I'm gonna rattle his bones for him!" The plane was already being hosed with water pumped out of the bay by the Naval fire service in case the fuel tank might explode. The men jumped back when they saw Ken Hale leap up onto the

empennage and scramble to the front. His huge fingers clutched the hatch and pulled. A bullet spray of rivets shot out as the entire cockpit ripped from the frame. The skeleton tried to evade his reach but Ken Hale soon had hold of its ribcage. As he pulled the pilot out he saw something behind it flashing in the morning sun. The skeleton's right arm rotated freely in its socket to reach for the flashing object, then returned quickly, plunging an ornate dagger into Gorilla Man's forearm.

"WAARRROOORRRHHH!!!" The beast roared in pain, whipping the skeleton completely from the plane and slinging it down onto the asphalt to smash into several pieces. The skull rolled several feet to stop before Jimmy Woo, who reached down to pick it up. The death face's last act was to open its mandible and clamp down with full force on Jimmy's hand. "YEEOOOWWW!" blurted Jimmy, who then swung his hand back to hit the plane's wing. The skull cracked into two sections and the jaw popped off. Jimmy held his throbbing hand against his chest and Venus ran closer to examine it.

"Did it break the skin?" she asked. "No," Jimmy said through a contorted expression. "But it smarts like the Dickens! It feels like I just put my hand in one of those oversized rat traps!"

"I bet it feels better than this," said Ken Hale through a row of clenched teeth. He grabbed the lavish hilt of the dagger sticking out of his arm, and pulled it free.

"Nuts," said Jimmy. "I wanted to try and get some info out of that pilot."

Marvel Boy made an attempt to ease his team leader's conscience. "From my experience with animated skeletons, and I have some, not many of them can speak anyway."

"Just what I was going to say," added Venus, whose voice helped take some of the sting out of the injuries. "The magic needed to move a skeleton servant is usually temporary. It would have probably gone inert in a few minutes, and wouldn't have made anything more than a clacking sound if it tried to talk. They're tough for me because my power doesn't work on them at all." Her observations shed little light on the matter but served her goal of soothing her friends' aches somewhat. A helpful officer brought a first aid kit over to treat Gorilla Man's wound, and another came to lead them to their original destination, the docking slip where the Coast Guard Cutter had been stolen. Marvel Boy flew over the deck of the Carrier to see if it held anymore kamikaze-style surprises. When he was satisfied that it didn't, he flew around the shipyard and pondered the history of sea vessels and how they laid the groundwork for spaceships like he often flew now. He saw the light cruiser USS San Diego being stripped of artillery in preparation for being sold into scrap. He thought he should probably update M-11's technology a bit more than he had a few months ago. Finally he rejoined his team who were talking to the crew members on duty at the time of the theft. They had witnessed nothing; their accounts led Jimmy to believe a sleeping gas had been used on them.

"That's all we know sir." finished the young yeoman. "Thanks," replied Jimmy Woo. "It's not much to go on, but maybe we'll scrape up some kind of a lead."

"To find the location of the stolen Cutter? Because I know where it is, if so," Bob said as he landed.

The gorilla rolled his eyes at the young man. "What was all that about not being able to track ships yet with our primitive technology, then?" Ken growled.

"I've found something like the transponder I mentioned," returned Marvel Boy, a bit happy at having flustered Ken Hale. "That dagger you're holding has rare earth minerals in its makeup — very distinctive. And I'm picking up similar objects about a hundred miles offshore. The chances are very good they're related and involve the stolen ship." Bob Grayson's wristbands began to glow again and he turned towards the ocean. "I'll go check it out and tell you what I find."

"Hold up, Bob," said Jimmy. "I know you're still used to years of tackling danger solo, but we do things as a team now. We're all going out there."

"Thanks Jimmy, but I think I'll be fine."

"And how fine would you have been earlier if M-11 hadn't been around to stop that plane from cutting us up?" The debate came from Venus, strangely enough. Jimmy was grateful that she anticipated his reasoning and put the idea out herself. Though Marvel Boy generally took Jimmy's advice without question, there was still always the chance that pride could be hurt or one of the team might feel manipulated. Coming from her, such statements never seemed unwanted. "Point taken," smiled Marvel Boy. "But I can't carry all of you with me. How will we get out there?"

"This baby right here!" shouted Ken with glee, scrambling up on top of a boat unlike any Jimmy had ever seen. "Lookit! This is a hovercraft! They've been working on small versions of this, but this looks like it's got real power behind it. I bet this'll get us out there in a hurry!"

"Uh — sir, that's off limits," stammered the formerly helpful officer. "That's a prototype we're fine tuning, and no civilians should even be near it... sir..."

"Except these civilians," boomed a voice from up the dock. Everyone turned to see a tower-straight man with graying hair marching toward them. The young officer turned perpendicular to the man and his body pulled up as if a cable had retracted over his head. The decorated speaker was Admiral Peter Noble, who didn't take his eyes off Jimmy Woo's team even when saying "At ease." The sea-hardened man rested his hand on the sword at his side and his face made something approaching an approving smile. It was uncharacteristic for swords to be worn, even at full-dress ceremonies, but Admiral Noble always sported his without question. It looked so appropriate that no one mentioned it, even in private.

"While I'm not at liberty to reveal specifics, this group recently did our country a great service," announced the military figure. "If they need to borrow one of our vessels, they can do so for as long as they wish with the Navy's blessings." It seemed perfectly natural for this man to speak for the Navy with full authority, and several sailors hustled to make sure the hovercraft was full of fuel.

"Thank you sir," said Jimmy. "The FBI appreciates your help."

The old sailor saluted, turned 90 degrees, and left.

* * * * *

Spray kicked up behind the hovercraft as it raced behind the flying figure of Marvel Boy. Beams of light aimed down in the water from his wristbands, and smaller beams fed up to his headband. He began to slow down, and Gorilla Man dropped speed accordingly. Soon the craft came to a rough stop, gliding around the area that Bob Grayson had pinpointed. The caped man flew over and landed on the boat's deck as if his task were done.

"I thought you said the Cutter would be right here, Bob."

Marvel Boy shrugged. "It is. Whoever stole it must have sunk it."

Ken moved his furry hands around on the controls to bring the fans to low throttle, and it became easier to hear his remarks. "Kids. Always stealing Coast Guard Cutters for joyrides and sinking 'em in the Pacific when they're done. Whatcha'ya gonna do."

"Shoot," said Jimmy. "I wish Namora were around. This would be the perfect time to have her along." Jimmy referred to the cousin of Prince Namor, known more commonly on the surface as the Submariner. Her actual name had been Aquaria, and she was one of the very rare Human-Merman hybrids like Namor.

"No use thinking about her, she sent you packing when you asked her for help rescuing the President. She ain't gonna show up to check out a shipwreck for us."

"Well, she is royalty in the undersea world," answered Marvel Boy. "I believe there was civil unrest in Lemuria and she felt she was needed more there after helping surface people for years."

"I'm betting she's got a fella down there," said Venus with a wink.

"Besides, she found M-11 for us — she's okay in my book," added Jimmy, still staring down at the waves. "How far down is the boat, Bob?"

Marvel Boy touched his hand to his headband. "It's only a little more than seven fathoms deep, at the top. We could pull it up with a trawler, or inflate gaseous bladders inside its hull to —" His speech stopped with the sound of a splash. Quick glances around revealed that the only person not on the hovercraft now was Venus. Everyone turned to look at a spot of foam on the water that was quickly growing calm.

"Hey, what gives? That water's freezing!"

"She musta got tired of hearin' Bob talk." Marvel Boy glared at Gorilla Man, largely in disbelief that anyone could joke when a team member was possibly in trouble. "I'm kidding, son. Remember our lesson on jokes and what they are? You all need to cool your jets. She's a goddess or whatever — they don't drown."

It would take a minute before her eyes would adjust to the dark sea. Daylight still had yet to take a foothold in the Pacific. She swam all the way down until she felt bottom, and began to move along gradually from there. Her hand felt masses of coral, part of a reef system. She hoped it hadn't been hurt by the ship. Schools of fish darted out of her way as she progressed, leaving a tickling sensation on her skin. Her hand came to rest on something that had a tough surface, yet was amorphous in shape. She drew her arm back immediately and the thing drifted down her side. She felt the octopus press against her leg, and its suckers began to adhere to her skin. "Hey, no getting fresh," she thought as she peeled the cephalopod from her. Doing so caused the creature to use its primary defense, and a cloud of black enveloped her.

Suddenly a light cut through the sea, penetrating even the natural defense of the octopus. "Thanks Bob," thought Venus, who could now make out the hull of the Coast Guard Cutter a mere twenty yards in front of her. She swam to its side and upward. Not at speeds like Namora, she thought, but she could get along pretty well underwater. There were no signs of life on deck, which sat at a slant. She coasted around a bit and then decided to venture into the pilot house. Without the aid of Bob Grayson's light her eyes would have to adjust again. It didn't take long—she was already starting to distinguish an instrument panel. On a round glass she saw the movement of a shape, and then a sparkle. Realizing she was seeing a reflection of something behind her, she spun around in time to see an alabaster hand brandishing a knife similar to the one Ken had pulled from his arm.

The chalky hand holding the dagger pushed through the water towards Venus. She darted from her position to another section of the pilot house. More shapes arose from the black, shapes she knew to be people possibly, but she couldn't make out anymore than that. She easily outmaneuvered them and found the door she swam in. One of the shapes was trying to close it, but Venus braced her foot against the wall and pulled with everything she had. Her would-be trapper fell away, and she made it back out to the Cutter's deck. Now the shapes started emerging from the doorway behind her, and she thought to ascend as fast as possible. Afraid these attackers would somehow be gone upon another investigation, she turned to get a look—maybe she would see something that would help her teammates with this stolen ship case. As they moved out into the light still being sent from Marvel Boy on the water's surface, their forms coalesced to reveal themselves. They were skeletons like the one who nearly ran the team down with a plane back at the shipyards. Upon visual identification, Venus' legs went stiff, and her arms stopped moving. The same hypnotic suggestion or whatever had bound them before was at work again. She also couldn't open her mouth to cry for help, and her friends likely wouldn't have heard that anyway.

The skeletons advanced. There were six—no, seven of them altogether. Three of them had daggers like the first had, one was carrying the blade clenched in its teeth. Venus thought of how much she relied on her sway over men in dealing with danger, and how at this moment it seemed to not even be a power at all. The skeletons now were only about fifteen feet away, lurching steadily forward. They had no ability to swim, but with little body mass to create resistance, they could walk almost as fast as they might on dry land. They were ten feet away when a large shape plunged between them and Venus, ringing a loud boom upon contacting the deck. As bubbles dispersed around it, it was clearly M-11. His torso turned to the side and his right arm extended twelve feet. Then his torso pivoted quickly in the opposite direction so that his arm shattered the skeletons in one movement. Skulls spun in an orbit and drifted out through the water. The effect on Venus ended and she began moving. Her first act was to try to hug the robot, but M-11's mass proved difficult to embrace. The robot turned its head and looked upward, and Venus realized that M-11 couldn't get back up to the ship. "Hang on," she said, though she wasn't sure if the robot could understand her speech here. She made her way quickly to the surface.

"Hey! Going my way?"

"Venus! Are you okay?"

"Yes, thanks to M-11. He came down just in time! There was a whole skeleton crew coming for me, and I couldn't move—just like before! But he broke up the party. Say, he can't swim—do we have a way to bring him up?"

Gorilla Man hopped over to grab a steel cable and hit the release on the winch. "Here ya go. Take this down there and wrap it around him—hook it good, he's heavy!"

Venus took the cable back down to the Coast Guard Cutter's deck where M-11 stood as before. She wound the line around him under the arms and pulled the hook tight onto it. After she gave the cable a couple of tugs, Ken Hale began cranking the winch, soon using both arms once the slack went out of the line. Marvel Boy helped Venus back onto the hovercraft and the robot

began to emerge from the sea. Jimmy Woo watched, and thought how much this reminded him of when he first salvaged M-11 alongside the Atlantean Princess Namora. The robot wasn't functioning then, and was covered with barnacles and other sea life that had attached to his body. This time was very different. Water rolled off the android, but none poured out from inside him. His head turned slightly to see where Gorilla Man was operating the much simpler machine that retrieved him now. The ape snapped his fingers as he held his hand out in the gesture of a pistol.

"That was a close one," said the woman as she raked salt water from her silvery hair.

"Yeah, sorry," said Jimmy Woo. "Not long after you went under, we were talking and then it occurred to us that if a skeleton could fly a plane, that might be what took the boat as well. Since M-11 clearly isn't affected, we elected him next to go down. Like Bob said earlier, he doesn't rust these days." Jimmy turned to the robot who was now coming to a stand on the hovercraft. "M-11, did you detect anything else down there—besides skeletons, I mean?"

The cyclopic eye glowed slightly as M-11 made a rare utterance. He could speak, but no one could predict when it might happen. Such communications were almost always directed to Jimmy Woo.

"NO CARGO. NO FOREIGN MATERIALS. FUEL TANK EMPTY."

"Thanks," said Jimmy. "Not sure what to make of this, gang. A bunch of skeletons steal a ship, go until they run out of gas, then sink it."

"I have a theory," said Ken Hale, retracting the winch completely. "I think they had a diabolical scheme involving a fast ship, they took it, then forgot what the plan was because they don't have any brains in their heads!"

"I'm feeling like I don't either, right now." said Jimmy. "Okay, I don't think there's any more we can do here. Let's get the Navy their vessel back and tell them where the Cutter is. Though they'll probably just leave it here to become a reef."

The gorilla pulled the throttle back and the engines roared. The hovercraft lifted up noticeably, and the team made their way back to the mainland.

* * * * *

Later Jimmy Woo and his unusual band of Federal agents were mulling over the events of the morning at Ling's Tea Room. Jimmy poured another round of hot tea as he went over the details again. Bob Grayson waved for their regular waiter to see that his bowl was empty. The young man nodded and disappeared into the kitchen. "I don't know why they don't have sizzling rice on Uranus," said Marvel Boy as he spooned out the last bit. "All our food there is the same texture." Since the formation of the team and establishing of the group in San Francisco where Jimmy had been based, Ling's had been a regular stop during their weekly duties. Ling was a family friend of Jimmy's and his restaurant was accessible through certain underground passages in the city that Marvel Boy and the Human Robot connected to their own base of the Federal Building. This allowed them to go to Ling's without too much attention, as the FBI had asked them to be discreet in public appearances. A private room in the back was always made ready for the group.

Jimmy took another sip of tea before speaking again. "Every time we get a straight-on look at one of them, the spell kicks in. Or hypnotic suggestion. Whatever it is, we need to shake this thing off so M-11 doesn't have to do all the work when a skeleton shows up."

Marvel Boy looked to be preoccupied, touching his headband often. Whatever his concern was, it was put aside as the waiter brought him another bowl of sizzling rice soup. "Thank you," said the young hero.

"I know someone who may be of help," said Venus. "This kind of thing is right up his alley. His alley is in Manhattan, though."

"No problem when one of our pals has a rocketship," said Gorilla Man through a mouthful of dumplings. Bob Grayson sat up more attentively, a bit surprised to hear Ken Hale refer to him as a pal. Maybe he had been taking the gorilla's ribbing too personally, as Jimmy often said. The colonists on Uranus didn't tease one another, as a rule, and the practice was alien to Bob.

"Great," said Jimmy. "Can you give him a call and let him know we'll be over soon?"

"He doesn't open for business until night time. And I don't think he has a phone, but he'll probably be there. I guarantee that when we show he'll say he was expecting us."

"Well, then we've got a few hours to kill. It may be a late night, so I'd suggest everyone take a nap when we get back to the building." Jimmy Woo then added: "Try not to dream."

* * * * *

No one saw Marvel Boy's rocket when it landed directly behind the Statue of Liberty. The Silver Bullet was a bit shorter than the copper-plated lady, and was well hidden by it at night. A private ferry came to take the group over to the main island, where a private cab was waiting to transport them the rest of the way. The driver had taken the odd bunch into town several times, but was still unsettled at having a gorilla in the front seat. He tried to focus instead on the young woman who smiled pleasantly at the sights outside her window. The oversized cab made its way up further to Midtown, and over to 387 Park Avenue. The Packard motored into an alley where it would wait for the five to return, and the team piled out.

Venus held Ken's arm on one side and M-11's on the other, and made a bounce like she wanted to skip down the street. "We're off to see the Wizard!" Hale made an amused grunt at her joke. "I ain't a lion, and I ain't cowardly. Or was he the one that needed a brain?"

"No, that was the Scarecrow — right?" offered Jimmy.

"Yes, and the Tin Man needed a heart," explained Venus.

"Just like ours," said Ken.

"Aw, ours does too have a heart!" said the young woman looking up at M-11. Marvel Boy didn't know what everyone was talking about, and made a mental note to ask later. He was more concerned that they were about to meet a practitioner of the occult, which he was never comfortable with. He liked things that were science-based, logical and orderly. After leaving Ling's he had confided in Venus that he felt he confused about his abilities. He thought he should have been able to undo the effect of the shared dream with his headband's help, but it seemed to be limited — unnaturally so. "It's an impressive piece of technology," he had told her. "But sometimes I think I'm not getting the full use out of it, like I'm wasting it." Venus assured him that everybody feels this way about their abilities at times. Bob Grayson thought that she didn't quite get his meaning and he didn't know how to express himself more clearly on the matter. Nonetheless, her assurance had consoled

him some. The group had reached the top of a stairway, and stood outside a door with an onyx plaque. Engraved golden letters stated simply and directly:

MAGAR THE MYSTIC

Jimmy reached out to knock on the door, and it swung open quietly before his knuckles could connect. He looked back at the group and then back to the door. "Come in," said a measured voice. "You have been expected."

A sophisticated man wearing a suitcoat and a dark green turban appeared from around the corner. He knelt to kiss the back of Venus' hand. "Good to see you again my dear. You honor me by bringing along such esteemed guests."

"These are my friends, Magar. I'm working with the FBI these days, and Jimmy Woo here is my team leader. The charming gorilla is Ken Hale, and you probably have heard of Marvel Boy before. Our personal Univac there is called M-11." Hands were shaken and the mystic led the group over to a round oaken table that had seven candles. Everyone but M-11 took a seat as Magar instructed. Magar said something quietly that no one could understand.

"Mister... Magar, we've recently been put under some kind of hoodoo," began Jimmy. "Somehow we all had the same dream of a skeleton, and now when we encounter them — which is surprisingly common lately — we freeze up. No one can move, except M-11 of course."

"Yes," replied the somber man. "You have been the targets of Dream Hypnosis — a very potent form of suggestion, since it is placed in the subconscious during deep sleep. I could see it when you entered, and I've already removed it."

"You saw it?" asked Marvel Boy.

"This practice leaves a psychic marker, if one is able to see such things. And I am. You each had a small floating skull beside the left temple. Dispelling the suggestion was a simple matter. And one that was more scientific in nature than magical, if that lessens your concern, Mr. Boy."

"It's actually Grayson," returned Marvel Boy, "and are you reading my mind, now?"

"No, I read your face. It is very revealing." Bob Grayson felt a little embarrassed and yet relieved that his telepathic abilities seemed to still be unchallenged. Magar opened a brass box and took something out. When he turned around, he was holding a human skull.

"Move your arms please."

Each of the agents was satisfied to find full motion in any tested body part even as they stared at the skull. "Not bad!" said Ken. "Jimmy, slip this guy an extra Hamilton. Wait 'til those bonebags try to get the drop on me again."

"Well great, I guess we don't need to take up anymore of your time, sir." Jimmy Woo started to push himself up from the table and Magar held out a halting hand. "No one comes to Magar for mere jinx and hex removal. Any gypsy witch could do that." Marvel Boy frowned. "No, whether you know it or not, you have sought me out for greater answers. Please, enlighten me to your quest."

Jimmy sat back down and turned more towards the mystic. "Well, we're investigating a number of stolen sea vessels, that all went missing at the same time. The one we've found so far was crewed by a group of living skeletons, I guess you'd call them."

"I have encountered such acolytes. In great numbers, they can be very dangerous."

"Tell me about it. I'm guessing the other ships were taken in a like fashion. So the reason for the hex is pretty clear. But we couldn't find a reason for the theft."

"Ah," said Magar, now reaching to remove a thick piece of red velvet from an object on the table. From the size, Ken expected to see another skull. What he did see was a crystal ball, reflecting the candlelight of the table. The glints of light seemed to swirl inside the orb, moving as if by choice. Magar put his fingertips on either side of the sphere without touching it, and the clear ball became opaque, not mirroring the candles at all. "Venus may have told you of my gift—the ability to commune with the formerly living."

"Dead people, I call 'em," said Ken.

"It depends on your point of view. That is not my greatest gift, however. More valuable is the ability to know which ones to talk to. Merely being in a spirit realm doesn't qualify a being to answer any question. More often than not, they seek answers from us. Since your mission concerns piracy, I believe it logical to go to the greatest of that number."

Magar began chanting words that Jimmy couldn't understand and that seemed to make Venus momentarily dizzy. Clouds of obsidian formed inside the crystal and began to swirl at great speed. On Magar's last word, the candles on the table flared a couple of feet high, producing a haze of smoke over everyone's heads. Though the window by the bookcase was open, the soft night breeze didn't affect the cloud, which now looked like the ones in the sphere. In the smoke a dark shape began to approach from some distance. Near its head were small flashes of light. At once the figure became clear, clothed in a long coat with its fists resting on a large belt around the middle. A scabbard hung from the being's left hip, and its head sported a large hat with a curling side brim. The flashes of light were now distinguishable as burning matches twisted into the man's thick black beard.

"YAHRR!!! Who be of such hardy stock that would summon the shade of Edward Teach!?"

"Dread specter, you are here at the request of Magar the Mystic. I summon you on behalf of these mighty heroes. They are the ones who have business with you."

"Ahrrh... such a motley bunch I've not seen in over two hundred years then," said the spirit, his eye widening as he looked around the table. Uncharacteristically, Ken Hale was unnerved by this development. He had assumed he was seeing something that worked like television, and wasn't expecting the vision to acknowledge his own presence. The pirate then made an expression similar to the ape's, and Ken followed his gaze to see that the object it studied was Venus. "Shiver me timbers."

"Great Captain," said Venus, even being sweet to the long dead Scourge of the Seas. "We are seeking stolen ships. We do not know the culprit, but he appears to be using magic. We cannot discern the motives either. The first vessel we found was sunk for no apparent reason. Can you offer insight?"

The thickly garbed spirit stared at her some more, and then resumed its former manner. "Remember lass, not all pirates steal for treasure, and not

all commandeers mean to keep the ship. When me crew and I fired upon the HMS Scarborough the first time, we were not after the King's Man O' War. Me other vessel plundered two Merchant ships right out of port! Ha-har, 'twas a good day!" Amused with his past victory, the pirate pulled out a long pistol and fired it off into the air with a loud report. Ken Hale noticed that an actual blast mark was left in Magar's vaulted ceiling.

The boisterous pirate then broke into laughter and his image faded into the murky smoke.

"Now I'm more confused than before," said Jimmy.

"Spirits and oracles are rarely direct in communication. Being cryptic is how they judge the tenacity of mortals. When you begin to understand them, you often earn the bond of the spirit."

"Do I really want a bond with a murderous pirate?" asked Bob.

"That is always a question worth asking," said Magar with a smile. The smoke over the table began to drift apart, then stopped and began swirling. Another dark shape drew closer and an aged woman's face appeared, her eyes wider than seemed possible. She had been groaning softly and now the sound built to a shriek as she blurted:

"WE RQSA JE MXUHU OEK VEKDT JXU HUT REN!"

The image then vanished and the smoke blew apart. The crystal ball became clear again.

"What was THAT?" asked Venus.

"Other spirits often invade openings to our world with their unwanted communications," explained Magar. "I would pay it no attention."

The team got up from the table, each shaking hands with Magar while mulling over the visions just seen. As they walked out the door, Jimmy turned suddenly. "Oh, I'm sorry. How much does that session cost?"

"My services are always free to friends of the lovely Venus. Were it not for her powers of influence, I would be but a shrunken head hanging from a tree in New Guinea today."

"Thanks again," said Jimmy from the bottom of the staircase. They exited onto the street where the cab waited, its driver leaned back and snoring. No one noticed the shadow across the street studying the team intently.

* * * * *

Jimmy Woo wound his watch as he and his team walked back to the cab that awaited them. "Okay everyone. Let's hightail it over to Lady Liberty and catch the Silver Bullet. We can put in some facetime at the Bureau in the morning, see if they've turned up anything." Suddenly a flash went off from across the street, and everyone but M-11 recoiled at the bright light. The robot shined a light of its own at the tall dark-haired man with the camera, and the beam grew brighter. "Wait M-11, it's just a photographer, turn down your ray." This came from Marvel Boy, whose eyes were used to adjusting fast to sudden changes in light. The man stood in place as the group approached him, realizing that fleeing would be useless anyway.

"Say, why are you lurking around here snapping our photo?" asked Jimmy Woo.

"Kind of obvious, isn't it? I mean, I don't know who you — people — are, but you look like news to me," answered the burly young man. "I haven't been back in the states for a while, but last I heard it was still a free country."

"You're... Pat, right?" asked Gorilla Man. The man with the camera was stunned.

"Uh. Yeah. That's right. How do you know — "

"You used to hang around Jann of the Jungle some, I think."

"Yeah, good ol' Jann!" said the man, relieved. "We saw some gorillas together, but never one who talked! I haven't seen her in a while, do you know how she's doing?"

"She seemed fine when I saw her last. She's the reason I'm working with this bunch. That's a nice one. Can I see that?" Surprised to have found someone who knew of him, the man called Pat handed over his camera with almost no consideration. Ken Hale looked at the device for a minute, then crushed it in his hand.

"You wanna shoot wildlife, head back to the Congo. Now beat it." Ken turned and climbed into the cab. Venus made an apologetic shrug before Pat, who stood with his mouth open. Jimmy Woo turned quickly so no one could see him stifle a laugh.

* * * * *

Upon touchdown at the secret location in Arlington, Virginia, a government driver pulled up to escort Jimmy Woo's team into the District of Columbia. Assistant Director Wall welcomed the five at the front door of the Department of Justice Building on Pennsylvania Avenue, making several quick asides to employees warning them not to stare. Once in Wall's office everyone sat down except M-11, who stood vigilantly at the window. "Good to see you again, Agent Woo. So what brings the FBI's top dog unit to our offices?"

"Thought we'd see if you boys have made any progress on this stolen ships case your agents brought to us," said Jimmy as he leaned back in the leather chair.

Wall stared at Jimmy Woo blankly as if waiting for more information that never came. "Stolen ships."

"Yeah, the ships that all went missing at once last week. Derskin and Oglethorpe gave us a file full of photos and notes."

"Derskin and Oglethorpe."

Gorilla Man was growing annoyed at Wall's unresponsiveness. "You know, that Abbot and Costello team who works outta here. Short stocky guy and a taller one."

"We don't have any men working out of this branch by that name."

"Could you look through your files?" asked Jimmy, now leaning forward in his chair.

"I don't have to. I know every agent in Washington, and we don't have any named Oglethorpe or Derskin. When did these men come to you?"

Jimmy felt blood drain from his face and was uncharacteristically uncomfortable. "I don't get it. The front desk in the Federal Building sent the guys up like business as usual." The arm of the chair Ken Hale sat in crunched under his grip. "Somebody played us like prize chumps! I knew I didn't like those guys. I should have shook 'em down for more I.D."

"I blame myself," said Marvel Boy. "I could have scanned their minds and picked up any deception."

"You came in late," reminded Venus. "When you arrived we were already talking to them like it was official business — you had no reason to be suspicious." Jimmy hopped up from his chair, now much more animated. "That's right. In fact, one of the men started in on an argument with Bob almost as soon as he got in. Probably to keep him on the defensive and too busy to use his headband." The young agent paced around the desk and came to a stop next to the Human Robot. "Somebody sent us on a wild goose chase. For what? We weren't working on a case at the moment."

"They wanted us dead," said Ken matter-of-factly. "The skeleton pilot was supposed to take us out, and if that didn't work, there was the backup of the ones on the Coast Guard Cutter. All ready to work because of the dream whammy they threw on us. Classic villain stuff — everybody wants us dead because we're good guys. End of story."

Venus countered in her manner that never gave offense. "No, anyone who would plan so well as to sneak in fake agents, plant a suggestion in our subconscious minds, and hide an animated skeleton at the Naval Shipyards — that planner would certainly take into account the robot on our team who wouldn't be affected by the magic."

Assistant Director Wall took a bromo-seltzer out of his desk drawer and poured it into a glass of water. "You people lost me back at the skeleton pilot."

* * * * *

The gleaming rocket soared above an ocean of clouds. Its chrome surface took on the golden hues of sunset — a sunset that stretched on much longer than usual since The Silver Bullet was on a westward trajectory. Inside the large cockpit of the craft, the pilot fussed with the instrument panel, though he had already programmed the course into the guidance system and didn't need to do anything else. Jimmy Woo sat in the copilot's seat with his face firmly lodged against his hand as he stared out the window. "If you look on Monitor 8 you'll see the Mississippi river below," said Marvel Boy.

"Fascinating," returned Ken Hale, who spun around in his seat and got up. He walked over to the Preservation Cell, a trunk-sized refrigerated chamber that Marvel Boy used when procuring organic samples for study. The ape reached his arm in and pulled out a small bottle of Coca-Cola. "Anyone else want one?"

Bob Grayson grimaced slightly at Ken Hale's misuse of his equipment, then raised his hand. The variety of flavors on Earth still fascinated him, and he rarely passed up an opportunity to taste anything. For some time no one said anything. Then Jimmy got up to go get a drink as well, and Venus smiled, realizing her team leader was starting to emerge from the dark mood he had been in since the D.C. visit.

"Sorry I've been such a pill, everybody." Jimmy said. "I've been worried that Jerry back in Washington thinks we're losing it. I guess it's inevitable when you get talked up as much as we do — everybody slips up some time. I just want you to know the blame lies squarely with me."

"Hey buddy, we're not worried what they think. Well, I'm not. And I'm sure the robot isn't."

Venus chimed in too. "Besides, we've got some clout built up. We did rescue the President after all. That should be good for something."

Ken grew more animated. "Yeah, the pressure oughta be on him! What's he been doing since then? All I ever hear about is new places he's played the back nine."

As usual, Bob Grayson missed the ape's gruff joke and gave an actual answer. "He does have a plan in effect to create a new highway system. If you ever plan to motor west, multiple interstate roads will allow for a straight drive."

"You sure get a lot of weird facts from The Silver Bullet," said Hale as he swigged his soda.

"I didn't get that from the ship's computer, I read it in the New York Times while we were there—after I finished the crossword. They need to make those puzzles tougher, I finished it too fast."

"Well they ought to post your mug on the cover of Popular Science. In fact, why not go on Twenty-One and make us a fortune."

"Well, I have a bit of an edge. It would kind of be cheating."

"Professor Van Doren can do it, so can you," said the gorilla.

"Aw, now that's just a rumor," said Jimmy. "You always think everyone's cheating, Ken."

"From my experience, everyone is. At least, everybody who looks to be the best at something. I'm not judging, I'm just saying."

Venus leaned back in her seat with a grin. Hearing her friends banter about news and trivia again meant the cloud had lifted and they would be ready to get back cracking on the mystery in no time. Their renewed enthusiasm would have to wait until morning though. Upon reaching San Francisco, Jimmy Woo insisted as usual that the group turn in for the night to get an early start the next day. Venus admired this tendency of Jimmy. Other crime-fighting organizations she had known were often insistent on burning the midnight oil, driving their people to the point of exhaustion. With exceptions, Jimmy always tried to keep his team well fed and rested, encouraging any practices that led to being more focused and sharp.

As the group retired to their rooms, M-11 stepped through the large window onto the ledge to begin his nightly surveillance.

* * * * *

Venus found herself running through a forest glade. Her feet were bare—in fact most of her was. She almost fell upon stepping onto a patch of damp moss, but managed to balance herself and slide on her feet down a steep but short hill. She began to run again, taking in deep draughts of spring air. She could almost taste honeysuckle with each breath. A field by a stream was thinly filled with grass nearly as tall as she was, and she immediately followed the urge to plunge into it. The blades of the plants wicked gently at her skin, producing tingles that enveloped her body. As the growth turned thicker, she changed direction and raced to the stream's edge, kicking up sheets of clear water. She enjoyed the mud through her toes until reaching a small lagoon. Arcing her body, Venus dived fully into the still water that had been warmed all afternoon by the sun. Minnows darted out of her path as she propelled herself with long kicks. She paused to watch the plantlife

flow slowly back and forth and felt her long hair matching the movements. The lengths of reed cast dazzling patterns of shadows that she could have watched until dark. Instead she pushed upwards to the shimmering surface, dotted with waterlilies. As she breached, several lily pads clung to her body like a garment. She didn't bother to remove them, they would fall off soon enough after drying out. Venus stepped carefully on her way to the edge to keep from breaking any of the reeds growing there. She soon stepped onto soft grass and sat down to let the sun dry her figure. After a few minutes on her back she rolled over on her stomach and rested her chin on crossed arms. Having indulged most of her senses, she closed her eyes to give her ears equal time with the wonders of nature. In this way she became aware of a family of birds fussing over their nearby nest, as well as a colony of frogs. The next animal to take her attention she wasn't sure had made a noise at all, but she could tell it was in front of her. She opened her eyes to see a small dog standing in front of her, wagging its tail. The woman smiled and patted at the ground in hopes the animal would take that as an invitation to come closer. It tilted its head, and then took a couple of steps nearer. Then Venus felt Marvel Boy's hand touch her shoulder, and she woke up.

"Ah. Um. I'm sorry to disturb you... but we're... ah, the dream suggestion. It's happening again."

Awash in moonlight from her bedside window, Bob Grayson could see Venus' startled expression turn to a soft smile. "Really? And I was having such a beautiful dream, too."

"Yes, you were. I mean—well, I watched some of it, to see where it was going. You know, to figure out what the goal of... whoever... was. You know, the people who made us dream about the skeletons."

Venus sat up now, gathering her silk sheet up against her. "Bob, I don't mind that you watched me."

"It was just work!" He stepped back from the bed some. "Then I thought maybe I better wake you up anyway, before some other suggestion was planted that might endanger you. Which could be happening to the others now, so we better go wake them up." Venus slipped a robe on and went to knock on Ken Hale's door as Marvel Boy went to Jimmy Woo's. Within minutes all of them were standing in the hallway.

"So how do you know this was another subconscious invasion?" asked Jimmy. Grayson tapped at the solid black band on his forehead. "Just as I was falling asleep it occurred to me that our mystery villains might try the trick again, so I took my headband off the nightstand and put it on. I usually don't sleep with it on. It leaves enough of a ring on my head having it on all day. But sure enough, as I was entering REM sleep, the band alerted me to impulses that didn't originate in my brain."

"Nice of you to see to Venus before the rest of us," Ken Hale smirked. Grayson's face grew flush, and Venus interjected. "Ladies first!" Jimmy looked around at the paneling on the walls and back to the young man. "Can you tell who did it—where it came from?"

Marvel Boy put his fingers to his temple. "It's still happening, actually. Like a broadcast." His blue cape made a swirling flourish as the hero turned to walk down the hall. He reminded Ken Hale of an uncle who used to seek out water sources with a divining rod made of tree branches. Bob turned into the office and walked forward until he realized he was about to hit a wall. Then he went over to the window and stepped up into it. On the ledge outside M-11 turned his eyebeam onto Grayson. "Turn that off, you're blinding me." The robot instantly complied. When the flashes disappeared from Marvel Boy's vision he looked forward as his headband directed. "There." He raised his arm and pointed at a window across the street. In the corner was a metallic object that looked to be an oscillating fan in the dark. Marvel Boy quietly lifted from the ledge and drifted across the canyon of buildings to hover outside the window. The glass was open, and inside the room a dark figure stood by a machine, busily adjusting controls. The round end of the device was what looked like a fan from a distance. The man's hands stopped, and he turned to discover the observer floating above him. He scrambled wildly, knocking over other pieces of equipment and kicking wires. Marvel Boy now came down into the room and his wristbands glowed to fill the area with light. The man pulled a gun off a table and began firing repeatedly at his pursuer. Marvel Boy flew quickly to the left in a twisting path that the gunman couldn't draw a bead on. Then he pointed his flat hand forward and and the weapon immediately grew too hot to hold. As it fell to the floor, the man doubled around to another window on the same wall. Just when Marvel Boy thought he would stop, the man leapt, smashing through the glass and beginning the long fall to the street. From the Federal Building M-11 extended his right arm with such force it seemed another gun had been fired. The expanding bands that made up his limb hit their maximum length just as the man was falling out of reach. M-11's fingers then also extended, which surprised Jimmy as he hadn't seen them do that before. The alloyed hand clamped onto the man's shirt and the robot's arm began to retract.

"Gotcha, goofball." Hale's long arm grabbed the man's collar as M-11 brought him to the ledge. He was short and wiry, and kicked and flailed with such energy that even the gorilla had trouble containing him. "Where do you think you're going, idiot? I don't see a parachute on your back."

"He was already headed to the street," said Venus. "He must really not want to be taken alive. Calm down, sir. We just want to talk to you." As usual Venus was casually employing her effect so as not to alert her target to what she was doing. If someone knew about Venus they might be able to employ a mental exercise to hold her influence at bay long enough to escape. The thrashing man seemed so completely unaffected that she dropped any subtlety and began to sing one of her favorite traveling songs covered by Nat King Cole a few years back. Jimmy instantly plugged his ears. Since Ken had one hand occupied with the culprit, he launched into a series of grunts and hoots as a natural ape might. Besides helping mask the infectious tones of his teammate, this would often frighten criminals to the point of excessive release of information. Jimmy relaxed slightly, expecting a long confession to begin pouring from the captive. Instead he saw a flash of moonlight glinting from an ornate dagger that was clearly of the same make that the skeleton pilot brandished the day before. Just as Venus reached the lyrics "looks mighty pretty," the small man's arm swung out, raking the same spot on Ken's arm that the pilot had hit with his own knife. The ape howled.

"SON OF A—"

Jimmy's leg fired upwards and his foot knocked the knife from the man's hand with such force that it stuck in the wall by the window. Continuing the motion, Jimmy's body turned with the kick in a complete spin, and his fist landed squarely between the man's eyes. Had M-11 not still been holding onto the man's shirt, the punch would have certainly sent him back out the window. Instead the man's head flopped forward and his body slumped towards the floor, still dangling in the robot's grip.

"Shucks, I didn't want to knock him out. Now we'll have to wait a while to get anything out of him. I was sure once you started singing he'd be spilling his guts to us in minutes."

"You have to get your kicks," joked Venus. Her smile dropped upon looking closer at the man. "Ooh. I don't think I could have had any effect

on him," said Venus with a look of repulsion. She knelt down next to the unconscious man and pointed to his ear. Like the other, it was disfigured with scar tissue as if someone had melted candlewax in it. "He's been made deaf," said Jimmy. "Look, there's some other scarring around his nose too. He either went to the world's worst face doctor or someone prepared him specifically to be immune to you."

"He'll get worse than that from me when he wakes up!" roared Hale as he closed the medicine cabinet. The gorilla poured the rest of a bottle of Witch Hazel onto his reopened wound. Marvel Boy floated through the open window, careful to not hit the glass with the long device he bore under his arm. He sat the machine down on Jimmy's desk and switched on the lamp. For better illumination he adjusted the bendable arm of the lamp, briefly thinking how it was a crude version of M-11's arms. The light revealed a device around four feet in length, with a conical dish at one end. The part that had looked like a fan from outside.

"It's a gun," growled Gorilla Man.

"Yeah, but what does it shoot?"

"Images. Ideas. Dreams." Marvel Boy peered around the device, nodding as he looked at various sections. "Impulse creation." Jimmy realized that in a strange way his Uranian-born friend was approving of the thought that had gone into making the machine, if not the purpose for which it was built. "It runs on standard current." He opened a small red box in the middle, then finding it of little use, closed it. Finally he came to the other end of the invention, which housed a glass canister full of liquid. Several wires ran into a small flexible shape that floated in the solution. It was roughly the size of a nearly-finished bar of soap. The space hero regarded this for a moment and then said simply, "Gosh."

"That looks kind of familiar," said Hale. "But I can't place it. You going to let us in on the gag?"

"Yes," answered Marvel Boy in a hollow voice. "You'd recognize it if it were in context of the whole thing it comes from, though." The others leaned in to see the floating object. Jimmy studied the creases running through it. Venus thought it looked like a sponge. "Well?" she asked.

"It's brain tissue."

"Brain tissue?" asked Venus, clearly repulsed.

"Yes—a brilliant if crude solution," replied Marvel Boy as he looked at the machine that had been influencing their dreaming minds. "Earth simply doesn't have very sophisticated means of computing yet. Your greatest computer is the size of a small house and can barely calculate a square root. Data is stored on tape reels and one has to enter commands with a punch card. Seriously, a child with an abacus can do as much."

Gorilla Man leered as he finished bandaging his arm. "Is all this anti-Earth propaganda going somewhere, or are you just cranky from being woke up at 3 AM?"

"I'm getting to it, Ken. So, to transmit specific imagery—as in a scenario where snakes bind you when a skeleton appears, say—you would need something to store those images. Dragging an enormous computer around would be nearly impossible. So what someone did with this device was use organic data storage from the greatest computer the planet has available... the human brain."

"Holy smokes," said Jimmy. "I wonder how they put the dream into the piece of brain in the first place?"

"The former owner of the brain merely observed the scenario. Then where the memory is stored, we extract tissue." Jimmy and the others turned in the direction of the new voice. It was the man Jimmy had knocked unconscious minutes ago. Ken Hale scooped him up and held him tightly by the shirt collar. The man's face looked considerably redder as he did so.

"All right, you! What's this all about? What are you trying to pull here?"

"I have very little hearing due to... alterations made upon me. So that I would not be susceptible to the young lady's power." The man seemed oddly calm, resigned in fact. "I can only read your lips and the gorilla is too difficult for me. If you have questions, they should come from one of the others."

"You say the brain tissue came from someone who saw the imagery?" asked Marvel Boy.

"Yes. We have many Datamen. They exist to use their senses to record information for us. Early on the process almost always necessitated the tissue donor's death, but now we have it refined. They all have artificial access ways riveted to the backs of their skulls, and special liquids help them regenerate new brain tissue. This works even better. After a few transfers, the Datamen have no memories of their own that could possibly interfere with the intended storage." The little man sat up more now, as if proud of this development.

Venus looked aghast. "Whoever you people are, you're monsters."

The man seemed puzzled at her judgment. "We only use indigents and drifters. No one who matters to society or the economy."

"Oh, well that's better." said Gorilla Man. "For a moment we were afraid you were up to no good. Okay Jimmy, let's turn him loose."

"Take that act to the Poconos, Ken. Okay pal, now who were these Derskin and Oglethorpe guys that started us on the goose chase?"

"Those are their names, Mister Woo. They just do not work for the Federal Bureau, as you have surmised by now. Their purpose was to lead you away from paths that would have crossed with our own. You cannot combat this organization as you might ordinary criminals. Our planning is very layered and has many fail-safes built in."

"For someone who was willing to kill himself to evade me, you're being pretty helpful now," said Marvel Boy.

"Because it doesn't matter now. Now that you have captured me, my life is forfeit. I may as well tell someone the wonders and horrors I have seen in my time with the Foundation. I don't think I realized until now just how much I wanted to share the arcane knowledge I have acquired." The strange man looked aside a moment, then spoke again. "It must be a similar thing with monks who have taken a similar vow of secrecy."

"Brother!" said the ape. "Now this guy thinks he's practically clergy! Come on, let's go introduce him to Jonas Salk and see if he'll share his Nobel Prize!"

"Salk didn't get the Nobel Prize, remember?" clarified Bob.

"Then he was robbed," grunted Ken.

"He is indeed a brilliant man, and we are already putting his immunization work to good use," countered the man, who was able to pick up on Hale's last statement thanks to the especially animated delivery. "I do envy him the public acknowledgment of his achievements. I shall die soon with no one knowing the leaps I made in developing the Dream Ray. Likely, the existence of the machine will never be public at all." The man seemed to be unaware of the others around him at this point, having a dialogue with only himself. "Still, I have always been well funded by the Foundation, and have had all the test subjects I needed. Not many scientists can say that."

"So what is this Foundation?" asked Jimmy, kneeling before the man. "What do they not want us to interfere with?" He waited what seemed an interminable period, staring at the man's glassy eyes. Jimmy finally realized that the eyes hadn't blinked in almost a minute. He reached out and touched the scientist's shoulder, and the man slumped over. In the moonlight from the still open window, the feathery plume of a dart could be seen at the middle of the man's neck.

Jimmy bolted up to look out the window, then stepped aside just as quick with the realization that he could be the next target of a dart. Bob Grayson raised his arm and projected a bright beam of light to the buildings across the street, scanning for movement in any of the windows. Seeing no movement he dived down to street level and began circling the blocks. The bustling city was unusually quiet. Finally he returned to the large open window to see Venus checking at the man's wrist and neck.

"I'm not finding the pulse."

"Well I couldn't find a suspect, so we're even," said Marvel Boy. "It's like a ghost killed him."

"So we're back to where we were, with diddly-squat to go on," said Ken, scratching at his itching forearm.

"No, we're not totally licked," said Jimmy Woo, walking over to shut the windows. "M-11, could you take this body downstairs to the infirmary?" The robot scooped up the corpse, carried it into the private elevator and down to the third floor. Jimmy stared out the window for a minute and then turned around.

"He said these people were worried about our paths crossing. What path were we on? It makes me think he was referring to what Bob was doing when he arrived the other night." Jimmy walked a few steps from the window as if he were retracing Marvel Boy's actions. "You had been to the new Space Administration in Huntsville."

Bob Grayson's headband pulsed quickly as he looked up at Jimmy. "You mean because I was advising on the space program."

"Right. I'm thinking that's what this is all about. Those fake FBI agents showed up, then I called for you to come back because there was suddenly a case to work on. Now, somebody is going to great lengths to pull off this caper, and they're obviously pretty dangerous with magic and science."

"That's for sure," said Venus. "If these people have the kind of science like this ray gun, they might not want competition like the new space agency will create."

"It's... the Russians..." said Ken, with his head much lower than usual. He wobbled forward as if his feet weren't finding the floor easily. His massive frame began to sway from side to side. "No good... I shoulda known... they got that Sputnik…" Hale then reached out his hand to Jimmy Woo's shoulder to steady himself, and fell anyway—bringing Jimmy to the floor with him.

"Ken! Are you okay?"

The gorilla's eyes rolled around, not focusing on any one thing. Jimmy looked at the bandage, which was pulled open a bit, enough to show Ken's blood bubbling into a froth around the knife wound.

"The knife!" shouted Venus. "It must have had poison on it!" She grabbed a glass of water from Jimmy's desk and poured it on the wound, trying to flush out the toxic chemical. Ken Hale's chest began to heave up and down in large motions.

"Bob! Can you do something?"

Marvel Boy looked at a loss, kneeling over his teammate. "I… I can't… it seems like I should know how but—"

Grayson was cut off by a loud howl, much higher pitched than any Gorilla Man had made before. The sound then receded as if he were moving into the distance. At the end of it, the team could only hear a small gurgling. The ape's eyes went still and his limbs stopped where they were. Jimmy grabbed one of the massive arms and shook it. "Come on, big guy! Come back! You can fight it!"

A strange sensation played at Jimmy's palm. Where he held the gorilla's arm, he began to feel less fur in his hand. The form he touched also seemed to be moving inward. Looking to Hale's face, Jimmy saw the massive brow begin to recede, along with all the dark hair. His snout sunk in and lips began to form. Ken's whole body shrunk in size, though the form it took was big for a man, with muscular forearms and a square jaw. Ken Hale had once showed Jimmy a picture of himself when he was still human, and that was the face they all now saw.

Venus looked up to Jimmy and Bob, her eyes shimmering with tears that hadn't yet escaped.

"He's dead."

The teammates stood in shock over the human form of Ken Hale, and Jimmy Woo became aware of an impact repeating against the floor. It was M-11, who had walked quickly across the room and now stood at Hale's feet. His arm extended down, the hand halting over Hale's chest. Then two of the robot's fingers extended as well, connecting at symmetrical points on the upper chest. The cyclopic eye began to glow.

"700 VOLTS."

Ken Hale's body lurched where current entered his body. Venus jumped.

"M-11! What are you doing!?"

Marvel Boy looked up, wide eyed. "Get out of his way! Let him do this!"

"1000 VOLTS."

The body now jerked up even more, causing Hale's arms to swing outward. Jimmy Woo's eyes raced between the figure on the floor and the machine known as the Human Robot.

"1400 VOLTS."

At this discharge, the body arched all the way up off the floor. The robot's eye grew brighter, and then his arm retracted to its regular position. Ken Hale's eyes began to flutter, and his arm slid to the side. He coughed a large burst of air, then drew in an equal volume of oxygen. His eyes opened to see his four teammates looming over him. Wiping at his face he realized he was using a very naked looking hand. He held it further away to focus better, and then brought his other hand up to his face as well. He looked over his forearms for the dark chestnut fur that usually covered his body to see nothing but the skin of a man.

"You did it, M-11!" shouted Venus, who tried to hug the large robot. Jimmy Woo ran over from his desk with a glass of water and held it to Hale's mouth.

"Here buddy, take a drink."

Ken Hale raised his head and neck and braced himself on one elbow. He drank the whole glass down in seconds and gasped, then wiped at his small brow again. "I'm… I'm…"

Before he could reach his next word, he felt the strange sensation of his neck growing wider. He felt his body raise from the point where his elbow rested on the oak wood planks as his upper arm lengthened. His mouth pushed out and his nose flattened as it did. He had the sensation of sinking into himself from his eyes as his brow protruded. His wide field of vision was again restricted to the point where he'd have to turn his head to easily see an object at his side. His wide nostrils issued a loud sigh and he raised himself up on his knuckles. The ape's head hung low for a moment, and then came back up. He moved a couple of steps forward to where M-11 stood and rested his massive hairy hand on the robot's shoulder. Venus wiped tears from her eyes with big motions of her arm and then buried her cheek in the furry shoulder of her friend. Marvel Boy stood up and smiled at the robot, resting his hands on his belt. Jimmy Woo leaned back from his position on the floor against the nearby chair and exhaled as if he hadn't been breathing for several minutes.

* * * * *

Morning began at the "It's Tops" Diner down on Market. M-11 had already left in the back of a truck with Bureau drivers who would take him to Chabot Observatory in Oakland, where Marvel Boy's rocket was hidden. There he would clamp his large feet into two recessed areas of the cockpit and await the others' arrival at the Silver Bullet. Back in the city, Venus lowered a new pair of sunglasses before her eyes. "Lamp my specs, boys, they're all the rage in Italy."

"Venus, you don't really have to tell people to stare at you. It just kind of happens." Ken Hale pulled his porkpie hat down lower on his head. "Don't hide yourself, I need you to draw attention away from me."

"Aw, thanks Ken."

Jimmy Woo's agents dressed in civilian apparel so as not to attract attention. Ken Hale wore a hat, sunglasses, and a trenchcoat with the collar flipped up, and he still got looks at 7 in the morning. Their favorite waitress Edie led them to the most private booth in the restaurant, though it still was near a window. Jimmy Woo tapped at his own forearm as he spoke to his friend. "How's that arm this morning, Ken?"

The gorilla pulled back his sleeve to show a nearly perfect simian arm. "Barely even a scar now."

"Whatever the poison was on that blade, it must not be as strong as the ancient curse that makes you a gorilla," said Bob Grayson.

"You mean the blessing that keeps me from having to be a man?" The ape worked his way into the clamshell booth and rested his long arms on the backs of the padded seats. Though it was no secret that Ken Hale longed to be human again, he almost never complained about his condition around the team. In his days as a Soldier of Fortune, Hale was known to walk around with serious injuries that he would hardly mention. Still, Jimmy knew that the brief moment of humanity had only rekindled Hale's hopes before dashing them again. Picking up a newspaper that someone had left on the table, Jimmy saw something that would surely take the ape man's mind off his condition for a bit.

"Hey Ken, you haven't seen the paper since we left the other day, have you?"

"Nah, I'm giving up on reading. It's overrated."

"You don't have to read. Here. Just look at this photograph."

Jimmy slid the sports section into the gorilla's field of view. Hale looked down to see a horse with a smiling jockey on its back, and a large horseshoe shaped collection of roses around the animal's neck. Ken Hale stared blankly at the image, and then his eyes widened to offer the rare view of white around his pupils.

"Tim Tam! He did it! Ho boy, look at that! YEAH!"

Any effort to be inconspicuous was dropped as Hale went on for the next ten minutes about the Kentucky Derby, horses and racing in general. Then he leapt over the table and grabbed his hat from the hook on the wall.

"Hey, where are you going?" asked Jimmy. "We've got to get to the rocket after breakfast and head out to the Space Center."

"I'll meet you there! My bookie has something for me—Scratch that. He's got a LOT of something for me!" With that the ape rushed out the door and loped quickly up the street. From the window Jimmy watched his friend amble away, and took a drink of his coffee. Over the edge of the cup he noticed something through the glass. Across the street, a man in a dark coat and cap watched the ape as well, and pulled his lapel out to speak discreetly. Jimmy could see a small transmitter with an antenna just inside the man's coat. Woo erupted from the booth and ran through the door.

"Jimmy, what's up?" asked Venus, too late to be heard.

The man with the transmitter saw Jimmy Woo coming through the doorway of the diner and ran. He made his way down the block and turned, and then crossed the street. Jimmy Woo was closing the distance quickly when the man ran into a small brick and iron structure. It was an entrance that led below street level, possibly a train access. The door clicked shut just as Jimmy reached it. Jimmy pulled on the handle but it wouldn't budge, having been locked from within. Marvel Boy flew down with Venus on his arm.

"Jimmy, what is it?"

"Some guy was spying on us, and reporting in to somebody," said Jimmy who was now kicking at the lock. Finally he produced his gun from his jacket and shot the handle. The door swung open.

The three ran down a long series of steps. The stairway was pitch black,

but Marvel Boy's wristbands soon made it as bright as the street above. "How deep does this go?" asked Venus.

"It's probably an old unused train entrance," said Jimmy, skipping steps to move faster. "We've gone much lower than the platform would be though. I know there's tunnels under the city, but they're not supposed to be this far down." The group emerged in a large area of tiled wall. A quick look around revealed no exits or even vent shafts that someone could climb through.

"We didn't run past any doors, did we?"

"No."

The three grew quiet and listened. No footfalls or breathing. Jimmy saw a faded image on the large wall. Walking closer he could see that it was an antiquated version of the globe, held by the kneeling god Atlas. He touched the wall, which was covered with dust.

"I feel like I should know some magic word. Open sesame." The wall and its artwork remained still and silent.

*　*　*　*　*

Outside the building in Huntsville, a silvery craft lowered gradually to the testing launch pad. From the windows, men in short sleeve dress shirts were scribbling madly upon notebooks and clipboards, noting details like the lack of smoke from the Silver Bullet's flaming retrorockets. The vessel then lowered forward slowly by means they couldn't determine and came to rest on the asphalt as an airplane might.

One female lab assistant gave the scientists an incredulous look and then scribbled on another piece of paper with a large marker. She then pressed the piece of paper against the glass so that Jimmy Woo's team might look up and see her brief but clear message of HELP. Jimmy was already looking at the source of her distress. For a second he had thought that the parking lot ended a ways from the Marshall Space Center, then realized that what he assumed was foliage was moving. The space between the scientists' cars and the front door was overrun by the dark green shapes of hundreds of alligators. Several engineers sat or stood atop their vehicles, unable to enter the workplace and now afraid to step down to open their driver's side doors.

"I didn't know alligators lived this far north," said Venus.

"You're not more impressed that they're all working together?" asked Ken Hale. Jimmy shouted over to one of the men perched nervously atop a Buick Sedan. "What's going on with all these gators?"

"This has happened a couple of times already this week," returned the man, steadying himself. "I don't know if they're looking for food or what, but we're losing valuable work time and falling behind schedule. I haven't heard of it happening anywhere else in town. Or the whole state, for that matter."

Jimmy turned to Marvel Boy. "Bob, could any of the equipment they're working with in there be attracting the animals?" Bob Grayson looked at the complex and his headband glowed briefly.

"No."

The dark green mass kept moving around the building's perimeter, forming what was essentially a reptilian moat. Jimmy looked around and noticed a pickup truck in the parking lot, its driver still inside. "Sir," called Jimmy. "May we use your truck for a minute? I think we can get you back to work." The man nodded anxiously. Jimmy spoke quickly to M-11, who then proceeded to where the truck was parked. The robot extended his arms and picked the truck up, walking carefully to not step on any of the alligators. His course took him by each trapped scientist, who then jumped into the bed of the truck. The ape shook his head.

"You know, years ago I would have just broke out the guns and we'd be cornering the market on alligator-skin boots right now. I guess I'm getting soft in my old age."

"Or maybe your perspective has changed a bit," said Venus. Having collected all the space center technicians, M-11 walked the truck over to the front steps and held the rear of it a few feet from the door. A woman inside opened the door and the engineers quickly rushed in. Marvel Boy held one arm around Venus and flew her into the entrance as well. "Wait up!" shouted Ken Hale, who took a running leap that got him to the branch of an oak tree by the entrance. He swung to and fro for a few seconds to build up momentum, then released to land on the hood of the truck. He climbed over into the building, making a mock salute at his mechanical teammate as he did so. Jimmy walked back to the edge of where the alligator mass began, having thoroughly checked the area for any more stranded workers.

"Looks like everyone's in the clear—hey! Some team you are, I'm still out here in gatorland!" Jimmy looked down as some of the reptiles began to advance in his direction. He knew one of the group would realize his absence in a minute, but decided not to wait. He ran forward and leapt into the swarm, using the backs of the alligators as stepping stones. It took him five jumps to reach the door, and he closed it from the inside as several very agitated beasts charged towards it.

* * * * *

Jimmy and his team spent the next hour going over the work the Space Center had been doing lately. "We've been expecting spies," explained Chief Engineer John Siuntres. "But we weren't quite ready for nature itself to turn against us. Mankind's quest into space is hitting enough snags without all these extra obstacles in our path."

The gorilla snorted as he drank coffee from a paper cup. "It's not just bad luck, Doc. The gators are someone's big idea of sabotage, it doesn't take a rocket scientist to see that." Ken Hale took another sip of coffee and then became aware of the leers aimed at him from around the operations center. "Oh yeah. I guess all you guys are rocket scientists."

"I agree with Ken, Doctor," said Jimmy Woo. "We've had a lot of unlikely stuff happen to us lately that has turned out to be related. I believe someone doesn't want you making any progress, and they don't want Bob here helping you out."

"We've barely even made use of Marvel Boy's knowledge," said the flustered scientist. "All we really asked was that he go up and check out the Sputnik satellites to see if the Soviets were much ahead of us." An aide entered the room and whispered something to Dr. Siuntres.

"It seems Assistant Director Wall from the FBI has sent a transmission for you," explained the doctor. "I'll go down to the radio room and bring back what the lab boys taped. Excuse me."

As the scientist left the room, Bob Grayson felt something tugging at the bottom of his cape. He turned to see a boy of about nine. "Mr. Marvel Boy!

Will you sign my comic?" His father leaned over from a nearby console. "Sorry. I bring him to work a lot and I guess he heard us mention that you were coming to visit. Caleb, they're here on important business."

"The future leaders of this planet are pretty important business too," said Marvel Boy with a big smile. He kneeled down and shook hands with the boy.

Ken Hale stared at the cover that had an image of his caped teammate fighting mutant cavemen. "Wha... you got a comic book? When did this happen?"

"It was a few years back," answered Grayson as he scribbled a message on the cover of the periodical. "The Uranian High Council suggested I try to appear in Earth media to build a good reputation in society. They thought it would make my work easier. While on a case in New York one time I ran into some nice gentlemen named Bill and Joe who said they'd love to create a book for me at the company they worked for. It was..." Marvel Boy searched his memory for a moment before rolling his eyes at how dense he was being. He looked down at the cover of the comic. "Timely. Anyway, the whole point was to let people know the Uranians were nothing to be scared of and that I'm available to help in really dangerous situations."

"I don't remember hearing about this," said Jimmy.

"That's because it didn't work. It had the opposite result. People who saw me assumed I was promoting the comic book, and that I was using special effects to fly. I thought once they saw it in print they would accept the facts, but it seems books work differently here."

"Welcome to Earth, headband. Can I see that, son?" Ken Hale reached for the comic and the boy handed it over, delighted that a gorilla had just spoken to him. As the ape flipped through it, the youngster walked around behind him and looked on his back for a zipper.

Ken was engrossed in the boy's comic. "Heh. Look, the speech bubbles have ya saying 'gosh' all the time."

"That's called a word balloon, Ken," corrected Venus.

"Oh yeah, you worked as an editor for a while, guess you'd know."

"Well, that was for Beauty magazine. That reminds me, I should check up on Whitney. I mainly focused on interviews, we didn't run any comics except single panel gags. I just remember that term from when Timely printed my comic book."

The gorilla looked around as if he just found himself in a new place. "What... you had one too? Next I'm gonna find out you guys all had movie deals and didn't tell me." He looked behind him at the robot that stood unmoving, and rapped his knuckles on M-11's chest. "I guess we don't rate, huh?" The mechanical man gave his usual response of silence. Dr. Siuntres returned to the room.

"Okay, Mr. Woo, here's the audio we were sent." The man with glasses opened what looked to be a briefcase and drew out a thick electrical cord which he plugged into the wall. A click of a toggle switch started two tape reels turning. Jimmy leaned in to listen. First there were hisses and pops, then several bursts of what sounded like a human voice underwater. It did indeed sound like gibberish or something that had been mangled in transmission. As the sounds faded out, the scientist shut off the tape player. "And that's it. I wouldn't have wasted your time with it, but we don't want the Bureau to think we're not trying to cooperate."

"Thanks," said Jimmy. "It wasn't a waste of time, Dr. Siuntres. That's the way they often send us transmissions. Okay, M-11, play it back, please."

The robot's visor flashed a couple of times, and then an internal speaker played the message from the tape, now unscrambled.

Jimmy Woo turned to Ken Hale. "Well, that's pretty interesting, huh?" The ape nodded. "We better check it out."

Dr. Siuntres pushed his glasses back up his nose as the strange crew departed.

* * * * *

The shining missile raced across 1200 miles of ocean, banked south, traveled 220 miles before heading east again. It kept up this path over the Aleutian Islands and the Gulf of Alaska in its search for the Natty Bumpo, the ship that had gone missing out of the Port of Seattle. At the port itself waited Jimmy Woo and his team of G-Men, investigating the area as Marvel Boy's headband periodically flashed to let him know another sector had been ruled out. All around the docks men lay back on whatever surface was comfortable, staring at the cloud formations.

When Jimmy Woo's team had arrived by rocket, the entire port buzzed with excitement, gathering around. Some had produced guns for fear of an attack. Unlike the similar visit at Hunter's Point, the Port of Seattle wasn't under Naval control and there were no orders given for the inhabitants to accept the strange visitors. When the hatch to the rocket opened and a one-eyed robot stepped out, every Saturday night drive-in movie with invaders from another world leapt to the minds of the Northwest workers. In seconds a hail of bullets ricocheted off M-11's body from all directions. The android's eye began to glow and its white light crossed the spectrum to red. The voice of Jimmy Woo blurted "M-11! Stand down! Do not attack!" The robot's eye returned to its usual dim glow.

Then Marvel Boy had exited next, flying. This alarmed the men further and immediately the bullets went towards the moving target. Bob Grayson poured on the speed and raced out of range. Ken Hale was about to leap out from the rocket when Jimmy Woo pulled at his shoulder. "Come on, Ken. What do you think they're going to do when they see a big gorilla jumping out at them? You're not bulletproof like M-11!"

"Yeah, but I can outshoot any of those dockjockeys. All I gotta do is get hold of one gun…"

"No. Leave this to me." Jimmy pulled out his FBI identification and climbed up over the edge of the hatch.

"Look! The Reds are behind this!"

The hail of bullets returned low and peppered the spaceship where Jimmy Woo had barely gotten to look out. "You idiots! I'm FBI!"

Venus spun around in her seat and smiled. "Would you like me to wrap this up, or are we going to play Wild West all day?"

"We get so deep into missions that I don't watch a lot of television or read the papers. I forget how Cold War crazy the world is. Go on, take 'em out."

Venus pushed her hair back and tilted her head up. Even before her mouth opened Jimmy and Ken could feel the ethereal voice ripple through them. The air seemed to shimmer and sparkle as Venus' lone chorus began to permeate

the port. Sounds of metal hitting the ground came from all around, and then she stepped out of the ship. The men who had been holding guns stood with their arms at their side or reaching before them. Their eyelids hung low, as did their jaws. Standing on the rocket Venus sang louder and the populace fell on their backs in a wave, like a stack of dominos that had been set in motion.

As the men of the area laid back seeing their deepest desires seemingly brought to life, Venus asked around about the ship that had gone missing the previous week. Within minutes she had ascertained the exact type of vessel that Bob Grayson would send his rocketship hunting. After that, the group looked around at the many ships and the massive cranes that would lower and raise their cargo. They only had to kill time for about ten minutes.

"I'm getting a message from the Silver Bullet!" said Marvel Boy. "It's located the ship about 650 miles to the southwest. It'll be back in a minute to pick us up." Jimmy got up and stretched. "That's one impressive wagon you have there, Bob."

Marvel Boy shrugged. "Actually it's kind of limiting. My father made it with the instructions he was given by the Uranian High Council, and I've improved upon it since. But I wouldn't have used the rocket design. I can't put it down just anywhere. The scanning range could be a lot better, and I could really use a meteor smasher on it. If I ever get some time, I'd probably start from scratch and work off the flying saucer model."

"Then everybody's gonna think you're a little green guy with a big head," returned Ken. "Stick to rockets, that's Earth-style." Grayson stood deep in thought as if he were planning the future saucer at that moment, and the Silver Bullet returned.

* * * * *

As the rocket approached the lifeless ship it slowed and fired hull nozzles so it could hover over the ocean surface, then went into a circling orbit around the vessel. At the next closest pass, the team jumped from the open hatch onto the ship's deck and the rocket pursued its elliptical course.

"See, if I had a saucer, it could just hover there indefinitely. Right over this boat."

"If ifs and buts were candy and nuts, we'd all have a wonderful Christmas, flyboy. Okay, what are we looking for here, Jimmy?"

"Whatever the real reason for stealing a ship on the west coast was, before we went on that wild goose chase. I gotta say, we're up against some pretty sharp cookies this time. Usually the bad guys just have one goal with any given operation. These people hit about two or three birds with one stone. They got Bob away from helping the Space Center scientists to go after one of the missing ships. Which turned out to be a trap that almost got us killed, since they put a whammy on us in our sleep. Then we find out the FBI agents we met were fakes, and write off the whole thing as a decoy. Then it turns out even that was a trick, because this ship, the Natty Bumpo, actually went out to sea. You really can't take anything for granted with this outfit, they think things through. But I think it was all about whatever this ship was supposed to do."

"I've been thinking about that myself," added Ken, leaning on his knuckles. "The fake agents fed us some of the truth, which made it so convincing. Ships from all up and down the seaboard were taken. I don't think it was for smuggling now though. It looks to me like they wanted ships in the water ready to go, but they didn't know where they'd need them. So

449

they covered all their bases. And whatever they were looking for, it turned up at this latitude."

Bob Grayson took mental notes as Jimmy and Ken threw out theories. Deceit and subversion were still largely foreign concepts to him, but his time on Earth was teaching him more on the matters every day. He still hadn't adopted what he thought of as the casual attitude his teammates seemed to have towards it all. Though he did like the problem-solving aspect that went with it.

Then skeletons began pouring over the deck, from the sides, hatches and pilot house.

"There's dozens of them!" shouted Venus.

"Hey bones!" blurted Gorilla Man as he grabbed a long pole. "Do I look frozen this time? Thought we'd be a bunch of sittin' ducks, huh?" The gorilla whipped the rod around quickly, knocking the skulls off six of the skeleton army. Several of the skeletons erupted from a deck door and began to lock their fingers around Venus' legs. "HEY! Someone! These guys don't have the right body parts for me to influence!" Within a second Venus felt something cold wrap around her waist, and then she rose quickly through the air. Once safely out of the grasp of her assailants, she realized that M-11 was holding her aloft with an extended arm. His other arm swept several of the undead off the side of the ship and into the waves. With no flesh on their frames, they sank into the deep blue.

One skull after another began to explode into white powder. Some were the result of Jimmy Woo's automatic gun, and others were from the laser blasts of Marvel Boy's wristbands. The skeletons stood briefly as if waiting for the return of their heads, then charged into battle again. Marvel Boy widened the field of his blasts and the tenuous cartilage that held the bodies together evaporated in the heat of his beams. Bones rolled over the entire deck until walking or running became perilous. Finally there was but one skeleton left, wielding an ornate dagger like the first one they had met, and the inventor of the Dream Ray later. Kenneth Hale leaped farther than his friends had thought possible and landed before the dagger's bearer. In one quick motion he pulled out the arm with the blade and slung it out into the sea. Then he brought his large forearm back and broke the creature's spine in half. Finally he grabbed the skull with a large hand and squeezed it. Bone shrapnel burst from the gorilla's grasp. Jimmy Woo winced as he touched at his own skull.

"Okay. I think we got the right boat this time," said Jimmy, stepping over bone shards. "Besides that it actually traveled a ways, our mysterious enemy made sure it had the most backup in case of trouble."

"I bet these creeps work cheap," said Hale, opening a deck door and poking his head down into it. His next words echoed in the hold. "If skeletons ever get unionized, then we'll have these bad guys where we want 'em. Hey, Living Laser—come over here and light up this cargo hold, please."

Bob Grayson floated over above the dark opening and drifted down, filling the area with golden light. He mused to himself how Ken's latest quip was in fact a pretty good name.

The hold was largely empty but for a couple of large pieces of metal at opposite ends of the room. As the team made their way inside, they took turns looking at what appeared to be wreckage of an odd sort.

Both pieces of metal were warped and charred on the outer surface. "It looks like it was blasted apart from the inside," said Ken. Marvel Boy put

his fingers to the scorched metal. "These are radiation burns." Jimmy raised his palm. "Hey, maybe you guys should back away from that, it might be radioactive."

Grayson shook his head. "My headband would have picked up on that right away. You're right, it should be radioactive if it was bombarded like this, but it's not for some reason. Maybe something absorbed the radiation." Marvel Boy leaned over and put one piece of the wreckage next to the other and looked back at his team. "I thought this looked familiar."

The caped man carried one piece of metal over to the next, and put the halves together. He turned around, holding the heavy assemblage in front of him.

"It's a cone." said Venus.

"A nose cone!" clarified Ken Hale.

"Right. It's the nose cone of a rocket. One I tried to locate for the folks at the Marshall Space Center. But when I went up to scout for it, it was gone. See, look." Marvel Boy pointed at the charred but still readable name stamped on the metal cone. It read:

СПУТНИК-2

* * * * *

The explosion blew a cloud of snow and steam for a kilometer and black clouds of birds emptied the surrounding forests. Several men in fur hats wiped moisture from their glasses and shook their heads towards the ground. Water trucks raced to the launchpad and began dousing the flames around the area. In the watchtower a burly man pulled off a pair of headphones and slung them at the nearby console. He tried to find a clear patch of sky through the tower window but it would be an hour before the haze would settle. The moisture provided perfect cover for the far more successful rocket now racing down to the remote sector of Siberia.

"Well that was lucky," said Venus. "I mean, not for them so much, but we could have been zipping around this country for hours without finding their launch facility."

Marvel Boy set the Silver Bullet guidance system for landing and turned to his attractive teammate. "I think our odds would have been pretty good to detect activity even without a failed liftoff. As I told the fellows at the Marshall Space Center when they were worried how far they were falling behind the Soviets' space program... my guess is they're putting more resources into their program and firing off many more rockets. And charting that on a bell curve would show a lot more disastrous attempts than they're probably letting on about."

"Well that would be none, because from what we hear, everything they try works like a charm," added Jimmy Woo. "Their main guy, the — what do they call him... Chief Designer? You'd think he's the Earth equivalent of you the way they go on about him and his knowledge of rocketry."

"Yeah, well we got Von Braun on the Disney show. We're gonna have cartoons in space before them." The gorilla grabbed onto the ring on the wall to steady himself as the rocket lurched backward and lowered behind a hill some distance from the Soviet scientists. Bob took off his cape and put on a coat, sweater, pants and boots over his usually sparse costume. Ken Hale whistled at the young hero. "Look at the ordinary Joe! Who'd know this kid grew up on a planet where they think capes and shorts is the style?"

Grayson pulled on a wool cap as well. "When in Siberia, to paraphrase your old saying. I could keep myself warm by powering my armbands up more, but then I'd be a spectacle — and I don't think Jimmy wants any extra attention on us."

"That's right," returned Jimmy, pulling on his own coat. "We're just here for some info, and this is a touchy situation. As an FBI team we're way out of line coming behind the Iron Curtain like this. Venus is going to take the lead on this one. I'll keep my trap shut and maybe they'll just think I'm Chinese."

"Hey, you set off a war between the U.S.S.R. and Red China, that would be something," said Hale.

"No one's getting hurt today, because we're doing things my way." Venus ran her hands through her long hair and its silver color took on a bluish hue. "Just to really play up the effect. Let's go."

The Soviet guards were discussing as always when they might be able to leave this temporary post, when one heard the crunching of feet upon snow. Their guns raised at the figures stepping out of the woods and walking towards them.

"M-11, incapacitate those gunmen, but leave them alive. And jam all transmissions from this area."

The robot marched forward and a hail of bullets rained upon his metal casing. Rather than ricochet off as the bullets in Seattle had, these stuck to the android, who now generated a magnetic field to protect the team members behind him from any stray fire. The guards emptied their clips and reloaded or grabbed extra guns from nearby vehicles. It was becoming difficult to distinguish the robot's form as the covering of rounds grew. One of M-11's arms was extended and wrapped around the fragments of rocket found in the Natty Bumpo. His free arm extended rapidly to its full length, followed by the fingers on that hand. From the tips of the fingers burst arcs of electric current that filled the clearing and connected all the Soviet gunmen for an instant. Briefly their grips contracted to force even more machine gun fire, and at once the attack stopped as they each collapsed in place. Jimmy, Ken and Bob turned over a few who had fallen face down in the snow to keep them from smothering, and the team continued forward. A telepathic scan by Marvel Boy revealed the Soviet scientists to be holed up inside the watchtower. Ken Hale pushed the locked door until it popped off its hinges and the troupe proceeded up a metal staircase.

At the door to the launchroom Jimmy turned and whispered. "Any guns in there, Bob?"

"Just one. They're all hiding behind tables and equipment."

"Okay, let's go. No one talks but Venus. It's your show." The men put their fingers to their ears.

She nodded, and began to hum. As she let her voice get louder, the thud of the gun being dropped could be heard. Ken then pushed this door open as well to let her step inside. Jimmy held a hand up to M-11 indicating for him to stand in the hall for the moment.

In the control room, several Russian and German engineers held onto whatever structures they were near as if on a ship that was rocking gently, yet steep. They were all delighted when the bearer of the unearthly voice entered. Venus kept singing and held out her arm as if to introduce those

that followed — a short asian man, a tall nordic man, and an extremely large gorilla. While her voice worked through their heads the entourage seemed perfectly normal. Then the singing stopped and the group seemed the oddest ensemble the scientists had ever seen. Still, they were no longer terrified of what the guards must have been firing upon, and the calm stayed with them.

--NOTE FROM AGENT WELLINGTON, TRANSCRIPTIONIST--

The following exchange between Agent Venus and the Soviet scientists has been translated from Russian. These have been triple-checked by Linguistics, who have the reels made from M-11's playback. -A.W.--

"Greetings, Earth Men. My crew and I are visitors to your world. It is our understanding that you seek to travel the reaches of outer space."

"You speak Russian?" asked a man with thick framed glasses. "Is our language like yours?"

"No," replied Venus, stifling a smile. "To speak our language you would need four more mouths and an extra octave range. We are appearing to you in bodies representative of your highest life forms for your own comfort. You are not ready to see beings such as us yet."

Two of the scientists looked at each other and spoke in their native German. "Gorillas are one of our highest life forms?"

"Yes, they are," Venus replied in their direction, which startled the men. She reminded herself for later to not share that part with Ken. "We are curious about certain parts of your space program. Last year you sent up your second capsule into orbit. I believe it had a passenger... a dog, you call it. Is this correct?"

A few of the men looked down in apparent shame. "Yes," said a thin man with a kind face. "Laika."

"Was the capsule designed to return to Earth with this passenger?"

The thin man wiped his eye. "No. Our instruments were to test if one could survive the gravity pull and weightlessness. She... would not have lived more than a few hours."

"Really." Venus turned towards the door. "Automaton, please bring in the debris we found."

The calm of the room evaporated as the massive form of M-11 walked in, his torso at 90 degrees to his advancing legs. Once he had cleared the doorway with the metal he carried, his body rotated back into alignment. The expanded arm retracted to place the two halves of the Sputnik II space capsule on the floor of the men who assumed they would never see the craft again.

"You brought it out of orbit!" The man turned to the others. "I knew it! I knew once we began going into the cosmos we would attract attention! We — we have only peaceful intentions with our program... we only seek to fly around our own planet! Please do not destroy us."

Venus raised an eyebrow at M-11. Naturally they were assumed to be peaceful emissaries until the menacing android appeared. "We are not angry with you, but something you're telling us doesn't make sense. We found this debris on Earth."

The burly man who had thrown his headphones in anger earlier stepped forward. "I am Korolyov — the Chief Designer." The man paused a minute to compose himself. He had never planned to tell this news to his superiors at the Kremlin, and assumed no one outside his immediate staff of engineers would believe it either. Now he found himself facing beings who would likely not find his story unusual, so he began.

"Sputnik II was not designed for reentry. We are not at that phase yet. But a month before launch, I had a dream... several of us had the dream, in fact. In the dream we were shown plans to fit the capsule for life support. Others were shown how to produce a chemical to be injected into Laika, as well as device to be implanted under her skin. The dreams recurred and compelled us to follow this new plan. It was only at liftoff that we all realized we had been influenced. We thought perhaps... creatures such as yourselves may have done this." As he explained in more detail the additions they had made, an engineer in the corner named Kragoff jotted down notes furiously on his clipboard.

"Perhaps," returned Venus. "It was not us, however."

Kragoff stepped a bit closer and spoke. "What do aliens want with such information? How do we know you are not spies?"

Marvel Boy floated up three feet and hovered over across the room to look down on Kragoff. The balding scientist retreated back to the desk where he had been scribbling notes.

"We do not want your secrets, we were only curious as to your motivation," answered Venus. "It is clear you were not under your own control during this mission."

The Chief Designer spoke again, feeling oddly free to share information as his audience was not a part of the politics that governed his life and work. "Please excuse him. We are forced to take great measures with our space program, such as moving our launch sites to different parts of the Union." He looked out the window at the bleak cold sky. "I would never have brought us here — I was sent here many years ago, to a gulag. I believe soon we will be able to build a permanent center outside of Moscow, where our program can proceed at full pace. We would welcome you to return then, to our Star City."

"Thank you. But we have many other planets to visit and document. Perhaps we will return one day. Now we must say farewell."

Marvel Boy's headband glowed quickly, surprising the engineers. Venus nodded his way and then asked a new question. "Yes. Do you have anything of the animal... a blood sample, perhaps?"

The thin man walked over to Venus, his head still hanging as he reached into his coat pocket. From the jacket he produced a small leather collar. Marvel Boy's headband pulsed again.

"May I keep this?" Venus asked. She politely kept the quality of her voice to a level that wouldn't coerce the man. He nodded his head.

"Thank you. We are very grateful."

As the strange visitors exited, Venus turned once more for a final question. "One more question. Why do you have so many people with weapons around this noble venture?"

"Our leaders fear that others on this planet will learn our methods... and possibly reach the heavens before us." Korolyov felt flush at what he had said. "That must sound quite ridiculous to beings such as yourselves."

"I wish it did," said Venus.

* * * * *

The small leather collar with the red metal star lay on a round glass surface. Colored lights from all across the spectrum raced around the object, and a transparent image of the collar appeared above the actual object. Strange text began to appear in the air as well, reading out from right to left, and from bottom to top. Jimmy Woo reached his fingers through the odd glyphs to see if he could feel them, but of course he did not. "So what's this gizmo doing, Bob?"

Marvel Boy flipped a switch on the console of the Silver Bullet that would keep it on a clear course, and rotated his seat to look at the analyzer his friends were gathered around in fascination. "It's analyzing traces of the animal's genetic structure. You can see that there are a few hairs to work with, and the leather has absorbed oils from the dog's skin."

"Sweat too, huh," added Jimmy, fixated on the holograms.

"No, dogs aspirate through their paws and by panting," said Ken Hale, equally transfixed. He felt the eyes of his team upon him in the way that generally irritated him. "Why is everybody surprised when I know a little science? I'm an ape of all trades! I could fly this rocket too, if pretty boy let me." Then a new hologram projected, of planet Earth. It began spinning quickly in the direction of the actual planet, then vertically. Hundreds of thin lines crossed through the image and more arcane text appeared.

"It's searching the planet now for a match," explained Grayson. The gorilla looked over at a container and turned back to them. "Hey! We should do this with one of those fancy daggers those skeletons couldn't stop stickin' me with! That oughta take us right to whoever's behind this nutty scheme."

"It won't work," explained Bob. "It's a good idea, and you're catching on quickly to how devices like this function, Ken, but even my technology isn't to that point yet. The only way this is going to work — if it does — is if there's an actual living creature somewhere with the corresponding DNA chain. For an instrument like this, living bodies function almost as transmitters, constantly broadcasting their code as they expend energy. The skeletons were animated by some other force, they weren't alive." Grayson's headband seemed to glow slightly as he mused on the point he just made. "It's probably just dumb luck on the bad guys' part. But using the skeletons was the perfect way to keep me off their trail." He had little time to think on the matter further as a light began pulsing on the projection of the globe, which then enlarged to show more detail. The glowing region then lifted out of position and produced an exploded view, showing in progressively greater relief the geographic location where the analyzer had found its match.

"It's found something!" said Venus. "Does this mean... the little dog is alive?"

"Yes. Though it's not the readout I expected to see. Something's... different. I'll put in a new course, I expect Jimmy wants to go there immediately."

Jimmy Woo leaned in closer and nodded a yes. He felt a cold wave pass over his skin as he saw the location.

"Washington, DC."

* * * * *

Grayson looked at his instrument panels. "Two objects are coming in almost as fast as we are." Kenneth Hale looked at the glowing dots on the round monitor. "Jets! We're a UFO coming into Washington airspace, they're gonna fire on us!

"Wag your wings!"

"Here, you take the helm since you're the ace pilot." Marvel Boy unclipped his seat latch and started for the rear of the rocket. "I've got to go draw them away while you land. If they start firing we'll never have a chance to explain ourselves."

Ken Hale leapt into the pilot's seat and took the stick as the young man opened a small airlock in the hull and closed it behind him. The Air Force pilots broke off immediately as Marvel Boy shot out of the side of the rocket—resembling a missile himself. The red and blue missile then looped in the opposite direction that Hale now took the Silver Bullet.

"Ken! At least fly rightside up so my stomach will go down!"

"Ha! Sorry Jimbo." The ape pulled the stick and turned their world back on the axis they preferred. "You guys are used to Bob, drivin' like my dad. I'll show those flyboys a thing or two."

"Let Bob deal with them, we need to get down to the National Mall pronto."

The gorilla rolled his eyes. "All right. Lemme give those crewcuts a signal, maybe it'll help." He brought the rocket around before the jets, which had just returned to formation. Coming in at eleven o'clock, he rocked the ship a number of times and then blasted away, leaving only a contrail for the jets to see.

"Did that UFO just wag its wings at us?"

"Roger that. Eyes up at two o' clock—the other one is up to something."

"Lordy. How does it turn that sharp? It looks like it's... skywriting."

Bob Grayson's wristbands glowed brightly as he raced several hundred yards and then took another abrupt turn. After two more such paths, the symbol he made was connected. He then flew back like a swimmer pushing himself away from a pool wall, and aimed his arms forward. The nearly solid beams of light he made filled the large shape to form an enormous white star. The jets radioed back to the tower.

"I think these guys are trying to tell us they're American," said the pilot. "Is this some new defense you didn't let us in on?"

"It's news to us too, Grigsby," called back the man at the tower. "But we just got a call from the Feds saying this is some of their people, believe it or not."

"They've got an air division now?"

"Appears so. Break off and resume a perimeter patrol so no more of those bogeys like before get through."

The National Guard had troops in place at each street before the Washington Mall Park. They had rolled out Howitzers, the quickest defense that could be assembled. As the creature advanced down 7th Street, the large guns fired on it, their report echoing through all of the District of Columbia. Jimmy Woo watched the shells impact the creature's skin, sending showers of sparks and flame off to each side. Four direct hits made no difference in the beast's approach. The soldiers manning one of the large guns scattered as the creature opened its cavernous mouth and bit down on the barrel, crumpling it like foil. It shook its head from side to side and the Howitzer flew into several sections, causing infantry to take cover behind their barricades. Jimmy Woo couldn't help but think of some of the movies he'd seen directed by George Pal in which he'd noticed the name of the special effects artist Ray Harryhausen. He thought that the films had been eerily accurate in depicting a large alien terror with the exception of always being shot from a level distance. From his own vantage point the beast towered six stories over his head. He looked over at Ken Hale who was uncharacteristically speechless.

"That's the little dog?" asked Venus.

"It grew," replied Jimmy.

A brave treasury agent on the way to work had pulled his Buick sedan to the side as a barricade for the juggernaut that made its way through 7th Street. He emptied his revolver at the creature, and each bullet was rejected by the thick skin. Having no further defense to offer, the agent ran from the car just as an enormous foot crushed it.

FBI officer Jerry Wall saw Woo and his odd team and ran to them. "Boy, you guys showed up at the right time, we couldn't even get anybody in place to call you this thing hit so fast! When I saw the rocket I called the Defense Department to get you clearance. You know what this thing is?"

"Remember that dog the Russians sent up last year?" said Jimmy Woo, still absorbed by the sight before him.

"Muttnik?"

"Yep. Its name was Laika, actually. It's been exposed to cosmic rays in a section of the Van Allen Belt, and this is what you get now."

"Holy... the Soviets are attacking us with monsters! I didn't see it happening that way."

"It's not them, they were manipulated. Whoever is behind this, I think wanted us to think this was a Communist attack. The creature was probably supposed to come down in the capsule so we'd see where it was from, but the radiation didn't work like they expected. This is Bob's notion—it took a lot longer to mutate than they thought, so they had to leave it in orbit several months. Then they had trouble controlling where the payload would come down, and that's why the plot with all the stolen boats. They had to cover the whole Pacific Ocean, more or less."

In front of Flynn's Irish Pub a group of leather-clad bikers made hoots and catcalls at the frenzied scene. They were too mesmerized to look back at the gruff voice speaking to them.

"Hey boys! Who's got the fastest bike of this bunch?"

The leader of the gang watched the giant beast shake a truck apart with its jaws. "I'm the big deal—mine flies, hero. Who wants to know?" The man felt his jacket tighten around the sewn emblem that said "SAINTS" inside a devil's head, and his body lifted from the motorcycle. He dropped into the sidecar and the large hand reached down to the linkage to separate it with one quick clench. The leader of Satan's Saints watched a gorilla kick-start his prized machine and turn to give him a thumbs up. "Your country thanks you," said the Gorilla Man, and the vehicle raced away toward the chaos.

Marvel Boy lowered to the creature's eye level.

"Don't hurt it, Bob!" yelled Venus.

"I don't think there's any danger of that!" Bob Grayson concentrated his light beams and sent a powerful flash at the creature's eyes. A piercing howl rang through the canyons of buildings as the beast squinted and shook its head. Its large eyes opened again, and a greenish membrane slid down over the obsidian pupils. Marvel Boy's bands pulsed again to make an even brighter flash that had no effect this time. The large lower jaw opened and a wave of flame erupted in the direction of Marvel Boy. The young hero propelled himself back at top speed, staying mere feet ahead of the pursuing flames. Several elm trees on the Mall caught the fire and began to burn.

Jimmy Woo ran to an overturned police car and picked up the megaphone he saw by the smashed window. "Venus! See if you can calm the creature down through this!" He threw the device to her and she fumbled with the switch. Clearing her throat, she aimed the cone up towards the beast. Venus thought for a moment, then made a brief whistle. The creature's scaly ears lifted.

"Laika! Here girl! Come on puppy... come on... who's a good doggie?"

A soldier grabbed the hand of his crew member about to drop another shell into the mortar barrel. The enormous beast's head cocked at an angle and its multi-nostriled nose began sniffing towards the woman below.

"That's a good Laika! Yeah, come on girl. Calm down... calm down..."

The beast had a tail roughly twenty feet long with several spiky protrusions along the sides. A jeep was sticking out of a second story window where the tail had smacked it. Now it began to wag. The various soldiers and federal agents in the area kept their guns up but didn't move or advance.

"Well I'll be... it looks like your girl may just do it," said Wall as he pushed his hat back.

"Beauty always trumps Beast," said Jimmy Woo. The two watched the enormous creature shuffle its legs and lean back into a sitting position while Venus kept cooing through the megaphone. Then a quick burst of sound cut through the ears of everyone on the Mall, becoming inaudible though Jimmy could feel a ringing in his head. The beast rose again and now stood on its haunches, towering over the buildings around it. A roar echoed around the DC buildings and caused several men to turn and run. They had been at the back of the line of defense and hadn't a clear idea of the size of the brownish green animal until that moment. The creature's head thrashed and spit more fire, and as it came down its foot plunged to the part of the street where Venus stood.

The horn ridged foot stopped at nine feet above Venus' head, held by the metal hands of M-11. The robot's extended arms twisted and pushed to keep the leg from coming down, and a red-blue blur raced through to remove Venus from the area. M-11 released his grip and the massive paw slammed down, buckling the street. Though the beast hadn't been aware of the goddess under its feet, it was now very concerned with the shining metal figure there, and released another torrent of fire. Jimmy Woo's eyes followed where Marvel Boy put Venus down, by the gate of the Smithsonian. As he turned to look back at the threat, his peripheral vision caught site of two men atop the museum. They had been in the position of snipers, which were no doubt everywhere now, but something struck him as odd. Looking back he saw that the two were manning something like a large gun, but of gleaming chrome. One of the men had headphones on that were wired to the gun. One of the men was tall, the other shorter and balding.

Ken Hale raced up to Jimmy. "How we doing?"

"We're losing. M-11! Shock it!"

The robot extended both arms and its fingers, and large arcs of electricity worked their way through the alien creature, much more current than had been used on the Russian soldiers the day before. The beast howled loudly again and spun around. The spiky tail swung with terrific force, launching the robot from the street over the flaming trees along the Mall. Even through all the commotion Ken Hale could hear the bang M-11's body made when it hit the ground. "That dog oughta play for the Red Sox."

Jimmy jumped on the back of the motorcycle. "I think the animal is being controlled, like those gators at the Marshall Center. Take me over to that entrance of the Smithsonian, and cut around so those guys on top don't see us!"

"Aye, aye." The gorilla turned the throttle and the machine raced around a barricade and by the building. Jimmy hopped off and gave a final order. "I hate to ask you to do this, but the monster looks pretty agitated now. I think it's going to start eating those soldiers if it's not distracted."

"Hey, you're talking to a guy who knows how to make animals hunt him down. Watch my smoke." The front of the motorcycle lurched upwards and Gorilla Man raced towards the rampaging beast.

Jimmy Woo ran up the steps of the museum and found the roof access. He quietly opened the door and walked around the brick structure to see the men aiming the long device and turning knobs. Below the creature opened its mouth to fire upon a troop of National Guardsmen who now had no cover. Its attention was then captured by a buzzing motor. A gorilla driving a motorcycle went through the beast's legs.

"C'mon pup! I'm right under your nose!" The ape raced between the front and hind legs, and turned sharply upon nearing the tail, remembering what that had done to M-11. The creature twisted and writhed as it looked under itself, and the bike jetted out from underneath. Ken Hale turned left and raced full speed down the Mall in the direction of the Washington Monument, the giant mutant in pursuit. The beast's gallop sounded like thunder and Hale tried to tune it out. Marvel Boy swooped down and matched speed alongside the motorcycle. "What's the plan, Ken?"

"I'm taking her for a walk! Who knows, maybe she's just got to go!"

"Where's Jimmy?"

"He's up on top of the Smithsonian checking out two guys who might be running this show. Why don't you go there, I got this under control!"

"Yes, you have her right where you want her," Marvel Boy smiled, and blasted off to find Jimmy. At this moment, Jimmy Woo had his FBI credentials and his gun out. "FBI! What are you men doing..." The men turned and Jimmy recognized them as the fake Federal agents who had visited his office that night a week ago. "Derskin! Oglethorpe!"

The one called Derskin lifted his own gun, only to feel a bullet pierce his upper arm. Oglethorpe now had his weapon up, a machine gun. Jimmy ducked back behind the roof access as a rain of bullets hit the bricks.

Ken and the creature were passing the Washington Monument now, which briefly caught the animal's attention, making it pause. "Hey! That ain't a fire hydrant! Down here — here!!!" Ken spun the back wheel of the bike to kick up a huge cloud of dust by the creature's snout, and it turned from the obelisk. The chase began again, with Ken Hale going downhill to the Reflecting Pool.

"You traitors! What were you trying to do, set off World War III?" Jimmy pulled his head back at the response, another hail of bullets. "We're not authorized with that kind of information — but we do have clearance to fire on you." More shots ate away at the brick. Oglethorpe's hands suddenly felt warm, then in intense pain. He dropped the machine gun which was glowing red. He looked up to see Marvel Boy coming in too fast to avoid and his next sensation was rolling across the roof of the museum, his jaw feeling less attached than usual. As the young hero landed, Derskin turned back to the machine and flipped a red switch. Jimmy was back out in the open, his gun levelled at Derskin's head. "What was that? What did you just do?"

Ken Hale raced along the Reflecting Pool and could feel water hitting him in steady bursts. The giant creature was running through the landmark, kicking up tall waves that washed over a few drifters who had been sleeping on the park benches nearby. The shrill sound cut through the air again and the beast stopped instantly. It turned as it stepped out of the pool, and shook itself vigorously as if it still had fur. By the time Hale realized he wasn't being chased anymore, the mutant was halfway back to the museum.

Marvel Boy held Derskin in the air by his coat collar. "Who do you work for?"

"The Foundation. Just like you will one day, space man!"

Jimmy tightened handcuffs on Oglethorpe and stood back up. "We'll get it out of you, once we've taken care of — "

His sentence stopped when he realized the source of warm air that was flowing over him. Jimmy Woo looked up to see the creature that was once a small mongrel, its dripping fangs a mere 15 feet away. Derskin reached towards the controlling device, but Marvel Boy still held him away even though he was captivated at the sight before him. The mutant's eyes were red orbs that reflected the four men. On its head were long antennae stalks that swayed constantly. It had been summoned, but now there were no more commands. No one moved.

Venus stepped out slowly from the roof access. She started to raise the megaphone she still held, then caught herself. Instead she whispered very calmly, "Bob."

Marvel Boy concentrated. It was difficult considering the looming threat, but he managed to put his response in Venus' mind.

"Don't speak, Venus. Just think what you have to say."

"Ooh, look who's in my head," thought Venus. "Don't go running around in here, now! I can't guarantee what you'll find."

"You were going to tell me something?" thought Bob, impatiently.

"Yes. Remember the Russian scientist who gave us Laika's collar? Can you project his image in light with your armbands? And make him stand by Jimmy."

"I can. It will take extreme concentration, so I'm ending this transmission." Marvel Boy broke off the communication and closed his eyes. His headband glowed white, and his armbands grew brighter. The effort caused him to loosen his grip on Derskin, who began to slide out of his coat. The beast began a low growl that shook the chests of everyone on the roof. The light of the

sky appeared to fold and shift in the space next to Jimmy, whose forehead beaded with sweat as the air from the creature's mouth grew still hotter. The animal's mouth popped open and its ears raised as the light completed its structure. Next to Jimmy stood the thin engineer who seemed so distraught as the Soviet scientists explained the fate of Laika. The monster's head tilted to the side.

The hologram took so much attention from Bob Grayson he was unaware that Derskin was now free of his grasp. Derskin grabbed the controlling device and Jimmy started for him. Before Jimmy Woo could grab the machine, Oglethorpe slammed into his back, knocking him into Bob Grayson. The two men got in each other's way as Derskin desperately grabbed for the switches that would bring the mutant back under their influence. The device vibrated from a nearby rumbling, making their task even more difficult. It became clear that the rumbling was a low, deep growl. The false agents looked up from their machine to find a cavern of teeth inches away from their heads. Oglethorpe's last moment of self-awareness came as he looked to the shimmering light around his shoulder. The two had stepped into the hologram Marvel Boy projected, disrupting it so that the gentle scientist was gone. The movement of the mouth snapping around them was so fast Venus thought for a moment they had been holograms too. The lump moving down the creature's throat dispelled that notion immediately.

"Where's the machine that controls it?" shouted Marvel Boy, looking around the roof.

"It went down with them," answered Jimmy Woo. The beast looked back to the two men and drew in a long breath as it had done before when about to belch flames. Marvel Boy aimed his palms at the creature's head and cut loose with two intense blasts of his own energy before it could strike. Then arcs of electric current contacted the beast's skull again and it let out a multi-octave howl. Jimmy looked over the edge of the roof.

"M-11! Get up here now!"

The robot extended its arms to clamp on the brickwork near Jimmy Woo and pulled itself up to their level. "The dog has swallowed a machine — a control device. Can you reach down its throat and retrieve that?"

The cyclopic eye of M-11 turned to the giant animal. It was shaking its head violently from the double sided attack and turned as if to move away. It continued to turn, again facing the group atop the museum, growling. Its mouth opened again and the robot's right arm fired into the maw. The beast made a gurgling sound as the extending arm kept feeding into it. The large teeth clamped down and the beast shook its head furiously, whipping the robot around the area and into the Smithsonian several times. The beast backed up several yards and lowered its body as it continued to thrash M-11 about. Grass, mud, and asphalt flew up depending on where the robot hit next. The beast rooted its muzzle into the ground in the attempt to tear the arm apart, and in doing so it laid its long tail down. Soldiers who had been standing by watching in amazement suddenly cleared a space as the gorilla on the motorcycle returned, yelling for them to scatter.

Ken Hale maneuvered the front wheel of the vehicle through an opening in the spikes and found the path up the center of the beast's tail clear. Pulling the throttle wide open, the ape drove straight up the tail and spine of the creature. The bike handled the scaly surface well until reaching a slimy frill around the beast's neck, and the ape pitched over the handle bars. Finding himself between the round red eyes, Ken Hale swung his long arm into the nearest one. "Let him GO!!!" The eye closed and the deadly mouth opened to howl again. M-11 retracted his arm at full speed, causing sheaths of yellowish-green mucus to fly from the animal's throat. The arm stopped before the hand could emerge. Marvel Boy flew fast at the robot, ramming into its side. The jolt caused the obstruction to break free, and the metal hand holding the control device emerged from the mouth before it could shut again. Grayson pulled away the muck covering the machine, wincing as he did so. "This is really nasty. Hope this still works."

He traced his finger around the controlboard, making quick judgments as to what the switches and knobs did. Warm air drifted over him, and the temperature rose dramatically. Bob Grayson looked up to find the cavern of teeth now poised over his own head. As the beast lurched, the young hero's finger turned a knob. The snout stopped as a shrill sound was emitted. Marvel Boy turned the knob back a few notches, and the creature rose up, sitting on its massive haunches. The long tongue poked from the mutant's mouth as it began to pant calmly. Grayson exhaled more air than he thought he had breathed all day. Lifting his head he saw Ken Hale on the ground giving him an upraised thumb.

Jimmy Woo and Venus were running at full speed across the museum lawn to the force that now advanced. Several tanks and trucks with rocket launchers had just arrived and were rolling into position. "Stop! Stop! The danger's over! We're in control!" If any of the military could hear Jimmy, they did not acknowledge him. Tank barrels raised and rocketmen cranked their missiles at the low angle trajectory of the mutated hound. Venus' hand grabbed Jimmy's shoulder as she pushed for him to step back. The silver haired beauty held the megaphone up to her mouth and began to sing the first thing that came to mind, Bali-Ha'i from South Pacific. The ethereal voice worked around the open area with a slightly different quality due to the megaphone, but within seconds the tanks came to a stop, their drivers and crew popping out of the hatches. The rocket crew on Truck 7 suddenly couldn't remember why they were preparing to ignite their missile, or why they were there at all since they had girlfriends at home waiting to embrace them. A few men fell from vehicles as they began to wander aimlessly. Venus stopped singing and began to speak.

"Please cease all hostilities. We have the situation under control. If any of you have the rank of general and can help us arrange transportation of a very large dog, please come forward."

A two-star general did step forward to respond with his own megaphone.

"How did you stop that thing... who ARE you people?"

Jimmy Woo held out his badge and said simply, "FBI."

* * * * *

From the deck of the tanker, Marvel Boy turned a knob on the signal device and Laika erupted from the cargo hold. The towering beast sniffed at the salt air and next turned its nose to the volcanic island off starboard. Grayson flipped a toggle switch and the creature leapt into the ocean, causing the oceangoing ship to rock violently for a few seconds. Jimmy Woo, Gorilla Man and Venus shielded their faces from the spray that accompanied the magnificent splash. Only Laika's head could be seen as she paddled to the island, leaving a wake as wide as the freighter they came to this part of the Pacific on. As she neared the beach, Jimmy Woo looked through a pair of binoculars at the island to see a pterodactyl fly by. Below what appeared to be a walking oak tree shuffled through the jungle.

"Good call, Bob. After our close call on this island a few weeks ago, I was sure we wouldn't be coming back anytime soon. But I can't think of a better place for the pup to call home now that she's in this condition."

"I hope she'll be okay," said Venus. "There's so many fierce monsters here."

"I don't think she's got much to worry about," added Ken Hale. "They're the ones that better stay clear of her." Marvel Boy walked over to the edge of the ship with the control device, stopped, and then looked at Hale.

"Ken, would you like to the honors?"

"Aw, thanks for thinkin' of me, kid." The caped hero handed the device to the gorilla, who bent it 90 degrees, sparks shooting from its console as he did. Hale then tossed the ruined machine into the ocean where it soon faded from sight.

Venus looked back at Jimmy, still studying the island through the binoculars. "I guess the fingerprints on the machine turned up nothing."

"Nope," replied Jimmy. "Whoever those fake agents really were, they're not in anyone's files. I may work on this in my spare time, but for now this trail has dried up completely. Everyone connected with this 'Foundation' is either dead or a skeleton. But, I guess we saved Washington, DC and the space race is back on. So that's something."

Venus smiled at his completely serious assessment. "How are they explaining to the public what happened in Washington?"

"The military told the press it was an elaborate defense simulation, like war games. And for any citizens who might have seen Laika, they explained that they let a Hollywood studio work in props with the exercise to use for a movie, in return for helping with the USO."

Hale snorted. "Are people really expected to buy that?"

"Well sure, Ken." answered Jimmy. "That's the story they're getting straight from the White House. Why wouldn't they believe it?"

The gorilla looked back at the island, where the giant mutant was running along the beach splashing in the surf and sampling the smells of its new home. Jimmy slapped Marvel Boy on the shoulder as he started across the deck.

"You can all start piling back in the Silver Bullet. I'm going to go thank the Captain for coming through this treacherous part of the Pacific."

"With my instructions," added Grayson, "he should still be able to safely navigate the strange currents that cut the island off from the sea lanes." Bob's headband flashed and the hatch of his spacecraft opened. As the odd team made their way to the rocket, Ken Hale looked around the deck of the freighter.

"I think I'm going to be paranoid for a while on ships. Keep expecting skeletons to jump out at me."

"We showed that mysterious Foundation what super-group they don't want to fool with!" Venus laughed, leaping up onto Ken's neck for a piggyback ride. "I doubt these bad guys have much interest in snooping on us anymore!"

The single eye of the Human Robot glowed briefly and M-11 turned to follow the team into the ship.

END MISSION G-4: "THE MENACE FROM SPACE"

“THE MENACE FROM SPACE” BACKGROUND ARTICLE, FROM THE *AGENTS OF ATLAS PREMIERE HC*

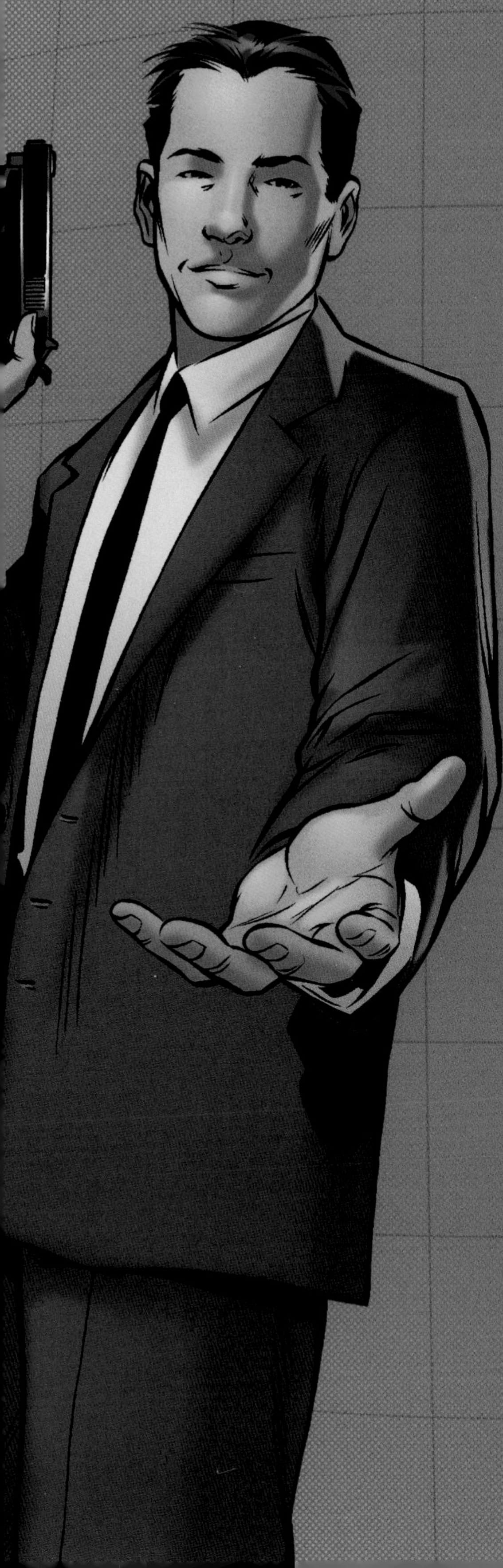

AGENTS OF ATLAS:
THE ONLINE STORY

Mark Paniccia wanted Nate Cosby and I to brainstorm ideas to promote *Agents* on a budget of...nothing. So while I was visiting the offices in New York we went around the corner to get pizza for lunch and discuss a mad scheme. I had recently worked with my studiomates on a section of an Alternate Reality Game that Sean Stewart (sci-fi writer and a pioneer of ARGs) directed, *Last Call Poker*. My thought was to introduce an enigmatic character who would make cryptic statements and leave trails on the internet, and players would have to solve these puzzles to release sections of an online story. The story premise would be that this was an appropriated FBI file documenting a secret mission of Jimmy Woo's team in 1958. Artist Steve Lieber suggested that we make some of the answers available at participating local comics shops, so there would be a “real-world” element to the gameplay. Marvel VP David Gabriel briefed retailers that they would be receiving passwords to give to customers, and John Dokes and Peter Olson set up the *Temple of Atlas* weblog where the story would run. Jim McCann got the word out to the online comics community that we needed co-conspirators to plant fake news stories and hide clues, and for most of the summer of 2006 we brought the “Menace From Space” story to the world.

Running the game story was exhilarating, fun and a lot of work. Dozens of people volunteered their time and web space, and many comics-shop owners lent their names to “news” stories that often implicated them in a vast conspiracy that mirrored the workings of the Atlas Foundation in our story. The game didn't virally spread as wide as I'd hoped, but I'm not sure I could have handled the workload if it had. Clever players were already devoting lots of energy and time to problem solving and searching for clues. I had to make clues harder and more obscure just to buy myself enough time to write the story each week. For instance, one week they had to follow clues embedded in the chapter to the *About* page of Newsarama.com and find text hidden in a black field at the bottom of the page, written in Greek. Then they had to translate that to get a password to take to a participating comics shop and return to the blog with the keyword the store gave them. Some played purely by armchair and handed off “field work” duties to others, and it evolved into a neat active community.

Ultimately, the game shaped the series profoundly. The dragon that attacks Woo's first strike force was originally going to be only a guard beast — but once I started planning out Mr. Lao's appearances, I realized he and the dragon should be one. As “Menace From Space” came together, I kept finding ways to refer to it in the series, and then a key scene near the end took place at the Naval shipyard from the online story. The serialized story is too long to reprint here, but can be found in total at Marvel.com. I'd like to revisit the ARG-style promotion again on a larger scale at some point, with a crew of writers and webmasters. I love problem-solving exercises, and the idea of following difficult and cryptic trails that actually lead to answers, so the entire time I was envious of the players. They were having fun!

Your Humble Servant,
Jeff Parker

THE TEMPLE OF ATLAS

2006-06-16 14:16:32

Welcome. As you have found this site, you are clearly one of those rare people who realize there's more to the world than what you see on the surface. You may qualify for membership in an organization of which I am involved. My name, at least one that you can pronounce, is Mr. Lao.

Some of you were promised a "decoder ring", yet you will receive something of more worth than a mere plastic decrypting toy. No, the Decoder Ring of which I speak is all of YOU- working together as a whole. If you are the first to reach the Temple, do sign in now.

What you'll receive are classified FBI documents, on a weekly schedule. (Needless to say, anyone who feels they should reveal this to the Bureau, will find themselves in a very wet climate lacking in oxygen) These records we've retrieved for you concern a mission from 1959, headed by a young firebrand named James "Jimmy" Woo. With special powers given him by your government, Special Agent Woo assembled a very unusual team that worked together for just more than six months. It is of relevance because this team has recently reunited. This is a team with which my organization is quite concerned. Our destinies are intertwined, and I believe will be coming to a resolution in the near future.

The story is broken up in separate entries, transcribed years ago by Federal Agent Angela Wellington, a young woman who clearly had a fondness for the old pulp magazines, as you'll see by her writing style. She left the agency in 1960 and became a full time science fiction writer. While she did take liberties in detailing the facts at hand, it does make the file a bit less dry than most government documents. Much of the information is reliable as it was taken from recordings made regularly by one of Woo's agents.

Now I shall leave you to the lost art of reading for a few minutes. After you've reviewed the excerpt, more direction will be offered. Enjoy.

That is all for now. You may respond in the Comments section of this web log, which will be at this website unless matters of urgency force us to relocate. Pick a code name and keep using it that I may track your progress. Please observe some decorum with name selection. We may be murderers, smugglers, dictators and charlatans, but we frown on vulgarity and will ignore such missives. You may be asked to solve a small problem and report back, and I will need your code name to distinguish your actions. A list of exceptional agents will likely be printed in the AGENTS OF ATLAS "comic book" later. We often pass on coded information through these fantastic periodicals, so I suggest you purchase them if you wish to stay abreast of our current machinations.

Our first exercise this week is ridiculously simple (though that will change). You need only locate a key phrase that I have placed in cyberspace. Once you've found it, share the link here. The path can be found in the first part of the classified mission!

--Mr. Lao

UPDATE: New arrivals- please continue to check in, though you do not need to mention the key phrase. There is, however, a successive post after this you may notice to your right (Timely's weblog archives immediately!) where you might wish to hazard a guess on the addition to Jimmy Woo's team of agents. As no one has guessed correctly, I fear we may not have psychic ability amongst our new recruits. There is also a piece of iconography in the next post you may wish to keep.

Agent's Response

It appears that I am the first to have reached the Temple of Atlas and, as commanded, I have signed in.

I believe the code Mr. Lao refers to is the scrambled words from the press release: helpmate, falsetto and bowleg. (The other words were comic book titles previously published by Timely.) Unscrambling the letters reveals where we are now: The Temple of Atlas Blog.

INTRODUCTION

"That would be one kick-ass hotdog stand."
— *Ken Hale, the Gorilla Man*

I know this is an intro, but maybe you should go ahead and read the story, and then come back to this. I don't want to spoil it, and it may all make more sense once you know where my head was. Go ahead, enjoy.

OK, welcome back. Did you like it? Great. So I was writing *Marvel Adventures Fantastic Four* when editor Mark Paniccia called and asked me to look at a book from the '70s, *What If #9*, featuring the "Secret Avengers." He had just come across it again and couldn't stop thinking, "There's something there." Immediately, I agreed: There *was* something there. The team broke down into archetypes of pulp adventure: A secret agent. A spaceman. A goddess. A gorilla. A robot. A guy who was like *three* guys. OK, they didn't all correlate so well — but one of them could sit this round out. Then, I looked into another character that appears briefly in the story and found out that cartooning legend Bill Everett conveniently left this superstrong Atlantean in a block of ice. A mermaid? This could be the greatest team *ever*.

Then, the hand of Fate and the hand of Paniccia conspired to place artist Leonard Kirk in the mix. Kirk immediately clicked with the story proposal and knew how to pull it off. Yes, it had wacky, over-the-top elements throughout — but under all the pulp trappings, the characters were real people. If we believed in them, readers would too. Even knowing Kirk's track record, we didn't realize his true range until now. Leonard can handle *any* genre of fiction, which comes in handy because we go through so many in our story. He invests something of himself into each of the cast, and they come to life completely. His character designs sing. The Atomic Age of Comics is still evident in the team's look, yet each has a timeless quality. They look like a group that belongs together.

During this planning stage, we went through about thirty names. "Secret Avengers" got claimed for something else, and no word combination could make all of us happy. Then, the obvious occurred: While we have this rare chance to acknowledge the earlier days of Marvel, we should put the company label of the 1950s, Atlas, in there. I called to say this and Assistant Editor Nate Cosby blurted, "Agents of Atlas!" From this point, the arcane and powerful Atlas Foundation began to emerge in full, and the mysterious Mr. Lao stepped out of the shadows. Tomm Coker started turning in iconic cover designs that would give the series a strong presence. Michelle Madsen brought her formidable color design to the House of Ideas (not warned about what unreasonable menaces Leonard and I are with color notes). We all labored over details that may never get noticed, and Kris Justice and Dave Lanphear were saddled with ridiculous windows to bring the final pages together. But it was happening, and it was exciting.

If I can speak for everyone else — and of course I can, because I'm writing the intro! — I think we all realized we were suddenly creating something special, something bigger than our individual efforts might produce. A big part of comic books, some say the biggest element, is wish fulfillment. For my part, I can say it's the driving impulse in *Agents of Atlas*. When Mark called me with his hunch about offbeat characters no one had seen in decades, I went straight for my greatest wish. I had only two weeks earlier given permission for my father to be taken off life support. My days were filled trying to make my deadlines from his house while poring through the artifacts of his whole life, looking through photos of him as a young man. If Ken Hale seeing Jimmy Woo in critical condition at S.H.I.E.L.D.'s Mojave Base has resonance, that's where it came from. I wasn't concerned with what was in vogue in mainstream comics. I wanted full-on, indulgent *escapism*. Wouldn't it be great if that idealistic young FBI agent got another chance at life? Any of us? To hell with the real world where we have to settle for one go-round, this is *comics*. It *could* happen, and *it was going to*.

This story is about returns and second chances, largely brought about by characters who aren't willing to let the past swallow up their old friends. There are moments in history when the right people connect at the right time. Jimmy Woo's secret team were only together for about half a year, 50 years ago. Yet that combination at that point *meant* something. When the reformed killer robot M-11 reappears with no explanation, Ken Hale takes it seriously. And as an immortal gorilla, Ken Hale does not take much seriously. Of course, as our Mr. Lao points out at the end of Book One, nothing returns alone, does it?

Maybe you'll recognize people you know in Jimmy Woo's team, like the winning young leader himself. The incredibly sweet-natured Venus, and the alienated and withdrawn Bob Grayson. The earthy and adventurous Ken Hale. Or the regal, honor-bound Namora. The inscrutable M-11 is probably the model we should all follow in our dealings with others. What little he says gives no insight, but his actions tell Jimmy Woo everything he needs to know about the oddly named "Human Robot." I'm also very fond of the team's unofficial member, Derek Khanata, the rational yet empathetic S.H.I.E.L.D. agent.

The Agents of Atlas took on a life of their own, and here's hoping they keep it. Should I ever find myself in real danger — and in the Marvel universe — I'd certainly welcome the help of any heroes shooting flames or webs. But I think I'd be most happy to see a beam projecting down from a Uranian flying saucer.

Jeff Parker
March 2007

CBR SPOTLIGHT ON AGENTS OF ATLAS

Posted: May 12 - June 16, 2006

BY DAVE RICHARDS, STAFF WRITER, COMICBOOKRESOURCES.COM

WEEK 1: EDITOR MARK PANICCIA
AGENT PROFILE: *GORILLA MAN*

Posted: May 12, 2006

SECRET AVENGERS REASSEMBLED?
PANICCIA TALKS "AGENTS OF ATLAS"

In the 1940's during one of the Marvel Universe's darkest hours, a legion of super powered heroes came forward. These heroes stood up to the menace of the Axis Powers and then seemingly disappeared until many like Captain America reappeared when the second age of Marvels began years later. What happened during those intervening years? Who protected the Marvel Universe from otherworldly threats? "Agents of Atlas," a new five issue mini-series by writer Jeff Parker and artist Leonard Kirk, will answer these questions and many more. The mini-series follows the modern day adventures of a reunited team of heroes who defended the Marvel Universe before The Avengers ever assembled. In part one of our spotlight on Agents of Atlas CBR News spoke with Editor Mark Paniccia about the series.

"Agents of Atlas" was born when Paniccia stumbled across an old 1978 issue of Marvel's "What If?" The issue #9, was "What If the Avengers Fought Evil During the 1950s?" and the cover depicted a number of characters from Marvel's past charging forward, while the present day members of The Avengers looked on. "That cover was intriguing," Paniccia told CBR News. "It instantly tickles the nostalgia bone."

The nostalgic characters that composed the 1950s Avengers: Marvel Boy, Gorilla-Man, Venus, 3-D Man, and the Human Robot, all first appeared during the Golden Age of Comics and were unlike any of the later Marvel Comics characters. "They are most definitely a product of a different era," Paniccia explained. "When you look at the original versions of these characters, they're like something out of an Ed Wood movie. That surface impression is what helps them stand out from the 'modern' Marvel hero, but there's more to all of them than meets the eye."

To help show off the hidden qualities of these characters, Paniccia enlisted Jeff Parker to chronicle their modern day adventures in "Agents of Atlas." "Jeff is cool," Paniccia said. "But besides that, he not only gets the appeal of bizarre characters like this, he understands how to apply them in contemporary terms without losing that nostalgic charm that they have. When I first saw these guys, I called him right away. We were both looking at the cover online and he started giving me this 'Doom Patrol' meets 'JSA' take — which was spot on."

And to bring Parker's take on the characters to life, Paniccia recruited the artistic talents of Leonard Kirk, "Leonard is a superb draftsman," Paniccia stated. "He can draw anything from a 1950s-style rocket to a lavish jungle scene to an alien cityscape. I ask, what makes him not perfect for this book?"

One thing Kirk won't be drawing in "Agents of Atlas" is 3-D Man. Paniccia told CBR News that there were no plans for 3-D Man

or his modern day counterpart the former Avengers member Triathlon to appear in "Agents of Atlas." The team, which was originally assembled by former FBI agent and current SHIELD agent Jimmy Woo, will include Gorilla Man, Marvel Boy, Venus, The Human Robot, and a fifth member whose identity Marvel wants to remain a mystery for the time being.

Readers looking for a good mystery set in the Marvel Universe will want to pick up "Agents of Atlas." "There are super powered beings in it, but there's a grand mystery involved here," Paniccia explained. "Part of the fun is going to be watching that mystery unravel - and see how it ties into the Marvel Universe."

The team members of Agents of Atlas all have ties to the early days of the Marvel Universe, but readers who may be unfamiliar with the characters' histories will have no problem understanding and enjoying the series. Paniccia said, "I think this is a good series for anyone who is looking for something a little different to jump into."

CBR's "Agents of Atlas" coverage continues next week with an in-depth interview with series writer Jeff Parker. Also, each week we'll bring you another Agent Profile, where Jeff Parker gives CBR News the inside info on the team members that compose the Agents of Atlas. Find below the first of those profiles as Jeff Parker tells us more about Gorilla-Man. In the weeks ahead, look for the identity of the mysterious fifth team member to be revealed exclusively here at CBR.

AGENTS OF ATLAS
KEN HALE
"PRE-GORILLA"

AGENT PROFILE: *GORILLA MAN*

When the Agents of Atlas reunite this August in the pages of their self titled mini-series, many readers will be meeting this bizarre and eclectic troop of heroes for the first time, even though they've been around for over fifty years. Many of the characters debuted in titles published by Atlas Comics, the company that would eventually become Marvel Comics. In order to better acquaint readers with the cast of "Agents of Atlas" and offer some insight into their roles in

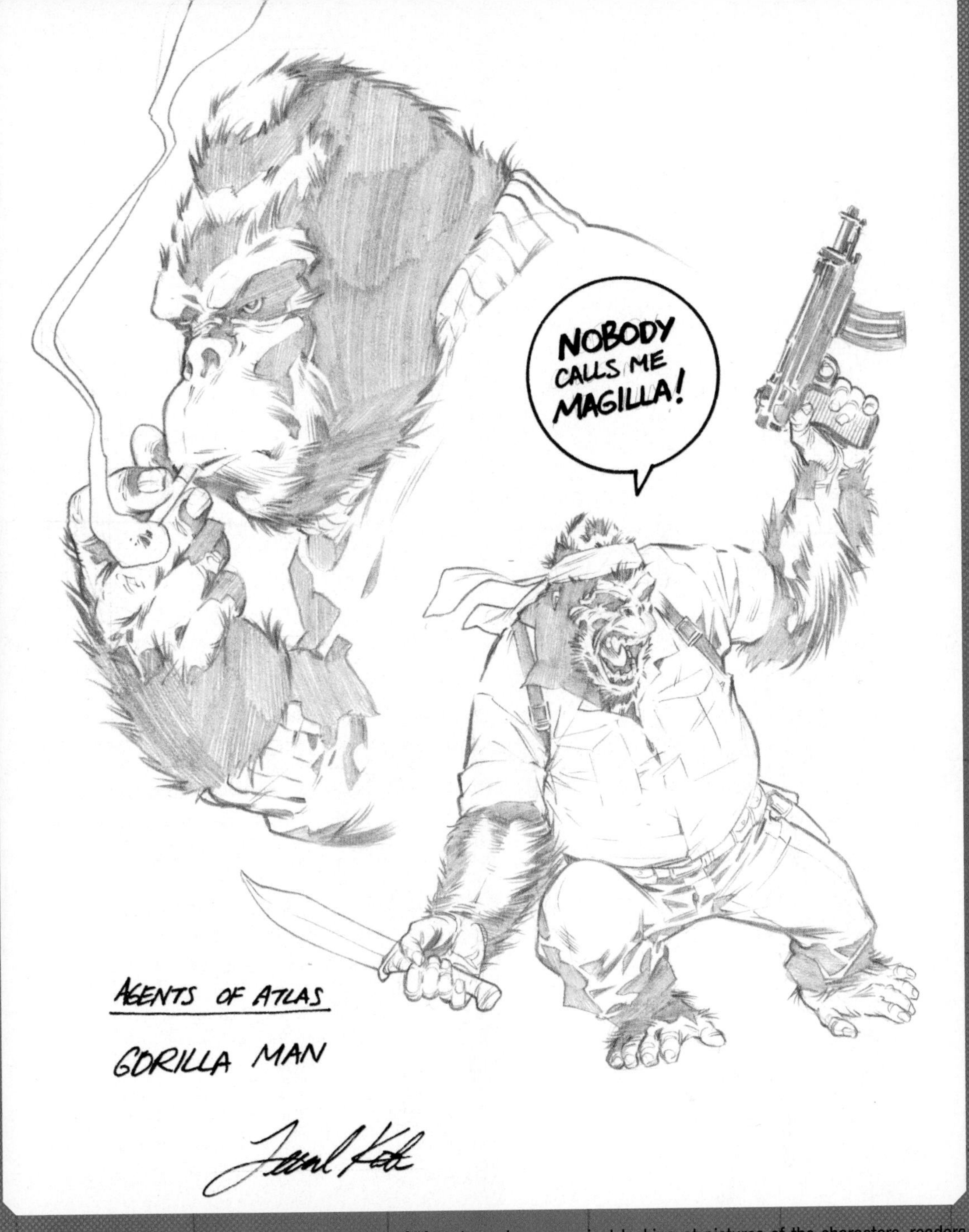
NOBODY CALLS ME MAGILLA!
AGENTS OF ATLAS
GORILLA MAN

the mini-series, CBR News has compiled a number of "Agent Profiles" by speaking with "Agents" writer Jeff Parker. The first Agent profiled is the team's expert on Guerilla warfare, Gorilla-Man.

There have actually been a number of Atlas/Marvel characters with the moniker of Gorilla-Man. "One was a mad scientist who was sure that taking the form of a gorilla would help him enslave the world," Parker told CBR News. "Ours is Ken Hale, the Gorilla Man who appeared in Men's Adventure #26. That version is credited to Stan Lee and Robert Q. Sale."

Like any good primate, Ken Hale has evolved since his debut appearance. "I think that what happens with a lot of good characters is that they slowly create themselves," Parker said. "What readers enjoy sticks, and what they don't falls by the wayside. At least that's the way it should work. It's interesting how even just looking at pictures of the characters, readers gravitate to Gorilla Man. Smart talking gorillas are a beloved staple of comic books, and people don't think of Marvel as having any. But we've got Gorilla Man, and that's better than a barrel full of monkeys."

To help distinguish Ken Hale from the band of other four color Gorilla characters, Parker has further defined Gorilla-Man's background and made him a simian super solider. "We've added more to his origin to help the logic of why he was brought into the group originally, and this is one of those cases where the character has become more of what people want him to be," Parker stated. "People like him being a big-action weapons expert, and now that's part of his back-story. We find out Ken was a Soldier of Fortune who was a force to reckon with even as a human. You curse him with the immortal body of a gorilla, and you have a major @$$-kicker.

"He's very strong, agile and proficient with all manner of weaponry. Actually, he's a bit bigger than a mountain gorilla. He also doesn't age, as you'll read more about in the story. His most valuable function in the group now is actually as the touchstone to the present day. Everyone else has been largely cut off from the modern world except for him."

Gorilla-Man was last seen interacting with the modern world in the pages of "Nick Fury's Howling Commandos" "The Howling Commandos unit has had him busy in secret operations so he doesn't know much about what's going on with specific things like say, the events of 'Civil War,'" Parker said.

When "Agents of Atlas" begins, Gorilla-Man is still serving as an agent of SHIELD, which will put him in an emotionally difficult spot. "He's got a really tough decision to make about his allegiances (not unlike 'Civil War', I guess!)," Parker explained." He's one of SHIELD's go-to guys, but being part of Jimmy Woo's team was a key time in his life. What you have to know about Ken is that loyalty is very important to him; he's pretty old-fashioned when it comes to values like that. Not the type to leave a man behind, definitely someone you want to have your back."

WEEK 2: WRITER JEFF PARKER
AGENT PROFILE: *VENUS*

Posted: May 19, 2006

THE MARVEL UNIVERSE NOW WITH EXTRA PULP: PARKER TALKS "AGENTS OF ATLAS."

AGENTS OF ATLAS

VENUS COSTUME

- NOT COMPLETELY TRANSPARENT BUT PRETTY DARN CLOSE.

9/7/06

In part one of our spotlight on "Agents of Atlas," CBR News got inside info on the background of the five issue mini-series from Editor Mark Paniccia. For part two of our in-depth look at Marvel's "Agents of Atlas," CBR News spoke with writer Jeff Parker for the scoop on the series, which reunites a group of heroes that defended the Marvel Universe of the 1950s for a modern day adventure.

As we revealed last time, "Agents of Atlas" was born out of a phone conversation between Parker and Paniccia after the editor rediscovered "What If?" issue number #9, which asked the question "What if the Avengers Fought Evil During the 1950s?" What impressed Parker and Paniccia the most about the issue was the unique characters. "He had a gut feeling about those characters," Parker told CBR News. "It's easy to see why — they're not simply older superheroes, they're pulp adventure icons.

"I'm a sucker more for what they represent — gorillas, spacemen, robots, etc.," Parker continued. "They're going to be a clean slate to lots of readers, so we'll be referencing their past adventures when we can. Okay, I'll admit I found Venus a little bit hot."

The name "Agents of Atlas" is a reference to the characters' past, but it also has plot significance. "The original name for the group of course was essentially The Secret Avengers," Parker said. "But since then Marvel has determined that no prior group called themselves that, so we couldn't use it. We were a bit bummed at first, and then when we realized we could mark out historical territory by using the Atlas name, we cheered up pretty fast! There's no need to ride the coattails of another team, 'AOA' should show that they deserve a book on their own strengths."

One man saw the strengths of the "Agents of Atlas" and brought them together as a group. "The glue is Jimmy Woo!" Parker stated. "They're from before the generations of bickering infighting teams. It's all about loyalty and honoring a connection they had together years ago. That said, they will run into a pretty huge intrateam conflict that there's no way of avoiding. That's when we'll see what Jimmy is really made of."

Jimmy is going to have to be made of some stern stuff to survive the perils he and his team will face in "Agents of Atlas." "Jimmy is in... pretty horrible shape at the beginning of the series," Parker explained. "His life has gone way off course from where it was in the 1950s. He's way up in SHIELD, in Directorate, but it's an ugly job and he hasn't seen field work in years. Unknown to the rest of SHIELD, he's been investigating a personal mystery for the past few years, and though he's in his twilight years, he heads an unauthorized mission that ends as bad as it possibly could.

"No one at SHIELD really knew Jimmy in his heyday: A young slang-talking firebrand who would routinely run into danger with impossible odds," Parker continued. "Had James Dean known about Woo at the time, he would have abandoned Hollywood to join the FBI and emulate Jimmy! Jimmy had such a strong sense of direction and self-assurance that he radiated leadership. People respond to that in a big way. It's almost like a superpower itself — better in some ways. Jimmy's short-lived team felt a sense of belonging and purpose in that few months together that none of them ever

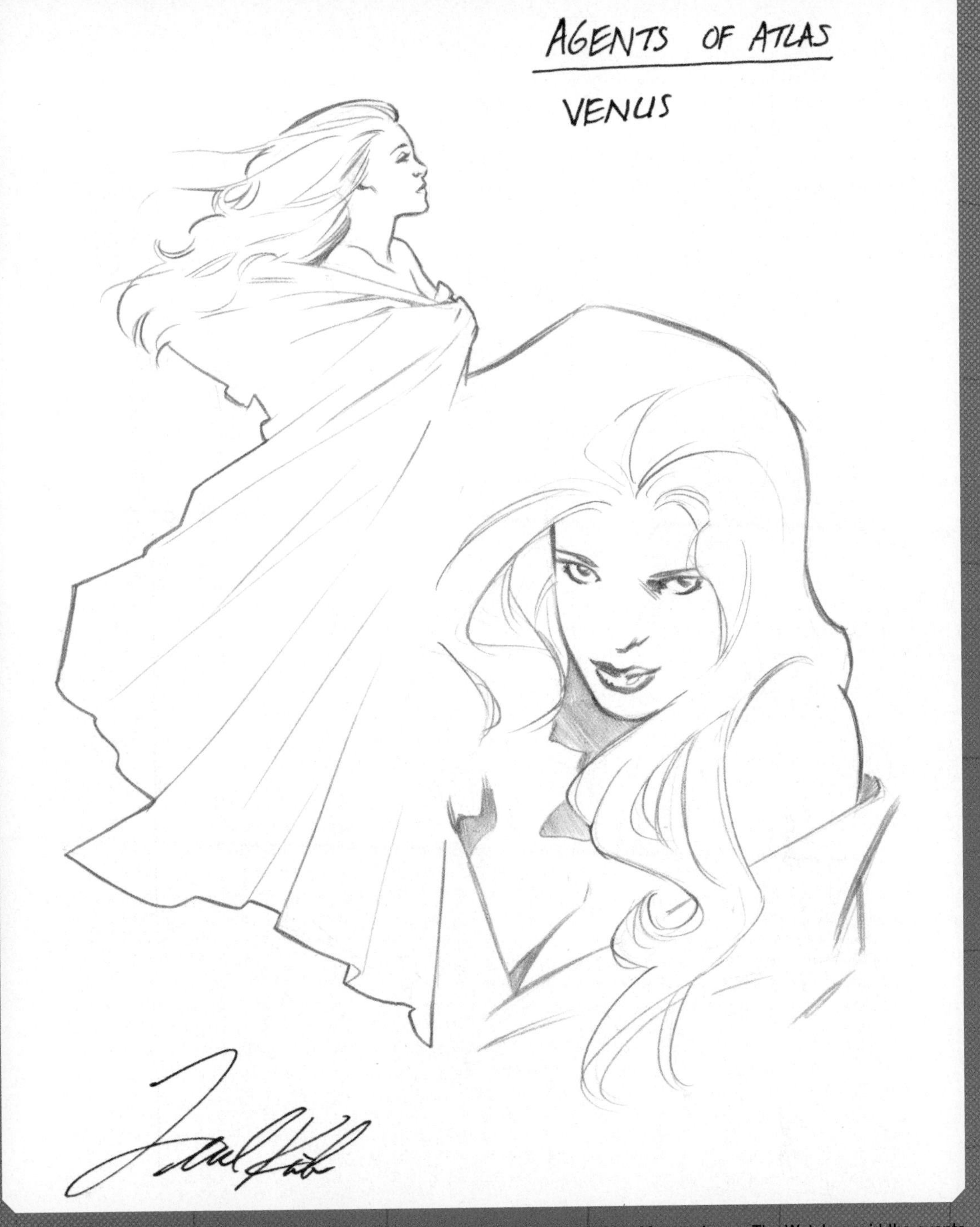
AGENTS OF ATLAS
VENUS

did afterward. And that's why even after almost fifty years, when word gets out that Jimmy's in trouble, the team comes back for him."

The team's quest to save Jimmy will have them traversing the globe. "This bounces around the world a bit, from the Mojave Desert, to Africa, and colder regions," Parker said. "That's another Golden Age difference — whereas '60s Marvel stories hang around Manhattan mostly, the '50s ones hopped the planet a lot. Our main American city is going to be San Francisco."

As the Agents trek around the world to save their friend, readers will learn more about them in a series of flashbacks to the Agents' original adventures. "Though the initial 'What If?' story said that the team was disbanded after their one successful rescue mission, we're establishing that they were together for about six months after that," Parker stated. "Remember, Iron Man and even The Watcher said the events being seen on the Avengers computer might not be the exact events from our (616) history! It could pick up things that happened in alternate realities. So this will determine how it all went down in our timeline."

When Jimmy Woo wasn't working with the Agents of Atlas in the 1950s, he was most likely serving as an agent of the FBI and working hard to foil the latest nefarious scheme of his arch-foe, the Yellow Claw. "If you want to dig up some of his bouts with the Yellow Claw affordably, they ran them later as back ups in 'Giant Size Master of Kung Fu.'" Parker said. "Someone re-lettered the parts that said 'FBI Agent Jimmy Woo' to 'S.H.I.E.L.D. Agent Jimmy Woo!' You couldn't really say there was a cohesive Marvel Universe then, but it's pretty interesting. The creators were trying all kinds of genres to see what would stick, and indulging their interests. When you look at the range of genres, you see the groundwork, the foundation of what the '60s books would be built upon. Look at the Fantastic Four as the best example of taking what came before. Reed and Sue are straight out of the Romance books with the science-fantasy added, Ben is a carryover from the Monster comics, and of course Johnny is an update of an earlier superhero. Bring them all together and you've got a quirky and exciting team that redefines what a superhero comic book is. This is why I think it's important to not dismiss those pre-Marvel years. Much of the success of the Silver Age grew out of the experimenting that happened then."

When Jimmy's old team reunites in the present day to rescue him, they'll find to save their friend they must confront his chief foe from the Pre-Marvel Years. "You're going to see the Yellow Claw, and just as there's more to each of our heroes, there's a lot more to him, too," Parker explained. "I mean, you know his name probably isn't really 'Yellow Claw,' right? And why would a diabolical mastermind even refer to himself with some stereotypical racist 'yellow peril'-style name anyway? In other words, there's a good chance everyone who fought him was being played in a major way! And as if he wasn't manipulative enough, we're going to be introduced to a mysterious advisor of his, essentially the consigliere to the mastermind."

The "Agents of Atlas" will also have advisors of their own; some of the agents of SHIELD that are part of the series supporting cast. "Besides our main heroes, we'll be seeing a stalwart of SHIELD, Dum Dum Dugan," Parker said. "Much of the investigation from their perspective will be handled by agent Derek Khanata, who appeared in 'Amazing Fantasy.' His Wakandan origins figure in very well with some aspects of our story. In a way, he sort of steps into the position Jimmy Woo had in the original 'Secret Avengers' story, where now Jimmy takes a much more active role with the team."

SHIELD might be able to offer some assistance, but the "Agents of Atlas" shouldn't count on any of the Marvel Universe's costumed champions to be of much help. "The other heroes have their hands full with 'Civil War,' but there'll be some brief communications with Reed Richards and King T'Challa," Parker explained.

The Agents of Atlas might not be directly involved in the epic conflict that is "Civil War," but the events of the mega story will affect the series. " 'Civil War' doesn't impact directly on our group; they're all very separated from current society- at least at first," Parker said. "Something that happens in 'Civil War' will affect one of them later, though. It's not something we were anticipating either, it just worked out that way."

Parker hopes things work out with "Agents of Atlas" because he has plenty more tales of the team that he'd love to tell. "As you'll see at the end of the series, if we continue their adventures, the dynamic will be pretty different than other hero-team books. We're counting on readers being ready for something different, because if we made the Agents of Atlas work in similar fashion to other superheroes, there really wouldn't be any point to bringing them back. What I'd like is for a threat to present itself, and readers to say 'Sure, the Avengers or the X-Men could deal with this menace... but I'd really like to see how these guys handle it.'"

AGENT PROFILE: *VENUS*

VENUS

Last week things got a little hairy around these parts as Jeff Parker brought us an Agent Profile on the "Agents of Atlas" member Gorilla-Man. This week love is in the air as Parker brings us the latest Agent Profile: Venus.

Venus made her debut in issue #1 of her self titled series in 1948. "I don't know who wrote the first story, but the first artist was Ken Bald, who Timely often went to for drawing heroines," Parker told CBR News. "She started out in stories that were more about cheesecake and humor. What's interesting is how that gradually started bending to the supernatural and horror, so more often than not Venus is having run-ins with living skeletons, monsters, and the undead, and so on. Our arc for her character is very much a tribute to that development. It's interesting to me that in today's adventure and superhero comics, most characters showing up on the scene are likely to cause some friction with other characters. By her very nature though, Venus doesn't do that. When she's around, people tend to forget why they were angry or fighting. What we want to show with her is that such an effect can be even more potent than destructive power."

Venus's potent powers allow her to influence even the most confident and self assured individuals. "On a small, human scale, you've probably experienced women like her," Parker explained. "An attractive woman with such presence that when she says the briefest of things to men-and looks them in the eye- they just lose it. They can't focus, they feel like they're underwater and even the most James Bond of the bunch can't keep his composure. It's generally pretty hard to say what's affecting the guys the most. Sure she's gorgeous, but so are other girls and they don't all make you walk into walls because you're trying to keep track of where she is in the room. Is it something in her eyes, or the unearthly quality of her voice?

"If you've encountered one of these mind-wiping women, then you have some limited idea of the effect Venus has on people she wants to influence," Parker continued. "Or even those whom she doesn't. She tries to rein in her effect when it's not needed, but it's so much a part of her nature that it's

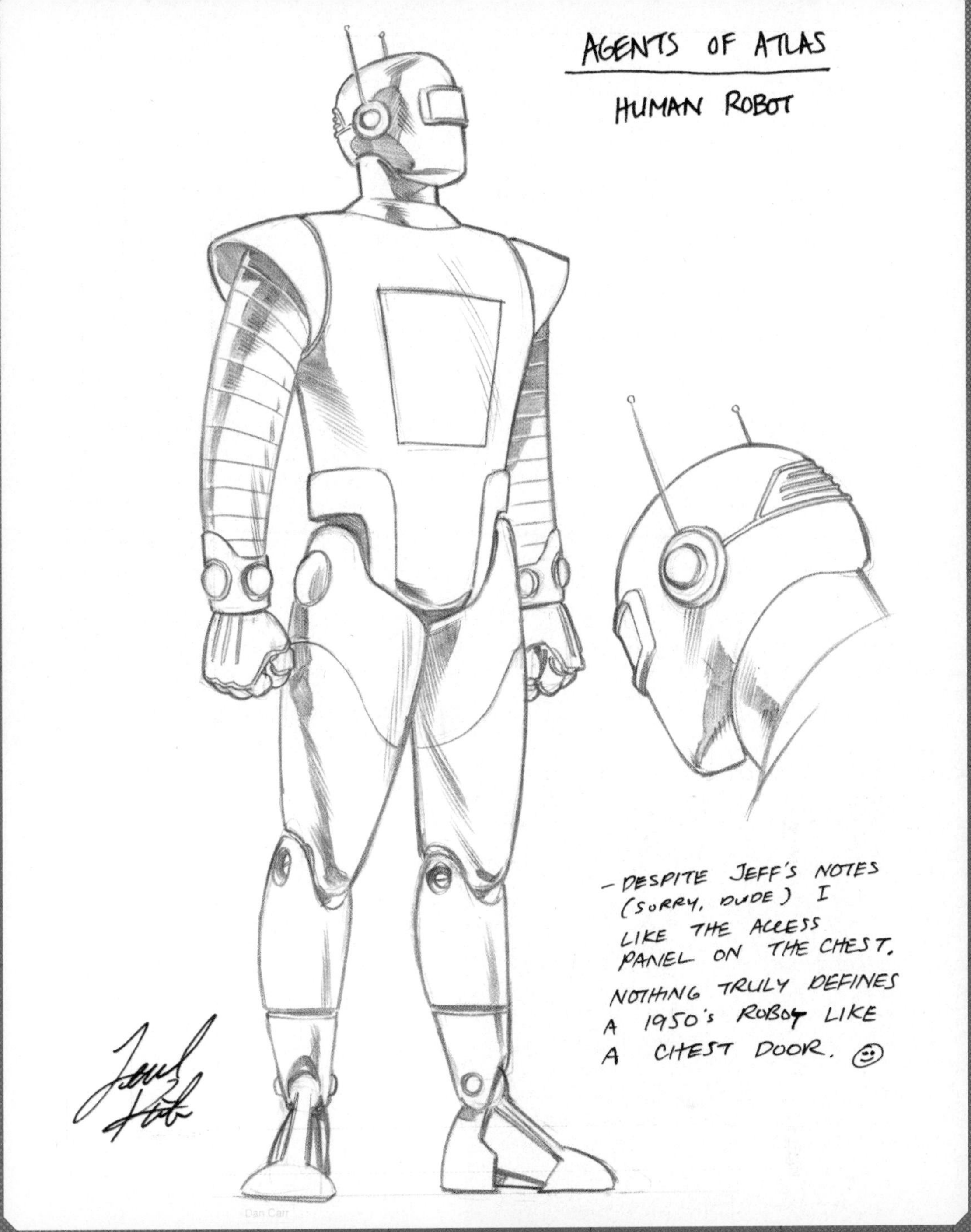
AGENTS OF ATLAS
HUMAN ROBOT
- DESPITE JEFF'S NOTES (SORRY, DUDE) I LIKE THE ACCESS PANEL ON THE CHEST. NOTHING TRULY DEFINES A 1950's ROBOT LIKE A CHEST DOOR.

not possible to muffle completely. Her own team has come up with various solutions to stay on course. Jimmy Woo often sticks his fingers in his ears when she's talking to dampen the vocal effect."

When "Agents of Atlas" begins, Venus isn't looking to dampen the effects of her powers, she's quite happy using them to spread joy. "She is still living among humans and using her abilities for good," Parker said. "But she's not bothering with the secret identity when we meet her again. That's not to say she won't use it in the future."

Vicki Starr is the secret identity Venus often employed in the past and she still maintains to actually be the goddess of love. When asked about Venus's claim of godhood Parker cryptically hinted, "As we've said, there's more to all of these characters than we may have thought."

WEEK 3: PENCILER LEONARD KIRK - AGENT PROFILE: *THE HUMAN ROBOT*

Posted: May 26, 2006

THE WEIGHT OF THE WORLD ON HIS PENCIL: KIRK TALKS "AGENTS OF ATLAS"

In part one of CBR News's focus on Marvel Comics' "Agents of Atlas" mini-series, Editor Mark Paniccia gave us the background and basics on the series. Last week, writer Jeff Parker gave us an in-depth look at the series. Today, in part three of our coverage, CBR News chats with the man responsible for bringing Parker's action packed scripts to life, artist Leonard Kirk.

"Agents of Atlas" is the first in a number of projects at Marvel for Kirk, who CBR News has learned recently signed an exclusive contract with the company. "In all honesty, this is the first time anyone has offered me an exclusive," Kirk told CBR News. "As for going with Marvel, I just felt it was time. DC has been great for me over the years and I'd love to work with them again someday but there are still some characters and projects that I'd like to work with that are only available through Marvel.

"After being offered the exclusive, I was already working on one project with Marvel when I got a call from Mark Paniccia about 'Agents of Atlas,'" Kirk continued, "That's about it. He described the project, sent me the outline and I jumped aboard."

It was the chance to illustrate an eclectic group of bizarre characters that drew Kirk to "Agents of Atlas." "The appeal for me was the histories of the characters themselves," Kirk said. "I'm not very familiar with them, but what I did learn from my research was what clinched the deal for me. How the hell do you say no to a project featuring characters named the Human Robot, Marvel Boy, Venus and Gorilla Man? Being a fan of 'Planet of the Apes,' I certainly wasn't going to pass up the chance at drawing a talking gorilla."

For Kirk, the chance to illustrate a talking gorilla and other offbeat and obscure characters was the most fun and rewarding aspect of "Agents of Atlas." "The term 'obscure' might bother some fans but, really, many of the gang you'll see in this series have made only sporadic appearances since their Atlas days. Some of them haven't shown up in comics for years," Kirk explained. "I like working with characters like this because I have a little more freedom with how they can be depicted. There aren't the kinds of restrictions in place that you might encounter when working with characters like Spider-Man or the X-Men."

The lack of restrictions has made "Agents of Atlas" an almost difficulty free assignment for Kirk. "I don't know that I'd call this a difficulty but Marvel has insisted that I turn in layouts of the pages before doing the finished pencils," Kirk stated. "I generally prefer to go straight to drawing on the board, but that's OK. The process adds a little time to my work week, but not much. Also, there are advantages to fleshing things out ahead of time. Aside from that, and digging up a bundle of reference, I can't really think of any difficulties I've had with this project so far."

For Kirk, collaborating with Jeff Parker was another difficulty free and fun part of "Agents of Atlas." "Working with Jeff has been great," Kirk said. "He's good to talk with, really open to suggestions and I can honestly say that he has given me fewer wedgies during the typical work week than any other writer (Peter David included). Also, he's so personable over e-mail that you'd never guess he had those huge Borg-like cybernetic implants imbedded in his skull unless you saw him in person. However, if you ever do see Jeff in person, I strongly suggest you stay on your side of the Plexiglas barrier. If you want an autograph, just pass your comic through the sliding panel to the right."

Kirk was greatly impressed by Parker's script and wanted to capture all the major elements, with the characters being the most important element. "Gorilla Man is probably the one character I most wanted to properly flesh out," Kirk said. "However, I really enjoy working with the rest of the cast as

well."

Fans of Kirk's other work on titles like "Freshmen" will be happy to hear that he's bringing the cast and action of "Agents of Atlas" to life with his usual artistic style. "I don't think my style is going to be all that different than what you've seen from me before," Kirk explained. "In my opinion, this isn't the kind of project that's really suited to something too radical. However, as far as backgrounds are concerned, especially when we find ourselves inside Marvel Boy's flying saucer, I will definitely be pulling some inspiration from Wally Wood and some of the great sci-fi backgrounds he did in the '50s and '60s."

Kirk already has another project lined up after "Agents of Atlas" which he had to remain mum about. "All I can say is that it stars some of my favorite Marvel characters," Kirk said. "I got started on it before 'Agents of Atlas' was dropped in my lap and one issue has already been finished."

Kirk hopes that when "Agents of Atlas" finishes with issue five that readers will want more because he'd love to depict the team's future exploits. "I hope that everyone enjoys 'Agents of Atlas' and that they go out and buy lots of copies. Lots and lots of copies," he joked. "Seriously, break the frickin' bank, people. Poppa needs a new car."

AGENT PROFILE: *THE HUMAN ROBOT*

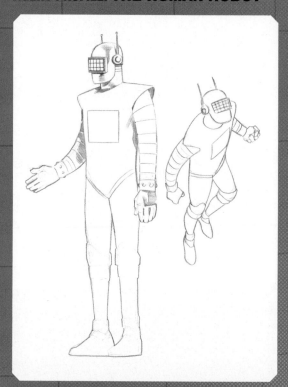

Last week CBR Readers felt the love as they learned about the Agents of Atlas member, Venus. This week readers will be saying, "Domo Arigato, Mr. Roboto," as CBR News again chats with "AOA" writer Jeff Parker for the latest Agent Profile: The Human Robot.

The Human Robot sprang to life for the first time in 1954 in the pages of "Menace" #11. "He was created by the team that would later make regular comics history, Stan Lee and John Romita!" Parker told CBR News. "It's a very brief horror

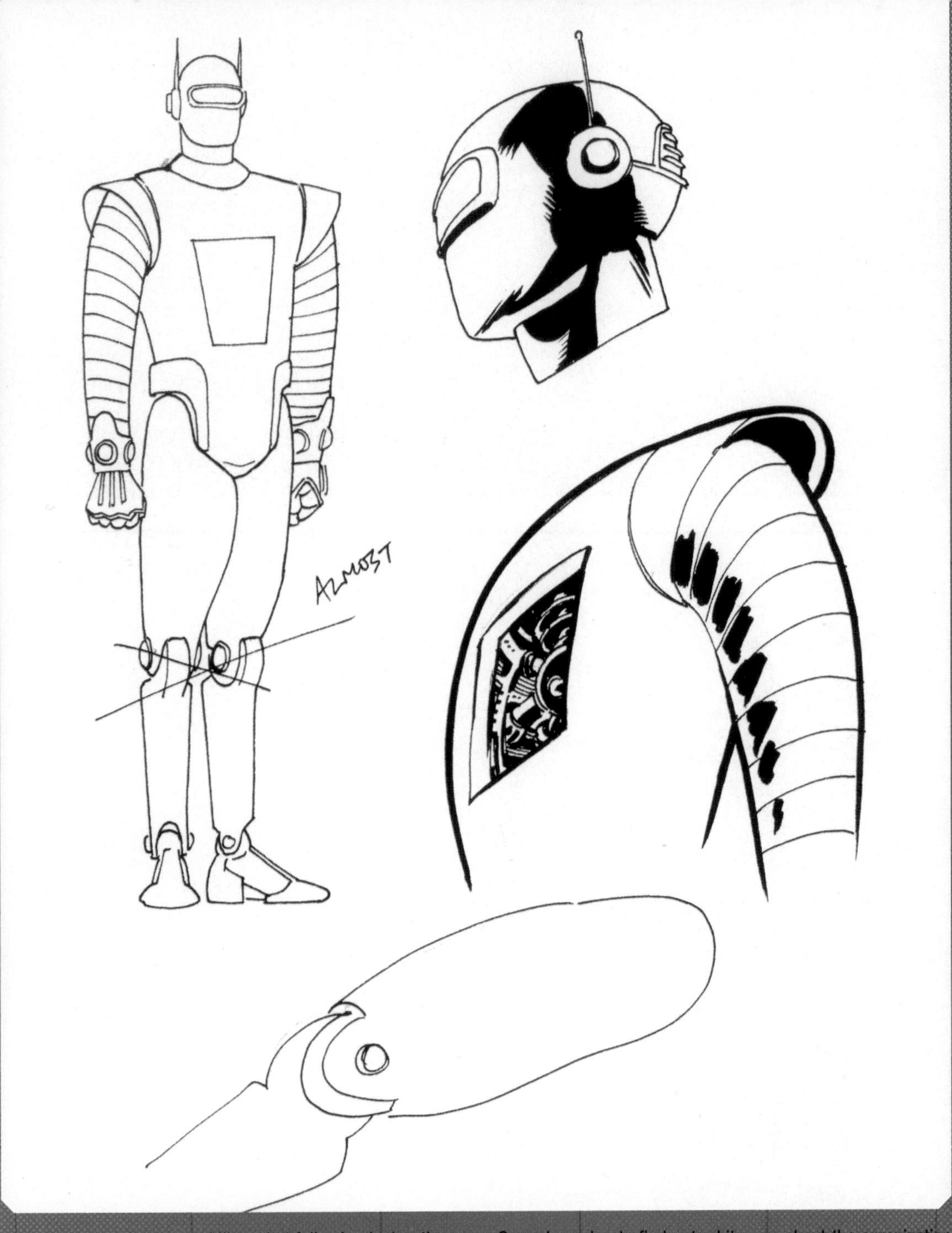
ALMOST

story that's simply about a killer robot following instructions a bit too literally after it was rushed into development. According to the letter column in 'What If' #9, when Roy Thomas was concocting the idea of a 1950s super team, it was writer Don Glut who remembered the 'Menace' story and suggested that the robot ended up sinking into the harbor. The choice of that robot in the 'Secret Avengers' story is the most interesting one they made, I think. I like the fact that Namora is the one who found it and put Jimmy Woo onto the robot, and that Marvel Boy restored it.

"Since the original story left out a lot of detail — it doesn't give you the name of the scientist who builds the robot, the company he works for, or why he's built what is apparently a killing machine — it gives us a nice blank slate to fill in," Parker continued. "You rarely get an opportunity like that! So we're going to find out a bit more about the organization responsible for building this machine in the first place. I'll give you a hint — it starts with an A!"

The organization responsible for the Robot's creation didn't build your garden variety automaton, as the character's name suggests, they built a Human Robot. "We're going to address exactly why he's called that, beyond being a bipedal construct," Parker explained. "Still, it's a bit ungainly when the group talks for everyone to say, 'Hey, The Human Robot, come here,' and simply referring to him as robot seemed too demeaning. So we've given him a designation as his builder would no doubt have done. His proper name is M-11, the reference of which will now be obvious to CBR readers, at least."

M-11 is equipped with a variety of awesome and mysterious capabilities which make him an asset to the Agents of Atlas.

"He's clearly very strong," Parker stated. "In the preview you saw him throw a tank through the door of the fortress they stormed. It's also revealing about his nature that he has a Death Ray that fires from his eye at various levels of intensity. We know it's a Death Ray because if you look on the inside of his chest plate there's a diagram that says 'Death Ray!' When Marvel Boy repaired M-11 originally, he changed the structure of the robot's metal to an alloy that will be near impossible to affect with earthly weapons. As the story goes on, we find some more modifications that weren't made by Marvel Boy, which begs the question: who made them? M-11 now seems to be able to infiltrate any computer system he wants. In fact, he's constantly accessing datastreams from the internet as well as many other normally secured systems around the world. What's he doing with all this information? Suddenly what everyone thought of as a relatively primitive killing machine seems to be a lot more sophisticated and versatile. Appropriately for the most cryptic member of the team though, his secrets are going to be revealed last."

In addition to being a walking arsenal shrouded in secrecy, Parker feels that the Human Robot will strike a chord with readers because of his retro style appearance. "Visually, the robot is cool because he embodies the robot menace of the pulp adventures," Parker said. "With that cyclopean eye, no mouth, the antennae — he's got a classic look that conjures up everything from Gort in 'The Day the Earth Stood Still' to the giant robots in 'Sky Captain.' His body is a bit more detailed than in the 'Menace' story — we kind of approach that as 'what would the artist have likely done had he more time than a weekend to design this guy' and so he gets a little more definition and a nice solid eyepiece instead of one that looks like a lightboard. I was originally suggesting that we leave off his chest door or move it to the back, but Leonard Kirk was adamant that he needed it up front to really convey 'classic robot.' He's right

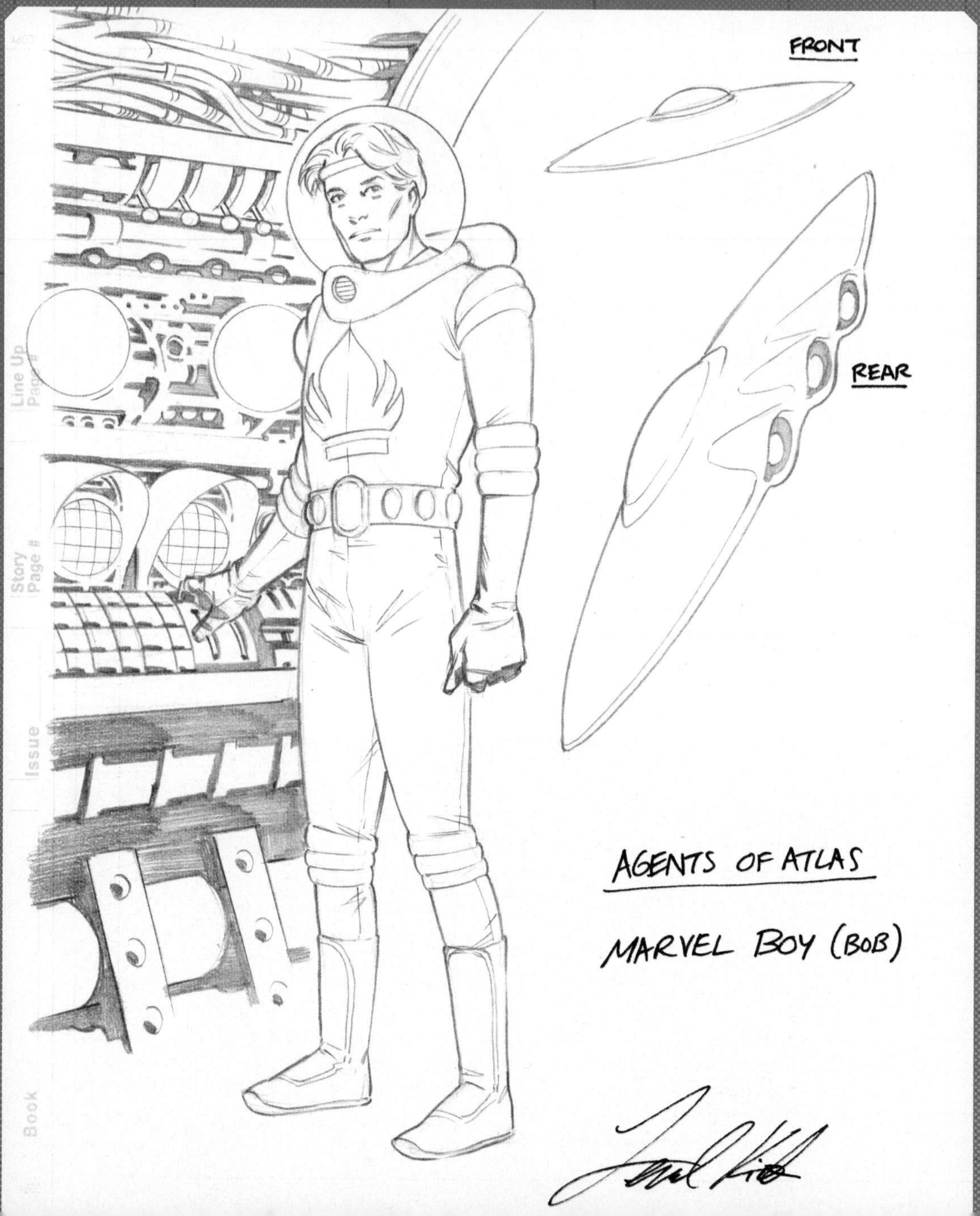
FRONT
REAR
AGENTS OF ATLAS
MARVEL BOY (BOB)
Line Up Page #
Story Page #
Issue
Book

of course."

That classic robot has been MIA for decades when "Agents of Atlas" begins. "No one has seen M-11 since the late 50's," Parker explained. "He was hanging out with Marvel Boy, but we're going to find out that Bob Grayson had to leave Earth in a hurry and didn't take the robot with him. So, where's he been all this time? He's a really tough nut to crack, because he doesn't say much. But he seems to respond to Jimmy Woo. He turns out to be very important in bringing the team back together, but it's going to very puzzling for a while. What's his agenda? Does he even have agendas? Should we even refer to him as 'he?'"

WEEK 4: AGENT PROFILE: MARVEL BOY & A CRYPTIC INVITATION

Posted: June 3, 2006

Last week CBR News was doing the robot as "Agents of Atlas" writer Jeff Parker acquainted us with M-11 AKA the Human Robot. This week Parker plays Ground Control to our Major Tom as he checks back in with the latest Agent Profile for Marvel Boy. Also CBR News feature on "AoA" has caught the eye of a mysterious stranger and we share with our readers the cryptic invitation that he sent us.

Marvel Boy made his debut in the 1950s in issues #3-6 of the Timely-Atlas title "Astonishing" and went on to star in his own self-titled series. It was the character's last known appearance that has many fans puzzled at Marvel Boy's inclusion in the modern day line up of the "Agents of Atlas." "He's probably the character that the most talk has been about since this project was announced," Parker told CBR News. "Didn't he die in 'Fantastic Four' #165? Doesn't the hero Quasar have his bands now- the Quantum Bands? How many Marvel Boys are there? Wasn't one a New Warrior? Wasn't one a Kree Warrior?

"Let's go back to the beginning," Parker continued. "Our Marvel Boy is Bob Grayson, who was born in Germany as the Nazi party was coming into power. His father Matthew was a scientist who built a rocketship so he and his son could flee the Earth for another more peaceful planet without dictators. And that planet turned out to be the 7th one in our solar system, Uranus. Not habitable you say? In fact there was a paradise full of other humans that existed in the life-supporting Omnidome, and they took the Graysons in."

The Graysons' benefactors turned out to be an offshoot of the immortal, earth born, aliens, The Eternals. "They were very advanced, and as Bob grew up they bestowed many of their technological gifts upon him," Parker explained. "As a teenager, he returned to Earth with strength enhanced by pills they gave him, and he could fly and manipulate light in powerful ways thanks to these armbands he wore. He also had a headband that allowed him extra mental abilities such as telepathy."

Bob Grayson returned to Earth and attempted to be a hero, but ultimately his return to his birth planet proved to be his downfall. "The last time we saw Bob he was giving the Fantastic Four a hard time, frothing at the mouth and calling himself The Crusader," Parker stated. "Apparently, the Uranian colonists were in need of medical supplies, so Grayson tried to borrow money from a bank to raise what he needed to help the colonists. It was for nothing, because a vaguely described cataclysm destroyed them. Here's a good webpage that fills in some of that info. Anyway, the wristbands themselves destroyed the Crusader, and that's the last we've seen of him."

The reason behind Bob's strange reappearance among the living in "Agents of Atlas" can be found by probing the mysteries of his past. "Rather than also vaporize continuity that doesn't work for our purposes, 'Agents of Atlas' takes into account all of these major points in Marvel Boy's history and treats it as a mystery story," Parker explained. "So many things don't add up. Why could Marvel Boy never make the bands work to the extent that Quasar could? Since when do ultra-advanced civilizations need our medical help? Weren't those colonists exiles, after all? Heck, how did Dr. Grayson manage to build a spaceship and find them in the first place? To get to the bottom of the mystery, we address practically everything!"

Whatever it was that caused Bob's return, he did not emerge from the process unscathed. "When we meet Bob in the present day, he's a little different," Parker stated. "It takes him a while to get the hang of English again. He's not flying around, he's no stronger than anyone else, and he sure doesn't have those wristbands. He has to wear a suit that keeps him in an environment he can live in — breathing a mixture of hydrogen, methane and helium — and a temperature a couple hundred degrees below what we can stand. That looks like a glass bubble helmet, but it's actually a field generated by the suit to hold in the cold and gases. He can reach through it to say, eat dinner. But trust us... you do not want to see Bob eat.

"Nonetheless, Jimmy Woo and the gang are very glad to have their interplanetary pal back even if he has changed," Parker continued. "And there do seem to be some pros to his new condition. His mental ability is much broader than what it was- he has lots of abilities you would associate with 'Grey' aliens. And he hasn't aged nearly as much as we would have expected him to by now. Is he still human? That will be determined by the end of the series."

It will also be determined by the end of the series whether or not Marvel Boy is still a fitting heroic moniker for the seemingly resurrected Bob Grayson. "Just as the team always refers to Gorilla Man as Ken, everyone calls him Bob," Parker said. "The title Marvel Boy seems a little young for him now (and of course, there are others as we mentioned), but we'll leave it to readers to ultimately decide how to refer to him. I like the term one of our yet-to-be-introduced characters uses to refer to him: The Uranian."

Speaking of mysterious characters, this reporter received an interesting bit of mail yesterday. Which is strange, because Comic Book Resources only lists my email address. I suppose since this person is that resourceful, I should share the message!

Mr. Richards.

It has not escaped my notice that you are documenting information relating to The Atlas Foundation. The thoroughness of this feature persuades me to extend an invitation to you and your readers. Stay alert next week. There will be an announcement made by one very loyal to my Order. Exceptional minds shall be led to an offering of what you might call a "decoder ring." I believe you are schooled enough in our methods that you will recognize the announcement when you see it.

Your Humble Servant

That was it. There was no name. The invitation arrived in an odd crimson envelope with a wax seal on the back. Now, I wish I hadn't opened it that way because the seal appeared to be some kind of symbol, but you can't make it out now.

WEEK 5: AGENT PROFILE: *JIMMY WOO*

Posted: June 12, 2006

For weeks now readers have been following CBR News's coverage of Marvel Comics "Agents of Atlas" mini-series and wondering who the mysterious fifth member of the team was. This week Jeff Parker declassifies the identity of the fifth team member, with the agent profile of former FBI and current SHIELD agent Jimmy Woo. Some readers might be thinking that that's not such a big revelation and they would be right. CBR News is proud to announce that its "Agents of Atlas" coverage will be expanded to one more part - this Friday we'll reveal for the first time anywhere the identity of the mysterious sixth team member of the Agents of Atlas.

Parker briefly discussed Jimmy with CBR News in his in-

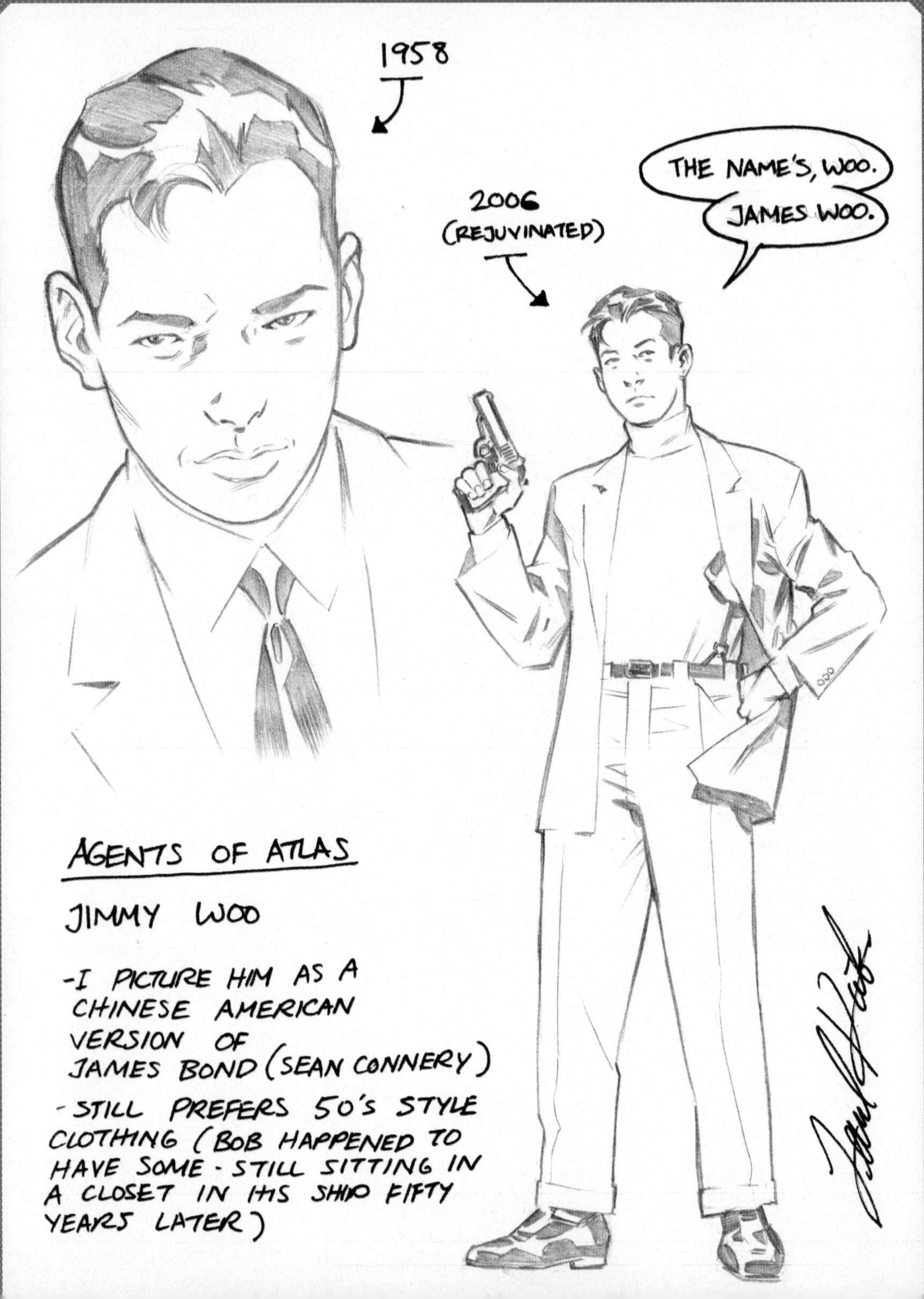
1958
2006 (REJUVINATED)
THE NAME'S, WOO. JAMES WOO.
AGENTS OF ATLAS
JIMMY WOO
-I PICTURE HIM AS A CHINESE AMERICAN VERSION OF JAMES BOND (SEAN CONNERY)
-STILL PREFERS 50'S STYLE CLOTHING (BOB HAPPENED TO HAVE SOME - STILL SITTING IN A CLOSET IN HIS SHIP FIFTY YEARS LATER)

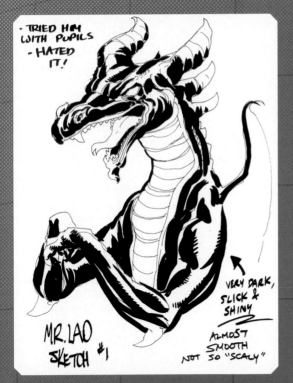

- TRIED HIM WITH PUPILS
- HATED IT!
VERY DARK, SLICK & SHINY
ALMOST SMOOTH NOT SO "SCALY"
MR. LAO SKETCH #1

depth interview weeks ago, but since Jimmy is a core, active member of the Agents, he felt that Woo merited an expanded Agent Profile.

Unlike the rest of his compatriots, many Marvel readers might be aware of Jimmy as a character, but not really know it. "Jimmy Woo is like one of those lovable character actors whose name you can't ever get," Parker told CBR News. "He's been backing up bigger names in the Marvel Universe for years, and he's one of the characters they allowed to age. Though that wasn't always played up — just a few years ago he appeared looking pretty young, but if you read his recent SHIELD profile, he's pretty advanced in years. No one gave him a formula to drink or dropped him in suspended animation, he just kept working. You've got to choose what's canon. For example, I'm fine with saying he was flying around with Dum Dum Dugan in the Helicarrier chasing Godzilla, but I'm thinking Marvel proper isn't!"

Like his other team mates, Jimmy was introduced to readers before there was a proper Marvel Universe. "Jimmy came from the 'Yellow Claw' comic book of the '50s, tirelessly on the case of the criminal mastermind," Parker stated. "I don't know if there was simply a mandate to put out a Fu Manchu-clone book, but what I find interesting is that they at least let the hero be of Chinese roots, in a time that being balanced towards minorities just wasn't a priority. That has to be due to Al Feldstein beginning the writing of the book. He was a forward thinker and dealt with a broad range of social issues in his work, especially at EC Comics. The first art by Joe Maneely is lush and evocative, using Asian imagery as a design element throughout. It's too bad they didn't keep doing it, because the book really had its own feel. Not that anyone can complain about who took over next — Jack Kirby! — but his stories were much more influenced by Doc Savage novels, a different thing altogether. Jim Steranko brought Jimmy into SHIELD a few years later because, hey, the Yellow Claw turned up. That turned out to be a robot, but it gave Jimmy another chance to shine, so it's worth it."

Since he was brought into SHIELD, Jimmy has had many scandalous experiences. "Jimmy Woo has been in SHIELD for years, and close to some ugly secrets," Parker said. "He's worked a lot in interrogation, and that's obviously not a pretty job. While he likely knew about the more questionable activities his own people were involved with, he wouldn't have much room to judge. He was hip deep in questionable activities of his own."

As "Agents of Atlas" begins, the chickens of Jimmy's questionable activities are coming home to roost. "At this point we're seeing a Woo near retirement, higher up in SHIELD hierarchy," Parker explained. "As we discussed before, at the beginning of' 'Agents' we find out Jimmy was running an investigation no one in SHIELD Directorate knew about, and an unauthorized mission he was in no condition for went horribly wrong. Had he been working on this secret for all those years, and what is this secret so big he didn't trust his own agency? But one of the themes of this whole storyline is the Second Chance. Life passes people by and windows of opportunity close. Maybe, just maybe, if you stick to your guns and never give up on your goal, even in the final inning a window will open again. And though you've been tainted by a grey world, that doesn't outweigh your time as a young optimistic idealist who could inspire some of the strangest people on Earth to charge into the demon pit with you. Somewhere in Jimmy Woo is that young, natural-born leader who some old buddies think is worth betraying allegiances and traveling 1.6 billion miles!"

Jimmy Woo will definitely need the help of his friends to survive his ordeal in the demon pit, but readers shouldn't think he's totally defenseless or dependant on them. "I'm sure some readers are wondering how Jimmy is supposed to hang with teammates who can control minds, fire death rays and the like. I don't think there'll be much doubt once he's back in action, and especially when his very grand destiny is revealed.

"And that's the team," Parker said. "Oh wait; we're forgetting

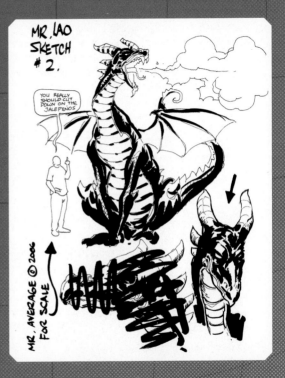

MR. LAO SKETCH # 2.
YOU REALLY SHOULD CUT DOWN ON THE JALEPEÑOS
MR. AVERAGE © 2006 FOR SCALE

someone, aren't we?"

Be sure to check back here on Friday when Parker remembers who we forgot and brings us the final agent profile, where we reveal his identity exclusively here on CBR!

NAMORA

"DEATH GOWN" COLOR SCHEME

WEEK 6: AGENT PROFILE: *NAMORA*

Posted: June 16, 2006

For weeks now writer Jeff Parker has been reintroducing CBR readers to a group of golden age Marvel Comics characters who will be reassembling in the present day to continue the fight against injustice in the pages of "Agents of Atlas," a six issue mini-series debuting in August. Readers have also been eagerly awaiting the revelation of the identity of the final mysterious member of the "Agents." Well the wait is over! But before we begin, this reporter must apologize for the accidental use of the pronoun "he" in last week's feature, which proved misleading to some readers trying to guess the identity of the final member. So, without further ado . . . Everybody out of the pool! Jeff Parker checks in again one last time with the final Agent Profile: Namora.

Readers not familiar with Namora might assume she has a connection with the Avenging Son of Atlantis, Prince Namor, and they would be right. "Namora is credited to Ken Bald, who we mentioned in talking about Venus, and I'm not sure if the writer was ever named," Parker told CBR News. "And of course, she was presented quite a bit by Bill Everett [creator of Namor]. She's Prince Namor's cousin, which makes her royalty as well. Namora was a name she gave herself to note her dedication to stomping evil — her original name is Aquaria Nautica Neptuna — quite possibly the most sea-related name a character could have!"

In the original "What If the Avengers Fought Evil in the 1950s"

story that inspired "Agents of Atlas," Namora makes a brief appearance and assists the group in the salvaging of an important find from the sea. "In the 'What If' story, Namora helps out the Secret Avengers by bringing them an interesting find — the Human Robot," Parker explained. "We mention in some of the preview pages that Jimmy asked her to join the team, but she declined. Though her excuse is the need to deal with her undersea affairs, it's worth noting the year always given for the birth of her daughter — 1958!

"When I reread the 'What If' story, I think I had the same reaction as a lot of readers. They bring Namora into the story for a minute and I immediately thought, 'Hey, why isn't she on the team? Then you'd have a lot of extra power, and a heroine with actual history!' The obvious reason is they were more concerned with making this team a counterpart of the current Avengers," Parker continued. "But if you have Namora on board, besides the fact that she was an actual character from the time, then you have a team of archetypes, pulp icons. I quickly went digging for her last appearance to see what became of her and lo and behold I found the issue of 'Sub-Mariner.' There she is, frozen in a block of ice. I don't know about you, but when I see a Golden Age Marvel hero in a block of ice . . ."

In her last appearance Namora was confined to a frozen prison, but much of the world believes her dead. "As Bill Everett later wrote, Namora was poisoned by her rival Llyra. Then all the info we have is from Namorita, who believes her mother is dead," Parker said. "So a 14 year old is convinced, but for some reason Submariner's enemy Byrrah kept her on ice. The popular complaint with this is that poison wouldn't take out Namor, so it's unlikely it would her either. I mean, she can survive a direct hit from a torpedo!

"It seemed clear to me that Everett wasn't just keeping her body around for decoration," Parker continued. "Then I found out, thanks to the posters over at the Invaders Message Board at Comicboards.com, that Roy Thomas even wrote that Bill Everett planned to bring her back — but of course Everett's health was deteriorating then. He died soon after, and Marvel had a rare full page tribute to him, which coincidentally Tom Spurgeon ran on the Comics Reporter site recently."

Unfortunately for Namora her resurfacing coincides with a tragic event for her. "I have to say this, since people will immediately wonder. When I told my editor (and subsequently other editors and executives) my intent to bring Namora back, I had no idea what was going to happen in 'Civil War.' By which I refer to her daughter Namorita being killed along with most of the New Warriors. I think some readers are going to assume it was planned, but when I found out that was happening, it was pretty bizarre — it felt like some cosmic trade-off was happening. It's a little strange because, as you'll see, our story is very much about grand manipulations, where destinies are being decided in secret, and though I'm still fairly sure bringing Namora back was my idea, it doesn't feel like it!"

Parker concluded the agent profile with a dedication. He said, "Bill, this one's for you."

That wraps up CBR News' spotlight on "Agents of Atlas." We would like to thank Jeff Parker, Leonard Kirk, Mark Paniccia, and Jim McCann for all their contributions to our multi part feature.

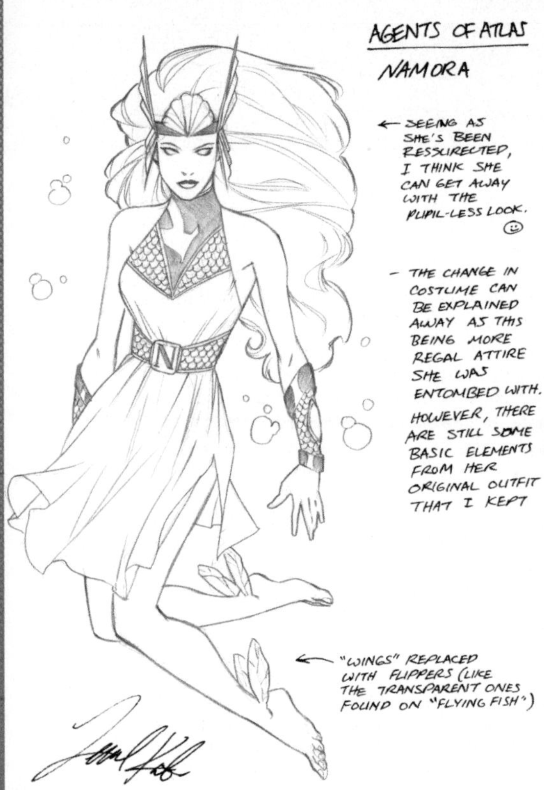
AGENTS OF ATLAS
NAMORA
← SEEING AS SHE'S BEEN RESSURECTED, I THINK SHE CAN GET AWAY WITH THE PUPIL-LESS LOOK. ☺
- THE CHANGE IN COSTUME CAN BE EXPLAINED AWAY AS THIS BEING MORE REGAL ATTIRE SHE WAS ENTOMBED WITH. HOWEVER, THERE ARE STILL SOME BASIC ELEMENTS FROM HER ORIGINAL OUTFIT THAT I KEPT
← "WINGS" REPLACED WITH FLIPPERS (LIKE THE TRANSPARENT ONES FOUND ON "FLYING FISH")

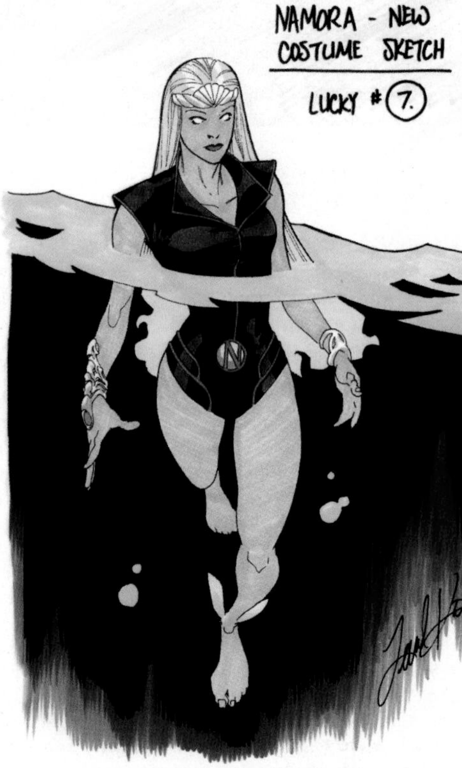
NAMORA - NEW COSTUME SKETCH
LUCKY # 7.

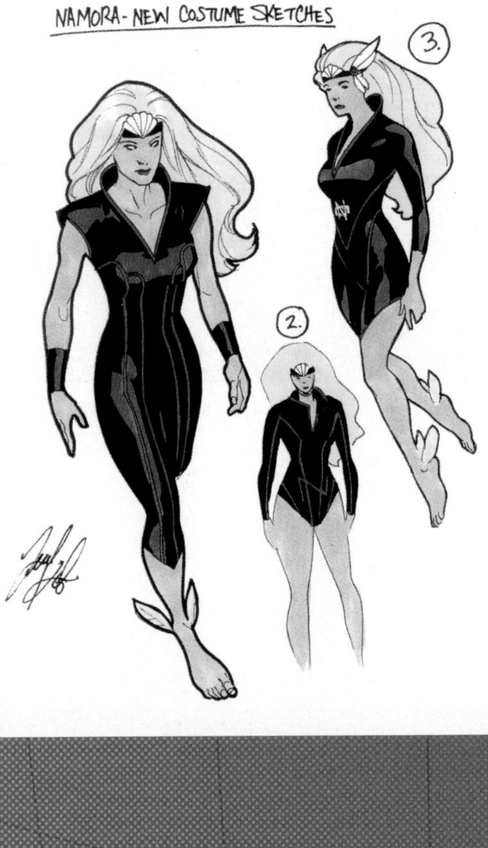
NAMORA - NEW COSTUME SKETCHES
3.
2.

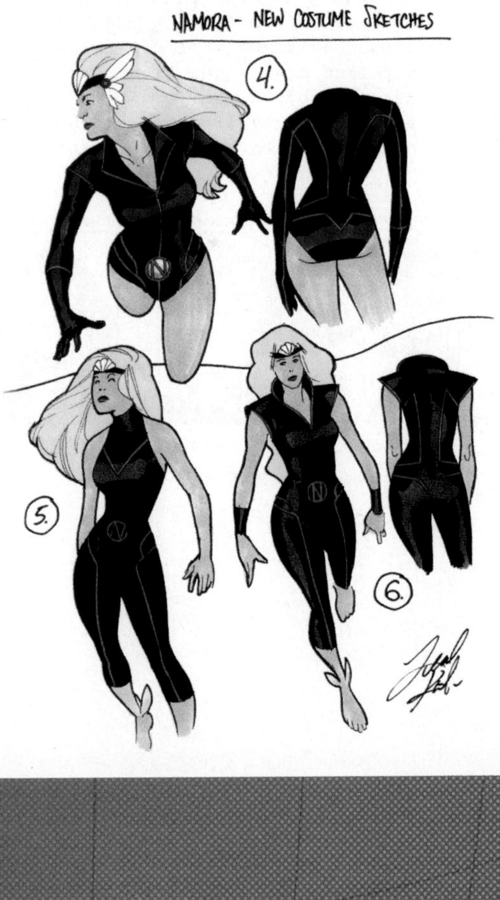
NAMORA - NEW COSTUME SKETCHES
4.
5.
6.

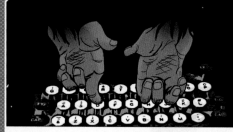

FROM THE CASE FILES OF KEN HALE

It's all going down tomorrow, baby! Can't believe the turns my life has taken in the last few weeks. Well, they're not "turning-into-a-gorilla" big, but still.

The last couple of years I've been working in this Special Ops section of S.H.I.E.L.D., kicking monster ass, when one day M-11, "The Human Robot," tracks me down. He and I used to work for Jimmy Woo on a secret FBI team in '58--I didn't know what happened with him after that. So M-11 tells me Jimmy's in S.H.I.E.L.D.'s Mojave Base on life support, and that our old bud Bob "Marvel Boy" Grayson can save him if we get in touch. Seems Jimmy had led some crazy secret mission against a group called "Atlas" and got his whole team killed. I couldn't stand the thought of my old boss going out like that, so the robot and I call up Uranus (heh). Ends up with me and the robot trashing the base and snatching Jimmy with Bob's new flying saucer.

Bob's gotten pretty weird over the years--he doesn't fly around in underpants shining lights in everyone's eyes anymore, and you DO NOT want to see him eat. But his headband is really powerful now, and he was able to restore Jimmy to the way he remembered him in the Fifties. That's as far as his memories go now, too. (Fun fact: Jimmy's Chinese name is Woo Yen Jet.)

Next thing I know, we're putting the band back together, finding Venus in Africa and even going to the bottom of the ocean and breaking Namora out of ice! All the while Yellow Claw...excuse me, GOLDEN Claw keeps popping up like he knows our every move. And he did, 'cause the damn robot kept TELLING him our every move! I'd bust his tin head, but apparently he can just rebuild himself from obliteration, so whatcha gonna do?

Anyway, Jimmy thinks we just need to go back to that underground room and say Open Sesame or something. Hell, the kid hasn't been wrong yet. We're heading down tomorrow. Now maybe I'll get to find out:
1. What that Eisenhower kidnapping was all about
2. Where the robot was for 50 years
3. And why Jimmy's life was spared when he attacked the Atlas Foundation
Or I'll get killed. One way or another, it's gonna be a big day.

the spy

JIMMY WOO

the spaceman

BOB GRAYSON
MARVEL BOY

the goddess

VENUS

the mermaid

NAMORA

the robot

M-11
HUMAN
ROBOT

the gorilla

KEN HALE
GORILLA
MAN

AND NOW FOR OUR FEATURE PRESENTATION!

THE STAR
OF THIS EVENING'S
SHOW...

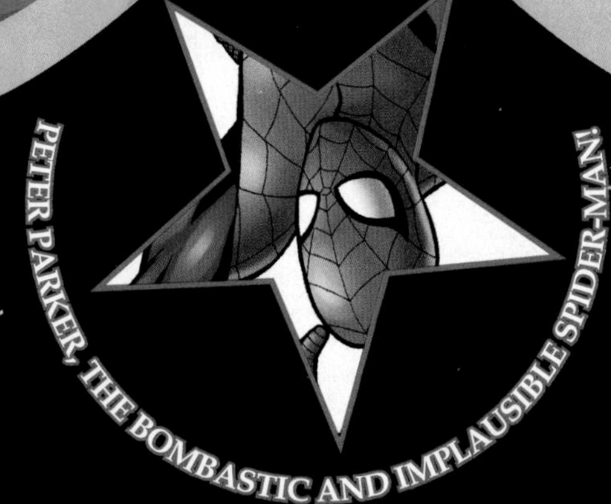
PETER PARKER, THE BOMBASTIC AND IMPLAUSIBLE SPIDER-MAN!

A radioactive spider bite gave brainy bookworm Peter incredible abilities! The Amazing Spider-Man can scale walls! Weave webs! And with his fantastic strength, knock out villains with a single body blow!

And our featured players...The Astounding Agents of Atlas!

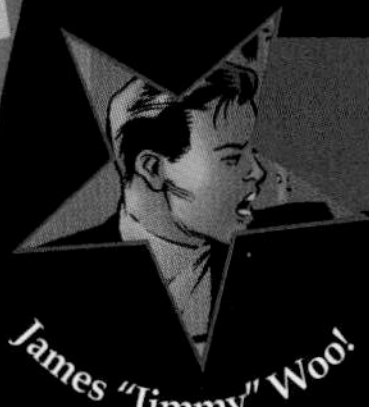
James "Jimmy" Woo!

A suave, swingin' FBI agent from the 50's, Woo's been de-aged and had all his old-guy memories wiped clean. Bad guys and hot ladies beware...Jimmy's on the loose!

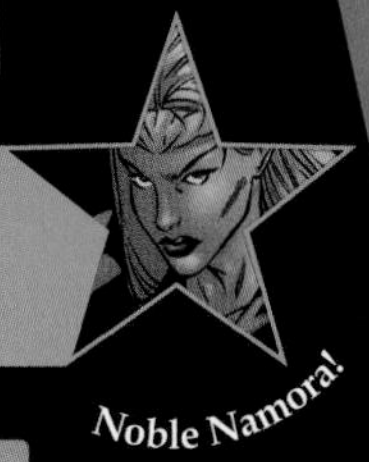
Noble Namora!

Fancy a looker with gills and ankle wings? Have we got a gal for you! This sultry seabreather took a fifty-year nap and has a hankerin' to stretch her super-strong muscles!

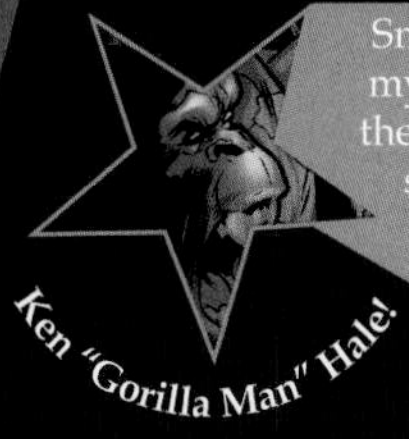
Ken "Gorilla Man" Hale!

Smart alecks don't get much smellier than this! Ol' Hale killed a mystical gorilla over in Africa...and wouldn't you know it, inherited the gorilla's curse himself! Now he uses his proportionate gorilla strength and speed, as well as his weird "Gorilla Sense," which warns him of danger! (note: Hale might be pulling our leg with the whole "Gorilla Sense" thing)

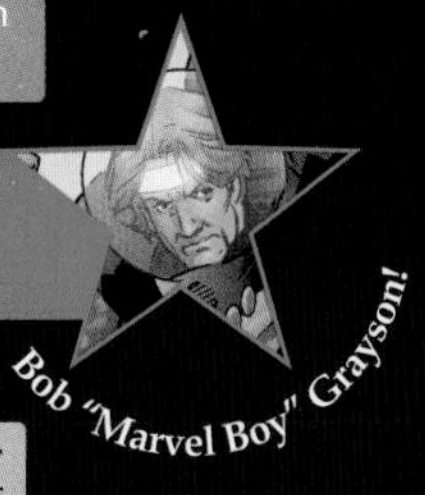
Bob "Marvel Boy" Grayson!

Comin' straight from Uranus (snicker), Mr. Grayson has a spaceship, weird alien powers and a bubble on his head. What more could ya want in a teammate?

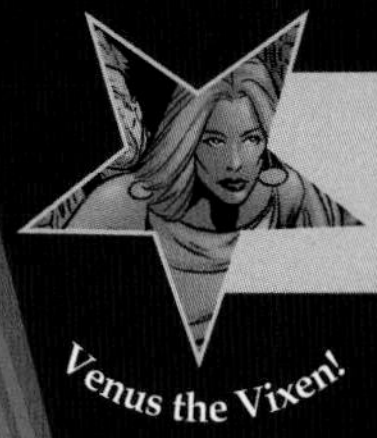
Venus the Vixen!

Check out those lips! Those eyes! Those...um, lips! But buyer beware, fellas: this beauty is actually an ancient Siren, capable of luring men to their deaths with but a word. Luckily, she's kicked the killing habit and's working on the side of angels!

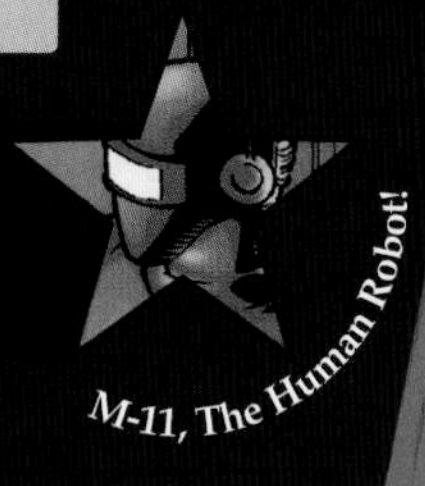
M-11, The Human Robot!

He's clunky! He's chunky! He likes to annoy that monkey! He's the oddball automaton that the Atlas cats depend on to steer 'em in the right direction. Archive, you crazy robot you. Archive.

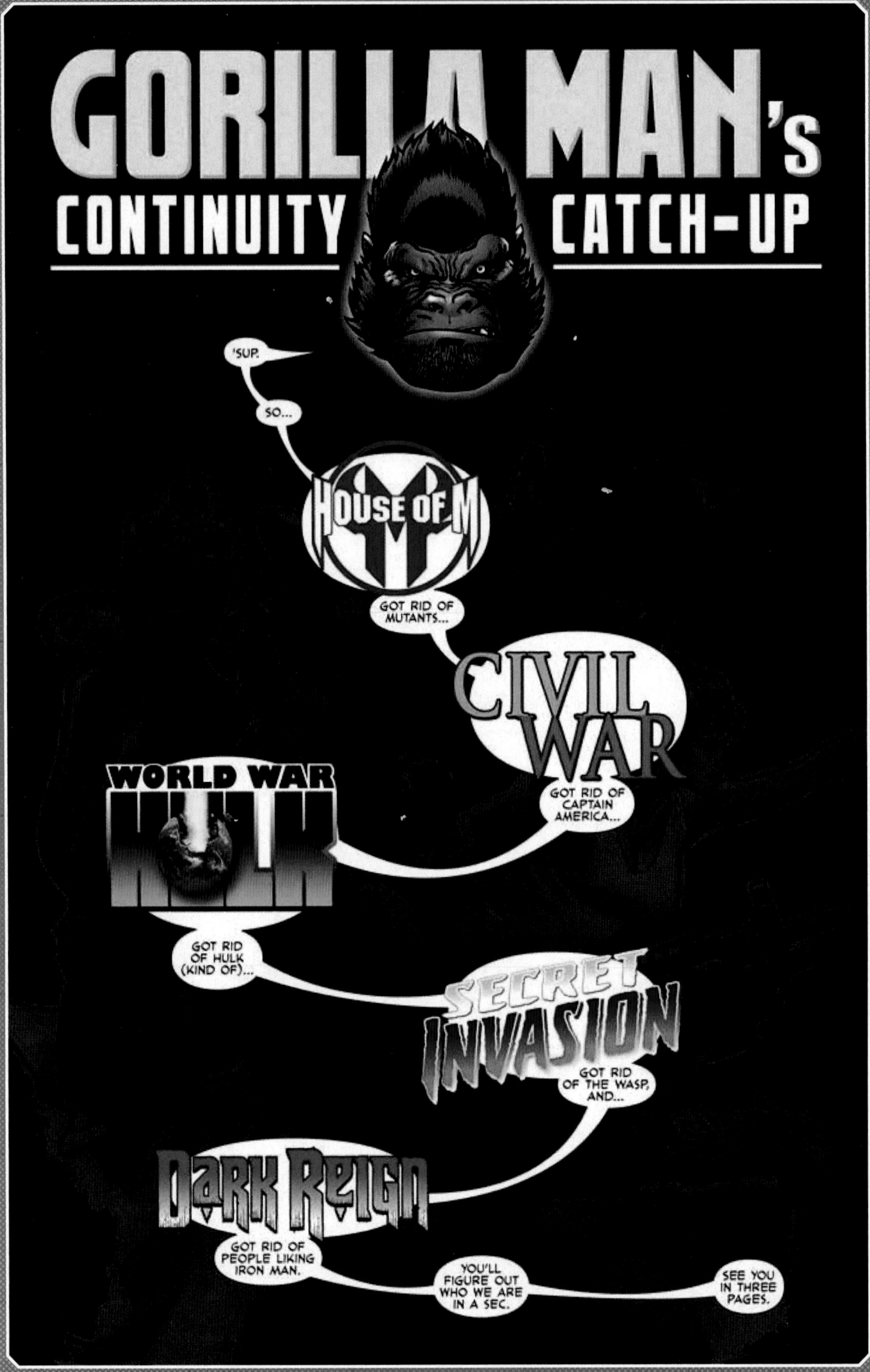
GORILLA MAN's
CONTINUITY CATCH-UP
'SUP.
SO...
HOUSE OF M
GOT RID OF MUTANTS...
CIVIL WAR
GOT RID OF CAPTAIN AMERICA...
WORLD WAR HULK
GOT RID OF HULK (KIND OF)...
SECRET INVASION
GOT RID OF THE WASP, AND...
DARK REIGN
GOT RID OF PEOPLE LIKING IRON MAN.
YOU'LL FIGURE OUT WHO WE ARE IN A SEC.
SEE YOU IN THREE PAGES.

AGENTS OF ATLAS (2009) #1-5 RECAP PAGES

Reunited in the present to save their leader Jimmy Woo, an incredible team of 1950s FBI agents discovered Woo was the heir to an ancient underground empire known as the Atlas Foundation! Assuming command of the worldwide syndicate, Woo and his fellow agents plan to use its far-reaching influence for good. Now Master Woo, Gorilla-Man, Namora, The Uranian, Venus, and the killer robot M-11 are regarded as global threats — and known to the underworld as the...

AGENTS OF ATLAS

M-11'S RECENT HISTORY LOGS

011011011101--RETRIEVING ARCHIVE: JAMES WOO'S "OPERATION TROJAN HORSE" SUCCESSFULLY FORMS TENTATIVE ALLIANCE WITH H.A.M.M.E.R. DIRECTOR NORMAN OSBORN00101110 OSBORN BELIEVES ATLAS INNER CIRCLE TO BE CRIMINAL OPERATIVES 00101110 VENUS' SEXUAL INFLUENCE SUCCESSFULLY CONTROLS THE SENTRY00101110 98.32% PROBABILITY OSBORN WILL OUTFIT SENTRY TO RESIST VENUS00101110 ATLAS GRANTS H.A.M.M.E.R. RECONNAISSANCE TEAM ACCESS TO HIDDEN CITY TO CONVINCE OSBORN OF ORGANIZATION SIZE00101110 ATF CREW LEADER MICHAEL MARKO STRAYS FROM PATH TO FOLLOW WOO POSING AS CAPTIVE00101110 MARKO DISCOVERS TRUE MOTIVES OF JAMES WOO AND TEAM00101110 MR. LAO CONSUMES MARKO FOR CALORIC NOURISHMENT00101110 LAO APPOINTS EMERGENCY SUCCESSOR TO WOO -- TEMUGIN SON OF WARLORD KNOWN AS THE MANDARIN00101110 **END TRANSMISSION**

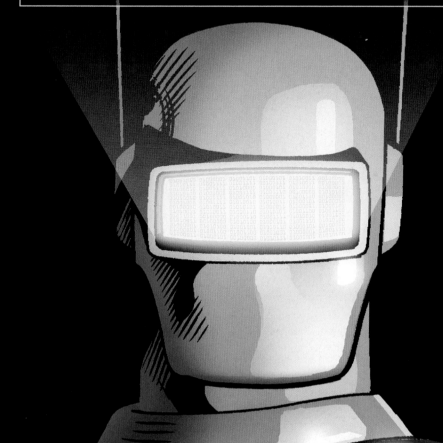

Reunited in the present to save their leader Jimmy Woo, an incredible team of 1950s FBI agents discovered Woo was the heir to an ancient underground empire known as the Atlas Foundation! Assuming command of the worldwide syndicate, Woo and his fellow agents plan to use its far-reaching influence for good. Now Master Woo, Gorilla-Man, Namora, The Uranian, Venus, and the killer robot M-11 are regarded as global threats – and known to the underworld as the...

AGENTS OF ATLAS

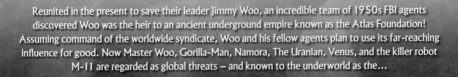

NAMORA'S SEA-NOPSIS

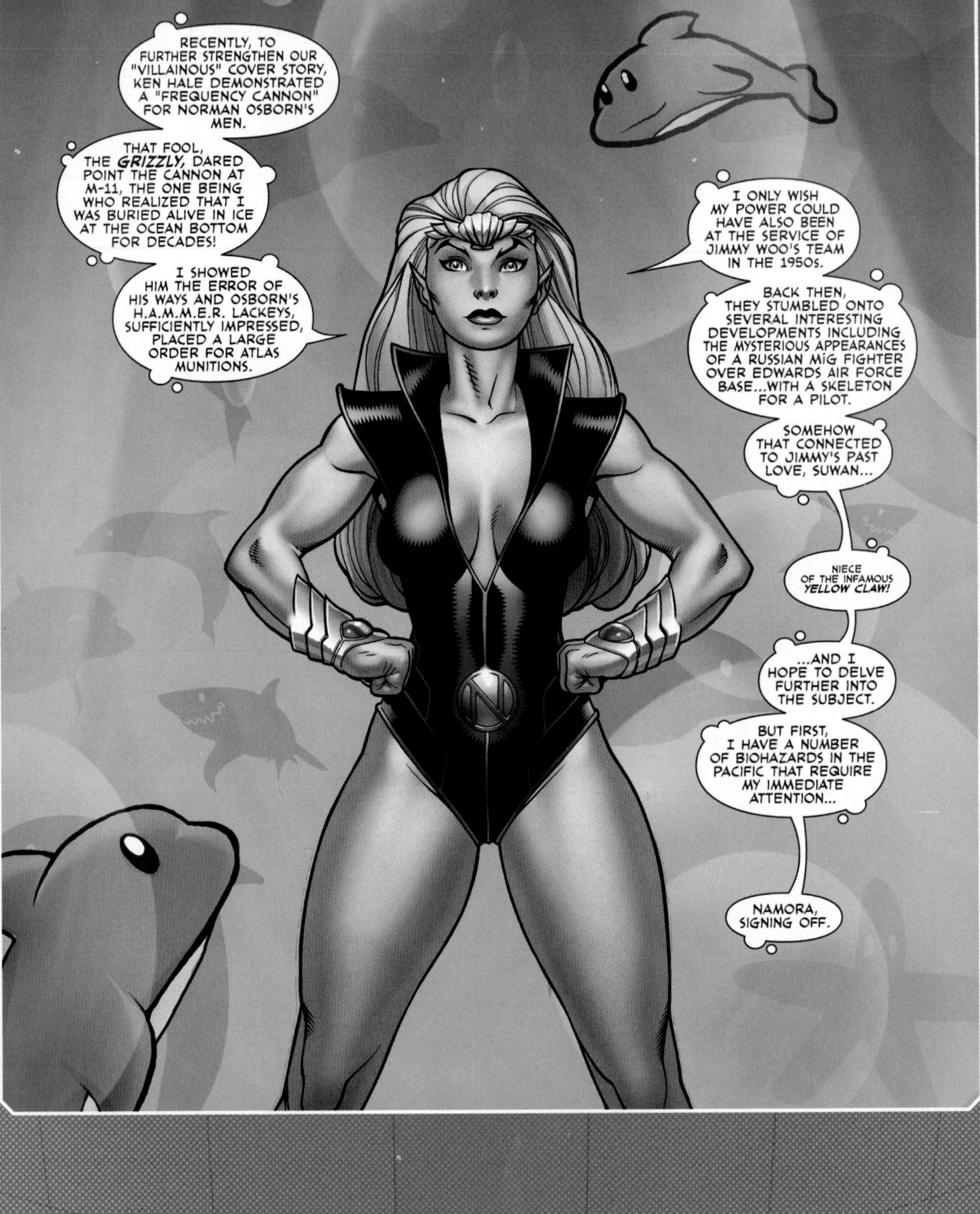
RECENTLY, TO FURTHER STRENGTHEN OUR "VILLAINOUS" COVER STORY, KEN HALE DEMONSTRATED A "FREQUENCY CANNON" FOR NORMAN OSBORN'S MEN.
THAT FOOL, THE *GRIZZLY,* DARED POINT THE CANNON AT M-11, THE ONE BEING WHO REALIZED THAT I WAS BURIED ALIVE IN ICE AT THE OCEAN BOTTOM FOR DECADES!
I SHOWED HIM THE ERROR OF HIS WAYS AND OSBORN'S H.A.M.M.E.R. LACKEYS, SUFFICIENTLY IMPRESSED, PLACED A LARGE ORDER FOR ATLAS MUNITIONS.
I ONLY WISH MY POWER COULD HAVE ALSO BEEN AT THE SERVICE OF JIMMY WOO'S TEAM IN THE 1950s.
BACK THEN, THEY STUMBLED ONTO SEVERAL INTERESTING DEVELOPMENTS INCLUDING THE MYSTERIOUS APPEARANCES OF A RUSSIAN MiG FIGHTER OVER EDWARDS AIR FORCE BASE...WITH A SKELETON FOR A PILOT.
SOMEHOW THAT CONNECTED TO JIMMY'S PAST LOVE, SUWAN...
NIECE OF THE INFAMOUS *YELLOW CLAW!*
...AND I HOPE TO DELVE FURTHER INTO THE SUBJECT.
BUT FIRST, I HAVE A NUMBER OF BIOHAZARDS IN THE PACIFIC THAT REQUIRE MY IMMEDIATE ATTENTION...
NAMORA, SIGNING OFF.

Reunited in the present to save their leader Jimmy Woo, an incredible team of 1950s FBI agents discovered Woo was the heir to an ancient underground empire known as the Atlas Foundation! Assuming command of the worldwide syndicate, Woo and his fellow agents plan to use its far-reaching influence for good. Now Master Woo, Gorilla-Man, Namora, The Uranian, Venus, and the killer robot M-11 are regarded as global threats – and known to the underworld as the...

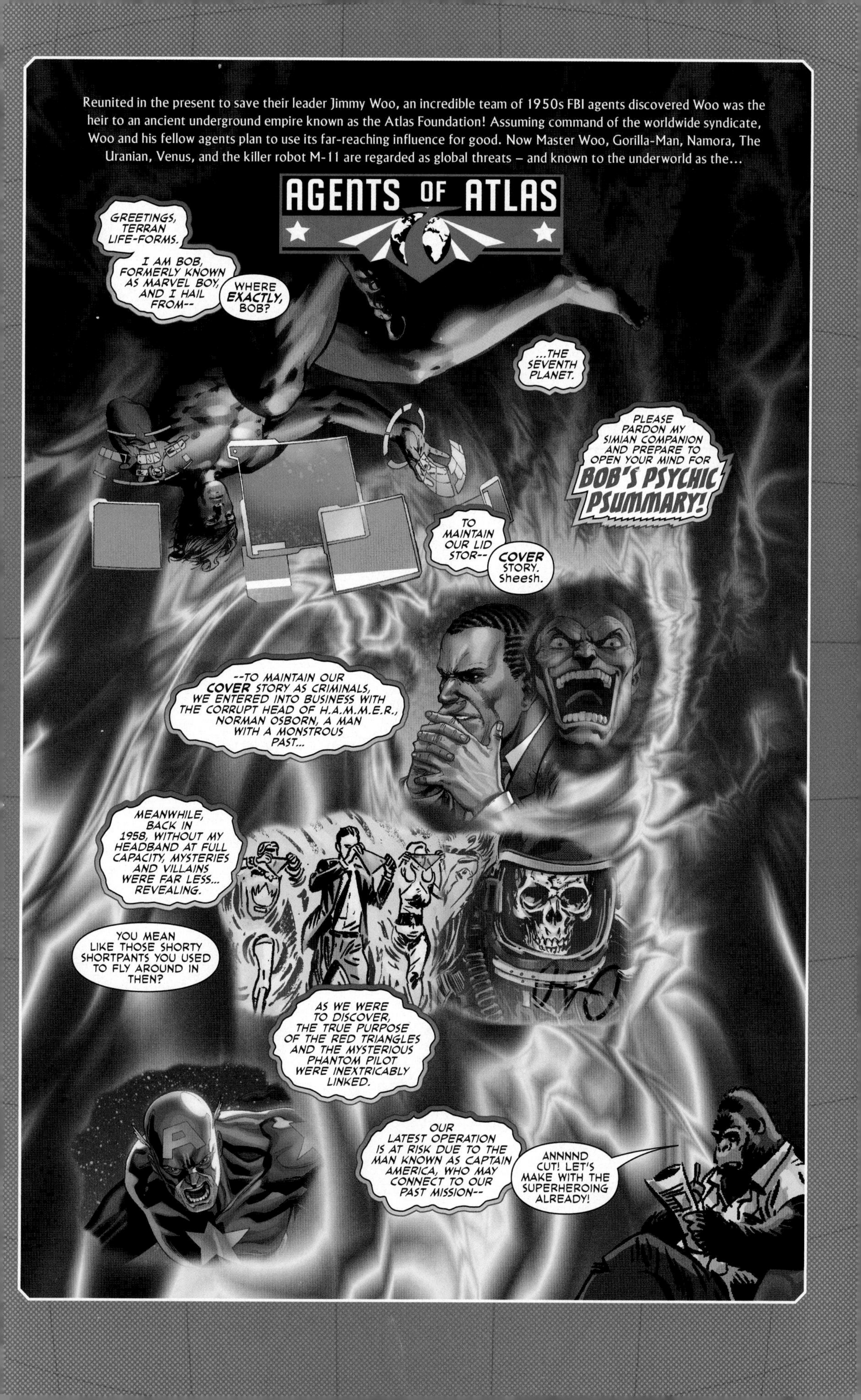
AGENTS OF ATLAS
GREETINGS, TERRAN LIFE-FORMS.
I AM BOB, FORMERLY KNOWN AS MARVEL BOY, AND I HAIL FROM--
WHERE EXACTLY, BOB?
...THE SEVENTH PLANET.
PLEASE PARDON MY SIMIAN COMPANION AND PREPARE TO OPEN YOUR MIND FOR
BOB'S PSYCHIC PSUMMARY!
TO MAINTAIN OUR LID STOR--
COVER STORY. Sheesh.
--TO MAINTAIN OUR COVER STORY AS CRIMINALS, WE ENTERED INTO BUSINESS WITH THE CORRUPT HEAD OF H.A.M.M.E.R., NORMAN OSBORN, A MAN WITH A MONSTROUS PAST...
MEANWHILE, BACK IN 1958, WITHOUT MY HEADBAND AT FULL CAPACITY, MYSTERIES AND VILLAINS WERE FAR LESS... REVEALING.
YOU MEAN LIKE THOSE SHORTY SHORTPANTS YOU USED TO FLY AROUND IN THEN?
AS WE WERE TO DISCOVER, THE TRUE PURPOSE OF THE RED TRIANGLES AND THE MYSTERIOUS PHANTOM PILOT WERE INEXTRICABLY LINKED.
OUR LATEST OPERATION IS AT RISK DUE TO THE MAN KNOWN AS CAPTAIN AMERICA, WHO MAY CONNECT TO OUR PAST MISSION--
ANNNND CUT! LET'S MAKE WITH THE SUPERHEROING ALREADY!

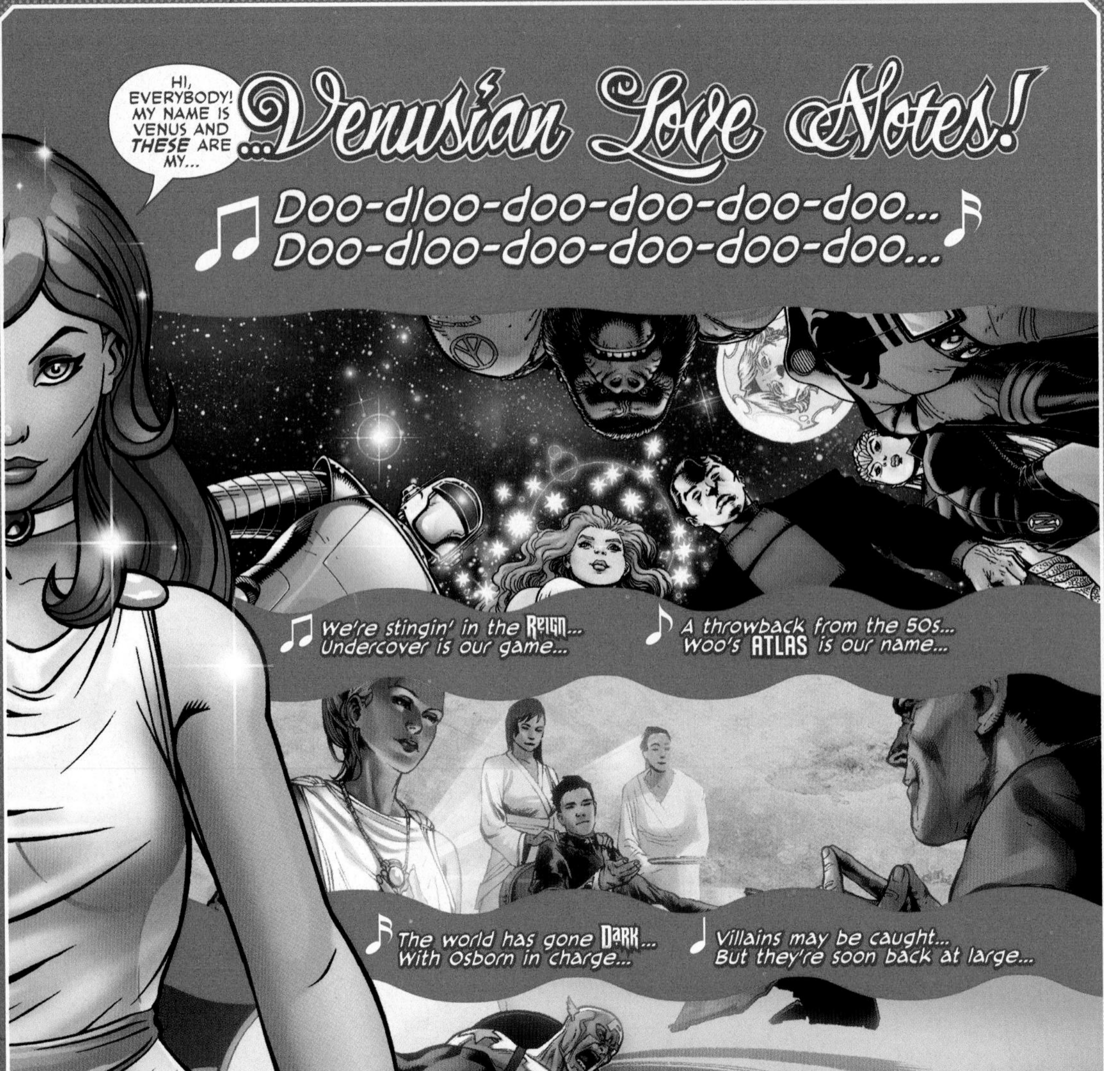

HI, EVERYBODY! MY NAME IS VENUS AND THESE ARE MY...
...Venusian Love Notes!
Doo-dloo-doo-doo-doo-doo...
Doo-dloo-doo-doo-doo-doo...
We're stingin' in the REIGN... Undercover is our game...
A throwback from the 50s... Woo's ATLAS is our name...
The world has gone DARK... With Osborn in charge...
Villains may be caught... But they're soon back at large...
Weapons deals they were made... Not intended to be paid...
Our plan worked so well, Cap's planning a raid!
Bob used the arcane... To plant suggestions in Cap's brain...
Avengers... They're bringing on the pain...

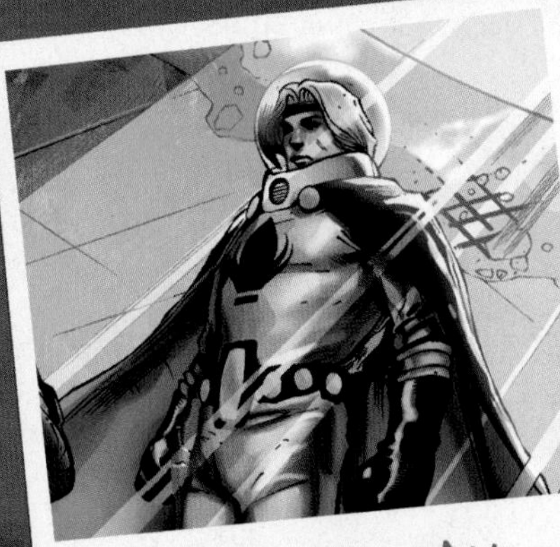

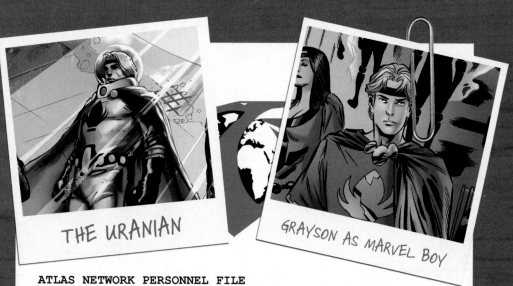

THE URANIAN

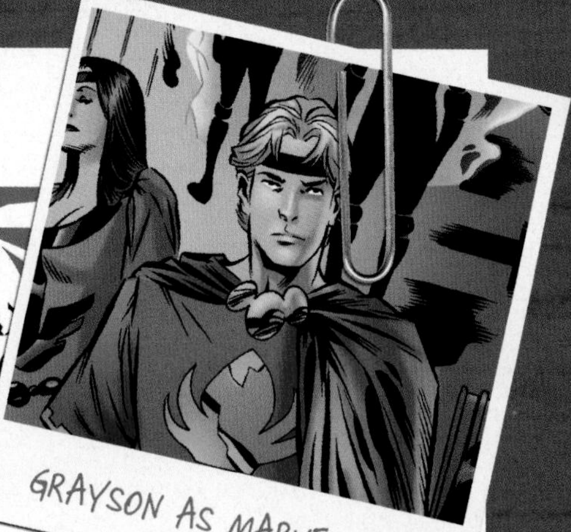

GRAYSON AS MARVEL BOY

ATLAS NETWORK PERSONNEL FILE
MASTER WOO'S INNER CIRCLE: GRAYSON, ROBERT "BOB"

MARVEL BOY - Raised on the Planet Uranus among a highly advanced race of humanoids, Bob Grayson was groomed to return to his birth planet Earth to fight injustice as the solar-powered hero Marvel Boy. His mind was conditioned to enhance psychic ability and work in conjunction with a sophisticated computer/scanner/projector in the form of a headband. Marvel Boy worked in the FBI's Department Zero under Jimmy Woo fighting world threatening menaces in secret.

THE URANIAN - Grayson later discovered that the people of Uranus were in truth a penal colony of Eternals who planned to return to Earth with his help, violating the terms of their exile. This transgression was lethally punished by the original Uranians, an amorphous race living under the planet's surface. Grayson was taken in by the Uranians and genetically altered to live in their environment. No longer limited by the colonists, his headband now functions at a much higher capacity, allowing Grayson to project psychic illusions and better connect to other minds.

FOR MORE INFORMATION ABOUT BOB GO TO MARVEL.COM

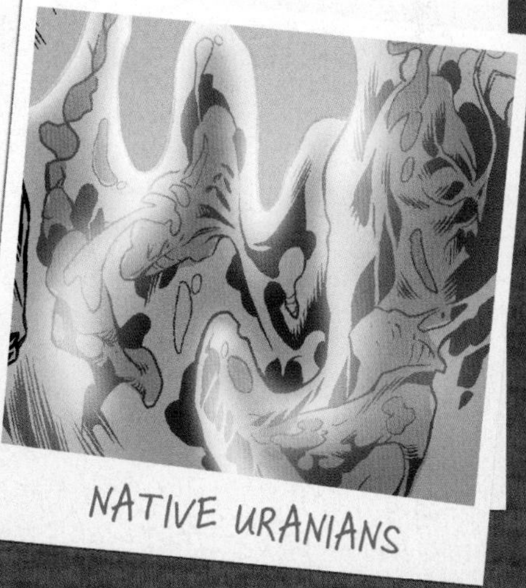

NATIVE URANIANS

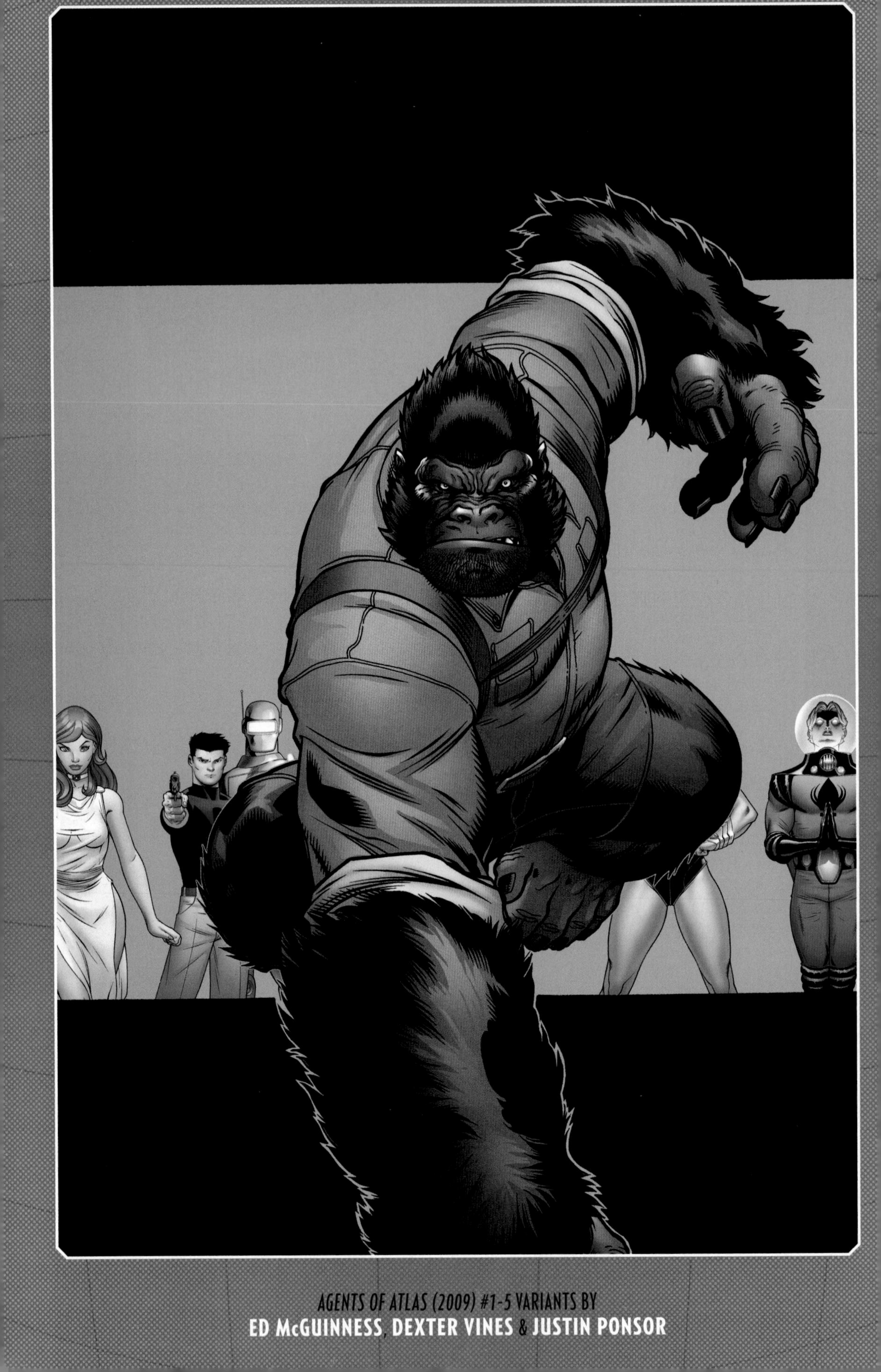

AGENTS OF ATLAS (2009) #1-5 VARIANTS BY
ED McGUINNESS, DEXTER VINES & JUSTIN PONSOR

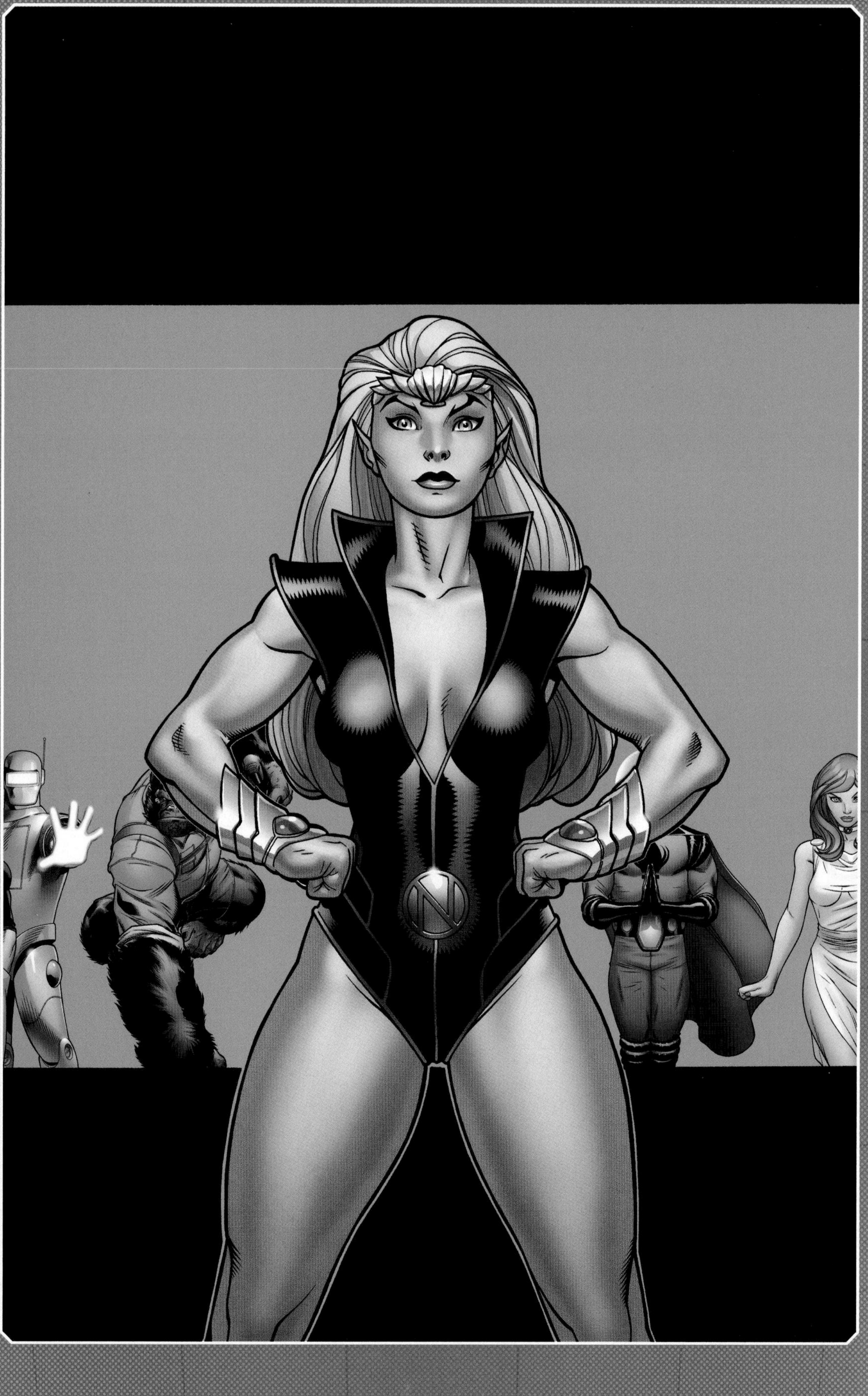

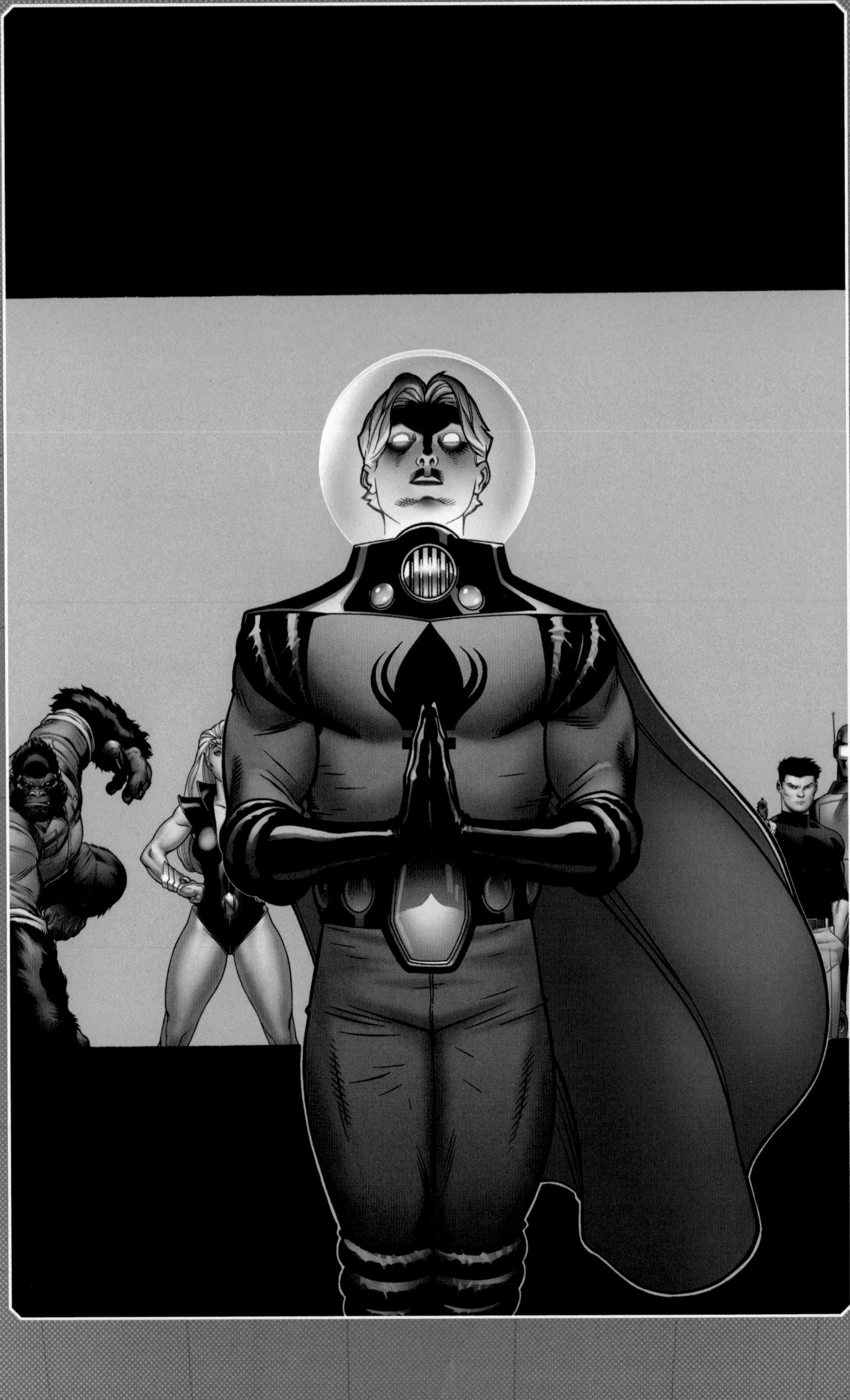

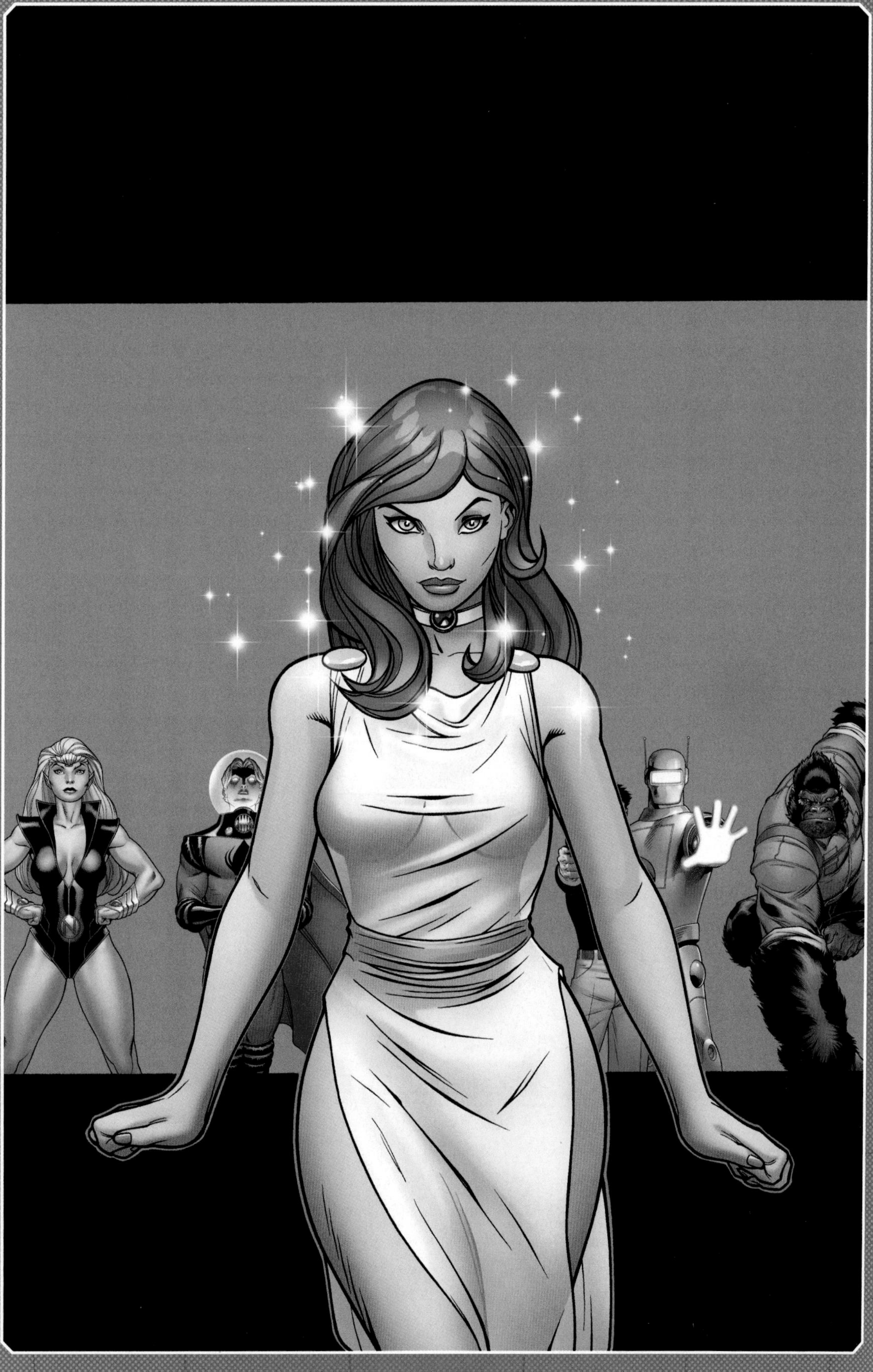

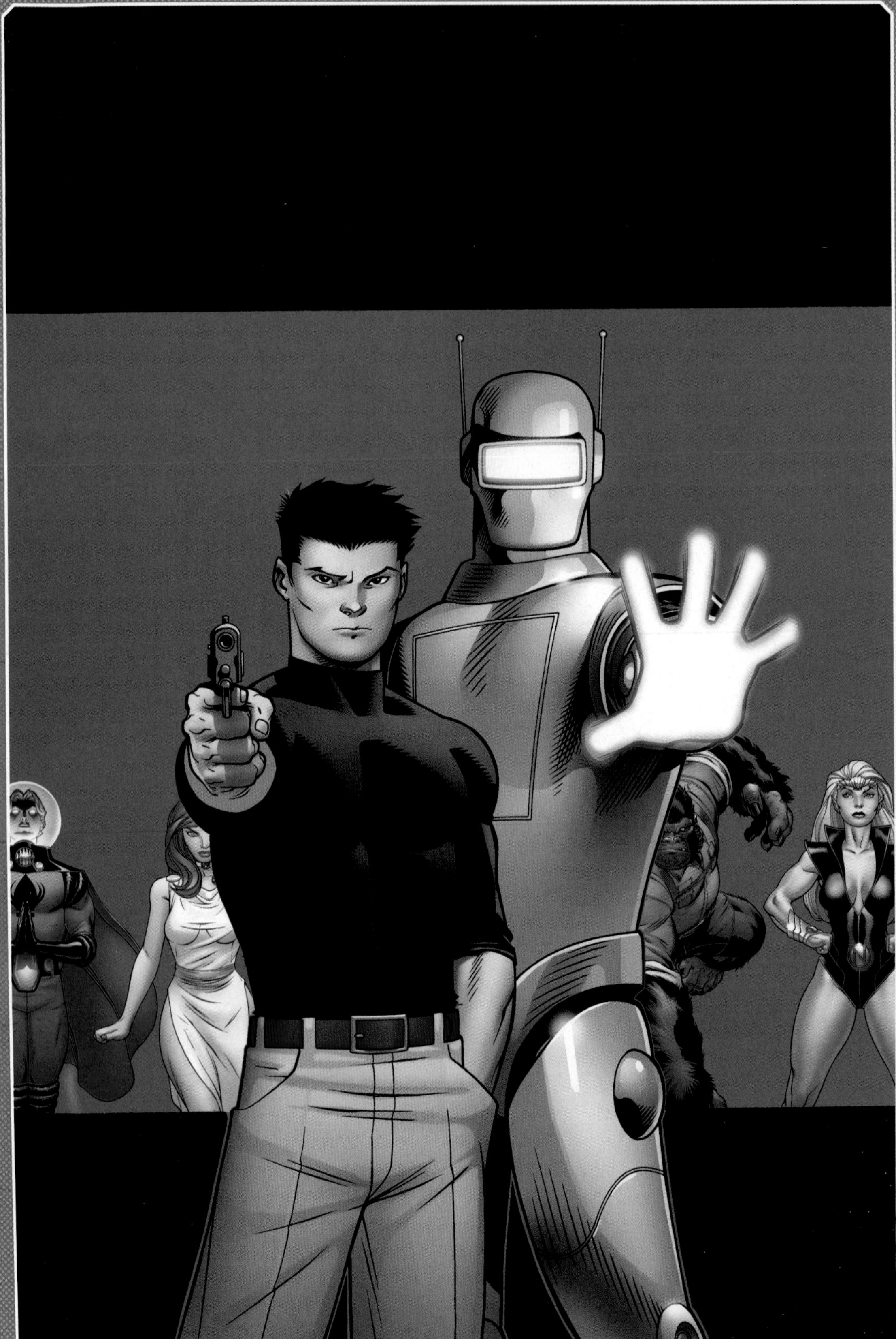

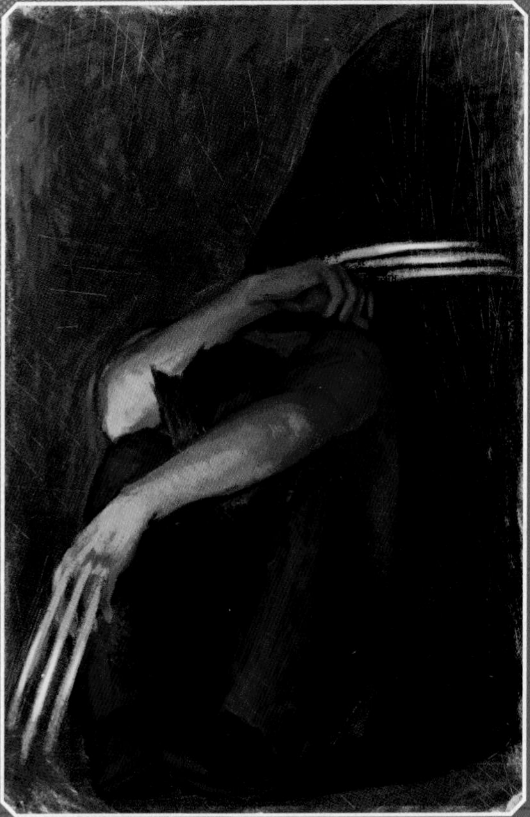

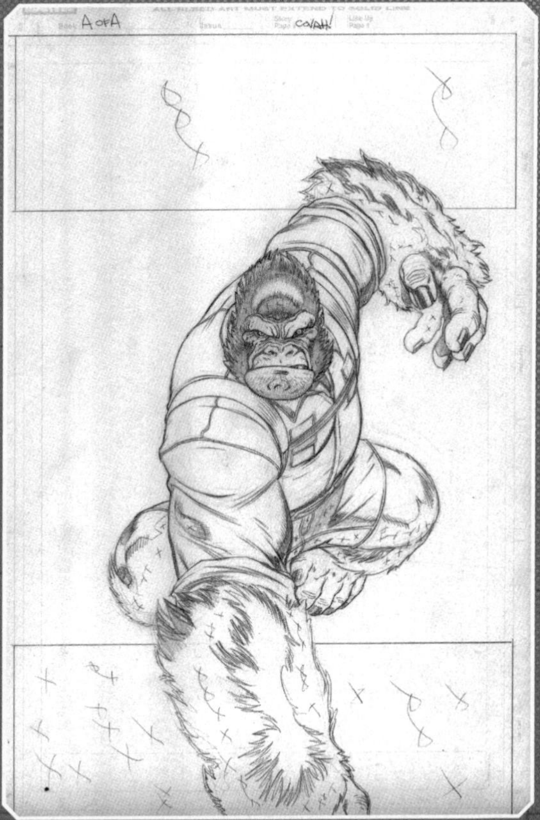

AGENTS OF ATLAS (2009) #3 WOLVERINE ART APPRECIATION VARIANT BY **GERALD PAREL**

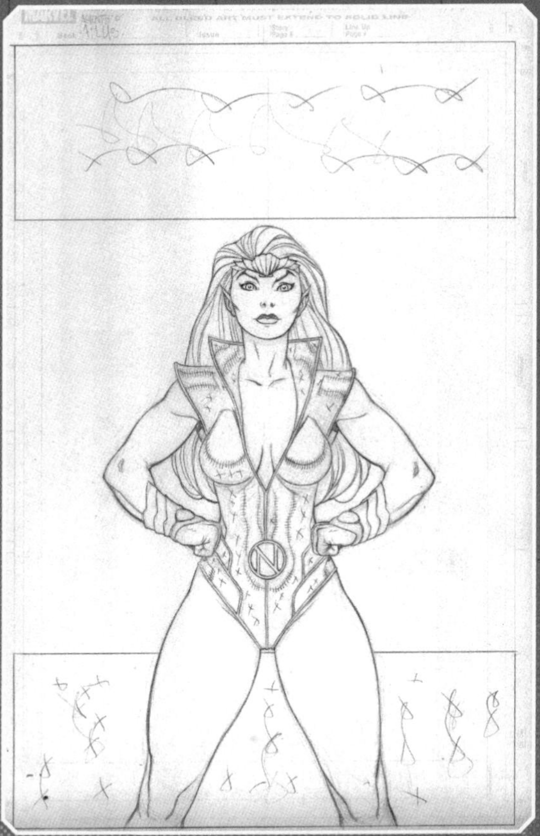

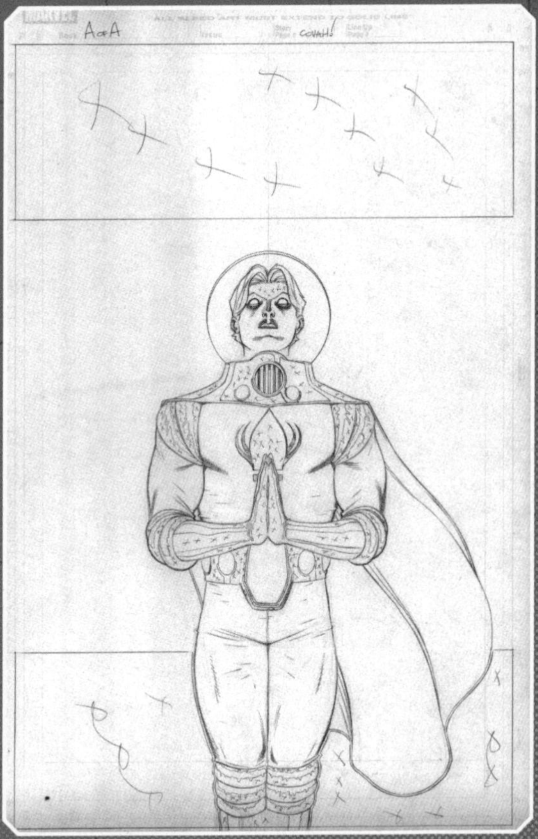

AGENTS OF ATLAS (2009) VARIANT COVER PENCILS BY **ED McGUINNESS**

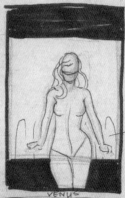

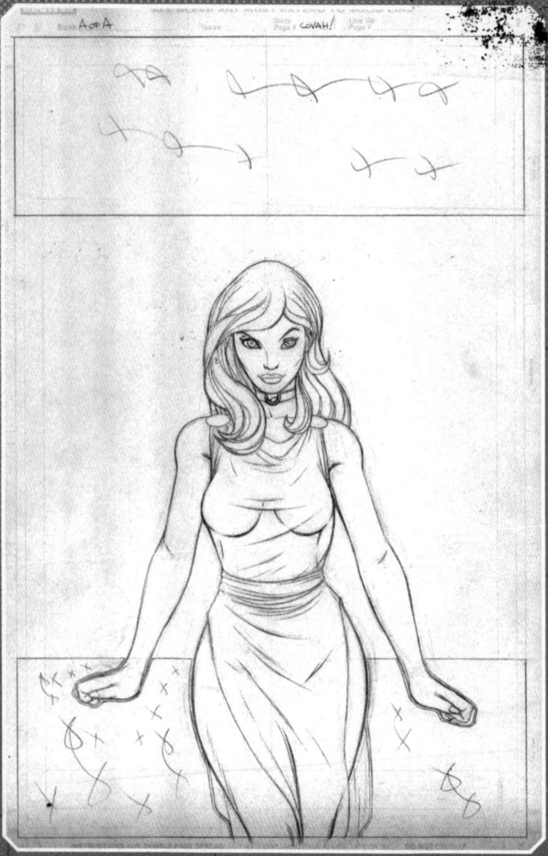
COVAH!
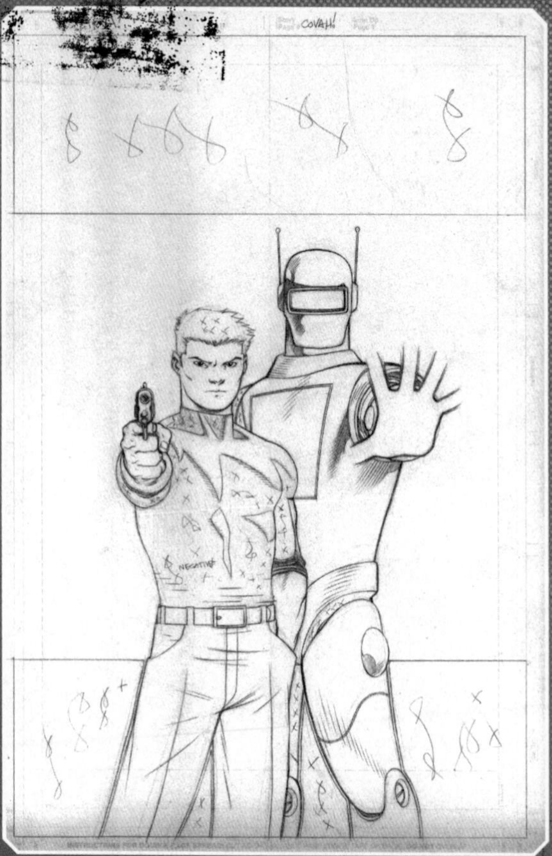
COVAH!
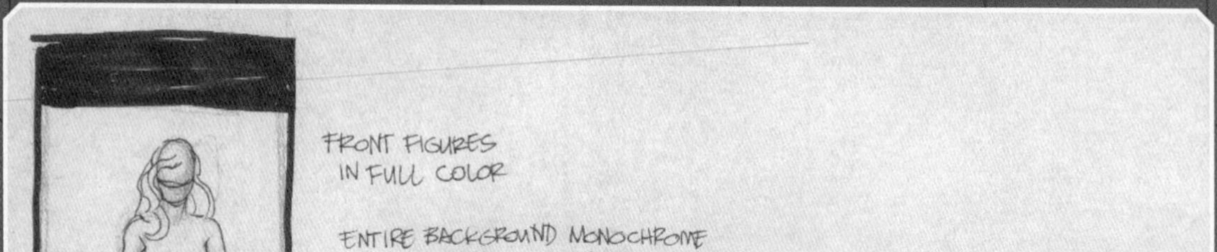
FRONT FIGURES IN FULL COLOR
ENTIRE BACKGROUND MONOCHROME IN A COLOR THAT BEST SUITS THE CHARACTER
EX. VENUS – PINK
STATS OF THE OTHER TEAM MEMBERS IN BACKGROUND
VENUS
GORILLA MAN

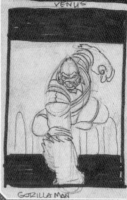

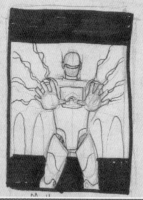

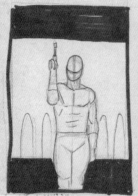

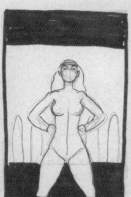

AGENTS OF ATLAS (2009) VARIANT COVER PENCILS & CONCEPT SKETCH BY **ED McGUINNESS**